Published by
Time Out Guides Limited
Universal House
251 Tottenham Court Road
London W1T 7AB
Tel +44 (0)20 7813 3000
Fax +44 (0)20 7813 6001
email guides@timeout.com
www.timeout.com

Editorial
Editors Cath Phillips, Guy Dimond
Deputy Editor Phil Harriss
Copy Editor Tom Lamont
Listings Editor Cathy Limb
Researchers Shane Armstrong, Alex Brown, James Cartwright, Alan Cheek, Francis Gooding, Gemma Pritchard
Proofer John Pym
Subject Index Jacqueline Brind

Managing Director Peter Fiennes
Financial Director Gareth Garner
Editorial Director Sarah Guy
Series Editor Cath Phillips
Editorial Manager Holly Pick
Assistant Management Accountant Ija Krasnikova

Design
Art Director Scott Moore
Art Editor Pinelope Kourmouzoglou
Senior Designer Henry Elphick
Graphic Designer Gemma Doyle
Junior Graphic Designer Kei Ishimaru
Digital Imaging Simon Foster
Ad Designer Jodi Sher

Picture Desk
Picture Editor Jael Marschner
Deputy Picture Editor Tracey Kerrigan
Picture Researcher Helen McFarland

Advertising
Sales Director & Sponsorship Mark Phillips
Sales Manager Alison Wallen
Advertising Sales Ben Holt, Alex Matthews, Jason Trotman
Advertising Assistant Kate Staddon
Copy Controller Declan Symington

Marketing
Group Marketing Director John Luck
Marketing Manager Yvonne Poon
Sales & Marketing Director North America Lisa Levinson

Production
Group Production Director Mark Lamond
Production Manager Brendan McKeown
Production Controller Caroline Bradford
Production Coordinator Susan Whittaker

Time Out Group
Chairman Tony Elliott
Financial Director Richard Waterlow
Group General Manager/Director Nichola Coulthard
Time Out Magazine Ltd MD Richard Waterlow
TO Communications Ltd MD David Pepper
Managing Director, Time Out International Cathy Runciman
Group Art Director John Oakey
Group IT Director Simon Chappell

Sections in this guide were written by
African & Caribbean Franka Philip (Caribbean); Guy Dimond, Haben Habteslasie, Michela Wrong (African); **The Americas** (North American) Christi Daugherty; (Latin American) Chris Moss, Christi Daugherty; **British** Sarah Guy, Ruth Jarvis; **Chinese** Antonia Bruce, Fuchsia Dunlop, Ian Fenn, Phil Harriss, Jane Hutcheon, Jennifer Lee, Sally Peck; **East European** Susan Low, Janet Zromczek; **Fish** Jan Fuscoe, Cath Phillips, Yolanda Zappaterra; **French** Simon Cropper, Guy Dimond, Peter Fiennes, Roopa Gulati, Ruth Jarvis, Nick Rider, Ethel Rimmer, Caroline Stacey, Simon Tillotson; **Gastropubs** Guy Dimond, Will Fulford-Jones, Jan Fuscoe, Sarah Guy, Tom Lamont, Patrick Marmion, Chris Moss, Jenni Muir, Veronica Simpson, Nick Rider, Ethel Rimmer; **Global** Phil Harriss, Caroline Hire; **Greek** Photini Philippidou; **Hotels & Haute Cuisine** Helen Barnard; **Indian** Robina Dam, Guy Dimond, Roopa Gulati, Phil Harriss, Seema Merchant, Amy Sohanpaul, Anjali Wason; **International** Claire Fogg, Nick Rider, Ethel Rimmer; **Italian** Elena Berton, Richard Ehrlich, Patrick Marmion, Jenni Muir; **Japanese** Kei Kikuchi, Susan Low, Rebecca Taylor; **Jewish** Judy Jackson; **Korean** Joe Bindloss; **Malaysian, Indonesian & Singaporean** Ian Fenn, Jennifer Lee; **Middle Eastern** Andrew Humphreys, Ros Sales, Cyrus Shahrad; **Modern European** Guy Dimond, Dominic Earle, Peter Fiennes, Will Fulford-Jones, Phil Harriss, Emma Howarth, Sarah Guy, Ruth Jarvis, Susan Low, Jenni Muir, Anna Norman, Cath Phillips, Nick Rider, Ethel Rimmer, Caroline Stacey, Elizabeth Winding; **North African** Andrew Humphreys, Janet Zmroczek; **Oriental** Terry Durack; **Portuguese** Amanda Smith; **Spanish** Andrew Staffell; **Thai** Guy Dimond, Jennifer Lee, Sally Peck; **Turkish** Ken Olende; **Vegetarian** Natasha Polyviou; **Vietnamese** Guy Dimond, Lam Thuy Vo; **Budget** Anna Norman, Jenny Rigby, Fiona Shield, Pete Watts; **Cafés** Richard Ehrlich, Roopa Gulati, Pendle Harte, Anna Norman, Holly Pick, Lisa Ritchie, Fiona Shield, Veronica Simpson; **Fish & Chips** Simon Cropper, Alexi Duggins, Holly Pick, Cyrus Shahrad; **Pizza & Pasta** Ronnie Haydon, Cathy Limb, Holly Pick, Cyrus Shahrad, Fiona Shield; **Wine Bars** James Aufenast; **Eating & Entertainment** Alex Brown, Cathy Limb, Gemma Pritchard.

Additional reviews by Ismay Atkins, Simone Baird, Simon Coppock, Simon Cropper, Guy Dimond, Dominic Earle, Peter Fiennes, Will Fulford-Jones, Viv Groskop, Roopa Gulati, Sarah Guy, Phil Harriss, Pendle Harte, Ronnie Haydon, Emma Howarth, Jane Hutcheon, Tom Lamont, Cathy Limb, Susan Low, Fiona McAuslan, Patrick Marmion, Tom Masters, Anna Norman, Simon Richmond, Jenny Rigby, Lisa Ritchie, Ros Sales, Sejal Sukhadwala, Cyrus Shahrad, Veronica Simpson, Daniel Smith, Caroline Stacey, Andrew Staffell, Gordon Thomson, Pete Watts, Elizabeth Winding, Janet Zromczek.

Interviews Jenni Muir, except Riaz Ali (Roopa Gulati), Felix Yu (Sally Peck).
Shelf Life boxes Jenni Muir (also Guy Dimond, Tom Lamont, Andrew Staffell).

The Editors would like to thank Katy Attfield, Jessica Cargill Thompson, Sarah Guy, Mike Harrison, Susan Low, Jenni Muir and our sponsor, Leffe.

Maps john@jsgraphics.co.uk

Cover photography by Nice Studios, plate by Wedgwood by Plato, www.wedgwood.com, stockist no. 0800 028 0026

Photography by pages 18, 19, 26, 48, 52, 63, 65, 81, 92, 100, 109, 116, 122, 123, 124, 128, 140, 141, 158, 176, 183, 190, 191, 228, 231, 236, 237, 254, 259, 263, 277, 279, 287, 291, 295, 342, 346, 347, 349 Ming Tang Evans; pages 19, 43, 70, 76, 78, 84, 91, 103, 136, 137, 161, 179, 213, 225, 233, 242, 247, 253, 284, 316, 317, 325, 351, 355 Heloise Bergman; pages 19, 51, 55, 73, 173, 301, 340 Alys Tomlinson; pages 26, 120, 200, 249 Martin Daly; pages 26, 221 Kate Peters; pages 28, 150, 198, 199, 205, 251, 265, 273, 280, 281, 309, 313, 320, 338, 341 Gemma Day; pages 30, 37, 41, 95, 98, 151, 155, 186, 293, 302, 306 Jitka Hynkova; pages 31, 105, 108, 112, 166, 189, 197, 299, 319, 339 Rob Greig; pages 57, 134, 210, 217, 268 Tricia de Courcy Ling; pages 58, 59, 60 Rogan MacDonald; pages 67, 106, 107, 132, 133 Michael Franke; pages 77, 80, 83, 331 Britta Jaschinski; pages 85, 89, 97, 127 Troy Bailey; page 119 Oliver Knight; page 143 Mark Jory; page 147 Paula Glassman; page 261 Dave Lyons.

The following images were provided by the featured establishment: pages 105, 189, 335.

Maps JS Graphics (john@jsgraphics.co.uk). Maps 1-18 & 24 are based on material supplied by Alan Collinson and Julie Snook through Copyright Exchange.

Printers Pindar Graphics, Shannon Way, Tewkesbury Industrial Centre, Tewkesbury, Gloucestershire GL20 8HB.

Time Out Group uses paper products that are environmentally friendly, from well managed forests and mills that use certified (PEFC) Chain of Custody pulp in their production.

ISBN 978-1-905042-30-2
ISBN 1-905042-30-2
ISSN 1750-4643
Distribution by Seymour Ltd (020 7429 4000)
For details of distribution in the Americas, see www.timeout.com

Introduction

How we compile the Time Out Eating & Drinking Guide

The restaurants, gastropubs, cafés, bars and pubs included in this guide are picked by the editors as the best of their type in London. Time Out always pays the bill; restaurants do not pay to be included in the guide, and can exert no pressure on us as to the content of their reviews.

Although our reviewers are often experts in their field, they are in one sense no different from other members of the public: they always visit restaurants anonymously. This is why the reviews here are more likely to match your own experience than reviews you might read elsewhere. Recognised critics receive preferential treatment, so it is much harder to trust their judgement. They get better treatment from the staff and more attention from the kitchen, which invariably colours their impressions of a restaurant. However, when Time Out reviews a restaurant for either this guide or the Food & Drink pages of the weekly magazine, we do so anonymously. There is no hob-nobbing with PRs, no freebies and no launch parties. We feel our readers have a right to know what eating at that restaurant might be like for them.

Our reviewers are journalists who have a passion for food, and for finding the best places to eat and drink. Many of them also have extraordinary expertise in specialist areas; a few are, or have been, chefs, but most are just enthusiasts. For example, we employ a Vietnamese speaker and food expert to review London's Vietnamese restaurants, and a number of Indian regional food experts for the Indian chapter, while the principal authors of the Chinese section are trained Chinese chefs who also speak Mandarin and/or Cantonese.

For the weekly *Time Out* magazine alone, our reviewers visit around 200 new places every year. The better discoveries are then included in this guide. On top of that, reviewers also check other new openings, as well as revisiting all the places included in the previous edition. As a result, at least 2,000 anonymous visits were made in the creation of this guide. We also pay attention to recommendations and feedback from readers and from users of our website. We then eliminate the also-rans to create the annual list of London's best eateries that this guide represents.

EDITION 25

timeout.com/restaurants

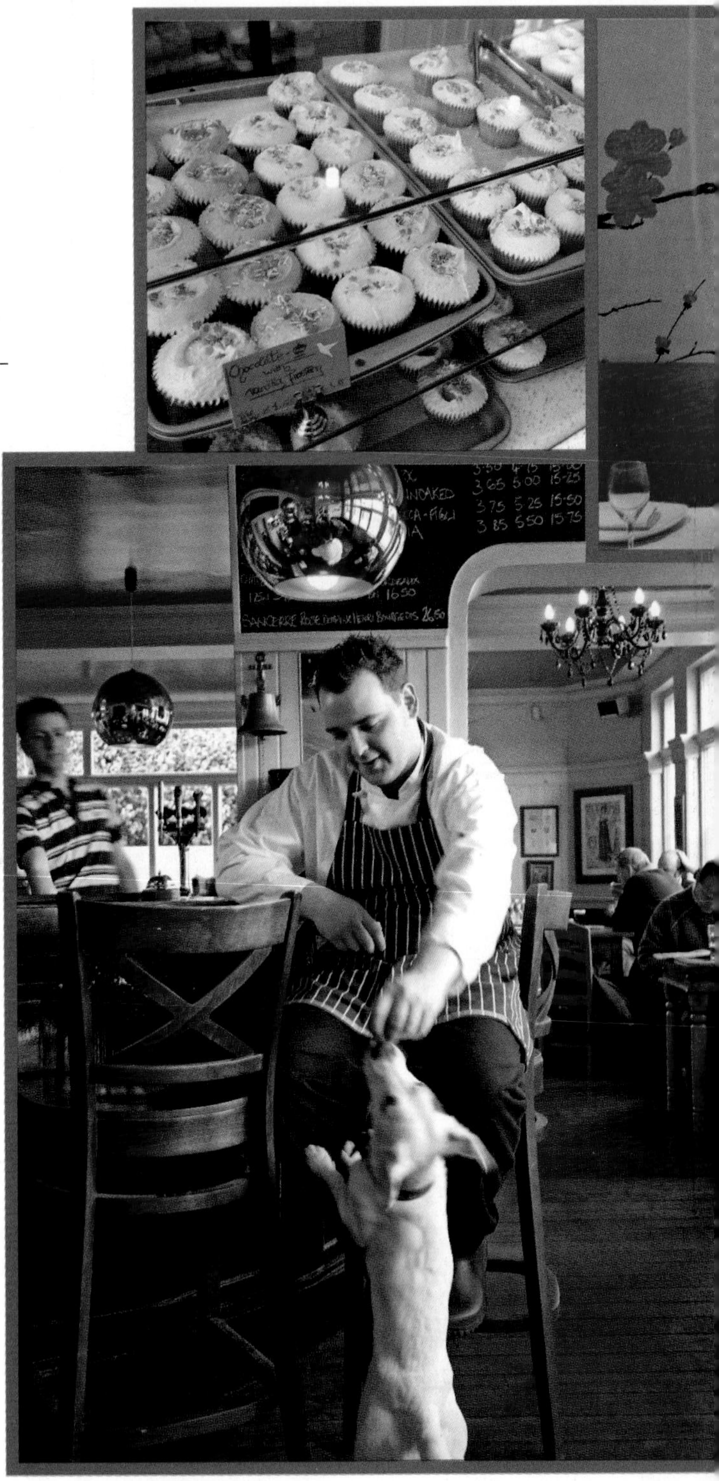

RESTAURANTS

CHEAP EATS

DRINKING

Eating & Drinking 2008

Contents

MAPS & INDEXES

FEATURES

100% INDEPENDENT
The reviews in the ***Time Out Eating & Drinking Guide*** are based on the experiences of Time Out restaurant reviewers. All restaurants, bars, gastropubs and cafés are visited anonymously, and Time Out pays the bill. No payment of any kind has secured or influenced a review.

So what do *you* think?

What's the best thing about eating out in London? What's the worst? Read the results of our readership survey to find out – you might be surprised.

WHAT IS YOUR FAVOURITE TYPE OF RESTAURANT?

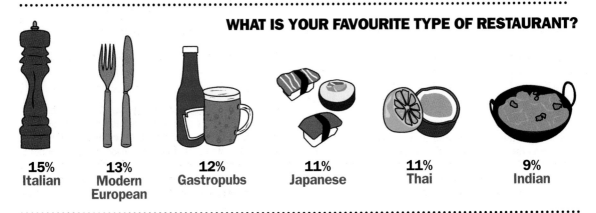

15%
Italian

13%
Modern European

12%
Gastropubs

11%
Japanese

11%
Thai

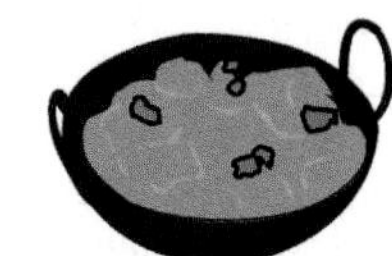

9%
Indian

Who are you, what are your experiences of eating out in London, and what do you expect? We already know that you, the reader, are very interested in food, and fairly food-literate – because if you weren't, you probably wouldn't be reading this guide. But we wanted to know more detail about your preferences, likes and dislikes. So during summer 2007 we posted an online questionnaire on Time Out's food website (www.timeout.com/london/restaurants) to find out more about you. More than 3,000 responded – three-quarters of whom claimed to also be *Eating & Drinking Guide* readers – and these are the results of that survey.

COMPETING CUISINES

Ooh la la! It seems that Londoners' centuries-long love affair with Gallic food is now well and truly over, with a mere five per cent of you citing French as your favourite cuisine when eating out. Top of the list was Italian, at 15 per cent. But close on its heels were Modern European restaurants (13 per cent), gastropubs (12 per cent) and then – wait for it – Japanese restaurants (11 per cent). The first three categories are to be expected, but Japanese? It's a trend we've noticed before: analysed by cuisine type, Japanese restaurants are among the most searched-for reviews on the Time Out website. Some cuisines haven't made nearly such an impact – Vietnamese got only 33 votes, Turkish 22 – but this is a vicious circle: the less likely you are to encounter an unfamiliar cuisine type, the less likely you are to seek it out.

What you spend when you eat out is also telling: most of the respondents said they pay between £25 and £40 per head, which is in line with our findings on the cost of dining in London, though a startling two per cent claim to typically spend more than £60 per head. So either you're eating out in smart Mayfair restaurants as a matter of course, or you're very fond of Turkish mangal restaurants and have a very, very large appetite.

The survey results made it clear you like the conviviality of Italian restaurants and the laid-back atmosphere of a gastropub, but it's also clear you like – and know about – Japanese food. What is your favourite dish? There was a clear winner: 'sushi'. Perhaps more significantly, many of you went into much more detail than that. Dozens specified the likes of yellowtail sashimi, chirashi sushi (raw fish on rice) and agedashi dofu (a simmered tofu dish). Londoners, it seems, are no longer scared of raw fish. Increasingly too, you know just what to order in Japanese restaurants.

DISHING THE DIRT

'What is your favourite dish?' The responses to this question were some of the most revealing in the survey. Fish 'n' chips and chicken tikka masala featured, of course – but the vast majority of answers were far less predictable. Razor clams, stuffed courgette flowers, roasted marrow bone, chicken feet in black bean sauce, okra curry, wood pigeon, roast belly of pork, and frogs' legs with chilli and lemongrass were some that caught our eye. Rabbits took a big hit – a fair few cited dishes such as lapin à la moutarde, or rabbit pie. Bye bye, Thumper, down the hatch. London still has a sizeable sweet-tooth, with 'dessert' proving popular; 'desert' got a few nods too. A few of the answers had us utterly flummoxed. We looked to Google to discover that panthe kaukswe is a Burmese dish of egg noodles with curry sauce, and that sayyadiya is a delicately spiced fish dish on rice from the Middle East. Some answers were thoughtful, though less specific: 'A dynamic salad, simple or complicated'; 'I select new things if possible, but filling and comfort-oriented works for me: fish and spuds, risotto, roasts, sticky toffee pudding'; and 'Just one? Aww, that's way too hard. But I did have an amazing lotus salad at a Vietnamese place on Kingsland Road last night.'

In short, you are deeply interested in food, remarkably food-literate and keen to try new things. Just as well you live in London.

LOCAL LEGENDS

We were pleased to see you're tough to fool, not easily taken in by hype or PR. When asked to nominate your favourite restaurant, the vast majority were good, small neighbourhood restaurants of the type that we at Time Out love to seek out and give the recognition they deserve (indeed, around 95 per cent of your favourites are listed in this very guide). Rather than opting for the big-buck, big-name haunts, you are deeply loyal to the consistent local restaurants that treat you well. That they charge a fair price was an important factor in your decision – 40 per cent cited expense as the factor most disliked about London dining.

In terms of sheer numbers, Chez Bruce in Wandsworth topped the poll for our question, 'What's your favourite London restaurant?' In second place, it was the Ivy… what was that we were saying about big-buck, big-name haunts? Don't worry – the Ivy's support was undermined by another statistic. A staggering 446 people (more than ten times the number who voted in its favour) consider the Ivy London's most overrated restaurant. Ouch. Nobu didn't come off too well (second most overrated, with 161 votes), and Jamie Oliver didn't escape either (Fifteen came third, with 98 votes).

Dish delights

These are some of the answers we got to the question 'What is your favourite dish?' Varied, huh.

pan-fried foie gras
macaroni pie
pizza
an excellent rump steak
buttermilk pudding
imam bayeldi
anything I've not tried before
black cod with miso
prawn tempura maki
such a hard question!
so many.. but tom yum soup is a good one
grilled eel sushi
fish pie
pimento di padron
braised pork belly
sea bass
stri-fried duck and tamarind with coconut
roasted bone marrow
calf's liver
oxtail
pierogi
soft-shell crab
razor clams
anything with duck
anything Italian
roast lobster
fish and chips
dim sum
Vietnamese pho
at present, ho fun
Moroccan tagine
lamb jalfrezi
salt and pepper squid
scallops
crème brûlée
guinea fowl
lentil dahl
mushrom risotto
fajitas
authentic kebabs from the Edgware Road
just one?

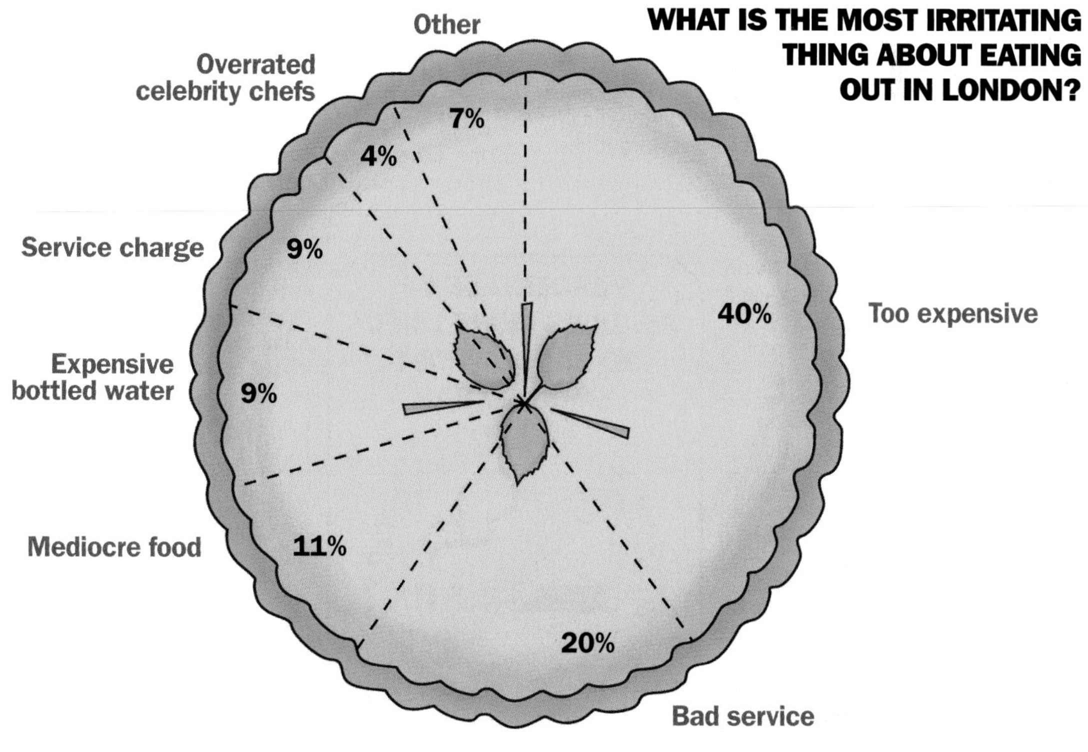

WHAT IS YOUR FAVOURITE DRINK?

45% Wine

13% Lager

12% Cocktails

12% Spirits

6% Ale

6% Non-alcoholic

BATTLE OF THE CHEFS

Wary of overhyped restaurants, you were less condemning of celebrity chefs in person. Little surprise, really – the higher a chef's media profile, the more likely people are to remember their name. The best-known and most popular chef was Gordon Ramsay, with 802 votes – the clear winner. Jamie Oliver also pulled a respectable 442 votes. Though chefs such as Tom Aikens and Giorgio Locatelli garnered praise, the message was clear: to become a really well-known chef, you need to be on TV.

Gordon, though, needn't feel too smug about topping the popularity poll. His restaurants drew a lot of negative feedback too, with various specific criticisms of Gordon Ramsay at Claridges, Gordon Ramsay (Royal Hospital Road), Boxwood Café, Angela Hartnett at The Connaught – and even the very general comment 'anything run by Gordon Ramsay'. Some of you resisted the lure of the big names – 'I don't go for celebrity chefs', was one response – while 'my boyfriend/girlfriend' was loyally voted favourite chef a number of times. Sweet.

YOU LIKE A DRINK

Although six per cent of you claim to drink alcohol seldom or never, 94 per cent do – and do so regularly. Wine is the favourite drink by a long margin, the preferred choice of 45 per cent of total respondents. Lager was no surprise either (13 per cent), but we were disappointed to see only six per cent cite real ale as a favourite. Cocktails (12 per cent) and spirits (11 per cent) had their devotees, but London's oenophiles were in the majority by far. And when you go out, most (42 per cent) spend around £10-£29 per week on drink; though a staggering two per cent said they spend more than £90 per week, every week, on drink. You'll be the ones ordering the rounds for Prince Harry and his mates, we can only assume.

PERCENTAGE OF READERS MORE LIKELY TO EAT OUT, POST SMOKING BAN

BREATHE EASILY

What about the thorny issue of cigarettes? Well, the world didn't end on 1 July 2007, as the pro-smoking lobby thundered it would. Instead, people carried on much as before going out to pubs and restaurants – only now breathing easier, accompanied by many who abstained before. A massive 85 per cent of you said you were more likely to go out drinking in pubs and bars post-ban; an even greater 91 per cent said you were more likely to go out to eat. But a small minority (14 per cent) said they were less likely to go out now that the smoking ban is in place.

YOU LOVE LONDON!

Which is the best city in the world for eating out? We believe it's London – and it turns out that you agree. Even *Gourmet* magazine – the world's top food magazine, based in New York – declared London 'the world's best place to eat' in 2006. More than 50 perc ent of survey respondents voted for London, with a mere 17 per cent opting for New York. Paris has a following, with a 19 per cent share of the vote. Melbourne and Sydney pulled in commendable support too; perhaps you felt you didn't know Hong Kong and Tokyo well enough to judge, though they also had their fans.

Those were our results, that fascinated and made us hungry in equal measure. What have we learned? That knowledge about food is important to Time Out readers. That many of you would rather eat at your friendly neighbourhood Italian or gastropub than pay through the nose to be in the latest West End hotspot, but you are always prepared to try new things. That Gordon Ramsay is loved and loathed in equal measure. So the next time we see someone eating sushi in front of their computer, who enjoys a glass of wine with dinner, and is more likely to be having a pot roast than a Pot Noodle for dinner – there's our typical reader.

OXO

Silver service

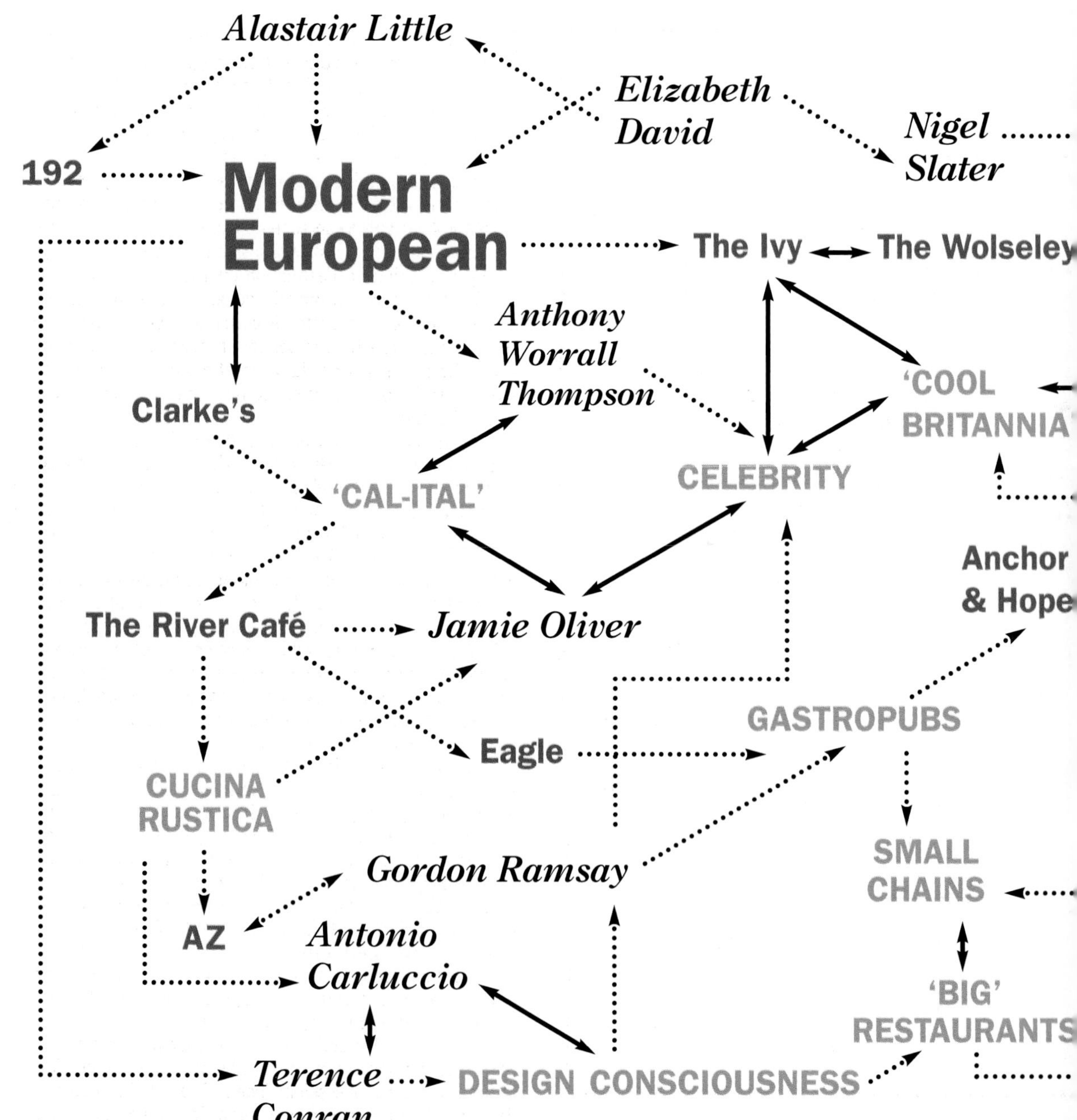

Alastair Little
Elizabeth David
Nigel Slater
192
Modern European
The Ivy
The Wolseley
Anthony Worrall Thompson
Clarke's
'COOL BRITANNIA'
CELEBRITY
'CAL-ITAL'
Anchor & Hope
The River Café
Jamie Oliver
GASTROPUBS
Eagle
CUCINA RUSTICA
SMALL CHAINS
Gordon Ramsay
AZ
Antonio Carluccio
'BIG' RESTAURANTS
Terence Conran
DESIGN CONSCIOUSNESS

Guy Dimond charts the revolution that has transformed London's restaurants, pubs and cafés over the past 25 years, turning the city into the world's most exciting place to eat and drink.

It's been 25 years since *Time Out* produced its first annual London restaurant guide – a 128-page, black and white paperback costing £1.25, listing 600 eating and drinking venues. Look back at the first edition and it's striking how far both London and the *Eating & Drinking Guide* have come (our readers' survey results, starting on page 4, reflect on what Londoners eat and drink right now). Apart from the obvious increase in the size and number of listings in the guide, we have also been able to document London's year-by-year rise from an also-ran to its present position as the most exciting dining and drinking destination on the planet. The key members of the team behind the guide have changed little in nearly two decades (has it really been that long?), so the long-running reviewers have experienced much of it first-hand: from Marco's meals at Harvey's, through the queues of Wagamama's opening weeks, to the current omnipresence of Gordon Ramsay.

Now, the *Time Out Eating & Drinking Guide* is the best-selling restaurant guide in the UK, and Time Out also produces restaurant guides to other great dining-out cities, such as Paris and New York. But the timing of the launch of the first London edition in 1983 was extremely fortunate. It was just ahead of the curve, just before the mid 1980s revolution of Modern British cooking that transformed the way we Londoners ate. Back in 1982, London's centuries-old love affair with old-school French cooking was clearly evident, both on menus and in our reviews; buttery sauces, heavy reductions and cream desserts were still the norm. Good wine lists were French, or perhaps Spanish and Italian; the New World was seen as a source of lamb chops, not somewhere that made potable wine.

Ethnic food was Indian or Chinese: low-budget, and not as well understood as it is today. Japanese and Thai cuisines were still largely mysteries of the Orient. Our tally of the city's Japanese restaurants totalled only seven places in the first edition; in this 25th edition, we have reviewed 55. The 'name' chefs of the day included the Rouxs at **Le Gavroche** in Mayfair (*see p145*), Nico Ladenis at Chez Nico in Battersea, and Pierre Koffman at La Tante Claire in Chelsea – all cooking bourgeois-style French haute cuisine. In Mayfair, Peter Langan was the host with the mostest. The leading fashionable restaurant in town, though, was the just-opened **Le Caprice** (*see p236*), where – if you could get a table – you could spend a tenner on lunch and enjoy a bit of celebrity-spotting (in the era before celebrity culture became a national obsession). The cocktail of the moment? Pina colada, often accompanying a deep-dish pizza. Ah, those were the days.

1983

In 1983, French 'nouvelle cuisine' is already the subject of ridicule, yet many of its elements are being assimilated into mainstream French-style food: lighter sauces, healthier cooking. Mediterranean approaches to dishes and ingredients are just starting to creep in. It's a heady time in London's West End, as the Thatcher years create a climate of conspicuous consumption – which includes customers throwing their money around in fashionable and smart restaurants. French restaurant **L'Escargot** (*see p107*), which opened in 1981, is the restaurant of choice for Soho's media darlings; more adventurous eaters try the Bombay Brasserie, London's first truly upmarket Indian restaurant, with a menu to match (it opened in 1982). The Zen Chinese restaurant chain boasts it is a monosodium glutamate-free zone, and sports strikingly modernist decor.

1984

The cool crowd flocks to (now defunct) bars such as Zanzibar and Moscow, while after-theatre luvvies pack into Covent Garden's **Joe Allen** (*see p43*). But a revolution is afoot in fine dining. Chef Sally Clarke, who had been inspired by Californian cookery, notably at Alice Waters' restaurant Chez Panisse in Berkeley, brings the same Cal-Ital approach back to the UK to set up her own restaurant, **Clarke's** (*see p238*). Dinner at Clarke's is from a no-choice menu (it remains so until 2007), using only the best seasonal ingredients.

Other chefs also start playing with their food. A talented 23-year-old called Antony Worrall Thompson opens a restaurant called Ménage à Trois, which (with no small irony for Prince Charles' wife) becomes a favourite choice of HRH the Princess of Wales; it is based on the premise that the best dishes are starters and desserts, but 'no intercourse'. French haute cuisine is still far from dead, however; Pierre Koffman's La Tante Claire steps up a few gears by moving premises to 68 Royal Hospital Road in Chelsea (now the location of **Gordon Ramsay** restaurant, *see p148*), and his way with pigs' trotters becomes the stuff of legends.

1985

Sally Clarke isn't the only one reinventing 'British' food. Another young chef called Alastair Little, who had cooked at a trendy Notting Hill bar, 192, sets up his own place on Frith Street in Soho. Restaurant critics are amazed and mystified by turns, unable to categorise this new cuisine: British ingredients simply prepared, such as warm red mullet on a bed of salad, or steamed brill with sorrel sauce. Little draws inspiration from the books of Elizabeth David (1913-92), the British food writer who was an early proselytiser of Mediterranean food. Eventually, a name is coined for this new style of cooking, 'Modern British', and a new era begins. (Little has since moved on, though the restaurant still called **Alastair Little** remains, *see p236*.)

A recently opened private members' club, the Groucho, becomes an immediate hit with London's media set. Soho's fine-dining scene is given added spice by Amin Ali's **Red Fort** (*see p157*), which helps shake off the assumption that Indian food must be cheap (the restaurant has since been reinvented, but both Ali and the Red Fort remain). Up to the mid 1980s, Chinese restaurants are more successful than Indian at serving good food in smart surroundings; **Mr Chow** (*see p77*) in Knightsbridge has combined Peking dishes with Italian service since the 1960s, while **Hunan** (*see p71*) and Ken Lo's Memories of China have kept Pimlico diners sated with delicate noodles and dumplings. Mediterranean, and particularly Italian food, starts to become mainstream too, with Marks & Spencer creating a new Italian-style bread that it calls ciabatta.

1986

London's variety of high-quality fast food has previously been quite limited, but this starts to change when a new sandwich shop, Pret A Manger, opens its first branch in Victoria. As Pret gains ground over the coming years, scores of emulators pop up. In Covent Garden, a branch of Joe Allen – Italian restaurant **Orso** (*see p181*) – is making waves by serving food all-day (how un-Italian!), but using proper, fresh ingredients for its *cucina rustica*. Brixton gets its first ever upmarket restaurant, Twenty Trinity Gardens, which serves a Modern British menu in a part of town that in 1986 is better known for its riots than its red snapper with lime. This is also the year that Spanish tapas bars start appearing – everywhere. Food is beginning to move away from being a niche interest towards the mainstream, as the new, glossy Sunday supplements (a result of improvements in printing technology) start producing pages of full-colour food photography; gastroporn comes of age.

1987

A young, little-known chef opens his own restaurant, Harvey's, overlooking Wandsworth Common. His name: Marco Pierre White. No young chef has ever received such immediate accolades for his cooking, and a book of photographs – *White Heat* – follows within a couple of years, showing him at work with his sous-chefs (including a young Gordon Ramsay). This quickly establishes White's reputation as a bad-boy chef (helped along by numerous articles on a similar theme). White helps propel British fine dining to a new level with dishes that place texture, flavour and freshness above appearance – such as roast rabbit with wild mushrooms or oyster tagliatelle.

Meanwhile, chef Simon Hopkinson, in partnership with Terence Conran, opens **Bibendum** (*see p237*) in the beautifully refurbished Michelin building in Brompton Cross. Up on Kensington Church Street, a more radical approach to restaurant design is heralded by architect Julyan Wickham. His design of **Kensington Place** (*see p238*) is hard-edged, hard-surfaced and relentlessly modernist. Simple, modern brasseries that are only vaguely inspired by France are also doing very well, such as Café Flo, Café Rouge, Dôme, Café Delancey and Le Café des Amis du Vin (now **Café des Amis**, *see p347*).

1988

More architects are at play, this time in Hammersmith. The location of Richard Rogers' architectural practice is a bit remote, so the company decides to set up its own café/restaurant on the ground floor; Rogers' wife, Ruth Rogers, goes into partnership with Rose Gray to start the **River Café** (*see p189*). At first the venue goes unrecognised – this was in the days before restaurant PR – but within a year or two it becomes the place to be, and within a decade

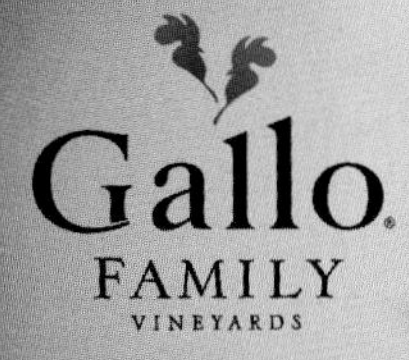
Gallo.
FAMILY
VINEYARDS

Gallo
FAMILY

is being described as the best Italian restaurant in Europe because of its home-style, Tuscan-like dishes. It soon spawns a series of bestselling cookbooks. The River Café's impact goes beyond selling bean soup and pasta salads; chefs such as Sam and Sam Clark (**Moro**, *see p258*), Jamie Oliver and Hugh Fearnley-Whittingstall are among its alumni.

1989

By now, Thai cafés and pubs are starting to pop up all over the capital. The trend was started by the Churchill Arms on Kensington Church Street (still home to the Churchill Thai Kitchen), which hired a Thai chef to prepare food to complement its beers. Another early arrival was the Bedlington Café in Chiswick, which was a greasy spoon caff by day, Thai bistro by night. It takes another decade before there's a Thai restaurant on every high street, but the rise is inexorable. Also in 1989, the first restaurant PR outfits reach maturity; it's a dark art that has since grown into a huge industry and is now (some might argue) more powerful than journalists in ensuring chefs and restaurants gain copious press coverage.

1990

The Ivy (*see p232*) is taken over by the team running Le Caprice restaurant. They refurbish it and quietly launch it as a place where celebrities can relax without the intrusion of paparazzi or gossip-mongers. The charm of the owners at the time, Jeremy King and Chris Corbin, also cements its pole position as the restaurant of the 1990s. The food is secondary, but the menu's not at all bad.

A new wave of eclectic restaurants is starting to emerge in boho districts such as Notting Hill, where First Floor and the Market Bar become the bar-restaurant hangouts of choice; One Ninety Queen's Gate, from chef Antony Worrall Thompson, is cooking an eclectic but more robust style that wins it *Time Out*'s gong for Best New Restaurant of the year.

1991

Terence Conran's ambitions start to be realised as his Butlers Wharf development opens, which includes **Le Pont de la Tour** (*see p245*). The revival of Clerkenwell – in those days, not the haven of loft apartments and DJ bars it is now – starts with the opening of the **Eagle** (*see p117*). This simple pub serves good ales, but is staffed by a group of enthusiastic young chefs who prepare simple but exciting meals in an open kitchen with a blackboard menu. Sounds familiar? The Eagle is the first real 'gastropub' (the term is yet to be coined in 1991), and the idea soon gets copied right across London. A year after the BSE scandal first breaks, diners are starting to show concern about the provenance of the meat they eat. New-wave Italian restaurants are by now rife, karaoke has arrived in London's pubs, and a handful of cheap Japanese cafés start to introduce Japanese food to a new, appreciative audience.

1992

A young unknown food writer called Nigel Slater is hired by *Marie Claire* magazine, where he stays for the next five years before being head-hunted by the *Observer* newspaper. **The Square** (*see p146*), the **Brackenbury** (*see p239*), Stephen Bull – all open: this is a great year for British cooking. **Pied à Terre** (*see p140*) also opens on Charlotte Street, under chef Richard Neat. **Chutney Mary** (*see p160*), a new-wave regional Indian restaurant, opens on the King's Road. One of the most significant openings of the year, however, is an oriental noodle bar in a basement near the British Museum: **Wagamama** (*see p252*). It's no exaggeration to say that Alan Yau's creation (which he no longer owns) completely shook up our ideas about oriental food, canteen dining and – of course – noodle dishes. September sees Black Wednesday, when the pound crashes against other currencies; this curbs the heady confidence (and expense accounts) of City spenders for months to come.

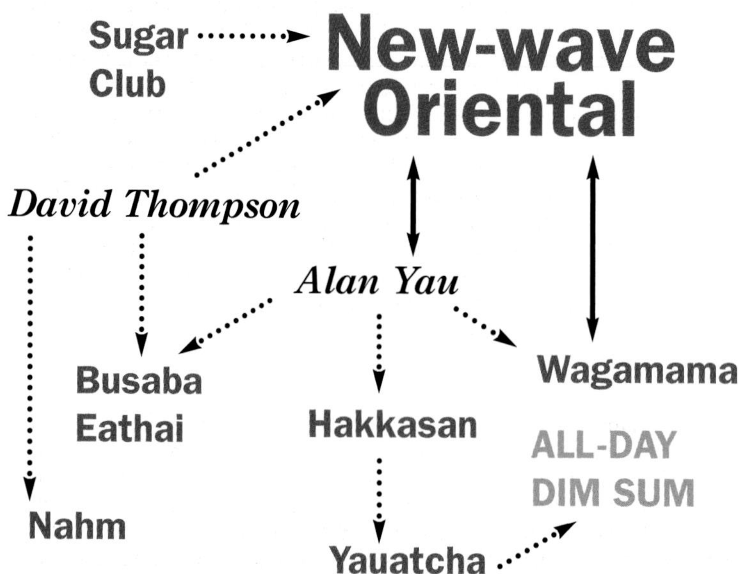

1993

Keith Floyd's latest TV series, *Far Flung Floyd*, picks up on the growing interest in the food of South-east Asia, particularly Thai food, which is by now commonplace in London. Terence Conran pushes the boat out with a startling revamp of **Quaglino's** (*see p236*), which immediately becomes one of the most glamorous restaurants of the year – and creates a huge demand for (stolen) ashtrays, taken as trophies of a visit. Conran also kick-starts the trend for super-sized restaurants, and becomes one of the largest employers of Australian staff in the capital.

Other notable openings of the year include: **Ransome's Dock** (*see p242*), **Banners** (*see p60*), Bistrot Bruno, the **Fifth Floor** (*see p233*), the Fire Station and, of course, Granita – famous for the Brown-Blair 'Deal' (hard to imagine then, but the Labour government has outlasted the restaurant). There is a growing number of low-budget, but excellent Turkish grills in Dalston, such as **Mangal Ocakbasi** (*see p281*); Vietnamese cafés such as **Viet Hoa** (*see p295*) are also starting to take root in Hackney. Beach Blanket Babylon was the Notting Hill bar causing a stir.

1994

Following on from Quaglino's, a load more large-scale restaurants open up; the addition of **Butlers Wharf Chop House** (*see p69*) brings the number of Conran seats at Butlers Wharf alone to 770. But right in the heart of Soho, it is Oliver Peyton's Atlantic Bar & Grill that makes a big splash. For a few months at least, the Atlantic is *the* bar to be seen in, with huge queues and a notorious, unpredictable door policy; it is also cocktail heaven – in Dick's Bar, at least, run by the legendary Dick Bradsell. The very first cybercafés start appearing; customers need careful instruction in how to use the interweb, as 'message boards', 'websites', 'email' and 'search engines' are still unknown to all but the geekiest of computer nerds.

1995

This is the year that American-style coffee bars begin cropping up everywhere, and new expressions such as 'caffè latte' start appearing in everyday language. Notting Hill is still maintaining some urban cool, greatly helped by a new restaurant on All Saints Road called the Sugar Club, which the highly original and talented chef Peter Gordon has brought all the way from New Zealand – together with his two business partners. The original Sugar Club's years of brilliance are numbered, but the restaurant has a huge impact as 'fusion' dishes start to become more common on London menus.

Meanwhile, on the fringes of Smithfield Market, a very different but equally creative approach is fully formed. Chef (and former architect) Fergus Henderson, formerly of the French House Dining Room, converts a former smokehouse into a new style of British restaurant: **St John** (*see p63*). With signature dishes such as roasted bone marrow with parsley salad, or eccles cakes served with lancashire cheese, St John quickly becomes one of the most critically acclaimed restaurants in the country. The original branch of the South Indian vegetarian restaurant **Rasa** (*see p166*) also opens, bringing real Keralite cooking to Stoke Newington.

1996

Restaurateur Oliver Peyton is nothing if not enterprising, and his latest Marc Newson-designed restaurant, Coast, wows the critics with its extraordinary futuristic interior and excellent cooking from chef Stephen Terry. However, the paying public are less convinced; Coast closes within a couple of years. Antony Worrall Thompson's growing empire – he's running 15 restaurants by this stage – appears to have clouded his business judgement, and he opens the vast but ill-fated Thunder Road, which closes within weeks. (These days, as well as a successful media career AWT runs some good little steak restaurants in west London.) A few of the other big openings find the going tough too: L'Odeon shuts, as does Richard Neat's Neat. Impressive new restaurants with greater longevity include **Tamarind** (*see p152*), a top-end Indian venue then under chef Atul Kochhar. Bank and the **Oxo Tower Restaurant, Bar & Brasserie** (*see p243*) are two of the year's other big openings.

1997

Gary Rhodes makes his first TV appearance, and will forever be remembered for his sticky-up hair (even though he's had it trimmed close for years now). In Hoxton and Shoreditch, the first cool bars start opening to cater for the influx of young designers, artists and their ilk moving into the areas in search of cheap rents. Trendy bar-restaurant **Cantaloupe** (*see p179*) becomes the focus for that community, along with nearby pub the Bricklayers' Arms. Exmouth Market sees a revival of its fortunes when a young couple, Sam and Samantha Clark (formerly of the River Café and the Eagle) start cheffing at their own Spanish-Moorish restaurant **Moro** (*see p258*). Terence Conran opens **Bluebird** (*see p239*) on the King's Road, while the peripatetic Jean-Christophe Novelli opens his ill-fated Maison Novelli in Clerkenwell; one of many such misadventures for the unlucky chef. North African **Momo** (*see p250*) becomes one of the West End's most fashionable joints. Conveyor-belt sushi is taking London by storm too, as it's introduced and popularised by the **Moshi Moshi Sushi** chain (*see p196*). But the restaurant that really shakes up Japanese food is **Nobu** (*see p199*); the Peruvian-Japanese flavour combinations really are like nothing seen before, and soon signature dishes such as black cod with miso and new-style sashimi start appearing on menus all over town.

1998

Cheeky chappie Jamie Oliver appears on TV for the first time as *The Naked Chef*, while Britart maverick Damien Hirst turns restaurateur with the opening of Pharmacy restaurant. The choice of name upsets pharmacists, and for a while the neon letters outside are switched to glow 'army chap', then 'archy ramp'. Fortunately, not too many people wander into the bar waving their prescriptions, and the name soon reverts. In Mayfair, the **Avenue** (*see p235*) opens – one of the last really big, austere restaurants. Shy, voluptuous food-writer-turned-TV-star Nigella Lawson publishes *How to Eat* and quickly becomes the first-ever female food writer pin-up. The first farmers' markets begin to appear in London. Gordon Ramsay has a spat with his employers at **Aubergine** (*see p148*), and leaves to set up his own little place – modestly called **Gordon Ramsay** (*see p148*) – less than a mile away; nearly all his staff go with him, but the resulting pressure on Ramsay is captured in the TV series *Boiling Point*, which makes Ramsay a household name. Alan Yau opens his first branch of the Thai restaurant chain **Busaba Eathai** (*see p269*), fighting back after losing ownership of Wagamama.

1999

A year of trends that appear and disappear like poppies in a field. At last, London picks up on the microbrewery trend that had already swept the US (where they are called brewpubs). Oliver Peyton's **Mash** (*see p175*) is the most ambitious, and the Soho Brewing Company is soon followed by several others over the next couple of years. The bar scene is unmistakably moving east, with new openings such as the Shoreditch Electricity Showrooms leading the way.

High-concept, 'big design' restaurants continue to open, but struggle; Oliver Peyton's Isola opens many months late, and the Belgo Group's Belgo Zuid closes just a couple of years after opening. Some chefs go back to basics instead; Theodore Kyriakou, who set up Livebait then sold it, starts the Real Greek in Hoxton (which he has now also sold). Juice bars and soup bars appear – and disappear.

2000

The Great Eastern Hotel at Liverpool Street is given a thorough revamp by Terence Conran in a hugely ambitious redevelopment of hotel, bars and restaurants. Ian Schrager's second hotel, the Sanderson, opens and immediately becomes the place of choice for the 'see and be seen' crowd – just like his first hotel, St Martins Lane, did in 1999. **Tate Modern** (with its spacious café, *see p58*) opens, and becomes the focal point of Bankside – though it will be months before you can reach it via the newly built Millennium Bridge, which is wobblier than a panna cotta. East London continues to blossom with ambitious new restaurant/bar complexes, such as **Smiths of Smithfield** (*see p232*) and the Light Bar in Shoreditch.

2001

A good year for Alan Yau as he opens **Hakkasan** (*see p76*): both press and diners are wowed by the stunning looks and stunning food of this highly original Chinese fine-dining restaurant. (Right to the present day Hakkasan is consistently near the top of nearly every 'favourite restaurant' poll.) This is one of the last successful 'big' restaurants to open, though; many subsequent ones flounder. A trend away from super-sized restaurants becomes evident with the likes of **La Trompette** in Chiswick (*see p108*): an excellent neighbourhood restaurant that sets the standard for others to follow. Even the master of the gastrodromes, Terence Conran, gets in on the act with his own version of a neighbourhood restaurant: **Almeida** (*see p113*), in Islington.

Shoreditch comes of age with its own, first (and arguably, still its only) outstanding neighbourhood restaurant, **Eyre Brothers** (*see p133*). Stephen Bull, one of the founding fathers of the Modern British food movement, closes his London restaurants to run a gastropub in Herefordshire – it's the end of an era. Gastropubs are at their zenith, with even the big pubco operators going gastro – and creating some impressive results, such as **Lots Road Pub & Dining Room** (*see p121*).

Iqbal Wahhab's **Cinnamon Club** (*see p158*) wows the critics with its Indian haute cuisine, and amuses TV viewers with the documentary about its late opening, *Trouble at the Top*. **Baltic** (*see p91*) reassesses Polish and Baltic food, years before Poland joins the EU. And last but not least, **Gourmet Burger Kitchen** (*see p300*) in Battersea kick-starts a new trend in (me-too) gourmet burger bars. A British outbreak of foot and mouth disease helps raise consciousness about the provenance of meat.

2002

Fifteen restaurant (*see p193*) opens in Shoreditch in a blaze of publicity resulting from the TV series *Jamie's Kitchen* – and reviews penned by Jamie Oliver's chums and fans. It's an instant success. Gordon Ramsay's influence continues to grow as he opens yet another hotel restaurant, this time in the Connaught hotel, fronted by Angela Hartnett, in a triumph of clever marketing that puts even Jamie Oliver to shame. (The resulting reviews are lukewarm, however.) It's a different story back in Shoreditch, where an old pub is bought by a visionary threesome and converted into a shabby-chic French restaurant, appropriately called **Les Trois Garçons** (*see p113*). *Time Out* reviews it a fortnight after it opens; it quickly becomes the hangout of choice for the Britart crowd, and remains the most fashionable local landmark to this day. Even further east, in Wapping, a more ambitious art/design/culinary project converts a former pumping station into the huge space that is **Wapping Food** (*see p246*).

Over in west London, chef Henry Harris sets up the perfect neighbourhood brasserie in **Racine** (*see p105*) on the Old Brompton Road. Rather more daring is Will Ricker's pan-oriental **E&O** (*see p253*), which gets very mixed reviews yet immediately fills with Notting Hill's beautiful people. But the restaurant that everyone has been anticipating – and is months overdue, and millions over budget – is **Sketch** (*see p177*). Costing an estimated £12 million, the interiors certainly don't disappoint; however, the elitist door policy, capricious service and exorbitant prices make some wonder if Sketch will survive. (Five years on, it's doing just fine.) Japanese food continues to grow and evolve, with fashionable new eaterie **Zuma** (*see p198*) opening in Knightsbridge.

2003

'Back to our roots!' seems to be the battle cry from Kevin Finch as he saves Alfredo's greasy spoon in Islington, with its splendid old interior of melamine, aged wood and polished metal, by converting it into a delightful **S&M Café** (meaning sausage and mash, of course; *see p303*). Heritage is also being preserved south of the river, as Borough Market is little by little being reclaimed by a bunch of fine-food enthusiasts and turned into London's most exciting food market; soon, Borough Market is to become one of London's top tourist attractions.

Chris Corbin and Jeremy King have long since sold their shares in Le Caprice and the Ivy, but they've not turned their backs on restaurants just yet; their renovation of the former Wolseley car showroom on Piccadilly becomes London's most dazzling European-style brasserie, the **Wolseley** (*see p235*). Celebrated chef Atul Kochhar (lately of *Great British Menu* fame) leaves Tamarind to set up his own place, **Benares** (*see p151*): yet another jewel in London's crown. Over in Shoreditch, the three garçons buck the trend for industrial bar interiors by opening the opulent, fantastic, and kitsch **Loungelover** bar (*see p338*).

2004

Good food can be found in the most unexpected places, as Skye Gyngell, chef at **Petersham Nurseries Café** (*see p247*) near Richmond, demonstrates. Her dishes are served in a garden centre café, but the cooking ticks all the right boxes: seasonal, simple, fresh. Simplicity seems one of the key trends of the year, with an unfussy fish and chip restaurant – **Fish Club**, in Battersea (*see p317*) – putting many long-established London chippies to shame with the quality of its ingredients and side dishes. In Islington, Yotam

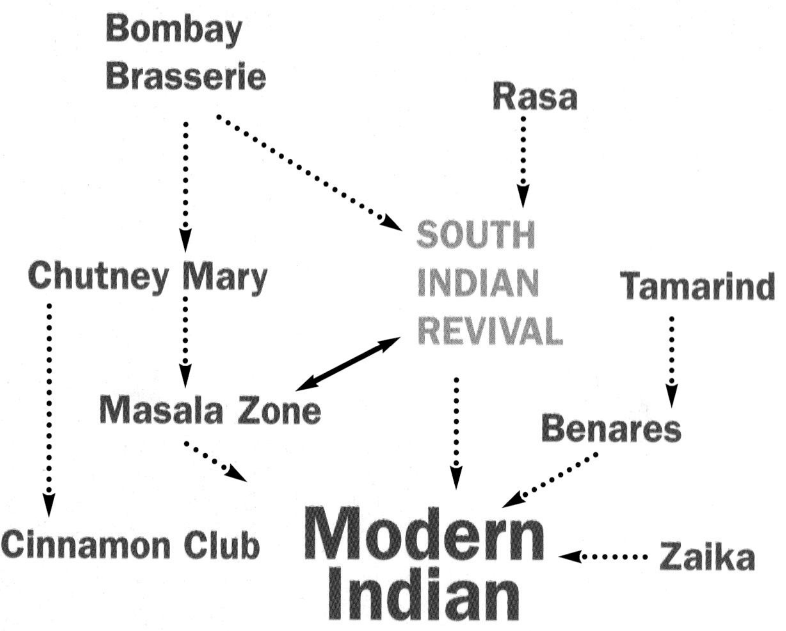

David Tang, who creates a vision of art deco Shanghai elegance with a slightly pedestrian Cantonese menu.

Korean cafés become more numerous, but moving upmarket proves difficult; fusion-Korean Wizzy closes within a couple of years, while **Asadal** (*see p216*) succeeds, despite its odd basement location next to Holborn tube station. Fine-dining restaurant Jason Atherton's **Maze** (*see p146*) picks up just about every gong going for its creative approach to canapé-like small dishes.

2006

A good year for Oliver Peyton, who seems to open a new restaurant or café as often as the rest of us open a newspaper. Pick of the bunch is the **National Dining Rooms** (*see p66*) – not for its tricky location in the National Gallery, but for chef Jess Dunford Wood's take on proper British ingredients. The reception is not as positive for **Konstam at the Prince Albert** (*see p64*), which restricts ingredient sourcing to within the tube network; many people feel this is a gimmick, though the cooking is generally good. Burlesque- and cabaret-style nightclubs such as **Pigalle Club** (*see p353*) start popping up, though in most the food and drink is definitely secondary to the entertainment. A very different approach to nightlife is taken by Favela Chic, which trashes a once-beautiful bar in Shoreditch to make it resemble a Brazilian slum. It then installs some good DJs, serves utterly basic drinks and food – and the queue stretches right around the corner. We're much more impressed with the food and drink at the **Ambassador** (*see p230*), a bistro/wine bar in Exmouth Market; it has an excellent wine list by the glass and good cooking too. It's pipped to the post of Best New Restaurant in the 2006 Time Out Eating & Drinking Awards by the all-round appeal of **Arbutus** (*see p236*), Anthony Demetre and Will Smith's new Modern European restaurant in Soho.

A sense of humour seems to be creeping back into eating and drinking venues. Pâtisserie-boulangerie **Macaron** (*see p310*) kits out its staff in burlesque-style uniforms, while **Gilgamesh** (*see p255*) creates a warehouse-sized restaurant with huge carvings copied from the British Museum – and adds a retractable roof for good measure (or should that read 'good weather'?). **Yakitoria** (*see p203*) gets off to a rocky start, but soon gathers pace with its modern Japanese menu and stunning modernist design; it goes on to win the Best Design category in the Time Out Eating & Drinking Awards. But it's **Bar Shu** (*see p79*) that is one of the most applauded new developments of the year – not for burlesque outfits or statues of Mesopotamian gods, but for introducing a convincing and extensive Sichuan menu to London.

2007

For a detailed account of what's happened in London in the year immediately preceding publication of this guide in September 2007, turn to page 18.

Ottolenghi's second café, **Ottolenghi** (*see p180*), becomes the flagship for his new style of modern Mediterranean food, which is colourful, vibrant and has particular appeal for vegetarians. It's not long before Ottolenghi is commissioned as a cookery columnist for the *Guardian*. The rise and rise of Indian food is consolidated by the opening of **Amaya** (*see p151*) in Knightsbridge: a high-end, design-conscious restaurant to pull in the Nobu/Zuma crowd. Alan Yau's Soho offshoot of Hakkasan, **Yauatcha** (*see p80*), kicks off a new trend by offering an all-day dim sum menu; soon, several other Chinese restaurants follow suit.

2005

Some experimental restaurant 'concepts' such as Pengelley's and Graze wither within months of opening, but occasionally the simplest ideas hit you between the eyes, making you wonder why no one thought of it before: one such is the Soho houmous bar **Hummus Bros** (*see p299*). A few tried-and-tested ideas from further afield do very well, including Argentinian grill Santa Maria del Buen Ayre (now called just **Buen Ayre**; *see p51*). At last, we see the Italian enoteca idea translated to the UK; **Vinoteca** (*see p346*) is one of the first casual wine bars that also allows you to buy bottles to take home.

Really good neighbourhood restaurants can never fail, it seems, such as **Sam's Brasserie & Bar** (*see p237*) in Chiswick. Chris and Jeff Galvin prove there's still life in good French restaurants too, with their **Galvin Bistrot de Luxe** (*see p105*). The British food revival is in full-flow, with exciting new restaurants such as **Roast** (*see p69*), but also old favourites such as Irish seafood bar **Bentley's Oyster Bar & Grill** (*see p95*) being given a brush up by chef Richard Corrigan. Overseas investors are taking a keen interest in London too; some perish, for instance, a steak-frites chain from Paris (Entrecôte de Café de Paris), but others blossom, such as pâtisserie **Ladurée** (*see p306*) in its Harrods hothouse. After Alan Yau pulls out, **China Tang** (*see p78*) in the Dorchester hotel proceeds with entrepreneur

GRANA PADANO
NATURAL
ORIGINAL
GENUINE
APPETIZING
ITALIAN
INIMITABLE
BUONO
GRANA PADANO
G
GRANA PADANO
P
Grana Padano.
The best-selling italian PDO cheese in the world.
Inimitabile dal 1135

The year that was

Guy Dimond takes a look at the openings, closures, movings and shakings in London's restaurant scene over the past 12 months.

For the last 25 years we've had a crack team of expert chowhounds combing the city for the most original bars, the best-value meals and the most welcoming service, and assessing every type of world cuisine. During that time we've seen what can only be described as a revolution in the dining habits of Londoners – and our reviewers have always been at the forefront of new discoveries and charting new trends.

It doesn't look as if London's eating-out boom is damping down in the slightest. Every survey, including Time Out's own, shows that Londoners are dining out more than ever before, and becoming more adventurous. Over the past 12 months, since the publication of our last *Eating & Drinking Guide,* we've seen plenty of new developments that are worth drawing attention to. Here are some of the best.

2006

SEPTEMBER

A total of £5 million is spent ripping out the (beautiful) interior of what used to be Christine Manfield's East@West, and turning it into the latest branch of the international chain **L'Atelier de Joël Robuchon** (*see p232*). The money certainly shows, with an elegant and stunning interior based on contemporary Tokyo fine-dining restaurants, though the cost of a meal here proves to be just as eyebrow-raising as the look. At around £150 for two for dinner, it's a 'one pound to one euro' exchange rate compared to the Paris branch.

Oliver Peyton's mission to transform London's museum caffs gathers pace as he wins the contract for the Wallace Collection, and turns the courtyard into a fine French restaurant called the **Wallace** (*see p106*); while over on Tottenham Court Road, his café inside the Heal's department store, called **Meals** (*see p306*), shows that department store cafés can do a lot more than cheese sandwiches and scones. Oh, and in the same month, Peyton also opens his British food shop at the entrance to Heal's, called Peyton & Byrne (Byrne being his mother's maiden name). The second **Peyton & Byrne** (*see p305*) is a proper sit-down café inside the Wellcome Collection, whereas the first is just a takeaway. A good year for Peyton, and a good year for people who like his sausage rolls too.

OCTOBER

'Molecular gastronomy' is one of those catchy terms with no clear definition, but chefs and commentators like to bandy it around. If it's done well, you get the alchemical magic of Heston Blumenthal; done badly, you get a dog's dinner. Our experience of Bacchus restaurant in Hoxton tends towards the latter, and many fellow reviewers agree.

The Narrow

A more straightforward approach to modern cooking is demonstrated at **Lola Rojo** (*see p265*), a modern Spanish restaurant in Battersea that's inspired by the wave of *nueva cocina* sweeping across Spain. Other formulas are better tested, but although not winning any points for originality, the **Big Chill House** (*see p331*) in King's Cross is just what most people want from a music bar: good music, good drinks, friendly vibe, not too expensive.

Odette's (*see p246*) in Primrose Hill takes a very different approach to produce what is also a successful outcome. For years it had languished as a romantic neighbourhood restaurant of modest ambition, but the new impresario owner, Vince Power, changes all that by installing a top-class chef (Bryn Williams) and giving the place a Shaun Clarkson makeover that would be the envy of *Changing Rooms*. Some people lament the loss of a timeless romantic spot; others are glad to see top-class cooking here at last.

And it seems Oliver Peyton is in danger of getting bored this month after frenetic activity in September, so he opens yet another gallery café – this time in the National Gallery, called the **National Café** (*see p56*).

NOVEMBER

November kicks off with the arrival of chef Tom Aikens' affordable brasserie, **Tom's Kitchen** (*see p57*), just round the corner from his haute-cuisine restaurant. It's just one of a number of new openings this year that sees big-name chefs moving into cheaper territory. We like the design and the food, but the service still leaves something to be desired.

Although past its prime, Notting Hill is an area thick with pretension and experimentation, and it can still put on a good

Snazz Sichuan

Odette's

L'Atelier de Joël Robuchon

show for people wanting an unusual dining experience. One such restaurant is **Bumpkin** (*see p239*), surely one of the most ridiculous concepts we've seen in a long time: an urban recreation of a rural pub idyll – except you can't actually pop in for a pint (it's a restaurant pretending to be a country pub). Needless to say, Bumpkin is a smash hit with Notting Hill folk from the first week. We wish them luck.

Although Shoreditch and Notting Hill have the liveliest bar scenes outside Soho, the more taciturn Mayfair can occasionally produce a winner. **Mahiki** (*see p333*) is the latest Polynesian-style tiki bar to open in town (around 50 years after the trend peaked in the US), and it quickly becomes the haunt of Princes Harry and William, Kate Middleton, Madonna and Guy Ritchie. Bus-loads of B-list celebs and wannabes soon fill the bar – we just hope it's not the Guilty Pleasures-style playlist that's pulling them in.

DECEMBER

We've always puzzled by how the population of Fulham seems to feel a spiritual bond with Tuscan peasants, as evidenced by the number of *River Café Cook Book*s seen on Fulham shelves. But now, even the international jet set is able to get in on the act with Italian peasant food at Mayfair prices in a Park Lane hotel. We love the food at **Theo Randall at the InterContinental** (*see p146*), we just think the setting is a bit odd – and with a meal for two costing around £140, we wonder how many Tuscan peasants are going to be eating this *cucina rustica*. We also like the new **Trenta** (*see p183*), a neighbourhood restaurant just off the Edgware Road that costs less than half the price of the InterContinental for expertly made, authentic Italian cooking.

Environmental consciousness now touches on every aspect of our daily lives, as it should. But few restaurants make such a concerted effort to do the right thing – from filtering their own-bottled drinking water to recycling everything they can, and buying local produce as much as possible – as **Acorn House** (*see p56*). It's a brilliant neighbourhood restaurant, and we hope to see similar operations elsewhere in London.

Just in time for Christmas, Jeremy King and Chris Corbin – who once ran the Ivy and now own the Wolseley – open a terrific new restaurant, **St Alban** (*see p132*). But, in a move more shocking than catching Santa Claus kissing mum, they

Goodbye

We bid farewell to the A-Z of restaurants that have changed hands or shut since the last edition of the guide. The following is just a choice selection of the year's closures.

Arkansas Café
Bubba's barbecue pit in Old Spitalfields Market baked its last hog – but Bubba's moving to the US Embassy to cater there instead.

Armadillo
Hackney's Broadway Market no longer steps to this Latin beat.

Astor Bar & Grill
The relaunch of the site that used to be Atlantic Bar & Grill failed.

Babes 'n' Burgers
Clearly not yummy enough for Notting Hill's mummies.

Ben's Thai
Thai restaurant above the Warrington pub in Maida Vale, now a Gordon Ramsay Holdings gastropub.

Blandford Street
Veggie-friendly Modern European restaurant.

Bluebird Dining Rooms
Chef Mark Broadbent's excellent British dining room at Bluebird has been turned into a private function room.

Boteca Carioca
London's best Brazilian food, for a few months.

Calabash
Covent Garden old-timer that closed along with the Africa Centre.

Canyon
Once-stylish Richmond riverside restaurant, now a branch of Gaucho Grill.

Deya
A Modern Indian venue that couldn't take the heat.

Fiore
This hothouse flower in St James's turned out to be an annual, not a perennial.

Found
A shebeen entrepreneur turned his hand to running a restaurant in Shoreditch for a few months, but balancing the books proved to be harder than pouring the drinks.

1492
In 1492 Christopher Columbus sailed the ocean blue, but in 2007 this Latin American restaurant in Fulham also set sail.

Globe
Swiss Cottage restaurant with a famous Thursday night cabaret act; what a drag it's now shut.

Hosteria del Pesce
Short-lived Italian seafood restaurant that was a fish out of water in Fulham.

Jack & Lulu's
The classroom bell rang on this children's play restaurant weeks after it opened.

Mawar
A budget Malaysian canteen on the Edgware Road that took a long wok in 2007.

Mocotó
Bar-restaurant that was as showy (but shorter-lived) than a Brazilian carnival costume.

Neal Street
Antonio Carluccio's flagship restaurant didn't have its lease renewed – but he'll be back, in the new Carluccio's (see *p23*).

Pescador
Portuguese fish restaurant – gone fishing.

Pizzeria Castello
Baking dough no more.

Tugga
Chelsea Portuguese bar and restaurant with less staying power than Jose Mourinho.

Vinifera
Clapham wine bar swallowed up by rival Green & Blue.

Wizzy
Modern Korean fusion food? We loved it, but Wizzy soon wozn't.

Xich Lo
Vietnamese-Norwegian fusion restaurant in Clerkenwell.

Zinc Bar & Grill
Sent down the plug-hole when D&D London took over.

adopt a modern Mediterranean menu and a curiously modern design that divides the critics (most of whom seem more interested in the various celebs the place attracts). We think St Alban is one of the best new places of the year, which is why it makes our shortlist for the Best New Restaurant Award in 2007.

2007

JANUARY

The reopening of **Scott's** (*see p95*), the latest splendid restaurant from Caprice Holdings (which owns Le Caprice, the Ivy and others), is running a bit late. In fact, quite a few weeks late, as its licence has been held up by complaints from a neighbour. But rather than call back hundreds of potential diners and cancel their bookings, the owners honour the bookings – and give diners a free meal. All of them. The loss to Caprice Holdings is estimated at £350,000 by some. We just wish all bungled openings were treated with such generosity by the proprietors. Scott's has since become an established favourite with Mayfair high society.

Another triumph for British stiff upper lip over adversity is the huge success of the **Empress of India** (*see p70*). Adversity? Well, it's a smart restaurant in Victoria Park, a location that could be considered risky for a heroically British menu containing the likes of oysters, roast duck and spotted dick. It's an instant hit.

Another recent Hackney success story is Santa Maria del Buen Ayre, a little Argentinian steak grill in Broadway Market. At the start of 2007 the owners open a branch in Battersea, then weeks later there's a falling-out, which leads to the original founders splitting the business in two, hence the Battersea branch taking a new name, **Santa Maria del Sur** (*see p51*). Whatever they call it, it's a great place for steak, with a menu that's very close to the Hackney original.

Santa Maria isn't the only example of restaurateurs taking a foreign concept and successfully adapting it to London; the team behind the much-praised Fino does this with **Barrafina** (*see p261*), a Soho tapas bar that they freely admit has been inspired by Barcelona's Cal Pep (though the prices here are very London).

FEBRUARY

The tiny Soho sandwich bar, **Fernandez & Wells**, is such a big hit that a second, coffee-bar branch (*see p307*) opens just around the corner a few months later. Unexpected parts of London see significant new openings too, such as Borough, now home to **Magdalen** (*see p69*). And the Paddington regeneration caused by the new Paddington Basin development gets a further boost with the arrival of beautiful Chinese restaurant **Pearl Liang** (*see p79*).

MARCH

To protect the consumer, it's the law in Britain that wine can only be served in fixed measurements: 125ml, 175ml and multiples thereof. Which is great for preventing you being ripped off by unscrupulous bartenders, but less useful if you want to try a selection of wines in small taster-sized measurements, called flights. Various methods have been tried to get around this restrictive law, but the Sampler – an off-licence in Islington – has come up with the clever idea of selling credit to customers, who can then try small measures of the dozens of wines on display in computerised dispensers. Quite brilliant. Not so brilliant when Selfridges tries to use the same idea and technology in their **Wonder Bar** (*see p347*) a few months later – the latter is a wine bar, not an off-licence, so Westminster Council forces Selfridges back to the standard glass measures. A great pity, we feel.

Copying ideas is rife in the restaurant world too, and we're pleased to see the growth of proper Sichuan restaurants in London, following on from the success of last year's Bar Shu. **Snazz Sichuan** (*see p76*) hits the right notes of chilli-heat and sichuan pepper numbingness, and has been welcomed by London's Chinese food enthusiasts.

Oriental food often has a more tortuous path to reach London, and **Haiku** (*see p252*) is one of the least expected. It's a branch of a restaurant in Cape Town, and the results are fairly successful; the Indian, Chinese and Japanese dishes on the menu are created by dedicated chefs working in separate kitchen areas, which seems to beat the 'jack of all cuisines, masters of none' approach that most pan-oriental restaurants adopt.

APRIL

Gordon Ramsay Holdings hasn't been idle in 2007, and its latest project is a departure from the norm: a gastropub. Most diners arrive sceptical, but leave converted by the excellent food and good service – those that can get a table at the **Narrow** (*see p125*), that is. **Great Queen Street** (*see p64*) is from the team behind the Anchor & Hope; here they take similar rustic, British-leaning gastropub food and put it in a restaurant setting.

Kingsland Road in Shoreditch has for many years been a Little Vietnam for people seeking cheap Vietnamese food, and while the food is certainly cheap, it isn't always authentic (the distinguished Song Que being an honourable exception). The arrival of **Thang Loi** (*see p294*) is, we hope, the way forward for the many Vietnamese cafés in the area. It serves an extensive Vietnamese menu centred on one region (Hanoi and the north), eschewing the usual Sino-Viet dishes dumbed-down for non-Vietnamese customers.

MAY

London's luxury hotel market continues to boom, as wealthy foreign visitors seem undeterred by the city's alarmingly high room rates. Sometimes, though, you've just got to say 'I'm worth it', and places like the Haymarket Hotel are clearly aimed at people who think they're worth quite a lot. Ostentatious, sure, but design hotels don't come much better than this; its bar and restaurant **Brumus** (*see p186*) doesn't quite live up to the same high standards as the design, but it's an appealing Italian restaurant nonetheless.

Nostalgia and regeneration are common themes in London restaurants, which are very often built on the site of a previous dining establishment. However, the new owners of **Geales** (*see p97*) don't see the need to change much; the name, the fact it's a fish restaurant, and even the 15p-a-head cover charge are all retained, while superchef Garry Hollihead ensures that the quality of the cooking is now never less than excellent.

But by far the biggest publicised takeover and reinvention of the month is the conversion of the Barkers department store in Kensington into the UK's first (and flagship) **Whole Foods Market** store (*see p289* **Shelf life**). This US chain champions organic produce, and it's quite extraordinary to see the Whole Foods machine being put into action with British producers and customers.

JUNE

The Swedes like a good *fika* (coffee break) and the Finns love their *suomi-kahvila* (coffeeshops) too. In June, **Nordic Bakery** (*see p308*) successfully transplants a Swedish-Finnish bakery and coffeeshop into the heart of Soho, complete with savoury snacks, alluring cakes and caffeine highs. As yet, Soho's hipsters don't seem to have heard the buzz about this delightful place; maybe they're hard of herring.

Ever wondered where the next new thing is going to be? Richard Bigg of the Cantaloupe Group clearly thinks it's King's Cross, as only months after selling his pioneering Cantaloupe bar in Shoreditch, he opens a Spanish tapas bar called **Camimo** (*see p261*) on what he hopes is now the right side of the tracks.

Gary Rhodes is one of the few top-level chefs who doesn't run his own restaurants; he prefers to work for a big company that runs restaurants inside hotels and other landmarks. His latest restaurant, confusingly called **Rhodes W1** (*see p143*) – just like the next-door brasserie of the same name – pulls out all the stops to impress: Kelly Hoppen design, Swarovski crystal chandeliers, pouffes to place your lap-dog on. It's a good restaurant, but expensive. And if what really decides a restaurant's success is location, location, location, then we're backing **Skylon** (*see p243*); housed in the front of the Royal Festival Hall, with spectacular night-time views of the Thames, this is D&D London's first new restaurant since its buyout from Conran Restaurants – and it's certainly one to wow visitors with.

JULY

It was the people running the Cumberland Hotel at Marble Arch who recruited the services of Gary Rhodes to manage their new restaurants. They're nothing if not ambitious, and have also opened a vast new bar that, they claim, is a 'Shoreditch-style bar': **Carbon** (*see p333*).

July 2007 is, of course, the summer of no summer at all, but as well as watching flood reports it's possible to enjoy a taste of the Sardinian seaside at **Olivomare** (*see p94*), the latest in Pimlico's Olivo chain. And the flavour of Tuscany arrives in Covent Garden with the opening of **Scoop** (*see p310* **Ice-cream shops**), a Tuscan-style ice-cream parlour in Shorts Gardens that brings with it a real flavour of summer.

Another foreign import we are pleased to welcome is **La Petite Maison** (*see p106*), a branch of a restaurant in Nice. Treasures that are more home-grown include the delightful West Dulwich pub the **Rosendale** (*see p125*), the charming **Shipp's Tea Rooms** (*see p311*), and **Wild Honey** (*see p235*), the magnificent new sibling to the Time Out award-winning Arbutus restaurant.

As we go to press in late August 2007, there are lots of exciting new openings to look forward to – you'll find these listed in the **Hello** box, which starts on p23.

See the latest restaurant and bar reviews at...
www.timeout.com/restaurants

Hello

As the guide went to press, scores of new restaurant openings were being planned. Dates may change – as may other details.

2007 SEPTEMBER

Fortnum & Mason

181 Piccadilly, W1 (7734 8040).
As part of Fortnum & Mason's refurbishment, a few new eating and drinking places will be opening. First to start trading is the Parlour, styled liked a 1950s ice-cream parlour; the Fountain will reopen as a brasserie, the Gallery will then open where Patio used to be; and eventually, at the end of October, the St James's restaurant will reopen.

Kenza

10 Devonshire Square, EC2 (7929 5533).
A new Lebanese restaurant from Tony Kitous, who also runs Moroccan restaurant Pasha in Gloucester Road and Lebanese Levant in Marylebone.

Beach Blanket Babylon

19-23 Bethnal Green Road, E1 (www.beachblanket.co.uk).
The Notting Hill bar of the 1990s, BBB is opening a new branch in Shoreditch, which will include a restaurant, cinema, contemporary art gallery, roof terrace and – planned for 2008 – a private members' lounge.

O2 Centre

Peninsula Square, SE10 (www.theo2.com).
The bars and a handful of chain eating places are already open, but three more slightly plusher restaurants – called Raan, Britain and America – open in September. Raan will serve grilled Indian food, while Britain and America will, unsurprisingly, serve the dishes of the UK and US.

Carluccio's

Corner of King Street and Garrick Street, WC2 (www.carluccios.com).
Antonio Carluccio's Neal Street restaurant closed in 2007, but he has bounced back with this venture. The ground floor houses a food shop and caffè, while upstairs is another caffè area and a bar/private dining room. The food shop will serve an extended range of fresh and packaged deli items, similar to the Carluccio's Caffès.

Sake No Hana

23 St James's Street, SW1 (020 7925 8988)
The unlucky site that used to be Shumi and before that Che restaurant is now in the far more capable hands of Alan Yau, who is turning it into an upscale Japanese restaurant and sushi bar.

Prince Arthur

95 Forest Road, E8.
This fine-dining restaurant/ gastropub is from brothers Tom and Ed Martin, who also run the Empress of India, the Gun and others.

Hereford Road

3 Hereford Road, W2 (7727 1144).
The former chef at St John Bread & Wine in Spitalfields is opening a British restaurant of his own in Notting Hill.

Tom's Place

1 Cale Street, SW3.
Top chef Tom Aikens opened brasserie Tom's Kitchen at the end of 2006, but is about to try an even cheaper 50-seater fish and chip shop.

Texture

34 Portman Street, W1 (7224 0028).
The former head chef at Le Manoir aux Quat' Saisons, Agnar Sverrisson, has left Raymond Blanc and is setting up his own place, along with Blanc's former sommelier Xavier Rousset.

Divo

12 Waterloo Place, SW1 (7484 1355).
The St James's site that used to be W'Sens is being turned into a Ukrainian restaurant, with an 18th-century baroque look and a mix of Ukrainian and Russian dishes.

The Only Running Footman

5 Charles Street, W1 (www.therunningfootman.biz).
The people behind gastropubs the House in Canonbury and the Bull in Highgate are refurbing this Mayfair boozer into a ground-floor pub and first-floor restaurant.

British Tea Rooms

Marylebone High Street, W1.
This collaboration between Hope & Greenwood and catering firm Ponti's will be a proper tea room and sweet shop with an ice-cream counter, designed along a 1950s theme.

Harrison's

15-19 Bedford Hill, SW12 9EX (8675 6900/www.harrisonsbalham.co.uk).
What used to be the Balham Kitchen & Bar has been bought by Sam Harrison (of Sam's Brasserie in Chiswick).

Almada

33 Dover Street, W1.
Almada is the working title of this yet-to-be-named and much-delayed restaurant next to Mayfair's Automat.

OCTOBER

Le Café Anglais

Whiteleys, 8 Porchester Gardens, W2.
Part of the ongoing revamp of Whiteleys shopping centre, this joint partnership between chef Rowley Leigh and Bush Bar & Grill owner Charlie McVeigh will be a 200-cover brasserie with Anglo-French food and a big rotisserie.

Hibiscus

29 Maddox Street, W1.
Chef/proprietor Claude Bosi used to run the top-rated haute cuisine restaurant Hibiscus in Ludlow, but is now moving to Mayfair.

The Landau

Langham Hotel, 1C Portland Place, W1 (7636 1000/ www.thelandau.com).
This new restaurant inside the Langham is employing a top-rated chef (Andrew Turner) and using David Collins as the interior designer.

Warrington

93 Warrington Crescent, W9 (7286 2929).
A lovely old boozer being given the once-over by Gordon Ramsay Holdings, to open as a poshed-up gastropub.

NOVEMBER

Ducasse at the Dorchester

53 Park Lane, W1 (7629 8888).
Alain Ducasse, one of the world's top 'superchefs', is putting his name to a dining room inside the Dorchester hotel as part of his large international portfolio.

Boundary Project

2-4 Boundary Street, E2 (www.theboundary.co.uk).
Sir Terence Conran may have sold his majority share in what used to be called Conran Restaurants, but he's not ready for retirement yet. Boundary Project is a new Shoreditch venture that will incorporate a café, restaurant and rooftop cocktail bar, together with 'some rooms'.

DECEMBER

Paramount

Centrepoint, New Oxford Street, W1 (www.paramount.uk.net).
Chef Pierre Condue, formerly of L'Odeon restaurant, is planning a fine-dining restaurant and bar on the 32nd floor of the 1964 Centrepoint building.

2008

Maze Grill

Marriott Hotel, Grosvenor Square, W1.
Jason Atherton's Maze restaurant (part of Gordon Ramsay Holdings) has proved such a hit that the Marriott Hotel is letting it extend a 'Maze-lite' restaurant into an adjacent space.

The Water House

Canalside Works, Orsman Road, N1 5QJ.
A spin-off from the eco-friendly restaurant Acorn House, this time in De Beauvoir. More of a café than a restaurant.

Westfield London

White City, W10.
White City is undergoing large-scale redevelopment, including the new Westfield London complex. Due to open during 2008, it will contain around 270 stores and a multiplex cinema. The high-end shopping mall is to be called the Village, with more than 40 places to eat and drink – including 15 'lifestyle restaurants'.

Zulu

Camden Stables Market, NW1.
The new owner of oriental bar-restaurant Gilgamesh is planning to convert the space below into an African-themed eaterie, two bars and an entertainment venue.

Time Out's Hot 100

The editors of the *Time Out Eating & Drinking Guide* have picked out 100 places, entirely subjectively, that we believe offer some of London's most interesting eating and drinking experiences. We're not saying these venues have the best food and drink in the capital, but we believe each of them adds something life-enhancing to our city. Here they are, in alphabetical order. Each review is marked with a (100) in the relevant chapter of the guide.

Adam's Café
North African p251.
Cherished Tunisian café in Shepherd's Bush.

Amaya
Indian p151.
Indian fine dining in Knightsbridge that sets a new standard.

Ambassador
Modern European p230.
Wine bar and brasserie in Exmouth Market.

Anchor & Hope
Gastropubs p123.
Proper pub on one side, no-bookings gastropub on the other, with rustic British and Med dishes by chef Jonathan Jones.

Arbutus
Modern European p236.
Highly creative cookery at fair prices in a relaxed setting in Soho.

Assaggi
Italian p187.
Proper Italian food in a light-filled room in Notting Hill.

Baker & Spice
Cafés p312.
Perfect pastries, lip-smacking salads and a bounty of breads.

Baltic
East European p91.
East European cooking that looks to the future, not the past, in a suitably modern setting near Tate Modern.

Bar Shu
Chinese p80.
Pucker up for the spicy heat of London's first fully Sichuan menu.

Barrafina
Spanish p261.
London-style homage to the great Barcelona seafood bar, Cal Pep.

Bentley's Oyster Bar & Grill
Fish p95.
Chef Richard Corrigan's back-to-basics revamp of a long-established Mayfair venue.

Bistrotheque
French p113; Bars p337.
Bar, cabaret room and bistro in a Bethnal Green backstreet.

Blue Bar
Bars p331.
The cocktail bar of the international jet set, being extended during 2008 as the Berkeley hotel refurbishes.

Buen Ayre
Latin American p51.
Original Hackney branch of the Argentinian parrillada, or steak-grill.

Busaba Eathai
Thai p269.
Queue for a shared table at a branch of this mini-chain of beautifully designed fast-food Thai restaurants.

Cah Chi
Korean p218.
Raynes Park Korean with extraordinary home-style cooking and friendly vibe.

Chez Bruce
French p111.
Wandsworth Common restaurant that's been a destination for food and wine for more than a decade.

China Tang
Chinese p78.
A clever recreation of 1930s China inside a Park Lane hotel, by designer David Tang.

Clarke's
Modern European p238.
Since the early 1980s, Sally Clarke's restaurant has been at the forefront of good food, proving that real quality never goes out of style.

Club Gascon
French p102.
Interpretations of the dishes of south-west France, served in tapas-sized portions.

Coach & Horses
Gastropubs p115.
Gastropub par excellence in Clerkenwell, with proper beers, friendly service and great food.

Cow
Gastropubs p121.
One of Notting Hill's nicest pubs, though it's busy on the ground floor; eat at the tables further back or in the smarter dining room upstairs.

Czechoslovak Restaurant
East European p88.
London's only Czech restaurant and bar dates back to the Cold War era: a piece of living history.

Eagle
Gastropubs p117.
Scholars of the gastropub movement should visit this Clerkenwell boozer to see where it all began.

Eyre Brothers
Global p133.
Iberian-accented Mediterranean cooking in Shoreditch.

Fish Club
Fish & Chips p317.
Top-quality ingredients, imaginative side orders and an unusual selection of seafood set this Battersea chippie apart.

Food for Thought
Vegetarian p287.
Squeeze into one of the shared tables for hearty portions of low-priced vegetarian food, right in the heart of Covent Garden.

La Fromagerie
Cafés p307.
Delightful café inside one of Marylebone's best food shops.

Le Gavroche
Hotels & Haute Cuisine p145.
Old-fashioned service in an old-fashioned setting, but – *mon dieu!* – they know how to do things properly.

Geales
Fish p97.
Former chip shop transformed into a stylish fish restaurant by top chef Garry Hollihead.

Gilgamesh
Oriental p255; Bars p338.
Where more is more – Mesopotamian carvings, a retractable roof, nightclub lighting – yet the oriental food is surprisingly good.

Golden Hind
Fish & Chips p315.
Traditional chippie in the heart of Marylebone, dating from World War I.

Gourmet Burger Kitchen
Budget p300.
The original branch in Battersea started a whole movement – we reckon it's still the best.

Greenhouse
Hotels & Haute Cuisine p146.
Fine-dining restaurant in a Mayfair mews.

Gun
Gastropubs p125.
Historic Thames-side pub gone gastro, but still serving great beers with the British dishes.

Hakkasan
Chinese p76; Bars p330.
Restaurateur Alan Yau's masterpiece: a stunning subterranean space, with equally impressive dim sum and modern Chinese menus.

Hawksmoor
Bars p330.
Cocktail maestro Nick Strangeway is a retro cocktail enthusiast; his bar and steakhouse is the place to go if you're tired of caipirinhas.

Hummus Bros
Budget p299.
Fast-food café with houmous at its core. So simple, so brilliant: why didn't someone think of it before?

Hunan
Chinese p71.
Veteran Chinese menu where it's best to let proprietor Mr Peng choose the Taiwanese-influenced Hunan dishes for you.

Inn The Park
British p64.
Oliver Peyton's design-savvy burrow of a restaurant in leafy St James's Park.

Jerusalem Tavern
Pubs p339.
Clever re-creation of an 18th-century tavern interior, with fine ales from St Peter's Brewery.

Lab
Bars p334.
That rare thing: a bar in Soho where the staff know how to make a good cocktail.

Lobby Bar
Bars p330.
A highly civilised hotel bar on the edge of Covent Garden.

Lola Rojo
Spanish p265.
Battersea tapas bar that's brought a taste of *nueva cocina* to Northcote Road.

Long Bar
Bars p330.
The bar is not as achingly hip as it once was, but the Philippe Starck interior is as eye-popping as ever.

Loungelover
Bars p338.
The first of the bars that countered Shoreditch minimalism with camp excess. Book a table and time before you go.

Macaron
Cafés p310.
Perfect neighbourhood tea room, pâtisserie and bakery.

Madhu's
Indian p171.
If you're keen to explore Southall's Indian restaurants, this smart East African Punjabi specialist makes a fine starting point.

Mandalay
Global p131.
Astonishing Burmese food in a basic caff on the Edgware Road.

Mangal Ocakbaşi
Turkish p281.
One of the first no-frills Turkish grills in Dalston, and still one of the best.

M Manze
Budget p304.
The granddaddy of pie and mash shops, all wooden benches and turn-of-the-century tiling.

Masa
Global p131.
Experienc Afghan cooking in Harrow's north-west frontier.

Maze
Hotels & Haute Cuisine p146.
Jason Atherton's canapé-style menus are a luxurious treat.

Milk & Honey
Bars p334.
'Exclusive' cocktail bar (you only need to phone them to gain entry) that's handy for Oxford Circus.

Momo
North African p250.
The Morocco straight out of *The Sheltering Sky*: a souk-like interior, exotic spices and Berber waiting staff.

Moro
Spanish p258.
Sam and Sam Clark's mix of North African and Spanish ingredients in a modern setting still holds its own against London's new wave of Spanish restaurants.

Nahm
Thai p269.
Proper Thai-style flavours and dishes masterminded by chef David Thompson in the Halkin hotel.

National Dining Rooms
British p66.
Arguably Oliver Peyton's best restaurant: a true Brit in a tourist-friendly setting overlooking Trafalgar Square from the National Gallery.

Nauroz
Indian p169.
The family behind this Eastcote eaterie creates the best Pakistani karahi restaurants, then sells them on; catch them while you can.

Nobu
Japanese p199.
Where would modern Japanese cuisine be if Nobu Matsuhisa hadn't brought his Peruvian-Japanese fusion food to London in 1997?

Ottolenghi
International p180.
Stunning modern Mediterranean food; we think the Islington branch is the best.

Patogh
Middle Eastern p224.
A little Iranian café just off the Edgware Road, serving tip-top grilled meat, rice, herb salads and huge wheels of flatbread.

E Pellicci
Budget p302.
A proper East End caff, serving proper East End caff food. Oh, and the lovely art deco interior is grade II-listed as well.

Plateau
Modern European p245.
Pretend you're in Gotham City inside the visionary bar-restaurant that Terence Conran built at Canary Wharf.

Racine
French p105.
More French than the Eiffel Tower, this is the place to come if you yearn for Parisian romance (and cooking).

Ram's
Indian p169.
Heavenly Gujarati vegetarian food in Kenton, Middlesex.

Ranoush Juice
Middle Eastern p224.
A late-night pitstop that's perfect for stoking up with falafel and fruit juice.

Riva
Italian p190.
Barnes-storming neighbourhood restaurant with imaginative Italian dishes.

The River Café
Italian p189.
Better Italian food than you find in Italy? Some people think so. Head to Hammersmith to find out.

Roast
British p69.
Borough Market is the perfect site for this handsomely porticoed meat specialist.

Royal China (Queensway)
Chinese p82.
The original Bayswater dim sum specialist, and still outstanding.

Royal Oak
Pubs p343.
A beer-drinkers' pub that's a short walk – but a world away – from Borough Market.

S&M Café
Budget p303.
What used to be Alfredo's greasy spoon in Islington, sympathetically renovated and turned into a sausage and mash specialist.

Sagar
Indian p158.
South Indian vegetarian dishes from Udipi, on the coast of Karnataka.

St Alban
Global p132.
Modern Mediterranean dishes in a svelte setting, from Chris Corbin and Jeremy King.

St John
British p63.
Chef Fergus Henderson reinvented the way we think about British food; and this former smokehouse next to Smithfield Market is still a fun place to sample his unusual dishes.

Sakonis
Indian p174.
The original Indian vegetarian chat (snack) house, catering to Wembley's Indian families with South Indian and Gujarati specialities.

Satay House
Malaysian p221.
An old-timer that's recently been given a makeover, but the food is as reliable as ever.

J Sheekey
Fish p95.
We prefer Sheekey's to its sister the Ivy for the lack of pretension, the urbane service and the appealing mix of traditional ingredients and comfort food.

Sketch: The Gallery
International p177.
The mid-priced place to eat at Sketch in the evening. If you go to gawp, make sure you visit both loos; the pods and the upstairs ones.

Skylon
Modern European p243.
Retro-sleek design and brilliant river views make this destination restaurant within the revamped Royal Festival Hall worth a visit.

Smiths of Smithfield
Modern European p232.
A multi-floored extravaganza of café, brasserie, cocktail bar and separate fine-dining steak restaurant (called Top Floor at Smiths).

Song Que
Vietnamese p294.
The finest of the numerous Vietnamese cafés on Kingsland Road, with an extensive list of proper Vietnamese dishes at bargain prices.

Story Deli
Budget p302.
Top pizzas and a friendly vibe, in a lively location on Brick Lane's busy Dray Walk.

Sushi-Hiro
Japanese p202.
No conveyor belt and no gimmicks: just an Ealing sushi bar that's one of the best, and easily the best value, in London.

Sweetings
Fish p94.
Barely changed since it opened in 1830, this City fish restaurant is a taste of what eating out in Victorian times was like.

The Table
Budget p301.
A stylish and highly appetising brunch or lunch spot on Bankside, handy for Tate Modern.

Tapas Brindisa
Spanish p267.
A Borough Market tapas bar that's perfect for a comfy seat and a first-rate grazing menu.

Tiroler Hut
Eating & Entertainment p355.
Decorated like a ski lodge in the Austrian Tyrol, this kitsch basement restaurant is perfect for parties (as long as you like accordion music and cowbell shows).

Tobia
African & Caribbean p39.
Outstanding Ethiopian cooking in a homely room above an Ethiopian cultural centre, just off Finchley Road.

Tre Viet
Vietnamese p295.
Currently the best of Hackney's many small Vietnamese restaurants.

Les Trois Garçons
French p113 .
French cooking accompanied by hippo heads and stuffed bulldogs in tiaras and fairy wings, in a former Whitechapel pub.

Vinoteca
Wine Bars p346.
A wine bar and Italian-style enoteca (shop and bar) on the edge of Smithfield Market.

Wagamama
Oriental p252.
The original 1992 design of this branch spawned a chain and many imitators – but 15 years on, it still seems cutting-edge.

Wapping Food
Modern European p246.
A former pumping station in the East End is the impressive location for this design-conscious restaurant.

White Horse
Pubs p341.
This Parsons Green pub is a prime destination for both beer and wine: hugely popular, but deservedly so.

The Wolseley
Modern European p235.
The listed interior of the former Wolseley car showroom on Piccadilly is a perfectly dapper setting for this European-style grand brasserie.

Yakitoria
Japanese p203.
Award-winning design, great food and the kind of bar in which you can linger, all in a modern Japanese restaurant in Paddington Basin.

Yoshino
Japanese p200.
Ever wanted to eat in a discreetly hidden, little-known, Zen-inspired Japanese sushi bar? Here it is.

Zuma
Japanese p198.
The place to watch the rich at play, in an absolutely fabulous Knightsbridge bar and modern Japanese restaurant.

AWARDS 2007
Eating & Drinking

Rounding up the capital's most impressive new restaurants, gastropubs and bars, Time Out, in association with Leffe, honoured the very best in ten categories in its 18th annual awards.

Here at Time Out we're proud of our reputation for championing the best of London's eating and drinking places. Not just those with the grandest credentials, either, but the little places too, the ones you're not likely to read about anywhere else, which are, in their own field, exceptional. This is the ethos behind our broad coverage of London's gastronomic delights – from weekly reviews in *Time Out London* magazine to our numerous guides. And this is why our annual Eating & Drinking Awards take in not only London's restaurant élite, but also representatives from neighbourhood restaurants, gastropubs and bargain eateries as independently selected by a panel of Time Out judges.

With a fresh crop of new reviews appearing each week in *Time Out London* magazine (and on our website, www.timeout.com/restaurants), the list of potential candidates can seem dauntingly long, but our panel of independent (and strictly anonymous) reviewers is able to whittle them down to a shortlist of 50 – five nominations in each of ten categories. These categories, which vary each year, reflect the diverse needs and tastes of London's diners and drinkers: this year we included new categories for Best Local Traiteur, Best Coffee Bar and Best British Restaurant, to reflect the recent emergence of several outstanding new places in all these areas. We then ask readers of the magazine and website for their feedback, which helps inform our judges' choices.

And there's more. The judges are sent out to revisit every shortlisted establishment as normal paying punters (we never accept PR invitations or freebies of any kind), so that a final decision can be reached. Finally, the results are announced – at a glittering ceremony on Monday 17 September 2007.

Wild Honey

Kiasu

National Dining Rooms

AND THE WINNERS ARE...

in alphabetical order...

BEST BAR

Winner
The Rake *See p337.*
Runners-up
Artesian *See p333.*
Big Chill House *See p331.*
Mocotó Closed 'for refurbishment' as we went to press.
Montgomery Place *See p335.*

BEST BRITISH RESTAURANT

Winner
National Dining Rooms (British) *See p66.*
Runners-up
Empress of India (British) *See p70.*
Geales (Fish) *See p97.*
Great Queen Street (British) *See p64.*
Magdalen (British) *See p69.*

BEST CHEAP EATS

Winner
Kiasu (Malaysian, Indonesian & Singaporean) *See p220.*
Runners-up
The Diner (North American) *See p45.*
Mother Mash (Budget) *See p299.*
Ooze (Budget) *See p298.*
Sufi (Middle Eastern) *See p228.*

BEST COFFEE BAR

Winner
Fernandez & Wells (Cafés) *See p307.*
Runners-up
Bullet (Cafés) *See p305.*
Flat White (Cafés) *See p307.*
Nordic Bakery (Cafés) *See p308.*
Sacred (Cafés) *See p308.*

BEST DESIGN

Winner
Skylon (Modern European) *See p243.*
Runners-up
L'Atelier de Joël Robuchon (Modern European) *See p232.*
High Road Brasserie (Brasseries) *See p56.*
Meals (Cafés) *See p306.*
Pearl Liang (Chinese) *See p79.*

BEST FAMILY RESTAURANT

Winner
Tate Modern Café: Level 2 (Brasseries) *See p59.*
Runners-up
Mudchute Kitchen (Cafés) *See p311.*
Munchkin Lane (Cafés) *See p310.*
Pick More Daisies (Brasseries) *See p60.*
Raviolo (Pizza & Pasta) *See p322.*

BEST GASTROPUB

Winner
Rosendale *See p125.*
Runners-up
Brown Dog *See p121.*
The Narrow *See p125.*
Roebuck *See p119.*
Waterfront *See p122.*

BEST LOCAL RESTAURANT

Winner
Trinity (French) *See p112.*
Runners-up
High Road Brasserie (Brasseries) *See p56.*
Lola Rojo (Spanish) *See p265.*
Tom's Kitchen (Brasseries) *See p57.*
Tapas y Vino (Spanish) *See p268.*

BEST LOCAL TRAITEUR

Winner
The Grocer on Elgin
Runners-up
Hand Made Food
Melrose & Morgan
Tavola
Trinity Stores
For details of all, see p111 **Best traiteurs**.

LEFFE BEST NEW RESTAURANT

Winner
Wild Honey (Modern European) *See p235.*
Runners-up
Barrafina (Spanish) *See p261.*
Odette's (Modern European) *See p246.*
Olivomare (Fish) *See p94.*
St Alban (Mediterranean) *See p132.*

This year's judges: Jessica Cargill Thompson, Richard Ehrlich, Sarah Guy, Ronnie Haydon, Ruth Jarvis, Tom Lamont, Jenni Muir, Cath Phillips, Andrew Staffell, Gordon Thomson.

in association with

Where to...

Looking for something more specific? Then consult the **Subject Index**, starting on p392.

GO FOR BREAKFAST

Breakfast is offered every day unless stated otherwise. *See also* **Cafés** and **Brasseries**.

WATERSIDE

See also the E14 branch of **Jamies** and the Southbank Centre branches of **Giraffe**, **Strada** and **Wagamama**.

TAKE THE KIDS

See also **Cafés**, **Brasseries**, **Fish & Chips**, **Pizza & Pasta**.

Smollensky's on the Strand
The Americas p46

Tate Modern *Brasseries p58*

Tootsies Grill *The Americas p47*

Victoria *Modern European p241*

Wagamama *Oriental p252*

ENJOY THE VIEW

Babylon *Modern European p238*

Bincho *Japanese p203*

Blueprint Café
Modern European p245

Butlers Wharf Chop House
British p69

Le Coq d'Argent *French p101*

Galvin at Windows
Hotels & Haute Cuisine p145

Oxo Tower Restaurant, Bar & Brasserie
Modern European p243

Ozu *Japanese p205*

Plateau *Modern European p245*

Le Pont de la Tour
Modern European p245

Roast *British p69*

Rhodes Twenty Four *British p61*

Skylon *Modern European p243*

Tamesa@oxo *Brasseries p58*

Thai Square *Thai p275*

Top Floor at Smiths *British p63*

Vertigo 42 Champagne Bar
Eating & Entertainment p356

TRY UNUSUAL DISHES

See also **Global**.

Abeno Too *Japanese p203*

Archipelago *International p175*

Asadal *Korean p216*

Bar Shu *Chinese p80*

Belgo Noord *Global p131*

Esarn Kheaw *Thai p271*

Hunan *Chinese p76*

Mandalay *Global 131*

Nahm *Thai p269*

The Providores & Tapa Room
International p175

St John *British p63*

Song Que *Vietnamese p294*

Snazz Sichuan *Chinese p76*

Tbilisi *East European p88*

Umu *Japanese p199*

DO BRUNCH

See also **Cafés** and **Brasseries**.

Ambassador (Sat, Sun)
Modern European p230

Bermondsey Kitchen (Sat, Sun)
Modern European p245

Bluebird (Sat, Sun)
Modern European p239

Brackenbury (Sat, Sun)
Modern European p239

Brasserie de Malmaison (Sun)
Brasseries p54

Christopher's (Sat, Sun)
The Americas p43

Clarke's (Sat) *Modern European p238*

Le Comptoir Gascon (Sat)
French p102

The Farm (Sat, Sun)
Modern European p241

Fifth Floor (Sun)
Modern European p233

High Road Brasserie (Sat, Sun)
Brasseries p56

Joe Allen (Sat, Sun) *The Americas p43*

Lundum's (Mon-Sat)
Scandinavian p134

Manna (Sun) *Vegetarian p291*

Notting Grill (Sat, Sun) *British p67*

Penk's (Sat) *International p180*

Ransome's Dock (Sun)
Modern European p242

Roast (Sat) *British p69*

Sabor (Sat, Sun) *Latin American p53*

Sam's Brasserie & Bar (daily)
Modern European p237

The Sequel (Sat, Sun)
International p197

The Terrace (WC2) (Sat)
Modern European p232

The Terrace (W8) (Sat, Sun)
Modern European p238

Tom's Kitchen *(Sat, Sun)*
Brasseries p57

Wapping Food (Sat, Sun)
Modern European p246

DINE ALFRESCO

See also p313 **Park cafés**.

Babylon *Modern European p238*

Back to Basics *Fish p94*

Bank Westminster
Modern European p237

Bull *Gastropubs p128*

Butlers Wharf Chop House
British p69

Cantina del Ponte *Italian p193*

Chez Kristof *French p109*

Le Coq d'Argent *French p101*

Curve *The Americas p48*

Deep *Fish p98*

Drapers Arms *Gastropubs p129*

Ealing Park Tavern
Gastropubs p119

fish! *Fish p99*

Franklins *British p67*

Geales *Fish p97*

Gordon's *Wine Bars p348*

Greek Affair *Greek p135*

Gun *Gastropubs p125*

High Road Brasserie
Brasseries p56

House *Gastropubs p129*

Hoxton Apprentice
Modern European p246

Inn The Park *British p64*

Lola Rojo *Spanish p265*

Manicomio *Italian p190*

The Narrow *Gastropubs p125*

Oxo Tower *Modern European p243*

Paternoster Chop House
British p61

Petersham Nurseries Café
Modern European p247

Phoenix Bar & Grill
Modern European p241

Plateau *Modern European p245*

Le Pont de la Tour
Modern European p245

Queens Pub & Dining Room
Gastropubs p128

RIBA Café *Brasseries p55*

The River Café *Italian p189*

Rochelle Canteen *British p70*

Roka *Japanese p197*

Rosmarino *Italian p195*

Royal China
Chinese (Docklands branch) *p85*

Saran Rom *Thai p272*

Scott's *Fish p95*

Where to... and what to drink?

Speciality Beer. The term is starting to be bandied about, with pubs and beers enticing you in to sample their extensive range, but chances are you may not actually have discovered a lot about them. When should they be drunk? Where should they be drunk? Most importantly, what exactly are they?

In a nutshell, Speciality Beers are brewed in their own country of origin (and often have been for hundreds of years. Leffe, for example, has been brewed in Belgium for over 800 years). They stand out from other beers through their authentic brewing heritage, special ingredients and unique brewing methods.

They each have a distinct appearance and character with specific aromas and flavours, which are often an appealing trait to those people who drink wine over beer. Speciality Beers can be described in similar terms to wine – 'full-bodied', 'fruity bouquet', 'earthy aroma' etc – and many people are surprised, pleasantly so, to discover the differences between them all.

Leffe, (pronounced 'Lef' or 'Leff-er' but never 'Leff-ee') the UK's No1 Speciality Beer, comes in 4 different varieties, each with a distinct taste of its own. Served in a unique chalice glass that enhances the aroma, Leffe's stemmed glass encourages you to enjoy it at leisure, taking time to savour the different character and complexities on the nose and palate – just like any wine.

Leffe Blonde has hints of quince, apple, bitter cherry and gooseberry, alongside cloves, allspice and nutmeg, to produce a well-balanced beer that demands to be savoured layer by layer. Sip by sip. Leffe Brune is flavoured with rich roasted malts and delivers caramel bitter sweetness with hints of warm fruit, whilst Leffe Triple takes it a step further with its secondary fermentation in the bottle, contributing to its spicy coriander and orange nose and palate. The last of the four, Leffe Radieuse, is the richest, with a taste that includes banana, citrus fruits, coriander and cloves alongside an earthy aroma. All of them are distinctly different, but what they do have in common with each other – and with many wines – is their superlative ability to be matched with food in a way that complements them both.

Many people haven't discovered that speciality beers can be the perfect match to a delicious meal. Forget the cliché of lager louts and curry, the tantalising aromas of the beer can actually lift and improve the food that it is accompanying in the same way a good wine can.

Specialist Beer Sommelier and Belgian Beer Ambassador, Marc Stroobandt says, 'People often think beer and food pairing is complicated, but you just need to think about it in terms of food and wine pairing. The culinary clout of beer is on the increase and speciality beer is a great compliment to a range of dishes.'

Leffe Blonde is ideally twinned with cured meats or subtle cheeses – or perhaps more memorably, with delicious creamy desserts such as crème brûlée. We recommend that you discover this combination for yourself at Belgo Noord, 72 Chalk Farm Road, Chalk Farm, NW1.

Leffe Radieuse works beautifully with robust meat and game dishes – but not just as an accompaniment. Why not put a generous splash or two into the next gravy you make?

Leffe Brune is a sublime combination with dark chocolate or full-flavoured meat and roasted vegetable dishes. Marc strongly recommends trying Leffe Brune at home with a sumptuously rich chocolate tart from Macaron, 22 The Pavement, Clapham Common, SW4 (winner of Best Pâtisserie at the Time Out Eating & Drinking Awards 2006). Try it once and you'll never look back.

Finally, Leffe Triple makes a great replacement for white wine dishes and is ideal with rustic vegetable pasta dishes as well as rich lamb or chicken casseroles. Discovering the joy of food and beer matching works as well in or out of the home. The beer can be savoured with the food, but works equally well as part of the dish itself. Why don't you give this recipe a whirl to find out for yourself?

ADVERTISEMENT

Leffe Brune Chocolate Tart

Preparation time: 10 minutes
Cooking time: 30-40 minutes

Ingredients:

For the pastry

500g plain flour
250g butter, diced and soft
150g sugar
1 egg

For the filling

400g dark chocolate (min 70% cocoa solids)
200g butter
5 egg yolks
3 whole eggs
100g sugar
100ml Leffe Brune

Method:

Pre-heat oven to 180°C/gas mark 4. If you have a food processor put in all the pastry ingredients and whizz for a few seconds until the pastry comes together in a ball. If not, sieve the flour into a bowl and work in the butter and sugar with your fingers. Make a well in the middle and add the beaten egg. Knead the mixture until smooth and amalgamated. Wrap in cling film and rest in the fridge for 30 minutes. Lightly flour a work surface and roll out the pastry as thin as possible. Lightly butter a flan tin (approx. 32cm diameter x 2.5cm deep) and lay the pastry inside leaving an overhang. You can trim this off later. Cut a circle of greaseproof paper to fit inside the tin and place on the pastry. Make a cling film parcel filled with rice or dry beans big enough to cover the surface area of the pastry and place on top. Bake in the oven. After about 15 minutes, remove the cling film parcel and greaseproof paper and continue to bake for a few more minutes.

While the pastry is blind-baking, make the filling. Break up the chocolate and butter and put in a heatproof bowl with the Leffe. Set over a pan of simmering water and melt. When melted, remove from the heat and stir well. Whisk the egg yolks, eggs and sugar until smooth. Stir the chocolate mixture into the egg mixture. Pour the mixture into the pastry case, turn the oven down to 150°C/gas mark 2 and bake for 8-10 minutes. Allow to cool and refrigerate overnight

Serves: 12

To find out more about Speciality Beers and try some perfect recipes, visit www.specialitybeerselection.com or www.leffe.com

www.drinkaware.co.uk

Stein's *Budget p304*
Strada *Pizza & Pasta p327*
Story Deli *Budget p302*
Suka *Oriental p252*
The Terrace (WC2) *Modern European p232*
The Terrace (W8) *Modern European p238*
La Trouvaille *French p108*
Victoria *Modern European p241*
Wapping Food *Modern European p246*
Waterfront *Gastropubs p122*
Yakitoria *Japanese p203*

PEOPLE-WATCHING

Blue Bar *Bars p331*
Embassy *Modern European p233*
Fifth Floor *Modern European p233*
The Ivy *Modern European p232*
Loungelover *Bars p338*
Mr Chow *Chinese p77*
Obika *Italian p183*
Papillon *French p108*
St Alban *Global p132*
Sketch: The Gallery *International p177*
The Wolseley *Modern European p235*
Zuma *Japanese p198*

TAKE A DATE

Andrew Edmunds *Modern European p236*
L'Atelier de Joël Robuchon *Modern European p232*
L'Aventure *French p114*
Bentley's Oyster Bar & Grill *Fish p95*
Café du Marché *French p102*
Club Gascon *French p102*
Fifth Floor *Modern European p233*
Le Gavroche *Hotels & Haute Cuisine p145*
Greenhouse *Hotels & Haute Cuisine p146*
Hakkasan *Chinese p76, Bars p330*
Kettners *Pizza & Pasta p321*
Lindsay House *British p64*
Momo *North African p250*
Nobu *Japanese p199*
Orrery *Modern European p233*
Petersham Nurseries *Modern European p247*
The River Café *Italian p189*
J Sheekey *Fish p95*
La Trouvaille *French p108*
Les Trois Garçons *French p113*
La Trompette *French p108*
Wild Honey *Modern European p235*

LOVE THE LOOK

Amaya *Indian p151*
Asia de Cuba *International p175*
L'Atelier de Joël Robuchon *Modern European p232*
Baltic *East European p91*
Benares *Indian p151*
Le Cercle *French p101*
China Tang *Chinese p78*
Cocoon *Oriental p253*
Dinings *Japanese p198*
Fifth Floor *Modern European p233*
Gilgamesh *Oriental p255*
Hakkasan *Chinese p78, Bars p330*
High Road Brasserie *Brasseries p56*
Inn The Park *British p64*
Jerusalem Tavern *Pubs p339*
Ladurée *Cafés p306*
Loungelover *Bars p338*
Macaron *Cafés p310*
Meals *Cafés p306*
Nobu Berkeley Street *Japanese p199*
Pearl Bar & Restaurant *Hotels & Haute Cuisine p140*
Pearl Liang *Chinese p79*
E Pellicci *Budget p302*
Petersham Nurseries *Modern European p247*
Pumphouse Dining Bar *Brasseries p60*
Rhodes W1 (restaurant) *Hotels & Haute Cuisine p143*
Roka *Japanese p197*
Saran Rom *Thai p272*
Shanghai Blues *Chinese p76*
Sketch: The Gallery *International p175*
Sketch: The Lecture Room *Hotels & Haute Cuisine p146*
Skylon *Modern European p243*
Trailer Happiness *Bars p335*
Les Trois Garçons *French p113*
Wapping Food *Modern European p246*
Yakitoria *Japanese p203*
Yauatcha *Chinese p80*
Zuma *Japanese p198*

GREAT COCKTAILS

Artesian *Bars p333*
Dukes Hotel *Bars p334*
Hakkasan *Chinese p80, Bars p330*
Hawksmoor *The Americas p42, Bars p330*
Lab *Bars p334*
Lonsdale *Bars p335*
Library *Bars p333*
Match Bar *Bars p330*
Montgomery Place *Bars p335*
Shochu Lounge *Bars p330*

EAT LATE

Balans *Brasseries p56*
Ed's Easy Diner *The Americas p45*
Fish in a Tie *Budget p301*
Hoxton Grille *Brasseries p59*
Joe Allen *The Americas p43*
Mangal II *Turkish p281*
Le Mercury *Budget p303*
New Mayflower *Chinese p74*
PJ's Grill *The Americas p45*
Planet Hollywood *The Americas p46*
Sariyer Balik *Turkish p281*
Tinseltown *Eating & Entertainment p356*
Vingt-Quatre *Eating & Entertainment p356*
The Wolseley *Modern European p235*

About the guide

LISTED BY AREA
The restaurants in this guide are listed by cuisine type: British, Chinese, Indian etc. Then, within each of chapter, they are listed by geographical area: ten main areas (in this example, Central), then by neighbourhood (Bloomsbury). If you are not sure where to look for a restaurant, there are two indexes at the back of the guide to help: an **A-Z Index** (starting on p417) listing restaurants by name, and an **Area Index** (starting on p398), where you can see all the places we list in a specific neighbourhood.

STARS
A red star ★ means that a restaurant is, of its type, very good indeed. A green star ★ identifies budget-conscious eateries – expect to pay an average of £20 (for a three-course meal or its equivalent, *not* including drinks or service).

AWARD NOMINEES
Winners and runners-up in Time Out's Eating & Drinking Awards 2007. For more information on the awards, *see p26*.

OPENING HOURS
Times given are for *last orders* rather than closing times (except in cafés and bars).

MAP REFERENCE
All restaurants that appear on our street maps (starting on p358) are given a reference to the map and grid square on which they can found.

Central
King's Cross

★ ★ Frugal NEW (100)

2007 RUNNER-UP BEST CHEAP EATS

251 Grim Road, W1T 7AB (9876 4321). King's Cross tube/rail. **Lunch served** noon-3pm, **dinner served** 6-11pm daily. **Main courses** £8-£13. **Set meal** (6-8pm Mon-Sat) £12 2 courses, £16 3 courses. **Cover** £1. **Credit** AmEx, DC, MC, V.

Frugal has cleverly taken two of the year's strongest restaurant trends – carbon footprint awareness, and nostalgia – and combined them into an eco-restaurant that also pays homage to the austerity years of British rationing. The Nissen Hut entrance opens on to the ominous sight of Home Guard trenchcoats, which you are advised to wear as the restaurant has no heating. The staff (clad in either demob suits or utility dresses) are a cheerful lot, and lead you through to the dining room, which resembles a works canteen, kept moodily dim by low-wattage bulbs and blackout curtains. 'Mustn't grumble', said our waitress, 'but the cream, bacon and sugar are off.' Ingredients are carefully sourced: dried egg replaces fresh, margarine is used in place of butter, tinned snoek (a South African fish) rather than cod. Starters might include split-pea soup, followed by corned beef with brussels sprouts a l'italienne. Our dessert of stewed fruit cooked with bicarbonate of soda and saccharin tasted as you might expect, but diners can feel smug in the knowledge that their carbon footprint remains scarcely touched by dining here. Staff cannot call you a taxi home, but bicycles may be borrowed.

Babies and children welcome: crayons; high chairs; tin soldiers. Disabled: toilet. Tables outdoors (10, air raid shelter). **Map 4 L3.**

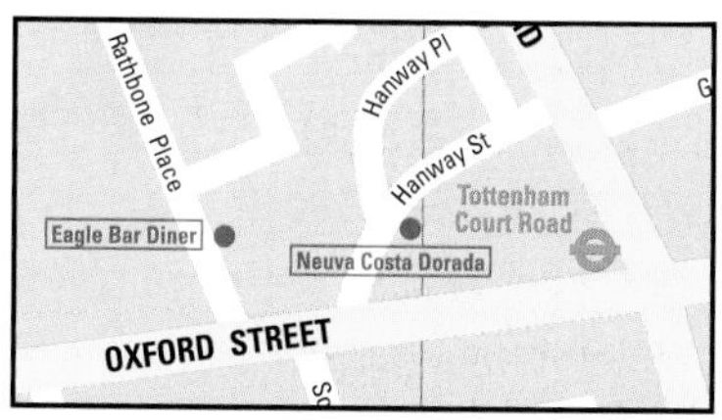

NEW ENTRIES
The NEW symbol means new to this edition of the *Eating & Drinking Guide*. In most cases, these are brand-new establishments; in some other instances we've included an existing restaurant for the first time.

THE TIME OUT 100
The (100) symbol means the venue is among what we consider to be London's top 100 iconic eating and drinking experiences. For details of the complete 100, *see p24*.

PRICES
We have listed the cheapest and most expensive main courses available in each restaurant. In the case of many oriental restaurants, prices may seem lower – but remember that you often need to order several such dishes to have a full meal.

COVER CHARGE
An old-fashioned fixed charge may be imposed by the restaurateur to cover the cost of rolls and butter, crudités, cleaning table linen and similar extras.

Anonymous, unbiased reviews
The reviews in the *Eating & Drinking Guide* are based on the experiences of Time Out restaurant reviewers. Restaurants, pubs, bars and cafés are always visited anonymously, and Time Out pays the bill. No payment or PR invitation of any kind has secured or influenced a review. The editors select which places are listed in this guide, and are not influenced in any way by the wishes of the restaurants themselves. Restaurants cannot volunteer or pay to be listed; we list only those we consider to be worthy of inclusion. Advertising and sponsorship has no effect whatsoever on the editorial content of the *Eating & Drinking Guide*. An advertiser may receive a bad review, or no review at all.

SERVICES
These are listed below the review.

Babies and children We've tried to reflect the degree of welcome extended to babies and children in restaurants. If you find no mention of either, take it that the restaurant is unsuitable.

Disabled: toilet means the restaurant has a specially adapted toilet, which implies that customers with walking disabilities or wheelchairs can get into the restaurant. However, we recommend phoning to double-check.

Vegetarian menu Most restaurants claim to have a vegetarian dish on the menu. We've highlighted those that have made a more concerted effort to attract and cater for vegetarian (and vegan) diners.

Restaurants

African & Caribbean

A continent, and a diaspora: that's a lot of cooking to cover. Yet the cooking of the black nations is still inadequately represented in London. There are remarkably few black head chefs, fewer still black-run restaurants, and fewer still that serve up good cooking true to culinary roots. The best ones we've included below, divided into the two main subdivisions of African and Caribbean.

AFRICAN

The food of east Africa is radically different from that of west Africa. Eritrean and Ethiopian cooking are very similar, often consisting of spicy stews served on a large injera bread; Nigerian restaurants tend to serve grilled meats with big helpings of carbohydrates. We've printed the relevant country of origin in red above each review. You can also refer to the Menu box for the low-down on injera, suya, berbere and other key ingredients and dishes. If you're looking for north African restaurants (Morocco and Tunisia), there are enough of them to merit their own chapter, starting on p248.

Central

King's Cross

★ Addis

42 Caledonian Road, N1 9DT (7278 0679/www.addisrestaurant.co.uk). King's Cross tube/rail/ 17, 91, 259 bus. **Meals served** noon-midnight Mon-Fri; 1pm-midnight Sat, Sun. **Main courses** £6.50-£8.50. **Credit** AmEx, MC, V. Ethiopian

'Ethiopia opens her arms to God,' reads a sign on the wall, painted in Amharic. Walking into Addis's welcoming yellow-ochre interior, decorated with photographs of the nation's many tribes, you feel as though you've left King's Cross and entered somewhere altogether warmer. The menu offers a few non-traditional options – falafel and houmous aren't exactly classic Ethiopian fare – and injera is made from rice flour rather than the grain teff; but there's little else to quibble about here. Kitfo, minced beef served either raw or lightly cooked and mixed in butter, is one of many typically Ethiopean dishes; though there are plenty of alternatives for those who prefer their food well-cooked. Try derek tibs (lamb cubes fried in onion) or chicken wot (a hot tomato-flavoured stew). The menu even stretches to Bati, a rather bland Ethiopian lager, and Ethiopian wine. Service can be patchy, as there aren't quite enough waiters to cope with the constant flow of customers, most of whom are Ethiopian. Dish prices are slashed by a quid at lunchtime, making an already bargain restaurant even easier on the wallet.

Babies and children welcome: high chairs. Booking advisable. Takeaway service. **Map 4 L2.**

★ New Merkato

196 Caledonian Road, N1 0SL (7713 8952). King's Cross tube/rail/17, 91, 259 bus. **Meals served** noon-midnight daily. **Main courses** £5-£10. **Credit** AmEx, MC, V. Ethiopian

Merkato is Amharic for 'market', but this intimate and friendly establishment carries few of the associations suggested by its name; the atmosphere is relaxed and quiet. The smell of incense burned continuously throughout our visit, but not overpoweringly so. Oil lamps hang from the bar, casting a soft glow on contrasting red and white walls; tables are lit by candles in bamboo holders. Brightly coloured Ethiopian fabric designs are used as both tablecloths and wall-mounted decorations. Customers with an interest can acquaint themselves with Ethiopian script, thanks to a framed scroll hanging next to the staircase displaying the Ethiopian alphabet. We were a little disappointed by the standard of cooking – perhaps because of the delicious, promising aroma that hit us as we entered. Atkilit (potatoes and cabbage cooked in onion and vegetable oil) was too oily, and the pulses in a misser wot (lentils with berbere in onion and vegetable oil) were undercooked. All meals are served with injera. But service was friendly and food was served promptly. All spices used are imported from Ethiopia.

Babies and children welcome: high chairs. Booking advisable Fri, Sat. Tables outdoors (2, pavement). Takeaway service. **Map 4 M1.**

West

Westbourne Park

★ Mosob

339 Harrow Road, W9 3RB (7266 2012/ www.mosob.co.uk). Westbourne Park tube. **Meals served** 1pm-midnight Mon-Sat; 1-11.30pm Sun. **Main courses** £6-£11. **Credit** AmEx, MC, V. Eritrean

Mosob was about to close for renovation around the time of publication of this guide, but the sons who run the place (with mum in the kitchen) say it will lose none of its funky charm and family-feel in the process. A modish Eritrean crowd attests to the restaurant's authentic menu and incredibly low prices. The house special is tender, garlic-flavoured lamb chops, but there are also a number of vegetarian dishes. These should be mixed and matched with traditional meaty fare such as zigni (a mild lamb stew) and quanta fitfit (dried meat in a spicy sauce). Courses are served on a communal plate of injera, the spongy fermented pancake peculiar to Eritrea and Ethiopia; you eat with your hands. Meiss (home-made honey wine) was off the menu when we visited, but there was plenty of Asmara beer – a miracle in itself, as these stumpy brown bottles are like gold dust in London. Fragrant with incense, quietly chic, Mosob is a great place to linger over your food; don't plan for a quick get-away. Service is leisurely, although the boys promise the renovation will slash the time between order and delivery.

Babies and children welcome: high chairs. Booking advisable. Separate room for parties, seats 22. Takeaway service. **Map 1 A4.**

South

Brixton

★ Asmara

386 Coldharbour Lane, SW9 8LF (7737 4144). Brixton tube/rail. **Dinner served** 5.30pm-midnight daily. **Main courses** £4.50-£8. **Set meal** vegetarian £25 per person (minimum 2) 6 courses; meat £27 per person (minimum 2) 7 courses. **Credit** MC, V. Eritrean

Plate-glass windows with no curtains give diners little respite from the bustle of Coldharbour Lane outside; only some homespun paintings on the glass obscure the view. The same artist has created the large landscapes of upland Eritrea, complete with carefully rendered paintings of donkeys. Embroidered tablecloths are trapped under glass, colourful raffia tables are ready to receive the mosob (communal eating plate). The set meals served on the mosob are a smart choice for novices, allowing a taste of several dishes – either a meat version, or vegetarian. The injera bread here is a pale golden colour, with an elastic, mop-like consistency, perfect for soaking up the wot (stew) of chicken and egg, or the mild-tasting dullet (chopped liver and 'tribes of lamb', as it says on the menu). We particularly liked the shiro (purée

SHELF LIFE

Street markets are the best place to look for both African and Caribbean provisions; here are three of the best, plus one shop.

Blue Mountain Peak

2A Craven Park Road, NW10 4AB (8965 3859). Willesden Junction tube/rail. **Open** 7.30am-6pm Mon-Thur; 6.30am-6.30pm Fri, Sat.

Owned by well-informed Indians, this enormous shop is crammed with African and Caribbean provisions. Fruit and veg includes white and yellow yams, sugar cane, mustard leaves, fresh pinto beans, jackfruit and Jamaican mangoes. Pulses include East African maganjo beans and Nigerian brown beans.

Brixton Market

Electric Avenue, Pope's Road, Brixton Station Road, Atlantic Road, SW9 (www.lambeth.gov.uk). Brixton tube/rail. **Open** 8am-6pm Mon, Tue, Thur-Sat; 8am-3pm Wed.

An outdoor market and several arcades selling exotic fruit and veg, halal meats, and fish.

Queen's Market

Off the junction of Green Street & Queen's Road, E13 (www.newham.gov.uk). Upton Park tube. **Open** 8am-noon Tue; 8am-5pm Thur-Sat.

Fish, and a huge range of exotic fruit and veg.

Ridley Road Market

Ridley Road, off Kingsland High Street, E8 (www.hackney.gov.uk). Dalston Kingsland rail/30, 38, 56, 67, 76, 242, 243, 277 bus. **Open** 8.30am-5.30pm Mon-Sat.

A lively street market, with stalls selling fruit, veg, fish and meat.

of finely ground chickpeas), but the mixed fried vegetables consisted mainly of cabbage. Ice-cream is the only dessert, but the coffee ceremony is worth the wait: cardamom-scented high-roast coffee is wafted around every diner in the room before appearing on your table with a big bowl of warm popcorn.
Babies and children welcome: high chairs. Booking advisable. Separate room for parties, seats 35. Takeaway service. Vegan dishes. Vegetarian menu. **Map 22 E2.**

Kennington

Adulis

44-46 Brixton Road, SW9 6BT (7587 0055/ www.adulis.co.uk). Oval tube/rail. **Open** 5pm-midnight Mon-Wed; 1pm-midnight Thur-Sun. **Main courses** £7.95-£9.95. **Credit** MC, V. Eritrean

The name derives from an ancient port on the Red Sea, and many of the ingredients used at Adulis – the spices, the finely ground chickpeas for the shiro, the teff grain in the injera bread – are directly imported from Eritrea. Traditionally spicy dishes are served mild, though the owner tells us you can specify the full spice kick if you want it (this isn't stated on the menu). Shimbra assa – chickpeas mashed into balls and roasted in an Eritrean tomato sauce called tsebhi – made up in its flavours of ginger and garlic what it lacked in berbere (traditional Eritrean spice mix). One dish that did not include any berbere was alicha, a dish of chopped potatoes and vegetables cooked in tomatoes and olive oil with a touch of ginger and garlic. All meals are served either with injera or rice, and bottles of Asmara beer are available. Chilled desserts are bought-in; the alternative is to order a coffee and enjoy the aroma of freshly ground beans taking charge of your nostrils. Walls are adorned with paintings of traditional Eritrean life and ornaments such as sandals, symbolising the struggle for independence (sandals were the only footwear worn by soldiers during the 30-year war of independence from Ethiopia).
Babies and children welcome: high chairs; nappy-changing facilities. Booking advisable. Entertainment: band 10pm-midnight Fri-Sun. Separate room for parties, seats 150. Takeway service. **Map 16 M13.**

South East

Peckham

★ 805 Bar Restaurant

805 Old Kent Road, SE15 1NX (7639 0808/ www.805restaurant.com). Elephant & Castle tube/rail then 53 bus. **Meals served** 2pm-midnight daily. **Main courses** £6-£15. **Credit** MC, V. Nigerian

Tucked away on a grim stretch of the Old Kent Road, 805 is a bit of a culinary Tardis: what lies within its golden interior bears little relation to its unprepossessing exterior. Inside, you're in upmarket Lagos, with afrobeat on the sound system and a spicy menu to warm your chilled London bones. Regarded by those in the know as the city's best Nigerian restaurant, 805 draws a sharply modish crowd, but the mood remains laid-back and boisterous; this is very much a family-friendly restaurant. Staff offer helpful guidance to non-initiates, ensuring that newcomers don't order tripe without meaning to; they will also ask whether you want to eat with your hands. The Nigerian menu (there are non-African dishes for the bland of palate) is fairly short, but nothing here comes small, so you won't want to order much. An authentically bracing pepper 'soup' came with a whole fish in it. Gamey goat stew in egusi (pounded melon seeds) had a strong smoky flavour and went well with the delightfully creamy pounded yam. There's a steady supply of chilled Star and Gulder beer on hand to cool overheated mouths.
Babies and children welcome: high chairs. Disabled: toilet. Separate room for parties, seats 60. Tables outdoors (6, pavement). Takeaway service.

805 Bar Restaurant

North East

Dalston

★ Suya Obalende

523 Kingsland Road, E8 4AR (7275 0171/ www.obalendesuya.com). Dalston Kingsland rail/38, 67, 76, 149 bus. **Meals served** noon-midnight Mon-Thur, Sun; noon-1am Fri, Sat. **Main courses** £7.95-£8.95. **Set buffet** (Sun) £9.95. **Credit** MC, V. Nigerian

Part of the Suya Express chain – an outfit that started life in a trailer in Elephant & Castle – this restaurant is almost totally hidden behind the counter of its streetfront takeaway. Dubbed the 'African McDonald's', it's hardly the place for a romantic tête-à-tête. The temperature, in true Nigerian style, is fridge-like, the crimson and black interior is chic but distinctly functional, and if the plasma screens aren't showing noisy footie, music is played stompingly loud. However, this is a great place for large groups, plus anyone more interested in the authentic flavours of downtown Lagos – and value for money – than a sophisticated dining experience. Suya (lamb, chicken or beef skewers grilled over a charcoal fire) is the speciality, but the menu also stretches to stewed snails, crab claws, chicken gizzards and the occasional crocodile. There's also asun (spicy goat chunks), pounded yam and moi-moi (steamed beancake). Meat dishes are accompanied by roast plantain, mounds of jollof rice, stewed spinach and a pungent chilli sauce. On Sunday there's a 'Grill Greedy' buffet; the management slaps a hilarious £2.50 surcharge on anyone failing to clear their plate, the money going to Oxfam.
Babies and children welcome: high chairs. Booking advisable. Takeaway service.
Map 25 B5.
For branch (Suya Express) see index.

North

Kentish Town

★ ★ Queen of Sheba

12 Fortess Road, NW5 2EU (7284 3947/ www.thequeenofsheba.co.uk). Kentish Town tube/rail. **Meals served** 6-11.30pm Mon-Sat; 1-10pm Sun. **Main courses** £5-£10.50. **Credit** MC, V. Ethiopian

The tiled floor and plain pale walls offset by assorted artefacts give little hint of the delights to come at this charming restaurant, where platters lined with injera come piled high with delicious meat or vegetarian selections, elegently served under a tagine-shaped basket. Impeccable food and funky music played a little too loud made for a cheerful evening, even before the restaurant filled up with Ethiopians later in the evening. From a menu that has as much to appeal to vegetarians as meat-eaters, everything was cooked with delicacy; alich'a minchet abish (minced beef warmly spiced with ginger, garlic and turmeric and laced with Ethiopian clarified butter) belied drab looks with its irresistibly rich and complex tastes: an exceptional dish. Paired with a selection of subtly and distinctively spiced wot (spelt here as we't) stews – one with green chilli-spiked yellow split peas and peppery brown lentils, the other a cabbage and potato wot – and accompanied by a zingy tomato salad, it made for a perfectly balanced feast. By the time we'd lost the attention of the notably beautiful waitress to the numerous arrivals, we were nicely sated and not much poorer.
Babies and children welcome: high chairs. Booking advisable. Restaurant available for hire. Tables outdoors (2, patio). Takeaway service. Vegetarian menu. **Map 26 B4.**

Tufnell Park

Lalibela

137 Fortess Road, NW5 2HR (7284 0600). Tufnell Park tube/134 bus. **Dinner served** 6pm-midnight daily. **Main courses** £8.50-£9.95. **Credit** MC, V. Ethiopian

Full of wonder and delight, Lalibela occupies two floors furnished with assorted chairs and tables of varying heights. Upstairs, in a room festooned with bric-a-brac, a loyal throng of Ethiopian and European customers sets a lively tone. As did refreshing starter salads of warm beetroot and potato, and shards of crisply fried fish mixed with tomato and lettuce. It then proved impossible to do justice to the shared vast expanse (two rolls apiece!) of injera, the spongy, pancake-like bread that substitutes both plate and cutlery. The otherwise rather uninterested waitress seemed surprised and disappointed we hadn't finished. Our defeat was in part due to fried strips of lamb spiked with rosemary and thyme – the house special – being

RESTAURANTS

Jerk CITY
The First and Original Caribbean Restaurant in Central London
Caribbean Cuisine at it's finest
HALAL MEAT
Monday-Sunday: 10:00am-10:00pm
189 WARDOUR STREET, LONDON, W1F 8ZD
112 WANDSWORTH HIGH STREET, LONDON SW18 4JP
020 7287 2878
020 7287 3121
• Halal meat used in all dishes
• Outside catering available
• No occasion too big or small

The Adelaide
The Adelaide is a spacious and comfortable bar that offers a warm and friendly atmosphere. We also boast one of the largest gardens from this exciting part of NW3.
What's On:
Regular live music session
DJ's all weekend
Upstairs @ The Adelaide:
Slowfoot Records host live acts once a month
Hampstead Comedy Club every Saturday
Album launches, private parties and much more...
Delicious modern European food available all day: Brunch, Lunch and A-La-Carte
For Room Hire and Reservations Contact Jo:
Swiss Cottage
C11
31
Adelaide Rd
Chalk Farm
The Adelaide, 143 Adelaide Rd, NW3 3NL
020 7722 3777
www.myspace.com/theadelaidenw3
www.helmshine.com

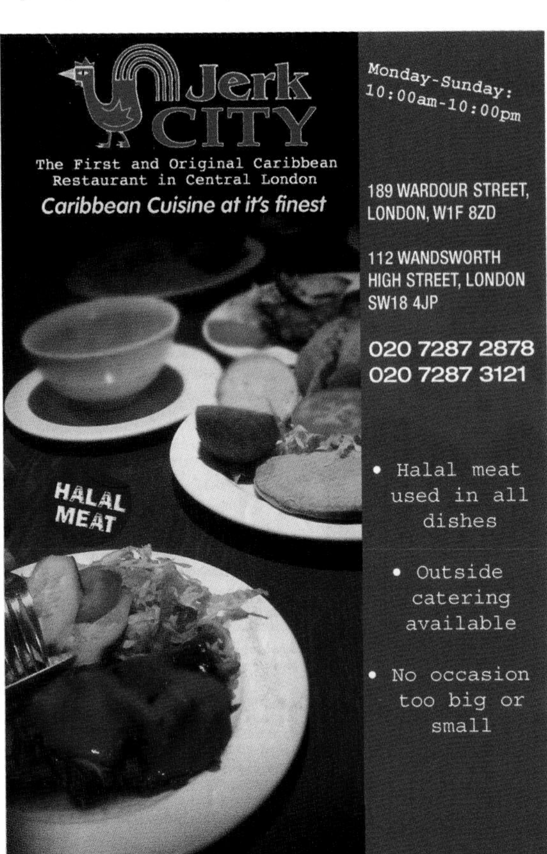

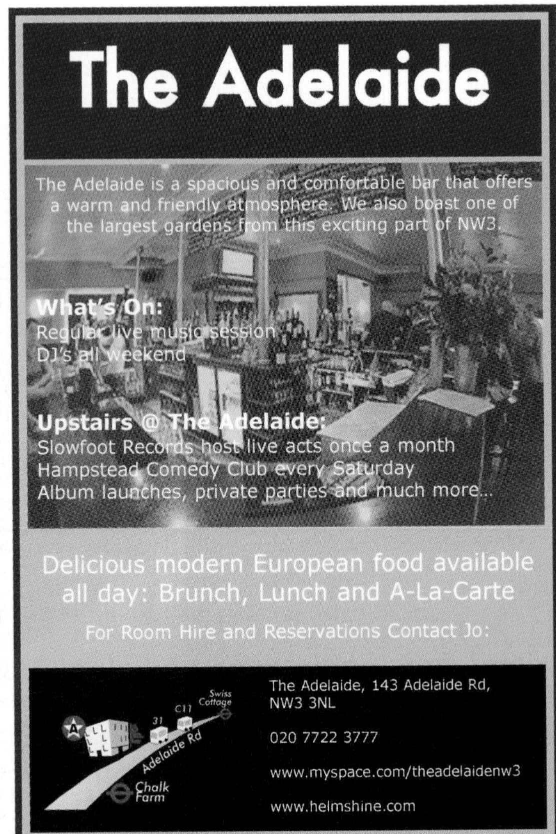

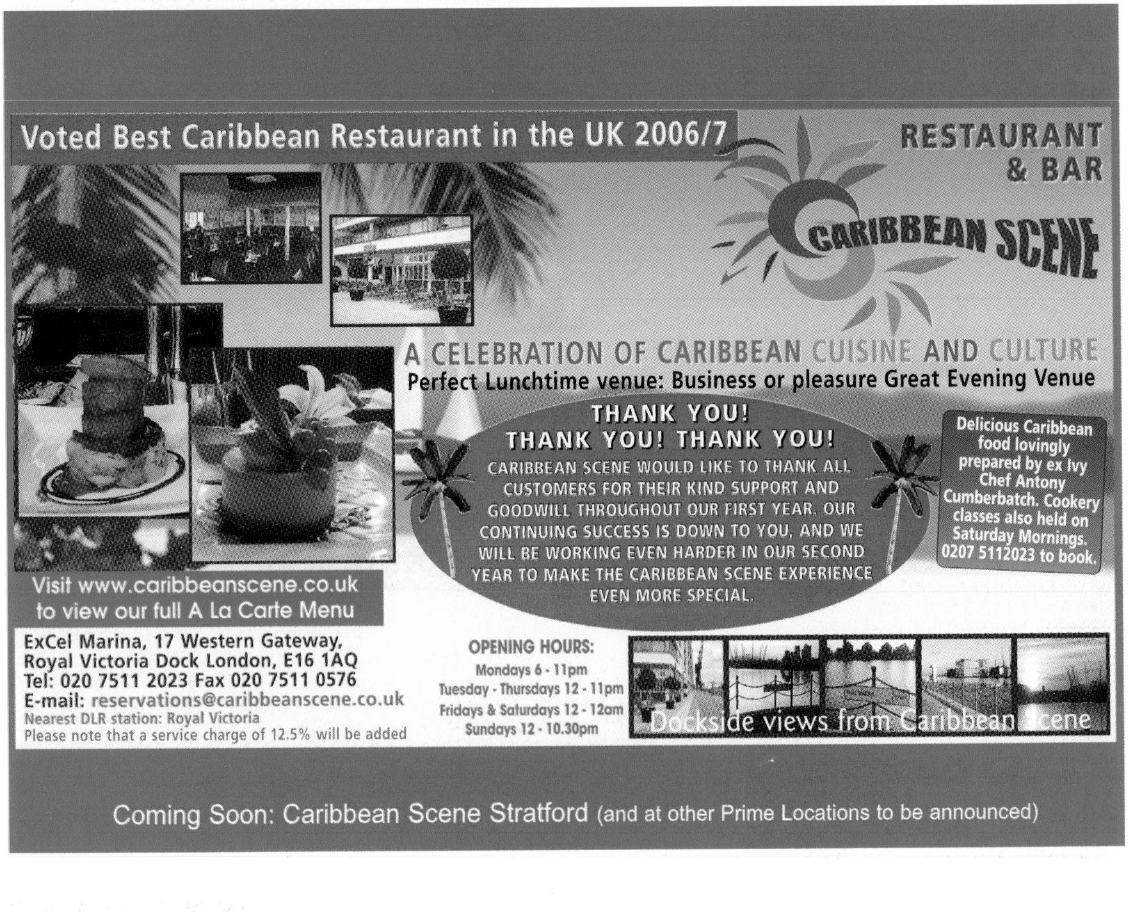

Voted Best Caribbean Restaurant in the UK 2006/7
RESTAURANT & BAR
CARIBBEAN SCENE
A CELEBRATION OF CARIBBEAN CUISINE AND CULTURE
Perfect Lunchtime venue: Business or pleasure Great Evening Venue
THANK YOU!
THANK YOU! THANK YOU!
CARIBBEAN SCENE WOULD LIKE TO THANK ALL CUSTOMERS FOR THEIR KIND SUPPORT AND GOODWILL THROUGHOUT OUR FIRST YEAR. OUR CONTINUING SUCCESS IS DOWN TO YOU, AND WE WILL BE WORKING EVEN HARDER IN OUR SECOND YEAR TO MAKE THE CARIBBEAN SCENE EXPERIENCE EVEN MORE SPECIAL.
Delicious Caribbean food lovingly prepared by ex Ivy Chef Antony Cumberbatch. Cookery classes also held on Saturday Mornings. 0207 5112023 to book.
Visit www.caribbeanscene.co.uk to view our full A La Carte Menu
ExCel Marina, 17 Western Gateway, Royal Victoria Dock London, E16 1AQ
Tel: 020 7511 2023 Fax 020 7511 0576
E-mail: reservations@caribbeanscene.co.uk
Nearest DLR station: Royal Victoria
Please note that a service charge of 12.5% will be added
OPENING HOURS:
Mondays 6 - 11pm
Tuesday - Thursdays 12 - 11pm
Fridays & Saturdays 12 - 12am
Sundays 12 - 10.30pm
Dockside views from Caribbean Scene
Coming Soon: Caribbean Scene Stratford (and at other Prime Locations to be announced)

too long and chewy to eat with dignity and no knife. Wimps who want cutlery can order turmeric rice instead of the versatile, terrifically tangy bread; this injera made the timidly spiced yellow split peas with courgettes and green pepper pale by comparison. Sprightly spring greens stewed with ginger, tomato and onion were a revelation, and the food was served with enough ceremony – mains sizzle over a nightlight in an unusual mask-like claypot – to make the experience thoroughly enjoyable, despite the odd disappointing dish.
Babies and children welcome: high chair. Booking advisable. Takeaway service. Vegetarian menu. Vegan dishes. **Map 26 B3.**

North West

Kilburn

Abyssinia

9 Cricklewood Broadway, NW2 3JX (8208 0110). Kilburn tube. **Meals served** noon-midnight Mon-Fri; 2pm-midnight Sat, Sun. **Main courses** £4.50-£10. **Credit** MC, V. Ethiopian

This smart Kilburn restaurant underwent a change of management in early 2007, though little has been altered in terms of menu or decor. The effort to present an 'authentic' Ethiopian style – paintings of Ethiopian countrymen and women cradling babies hang on the cream walls – is still compromised by minimalist glass mirrors that run in strips alongside them, but the restaurant is none the worse for the contrast. The menu promises an 'Abyssinian culinary experience', helped by Ethiopian music playing in the background, incense burning throughout the evening and a mouth-watering aroma of spices wafting from the kitchen. We tried various vegetarian dishes. Kik wot (boiled split yellow peas) was deliciously mild and delicately spiced, but misser wot (puréed split red lentils, simmered in berbere sauce) was a little too rich and overpowering. Cinnamon-hinted tea was served with dabo, a thick Ethiopian bread that's eaten with savoury food as well as tea. It made for a refreshing end to a rich and enjoyable meal. Food arrived in reasonable time and service was extremely friendly.
Babies and children admitted: high chairs. Booking advisable. Separate room for parties, seats 30. Tables outdoors (6, garden). Takeaway service.

West Hampstead

★ ★ Tobia (100)

1st floor, Ethiopian Community Centre, 2A Lithos Road, NW3 6EF (7431 4213/ www.tobiarestaurant.co.uk). Finchley Road tube. **Meals served** noon-midnight Tue-Sun. **Main courses** £5-£9. **Credit** AmEx, DC, MC, V. Ethiopian

Down a side street, through a grubby garage entrance and up some stairs past a cavernous function room is London's best east African restaurant. True, it might not look like much – especially if (as on our visit) the staff have left the unwatched big-screen TV blaring away, while a family friend sat at a dining table tapping away on his laptop – but for the real tastes of Ethiopia, this is the place. We marvelled at the coffee-coloured injera bread: this version made with pure teff (an east African grain), slightly sour and perfectly elastic and spongy. On this a succession of sublime dishes were served, from lamb with clarified butter, through garlicky spring-green stir-fries, to dal-like lentil dishes. We were wowed by the traditional marinated raw tuna dish, well spiced and unusually textured; and an extraordinary cold 'omelette' of broad-bean flour. Tobia has an extensive selection of appealing vegetarian dishes – Ethiopia's Coptic Christians are vegetarian for most of the year – and every Wednesday and Friday offers meat- and dairy-free menus, though seafood is also served. Chef-proprietor Sophie Sirak-Kebede is a very genial hostess and happy to explain the dishes and cooking.
Babies and children admitted: high chair. Booking advisable weekends. Takeaway service. Vegan dishes. Vegetarian menu. **Map 28 A3.**

Menu

AFRICAN

Accra or **akara**: bean fritters.
Aloco: fried plantain with hot tomato sauce.
Asaro: yam and sweet potato porridge.
Ayeb or **iab**: fresh yoghurt cheese made from strained yoghurt.
Berbere: an Ethiopian spice mix made with many hot and aromatic spices.
Cassava, manioc or **yuca**: a family of coarse roots that are boiled and pounded to make bread and various other farinaceous dishes. There are bitter and sweet varieties (note that the bitter variety is poisonous until cooked).
Egusi: ground melon seeds, added to stews and soups as a thickening agent.
Enjera, enjerra or **injera**: a soft, spongy Ethiopian and Eritrean flatbread made with teff/tef (a grain originally from Ethiopia), wheat, barley, oats or cornmeal. Fermented with yeast, it should have a distinct sour tang.
Froi: fish and shrimp aubergine stew.
Fufu: a stiff pudding of maize or cassava (qv) flour, or pounded yam (qv).
Gari: a solid, heavy pudding made from ground fermented cassava (qv), served with thick soups.
Ground rice: a kind of stiff rice pudding served to accompany soup.
Jollof rice: like a hot, spicy risotto, with tomatoes, onions and (usually) chicken.
Kanyah: a sweet snack from Sierra Leone made from rice, peanuts and sugar.
Kelewele or **do-do**: fried plantain.
Kenkey: a starchy pudding that's prepared by pounding dried maize and water into a paste, then steaming inside plantain leaves. Usually eaten with meat, fish or vegetable stews.
Moi-moi, moin-moin or **moyin moyin**: steamed beancake, served with meat or fish.
Ogbono: a large seed similar to egusi (qv). Although it doesn't thicken as much, it is used in a similar way.
Pepper soup: a light, peppery soup made with either fish or meat.
Shito: a dark red-hot pepper paste from Ghana, made from dried shrimps blended with onions and tomatoes.
Suya: a spicy Nigerian meat kebab.
Tuo or **tuwo**: a stiff rice pudding, sometimes served as rice balls to accompany soup.
Ugali: a Swahili word for bread made from cornmeal and water.
Ugba: Nigerian soy beans; also called oil beans.
Waakye: a dish of rice and black-eyed beans mixed with meat or chicken in gravy.
Waatse: rice and black-eyed beans cooked together.
Wot: a thick, dark sauce made from slowly cooked onions, garlic, butter and spices – an essential component in the aromatic stews of East Africa. (**Doro wot**, a stew containing chicken and hard-boiled eggs, is a particularly common dish.)

CARIBBEAN

Ackee: a red-skinned fruit with yellow flesh that looks and tastes like scrambled eggs when cooked; traditionally served in a Jamaican dish of salt cod, onion and peppers.
Bammy or **bammie**: pancake-shaped, deep-fried cassava bread, commonly served with fried fish.
Breadfruit: this football-sized fruit has sweet, creamy flesh that's a cross between sweet potato and chestnut. Eaten as a vegetable.
Bush tea: herbal tea made from cerese (a Jamaican vine plant), mint or fennel.
Callaloo: the spinach-like leaves of either taro or malanga, often used as a base for a thick soup flavoured with pork or crab meat.
Coo-coo: a polenta-like cake of cornmeal and okra.
Cow foot: a stew made from the hoof of the cow, which is boiled with vegetables. The cartilage gives the stew a gummy or gelatinous texture.
Curried (or **curry**) **goat**: more usually lamb in London; the meat is marinated and slow-cooked until tender.
Dasheen: a root vegetable with a texture similar to yam (qv).
Escoveitched (or **escovitch**) **fish**: fish fried or grilled then pickled in a tangy sauce with onions, sweet peppers and vinegar; similar to escabèche.
Festival: deep-fried, slightly sweet dumpling often served with fried fish.
Foo-foo: a Barbadian dish of pounded plantains, seasoned, rolled into balls and served hot.
Jerk: chicken or pork marinated in chilli spices, slowly roasted or barbecued.
Patty or **pattie**: a savoury pastry snack similar to a pasty, made with turmeric-coloured short-crust pastry, usually filled with beef, saltfish or vegetables.
Peas or **beans**: black-eyed beans, black beans, green peas and red kidney beans (the names are interchangeable).
Pepperpot: traditionally a stew of meat and cassereep, a juice obtained from cassava; in London it's more likely to be a meat or vegetable stew with cassava.
Phoulorie: a Trinidadian snack of fried doughballs often eaten with a sweet tamarind sauce.
Plantain or **plantin**: a savoury variety of banana that is cooked like potato.
Rice and peas: rice cooked with kidney or gungo beans, pepper seasoning and coconut milk.
Roti: the Indian flatbread, usually filled with curried fish, meat or vegetables.
Saltfish: salt cod, classically combined with ackee (qv) or callaloo (qv).
Sorrel: not the European herb but a type of hibiscus with a sour-sweet flavour.
Soursop: a dark green, slightly spiny fruit; the pulp, blended with milk and sugar, is a refreshing drink.
Yam: a large tuber, with a yellow or white flesh and slightly nutty flavour.

CARIBBEAN

Caribbean cuisine in London is largely the domain of takeaway establishments in areas with a particularly high Afro-Caribbean population. **Wadada's** (161 Askew Road, W12 9AU, 8740 3452) offers Grenadian-inspired cuisine, while **Roti Joupa** (12 Clapham High Street, SW4 7UT, 7627 8637) specialises in Indo-Trinidadian food. Both are excellent, though standards can be variable in other Caribbean takeaways. As far as the few smarter Caribbean restaurants go, **Glistening Waters** in Brentford is perhaps the best that we've discovered recently; **Caribbean Scene** in east London also helps raise the bar, and **Brown Sugar** knows how to get the ambience right. Soho's Mr Jerk has split into two very similar (and similarly named) operations; **Original Mr Jerk** and **Jerk City**. Other old favourites might need to do some rethinking and step up their game.

Central

Clerkenwell & Farringdon

★ Cottons

70 Exmouth Market, EC1R 4QP (7833 3332/ www.cottons-restaurant.co.uk). Farringdon tube/ rail/19, 38, 341 bus. **Lunch served** noon-4pm Mon-Fri. **Dinner served** 5.30-11pm Mon-Thur; 6-11.30pm Fri, Sat. **Meals served** noon-11pm Sun. **Main courses** £7.50-£8. **Credit** AmEx, MC, V.

The high standard that Caribbean food lovers have come to expect at the Cottons flagship in Chalk Farm has finally been replicated at its second branch on Exmouth Market. It's got a groovy tropical feel to it and although the decor hardly screams of beach shacks and sundowners, there's a definite appeal in the laid-back atmosphere and gentle rock soundtrack. Service isn't as relaxed as the vibe; we found staff attentive and extremely patient. A starter of deliciously light saltfish fritters was a good indication of the quality that was to follow. Although coq au rhum (chicken marinated in a peppercorn and cream sauce) sounded retro, there was no doubting – once we'd tasted it – why this dish has become a signature dish. The chicken (a very substantial portion) was well seasoned and perfectly cooked. Impressively, the bar has built up a drinks range that features more than 150 rums from around the world; they can be sampled in the restaurant itself, or in the basement Rum Jungle Bar. Here, on Friday and Saturday nights, a DJ spins the latest Caribbean hits until the small hours.

Babies and children admitted: high chairs. Booking advisable. Disabled: toilet. Entertainment: singer 6.30-10pm, DJs 10.30pm-1am Fri, Sat. Separate room available for parties, seating 70 (Mon-Thur). Outdoor tables (7, patio). Takeaway service. **Map 5 N4.**

For branch see index.

Soho

★ Jerk City NEW

189 Wardour Street, W1F 8ZD (7287 2878/ www.jerkcity.co.uk). Tottenham Court Road tube. **Meals served** 10am-10.30pm Mon-Wed; 10am-11pm Thur-Sat; noon-8pm Sun. **Main courses** £6-£8.50. **Credit** MC, V.

The site that used to be called Mr Jerk has changed name and management, but it's still as Caribbean as calypso music. The sound system plays Lovers' Rock; the cooler cabinet is stocked with Supermalt, Old Jamaica Ginger Beer and 'Authentic Zion Roots Drink'; a cluster of people hang around the entrance waiting for their takeaways. The menu is near-identical to the adjacent Original Mr Jerk (*see below*), and there's not that much to choose between the two, though Jerk City is brisker, with orders taken and paid for at the counter. Don't over-order: on our many visits we've never managed to finish our 'medium' portions, so we wonder who orders 'large' – Mike Tyson? And it's a shame to waste food when it's as good as the curried mutton, with complex flavours and unctuous textures that would be the pride of any Trinidadian Indian; the soft roti is also the real thing. The saltfish and ackee should also nice-'em-up, but is so rich that the accompanying rice 'n' peas (long-grain rice stained auburn with red kidney beans) seems like welcome relief. Soursop juice (resembling a thick milkshake) makes a refreshing accompaniment, but is also so intense that it might play havoc with your cholesterol level.

Babies and children welcome: high chairs; nappy-changing facilities. Takeaway service. **Map 17 B3.**

For branch see index.

★ Original Mr Jerk NEW

187 Wardour Street, W1F 8ZB (7437 7770/ www.mrjerk.co.uk). Tottenham Court Road tube. **Meals served** 11am-11pm Mon-Sat; noon-8pm Sun. **Main courses** £7-£9. **Credit** AmEx, DC, MC, V.

Mr Jerk on Wardour Street used to be *the* place for good Caribbean food in central London. Although it was small, cramped and uncomfortable, no one really minded because the food was so good. In late 2006, a split between the original business partners saw two Mr Jerks appear: Jerk City (*see above*) on the old site, and Original Mr Jerk right next door. The latter is a spacious new restaurant with a good atmosphere and great food that's still affordable. In the front, there's a decent-sized bar area that's ideal for chilling out with a cocktail. The separate dining area is comfortable, with room for about 20 people. The menu is much as before; perhaps the portions are a little smaller (once enormous, they now rate as big), but they're still tasty. The signature dish – jerk chicken with rice and peas and steamed vegetables – was good; the chicken spot-on, though the vegetables could have been prepared with more attention. There's a definite buzz around the place; improvements in the friendliness and smoothness of staff will impress old customers and should attract many new ones.

Babies and children admitted. No bookings. Takeaway service. **Map 17 B3.**

South

Battersea

Brown Sugar NEW

165-167 St John's Hill, SW11 1TQ (7228 7713/ www.brownsugarlondon.com). Clapham Junction rail. **Dinner served** 6-11pm Mon-Thur; 6pm-midnight Fri; 4pm-midnight Sat; 2-11pm Sun. **Main courses** £11.25-£13.95. **Credit** AmEx, MC, V.

Brown Sugar's spacious interior and chic looks create an excellent first impression – which isn't always the case with Caribbean restaurants. On the food side, they aren't doing too badly either. The menu, which is described as 'classic' with a 'unique contemporary slant', offers something for everyone, including a fair share of options for vegetarians. The most enticing-sounding starter was 'spicy pepper medley' (sautéed sweet peppers served on hardough bread), but the irresistible combination of green banana and saltfish – in this instance as a salad – won out. Tempting main courses included Caribbean cod with green banana, spinach and okra, okra medley (sautéed okra with sweet peppers, shallots, garlic and scotch bonnet peppers) and the ubiquitous jerk chicken with rice and peas. Our chosen dishes of curried goat and callaloo royale (callaloo greens stir-fried with sweet peppers, chilli, garlic and shallots) were delicious, but a little too spicy. Brown Sugar offers a good dining experience – the decor, service and atmosphere are all great – but the food, though tasty, doesn't quite have the wow factor to match.

Babies and children admitted. Booking advisable. Disabled: toilet. Entertainment: DJ 7pm Sat. Tables outdoors (4, pavement). Takeaway service. **Map 21 B4.**

Brixton

★ Bamboula

12 Acre Lane, SW2 5SG (7737 6633/www. walkerswood.com). Brixton tube/rail. **Meals served** 11am-11pm Mon-Sat; 1-9pm Sun. **Main courses** £7-£9. **Credit** MC, V.

This popular Brixton spot has a reputation for tasty, well-priced Caribbean food. But while the cost remained reasonable, a recent meal wasn't as satisfying as in the past. Although Bamboula's food is still flavourful, there no longer appears to be as much passion, imagination or attention to detail in the kitchen. There were problems with both presentation and execution. For example, a portion of curried goat (excellent) came on a cold plate with a cold portion of 'Caribbean salad'; the salad itself was an uninspiring combination of shredded iceberg lettuce, cabbage and sliced tomatoes. The exotically named 'Ring of Nubian Queen' (saltfish and red beans in a coconut sauce with banana chips) failed to live up to its exciting billing, the saltfish being bland. The small restaurant (20 or so seats) was full on a Friday night, which meant abrupt service from a clearly stretched two-person waiting team. Bamboula was once a real beacon for Caribbean cuisine and could be again, but there needs to be a rethink to resurrect that old glory.

Babies and children admitted. Booking advisable Fri, Sat (£5 deposit required over 4 people). Tables outdoors (2, garden). Takeaway service. **Map 22 D2.**

East

Docklands

Caribbean Scene NEW

ExCel Marina, 17 Western Gateway, Royal Victoria Dock, E16 1AQ (7511 2023/www. caribbeanscene.co.uk). Royal Victoria DLR. **Meals served** noon-10.30pm daily. **Main courses** £11.50-£35.50. **Credit** AmEx, MC,V.

Despite the name, Caribbean Scene is savvy enough to avoid hackneyed tropical references. The understated decor (smart leather seating, serene views over Royal Victoria Dock and an open kitchen fringed with palms) creates a comfortable but slick space – more uptown Kingston than Montego Bay. Both lunch and dinner menus feature classic fare from the region alongside more experimental dishes prepared to varying degrees of success. A starter of succulent king prawns, grilled and served with a fresh and zesty mango salsa, was innovative and successful; 'plantain drops' sounded more intriguing than the reality of deep-fried mashed plantain balls served with an abrasive barbecue dip. Mains were consistently good, the restaurant's expertise most evident in its well-crafted versions of traditional dishes. Jerk chicken was marinated in a pleasantly peppery sauce that managed to be both sweet and tangy; a brown fish stew was full of flavour, the 'stew' a richly reduced sauce laced with scotch bonnet pepper and garlic. First-class presentation and attentive service give CS personality aplenty. Even on a rainy Monday evening, the restaurant managed to draw a crowd that included laid-back diners and business folk, far outstretching its corporate Docklands surrounds.

Babies and children welcome: high chairs. Booking advisable Fri-Sun. Disabled: toilet. Entertainment: band 8-10.30pm Fri, Sat. Tables outdoors (16, patio). Takeaway service.

North

Camden Town & Chalk Farm

Mango Room

10-12 Kentish Town Road, NW1 8NH (7482 5065/www.mangoroom.co.uk). Camden Town tube. **Lunch served** noon-4pm, **dinner served** 4-11pm Mon-Sat. **Meals served** noon-11pm Sun. **Main courses** £10-£13. **Credit** AmEx, MC, V.

Glistening Waters

Mango Room's menu abandons cliché in favour of a modern approach to Caribbean cuisine. Based on the superb cooking we've usually enjoyed here in the past, we had high expectations of starters such as 'ebony' chicken and grilled prawns skewered with rosemary. But on this occasion both dishes were decidedly ordinary; the chicken lacked flavour and the rosemary overpowered the seafood with its strong flavour. A chargrilled pork loin lacked depth or character; the meat didn't taste as if it was of especially high quality, and no amount of spicy sauce can make up for that. But things improved with a perfectly grilled main of entrecote steak garnished with mango salsa. Caribbean fruit cake is always a popular option for dessert, so we ordered that and were not disappointed. Service too was just right: friendly and attentive but not intrusive. Mango Room is to be applauded for having a go at mirroring the kind of modern, sophisticated vibe that one finds in the Caribbean's best restaurants; it's just a pity that the results were so variable.

Babies and children welcome: high chairs. Booking advisable weekends. Separate rooms for parties, seat 10, 20. **Map 27 D2**.

Outer London

Brentford, Middlesex

★ Glistening Waters NEW

5 Ferry Lane, Ferry Quays, High Street, Brentford, Middx TW8 0AT (8758 1616). Brentford or Kew Bridge rail. **Meals served** 6pm-11.30pm Tue-Fri; 3pm-midnight Sat; 1-10.30pm Sun. **Main courses** £9.95-£50. **Credit** MC, V.

Brentford isn't the most obvious location for an upmarket Caribbean restaurant. But tucked beside the Thames and just across the river from Kew Gardens, newcomer Glistening Waters is already one of London's best. White walls, modern paintings and African sculpture create an elegant yet funky vibe. Heady smells fill the dining room every time a sizzling platter emerges; 'bassa bassa chicken', for example, brought with it the delicious aroma of tamarind. Satisfied 'mmm's and 'aah's from those who had ordered it fuelled our excitement before our own meal had arrived. An exquisitely presented starter of plantain rounds (strips of plantain bent into circles) filled with ackee and callaloo did not disappoint; it was one of the best ackee dishes we've found in London. A main of 'coconut rundown' (prawns cooked in coconut sauce with noodles) was also good. Though full after two courses, meringues filled with cream, sweet mango chunks and passionfruit proved irresistible. Prices here are a bit higher than at other Caribbean restaurants, but the quality of the cooking justifies them. Glistening Waters have definitely raised the bar in this genre, thanks to an uncomplicated but well-executed menu, assisted by faultless service.

Babies and children welcome: high chairs. Bookings advisable. Tables outdoors (2, pavement).

The Americas

NORTH AMERICAN

London's North American restaurant sector has been active during the past couple of years. New establishments such as the excellent **Hawksmoor** and the **Diner** (contender for Best Cheap Eats in the 2007 Time Out Eating & Drinking Awards) have opened to rave reviews, while old friends, including the late and much lamented Arkansas Café, have left the scene (though we're hoping that gregarious chef/owner Bubba will find a new site soon).

There's much similarity between the places in this chapter – the vast majority of American restaurants have some sort of hamburger or steak at the heart of their menus – but there's also increasing variety. Newcomer **Rhodes B-B-Q Shack** has joined the estimable **Bodean's** in offering great smoky cuisine. **Pacific Bar & Grill** and the **Coyote** are both excellent local joints featuring adventurous cuisine, while **Curve** and **Christopher's** keep us keen with regular menu revisions. There's plenty offered in a wide spectrum of price ranges, proving that not all American cuisine fits neatly in a bun with a dollop of relish.

Central

City

Missouri Grill

76 Aldgate High Street, EC3N 1BD (7481 4010/ www.missourigrill.com). Aldgate or Aldgate East tube. **Lunch served** noon-3pm, **dinner served** 5-10pm Mon-Fri. **Main courses** £10-£19.50. **Set dinner** £12 2 courses, £16 3 courses. **Credit** AmEx, MC, V.

A small, low-key restaurant almost directly across from Aldgate tube station, the Missouri attracts local office workers as regulars. They gather here for business lunches and after-work steaks and cocktails. Perhaps because of this the atmosphere is restrained; customers tend to be puzzling over complex-looking documents and making deals. Nobody gets particularly rowdy. The look of the place is also unstartling: white tablecloths and plain walls. The menu reads like a who's who of upmarket US cuisine. Starters include a creamy New England clam chowder, grilled asparagus topped with a fried egg, beef carpaccio, and crab cakes. Mains are heavy on the steak (perfectly grilled to order, but nothing unusual), yet there are plenty of other options including the blackened salmon, Cornish chicken with chipotle crème fraîche, and rack of lamb. Everything's precisely as you might expect, given the locale. Puddings are also straightforward: cheesecake with blueberries, tooth-achingly sweet pecan maple tart and tangy lemon custard. So, no surprises – but that can be a good thing.

Babies and children welcome: children's portions; high chairs. Booking essential lunch. Separate room for parties, seats 14. **Map 12 R6.**

★ Hawksmoor

157 Commercial Street, E1 6BJ (7247 7392/ www.thehawksmoor.com). Liverpool Street tube/ rail. **Lunch served** noon-2.30pm Mon-Fri. **Dinner served** 6-10.30pm Mon-Sat. **Main courses** £14.50-£25.50. **Credit** AmEx, MC, V.

Just up the road from the titular architect's iconic Christ Church, Hawksmoor is all about subtlety. Its sign is easy to miss, the dining room is subdued, the decor self-effacing. In fact, there are only two things that really stand out: the gregarious, skilled bartenders and the incredible steaks – no surprise, perhaps, as it was runner-up for both Best Bar and Best Steak Restaurant in the 2006 Time Out Eating & Drinking Awards. Great, thick slabs of impossibly tender beef – from Longhorn cattle reared, the restaurant claims, in 'sunny North Yorkshire' – arrive alone on a plate, as if any garnish would be gilding the lily. And so it would. The quality sirloins, ribeyes and T-bones are chargrilled precisely to order. There are also racks of lamb from Swaledale sheep raised on heather moorland, pork chops from pedigree Tamworth pigs, and chicken, along with meat-free aubergine parmigiana. Nevertheless, this place is really a culinary love song to beef. Fries are hand-cut, cooked to a crisp and served in glasses. Vegetables are offered in tiny amounts: all the better not to distract you from the meat at the heart of the matter.

Babies and children admitted. Disabled: toilet. **Map 6 R5.**

Clerkenwell & Farringdon

The Bar & Grill

2-3 West Smithfield, EC1A 9JX (7246 0900/ www.blackhousegrills.com). Farringdon tube/rail. **Meals served** noon-11pm daily. **Main courses** £8.50-£50. **Credit** AmEx, MC, V.

Part of the Blackhouse Grills mini chain (based in north-west England), this Farringdon eat-and-drinkerie has endeared itself to the area's office workers. They cram into its stylish bar, then stumble into the busy dining room where (on recent visits) they could be seen lustily conversing about office politics and snogging in the curvy dark leather booths. The attractions are obvious: the cocktails are excellent and well priced, and the menu is varied and not outrageously expensive. Starters tend to be hearty, including gnocchi with three-cheese sauce, and shellfish marinière (with clams, crab claws and mussels). Most mains are similarly sturdy: steak (from chateaubriand to rump), mixed grills, and virtually anything else meaty (lamb, suckling pig, ostrich) that can be sliced and roasted. There's also plenty of seafood, but the restaurant's eyebrow-raiser is the Kobe beef fillet (£50): a big hunk of incredibly tender meat from happy, massaged, classically raised cows. We reckon the menu has become slightly too diverse of late, and the quality of the meat has slipped. It would be nice to see the B&G refocus on simple, excellent food.

Babies and children welcome: high chairs. Booking advisable. Disabled: toilet. Separate area for parties, seats 10. **Map 11 O5.**

Dollar Grills & Martinis

2 Exmouth Market, EC1R 4PX (7278 0077). Angel tube/Farringdon tube/rail/19, 38 bus.
Bar **Open** 6pm-1am Mon-Sat; 6pm-midnight Sun. **Meals served** 6-11pm Mon-Sat; 6-10pm Sun. **Main courses** £4.50-£9.
Restaurant **Lunch served** noon-4pm Mon-Sat; noon-5pm Sun. **Dinner served** 6-11pm Mon-Sat; 6-10pm Sun. **Main courses** £8.50-£22.50. **Set lunch** (Mon-Fri) £8.95 2 courses
Both **Credit** AmEx, MC, V.

This colourful, flamboyant disco ball of a venue is brought to you by the people behind Notting Hill's Beach Blanket Babylon. Inside, the walls are covered in mirrors and big, bright art. Rows of windows overlook Exmouth Market. The waiters flounce by with Technicolor cocktails trailing strands of fresh lemongrass or piled high with raspberries. The dinner menu emphasises the burgers – which arrive so thick that it's hard to bite into them. The sweet-cure bacon and mozzarella burger is one of the less towering options. If you're not in the mood for a beef sandwich, try one of the many alternatives: lighter options such as a grilled goat's cheese and asparagus salad, wild mushroom and pea tagliatelle, or grilled salmon with caper butter. Heavier mains include butter-rich monkfish served with spinach, mustard mash and prawns, or roast leg of lamb with grilled aubergine and a pesto-stuffed tomato. Everything takes place in a jovial, lively atmosphere that

BEST NORTH AMERICAN

Stunning steaks

Beef it up at **Black & Blue** (*see p45*), **Hawksmoor** (*see left*) and **Sophie's Steakhouse & Bar** (*see p47*).

What a burger!

Prime patties at **Dollar Grills & Martinis** (*see above*), **The Diner** (*see p45*), **Eagle Bar Diner** (*see right*) and **Lucky 7** (*see p47*).

Good times

Let 'em roll at **The Bar & Grill** (*see left*), **Big Easy** (*see p47*), **The Coyote** (*see p46*), **Dollar Grills & Martinis** (*see above*) and **PJ's Grill** (*see p45*).

Upscale dining

Best bib and tucker at **Christopher's** (*see right*), **Curve** (*see p48*), **Hawksmoor** (*see left*) and **Pacific Bar & Grill** (*see p46*).

Breakfast

Kick off the day in style at **Automat** (*see p45*), **Curve** (*see p48*), **The Diner** (*see p45*), **Eagle Bar Diner** (*see right*), **Joe Allen** (*see right*) and **Lucky 7** (*see p47*).

Kid-tastic!

Jolly-up Junior at **Dexter's Grill & Bar** (*see p46*), **Ed's Easy Diner** (*see p45*), **Hard Rock Café** (*see p46*), **Jo Shmo's** (*see p47*), **Planet Hollywood** (*see p46*), **Sticky Fingers** (*see p47*), **TGI Friday's** (*see p46*) and **Tootsies Grill** (*see p47*).

makes you feel like putting on your high heels and heading out to the ball. If the Scissor Sisters owned a restaurant, it would look like this.
Babies and children admitted. Bar available for hire. Entertainment: DJs 8pm Fri, Sat. Tables outdoors (10, pavement). **Map 5 N4.**

Covent Garden

Christopher's

18 Wellington Street, WC2E 7DD (7240 4222/ www.christophersgrill.com). Covent Garden tube. Bar **Open/snacks served** noon-midnight Mon-Fri; noon-1am Sat; noon-10.30pm Sun. *Restaurant* **Brunch served** 11.30am-3.30pm Sat, Sun. **Lunch served** noon-3pm Mon-Fri. **Dinner served** 5-11.30pm Mon-Sat. **Main courses** £12-£34. **Set brunch** £15.25 2 courses, £18 3 courses. **Set meal** (5.30-7pm, 10-11.15pm Mon-Sat) £14.50 2 courses, £17 3 courses. *Both* **Credit** AmEx, DC, MC, V.

Christopher's is an attractive spot, with its creamy decor and wide windows letting in light and air. The restaurant has long staked out a position on the first floor of one of Covent Garden's prettier buildings. Below is a newly trendy ground-floor bar, and a marble Italianate staircase that leads up to the dining room. The menu is consistently excellent, featuring some of the best US cuisine – juicy steaks from Nebraskan cattle, lobster from Maine – as well as more elaborate dishes such as pan-fried sea bass with fennel and chorizo, halibut cooked in red wine with roast salsify, and roast pumpkin mousse with shiitake mushrooms and pumpkin salsa. The restaurant still has too much expense-account padding (£22 for the burger with lobster, for example, and £27.50 for a 14oz sirloin), but it also has more affordable dishes, and creative options such as fillet steak served 'carpetbag style': with fried oysters. Desserts are always outstanding; the chefs do things with peach melba your grandma never thought of. The atmosphere is just slightly formal, but never uncomfortable. Service verges on impeccable, and the wine list is seductive.
Babies and children welcome: children's menu; high chairs. Booking advisable. Separate room for parties, seats 40. **Map 18 F4.**

Joe Allen

13 Exeter Street, WC2E 7DT (7836 0651/www.joeallen.co.uk). Covent Garden tube. **Breakfast served** 8-11.30am Mon-Fri. **Brunch served** 11.30am-4.30pm Sat, Sun. **Meals served** noon-12.30am Mon-Fri; 11.30am-12.30am Sat; 11.30am-11.30pm Sun. **Main courses** £8-£18. **Set brunch** £18.50 2 courses, £20.50 3 courses incl drink. **Set meal** (noon-3pm Mon-Fri, 5-6.45pm Mon-Sat) £15 2 courses, £17 3 courses. **Credit** AmEx, MC, V.

Tucked away in a basement at the edge of Covent Garden, Joe Allen has been packing in the theatre crowds for as long, it seems, as there have been theatres. It's one of the places where you're most likely to see the cast and crew of a musical carousing in a corner – sometimes still in their stage make-up. It's always full, and always buzzing. That's what lures people. Not the service, which runs the gamut from flounce to snarl, and certainly not the food, which is far from memorable. With starters such as chopped chicken liver, and anchovy and black olive salad, this menu is all about the 1970s, only without the knowing wink. There's nothing ironic about the side order of mangetouts with toasted almonds, the minted new potatoes or the pan-fried calf's liver main course. Generally speaking, the more adventurous the menu gets, the more hit and miss the food, so it's best to go for basics such as sirloin steak with fries, or grilled tuna with roasted baby corn, and cross your fingers.
Babies and children welcome: booster seats. Booking advisable. Entertainment: pianist 9pm-1am Mon-Sat. **Map 18 E4.**

Fitzrovia

Eagle Bar Diner

3-5 Rathbone Place, W1T 1HJ (7637 1418/ www.eaglebardiner.com). Tottenham Court Road tube. **Open** noon-11pm Mon-Wed; noon-1am

Hawksmoor

Thur, Fri; 10am-1am Sat; 10am-6pm Sun.
Main courses £5.95-£12.95. **Credit** MC, V.
The Eagle was one of London's first gourmet burger restaurants – possibly the first. The polished pine floors, leather banquettes, arty lighting and knowing approach to revising the burger ethic were revolutionary when it opened a few years ago. Now the place is starting to look just a little worn around the edges. Still, there aren't too many better lunch options at the ugly, eastern end of Oxford Street. The food still works: big juicy burgers (made with anything you wish, from beef to chicken to tuna to bison to emu… you get the picture), thick sandwiches, big leafy salads and all-day American-style breakfasts with stacks of pancakes or waffles. The milkshakes are creamy and served in large glasses, and soft-drinks come in glass bottles, as they should. One problem is the service, which runs from indifferent to resentful. The other problem is the restaurant's penchant for pounding club music at dinner time: played so loud it's virtually impossible to sustain a conversation. Lunches, blessedly, are free of that scourge, though the service could still be better.
Babies and children admitted (until 9pm if dining). Disabled: toilet. Entertainment: DJs 7.30pm Wed-Sat. Takeaway service.
Map 17 B2.

Marylebone

Black & Blue
90-92 Wigmore Street, W1V 3RD (7486 1912/ www.blackandblue.biz). Bond Street tube. **Meals served** noon-11pm daily. **Main courses** £8-£25. **Credit** AmEx, MC, V.
This slick, reliable steakhouse chain – with five outlets around London – has spent the last few years contentedly making it look easy. Walk into the small, modern dining room, with its rows of deep booths, and you get the impression that knocking out juicy sirloins, ribeyes and fillets, then serving them up with crispy fries, is a simple thing. There's chargrilled tuna when you don't feel like meat, as well as roasted chicken and big salads. The large portions and reasonable prices, combined with the sophisticated look of the restaurants, and the convivial first-date-friendly ambience keep the crowds rolling in. The only criticisms are that it's all a bit suburban and unadventurous – and the easy-listening music would be excruciating if it was turned up loud enough to be properly audible. But the food is straightforward and reliable, the shortish wine list is well chosen and kindly priced (with plenty of bottles for less than £20), and the artichoke and spinach dip starter is perfect for sharing (just don't smile until you've checked your teeth).
Babies and children admitted. Bookings not accepted. Tables outdoors (2, pavement).
Map 9 G6.
For branches see index.

Mayfair

Automat
33 Dover Street, W1S 4NF (7499 3033/ www.automat-london.com). Green Park tube.
Breakfast served 7-11am Mon-Fri. **Meals served** noon-midnight Mon-Fri; 11am-midnight Sat; 11am-4pm Sun. **Main courses** £7-£25. **Credit** AmEx, JCB, MC, V.
According to the gossip columns, this hyper-trendy Mayfair eaterie is a favourite with celebrities. We suppose they must be seated in the lovely front section, with its symmetrical rows of leather-covered booths, since we've never seen them from our usual seats in the soulless back room. Here, the tables are shoved too closely together, and the smells from the open kitchen soak into your clothing as a lasting reminder of this indifferent restaurant. The attraction at Automat must be the tasty cocktails and the star-spotting, as it's surely not the roadside-diner-style food. The nudge-nudge 1970s menu fails to update creatively the boring, stodgy food of that unlamented decade. Our bland, greasy macaroni cheese remindes us a little too vividly of real roadside diners, as did the dull pasta primavera (it was boring then, and it's boring now). The knowing kitsch value of serving baked lobster with cauliflower cheese might have worked, if it wasn't all so bland. The safest bets here are the steaks and fries, if you must.
Babies and children admitted. Booking advisable. Disabled: toilet. Takeaway service. **Map 9 H7**.

Soho

★ Bodean's
10 Poland Street, W1F 8PZ (7287 7575/ www.bodeansbbq.com). Oxford Circus or Piccadilly Circus tube.
Deli **Open** noon-11pm Mon-Sat; noon-10.30pm Sun. *Restaurant* **Lunch served** noon-3pm, **dinner served** 6-11pm Mon-Fri. **Meals served** noon-11pm Sat; noon-10.30pm Sun. **Main courses** £6.95-£17.95. **Set meal** (minimum 8) £16.95 2 courses.
Both **Credit** AmEx, MC, V.
Never before has anybody successfully paired barbecue with sophistication, but somehow Bodean's pulls it off. Not on the ground floor, though – that's a casual walk-in diner, where crowds of US and Canadian expats gather to watch football and baseball games on the numerous TVs, and the door-handles are shaped like pigs' heads. The basement, on the other hand, is another world, with leather banquettes and booths, soothing lighting, wood panelling… and televisions showing football and baseball. Oh well, you can't have it all. The main attraction is the (short) menu of spare, baby-back and beef ribs, big grilled steaks, pulled pork, chicken and brisket, and the sheer fun of eating down-home barbecue food in oh-so-sophisticated Soho (there are also branches in Clapham and Fulham). The grill is used expertly; all our meat was perfectly cooked. Sides of sweet baked beans and fries are almost superfluous, given the huge plates of meat. It's virtually impossible to save room for a slice of cool key lime pie for dessert. Not for vegetarians.
Babies and children welcome: children's area; children's menu; high chairs; nappy-changing facilities. Booking advisable (restaurant). Restaurant & deli available for hire. Tables outdoors (10, pavement). Takeaway service.
Map 17 A3.
For branches see index.

★ The Diner NEW
2007 RUNNER-UP BEST CHEAP EATS
18-20 Ganton Street, W1F 7BU (7287 8962/ www.thedinersoho.com). Oxford Circus or Piccadilly Circus tube. **Meals served** 8am-12.30pm Mon-Fri; 9am-12.30pm Sat; 9am-11am Sun. **Main courses** £5-£9. **Credit** AmEx, MC, V.
How do you sex up American food in the wake of all the bad press? If you thought it couldn't be done, take a look at this artfully reconstructed US diner newly arrived in Soho. A calculated hotchpotch of retro styles gives the place the air of knowing irony needed to maintain credibility among its trendy neighbours. A fun and friendly attitude, ample space, great drinks and hearty, good-quality scoff also help the Diner compete. It's a rare pleasure to eat a burger that tastes as if you've just made it yourself, with no trace of mass production or mechanical preparation. Such was our delight as we bit into the pleasingly amorphous patty that came with cheese, bacon, fresh leaves and a good, firm bun. Some crunchy-out, fluffy-in chips scattered with cajun spice, and a moreish red cabbage coleslaw provided worthy sides. 'Mexican breakfast' from the all-day breakfast menu was a filling plate of scrambled eggs, guacamole, refried beans, salsa and chorizo lardons. Only a weak, watery bloody mary let the side down; we shouldn't have shunned the house cocktail menu. But overall, this is a first-rate supplier of straight-down-the-line, unfussy comfort food and drink.
Babies and children welcome: booster seats; children's portions. Tables outdoors (7, pavement). Takeaway service. **Map 17 A4**.

★ Ed's Easy Diner
12 Moor Street, W1V 5LH (7434 4439/ www.edseasydiner.co.uk). Leicester Square or Tottenham Court Road tube. **Meals served** noon-midnight daily. **Main courses** £4.40-£5.75. **Minimum** (6pm-midnight Fri-Sun) £4.55. **Credit** MC, V.
This popular, four-strong chain of *Happy Days*-style red and white diners lives in a weird world where American 1950s cuisine meets a British 1970s jukebox in 21st-century London. The concept is undeniably strange, but the food is good and cheap, and the venues are both fun and handy (three are in the West End, one in Chelsea). And it's obviously doing something right, as it celebrates its 20th birthday in 2007. The menu is all about burgers – with cheese, or without – piled with lettuce, pickles and all the trimmings. If you're not in the mood for burgers, try a hot dog, onion rings or even a green salad. The shakes and malts are legendary, and the food is fresh and served quickly by the laid-back staff (the fries arrive so hot you have to let them cool before you can eat them – that doesn't happen in many London restaurants). The music (played for loose change, from table-top jukeboxes) can be a bit cloying, but Ed's is great for families and big groups who don't want to spend a lot.
Babies and children welcome: children's menu. Tables outdoors (2, pavement). Takeaway service.
Map 17 C3.
For branches see index.

South Kensington

PJ's Grill
52 Fulham Road, SW3 6HH (7581 0025/ www.pjsgrill.net). South Kensington tube.
Meals served noon-11.45pm Mon-Fri; 10am-11.45pm Sat; 10am-11.15pm Sun. **Main courses** £11.95-£25. **Credit** AmEx, MC, V.
This great-looking place seems to have stepped straight out of the 1930s. It sports glossy, dark wood-panelled walls and high ceilings, and has a polo-loving ethos that carries through virtually every piece of art in the room (the name stands for 'Polo Joe's'). The crowd is a mix of young wealthy South Ken types, and older wealthy South

SHELF LIFE

For the best of American home baking, visit **Hummingbird Bakery** (*see p308*).

Panzer's
13-19 Circus Road, NW8 6PB (7722 8596/www.panzers.co.uk). St John's Wood tube. **Open** 8am-7pm Mon-Fri; 8am-6pm Sat; 8am-2pm Sun.
Whether you want to bake an apple pie, feast on the foods of the Deep South or find the right treats for Halloween, this deli-supermarket is the Big Apple.

Partridges
2-5 Duke of York Square, SW3 4LY (7730 0651/www.partidges.co.uk). Sloane Square tube. **Open** 8am-10pm daily.
Plenty to soothe the homesick diplomat or businessman, including instant grits, Oreo O's cereal with marshmallow bits, and Goober Grape peanut butter and jelly.

Rosslyn Delicatessen
56 Rosslyn Hill, NW3 1ND (7794 9210/www.delirosslyn.co.uk). Belsize Park or Hampstead tube. **Open** 8.30am-8.30pm Mon-Sat; 8.30am-8pm Sun.
Suppliers of essential groceries such as Karo syrup and cornbread mix, this sophisticated deli will also roast your turkey and bake your pumpkin pie for Thanksgiving.

Chain reaction

London is blessed – or perhaps cursed – with a host of bright, noisy, often celebrity-oriented American chain restaurants. Here's the lowdown on what's on offer.

Cheers

72 Regent Street, W1R 6EL (7494 3322/ www.cheersbarlondon.com). Piccadilly Circus tube.
Bar **Open/snacks served** noon-3am Mon-Sat; noon-12.30am Sun. **Snacks** £6-£8.
Restaurant **Meals served** noon-10pm daily. **Main courses** £6.95-£12.90. **Set lunch** (noon-5pm Mon-Fri) £2.95-£5.95 1 course. **Minimum** £7.
Both **Credit** AmEx, MC, V.

A dark, warehouse-sized space, Cheers is loosely based on the old TV show of the same name, but the relationship between the two is hard to see (outside of the souvenir T-shirts and mugs bearing the familiar *Cheers* logo). Dishes are named seemingly randomly after characters from the show, but there the crossover ends. This place is known for showing major sporting events on big TVs, when it gets so packed you can hardly move. The food is mostly an afterthought: the burgers are tough, the fries flaccid and the salads generally flavourless.
Babies and children welcome (until 6pm in restaurant): children's menu; high chairs; nappy-changing facilities. Disabled: toilet. Entertainment: DJ 10pm daily. Vegetarian menu. **Map 17 A5.**

Dexter's Grill & Bar

20 Bellevue Road, SW17 7EB (8767 1858/www.tootsiesrestaurants.co.uk). Wandsworth Common rail/319 bus. **Meals served** noon-11pm Mon-Fri; 10am-11pm Sat; 10am-10.30pm Sun. **Main courses** £7.25-£14.50. **Credit** AmEx, MC, V.

Part of the Tootsies corporate family, Dexter's shares the same kid-tastic attitude (and a very similar menu). This branch even has a candy-and-sundaes section to add to the child-friendly menu. The staff are used to tantrums and fussing, so nobody will glare at you if the little one's in a bad mood. And the menu is full of pacifying finger food. Adults can choose from a lengthy list of burgers and sandwiches, as well as big creative salads, and steaks. There are lots of ice-cream-based desserts that will appeal to the kid in anyone.
Babies and children welcome: children's menu; crayons; high chairs. Booking advisable weekends. Disabled: toilet. Separate room for parties, seats 40. Tables outdoors (9, patio). Takeaway service.

Hard Rock Café

150 Old Park Lane, W1K 1QZ (7629 0382/www.hardrock.com). Green Park or Hyde Park Corner tube. **Meals served** 11.30am-midnight Mon-Thur, Sun; 11.30am-1am Fri, Sat. **Main courses** £8.50-£15. **Credit** AmEx, MC, V.

One of the most famous of the American chains, Hard Rock continues to thrive. Just as you'd expect, rock memorabilia covers the walls from floor to ceiling, and music (more pop than rock) blasts out of hidden speakers. This place is ideal for children, as nobody can hear them scream. If it's any comfort, the food is excellent, which forms a troubling dichotomy – going to Hard Rock for the food is a bit like buying *Playboy* magazine for the articles. Still, the burgers are big and juicy, the nachos are gooey and spicy, the salads are enormous and fresh, and the sandwiches are huge and creative.
Babies and children welcome: children's menu; high chairs; toys. Disabled: toilet. Booking advisable. Restaurant available for hire. Tables outdoors (18, pavement). **Map 9 H8.**

Planet Hollywood

Trocadero, 13 Coventry Street, W1D 7DH (7287 1000/www.planethollywood.co.uk). Piccadilly Circus tube. **Meals served** 11.30am-1am Mon-Sat; 11.30am-12.30am Sun. **Main courses** £8.95-£21.95. **Credit** AmEx, DC, MC, V.

The Hollywood version of the Hard Rock Café (*see above*), famously co-owned by Bruce Willis, this enormous place seems to be made entirely of plastic. It simulates the red-carpet atmosphere with flashing lights, and incredibly loud movie soundtracks and trailers blasted from numerous hidden speakers. The menu is slightly more adventurous than Hard Rock's, with fewer burgers and more rotisserie chicken, but it's still largely geared at providing finger food for kids.
Babies and children welcome: children's menu; high chairs; nappy-changing facilities. Booking advisable. Disabled: toilet. Separate room for parties, seats 80. **Map 17 B5.**

Smollensky's on the Strand

105 Strand, WC2R 0AA (7497 2101/ www.smollenskys.co.uk). Covent Garden, Embankment or Temple tube/Charing Cross tube/rail.
Bar **Open** noon-11pm Mon-Thur; noon-1am Fri, Sat; noon-5.30pm, 6.30-10.30pm Sun.
Restaurant **Meals served** noon-11pm Mon-Sat; noon-10pm Sun. **Main courses** £8.95-£21.95. **Set meal** (noon-6.30pm Mon-Fri) £10.95 2 courses, £12.95 3 courses.
Both **Credit** AmEx, DC, MC, V.

Of late, this Chicago-style chain has been looking for an identity, opening mini steakhouses and turning them into mini hamburger joints (hey presto!). In the meantime, Smollensky's has renovated this flagship branch out of recognition (it's all but wandering around mumbling to itself). Still, who cares? It's a nice, reasonably priced place, with a newly sleek bar, and great steaks on the menu. In fact, steaks are the raison d'être – any size, any shape. Staff are friendly, and the wine list is small but not bad, which all helps create a great venue for dining with a friend. So what, if they keep moving the furniture?
Babies and children welcome: booster seats; children's menu; entertainment (noon-3pm Sat, Sun); high chairs; toys. Booking advisable. Disabled: toilet. Entertainment: musicians 7.15-9.30pm Tue-Thur; 7.45-10.30pm Fri, Sat. Tables outdoors (4, pavement). **Map 18 E5.**
For branches see index.

TGI Friday's

6 Bedford Street, WC2E 9HZ (7379 0585/www.tgifridays.co.uk). Covent Garden tube/Charing Cross tube/rail.
Bar **Open** noon-11pm Mon-Sat; noon-10.30pm Sun.
Restaurant **Meals served** noon-11.30pm Mon-Sat; noon-11pm Sun. **Main courses** £7.95-£17.95.
Both **Credit** AmEx, MC, V.

Ken types – so they all have something in common. The staff are friendly, and the restaurant always seems packed. PJ's is famed for both its bloody marys and its Sunday brunch, seemingly designed to end one hangover and help you start the next. The menu is a pleasant, uncontroversial something-for-everyone mix of organic steaks and burgers and other familiar dishes. Starters include creamy seared foie gras, tangy crispy duck pancakes, and zesty and light chargrilled squid. Mains tend towards the sturdy meaty variety, such as roast rack of lamb with dauphinoise potatoes and crisp french beans. But you'll also find grilled whole dover sole with lemon, and a delicate but rich lobster risotto. Puddings are similarly hearty; the apple crumble is comfortable perfection. It's all highly civilised, with a nice, uncomplicated but undeniably sophisticated buzz.
Babies and children welcome: children's portions; high chairs. Booking advisable. Separate room for parties, seating 20-82. Tables outdoors (3, pavement). **Map 14 E11.**
For branch see index.

West

Chiswick

The Coyote

2 Fauconberg Road, W4 3JY (8742 8545/ www.thecoyote.co.uk). Chiswick Park tube/ Gunnersbury tube/rail. **Dinner served** 5-11pm Mon-Fri. **Meals served** 11am-11pm Sat; 11am-10.30pm Sun. **Main courses** £8.95-£15.50. **Credit** AmEx, MC, V.

This busy local restaurant has been packing in Chiswick's finest for years, all drawn by its excellent Southwestern US menu that ranges from the ordinary (cheesy nachos) to the extraordinary (blackened ribeye in rich chipotle sauce). The atmosphere is almost always lively, although the acoustics of the building mean it can get a little deafening, despite the fact the dining room is quite small. The menu is consistently creative, and the daily specials are unpredictable and innovative. The chef uses excellently sourced game in dishes such as peppered ostrich steak with caramelised vegetables. Other exceptional choices include: the Oaxacan rack of lamb rubbed with dried spices and coated in roasted pecans; baby pork ribs crusted with spices, and served with tobacco onions; and duck breast stuffed with poblano chillies and coriander pesto, served with a bright lime and mango sauce. There are ample, equally creative vegetarian dishes too (especially the spicy moroccan vegetable stew, with haricot beans, chickpeas, carrots, celery and lentils, served with saffron rice), as well as huge fresh salads. Although a neighbourhood restaurant, the Coyote is unusual and merits a detour.
Babies and children welcome: children's menu; high chairs. Booking advisable. Disabled: toilet. Tables outdoors (7, pavement).

Hammersmith

Pacific Bar & Grill

320 Goldhawk Road, W6 0XF (8741 1994). Stamford Brook tube. **Meals served** noon-11.30pm Mon-Sat; noon-11pm Sun. **Main courses** £9.95-£16.50. **Credit** AmEx, MC, V.

This bright, determinedly cheery, candy-striped chain is the most child-focused of the US options, and it has plenty of time for big, noisy birthday parties. Strangely juxtaposed against that, however, is a popular bar serving big, alco-rific cocktails of the multicoloured variety. The music and the unfortunate outfits forced on the waiters give the impression that somewhere somebody in charge really liked 1984. But the food is varied and reliably good, with lots of sticky barbecue choices, plenty of Tex-Mex dishes and the inevitable burgers and fries. And the puddings are excellent.
Babies and children welcome: children's menu; crayons; high chairs. Disabled: toilet. Takeaway service.
Map 18 D5.
For branches see index.

Tootsies Grill

48 High Street, SW19 5AX (8946 4135/www.tootsiesrestaurants.com). Wimbledon tube/rail. **Meals served** noon-10.30pm Mon-Thur; 11am-11pm Fri; 9am-11pm Sat; 9am-10.30pm Sun. **Main courses** £6.25-£13.50. **Credit** AmEx, MC, V.
The Tootsies chain is so family-friendly that waiters all but take your order in colouring books with crayons. The restaurants are bright, with big windows and light pine furniture. Staff are young and laid-back about prams blocking walkways or kids dashing about looking for lost teddies. The menu has nearly a dozen kinds of burgers, from a cheeseburger down to a burger with no burger at all (aka a veggie burger). Then there are chicken sandwiches, big filling salads, and lots of ice-cream desserts. But what keeps drawing us back are the butterscotch milkshakes – worth the heart attack later in life.
Babies and children welcome: children's menu; crayons; high chairs. Tables outdoors (4, pavement). Takeaway service.
For branches see index.

Lucky Hammersmith to have this restaurant right in its own backyard. The clean, cream lines of the dining space are dappled with big windows, and a corner fireplace that has a blaze crackling away on cold evenings. For warm nights there's a courtyard patio with a cluster of tables. The menu covers the gamut of California's polyglot upscale cuisine, encompassing both Far Eastern influences and Southwestern US flavours. Starters include cool, light salads (such as pear and rocket, or tangy ham and fig); there are also daily specials, among which we sampled a delightful, warming ham and parmesan risotto. Steaks and burgers are popular main-course options, as is the house special, lime chilli chicken – which arrived drowned in an overly sweet sauce. The naked lamb burger was precisely that: no bread, no salad, nothing. Add a big side order of crispy, hand-cut fries and you might ruin an Atkins Diet, but who cares? They're so light they must be good for you. Puddings are excellent: the banoffi pie is light and tasty, the apple pie fresh and tangy. The wine list may be short but it's good, and the bar staff mix a mean cosmopolitan.
Babies and children welcome: children's menu; crayons; high chairs; magician/entertainer (1-3pm Sun). Tables outdoors (12, terrace).
Map 20 A3.

Kensington

Sticky Fingers

1A Phillimore Gardens, W8 7QG (7938 5338/ www.stickyfingers.co.uk). High Street Kensington tube.
Bar **Open** noon-10pm Mon-Sat.
Restaurant **Meals served** noon-11pm Mon-Sat; noon-10.30pm Sun. **Main courses** £9.25-£17.95.
Both **Credit** AmEx, JCB, MC, V.
After a renovation that opened up the place and let in more sunshine, Sticky Fingers is looking better than it has in some time. This rambunctious restaurant, part-owned by ex-Rolling Stone Bill Wyman, is a haven for west London yummy mummies who pack the place with their offspring throughout the day, but tend to scamper off at night when the young office crowd moves in. The walls may be covered in Stones memorabilia, but the music is a varied menu of rock 'n' roll classics. The food menu (which is big, but slightly less extensive than the vast cocktail list) is full of family-friendly fare, with starters such as potato skins, a half-rack of barbecue ribs, nachos and deep-fried camembert. Mains have a Southwestern bent, with six kinds of burgers (including the 'californian' with bacon, guacamole, salsa, cheese and sour cream). There's also a seared fillet of salmon with crayfish cream; blackened steak with tortillas; and asparagus and mushroom enchilada. If you can't decide, you could choose the 'beggars banquet' selection, featuring eight kinds of starters spread out, rock-star style.
Babies and children welcome: children's menu; entertainment (face-painting & magician 1.30-3.30pm Sat, Sun); high chairs. Booking advisable. Takeaway service. **Map 7 A9.**

Westbourne Park

★ Lucky 7

127 Westbourne Park Road, W2 5QL (7727 6771). Royal Oak or Westbourne Park tube.
Meals served 10am-11pm Mon-Thur; 9am-11pm Fri, Sat; 9am-10.30pm Sun.
Main courses £5.45-£12.95. **Credit** MC, V.
This tiny, laid-back diner has a short menu and a lengthy list of fans. Every day it packs customers into its six long booths; you'll usually have to share with strangers. The burgers are undeniably the big attraction; they're large, heavy and made to order. There's a fairly good selection, including plenty for vegetarians, and a 'foghorn-leghorn' chicken burger. Sizeable orders of crispy fries and onion rings sit neatly alongside the burgers; for a healthier option, choose one of the half-dozen salads. The menu also features a handful of sandwiches, and a wide variety of shakes and malts priced according to their levels of thickness. Excellent calorific breakfasts of pancakes, eggs and bacon are available too. Aside from the lack of seating, the only area where this diner tends to fall down is in its service, which is nonchalant to the point of somnolence – never good when you've got a hunger only a burger can remedy.
Babies and children welcome: booster seats. Bookings not accepted. Separate room for parties, seats 35. Tables outdoors (1, pavement). Takeaway service. **Map 7 A5.**

South West

Chelsea

Big Easy

332-334 King's Road, SW3 5UR (7352 4071/ www.bigeasy.uk.com). Sloane Square tube then 11, 19, 22 bus.
Bar **Open** noon-11pm Mon-Fri; 11am-11pm Sat; 11am-10.30pm Sun. **Main courses** £7.95-£14.95.
Restaurant **Meals served** noon-11.30pm Mon-Thur, Sun; noon-12.30am Fri; 11am-12.30am Sat. **Main courses** £9.95-£22.95. **Set lunch** (noon-5pm Mon-Fri) £7.95 2 courses.
Both **Credit** AmEx, DC, JCB, MC, V.
This raucous barn of a restaurant takes a 'there goes the neighbourhood' approach towards the snooty stretch of the King's Road where it sits, legs akimbo: a Yankee in the Sloanes' court. It's certainly a loud joint, with a band playing downstairs, so it's not the best choice if you're looking for a romantic night out. Nevertheless, with a few friends and a few beers, it's the ideal location for reasonably priced, well-cooked, substantial plates of food. The place looks like a bayou-side Cajun diner in southern Louisiana, with a rough wooden floor, big wooden tables, and metal signs on the wall with pithy sayings like: 'Oysters: fried, stewed and nude'. Starters are made for sharing: jalapeño peppers stuffed with cream cheese, deep-fried calamares, and leggy Alaskan snow crab claws. Mains are made for gorging: large, fire-grilled steaks, enormous burgers, broiled lobster, and sticky barbecue ribs. A party atmosphere prevails. Rumour has it that Prince William has been here, but that's hard to imagine. If you're after a down-to-earth place in posh Chelsea, this could be it.
Babies and children welcome: children's menu; crayons; high chairs. Entertainment: musicians 8.30pm Mon-Thur; 9.30pm Fri-Sun. Tables outdoors (5, pavement). Takeaway service.
Map 14 D12.

Fulham

Sophie's Steakhouse & Bar

311-313 Fulham Road, SW10 9QH (7352 0088/ www.sophiessteakhouse.com). South Kensington tube then 14, 211, 414 bus. **Meals served** noon-11.45pm Mon-Fri; 11am-11.45pm Sat; 11am-11.15pm Sun. **Main courses** £6.95-£34.95. **Set meal** (noon-6pm Mon-Fri) £11.95 2 courses. **Credit** AmEx, MC, V.
A Chelsea-style approach to selling steak is taken here. Sophie's is glossy: all polished wood, big windows (spilling sunlight everywhere) and expensive light fixtures. The staff look like they've never eaten red meat; chardonnay is a more common beverage than beer. Ladies-who-lunch come to receive their protein. The menu reflects the airbrushed clientele. Starters include light, citrusy baby spinach salad with crisp bacon and creamy avocado; a smoky dish of sautéed field mushrooms with rocket and goat's cheese on toasted brioche; and light, cool, dressed Cornish crab salad. Every form of steak is listed among the main courses, including a breathtaking 27oz porterhouse, and a 24oz côte de boeuf. For lesser appetites there are juicy 10oz cuts, and a thick 8oz fillet. All come with the sauce of your choice. Alternatives include juicy Welsh lamb steak with red berry jus; or light, tasty chargrilled tuna steak with marinated avocado, tomato and red onion salsa. There are several sandwich and salad options, the trademark lobster and avocado club, and the tangy grilled goat's cheese salad among them. Desserts are the usuals: sticky toffee pudding, crème brûlée and a luscious banana cream pie.
Babies and children welcome: children's menu; high chairs. Disabled: toilet.
Map 14 D12.

Wimbledon

★ Jo Shmo's

33 High Street, SW19 5BY (8879 3845/ www.joshmos.com). Wimbledon tube/rail then 93 bus. **Meals served** noon-11pm Mon-Thur, Sun; noon-11.30pm Fri, Sat. **Main courses** £6.95-£13.50. **Credit** AmEx, MC, V.
A tale of two restaurants. The bar section of this sunny, pleasant establishment has a sophisticated edge, with wooden floors, leather furniture and big windows. The back section is what life would be like if kids were in charge. A busy open kitchen adds heat and noise. The place tends to get packed with beleaguered parents and their energetic little darlings who have an occasional tendency to run amok, dashing between tables. Volume control is a problem, so if that matters to you, sit up front. That said, the menu is a happy mix of food that will please the young ones (hot dogs, kid-sized burgers,

The Diner. See p45.

shakes) added to the kind of thing likely to soothe an adult's fevered soul (cocktails, for example). The grown-up menu has shareable starters such as gooey nachos and popcorn crayfish. Mains vary from 'eat with your hands' choices (burgers, ribs, fried onion 'strings') to date-food (juicy steaks, big salads, grilled chicken). Jo Shmo's isn't the most inventive restaurant in the world, but it has a good atmosphere, friendly and capable staff – and memorable chocolate shakes.
Babies and children welcome: children's menu; high chairs. Disabled: toilet. Tables outdoors (2, pavement).
For branch see index.

East

Docklands

★ Curve

London Marriott, West India Quay, 22 Hertsmere Road, E14 4ED (7093 1000 ext 2622/www.marriotthotels.com). Canary Wharf tube/DLR/West India Quay DLR. **Breakfast served** 6.30-11am Mon-Fri; 7-11am Sat, Sun. **Lunch served** noon-2.30pm daily. **Dinner served** 5-10.30pm Mon-Sat; 5-10pm Sun. **Main courses** £9.50-£22.50. **Credit** AmEx, DC, JCB, MC, V.

A sleek operation on the ground floor of the five-star Marriott West India Quay hotel, Curve has found a willing crowd of regulars among the besuited office workers of Docklands. It certainly makes the most of its prime waterside setting. On sunny days you can sit outside with a pre-dinner cocktail, with no traffic noise and the water lapping peacefully at the land's edge. It's difficult to believe you're still in London. Over the last year Curve has refocused on seafood (always a forte). Also, diners now have the option of eating a more casual meal at the 'crustacean bar', where oysters are served on the half-shell, and prawns by the (artful) bucketful.

The full, fine-dining experience is still provided in the glossy main dining room, where you can feast on a seafood-heavy menu including rich New England clam chowder, characterful and chunky fish stew, or delicate, melt-in-your-mouth diver-caught scallops – fresh each day from Billingsgate Market. Puddings are as gorgeous as ever; witness the light pistachio cheesecake, served like a piece of pale-green rectangular art. Staff are observant and friendly, and the wine list is excellent.
Babies and children welcome: children's menu; crayons; high chairs. Booking advisable. Disabled: toilet (in hotel). Tables outdoors (20, terrace). Vegetarian menu.

Wapping

Rhodes B-B-Q Shack NEW

61 Wapping Wall, E1W 3SJ (7474 4289/ www.rhodesbbq.com). Wapping tube. **Meals served** 6-11pm Mon-Thur; 6pm-midnight Fri; 5-11pm Sat, Sun. **Main courses** £6.95-£16.95. **Credit** AmEx, MC, V.

As casual barbecue joints go, they don't get more casual and barbecuey than this new joint, which sits incongruously in quiet, upmarket Wapping. Its design is simple; plain whitewashed brick walls are covered in brightly coloured reviews written by customers (ask for a pen to add your own). There's a tiny kitchen tucked away among the unornamented tables and chairs, but not much else to distinguish the place except the sweet, smoky smell of barbecue. All cooking is done offsite in an enormous smokehouse, but that sweet smell pervades the place all the same. The offsite grilling causes purists to raise eyebrows sharply, but if you didn't know the meat was cooked elsewhere you'd be hard-pressed to guess it. Chicken, beef and pork are all barbecued well. The sauce is the perfect mix of sweet with a tangy edge. The cuts of meat are generally good; tender pork shoulder and juicy beef ribs didn't disappoint, although the beef was the tiniest bit chewy. Platters are served with flavourful beans and fresh, cold coleslaw – as all good barbecue should be. Desserts are largely limited to delightfully strange smoked fruit: light and unique. Certainly worth the trip to Wapping.
Babies and children welcome: children's portions. Booking advisable.

North East

South Woodford

Yellow Book Californian Café

190 George Lane, E18 1AY (8989 3999/ www.theyellowbook.co.uk). South Woodford tube. **Lunch served** noon-2.30pm Mon-Fri. **Dinner served** 6-10pm Mon; 6-11pm Tue-Fri. **Meals served** noon-11pm Sat; noon-10pm Sun. **Main courses** £6.95-£15.45. **Set lunch** (Mon-Fri) £6.75 1 course incl drink. **Credit** AmEx, MC, V.

This sweet place is a great option for those who live in far-east London. The main dining room is long and roomy, with wooden floors and lemon-hued walls, but there's more cosy dining outside in the breezy courtyard when the weather allows. The Yellow Book tends to fill up early and stay packed, as locals pile in for crisp, thin-crust pizzas baked in wood-fired ovens, or for starters that take advantage of California's Pacific Rim connections to bring in soy-dipped chicken skewers, sweet thai fish cakes and baby squid stuffed with prawns. If you don't feel like pizza, try the sizzling fajitas (chicken, veg, prawn or beef), or a big oven-baked burrito – with lots of vegetables wrapped in a flour tortilla. The menu is capacious: there's also pasta, burgers, and even veal steaks, grilled salmon and tasty sesame-crusted tuna steak served with ginger soy noodles. The atmosphere is jovial, the staff are so friendly you'll want to take them home, and the food is good and generously portioned. All in all, an excellent option.
Babies and children welcome: high chairs. Tables outdoors (8, patio). Takeaway service (pizza only).

LATIN AMERICAN

London's Latin restaurants are fuelled by a heady mix of vivacious Central and South American expat communities, prime ingredients (especially in the case of Argentinian beef), and potent national drinks – from tequilas to caipirinhas. Unfortunately, there are several 'Latino' venues in town that strive for the office-party market, yet offer food that is at best mediocre. Consequently, we've pruned some establishments from the section this year. Numbers have also decreased with the closure of two Pan-American restaurants in the past 12 months: Hackney's Armadillo and Fulham's 1492. Fear not: there were openings too. The ranks of Brazilian restaurants have been swelled by homely **Casa Brasil**; Argentinian food has a new advocate in the shape of Battersea's **Santa Maria del Sur**; stylish-looking **Wahaca** is flying the flag for Mexico; and a Cuban restaurant has started trading, though perhaps the mojitos and daiquiris surpass the food at **La Bodeguita del Medio**.

Argentinian

Central

Piccadilly

★ Gaucho Piccadilly

25 Swallow Street, W1B 4DJ (7734 4040/www. gauchorestaurants.co.uk). Piccadilly Circus tube.
Bar **Open** noon-midnight Mon-Sat; noon-11pm Sun.
Shop **Open** 10am-6pm Mon-Sat.
First-floor restaurant **Meals served** noon-midnight Mon-Sat; noon-11pm Sun.
Top-floor restaurant **Dinner served** 6pm-1am Mon-Fri; noon-1am Sat; 6-11pm Sun. **Main courses** £8.50-£32.
All **Credit** AmEx, DC, MC, V.

Steakhouse chic is what this flagship branch of the Gaucho chain is all about – from its well-stocked Cavas wine shop to its pitch-dark cocktail bar and its penchant for cowskin wallpaper and pouffes. The place won the Best Steak Restaurant category in the 2006 Time Out Eating & Drinking Awards, so, as you'd expect, its steaks are always good-to-great; the bife de lomo (fillet) can be outstanding. The menu also stretches to dishes containing Ecuadorian prawns and Peruvian hake, and a sausage platter with Mexican dips. These 'nationality' tags are, in truth, absolute *pelotas*; the 'Argentine-style' sausage coming with jalapeños is proof of that. The whole Gaucho brand seems to be drifting between cow theme-park and pan-Latin glam bar. But the food is tasty and well presented, if pricey – £18.50 for a sirloin – and the Argentina-dominated wine list is fantastic. Desserts range from fruit and cheesecakes to Argentinian classics such as dulce de leche pancake and Don Pedro (ice-cream and whisky). Service is a touch too slick, but that's the nature of smart chains. And Gaucho is expanding, with new branches near Tower Bridge and on the river in Richmond.
Babies and children welcome: high chairs. Booking advisable. Entertainment: band/musician 8pm daily (top-floor restaurant). Top-floor restaurant available for hire. Wine cellar available for hire, seats 100. **Map 17 A5.**
For branches see index.

South West

Chelsea

El Gaucho

Chelsea Farmers' Market, 125 Sydney Street, SW3 6NR (7376 8514/www.elgaucho.co.uk). Sloane Square or South Kensington tube. **Meals served** noon-5.30pm Mon-Fri; noon-6.30pm Sat, Sun. **Main courses** £7.90-£14.90. **Credit** AmEx, MC, V.

This Chelsea Market outlet of El Gaucho looks like the genuine Argentinian article. It's a small shack-like affair, with a grill on view to all just a few feet from the tables. These are lined up so that everyone eats communally. The house malbec wine is served by the glass and pairs very well with the juicy chicken empanadas – perhaps the best in London. Nice cobs of bread, olives and a pot of chimichurri sauce arrive as standard. Our chorizo sausage was a bit dull; it's the one starter worth skipping. In contrast, the beef was excellent: slightly fattier than at other Latin American steakhouses, but charred to give it a smoky bite. More salt would have helped, but perhaps the Chelsea clientele likes to control the condiments. The experience here is no frills, no fuss, no extras, but the atmosphere is convivial and, thanks to the energetic maître d' from Buenos Aires, just like being in a little place on the River Plate. Note that this branch is not open in the evening, though it's far more fun than the South Kensington basement outlet, which always feels tired and lacklustre.
Children admitted. Tables outdoors (14, pavement). Takeaway service. **Map 14 E12.**
For branch see index.

South

Battersea

La Pampa Grill

60 Battersea Rise, SW11 1EG (7924 4774). Clapham Junction rail. **Dinner served** 6-11pm Mon-Fri; 6-11.30pm Sat. **Main courses** £7.95-£15.50. **Credit** AmEx, MC, V.

Tuesday night in Clapham Junction is about as far as it gets (in terms of atmosphere, architecture and *alegría*) from Buenos Aires. La Pampa is a rather unexciting experience, and on our visit the waiters were almost as tired as the decor (unchanged for years – a mix of Spanish bull-fighting posters, *Blues Brothers* memorabilia and farmyard animals on a faux-rustic rooftop tableau). The music was mainly Colombian, with the odd Cuban number. There was an unmistakeable whiff of bleach in the air, which again, has been here for years. The sole means of salvation is to attack a piece of meat. Both the strip loin (porterhouse) and fillet were magnificent, the latter (at least when grilled to medium) as soft as butter and as tasty as a steak gets. The chips were good too: chunky, crisp and nicely browned. Everything else, though, was either below par (the chorizos lacked a peppery bite) or non-existent. Such basics of pampas cuisine as black pudding,

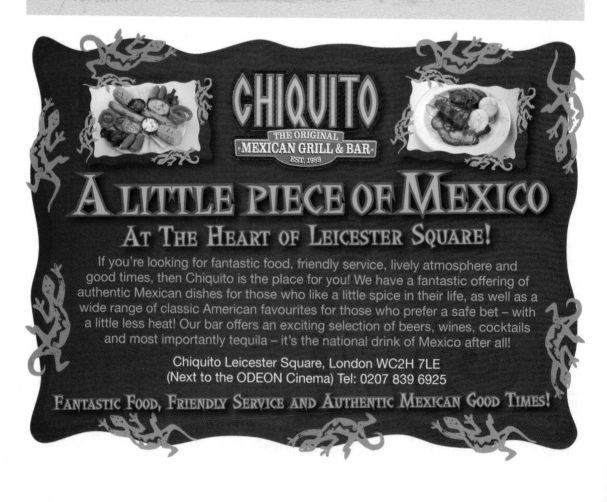

kidneys, sweetbreads, provolone cheese and mixed salad were absent. La Pampa has the feel of a chain that relies on pulling in passing trade.
Booking advisable; essential Sat. Separate area for parties, seats 25. Tables outdoors (2, pavement).
For branch see index.

★ Santa Maria del Sur NEW

129 Queenstown Road, SW8 3RH (7622 2088/ www.santamariadelsur.co.uk). Queenstown Road rail. **Dinner served** 6-10.30pm Mon-Fri. **Meals served** noon-10.30pm Sat, Sun. **Main courses** £8-£17.50. **Credit** MC, V.

Santa Maria del Sur is modelled on Hackney's Buen Ayre (*see below*), from which it split in early 2007 – but it's a bit posher, to suit its Battersea clientele. Located on a rather desolate stretch of Queenstown Road, it's not that convenient unless you live locally – though the welcome you receive compensates. It's not just the warmth of the coals (the grill is cannily placed in the window to tempt passers-by). The staff, from the cheery waiters to the grill chefs, have time for a '*¿cómo estás?*' and, Argentinian natives all, are happy to show off their wines and national dishes. The food is classic: steaming hot meat empanadas; sweet Spanish-style blood sausage; excellent bife de chorizo (with rump steak from Argentina); and sides of thick, well-tanned chips (ask for the garlic-laced option) and crisp salad. Non-carnivores can indulge in giant mushrooms or a grilled slab of tuna. The wine list is extensive: from £15 basic reds to a Catena rarity costing a ton; the £20 malbec reservas are outstanding. Dessert after such a meat-fest is excessive, but the Don Pedro (an ice-cream, walnut and whisky creation) usually goes down easily enough.
Babies and children welcome: children's portions; high chairs. Booking advisable weekends.

North East

Hackney

★ Buen Ayre (100)

50 Broadway Market, E8 4QJ (7275 9900/ www.buenayre.co.uk). London Fields rail/26, 48, 55, 106, 236 bus. **Lunch served** noon-5pm Sat, Sun. **Dinner served** 6-10.30pm Mon-Fri; 6-10.30pm Sat, Sun. **Main courses** £7-£19. **Credit** AmEx, MC, V.

Having seduced Hackney's meat-eating middle classes over the past couple of years, Buen Ayre is a firm favourite in that *barrio*. Original co-owners John Rattagan and Alberto Abbate went their separate ways in early 2007; Abbate now runs Santa Maria (*see above*) in Battersea. Buen Ayre's Ikea-style light wood furnishings and modern art on the walls may not suggest a gaucho ranch, but the place is in harmony with the new-look restaurants of Buenos Aires: bright, clean, young and cliché-free. Most diners dive into the parrilladas (mixed grills): a carefully sourced array of steak, chorizo sausages, black pudding, offal and/or melted provolone cheese. The lomos (fillet steaks) are also top class; fresh salads (from a good selection) provide the ideal accompaniment. It doesn't try to offer more than a neighbourhood steakhouse, but there's attention to detail. Chorizo is made specially, using Argentinian red pepper; the meat is basted with salmuera (salty water), which penetrates it better than salt crystals. The delicious flans (crème caramel) are made according to an old family recipe. Liquor and beer from Argentina are now offered, as well as an excellent selection of fair-priced malbecs. A night here is about as close as you get to a Latino family fiesta.
Babies and children welcome: high chairs. Booking advisable. Disabled: toilet. Tables outdoors (5, garden).

Brazilian

North

Finchley

Casa Brasil NEW

289A Regents Park Road, N3 3JY (8371 1999). Finchley Central tube. **Meals served** 11am-6pm Tue-Thur; 11am-9pm Fri-Sun. **Main courses** £6.40-£9.40. **Unlicensed. Corkage** £5. **No credit cards.**

This certainly felt like a 'casa' on the night we went: it was full of chatting mothers and their kids, couples, and locals stopping by for a quick bite. A blackboard outside tells you it's a deli, a snack bar, a restaurant and a place to indulge in the Brazilian classic, feijoada. Edir, who hails from the state of Minas Gerais, prepares Brazilian standards just as she would at home. Starters tend to be carb-loaded, but we devoured the pão de queijo (cheese puffs) and two small (but filling) empanadas with our guaraná aperitif. Haddock moqueca was a nice light main dish to follow, the crisp, tender fish subtly enlivened by coriander and coconut oil. The feijoada was far heavier, with good-sized chunks of pork in a rich broth of beans, onion and garlic. The pot looked small, but, combined with rice and a large portion of farofa (toasted manioc flour) was ample for two. As our chosen juice – açai, from açai palm fruit (there's no alcohol licence, though you can BYO) – was akin to a meal-replacement drink, we left wondering how Brazilians manage to wear those tiny bikinis given such a diet.
Babies and children welcome: high chairs. Booking advisable Fri, Sat. Tables outdoors (6, patio).

Islington

Rodizio Rico

77-78 Upper Street, N1 0NU (7354 1076/ www.rodiziorico.com). Angel tube. **Lunch served** noon-3.30pm Mon-Fri. **Dinner served** 6-11.30pm Mon-Fri. **Meals served** noon-11.30pm Sat, Sun. **Buffet** £13 vegetarian, £19 meat, £24.90 seafood. **Credit** AmEx, DC, JCB, MC, V.

The 'rodizio' style of dining suits the Brazilian flair for informal fun. Waiters dash round the room with long, sword-like skewers of meat. The only way to enjoy the experience is to chat with them and ensure you get the best cuts. The meal is constantly interrupted. To get anything else (salad, black beans, rice, fried fish), you have to visit the self-service buffet. The Islington branch is a lively, bustling place; on a Friday night, we beat the rush (just) by arriving at 7.30pm. Though we were relatively alone in a semi-secluded corner, the friendly waiters came and went every few minutes bringing chicken hearts, garlic-laced lamb, pork sausages, tender sirloin, chicken wings and assorted other meaty delicacies. Everything was tasty, well salted and generally well grilled. When the maître d' asked how things were going, we requested a medium-rare slice of steak, and in a trice it was delivered. The fixed price – £19 a head for meats only; £24.90 for the seafood option (not available in the Westbourne Grove branch) – is on the high side, so try to come here when you're very hungry and fancy a boisterous chat.
Babies and children welcome: booster chairs. Booking advisable. Disabled: toilet. Vegetarian menu. **Map 5 O2.**
For branch see index.

Cuban

Central

Soho

Floridita

100 Wardour Street, W1F 0TN (7314 4000/ www.floriditalondon.com). Tottenham Court Road tube.

Gaucho Piccadilly. See p49.

RESTAURANTS

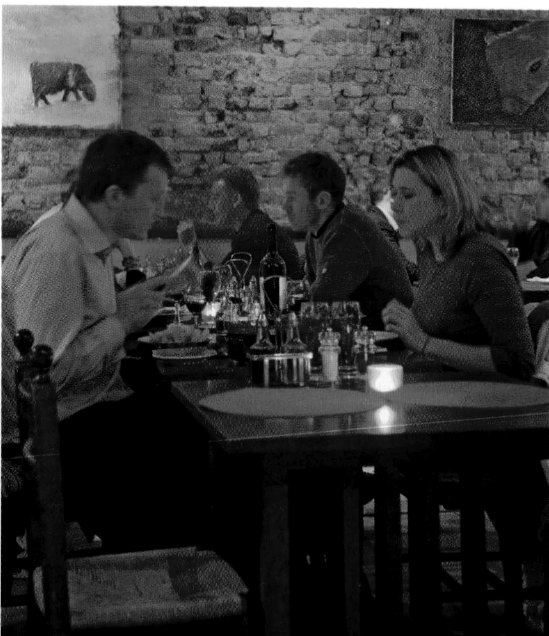

Santa Maria del Sur. See p51.

Bar **Open** 5.30pm-2am Mon-Wed; 5.30pm-3am Thur-Sat.
Restaurant **Dinner served** 5.30pm-1am Mon-Wed; 5.30pm-1.30am Thur-Sat. **Main courses** £11-£35. **Admission** (after 7pm Thur-Sat) £15. **Credit** AmEx, DC, MC, V.

Dinners at this dark, glitzy Cuban theme-bar/restaurant tend to involve a scrum of after-office boozers, curious tourists, and, from Thursday to Saturday, Floridita club members bagging the best tables. The rousing live music also makes conversation improbable. Wisest move is to accept the vibe, take a stool at the bar and dip into the tapas-style bar menu. Tasty cold bites include Brazilian cheesy bread, crispy pork skins and red snapper ceviche; there are equally appetising hot plates of suckling pig, crab croquettes and plantain fritter. These cost just £1.50 to £3 each. True, they're more comfort food than haute cuisine, but they make great accompaniments to the icy beers and top-notch cocktails. Larger mains include decent burgers, mozzarella and aubergine quesadilla (with a nice basil kick) and a crisp salad tossed with oranges and palm hearts. If you'd prefer something closer to what you'd find at the original Floridita in Havana, opt for the lobster l'armoricaine on the pricey à la carte menu. Desserts are the most exotic part; fancy an Amazonian palm berry and banana sorbet? It's delicious. Floridita doesn't quite work, but it makes a good alternative to the pub and is always lively.
Booking advisable. Disabled: toilet. Entertainment: Cuban band, DJ 8pm Mon-Sat. Dress: funky/glam. Separate room for parties, seats 40-60.
Map 17 B3.

West

Kensington

La Bodeguita del Medio NEW

47 Kensington Court, W8 5DA (7938 4147/ www.bdelmlondon.com). High Street Kensington tube. **Meals served** noon-11pm Mon-Sat;

noon-10.30pm Sun. **Main courses** £9.50-£14. **Set lunch** (noon-6pm) £10 2 courses. **Credit** AmEx, DC, MC, V.
Havana's Bodeguita del Medio started life as an ordinary bar, busy with local bohos and rough sailors knocking back cheap beers and mojitos, and eating hangover-padding such as moros y cristianos (beans and rice). But Hemingway dropped by for a few litres of daiquiri and the bar became a tourist trap. This London franchise starts off at the end of the story, hence the distressed paintwork, faux faded posters and piped salsa music – which you can't hear as the acoustics are dire. As theme bars go, the food's not exactly bad (crispy salmon ceviche, nicely grilled artichokes, tasty burgers and a gently spiced chicken main course), but it's only a notch above catering fodder. Portions are rather small too. Service is well intentioned, but was shoddy on a busy Friday night, and the tables are placed too close together. The Cuban booze is good, though; the mojito mix was a finely balanced affair, and a mango daiquiri was like a smoothie, but with a mean kick. This is a place to drink and chat (or shout). If you want a memorable meal, you'll have to go to Havana, circa 1955.
Babies and children admitted. Tables outdoors (3, pavement). Takeaway service. **Map 7 B8/9.**

Mexican & Tex-Mex

Central

Covent Garden

Wahaca NEW

66 Chandos Place, WC2N 4HG (7240 1883/ www.wahaca.co.uk). Covent Garden or Leicester Square tube. **Meals served** noon-11.30pm daily. **Main courses** £5.50-£10. **Set meal** £9.75 per person (minimum 2). **Credit** AmEx, MC, V.
This latest Latino venue is keen to show that Mexican food can be cool and stylish, as well as great with cold beer. Food arrives as it's cooked. We were given some nachos and guacamole, then came the 'sides' of green, coriander-laced rice, which was delicious, and some rich, smoky frijoles, and then our main course choice: a scrumptious 'street food selection'. For £19.50 we got two lean steak tacos, two small chicken tacos, two chorizo quesadillas, two aubergine and goat's cheese quesadillas and, best of all, two tacos full of tender fish in an achiote (annatto seed) marinade. The menu contains none of the classics such as chiles en nogada, no escabeches, no stews and – a real sin – nothing accompanied by mole. We suspect ambition has been reigned in to keep prices low and clients flowing in. Was the taco fest better than mere beer food? Just about. Awful acoustics make this a noisy place; with no reservations unless you're a group of eight or more, be prepared to stand around while others tuck in (there's no boozing at the bar either). The lime and yellow interior is visually impressive and the menu is quirky, but Wahaca isn't going to transform the way Londoners see Mexican food.
Babies and children welcome: high chairs. Booking not accepted (except for groups). Disabled: lift. **Map 18 D5.**

Fitzrovia

★ Mestizo

103 Hampstead Road, NW1 3EL (7387 4064/ www.mestizomx.com). Warren Street tube/ Euston tube/rail. **Lunch served** noon-4pm Mon-Sat. **Dinner served** 6-11.30pm Mon-Sat; 6-10.30pm Sun. **Main courses** £9.50-£14.50. **Credit** MC, V.
A small, classy restaurant tucked away near Warren Street tube station, Mestizo has quickly become a favourite with office workers, drawn by its Mexican beers and tequilas. The place looks great – with Mexican artworks, wooden floors, and tables in clusters – but the food's the star. Here you'll encounter authentic, high-end Mexican cuisine that's rarely found so far from the Americas. The menu is divided in two. Start by choosing from the starters and tacos menu, which lures you to fresh, mild tamales (shredded chicken, vegetables or pork, wrapped in corn meal and steamed inside a corn husk); queso fundido (melted cheese that you spoon into flour tortillas); or tacos (corn and flour tortillas loaded with anything from cactus leaf and cheese to roast lamb, shredded beef or juicy pork). Then move on to larger mains, such as the house special molcajete: a stone bowl filled with spiced beef, chicken or vegetables, with cheese, chorizo, spring onions, avocado and salsa. There are also dishes made with subtle Mexican mole sauce (dried chillies, herbs, spices, almonds and chocolate), and rich crêpes filled with mushrooms, sweetcorn and onions in a tequila cream sauce.
Babies and children welcome: high chairs. Booking advisable weekends. Disabled: toilet. Separate room for parties, holds 150. Takeaway service.

West

Notting Hill

★ Taqueria

139-143 Westbourne Grove, W11 2RS (7229 4734). Notting Hill Gate tube. **Meals served** noon-11pm Mon-Thur; noon-11.30pm Fri, Sat; noon-10.30pm Sun. **Main courses** £3.50-£6.50. **Set lunch** (noon-4.30pm daily) £5.50 1 course. **Credit** MC, V.
This little diner now has legions of devoted fans, who line up at the door for the cheap and cheerful taco menu. The roll-'em-and-eat-'em tacos at Taqueria aren't the crispy kind you might be familiar with, but are made with soft corn tortillas and filled with a huge variety of ingredients. You can choose from an extensive menu, ranging from chargrilled steak to prawns, chorizo, pork, sea bass – you name it. Portions are small, but so are the prices and you're encouraged to order an array. Aside from tacos, other enticing options include torta de pulpo (sourdough bread filled with octopus) and flautas (corn tortillas filled with beef, rolled up like a cigar and fried to a crisp). To imbibe, there are aguas frescas (fresh fruit juice drinks), Mexican coffee (café con leche) or a great menu of Mexican beers; the chelada – a Pacifico beer served with lime juice in a glass with a salted rim – is particularly refreshing on a hot day. Service has always been a weak spot here, and it's difficult to convince a waiter to pay attention to you. Still, the crowds keep coming.
Babies and children welcome: high chairs. Bookings not accepted. Takeaway service. **Map 7 A6.**

South

Clapham

Café Sol

56 Clapham High Street, SW4 7UL (7498 8558/ www.cafesol.net). Clapham Common or Clapham North tube. **Meals served** noon-midnight Mon-Thur, Sun; noon-1am Fri, Sat. **Main courses** £5.95-£11.95. **Credit** AmEx, DC, MC, V.
This busy, friendly restaurant seems to be packed to the gills every night from about 8pm. We can see why. Café Sol is perfect for Clapham: the food is ideal for post-pub sharing; the bartenders make excellent margaritas; and the place is open late enough for you not to feel rushed if you come through the door at 10pm with a mad nacho craving. The look is pure Texas border: rough wooden floors, and walls painted with clichéd Mexican village scenes of glossy-haired señoritas going about their daily business in traditional Indian garb. Food arrives fast and hot from the kitchen (you get the feeling nothing sits under a heat lamp here): steaming plates of enchiladas (rolled-up corn tortillas filled with cheese and vegetables, or beef and chicken) with rice and beans; big, meaty tacos with crispy corn tortillas; burritos (meat and beans wrapped in a flour tortilla); and chimichangas (similar to burritos, only grilled or deep-fried). The nachos are memorable – piled high with meat, cheese and guacamole. There are hamburgers and ribs too, but it's worth diving in and trying the humble but tasty Tex-Mex cooking.
Babies and children welcome: high chairs. Booking essential dinner Fri, Sat. Disabled: toilet. Entertainment: DJ 11pm Fri, Sat. Tables outdoors (6, pavement). Takeaway service. **Map 22 B1.**

East

Shoreditch

★ Green & Red

51 Bethnal Green Road, E1 6LA (7749 9670/ www.greenred.co.uk). Liverpool Street tube/rail. **Dinner served** 6-11pm Mon-Sat; 6-10.30pm Sun. **Main courses** £10.50-£14.50. **Credit** AmEx, MC, V.
A combination of Mexican cantina and tequila bar, with wooden floors and panelling, Green & Red looks like a set from a Sergio Leone film, only nicer. It has a vibrant atmosphere, with crowds of loyalists vying for space in the ground-floor eaterie and basement bar. The tequila list seems virtually limitless; aficionados will be in cactus-juice heaven. Happily, the food is just as good, and creative. The owners are fans of food from Jalisco, the Mexican province where most tequila is produced. So the menu incorporates smoky ancho chillies stuffed with crumbly cheese; ceviche (fish marinated in citrus juices) with pomegranate seeds; and pork belly with grilled ribs rubbed with orange salt. Mains are served with steamed corn tortillas, fresh beans and shredded cabbage, as well as freshly made salsas. Desserts continue the authentic theme; one of the best options is the churros (doughnuts) served with spiced chocolate sauce. The atmosphere can get raucous – and the music is sometimes too loud – but the food makes up for such shortcomings.
Babies and children welcome: high chairs. Disabled: toilet. Entertainment: DJs 9pm-1am Fri, Sat. Tables outdoors (1, terrace). **Map 6 S4.**

Pan-American

North

Islington

Sabor

108 Essex Road, N1 8LX (7226 5551/ www.sabor.co.uk). Angel tube/Essex Road rail/ 38, 73 bus. **Brunch served** 10am-3pm Sat, Sun. **Lunch served** noon-2.30pm Mon-Fri. **Dinner served** 5-11pm Mon-Fri; 5pm-1am Sat; 5-11pm Sun. **Main courses** £8-£19.50. **Set lunch** £10 2 courses, £12.50 3 courses. **Credit** MC, V.
Sabor's chef is from France, not South America – but he's well informed and has produced a tantalising menu, full of dishes laced with tropical fruits, spices, lime, guacamole and subtle salsas. The weekend brunch menu features some of the best dishes from the evening carta. As there's so much to explore, it's wise to come in a party and share dishes; a group of four will be satisfied with three choices. The classic Peruvian starter, monkfish ceviche, was tangy and mouth-watering; lamb empanadas oozed with meaty juices that worked well with the mint-based salsa; the weakest dish was duck and cheese quesadillas (tasty but not hot enough). Mains were equally appetising, especially the healthy quinoa pie (enlivened by red onions and thyme), and the tarta de choclo (a delicious corn wrap, with lime and avocado dressing). Several desserts were unavailable, but the passionfruit cake and a Latin version of trifle (which delivered a tart, fruity kick and a shot of liqueur) were perfect. Excellent Argentinian vintages and good by-the-glass options are features of the extensive wine list. There was zero atmosphere at the lunchtime sitting, but this funky little cantina is buzzing at night.
Babies and children welcome: high chairs. Booking advisable. Disabled: toilet. **Map 5 P1.**

Brasseries

London was a late starter in the European brasserie stakes. Until 20 years ago, few establishments were allowed to serve alcohol through the afternoon. Now, it's easy to find a meal and a drink in central London at 4pm, whether at inexpensive caffs specialising in Middle Eastern kebabs, Japanese noodles, Chinese dim sum or home-grown pie and mash – or at purpose-built brasseries. Over the past decade or so, the city's brasseries have developed their own characters, becoming something more than simply wine bars with food.

Some, like **Banners**, **Butcher & Grill**, the **Giraffe** chain, **Tate Modern Café** and **Pick More Daisies** (the last two were both contenders for Best Family Restaurant in the 2007 Time Out Eating & Drinking Awards), aim at providing family-friendly environs where both children and parents get decent food, and the grown-ups can have a relaxing drink. Others, such as **Flâneur Food Hall** and the new **Larder** concentrate on first-rate ingredients, either assembled on a plate or for sale in a shop. Others still major in cocktails or brunches: **Electric Brasserie**, **High Road Brasserie** (a contender for both Best Design and Best Local Restaurant) and **Joanna's**. Mention too should be made of **Acorn House**, a laudable new enterprise that, though providing training opportunities for local youngsters, is anything but grimly worthy. Finally, we've noticed this year what might become a new trend: high-class restaurants offering a simpler menu in brasserie-style offshoots, the **National Café**, the brasserie in **Rhodes W1** (*see p143*) and **Tom's Kitchen** (also a contender for Best Local Restaurant) being pioneers.

Central

Belgravia

Chelsea Brasserie NEW

Sloane Square Hotel, 7-12 Sloane Square, SW1W 8EG (7881 5999/www.sloanesquarehotel.co.uk). Sloane Square tube. **Lunch served** noon-3pm daily. **Dinner served** 6-10.30pm Mon-Sat; 6-10pm Sun. **Main courses** £12.75-£17.75. **Set meal** (lunch, 6-7.30pm) £17.50 2 courses, £20.50 3 courses. **Credit** AmEx, MC, V.

A head chef who's come from Racine and a manager from Galvin Bistrot de Luxe boded well for the Sloane Square Hotel's new brasserie, though so far it hasn't managed to scale the heights of those two stellar French restaurants. The short, daily-changing menu is French-biased with an emphasis on British ingredients. A perfectly fresh mixed-leaf salad came with a generous assortment of smoked duck slivers, duck rillons and cubes of foie gras; also generous was the pile of pickled crab served with avocado and cucumber. A main course of sea bream fillet with mussels and wild mushrooms couldn't be faulted, but a confit duck leg, though tasty, sounded a couple of bum notes: the skin was overcharred, and the accompanying raw carrot with sweet chilli sauce was an amateurish, redundant extra. Still, we had a great bottle of 2006 Domaine de la Prade rosé, typical of the concise, well-chosen wine list. What's more, prices are reasonable (most mains cost under £15), service precise, and the room bright, spacious and pleasantly decorated (a Chelsea version of edgy, with exposed bricks, abstract art and green ceiling lanterns). Worth considering for a reliable, civilised, good-value meal if you're in the area.

Babies and children welcome: high chairs. Booking advisable. Disabled: toilet. Separate room for parties, seats 12. **Map 15 G10.**

City

Royal Exchange Grand Café & Bar

The Royal Exchange, EC3V 3LR (7618 2480/ www.danddlondon.co.uk). Bank tube/DLR. **Breakfast served** 8-11am, **meals served** 11.30am-10pm Mon-Fri. **Main courses** £6.50-£14.50. **Credit** AmEx, DC, MC, V.

The setting is magnificent: the soaring, arched interior of the grade I-listed Royal Exchange, surrounded by jewellery shops and huge 19th-century paintings depicting the City's history. There are brasserie-style tables in the courtyard, next to the oval bar with its crustacea displays and flower arrangements. Alternatively, choose a leather chair in the quieter upstairs gallery, where some tables overlook the action below (French restaurant Sauterelle is also here). You can come for breakfast (pastries, muesli or a bacon sarnie), dinner or a drink after work, but lunchtimes are busiest – when the no-bookings policy means you may have to wait. Charcuterie, steak and caesar salad are typical offerings, though seafood is a strength, and probably the wisest choice: oysters, plateau de fruits de mer and caviar (City fat-cats can celebrate bonuses with Iranian beluga at £135/30g). Other dishes were mediocre. Lobster bisque was flavourful yet thin. A main of 'Thai-baked sea bass in banana leaf' was a sorry affair: a miserably small fillet with a single red chilli and sprig of coriander as garnish, plus a bowl of distinctly unaromatic rice. Nice to see seasonal samphire as a side dish; a pity its delicate briny flavour was swamped by the accompanying horse mushrooms. Crème brûlée and panna cotta are typical puddings.

Babies and children admitted (restaurant). Bookings not accepted. Disabled: toilet. Dress: smart casual. **Map 12 Q6.**

Clerkenwell & Farringdon

Brasserie de Malmaison

Malmaison, 18-21 Charterhouse Square, EC1M 6AH (7012 3700/www.malmaison-london.com). Barbican tube/Farringdon tube/rail. **Breakfast served** 7-10am Mon-Fri; 8-10.30am Sat, Sun. **Brunch served** 11am-3pm Sun. **Lunch served** noon-2.30pm Mon-Sat. **Dinner served** 6-10.30pm daily. **Main courses** £12-£20. **Set meal** £15.50 2 courses, £17.50 3 courses. **Credit** AmEx, DC, JCB, MC, V.

This dimly lit brasserie, inside the London outpost of the mini Malmaison hotel chain, has a romantic (if slightly formal) vibe, with big, comfy chairs and lots of secluded corners. These were being put to good use on our Friday night visit by couples tucking into a menu of crowd-pleasing brasserie basics (salads, steaks, lots of fish dishes). Pan-fried red mullet was a well presented dish let down by an overdose of bland black olives. A tomato and mozzarella starter had a similar discrepancy; it looked fabulous, but the cheese portion was tiny and the tomatoes lacked flavour. A classic steak was more successful, and the fries served with a bloody mary sauce were spot-on. Other nice touches include the boards of bread, butter and tapenade, good olive oil at each table and coffees served with shots of chocolate mousse. Service was slick and friendly, though staff outnumbered diners – even when we left at 9.30pm. For a safe business lunch, or dinner with fussy relatives, this hotel offers the right kind of smooth-running professionalism. If you're after something special, the bland background music (at best funk, at worst a cringe-worthy swing/soul mix) and formulaic, 'could be anywhere' vibe don't quite cut it.

Babies and children welcome: high chairs. Booking advisable. Disabled: toilet. Separate rooms for parties, seating 6, 16 and 30. **Map 5 O5.**

★ Flâneur Food Hall

41 Farringdon Road, EC1M 3JB (7404 4422/ www.flaneur.com). Farringdon tube/rail. **Breakfast served** 8.30-10.30am Mon-Sat. **Lunch served** noon-3pm Mon-Fri. **Brunch served** 10am-4pm Sat, Sun. **Dinner served** 6-10pm Mon-Sat. **Main courses** £12-£14.50. **Set menu** £19.50 2 courses, £24.50 3 courses. **Credit** AmEx, DC, JCB, MC, V.

Flâneur's two sides – restaurant and food hall – complement each other beautifully. Ceiling-height shelves packed with neatly arranged tins and jars provide the restaurant with a novel backdrop, while diners inspired by lunch can pick up ingredients on their way out. At the set-price, multi-choice lunch or dinner, charcuterie or cured fish might be followed by roast breast of Barbary duck, or fish stew. The top-notch full english and veggie breakfasts we tucked into at Sunday brunch required a chef of exacting talents to construct. Mushrooms, tomatoes and bubble and squeak were flavoursome, fried manouri cheese was a break from the veggie-sausage norm, and the cumberland sausage, bacon and black pudding were clearly carefully sourced. Our only complaint concerned slightly overcooked eggs. A side order of unnecessary but delicious chargrilled sourdough meant we failed to try one of the much-lauded desserts (pineapple upside-down cake, chocolate tart, poppy-seed cake) served with lashings of cream. Flâneur has a relaxed, slightly otherworldly feel – created by Goldilocks and the Three Bears-style giant chairs and dim lighting – that also works well for lunchtime escapes and foodie romantic dinners. Service was efficient and helpful.

Babies and children admitted. Booking advisable. Separate room for parties, seats 20. Takeaway service. **Map 5 N5.**

The Larder NEW

91-93 St John Street, EC1M 4NU (7608 1558/ www.thelarderrestaurant.com). Barbican tube/ Farringdon tube/rail. **Breakfast served** 8-11am, **lunch served** 11am-3pm, **dinner served** 6-10.30pm Mon-Sat. **Main courses** £9-£17.90. **Credit** MC, V.

Set across a curious mix of old and new properties, the Larder's gigantic dining area has 110 covers and a large open kitchen. The menu is Middlesbrough-meets-Mediterranean, with Yorkshire ham, Swaledale cheese and cumberland sauce lining up against chorizo, duck confit and tapenade. Meat is extraordinarily good, so it's a shame the accompaniments weren't more impressive. Barnsley chop was pinky-red at the centre – a little underdone for many tastes, but nothing to grumble about; it was the undercooked aubergine that let the dish down. Luscious pork loin was lightly gratinéed with cheese, but while the apple sauce was welcome in this rich mix, the caramelised fruit on the side was bland and superfluous. A classic prawn cocktail starter, served in a porcelain beaker, was a success. Of the desserts, fondant-style chocolate pudding had a slightly burnt crust and soupy interior, but vanilla cheesecake topped with caramelised bananas was surprisingly light and delicious. We also liked the international selection of wines (18 by the glass), helpfully divided into stylistic categories. Despite the incorporation of a bar and shop, there has been little attempt to divide the space, so looking busy will always be a challenge here.

Babies and children welcome: high chairs. Separate room for parties, seats 16. Takeaway service. **Map 5 O4.**

Fitzrovia

RIBA Café

66 Portland Place, W1B 1AD (7631 0467/ www.riba.org). Great Portland Street or Oxford Circus tube. **Meals served** 8am-6pm Mon-Fri; 9am-4pm Sat. **Main courses** £8.50-£19.50. **Set meal** £23.50 3 courses. **Credit** AmEx, DC, MC, V.

Located on the first floor of the Royal Institute of British Architects' headquarters, this brasserie is run by Charlton House Catering. Most diners are business lunchers, appreciating the grand surroundings. The setting is terrific: gorgeous curved couches inside, and a delightful roof terrace for summer. Parasol-topped tables are surrounded by zinc planters and a water feature, with an apt backdrop of mixed-period buildings. Breakfast, salads and sandwiches are offered alongside a lunch menu of Modern European classics. It's a shame all the effort appears to have gone into presentation (painstaking arrangements on oversized white crockery) rather than the food. Greek salad with olive and feta tarte tatin was fine, but pricey at £10.50 for what was largely salad leaves. Goat's cheese tart with aubergine caviar featured a generous disc of cheese atop nicely flaky pastry, but the artichoke tasted sharp and the aubergine smears were more embellishment than nourishment. Fancy desserts include chocolate pyramids with good raspberry ice-cream, but poached rhubarb comprised cold, almost-raw sticks in syrup, topped with toothpaste-tasting mint sorbet. Waitresses favoured the suits before serving others. A great spot, let down by uninspired corporate catering and unprofessional service.

Babies and children welcome: high chairs. Booking advisable. Disabled: lift; toilet. Tables outdoors (20, terrace). Separate rooms for parties, seating 6-270. **Map 3 H4.**

BEST BRASSERIES

For taking the kids

Most brasseries accommodate kids happily, but **Banners** (*see p60*), the **Giraffe** chain (*see p58*), **Pick More Daisies** (*see p60*) and **Tate Modern Café** (*see p58*) all deserve praise for making a special effort.

A sunny outlook

When the weather permits, enjoy alfresco dining at **Giraffe** (*see p58*), **High Road Brasserie** (*see p56*), **Hoxton Grille** (*see p59*), the **Market Place** (*see p57*), **Newtons** (*see p58*) and **RIBA Café** (*see left*).

When looks matter

For stylish surroundings, check out the **Electric Brasserie** (*see p56*), **High Road Brasserie** (*see p56*), **Napket** (*see p57*) and the **Royal Exchange Grand Café & Bar** (*see left*).

Midnight feasts

You can eat until midnight on Friday and Saturday at **Banners** (*see p60*) and **High Road Brasserie** (*see p56*) and every day at **Hoxton Grille** (*see p59*) and **Tom's Kitchen** (*see p57*), but **Balans** (*see p56*) is the winner of the night owl award: it's open until 5am six nights a week and 2am on Sunday.

Hoxton Grille. See p59.

King's Cross

★ Acorn House NEW

69 Swinton Street, WC1X 9NT (7812 1842/ www.acornhouserestaurant.com). King's Cross tube/rail. **Breakfast served** 8-11am Mon-Fri; 10am-noon Sat. **Lunch served** noon-3pm, **dinner served** 6-10.30pm Mon-Sat. **Main courses** £12-£18. **Credit** AmEx, MC, V.

'Eco-friendly training restaurant' doesn't successfully convey the charm of Acorn House. The engaging interior – furnished with modern tables and chairs, and decorated in white and brown with splashes of apple green – makes it easy to shake off grimy Gray's Inn Road. The restaurant is committed to seasonal menus and environmental responsibility. It runs a training programme too (ten local young adults a year), but the experience of dining here is anything but worthy. Breakfast (power shakes through to pastries) and an all-day roster of sandwiches, paninis and coffees are served, but the real pleasure lies in the flavour-packed cooked dishes and simple assemblies for lunch and dinner. There are soups (pea and broad bean); cured meats; a choice of sprightly, multicoloured salads; a pasta dish and a risotto; plus five or so major mains, such as roast pork chop with soy honey and thyme, or chargrilled sea bream with salad. Rice pudding with strawberry jam and hazelnut biscotti was a rich treat, though chocolate cake with ginger ice-cream also appealed; there are English cheeses too. Add a tempting wine list (plenty by the glass) and warm, friendly staff, and you have a great local.

Babies and children welcome: high chairs; nappy-changing facilities. Disabled: toilet. Takeaway service (lunch). **Map 4 M3.**

Mayfair

Truc Vert

42 North Audley Street, W1K 6ZR (7491 9988/ www.trucvert.co.uk). Bond Street tube. **Meals served** 7.30am-10pm Mon-Sat; 9.30am-3pm Sun. **Main courses** £12.50-£17. **Credit** AmEx, MC, V.

Despite its Mayfair address, there's nothing stiff and starchy about this diminutive brasserie. Rustic wooden tables and airy, light-flooded surrounds make Truc Vert an inviting spot for a leisurely breakfast or lunch. White tablecloths and flowers mark the change from daytime to evening, but a laid-back feel persists; it's more a place for casual early-evening suppers than a romantic rendezvous. From the succinct, daily-changing menu, duck confit salad with chorizo, new potato, rocket and tangy own-made tomato chutney was a satisfyingly substantial starter. Equally hearty, if slightly overcooked, was hot smoked salmon served with potato and feta cake, mixed leaves and dill sour cream. To follow, deliciously fresh and simple grilled sea trout with chilli salsa easily outshone an unremarkable slab of lamb accompanied by roasted root vegetables and fiercely salty fried polenta (as greasy as the hash brown it resembled). Happily, a chocolate pudding with an oozing molten centre made some amends. The kitchen's lapses may, like the charming but rather inattentive service, be forgivable, but neither is really excusable at these prices.

Babies and children welcome: high chairs. Booking advisable. Tables outdoors (6, pavement). Takeaway service. **Map 9 G6.**

Soho

Balans

60 Old Compton Street, W1D 4UG (7437 5212/ www.balans.co.uk). Leicester Square or Piccadilly Circus tube. **Meals served** 8am-5am Mon-Sat; 8am-2am Sun. **Main courses** £8-£17.50. **Credit** AmEx, MC, V.

Balans may be a bit late 1990s in terms of decor (red leather walls, metal chairs, blackboards and mirrors), but it's still a deservedly popular spot with both Londoners and tourists. The large, split-level space was almost full on the Tuesday night of our visit. The concept is New York-style brasserie (with good-looking, efficient waiters, an eclectic, flexible menu and wi-fi) meets hedonistic Soho bar (it's open until 5am most nights, and a clubby vibe prevails). Dishes run the gamut from American brunch-style breakfast food – the likes of eggs benedict, blueberry pancakes, granola, and breakfast burrito – to well-prepared late-night fillers such as sesame tuna steak and thai chicken curry. There's also an extensive range of meat dishes from the grill, fresh fish and seafood options, pasta, pastry-based dishes, salads, daily specials, desserts and a huge choice of sides. In fact, whatever flavours you're craving, it's likely Balans will deliver. The same applies to drinks, with a selection of aperitifs (prosecco, bellini, kir royale) complementing the diverse wine list and extensive (and reasonably priced) cocktail menu. An essential part of Old Compton Street.

Babies and children admitted (until 6pm). Bookings not accepted Fri, Sat. **Map 17 B4.**
For branches see index.

Trafalgar Square

National Café NEW

East Wing, National Gallery, Trafalgar Square, WC2N 5DN (7747 2525/www.thenationalcafe.com). Charing Cross tube/rail. **Breakfast served** 8am-11.30am, **lunch served** noon-5pm, **dinner served** 5.30-11pm Mon-Sat. **Afternoon tea served** 3-5.30pm daily. **Meals served** 10am-6pm Sun. **Main courses** £8.50-£16.50. **Set dinner** (5.30-7pm) £14.50 2 courses; £17.50 3 courses. **Credit** MC, V.

Tucked into the east wing of the National Gallery, this relaxed café-cum-brasserie makes a pleasing, informal alternative to its classy British elder sister, the National Dining Rooms. Opening hours are more appealing too (the Café stays open until 11pm, except on Sunday). It's an attractive, high-ceilinged space, with a marble-topped bar running the length of one wall. Left a long time before being seated, we weren't overwhelmed by the service; plentiful staff seemed oddly overrun by a quiet lunchtime crowd. As our starters were taken away, a waiter asked if we would care to order dessert – bizarre, but the food saved the day. An opener of gorgeously creamy mozzarella, tempered by scattered salad leaves and lemon rind, was superb; same too a platter of rabbit rillettes. A main of haddock fish cakes (topped by a just-right egg and professional hollandaise) maintained standards. Dressed dorset crab was let down by a dollop of lacklustre dill sauce; the dish needed more punch. Adjoining the Café's main room is a bustling self-service area, with salads and sandwiches: a nod to the dreary museum-café clichés that proprietor Oliver Peyton is slowly eroding, perhaps.

Babies and children welcome: high chairs. Booking advisable. Disabled: toilet. Separate room for parties, seats 30. Restaurant available for hire. **Map 10 K7.**

West

Chiswick

★ High Road Brasserie

2007 RUNNER-UP BEST LOCAL RESTAURANT
2007 RUNNER-UP BEST DESIGN

162-166 Chiswick High Road, W4 1PR (8742 7474/www.highroadhouse.co.uk). Turnham Green tube. **Breakfast served** 7am-noon Mon-Fri; 8am-noon Sat, Sun. **Brunch served** noon-5pm Sat, Sun. **Dinner served** 5pm-midnight Sat; 5-10pm Sun. **Meals served** noon-11pm Mon-Thur; noon-midnight Fri. **Main courses** £10-£22. **Set lunch** £13 2 courses, £16 3 courses. **Credit** AmEx, MC, V.

An offshoot of Nick Jones' Soho House (there's a members club and hotel upstairs), this is a slick and seductive operation that wouldn't look out of place in central London, Paris or New York. It's a good-looking (if noisy) space, with dark wood furniture, green banquettes, and a dove-grey awning over the pavement tables; the colourful, multi-patterned ceramic floor tiles are particularly striking. The classic brasserie menu caters for all appetites, at all hours. It covers everything from seafood (oysters, seafood platters) to sandwiches, burgers and grilled fare (ribeye, chateaubriand), plus regular starters, mains and desserts. You could drop in for breakfast or for cocktails. The food didn't quite live up to the promise of the menu; it's good but not flawless. Potted shrimps were excellent (buttery, creamy, packed with flavour), as was a summery chicken casserole with baby turnips, carrots, peas, broad beans and potatoes. However, a main of skate was overcooked, and the accompanying salad was dreary. The shallot vinegar – to go with good-quality oysters – came in a bottle, which made it almost impossible to use. The wine list is appealing, though there's not much choice by the glass. Impeccable service from staff dressed in long white aprons and black waistcoats, and a buzzing atmosphere compensated; the attraction here is more about generosity of spirit than perfect, finicky food.

Babies and children welcome: children's menu; crayons; high chairs; toys. Booking advisable. Disabled: toilet. Tables outdoors (14, terrace).

Notting Hill

Electric Brasserie

191 Portobello Road, W11 2ED (7908 9696/ www.the-electric.co.uk). Ladbroke Grove tube. **Meals served** 8am-11pm Mon-Fri; 8am-5pm, 6-11pm Sat; 8am-5pm, 6-10pm Sun. **Main courses** £9-£28. **Set lunch** (noon-4.45pm Mon-Fri) £12 2 courses, £15 3 courses. **Credit** AmEx, DC, MC, V.

The Electric Brasserie remains a buzzing venue with its busy terrace overlooking Portobello market and its folding doors adjoining the refurbished Electric cinema. Panoramic people-watching opportunities are offered. The New York diner-like menu has, over the years, proved a real crowd-pleaser, with breakfast served until noon daily, and brunch at the weekend. Whether you're after something light and slimming like a caesar salad, or something big and filling like a steak sandwich, or even something chic and tempting like baked lobster – this is the place. Sometimes, though, a set lunch menu is a welcome relief as you pull up a heavy chair on the concrete floor by the chrome bar, and flag down one of the scurrying aproned staff. Squid, fennel and gremolata began our meal as nicely as the chicken and bacon salad, while a warm lamb sandwich made with ciabatta was a juicy, oozing highlight. Mackerel served with sage potatoes provided a fresh, simple treat. Strawberry mousse with mango sauce, and banana almond strudel with honey chocolate ice-cream begged to be eaten, and at the bargain set-lunch prices probably should have been. A considerable wine list also boosts the Electric's well-deserved popularity.

Babies and children welcome: high chairs. Disabled: toilet. Tables outdoors (8, pavement). **Map 19 B3.**

South West

Barnes

The Depot

Tideway Yard, 125 Mortlake High Street, SW14 8SN (8878 9462/www.depotbrasserie.co.uk). Barnes, Barnes Bridge or Mortlake rail/209 bus. **Lunch served** noon-3pm Mon-Fri; noon-4pm Sat, Sun. **Dinner served** 6-11pm Mon-Sat; 6-10.30pm Sun. **Main courses** £9.95-£17.95. **Set meal** (noon-7.30pm Mon-Fri) £13.50 2 courses, £15.50 3 courses; (Oct-Nov, Jan-Feb) £10 2 courses. **Credit** AmEx, DC, JCB, MC, V.

This long-standing brasserie by the Thames (the sought-after window tables make for perfect sunset-viewing) is as popular as ever with the well-heeled denizens of Barnes and Mortlake. The smart-cas look (all polished wooden tables and chairs, and striped-top banquettes) suits the demographic to a T. It works just as well for family get-togethers as intimate dinners à deux. The food has got smarter of late – and more expensive, with most mains hovering around £15 – but remains determinedly seasonal (white and green asparagus with Jersey Royals and mousserons on our visit), though by no means exclusively British (witness the shiitake broth and chinese greens with slow-

roast pork belly). Cooking is generally deft, yet there were a few low points: a starter of oat-crusted smoked eel and fried scallops yielded high-quality scallops, but the eel pieces were too small for their heavy coating, and the accompanying horseradish cream was overpowering. Crayfish, tarragon and spinach risotto was too reminiscent of a Pret sandwich filling, but the sea bass on top was cooked just right. The childish delights of eton mess made an enjoyable conclusion. Staff tend to be on the ball, though our waiter forgot a side dish.
Babies and children welcome: children's menu; crayons; high chairs. Booking advisable. Tables outdoors (8, patio).

Chelsea

The Market Place

Chelsea Farmers' Market, 125 Sydney Street, SW3 6NR (7352 5600). South Kensington tube/11, 19, 22, 49 bus. **Meals served** *Apr-Sept* 9.30am-5pm Mon-Fri; 9.30am-6pm Sat, Sun. *Oct-Mar* 9.30am-5pm daily. **Main courses** £8-£12. **Credit** AmEx, MC, V.

On a sunny Saturday lunchtime, the outside tables at this Med-influenced brasserie in Chelsea Farmers' Market make a seemingly perfect setting for an alfresco lunch break from the rigours of King's Road shopping. But there the illusion ends. First, the lack of a booking system meant we had to wait behind a rope, while the waiters ignored the queue. Once across the divide, we were squeezed on to a café table barely fit for one. A simple request for tap water entailed a ten-minute wait and five reminders – until, in true Fawlty Towers style, two glasses arrived at once. And the food? Suffice to say, it is fine and no more, with an uneventful line-up of gourmet burgers, fish cakes and assorted Med salads. The kids' menu is equally dull: chicken and chips or goujons and peas. A request for goujons and chips was met with consternation (the child on the next table had already had this request turned down and coughed up an extra £3.50 for chips), until the waiter gave in and agreed to the swap. A half-decent tiramisu raised the spirits, but the service was enough to dampen the sunniest weekend.
Babies and children welcome: children's menu; high chairs. Bookings not accepted summer. Tables outdoors (30, patio). **Map 14 E12**.

Napket NEW

342 King's Road, SW3 5UR (7352 9832/ www.napket.com). Sloane Square tube then 11, 19, 22 bus. **Meals served** 8am-9pm Mon-Thur; 8am-10pm Fri-Sun. **Main courses** £2.95-£5.85. **Credit** MC, V.

Remember Fashion Café? A group of supermodels launched a restaurant chain along the lines of Planet Hollywood, but it faded faster than last season's colours. Napket is what Fashion Café might have been, if done with style – and it clearly has dreams of expansion. 'Snob food' is the strapline, used ironically, but that doesn't mean the place isn't pretentious. Pictures of pretty girls wearing prettier dresses line the walls; there are low-slung chandeliers covered in brown gauze, iPod sockets in the communal table, Philippe Starck chairs and much black gloss. Various cakes are available, from savoury cheddar with fig and rocket, to a Schiaparelli-pink 'candy' number, but if our dry, thick-crusted coconut pound cake was fair indication, they're not even D-list. Staff compile each meal from an open serving cabinet. An altar of ham, cheese and white flour, this is lined with luscious salads of plump mozzarella and tangy serrano, daintily cut sandwiches, flaky croissants (very good) and pots of yoghurt and granola. Your order is placed on a tray and delivered to your seat. To drink, choose from freshly squeezed juices (the watermelon was bitter), Illy coffee, herbal teas and 'Frapkets' in flavours such as caramel, chocolate and strawberry.
Babies and children admitted. Takeaway service; delivery service (over £25 within SW3). **Map 14 D12**.

Tom's Kitchen NEW

2007 RUNNER-UP BEST LOCAL RESTAURANT

27 Cale Street, SW3 3QP (7349 0202/ www.tomskitchen.co.uk). South Kensington or Sloane Square tube. **Breakfast served** 7-10am, **lunch served** noon-3pm Mon-Fri. **Brunch served** 10am-3pm Sat; 11am-3pm Sun. **Dinner served** 6pm-midnight daily. **Main courses** £14-£25. Credit AmEx, MC, V.

Tom is acclaimed young British chef Tom Aikens, who runs his own haute cuisine restaurant just round the corner. This is his simpler, cheaper restaurant for the masses (it's certainly popular with the well-groomed Chelsea masses). With white-tiled walls, a big skylight and a marble counter along one side (behind which you can see the chefs in action), it's a bright and attractive space – though noisy. The pale wood tables are too close for comfort, however, and the oversized sepia photos of butchers in moody poses are a bit pretentious. You can visit for breakfast (porridge, full english and, absurdly, Weetabix for £2), lunch, dinner or, at the weekend, brunch – though many dishes appear throughout the day. The menu is a crowd-pleasing mix of British and French influences, with plenty of meaty options (steak tartare, cumberland sausages with mash and onion gravy, roast rump of beef with yorkshire pudding) as well as the likes of lemon sole 'à la française' and macaroni cheese. We enjoyed excellent eggs benedict (perfectly cooked eggs, crispy bacon), less so a burger with all the trimmings, though the thick-cut chips were spot-on. Best were the puds: chocolate profiteroles with vanilla ice-cream and a sumptuous chocolate sauce; and own-made vanilla yoghurt with sugared churros. The black-shirted staff were scatty and didn't smile much.
Babies and children welcome: high chairs. Disabled: toilet. Separate room for parties, seats 22. **Map 14 E11**.

South

Battersea

Butcher & Grill

39-41 Parkgate Road, SW11 4NP (7924 3999/ www.thebutcherandgrill.com). Clapham Junction or Queenstown Road rail/49, 319, 345 bus.
Bar **Open** 9am-11pm Mon-Sat; 9am-4pm Sun. **Breakfast served** 9-11am Mon-Sat; 9.30am-noon Sun.
Restaurant **Lunch served** noon-3.30pm Mon-Sat; noon-4pm Sun. **Dinner served** 6-11pm Mon-Sat. **Main courses** £8.50-£25.
Both **Credit** AmEx, MC, V.

A barn-like space identifiable by a jaunty blue and white awning, B&G is a shop, bar and restaurant on two levels, with a tiny deck overlooking Ransome's Dock. Despite its size, it gets hot inside thanks to all the grill action (everything from burgers and sausages to various steaks) and

ineffectual air-conditioning. It's a real locals' hangout; at weekends this means families, lured by the easy-going attitude and a £5.25 kids' menu (on Sundays there's a mini roast too). Apart from the grills, the menu is an undemanding mix of caesar salads, charcuterie, fish of the day and a vegetarian pasta, but meat is the point – so we were disappointed when our worst dish was the 8oz burger. It cost £9.50 (decent chips are another £2.75) for a dry patty with an unpleasant after-taste. (We left most, told the waitress it wasn't nice, yet it stayed on the bill.) Grilled squid with chilli fennel and rocket tasted much better, but was a tad chewy. Our meal was redeemed by the odd-sounding but delicious salt-and-pepper duck breast with crushed Jersey Royals and sweet black bacon sauce; and a tangy, refreshing passionfruit jelly with mandarin sorbet. A likeable brasserie that could try a bit harder for the price.
Babies and children welcome: children's menu; high chairs. Booking advisable weekends. Disabled: ramp; toilet. Tables outdoors (5 pavement, 6 terrace). **Map 21 C1**.

Clapham

Newtons

33-35 Abbeville Road, SW4 9LA (8673 0977/ www.newtonsrestaurants.co.uk). Clapham South tube. **Lunch served** noon-4pm daily. **Dinner served** 6-11pm Mon-Sat; 6-10.30pm Sun. **Main courses** £9.50-£16. **Set lunch** (noon-4pm Mon-Sat) £8 2 courses, £10.50 3 courses; (Sun) £16.50 3 courses. **Set dinner** (Mon-Sat) £15 2 courses, £18.50 3 courses. **Credit** AmEx, MC, V.
This stalwart of chichi Abbeville Road's dining scene continues to be a classy performer. The two-room brasserie has bentwood chairs, quirky treasures from global travels, and exposed brick walls painted pale cream. The look is further enlivened by the arresting portrait photography of the owner's husband. The good-value set dinner has enough choices for both starters and mains. Marshmallowy mozzarella paired with warm caramelised onions and tomato worked a treat; the overcooked and salty fillets of plaice with fresh pasta in a creamy sauce, less so. The hearty beefburger and feathery-light bread and butter pudding were standards done well. What's more, we were pleasantly surprised at the high quality of the handful of Asian dishes on the menu (such as a thai green curry packed with juicy chunks of chicken). Service was friendly and professional; a possibly corked bottle of wine was replaced without asking, and a major wine spill at the next table was cleaned up with the minimum of fuss. No wonder Newtons has a faithful following.
Babies and children welcome: crayons; high chairs. Booking advisable. Tables outdoors (8, terrace). **Map 22 A3**.

Waterloo

★ Giraffe

Riverside Level 1, Royal Festival Hall, Belvedere Road, SE1 8XX (7928 2004/www.giraffe.net). Embankment tube/Waterloo tube/rail. **Meals served** 8am-10.45pm Mon-Fri; 9am-10.45pm Sat; 9am-10.30pm Sun. **Main courses** £6.95-£12.95. **Set meal** (5-7pm Mon-Fri) £6.95 2 courses. **Credit** AmEx, MC, V.
If there's one chain that's reliable on all fronts – food, service, atmosphere, family-friendliness, value for money – it's Giraffe. This branch could be marked down for being just too popular, though. On our most recent visit (to escape inclement weather during a Sunday walk on the South Bank) there was a queue for a table. Nonetheless, the short wait sharpened our appetite for starters of sticky chicken wings and a colourful bruschetta in which cherry tomatoes, avocado, red pepper and mozzarella all played a part. Many of the dishes are ensemble pieces. Our favourite main course, the falafel burger, comes with grilled pepper, beetroot, rocket, halloumi and tzatziki; the Aberdeen Angus steak burger is less dressed up but adequately juicy. Another great main is the firecracker chicken with mushrooms, greens, pineapple, chilli sambal and noodles: all the food groups on one plate. With top puds (the fruit crumble is made for sharing), smashing sides, a hugely popular brunch menu, a sensible list for children (egg and soldiers, beans on toast, as well as proper mains), feel-good cocktails (especially the mango lime daiquiri) and feel-worthy smoothies – the ubiquitous Giraffe always cheers, whatever the weather.
Babies and children welcome: children's menu; crayons; high chairs. Disabled: toilets. Tables outdoors (30, terrace). Takeaway service. **Map 10 M8**.
For branches see index.

Tamesa@oxo

2nd floor, Oxo Tower Wharf, Barge House Street, SE1 9PH (7633 0088/www.oxotower.co.uk). Blackfriars or Waterloo tube/rail. **Lunch served** noon-3.30pm, **dinner served** 5.30-11.30pm Mon-Fri. **Meals served** noon-11.30pm Sat; noon-4pm Sun. **Main courses** £12-£15.75. **Set meal** (lunch, 5.30-7pm, 10-11.30pm Mon-Sat) £14.50 2 courses, £17.50 3 courses. **Credit** AmEx, MC, V.
The second floor of the Oxo Tower has been a notoriously difficult place to pacify, and several restaurants have come and gone. Tamesa has lasted longer than many, and has done so by making the most of the space, opening up even more views of the river and encouraging walk-up custom from the South Bank. Food isn't the prime draw. Brasserie standards dominate – beer-battered cod and chips, daube of Angus beef, roast sea bass, spinach and ricotta cannelloni – and your meal is more likely to be expensive than it is memorable. Lamb rump was over-peppered, while steamed mussels were under-sauced. Breast of Barbary duck with red onion tatin was better, and the cold chocolate fondant with orange sauce was at least a nice way to end an otherwise unimpressive meal. The long, thin space (with the majority of tables crammed up against the riverside windows) has the clean, uncluttered feel of a canteen from *Star Trek*: in other words a rather dated, but not unpleasant, notion of the future. Tamesa also doubles as a cocktail bar.
Babies and children welcome: children's menu; crayons; high chairs. Booking advisable. Disabled: lift; toilet. Separate room for parties, seats 28. **Map 11 N7**.

South East

Bankside

★ Tate Modern Café: Level 2

2007 WINNER BEST FAMILY RESTAURANT

2nd floor, Tate Modern, Sumner Street, SE1 9TG (7401 5014/www.tate.org.uk). Southwark

National Café. See p56.

tube/London Bridge tube/rail. **Breakfast served** 10-11.30am, **lunch served** 11.30am-3pm, **afternoon tea served** 3-5.30pm daily. **Dinner served** 6.30-9.30pm Fri. **Main courses** £9.95. **Credit** AmEx, DC, MC, V.
Super-efficient waiters soon put you at ease here, tempering what might be a slightly austere venue: a large, clattery space clad in shiny black and plate-glass. Children especially are greeted with much enthusiasm. The kids' menu (handed out with a pot of wax crayons, and including art and literacy activities) offers haddock goujons, spaghetti and meatballs or pasta and tomato bake, with a choice of drink and an ice-creamy or fruit pudding. Or they can order half-price mains from the adult menu. This features some inspirational light lunches; our favourite was the vivid vegetarian meze plate (houmous, beetroot, dips, goat's cheese, lentils, roasted vegetables with grilled flatbread). Alternatives range from snacks such as potted devilled crab to mains like grilled polenta with wild mushrooms, spinach and parmesan. You can also get breakfast (organic muffins, sausage ciabatta) afternoon tea and, on Tate Modern's late-closing nights, dinner (roasted salmon with cauliflower champ and asparagus, say). It's all about quality (the fish is the catch of the day from Newlyn, the ice-cream is Roskilly's) over quantity – always a good idea, especially where kids are concerned. A knickerbocker glory was a mini masterpiece of vanilla ice-cream, berry jelly and chocolate and raspberry sauces.
Babies and children welcome: children's menu; crayons; high chairs. Bookings not accepted Sat, Sun. Disabled: toilet. **Map 11 O7.**

Crystal Palace

Joanna's

56 Westow Hill, SE19 1RX (8670 4052/www.joannas.uk.com). Crystal Palace or Gipsy Hill rail. **Breakfast served** 10am-noon daily. **Meals served** noon-11pm Mon-Sat; noon-10.30pm Sun. **Main courses** £9-£17.75. **Credit** AmEx, MC, V.
Much has changed in the 30-odd years since John and Christina Ellner opened Joanna's. It was then an American-themed diner named in rhyming slang after the ivories tinkled between blasts of John's Rat Pack records. Music these days leans towards sedate jazz, which complements the warm wooden panelling, oversized mirrors and well-spaced tables draped in white linen (window tables enjoy sweeping city views). An air of unpretentious exclusivity is generated. But it's the food that keeps Joanna's at the centre of hearts both local and less so. The culinary flag is now firmly planted in the British Isles; hearty brunches remain a big draw alongside trademark roasts (crowned with perfectly cooked yorkshire puds of intimidating proportions). The à la carte is excellent too; dishes betray a keen eye for flavour combinations, be they starters such as delightfully flaky sweet onion and parmesan tart, or mains such as sea trout with avocado and chilli cream. It's not all artful invention; meat dishes tend towards simplicity, from juicy Joanna burgers (a throwback to diner days) to a slow-cooked pork belly with melt-in-the-mouth crackling. Quiet weekday lunches are guaranteed, but be prepared to wait at weekends.
Babies and children welcome (before 6pm): high chairs. Separate room for parties, seats 6. Tables outdoors (4, patio).

East

Shoreditch

Hoxton Grille NEW

81 Great Eastern Street, EC2A 3HU (7739 9111/www.grillerestaurants.com). Old Street tube/rail/55 bus. **Meals served** 7am-midnight daily. **Main courses** £7-£20. **Credit** AmEx, MC, V.
Although housed within the Hoxton Hotel, opened in September 2006 by Pret a Manger co-founder Sinclair Beecham, the Hoxton Grille is operated independently: it's the first London spot from the small Room Restaurants group, which has previously found success in Manchester and Leeds, so has rather more incentive to impress than eateries in similarly priced hotels (rooms are often under £100). It generally delivers on its promise. Served in an airy room dominated by bare-brick walls and exposed piping, the menu is made up of uncomplicated brasserie fare, such as a nicely executed prawn cocktail with mellow avocado sauce, but with a few lively, lovely touches. A starter of oyster mushrooms came with a delectable creamy sauce flavoured with vermouth and saffron, while a perfectly tender grilled pork cutlet was coloured by a more-delicate-than-it-sounds cider and parsley sauce. Devoid of flavour and charisma, linguini vongole let the side down badly, but the faultless service and decent wine list made it that much easier to swallow. Good stuff.
Disabled: toilet. Entertainment: DJ 7pm Sat, Sun. Separate rooms for parties, seating up to 25. Tables outdoors (20, courtyard). **Map 6 Q4.**

North

Camden Town & Chalk Farm

The Roundhouse

Roundhouse, Chalk Farm Road, NW1 8EH (0870 389 9920). Chalk Farm tube. **Meals served** 11am-11pm Tue-Sat; 11am-5pm Sun. **Main courses** £8-£10. **Credit** JCB, MC, V.
Before a performance, this place can be a nightmare. After standing in a shambolic queue for ten minutes, ignored by the harried waiters, we beat a hasty retreat. On a quiet Saturday afternoon, it was a different story. The trappings of contemporary cool (sleek white plastic tables and chairs, and cheery orange walls dotted with blow-up Peter Blake photographs) provide a laid-back, modern feel. Light streams in through the floor-to-ceiling windows. The succinct, appealingly simple menu focuses on fresh, seasonal ingredients, offering chunky, poshed-up sandwiches, salads and Welsh Black Angus burgers. A superb deli plate featured deliciously smooth, smoky moutabal (puréed aubergine), nutty own-made houmous, glistening pickled anchovies, tabouleh salad, olives and warm chargrilled artichoke hearts – the best we've eaten in ages. Grilled chicken served with nan and topped with cool, minty raita and a feta and mixed leaf Roundhouse big salad were both generously proportioned but slightly bland. We wished we'd gone for the safer bet of smoked salmon on sourdough, or focaccia with breaded lemon sole and tartare sauce. Service was exemplary; the waitress even squeezed our orange juice by hand

Tom's Kitchen. See p57.

after the machine fused. Note that the terrace is for beer and barbecue only, and is usually only open on Saturday and Sunday.
Babies and children welcome: high chairs. Booking advisable. Disabled: toilet. Separate room for parties, seats 40. Tables outdoors (10, terrace).
Map 27 B1.

Crouch End

Banners

21 Park Road, N8 8TE (8348 2930/www.banners restaurant.co.uk). Finsbury Park tube/rail then W7 bus. **Meals served** 9am-11.30pm Mon-Thur; 9am-midnight Fri; 10am-4pm, 5pm-midnight Sat; 10am-4pm, 5-11pm Sun. **Main courses** £10-£15. **Credit** MC, V.

A Crouch End institution, beloved of families, Banners sports its boho credentials proudly. World music plays in the background, a glass of tap water incurs a 15p donation to WaterAid, and the menu cover is a child's colourful drawing. At weekends, grown-ups talk playground politics and tackle the famous fry-up, while their offspring devour burgers, pasta or the kids' meze plate. After dark, when the lights dim, the wooden tables fill with convivial locals and wine-quaffing escapee parents. The concertedly global menu ranges from haddock fish cakes to jerk chicken and malay pumpkin curry, but the adventurous flavour combinations don't always come off. Wasabi mayonnaise was too fierce a pairing for subtly spiced goan fish cakes (from the specials board), and garlic-marinated chips proved inedibly potent. Portions are generous. A thai red curry brimmed with plump, shell-on king prawns. Service can be high-handed; even though plain chips quickly appeared to replace the garlic versions, the waitress radiated disapproval ('well, they are garlic chips'). The evening ended with French *chansons* and a huge slice of mango and white chocolate cheesecake – which sweetened us up for the long wait for the bill.
Babies and children welcome: children's menu (until 7pm); high chairs. Booking advisable.

Pick More Daisies NEW

2007 RUNNER-UP BEST FAMILY RESTAURANT

12 Crouch End Hill, N8 8AA (8340 2288/ www.pickmoredaisies.com). Finsbury Park tube/ rail then W7 bus. **Meals served** 9am-10pm Mon-Thur; 9am-10.30pm Fri, Sat; 10am-9pm Sun. **Main courses** £6.50-£18.50. **Credit** MC, V.

The philosophy expressed in the name, about living life better, is borne out in this friendly Californian diner, where families make up much of the daytime clientele, and toddlers can toddle with impunity. The gourmet burgers are the business: chunky, juicy and made with Charolais beef, or, in the case of the 'yummy mummy' burger, Kobe beef. They arrive between two blankets of arctic flatbread – like a quilted pitta: very nice. Skin-on fries are an essential side order (the burgers come with melon and a rather soggy coleslaw). The children's menu is pleasingly all-American: peanut butter and jelly grilled sandwiches, pancakes and baked macaroni cheese. The ice-cream sundae to share, with marshmallows, various sauces and M&Ms, is the star pudding. Come evening, the atmosphere becomes more grown-up, and the menu offers grilled meat, fish, hearty salads and Mexican-style dishes (nachos, quesadillas). To drink, there's a short wine list, Anchor Steam beer and creamy alcoholic shakes. Everything is presented with care and a sense of fun. Even the bill comes with M&Ms.
Babies and children welcome: children's menu; crayons; high chairs; nappy-changing facilities; toys. Booking advisable.

Hornsey

Pumphouse Dining Bar

1 New River Avenue, N8 7QD (8340 0400/www. phn8.co.uk). Turnpike Lane tube/Hornsey rail.
Bar **Open** 11.30am-11pm Mon-Sat; noon-10.30pm Sun.
Restaurant **Lunch served** noon-2.30pm Mon-Sat; 1-4pm Sun. **Dinner served** 6.30-9.30pm Mon-Thur, Sun; 6.30-10pm Fri, Sat. **Main courses** £10-£16.
Both **Credit** AmEx, DC, JCB, MC, V.

The once grand interior of this once grand pumping station (with what looks like original tiling, and old haulage machinery hanging from the soaring ceiling) has, sadly, been turned into a bit of a dog's dinner, with incongruous dark wood Indonesian furnishing, a blond-wood bar that looks as if it's straight out of Ikea and, over half the space, a false ceiling with plasticky circle effects. But this does nothing to dent the place's popularity with locals, who recognise the benefit of a spacious bar area that serves proper cocktails, and a restaurant with good, honest food. A starter of soft, coconut-infused shell-on prawns on layers of fried won tons, with a zingy salsa of avocado, red onion, coriander and lime, showed a sure hand with a great mix of flavours. Scallops were pretty faultless too. More quality came with the mains: very fresh haddock in a luxurious, non-greasy batter, with lashings of chunky chips; and tender sirloin steak, cooked exactly as requested, with more of those chips and a béarnaise sauce. Pleasant staff helped along the relaxed ambience.
Babies and children welcome (restaurant and patio only): high chairs. Booking advisable. Disabled: toilet. Tables outdoors (10, patio).
For branch (Mosaica @ the factory) see index.

Muswell Hill

Café on the Hill

46 Fortis Green Road, N10 3HN (8444 4957). East Finchley tube or Highgate tube then 43, 134 bus. **Meals served** 8am-4pm Mon, Sun; 8am-10pm Tue-Sat. **Main courses** £6.95-£15. **Credit** AmEx, MC, V.

With its dark wood tables, airy interior and white-painted brick walls (hung with Jack Vettriano prints), this is a laid-back daytime hangout. It provides well-heeled locals with salads, panini and steeply priced breakfasts (£7.90 for a fry-up). In the evening the place becomes an elegant little neighbourhood eaterie, offering a concise but appealing menu of brasserie classics: duck confit terrine; poached lemon sole; fig, mozzarella and parma ham salad. Service is friendly and efficient, but impatient diners should heed the menu's warning that the freshly cooked food may take a while. Fortunately, it's worth the wait. Asparagus and pea risotto was creamy without being overly rich; grilled lamb cutlets, served with feta and chickpea salad, were plump and juicy, with a hint of rosemary. From the short wine list (five reds and five whites), Vallobera Anada Rioja blanco was fresh and floral. For afters, we tried a marvellously tangy lemon and lime cheesecake with ginger biscuit base, and a dark chocolate mousse cake with a slightly cloying pool of Baileys cream.
Babies and children welcome: high chairs; toys. Entertainment: jazz 8pm Sat. Tables outdoors (4, pavement).

British

The great British food revival (flagship restaurant and founder member: **St John**) continues. The sheer number of new, exciting restaurants under the British banner – **Empress of India**, **Magdalen**, **Stanza**, **Great Queen Street** – tells part of the story; and to celebrate this ongoing renaissance we've included a Best British Restaurant in the 2007 Time Out Eating & Drinking Awards. Another indicator is the sight of old-stagers reinventing themselves: our favourite makeover so far is the **Goring Hotel**. We suspect that the most spectacular example this year will be **Fortnum & Mason** (7734 8040), where all three restaurants are being transformed by David Collins in anticipation of the firm's 300th anniversary celebrations: all should have reopened by late autumn 2007; St James's and the Fountain will retain their names, while the Patio will become the Gallery. Note that the **Savoy Grill** (7592 1600) is to close in December 2007 for a year because of building work at the Savoy hotel.

More fundamental than mere refurbishment, however, is that over the past ten years the places that have been cynically coasting, charging high prices for poorly executed dishes in moribund surroundings, have been outnumbered by a growing roster of establishments that care about innovative cooking, thoughtfully sourced ingredients and their customers' well-being. And while we greatly admire the charming, extravagant world of **Wiltons**, it's refreshing to be able to enjoy British dishes in more casual surroundings at a fraction of the price. Notable this year for combining value for money, good food and the option of wearing jeans are **Konstam at the Prince Albert**, **Rochelle Canteen** and **Medcalf**, as well as many of the aforementioned new openings.

Central

City

Canteen

2 Crispin Place, off Brushfield Street, E1 6DW (0845 686 1122/www.canteen.co.uk). Liverpool Street tube/rail. **Meals served** 8am-11pm Mon-Fri; 9am-11pm Sat; 9am-10.30pm Sun. **Main courses** £7-£16. **Credit** AmEx, MC, V.

A couple of recent meals (one lunch, one dinner) at this bare, modern restaurant in the new part of Spitalfields Market confirmed last year's first impressions. That is, it all looks spiffy – three walls of glass, big oak tables and booths, an open kitchen, an outdoor space at the front – but food and service don't match up. Staff are smiley but dopey, and much of the pleasure drains from a meal when you keep having to ask for things. The menu is a great read; dishes range from a bacon sandwich or hot buttered arbroath smokie (breakfast is served all day) through to smoked haddock with spinach and mash, or pie of the day (always a meat and a veg option). Some dishes work a treat: a moreish special of grilled skate with spiced shrimp butter, and a zingy watercress and fennel salad, for example. But there are too many off-notes: fish and chips that resembled old-style canteen fare, or uninspiring roast beef, or gloopy mash served with the smoked haddock. Prices are reasonable, yes, but with more attention to detail, Canteen could do much better. It will be interesting to see how the newer South Bank branch fares.

Babies and children welcome: children's portions; high chairs. Disabled: toilet. Tables outdoors (10, plaza). **Map 12 R5.**

For branch see index.

Paternoster Chop House

Warwick Court, Paternoster Square, EC4M 7DX (7029 9400/www.danddlondon.co.uk). St Paul's tube. **Lunch served** noon-3pm Mon-Fri; 11am-5pm Sun. **Dinner served** 5.30-10.30pm Mon-Fri. **Main courses** £11.50-£20. **Set lunch** (noon-4pm Sun) £16.50 2 courses, £20 3 courses. **Credit** AmEx, DC, MC, V.

A big, white upmarket canteen aimed both at City folk and the tourist trade (tea and sponge cake is served in the afternoon). Prices are stiff, though service is anything but, and the place is full of chatter. A very British menu changes seasonally, but there are some constants (such as starters of onion tart or smoked salmon). The 'beast of the day' option is always worth ordering; we enjoyed a rich, vast serving of Longhorn beef with fresh horseradish and pulled beef. Lamb with haggis was more than its match. More delicate-tasting, but still covering a lot of plate, was pan-fried Cornish pollack with wild garlic champ. Puddings – if you get that far – are the likes of lemon posset with shortbread, or sticky toffee pudding with caramel sauce. There are also cheeses and savouries, and a top drinks list. Alongside the expected wide-ranging selection of wines, there are cocktails (including an after-dinner option featuring Hovis biscuit) and a fine choice of beers, ales and cider, most of them English. Good though the dinner was, we cherish most the memory of the couple next to us, one on a mobile and one on a BlackBerry throughout most of their meal.

Babies and children welcome: children's portions; games; high chairs. Booking advisable. Disabled: toilet. Tables outdoors (25, courtyard). **Map 11 O6.**

Rhodes Twenty Four

24th floor, Tower 42, Old Broad Street, EC2N 1HQ (7877 7703/www.rhodes24.co.uk). Bank tube/ Liverpool Street tube/rail. **Lunch served** noon-2.15pm, **dinner served** 6-8.30pm Mon-Fri. **Main courses** £15.90-£29.50. **Credit** AmEx, DC, MC, V.

If you've the choice, visit Rhodes Twenty Four at night, when the view eastwards over London twinkles prettily, and the room acquires a veneer of glamour. It's all much more grey and corporate at lunch. The kitchen is currently on good form: almost everything we tried was excellent, from the pre-starter chilled gazpacho to the final petits fours. A succulent warm smoked eel with poached egg hollandaise and confit pork belly starter deserves singling out for particular praise; also fabulously tasty was a main of roast beef fillet with red wine onions and oxtail hash. Seared scallops with shallot mustard sauce and a whirl of mashed potato was good too. The only blot on the horizon was asparagus risotto with artichoke and summer truffle salad; the risotto was a beautiful green but had a harsh aftertaste, while the wonderful truffle flavour struggled to emerge from a woefully oversalted salad. But puddings (notably a dreamy bread and butter number) put matters back on track. Not a fun restaurant, but a very safe bet for a haute-ish meal in talking-point surroundings.

Babies and children admitted. Booking essential, 2-4 weeks in advance. Disabled: toilet. Dress: smart casual. **Map 12 Q6.**

★ St John Bread & Wine

94-96 Commercial Street, E1 6LZ (7251 0848/ www.stjohnbreadandwine.com). Liverpool Street tube/rail. **Breakfast served** 9-11am Mon-Fri; 10-11am Sat, Sun. **Lunch served** noon-4pm, **dinner served** 5-10.30pm daily. **Main courses** £12-£15. **Credit** AmEx, MC, V.

The Spitalfields outpost of St John (*see p63*) is decorated in much the same way as the Smithfield original, with whitewashed walls and simple wooden chairs and tables. Similarly, service is both friendly and professional, and many dishes appear on both menus. The atmosphere here is somewhere between bar and restaurant, making it the perfect

BEST BRITISH

Laid-back fun

Kick back in clean, white spaces at **Canteen** (*see left*), **Rochelle Canteen** (*see p70*) and **St John Bread & Wine** (*see above*); in modishly converted pubs at the **Empress of India** (*see p70*) and **Konstam at the Prince Albert** (*see p64*), and in transformed butcher's premises at **Medcalf** (*see p63*).

A room with a view

Gaze out over: the river at **Butlers Wharf Chop House** (*see p69*), London's prettiest park at **Inn The Park** (*see p64*), Trafalgar Square at **National Dining Rooms** (*see p66*), the City at **Rhodes Twenty Four** (*see above*), Borough Market at **Roast** (*see p69*) and Smithfield's rooftops at **Top Floor at Smiths** (*see p63*).

Impeccable service

Boisdale (*see p67*), the **Goring Hotel** (*see p67*) and **Lindsay House** (*see p64*) are all a cut above, but for total coddling, it has to be **Wiltons** (*see p64*). For casual but totally on-the-ball professionalism, try **St John** (*see p63*).

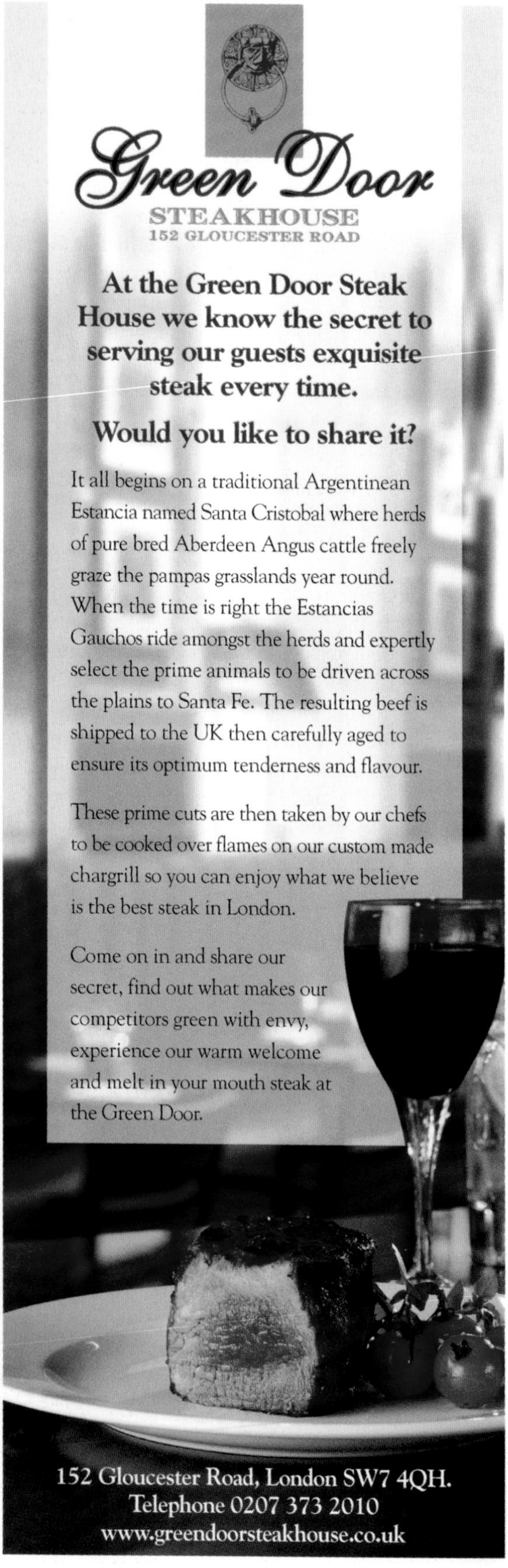

place to drink a glass or two of wine while picking away at smoked sprats and horseradish or the wonderfully chewy own-made bread, or trying something more substantial such as grilled plaice, duck livers on toast, or beautifully savoury lentils with courgettes and crème fraîche. Sweet things run from half a dozen madeleines to chocolate terrine with cherries, though we rarely make it past the divine eccles cake with lancashire cheese. Breakfast has a Middle White bacon sandwich for under a fiver, though you could have porridge, or toast and honey. From 11am, seed cake with a glass of Madeira becomes a possibility. The French wine list is unintimidating and there's plenty of help on hand if you can't decide. As with the bread and cakes, bottles are available as off-sales.
Babies and children welcome: high chairs. Booking advisable. Takeaway service. **Map 12 S5.**

Clerkenwell & Farringdon

Medcalf

38-40 Exmouth Market, EC1R 4QE (7833 3533/ www.medcalfbar.co.uk). Farringdon tube/rail/19, 38, 341 bus. **Lunch served** noon-3pm Mon-Fri; noon-4pm Sat, Sun. **Dinner served** 6-10pm Mon-Thur, Sat. **Main courses** £10.50-£15. **Credit** MC, V.
Since the last edition, Medcalf has expanded into the next-door premises, but the slightly harum-scarum nature of the place remains, and it's still just as much bar as restaurant. The menu is more serious than the laid-back attitude of the staff and the slightly scruffy decor might suggest. Food is generally hearty stuff. For every beetroot, watercress and goat's cheese salad, a more typical meal would be faggots or half a pint of prawns with mayo and brown bread, followed by grilled calf's liver with bacon and bubble and squeak, or battered plaice with chips and mushy peas, topped off by apple crumble and custard or British cheeses with oatcakes and chutney. Judging by a recent lunch, robust is the way to go. The calf's liver was meltingly tender while roast beetroot, red onion and goat's cheese tart had the looks but no taste, and disappointing puff pastry. And it cost £10.50, which seemed off kilter with the good value of most other dishes here. Mellow during the day, Medcalf gets more hectic at night, particularly when there's a DJ set in swing.
Babies and children welcome (until 7pm). Disabled: toilet. Entertainment: DJs 7pm Fri. Separate room for parties, seats 50. Tables outdoors (5, garden; 4, pavement). **Map 5 N4.**

Quality Chop House

92-94 Farringdon Road, EC1R 3EA (7837 5093/ www.qualitychophouse.co.uk). Farringdon tube/ rail/19, 38 bus. **Lunch served** noon-3pm Mon-Fri; noon-4pm Sun. **Dinner served** 6-11pm Mon-Fri; 6-11.30pm Sat; 6-10pm Sun. **Main courses** £6.95-£19.95. **Set meal** (lunch Mon-Fri, 6-7.45pm Mon-Sat; Sun) £9.95 2 courses. **Credit** AmEx, JCB, MC, V.
'Progressive caterers for the working class' are the words etched on the glass of this gorgeous little revamped chop house. It's now trad food for the middle classes, along the lines of potted shrimps or steak tartare to start, pork chop with black pudding hash or battered haddock and chips for mains, and rice pudding with apricot jam to finish. There's no doubting the quality of the ingredients – grilled calf's liver (with bacon, mash and onion gravy) was deliciously dense without being rubbery, jellied Irish eels robust but not overwhelming – but there's sometimes room for improvement in the cooking; our pork chop, for example, was badly burned in parts. A sure-fire main is the salmon fish cake with sorrel sauce; it's a modern classic. Prices are very reasonable. Lovely staff contribute to the warm, intimate ambience; the place oozes charm, though it's hard to settle in for a long session if you're perched on the narrow benches in one of the nine oak booths. You'll be shown how to arrange the cushions to make the seating more comfortable, but a certain amount of wriggling is inevitable. Nice at any time of day, QCH makes an especially good brunch destination.
Babies and children admitted. Booking advisable. Separate room for parties, seats 40. **Map 5 N4.**

★ St John (100)

26 St John Street, EC1M 4AY (7251 0848/4998/ www.stjohnrestaurant.com). Barbican tube/ Farringdon tube/rail. **Lunch served** noon-3pm Mon-Fri. **Dinner served** 6-11pm Mon-Sat. **Main courses** £13.50-£22.50. **Credit** AmEx, DC, MC, V.
Fergus Henderson's St John has become a world-class, world-famous restaurant while managing to remain an extremely congenial venue where you can still get a table. It looks the same as ever: a beautifully white airy dining room with a semi-open kitchen, reached through a spacious bar with an even loftier ceiling. The menu changes daily, but there are recurring treats – roast bone marrow and parsley salad being the most renowned. Typical starters might be langoustines and mayonnaise, or bacon with eggs and beans (not a campfire supper but a robust salad), while mains might be chitterlings and dandelion, or brill with cucumber and dill. St John's reputation may derive from its meat offerings, but vegetables are treated with equal reverence: peas in the pod made a perfectly self-sufficient appetiser; Bugs Bunny-esque sprouting carrots came with a creamy, punchy aïoli. Down in the bar, welsh rarebit is enough to answer most hunger pangs. In the course of several recent meals we've only had one duff dish (summer vegetables in a bland broth). The majority had us scraping our plates – most memorably a peach jelly with shortbread and cream, and (from the summer feasting menu, which has to be booked in advance) grilled squid with fennel and green sauce. An inspirational, admirable restaurant.
Babies and children welcome: high chairs. Disabled: toilet (bar). Separate room for parties, seats 18. **Map 5 O5.**

Top Floor at Smiths

Smiths of Smithfield, 67-77 Charterhouse Street, EC1M 6HJ (7251 7950/www.smithsofsmithfield. co.uk). Barbican tube/Farringdon tube/rail. **Lunch served** noon-3pm Mon-Fri; 12.30-3.45pm Sun. **Dinner served** 6.30-10.45pm Mon-Sat; 7-10.15pm Sun. **Main courses** £12-£28. **Credit** AmEx, DC, MC, V.
Unlike the rest of this busy bar and restaurant complex, the dining room on the top floor is a calm retreat, where waiting staff are attentive, and conversation is at a moderate pitch. The room is modern and pleasant-looking, but plainly decorated; quite rightly, all the focus is on the view. Diners look out over Smithfield's rooftops and towards St Paul's through sliding glass doors or, if they're lucky, from one of the coveted tables on the terrace. The menu (overseen by John Torode) makes much of its suppliers, and 'rare-breed, organic, additive-free meat'. Steak is indeed first-class, but unusually, on a recent visit, some of the other dishes were below par. Salt and pepper squid with roast chilli dressing (a menu stalwart) was so-so. It appeared unnervingly quickly, as did another underwhelming dish of dorset crab on toast. Mains – pork three ways (fillet, roast belly, braised shoulder, served with veg and salsa verde), and a special, dover sole – were much more dynamic, but didn't quite achieve the giddy heights of past meals here: a pity at these prices (the pork main cost £19). Still, we'll return to sample a 10oz Longhorn sirloin; Top Floor remains a gem even in a competitive area.
Babies and children welcome: high chairs. Booking advisable. Disabled: lift; toilet. Tables outdoors (8, terrace). Separate room for parties, seats 24. **Map 11 O5.**

Covent Garden

Rules

35 Maiden Lane, WC2E 7LB (7836 5314/ www.rules.co.uk). Covent Garden tube. **Meals served** noon-11.30pm Mon-Sat; noon-10.30pm Sun. **Main courses** £16.95-£27.95. **Set meal** (after 10pm Mon-Thur) £16.95-£27.95 2 courses. **Credit** AmEx, JCB, MC, V.
'London's Oldest Restaurant' offers a theme-park experience, and an increasingly dispiriting one. The tone was set when we were left to kick our heels in a holding lobby too small for all the would-be diners, and the evening ended with the off-hand waiter briskly clearing away our not-quite-empty wine glasses. In between there were some good dishes – such as a hard-to-get-wrong Isle of Lewis smoked salmon with capers and soda bread, and a pretty, delicate raspberry blancmange with 'candy floss' (spun sugar) and macaroons – but they were outnumbered by lacklustre ones. Fish and chips was cutely presented, wrapped in a paper bucket made of pages from the *FT*, but the chips were soggy, the batter greasy and the haddock pretty tasteless. First impressions of steak and kidney pie with green beans were positive too, but both steak and kidneys were tough, the gravy too thin, and the pastry no better than you'd get on a shop-bought pie; what's more, the beans were stringy. Some solace can be found in the decent wine list and OTT decor (all mounted heads, framed prints and stained glass), but overall this is tourist food at tourist prices.
Babies and children welcome: children's portions; high chairs. Booking advisable. Dress: smart casual. Separate rooms for parties (7379 0258), seating 8, 10, 14 and 18. **Map 18 E5.**

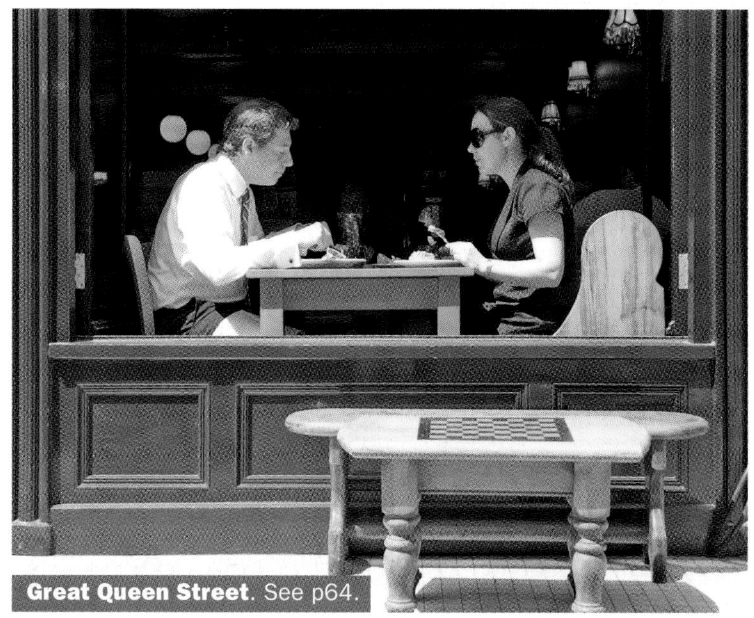

Great Queen Street. See p64.

Holborn

★ Great Queen Street NEW

2007 RUNNER-UP BEST BRITISH RESTAURANT

32 Great Queen Street, WC2B 5AA (7242 0622). Covent Garden or Holborn tube. **Lunch served** noon-2.30pm Tue-Sat. **Dinner served** 6-10.30pm Mon-Sat. **Main courses** £9-£18. **Credit** MC, V.

Sister restaurant to the rated Anchor & Hope in Waterloo, 32 Great Queen Street shares that gastropub's unpretentious, buzzy air. The pub-style room, done up in classic gastropub burgundy, positively thrums with conversation and bonhomie – though the small, tightly spaced tables can make this an irritant. Ranging from snacks and starters to main courses to share, the menu is approachably modern British; it's food to tempt and satisfy rather than educate or impress. Brawn was subtle but enjoyable; arbroath smokie deliciously savoury; rabbit saddle appropriately rustic; artichokes enormous. Pies are encased in shortcrust pastry that released a rush of aroma when breached. Bottled octopus (a kind of salad) could have been more interesting, and the gooseberries in an otherwise lovely fool tasted woody, but in general the food was excellent and well-priced. It was let down, however, by service that was disorganised and a little full of itself. And it's a real shame there were no British beers available on this occasion, although we're told that sometimes a barrel is bought in. Not that it's any excuse, but this isn't really a drinking establishment, with only the bar and outside tables currently available to non-eaters.

Babies and children admitted. Booking advisable. Disabled: toilet. Tables outdoors (3, pavement). **Map 18 E3**.

King's Cross

Konstam at the Prince Albert

2 Acton Street, WC1X 9NA (7833 5040/ www.konstam.co.uk). King's Cross tube/rail. **Lunch served** 12.30-3pm Mon-Fri. **Dinner served** 6.30-10.30pm Mon-Sat. **Main courses** £10.50-£15.50. **Credit** AmEx, MC, V.

There's a lot to like here, from the super-attentive maître d' (who worked the small room like it was the Ivy) to the fact there was no pressure to leave, even though the restaurant was packed all evening. The slightly wild decor – dark green paint, even on the floor, and talking-point lights made by Thomas Heatherwick from plug chains – is a welcome change after so many identikit interiors. Chef-owner Oliver Rowe's menu doesn't play safe either. About 90 per cent of the ingredients come from within reach of the tube network (*not* from within the M25 as has been widely reported), and wines come from no farther afield than Europe, with plenty of English bottles on the list. The sourcing policy results in dishes like pan-fried Mersea plaice with braised spring onions, potatoes and beurre blanc, or Waltham Abbey chicken with braised chicory and goat's cheese spätzle. Dishes don't always deliver; nettle and crème fraîche tart with leek, mushroom and parsley salad had a sloppy filling and a taste so delicate it was scarcely there. But mostly they do, and in some instances (a very moreish starter of beer-battered herring roe with mustard sauce) they're excellent. Konstam is very much not resting on its laurels.

Babies and children admitted. Booking advisable. Disabled: toilet. Tables outdoors (2, pavement). **Map 4 M3**.

Mayfair

Dorchester Grill Room

The Dorchester, 53 Park Lane, W1K 1QA (7629 8888/www.thedorchester.com). Hyde Park Corner tube. **Breakfast served** 7-10.30am Mon-Fri; 8-11am Sat, Sun. **Lunch served** noon-2.30pm Mon-Sat; 12.30-3pm Sun. **Dinner served** 6.30-10.30pm Mon-Fri; 6-11pm Sat; 7-10pm Sun. **Main courses** £19.50-£35. **Set lunch** (Mon-Sat) £25 2 courses incl coffee, £27.50 3 courses incl coffee; (Sun) £35 3 courses. **Credit** AmEx, DC, JCB, MC, V.

Brace yourself. Many-hued tartans cover almost every surface except the walls, which are mustard yellow embellished with strident murals of Scotsmen and women. High-backed gothic banquettes, deep-buttoned crimson and black, stand against tartan room dividers, and the only colour lacking is natural daylight. A waiter explained that the designer took his inspiration from the restaurant's signature ingredients: Aberdeen Angus beef and smoked salmon. We felt obliged to try one of these rich sources of artistic licence, in the form of roast beef and yorkshire pudding from the reasonably priced set lunch menu. Carved from a great hunk of flesh on a silver domed trolley wheeled to our table, this was extremely tasty, yet let down by fussy turned carrots coated in thick orange juice, woolly roast potatoes, and broccoli under gloopy hollandaise. Dishes plated in the kitchen, such as red mullet on squid ink risotto, and a pleasant pear tarte tatin with ginger ice-cream, were better. Better still are the à la carte options, which might include fillet steak served with blue cheese potatoes, bone marrow and wild garlic. A cheerful place to go – with money – to liven a cold grey day.

Babies and children welcome (Sat, Sun): high chairs. Booking advisable; essential weekends. Disabled: toilet. Dress: smart casual. **Map 9 G7**.

St James's

Inn The Park (100)

St James's Park, SW1A 2BJ (7451 9999/ www.innthepark.com). St James's Park tube. **Breakfast served** 8-11am Mon-Fri; 9-11am Sat, Sun. **Lunch served** noon-3pm Mon-Sat; noon-4pm Sun. **Tea served** 3-5pm Mon-Fri. **Dinner served** 5-9pm daily. **Main courses** £14.50-£23. **Credit** AmEx, MC, V.

Oliver Peyton's all-day lakeside 'café' has everything going for it: a stunning location in the middle of St James's Park; a beautiful building whose fluid organic lines and natural materials ensure it's perfectly in tune with its setting; interiors by Habitat head honcho Tom Dixon; and a tempting, nicely varied modern English menu from chef Oliver Smith. So why didn't the enormous barnsley lamb chop have us gambolling with delight? What let down the impressively teetering organic salmon and smoked haddock fish cake with spinach and poached egg? Both looked fantastic, and were served with panache, but the lamb lacked flavour, and the fish cake was dry and, again, missed the punchy flavours expected of such ingredients. Maybe the oft-mentioned poached egg and soldiers breakfasts, or the newly opened barbecue (available on the terrace until 9pm in summer months), pass muster, but the à la carte menu left us underwhelmed. Despite the place having one of London's nicest settings, visited on one of those summer evenings when you feel nothing but bonhomie and largesse towards the city and its inhabitants, we left feeling disappointed.

Babies and children welcome: children's menu; high chairs. Booking advisable. Disabled: toilet. Tables outdoors (23, terrace). Takeaway service. **Map 10 K8**.

★ Wiltons

55 Jermyn Street, SW1Y 6LX (7629 9955/ www.wiltons.co.uk). Green Park or Piccadilly Circus tube. **Lunch served** noon-2.30pm, **dinner served** 6-10.30pm Mon-Fri. **Main courses** £15-£50. **Credit** AmEx, DC, JCB, MC, V.

Wiltons offers a retreat from the rigours of real life. Sink into one of its upholstered chairs, prepare to be cosseted (but not irritated or patronised) by maître d', waiter and sommelier, and marvel at the classic, fish-heavy menu. Just try not to focus on the prices. From the carte there are starters such as dressed crab, potted shrimps and hot or cold beef consommé; mains include grilled meats and fish cooked in a variety of ways, plus savouries, cheeses or stalwart puddings such as sherry trifle or apple and rhubarb crumble. This menu is supplemented by a substantial daily changing list, from which cold poached salmon and pink roast beef with yorkshire pudding were stand-out dishes, though summer pudding wasn't to be sniffed at either. The little extras are also first-rate: for example, scrumptious roast potatoes (sadly, only two of them), a spoon-lickingly creamy celeriac purée and irresistible petits fours. Wiltons is what it is, right down to the besuited clientele and hefty wine list. Don't expect innovation or a bargain, and you'll have a fine old time.

Babies and children admitted. Booking advisable. Disabled: lift; toilet. Dress: smart; jacket preferred. Separate room for parties, seats 18. **Map 17 B5**.

Soho

★ Lindsay House

21 Romilly Street, W1D 5AF (7439 0450/ www.lindsayhouse.co.uk). Leicester Square tube. **Lunch served** noon-2.30pm Mon-Fri. **Dinner served** 6-11pm Mon-Sat. **Set dinner** (6-6.30pm) £27 3 courses; £56 3 courses, £68 tasting menu (£110 incl wine). **Credit** AmEx, DC, MC, V.

The Irish element at Richard Corrigan's charming restaurant is low-key indeed: noticeable only in the odd ingredient (Carlingford Lough oysters, say) and the occasional overheard accent. Lindsay House is an 18th-century Soho townhouse, with intimate dining rooms on the ground and first floors (plus several private rooms); it really comes into its own in the evening. Elegant restraint rules – drawing-room decor, impeccable service, quietly spoken diners – until the food arrives. An amuse-gueule of a tiny duck pasty with chutney produced squeaks of pleasure. It set the tone for the rest of the meal, as one perfect, gutsily flavoured course followed another. Smoked eel salad with cider apple jelly and crispy bacon gave way to onglet of beef with roast garlic mash and sautéed girolles, followed by peanut parfait with roast banana and caramel ice-cream: a grand and indulgent finale. The wine list doesn't have a dull bottle on it – organised stylistically, it contains unusual varieties and styles plus top-grade producers, and there's an emphasis on food-friendliness. All this comes at a price, of course: the set dinner is £56 (you pay for three courses even if you only eat two); the tasting menus are even more, though it's worth noting that one of them is vegetarian. And an espresso is £4.95. But if you're prepared to swallow the financial hit, then this is a real treat.

Babies and children admitted. Booking advisable. Dress: smart casual. Separate rooms for parties, seating 6, 12 and 18. Vegetarian menu. **Map 17 C4**.

Stanza NEW

93-107 Shaftesbury Avenue, W1D 5DY (7494 3020/www.stanzalondon.co.uk). Leicester Square tube.
Bar **Open** noon-3am, **meals served** noon-1am Mon-Sat. **Main courses** £5.50-£8.50.
Restaurant **Lunch served** noon-3pm, **dinner served** 5.30-11pm Mon-Sat. **Main courses** £9-£16.50. **Set lunch** £12.50 2 courses, £14 3 courses. **Set dinner** (5.30-7.30pm) £16.50 2 courses, £18.50 3 courses.
Both **Admission** £5-£10 after 10pm Fri, Sat. **Credit** MC, V.

Stanza occupies most of the former site of members' club Teatro, and while the room has been given a revamp with pretty ironwork, table orchids and mirrors, it still has the air of a not terribly cool nightclub. All the more surprising, then, to encounter some very good modern British cooking based on carefully sourced, high-quality ingredients. On our visit, starters included scallops with pea blancmange, a crayfish cocktail served retro-style in a sundae glass, and a plate of Cumbrian charcuterie that compared favourably with its Italian equivalent. Pork belly with dripping-roast potatoes, rib of beef with triple-cooked chips, salmon fish cake, and a rich fish pie were among the gastropubby main courses. Our favourite dessert was a deconstructed cheesecake comprising macerated strawberries, whipped cream cheese and a piece of shortbread. Service was assiduous, sometimes excessively so – our conversation was interrupted by a waiter enquiring after our enjoyment – but overall the efficiency is an asset. This is a hard site to inhabit successfully, but Stanza's food, prices and Theatreland location might just make it work.

Goring Hotel. See p67.

Babies and children admitted. Booking advisable. Entertainment: DJs 10pm Wed-Sat. Separate room for parties, seats 38. **Map 17 C4**.

Strand

Simpson's-in-the-Strand

100 Strand, WC2R 0EW (7836 9112/www.simpsons-in-the-strand.com). Embankment tube/Charing Cross tube/rail. **Breakfast served** 7.15-10.30am Mon-Fri. **Lunch served** 12.15-2.45pm Mon-Sat; noon-3pm Sun. **Dinner served** 5.45-10.45pm Mon-Sat; (Grand Divan) 6-9pm Sun. **Main courses** £15.95-£23.95. **Set breakfast** £17.95-£19.95. **Set meal** (5.45-6.45pm) £24.50 2 courses, £29.50 3 courses. **Credit** AmEx, DC, JCB, MC, V.

It's hard not to feel that Simpson's is trading on its past. The Grand Divan dining room is glorious – all dark panelling, lofty ceiling and crystal chandeliers – but a little faded around the edges. Service is decent enough, but not exemplary, and staff uniforms leave a lot to be desired: odd when diners are given a strict dress code. In short, the whole place could be an upmarket Berni Inn, apart from the food. A resolutely traditional menu includes Forman's London-cured Scottish salmon, Cornish crab cakes and dover sole, but these are mere satellites to the roast meats. Roast rib of Scottish beef came with roast potatoes, buttery savoy cabbage and a nice big yorkshire pudding, but wasn't as warm as it might be (the ceremony of carving at the tableside trolley takes its toll). Roast saddle of lamb wasn't quite as splendid, but was still a fine plateful. Treacle sponge with vanilla custard is our pick of the puddings. It's unlikely that much will change here; we can only assume the largely male clientele don't notice the surroundings, don't have to pay their own bills, and focus on the first-class comfort food.

Babies and children admitted: high chairs. Booking advisable. Disabled: toilet. Dress: smart casual; no jeans, T-shirts or sportswear. Separate rooms for parties, seating 15 and 120. **Map 18 E5**.

Trafalgar Square

Albannach

66 Trafalgar Square, WC2N 5DS (7930 0066/www.albannach.co.uk). Charing Cross tube/rail.
Bar **Open/snacks served** noon-1am Mon-Wed; noon-3am Thur-Sat.
Restaurant **Lunch served** noon-3pm, **dinner served** 5-10.30pm Mon-Sat. **Main courses** £15-£25. **Set lunch** £15 2 courses, £18 3 courses. **Set dinner** £27.50 2 courses, £32.50 3 courses.
Both **Credit** AmEx, MC, V.

The Scottish theme at Albannach is applied with a light touch. Apart from the young waiters' kilts (in a subdued tartan), a splendid antler chandelier and a modish stag's head lampshade, it looks like any other smart, central London bar-restaurant. The dining room is on the first floor, but only has views of the ground-floor bar (where you can also eat) and glimpses of Trafalgar Square. Which is a shame, as the food on our most recent visit wasn't diverting. The express lunch menu certainly lived up to its name, starters appearing before drinks or bread. An enticing-sounding Shetland smoked salmon pâté (with citrus jelly and toasted spinach loaf) tasted no better than if it had came from a supermarket tub; slightly better was a chilled soup of roasted pepper and plum tomato with crème fraîche. The main courses appeared the second we put down our cutlery. Scottish smoked haddock on spinach with a poached egg was a small, pretty portion. It beat a dull smoked cheddar, Scottish brie and cream cheese tart, served with salad and quince and grape chutney, hands down in the taste stakes. We've had better meals here, but on this showing, we can only assume Albannach has decided to concentrate on the bar side of its operation (with whisky the focus, of course).

Babies and children admitted (until 5pm). Disabled: toilet. Separate room for parties, seats 20. Tables outdoors (3, pavement). **Map 10 K7**.

★ National Dining Rooms (100)

2007 WINNER BEST BRITISH RESTAURANT

Sainsbury Wing, National Gallery, Trafalgar Square, WC2N 5DN (7747 2525/www.nationalgallery.co.uk). Charing Cross tube/rail.
Bakery **Snacks served** 10am-5.30pm Mon, Tue, Thur-Sun; 10am-8.30pm Wed.
Restaurant **Lunch served** noon-3.30pm daily. **Dinner served** 5-7.15pm Wed. **Set meal** £17.50 1 course, £24.50 2 courses, £29.50 3 courses.
Both **Credit** AmEx, JCB, MC, V.

The dark colours and low ceilings of the National Gallery's Sainsbury Wing make for a subdued first impression, not aided by a slightly institutional feel. But the food here is the other end of the scale: individual, delicate and inspiring. This is an Oliver Peyton restaurant, and in culinary terms his best yet. Like Peyton's earlier venues, it caters to various feeding whims – particularly appropriate given the mixed needs of the clientele here. There's a prix fixe, an afternoon tea, a bar menu and a café counter of appetising pies, tarts and cakes. The prix fixe takes British food to an advanced level of finesse. Tiny crab cakes came in a clear tomato soup of intense flavour, beautifully garnished; and even the piccalilli that ringed the chicken liver mousse was pretty. The flavours in the beetroot and wensleydale tart were brilliantly realised, and the quality of ingredients in boiled and roast chicken and foraged mushrooms had been encouraged to shine through. Puds were less impressive, but points for the seasonal sundaes – and also for the Trafalgar Tap ale and a good British rosé. Service is polite and enthusiastic once you're seated (less so front of house) and acoustics are good. Most customers seem to be gallery-goers from out of town, suggesting that Londoners are missing a trick. Dinner is served only once a week, but lunch here can be a revelation.

Babies and children welcome: children's menu; high chairs. Booking advisable. Disabled: lift; toilet. **Map 17 C5**.

Victoria

Boisdale

13 Eccleston Street, SW1W 9LX (7730 6922/ www.boisdale.co.uk). Victoria tube/rail.
Bar **Open** noon-1am Mon-Fri.
Restaurant **Lunch served** noon-2.30pm Mon-Fri. **Dinner served** 7-11.15pm Mon-Sat. **Main courses** £14.50-£36. **Set meal** £17.80 2 courses.
Both **Credit** AmEx, DC, MC, V.
Boisdale's central London branch inevitably draws a more diverse crowd than the City outlet, though both share a Scottish menu and decor, and a focus on whisky and jazz, as well as a high quotient of business diners. Here a light-filled room is buzzing at lunch and positively hopping at night. Central to the menu is 21-day matured Scottish beef, served in a variety of cuts (costing £19.50-£36) with a choice of accompaniments. The rest of the menu is also pricey, though there are deals to be had, and portions are large. Cooking is good though not stellar; some (imported) asparagus served with a sea bass was singed, and green beans were swimming in butter. Excellent haggis with a noggin of Famous Grouse similarly suffered from butter-heavy mash and neeps. Still, diners aren't here for the comforting cuisine alone – though perhaps some come for the bread and butter pudding with brandy custard. It's the whole package that appeals, from the personable but efficient service through to the merrily unfashionable decor: all dark red and green tartan, hunting scenes and trophy heads. Havana cigars can still be purchased, but since the smoking ban can only be smoked at the outdoor bar tables.
Babies and children admitted. Booking advisable. Dress: smart casual. Entertainment: jazz 10pm Mon-Sat. Separate rooms for parties, seating 16-34. **Map 15 H10.**
For branch (Boisdale Bishopsgate) see index.

★ Goring Hotel

Beeston Place, Grosvenor Gardens, SW1W 0JW (7396 9000/www.goringhotel.co.uk). Victoria tube/rail. **Breakfast served** 7-10am Mon-Sat; 7.30-10.30am Sun. **Lunch served** 12.30-2.30pm Mon-Fri, Sun. **Dinner served** 6-10pm daily. **Set lunch** £32.50 3 courses. **Set dinner** (6-6.30pm) £32 2 courses, £44 3 courses. **Credit** AmEx, DC, JCB, MC, V.
Still one of the prettiest dining rooms in town after its 2005 makeover (design by David Linley with delicate, exquisite Swarovski chandeliers), the Goring continues to please in other areas too. Staff are a smooth bunch in very natty uniforms, and the monthly changing menu is a treat to read. For every classic dish (chilled watercress soup, dover sole, raspberries with cream), there's one that's a little bit different: a trait exemplified by the inclusion of hogweed (a slightly scratchy but intriguing-tasting plant) among the vegetables. Isle of Sheppey wild rocket with goat's cheese, apple and celery salad was an undemanding starter. Punchier (though not as good as the version at St John, *see p63*) was roast bone marrow with breadcrumbs, parsley and toasted onion bread. Cod, chips and peas (a special) was a top-notch version, and a large steak and kidney pie with creamed potatoes disappeared just as rapidly. Custard tart with nutmeg ice-cream made a fine finale. There's a long wine list and accompanying sommelier. Judging by its performance over the past year, the Goring has made the transition into the 21st century with aplomb.
Babies and children admitted. Booking essential. Disabled: toilet (in hotel). Dress: smart casual. Separate rooms for parties, seating 6, 12 and 40. Tables outdoors (9, terrace). **Map 15 H9.**

West

Holland Park

Notting Grill

123A Clarendon Road, W11 4JG (7229 1500/ www.awtrestaurants.com). Holland Park tube.
Bar **Open** 6.30-11pm Mon-Thur; 6.30pm-midnight Fri, Sat; noon-10pm Sun.
Restaurant **Brunch served** noon-4pm Sat, Sun. **Lunch served** noon-2.30pm Tue-Fri. **Dinner served** 6.30-10.30pm Mon-Thur; 6.30-11.30pm Fri, Sat. **Meals served** noon-10pm Sun. **Main courses** £12.50-£34.95. **Set lunch** £15.95 2 courses, £18.95 3 courses. **Credit** AmEx, DC, JCB, MC, V.
This branch of the Antony Worrall Thompson mini-chain feels a little tired and could do with a refurbishment; the faintly Arabian decor looks old-fashioned (not in a good way) and a bit bashed about. The waiting staff, though willing, don't constitute a crack team. And the food – apart from a top-notch 6oz fillet steak – was lacklustre on our visit, especially a very bland fish cake and an almost slimy dish of Mediterranean vegetables. On the plus side, Notting Grill is a very relaxed, unstuffy venue, so a perfect choice for groups and families; and everyone likes the outdoor tables on the roomy first-floor terrace. Wait for a sunny day, don't be in a hurry, and order meat, preferably a steak (popeseye, ribeye, sirloin, fillet or T-bone, all 35-day-aged Aberdeen Angus beef, served with chunky chips). The 10oz burgers are worth trying too; they're made from the same quality meat, and are available in half portions for children. Alternatives include a salmon platter, or Middle White pork sausages and mash with onion gravy. The other branches are in Barnes and Kew, both districts with fewer restaurants than Notting Hill, so with customers that are perhaps more forgiving of transgressions.
Babies and children welcome: high chairs. Booking advisable. Separate room for parties, seats 60. Tables outdoors (6, terrace; closes 10pm).
Map 19 A4.
For branches (Barnes Grill, Kew Grill) see index.

Olympia

Popeseye Steak House

108 Blythe Road, W14 0HD (7610 4578/ www.popeseye.com). Kensington (Olympia) tube/rail. **Dinner served** 7-10.30pm Mon-Sat. **Main courses** £10.95-£46.45. **No credit cards.**
Steak is the only dish served at Popeseye – until you get to dessert stage, when there's a choice of cheese or own-made puddings such as rhubarb crumble or white chocolate cheesecake. There are no starters, no fish dishes and most definitely no vegetarian options. It makes for an uncomplicated meal, where the only decisions are whether to have rump (popeseye), sirloin or fillet steak, what size to plump for (from 6oz right up to 30oz), and whether or not to go wild and order a side salad (all steaks come with chips). The salad was so-so (lettuce and tomato in an unsubtle vinaigrette) and the chips were OK, but the Aberdeen Angus steaks were good, cooked as requested and served with an array of sauces and mustards. The wine list is a straightforward one, with no annotation. The room is similarly pared down – just a stripped-wood floor, wooden tables and chairs and the kitchen in one corner, with a few fairy lights and paintings as decoration. Staff are young and friendly. In short, a great little local – as long as you like steak. Note that they don't accept credit cards, and it's a bit of a walk to the nearest cash machine.
Babies and children admitted. Booking advisable.
Map 20 C3.

South

Kennington

Franklins

205-209 Kennington Lane, SE11 5QS (7793 8313/www.franklinsrestaurant.com). Vauxhall tube/rail. **Meals served** noon-10.30pm Mon-Sat; 1-10pm Sun. **Main courses** £12.50-£18. **Set meal** (noon-7pm Mon-Sat) £11.50 2 courses, £15 3 courses. **Credit** AmEx, MC, V.
Deserved success in converted pub premises in East Dulwich has led Franklins to open a second venue in Kennington. This one is much more of a restaurant, with tables outside in a pleasant

Interview
RODNEY FRANKLIN & TIM SHEEHAN

Who are you?
Rodney (pictured right) and chef Tim, co-owners of the **Franklins** restaurants in Dulwich and Kennington (*see left*).
Eating in London: what's good about it?
The availability and relative cheapness of local/British ingredients.
What's bad about it?
We hate the ever-spreading chains that serve sub-standard food with sub-standard service at so-called cheap prices. We hate snooty maître d's and wine waiters. We hate that they have not been consigned to history, as they do nothing to encourage a new generation of restaurant-goers.
Which are your favourite London restaurants?
Places like **Tapas Brindisa** (*see p267*) and **Wright Brothers** (*see p99*) in Borough Market provide good food in an atmosphere we like, and the interior of the **Wolseley** (*see p235*) is one of the most exciting spaces in the capital.
Who or what has had the biggest impact on London's restaurant scene in the past 25 years?
We've enjoyed witnessing the transition of pubs serving tired scotch eggs and pork scratchings to numerous neighbourhood pubs offering such delights as Middle White pork terrine with piccalilli.
Any hot tips for the coming year?
Customers will care more about where their food has come from, which can only benefit the growing number of pubs and restaurants serving British food. We predict smokers getting used to cold food served alfresco in December and mulled wine on drinks lists throughout the winter. And we look forward to the next generation of young chefs inspired by the likes of Rick Stein to take British cooking and restaurants to the next level.

courtyard, and a small bar area near the entrance. The mint-green decor feels a little dated, but it's nice enough, with comfortable chairs, leather banquettes and lots of light. Lunch or dinner, the focus remains British; as well as puddings such as rhubarb trifle or treacle sponge, there's a choice of savouries. Smoked eel with caramelised apple and bacon vied with summer truffle risotto for best starter, and a main of wild rabbit with girolles, peas and bacon also went down a treat. The odd dish out was fennel, artichoke and tomato tart – the ingredients sitting on a disc of unappetising pastry. We wished we'd ordered smoked Old Spot chop with a fried duck's egg instead. Many of the simpler dishes are available on the blackboard bar menu. It's perhaps too early to tell, but on this year's showing we prefer the East Dulwich branch; the standard of cooking and service is similar at both, but there seems a jollier atmosphere in SE22.
Babies and children welcome: high chairs. Booking advisable. Separate room for parties, seats 25. Tables outdoors (15, courtyard).
For branch see index.

South East

Greenwich

Rivington Greenwich

178 Greenwich High Road, SE10 8NN (8293 9270/www.rivingtongrill.co.uk). Greenwich DLR/rail.
Bar **Open/snacks served** 5pm-midnight Tue, Wed; noon-midnight Thur-Sun.
Restaurant **Breakfast served** 10am-noon Thur-Sun. **Lunch served** noon-3pm Thur, Fri; noon-4pm Sat, Sun. **Dinner served** 6-11pm Tue-Sat; 6-10pm Sun. **Main courses** £9.25-£25.50. **Set lunch** (Sun) £18.50 3 courses.
No credit cards.
Diners eat the same kind of dishes at the two Rivington Grills, amid pretty similar decor (plainly furnished rooms, with light painted wood, blackboards and a welcoming bar area), but in very different atmospheres. Unsurprisingly, the Shoreditch branch has an edgier, more look-at-me vibe, whereas the two floors of the Greenwich restaurant are full of local couples and families. It's much more relaxed, but, regrettably, so is the service. We waited a long time for any drinks to appear, and a suspicion that our waitress wasn't cut out for the job was confirmed when she attempted to take a corkscrew to a screw-top bottle (Grüner Veltliner Spiegel 2006 Weingut Heidler from a resolutely un-English list). We took refuge in the menu, an undemanding list of Brit classics at a range of prices – from whole dorset crab with mayonnaise, and lots of tasty things on toast (own-made baked beans, for example), to fish and chips with mushy peas, or roast suckling pig with greens and apple sauce. Many dishes are served as all-day snacks in the bar. Given the service, the food was considerably better than we'd expected, notably a lovely sea trout. A happy addition to a part of town largely overrun by chains.
Babies and children welcome: children's menu; high chairs. Booking advisable. Disabled: toilet. Separate room for parties, seats 40. Tables outdoors (8, courtyard).
For branch (Rivington Bar & Grill) see index.

London Bridge & Borough

★ Magdalen NEW

2007 RUNNER-UP BEST BRITISH RESTAURANT

152 Tooley Street, SE1 2TU (7403 1342/ www.magdalenrestaurant.co.uk). London Bridge tube/rail. **Lunch served** noon-2.30pm Mon-Fri. **Dinner served** 6.30-10.30pm Mon-Sat. **Main courses** £12-£21. **Credit** AmEx, MC, V.
Magdalen's very civilised interior – all dark wood, aubergine paintwork and florally accessorised elegance – leads you to suspect that its food will be as well-mannered as its staff. A pleasant surprise, then, to be ambushed by some spirited flavours on the daily-changing, largely British menu. Artichoke soup was as glossy in taste as in texture. Salade gourmande arrived thickly dressed: an enjoyably to-hell-with-it assembly of endive, foie gras, house-made duck ham, walnuts, radish, more duck and french beans. Rump of Hereford beef was a fine piece of meat, served with dripping toast too crisp for authenticity but perfect for the dish. It's a meaty menu (also featuring veal offal, sliced pig's head and too-bland milk-fed lamb); the fish we tried wasn't up to the standard of the beef, and no vegetarian main was offered. Still, an outstanding french toast with strawberry jam helped make amends. A very good restaurant, Magdalen is occasionally let down by inconsistency (a previous meal was worse; perhaps it depends which of the three chef-owners is helming), atmosphere (strangely subdued despite being nearly full on a Saturday night) and the wine list (everything we tried seemed quite heavy, including the supposedly lighter choices).
Babies and children admitted. Disabled: toilet.
Map 12 Q8.

Roast (100)

The Floral Hall, Borough Market, Stoney Street, SE1 1TL (7940 1300/www.roast-restaurant.com). London Bridge tube/rail. **Breakfast served** 7-9.30am Mon-Fri; 8-10.30am Sat. **Lunch served** noon-2.30pm Mon-Thur; noon-3pm Fri; noon-3.30pm Sun. **Brunch served** 11.30am-3.30pm Sat. **Dinner served** 5.30-10.30pm Mon-Fri; 6-10.30pm Sat. **Main courses** £12.50-£20. **Set meal** (Sun) £22 2 courses, £26 3 courses. **Credit** AmEx, MC, V.
Looking out over Borough Market, Roast consists of a comfortable bar area giving way to a handsome, high-ceilinged restaurant with views of St Paul's and the railway line through huge windows. If it's a really sunny day, the room gets a bit too hot to handle, but most of the time it's a boon to have so much natural light. The place never stops: it's open for breakfast (smoked bacon and fried egg butty) and tea (coronation chicken sandwiches) as well as lunch and dinner, plus there's now a takeaway outlet at the ground-floor entrance. We like the attention to detail: for example, there's just as much emphasis on specialist teas as on cocktails, and there's a roll call of British suppliers on the menu. But our meal lacked oomph. From herring roes on toast to grilled barnsley chop with peas, broad beans and lovage cream, it was all a little bland. Even a splendid-looking roast rump of rare beef with girolles and onion sauce was merely average, with neither texture nor taste standing out. Service started slowly, and only snapped to when the charming maitre d' came on the scene. A good restaurant that's currently underperforming.
Babies and children welcome: children's menu; high chairs. Booking advisable. Disabled: lift; toilet. Dress: smart casual.
Map 11 P8.

Tower Bridge

Butlers Wharf Chop House

Butlers Wharf Building, 36E Shad Thames, SE1 2YE (7403 3403/www.danddlondon.co.uk). London Bridge tube/rail/Tower Gateway DLR/ 47, 78, 142, 188 bus.
Bar **Open** 8am-3pm, 6-11pm Mon-Fri; 8am-4pm, 6-11pm Sat; 8am-4pm, 6-10pm Sun. **Breakfast served** 8am-noon Mon-Fri; 8-11.30am Sat, Sun. **Set meal** (noon-3pm, 6-11pm) £10 2 courses, £12 3 courses.
Restaurant **Lunch served** noon-3pm, **dinner served** 6-11pm daily. **Main courses** £14-£26. **Set lunch** £22 2 courses, £26 3 courses.
Both **Credit** AmEx, DC, JCB, MC, V.
First the positives. The setting is unarguably impressive: there are great views over the Thames, with a close-up on Tower Bridge. The tables on the river terrace are alluring, especially at night. Inside, the decor (generally quite plain and modern but with a few French country-kitchen bits and pieces dotted about) is inoffensive. And staff are welcoming. But that's about it. Our most recent meal here saw a really slack performance. It wasn't until the waiter came to take our order that he revealed many, many dishes from an initially tempting menu were off – including such basics as chips. We ended up having mash with our (very average) fish. Dressed crab and potted shrimps were passable, shallot tart was a huge quiche-like wedge, leaving fisherman's pie as the best of a bad lot. Hopes of better things for dessert were dashed by treacle sponge that was dry around the edges and needed every bit of custard it came with. Service was generally chaotic, if willing. Even if we experienced an off-night, at these prices (roast beef with yorkshire pudding cost £18.50) our meal was unacceptable. New owners D&D London need to take heed.

SHELF LIFE

London's independent butchers are a dying breed, thanks to the rise of the all-powerful supermarket giants. But for top-class, organic and free-range meat, you really need a proper butcher, like these.

Ginger Pig

8-10 Moxon Street, W1U 4EW (7935 7788). Bond Street or Baker Street tube/Marylebone tube/rail. **Open** 9am-6pm Mon-Thur; 9am-6.30pm Fri, Sat; 9am-3pm Sun.
The Ginger Pig's North Yorkshire farm is the source of much of the meat for this Marylebone shop, where an old-fashioned cream Aga churns out rustic pies and other savoury treats. There's also a branch in Borough Market.

C Lidgate

110 Holland Park Avenue, W11 4UA (7727 8243). Holland Park tube. **Open** 7am-7.30pm Mon-Fri; 6.30am-6.30pm Sat.
The decor and service are thoroughly traditional, but Lidgate's is always at the cutting edge of butchery with organic meats from royal estates and an exciting range of own-made recipe dishes.

M Moen & Sons

24 The Pavement, SW4 0JA (7622 1624/www.moen.co.uk). Clapham Common tube. **Open** 8.30am-6.30pm Mon-Fri; 8.30am-5pm Sat.
Legs of lamb tied with rosemary, and skinned rabbits hang in the window of this gloriously old-fashioned shop specialising in organic and free-range meats.

Sheepdrove Organic Farm Family Butcher

5 Clifton Road, W9 1SZ (7266 3838/ www.sheepdrove.com). Warwick Avenue tube. **Open** 9am-7pm Mon-Fri; 9am-5pm Sat; 10am-4pm Sun.
From one of the leading players in the organic movement, this butcher sells meat from Sheepdrove's large Berkshire estate and is particularly renowned for its chickens.

Wyndham House Butchers

339 Fulham Road, SW10 9TW (7352 7888). Gloucester Road tube. **Open** 7am-7pm Mon-Fri; 7am-5.30pm Sat; 10am-4pm Sun.
Related to the well-known poultry shop at Borough Market, this is an excellent source of expertly prepared game, meat and sausages.

Empress of India

Babies and children welcome: high chairs. Booking advisable. Dress: smart casual. Tables outdoors (12, terrace). **Map 12 R8.**

East

Shoreditch

Rochelle Canteen NEW

The Canteen, Old School Building, Arnold Circus, E2 7ES (7729 5677/www.arnoldandhenderson.com). Old Street tube/rail. **Breakfast served** 9-11am, **lunch served** noon-3pm Mon-Fri. **Main courses** £9-£12. **Unlicensed. Corkage** £3.50-£5. **Credit** MC, V.

A curious but charming restaurant that operates as the canteen for the next-door art studios, yet also happily accepts outside diners. Rochelle is part-run by Margot Henderson, wife of Fergus who co-owns St John (*see p63*). It shares many of that restaurant's characteristics, including the motto 'nose-to-tail eating'. The short, daily changing menu reads like a cut-down version of St John's (with entries such as artichoke vinaigrette, jellied ham, poached chicken with carrots and aïoli), but while the cooking may not be as sure-fire, the prices are kinder. There's a touch of the Mediterranean in food such as tomato bruschetta, or aubergine with polenta and goat's curd (the least successful dish we tried). Puddings, though, are reassuringly back-to-British: gooseberry fool and shortbread, chocolate pot, or wigmore cheese with chutney (only £3.50 each: about half the price of St John's). The small, stark, white premises are the former school bike sheds. Inside there are long white tables; outside, beside an immaculate lawn, are café tables. Service is warm and friendly but can be dippy. Note that the Canteen is unlicensed; BYO or sip on a ginger beer or apple juice. And remember to book: word has spread and Rochelle's charms are no longer a secret.

Babies and children admitted. Booking advisable. Disabled: toilet. Tables outdoors (6, courtyard). Vegetarian menu. **Map 6 S4.**

Victoria Park

★ Empress of India NEW

2007 RUNNER-UP BEST BRITISH RESTAURANT

130 Lauriston Road, E9 7LH (8533 5123/www.theempressofindia.com). Mile End tube then 277 bus. **Breakfast served** 8.30-11.30am Mon-Fri; 9-11.30am Sat; 9am-11am Sun. **Lunch served** noon-3pm Mon-Sat; noon-4pm Sun. **Tea served** 3-6pm Mon-Sat. **Dinner served** 6-10pm Mon-Fri; 6.30-10pm Sat; 6.30-9.30pm Sun. **Main courses** £9.50-£15.50. **Credit** AmEx, MC, V.

Opened in late 2006 by the people behind the Gun, the Well and the White Swan Pub & Dining Room gastropubs, the Empress has swiftly become a destination restaurant for east Londoners. It has managed this only by first succeeding as a great local, catering to the day-long sustenance and social needs of a varied clientele. With large windows, a mosaic floor, substantial bar and intriguing talking-point shell chandeliers, in looks it refers to pub, restaurant and grand café – and works as all three. Food is finessed British gastropub fare, in pleasing combinations: grilled sardines so fresh they might have swum on to their sourdough toast (served with tapenade and gremolata); a flavourful barnsley chop with broad bean bubble, cooked with the ability it deserved. Raspberry cranachan, and plum and frangipane tart, were less involving; this is definitely somewhere that does sturdy better than sweet, notably on the rotisserie, which turns out all manner of meats (including game and rare breeds) for diners to pull apart on wooden boards. Craft beers include two from Greenwich's Meantime brewery. Chapel Down's rated Brut NV is one of two house fizzes available by the glass (though the more expensive Roederer is the one eager staff suggest to undecided drinkers).

Babies and children welcome: children's menu; high chairs; nappy-changing facilities. Disabled: toilet. Tables outdoors (15, pavement).

Chinese

The last few years have seen a growing glamour about Chinese dining in London. The **Royal China Club** has established itself as one of the capital's premier Chinese restaurants with its exquisite dim sum, fine teas and friendly service: a classically Cantonese retort to the challenge thrown down a few years ago by **Hakkasan** and **Yauatcha**. **Pearl Liang** (a contender for Best Design in the 2007 Time Out Eating & Drinking Awards) is a new jewel in the crown of the London dim sum scene; head there for fabulous Cantonese food in luxurious surroundings. New arrival **Hoazhan** bucks the Chinatown norm, with its very modern take on Chinese food and attentive service. Meanwhile, the expansion of the **Royal China** chain continues, with a new branch in Fulham, a sure sign that high-quality, authentic Chinese food is moving into the mainstream.

Sichuanese cookery, arguably China's most exciting regional cuisine, has been making further inroads after the stir created by last year's hot opening, **Bar Shu** – an echo of the recent fashion for spicy dining out in mainland China. Newcomer **Snazz Sichuan**, near the British Library, is offering hearty folk favourites such as numbing-and-hot rabbit, and a number of Chinatown restaurants are trying to join in the fun, producing their own lists of Sichuanese specials.

With the Beijing Olympics coming up in 2008, China is attracting international attention as never before. Shanghai has become a fashionable tourist destination, and European travellers are coming home from their holidays with higher expectations of Chinese food. In Britain, a nationwide festival in 2008, China Now (www.chinanow.org.uk), will showcase contemporary Chinese culture, including its cuisine. With luck, all this will feed into the increasing authenticity and regionalisation of the capital's Chinese dining scene.

A FEW TIPS

Most set menus in Chinese restaurants pander to outdated Western stereotypes of Chinese food, yet main menus can be daunting if you're unused to the cuisine. Here are a few pointers.

The art of ordering a Chinese meal lies in assembling a variety of dishes, differing from one another in terms of ingredients, cooking methods and flavours. Thus, if you're dining with a group, it's best to coordinate your ordering; if each guest insists on a personal favourite, you may end up with a lopsided meal. Starters are easy: just order as you please and remember there is life beyond the usual deep-fried snacks (a cold-meat platter or steamed scallops can make a delicious beginning to a meal).

For main courses, aim to order about one dish for every person in your party, and then one extra, and share everything. Make sure you choose a variety of main ingredients so that things don't get repetitive. Then try to balance dry, deep-fried dishes with slow hotpots and crisp stir-fries; rich roast duck with fresh vegetables; gentle tastes with spicy flavours. And ask your waiter about seasonal greens; you may find the restaurant has pak choi, gai lan (chinese broccoli), pea shoots, water spinach and other marvellous Chinese treats.

Most Chinese fill up on plain steamed rice, which makes a good foil to the flavours of the other food and is much more comfortable than that old takeaway staple, egg-fried rice. Desserts aren't a forte of Chinese cuisine, and you rarely find much beyond the old clichés of red-bean paste pancakes and toffee bananas – **Hakkasan** and **Yauatcha** make their own exceptional pâtisserie, while **Mr Chow** buys in French pastries from an outside pâtisserie. Better, in most cases, to order an extra savoury dish and stop at a café afterwards if you want something sweet.

Central

Belgravia

Hunan (100)

51 Pimlico Road, SW1W 8NE (7730 5712). Sloane Square tube. **Lunch served** 12.30-2pm, **dinner served** 6-11pm Mon-Sat. **Set meal** £35-£150 per person (minimum 2). **Credit** AmEx, DC, MC, V.

While an à la carte menu is available on request, the best option at Hunan is the 'leave it to us feast': a series of small dishes that can be adjusted to suit dietary requirements or allergies, rather like a Chinese tasting menu. On our visit, the son of owner Mr Peng (who hails from Taiwan) was a charming host and very helpful in deciphering the ten or so little dishes that arrived at our table in swift succession. Highlights included a delicious savoury broth with steamed minced pork and water chestnuts; hot spicy beef flavoured with dried mandarin peel; a meltingly tender cube of red roast pork belly; and sesame crispy octopus with plum jam. Other dishes were less enjoyable, such as an overcooked steamed salmon and snapper roll, but the meal's variety of taste combinations was interesting and fun, if not always authentically Chinese. We finished with a larger plate: pork shoulder wrapped in lotus leaves, which arrived with sautéed chinese broccoli and stir-fried rice. Hunan's small interior is charmingly decorated with cream walls, brush paintings and other Chinese works of art. It's a hospitable place, which has given it a loyal following.

Babies and children admitted (lunch only). Booking essential. Vegetarian menu.
Map 15 G11.

Chinatown

Chinese Experience

118 Shaftesbury Avenue, W1D 5EP (7437 0377/ www.chineseexperience.com). Leicester Square or Piccadilly Circus tube. **Meals served** noon-11pm Mon-Thur; noon-11.30pm Fri, Sat; noon-10.30pm Sun. **Main courses** £6-£22. **Set meal** £19-£23 per person (minimum 2). **Credit** AmEx, MC, V.

The modern interior (with a striking red feature wall and contemporary calligraphy) sets Chinese Experience apart from many of its Chinatown competitors. The menu includes a long list of chef's recommendations, with intriguing dishes such as spare ribs with strawberry sauce and grilled ice fish with lotus. We began with salt and pepper soft-shell crab, which appeared in under five minutes, clearly straight from the wok.

BEST CHINESE

For glamour
Dress up to the nines at **China Tang** (*see p78*), **Hakkasan** (*see p76*), **Kai Mayfair** (*see p79*), **Mr Chow** (*see p77*) and **Pearl Liang** (*see p79*).

For a hot date
You'll find chilli aplenty at London's batch of Hunanese and Sichuan restaurants: **Bar Shu** (*see p79*), **Hunan** (*see left*), **Shangri-La** (*see p87*) and **Snazz Sichuan** (*see p76*).

For Chinatown's choicest
The best Chinese restaurants in Soho's famous Sino-strip include authentic Cantonese outfit **Feng Shui Inn** (*see p72*), little Fujianese caff **Fook Sing** (*see p73*), dim sum expert **Imperial China** (*see p73*), Gerrard Street's finest **Golden Dragon** (*see p73*) and new-wave newcomer **Haozhan** (*see p73*).

For roast meat
For succulent duck and other meaty fare, try **Four Seasons** (*see p81*), **Gold Mine** (*see p82*), **Green Cottage** (*see p87*) and **North China** (*see p81*).

For all the tea in China
Well, not quite, but you'll find an exciting choice of brews at **Royal China Club** (*see p78*) and **Yauatcha** (*see p80*).

Chinatown cafés

These days, most of London's best Chinese restaurants aren't found in Chinatown. Yet this little segment of southern Soho still contains a wealth of cheap cafés where you'll can enjoy a swift snack amid the bustle. These pit-stops are much used by Chinese Londoners, and some of the food can be extremely good – the dumplings at **Jen Café** and the seasonal greens at **HK Diner** spring to mind.

The establishments can be roughly divided into three: bakeries selling various cakes, biscuits and buns (both savoury and sweet); old-style caffs specialising in noodle and rice plates (**Canton** and **Hing Loon** are two of our favourites); and a newer breed of Hong Kong-style cafés that serve a wider array of dishes (including, perhaps, Chinese versions of borscht, or barbecued meat and scrambled egg sandwiches), as well as the old standards. This latter category, which includes **Café de HK**, **Café TPT** and **HK Diner**, is favoured by young Asian students, especially those originating from Malaysia and China. Popular drinks at these venues include Taiwanese-style 'bubble teas': sweet, icy concoctions filled with gelatinous balls of jelly that have to be sucked up through large straws. Slurp them proudly – it's the only way.

★ Café de HK

47-49 Charing Cross Road, WC2H 0AN (7534 9898). Leicester Square or Piccadilly Circus tube. **Meals served** 11.30am-11pm daily. **Main courses** £5-£6. **Credit** (over £10) MC, V.

Ease past the ground-floor throng of takeaway punters to the mezzanine, where tiled flooring, benches and glass-topped tables are soon forgotten when you see the menu. This vast list ranges from borscht to spag bol, via Chinese rice and noodle dishes, barbecue meats and snacks (such as cold slices of boneless pig's trotter served with shredded jellyfish). The 'hawker soup noodles' deal is a good one: choose your noodles, sauce and three toppings for £5.80. Drink iced bubble tea (sesame with milk is recommended, despite looking like mud). Service is fast and friendly.

Booking not accepted. Vegetarian menu. **Map 17 C4.**

★ Café TPT

21 Wardour Street, W1D 6PN (7734 7980). Leicester Square or Piccadilly Circus tube. **Meals served** noon-1am daily. **Main courses** £6.50-£24. **Set meal** £9.50-£19.50 per person (minimum 2). **Credit** MC, V.

This tiny pit-stop has all dishes translated into English (though 'whatever, £9.80' is a touch esoteric). The choice is immense, including chinese mushroom with frogs' legs congee, and some Malaysian food, though the regulars (Chinese students, office workers) invariably order meal-in-one rice or noodle dishes. Vermicelli with minced beef and gelatinous '1,000-year-old egg' in a steaming stock tasting of Bovril laced with rice wine was fabulous. Grab a menu from the counter if necessary; the terse yet speedy staff can be a bit lax.

Babies and children admitted. Takeaway service. Vegetarian menu. **Map 17 B5.**

★ Canton

11 Newport Place, WC2H 7JR (7437 6220). Leicester Square or Piccadilly Circus tube. **Meals served** noon-11.30pm Mon-Thur, Sun; noon-12.30am Fri, Sat. **Main courses** £5.20-£9. **Set meal** £9-£15 per person (minimum 2). **Credit** AmEx, JCB, MC, V.

In the same mould as Hing Loon (*see below*), Canton is a diminutive old-school café offering a huge menu. Be guided by the window display of dangling ducks, glistening and bronzed like sun-tanned bodybuilders. The hot roast duck meat is succulent indeed. Mouth-watering too is the luscious pork belly on rice – one of many meal-in-one rice and noodles dishes, and a whopping portion for a fiver. Order it with a crunchy-fresh portion of gai lan (chinese broccoli) with garlic. Late-night couples, students and solo diners venture into the brightly lit interior to wolf down a plateful.

Babies and children admitted. Booking advisable. Separate room for parties, seats 22. Takeaway service. **Map 17 C4.**

★ Hing Loon

25 Lisle Street, WC2H 7BA (7437 3602/7287 0419). Leicester Square or Piccadilly Circus tube. **Meals served** noon-11.30pm Mon-Thur; noon-midnight Fri, Sat; noon-11pm Sun. **Main courses** £3.70-£7.50. **Set lunch** £4.50 2 courses. **Set dinner** £5.80-£9.50 per person (minimum 2). **Credit** AmEx, MC, V.

With its small tables and modest decor (don't miss the display of world banknotes), this tiny stalwart is a 'head down, chopsticks shovelling' joint. It caters admirably for single diners with its one-plate meals, though there are many more complex dishes too (braised eel with crispy pork, say). To find the 'economic meals' advertised in the window, look for the rice and noodle dishes on the main menu. Beef brisket on boiled rice was a tender plateful of meat in a cinnamon-tinged stew – and cost just £3.80.

Babies and children admitted. Separate room for parties, seats 50 (Fri, Sat eve). Takeaway service. Vegetarian menu. **Map 17 C4.**

★ HK Diner

22 Wardour Street, W1D 6QQ (7434 9544). Leicester Square or Piccadilly Circus tube. **Meals served** 11am-4am daily. **Main courses** £5-£25. **Set meal** £10-£30 per person (minimum 2). **Credit** AmEx, MC, V.

Disappointingly, the crab was covered in an oily batter; the salty fried garlic and chilli sprinkled over it were the dominant flavours. Braised pork belly in five-spice sauce was attractively presented on a thick bamboo skewer flanked by several stems of choi sum; the salty/sweet five-spice sauce complemented the tasty yet slightly dry pork. Shanghai stir-fried noodles and sichuan stir-fried string beans were both authentic and full of flavour. We also liked the tangy home-style beancurd, topped with pork, peppers and fresh baby corn. Our Chinese experience was definitely positive. This is a deservedly popular place (look out for regular special discounts too, such as a half-price weekday lunchtime dim sum deal).

Babies and children welcome: high chairs. Booking advisable. Separate room for parties, seats 30. Takeaway service. Vegetarian menu. **Map 17 C4.**

Crispy Duck NEW

27 Wardour Street, W1D 6PR (7287 6578). Leicester Square or Piccadilly Circus tube. **Meals served** 9am-4am daily. **Main courses** £5-£18. **Set meal** £10.50; £11.50-£12.50 per person (minimum 2). **Credit** AmEx, MC, V.

With a plethora of grimy-looking restaurants sporting battered menus, Chinatown is awash with mediocrity. There are surprises, though, and while it might not appeal at first glance, Crispy Duck on Wardour Street (it has a more upmarket branch on Gerrard Street) is one such surprise. The ground floor is deceptively small. With just six to eight tables, it looks like a fast noodle café, but there are two other floors above this. A huge menu caters to Western and Chinese tastes. An appetiser of salt and chilli soft-shell crab provided a crunchy hit of salt, spice and sweet crab flavour. We stuck to seafood for the main course, choosing a whole, steamed sea bass finished with soy, ginger and spring onions; the delicately seasoned flesh was tender and succulent. As a contrast, the waiter suggested a spicy medley of green peppers, aubergine and beancurd, stuffed with minced prawn in black bean sauce. A generous portion of stir-fried mangetouts was the perfect complement. Crispy Duck isn't stylish, but it offers good cooking and efficient service.

Babies and children welcome. Separate room for parties, seats 20. Takeaway service. Vegetarian menu. **Map 17 B4.**

For branch see index.

Feng Shui Inn

4-6 Gerrard Street, W1D 5PG (7734 6778/www.fengshuiinn.co.uk). Leicester Square or Piccadilly Circus tube. **Meals served** noon-11.30pm Mon-Sat; noon-10.30pm Sun. **Main courses** £6.80-£24.80. **Set lunch** (noon-4.30pm) £3.90 1 course incl tea, £5.90-£10.90 2 courses incl tea. **Set meal** £12.80-£26.80 per person (minimum 2). **Credit** AmEx, MC, V.

Located between the gilded arches of Chinatown's main drag, and named after the new-age fad based on an ancient Chinese art, this Cantonese restaurant festooned with red lanterns may not appear a promising option. Don't be quick to dismiss it. Feng Shui Inn is a self-styled family restaurant and serves some of the best and truest dishes in the neighbourhood, with friendly prices too. Like a quintessential Chinese host, our waitress recommended her favourite dishes with pride, describing ingredients and cooking methods with enthusiasm. The Cantonese-style steamed whole sea bass was faultless, its perfectly cooked flesh sliding off the bone with the nudge of a chopstick. Deep-fried salt and pepper squid succeeded where so many others fail: chewy yet soft, crisp without being oily. The best testament to the restaurant's authenticity was the steamed tofu custard topped with seafood and vegetables. Listed only on the Chinese menu, it was a silky, subtle, sensory delight. Service was warm, efficient and relaxed, allowing us to linger over a bottomless pot of tea despite the crowds forming at the door.

Babies and children admitted. Booking essential weekends. Entertainment: karaoke (call for details). Separate rooms for parties, seating 12, 20 and 40. Vegetarian menu. **Map 17 C4.**

Wardour Street's HK Diner is the current late-night venue of choice for young Chinese Londoners. Its catch-all menu helps, though most soup noodle dishes are on the untranslated list; non-Chinese readers should flip this over (ignore the menu of bland stir-fries you'll be given on arrival) to find an enticing choice of specials: for example, chitterling with preserved cabbage; a huge helping of tender beef brisket in profoundly pleasing gravy; deep-fried oysters (17 of them); and a superb selection of seasonal veg. Staff are bright and breezy, the restaurant design is bright and minimalist, and bright Hong Kong pop provides the soundtrack.
Babies and children welcome: high chairs. Booking not accepted. Disabled: toilet. Takeaway service. Vegetarian menu. **Map 17 C4.**

★ Jen Café

4-8 Newport Place, WC2H 7JP (no phone). Leicester Square or Piccadilly Circus tube.
Meals served noon-8pm Mon-Fri; noon-8.30pm Sat, Sun. **Main courses** £4-£16. **No credit cards.**
Here's the gen on Jen: it's a basic corner caff with seating at easy-wipe tables or on high stools by the entrance. In the window, if you're lucky, a woman will be making fresh dumplings. Order these grilled and savour the juicy, aromatic pork and chive fillings and nicely chewy wrappings – first-rate. Noodles and rice plates fill the menu. An order for soup noodles will produce a big warming bowlful; ho fun with shredded pork and preserved cabbage is a winner. Bubble teas and unusual hot drinks (a faintly medicinal-tasting honey and watercress) are further fortes. Prices are minuscule.
Babies and children admitted. Takeaway service. **Map 17 C4.**

★ Fook Sing

25-26 Newport Court, WC2H 7JS (7287 0188). Leicester Square or Piccadilly Circus tube.
Meals served 11am-10pm daily. **Main courses** £3.90-£4.30. **Unlicensed.** No alcohol allowed. **No credit cards.**
The unassuming premises of little Fook Sing might lead you to think this is just another unremarkable Chinatown caff. Flick to the back page of the menu, however, and there are Fujianese specialities. Fried pig's stomach may not be for the faint-hearted, but this was easily our favourite dish: thin slices of tender stomach combined with crunchy vegetables and a light savoury sauce. Intrepid diners might also try the hotchpotch soup, a peppery sour soup packed with a bewildering assortment of ingredients; ours included (among others) pig's stomach, liver, beef ribs, beancurd, taro and mussels. Braised 'pig's hoof' came in a lovely sweet and lightly spicy sauce, but was tough, as though it had not been cooked for long enough. Fujian-style vermicelli was also variable; the shellfish were overcooked and uninspiring, but the noodles were delicious – infused with seafood flavour and mixed with chinese cabbage to provide a pleasing textural contrast. Don't miss the oyster cakes; these crisp patties of oyster and shredded vegetables make a tasty snack for just £1.
Babies and children admitted. **Map 17 C4.**

Golden Dragon

28-29 Gerrard Street, W1D 6JW (7734 2763). Leicester Square or Piccadilly Circus tube.
Meals served noon-11.30pm Mon-Thur; noon-midnight Fri, Sat; 11am-11pm Sun. **Dim sum served** noon-5pm Mon-Sat; 11am-5pm Sun. **Dim sum** £2.20-£4. **Main courses** £6-£25. **Set meal** £12.50-£35 per person (minimum 2). **Credit** AmEx, MC, V.
With its choice location along the spine of Chinatown, Golden Dragon draws in the tourists. If it hadn't been for English football on the restaurant's TV screens, the place would have felt like an older-style Hong Kong establishment. Portion sizes are generous. We chose the sizzling fillet steak with black pepper: extremely tender beef swimming in an overly thick, rich, but nicely fiery sauce. A highlight of the meal was the crab and glass noodles hotpot, a delightful combination of a whole crab (broken into segments) and slippery vermicelli noodles in a light satay sauce with chilli thrown in for extra zing. Stir-fried pak choi was crisp and flavourful. The only disappointment was fried stuffed braised beancurd, where the prawn filling was mean and bland. Many Gerrard Street restaurants tend to dumb down flavours for the Western palate, but Golden Dragon's chefs clearly have some flair (although the menu does cater to all tastes). On our visit, we found the service very helpful and friendly, with the waiter full of suggestions.
Babies and children welcome: high chairs. Booking advisable. Separate rooms for parties, seating 20 and 40. Takeaway service. **Map 17 C4.**

★ Haozhan NEW

8 Gerrard Street, W1D 5PJ (7434 3838). Leicester Square or Piccadilly Circus tube.
Meals served noon-11.30pm Mon-Thur; noon-midnight Fri, Sat; noon-10.30pm Sun. **Main courses** £6-£26. **Credit** AmEx, MC, V.
It's easy to get blasé about Chinatown restaurants, as so often they disappoint; but just occasionally you get a nice surprise – such as Haozhan. This modern-looking venue has a contemporary, globally ranging menu, produced by a chef who was at Hakkasan (*see p76*). The techniques here are impeccable, and there's great attention to detail. Many dishes are textural masterpieces. The centrepiece of our meal was a Japanese-style platter of soft tofu cubes, deep-fried to give them a contrast of texture and topped with firm sweet scallops. This was garnished with puréed spinach and red flying fish roe, for visual flair. Haozhan's fish soup follows a Malaysian rice noodle approach, though big chunks of fresh cod are used together with the fish-head stock; its coconutty liquid was given added spice by chilli, tomato and spring onion, which masked any fish oil smells. The bowl was big enough to be a meal in itself; Wagamama doesn't even come close for soup-noodles. There are plenty of other attention-grabbing dishes, but even simple 'Sichuan vegetables' wowed us. Our waiters were attentive to the point of being almost chummy, and, importantly, knew a lot about the dishes. And the low bill was yet another pleasant surprise.
Babies and children welcome: high chairs. **Map 17 C4.**

Imperial China

White Bear Yard, 25A Lisle Street, WC2H 7BA (7734 3388/www.imperial-china.co.uk). Leicester Square or Piccadilly Circus tube. **Meals served** noon-11.30pm Mon-Sat; 11.30am-10.30pm Sun. **Dim sum served** noon-5pm daily. **Dim sum** £2.30-£3.60. **Main courses** £5.90-£26.50. **Set meal** £14.95-£31.50 per person (minimum 2). **Minimum** £10. **Credit** AmEx, JCB, MC, V.
Imperial China offers superior dim sum in an attractive, light-drenched, wood-panelled setting. The quality and freshness of ingredients is notable, and the food is authentic and reasonably priced (although menu translations can be misleading). Siu mai (pork dumplings) can be bland elsewhere, but here came alive with a crab roe topping that gave a sharp hint of the sea. Pork and egg congee (rice porridge) – which, along with chicken's feet is 'not recommended' to English-

Snazz Sichuan. See p76.

RESTAURANTS

reading diners, according to the menu – was cooked in a rich broth, and boosted by a coriander and spring onion garnish. Beef and pineapple dumplings may sound questionable, but were delicious, presented in an exquisite butterfly shape with two coriander stalks as antennae. There were serious problems with the service on our visit, however. Staff had limited English (the weekend crowd was 70% Chinese), and we waited over an hour for some dishes, despite frequent reminders. One dish was even brought after the bill. Soundproofing the karaoke room adjacent to the first-floor dining room would be a good investment too; on a Sunday afternoon, we suffered all of Whitney Houston's greatest hits.
Babies and children welcome: high chairs. Booking advisable. Disabled: toilet. Entertainment: pianist 7.30-10.30pm Wed-Fri. Separate rooms for parties, seating 10-70. Tables outdoors (5, courtyard). Vegetarian menu. **Map 17 C4.**

Joy King Lau

3 Leicester Street, WC2H 7BL (7437 1132/1133). Leicester Square or Piccadilly Circus tube. **Meals served** noon-11.30pm Mon-Sat; 11am-10.30pm Sun. **Dim sum served** noon-4.45pm Mon-Sat; 11am-4.45pm Sun. **Dim sum** £1.90-£2.90. **Main courses** £6.50-£20. **Set meal** £9.80-£35 per person (minimum 2). **Credit** AmEx, DC, MC, V.
Located off Lisle Street, away from the hustle of Gerrard Street, Joy King Lau is made up of four floors of narrow dining rooms, serving the usual Cantonese fare of Chinatown. We visited for lunch to order from the dim sum menu. Of our choices, we most enjoyed the scallop cheung fun; the silky steamed sheets of rice pasta made a perfect foil for the tender scallops wrapped inside. We also liked the crisp, wafer-wrapped prawns for their fresh, minced prawn filling and tangy dipping sauce. Other dishes were less successful. Fried taro dumplings looked perfectly cooked with their trademark lace-like shells, but were tough to bite into, not soft and yielding as they should be. Turnip paste patties were underseasoned and stodgy, while prawn fun gwor had been over-steamed so the pastry was gluey; the filling tasted overwhelmingly of carrot instead of prawn. From the main menu, fried oysters with crispy pork was an interesting combination, but let down by tough meat and soggy batter on the oysters, which would have been better without any coating.
Babies and children welcome: high chairs. Booking advisable weekend. Takeaway service. **Map 17 C5.**

Laureate

64 Shaftesbury Avenue, W1D 6LU (7437 5088). Leicester Square or Piccadilly Circus tube. **Meals served** noon-11.30pm Mon-Sat; 11am-10.30pm Sun. **Main courses** £7.50-£25. **Set meal** £11.80-£14.50 per person (minimum 2). **Credit** AmEx, MC, V.
This spacious, bright restaurant has a first-rate corner location close to West End theatres. It offers speedy service and a mix of Cantonese and Peking-style cuisine. Deep-fried squid in chilli and salt appeared within five minutes of our order being taken. Moments later, ho fun Malaysian-style noodles, and lo hon vegetables and beancurd were served. Unfortunately, speed of service wasn't matched by culinary flair. The thick ho fun rice noodles were decent enough, and came with a strong curry flavouring and a few fresh prawns, but the lo hon vegetables were limp and bland (the medley, including mushrooms, bamboo shoots and baby corn, tasted as if it came out of a tin). The squid was covered in a floury, undercooked batter. We also chose a more expensive dish (£13.50) of deep-fried stuffed crispy duck with yam paste. Here too, the experience was mixed. The oily yam stuffing lacked seasoning, although the crispy duck had plenty of flavour. Service on our visit was somewhat brisk and inexperienced. If you prefer mild food served quickly, Laureate fits the bill; for a more leisurely gourmet experience, head elsewhere.
Babies and children welcome: high chairs. Booking advisable. Separate rooms for parties, seating 14-30. Takeaway service. Vegetarian menu. **Map 17 B4.**

London Hong Kong

6-7 Lisle Street, WC2H 7BG (7287 0352/www.london-hk.co.uk). Leicester Square or Piccadilly Circus tube. **Meals served** noon-11.30pm Mon-Thur; noon-midnight Fri, Sat; 11am-11pm Sun. **Dim sum served** noon-5pm daily. **Dim sum** £2-£3.50. **Main courses** £6-£9. **Set meal** £11.80-£15.80 per person (minimum 2). **Credit** AmEx, JCB, MC, V.
Diners from both inside and outside London's Chinese community are catered for at this gold- and burgundy-coloured restaurant. There are two menus: one containing the Cantonese and northern Chinese dishes common in Chinatown, the other a smaller list of dim sum. Following the lead of the Chinese customers around us, we chose from the dim sum photo-menu. The dumplings, like the photos, were extremely small. Prawn cheung fun was distinctly lacking in prawn; and siu loon bao (minced pork in broth encased in a dumpling) was bland. The barbecued pork buns were passably tangy. From the same menu, we ordered mixed seafood udon with XO sauce; this had more flavour than any of the dim sum, but contained tough, virtually raw cabbage in the seafood and noodle mix. Pea shoot dumplings took almost half an hour to arrive, well after the rest of the food had been eaten – with little of the delicate pea shoot filling, they weren't worth the wait. Even the bo lay (pu-er) tea was lacklustre. At least a meal here won't break the bank; our lunch for two (without alcohol) cost £26.
Babies and children welcome: high chairs. Booking advisable. Separate room for parties, seats 60. Takeaway service. Vegetarian menu. **Map 17 C4.**

Mr Kong

21 Lisle Street, WC2H 7BA (7437 7341/9679). Leicester Square or Piccadilly Circus tube. **Meals served** noon-2.45am Mon-Sat; noon-1.45am Sun. **Main courses** £6.20-£26. **Set meal** £10 per person (minimum 2); £16-£22 per person (minimum 4). **Minimum** £7 after 5pm. **Credit** AmEx, DC, JCB, MC, V.
Following a minor fire, Mr Kong underwent a revamp in 2007: the kitchen was moved to the basement, allowing the ground floor to have two dining rooms (there's a third on the first floor). The affable manager continues to greet every customer like an old friend. Many probably are. People return here repeatedly – whether for the familiar welcome or the cooking. An epic menu ensures variety. The best strategy, though, is to avoid it and ask the manager for recommendations. Of the more than dozen dishes we tried, all were OK, though none exceptional: a typical drawback of having too much choice. Steamed razor clams with garlic served with chilli soy sauce and spring onions were impressively oversized, but also overcooked. In contrast, a casserole of pork belly with preserved cabbage needed longer cooking; while the flavours were correct, the meat was hardly melt-in-the-mouth. Crispy aromatic duck was a better rendition: neither dry nor greasy, and tender enough to be fork-shredded. A blur of other dishes, including a steamed sea bass, were unobjectionable and unremarkable. At least the place is now looking far more presentable.
Babies and children welcome: high chairs. Booking advisable. Separate room for parties, seats 30. Takeaway service. Vegetarian menu. **Map 17 C4.**

New Mayflower

68-70 Shaftesbury Avenue, W1D 6LY (7734 9207). Leicester Square or Piccadilly Circus tube. **Meals served** 5pm-4am daily. **Main courses** £7-£48. **Set meal** £11.50-£22 per person (minimum 2). **Minimum** £8. **Credit** MC, V.
New Mayflower is a Chinatown stalwart, popular both inside and outside the Chinese community. Its lengthy Anglo-Cantonese menu provides many familiar dishes, plus a few more esoteric concoctions. The decor is slightly rough around the edges, especially in the basement where we ate on a typically crowded night. Waits for tables are frequently long. Bored by the English menu, we asked for advice from the Chinese list. From this, we ate fried eel with honey and pepper sauce (perfectly firm, sweet and spiky), and pork with chinese broccoli and ginger. Crispy duck was OK, with crunchy skin, flavourful meat and generous portions of pancakes, cucumber and spring onion. In contrast, wun tun soup was disappointing, with bland broth and dumplings that relied too much on prawns and tasted fishy. The set meals are reasonably priced, and slightly more balanced than the norm, though a dinner of crispy duck, chicken with black bean and chilli, fried crispy beef with carrot, mangetouts with beansprouts and egg fried rice (£14.50) still contained too much fried food. New Mayflower's particularly friendly staff set it apart from nearby competitors, and this will keep us returning. The very late hours are a bonus too.
Babies and children welcome: high chairs. Booking essential. Separate room for parties, seats 30. Takeaway service. Vegetarian menu. **Map 17 B4.**

New World

1 Gerrard Place, W1D 5PA (7734 0396). Leicester Square or Piccadilly Circus tube. **Meals served** 11am-11.45pm Mon-Sat; 11am-11pm Sun. **Dim sum served** 11am-11pm daily. **Dim sum** £2-£5. **Main courses** £4.90-£10.50. **Set meal** £12-£50 per person (minimum 2). **Minimum** (after 6pm) £5. **Credit** AmEx, DC, MC, V.
This is one of Chinatown's most popular dim sum venues – though not necessarily for the food (which is generally of average standard) or the service (somewhere between indifferent and rude, in our experience). No, the appeal of New World lies in the old-world trolley service, a disappearing custom that allows diners to glimpse the dishes before ordering. That these trolleys continue to trundle along the well-worn floors of this immense, three-roomed restaurant until 11pm is another draw. Toss in reasonable prices and you have a hit, especially among diners seeking an authentic, no-nonsense bite. All the dim sum staples – from prawn dumplings to chickens' feet – are faithfully executed. Whether the food is steamed, deep-fried, braised or stir-fried, the flavours are real: the oiliness often too real. Hits and misses range from well-seasoned, well-cooked dry-fried beef noodles, to disappointingly dry xiao long bao (shanghai steamed 'soup' dumplings). The extensive full menu is packed with stir-fries and more esoteric Cantonese dishes. Given the variety, convenience, authentic bustle and the cost, this crowd-pleaser is worth a visit.
Babies and children welcome: high chairs. Booking not accepted lunch Sun. Takeaway service. Vegetarian menu. **Map 17 C4.**

Royal Dragon

30 Gerrard Street, W1D 6JS (7734 1388). Leicester Square or Piccadilly Circus tube. **Meals served** noon-3am, **dim sum served** noon-5pm daily. **Dim sum** £2.10-£3. **Main courses** £6.50-£15. **Set meal** £12.50-£25 per person (minimum 2). **Credit** AmEx, MC, V.
Refurbished a few years ago, Royal Dragon has a much more modern feel than its sibling next door, well-known tourist haunt Golden Dragon (*see p73*). Simply decorated with black and white photos, the mean and moody interior is strangely cool, with exposed metal air-conditioning tubes and bare, rectangular dark wood tables. Even the efficient staff wear black. Good dim sum can be eaten here at lunchtime, but most diners (particularly young Chinese) scour the 350-dish menu for Hong Kong-style tea house options, such as minestrone soup, french toast or mixed-sausage spaghetti. Our bowl of Portuguese-style 'baked' rice was bright yellow in colour, sweet with coconut milk and generously topped with mixed seafood, potato and plenty of carrot. However, an otherwise excellent hotpot of stewed pork belly with preserved vegetable was lukewarm in places; we assumed it had been badly microwaved. A large, own-made crème brûlée, one of a batch of Western-style desserts, helped to cheer us up. If you're looking for a meal in the early hours, this is a good spot: it's open until 3am.
Babies and children welcome: high chairs. Booking advisable weekends. Entertainment: karaoke (phone for details). Takeaway service. Vegetarian menu. **Map 17 C4.**

金龍堡
Dragon Castle
This is an outpost of fine Guangzhou cuisine in a part of the metropolis, long denigrated but soon to be made new.
This is an oasis of taste fortified with the sure touch to provide pleasures to the palate and satisfaction to the being.
This is the watering hole where dire thirst is quenched by tea and the fermented grape juice intoxicates.
This is where your heart is touched (dim sum) and your spirit is replete.
This is
Dragon Castle
Dragon Castle
100 Walworth Road
Elephant & Castle
London SE17 1JL
020 7277 3388
info@dragoncastle.eu
www.dragoncastle.eu
金龍堡

Phoenix Palace

Clerkenwell & Farringdon

Old China Hand

8 Tysoe Street, EC1R 4RQ (7278 7678/www.oldchinahand.co.uk). Angel tube/19, 38, 341 bus. **Lunch/dim sum served** noon-3pm Tue-Fri. **Dinner/dim sum served** 6-10pm Tue-Sat. **Meals/dim sum served** noon-6pm Sun. **Dim sum** £4-£4.80. **Main courses** £6.80-£7.80. **Credit** MC, V.

Is there anywhere better in London to drink beer, watch football and feast on dim sum? This pub/Chinese restaurant is steered and cheffed by Ngan Tung Cheung, formerly of the Dorchester hotel's (now closed) Michelin-starred Oriental restaurant. The business began with great promise in 2006, yet has spent its second year searching for its feet. The decor is pub-like – the walls an industrial slate grey, the furniture cobbled together out of bits of trees. Food on our visit ranged from the sublime to the disappointing. Steamed vegetable dumplings with wrappers coloured green by broccoli had a subtlety that betrayed the pedigree of the chef; honey-barbecued pork was wonderfully sweet; and pork and prawn dumplings tasted far fresher than in many Chinatown spots. However, pan-fried and steamed chilli chicken was sickly sweet, and drowned in a red sauce that tasted of tomato paste. Vegetable chow mein was a mass of bland fried noodles with very few vegetables; it required a heavy dose of chilli sauce to muster any flavour. We might head here for the football and the unusual atmosphere, but Old China Hand isn't yet a destination for dim sum.

Babies and children admitted (until 6pm). Bar available for hire. Separate room for parties, seats 30. Tables outdoors (4, pavement). Takeaway service. **Map 5 N3.**

Euston

Snazz Sichuan NEW

New China Club, 37 Chalton Street, NW1 1JD (7388 0808). Euston tube/rail. **Meals served** 12.30-10.30pm daily. **Main courses** £6.50-£26.80. **Set meal** £14.80-£18.80 per person (minimum 2). **Credit** MC, V.

The bizarre tone of the decor, the enthusiasm of the staff, the skill and exuberance of the chef (Yang Xiukui, from Chengdu) and the wonderful aromas are testament to the authenticity of London's latest exponent of Sichuanese food. The two-tier dining room is decorated with flimsy magenta curtains, bold paintings and a Cultural Revolution poster. Surrounded by hip Chinese students, we enjoyed the fiery, ma-la (hot and numbing) fare. Sichuan-style beef, cold thin slices of lung swimming in chilli oil and peanut pieces, was sensational. Equally good was white-braised pork belly in a spicy sesame oil and garlic sauce. Next, ma po dofu had firm beancurd with spring onions in a spicy, aromatic sauce accented with numbing sichuan peppercorns. Gong bao intestines was pig's offal with peanuts and red chillies in a sweet-and-sour sauce. Yu xiang qiezi (fish-flavoured aubergine) was given depth by pickled chillies, garlic and ginger – sweet, sour, spicy and hot, this dish is a gem of Sichuanese cuisine and was perfectly prepared. Sadly, the hotpot menu is not translated into English, but don't let that deter you from trying this DIY treat where you add ingredients to a bubbling cauldron.

Babies and children welcome: high chairs. Disabled: toilet. Takeaway service. Vegetarian menu. **Map 4 K3.**

Fitzrovia

★ Hakkasan (100)

8 Hanway Place, W1T 1HD (7907 1888). Tottenham Court Road tube.
Bar **Open** noon-12.30am Mon-Wed; noon-1.30am Thur-Sat; noon-midnight Sun.
Restaurant **Lunch/dim sum served** noon-3pm Mon-Fri; noon-4pm Sat, Sun. **Dinner served** 6-11.30pm Mon-Wed, Sun; 6pm-12.30am Thur-Sat. **Dim sum** £3-£20. **Main courses** £9.50-£58.
Both **Credit** AmEx, MC, V.

Eating at Hakkasan – Alan's Yau's other Michelin-starred restaurant, in addition to Yauatcha (*see p80*) – is still a glamorous affair. Getting past the bouncer might puff up your ego a bit, and the sense of occasion will only be reinforced when you slide into the moody 1930s Shanghai-style basement dining room. Tables are separated by geometric wooden screens, the lighting is low, and diners tend to be fashionable or on expense accounts. Stop at the bar for a cocktail or go straight for the food, which is exceptional 'creative Chinese' (as our server put it). Braised Duke of Berkshire pork belly in a clay pot was typical: perfectly cooked, top-notch ingredients. Deep-fried soft-shell crab had been beautifully spiked with chillies; hot and sour soup, with abalone and tofu, was far more delicate than its Chinatown counterparts. Pi pa duck had the crispest of skin in a classy spiced plum sauce; and braised tofu in broth was a study in textural contrasts, with smooth deep-fried own-made beancurd juxtaposed with rubbery fungi and expertly cooked spinach. This is sophisticated and thought-provoking Chinese-inspired food, and must qualify as one of the chicest nights out in the capital. Pity, then, that the wine list is pretentious; luckily, the staff are friendly and can advise.

Babies and children admitted (until 7.30pm). Disabled: toilet. Entertainment: DJs 9pm daily. Restaurant available for hire. Separate room for parties, seats 65. **Map 17 C2.**

Holborn

Shanghai Blues

193-197 High Holborn, WC1V 7BD (7404 1668/www.shanghaiblues.co.uk). Holborn tube.
Bar **Open/dim sum served** noon-11.30pm daily.

Restaurant **Meals served** noon-11.30pm, **dim sum served** noon-5pm daily. **Main courses** £7-£40. **Set lunch** £15 per person (minimum 2). *Both* **Dim sum** £3-£20. **Credit** AmEx, JCB, MC, V.
Evoking the decadence of 1920s Shanghai with its high ceilings, oversized lanterns and silk panels, Shanghai Blues exudes elegance yet has the intimacy of a tea house. It encompasses Cantonese, Shanghainese and Sichuanese cuisine in an extensive menu that's refreshingly different. As well as classics such as sweet and sour pork and dim sum appetisers, there is – at the other end of the scale – foie gras with Chilean sea bass in soy sauce. We started with fresh, tangy shanghai xiao long pork dumplings, and, from the chef's specials, an unusual dish of assorted mushrooms served cold; we loved the delicate sauce with a hint of fresh chilli and star anise combining with the crunchy texture of the mushrooms. Steamed dover sole with ginger and shiitake mushroom (a main course) was subtly flavoured and beautifully presented, but the real highlight was a meltingly-tender braised pork belly cooked in herbs and sweet vinegar. Vegetarians are amply catered for with creative variations on classic Chinese Buddhist fare. Service was extremely friendly and efficient, despite a huge birthday party taking place in the restaurant's trendy bar. Wine lovers should be pleased with the extensive choice too.
Booking essential dinner. Disabled: toilet. Dress: smart casual. Entertainment: jazz 6.30-9.30pm Fri, 9pm-late Sat. Separate room for parties, seats 30. Takeaway service. Vegetarian menu. **Map 18 E2.**

Knightsbridge

Mr Chow

151 Knightsbridge, SW1X 7PA (7589 7347/ www.mrchow.com). Knightsbridge tube. **Lunch served** 12.30-3pm, **dinner served** 7pm-midnight daily. **Main courses** £12.50-£25. **Set lunch** £25. **Set dinner** £35; £40 per person (minimum 3). **Credit** AmEx, DC, MC, V.
A glamorous institution in its late 20th-century heyday, Mr Chow still draws a pedigree crowd. Its chic interior has a retro elegance that's offset by modern art on the walls. The food may be Chinese, but the waiters are Italian, there's a champagne trolley and you can have tiramisu for dessert. The unusually short menu is geared towards Western palates, but is nevertheless competently executed. Salt and pepper prawns were salty and crisp, topped with a moreish combination of spring onions, sliced chilli and fried garlic. Shanghai 'little dragon' buns were innocent-looking small steamed parcels that burst to release hot savoury stock and a beautifully moist porky filling – delicious. Glazed pork comprised two small, wonderfully tender and sweet cubes of pork belly. 'Gambler's duck' (better known as crispy aromatic duck) was also excellent, and notable for the translucent pancakes with which it was served. Mr Chow has everything you would expect from dining in Knightsbridge: smartly appointed surroundings, slick service, dependably good food – and elevated prices.
Babies and children admitted. Booking advisable lunch; essential dinner. Separate rooms for parties, seating 20, 50 and 75. **Map 8 F9.**

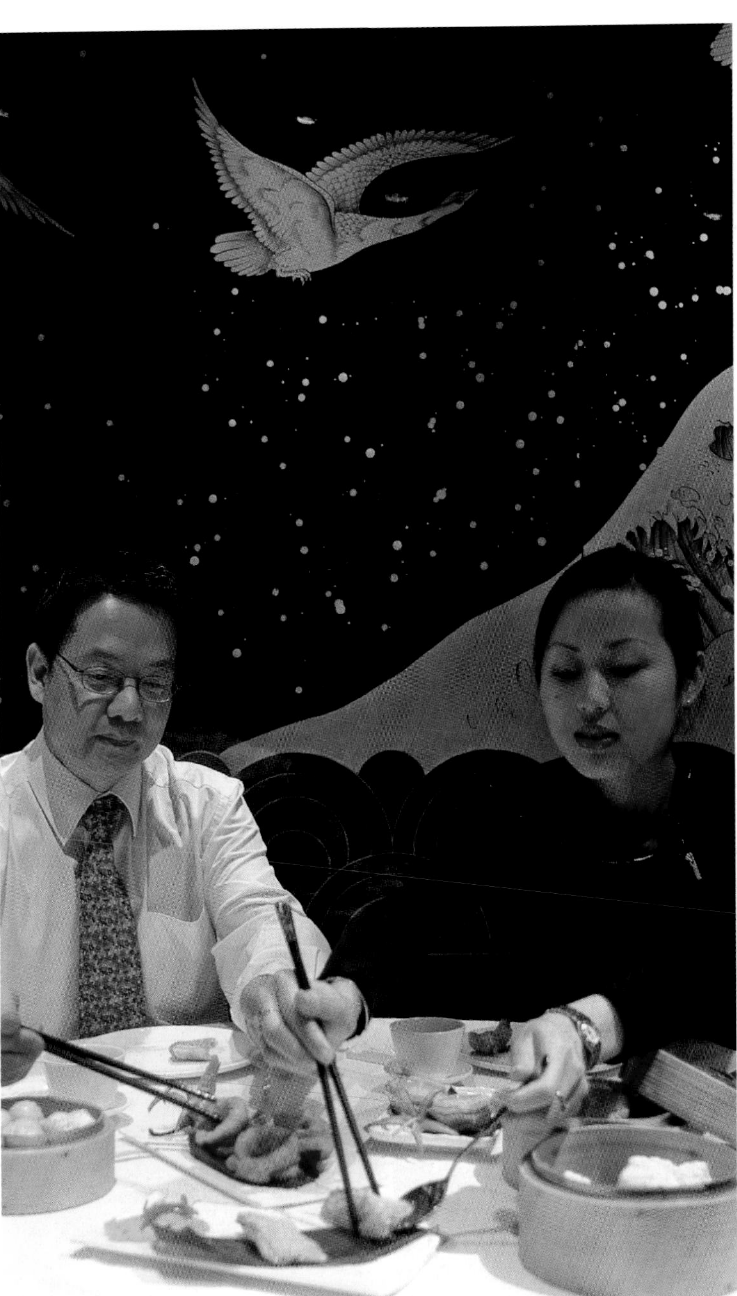

Royal China Fulham. See p82.

Marylebone

★ Phoenix Palace

5 Glentworth Street, NW1 5PG (7486 3515). Baker Street tube. **Meals served** noon-11.30pm Mon-Sat; 11am-10.30pm Sun. **Dim sum served** noon-5pm Mon-Sat; 11am-5pm Sun. **Dim sum** £2-£3.80. **Main courses** £6.50-£25. **Set meal** £24 per person (minimum 2). **Credit** AmEx, JCB, MC, V.
One of London's most consistently excellent Chinese restaurants, located conveniently near the Chinese Embassy, Phoenix Palace is frequented by the capital's smarter Chinese residents. It's also popular with the British establishment, judging by the photos of visiting grandees (Tony Blair among them). The dim sum are superb – on a par with, and at times eclipsing, those served at the Royal China restaurants – and terrifically good value. On our most recent visit, crispy scallop dumplings melted in the mouth, while the pork and prawn turnip patty (aka turnip paste) was possibly the best we've had in London. Parcels of glutinous rice in lotus leaves were unusually interesting, with chunks of duck accompanying the usual chicken and wind-dried sausage. Steamed prawn and pea-shoot dumplings were fresh and vibrant. Minor off-notes included the cheung fun, with a dough-stick stuffing that had been over-fried and was greasy. The main menu sings too: look out, in particular, for the chef's specials. The dining room is smart and comfortable (think upmarket Hong Kong), and service generally friendly, if a little scatty.
Babies and children welcome: high chairs. Booking advisable. Separate rooms for parties, seating 10 and 20. Takeaway service; delivery service (over £10 within 1-mile radius). Vegetarian menu. **Map 2 F4.**

Royal China

24-26 Baker Street, W1U 3BZ (7487 4688/ www.royalchinagroup.co.uk). Baker Street or Marble Arch tube. **Meals served** noon-11pm Mon-Thur; noon-11.30pm Fri, Sat; 11am-10pm Sun. **Dim sum served** noon-5pm daily. **Dim sum** £2.30-£4.60. **Main courses** £7.50-£26. **Set meal** £30-£38 per person (minimum 2). **Credit** AmEx, MC, V.
Comfortably furnished in chic shades of taupe and gold, the classy dining room and gleaming crockery at the Baker Street branch of this well-regarded chain promise a fine-dining experience. Normally the Royal Chinas can be relied on for top-notch dim sum. How disappointing then, to be so let down by the food on our last visit. With the exception of a chef's special of sea bass and mango rolls, which proved to be an unusual but

Gold Mine. See p82.

lovely blend of flavours, the other dim sum dishes we tried were painfully mediocre. Glutinous rice in lotus leaf, pan-fried turnip cakes, beef cheung fun rice rolls and prawn dumplings were fine but forgettable; greasy sesame-coated duck spring rolls and barbecued spare ribs coated in sauce, less so (bad dim sum is rare enough to be memorable). Dishes seemed also to be abnormally saturated with MSG, and service was cold and indifferent to the point of rudeness. We were baffled by the experience and hope it was an aberration. Otherwise, a return to form is needed.
Babies and children welcome: high chairs. Booking essential. Separate room for parties, seats 15. Takeaway service. Vegetarian menu. **Map 9 G5.**

★ Royal China Club

40-42 Baker Street, W1U 7AJ (7486 3898/ www.royalchinaclub.co.uk). Baker Street or Marble Arch tube. **Meals/dim sum served** noon-11pm Mon-Thur; noon-11.30pm Fri, Sat; noon-10.30pm Sun. **Dim sum** £2.60-£6.80. **Main courses** £9.50-£28. **Set lunch** £15. **Set meal** £17-£45 per person (minimum 2). **Credit** AmEx, JCB, MC, V.

The sleek dining room contains fish tanks, where enormous lobsters and crabs creep around; the shiny black bar is stocked with an array of impressive wines and beers; and polite servers bustle around in smart black suits. This is all very pleasant, but nothing extraordinary – unlike the food. Royal China Club serves some of the best and most interesting dim sum in London, with a forte in shellfish. The xiao long bao were exceptional: extra-large soup dumplings filled with a gingery ball of pork and crab surrounded by broth. Exquisite triangular dumplings with a subtle vegetable medley of mushrooms and cabbage were infused with the pungent flavour of fermented beancurd. Lighter-than-air scallop dumplings had their fillings boosted by fragments of water chestnut, spring onions and coriander. Soups from the dinner menu – lobster and spinach soup, brilliantly green and with a thickened, rich broth of unmistakable lobster flavour; and bamboo and coriander sliced fish soup – were perfect examples of the intelligent combinations and delicate flavours the kitchen can produce. The wide range of teas is also a highlight. The menu contains too many items accompanied by salad cream (though this is a favourite dip in Hong Kong) – but Royal China Club is a treat.
Babies and children welcome: high chairs. Booking advisable Sat, Sun. Disabled: toilet. Separate room for parties, seats 24. Takeaway service. **Map 9 G5.**

Mayfair

China Tang (100)

The Dorchester, 53 Park Lane, W1K 1QA (7629 9988/www.thedorchester.com). Hyde Park Corner tube.
Bar **Open/dim sum served** 11am-1am Mon-Sat; 11am-midnight Sun.
Restaurant **Meals/dim sum served** 11am-midnight daily. **Main courses** £16-£45.
Both **Dim sum** £4-£22. **Credit** AmEx, DC, MC, V.

Entrepreneur David Tang's opulently decorated restaurant combines 1930s Shanghai art deco with modern art and chinoiserie to create a space as grand as the Dorchester hotel in which it is housed. With such lavish surroundings, it's surprising the menu features casual home-style Cantonese dishes, such as congee (rice porridge), alongside such banquet dishes as three courses of peking duck (which consistently rates among London's best). Add an all-day dim sum menu and you have the potential for a meal consisting of an eclectic mix of dishes that may appeal more to Westerners than Chinese diners. The cooking is of a high standard and proudly MSG-free. Fried prawns with spicy salt and pepper were bouncy, coated in crisp batter and delectably moreish. Shanghai dumplings were delicately formed and juicy, but let down a little by a pork filling that was grainy in texture. We loved the deeply flavourful pi pa duck – roasted duck flattened to look like a pi pa (Chinese stringed instrument). Prices are high, as you might expect, but service was abysmal on our visit. We were

given a wine list that was unaccountably missing the pages of lower-priced wines; staff were incapable of explaining dishes; there were lengthy waits; and our bill was presented incorrectly – twice.
Babies and children welcome: high chairs. Disabled: lift; toilet. Dress: smart casual. Separate rooms for parties, seating 18-50. **Map 9 G7.**

Kai Mayfair

65 South Audley Street, W1K 2QU (7493 8988/ www.kaimayfair.co.uk). Bond Street or Marble Arch tube. **Lunch served** noon-2.15pm Mon-Fri; 12.30-3pm Sat, Sun. **Dinner served** 6.30-10.45pm Mon-Sat; 6.30-10.30pm Sun. **Main courses** £13-£54. **Set lunch** £24 3 courses. **Credit** AmEx, DC, JCB, MC, V.
Kai aims to show off the breadth of China's culinary possibilities, and the depth of customers' pockets. Extravagantly named dishes ('parcels of prosperity' are prawn and vegetable dumplings), at extravagant prices (£108 for shark's fin and abalone soup), are served to diners who scream wealth, in a dining room that whispers luxury. The menu combines classic dishes (peking duck, sweet and sour pork) and unconventional ingredients (wasabi prawns, stir-fried ostrich with three chillies) with mixed success. A signature dish of braised peking chicken boasted remarkably soft slices of chicken breast in a lovely ginger stock reduction, but was marred by an over-zealous squeeze of lemon. Ostrich with three chillies was perfectly cooked and intensely spiced, but tasted as if saturated with MSG. Beancurd and vegetable chai chang sah, however, was faultless: lively flavours, delicate textures. Staff attempted to be solicitous, but didn't quite succeed. A glass of corked white wine was graciously replaced – by an equally corked substitute. Still, given the quality and variety of the food, this is an experience worth repeating – assuming you've got a generous expense account.
Babies and children welcome: high chairs. Booking advisable. Entertainment: harpist (twice weekly; phone for details). Separate rooms for parties, seating 6 and 12. **Map 9 G7.**

Princess Garden

8-10 North Audley Street, W1K 6ZD (7493 3223/ www.princessgardenofmayfair.com). Bond Street tube. **Lunch served** noon-4pm Mon-Fri; noon-4.30pm Sat, Sun. **Dinner served** 6.30pm-midnight Mon-Sat; 6.30-11pm Sun. **Dim sum served** noon-4pm daily. **Dim sum** £2.30-£3.80. **Main courses** £7.50-£12. **Set lunch** £12 per person (minimum 2). **Set dinner** £30-£45 per person (minimum 2). **Credit** AmEx, DC, JCB, MC, V.
Princess Garden celebrated its silver anniversary in 2007, but a recent refurbishment means it doesn't look its age. The dining room – now bright, airy and elegant – wasn't the only thing to change. The new management has also introduced daily dim sum, which now rates among the best in London. Nicely handmade standards such as har gau (prawn dumplings) and siu mai (pork dumplings) proved good choices, but we also enjoyed less common versions such as pak choi with seafood, and scallop with gai lan (chinese broccoli). Prawn cheung fun were also up to par: soft, silky, translucent wrappers enveloping crisp king prawn. Competently prepared Anglo-Chinese dishes dominate the short à la carte menu, so aficionados may be disappointed. With a good wine list and polite, if occasionally stiff, service, this is a good choice for business dining. It will also be enjoyed by diners looking for fine weekend dim sum without the usual crowds.
Babies and children welcome: high chairs. Booking advisable. Separate rooms for parties, seating 6-50. Takeaway service. **Map 9 G6.**

Paddington

★ Pearl Liang NEW

2007 RUNNER-UP BEST DESIGN

8 Sheldon Square, W2 6EZ (7289 7000). Paddington tube/rail. **Meals served** noon-11pm daily. **Main courses** £6.80-£28. **Set meal** £20 per person (minimum 2); £35-£65 per person (minimum 4). **Credit** MC, V.
The new plaza in the Paddington Central development, where Pearl Liang is located, was deserted on our evening visit, but the restaurant was welcoming. A sumptuous black marble bar, floor-to-ceiling bamboo poles, a dark wooden screen and a giant wooden abacus, as well as the all-important fountain and fish pond (a portent of money), greet diners on arrival. Banquettes and chairs are fuchsia-pink, and frosted glass panels are decorated with golden motifs from Shang dynasty bronzes. Staff were friendly and solicitous, and the dim sum is rightly famed. We ordered courgette prawn dumplings as a starter and weren't disappointed; the wrappers were silk-thin, the stuffings a delightful melange of titbits with pleasing tastes and textures. Duck slices chiu chow-style was an unusual treat: five-spiced duck with beancurd in a rich gravy (off-menu, we asked for the traditional accompaniment of garlic-in-vinegar, which wasn't provided). The quality of the food suggested we'd be safe with a five-willow, sweet and sour dover sole; it was skilfully cooked, but the sauce looked as if it had been coloured artificially. Gai lan (chinese broccoli) with ginger was superbly wokked, and the unusual fried rice with dried scallop and egg white splendidly light and fragrant. There's some top-class talent in the kitchen here – we'll be back soon for a lunchtime dumpling extravaganza.
Babies and children welcome: high chairs. Booking advisable. Separate room for parties, seats 40. Takeaway service. **Map 8 D5.**

Soho

★ Bar Shu (100)

28 Frith Street, W1D 5LF (7287 6688). Leicester Square or Tottenham Court Road tube. **Meals served** noon-11.30pm Mon-Sat; noon-11pm Sun. **Main courses** £7-£28. **Credit** AmEx, MC, V.
Dramatic Chinese opera masks, big lanterns and ornate wooden screens help create excitement in this corner restaurant in the bustling heart of Soho. So too does the menu. Bar Shu is one of the few London restaurants dedicated to Sichuanese

food: a cuisine characterised by fiery chilli and numbing sichuan pepper. The menu provides clear descriptions and photographs of most dishes, but (thankfully) all our food looked better than portrayed. We began with a cold dish of cucumber, wood-ear fungus, bean-jelly ribbon (like a chewy noodle) and beancurd skin. This came with spicy pork, which the waitress told us about when we ordered, and a delicious sauce of chinkiang vinegar, soy sauce and sugar to toss through the salad. Hot and sour soup was thick but more peppery than sour, while fiery dan dan noodles were delightfully tangy. Next, chengdu dry-braised sea bass combined meltingly tender fish with a complex spicy sauce. Flavoursome gong bao chicken had crunch provided by peanuts and thick, dried sichuan chillies.There was a great choice of Chinese greens, and service was extremely helpful. Bar Shu isn't for the faint-hearted, but it's a joy to taste such wonderfully authentic flavours.
Babies and children welcome: high chairs. Booking advisable. Disabled: toilet. Separate room for parties, seats 15. **Map 17 C3**.

★ Yauatcha

15 Broadwick Street, W1F 0DL (7494 8888). Leicester Square, Oxford Circus, Piccadilly Circus or Tottenham Court Road tube.
Tea house **Tea/snacks served** 11am-11.45pm Mon-Sat; 11am-10.45pm Sun. **Set tea** £19-£26.50.
Restaurant **Meals served** noon-11.45pm Mon-Sat; noon-10.45pm Sun.
Both **Dim sum served** noon-11.45pm Mon-Sat; noon-10.45pm Sun. **Dim sum** £3-£14.50. **Main courses** £7.80-£38. **Credit** AmEx, JCB, MC, V.
Alan Yau's Michelin-starred Yauatcha is still shockingly popular. At dinnertime you must fight through crowds waiting in the small space inside the entrance to reach the basement restaurant, which is a cacophony of media chatter and loud, pulsing music. The decor is dark and star-spangled; the ground-floor space, where you can eat dim sum as well as first-class pâtisserie, blends cool minimalism with the ranked jars of a traditional Chinese tea house. The food is excellent, whether you order from the extensive dim sum menu (served until late into the evening) or the smaller selection of main courses. Our lobster dumplings and chive dumplings, stained green by chive juice, were devastatingly beautiful and delicately flavoured. Mushroom cheung fun slid down sexily; mango and prawn rolls were crisp and juicy. Main dishes were a little oversalted, but good nonetheless: crispy lamb with an arresting shiso and sour plum dip; and baby pak choi stir-fried briskly with morsels of salted fish. The only blight was the mooli puffs stuffed with prawn, sweet potato and dried scallop, which had an odour of ammonia – just as they did last time we ate here. The tea menu is a highlight, although infusions are served without tea leaves, so you can't enjoy subsequent brewings. Service can be aloof or friendly: pot-luck, it seems.
Babies and children admitted. Booking advisable (restaurant). Disabled: lift; toilet. Takeaway service (tea house). **Map 17 B3**.

Yming

35-36 Greek Street, W1D 5DL (7734 2721/ www.yminglondon.com). Leicester Square, Piccadilly Circus or Tottenham Court Road tube.
Meals served noon-11.45pm Mon-Sat. **Main courses** £7-£15. **Set lunch** (noon-6pm) £10. **Set meal** £16-£22 per person (minimum 2). **Credit** AmEx, DC, JCB, MC, V.
This long-time favourite has earned many accolades for its cooking, which focuses on northern Chinese dishes such as anise-scented gansu duck. Its location in the heart of Soho adds to the allure, particularly among Western diners, who see Yming as a refreshing counterpoint to the gaudy eateries of nearby Chinatown. Certainly, the friendly, efficient staff distinguish this venue from its cantankerous cousins. A request for rapid, pre-theatre service was impressively fulfilled; dishes arrived hot on the table minutes after we were seated. The cooking evinced a similarly no-nonsense approach: tasty, authentic, but hardly grand. A house speciality of double-braised pork

The art of dim sum

The Cantonese term 'dim sum' can be translated as 'touch the heart'. It is used to refer to the vast array of dumplings and other titbits that southern Chinese people like to eat with their tea for breakfast or at lunchtime. This eating ritual is simply known as 'yum cha', or 'drinking tea' in Hong Kong. Many of London's Chinese restaurants have a lunchtime dim sum menu, and at weekends you'll find them packed with Cantonese families. A dim sum feast is one of London's most extraordinary gastronomic bargains: how else can you lunch lavishly in one of the capital's premier restaurants for as little as £15 a head?

Dim sum are served as a series of tiny dishes, each bearing two or three dumplings, perhaps, or a small helping of steamed spare ribs or seafood. Think of it as a Chinese version of tapas, served with tea. You can order according to appetite or curiosity; a couple of moderate eaters might be satisfied with half a dozen dishes, while Time Out's greedy reviewers always end up with a table laden with little snacks. Some people like to fill up with a plateful of stir-fried noodles, others to complement the meal with stir-fried greens from the main menu. But however wildly you order, if you stick to the dim sum menu and avoid more expensive specials that waiting staff may wave under your nose, the modesty of the bill is sure to come as a pleasant surprise. The low price of individual dishes (most cost between £1.80 and £3) makes eating dim sum the perfect opportunity to try more unusual delicacies: chicken's feet, anyone?

Two of London's Chinese restaurants serve dim sum Hong Kong-style, from circulating trollies: the cheerful **New World** (*see p74*) and the less-cheerful **Chuen Cheng Ku** (17 Wardour Street, W1D 6PJ, 7437 1398, map 17 B/C5). Some of the snacks are wheeled out from the kitchen after being cooked; others gently steam as they go or are finished on the trolley to order. The trolley system has the great advantage that you see exactly what's offered, but if you go at a quiet lunchtime some of the food may be a little jaded by the time it reaches you. Other places offer snacks à la carte, so everything should be freshly cooked.

Dim sum lunches at the weekend tend to be boisterous occasions, so they are great for children (take care, though, as adventurous toddlers and hot dumpling trollies are not a happy combination). Strict vegetarians are likely to be very limited in their menu choices, as most snacks contain either meat or seafood – honourable exceptions include **Golden Palace** and **Local Friends**, which have generous selections of vegetarian snacks.

HOW TO EAT DIM SUM

Restaurants used to cease serving dim sum at 4pm or 5pm, when the rice-based evening menus took over. These days, however, since dim sum became fashionable outside the Chinese community, several establishments serve them all day and into the night. Dim sum specialists always list the snacks on separate, smaller menus, which are roughly divided into steamed dumplings, deep-fried dumplings, sweet dishes and so on. Try to order a selection of different types of food, with plenty of light steamed dumplings to counterbalance the heavier deep-fried

snacks. If you are lunching with a large group, make sure you order multiples of everything, as most portions consist of about three dumplings.

Tea is the traditional accompaniment. Some restaurants offer a selection of teas, although they may not tell you this unless you ask. Musty bo lay (pu'er in Mandarin Chinese), grassy Dragon Well (long jing) or fragrant Iron Buddha (tie guan yin) are delicious alternatives to the jasmine blossom that is usually served by default to non-Chinese guests. Waiters should keep teapots filled throughout the meal; leave the teapot lid tilted at an angle or upside down to signal that you want a top-up. **Royal China Club** and **Yauatcha** have the most extensive lists of Chinese teas, with many fine leaves.

WHERE TO EAT DIM SUM

London's best dim sum are found at the **Royal China Club** (*see p78*), **Hakkasan** (*see p76*), **Yauatcha** (*see left*) and newcomer **Pearl Liang** (*see p79*), which offer sublime dumplings in glamorous settings; at the typically Cantonese **Phoenix Palace** (*see p77*) or **Dragon Castle** (*see p84*); and at any of the other **Royal China** restaurants – in Marylebone (*see p77*), Bayswater (*see p82*), Fulham (*see p82*), Docklands (*see p85*) and St John's Wood (*see p87*), which all have particularly exciting specials. If you're eating in Chinatown, **Royal Dragon** (*see p74*) and **Imperial China** (*see p73*) are a cut above the rest. Outside central London, try **Shanghai** (*see p85*) in Dalston, **Peninsula** (*see p84*) in Greenwich, **Royal China** in Putney (*see p84* – no longer part of the Royal China chain), **Golden Palace** (*see p87*) in Harrow and **Mandarin Palace** (*see p87*) in Gants Hill. Also, **Super Star** (*see p85*) in Docklands now has a renowned dim sum specialist in the kitchen.

Below is a a guide to the basic canon of dim sum served in London:

Char siu bao: fluffy steamed bun stuffed with barbecued pork in a sweet-savoury sauce.
Char siu puff pastry or **roast pork puff**: triangular puff-pastry snack, filled with barbecued pork, scattered with sesame seeds and baked in an oven.
Cheung fun: slithery sheets of steamed rice pasta wrapped around fresh prawns, barbecued pork, deep-fried dough sticks, or other fillings, splashed with a sweet soy-based sauce. For some non-Chinese the texture is an acquired taste.
Chiu chow fun gwor: soft steamed dumpling with a wheat-starch wrapper, filled with pork, vegetables and peanuts. Chiu chow is a regional Chinese cooking style popular in Hong Kong.
Chive dumpling: steamed prawn meat and chinese chives in a translucent wrapper.
Har gau: steamed minced prawn dumpling with a translucent wheat-starch wrapper.
Nor mai gai or **steamed glutinous rice in lotus leaf**: lotus-leaf parcel enclosing moist sticky rice with chicken, mushrooms, salty duck-egg yolks and other bits and pieces, infused with the herby fragrance of the leaf.
Paper-wrapped prawns: tissue-thin rice paper enclosing plump prawn meat, sometimes scattered with sesame seeds, deep-fried.
Sago cream with yam: cool, sweet soup of coconut milk with sago pearls and morsels of taro.
Scallop dumpling: delicate steamed dumpling filled with scallop (sometimes prawn) and vegetables.
Shark's fin dumpling: small steamed dumpling with a wheaten wrapper pinched into a frilly cockscomb shape on top, stuffed with a mix of pork, prawn and slippery strands of shark's fin.
Siu loon bao or **xiao long bao**: Shanghai-style round dumpling with a whirled pattern on top and a juicy minced pork and soup filling.
Siu mai: little dumpling with an open top, a wheat-flour wrapper and a minced pork filling. Traditionally topped with crab coral, although minced carrot and other substitutes are common.
Taro croquette or **yam croquette**: egg-shaped, deep-fried dumpling with a frizzy, melt-in-your mouth outer layer made of mashed taro, and a savoury minced pork filling.
Turnip paste: a heavy slab of creamy paste made from glutinous rice flour and white oriental radishes, studded with fragments of wind-dried pork, sausage and dried shrimps and fried to a golden brown on either side.

with preserved vegetables could have benefited from a longer simmer in more robust juices; salt and pepper squid could have done with a lighter touch at the deep fryer. However, stir-fried braised aubergines were roundly satisfying in flavour and structure. The speedy service may have compromised the quality of cooking, but not enough to detract from the overall impression of a down-to-earth restaurant that delivers reliable and reasonably good food.
Babies and children admitted. Booking essential weekends. Separate rooms for parties, seating 10 and 18. Takeaway service. **Map 17 C4**.

West

Acton

North China

305 Uxbridge Road, W3 9QU (8992 9183/ www.northchina.co.uk). Acton Town tube/207 bus. **Lunch served** noon-2.30pm, **dinner served** 6-11pm daily. **Main courses** £5-£12.80. **Set meal** £14-£22.50 per person (minimum 2). **Credit** AmEx, MC, V.

Although its mottled orange walls aren't much to look at, this little outpost of northern Chinese cooking is well worth a visit. The simple, robust flavours of the region are mild compared to those of the spicy-hot western provinces, but no less interesting. Ask for the special menu to see for yourself. We started with grilled dumplings and a selection of cold starters. The dumplings were juicy and delicious, stuffed with seasoned pork, cabbage and ginger, and fried until crisp on one side. Smoked fish, jelly of pork with garlic and soy sauces and vegetarian goose (beancurd skin roll) were all commendable, and had a pleasing contrast of sweet, smoky, savoury and sour tastes with various textures. Chinese cabbage Shantung-style used rice vinegar to create a piquant sauce for the crunchy leaves, and was spiked with tiny, chewy cubes of salty Hunan ham and dried shrimp. Own-made noodles with soya beans – noodles dressed with whole yellow beans and paste, small cubes of pork, pickled green beans and cucumber shreds – was earthy and satisfying. North China is also famous for its excellent peking duck, prepared using only natural ingredients.
Babies and children welcome: high chairs. Booking advisable; essential dinner Fri, Sat. Separate room for parties, seats 36. Takeaway service; delivery service (within 2-mile radius). Vegetarian menu.

Bayswater

Four Seasons

84 Queensway, W2 3RL (7229 4320). Bayswater or Queensway tube. **Meals served** noon-11.15pm Mon-Sat; noon-10.45pm Sun. **Main courses** £5.80-£25. **Set meal** £15.50-£20 per person (minimum 2). **Credit** MC, V.

Despite barbecue chef Zhi Man Wong leaving a couple of years ago (he's now at Gold Mine, *see p82*), Four Seasons remains packed. Its popularity is evident from the collection of regulars, Chinese students and families from all cultures found queuing in the cramped reception area. Even booking doesn't guarantee immediate seating. The restaurant's speciality hangs in the front window: roasted ducks with crisp, lacquered skins and moist, tender meat. Order a whole one for a large group and watch it skilfully sliced then covered with rich, savoury roasting juices. Other dishes on the large menu are worth exploring, particularly the chef's recommendations. We dined like kings on generous portions of duck; double-cooked pork belly with yam; fat, juicy sizzling mussels with green peppers and salty black bean sauce; and a hotpot of braised aubergine with minced pork. Most notable was the pork belly – a heart-warming bowl of tender slices of belly, cushioned on sweet yams that soaked up the meaty juices. Least impressive was the braised aubergines, their charred skins giving the dish a burnt tang that interfered with the flavour of the minced pork. But order wisely, and the food here is a treat.
Babies and children admitted. Booking advisable. Takeaway service. **Map7 C6**.

SHELF LIFE

Chinatown is still the best place to look for Chinese ingredients, especially fresh produce, with several specialist supermarkets vying for your attention. But don't despair if you're not close to the West End: the two London branches of **Wing Yip** are destinations in themselves, and the principal Chinese ingredients are now readily available in big supermarkets.

Golden Gate

100 Shaftesbury Avenue, WC2H 7PR (7437 0014). Leicester Square tube. **Open** 10am-9pm daily.

This shop, located away from the main bustle of Gerrard Street, sells mainly Chinese groceries.

Loon Fung

42-44 Gerrard Street, W1V 7LP (7437 7332). Leicester Square tube. **Open** 10am-8pm daily.

This Chinese food hall has a resident butcher, but pork and pork spare parts are the only meats available. There is a wide range of processed fish products. A separate section stocks a variety of spice pastes, dry noodles, flours, sauces, canned pickles, dried spices and Chinese cooking utensils.

Wing Yip

544 Purley Way, Croydon, Surrey CR0 4NZ (8688 4880/www.wingyip.com). Waddon rail. **Open** 9.30am-7pm Mon-Sat; 11.30am-5.30pm Sun.

This massive Chinese superstore in Croydon also has a substantial selection of Vietnamese products. There's another branch in north London, in Cricklewood (as well as Manchester and Birmingham).

RESTAURANTS

Gold Mine NEW

102 Queensway, W2 3RR (7792 8331). Bayswater tube. **Meals served** noon-11.15pm daily. **Main courses** £6-£20. **Set meal** £13.50-£18. **Credit** JCB MC V.

This is the new home of barbecue chef Zhi Man Wong, who helped build the reputation of Four Seasons (*see p81*) just down the road. Large Cantonese roast ducks hang in the window – gloriously attractive, with the same shiny golden-brown colour throughout. Served cold, the duck tastes wonderful: slightly crisp, sweet skin gives way to a layer of fat that ensures moist flesh and intensely rich flavour. Wong's roast meat is similarly flawless. Char siu (honey-roast) pork was appropriately lean, with a caramelised crust. Gorgeously crisp siu yuk (roast pork belly) had the correct proportion of fat to flesh, pleasing roast connoisseurs if not dieters. The rest of the menu isn't as thrilling, but with such great barbecued meat, we're not sure we care. From the chef's specialities at the back of the menu, we selected braised aubergine and fish hotpot. It was good, with large pieces of battered fish, whole chinese dried mushrooms and large wedges of aubergine in oyster sauce. And Cantonese-style fillet steak was marvellous: tender medallions of beef sizzling in a sweet but spicy, deep-red sauce. Service was efficient rather than friendly. Tables in the brightly lit dining room can be somewhat cramped, but Gold Mine is no lame duck.

Babies and children admitted. Booking advisable weekends. **Map 7 C6**.

Magic Wok

100 Queensway, W2 3RR (7792 9767). Bayswater or Queensway tube. **Meals served** noon-11pm daily. **Main courses** £6-£14. **Set meal** £11.50-£24 per person (minimum 2). **Credit** AmEx, MC, V.

This long-established, traditionally decorated restaurant is unashamedly old-fashioned, and a great place for dishes that might be considered tired and pedestrian elsewhere. Its loyal following includes retired Chinese chefs keen to return to the good old days. Sweet and sour pork arrived surrounded by crisp batter and a bright red sauce that had a perfect (and rarely found) blend of sugar and vinegar; beef brisket noodle soup featured tender meat, rich stock and firm, thin noodles. Less common choices from the extensive, fully translated menu worked well too. Grilled minced pork and squid with salted fish, for example, was exemplary: tender patties with a smoky, crisp exterior. We also loved the braised winter melon bathed in a delicious sauce of crabmeat and egg white. The chefs are clearly capable of conjuring up the kind of superior Cantonese food that was once found on Lisle Street (when Chinatown was at its peak many years ago). Service is organised, efficient and rarely brusque, but expect the bill to appear without prompting when prospective diners are queuing outside.

Babies and children admitted. Booking advisable dinner. Separate room for parties, seats 30. Takeaway service. Vegetarian menu. **Map 7 C6**.

Mandarin Kitchen

14-16 Queensway, W2 3RX (7727 9012). Bayswater or Queensway tube. **Meals served** noon-11.30pm daily. **Main courses** £5.90-£28. **Set meal** £10.90 per person (minimum 2). **Credit** AmEx, DC, MC, V.

Queues are common at this long-established restaurant, even for diners with reservations; such is its reputation for seafood. After taking our place in line, it was surprising to see the majority of diners (mostly tourists) dodging the restaurant's renowned lobster noodles and opting instead for crispy aromatic duck. Perhaps this explains the apparent fall in standards we experienced. The meal began well. XO jellyfish with smoked chicken and arctic clam wrap was crunchy and refreshing; a couple of steamed razor clams also hit the mark. But then things went downhill. The lobster noodles with ginger and spring onion were let down by sloppy preparation; the lobster had been harshly chopped, and getting at the meat was a battle. The crustacean was also far too salty, as were companion dishes of minced prawn with gai lan (chinese broccoli) and black pepper steak. With frequently abrupt service and a cramped, dated dining room, Mandarin needs to try harder to maintain its reputation.

Babies and children welcome: high chair. Booking essential dinner. Takeaway service. **Map 7 C7**.

Ping Pong

74-76 Westbourne Grove, W2 5SH (7313 9832/www.pingpongdimsum.com). Bayswater tube. **Dim sum served** noon-11pm Mon-Wed; noon-midnight Thur-Sat; noon-10.30pm Sun. **Dim sum** £2.99-£3.99. **Set meal** £9.90-£11.90. **Credit** AmEx, MC, V.

Now with half a dozen branches, the Ping Pong chain is sweeping the capital, putting a different face on dim sum – a sleeker, more chic, but slightly sanitised face. It's a good choice for a fun night out with creative cocktails and dumpling snacks. During a recent lunch, har gau (prawn and bamboo in translucent pastry) required chilli sauce to coax out any flavour; and 'jasmine-infused chicken' came in a spring roll casing that tasted so strongly of the frying process that any subtle flavour in the chicken was undetectable. On the other hand, Ping Pong's version of shanghai pork buns, while lacking the traditional soup inside, had a pleasing note of ginger. Organic spinach wrapped around prawns with egg white was a very pleasant and light dish, typical of the chain's movement towards healthier versions of traditional dim sum. Jasmine tea was served in a tall glass, which perfectly showcased the ball of tea leaves as they unfurled and danced. The Bayswater branch is an elegant joint, where fashionable people can enjoy healthy designer (and remarkably unsalty) dim sum – but don't expect typical Chinese earthiness.

Babies and children welcome: high chairs. Booking accepted for 8 or more only. Vegetarian menu. **Map 7 B6.**

For branches see index.

Royal China (100)

13 Queensway, W2 4QJ (7221 2535/www.royalchinagroup.co.uk). Bayswater or Queensway tube. **Meals served** noon-11pm Mon-Thur; noon-11.30pm Fri, Sat; 11am-10pm Sun. **Dim sum served** noon-5pm Mon-Sat; 11am-5pm Sun. **Dim sum** £2.30-£5. **Main courses** £7.50-£50. **Set meal** £30-£38 per person (minimum 2). **Credit** AmEx, MC, V.

A glimpse into the kitchen at Royal China's flagship Queensway branch revealed energetic chefs chopping and stuffing amid a steamy haze of bamboo baskets. The restaurant is renowned for its dim sum, which include à la carte snacks as well as daily specials brought out on trays. Of the latter, we tried a cold dish of squid, coloured bright orange by chilli marinade. It made a spicy, enticing start to the meal. A serving of stir-fried morning glory helped pass the minutes before a parade of steamed delights appeared. Green dumplings filled with prawns in XO sauce, from the specials list, were a tangy departure from traditional favourites such as har gau and siu mai. Plump barbecue pork buns (char siu bao) had just the right mix of succulent pork and steamed bread; prawn cheung fun were fresh, tasty and tender. Chinese desserts are often uninspiring, but black sesame dumplings were warm, nutty, rich and totally moreish. Despite its popularity, Royal China, with its trademark mirrored interior in black and gold, isn't as noisy as many busy restaurants. Service was efficient and friendly.

Babies and children welcome: booster chairs. Booking essential Fri, Sat (not accepted lunch Sat, Sun). Separate room for parties, seats 40. Takeaway service. Vegetarian menu. **Map 7 C7.**

South West

Barnes

Chinoise

190 Castelnau, SW13 9DH (8222 8666/8748 3437). Hammersmith tube then 33, 72, 209 or 283 bus. **Lunch served** noon-2pm, **dinner served** 4.30-11pm Mon-Sat. **Meals served** noon-10pm Sun. **Main courses** £5.80-£14. **Set meal** £15.50-£19.50 per person (minimum 2). **Credit** AmEx, MC, V.

The Gallic name isn't the only surprise at this neighbourhood restaurant. At such a small, simply decorated establishment we were intrigued to find table settings befitting a banquet (gold-effect chopstick holders, fan-folded napkins) and a menu clearly divided into standard 'tourist' dishes and a section of regional north-eastern specialities. Unfortunately, on our visit the star chef wasn't on duty to do justice to the latter. Other fancy flourishes hinted at ambition in the kitchen. Our plates and bowls were warmed, and dishes arrived on heated stands; simple prawn crackers came with a sweet chilli dip, pickled vegetables and chilli-pickled chinese cabbage. The winning dish was hongshao dupian, soft slices of pig's stomach with bamboo shoots in a rich brown sauce. We also enjoyed the sanxian dumplings: own-made in a classic northern style (where the pastry is thick and comforting), served with chilli sauce and vinegar for dipping. Chinese leaves with mu'er (wood-ear mushrooms) came in a clear sweet-sour sauce and tasted just right – unlike the over-dry cumin lamb, which had been dry-fried with a surplus of overpowering cumin seeds.

Babies and children welcome: high chairs. Booking advisable. Tables outdoors (2, pavement). Takeaway service; delivery service (within 2-mile radius).

Fulham

Royal China NEW

805 Fulham Road, SW6 5HE (7731 0081/www.royalchinagroup.co.uk). Parsons Green tube. **Meals served** noon-11pm Mon-Sat; 11am-10pm

Pearl Liang. See p79.

Sun. **Dim sum served** noon-5pm Mon-Sat; 11am-5pm Sun. **Dim sum** £2.30-£4.80. **Main courses** £7.20-£28. **Set meal** £30-£38 per person (minimum 2). **Credit** AmEx, MC, V.
In 2007 Royal China Group closed Yuzu Oriental Diner, its attempt to blend Japanese and Chinese cuisines, and returned to what it knows best: Cantonese classics and dim sum in elegant surroundings. Now carrying the black and gold livery of the other Royal China siblings, this Fulham branch is much less spacious and attracts fewer Chinese diners. Even so, the kitchen seems to be maintaining high standards, albeit with a shorter menu focused on Anglo-Chinese favourites. The ubiquitous crispy aromatic duck was a little oily, but the portion was generous and perfectly seasoned. Sweet and sour pork had crisp batter, tasty meat and just enough bright red sauce to go round. A chef's special, prawn with salted egg yolk, ham and green vegetable was a revelation, the intensely flavoured salty egg giving way to crisp prawn, chewy ham and nicely perfumed choi sum. Crispy noodles topped with seafood completed an excellent meal. With the bonus of friendly and attentive service, this is the kind of high-street Chinese about which many London neighbourhoods can only dream.
Babies and children welcome: high chairs; nappy-changing facilities. Booking advisable. Disabled: toilet. Takeaway service. Vegetarian menu.

Putney

Royal China

3 Chelverton Road, SW15 1RN (8788 0907). East Putney tube/Putney rail/14, 37, 74 bus. **Lunch served** noon-3.30pm Mon-Sat; noon-4pm Sun. **Dinner served** 6.30-11pm Mon-Sat; 6.30-10.30pm Sun. **Dim sum served** noon-3.30pm daily. **Dim sum** £1.80-£5. **Main courses** £5.50-£40. **Set meal** £23-£35 per person (minimum 2). **Credit** AmEx, DC.
This Putney restaurant is no longer affiliated to the Royal China chain, but that's not immediately apparent. From the decor (glossy black lacquered walls) to the flavoursome food, it has retained many qualities that guarantee widespread appeal. However, our dim sum, though generally reliable, weren't of the highest order. The cheung fun enrobed perfectly tender prawns, but arrived lukewarm with an underseasoned sauce. Standards such as har gau (prawn dumplings), siu mai (pork dumplings), char siu bao (barbecue pork buns) and woo tau gok (taro root croquettes) satisfied, yet caused no surprises. Some dishes were simply a let-down, such as dao miu (pea shoots) that were too fibrous, and stir-fried beef with rice noodles that was tough. Going à la carte, however, yielded more rewards. The day's special of roasted pork belly was first-rate: the deliciously crunchy skin provided a wonderful counterpoint to the succulent meat, with both flavour and texture sinfully enhanced by an audacious layer of fat. The wide variety of dishes and the pleasant surroundings make this Putney stalwart a decent option for those in the neighbourhood. For anyone else, though, it might not be worth the journey.
Babies and children admitted. Booking advisable (not accepted lunch Sun). Takeaway service; delivery service (within 3.5-mile radius).

South East

Elephant & Castle

★ Dragon Castle

100 Walworth Road, SE17 1JL (7277 3388/ www.dragoncastle.co.uk). Elephant & Castle tube/ rail. **Meals served** noon-11pm Mon-Thur; noon-11.30pm Fri, Sat; 11.30am-10.30pm Sun. **Main courses** £4.50-£90. **Set meals** £14.50-£33 per person (minimum 2). **Credit** AmEx, JCB, MC, V.
Amid a grim landscape of council estates, this large, brightly lit place hasn't the most auspicious of locations. Yet despite such a handicap, Dragon Castle has become one of the best Chinese restaurants in London, offering a wealth of skilfully crafted dishes that won't break the bank – including many so authentic they're not available elsewhere. Service is thoughtful and intelligent too. Our waiter patiently guided us through the vast menu, then recommended a range of faultless dishes. A cold platter to start included jellyfish tossed in sesame seeds, given sharpness by grated raw garlic. To follow, fried crispy pork with golden crushed garlic was meaty but not heavy; salt and pepper fried squid was soft but not soggy. Steamed corn-fed chicken in ginger stock was a memorable highlight: tender and fragrant meat enhanced by a powerful sauce intensified by white pepper and star-anise. Even the proverbial rice bowl was special – perfumed with shredded dried scallop and the smoke of a fiery wok. For lovers of authentic Chinese cooking, this is one destination that definitely repays the journey.
Babies and children welcome: high chairs. Booking advisable Fri, Sat. Disabled: toilet. Separate room for parties, seats 60. Takeaway service. Vegetarian menu.

Greenwich

Peninsula

Holiday Inn Express, 85 Bugsby's Way, SE10 0GD (8858 2028/www.mychinesefood.co.uk). North Greenwich tube. **Meals served** noon-11.15pm Mon-Fri; 11am-11.15pm Sat; 11am-10.45pm Sun. **Dim sum served** noon-5pm daily. **Dim sum** £2.10-£6. **Main courses** £6.20-£11. **Set meal** £15-£19 per person (minimum 2). **Credit** AmEx, MC, V.
Situated on the ground floor of the Holiday Inn Express near the O2 (formerly the Millennium Dome), this dim sum restaurant (which offers free parking) has seating for up to 450 people. It is popular with Chinese families at weekends. The decor is neutral and reminiscent of Hong Kong several decades ago. Large (and thankfully mute) TV screens dotted around the restaurant show corny food ads. The menu is written in both Chinese and English, but unless you're familiar with Chinese characters you'll need help filling in the dim sum order form. Luckily there's no shortage of staff, and service was efficient on our

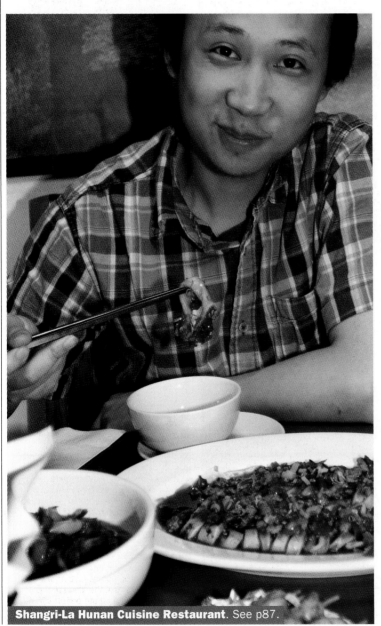

Shangri-La Hunan Cuisine Restaurant. See p87.

visit. We enjoyed the shanghai xiao long bao (tangy pork mince and broth within a dumpling), but other choices were disappointing. Scallop cheung fun was predominantly rice noodle with hardly any scallop and little flavour. Siu mai, and pork and prawn beancurd rolls, were dull. The glutinous rice in a lotus leaf was soggy, and mangetouts stir-fried with ginger were bland. Even the dessert, warm peanut-covered sesame balls, lacked inspiration. Peninsula is popular for its fresh dim sum and reasonable pricing, but the quality is no more than average.
Babies and children welcome: high chairs. Booking advisable. Disabled: toilet. Separate rooms for parties, seating 40 and 60. Takeaway service. Vegetarian menu.

East

Docklands

Royal China

30 Westferry Circus, E14 8RR (7719 0888/ www.royalchinagroup.co.uk). Canary Wharf tube/DLR/Westferry DLR. **Meals served** noon-11pm Mon-Thur; noon-11.30pm Fri, Sat; 11am-10pm Sun. **Dim sum served** noon-5pm daily. **Dim sum** £2.20-£4.50. **Main courses** £7-£40. **Set meal** £30-£38 per person (minimum 2). **Credit** AmEx, DC, JCB, MC, V.
There will always be hits and misses on a menu as extensive as Royal China's, but the group deserves its reputation for consistently reliable standards of cooking, particularly its wonderful dim sum. Hot, deep-fried starters of spicy squid, smoked chicken slivers, prawn balls and vietnamese pancake rolls were tasty, if a little greasy. Grilled stuffed minced prawn with scallops came with a tangy dipping sauce and were pleasingly bouncy in texture, with a crisp exterior. We also relished a wonderfully rich, soft and savoury dish of beef brisket and turnip – chunks of beef slowly braised and served bubbling in its clay pot. (Turnips are a delicious addition as they soak up the rich juices without losing shape, forming the perfect partner for the tender meat.) Beansprouts are notoriously hard to fry to crunchy tenderness, due to their high water content; ours were satisfyingly dry and crisp and spiked with small pieces of salted fish that provided a flavour punch. The location is superb too, especially the capacious terrace; there are few Chinese restaurants in London where you can sit outside next to the Thames in good weather.
Babies and children welcome: booster chairs. Booking advisable; essential lunch Mon-Fri. Disabled: toilet. Separate room for parties, seats 40. Tables outdoors (26, terrace). Takeaway service. **Map 24 A2.**

Super Star NEW

2 Western Gateway, Royal Victoria Dock North, E16 1DR (7474 0808/www.superstar london.com). Custom House DLR. **Meals served** noon-11pm Mon-Thur, Sun; noon-11.30pm Fri, Sat. **Dim sum served** noon-5pm daily. **Dim sum** £1.10-£2.40. **Main courses** £6.50-£28. **Set meal** £16.50-£28.50 per person (minimum 2). **Credit** AmEx, MC, V.
Until recently, this spacious restaurant was merely surviving, turning out competent Cantonese classics to irregular conference visitors. But its fortunes have been transformed by the arrival of a true superstar: dim sum chef Man Wai Lau, formerly of the renowned Golden Palace (*see p87*) in Harrow. Queues of Chinese aficionados started forming on the first weekend after his arrival. From our recent visit, it's easy to see why; everything we tried was faultless. Har gau contained crisp prawn, and had wrappers with the correct amount of bite; Thai-style cuttlefish cakes were tasty and golden brown in colour; chiu chow fun gwor (dumplings stuffed with pork, vegetables and peanuts) were packed with a crunchy, spicy filling. Special praise must be reserved for the siu loon bao. The thin, almost translucent wrappers flexed as we gingerly removed them from the steaming basket; moments later, they revealed a plentiful supply of soup stock as well as minced pork – easily the best rendition of the dish in London. The restaurant's sudden popularity seems to have caught its owners off guard: there simply weren't enough staff to go round, leading to inevitable delays. This, however, was dim sum worth waiting for.
Babies and children welcome: high chairs. Booking advisable. Takeaway service.

Yi-Ban

London Regatta Centre, Dockside Road, E16 2QT (7473 6699/www.yi-ban.co.uk). Royal Albert DLR. **Meals served** noon-11pm Mon-Sat; 11am-10.30pm Sun. **Dim sum served** noon-5pm daily. **Dim sum** £2-£3.50. **Main courses** £6-£25. **Set meal** £18-£37. **Credit** AmEx, MC, V.
Despite its location in an isolated area of post-industrial E16, Yi-Ban has managed to attract a loyal following since it opened a few years ago. During the day it's a popular dim sum destination, offering fantastic views of the Royal Albert Dock and London City Airport. At night the elegant first-floor dining room is transformed by multicoloured lighting and translucent white fabric into a much more lively affair, particularly on Friday and Saturday nights when meals are accompanied by jazz music. There are three menus. The first, available until 5pm, deals with dim sum, offering competently prepared standards such as siu mai and prawn cheung fun. The second covers Anglo-Chinese favourites, including sweet and sour pork, while a third (which we've always had to request specifically) offers more unusual choices. Double-steamed daily, the intensely flavoured lai tong (house soup) proved a refreshing appetiser. Other highlights included wonderfully fragrant steamed king prawn with Chinese wine, and some moist, juicy 'quay fay' chicken, served cold and on the bone. Service has improved immensely since the restaurant's opening; our tea cups were regularly refilled, even though the place was busy.
Babies and children welcome; high chairs. Disabled: toilet. Takeaway service. Vegetarian menu.
For branch see index.

North East

Dalston

Shanghai

41 Kingsland High Street, E8 2JS (7254 2878). Dalston Kingsland rail/38, 67, 76, 149 bus. **Meals served** noon-11pm, **dim sum served** noon-5pm daily. **Dim sum** £2-£3.90. **Main courses** £5.20-£7.20. **Set meal** £13.50-£15.20 per person (minimum 2). **Credit** AmEx, MC, V.
The front room of this Dalston local used to be an eel and pie shop and much of the old decor remains. The contrast of blue-green and cream tiles, marble-topped bar and wrought-metal mirrors, with wooden booths set with china bowls and chopsticks, is reminiscent of early 20th-century Shanghai chinoiserie. The back room is less interesting, but dome skylights of stained glass lend it warmth. Snatches of pop music drifting in from the karaoke room add to the eccentric but likeable ambience. The menu claims to be 'modern Shanghai' and certainly there are some evolved dishes, although the cuisine is not strictly Shanghainese. Our most successful choice was 'moon in king prawn's tummy': minced prawn wrapped around a whole salted duck egg yolk and deep-fried, like a sort of seafood scotch egg. Not only was the presentation beautiful, the flavour was delicious. A starter of lotus root sandwich (a classic Shanghai street snack) tasted a little dry, but braised scallops stuffed with mashed prawns, with a crabmeat sauce, was full of delicate flavours and textures. We also enjoyed silky-soft steamed chicken with shiitake mushrooms.
Babies and children welcome: high chairs. Booking advisable. Disabled: toilet. Separate rooms for parties, both seating 45. Takeaway service.
Map 25 B5.

Interview

FELIX YU

Who are you?
Head chef at **Dragon Castle** (*see left*).
Eating in London: what's good about it?
There's a lot of competition in London now. Everyone is trying to create something different. At **Hakkasan** (*see p76*) they use a lot of Western ingredients to create new dishes – not authentic, but definitely interesting.
What's bad about it?
The cost. Some Chinese restaurants charge £4 for a pot of tea, and then won't even top it up! Also, various chains puport to serve dim sum, but they don't have experts running the kitchens. The most crucial part of dim sum is the timing. If people in the kitchen don't understand timing, the food suffers.
Which are your favourite London restaurants?
I know the chef at **Super Star** (*see left*), and I go to talk about Cantonese food with him. The food at **Bar Shu** (*see p79*) is excellent, but the last time I went the chillies were a bit different. It can be difficult to source authentic ingredients in London.
What single thing would most improve London's restaurant scene?
In the past five or so years, the government has allowed restaurants to bring in chefs from Hong Kong and China, which has much improved the authenticity and quality of Chinese food in London. Food has become more sophisticated, traditional and refined. It would be great if restaurants could recruit more workers with knowledge of authentic Chinese food.
Who or what has had the biggest impact on London's restaurant scene in the past 25 years?
The increasing sophistication of diners. Years ago, the skin and fat on pork belly would put people off. Now they even eat feet.

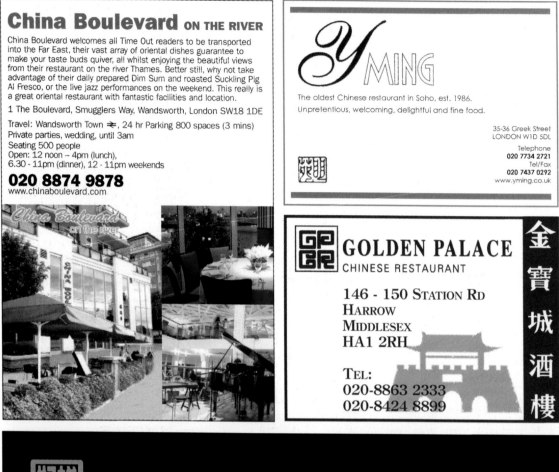

North West

Colindale

★ Shangri-La Hunan Cuisine Restaurant NEW

Oriental City, 399 Edgware Road, NW9 0JJ (8200 9838). Colindale tube. **Lunch served** 10.30am-2.30pm, **dinner served** 5-11pm Mon-Fri. **Meals served** 11am-11pm Sat, Sun. **Main courses** £1.50-£16. **Credit** MC, V.

This is the aficionado's dream – and perhaps the amateur's nightmare. A trek to Colindale and a walk through the vast Oriental City mall may make you think you're on a futile treasure hunt, but Shangri-La is, indeed, worthy of its name. Not much to look at, the restaurant occupies an unlikely corner of the mall's top floor. It's decorated with kitsch tiles and red plastic-covered tables, all evocative of a typical hole-in-the-wall restaurant in a Chinese city. As with the decor, so with the food: this is the most authentic, earthy Hunan-style cooking we've had in London. The cuisine from Chairman Mao's home province is characterised by bold chilli-laced flavours. Shangri-La's friendly staff are happy to advise in Chinese or English. Starters of cucumber with salted chillies, and five-spice beef slices made a perfect prelude to warm dishes of simple hand-shredded cabbage with pork belly, and an outstanding pot of lamb laced with hot green chillies, black beans and coriander, and cooked in paper. Reports of Oriental City's impending demise have circulated for some time, but it looks like it will finally be closing in summer 2008 – so visit while you can.

Babies and children admitted. Booking advisable. Takeaway service.

St John's Wood

Royal China

68 Queen's Grove, NW8 6ER (7586 4280/ www.royalchinagroup.co.uk). St John's Wood tube. **Meals served** noon-11pm Mon-Sat; 11am-10pm Sun. **Dim sum served** noon-4.45pm Mon-Sat; 11am-4.45pm Sun. **Dim sum** £2.30-£5. **Main courses** £7.50-£50. **Set meal** £30-£38 per person (minimum 2). **Credit** AmEx, MC, V.

In looks, the St John's Wood branch of Royal China offers 1980s oriental chic. Reflective black dropped ceiling, mirrored bar, windowless room lined in gold screens, and swirling waves on the carpet – all jar slightly with the traditional white north London building. If you can ignore this, and the offhand service, you'll have a generally enjoyable evening filled with delicate flavours. On arrival, bowls of salted peanuts and pickled cabbage are placed on each table. To start, grilled meat dumplings were plain stodge of the sort found in most local Chinese restaurants, but a soup of mustard greens, salted egg and sliced pork was a divine, light, gingery broth with delicate poached meat and generous amounts of greens. Less pleasing were the green beans (gan bian si ji dou), on the list of chef's specialities; supposedly in the Sichuanese style, they weren't at all authentic, with mushrooms, an overpowering flavour of Shaoxing wine and large pieces of pork. In contrast, succulent empress chicken was excellent, served in its own salty rich broth, with a pungent ginger-salt dipping sauce. So, a variable evening meal; it's probably better to stick with the daytime dim sum menu, which remains highly popular with Chinese and Western diners.

Babies and children welcome: high chairs. Booking advisable dinner Mon-Fri (not accepted lunch Sat, Sun). Separate rooms for parties, seating 14 and 21. Takeaway service. Vegetarian menu. **Map 2 D1**.

Swiss Cottage

★ Green Cottage

9 New College Parade, Finchley Road, NW3 5EP (7722 5305/7892). Finchley Road or Swiss Cottage tube. **Meals served** noon-11pm Mon-Sat; noon-10pm Sun. **Main courses** £5.80-£25. **Set meal** £12.50-£25 per person (minimum 2). **Credit** (over £10) AmEx, MC, V.

This traditional Cantonese restaurant is a treat. It has been feeding Swiss Cottage's Chinese population, and others, for donkey's years. The menu contains many chicken and duck dishes, a variety of offal, and the perennially popular and highly reputed roast meats. To start, paper-wrapped spare ribs were succulent and sweet; and shredded smoked chicken was well worth breaking a diet for. The meat was battered and then perfectly fried, yet still retained an infusion of smoky flavour, intelligently accented with chilli, spring onion, salt and pepper. We also enjoyed baked king prawns in salt and pepper, which arrived in their shells, providing a nice crunchy contrast to the moist meat within. The outstanding dish of our meal was roasted Cantonese duck, from the assortment displayed in the restaurant's window. The meat was served with the sauce on top, making the skin less crispy than in other restaurants, but the sweet sauce so perfectly complemented the dark meat that all was forgiven.

Babies and children admitted. Booking advisable; essential dinner. Restaurant available for hire. Takeaway service. **Map 28 B4.**

Regional cooking

Chinese cuisine is conventionally divided into four major schools: the fresh stir-fries of Cantonese cooking in the south; the sweeter, oilier food of Shanghai and the east; the strong spicy cuisine of western China (especially Sichuan and Hunan provinces); and northern cookery, which is typified by a reliance on breads and noodles, and by famous dishes such as mongolian hotpot and peking duck. Beyond these four great culinary regions, many provinces, not to mention cities and towns, have their own special dishes.

London's restaurant scene is still dominated by the Cantonese, many of whom originated in Hong Kong. Cantonese tastes have inevitably influenced the whole development of British Chinese cooking (many Cantonese people don't, for example, like spicy food, and they tend to tone down the flavours of the Sichuanese specialities on their menus).

A growing number of restaurants, however, are offering genuine regional specialities. **Bar Shu** (*see p79*) attracted widespread attention for its authentic Sichuan flavours when it opened in 2006; it has since been followed by **Snazz Sichuan** (*see p76*) and **Red'N'Hot** (59 Charing Cross Road, WC2H 0NE, 7734 8796, www.rednhotgroup.com, map 17 C4 – though not all dishes are translated on to the English menu). There's a modest but real Hunanese venue, **Shangri-La Hunan** (*see left*) in Colindale's Oriental City shopping complex, and **Hunan** (*see p71*) serves a sophisticated, Taiwanese version of Hunanese cuisine.

North China (*see p81*) serves a great cold-meat platter and a fine peking duck (prepared in three courses, including not only the familiar duck skin with pancakes, but also a duck-and-vegetable stir-fry and a final duck soup). **Mr Chow** (*see p77*) serves hand-pulled pasta (well loved by the Muslims of northern China) in spectacular fashion; watch as a chef comes out of the kitchen to whack a ball of dough into a delicate skein of noodles. For Fujianese food, visit **Fook Sing** (*see p73*) and **Rong Cheng** (72 Shaftesbury Avenue, W1D 6NA, 7287 8078, map 17 C4).

Outer London

Harrow, Middlesex

Golden Palace

146-150 Station Road, Harrow, Middx HA1 2RH (8863 2333). Harrow-on-the-Hill tube/rail. **Meals served** noon-11.30pm Mon-Sat; 11am-10.30pm Sun. **Dim sum served** noon-5pm Mon-Sat; 11am-5pm Sun. **Dim sum** £2.30-£3.20. **Main courses** £5.20-£8.50. **Set meal** £18-£26.50 per person (minimum 2). **Credit** AmEx, DC, MC, V.

Much used by local Chinese (and others from further afield), Golden Palace is widely known for the quality of its dim sum. On our last visit, however, we were disappointed by the evening menu. This makes claim to having strengths in Sichuanese and Malaysian cuisine, in addition to Cantonese food. To start, fried chilli meats and fish promised chicken, duck, squid and prawn, but the thickness of the batter made it remarkably difficult to distinguish prawn from chicken from duck. Wun tun soup was bland; the stuffing of the wun tuns was uniform and lacked the depth of flavour of either pork or prawn. Taking the server's advice, we tried a Sichuanese dish: fish-fragrant aubergine, which was a lacklustre Anglo-Canto attempt at the fiery Sichuanese original. Charcoal-roast honey pork had good flavour, but was unpleasantly tough. The hakka stuffed beancurd (a platter of tofu, green pepper and aubergine stuffed with a prawn mixture) lacked flavour. The large, ordinary-looking dining room is no reflection on the exceptional quality of the dim sum, but we suggest you skip the evening fare.

Babies and children welcome: high chairs. Booking advisable dinner. Disabled: toilet. Separate rooms for parties, seating 60 and 100. Takeaway service. Vegetarian menu.

Ilford, Essex

★ Mandarin Palace

559-561 Cranbrook Road, Gants Hill, Ilford, Essex IG2 6JZ (8550 7661). Gants Hill tube. **Lunch served** noon-4pm, **dinner served** 6.30-11.30pm Mon-Sat. **Meals served** noon-midnight Sun. **Dim sum served** noon-4pm Mon-Sat; noon-5pm Sun. **Dim sum** £2-£3.80. **Main courses** £2.50-£22. **Set dinner** £19.50-£39 per person (minimum 2). **Credit** AmEx, DC, MC, V.

From the red lanterns and faux-antique furniture to the drinks menu featuring such cocktails as brandy alexander, nothing seems to have changed at this comfortable, kitsch restaurant since it opened 30 years ago. The long menu lists more than 200 dishes, including many classics of Cantonese, Beijing and Sichuan cuisine. Almost all our food was superb. Roast duck was juicy and grease-free, with a full yet clean flavour. Pe pa special beancurd consisted of hot pillows of bland bliss, the crispy batter contrasting sublimely with the tofu's soft, fluffy interior. Cod in honey was also excellent: two perfectly cooked fillets that melted in the mouth, helped by a light, almost floral sauce. A simple dish of stir-fried morning glory stirred the senses, bathed as it was in intense (yet not overpowering) fermented beancurd. Even the humble shanghainese bun (for mopping up the juices) achieved perfection: deep-fried to a delicate, golden crisp outside, fluffy inside. The only let-down was a hotpot of braised beef brisket; the meat had not been braised for long enough, remaining tough and dry – a shame given its complex, well-balanced sauce. Service throughout was efficient and helpful.

Babies and children welcome: high chairs. Separate room for parties, seats 30. Takeaway service; delivery service (within 2-mile radius). Vegetarian menu.

For branch see index.

East European

Yes, we know these things take time, but we're getting impatient. Another year passes with precious little that is new appearing on London's east European restaurant roster. This is at odds with the number of new Europeans that have come to live and work here. True, eastern European cuisine is starting to influence our food culture – even national supermarket chains are stocking instant barszcz and Zywiec beer – yet few of the new arrivals have so far managed to set up restaurants providing the food of their homeland.

So, thank goodness this year we've had Georgia on our minds. **Tbilisi** had been flying the flag alone, then along came the fledgling **Mimino**, followed by **Little Georgia** reopening in a new location. Mimino stands out for its range of Georgian wines. Previously, these were rarely available in the UK, as most were exported to Russia; however, following a Russian import ban, Georgian wine makers have sought to widen their appeal.

Otherwise, there is stasis. **Baltic** remains the only truly glam east European destination. For a retro home-style calorie-fest, try **Daquise**, the **Czechoslovak Restaurant** or the **Polish White Eagle Club**. And you'll not do better than **Bar Polski** for quality bar food, an awesome range of vodkas and beers, and a cool stylish vibe. In contrast, old-school formality (with a friendly face) awaits at the **Gay Hussar**, London's only Hungarian restaurant. But where, oh where are the Russians? The well-established **Potemkin** remains the only serious contender, yet even this restaurant needs an injection of character.

Czech

North West

West Hampstead

★ Czechoslovak Restaurant (100)

Czech & Slovak House, 74 West End Lane, NW6 2LX (7372 1193/www.czechoslovak-restaurant.co.uk). West Hampstead tube. **Dinner served** 5-11pm Tue-Fri. **Meals served** noon-11pm Sat; noon-10.30pm Sun. **Main courses** £4.50-£12. **No credit cards.**

Come to this Hampstead stalwart for London's ultimate retro eastern European dining experience. In communist times, this was a community club for Czech and Slovak exiles, but it has now been given a boost by new arrivals in the capital yearning for a taste of home. The restaurant occupies a slightly tired-looking house awash with swirly carpets, embossed wallpaper and patriotic portraits. The food is the real deal: a chic modernist take on Czech cooking it is not. The stolid, rich dishes are perfect for pairing with Czech beers. Starters include a tasty utopenec v octe (pickled sausage), a vast juicy klobasa (frankfurter-style sausage) with piquant mustard, and a scrumptiously greasy bramborák se slaninou (potato pancake with herbs and streaky bacon). Next, you could try vepro knedlo zelo (succulent roast pork with sauerkraut and dumplings) or svícková (melt-in-the-mouth beef tenderloin drowning in an outrageously creamy vegetable sauce), which also comes with Czech dumplings (sliced, dense and torpedo-like, and fairly dry, for mopping up the sauces). Then there are yet more dumplings with apricots, swimming in butter, or pancakes with strawberry sauce swathed in thick cream. Staff are friendly and helpful, prices a bargain. A gem for nostalgia lovers.

Babies and children welcome: high chairs. Booking advisable weekends. Disabled: toilet. Separate room for parties, seats 25. Tables outdoors (4, terrace). Takeaway service. Vegetarian menu. **Map 28 A3.**

Georgian

West

Kensington

Mimino

197C Kensington High Street, W8 6BA (7937 1551/www.mimino.co.uk). Kensington High Street tube. **Dinner served** 7-11pm Mon-Thur; 6pm-midnight Fri, Sat. **Main courses** £10-£15. **Credit** AmEx, MC, V.

When Mimino opened, its characterless decor and rather grave approach to promoting Georgian culture didn't really work. One year on, the place has cheered up splendidly with the addition of bright Chagall-esque paintings, friendly relaxed staff, an eclectic mix of Georgian and Russian music, and a table displaying exotic Georgian wines. The wine list is well chosen and informative, including some rarely found Georgian bottles. Two semi-sweet reds, blueish-purple Kindzmarauli and heavy Khvanchkara, marry perfectly with khmeli suneli (the dried Georgian herb and spice mix) and the pounded-walnut sauces that are key elements of this fascinating, under-exposed cuisine. If they sound too heavy, try fruity, refreshing white Tsinandali or Mtatsminda rosé. Mimino's magnificent meze – rich and warmly spiced aubergine, phkali (leeks), espanakhi (spinach) and lobio (vibrant, flavoursome red beans with walnuts) – plus some excellent imereti khachapuri (yeasty bread stuffed with cheese), would make a feast by themselves: perfect for vegetarians. Mains of flattened chicken tabaka with plum sauce, and lamb kebabs (mtsvadi) were overwhelmingly large and dry; one between two would suffice after the copious delights of the meze. There's still room for improvement here, but we'll certainly be back.

Babies and children admitted. **Map 7 A9.**

East

Bethnal Green

Little Georgia NEW

87 Goldsmiths Row, E2 8QR (7739 8154). Liverpool Street tube/rail then 26, 48 bus. **Open** 9am-6pm Mon, Tue; 9am-10pm Wed-Sun. **Main courses** £10-£11. **Unlicensed. Corkage** no charge. **Credit** MC, V.

The revived Little Georgia – relocated not far from its previous site on Broadway Market – has retained much of the atmosphere we loved, with cream and mossy green painted tongue-and-groove, unfussy wooden furniture, jazzy Georgian music and low lighting lending a calm, laid-back vibe. Visiting soon after the reopening, there wasn't yet a licence: we rued the lack of opportunity to indulge in some of Georgia's exuberantly robust wines, rarely found in London. By day a café with some Georgian specials, the evening menu is still short and to the point. For the truly hungry, Georgian meze offers a combination of spinach phkali (a dense pâté with walnuts and cheese), a simple grated carrot salad with garlic and mayo, a good multi-textured russian salad and nigziani, a rich salad of peppers, aubergine and walnut served with the ubiquitous khachapuri (cheese bread). As in earlier times, we found it all a touch too heavy: the khachapuri (usually everyone's favourite) was so overstuffed with cheese that it soon collapsed into an unappealing, soggy mess. After the over-rich meze, mains of kebab and meatballs served with light rice and fresh tomato sauce were pleasingly simple.

Babies and childen welcome: high chairs. Separate room for parties, seats 25. Tables outdoors (2, pavement). Takeaway service. **Map 6 S3.**

North

Holloway

★ Tbilisi

91 Holloway Road, N7 8LT (7607 2536). Highbury & Islington tube/rail. **Dinner served** 6.30-11pm Mon-Fri; 6pm-midnight Sat, Sun. **Main courses** £6.95-£8.45. **Credit** MC, V.

Tbilisi is still flying the Georgian flag with more panache than its two London rivals, despite an unpromising location on a grimy strip of Holloway Road and ongoing debates among Georgians as to its authenticity. Who are we to argue, but a certain lightness of touch here suits us better. Step over the threshold to find glamorous dark red decor, gleaming glassware and cool jazzy sounds. Sometimes slightly empty midweek, it's more atmospheric at weekends. Seize the rare chance to indulge in Georgia's characteristically rich, semi-sweet wines such as Kindzmarauli, whose intense, dark, pomegranate hue marries so well with the aromatic dishes. Start with one of the mixed platters – more than enough for two. The kaheti combination features sparkily fresh carrot salad, beetroot with that most characteristic of Georgian ingredients, spicy walnut sauce, and khachapuri – soft yeasty bread stuffed with cheese. Or opt for kolheti, where spinach phkali (an intense, walnut-flavoured pâté) replaces the carrot. Of the mains, we always enjoy tabaka, flattened spring chicken with walnut or plum sauce, or one of the robust, tomatoey stews, such as the tagine-like lamb

chanakhi with aubergine, basil and parsley. Still a well-kept north London secret, Tbilisi is well worth seeking out – note it's open evenings only.
Babies and children admitted. Booking advisable Fri, Sat. Restaurant available for hire. Separate room for parties, seats 40. Takeaway service.

Hungarian

Central

Soho

Gay Hussar
2 Greek Street, W1D 4NB (7437 0973/ www.gayhussar.co.uk). Tottenham Court Road tube. **Lunch served** 12.15-2.30pm, **dinner served** 5.30-10.45pm Mon-Sat. **Main courses** £9.50-£16.50. **Set lunch** £16.50 2 courses, £18.50 3 courses. **Set meal** £45 tasting menu. **Credit** AmEx, DC, JCB, MC, V.
Enter the Gay Hussar's wood-panelled downstairs room and you feel teleported back to another time-zone. The place is jam-packed with political cartoons, both old and contemporary, many apparently sketched in situ. Service is old-school, but friendly and solicitous. Together with retro dishes, starched tablecloths and a soundtrack of wistful Hungarian violin music, it creates the feeling that all is well in a more certain world. We've worried before about the authenticity of the menu, but our Hungarian companion gave it a general thumbs-up. Lovers of scarily rich food should sample the velvety cold wild cherry soup with sour cream, or the crunchy breaded fried mushrooms with tartare sauce (quite Hungarian, apparently). Chicken pancakes were fine but scored low on the authenticity index, whereas serbian chicken in a hearty paprika and tomato sauce (lecso) with tarhonya (an own-made pasta resembling barley grains) set things right again. From the extensive Hungarian wine list, our fruity golden Bátaapáti Tramini was a real find. To finish, we were exhorted to indulge in that most Hungarian of gateaux, decadent chocolatey dobos torta, or poppy-seed strudel with ice-cream. How to refuse?
Babies and children welcome: children's portions; high chairs. Book dinner. Separate rooms for parties, seating 12 and 24. **Map 17 C3.**

Polish

Central

Holborn

★ Bar Polski
11 Little Turnstile, WC1V 7DX (7831 9679). Holborn tube. **Meals served** 4-10pm Mon; 12.30-10pm Tue-Fri. **Dinner served** 6-10pm Sat. **Main courses** £5-£7.50. **Credit** MC, V.
How often do you hit on that perfect spot that gets everything right, over and over again? Small but perfectly formed, Bar Polski (formerly Na Zdrowie) does just that. We're almost loath to sing the praises of its fine range of Polish beers, impressive menu of over 60 lovingly described vodkas and straightforward homestyle cooking, for fear it'll get so popular we won't be able to squeeze in. Go early in the week for a seat. On the vodka front, try woody Siwucha, Kminkowa (caraway seed) or Czarna Porzeczka (blackcurrant). With Polish beers now on sale in most London corner shops, Tyskie, Lech and Okocim aren't so unusual, but seekers of the exotic can always add a shot of delicious raspberry syrup, or go for one of the less common dark beers. All this and perfect drinking food too. Choose from herring and beetroot salad, potato pancakes with mushroom sauce, tender pierogi or garlicky kielbasa with mustard and mash. Decor comprises blond wood and a stylish take on Polish folk art, with bold wycinianki (paper cut-out designs) of cockerels and the like, while sounds are eclectic and laid-back and service friendly. Who could ask for more?
Babies and children admitted. Booking not accepted. Takeaway service. **Map 18 F2.**

Marylebone

Stara Polska NEW
69 Marylebone Lane, W1U 2PH (7486 1333/ www.starapolska.co.uk). Bond Street tube. **Lunch served** noon-3pm, **dinner served** 6-11pm Mon-Thur. **Meals served** noon-11.30pm Fri, Sat. **Main courses** £6.95-£11.90. **Set lunch** £9.95 2 courses. **Credit** MC, V.
The name means 'Old Poland', and they're not kidding. The furnishings could have been brought from central Europe by golems, possibly on the back of the giant sleigh we used as a dining table. Rustic knick-knacks cover every surface. The menu shows little modernity; this is not the Poland of plumbers driving Mercedes and ordering Thai takeaways, but the Poland of rivers and plains, long winters, home stills and Pope John Paul II. 'You are late! We have given your table away,' the manager barked. But then her accomplice, Mr Good Cop, found us another cosy table further back in the labyrinth of poky rooms. Our goulash was cooked in the traditional way, using little meat and with an unappetising glutinous sauce; the accompanying light and savoury buckwheat saved the dish. The pierogi were more consistent: ravioli-like dumplings filled with meat, sauerkraut and mushroom, or cheese and potato. Lots of classic dishes are also served in starter-sized portions: all the better for drinking with. Klopsy (meatballs in tomato sauce), kielbasa, bigos, and potatoes a dozen ways are among the simple delights, along with poppyseed cake for dessert. The house wines are cheap plonk; stick to the beers or vodka, and leave before the golem gets you.
Babies and children admitted. Separate room for parties, seats 9. Takeaway service. **Map 9 G5.**

South Kensington

Daquise
20 Thurloe Street, SW7 2LP (7589 6117). South Kensington tube. **Meals served** 11.30am-11pm daily. **Main courses** £5.50-£12.50. **Set lunch** (noon-3pm Mon-Fri) £7.50 2 courses incl glass of wine, coffee. **Credit** MC, V.
South Ken institution Daquise has been packing in a mix of faithful London Poles, bright young things with an eye for a bargain and passing tourist trade for over 50 years. Who needs sleek designer decor and chilly, distant service when plastic tablecloths, well-worn banquettes and friendly but stern waiting staff keep us coming back for more? From coffee and cake in the morning to nalesniki for lunch or the full works for dinner, Daquise won't disappoint those looking for the real deal, retro Polish style. Rich, peppery barszcz z uszkami (tender little wild mushroom ravioli) and melting herring with sour cream set the tone. Polish platters are a great idea if you want to try a range of homestyle favourites: pierogi, bigos, golabki and potato pancakes – heavy, slightly greasy, scarily calorific but deeply satisfying. Other classics include duck with apples and zrazy with nutty kasza gryczana (roasted buckwheat). To help all this down, there's the usual range of Polish beers (Zywiec, Okocim) and clear and flavoured vodkas. If you've still got room, don't miss the sweet cheese pancakes or szarlotka (apple cake).
Babies and children admitted. Booking advisable. Separate room for parties, seats 25. **Map 14 D10.**

West

Bayswater

Antony's
54 Porchester Road, W2 6ET (7243 8743/ www.antonysrestaurant.com). Royal Oak tube. **Dinner served** 6-11pm Mon-Sat. **Main courses** £7.90-£13.80. **Cover** 70p. **Credit** MC, V.
Pink walls, cleverly placed mirrors, soft candlelight and a mellow jazz soundtrack lend Antony's a rosy glow. A retro romantic vibe is created – ideal for couples, young and old, who seem to make up most

Interview
JAN WORONIECKI

Who are you?
Owner of **Baltic** (*see p91*), **Wódka** (*see p90*) and **Chez Kristof** (*see p109*). I'm also planning to open a new place in the middle of 2008.
Eating in London: what's good about it?
Diversity, increasing quality, simplicity and lessening pretension. Londoners are much more sophisticated in their approach to food, more confident and less reliant on outward displays of restaurant style.
What's bad about it?
It's often too expensive. There is an inevitability to that, but it's also still too expensive in relation to the other things in life. Not enough quality has spread out from the epicentre. For restaurateurs there is also the impossibility of finding well-trained staff, especially in the kitchen.
Which are your favourite London restaurants?
I'm going to sound like a hackneyed old restaurateur here, but I love the pared-down simplicity of **St John** (*see p63*), the total lack of pretension, that very austere vision of food, the way they under-explain the dishes. And I quite like **Scott's** (*see p95*) for its vulgarity – they've thrown money at it and you can see it sticking to the walls.
Who or what has had the biggest impact on London's restaurant scene in the past 25 years?
Terence Conran opening **Quaglino's** (*see p236*) was the seismic shift. More than anybody else, he started the whole modern eating ethos.
Any hot tips for the coming year?
A rather self-conscious lack of style is the current trend. I think we'll see more anti-restaurant restaurants, Michelin-level food in basic environs, less style with more content. More places like **Arbutus** (*see p236*), and restaurants tapping into the interest in casual dining and sharing dishes.

SHELF LIFE

With the huge influx of east European workers to the UK since 2004, *Polski skleps* have been appearing in every neighbourhood. But for more specialist and better quality produce, try these shops.

Fortune Foods

387-389 Hendon Way, NW4 3LP (8203 9325). Hendon Central tube. **Open** 10am-10pm daily.
Lithuanian, Slovakian, Russian and Polish foods can all be found here, and staff are multilingual. Great range of frozen dumplings.

Kalinka

35 Queensway, W2 4QP (7243 6125). Queensway or Bayswater tube. **Open** 11am-8pm daily.
Ukranian pig fat, herrings, tvarog cream cheese, Red October chocolates and sukhariki biscuits are the essentials of daily Russian life that you can find here.

Morawski

157 High Street, NW10 4TR (8965 5340/www.polskiesklepy.co.uk). Willesden Junction tube/rail. **Open** 8am-7pm daily.
Distinctively old-school Polish deli selling excellent golabki, pierogi, zurek and potato dumplings, plus some Romanian items such as beer and bacon.

Parade Delicatessen

8 Central Buildings, The Broadway, W5 2NT (8567 9066). Ealing Broadway tube. **Open** 2-7pm Mon-Fri; 2-5pm Sat; 2-4pm Sun.
Ealing has no shortage of Polish delicatessens, and this large outlet is at the heart of the community.

Polsmak

39 Balls Pond Road, N1 4BW (7275 7045/www.polsmak.co.uk). Dalston Kingsland rail/38 bus. **Open** 9am-8pm Mon-Fri; 9am-6pm Sat, Sun.
New-wave Polish deli in Dalston with an inviting range of specialities and down-home favourites, including cooked and smoked sausages, sauerkraut, carrot juice and packets of instant soup.

customers. The welcoming Polish owner will instantly make you feel looked after and cocooned from busy Westway (just up the street). A mix of Polish and classic international dishes is served. The cooking style is slightly old-fashioned, with rich sauces, but none the worse for it. Good peppery barszcz was let down by slightly undercooked uszka dumplings, but usually the Polish staples here are great: crispy, chewy-centred potato pancakes with mushroom sauce; tender herring fillet; and juicy grilled Polish kielbasa with mustard sauce. Mains come with a varied selection of plain vegetables: roast potatoes, red cabbage, courgette fritters and carrots. Our zrazy (rolled beef fillet stuffed with dill, cucumber and bread sauce in a rich red-wine gravy) was flavoursome and tender. Chicken wrapped in parma ham (very 1970s) was carried off with a light touch. No-nonsense puds, such as sweet-cheese pancakes or baked apple with ice-cream, go splendidly with a sweet wisniowka (cherry vodka) to finish.
Babies and children welcome: high chairs. Booking advisable weekends. Restaurant available for hire. Separate room for parties, seats 25. **Map 7 C5.**

Hammersmith

★ Polanka

258 King Street, W6 0SP (8741 8268). Ravenscourt Park tube. **Meals served** noon-10pm Mon-Sat; noon-8pm Sun. **Main courses** £4.90-£11.50. **Unlicensed. Corkage** £2 wine; £5 spirits. **Credit** MC, V.
Hidden away at the back of a deli in one of west London's longest-established Polish colonies, Polanka offers honest-to-goodness traditional Polish cooking. You'll waddle out, feeling replete and comforted, with no great dent to your wallet. The simple decor of light pine, artificial sunflowers and straw dolls has a nostalgic charm, reminiscent of a small-town restaurant at the time private enterprise really took off in Poland. Harsh lighting and no licence (though you can BYO) mean you're unlikely to linger, despite bright and cheery service from the sweet waitress. No surprises on the menu here, with herrings, pierogi and golabki – just as your fellow diners (mainly young Polish couples and after-work single chaps) would expect to find back home. Tender herring with beetroot was spot on, but the barszcz was slightly vinegary. Workman-sized portions of bigos and mash and good, meaty kielbasa with chips and salad were fine but unremarkable. With mains like these, dessert is hardly necessary, but for the reckless there's a fine array of cakes in the shop, including makowiec and sernik (cheesecake). Admitting defeat, we had no choice but to take ours home.
Babies and children welcome: high chairs. Booking advisable. Separate room for parties, seats 8. Takeaway service. **Map 20 A4.**

Kensington

Wódka

12 St Alban's Grove, W8 5PN (7937 6513/ www.wodka.co.uk). High Street Kensington tube. **Lunch served** noon-3pm Mon-Fri. **Dinner served** 6.30-11.15pm daily. **Main courses** £12.90-£17. **Set lunch** £8.50 1 course, £13.50 2 courses, £17 3 courses. **Set meal** £24.50-£28 3 courses. **Credit** AmEx, MC, V.
Our soft spot for Wódka – Jan Woroniecki's first restaurant, which paved the way for his grand project, Baltic (*see p91*) – is being sorely tested. Most recently, we waited an interminable time for drinks, then were told in an offhand way that our choice of sweet-cheese pancake was off. Our exasperation grew as three requests over 15 minutes to pay our bill went unheeded. Only at the bar was it revealed the machine wasn't working. But the kitchen is still getting it right. Puffy-light buckwheat blinis, with meltingly tender smoked salmon, herring, keta caviar and aubergine purée, were among the best we've eaten in London. Robust, warm smoked eel salad in a honey and caper sauce was a fab fusion of flavours. Both our main courses – simple pan-fried trout and almonds, and a 'Georgian-style' rump of lamb with aubergines and carrot salad – were spot-on. Combine such food with an interesting wine list (we loved our unusual Slovenian Janez from Jarenina, a spicy riesling/ sauvignon blend) and a great choice of vodkas (from classic clear to own-flavoured curiosities such as horseradish), and Wódka has everything going for it – except diligent service.
Babies and children admitted. Booking advisable. Separate room for parties, seats 30. Tables outdoors (3, pavement). **Map 7 C9.**

Shepherd's Bush

★ Patio

5 Goldhawk Road, W12 8QQ (8743 5194). Goldhawk Road tube. **Lunch served** noon-3pm Mon-Fri. **Dinner served** 6-11.30pm daily. **Main courses** £7-£9.50. **Set meal** £15.99 4 courses incl vodka shot. **Credit** AmEx, DC, MC, V.
With heavy velvet drapes, antique clutter and a welcoming Polish owner, Patio oozes old-school charm. It's one of three strikingly unreconstructed restaurants on an unpromising strip of busy Goldhawk Road. Three courses, complimentary coconut cake, fruit and a shot of vodka cost just £15.99, so too much quibbling is probably misplaced, but we feel standards have slipped a notch recently. If you're after whopping portions of hearty home-cooking, you're unlikely to be disappointed, but subtlety is rare. Reliable starters included a thick slab of Polish ham with beetroot and horseradish, tender herring, and decent clear barszcz. Mains were less consistent and more disappointing. Our pork schnitzel was a dense torpedo of minced pork: tasty, but a lot to wade through. Chicken walewska (breast in a dull tomato sauce) was uninspiring. Usually, delicious fresh vegetable side dishes save the day here – red and green cabbage, fried potatoes and raw carrot often feature – but this time all were a bit tired. For pudding (if you can manage it after the calorie assault), hefty portions of properly dense baked cheesecake or rum-infused sweet-cheese pancakes will leave you truly replete. Somewhat hit and miss then, but not bad if you're on a tight budget.
Book dinner Fri, Sat. Separate room for parties, seats 45. Takeaway service. **Map 20 C2.**

South

Balham

★ Polish White Eagle Club

211 Balham High Road, SW17 7BQ (8672 1723). Tooting Bec tube/Balham tube/rail/49, 155, 181, 319 bus.
Bar **Open** noon-3pm, 6-11pm Mon-Fri; noon-2am Sat; 11am-10.30pm Sun.
Restaurant **Lunch served** 11.30am-3pm, **dinner served** 6-10pm Mon-Sat. **Meals served** 11.30am-10pm Sun. **Main courses** £6.90-£10.95. **Set lunch** £7 2 courses. **Set dinner** £9.90 2 courses.
Both **Credit** MC, V.
The influx of Polish immigrants into the capital has revivified this old-style social club, and you're as likely to hear Polish karaoke in the bar as you are to hear a Polish choir practising in the ballroom. Although we've been PWEC fans for years, we've been rather disappointed with the food on recent visits. A main course of potato pancake with beef goulash featured nicely flavoured meat, but the pancake was quite obviously blackened and tasted burnt, while mixed pierogi had to be sent back because they were cold in the middle. Bread was less than fresh, while side dishes of sauerkraut and mixed peas and carrots tasted as though they could have come from a tin or freezer pack. More successful was a starter of zurek (sour soup, made with a base of fermented rye flour and water), flavoured with smoky kielbasa, juniper berries and pieces of ham. Salty herrings, served with smetana mixed with lots of raw onion, were firm and flavourful. The prices are very fair, especially given the generosity of the portions – and we know the kitchen can perform well when it tries.
Babies and children welcome: high chairs. Booking advisable. Separate rooms for parties, seating 30 and 120. Takeaway service.

Clapham

Café Wanda

153 Clapham High Street, SW4 7SS (7738 8760). Clapham Common tube. **Meals served** noon-11pm Mon-Fri; 11am-11pm Sat, Sun. **Main courses** £6.95-£14.95. **Credit** MC, V.
By day, head to Café Wanda for coffee and decadent, own-made Polish cheesecakes. In the evening, out come the candles and the place transforms into an old-fashioned, slightly eccentric neighbourhood restaurant. There are hanging spider plants not seen since the 1970s and an unashamedly '80s soundtrack. Café Wanda attracts local Poles, many of whom seem to be regulars, and the sorts of young Claphamites who value the place's individuality. The menu roams

from western to eastern Europe, where the attention focuses on a short list of Polish specialities. We were most impressed by a shared starter of intensely flavoured, tender little mixed pierogi, good enough to make a homesick Pole shed a nostalgic tear. Main courses are of generous proportions. Klopsy – big pork meatballs stuffed with mushrooms – served with aromatic kasha and topped with mushroom sauce, was a luscious winter chill-chaser. Golabki had a high rice-to-meat ratio in the stuffing, but were lighter for it; our only grumble was the blandness of the mashed potato that accompanied it. For afters, those afore-mentioned homemade cheesecakes will easily fill any empty spaces that might remain.
Babies and children admitted. Booking advisable. Entertainment: pianist 8.30-11pm Fri, Sat. Tables outdoors (2, pavement). Takeaway service. Vegetarian menu. **Map 22 B2**.

Waterloo

★ Baltic (100)

74 Blackfriars Road, SE1 8HA (7928 1111/ www.balticrestaurant.co.uk). Southwark tube/rail. **Lunch served** noon-3pm daily. **Dinner served** 6-11pm Mon-Sat; 6-10pm Sun. **Main courses** £10.50-£16.50. **Set meal** £14 2 courses, £17 3 courses. **Credit** AmEx, MC, V.

As Polish and Russian influences increase in London, it's perhaps surprising that Baltic has no serious competition to be the city's most glamorous eastern European restaurant. Its wow factor is indisputable. High ceilings, white walls, contrasting exposed red brickwork and a spectacular chandelier (aglow with hundreds of amber shards) aptly reference the architecture of Gdansk and other Baltic cities. The noise can be overwhelming, especially if you're hoping for some intimacy. Service is sometimes patchy too, but even that we'll forgive. The menu offers modern takes on traditional food. Begin with nutty buckwheat blini with smoked fish or caviar, or try more unusual dishes such as szczawiowa (sorrel soup) or kaszanka (Polish black pudding) with pickled cabbage and pear purée. Fish is excellent. We chose flaky roast halibut with tender fennel and white beans; and spatchcocked, paprika-roasted baby chicken. Portions aren't huge, so you might manage one of the top-rate puds, such as cherry vodka ice-cream with warm chocolate sauce. Don't forget the vodkas (to drink with your meal, or at the bar) – choose from over a dozen clear varieties or home-infused specialities like ginger or dill. Baltic bliss.
Babies and children admitted. Disabled: toilet. Entertainment: jazz 7pm Sun. Separate room for parties, seats 30. Tables outdoors (4, terrace). **Map 11 N8**.

Tbilisi. See p88.

Russian

Central

Clerkenwell & Farringdon

Potemkin

144 Clerkenwell Road, EC1R 5DP (7278 6661/ www.potemkin.co.uk). Farringdon tube/rail. **Meals served** noon-11pm Mon-Fri. **Dinner served** 6-11pm Sat. **Main courses** £9.50-£17. **Set dinner** £20 3 courses. **Credit** AmEx, DC, MC, V.

Although the upstairs vodka bar can get lively, the stylish but overly formal ground-floor restaurant at Potemkin often has a solemn air. It attracts well-heeled City folk who talk in hushed tones about their latest deals. The place looks glam (if slightly corporate) with its regal red and blue decor and gold-flecked khokhloma (painted-wood handicrafts) gleaming under artful lighting, but it never strikes us as a place for an atmospheric Russian night out. That said, we've been much more impressed of late by what's going on in the kitchen. Smoked salmon blinis were appropriately light and puffy (though very tiny); buzhenina (gently spiced roast pork with horseradish) was a bit too plain – but both went splendidly with a shot of basil or lemon vodka. Main courses were the shining stars of the meal. A dish of slightly crisp-skinned red mullet fillets in a subtle mustard sauce with shallots was sensational, both in texture and flavour. Rabbit in a peppery tomato sauce was equally appetising. Enticing-sounding cocktails such as Tuscan Mule (moscow mule with added vanilla vodka) tend towards the sickly sweet, so stick to the shots, clean Baltika lager or wine.

Babies and children admitted (lunch). Booking advisable. Takeaway service. **Map 5 N4.**

West

Acton

Rasputin

265 High Street, W3 9BY (8993 5802). Acton Town tube/70, 72, 207, 266 bus. **Meals served** 6pm-midnight daily. **Main courses** £7.50-£12.95. **Credit** MC, V.

In an unpromising spot opposite a dodgy-looking pub and a police station, Rasputin is full of surprises. The attractive large blue room (with photos of the Russian royal family, portraits of Rasputin and other arty *objets*) was terribly quiet. We were soon in conversation with the delightful chatty Montenegrin owner and her Croatian husband (who used to cater for Yugoslavian Embassy events), over orahovac (green-walnut vodka) and a complimentary mound of pickled vegetables. Russian, Polish, Ukrainian and Balkan dishes are on the menu, including good starters such as borscht (Ukrainian-style with veg and sour cream), moistly stuffed pelmeni and light smoked salmon blinis with sour cream and dill. We then hazarded hearty mains of peppers stuffed with rice, a honey-marinated fillet of salmon and a somewhat overfried 'schnytzel po evropeiskii', compromised by tired vegetables: greasy fried potatoes with onions, carrots and red cabbage. Clean-tasting Baltika lager, from an intriguing drinks list, made an admirable accompaniment. We ended with more complimentary vodkas and warm embraces from our hostess. The world seemed a better place. Note that's it's only open for dinner.

Babies and children admitted. Booking advisable. Separate room for parties, seats 45.

North

Camden Town & Chalk Farm

Trojka

101 Regents Park Road, NW1 8UR (7483 3765/ www.troykarestaurant.co.uk). Chalk Farm tube. **Meals served** 9am-10.30pm daily. **Main courses** £6.95-£11.95. **Set lunch** (noon-4pm) £9.95 2 courses. **Licensed. Corkage** £3 wine; £15 spirits. **Credit** MC, V.

Things got off to a bad start at Trojka when none of the drinks we wanted (from Georgian wine to Ukrainian beer) were available. But once ensconced with a light, flavoursome Cesu beer (from Latvia), we began to enjoy the relaxed atmosphere and mixed company – from grannies enjoying a cup of tea and cake to aspiring starlets on black coffee and cigarettes. For those not aiming for size zero, a plethora of temptations abound. Our Ukrainian borscht was oversalted, but buckwheat blini with just the right degree of chewiness went down a treat with smoked salmon and tender herring. For the sleek chaps squiring the starlets, a variety of caviars are also on offer. No surprises with the mains, with the usual hearty fare much in evidence – potato pancakes, goulash, coulebiac (salmon, rice and mushrooms in pastry). All are straightforward and satisfying, just like babushka used to make. Forget your too-skinny neighbours and indulge in toothsome pancakes with sweet cheese or blueberries. Given the chi-chi location, we're always pleasantly surprised to find such good, honest food at such reasonable prices.

Babies and children welcome: high chair. Book dinner Fri, Sat. Entertainment: Russian folk music 8-10.30pm Fri, Sat. Tables outdoors (3, pavement). Takeaway service. **Map 27 A1.**

Menu

Dishes followed by (Cz) indicate a Czechoslovak dish; (G) Georgian; (H) Hungarian; (P) Polish; (R) Russian; (Uk) Ukrainian. Others have no particular affiliation.

Bigos (P): hunter's stew made with sauerkraut, various meats and sausage, mushrooms and juniper.
Blini: yeast-leavened pancake made from buckwheat flour, traditionally served smothered in butter and sour cream; **blinchiki** are mini blinis.
Borscht: classic beetroot soup. There are many varieties: Ukrainian borscht is thick with vegetables; the Polish version (**barszcz**) is clear. There are also white and green types. Often garnished with sour cream, boiled egg or little dumplings.
Caviar: fish roe. Most highly prized is that of the sturgeon (**beluga**, **oscietra** and **sevruga**, in descending order of expense), though **keta** or salmon caviar is underrated.
Chlodnik (P): cold beetroot soup, bright pink in colour, served with sour cream.
Coulebiac (R): see koulebiaka.
Galabki, **golabki** or **golubtsy**: cabbage parcels, usually stuffed with rice or kasha (qv) and sometimes meat.
Golonka (P): pork knuckle, often cooked in beer.
Goulash or **gulasz (H)**: rich beef soup.
Kasha or **kasza**: buckwheat, delicious roasted: light and fluffy with a nutty flavour.
Kaszanka (P): blood sausage made with buckwheat.
Khachapuri (G): flatbread; sometimes called Georgian pizza.
Kielbasa (P): sausage; Poland had dozens of widely differing styles.
Knedliky (Cz): bread dumplings.
Kolduny (P): small meat-filled dumplings (scaled-down pierogi, qv) often served in beetroot soup.
Kotlet schabowy (P): breaded pork chops.
Koulebiaka or **kulebiak (R)**: layered salmon or sturgeon pie with eggs, dill, rice and mushrooms.
Krupnik (P): barley soup, and the name of a honey vodka (because of the golden colour of barley).
Latke: grated potato pancakes, fried.
Makowiec or **makietki (P)**: poppy seed cake.
Mizeria (P): cucumber salad; very thinly sliced and dressed with sour cream.
Nalesniki (P): cream cheese pancakes.
Paczki (P): doughnuts, often filled with plum jam.
Pelmeni (R): Siberian-style ravioli dumplings.
Pierogi (P): ravioli-style dumplings. Typical fillings are sauerkraut and mushroom, curd cheese or fruit (cherries, apples).
Pirogi (large) or **pirozhki** (small) **(R)**: filled pies made with yeasty dough.
Placki (P): potato pancakes.
Shashlik: Caucasian spit-roasted meat.
Shchi (R): soup made from sauerkraut.
Stroganoff (R): beef slices, served in a rich sour cream and mushroom sauce.
Surowka (P): salad made of raw shredded vegetables.
Uszka or **ushka**: small ear-shaped dumplings served in soup.
Vareniki (Uk): Ukrainian version of pierogi (qv).
Zakuski (R) or **zakaski (P)**: starters, traditionally covering a whole table. The many dishes can include pickles, marinated vegetables and fish, herring, smoked eel, aspic, mushrooms, radishes with butter, salads and caviar.
Zrazy (P): beef rolls stuffed with bacon, pickled cucumber and mustard.
Zurek (P): sour rye soup.

GREAT RUSSIAN
FOOD DESERVES
RUSSIA'S №1 BEER
BALTIKA
3
BALTIKA
БАЛТИКА
3
Classic beer
ALC 5.1% VOL
SINCE
1992

Fish

Some of London's longest-running and best-loved restaurants are fish and seafood specialists. **Scott's** is the oldest, having started life as an oyster warehouse in 1851, while seafood market stall holder Joseph Sheekey set up what became **J Sheekey** in 1896; now both are thriving under the ownership of Caprice Holdings. **Sweetings** has been feeding City gents in the same premises since 1889, and **Bentley's Oyster Bar & Grill** (established 1916) is enjoying a new lease of life under chef Richard Corrigan. **Geales** is a relative upstart, having opened on the eve of World War II; it's also had a recent makeover but without betraying its chippie origins, and was a contender for Best British Restaurant in the 2007 Time Out Eating & Drinking Awards.

These old-timers are all resolutely English in their various ways, but you can have foreign flavours with your fish too. New this year is Sardinian operation **Olivomare** (nominated for Best New Restaurant in 2007); Italian accents are also in evidence at **Signor Zilli**. Or how about French (**Lobster Pot, Lou Pescadou**), Scandinavian (**Deep**) or even Mauritian (**Chez Liline**)? For simply a great neighbourhood restaurant, of no particular nationality, try **Fish Hook** in the west or **Applebee's** in the east.

RESTAURANTS

Central

Belgravia

★ Olivomare NEW

2007 RUNNER-UP LEFFE BEST NEW RESTAURANT

10 Lower Belgrave Street, SW1W 0LJ (7730 9022). Victoria tube/rail. **Lunch served** noon-2.30pm, **dinner served** 7-11pm Mon-Sat. **Main courses** £14-£19. **Credit** AmEx, DC, MC, V.

A vision in white (and everything is white – floor, tables, chairs, lighting, except for one wallpapered wall) that gleams even when the lights are dimmed at dinner, this is one sleek restaurant. The food – a happy marriage of Sardinian recipes, fish and seafood – also looks a treat; it may be rustic in origin, but it's served in a very suave fashion, and the ingredients are good quality. Spaghetti alla bottarga (with thinly sliced grey mullet roe) looked simple, but was deceptively rich. Chargrilled monkfish with marinated courgettes was a large, meaty portion in delicious juices. Starters are even less complicated, but equally appetising: grilled squid with marinated tomatoes, pickled white anchovies on rocket and courgette salad, sparklingly fresh rock oysters. The little touches are well done too – witness the variety of breads and olives served gratis. Puddings include sebada (Sardinian cheese fritters with honey); the wine list is short and Italian. The staff are a charming, welcoming bunch, though if you're not a Sloane or a Euro-banker, you may feel the odd one out. Owner Mauro Sanna also runs nearby Italian restaurants Olivo and Olivetio.

Booking essential. Children admitted. Disabled: toilet. Tables outdoors (4, terrace). **Map 15 H10.**

For branches (Olivetto, Olivo) see index.

City

Chamberlain's

23-25 Leadenhall Market, EC3V 1LR (7648 8690/www.chamberlains.org). Bank tube/DLR/ Liverpool Street tube/rail.

Bar **Open** noon-11pm Mon-Fri.

Restaurant **Meals served** noon-9.30pm Mon-Fri. **Main courses** £17-£35. **Set dinner** £19.95 3 courses.

Both **Credit** AmEx, DC, MC, V.

Historic Leadenhall Market is an enticing spot for a meal, with its elegant wrought-iron and glass architecture and smart cream and red paintwork. At lunchtime the shops and restaurants are buzzing with City workers. You'll find the richer ones in this upmarket fish restaurant, where prices are clearly aimed at expense-accounters (dover sole £32, rump of lamb £29.95). You can eat in the light-flooded ground-floor restaurant overlooked by a small mezzanine, on the cobbled street outside beneath the market roof, or in the first-floor dining room, where smart table linen, leather-covered chairs and chilly air-con provide a more formal setting (there's also a brick-vaulted basement bar). The quality of the ingredients is beyond doubt; a half-dozen Irish oysters and a cylinder of dill-flecked crab meat encased in a parmesan crisp were top-quality starters. But a main of pan-fried salmon on a bed of sprightly samphire was severely undercooked. Po-faced staff offered no apology, but quickly brought a replacement: which was cooked just right. The wine list allows for blowouts, but the house offerings are perfectly acceptable. Puddingss – English strawberries and cream (for a stonking £7.50), crème brûlée and cheese – seem an afterthought.

Babies and children admitted. Restaurant available for hire. Tables outdoors (18, pavement). **Map 12 Q7.**

Sweetings (100)

39 Queen Victoria Street, EC4N 4SA (7248 3062). Mansion House tube. **Lunch served** 11.30am-3pm Mon-Fri. **Main courses** £11.50-£27.50. **Credit** AmEx, JCB, MC, V.

You don't have to have gone to public school to appreciate this City institution, though many of its customers obviously have. The small, wedge-shaped space is spartan (apart from the lovely mosaic-tiled floor), with most of the seating at linen-covered counters around the edge, behind which the amiable serving staff are trapped for the lunchtime sitting (the doors shut at 3pm). Crockery and glassware are functional, vegetables come in old-style metal dishes, the wine list is short to the point of brevity (there's also Guinness and bitter served in pewter tankards) and the cooking is determinedly old-fashioned – but we wouldn't have it any other way. Start with potted shrimps, say, smoked eel or herring roe (soft and creamy, laced with butter, on brown toast), followed by the likes of fish pie, skate wing with black butter or whole fish grilled, poached or fried. Smoked haddock was a big slab of perfectly cooked fish, unadorned save for a poached egg on top: simple, but satisfying. Complete the schoolyard fantasies with spotted dick, bread and butter pudding or fruit crumble. Sweetings has lasted over a century so far, and long may it continue.

Babies and children admitted. Bookings not accepted. Restaurant available for hire, seats 30 (dinner only). Takeaway service.

Map 11 P6.

Covent Garden

Loch Fyne Restaurant

2-4 Catherine Street, WC2B 5JS (7240 4999/ www.lochfyne.com). Covent Garden tube. **Meals served** 10am-11pm daily. **Main courses** £8.95-£17.95. **Set meal** (noon-6.30pm, 10-11pm) £11 2 courses. **Credit** AmEx, MC, V.

Loch Fyne's own fisheries and smokehouse provide its 30-plus restaurants countrywide with fresh fishy ingredients; we've always found dishes here competently and satisfyingly prepared, if a little by-the-numbers unadventurous. A starter of brandan orach smoked salmon was moist and densely flavoured, set off well by a garlicky aïoli. Three of the four kinds of marinated herring in a sampler platter tasted rather too much the same (essentially: vinegary), but were attractively presented on a moulded plate. Also pretty was a main of moules marinières, served in a heavy black dish, its lid removed with a flourish by a chummy, knowledgeable waiter. The highlight? The oysters: plump, delicious and tasting as if just plucked from the sea, served simply on crushed ice. The wine list is adequate – expectedly white-heavy, with plenty of choice by the glass. This branch in Covent Garden, like its sister restaurants, is styled with Fyne's trademark pine-wood blandness: simple furniture, chalkboarded specials, nautical watercolours. But then simple is what Loch Fyne does best.

Babies and children welcome: children's menu; high chairs; nappy-changing facilities. Booking advisable. Disabled: toilet. **Map 18 E4.**

For branches see index.

Fitzrovia

Back to Basics

21A Foley Street, W1W 6DS (7436 2181/ www.backtobasics.uk.com). Goodge Street or Oxford Circus tube. **Lunch served** noon-3pm, **dinner served** 6-10.30pm Mon-Sat. **Main courses** £12.75-£21.75. **Credit** AmEx, DC, MC, V.

Neighbourhood restaurants in the heart of central London are always fun to discover, doubly so when they're as intimate and warm as Back to Basics. Pavement tables, delicate glass flowers, colourful globe lampshades and a wall-sized blackboard listing the 15 or so daily fish specials combine to make for a charming experience marred by just one thing: the consistency in food quality. In a Jekyll and Hyde lunch, dressed crab with watercress mayonnaise, toast and boiled egg was huge, delicate and delicious, but a main of monkfish cheeks, king prawn kebab and spicy couscous veered from fluffy and delicious (the couscous) to oversalted (the prawns); and from dense, meaty fish to a greasy batter coating. The variety of both shellfish and fish is impressive; barracuda, sea bream, swordfish, cod, salmon, mussels, clams, oysters, prawns, and crab in several guises were all on the board on our visit. There's a tendency towards overly complex combinations, but with friendly staff, a laid-back ambience and super-fresh

fish, this is neighbourhood dining at its nicest. And most generous: vast portions left no room for the small but tempting selection of puds (bread and butter pudding, apple tart and the like).
Babies and children welcome: high chair. Booking essential. Tables outdoors (17, pavement). Takeaway service. **Map 17 A1**.

Leicester Square

J Sheekey (100)

28-32 St Martin's Court, WC2N 4AL (7240 2565/www.caprice-holdings.co.uk). Leicester Square tube. **Lunch served** noon-3pm Mon-Sat; noon-3.30pm Sun. **Dinner served** 5.30pm-midnight Mon-Sat; 6pm-midnight Sun. **Main courses** £12.75-£39.50. **Set lunch** (Sat, Sun) £24.75 3 courses. **Cover** £2. **Credit** AmEx, DC, MC, V.

There's a faintly unloved air to Sheekey's exterior, but the mirrored windows are there simply to put off onlookers. Inside, this favoured haunt of the well known is intimate and gentlemen's-club posh: a succession of little rooms (including a discreet bar) with polished wooden floors, monochrome photos of theatre stars, sea-shell light fittings and immaculately turned-out waiters. The large menu incorporates specials, caviar, stupendous seafood platters and even a few meat dishes (confit duck leg) and a vegetarian section (leek and girolle tart). Fish is ultra-fresh, and the cooking shows great flair – witness a perfectly constructed starter of arbroath smokie matched with bitter endive, soft-boiled quails' eggs and a tart dressing; and an exemplary haddock and chips with mushed fresh peas and chunky tartare sauce. But faults aren't unknown. Deep-fried sand-eels and brown shrimps with sauce gribiche wasn't sufficiently different from whitebait to merit depriving puffins of their favourite food; and although fish pie had a wondrously light mash topping and creamy filling, too much smoked fish (mainly haddock) and the addition of mustard made it very salty. Summer pudding and mirabelle jelly stood out as seasonal stars on the dessert list. The white-heavy wine list features half a dozen options by the glass.
Babies and children welcome: booster seats; colouring books; high chairs. Booking essential. Vegetarian menu. Vegan dishes. **Map 18 D5**.

Mayfair

Scott's NEW

20 Mount Street, W1K 2HE (7495 7309/ www.caprice-holdings.co.uk). Bond Street or Green Park tube. **Meals served** noon-10.30pm daily. **Main courses** £8-£23. **Cover** £2. **Credit** AmEx, DC, JCB, MC, V.

From the same stable as the Ivy and J Sheekey (*see above*), Scott's is a similarly smooth operation. The old-timer has been refurbed and buffed to a high sheen; it's all fairly trad, decorated in shades of grey and maroon, with occasional flashes of modernity – the art on the walls, for example, and the space-age seafood platter that takes pride of place at the bar. Diners can sit here on high stools for a more casual (though no less expensive) meal; or take a well-padded leather seat in the restaurant. Meat and vegetarian dishes are available, but that would be to miss the point. The showiest starters are the assorted crustacea, but there's also caviar as well as dishes such as griddled cuttlefish, sautéed skate knobs with peas and bacon (very moreish), and smoked eel with horseradish (nice enough). Mains run from prole (deep-fried haddock with mushy peas) to posh (dover sole meunière). Our most interesting main was a delightfully springy shrimp burger with a decent chilli kick, while golden-battered haddock with rather pale chips was merely fine – and the 'mushy peas' were, in fact, minted, puréed peas. Recover from any such let-downs with a cherry bakewell pudding with almond ice-cream. Dig deep for most of the wine list and try not to resent the £2 cover charge. In short, for the money, good but not stellar.
Babies and children welcome: high chairs. Booking advisable. Separate room for parties, seats 40. Tables outdoors (7, pavement). **Map 9 G7**.

Piccadilly

★ Bentley's Oyster Bar & Grill (100)

11-15 Swallow Street, W1B 4DG (7734 4756/ www.bentleysoysterbarandgrill.co.uk). Piccadilly Circus tube.
Oyster Bar **Meals served** noon-midnight Mon-Sat; noon-10pm Sun. **Main courses** £8.50-£24.
Restaurant **Lunch served** noon-3pm daily. **Dinner served** 6-11pm Mon-Sat; 6-10pm Sun. **Main courses** £16.50-£38.
Both **Credit** AmEx, MC, V.

Irish chef Richard Corrigan (of famed British restaurant Lindsay House) relaunched this old-timer a couple of years ago, and it's been a great success. Still occupying the same lovely Victorian building that it's been in for more than 90 years, Bentley's is a popular haunt for besuited gents; women were conspicuous by their absence on our lunchtime visit, but it's not stuffy or overly masculine. The oyster bar on the ground floor is the more relaxed space with its red leather banquettes, elegant scallop lights and marble-topped bar; the grill on the first floor (comprising three separate rooms) is smarter, with a blue and white colour scheme, polished oak flooring and crisp linen. Premium-quality oysters are almost compulsory, but there's much to please on the bar menu, from lighter dishes (shellfish bisque, Atlantic prawns with egg mayonnaise, salmon tartare) to more substantial fare (fish pie, smoked haddock with greens and potatoes). Prices are Mayfair-high, but ingredients and cooking are generally first-rate – our only complaint was with a dessert of pale pink spring rhubarb that was barely cooked. The grander grill menu offers the likes of sauté of lobster and West Cork beef. The globetrotting wine list is a treat, specialising in small regional producers. The maître d' was peerless on our visit, but other staff had a vague, distracted air.
Booking essential. Disabled: toilet. Dress: smart casual; no shorts. Separate rooms for parties, seating 14 and 60. **Map 17 A5**.

St James's

Green's

36 Duke Street, SW1Y 6DF (7930 4566/ www.greens.org.uk). Green Park or Piccadilly Circus tube. **Lunch served** noon-2.30pm, **dinner served** 5.30-11pm Mon-Sat. **Main courses** £11-£40. **Cover** £2. **Credit** AmEx, DC, MC, V.

While 'traditional' and 'English' are two ideas to treasure, put these together with 'decor' and you get Green's. It almost resembles a parody of an Angus Steak House, with its British Racing Green colour scheme, booth seating, and brassy fittings that can look MFI circa 1981 unless you're paying attention. The menu also clings to the past, though some dangerously modern rocket salad is discernible. So who eats here? At the seafood bar, Colonel Mustard and Professor Plum. Seated at a banquette, Miss Scarlet and the Detective. These English stereotypes still exist in St James's, seemingly happy to pay about a tenner for a starter and £15-£20 for most main courses. The food is fine: potted shrimps with toast was enjoyable, and

Sweetings

a tomato-rich crab bisque had good stock. But nothing on the menu surprised us. Salmon fish cakes were packed with good fish; cod was fresh and nicely crumbed on top, with braised lettuce below – yet such cooking belongs to a bygone era. Ah, that's why people come here: for reassurance that the England before hoodies, mobile phones and CCTV still exists. Mystery solved: it was Mr Parker-Bowles, in the kitchen, with a bain-marie and blowtorch.
Babies and children admitted. Booking advisable. Dress: smart casual; no trainers. Separate room for parties, seats 36. **Map 9 J7.**

Soho

Zilli Fish

36-40 Brewer Street, W1F 9TA (7734 8649/ www.zillialdo.com). Piccadilly Circus tube. **Meals served** noon-11.30pm Mon-Sat. **Main courses** £8.70-£32. **Set dinner** (5-6.30pm, after 10pm Mon-Sat) £25 2 courses, £30 3 courses. **Credit** AmEx, MC, V.
Aldo Zilli's mini Soho chain comprises this decade-old fish specialist, the adjacent Zilli Café and Italian restaurant Signor Zilli. Zilli Fish has the feel of an upmarket brasserie, with a sliding glass frontage that can be opened on hot days (though why you'd want to let in the cacophony of Brewer Street is beyond us). Piscine pleasures, 'fresh from Billingsgate Market', are the thing. We couldn't fault the presentation, nor the quality of the ingredients: tuna carpaccio with rocket, parmesan, olive oil and lemon juice was heavenly; monkfish wrapped in pancetta with sautéed wild mushrooms was a worthy follow-on; and the tuna steak, served with purple broccoli scented with garlic and chilli, was a lovely piece of fish, perfectly cooked. Staff were polished and effusive, the evening crowd the usual mix for this sort of establishment – well-to-do families and earnest couples. The shortish wine list has the expected lean towards Italy; the house white, a Trebbiano, was light, crisp and a fair bargain. For those who want to continue the Zilliness at home, Aldo's cookbook is for sale at the counter. His master classes are accessible through the website.
Babies and children welcome: high chairs. Booking advisable. Tables outdoors (2, patio). Takeaway service. **Map 17 B4.**
For branch (Signor Zilli, Zilli Café) see index.

South Kensington

Bibendum Oyster Bar

Michelin House, 81 Fulham Road, SW3 6RD (7589 1480/www.bibendum.co.uk). South Kensington tube. **Meals served** noon-10.30pm Mon-Sat; noon-10pm Sun. **Main courses** £8-£15. **Credit** AmEx, DC, MC, V.
'Nunc est bibendum' is the motto around the floor mosaic of the tyre-plump Michelin man, and this casual café/bar in the lovely tiled foyer of the Michelin building is indeed a good place for a drink, at any time. And good for premium-quality oysters too: four native and rock varieties on our visit, including premium-priced Colchester No.2s. You can sit in the foyer (a thoroughfare for customers to the adjoining Conran shop or first-floor Bibendum restaurant), in the small café to the side, or outside sandwiched between the oyster and flower stalls. Shellfish is a speciality, with the likes of lobster or crab mayonnaise, crevettes grises and a towering crustacea platter (minimum two people), but there are other fishy options (smoked salmon, gravadlax, rollmop herrings with onion salad) and salads on the regular menu. Most are small, light dishes perfect for the figure-conscious ladies who dine here at lunchtime. A small daily specials list adds variety; on our visit it included carpaccio-like slices of spiced pineapple with basil chantilly cream. Whites dominate the wine list; the house varieties are helpfully available in 450ml pots as well as by the glass and bottle. Staff are polished and professional.
Babies and children welcome: high chairs. Bookings not accepted. Disabled: ramp; toilet. Dress: smart casual. Tables outdoors (5, pavement). **Map 14 E10.**

Poissonnerie de l'Avenue

82 Sloane Avenue, SW3 3DZ (7589 2457/ www.poissonneriedelavenue.co.uk). South Kensington tube. **Lunch served** noon-3pm, **dinner served** 7-11.30pm Mon-Sat. **Main courses** £12.50-£25. **Set lunch** £14 1 course, £20 2 courses, £24 3 courses. **Cover** £1.50. **Credit** AmEx, DC, JCB, MC, V.
Poissonnerie de l'Avenue is over 40 years old, though its clientele tends to be older still. Expect bouffant hairstyles on the women, gold-buttoned blazers on the men and a certain type of famous face to appear – Raine Spencer, Princess Di's stepmum, swept in at one point during our midweek dinner. Back in the Swinging Sixties, it would have been Mary Quant and Mick Jagger. And expect the regulars (there are plenty) to get preferential treatment. The place wasn't full, but we were given the worst table (adjacent to the kitchen, with seats next to rather than facing each other) – though staff were happy to move us to a better position when asked. The decor is suitably time-warped, all nautical prints and wood panelling, as is the cooking – but then keeping up with the latest trends isn't the point here. Owner Peter Rosignoli's Italian background is evident in the smattering of pasta dishes, though the menu is mainly French, majoring in classics such as lobster thermidor, sole véronique and grilled dover sole. Rubbery squid was almost inedible, but grilled turbot was excellent, and smoked haddock 'monte carlo' with poached egg and beurre blanc was the ultimate in comfort food – and looking after the comfort of its customers is what Poissonnerie is all about.
Booking advisable dinner. Children admitted (babies admitted lunch only). Dress: smart casual. Separate room for parties, seats 20. Tables outdoors (4, pavement). **Map 14 E10.**

West

Chiswick

★ Fish Hook

8 Elliott Road, W4 1PE (8742 0766/www.fish hook.co.uk). Turnham Green tube. **Lunch served** noon-2.30pm Mon-Fri; noon-3.30pm Sat, Sun. **Dinner served** 6-10.30pm Mon-Sat; 6-10pm Sun. **Main courses** £16-£28. **Set lunch** £10 2 courses, £13.50 3 courses. **Credit** AmEx, JCB, MC, V.
The interior of this excellent Turnham Green local hasn't altered much since its previous incarnation as South African fish restaurant Fish Hoek. You'll still find a soothing environment of cream walls and dark flagstone floor, soft lighting and moody black and white piscine photos – and all that's changed on the logo is the 'e'. But the menu is much shorter, and no longer specialises in South African fish and flavours. Straightforward pricing (starters £8, mains £16, with the occasional supplement, puds £5.50) keeps things simple, though the cooking (courtesy of chef-proprietor Michael Nadra) tends towards the elaborate. A starter of warm octopus salad with purple broccoli, ratte potatoes and a delicate dill and lemon dressing was a finely balanced combination of flavours, with supremely tender octopus. Equally good were our main courses: ragout of scallops with baby squid and black tiger prawns, with tomato, sweet potato and basil; and crispy-skinned sea bass with crab ravioli, bisque sauce and courgettes. Good to see pollock as an alternative to endangered cod too. Desserts have a fruity, seasonal edge (poached peaches or strawberry millefeuille in summer, rhubarb in spring), though English and French cheeses are always available. The carefully chosen, well-priced wine list includes a lovely flinty Disznókó dry furmint from Hungary.
Babies and children admitted. Booking advisable.

Notting Hill

★ Geales (100)

2007 RUNNER-UP BEST BRITISH RESTAURANT

2 Farmer Street, W8 7SN (7727 7528/ www.geales.com). Notting Hill Gate tube. **Lunch served** noon-2.30pm Tue-Sun. **Dinner served**

Interview
ROBIN HANCOCK

Who are you?
Co-owner of **Wright Brothers Oyster & Porter House** (*see p99*). We also have a wholesale company that supplies many of London's finest restaurants, and we have the rights to the Duchy of Cornwall oyster farm on the Helford River.
Eating in London: what's good about it?
There's such an eclectic selection of food. London has become a centre for excellence, with some of the most innovative chefs in the world. With all the great food markets here, chefs have access to the finest ingredients.
What's bad about it?
Apart from the rather ancient transport system and parking difficulties, I am still amazed to find low-end restaurants and pubs with menus that are far too long; as a result, they must have kitchens full of freezers and microwaves. I love modest establishments with half a dozen dishes comprising fresh, local produce that is well cooked.
Which are your favourite London restaurants?
Racine (*see p105*) has very honest and delicious French bistro de luxe cuisine. I'm a big Mark Hix fan and love all the Caprice restaurants, particularly **Scott's** (*see p95*), which is a buzzing place to eat. I also love the steak tartare at the **Wolseley** (*see p235*) with a bottle of Côtes du Rhône!
Who or what has had the biggest impact on London's restaurant scene in the past 25 years?
From a British perspective, it has to be places like **Bibendum** (*see p237*), **Kensington Place** (*see p238*) and **Le Caprice** (*see p236*). Chefs like Simon Hopkinson, Graham Williams, Rowley Leigh and Marco Pierre White, to name a few, inspired and created the foundations of what makes London eating great today.

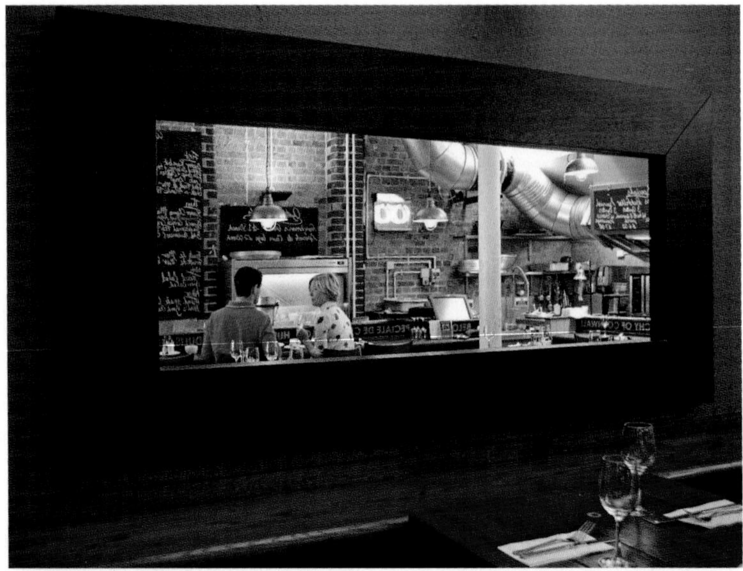

Wright Brothers

6-11pm Mon-Fri; 6-10.30pm Sun. **Meals served** noon-11pm Sat. **Main courses** £9-£14. **Cover** 15p. **Credit** AmEx, MC, V.

This long-time favourite local chippie (est. 1939) always had aspirations, and now new owners (including chef Garry Hollihead) have turned it into a suave and spacious fish restaurant. Its roots haven't been forgotten, though; the ketchup might come in porcelain jugs rather than squeezy bottles, but the core of the menu remains fish in batter, and grilled or fried market specials sourced from Devon and Cornwall. And they've retained the original cover charge (15p!). There are adjustments for gentrification; starters include sea scallops with burnt orange dressing, and thai soft-shell crab (recommended), along with dressed crab and pots of prawns. Cod, hake, haddock and sole arrived beautifully battered, and fresh as the new tide. From the specials, our whole dover sole, which requires an expert hand, was exquisite. Chips and onion rings didn't let dishes down, nor did the classy mushy peas, though we'd have preferred them unreconstructedly lurid. Desserts aren't really the point, but order the light, fresh jam roly-poly over the cloying mocha tart. Service was friendly and expert, with the caveat that we weren't told the prices of the market fish when ordering – disingenuous at best since the dover sole was, at £26, more than twice the £12 stated on the menu (small print warned only that 'some prices may vary').

Babies and children admitted. Booking advisable. Tables outdoors (6, pavement). Takeaway service. **Map 7 A7.**

South West

Earl's Court

Lou Pescadou

241 Old Brompton Road, SW5 9HP (7370 1057). Earl's Court tube. **Lunch served** noon-3pm daily. **Dinner served** 7pm-midnight Mon-Fri; 6.30pm-midnight Sat, Sun. **Main courses** £8.90-£18. **Set lunch** (Mon-Fri) £10.90 3 courses. **Set meal** (until 8pm Sat, all day Sun) £14.50 3 courses. **Credit** AmEx, DC, MC, V.

The pleasure of an authentic French restaurant is not to be underestimated. While so many are so *faux*, there is something *parfait* about this one, which could be found almost anywhere in France. As well as offering a typically good-value three-course lunch (only £10.90, with two options at each course), Lou Pescadou has a strong line in seafood starters, from crab salad or langoustines (fished in Scotland and Ireland, yet tough to find in the UK) to a classic fish soup with croûtons and aïoli. The choice of about five fish (such as a crispy salmon fillet) is typically accompanied by spinach and sautéed potatoes; there's a handful of seafood-based pastas too. What's more, with pork, steak and chicken (as well as vegetarian) dishes, you can even take your non-pescetarian friends. House wine is respectable, although most bottles from a select (not entirely French) list cost over £20. Service is relaxed, but uniformed and courteous – also very French. The stark white walls with bright paintings and the plain pine furnishing could do with updating to something cosier. Yet there's a classic simplicity about this place that other restaurants would do well to emulate.

Babies and children welcome: children's menu; high chairs. Booking advisable. Tables outdoors (8, terrace). Takeaway service. **Map 13 B11.**
For branch (Chez Patrick) see index.

Fulham

Deep

The Boulevard, Imperial Wharf, SW6 2UB (7736 3337/www.deeplondon.co.uk). Fulham Broadway tube then 391, C3 bus.
Bar **Open/snacks served** noon-11pm Tue-Fri; 5-11pm Sat. **Snacks** £4-£11.50.
Restaurant **Lunch served** noon-3pm Tue-Fri; Sun. **Dinner served** 7-11pm Tue-Sat. **Main courses** £12.50-£24. **Set lunch** £12.50 1 course, £15.50 2 courses, £19.50 3 courses.
Both **Credit** AmEx, JCB, MC, V.

The lifeless Imperial Wharf location does Deep no favours. Without any streetside bustle, the large, modern restaurant – all glass windows, white linen and fabric-covered chairs – seems stark if devoid of diners, as it was on our visit. The bar and two outside terraces were also empty, though amiable staff did their best to liven the atmosphere. The menu is rather unbalanced: there are starters galore (including prawns, oysters and lobster at market prices), but a much shorter list of mains and no side dishes. A pity, as the Scandinavian-influenced cooking – thanks to Swedish owners Christian and Kerstin Sandefeldt – can be good. To start, tuna tartare with Arctic caviar was sparkily sea-fresh; three kinds of marinated herring arrived in little bowls, with new potatoes, nutty cheese and crispbread. Presentation is striking. Perfectly cooked hot-smoked trout was served as three chunky pieces, each balanced on a disc of beetroot, interspersed with two blobs of mash topped with asparagus. But a deconstructed paella – salmon, prawns and mussels in separate piles, with the rice in its own copper pan – was an example of style over substance. The meal finished on a high with intensely flavoured sorbets (apple, mandarin, mango) and a couple of excellent akvavits from the 20-strong list.
Babies and children welcome: high chairs. Booking advisable. Disabled: toilet. Dress: smart casual. Entertainment: DJ 7pm Fri (bar). Tables outdoors (16, terrace). **Map 21 A2.**

South

Kennington

Lobster Pot

3 Kennington Lane, SE11 4RG (7582 5556/ www.lobsterpotrestaurant.co.uk). Kennington tube. **Lunch served** noon-2.30pm, **dinner served** 7-10.45pm Tue-Sat. **Main courses** £14.50-£32.50. **Minimum** (8-10pm) £23. **Set lunch** £11.50 2 courses, £14.50 3 courses. **Set meal** £21.50 3 courses, £39.50 tasting menu. **Credit** AmEx, JCB, MC, V.
For years the Lobster Pot, run by Breton chef Hervé Regent and his wife Michelle (on front-of-house duties), has provided a warm Gallic refuge from the grim surrounds of the Elephant & Castle hinterland. The two-level interior is an eccentric mishmash: fishing nets and lobster pots clutter the wood-panelled walls, real fish swim behind portholes – all to a soundtrack of seagulls and fog horns. It's a bit like being in a Jules Verne novel. The cooking is determinedly French and very good. Lobster is a speciality, as you'd expect, but there's also a popular seafood platter, classics such as skate wing with brown butter and capers, and even rabbit, duck, steak and chicken for die-hard meat eaters. An eight-course 'surprise menu' (with or without lobster) is also available, plus a handful of daily specials. A generous starter of poached prawns and scallops, served in a mini copper saucepan, came with a lovely mushroom, cream and Pernod sauce (much lighter than it sounds), while a main-course bouillabaisse was a richly flavoured, fish-packed treat, including an ultra-garlicky rouille. If you've room, finish with profiteroles with chocolate sauce, or pancake with raspberry sauce. The wine list is very short but does the job.
Babies and children welcome: booster seat. Booking advisable. Dress: smart casual. Separate rooms for parties, seating 20 and 28.

Waterloo

Livebait

43 The Cut, SE1 8LF (7928 7211/www.santeonline.co.uk/livebait). Southwark tube/Waterloo tube/rail. **Meals served** noon-11pm Mon-Sat; 12.30-9pm Sun. **Main courses** £9.95-£36. **Set meal** (noon-7pm) £14.50 2 courses, £18.50 3 courses. **Credit** AmEx, DC, JCB, MC, V.
Livebait's fishmonger aesthetic (walls covered in green and white tiles, too-bright lighting, ramped-up air-con) may thematically suit a fish restaurant, but it does make for rather chilly dining. The Vics Young and Old are just down the road, so theatregoers eat here, though there were plenty of other customers on our midweek visit. Hard to fathom why really, as the cooking is pretty dismal. Originally independent, Livebait is now part of the Chez Gérard group – and it shows. Staff are competent, but lack the personal touch. Stick with the simpler dishes (oysters, fish and chips, grilled fish with a choice of one side dish) and you should be satisfied, but anything more elaborate is to be avoided. The poached egg and buttered spinach were the best things about a starter of hot-smoked salmon; the fish was dry and chewy, and the accompanying parsnip and potato rösti was grey in colour and stringy in texture. Mini louisiana crab cakes came with a too-cold potato salad devoid of the promised 'Cajun' spicing. Even a shellfish plate was a failure: wizened mussels, dried-out winkles, flavourless prawns; only the cockles and oysters tasted fresh. The wine list is expensive too.
Babies and children welcome: children's menu; booster seats; high chairs. Booking advisable. Disabled: toilet. **Map 11 N8.**
For branch see index.

South East

London Bridge & Borough

fish!

Cathedral Street, Borough Market, SE1 9AL (7407 3803/www.fishdiner.co.uk). London Bridge tube/rail. **Meals served** 11.30am-11pm Mon-Thur; noon-11pm Fri, Sat; noon-10.30pm Sun. **Main courses** £9.95-£24.95. **Credit** AmEx, DC, MC, V.
That exclamation mark at the end of fish! says it all – this is a lively, vibrant place with an everyman approach that has both ups and downs. It's a pleasantly open space in a great location in Borough Market, the glass and steel structure enabling you to enjoy old London outside and new Londoners inside, among them families, groups of friends and couples all relishing their starters. From an impressive selection, we chose crispy yet succulent devilled whitebait, classic prawn cocktail (with a tart marie rose sauce), and baby octopus and borlotti bean salad (the sharpness of the pickled octopus contrasting wonderfully with the creaminess of the beans). Mains were less enjoyable. Grilled monkfish (from the 'choose your own' selection of steamed or grilled fish and sauces) was unappetising, though the salsa verde and steamed pak choi with sweet carrots that came alongside lifted the sad morsels of fish. Haddock and chips with mushy peas was better, but a meagre portion for £13.95. Still, it left room for a warm chocolate fondant dessert: delicious and filling. Fish! may be loud and brash, but it does what it does well, with efficient, good-natured service to boot. A decent house white, Trebbiano, was correctly chilled and, at £13.95, fairly priced.
Babies and children welcome: children's menu; crayons; high chairs. Booking advisable. Disabled: toilet. Tables outdoors (35, pavement). **Map 11 P8.**

★ Wright Brothers Oyster & Porter House

11 Stoney Street, SE1 9AD (7403 9554/ www.wrightbros.eu.com). Borough tube/London Bridge tube/rail. **Meals served** noon-10.30pm Mon-Sat. **Main courses** £8.75-£16.70. **Credit** AmEx, MC, V.
The world is your oyster at Wright Brothers; or, more accurately, the oyster is your world: this vibrant, characterful bar on the edge of Borough Market must have the widest range of the plump molluscs in London. September to April is the best time to visit (when native oysters are in season), but even in high summer the choice is immense: French, Irish and Scottish rocks, plus oyster specials (how about Japanese with wasabi, or Spanish with chorizo?), alongside the regular menu (dressed crab, fish soup, fish pie) and daily specials – all chalked up on assorted blackboards around the room. You can sit at shared tables with high stools or at a few oyster barrels on the pavement, but the ringside seats are the best: along the L-shaped counter, from where you can watch the chefs in their striped aprons shucking oysters, pouring wine, generally adding to the air of noisy bonhomie. The oysters are first-class, of course, but scallops baked on the shell with tomato, basil and mash, and harissa-tinged grilled prawns with coriander (both specials) were also excellent. Finish with crème brûlée (a brittle-topped, creamy-centred rendition) or perhaps Cointreau and chocolate truffles. The wine list is more than adequate, and on the night we visited staff seemed to be having as much fun as the customers.
Booking advisable. Disabled: toilet. Tables outdoors (3, pavement). **Map 11 P8.**

SHELF LIFE

All the restaurants in the **FishWorks** chain (*see p100*) have a wet fish counter attached.

Steve Hatt
88-90 Essex Road, N1 8LU (7226 3963). Angel tube. **Open** 8am-5pm Tue-Thur; 7am-5pm Fri, Sat.
Probably the capital's best-known independent fishmonger, renowned for expert gutting and filleting, as well as authoritative advice on cooking. Game is also available in season.

Golborne Fisheries
75-77 Golborne Road, W10 5NP (8960 3100). Ladbroke Grove tube. **Open** 9am-5pm Mon; 8.30am-6pm Tue-Sat.
This spacious store is the place to go if you're after exotic lines such as fresh abalone, live eels, conch meat, clams and frogs' legs – all at keen prices.

Walter Purkis & Sons
52 Muswell Hill Broadway, N10 3RT (8883 4355/www.purkis4fish.com). Highgate tube/134 bus. **Open** 8.30am-5pm Tue-Sat.
This family-run operation has been involved in the seafood business for around 200 years. Stock comes from all the UK's major fishing ports, from Aberdeenshire to Cornwall. There's also a branch in Crouch End.

Sandy's
56 King Street, Twickenham, Middx TW1 3SH (8892 5788/www.sandysfish.net). Twickenham rail. **Open** 7.30am-6pm Mon-Wed, Sat; 7.30am-8pm Thur; 7.30am-7pm Fri.
One of London's largest independent fishmongers, Sandy's supports sustainable fishing practices and offers a huge selection of attractively displayed fish and shellfish, plus some game.

North East

South Woodford

Ark Fish Restaurant

142 Hermon Hill, E18 1QH (8989 5345/ www.arkfishrestaurant.com). South Woodford tube. **Lunch served** noon-2.15pm Tue-Sat. **Dinner served** 5.30-9.45pm Tue-Thur; 5.30-10.15pm Fri, Sat. **Meals served** noon-8.45pm Sun. **Main courses** £8.75-£22.50. **Credit** MC, V.
Thanks to a no-bookings policy, shoals of famished fish-lovers can often be found swirling around the bar at the Ark, waiting for a bite. The

Geales. See p97.

secret to its success is simplicity: fresh fish bought daily from Billingsgate, grilled or deep-fried and served with chips, new potatoes or mash. Specials are chalked on a board. Smoked mackerel and salmon pâté made a rich and creamy starter, and scallops were wonderfully moist and tender, though too much garlic butter made the accompanying salad soggy. Rock eel (a main-course special) was a splendid specimen, perfectly cooked and strongly flavoured. Portions are generous: a piece of firm-fleshed yellow fin tuna, taking up half the plate, was a definite hit. Desserts are old-school, including a great sticky toffee pudding – an island of syrupy brown sponge surrounded by a moat of creamy custard. We had a few gripes: the space got very noisy as it filled up, some dishes were more successful than others (mushy peas beat mediterranean veg hands down) and the chips weren't as crispy as on previous visits. Still, service is exemplary and prices are very reasonable.
Babies and children welcome: children's menu; high chairs. Bookings not accepted.

Wanstead

★ Applebee's

17 Cambridge Park, E11 2PU (8989 1977). Wanstead tube. **Lunch served** noon-3pm Tue-Fri. **Dinner served** 6.30-10.30pm Tue-Sat; noon-9pm Sun. **Main courses** £13-£17.50. **Set lunch** £11.50 2 courses, £15.50 3 courses. **Set dinner** £21.50 3 courses. **Credit** AmEx, JCB, MC, V.
Lucky Wanstead to have Applebee's. The look is modern with a Mediterranean feel, enhanced by orange mosaic tiles; the atmosphere is relaxed; the service is friendly and expert. The menu favours fresh fish – scallops, prawns, crab, sea bass, tuna – but there is plenty to excite a carnivore's palate too. From a wide-ranging wine list, a fine, reasonably priced bottle of Nero d'Avola arrived with amuse-bouches of red pepper mousse on balsamic, setting the tone for a memorable meal. Smoked mackerel mousse piped on to new potatoes arrived with a creamy, mozzarella-filled tomato, countering the salty fish well. Beef carpaccio was as fine a cut as we've tasted, complemented by sweet roasted tomatoes. The faultless cooking continued with chunky, moist halibut that had been poached in red wine, served with saffron potatoes and grilled asparagus, and excellent ribeye married well with nutty truffle mash and grilled artichokes. With no room for dessert (plenty of berries, brûlées and chocolate), we were still happy to see the mini pastry cases filled with choux cream, each topped with a blueberry, that came with coffee. Prices are remarkably fair for food this good, and the set menus are a steal.
Babies and children welcome: children's portions; high chair. Booking advisable dinner. Tables outdoors (5, courtyard).

North

Camden Town & Chalk Farm

FishWorks

57 Regents Park Road, NW1 8XD (7586 9760/ www.fishworks.co.uk). Chalk Farm tube. **Lunch served** noon-3pm daily. **Dinner served** 6-10.30pm Mon-Sat. **Main courses** £9.50-£25. **Credit** AmEx, DC, MC, V.
After a period of fairly furious growth in 2005 and 2006, Mitchell Tonks' mini-chain seems to have spent the past year consolidating its operations. The group now runs ten restaurants in London, all in affluent areas with a larger than average population of yummy mummies. All offer a wet fish counter alongside the full restaurant menu. You can order direct from the counter, though we stuck to the menu and a brief specials board. A starter of grilled squid came with a nicely spicy piri-piri tang, but the squid itself was too chewy for comfort. A crab salad was dry and tasteless. Mains, though, were far better: grilled sea bass, filleted by request, was positively succulent, while a princely halibut special arrived on a throne of crushed, heavily oiled and decidedly moreish potatoes. Extra marks too for the lovely pinot grigio rosé accompaniment. The decor is the same in each outlet – royal blue and white colour scheme, cheery seaside paintings – so you're always very aware that you're in a chain eaterie. But if that's not a problem, there's plenty here to like.
Babies and children welcome: children's menu; high chairs. Booking advisable. Fishmonger. Tables outdoors (3, pavement). **Map 27 A2.**
For branches see index.

Finsbury Park

Chez Liline

101 Stroud Green Road, N4 3PX (7263 6550). Finsbury Park tube/rail. **Dinner served** 6.30-11pm Tue-Sun. **Main courses** £10.95-£17.75. **Set dinner** £15 3 courses. **Credit** AmEx, MC, V.
Resolutely urban Stroud Green Road may not be the best starting point from which to be transported to the Indian Ocean island of Mauritius, but Chez Liline succeeds in whisking you away. It does so not by dint of its decor – the small room is furnished with simple tables and chairs, bamboo screens and generic tropical island posters – but by its menu of Mauritian seafood. Most ingredients come fresh via the fishmonger next door (also owned by Chez Liline). On our visit they included native lobster, queen scallops, prawns and various sea fish – cooked in sauces that, despite familiar flavourings like chilli and ginger, tasted unlike anything we've eaten. A mix of the rich sauces of French Creole cuisine and the hotter, spicier end of Chinese and African cooking resulted in a plate of creole fish in tomatoes and chilli that was substantial yet delicate; we could easily discern individual spices and flavours. Garlic and chilli perfectly complemented the meatiness of lobster, but didn't overpower its subtle fresh flavours; a dark and glossy-brown fish curry was rich and powerful, though retained the delicacy of the fish. Desserts are standard French with a twist: crêpe, crème brûlée and papaya tart.
Babies and children welcome: high chairs. Booking advisable. Restaurant available for hire.

Islington

The Fish Shop

360-362 St John Street, EC1V 4NR (7837 1199/ www.thefishshop.net). Angel tube/19, 38, 341 bus. **Lunch served** noon-3pm, **dinner served** 5.30-11pm Tue-Sat. **Meals served** noon-8pm Sun. **Main courses** £11-£36. **Set meal** (noon-3pm, 5.30-7pm Tue-Sat, all Sun) £13.50 2 courses, £17 3 courses. **Credit** AmEx, DC, MC, V.
A couple of pirouettes from Sadler's Wells, the Fish Shop is an attractive spot, set over three levels, with yellow walls, pale wooden furniture and large windows, including a glass wall overlooking a pretty back garden (out of bounds, sadly). It's hard to believe it was once a pub. The atmosphere is relaxed, sedate even: partly because the place was only half-full on our Friday night visit. The menu is straightforward, running from crustacea – oysters, prawns, whelks, seafood platters – to soups, fish and chips (available deep-fried in batter or matzo meal, steamed or grilled, and with mash or chips), along with more elaborate dishes. We've complained about lacklustre cooking in the past, and there were some duff dishes this time too: salt and pepper squid was rubbery and lacked piquancy; haddock, salmon and tarragon fish cakes were stodgy. But the oysters (£1.75 a pop) were good quality, and a main of pan-fried sea trout was a fine specimen, well matched with braised fennel, cherry tomatoes and saffron sauce. Puds tend towards the homely (sticky toffee pudding, crumble, treacle tart), not that we're complaining; lemon tart was a creamy, tangy treat. An impressive choice of bottled beers supplements the well-priced wine list.
Babies and children welcome: children's portions. Booking advisable dinner Fri, Sat. Disabled: toilet. Tables outdoors (10, terrace). **Map 5 O3.**

French

French dining establishments in London stretch from neighbourhood bistros offering boeuf bourguignon and its traditional bedfellows, to the stellar gastronomic venues that we list in **Hotels & Haute Cuisine** (starting on p139). For many years, the scene had a rather blunt cutting edge, as innovative chefs moved into Modern European territory instead. More recently, though, adventurous cooking has returned, whether it be the inspiring creations at Alexis Gauthier's **Roussillon**, Morgan Meunier's **Morgan M**, the Galvin Brothers' sumptuous cuisine at **Galvin Bistrot de Luxe** or the cooking of south-west France developed at **Club Gascon** – continued at its siblings **Le Comptoir Gascon** and **Le Cercle**.

There are three significant new openings to report this year: **Trinity**, offering classical cuisine in Clapham – and contender for Best Local Restaurant in the 2007 Time Out Eating & Drinking Awards; Mayfair's **La Petite Maison**, out of the same stable as Japanese stars Roka and Zuma, and already attracting the beau monde; and the **Wallace**, Oliver Peyton's latest foray into revitalising art gallery dining.

Central

Belgravia

Le Cercle

1 Wilbraham Place, SW1X 9AE (7901 9999/ www.lecercle.co.uk). Sloane Square tube.
Bar **Open/snacks served** noon-midnight Tue-Sat.
Restaurant **Lunch served** noon-3pm, **tea served** 3-5.30pm, **dinner served** 6-11pm Tue-Sat. **Set lunch** £15 3 dishes incl coffee, £19.50 4 dishes. **Set dinner** (6-7pm, 10-11pm Tue-Sat) £17.50 3 dishes incl coffee, £21.50 4 dishes. **Tapas** £4-£16. **Credit** AmEx, JCB, MC, V.

The owners of Club Gascon (*see p102*), Le Comptoir Gascon (*see p102*) and wine bar Cellar Gascon have won acclaim for the smart, French-style tapas menu they've devised at this stylish basement restaurant. A discreet entrance leads downstairs to an impressive, high-ceilinged dining area, graced with billowy full-length curtains, dark wood and leather fixtures, and exposed brick walls. A parade of perfectly executed and presented morsels lived up to our consequent expectations. High points included a juicy fillet steak, served with buttery wild asparagus and delectable toasted garlic purée. Ravioli also delivered delicacy and balance, with a meltingly soft cheese filling enhanced by a veil of creamy, aniseed-scented sauce. Simple numbers didn't quite make the grade; a crisp spring vegetable salad betrayed no hint of the promised lavender in its lemony dressing. Neither were we convinced by the braised lamb, which needed an infusion of meaty juices to rescue it from ordinariness. Our waiter, although well intentioned, was a touch too eager to clear dishes away as soon as we paused for breath. But despite the stumbles, this spot provides rich pickings for well-heeled tourists and monied Chelsea residents.

Babies and children welcome: children's menu; high chairs. Booking advisable. Disabled: toilet. Takeaway service. **Map 15 G10**.

La Poule au Pot

231 Ebury Street, SW1W 8UT (7730 7763). Sloane Square tube. **Lunch served** 12.30-2.30pm Mon-Fri; 12.30-3.30pm Sat, Sun. **Dinner served** 6.45-11pm Mon-Sat; 6.45-10pm Sun. **Main courses** £15.50-£21. **Set lunch** £16.75 2 courses, £18.75 3 courses. **Credit** AmEx, DC, MC, V.

Festooned with wicker baskets and bunches of dried flowers, this retro French bistro is a much-loved icon for wealthy Chelsea residents. Although a tad cramped and a trifle dark, the rustic decor creates an inviting, intimate vibe, at odds with its top-end prices. There are no English translations on the all-French menu, but friendly waiters are helpful enough. This is coq au vin and bourguignon territory; expect no new-wave punches. Starters were impressive: a steamy helping of French onion soup delivered sweetly mellow notes, emboldened by meltingly soft onions. Equally delectable was a deep bowl of delicately scented, herby fish broth populated by a medley of juicy scallops, mussels and white fish morsels. Mains were robust: a huge helping of succulent rabbit cloaked in creamy, mustardy sauce worked especially well with homely boulangère potatoes. Deliciously rosy magret duck breast didn't reach the same heights, and was let down by a surfeit of lime-infused meaty jus; and crème brûlée lacked the vanilla it needed to tickle the taste buds. House wines are excellent, fairly priced and flow freely from magnums.

Babies and children welcome: high chairs. Booking essential. Disabled: toilet. Separate room for parties, seats 16. Tables outdoors (12, terrace). **Map 15 G11**.

★ Roussillon

16 St Barnabas Street, SW1W 8PE (7730 5550/ www.roussillon.co.uk). Sloane Square tube.
Lunch served noon-2.30pm Mon-Fri. **Dinner served** 6.30-10.30pm Mon-Sat. **Set lunch** £35 3 courses incl half bottle of wine and coffee. **Set dinner** £55 3 courses incl coffee. **Set meal** £65 tasting menu. **Credit** AmEx, MC, V.

A neutral colour scheme, punctuated by occasional flower arrangements, epitomises the restrained elegance of this fine-dining restaurant. The ambience is matched by a clientele of deep-pocketed local residents and crisp business suits. Chef-patron Alexis Gauthier's adventurous menu celebrates classic French cooking, fresh British produce and seasonal global specialities. Starters of light gnocchi worked well with the stridency of soft gorgonzola cheese and contrasting sweetness of balsamic vinegar. Equally superlative were plump seared scallops, garnished with a swirl of aromatic shellfish jus and wisps of black truffle: a marvellous combination. Main courses also lived up to expectation: tender Angus beef fillet, cooked to retain a perfect pinkness, scored top marks for succulence and was enhanced by butter-kissed purple artichokes and the bite of black olives. After polishing off a pre-dessert tease of tart lemon jelly topped with shards of grapefruit granita, we sunk our spoons into Indian mangoes and silken jasmine sorbet, and demolished a delectable chocolate parfait. You don't need to stray far from Languedoc-Roussillon in the wine list, or to spend more than around £30, but ample pleasures await if you do. Set menu options appease the pampered palates of young 'uns, and cater for vegetarians too.

Children over 8 years welcome: children's menu. Booking advisable. Dress: smart casual. Restaurant available for hire. Separate room for parties, seats 26. Vegetarian menu.
Map 15 G11.

City

★ 1 Lombard Street

1 Lombard Street, EC3V 9AA (7929 6611/ www.1lombardstreet.com). Bank tube/DLR.
Bar **Open/tapas served** 11am-11pm Mon-Fri. **Tapas** £7.50-£14.50.
Brasserie **Breakfast served** 7.30-11am, **meals served** 11.30am-10pm Mon-Fri. **Main courses** £16.50-£25.50. **Set meal** £16.50 2 courses, £19.50 3 courses.
Restaurant **Lunch served** noon-3pm, **dinner served** 6-9.45pm Mon-Fri. **Main courses** £24-£34.50.
All **Credit** AmEx, DC, MC, V.

If you're going to dine in the City, you may as well go the whole hog and dine in a bank. This particular temple of Mammon (deconsecrated) is a Grade II-listed building opposite the Old Lady of Threadneedle Street, made bright and welcoming by white walls, white table linen, big windows and Pietro Agostini's neoclassical domed skylights. Overseen by executive chef Herbert Berger, the food has won a Michelin star, which seemed merited at our high-end lunch in the swish brasserie section. The restaurant area to the side serves more expensive haute cuisine. After delicious, still-warm bread rolls, we chose seared pink salmon with thai aubergine caviar, and a sublime carpaccio of tuna with toasted sesame seeds (plus a balsamic sauce that criss-crossed the plate in a pretty weave of thin lines). Mains were fine poached salmon served with crushed new potatoes scented with caraway, and an immaculately cooked ribeye with chips. Most of the long, mainly French wine list is aimed at expense accounts, but the surprisingly lengthy choice of house wines will satisfy most needs for those on a more limited budget. Service is friendly and polished, and beneath the skylight is a dramatic, well-stocked circular bar.

Children over 10 years admitted. Booking advisable. Disabled: toilet. Entertainment: pianist and singer 6.30pm Fri. Restaurant available for hire. Separate room for parties, seats 40.
Map 12 Q6.

Le Coq d'Argent

No.1 Poultry, EC2R 8EJ (7395 5000/ www.danddlondon.com). Bank tube/DLR.
Bar & Grill **Lunch served** 11.30am-3pm Mon-Fri. **Main courses** £12-£16.
Restaurant **Breakfast served** 7.30-10am Mon-Fri. **Lunch served** 11.30am-3pm Mon-Fri; noon-3pm Sun. **Dinner served** 6-10pm Mon-Fri; 6.30-10pm Sat. **Main courses** £15-£25. **Set lunch** £24 2 courses, £28.50 3 courses.
Both **Credit** AmEx, DC, JCB, MC, V.

The Conran group may now be under the D&D banner, but nothing seems to have changed at this City favourite. Perched atop the striped behemoth that is No.1 Poultry, it's an architecturally imposing spot. You ascend by lift to a central, circular bar, lush with greenery. Leading off this

is the dining area, and a large wedge-shaped lawn offering striking views of the surrounding buildings. Tablecloths and comfortable club chairs mark out the restaurant from the smaller brasserie (where tables verge on too small and elbows are wedged), but both spaces have attractive, canopy-covered terraces. Polite, black-clad staff dash busily about, though service can be slow. Judging by the number of suits at lunchtime, the Square Mile expense account is in no danger of imminent extinction. Perhaps that's why the chefs don't have to try too hard with the food. From the brasserie menu, a main of tuna brochettes produced three skewers of perfectly cooked fish, but the accompanying ratatouille was watery. A hefty ribeye with béarnaise and chunky chips was pleasant, yet nothing special. Marine life is a strength, including oysters, langoustines, seafood platters and caviar. Best was a silky passionfruit tart with crème fraîche. The restaurant menu is longer, more elaborate and pricier, with most mains around £20.
Babies and children welcome: high chairs. Booking advisable. Disabled: lift; toilet. Entertainment: jazz noon-4pm Sun. Restaurant available for hire. Tables outdoors (14, restaurant terrace; 14, bar terrace). **Map 11 P6.**

★ Rosemary Lane

61 Royal Mint Street, E1 8LG (7481 2602/ www.rosemarylane.btinternet.co.uk). Tower Hill tube/Fenchurch Street rail/Tower Gateway DLR.
Lunch served noon-2.30pm Mon-Fri. **Dinner served** 5.30-10pm Mon-Fri; 6-10pm Sat. **Main courses** £13-£19. **Set meal** £14 2 courses, £17 3 courses. **Set dinner** (Sat) £30 tasting menu. **Credit** AmEx, MC, V.
A busy lunchtime destination, Rosemary Lane provides a stress-free retreat for its regular clientele – mainly smart City suits. The restaurant overcomes a dreary street location with an elegant interior of dark wood panelling, weighty drapes and white table linen. Its modern French-fusion menu is complemented by an adventurous wine selection; a 'very berry' Californian pinot noir worked well with our meal. Pre-meal teasers impressed: figs, sitting pretty on a bed of balsamic-dressed beetroot and topped with goat's cheese, provided a creative contrast of flavours. Equally enjoyable was a zesty first course of rare-cooked wisps of beef, rolled around avocado and cucumber strips and anointed with zingy orange dressing. Our mains were also top-notch: roast pork belly, infused with plum wine and finished with a dark soy glaze, was a showstopper thanks to its meaty succulence and crisp crackling. But it's not all about new-wave inspirations; indeed, nothing could be more authentic than a juicy ribeye steak, glazed in rich red wine sauce. If you like ices, finish with the pink guava sorbet – intensely aromatic and as light as air. In a virtually faultless meal, our only criticism was that portion sizes were rather on the substantial side.
Booking advisable lunch. Dress: smart casual. Restaurant available for hire. **Map 12 S7.**

★ Sauterelle

Royal Exchange, EC3V 3LR (7618 2483/ www.danddlondon.com). Bank tube/DLR.
Lunch served noon-2.30pm, **dinner served** 6-10pm Mon-Fri. **Main courses** £16.50-£19. **Credit** AmEx, DC, MC, V.
With its stunning location around the gallery of the lovely Royal Exchange, this ex-Conran operation (now owned by D&D London) doesn't have to worry about wow factor. It lays on quality linen and super-comfortable chairs and then focuses its energy on what matters: food and service. The former comes from a menu that is French at the intersection with Modern European: not so haute – nor expensive – as to discourage the middle management among its relatively relaxed City clientele. That's not to say it compromises on technique or quality: now, as in the Conran days, we were impressed by the precise rendition of every element of a dish and seduced by the overall effect. Scallops were enhanced, not overwhelmed, by a delicate, vanilla-infused jerusalem artichoke purée; goat's cheese tart was crispy and creamy in all the right places; duck magret with foie gras a textural treat. The mild disappointment of an ordinary tuna with tapenade was a blip rescued by a good Fleurie for £26, chosen from a short, well-balanced wine list. This positively delighted our waitress, who complimented us fulsomely on our good taste, service being an enjoyable mix of subtle sycophancy and informed professionalism.
Babies and children admitted. Disabled: toilet. **Map 12 Q6.**

Clerkenwell & Farringdon

Café du Marché

22 Charterhouse Square, Charterhouse Mews, EC1M 6AH (7608 1609/www.cafedumarche.co.uk). Barbican tube/Farringdon tube/rail.
Le Café **Lunch served** noon-2.30pm Mon-Fri. **Dinner served** 6-10pm Mon-Sat. **Set meal** £31.50 3 courses.
Le Grenier **Lunch served** noon-2.30pm Mon-Fri. **Dinner served** 7-10pm Mon-Sat. **Set meal** £31.50 3 courses.
Le Rendezvous **Lunch served** noon-2.30pm Mon-Fri. **Main courses** £6-£14.
All **Credit** MC, V.
An old warehouse a skip from Smithfield Market is home to this rather charming three-in-one restaurant: Le Grenier, up a corkscrew staircase on the first floor; at ground level, the brasserie-style Le Rendezvous that specialises in grills and frites; and Le Café, where we had our merry evening meal. The first thing you notice is the cheerfulness of the all-French staff, and (telling sign) how well they enjoy each other's company. Their good mood swells the rising enjoyment among diners, which is further boosted by a jazz pianist, romantic lighting and a commendably gentle touch with the decorations of Gallic bric-a-brac (this place is French, but it doesn't feel the need to ram the fact down your gullet). We went for the set meal, kicking off with venison carpaccio and grilled sardines with a fennel risotto – both excellent – and moving on to succulent guinea hen, and quasi d'agneau with girolle mushrooms. In lieu of dessert, we spent the extra £4 on a wonderfully whiffy cheeseboard. The wine list is strong on good, assertive French reds (our Gigondas nicely cut the mustard), and the digestif list includes a silky smooth calvados. Great fun.
Babies and children admitted. Booking advisable (not accepted Le Rendezvous). Entertainment (Le Café): jazz duo 8pm Mon-Thur; pianist 8pm Fri, Sat. Separate rooms for parties, seating 35 and 50. **Map 5 O5.**

★ Club Gascon (100)

57 West Smithfield, EC1A 9DS (7796 0600/ www.clubgascon.com). Barbican tube/Farringdon tube/rail. **Lunch served** noon-2pm Mon-Fri. **Dinner served** 7-10pm Mon-Thur; 7-10.30pm Fri, Sat. **Tapas** £8-£28. **Set lunch** £35 3 courses. **Set meal** £39 5 courses (£60 incl wine). **Credit** AmEx, MC, V.
Bijou in the best possible way, Club Gascon was the original of the Smithfield cluster of gems – Le Comptoir Gascon (*see below*), Le Cercle (*see p101*) and wine bar Cellar Gascon complete the set – offering food and wine of south-west France. But this is not the menu of wanton, calorie-laden luxury you might expect. It's grouped according to dishes' key ingredients (with headings of vegetables, seafood, lamb/beef and, famously, foie gras), and the idea is to have three or four of the starter-size dishes. Expect a succession of dazzling flavours, and for the fabulous bread to be the main carbohydrate. Occasionally odd, but more often than not plate-lickingly good, dishes included a classic duck foie gras and rabbit terrine with pickled cherries, brioche and pea-shoot salad, and morels served with tiny peeled broad beans. After that, try cheeses stunningly matched with different relishes, such as roquefort with clementine and kumquat pulp, or a bold dessert. Raspberries and red peppers – the berries in a capscicum-flavoured millefeuille – was a rare mismatch. With a silver ceiling and marbled walls from a previous life the handsome room has a subtle, luxurious lustre. Adept service comes from a team as young, good-looking, skilled and French as Arsenal once was. The wine list is all French too, leaning to the south-west – but don't expect bargains.
Booking essential. Restaurant available for hire. **Map 11 O5.**

Le Comptoir Gascon

61-63 Charterhouse Street, EC1M 6HJ (7608 0851/www.comptoirgascon.com). Farringdon tube/rail. **Brunch served** 10.30am-2pm Sat. **Lunch served** noon-2pm Tue-Fri. **Dinner served** 7-11pm Tue-Sat. **Main courses** £7.50-£13.50. **Credit** AmEx, MC, V.
This cosy corner of Smithfield is a temple to the products of south-west France, many of them unashamedly and delectably carnivorous, the rest of comparably impeccable provenance and flavour. There are, admittedly, sections on the menu for fish and vegetables, and we're sure they're delicious – the carrot, fennel and artichoke barigoule, squid and pearl barley, and Landes asparagus certainly were – but what keeps the punters perceptibly happy is the meat. The blackboard proffers the likes of veal kidneys, quail salad and suckling pig; there's a whole section of the menu devoted to duck derivations, foie gras included; and the classic starter is 'piggy treats', a board of wide-ranging charcuterie. Chips are fried in duck fat and are sublimely better off for it. With its brick walls, sausages hanging to dry and deli counter, the place has the feel of a working larder and generates a warm, personal atmosphere. This, the quality of the food and the very fair prices ensure it's usually very busy. The only blot on the landscape on our last visit was a gormless waiter, but the rest of the staff rallied around to compensate.
Babies and children welcome: high chairs. Bookings advisable. Tables outdoors (4, pavement). **Map 11 O5.**

Covent Garden

Mon Plaisir

19-21 Monmouth Street, WC2H 9DD (7836 7243/www.monplaisir.co.uk). Covent Garden tube.
Meals served noon-11.15pm Mon-Fri; 5.45-11.15pm Sat. **Main courses** £13.95-£22. **Set lunch** £14.50 2 courses, £16.50 3 courses. **Set meal** (5.45-7pm Mon-Sat; after 10pm Mon-Thur) £13.50 2 courses, £15.50 3 courses incl glass of wine and coffee. **Credit** AmEx, MC, V.
A more French-looking restaurant it's hard to imagine: outside, a whopping tricolour; inside, four snug little niches of Gaulish glory decked with Gauloise ads, an old Métro map, bric-a-brac by the cartload and a honeyed glow straight out of

BEST FRENCH

Gorgeous and Gallic

Savour the classiest cuisine at **La Belvedere** (*see p109*), **Chez Bruce** (*see p111*), **Club Gascon** (*see right*), **Galvin Bistrot de Luxe** (*see p105*), **The Ledbury** (*see p111*), **1 Lombard Street** (*see p101*), **Morgan M** (*see p113*), **Racine** (*see p105*), **Roussillon** (*see p101*), **RSJ** (*see p112*), **Sauterelle** (*see right*), **La Trompette** (*see p108*) and **La Trouvaille** (*see p108*).

Meat-free *manger*

Feast on vegetarian *délices* at **L'Escargot Marco Pierre White** (*see p107*), **Morgan M** (*see p113*) and **Roussillon** (*see p101*).

French dressing

Dress up to the *neufs* for **The Admiralty** (*see p108*), **The Belvedere** (*see p109*), **Criterion** (*see p107*), **L'Escargot Marco Pierre White** (*see p107*) and **Mirabelle** (*see p106*).

Vin extraordinaire

Try the terrific wine lists at **Chez Bruce** (*see p111*), **The Ledbury** (*see p109*), **1 Lombard Street** (*see p101*), **Papillon** (*see p108*), **RSJ** (*see p111*) and **La Trompette** (*see p108*).

Le Comptoir Gascon

BRASSERIE
ROUX

Enjoy a true French Brasserie in an atmosphere of informal elegance with special menus devised by Albert Roux

Sofitel St James London
Open seven days a week for breakfast, lunch and dinner

8 Pall Mall, London SW1Y 5NG
Tel. 020 7968 2900
www.sofitelstjames.com
brasserieroux@sofitelstjames.com

Booking / Information > 020 7253 1100
booking@danslenoir.com

Also enjoy ***Dans le Noir?*** *for unique* ***Corporate, marketing and PR events****, Christmas or New Year parties, private party,... Book now also for Halloween and the Dans le Noir? famous "Most horrible cry contest"! Register also for the "cooking lessons" with our chef or our "Dark Monday"(blind Date Bar). We highly recommend to book at least a week in advance.*

Restaurant / Bar / Lounge
30 – 31 Clerkenwell Green
London – EC1R 0DU
tel: 020 7253 1100
Metro : Farringdon (or Chancery Lane)
Bus : 243 – 55 – 63 – N35
Fax : 020 3217 2072

Bring this page from Time Out and get £3 off your full menu.
Discount on presentation of this voucher from Time Out. Offer till december 2008

Montmartre. Claiming to be London's oldest French restaurant, Mon Plaisir is powerfully evocative – and still disappointing. Though the staff are many, there's a distinct fluster in the service: cutlery shoved aside with the plate and an artful doodle of sauce unapologetically smudged before our eyes; a waitress who wouldn't give us her undivided attention; the bill that listed a dish at a higher price than the menu. The food, bistro fare, is so-so. Ravioles de royan were tasty, and entrecôte well cooked; from the specials menu, lamb with a herb 'crust' (soggy) came with good broad beans in a thyme sauce; lobster feuilleté was startlingly bland. Not a word of French did we hear among the diners, and there's your clue; this could be a great place, but at present it simply isn't making enough of an effort.
Babies and children admitted. Booking advisable. **Map 18 L6**.

Fitzrovia

Elena's L'Étoile

30 Charlotte Street, W1T 2NG (7636 7189/ www.elenasletoile.co.uk). Goodge Street or Tottenham Court Road tube. **Lunch served** noon-2.30pm Mon-Fri. **Dinner served** 6-10.30pm Mon-Sat. **Main courses** £15.75-£20.25. **Set meal** £19 2 courses, £22 3 courses. **Credit** AmEx, DC, JCB, MC, V.

She's now closer to 90 than 80, but Elena Salvoni continues to work the room as expertly as ever. The most beloved maître d' in town, Elena has been gliding around a succession of London dining rooms for more than six decades. In the century-old L'Étoile, which has carried her name since the mid 1990s, she's found her perfect match: a restaurant as cosy and comfortably old-fashioned as her warm but not over-familiar manner. Beneath walls lined with portraits of vintage stars (Ingrid Bergman, Maria Callas), efficient waiters serve crowds of cultured Fitzrovians with sturdy cuisine. The few breaks from French tradition aren't rendered with great skill: a starter of duck confit with soy dressing and ginger packed only a slight punch, and mushroom risotto was forgettable. It's all a bit better when you know what to expect: a straightforward duck à l'orange, for example, or monkfish in a gentle red wine sauce. The cuisine won't win any awards, but nor is it any disgrace to the room in which it's served, or the woman who sees everything that goes on within it. Long may Elena – and her empire – thrive.
Babies and children admitted. Booking advisable; essential lunch. Separate rooms for parties, seating 10, 16 and 32. **Map 9 J5**.

Knightsbridge

Brasserie St Quentin

243 Brompton Road, SW3 2EP (7589 8005/ www.brasseriestquentin.co.uk). Knightsbridge or South Kensington tube/14, 74 bus. **Lunch served** noon-3pm daily. **Dinner served** 6-10.30pm Mon-Sat; 6-10pm Sun. **Main courses** £12.50-£23.50. **Set lunch** (noon-3pm) £16.50 2 courses, £18.50 3 courses. **Credit** AmEx, MC, V.

Mirrors across the walls, maroon banquettes and red leatherette-upholstered chairs create an 1980s brasserie feel at this inviting restaurant, offset by fresh flower arrangements. It's an unstuffy atmosphere, buoyed by a charming and attentive service team. Although the menu is based on a French theme, there's a nod to Mediterranean classics and Modern British cooking – and British seasonal produce takes a starring role. We started with a pleasingly crisp puff pastry tart, slathered with pesto and topped with olive-oil slicked tomatoes. Creamy fish soup didn't quite hit the same heights, its delicate character masked by an overabundance of acidic tomatoes. The gold star went to a gloriously fresh wild sea bass fillet, accompanied by slow-cooked, garlicky peppers and deliciously herby salsa verde. Only the calf's liver disappointed, with its fibrous texture and undercooked garnish of whole shallots in balsamic vinegar and port – a blot on an otherwise enjoyable meal. The wine list is pricey at the top end, but includes quaffable entry-level choices for under £20. A prime location makes this place a popular destination for monied tourists and affluent Knightsbridge shoppers.
Babies and children welcome: high chairs. Booking advisable. Separate room for parties, seats 20. **Map 14 E10**.

Drones

1 Pont Street, SW1X 9EJ (7235 9555/ www.whitestarline.org.uk). Knightsbridge or Sloane Square tube. **Lunch served** noon-2.30pm Mon-Fri; noon-3.30pm Sun. **Dinner served** 6-11pm Mon-Sat. **Main courses** £14.50-£24.50. **Set lunch** (Mon-Fri) £15.95 2 courses, £18.50 3 courses; (Sun) £22.50 3 courses. **Credit** AmEx, DC, MC, V.

Drones is a place very much at ease with itself, providing a sense of the good life for diners outside the immediate area and a home from home for wealthy Belgravia regulars using this branch of the Marco Pierre White empire like a gilded canteen. The decor is suitably sumptuous, with brown leather seats, bronzed walls, thick white tablecloths, tall aspidistras and, everywhere, black and white photos of stars from the 1950s. Occasionally you find the odd buffer, ordering from memory from the wine list but, in general, the diners are interesting, colourful and varied, making for a surprisingly fun, friendly atmosphere. The food is remarkably good too, served in a French style but with recognisably British components: shredded crab piled high; dense duck liver pâté with tart cumberland sauce; savoury pink calf's liver; tender Welsh lamb. All the ingredients were of outstanding quality: fresh and full of the right flavours. Cheeses are English too, served with Bath Oliver biscuits, and no French cheese or baguettes to be seen. If you get the chance, look at the unique Michael Winner room downstairs and try not to let the good-humoured French staff see you smile.
Babies and children admitted. Booking essential. Restaurant available for hire. Separate room for parties, seats 40. **Map 15 G10**.

★ Racine (100)

239 Brompton Road, SW3 2EP (7584 4477). Knightsbridge or South Kensington tube/14, 74 bus. **Lunch served** noon-3pm Mon-Fri; noon-3.30pm Sat, Sun. **Dinner served** 6-10.30pm Mon-Sat; 6-10pm Sun. **Main courses** £12.50-£20.75. **Set meal** (lunch, 6-7.30pm) £17.50 2 courses, £19.50 3 courses. **Credit** AmEx, MC, V.

Push aside the heavy velvet curtains shielding the entrance door and you enter a lost world. Well-padded gents and their comfortable female consorts, francophiles and francophones alike, come here to revel in the bourgeois French cooking, and the timeless interior and atmosphere. There aren't many places where you can order calves' brains cooked with black butter and capers, but you can here; the pale brains are the texture of set custard, but the dressing gives a sharp bite to cut through the rich fat and protein. Main course? More brains: this time as part of a deboned tête de veau. The capers, onion and seasoning of the accompanying ravigote sauce provided a distraction from the odd textures of the calf's head, just as they are supposed to. It's not all offal: an escabeche of red mullet was winningly combined with lentils, globe artichoke and little toasts; another dish of baby leeks with a perfectly poached egg balanced on top was almost enough to make us renounce the sins of the flesh. You pay for the privilege of eating here, though – the figures on everything, from the puddings to the wines, feel as though they should be in euros, not pounds.
Babies and children welcome: high chairs. Booking advisable. Dress: smart casual. **Map 14 E10**.

Marylebone

★ Galvin Bistrot de Luxe

66 Baker Street, W1U 7DH (7935 4007/ www.galvinbistrotdeluxe.co.uk). Baker Street tube. **Lunch served** noon-2.30pm Mon-Sat; noon-3pm Sun. **Dinner served** 6-11pm Mon-Sat; 6-10.30pm Sun. **Main courses** £10.50-£21. **Set lunch** £15.50 3 courses. **Set dinner** (6-7pm) £17.50 3 courses. **Credit** AmEx, MC, V.

Interview
ADAM BYATT

Who are you?
Chef-proprietor of **Trinity** (*see p112*) in Clapham.

Eating in London: what's good about it?
I love the sheer diversity of cuisine, the volume of talented chefs, and the recent upsurge of restaurants that are chef- and food-driven. While classical French cooking underpins a lot of high-end restaurants, there is a definitive willingness among younger English chefs to modernise, personalising the cuisine they offer.

What's bad about it?
There is still a lot of mediocre food, which is overpriced and badly served – this, I suspect, is due to a large tourist market where customer loyalty is not the main concern.

Which are your favourite London restaurants?
Roka (*see p197*) for a great night out; **Yauatcha** (*see p80*) for lunch. I rarely eat similar food to mine, but, for a great local, **Chez Bruce** (*see p111*) is as good as it gets. I had a great meal and amazing service at **Foliage** (*see p141*) – Chris Staines is a real talent.

Who or what has had the biggest impact on London's restaurant scene in the past 25 years?
Marco Pierre White started the modern restaurant approach at Harvey's, which spawned many of London's leading chefs. It was a turning point for chefs to emerge from the kitchen and have a recognised viewpoint. On a local level, better food press and shops have helped to raise the culture of food; as consumers drive demand and sales this has upped the standard of sourcing and produce available mainstream.

Any hot tips for the coming year?
Refined cooking, well-sourced produce and talented chefs will no longer be out of reach for the mainstream public.

Trinity. See p112.

The location, on a bleak stretch of Baker Street, is unpromising. Yet the Galvin brothers (Chris and Jeff) have created a phenomenon: an outstanding restaurant, which was packed with enthusiastic customers on our midweek visit, many of them, we suspected, locals from buoyant Marylebone. The L-shaped room looks good too – high ceilings at the front with fans slowly rotating, brown leather seats, thick white tablecloths – and a window through to the kitchen at the elbow of the L, so you can see the food being plated. The service was slightly frantic – we rarely saw the same waiter twice – but the cooking was of exceptionally high quality. Highlights included a slab of Scottish beef that was more tender and delicious than we had previously imagined possible (seared then slow-roasted), served with a fried duck egg and crunchy straw potatoes; a confit duck leg that was both crisp and moist; a light and highly flavoured cauliflower soup with slices of scallop; and, in terms of presentation, a simple salad of endive leaves piled up, each one containing pieces of roquefort and walnut. The wine list is interesting too, with an additional, exclusive selection for the deep-pocketed.
Babies and children welcome: high chairs. Booking advisable. Disabled: toilet. **Map 9 G5.**

Le Relais de Venise l'entrecôte

120 Marylebone Lane, W1U 2QG (7486 0878/ www.relaisdevenise.com). Bond Street tube.
Lunch served noon-2.30pm Mon-Fri; 12.30-3.30pm Sat, Sun. **Dinner served** 6-10.45pm Mon-Fri; 6.30-10.45pm Sat; 6.30-10.30pm Sun. **Set meal** £18 2 courses. **Credit** AmEx, MC, V.
Choice is something we all crave, so we are told. How do you explain, then, that a restaurant like this has people queueing out of the door (you can't book)? It's a near-exact copy of its mother-brasserie in Paris, down to the waitresses in black dresses and little white aprons, who are brisk, in time-honoured Parisian style, but (in our experience) friendly and helpful too. There's no choice of first or second courses: just a simple green salad with walnuts and a punchy vinaigrette to start, followed by entrecôte steak (served in two 'rounds', so it doesn't get cold) with fries and Le Relais's 'famous sauce', the recipe for which is supposedly as secret as the Coke formula. Happily, the steak is first rate, and cooked exactly as ordered; so good, in fact, that it would be nice to try it without that sauce (a rich, herby, mustardy concoction) – but that's not an option. The potatoes are definitive, perfect frites (no one could call them 'chips'), and the good-value house Bordeaux washes it all down nicely. Choice reappears with the desserts: classic pâtisserie and a very correct cheeseboard. Very enjoyable.
Babies and children welcome: high chairs. Bookings not accepted. Disabled: toilet. Tables outdoors (7, pavement). **Map 9 G5.**

The Wallace NEW

Wallace Collection, Hertford House, Manchester Square, W1U 3BN (7563 9505/www.thewallace restaurant.com). Bond Street tube.
Cafe **Meals served** 10am-4.30pm daily. *Restaurant* **Lunch served** noon-3pm daily. *Both* **Dinner served** 5-9.30pm Fri, Sat. **Main courses** £13.50-£18.50. **Credit** AmEx, DC, JCB, MC, V.
His profile is lower than it was during the 1990s, but Oliver Peyton is busier than ever. These days, though, he's opening his restaurants in partnership with others: Royal Parks, Heal's, the National Gallery and now the Wallace Collection, which invited him to revitalise its catering in 2006. It's a curious endeavour: unusually for a Peyton place, it seems rather unsure of itself. The glass-topped courtyard space is undeniably dramatic, but it's ill served by furniture that can't decide whether it's built for the garden or the dining room. Service wanders between helpful and distracted. Even the menus strike a precarious balance between casual informality and old-world Marylebonian haughtiness (ice-cream desserts for £6.50, afternoon tea with champagne for £27), and the pricey, French-slanted food is almost as variable. Some ingredients were beautifully sourced, as with a starter of asparagus and poached egg served with a slightly gloopy mustard emulsion; others, though, were poor, as with the very drab beef tomato served with a more impressive fillet of sea bass. A tasty starter salad of frogs' legs, chorizo and artichoke was rather better, as was an appetising tomato tart, but this isn't Peyton's finest hour.
Babies and children welcome: children's menu, high chairs. Booking advisable. Disabled: lift; toilet. Restaurant available for hire. **Map 9 G5.**

Mayfair

Mirabelle

56 Curzon Street, W1J 8PA (7499 4636/ www.whitestarline.org.uk). Green Park tube.
Lunch served noon-2.30pm Mon-Sat; noon-3pm Sun. **Dinner served** 6-11.30pm Mon-Sat; 6-10.30pm Sun. **Main courses** £17.50-£28.95. **Set lunch** (Mon-Sat) £19.50 2 courses, £23 3 courses; (Sun) £24 3 courses. **Credit** AmEx, MC, V.
Past the doorman in his brown bowler hat and down the stairs awaits Marco Pierre White's 1930s fantasy world of glamour, glitterballs and, with luck, not too many local businessmen. Even in your finery it would be hard to appear overdressed here, next to the long bar, grand piano, mirrored room dividers and cocktail-quaffing clientele. Turn right into the spacious dining room, with its four long rows of tables, brown leather chairs and thick white tablecloths, where splendidly professional French staff reinforce the impression that you're in good hands. A decadent foie gras and truffle parfait with sticky, sharp jelly was enjoyable enough, but outshone by an outstanding scallop and endive tarte tatin, the sliced, caramelised scallops fragrant with orange butter and candied peel. Mains tend towards the elaborate. Bresse pigeon breasts were tender, bloody and succulent, wrapped in savoy cabbage and stuffed with more foie gras; a thick skate wing was cooked to perfection, scattered with tiny winkles and served with a tightly packed ball of spinach, dense as a lettuce heart. One small complaint: why, when the sauces are so rich, must the creamed potatoes be this buttery?
Babies and children welcome: high chairs. Booking advisable. Dress: smart casual. Entertainment: pianist dinner Tue-Sat, lunch Sun. Restaurant available for hire. Separate rooms for parties, seating 33 and 48. Tables outdoors (14, patio). **Map 9 H7.**

La Petite Maison NEW

54 Brooks Mews, W1K 4EG (7495 4774). Bond Street tube. **Lunch served** noon-3pm, **dinner served** 7-11.30pm Mon-Sat. **Main courses** £9-£35. **Credit** AmEx, MC, V.
Imported from a Nice original by Arjun Waney, principal owner of Japanese hotspots Zuma and Roka, La Petite Maison has become a hotspot too.

Inside, linen curtains and frosted glass block out the ugly road, but allow in much natural light. Chairs and tables are close together. You're meant to order many dishes to share. Deep-fried courgette flowers were great, with pale, gauzy batter, but were trumped by sage leaves and anchovies sandwiched together and deep-fried with the same coating; intense red pepper sauce paired well with the onion rings on the same 'trois saveurs de beignets' platter. On the next table, a bowl of bright, squeaky fine beans studded with tiny cubes of foie gras looked so good we had to order it; chopped shallots worked a treat in the salty, crunchy dressing. To follow, there are several fish and seafood options. We opted for scallop carpaccio, the silky discs topped with herbs, lemon zest and almond flakes: marvellous. A small filleted, salt-baked sea bass came secreted under deep-fried artichoke, tomato and teeny girolles mushrooms: excellent, but costly at £28. Staff were bright, chatty and vivacious. The France-dominated wine list contains seven Provence rosés, including an elegantly fruity Château de Roquefort Carail 2006. For dessert, the huge crème brûlée ranks among London's best.
Babies and children admitted. Booking advisable. **Map 9 H6**.

Piccadilly

Criterion

224 Piccadilly, W1J 9HP (7930 0488/ www.whitestarline.org.uk). Piccadilly Circus tube. **Lunch served** noon-2.30pm Mon-Sat; noon-3.30pm Sun. **Dinner served** 5.30-11.30pm Mon-Sat; 5.30-10.30pm Sun. **Main courses** £12.50-£28.50. **Set meal** (lunch, 5.30-7pm Mon-Sat) £14.95 2 courses, £17.95 3 courses; (lunch, 5.30-7pm Sun) £20 2 courses, £25 3 courses. **Credit** AmEx, DC, JCB, MC, V.

With its brief incarnation as just another outlet of Frankie's Italian Bar & Grill now over, Marco Pierre White's Criterion is back to what it does best: serving up a sense of occasion on demand with its stunning neo-Byzantine 1870s brasserie decor and its comfortingly familiar French menu. This avenue-like space can feel overwhelming unless it's busy, but on a Wednesday evening the place was fully booked with theatre-goers and tourists after 'affordable glamour', the restaurant's tag line. The meal itself was a mixed affair; a starter of quail's eggs was perfect, the eggs warm and runny inside and beautifully served, but a good-enough carpaccio of beef was a very measly portion for £9.95. Grilled lobster in garlic butter was drowning in too much béarnaise sauce to the extent that the lobster could hardly be tasted; in contrast, grilled dover sole was perfect, with rich and subtle multi-layered flavours. The wine list offers few bargains, but there's an excellent choice for those with plenty of cash. The Criterion may need to up its game when it comes to its food, but even the biggest cynic can't help enjoying the glittering setting.
Babies and children welcome: high chairs. Booking advisable. Dress: smart casual. Separate room for parties, seats 70. **Map 17 B5.**

St James's

Brasserie Roux

Sofitel St James, 8 Pall Mall, SW1Y 5NG (7968 2900/www.sofitelstjames.com). Piccadilly Circus tube. **Lunch served** noon-3pm Mon-Fri; 12.30-3pm Sat, Sun. **Dinner served** 5.30-11pm Mon-Sat; 5.30-10.30pm Sun. **Main courses** £9.50-£21.50. **Set meal** £24.50 3 courses incl 2 glasses of wine, water and coffee. **Set dinner** (5.30-7pm Mon-Sat) £15 3 courses, £20 3 courses incl 2 glasses of wine. **Credit** AmEx, DC, JCB, MC, V.

Sited in the Sofitel Hotel, this expansive restaurant attempts to liven up its dark wood decor with a cheery yellow and green colour scheme and quirky oversized lamps. We're not convinced it has managed to shake off the look and feel of an international hotel coffee shop. On our weekday evening visit, diners were sparse – mostly suited business types and well-to-do American visitors. Popular choices include roasts, grills and pastas, and retro classics in the line of vol-au-vents, saucy scallops and rum babas. Mediterranean-style dishes are impressive: the welcome chill of gazpacho delivered a bold medley of full-flavoured tomatoes, peppers and garlicky tartness, rivalled only by the simplicity of a buffalo mozzarella and tomato salad, dressed with syrupy balsamic vinegar. Mains weren't as illustrious: fried sea bass fillets were overcooked, although the addition of buttery, super-fresh samphire, tossed with crisp asparagus, lifted an otherwise underwhelming dish. A fairly priced wine list embraces New World selections alongside well-chosen classics. Service is attentive, if a tad detached. Early diners should check out the excellent-value set menus.
Babies and children welcome: children's menu; high chairs. Booking advisable. Disabled: toilet (hotel). Dress: smart casual. **Map 10 K7.**

Soho

L'Escargot Marco Pierre White

48 Greek Street, W1D 4EF (7437 2679/ www.whitestarline.org.uk). Leicester Square or Tottenham Court Road tube.
Ground-floor restaurant **Lunch served** noon-2.15pm Mon-Fri. **Dinner served** 6-11.30pm Mon-Fri; 5.30-11.30pm Sat. **Main courses** £12.95-£14.95. **Set meal** (lunch, 6-7pm Mon-Fri) £15 2 courses, £18 3 courses.
Picasso Room **Lunch served** 12.15-2pm Tue-Fri. **Dinner served** 7-11pm Tue-Sat. **Set lunch** £20.50 2 courses, £25.50 3 courses. **Set meal** £42 3 courses.
Both **Credit** AmEx, DC, JCB, MC, V.

L'Escargot is divided into two distinct venues. The ground-floor restaurant is consistently fun and stylish, serving food that is almost invariably outstanding. The Picasso Room upstairs, where we chose to eat, is better still in almost every way, although what you gain in sleekness, exclusivity and culinary ambition, you lose in bustle and brightness. The mirrors and banquettes on the ground floor give way to a more hallowed space with genuine Picasso sketches on the walls and ceramics in glass cases. On our gilt-rimmed plates came a succession of exquisite courses, including squab pigeon breasts, pink and tender with crisp skin, on a disc of duck pâté, surrounded by eccentric pickles; scallops with pear purée and caramelised pork belly; a coffee cup of vichyssoise with grated truffle; and a tall white peach soufflé that somehow managed to be rich, dense and light at the same time. It was a shame that there were few other diners – a party celebrating a business deal was the largest contingent – though this did mean we lucked out with free petits fours that might otherwise have gone to waste.
Babies and children admitted (ground-floor restaurant). Booking essential weekends. Dress: smart casual. Separate rooms for parties, seating 24 and 60. Vegetarian menu. **Map 17 C3.**

★ La Trouvaille

12A Newburgh Street, W1F 7RR (7287 8488/ www.latrouvaille.co.uk). Oxford Circus tube. **Lunch served** noon-3pm Mon-Fri. **Dinner served** 6-11pm Mon-Sat. **Set lunch** £15.50 2 courses, £18 3 courses. **Set dinner** £27.50 2 courses, £33 3 courses. **Credit** AmEx, MC, V.

It has been a couple of years since the first-floor dining room was redesigned to create a greater feeling of space (light walls, ornate mirrors, unobtrusive Perspex chairs), so it's time that longer-standing customers got over the consequent loss of some cosiness. La Trouvaille remains a treat. There's clearly someone in the kitchen with the keenest of taste buds, who uses the best ingredients and knows how to combine them into delicious food. To start, finest-quality lamb sweetbreads, from the heart not the throat, were firm and smooth, balanced with a crisp almond coating. Scallops in a filo parcel were perfectly fresh and tangy, accompanied by a salty sea urchin sauce. Mains were even better. Close-grained Herdwick lamb rump was tender and luxurious, perched on a velvety puy lentil cake and cassoulet-style white beans. Galloway beef fillet was also meltingly soft, cooked in broth with turnips and spots of sharp wasabi. The French staff were efficient, attentive and knowledgeable, the vibe relaxed and quietly convivial. Careful wine buying in the South and South-west of France (the buyer must know these areas intimately) means you can drink well for around £20, and there are some interesting bottles for between £35 and £40.

Babies and children admitted. Booking advisable. Tables outdoors (10, pavement). **Map 17 A3.**

South Kensington

Papillon

96 Draycott Avenue, SW3 3AD (7225 2555/ www.papillonchelsea.co.uk). South Kensington tube. **Lunch served** noon-3pm Mon-Sat; noon-4pm Sun. **Dinner served** 6-11.30pm Mon-Sat; 7-10pm Sun. **Main courses** £15-£25. **Set lunch** £14.50 2 courses, £16.50 3 courses. **Credit** AmEx, DC, MC, V.

Inhale upon entering this popular South Ken spot and you'll catch the whiff of fine food, good perfume and money. Around you, elegant people discreetly part with stacks of cash, for a few hours of serenity. Sebastien, the lovely sommelier (Philippe Messey, Papillon's former wine star, no longer works the floor), will help you wade through the 36-page, primarily French wine list (comprising hundreds of bins), and will ascertain your budget with sensitivity and advise accordingly – though low prices aren't a feature. Superb pan-fried foie gras, often excessively fussed over, was allowed to shine with a beautifully spiced half of poached pear, sugared fat and rocket; it was well paired with a generous sweet Jurançon, the cheapest dessert wine. A leaner white from the South-west went well with deep-fried pig's trotters, which were undersalted and tasted of deep-frying. Mains of lamb saddle and filet of steak were very French, and excellent. A young tannic red from the Basque appellation Irouléguy benefited from the restaurant's arsenal of Riedel stemware. Papillon clearly has the high end of the market well covered; go to this beautiful restaurant to check out of the real world for a while.

Babies and children welcome: high chairs. Booking advisable. Dress: smart casual. Separate room for parties, seats 18. Tables outdoors (6, pavement). **Map 14 E10.**

La Petite Maison. See p106.

Strand

The Admiralty

Somerset House, Strand, WC2R 1LA (7845 4646/www.somerset-house.org.uk). Embankment or Temple tube/Charing Cross tube/rail. **Lunch served** noon-2.30pm daily. **Dinner served** 6-10.30pm Mon-Sat. **Set meal** (lunch, 6-7pm) £15.50 2 courses, £19.50 3 courses. **Credit** AmEx, DC, JCB, MC, V.

The sense of occasion starts with your walk under the archway from the Strand, across the courtyard and past rows of fountains, then into the high-ceilinged dining room. Here you'll encounter tall windows, sea-green leather seats and (a playful reminder of the building's naval past), ship-shaped chandeliers. On our visit, other diners tended towards middle age: managers from the neighbouring Inland Revenue and execs from the BBC World Service. Starters of beetroot tarte tatin and gratin of Burgundy snails were good in parts (the beetroot was warm and fresh, the snails abundant), but let down by careless oversights; the tart's pastry was dry and hard, while the breadcrumb layer on the snails was so deep and biscuity it made a stodge with the tomato-based sauce. An entrecôte was rather tough and a rump of Cornish lamb even more so – both were cooked for far longer than requested. The Admiralty is usually better than this. In summer, if you want to eat somewhere with more of a riverside feel, check out the separate River Terrace Café where the menu runs from breakfasts to evening antipasto and hot mixed platters, via all-day brasserie dishes and tea and cakes.

Babies and children admitted. Booking advisable. Disabled: lift; toilet. Dress: smart casual. Restaurant available for hire. Separate room for parties, seats 30. **Map 10 M7.**

West

Chiswick

★ La Trompette

5-7 Devonshire Road, W4 2EU (8747 1836/ www.latrompette.co.uk). Turnham Green tube. **Lunch served** noon-2.30pm Mon-Sat; 12.30-3pm Sun. **Dinner served** 6.30-10.30pm Mon-Sat; 7-10pm Sun. **Set lunch** (Mon-Fri) £23.50 3 courses; (Sat) £25 3 courses; (Sun) £29.50 3 courses. **Set dinner** £35 3 courses, £45 4 courses. **Credit** AmEx, JCB, MC, V.

Completing a chic trio of restaurants run by Nigel Platts-Martin and Bruce Poole (alongside Chez Bruce, *see p111*, and Modern European restaurant the Glasshouse), La Trompette is deservedly popular. The linen-covered tables in the neutrally toned dining room were packed with wealthy diners on a Tuesday night. Service was unusually slow (a chef had fallen ill), but the food, full of intense flavour, just about made up for the wait. Vividly fresh seared tuna, enhanced with sesame and coriander and tingling with wasabi, set the

Galvin Bistrot de Luxe. See p105.

standard; it was equalled by a more classic boudin blanc with Madeira sauce, flecked with pistachios. Mains were even better. Rosy pink veal was fantastic at every mouthful, its juices soaking into a bright broad bean, morel and asparagus risotto; tender lamb rump with braised peas was equally fine. The wait slightly took the edge off our appetite for an eggy crème brûlée, and its rhubarb layer seemed to have lost some tartness, though a lime and tequila sorbet was deliciously sharp. The wine list, brought by an admirably patient sommelier, is extensive, even outside France. There's an interesting selection by the glass, but more choice under £30 would be useful.
Babies and children welcome: high chairs. Booking advisable. Disabled: toilet. Tables outdoors (7, terrace).

Le Vacherin

76-77 South Parade, W4 5LF (8742 2121/ www.levacherin.co.uk). Chiswick Park tube/rail. **Lunch served** noon-3pm Tue-Sun. **Dinner served** 6-10.30pm Mon-Thur; 6-11pm Fri, Sat; 6-10pm Sun. **Main courses** £12.50-£19. **Credit** MC, V.

Words like poulet, foie gras and spécialités de la mer etched into glass windows bode well for a taste of provincial France. Inside, banquettes, could-be-more-comfortable chairs, strip mirrors and white tablecloths in the suprisingly spacious pair of rooms create the impression of a genuine bistro. With snails, navarin of lamb, chateaubriand, crème brûlée and île flottante, the main menu is gratifyingly traditional. Dairy predictably plays a major part in a restaurant named after one of France's finest cheeses, and when it's in season you can have vacherin mont d'or baked as a starter or to finish. All the elements in a first-course salad of asparagus, quail's eggs and tiny purple leaves were just-so, and a fig tart with goat's cheese ice-cream was an outstanding ending. Standards dipped slightly in the middle. Chicken fricassee comprised substantial pieces of fine – but overcooked – fowl in a beautifully made, deeply flavoured creamy sauce with morels and broad beans (which were peeled: always a sign of a dedicated kitchen). A thick slice of plaice on the bone could also have been a little firmer. Wines are all French and well priced. Music as cheesy as brie adds to a pleasingly full-fat and very Gallic experience.
Babies and children welcome: high chairs. Booking advisable. Separate room for parties, seats 20.

Hammersmith

Chez Kristof

111 Hammersmith Grove, W6 0NQ (8741 1177/www.chezkristof.co.uk). Goldhawk Road or Hammersmith tube.
Deli **Open** 8am-7.30pm Mon-Fri; 8.30am-7pm Sat; 9am-6pm Sun.
Restaurant **Lunch served** noon-3pm Mon-Fri; noon-4pm Sat, Sun. **Dinner served** 6-11pm Mon-Sat; 6-10.30pm Sun. **Main courses** £12.50-£17.50.
Both **Credit** AmEx, JCB, MC, V.

This is the third of Jan Woroniecki's restaurants, though the others (Baltic, Wódka) are Polish rather than French. The single room is attractive, with a subuded colour scheme of maroon, grey and brown, and atmospheric low lighting, including a curtain of twinkling fairy lights in one window. The front terrace is a bonus, despite the distinctly uncomfortable low-slung canvas chairs, and was full on our visit. The menu reads a treat, promising plenty of strong, earthy flavours (clam and bean stew with chorizo, devilled lamb's kidneys, confit pig's head with pickled cabbages, bouillabaisse). Usefully, half a dozen dishes are available in starter or main course sizes, though vegetarians don't get much choice. Execution doesn't match expectation, however. Good to see herring roe on the menu (as a starter), but it was served on tough toast and swamped by a dressing of buerre noisette and capers. A smilar lack of finesse affected most of our dishes, especially a main of hake and clams in a far too oily sauce (almost a soup); better were a tangy steak tartare starter and a main of nicely cooked lamb on a bed of aubergine and shallots. Portions are big. Plus points for the all-French wine list and capable staff, but we'd like a more delicacte hand in the kitchen.
Babies and children welcome: children's menu; films; high chairs. Booking advisable. Disabled: toilet. Separate room for parties, seats 45. Tables outdoors (15, terrace). Takeaway service (deli). **Map 20 B3.**

Holland Park

★ The Belvedere

Holland House, off Abbotsbury Road, in Holland Park, W8 6LU (7602 1238/www.whitestarline.org.uk). Holland Park tube. **Lunch served** noon-2.30pm Mon-Sat; noon-2pm, 2.30-4pm Sun. **Dinner served** 6-10pm Mon-Sat. **Main courses** £10-£18. **Set lunch** (Mon-Fri) £14.95 2 courses, £17.95 3 courses; (Sat, Sun) £24.95 3 courses. **Credit** AmEx, MC, V.

Sequestered in one of London's lovelier parks, the Belvedere occupies a former summer ballroom of Holland House reached past honking peacocks and formal parterres. Inside, decor takes a dramatic Edwardian turn with bevelled mirrors, potted palms and florid wallpaper making a glamorous backdrop for all seasons. With a pianist among the well-orchestrated staff, expectations for a show that lives up to the setting are high. The brasserie-length menu ranges from comfort food to highly evolved luxuries. These two strands came together beautifully in a silky-smooth, thick and rich chicken liver and foie gras parfait served with brioche swaddled in a napkin. Crab risotto was simple perfection. A humble plaice fillet, classically matched with spinach, could have passed for a more expensive species; and ribeye beef, a notably fine and deeply flavoured piece of meat, was cooked exactly as ordered. Portions – four scallops for a starter –

L'Aventure
L'Aventure
Restaurant
Classic French cuisine in the heart of St. John's Wood.
5 mins from Abbey Road Studios.
3 Blenheim Terrace, London NW8 0EH
020 7624 6232

CAFÉ ROUGE
RESTAURANT BAR CAFÉ
Escape London with
a taste of France
any time of the day
www.caferouge.co.uk

were surprisingly generous. Minor let-downs include some fat 'pont neuf'-style chips, which could have been firmer, and a dull and heavy slab of walnut and date sticky (supposedly) toffee pudding. The Belvedere doesn't trade on its situation but actually delivers, and without charging as much as you might expect.
Babies and children welcome: high chairs. Booking essential. Entertainment: pianist. Restaurant available for hire. Tables outdoors (5, terrace).

Westbourne Grove

★ The Ledbury

127 Ledbury Road, W11 2AQ (7792 9090/ www.theledbury.com). Westbourne Park tube.
Lunch served noon-2pm Mon-Fri; noon-3pm Sat, Sun. **Dinner served** 6.30-10.15pm daily. **Set lunch** (Mon-Sat) £19.50 2 courses, £24.50 courses; (Sun) £35 3 courses. **Set dinner** £50 3 courses. **Credit** AmEx, JCB, MC, V.
No restaurant can be perfect, but the Ledbury is as near as damn it. The tone is set by plush parquet and swish leather seats, while all around drapes and mirrors create space and intimacy. Even the loos seduce, with black marble and wallpaper lined with golden trees. The lawyers, tycoons, moguls and trustafarians of Notting Hill consume here. The first thing that strikes you, after the £50 set dinner price tag, is the depth and breadth of the menu. Good old grilled mackerel becomes a subtle delight when served with avocado and shiso, while foie gras is reinvented with date purée, earl grey jelly, duck canapés and sundry toast melba. These two of seven starters were followed by a sublime amuse-bouche of chilled courgette soup. Then came seven classic mains, including monkfish and john dory, each made intriguing with the addition of truffle schnitzel and potato risotto respectively. Standards never slipped; another amuse-bouche (passionfruit jelly) was followed by desserts that included a terrific blueberry soufflé and gorgeous date and vanilla tart. So, what faults? Well, service is courteous to the point of asepsis, and the encyclopaedic world-wine list could contain a few more bottles under £50. Co-owners Nigel Platts-Martin and Philip Howard also run haute-cusine restaurant the Square, while Platts-Martin, with Bruce Poole, is behind the critically acclaimed trio of Chez Bruce (*see below*), La Trompette (*see p108*) and the Glasshouse (Modern European).
Babies and children admitted. Booking advisable; essential dinner. Disabled: toilet. Tables outdoors (9, pavement). **Map 7 A5/6.**

South West

Putney

L'Auberge

22 Upper Richmond Road, SW15 2RX (8874 3593/www.ardillys.com). East Putney tube.
Dinner served 7-10pm Tue-Sat. **Main courses** £11.95-£15.75. **Set dinner** £12.95 2 courses, £16 3 courses. **Credit** MC, V.
It's a minor miracle that a restaurant of this kind has survived for so many years on this difficult stretch of the South Circular. Yet L'Auberge seems to improve with age, now displaying fresh self-confidence along with staunch resilience. It was half-full on a Saturday night (though it's just as likely to be full) with diners both young and old. The decor – defined by *belle époque* prints on pale walls with 1970s trattoria plasterwork – remains comfortable rather than cutting-edge, but it works. The puddings remain the real highlight. A raspberry crème brûlée, with fresh fruit and crisp warm caramelised sugar, confirmed our view that chef-owner Pascal Ardilly makes the most moreish crèmes brûlées in London. The mains (red mullet with buttery rice and ratatouille; rabbit with tarragon and dijon mustard sauce) were high on flavour if, as ever, lower on presentation. The occasional themed menus (Provençale, on our visit) are really good value, although details such as the tinned tuna in our salade niçoise help to explain how prices are kept down.
Babies and children admitted.

Wandsworth

★ Chez Bruce (100)

2 Bellevue Road, SW17 7EG (8672 0114/ www.chezbruce.co.uk). Wandsworth Common rail.
Lunch served noon-2pm Mon-Fri; 12.30-2.30pm Sat; noon-3pm Sun. **Dinner served** 6.30-10.30pm Mon-Sat; 7-10pm Sun. **Set lunch** (Mon-Fri) £25.50 3 courses; (Sat) £27.50 3 courses; (Sun) £32.50 3 courses. **Set dinner** £37.50 3 courses. **Credit** AmEx, DC, JCB, MC, V.
Chef-patron Bruce Poole's ever-popular restaurant continues to strive to serve the best quality food at relatively reasonable prices. Sure, the menu doesn't change very often, and the decor only rarely gets an update (there's some colourful art on the walls this year), but the place still feels fresh and vital. Sit downstairs if you can and seek immediate help from the smooth-talking sommelier: oenophiles love Chez Bruce – its list shows care and flair in every country and every region. France dominates, and you can drink well for £30 or less. The set menu (half a dozen choices for each course) has modern flourishes but very French roots. We tried a sumptuous pig's trotter and ham hock salad; the meats were piled in a dainty tower and served with shreds of dandelion and beetroot. Gazpacho had great flavour, but came with an improbably huge, bobbing ball of mozzarella. A pea and mint risotto was a little too buttery, despite some lovely fresh young veg, but sea bream served with baby squid and salted almonds could not have been better. The well-heeled Wandsworth set that packs out the place most days can't believe their luck that an ambitious London restaurant has chosen to ply its trade on their leafy doorstep.
Babies and children welcome (lunch): high chairs. Booking essential. Separate room for parties, seats 16.

South

Battersea

Le Bouchon Bordelais

5-9 Battersea Rise, SW11 1HG (7738 0307/ www.lebouchon.co.uk). Clapham Junction rail/ 35, 37 bus.
Bar **Open** 10am-11.30pm Mon-Thur; 10am-midnight Fri, Sat; 10am-11pm Sun. **Breakfast served** 10am-2pm, **meals served** noon-10.30pm daily. **Main courses** £4.75-£16.95. **Set meal** £5.50 1 course.
Restaurant **Lunch served** noon-3pm, **dinner served** 6-11pm Mon-Fri. **Meals served** noon-11pm Sat; 12.30-10.30pm Sun. **Main courses**

Best traiteurs

If the restaurant revolution has given you a taste for good food, but work and family commitments make eating well at home as elusive as world peace, London's emerging army of traiteurs will seem a godsend. You can buy a full restaurant-quality meal to take home, without resorting to the mass-produced microwave monstrosities sold in the supermarkets. Some stores have café tables too. To celebrate this growing trend, we introduced a Best Traiteur category in the 2007 Time Out Eating & Drinking Awards. Here are the results.

The Grocer on Elgin

2007 WINNER BEST LOCAL TRAITEUR

6 Elgin Crescent, W11 2HX (7221 3844/ www.thegroceron.com). Ladbroke Grove tube. **Open** 7.30am-8pm Mon-Fri; 8am-6pm Sat, Sun.
It's hard to beat Ashley Sumner and Vivienne Hayman's cleverly conceived range of packaged meals for variety and quality. No matter whether your tastes are for classic comforts (meatballs and mustard mash, followed by thick vanilla custard) or exotic creations (miso-marinated cod, beetroot pesto), you'll find something inexorably delicious. And they sell Tim Tams!

Hand Made Food

2007 RUNNER-UP BEST LOCAL TRAITEUR

40 Tranquil Vale, SE3 0BD (8297 9966/ www.handmadefood.com). Blackheath rail. **Open** 9am-6pm Mon-Fri; 9am-5.30pm Sat; 9am-3.30pm Sun.
An exuberant outfit, with chefs working at the back in a semi-open kitchen. Dishes of the day – maybe valencia rice with seafood and chicken, or slow-roast pork with apricot and sage – are displayed in a cabinet at the front, with portions packed to order by caring staff. Local sourcing is a priority. The company also offers event catering.

Melrose & Morgan

2007 RUNNER-UP BEST LOCAL TRAITEUR

42 Gloucester Avenue, NW1 8JD (7722 0011/www.melroseandmorgan.com). Chalk Farm tube. **Open** 8am-8pm Mon-Fri; 9am-6pm Sat; 10am-4pm Sun.
A long central table is piled high with everything from pasties to crumbed chicken joints and lentil salads. Turn to the chiller cabinets and you'll find even more possibilities for supper: simple, but carefully sourced and cooked. We loved the own-made strawberry jelly and chocolate mousse, and the roast ham is some of the finest you'll ever taste.

Tavola

2007 RUNNER-UP BEST LOCAL TRAITEUR

155 Westbourne Grove, W11 2RS (7229 0571). Notting Hill Gate tube. **Open** 10am-7.30pm Mon-Fri; 10am-6pm Sat.
Renowned chef Alastair Little has a passion for 'food of the sun' and the range at his store stretches right along the Mediterranean, then over to Vietnam. The likes of rabbit sauce for pasta, and pho noodle soup show that Tavola is confident in its customers' sophisticated tastes. A discerning selection of packaged groceries, bought-in baked goods and kitchenware is available too.

Trinity Stores

2007 RUNNER-UP BEST LOCAL TRAITEUR

5&6 Balham Station Road, SW12 9SG (8673 3773/www.trinitystores.co.uk). Balham tube/rail. **Open** 8am-8pm Mon-Fri; 9am-5.30pm Sat; 9.30am-4pm Sun.
A cheerful deli-café where dishes of the day might include honey and mustard chicken skewers with yoghurt sauce, lasagne or lemon posset. Add bought-in produce such as delicate La Tua pastas (made in London), Helsett Farm Cornish ice-cream, and fine continental cheeses and charcuterie – and a walk home from the station has never been so mouth-watering.

£14.50-£19.50. **Set meal** (lunch, 6-7pm Mon-Fri) £15 3 courses.
Both **Credit** AmEx, MC, V.
A thriving bar (with its own brisk menu) occupies the main two rooms at this established Battersea Rise site: here you can savour wines by the glass in front of the spectacularly mirrored bar or on the small front patio, while catching up with the latest sports on TV. The restaurant occupies a long, narrow room to one side. It has its own bar, frenchified memorabilia on the walls and white tablecloths on the close-packed tables. Generally, the food is good enough, but rarely better than that. A starter of moules marinière was fresh but unexciting; the version with cream was better. French onion soup was competent enough, but lacked punch. Of the main courses, a succulent steak frites was the star, but steak tartare had little spice or flavour. And for dessert, a rather tired chocolate mousse was trumped by the far creamier, fresher crème brûlée. We had the impression that the place was just coasting, a feeling reinforced by erratic service. The substantial wine list is very French and worth exploring; although you may choose to do that in the bar.
Babies and children welcome: children's menu; crèche (Sat, Sun); high chairs. Disabled: toilet. Separate room for parties, seats 30. Tables outdoors (11, terrace). **Map 21 C5.**
For branch (Le Pot Lyonnais) see index.

Clapham

Gastro

67 Venn Street, SW4 0BD (7627 0222). Clapham Common tube. **Breakfast served** 8am-3pm, **meals served** noon-midnight daily. **Main courses** £12.95-£16.75. **Set lunch** (noon-3pm Mon-Fri) £9.95 2 courses incl coffee. **Credit** MC, V.
Reproducing an authentic French brasserie in London has proved tricky, but Gastro is as close to the real deal as you'll find. It's the kind of dark and casually efficient place found all over France, dispensing thick coffee, sweet jam and croissants for breakfast, croque monsieurs through the day, and hefty (if at times erratic) standards for lunch and dinner. Apart from the fact no one's smoking, everything is as it should be: plastic lobsters hang from the ceilings of the two rooms; a curved bar is staffed by a supercilious (but Byronic) Frenchman who will only reluctantly converse in English; families and couples spread themselves over the rickety tables; the menu displays an utter contempt for vegetarians; and the toilets need urgent attention. The food, cooked in an open kitchen and served with panache, is generally good. Moules marinière were wine-rich, plump and piping-hot; rib-sticking vegetable soup was, unfortunately, bland. Steak frites (with organic Scotch beef) was fabulous, and a sprightly salad came with slightly dry goat's cheese on toasted baguette rounds. Puddings are ineffably French (île flottante, crème brûlée, tarte tatin) and just the right side of overwhelming. In short, a great local asset.
Babies and children admitted. Booking advisable. Separate area for parties, seats 25. Tables outdoors (4, pavement). **Map 22 A2.**

★ Trinity NEW

2007 WINNER BEST LOCAL RESTAURANT

4 The Polygon, SW4 0JG (7622 1199/ www.trinityrestaurant.co.uk). Clapham Common tube. **Lunch served** 12.30-2.30pm Tue-Sun. **Dinner served** 6.30-10.30pm Mon-Sat; 7-10pm Sun. **Main courses** £15-£20. **Set lunch** £12 2 courses, £18 3 courses. **Set meal** (Sun) £25 3 courses. **Credit** AmEx, MC, V.
Chef/owner Adam Byatt ran Clapham's much-acclaimed Thyme a few years ago; he's returned to the area – and to form – with Trinity, a textbook model of a great local restaurant. The room is stylish but not flashy, with well-spaced circular tables and foldback windows that are a boon on warm evenings. Staff were impeccable: informed, attentive, with a personal touch that makes every diner feel special. The judiciously chosen wine list caters for all price points. And the food was sublime. Hardened carnivores fare well (braised pig's head), as do lovers of the luxurious (lobster, truffles), but vegetarians get a look-in too. Each dish is listed by its three main ingredients: a starter of 'mackerel, cucumber, horseradish' involved sweet, juicy mackerel fillets, with a smear of not-too-strong horseradish cream plus pickled cucumber in the form of tiny cubes and little curls (dishes look as good as they taste). 'Beef, oxtail, bone marrow' (a main) comprised pot au feu of longhorn beef – soft as butter – with punchy oxtail ravioli, bone marrow and a stew of summer vegetables. For dessert, we bravely resisted the temptation of 'chocolate, chocolate, chocolate' in favour of passionfruit sorbet (intensely flavoured, perfect texture). Pricing is very reasonable for cooking of this quality, and the set menus, especially the lunch offering, are an absolute bargain. A holy Trinity, indeed.
Babies and children welcome: children's portions; high chairs. Booking essential. Disabled: toilet. **Map 22 A1.**

Waterloo

★ RSJ

33 Coin Street, SE1 9NR (7928 4554/ www.rsj.uk.com). Waterloo tube/rail. **Lunch served** noon-2pm Mon-Fri. **Dinner served** 5.30-11pm Mon-Sat. **Main courses** £12-£17. **Set meal** £15.95 2 courses, £18.95 3 courses. **Credit** AmEx, DC, MC, V.
Still fresh as just-dried paint after 25 years, RSJ's first-floor dining room on the corner of a Waterloo street is plain but attractive and smart. Its reputation rests principally on its cellar of Loire wines; as well as an evening's worth of enjoyable reading between hard covers, there's a regularly changing list of a dozen wines by the glass for entry-level oenophiles. The concise menu is broadly French, but owes much of its zesty appeal to English ingredients. Fish and vegetable dishes

The Wallace. See p106.

suit the Saumurs, but the Loire's light reds are also well served by deftly cooked meat. Soft pillows of home-made gnocchi with a fragrant flotilla of young broad beans, peas, mussels, pea shoots and marjoram floating on a deeply delicious shellfish bisque was a flying start to a set dinner. They kept it up with a fine fillet of organically farmed salmon cooked to retain some firmness, with caramelised endive, a zingy herb sauce and baby beets. Don't miss – as an excuse for a pudding wine or not – the often fruit-based desserts, such as an exceptional chocolate and raspberry roulade. We're confident the neighbouring French diners were as impressed as we were.
Babies and children admitted. Booking advisable. Separate room for parties, seats 25. **Map 11 N8.**

East

Bethnal Green

Bistrotheque (100)
23-27 Wadeson Street, E2 9DR (8983 7900/ www.bistrotheque.com). Bethnal Green tube/ rail/Cambridge Heath rail/55 bus.
Bar **Open** 6pm-midnight Mon-Sat; 1pm-midnight Sun.
Restaurant **Lunch served** 11am-4pm Sat, Sun. **Dinner served** 6.30-10.30pm Mon-Thur, Sun; 6.30-11pm Fri, Sat. **Main courses** £10-£21. **Set lunch** £21 3 courses. **Set dinner** (6.30-7.30pm Mon-Fri) £12 2 courses, £15 3 courses.
Both **Credit** AmEx, MC, V.
An all-white warehouse space, with louche cabaret and a classily funky bar downstairs, Bistrotheque hit Hackney's new demographic on the head when it opened in 2004, blending sophistication with a dash of streetwise cool. It's stood the test of time, making remarkably few changes along the way: the service is still commited and friendly, the clientele relaxed and happy and the menu crafted to their whims, with a cocktail list, grazing dishes (croque monsieur, moules) and a good prix-fixe that extends to weekend lunch, when there's brunch too. The kitchen is characterised by bold flavours: roasted vine tomatoes, black pudding, steak, foie gras and chunky, no-nonsense chips give the idea. That's not to say the cooking is primitive: apart from a couple of lapses with I-could-do-that-better assemblages (such as apricot, stilton and baby gem salad), the flavours and presentation are well realised. Our half roast chicken was fabulously garlicky, while lemon tart with blood orange sorbet teetered satisfying on the sweet/sour edge. The open-plan space can be a disadvantage if there's a large party dining: just ask to move.
Babies and children admitted. Booking advisable. Disabled: toilet. Entertainment: cabaret (check website or phone for details); pianist noon-4pm Sun. Separate room for parties, seats 50.

Brick Lane

Les Trois Garçons (100)
1 Club Row, E1 6JX (7613 1924/www.lestrois garcons.com). Liverpool Street tube/rail/ 8, 388 bus. **Dinner served** 7-10pm Mon-Thur; 7-10.30pm Fri, Sat. **Main courses** £18-£32. **Set dinner** (Mon-Wed) £25 2 courses, £29 3 courses. **Credit** AmEx, DC, JCB, MC, V.
Les Trois Garçons laughs in the face of simplicity with a dramatic room that Salvador Dalí might have co-conceived with Miss Havisham, filled with tiara-ed taxidermy and a multitude of bizarre *objets trouvés*. Food is similarly bold and complex, offering technically demanding, multi-element dishes in artistic (perhaps sometimes pretentious) presentations. Were it to fail in its ambitions, this would be no more than a novelty restaurant – but it dazzles more often than it disappoints. There was a 'Surreal Things' menu on offer when we visited, to tie in with a V&A exhibition; we tried the 'Table With Bird's Legs' (in tribute to Meret Oppenheim), which turned out to be frogs' legs with asparagus, quail eggs and brioche. It was subtle and exotic. Another starter of foie gras was deliquescent, pleasingly teamed with green apples and rhubarb. For mains, veal sweetbreads with cannelono and salsify was excellent, but salmon was less good, its accompaniments confused in an unnecessary carrot velouté. The service is formal but can be abstracted; the clientele a mix of special-occasion diners and a vaguely mysterious international crowd. Dishes are expensive, so too the wine (though an £8 glass of pinot noir was excellent), but you do get a side of glamour with your grub.
Booking advisable. Restaurant available for hire. Separate room for parties, seats 10. **Map 6 S4.**

North

Crouch End

Les Associés
172 Park Road, N8 8JT (8348 8944/ www.lesassocies.co.uk). Finsbury Park tube/rail then W7 bus. **Lunch served** by appointment Wed-Fri; 1-3pm Sun. **Dinner served** 7.30-10pm Tue-Sat. **Main courses** £12.50-£17. **Set lunch** (Sun) £14 3 courses. **Set dinner** (Tue-Fri) £11 2 courses, £14.50 3 courses. **Credit** AmEx, MC, V.
Fad-following restaurants are not scarce in north London, but 'the Associates' know what they're doing and stick to it: classic French cuisine. And that's no bad thing, when the traditional virtues of French cooking – attention to detail, careful sourcing of good ingredients, deliciously crisp bread – are so closely observed. The ambience exactly matches the food: tranquillity itself, with a slightly chichi, very comfortable little dining room, a pretty front terrace, *chanson* wafting in the background and charming, vaguely cranky but ineffably French service. Prices are reasonable, and our three-course Sunday lunch was a steal. Starters of a tartare of avocado au pistou and rabbit terrine were lovely, combining strong and delicate flavours to great effect. To follow, confit of duck in cassis and a trio of fish in leek sauce were also enjoyable, though not as impressive as some evening meals we've had here. The highlights of the main menus are the daily specials, especially if they combine seafood and herbs. The berry-full house red is great value, but there are plenty of fine labels too.
Babies and children admitted. Booking advisable. Restaurant available for hire. Tables outdoors (8, garden).

Hornsey

Le Bistro
36 High Street, N8 7NX (8340 2116). Turnpike Lane tube/Hornsey rail/41, W3 bus. **Brunch served** 12.30-5pm Sun. **Dinner served** 6.30-11pm Mon-Sat; 5-10pm Sun. **Main courses** £10.50-£16. **Set meal** £10.95 2 courses, £12.95 3 courses. **Credit** MC, V.
It's not just the cooking that is resolutely French at this established neighbourhood local – the decor is too. Parisian posters, Gallic knick-knacks and framed mirrors lend a cosy charm, complemented by the friendly service. A first course of chilled trout and chive mousse brought summer flavours to the table with its delicate, herby notes. Deep-fried goat's cheese also delivered the goods, with a crisp crumb coating yielding to mild, pleasantly acidic warm cheese, well matched with a dab of sweet blackcurrant purée. Main courses were almost as satisfying: our succulent steak, cooked to perfect pinkness, was enhanced by perky green peppercorns swirled around in a toasted buttery glaze. A glistening chicken breast perched atop buttery mash was let down only by a stingy drizzle of delicately flavoured mushroom sauce. Puds are mainly indulgent. We opted for crème caramel; a fair rendition, but its sauce would have benefited from longer cooking to give it more kick. Set menus are a snip, while the well-chosen wine list includes special price offers to match – you'll find something very decent for under £20.
Babies and children welcome: high chairs. Booking advisable. Tables outdoors (18, garden).

Islington

Almeida
30 Almeida Street, N1 1AD (7354 4777/ www.danddlondon.com). Angel tube/Highbury & Islington tube/rail. **Lunch served** noon-2.30pm, **dinner served** 5.30-10.45pm Mon-Sat. **Meals served** 1-8.30pm Sun. **Set lunch** £20 2 courses, £22 3 courses. **Set dinner** £25 2 courses, £27 3 courses. **Set meal** (lunch, 5.30-7pm daily; 10-10.45pm Mon-Sat) £14.50 2 courses, £17.50 3 courses. **Credit** AmEx, MC, V.
Now that the Conran empire has been bought out by former managers and rebranded D&D London, changes may be on the way. For the moment, however, the Conran characteristics still seem to be in place at Almeida: some things are excellent, others not, and the whole experience – above all the service – comes with an air of corporate charmlessness, a lack of any real distinctiveness or individual involvement. Decor and lighting are discreetly contemporary rather than full-on designer, creating a more placid feel. The prix-fixe menus are decent value, and there are well-priced quality wines as well as grand crus on the hefty wine list. Starters were a high point: crayfish with coriander salad and saffron dressing, and seared tuna with chervil and parsley salad were both delicious, infused with delicate flavours. Breast of landaise chicken with piquillo peppers, chorizo and parsley, and roast cod with sauté potatoes, lentils and chives weren't quite on the same level: the sweet peppers were not matched by the blandish chicken, and the nicely done fish was overpowered by heavily salted vegetables. Enjoyable enough, but with nothing like the kind of buzz one should expect from fine dining.
Babies and children welcome: high chairs. Booking advisable. Disabled: toilet. Restaurant available for hire. Separate room for parties, seats 20. Tables outdoors (8, pavement). **Map 5 O1.**

★ Morgan M
489 Liverpool Road, N7 8NS (7609 3560/ www.morganm.com). Highbury & Islington tube/ rail. **Lunch served** noon-2.30pm Wed-Fri, Sun. **Dinner served** 7-10pm Tue-Sat. **Set lunch**

£19.50 2 courses, £23.50 3 courses. **Set dinner** £34 3 courses. **Set meal** £36 (vegetarian), £43 (non-vegetarian) tasting menu. **Credit** DC, MC, V.
The real deal. After so many overhyped but essentially ordinary restaurants, it's a delight to find one that really delivers. Morgan Meunier's cooking is supremely skilful; painstakingly intricate but without any just-to-impress gestures, producing multiple layers of subtle flavours. As in any first-cru French restaurant, the delicacies begin with the extras – on our visit, an appetiser of wonderfully fragrant beetroot soup (no relation whatsoever to borscht) with roquefort mousse. We could have stayed to contemplate that, but moved on to earthy foie gras and artichoke terrine, and perfect-quality seared tuna with a gorgeous, genuinely innovative red pepper sorbet. Every course produced unannounced delights: sea bass arrived with an elusively sweet saffron sauce, fillet of veal with a woody taste of morels. And the £34 set dinner (an extraordinary bargain) comprises three courses, so you carry on to the irresistible desserts, such as the chocolate platter with a Valrhona sorbet. Meunier is also known for his vegetarian creations, and there's an all-vegetarian menu. The wine list is on a par with the food, and service is utterly charming. An experience that stays in the mind, and lures you to return.
Babies and children admitted (lunch). Booking essential. Dress: smart casual. Separate room for parties, seats 12. Vegetarian menu.

Palmers Green

Café Anjou

394 Green Lanes, N13 5PD (8886 7267). Wood Green tube then 329 bus/Palmers Green rail. **Lunch served** noon-2.30pm, **dinner served** 6.30-10.30pm Tue-Sun. **Main courses** £8.95-£11.45. **Set lunch** (noon-2pm Tue-Sat) £7.45 1 course incl glass of wine and coffee. **Set meal** (Tue-Fri, lunch Sat) £12.95 2 courses, £14.45 3 courses. **Credit** AmEx, MC, V.
Decent prices and a relaxed atmosphere, akin to that of a real small-town French bistro, have kept this local in favour with Palmers Green residents. The food follows the neighbourhood bistro style too: nothing exceptional or overly adventurous, but enjoyable enough and with a freshly prepared feel. A mushroom and bacon salad came with a tangy, sweet but subtle dressing and flavoursome bacon, which offset the ordinary mushrooms; a salad of poulet fumé had a satisfying full-on smokiness. To follow, pork medallions in Calvados was, again, quite decent, even if the sauce could have done with more of a Calvados tang. Lamb brochette à la menthe featured another interesting, rich sauce, with garlic and redcurrants as well as mint, but was a tad overcooked. French details are well observed, with excellent bread and a varied cheese course, and there's a short but good-value wine selection. Our chief grouses were that the cheese was too cold, and that we thought we'd ordered a selection of 'legumes du jour' for £1.25 – which turned out to be the price of each vegetable.
Babies and children welcome: children's portions; high chairs. Booking essential dinner Fri, Sat. Restaurant available for hire.

North West

St John's Wood

L'Aventure

3 Blenheim Terrace, NW8 0EH (7624 6232). St John's Wood tube/139, 189 bus. **Lunch served** 12.30-2.30pm Mon-Fri. **Dinner served** 7-11pm Mon-Sat. **Set lunch** £15 2 courses, £18.50 3 courses incl coffee. **Set dinner** £27.50 2 courses, £32.50 3 courses. **Credit** AmEx, MC, V.
This place would be ideal for owners of a pied-à-terre in the French countryside needing to polish their language skills: at moments of maximum exuberance (which occur frequently), *la patronne* forgets the use of English completely. All this, though, is just grist to the mill for L'Aventure's cosmopolitan, well-heeled, mostly older clientele. With the traditional vague opulence of a French bourgeois restaurant (tapestries, plush seating, very proper table settings) and a leafy front terrace, it's very pretty and cosy – if slightly cramped in parts. The food on the regularly changing set menus (great value for lunch, much pricier for dinner) is as classically French as the setting. Artichoke salad came with a delicious pomegranate dressing, while a croustillant of wild mushrooms had a beautifully earthy flavour and a just-so crust. Mains – rack of lamb with garlic, monkfish medallions with sauce vièrge – were less distinctive, but pleasant. The wine list is expensive, but the lower-priced house wines are superior quality. L'Aventure has its inconsistencies – a cheese course was served too cold, and while some of the staff exhibit a proper French culinary training, others are just sloppy – but its regulars are clearly happy to forgive them.
Babies and children welcome: high chairs. Booking advisable dinner. Tables outdoors (6, terrace). **Map 1 C2.**

Outer London

Kew, Surrey

Ma Cuisine Le Petit Bistrot

9 Station Approach, Kew, Surrey TW9 3QB (8332 1923/www.macuisinekew.co.uk). Kew Gardens tube/rail. **Meals served** 10am-10.30pm daily. **Main courses** £8.95-£14.50. **Set lunch** (noon-3pm Mon-Sat) £12.95 2 courses, £15.50 3 courses; (noon-4pm Sun) £15 2 courses, £18 3 courses. **Credit** MC, V.
Ma Cuisine has two sites: this one near Kew Gardens station and another near Twickenham station. Outside, there are freshly written lists of typically French dishes (some of which, oddly, were not on the actual menu). Within, red gingham tablecloths, a smattering of *belle époque* posters and multicoloured lampshades make for a reasonable pastiche rather than replica of a real French bistrot. The starters raised expectations: crab soup was excellent, with grated gruyère, confit garlic and a sharp, garlicky rouille; a plate of charcuterie was outstanding, including more variations on foie gras than were mentioned on the menu and a particularly tangy sherry jelly. Then came a gaffe, as a main of 'marmite of scallops, salmon and bass with Pernod broth' turned out to consist of just three overgrilled pieces of the (named) fish with a small portion of that same crab soup as a separate sauce. A plate of warm tongue, oxtail and boned pig's trotter was sticky and earthy, providing some compensation. The French staff were cheerful; the waiter replaced our corked wine readily enough.
Babies and children welcome: children's menu (Sunday lunch); high chairs. Booking advisable. Tables outdoors (6, pavement).
For branch see index.

Richmond, Surrey

Chez Lindsay

11 Hill Rise, Richmond, Surrey TW10 6UQ (8948 7473/www.chez-lindsay.co.uk). Richmond tube/rail.
Crêperie **Meals served** noon-10.45pm Mon-Sat; noon-9.45pm Sun. **Main courses** £7.45-£9.45. *Restaurant* **Meals served** noon-10.45pm Mon-Sat; noon-9.45pm Sun. **Main courses** £12.75-£16.75. **Set lunch** (noon-3pm Mon-Sat) £14.50 2 courses, £17.50 3 courses. **Set dinner** (after 6pm) £16.50 2 courses, £19.50 3 courses. *Both* **Credit** MC, V.
There's a sunny vibe to Lindsay Wotton's low-key restaurant, with its yellow-painted brick walls, pale-wood tables, convivial atmosphere and smiling staff. The place was busy on a Monday night – always a good sign. Breton food and drink is the speciality, particularly seafood and galettes (crêpe-like pancakes made with buckwheat flour, served with savoury or sweet fillings), French sparkling ciders and wines from the Loire. Galettes are available as a starter, main and dessert, in versions both classic (ham and cheese, cheese and tomato), more unusual (scallops and leeks; chitterling sausage, onions and mustard sauce) and sweet (with just butter and sugar, or banana and chocolate sauce). They're quite hefty, even as a first course. But there are plenty of alternatives on the long menu, including lots of salads; you could visit for just a snack or a full-blown meal. Choucroute de la mer featured smoked haddock, salmon, mussels, clams and a huge langoustine with potatoes and a big heap of sauerkraut in a fishy broth; the waitress warned us that the sauerkraut dominated, and it did. Sirloin steak with tarragon butter, frites and a tasty green salad was a decent rendition. Great-value set lunches are a bonus.
Babies and children welcome: high chairs. Booking advisable. Separate room for parties, seats 35.

Surbiton, Surrey

The French Table

85 Maple Road, Surbiton, Surrey KT6 4AW (8399 2365/www.thefrenchtable.co.uk). Surbiton rail. **Lunch served** noon-2.30pm Tue-Fri, Sun. **Dinner served** 7-10.30pm Tue-Sat. **Main courses** £10.50-£15.50. **Set lunch** (Tue-Fri) £14.50 2 courses, £17.50 3 courses; (Sun) £17.50 3 courses. **Credit** MC, V.
The French Table team tries extremely hard to give local diners an outstanding experience – and most of the time they pull it off while still maintaining an air of casual ease. The small dining room is usually packed with groups of friends and dating couples, though the mirrors and pale walls help to increase the sense of space. The waiting staff had the kitchen details at their fingertips, explaining which dishes might arrive differently from the way the menu suggests ('this risotto is cold', 'this lamb comes cooked five ways') and were impressively attentive (phoning, as requested, when our table became available earlier, replenishing tap water without being asked). Food was fresh, inventive and invariably delicious – if a little fussier than it needed to be given the high quality of ingredients and cooking. Fried plaice in tempura batter with warm, tangy, sauce gribiche provided strong contrasts; also fun was a tumbler containing layers of livid pink foamed crab purée, creamed avocado, crab and that (cold) risotto. However, the lamb was a bit contrived; the effort that had gone into devising its 'five ways' was far more remarkable than the actual flavours and textures. Nevertheless, the French Table is worth a detour.
Babies and children welcome: children's portions; high chairs. Booking advisable; essential weekends.
For branch (The French Room) see index.

Twickenham, Middlesex

Brula

43 Crown Road, Twickenham, Middx TW1 3EJ (8892 0602/www.brulabistrot.co.uk). St Margarets rail. **Lunch served** noon-3pm, **dinner served** 6-10.30pm daily. **Main courses** £10-£19. **Set lunch** £12 2 courses, £14 3 courses. **Set dinner** (6-10.30pm Mon-Thur; 6-7pm Fri-Sat) £17 3 courses. **Credit** AmEx, MC, V.
Usually we are big fans of Brula. It is on a corner in upmarket St Margarets and, inside the small dining area, the stained glass windows, dark wood and drapes create an intimate, colourful feeling. There are photos of David Suchet as Poirot lunching genteelly in this room almost 20 years ago (it's near Twickenham Studios) and, on weekdays, Brula can still feel refined. On a Saturday, though, it was a nearly unbearable box of sound: with the windows closed, the noise from the enthusiastic locals made it sometimes impossible to hear the waiters. The food was close to its normal high standard, though aspects of the cooking suggested the kitchen was under stress. Sorrel soup was served at a scalding temperature, too hot for any complexity of flavour to come through, while a good, thick slice of halibut was a little undercooked (admittedly, that's preferable to overcooked) and duck confit was too salty. Only a rich and sweet foie gras with pineau jelly was at its best. You can buy wine in 50cl carafes, but be warned that you can pay the equivalent of almost £30 a bottle this way and still not see the label.
Babies and children admitted. Booking advisable. Separate rooms for parties, seating 8, 10 and 24. Tables outdoors (6, pavement).
For branches (La Buvette, La Saveur) see index.

Gastropubs

London's gastropub revolution may have started with the **Eagle** in Farringdon in 1991, but it's come a long way since. The initial impetus behind the wave of new gastropubs was the break-up of pubs tied to breweries, and the subsequent sell-off of licensed properties. This presented a great opportunity for young chefs who wanted to run their own place, but didn't have enough money to take on a fancy restaurant. Gastropubs boomed. Diversification, away from the initial formula of bare floorboards, blackboard menu and mismatched furniture, followed soon after. Some gastropubs segregated the dining area; some went as far as putting the dining room on another floor. Wine lists started to take greater prominence, and real ales far less. Wealthier operators moved into the growing market; some outfits started to be very plush indeed, with prices and menus virtually indistinguishable from a smart restaurant. And so we've arrived at the situation right now: gastropubs everywhere, some basic but many quite smart, and often with prices close to or exceeding restaurant menus. But to be a proper gastropub, it still has to have these essential elements: a bar where you can just drink, and a decent selection of ales. Cheers to that.

And there's no shortage of newcomers this year. Some have sprung up miles away from the traditional gastro heartlands of Islington and Clerkenwell in previously untouched districts, such as the **Dark Horse** (in Camberwell), **Old Nun's Head** (Peckham) and the **Queen's Arms** (Barons Court). Others are siblings to existing operations, such as the **Brown Dog** and the **Rosendale**; and others mark the first foray of corporate backers into the gastropub world: Gordon Ramsay in the case of the **Narrow**, Young's brewery in the case of the **Waterfront**. Many of these new arrivals are excellent operations, if different from the original blueprint – which is why we've again included a Best Gastropub category in the 2007 Time Out Eating & Drinking Awards.

Central

Belgravia

Ebury

11 Pimlico Road, SW1W 8NA (7730 6784/ www.theebury.co.uk). Sloane Square tube/ Victoria tube/rail/11, 211, 239 bus.
Brasserie **Open** noon-11pm Mon-Sat; noon-10.30pm Sun. **Lunch served** noon-3.30pm Mon-Fri, Sun. **Dinner served** 6-10.30pm Mon-Sat; 6-10pm Sun. **Set lunch** £11.50 1 course, £16.50 2 courses, £19.50 3 courses.
Dining room **Dinner served** 7-10.30pm Tue-Sat.
Both **Main courses** £10.50-£18.50. **Credit** AmEx, MC, V.

Very much at the restaurant end of the gastropub spectrum, the Ebury occupies a prominent corner site where Victoria coach station gives way to a swankier neighbourhood. A handsome ground-floor bar and restaurant is furnished in wood and dark leather, lightened by white walls and huge windows; upstairs is a more formal dining room. Wine and cocktails are to the fore, though you can get a pint of London Pride. The menu aspires to more than gastropub staples too – not always successfully, as demonstrated by an over-rich herb risotto, and an unctuous spiced pork belly with mashed potatoes, sautéed black pudding and star anise (it wasn't very spicy and we couldn't spot the black pudding). Much better were a delightfully fresh pea mousse with pea shoots and truffle dressing, and a moreish roast cod with puy lentils. Pricing is a concern; side orders are £3.50 apiece, and while white and dark chocolate mousse with orange and kumquat salad was good, it cost £5.50, like all the desserts. Presumably locals can happily swallow these prices, but given the variable quality, we weren't so sanguine. At the end of 2006 the Ebury was bought by Carlo Spetale, who also owns the Modern European Notting Hill Brasserie; one of his innovations has been the introduction of jazz evenings.
Babies and children admitted. Disabled: toilets. Separate room for parties, seats 60. **Map 15 G11.**

Bloomsbury

Norfolk Arms

28 Leigh Street, WC1H 9EP (7388 3937/ www.norfolkarms.co.uk). Euston tube/rail. **Open** 11am-11pm Mon-Sat; 11am-10.30pm Sun. **Lunch served** noon-3pm, **dinner served** 6.30-10.15pm daily. **Main courses** £8.50-£14.50. **Credit** AmEx, MC, V.

Despite its large and enticing central bar, we were told to go and sit down at our table like naughty school children when we went up to order a drink at the Norfolk Arms. The place is very tastefully fitted out with curvy French tables, a green marble fireplace with art nouveau tiling, lacy etched glass and an ornate ceiling. The bar looks like a deli counter, with hanging salamis, dried chillies and a professional rotary slicer, all the better to cut the pata negra ham, lomo, mortadella and fennel salami featured on the alluring list of 30 tapas and traditional pub snacks such as scotch eggs. A main course of toothsome valencia rice, featuring juicy razor clams, prawns, mussels, clams and vegetables continued the Spanish theme, while slow-roast ribeye doffed its cap to British pub grub. Desserts of Pedro Ximénez semifreddo with pine nut nougatine, and polenta cake with greek yogurt were tempting but impossible after such hearty mains. A summer pudding-style Spanish rosé cost a very reasonable £17 (the wine list starts at £12). Service fell off when it came to the bill, but now we've got used to the idea that we're not allowed to approach the bar, we'd happily return.
Babies and children admitted. Booking advisable. Separate room for parties, seats 25. Tables outdoors (15, pavement). **Map 4 L3.**

Clerkenwell & Farringdon

Coach & Horses (100)

26-28 Ray Street, EC1R 3DJ (7278 8990/ www.thecoachandhorses.com). Farringdon tube/rail. **Open** 11am-11pm Mon-Fri; 6-11pm Sat; noon-4pm Sun. **Lunch served** noon-3pm Mon-Fri, Sun. **Dinner served** 6-10pm Mon-Sat. **Main courses** £9.50-£14. **Credit** AmEx, MC, V.

Fancy design has never been the order of the day at the Coach & Horses, but recently part of the outdoor area has been converted into a dining room, and the garden now has only four tables. A large group of friends made a beeline there, leaving the rather plain white and brown dining area to couples and pairs of work colleagues. We were stuck listening to overbearing academic types who fancied themselves in the glamorous world of the media (the *Guardian*'s offices are nearby). The menu is dominated by French and British country cooking: a juicy pink duck breast with sautéed

BEST GASTROPUBS

Perfect pints

For interesting or varied real ales, try the **Charles Lamb** (*see p129*), **Drapers Arms** (*see p129*), **Duke of Cambridge** (*see p129*), **Earl Spencer** (*see p122*), **Horseshoe** (*see p130*), **Junction Tavern** (*see p129*) and **St John's** (*see p127*). The **Roebuck** (*see p119*) gets extra ale-head points for including tasting notes.

A restaurant vibe

Enjoy expert, upmarket fare in a smart (often separate) setting at the **Bull** (*see p128*), **Cow** (*see p121*), **Ebury** (*see p115*), **Greyhound** (*see p122*), **House** (*see p129*), the **Narrow** (*see p125*), **Peasant** (*see p117*), **Pig's Ear** (*see p121*) **Princess** (*see p127*), **Rosendale** (*see p125*), **Wells** (*see p130*) and **White Swan** (*see p117*).

Grape delights

Both the **Greyhound** (*see p122*) and **Rosendale** (*see p125*) are owned by sommelier Mark Van der Goot, so the wine lists are exceptional.

Riverside dining

For fine views of Mother Thames, secure an outdoor table at the **Gun** (*see p125*), the **Narrow** (*see p125*) or the aptly named **Waterfront** (*see p122*).

Queen's Arms. See p119.

vegetables or braised ox cheek might be preceded by, say, rabbit rillettes, while desserts could include chocolate tart, rhubarb mess and assorted ice-creams. Sourcing quality meat is a concern here and the rare breeds, such as our Gloucester Old Spot chop, come from Long Ghyll Farms in Lancashire. Over the past five years the C&H's chips have acquired quite a reputation, served with a powerful aïoli loaded with crushed garlic (the taste lingers along with the memories). Service was exceptionally sweet, and staff kept us well supplied with large glasses of decent red and rosé: unusually, the house wines are not the cheapest on the list. The beer is fine too, with the likes of Adnams, London Pride and Timothy Taylor.
Babies and children welcome: high chairs. Tables outdoors (4, garden). **Map 5 N4.**

Eagle (100)

159 Farringdon Road, EC1R 3AL (7837 1353). Farringdon tube/rail. **Open** noon-11pm Mon-Sat; noon-5pm Sun. **Lunch served** 12.30-3pm Mon-Fri; 12.30-3.30pm Sat, Sun. **Dinner served** 6.30-10.30pm Mon-Sat. **Main courses** £5-£14.50 **Credit** MC, V.
The Eagle's renown as birthplace of the modern gastropub movement seems to have resulted in an influx of tourists. Aside from the nearby Holiday Inn, this stretch of Farringdon Road is a curious destination for travellers, though they won't find a finer view of an NCP carpark anywhere in London. While a staff member is likely to allocate you a table, the service all but stops there. For drinks and food you need to order and pay at the bar, which also houses the open kitchen. Here, black-shirted cooks throw the likes of sardines, gilt-head bream and bruschetta on the chargrill. The blackboard menu is not well balanced in the three-course sense. There was a list of possible tapas (chicken wings, speck and melon, olives, chicken liver pâté), yet gazpacho soup and beetroot and feta salads seemed to be classified as main courses – once we saw the large servings we understood why. We couldn't fault the sourcing of peppery napoli sausages, barbecued and served on American-style home-baked beans, though the charred string binding them was an off-putting garnish. Draught beers included Kirin, Leffe, Eagle IPA (natch) and Bombardier, but on a hot evening we opted for chilled Fleurie.
Babies and children welcome: children's portions. Tables outdoors (4, pavement). **Map 5 N4.**

Easton

22 Easton Street, WC1X 0DS (7278 7608). Farringdon tube/rail. **Open** noon-11pm Mon-Thur; noon-1am Fri; 5.30pm-1am Sat; noon-10.30pm Sun. **Lunch served** 12.30-3pm Mon-Fri; 1-4pm Sun. **Dinner served** 6.30-10pm Mon-Fri, Sat; 6.30-9pm Sun. **Main courses** £8.95-£13.50. **Credit** MC, V.
The first of Andrew Veever and Jeremy Sutton's venues (the other is the Princess, *see p127*) is a wide-open, well-lit room with plush red banquettes and old chairs that are tattier than you find in most gastropubs. It's not a look that's been carelessly flung together: the Australian duo seem to have a penchant for the flamboyant wallpaper designs of Florence Broadhurst, and the Easton features one of green and cream birds. The menu focuses on a long list of mains (with vegetarians well looked after), plus a few chalked-up nibbles and just two desserts. Potted North Atlantic prawns spiked with capers and fresh chives featured plenty of chunky prawn pieces and tasted wonderful, despite being served too cold. Halibut came on a king-size bed of artichoke mash, topped with a summery salsa rosso. Ribeye steak was an apotheosis of its kind, given a judicious saucing with gorgonzola butter and accompanied by fat chips. There's a terrific list of wines by the glass (two sizes) and bottle; we were very impressed by the rosé and viognier-chardonnay blend. And we're glad to see there's now a real ale among the roster of lagers and continental beers. Staff are friendly and easy-going.
Babies and children admitted (until 9pm). Entertainment: DJs 9pm Fri. Tables outdoors (4, pavement). **Map 5 N4.**

Hat & Feathers NEW

2 Clerkenwell Road, EC1M 5PQ (7490 2244). Barbican tube/Farringdon tube/rail/55, 243 bus. **Open** noon-midnight Mon-Sat. **Lunch served** noon-2.30pm Mon-Fri. **Dinner served** 6-10pm Mon-Sat. **Credit** AmEx, MC, V.
The name of this large corner boozer hints at an age when hat-makers abounded in Clerkenwell. Derelict for years, the H&F reopened as a two-floor gastropub in 2006, the new management retaining its lovely acid-etched windows and wood panelling. Modern European cuisine is served on the first floor, where chef Adam Culverwell has created an interesting menu that hits more often than it misses. Pan-fried scallops with parsnip purée, lemon dressing and pea shoots was a well-presented, successful combination of moist, sweet and tart ingredients. However, caramelised onion tart was disappointing; the onions weren't caramelised, and had simply been piled on to a puff-pastry base. The kitchen had run out of fillet of beef with anchovy crumb and horseradish, so we opted for lamb rump with sweetbreads, butternut and mint purée – a fine chunk of juicy meat swimming in delicious Madeira gravy. We passed on dessert, though were tempted by banana split and tiramisu. The wine list is admirably broad, with 12 bottles under £20 and five wines by the glass, and the French waiters were warm and welcoming. A massive new outdoor terrace was added in time for summer 2007.
Babies and children admitted. Bar available for hire. Disabled: toilet. **Map 5 O4.**

Peasant

240 St John Street, EC1V 4PH (7336 7726/ www.thepeasant.co.uk). Angel tube/Farringdon tube/rail/19, 38 bus.
Bar **Open** noon-11pm Mon-Sat; noon-10.30pm Sun. **Meals served** noon-10.45pm Mon-Sat; noon-9.30pm Sun. **Main courses** £8.50-£9.50.
Restaurant **Brunch served** noon-3pm Sun. **Lunch served** noon-3pm Mon-Fri. **Dinner served** 6-11pm Mon-Sat. **Main courses** £9.70-£18. **Set lunch** (Mon-Thur) £14 2 courses, £18 3 courses.
Both **Credit** AmEx, MC, V.
Despite many gastro rivals in Clerkenwell, the Peasant is by no means a poor choice. The cosy bar area has bright red walls, a lovely old mosaic floor, illustrated tiles, pretty pink flower arrangements and burnished leather sofas. The range of draught beers is similarly inviting, with the Peasant's own lager, Cruz Campo, Bombardier and the little-seen Crouch Vale's Brewers Gold. Upstairs is a smartish restaurant, but we ate in the bar, tempted by the range of sharing platters and tapas featuring everything from edamame and oysters to lomo iberico. Steak sandwich with rocket and tomatoes on a Portuguese roll was let down by average fries. Organic salmon came in cartoccio (a bag) with leeks, herbs and chilli – an Italian dish with all the tongue-tingling qualities of an Asian recipe. Desserts, however, were poorly executed. Baked peach was lost in a chewy hunk of puff pastry billed as millefeuille, though the vanilla ice-cream on the side was lovely. Ice-cream would also have made a much better partner for the saggy chocolate and almond fondant than its praline-flavoured goo. Staff were friendly; though they repeatedly asked for our food order while we were having a drink, we can't fault their efficiency.
Babies and children welcome (until 9pm): high chairs. Booking advisable. Tables outdoors (4, garden terrace; 5, pavement). **Map 5 O4.**

Well

180 St John Street, EC1V 4JY (7251 9363/ www.downthewell.com). Farringdon tube/rail. **Open** 11am-midnight Mon-Thur; 11am-1am Fri; 10.30am-1am Sat; 10.30am-11pm Sun. **Meals served** noon-3pm, 6-10.30pm Mon-Fri; 10.30am-4pm, 6-10.30pm Sat; 10.30am-4pm, 6-10pm Sun. **Main courses** £9.95-£16.50. **Credit** AmEx, MC, V.
The Well is a small gastropub with large windows and heavy blue awnings, providing a voyeur's perspective of this corner of university land. It's owned by Tom and Ed Martin – who also run the Gun (*see p125*), White Swan (*see below*) and British newcomer Empress of India – so it's a surprise that no real ales are served. Instead there are premium lagers (Meantime's organic Helles, Leffe, Amstel, Paulaner), seven house cocktails and eight freshly made juices and smoothies – including such options as raspberry and mint, and pear and cinnamon. Tables are crammed in and the bar, overseen by a large bunch of crimson lilies and serenaded by dance music on our visit, can be hectic; table service is a necessity, and staff are mostly efficient and friendly. Food options span classic pub grub (a comforting fish pie, Gloucester Old Spot sausages with mash, pint o' prawns and mayonnaise) and more fanciful creations. We loved the special starter of beetroot-cured salmon with horseradish chantilly, though the portion was a little mean. A large bowl of white bean soup was too heavy-handed with cream, making it difficult to finish. Pork chop 'crépinette' came bundled with crushed potatoes in a caul wrap – needless, in truth, as the good ingredients didn't need such pretentious fiddling.
Babies and children welcome: high chairs. Booking advisable. Separate room for parties, seats 70. Tables outdoors (6, pavement). **Map 5 O4.**

Holborn

White Swan Pub & Dining Room

108 Fetter Lane, EC4A 1ES (7242 9696/ www.thewhiteswanlondon.com). Chancery Lane or Holborn tube. **Open** 11am-11pm Mon; 11am-midnight Tue-Thur; 11am-1am Fri. **Lunch served** noon-3pm, **dinner served** 6-10pm Mon-Fri. **Main courses** £13-£20. **Set lunch** (noon-1pm) £15 2 courses; £18 1 course, £24 2 courses, £29 3 courses. **Credit** AmEx, MC, V.
This spotless pub holds plenty to shield its fund manager customers from the atmosphere of a real boozer – lots of clubby dark wood, loos with posh flowers and hand towels, mirrors hinting at the art deco period, a classy carpet. Part of the burgeoning gastropub empire run by brothers Ed and Tom Martin – the others are the Well in St John Street (*see above*), the Gun in Docklands (*see p125*) and new British restaurant the Empress of India, in Hackney – it attracts a hip (rather than braying) City crowd. Beers on tap include Adnams Bitter and Broadside, and Guinness Extra Cold; there are some appealing bottled beers too. If you're interested in wine, there are around 150 on offer. A ribeye was deliciously tender and came with chips; we were advised side dishes were necessary, so opted for runner beans in preference to salad. Salmon fish cake, however, came with a mound of gritty spinach. A boring dish of ice-cream aside, desserts were impressive: strawberry sundae served in a martini glass, and a light, puffy and deliciously eggy apricot clafoutis with almond ice-cream. Service is charming at times, but prone to distraction and rather too keen on encouraging customers to order extras such as coffee. We ate downstairs; the mirrored and panelled dining room upstairs serves a different, smarter menu, with set meals at lunchtime, à la carte in the evening.
Babies and children welcome: children's portions; high chairs. Booking advisable, essential lunch. Restaurant available for hire. Tables outdoors (2, pavement). **Map 11 N5.**

Marylebone

Queen's Head & Artichoke

30-32 Albany Street, NW1 4EA (7916 6206/ www.theartichoke.net). Great Portland Street or Regent's Park tube. **Open** 11am-11pm Mon-Sat; noon-10.30pm Sun. **Meals served** 12.30-10pm daily. **Main courses** £9.50-£13.50. **Credit** AmEx, MC, V.
Away from the glass mausoleums of commercial property around the Euston Road corridor lies this thoroughly agreeable haven. A wood-panelled Victorian boozer, restored to create an easy-going ambience, the QH&A is a solid gastropub that performs its chosen tasks well and without pretension. Food from the main menu can be eaten at pavement tables, inside the light ground-floor bar, outside on a small Moroccan-styled patio, or

upstairs in the smarter, more intimate dining room. Snackers are spoilt with an A-Z of tapas, and not just typical Spanish dishes either: there's foie gras, English cheeses and greek salad too. Gazpacho was refreshing and summery; another starter of grilled lamb chop, beetroot couscous, lettuce and tzatziki pleased as well. Mains cost up to £13.50 (for ribeye steak); crispy organic salmon with fennel, asparagus and new potatoes was beyond reproach. Resisting desserts seemed pointless, and cape gooseberry frangipane tart rewarded a bit of indulgence. Add to the equation well-kept real ales (Marston's Pedigree, Adnams Best), a pleasingly balanced wine list and characterful multinational service and you have good reason to tarry.
Babies and children admitted. Separate room for parties, seats 45. Tables outdoors (6, garden; 8, pavement). **Map 3 H4.**

Temperance NEW

74-76 York Street, W1H 1QN (7262 1513). Baker Street or Marble Arch tube. **Open** noon-11pm Mon-Sat; noon-10.30pm Sun. **Lunch served** noon-3pm Mon-Sat; noon-5pm Sun. **Dinner served** 6-10pm Mon-Sat. **Main courses** £7.95-£15. **Credit** AmEx, MC, V.
Despite its name, the Temperance hasn't gone off the sauce. On our visit, there was Greene King IPA and Adnams Broadside on draught, and decent wines by the glass. The decor is as fresh as spring rain and the smell of varnish wafts about the dark wood and blood-red interior. On the ground floor you'll find upmarket bar snacks, like British tapas: paprika chicken, soused herrings, fried artichoke and beetroot (all £3.50). On the first floor, the small dining room looks like a Victorian lady's boudoir, with gold-toned flock wallpaper and a lavish flower arrangement. The only touch of restraint comes from the no-nonsense menu, comprising about four starters and puds, plus six or so main courses and a few side dishes. 'Tomato, purple basil and brie tart' was served tepid and, though the combination of flavours was good, the dish lacked character. 'Leg of lamb steak, boulangère potato' was underseasoned, the meat overcooked. 'Swordfish loin, beetroot, rocket pesto' lacked verve and cried out for sharpness – lemon juice or capers, say. More thought seems to have gone into the decor than the food, but the Temperance is a safe bet for a drink.
Babies and children admitted. Separate room for parties, seats 40. **Map 2 F5.**

Victoria

Phoenix

14 Palace Street, SW1E 5JA (7828 8136/ www.geronimo-inns.co.uk). Victoria tube/rail. **Open** 11am-11pm Mon-Sat; noon-10.30pm Sun. **Lunch served** noon-3pm Mon-Fri; noon-4pm Sat. **Dinner served** 6-10pm Mon-Sat. **Meals served** noon-8pm Sun. **Main courses** £9-£14. **Set lunch** (Mon-Fri) £7.50 2 courses, £10.50 3 courses. **Credit** AmEx, MC, V.
Chaos reigned on our Friday night visit to this branch of Geronimo Inns. The noisy saloon and smart outside areas were busy with an after-work crowd, and all the bitters (including Adnams, Sharp's Doom Bar and Hogs Back's toasty-flavoured Tea) were off when we first went up to the faux-Shaker bar. The dining room is tiny, making advance booking essential; with nearly all main courses costing under a tenner, steady custom is assured. The Phoenix and its Geronimo cohorts try to up their gastro credentials with dishes of olive oil and balsamic vinegar served with granary-style bread, but the basic quality of ingredients highlights this as pretension. Still, our cheeseburger was decent, and the meat filling in a steak and ale pie had a satisfyingly deep flavour. A honeyed fig failed to dispel the sense that a plate of cured meats had come straight from a packet, but we liked the rich smoked mackerel pâté, and the quality of add-ons such as mash and chips. Wines by the glass include a Rioja tempranillo, Margaret River shiraz and a cabernet sauvignon rosé. Our waitress said it was her first night so we forgive not being advised the prawn cocktail had run out until after we'd ordered.
Babies and children admitted. Booking essential. Separate room for parties, seats 30. Tables outdoors (5, garden). **Map 15 J9.**

West

Barons Court

Queen's Arms NEW

171 Greyhound Road, W6 8NL (7386 5078). Barons Court tube. **Open** noon-11pm Mon-Thur, Sun; noon-midnight Fri, Sat. **Lunch served** noon-3pm Mon-Fri; noon-3.30pm Sat; 12.30-4pm Sun. **Dinner served** 6.30-10pm Mon-Sat; 6.30-9.30pm Sun. **Main courses** £8.95-£15.95. **Set lunch** (Mon-Fri) £10 2 courses, £14 3 courses. **Credit** MC, V.
Little remains of the grubby pub the Queen's Arms once was. The interior has been completely refitted; it's now light-wooded, adorned with flatscreen TVs and spotlessly clean. Though there's a bar menu, most customers head upstairs to eat in the posher dining room. The food is too intricate at times – the menu boasts Italian, French, Thai, Turkish and British flavours – but generally impressive. A starter of fried soft-shell crab with brioche and tomato confit was intriguing and full of flavour, the crab in particular. Smoked haddock fish cakes were dense and professionally made. Then came the mains. A dish of high-quality lamb was rather over-complex: not only cannon and shank and cutlet, but also a 'roquefort tart' (a pedestrian mini-quiche that didn't fit at all). Likewise, roast halibut with gnocchi worked in part, the white flesh tender, but scallops wrapped in ham were a distracting addition. A huge cone of 'cookies and cream' ice-cream almost drew a laugh when it arrived; we were too full. A total of 15 wines are served by the glass. Staff were lovely, untroubled by a sizeable crowd.
Babies and children welcome: high chairs. Booking advisable. Disabled: toilet.

Chiswick

Roebuck NEW

2007 RUNNER-UP BEST GASTROPUB

122 Chiswick High Road, W4 1PU (8995 4392). Turnham Green tube. **Open** 11am-11pm Mon-Sat; noon-10.30pm Sun. **Meals served** noon-10.30pm Mon-Sat; noon-10pm Sun. **Main courses** £8.50-£17.50. **Credit** AmEx, DC, MC, V.
Part of a small gastropub group that includes the Queens (*see p128*) in Crouch End and Lots Road (*see p121*) in Chelsea, the Roebuck is bright and family-friendly: a worthwhile addition to restaurant-heavy Chiswick High Road. It's deceptively large, stretching back from a front bar to a big, well-lit dining room (centred around a table display of wines) and a paved garden beyond. A starter of cured Orkney salmon was almost sashimi-like in texture and freshness; it was set off by a sharp dill vinaigrette. Ham and rabbit terrine was just right, the flavour of the meats distinctive yet complementary. A main of three cumberland sausages with creamy mash and gravy was as good as that dish gets. It was bettered by roast pork, from a pig grilled whole, metres from the garden tables. We enjoyed the tender meat, and the spectacle. Strawberry and almond cake for pud came recommended by a bubbly Antipodean waitress; paired with hazelnut ice-cream, it was superb. Wines are grouped by style, with over a dozen by the glass. Changing real ales (Mauldons Suffolk Pride, Caledonian Top Banana and Adnams Regatta on our visit) are listed alongside the food, with tasting notes – an excellent touch.
Babies and children welcome: children's menu; high chairs. Disabled: toilet. Tables outdoors (14, garden; 3, pavement).

Ealing

★ Ealing Park Tavern

222 South Ealing Road, W5 4RL (8758 1879). South Ealing tube. **Open** 5-11pm Mon; 11am-11pm Tue-Sat; noon-10.30pm Sun. **Lunch served** noon-3pm Tue-Sat; noon-3.45pm Sun. **Dinner served** 6-10pm Mon-Sat; 6-9.30pm Sun. **Main courses** £5-£14. **Credit** AmEx, MC, V.

Roebuck

RESTAURANTS

We're impressed by the consistently warm welcome in both bar and restaurant at this cathedral-like establishment, which is surprisingly cosy for such a huge place (it's always been a pub, built in 1886, with the dining room added in 1939 at the grand cost of £2,400). The spacious garden is a treat, and staff are smart, sassy and great with kids – and dogs. Beers on offer may include Crane Sundancer from Twickenham Ales, Timothy Taylor Landlord and Leffe, while the wine list (starting at £12), is European with a strong French showing and some intriguing bottles from Spain. On the wide-ranging menu we counted six vegetarian dishes and six from the sea, plus meat options. Salmon with asparagus, broad beans and peas was undeniably delicious, but came with a lurid beetroot hollandaise that some of our party found off-putting. No complaints, though, about seared scallops with broccoli purée and chilli dressing, or the generous bowl of moules. Roast pork loin had all the trappings of a fully-fledged restaurant dish, with apricot, sage and pistachio stuffing, mash and an apple jus. The winning British cheeseboard featured expertly matured barkam blue, kelston park brie, sharpham rustic and boffard, though dessert options of chocolate tart and lemon mousse brûlée also appealed. A great destination for groups.
Babies and children welcome (until 8.30pm): high chairs. Entertainment: jazz 8.30pm alternate Wed. Tables outdoors (25, garden).

Ladbroke Grove

Fat Badger NEW

310 Portobello Road, W10 5TA (8969 4500/ www.thefatbadger.com). Ladbroke Grove or Westbourne Park tube. **Open** noon-11pm Mon-Thur; 11am-midnight Fri, Sat; noon-10.30pm Sun. **Lunch served** noon-3pm, **dinner served** 6-10pm Mon-Sat. **Meals served** noon-10pm Sun. **Main courses** £10-£15. **Credit** AmEx, DC, MC, V.

You could walk past the Fat Badger's uninspiring ground floor – sofas and newspapers scattered in equal measure, self-conscious punters selecting from numerous expensive lagers but only one real ale – without realising that the restaurant upstairs is something of a gem. A large sweeping corner staircase leads you to this airy room, decorated in clever-clever 'Shoreditch' flock wallpaper (repeated motifs of muggings and alkies on park benches); leading off is a small but sweet roof garden. The weekend menu offers brunch staples such as kipper and fried eggs; or black pudding, pea purée and poached egg. There are also lunch classics like roast halibut with braised summer veg and bacon, and a superb roast featuring Welsh beef and yorkshires. While we would have been happier with slightly larger main-course portions, we were grateful for the space to tuck in to an immense sticky toffee pudding: the largest we've ever had placed before us. A chocolate brownie, served with vanilla ice-cream, was also filling. Two great ways to treat yourself after a long Sunday haul along Portobello Market.
Babies and children admitted. Tables outdoors (6, terrace; 2, pavement). **Map 19 B1**.

Olympia

Cumberland Arms

29 North End Road, W14 8SZ (7371 6806/ www.thecumberlandarmspub.co.uk). West Kensington tube/Kensington (Olympia) tube/ rail. **Open** noon-11pm Mon-Sat; noon-10.30pm Sun. **Lunch served** noon-3pm Mon-Sat; noon-4pm Sun. **Dinner served** 7-10.30pm Mon-Sat; 7-10pm Sun. **Main courses** £8.50-£13.50. **Credit** MC, V.

Summer sees the Cumberland Arms' bottle-blue exterior obscured by the blooms of countless colourful window boxes. Its stripped wooden floors and artfully distressed tables and chairs take on a more homely glow during cold winter evenings. Regardless of the season, the daily changing menu mixes Mediterranean and North African influences with gusto. Risottos and pastas are always on hand as either starters or main courses, as are innovative salads such as smoked duck, artichoke and potato with own-made pesto. Portions tend towards the gargantuan: an antipasti platter to share came loaded with houmous, smoked salmon, parma ham and spare ribs; a main of expertly roasted salmon fillet was presented on a mountain of crushed potato; and the trio of grilled Italian sausages (some of the meatiest we've tasted) were paired with garlic mash and given an almighty kick by a fiery tomato chilli jam. There's also a well-edited wine list favouring France and the New World, with a dozen or so choices by the glass, plus London Pride, Deuchars IPA and Timothy Taylor Landlord on draught. Beyond a staff penchant for Razorlight, only the patented chocolate and almond cake failed to inspire: dry and flavourless despite being a local legend.
Babies and children admitted (until 7pm). Tables outdoors (9, pavement).

Shepherd's Bush

Anglesea Arms

35 Wingate Road, W6 0UR (8749 1291). Goldhawk Road or Ravenscourt Park tube. **Open** 11am-11pm Mon-Sat; noon-10.30pm Sun. **Lunch served** 12.30-2.45pm Mon-Sat; 12.30-3.30pm Sun. **Dinner served** 7-10.30pm Mon-Sat; 7-10pm Sun. **Main courses** £11.50-£19. **Credit** MC, V.

This small corner pub sticks to the original gastropub blueprint: no fancy separate dining room, tablecloths or leather-bound menus here. Instead, you can eat where you like: amid the hodgepodge of tables and sofas in the dark front section; in the sky-lit dining area at the back next to the open kitchen; or at awning-covered tables on the pavement. The regularly changing menu is chalked on a blackboard (a trim selection of five or so starters and mains apiece, plus a handful of puds). You can't book – which means you may have to wait, but that's no great hardship with real ales and a long wine list to savour. The food is consistently good, inventive and makes sterling use of seasonal ingredients. Highlights of a recent meal included good-quality oysters (French, Irish and Colchester); a seasonal salad of beetroot, assorted leaves and a perfect soft-boiled egg (neither runny nor set), with a horseradish and chive dressing; warm feta, spinach and pine nut roulade; simple roast plaice with chips; and a tangy gooseberry fool, stuffed with fruit. The only thing lacking is the huge, Stanley Spencer-esque painting that used

Rosendale. See p125.

to dominate the dining area. And service can get stretched when the place is busy.
Babies and children welcome: high chairs. Tables outdoors (5, pavement). **Map 20 A3**.

Havelock Tavern

57 Masbro Road, W14 0LS (7603 5374/ www.thehavelocktavern.co.uk). Hammersmith or Shepherd's Bush tube/Kensington (Olympia) tube/rail. **Open** 11am-11pm Mon-Sat; noon-10.30pm Sun. **Lunch served** 12.30-2.30pm Mon-Sat; 12.30-3pm Sun. **Dinner served** 7-10pm Mon-Sat; 7-9.30pm Sun. **Main courses** £10-£14. **No credit cards**.

It all depends on how you feel. Should you be after a loud, buzzy evening's mingling, you'll probably love the Havelock. If, on the other hand, you want a relaxed meal, and to lean back and talk without having to shout, you may hate the place. A tremendous volume builds up even early in the week, despite there being no music. The pub is the social hub of a very gentrified little enclave between Shepherd's Bush and Hammersmith, yet it's rather self-consciously basic – so no credit cards, no table reservations and the service is sometimes frantic. In such a busy venue it's hard to focus on the food, but there are imaginative options on the oft-changing menu, such as a pleasant salad of sautéed squid with chorizo, fennel, rocket and parsley; or fricassee of chicken, leeks and deliciously gammony bacon (one of several dishes that seemed hefty in summer). There's only one vegetarian main course, however. The wine list offers some high-quality bargains, and draught beers include London Pride, Marston's Pedigree, Brakspear and Staropramen.
Babies and children welcome: high chairs. Bar available for hire. Tables outdoors (6, garden; 2, pavement). **Map 20 C3**.

Westbourne Grove

★ Cow (100)

89 Westbourne Park Road, W2 5QH (7221 0021/www.thecowlondon.co.uk). Royal Oak or Westbourne Park tube. **Open** noon-11pm Mon-Thur; noon-midnight Fri, Sat; noon-10.30pm Sun. **Lunch served** noon-3pm daily. **Dinner served** 7-10.30pm Mon-Sat; 6-10pm Sun. **Main courses** £9-£19. **Set lunch** (Sun) £24 3 courses. **Credit** MC, V.

The Cow is to Notting Hill as Aberdeen Angus is to prime beef: still one of the best breeds in its field. This room above a pub was one of the smokiest eateries in west London, so we hope the pocket-sized, 1950s retro-Irish restaurant doesn't lose all its atmosphere post-ban. The pay-off could be that smoke-free environs will allow sharper appreciation of the cooking. Although the menu specialises in oysters, there's real finesse in starters ranging from new-season garlic leaf soup to sublimely simple scallops with herbs and tomatoes. There's imagination too in mains such as Barbary duck breast served with baby spinach leaves and a big, fat, gorgeously ripe quince. Elwy Valley lamb served with pea shoots and mint pesto was no less divine. Such quality doesn't come cheap – but for the time being all mains cost under £20. To finish, baked vanilla cheesecake and raspberries had the last word on that stout dessert. If you want a dependable, not over-articulated and acceptably priced wine list this is the place to come too – although a pint of finely kept London Pride can be ferried up from downstairs.
Babies and children admitted (lunch). Restaurant available for hire. Tables outdoors (2, pavement). **Map 7 A5**.

South West

Barnes

★ Brown Dog NEW

2007 RUNNER-UP BEST GASTROPUB

28 Cross Street, SW13 0AP (8392 2200/ www.thebrowndog.co.uk). Barnes Bridge rail. **Open** noon-11pm Mon-Sat; noon-10pm Sun. **Lunch served** noon-3pm Mon-Fri; noon-5pm Sat, Sun. **Dinner served** 7-10pm daily. **Main courses** £9.50-£17.50. **Credit** AmEx, MC, V.

Charmingly small, like the cottages of Barnes surrounding it, the Brown Dog makes good use of its 150-year-old space. To the left is a cosy bar (ales include Adnams Bitter, London Pride and Harveys Sussex Ale). To the right is a modestly proportioned dining area, filled with sturdy wooden tables. A main of boneless quail was one of the best gastropub dishes we've had: juicy meat, perfect crisp skin, served in a complex sauce stirred with peas and pancetta. A pint of prawns to start was, in pleasant contrast, as simple as could be: the prawns wonderfully fresh, a tart mayonnaise the only accompaniment needed. A satisfied customer on one side of the table then; our companion was not so lucky. Vegetarian, he had only one choice of main (a rather lifeless feuilleté atop mushrooms and spinach) and not a single choice of starter; he was left to order the cheese plate. A good-natured waitress did her best to minimise the gloom – 'And you'll be having the feuilleté... obviously!' A toffee pud for dessert (sticky, dense, excellent) returned smiles to our faces. The wine list is brief and wallet-friendly. An excellent gastropub, but one that needs to cater better for vegetarians.
Babies and children welcome: children's portions; high chairs. Disabled: toilet. Tables outdoors (12, garden).

Chelsea

Lots Road Pub & Dining Room

114 Lots Road, SW10 0RJ (7352 6645/ www.thespiritgroup.com). Fulham Broadway tube then 11 bus/Sloane Square tube then 11, 19, 22 bus. **Open** 11am-11pm Mon-Thur; 11am-midnight Fri, Sat; noon-10.30pm Sun. **Lunch served** noon-3pm, **dinner served** 5.30-10pm Mon-Fri. **Meals served** noon-10pm Sat, Sun. **Main courses** £6.50-£15.50. **Credit** AmEx, MC, V.

Several years ago, the opening of Lots Road Pub & Dining Room marked a significant departure. A plucky new pubco (the Spirit Group) entered the market and successfully mimicked the winning formula of independent, chef-run gastropubs by giving the resident chef almost free rein in the kitchen. Several years on, Lots Road is still pulling in immaculately coiffed Fulham folk and is still an appealing and friendly gastropub, but on our most recent visit we felt standards had slipped. The new team in charge were running a British food festival, so we were able to tuck in to the likes of black pudding, woodpigeon breast, confit lamb shoulder and seared scallops. Corners were cut, though: advertised 'fennel purée' with the scallops was the same mashed potato as served with the lamb shoulder, where it was incorrectly described as Scottish dish clapshot (if this 'clapshot' had any of the requisite swede in it, then call us neeps). Prices are still fair for this part of town, and the selection of guest ales was impressive: Tanglefoot, Spitfire and Old Speckled Hen. Most of our fellow diners seemed more keen on the smart wine list, with sparkling wines selling particularly well.
Babies and children welcome: children's portions; high chairs; nappy-changing facilities. Booking advisable. Disabled: toilet. Separate room for parties, seats 30. **Map 13 C13**.

★ Pig's Ear

35 Old Church Street, SW3 5BS (7352 2908/ www.thepigsear.co.uk). Sloane Square tube then 11, 19, 22 bus/South Kensington tube then 49 bus. **Open** noon-11pm Mon-Sat; noon-10.30pm Sun. **Lunch served** 12.30-3pm Mon-Fri; 12.30-4pm Sat, Sun. **Dinner served** 7-10pm Mon-Sat; 7-9.30pm Sun. **Main courses** £10.50-£18.50. **Credit** AmEx, MC, V.

A curiously un-Chelsea establishment, the Pig's Ear has a mellow vibe that makes you want to linger, either in the white-tableclothed first-floor dining room, or in the comfortable ground-floor bar. The menus are pretty similar in both and, despite the casual surroundings (the bar stops just short of cluttered), food is upmarket fare. There are indeed pig's ears, served as a starter with sauce ravigote; a hint that the menu has limited appeal for vegetarians, though a smooth, spicy gazpacho was a triumph. More typical are roast bone marrow with parsley and shallot salad, or ribeye steak (wickedly good, served with an almost sweet red wine and shallot butter, as well as slightly anaemic fries). Fish makes a decent showing too; pickled herrings with leek vinaigrette and soft boiled egg was a generous, flavour-packed helping. Fillet of sea bass was fine, but what really made the dish shine was the puy lentil and chorizo salsa accompaniment. A well-made macciato and a lovely white peach and frangipane tart with stem ginger ice-cream rounded things off nicely. The French-biased wine list will more than cover most people's needs, while ale fans get Pig's Ear (natch) and Deuchars IPA on draught. And we can't imagine many customers finding fault with the accommodating staff. A firm favourite.
Babies and children welcome: booster chairs. Booking advisable (dining room). **Map 14 E12**.

Putney

Spencer Arms

237 Lower Richmond Road, SW15 1HJ (8788 0640/www.thespencerarms.co.uk). Putney Bridge tube/22, 265, 485 bus. **Open** 10am-midnight daily. **Lunch served** noon-2.30pm Mon-Fri; noon-3pm Sat; noon-4pm Sun. **Dinner served** 6.30-10pm Mon-Sat; 6.30-9.45pm Sun. **Main courses** £7.50-£18. **Credit** MC, V.

'Gutsy grub' says the sign in the window, and that's a fair description of what this attractive corner pub offers. Unlike many gastropubs, the eating hasn't supplanted the drinking. There are nicely kept real ales and a longish wine list, and there's no pressure for customers to dine. The light-flooded main room is fitted with the usual mismatched wooden tables and chairs, but there's a side area – with worn leather sofas, a fireplace and even a bookshelf – that's more conducive to slumming with the papers. Picnic tables hug the road outside. The look (burgundy and sage paintwork, warm wood, silver dome lights above the bar) is casually rather than oppressively stylish. As is the food. A quirky, homely British slant is evident on the daily changing menu. You can have a black pudding toasty with HP sauce, macaroni cheese, or roast chicken with bread sauce and bacon (for two), as well as more elaborate concoctions. Fish soup, and warm smoked mackerel with lime pickle-tinged crushed potatoes, were suitably gutsy, while risotto with wild garlic leaves and pea shoots was a more delicate affair. The perfect spot for a pint and some nosh after a ramble by the river or on Barnes Common.
Babies and children welcome (until 9pm): children's portions; high chairs. Disabled: toilet. Entertainment: jazz duo 9pm occasional Tue-Thur. Tables outdoors (8, pavement).

Wandsworth

Freemasons

2 Wandsworth Common Northside, SW18 2SS (7326 8580/www.freemasonspub.com). Clapham Junction rail. **Open** noon-11pm Mon-Thur; noon-midnight Fri, Sat; noon-10.30pm Sun. **Lunch served** noon-3pm, **dinner served** 6.30-10pm Mon-Fri. **Meals served** 12.30-10pm Sat; 12.30-9pm Sun. **Main courses** £9.50-£12.95. **Credit** AmEx, MC, V.

This is a textbook neighbourhood gastropub. Bare wooden floors, kitchen on view, straightforward menu, good selection of affordable wines and great beers on tap. Too many gastropubs forget about the beer, but not the Freemasons: Timothy Taylor Landlord, Everards Tiger, Leffe and Franziskaner Weissbier were all being quaffed with alacrity on our Monday night visit, which was pub quiz time. The shrieks and whoops, plus a man with a mic, drove us away. Returning midweek, we secured a quiet table without problem and enjoyed a starter of own-made fish fingers with tartare sauce. Portions are generous; honey-roasted pork belly with a moat of red wine jus surrounding mash was so generous we had no room for pudding. Although most dishes are predictable (sausage and mash is a favourite), there are a few surprises, such

Brown Dog. See p121.

as the salmon gravadlax dyed with beetroot, served with a beetroot-coloured horseradish sauce. The salad-from-a-bag that comes with many dishes is a bit disappointing, but with main course prices mostly under a tenner, no one's complaining.
Babies and children welcome: high chairs. Tables outdoors (11, patio). **Map 21 B4.**

Waterfront

2007 RUNNER-UP BEST GASTROPUB
Baltimore House, Juniper Drive, SW18 1TS (7228 4297/www.waterfrontlondon.co.uk). Fulham Broadway tube/Wandsworth Town rail.
Open 11am-11.30pm Mon-Sat; 11am-11pm Sun. **Meals served** 11am-11pm Mon-Sat; 11am-10.30pm Sun. **Main courses** £9.95-£16.50. **Credit** AmEx, MC, V.

Part of Young's expanding portfolio of riverside gastropubs, the Waterfront follows the Waterside in Chelsea, the Duke's Head in Putney and the Riverside in Vauxhall. Here, the huge, multi-levelled room is decorated in a mishmash of modern styles. It looks more bar than gastropub: floor-to-ceiling windows, chandeliers, centrepiece leather booths, and tables of different shapes. Numerous outdoor benches overlook an unlovely stretch of the Thames, nice in summer nonetheless. Starters were above average: an interesting (if fridge-cold) terrine made with aubergines and puréed tomato, and high-quality gravadlax. Mains were unremarkable, though perhaps we chose badly; mushroom risotto was bland. A caesar salad with grilled chicken was fresh-tasting and generously portioned; we had no complaints. The meal might have been improved had we room for dessert; in the past we've been impressed by an exciting apple crumble, drizzled with crème anglaise. Young's beers and wines are of the usual excellent class. Staff in sleek black shirts were charming. It's hard to imagine anyone travelling far to come here – this corner of SW18 has all the character of a supermarket car park – but for residents of the new Battersea Reach development in which it's housed, the Waterfront will be a wonderful boon.
Babies and children admitted. Booking advisable. Tables outdoors (45, riverside deck). **Map 21 A4.**

Wimbledon

Earl Spencer

260-262 Merton Road, SW18 5JL (8870 9244/www.theearlspencer.co.uk). Southfields tube.
Open 11am-11pm Mon-Thur; 11am-midnight Fri, Sat; noon-10.30pm Sun. **Lunch served** 12.30-2.30pm Mon-Sat; 12.30-3pm Sun. **Dinner served** 7-10pm Mon-Sat; 7-9.30pm Sun. **Main courses** £8.50-£12. **Credit** AmEx, MC, V.

The Earl Spencer was a runner-up for Time Out's Best Gastropub award when it opened in 2003, and it still hits all the right gastro-buttons. The decor maintains a sense of tradition, from the old fireplaces and well-worn tables and chairs to the loaves of bread and huge jars of olives gracing the bar. Draught ales might be Badger's Tanglefoot, Deuchars IPA, Hook Norton's Hooky Bitter or Fuller's London Pride. The menu has taken on a 'world food' focus, with Thai, Chinese and North African influences popping up among trad dishes, such as a half-pint of smoked prawns or steak and chips. Pork rillettes was flavourful, but we'd have liked a chunkier texture. Portions are big; roast saddle of lamb was a thick slab, served atop (slightly soggy) couscous and a chickpea and tomato stew, with garlicky spinach and minted yoghurt. Thought is given to vegetarian mains, such as pancakes stuffed with 'home-smoked' ricotta and broccoli, served with taleggio sauce. Desserts, including banana and dulce de leche baked cheesecake, are rich and indulgent. No bookings are taken, so get in Earl-y at the weekend.
Babies and children welcome: children's portions; high chairs. Bookings not accepted. Separate room for parties, seats 70. Tables outdoors (10, patio).

South

Battersea

Greyhound

136 Battersea High Street, SW11 3JR (7978 7021/www.thegreyhoundatbattersea.co.uk). Clapham Junction rail/49, 319, 344, 345 bus.
Open noon-11pm Tue-Sat; noon-5pm Sun. **Lunch served** noon-3pm Tue-Sun. **Dinner served** 7-10pm Tue-Sat. **Main courses** £16.50-£19.50. **Set meal** (Sun) £16.50 2 courses, £20 3 courses. **Credit** AmEx, MC, V.

The Greyhound occupies beautifully restored premises on a cobbled street. There's a bar and tables at the front, but the main action takes place in the rear dining room. This is very much a gastropub with the focus on 'gastro'. It's also a magnet for wine lovers. Owner Mark Van der Goot had a distinguished career as a sommelier and his passion for wine pervades the list. You'll find big-name Bordeaux beside obscure Greek varietals, made the more appealing by low mark-ups. Some real ale would be welcome, though. The dining room combines bare brick with chandeliers and attracts pearl-bedecked blondes and suited men. The menu is brief and less studiedly British than many (pumpkin ravioli with sage and parmesan, for example). Our star dish was grilled octopus salad: a purple question mark of tender, tentacled flesh curled over a broad bean and tomato salad. For mains, pink duck breast came with smoky aubergine purée and, somewhat oddly, foie gras. Large gnocchi were stuffed with a gutsy ragout of Herdwick lamb, with crisp fried lamb sweetbreads. Desserts such as delectable black pepper ice-cream, and chocolate tortellini with strawberries were definitely more restauranty than pubby. Service is laid-back and friendly – as it should be when 12.5% is automatically added to the bill.

Booking advisable. Disabled: toilet. Restaurant available for hire. Separate room for parties, seats 25. Tables outdoors (6, patio; 6, garden). **Map 21 B2**.

Waterloo

Anchor & Hope (100)

36 The Cut, SE1 8LP (7928 9898). Southwark or Waterloo tube/rail. **Open** 5-11pm Mon; 11am-11pm Tue-Sat; 12.30-5pm Sun. **Lunch served** noon-2.30pm Tue-Sat; 2pm sitting Sun. **Dinner served** 6-10.30pm Mon-Sat. **Main courses** £11-£16. **Set lunch** (Sun) £30 4 courses. **Credit** MC, V.

Heck knows how the young, clued-up staff here keep their cool. Even on a Monday, the wait for a table was 50 minutes at 8pm (no bookings are taken). We took up the offer of immediate food at the bar counter – and regretted it. Crammed between after-work drinkers, we endured a joyless meal as prospective diners pleaded for a table in the adjacent burgundy-hued dining room. Most waited: such is the reputation of the rustic, Med-slanted food. Alcohol aids the endurance; Young's Bitter and Bombardier are joined by an impressive line-up of draught lagers (Red Stripe, Kirin, Crest) and a varied wine list. The worn floorboards and high ceilings are appealing too: this is a proper boozer. We bypassed the tempting starters (the likes of snails, bacon and laver bread on duck fat toast; or octopus, chickpeas, roast tomatoes and aïoli) heading straight for mains. Duck and mirabelles wasn't successful, the little plums too sweet for the tender duck leg, the dish lukewarm, and the tasty lentil side plate (£2.60 extra) arriving late. Several dishes on the daily-changing list ('seven-hour lamb shoulder', say) are designed for couples or group dining. Some redemption was found in a pistachio cake (moist, dense, fresh, nutty) with creamy lemon curd.

Babies and children admitted. Bookings not accepted. Tables outdoors (4, pavement). **Map 11 N8**.

South East

Bermondsey

Garrison

99-101 Bermondsey Street, SE1 3XB (7089 9355/www.thegarrison.co.uk). London Bridge tube/rail. **Open** 8am-11pm Mon-Fri; 9am-11pm Sat; 9am-10.30pm Sun. **Breakfast served** 8-11.30am Mon-Fri; 9-11.30am Sat, Sun. **Lunch served** noon-3.30pm Mon-Fri; 12.30-4pm Sat, Sun. **Dinner served** 6.30-10pm Mon-Sat; 6-9.30pm Sun. **Main courses** £10.30-£15.50. **Credit** AmEx, MC, V.

The buzzy, bustling Garrison certainly makes a good first impression. Crammed (indeed, slightly too crammed) with funkily jumbled furniture, from distressed farmhouse tables to modish 1970s stool-chairs (and with a mix of ornate lampshades and bare bulbs hanging from the ceiling), the characterful, shabby-chic room is pleasingly removed from hackneyed gastropub style. The cooking is just as eager to impress: sometimes too eager, as with a rather busy starter salad of honey-roasted parsnip, goat's cheese, pine nuts and raspberry vinaigrette; and a dessert of pistachio crème brûlée, a slightly unhappy collision of flavours. But when the kitchen keeps it a little simpler, as with a starter of salmon on a potato pancake, the food is far more successful. Both our mains were straightforward, comforting and beautifully tender: a special of seared tuna topped with tomato sauce and served on a bed of tapenade potato; and a particularly moreish portion of braised lamb shoulder with spring greens and Jersey Royals. Add in solid service and decent drinks (Adnams on draught; bottled St Peter's Organic Best Bitter), and it's easy to see why this likeable spot is packed most nights.

Babies and children admitted (lunch Sat, Sun). Booking advisable. Disabled: toilet. Separate room for parties, seats 25. **Map 12 Q9**.

Hartley

64 Tower Bridge Road, SE1 4TR (7394 7023/www.thehartley.com). Borough tube/London Bridge tube/rail. **Open** noon-midnight Mon-Thur; noon-2am Fri; 11am-2am Sat; noon-10.30pm Sun. **Lunch served** noon-3pm Mon-Fri; 11am-4pm Sat. **Dinner served** 6-10pm Mon-Sat. **Meals served** noon-6pm Sun. **Main courses** £8-£14.50. **Credit** AmEx, DC, MC, V.

The owners of this relatively recent addition to the genre have what amounts to a captive local market; it's a pity they don't do more with it. When the Hartley opened on this dreary road, it showed pleasing ambition in its menus. However, the one-room hangout has since settled into life as a by-rote gastropub, complete with metallic bar top, ropey art, friendly service and, on our visit, only fleetingly impressive food. Both starters were overwhelmed by their accompaniments, as if the kitchen lacked confidence in the raw ingredients. So it proved: beneath a confusion of pesto, rocket, cherry tomatoes and balsamic, the pan-fried scallops were uneven, while the asparagus that lurked under a fried egg and yet more balsamic was only slightly fresher than the less-than-dynamic bread. Marlin steak was fine, if slightly stringy; the best dish was one of the daily specials: duck confit with delicious mash. Partial compensation for the lack of ales arrived in the shape of Adnams' new quasi-lager Spindrift, albeit at £3.75 a pint. Prices are otherwise fair.

Babies and children welcome: children's portions; high chairs. Booking advisable. Entertainment: musicians 8pm Tue, alternate Fri. Separate room for parties, seats 50.

Camberwell

Castle

65 Camberwell Church Street, SE5 8TR (7277 2601). Denmark Hill rail/12, 36, 68, 68A, 171, 176, 185, 345 bus. **Open** noon-midnight Mon-

Thur, Sun; noon-2am Fri, Sat. **Meals served** noon-10pm Mon-Sat; noon-9.30pm Sun. **Main courses** £7.25-£10.85. **Credit** MC, V.

More a gastrobar than a pub, the Castle has a funky glamour that's wearing well. Scuffed leather banquettes, huge chandeliers and fairy lights combine with a massive music-video screen (silent) and chilled, offbeat soundtrack to pull in the local art students and slightly older bohemians with which Camberwell is richly populated. Many come for the vibe, the real ale (Adnams Explorer and Flowers IPA) and the generous wine list. The new owners have introduced more than 22 wines sold by the glass, and also expanded the food to include more European flavours. Chef/co-owner Michael Knight and his multinational team have created an eclectic menu that encompasses oysters, classic salads, mussel dishes, steaks and some can-I-have-seconds puddings. A slab of just-crisp bruschetta arrived piled high with flavoursome tomatoes, herbs and onions. Next, salmon in a Jack Daniel's sauce with soya and ginger was a wonderful combination. To finish, Belgian chocolate polenta pudding was deliciously moist and light, coated in a thick, chocolate glaze. Service was friendly and eager. The injection of new management and kitchen talent seems to be working very nicely; the Castle buzzes all week long.

Babies and children welcome: high chairs. Booking advisable. Entertainment: DJs 10pm Fri, Sat. Separate room for parties, seats 30. **Map 23 B2.**

Dark Horse NEW

16 Grove Lane, SE5 8SY (7703 9990). Denmark Hill rail. **Open** 11am-11pm Mon, Tue, Sun; 11am-midnight Wed-Thur; 11am-1am Fri, Sat. **Meals served** noon-10pm Mon-Fri; 11am-5pm Sat, Sun. **Main courses** £8.95-£15.95. **Credit** AmEx, DC, MC, V.

With its gleaming dark wood flanks, the Horse is a well-groomed beast. You'd never mistake it for an ordinary boozer, even before reading the menu – what with the huge candelabra, ornate mirror and cantering horses behind the bar. This equine-themed sister to the Black Sheep pubs (near the Oval and at Crystal Palace) has Black Sheep bitter on draught, alongside Belgian brews Hoegaarden, Leffe and Staropramen. The lunch menu is extremely cheap – all dishes are £3.50 or £4.50 – yet has a gastro slant. Spicy thai chicken curry with rice was a modest portion, not over-subtle in flavour, but great value. Portobello mushroom burger with onion marmalade and gorgonzola was a challenging contrast of flavours, the nicest being sweet red onions. It arrived tepid, with rapidly cooling, skin-on fries, but our complaint yielded a hot replacement served with good grace by the friendly staff. Dinner is fancier and pricier. Fried mackerel, organic salmon, risottos and seasonal salad starters precede mains such as crispy pork belly (with champ and summer veg), aged Scottish steak, or new-season lamb. Our witty pudding of caramelised peaches with Tic Tac (orange flavour) dust and pistachio ice-cream was marred by one half of the fruit being under-ripe.

Babies and children admitted. Disabled: toilet. Tables outdoors (6, pavement). **Map 23 A2.**

Dulwich

Herne Tavern NEW

2 Forest Hill Road , SE22 0RR (8299 9521/ www.theherne.net). East Dulwich or Peckham rail/12, 197 bus. **Open** noon-11pm Mon-Thur; noon-1am Fri, Sat; noon-10.30pm Sun. **Lunch served** noon-2.30pm Mon-Fri; noon-3pm Sat, Sun. **Dinner served** 6.30-9.45pm Mon-Sat; 6.30-9.30pm Sun. **Main courses** £8.50-£12. **Credit** MC, V.

The Herne is the affordable, family-friendly sister to the Palmerston (*see below*) in East Dulwich, and is helmed by an ex-Bibendum chef, Ben Hoggatt. You'll find the same consistently high quality of food and service, and the same kind of tempting and inventive dishes – only simpler and cheaper. The frequently changing, seasonal menu included, on our late-spring visit, crab salad, pork belly with pak choi, juicy and flavourful beefburger with excellent slim and crunchy chips, and fat fish cakes packed with tasty flesh. A dark-timber interior, plus original stained-glass windows, create an atmospheric setting, often enjoyed by old geezers drinking solitary pints. Despite its notable food, the Herne retains the feel of a quintessential and inclusive pub. Families and young drinkers relish the massive outdoor area at the back, landscaped to resemble the Teletubbies garden. Grassy mounds of earth create runways for excitable five-year-olds, while their parents consume Courage ales and succulent food. Outbuildings were transformed in summer 2007 to create an outdoor kitchen and bar area, for weekend feasts of barbecued pork and hot chorizo sandwiches.

Babies and children welcome: high chairs; nappy-changing facilities. Separate room for parties, seats 60. Tables outdoors (25, garden).

★ Palmerston

91 Lordship Lane, SE22 8EP (8693 1629). East Dulwich rail/185, 176, P13 bus. **Open** noon-11pm Mon-Thur; noon-midnight Fri, Sat; noon-10.30pm Sun. **Lunch served** noon-2.30pm Mon-Fri; noon-3pm Sat; noon-3.30pm Sun. **Dinner served** 7-10pm Mon-Sat; 7-9pm Sun. **Main courses** £12-£14. **Set lunch** (Mon-Fri) £10 2 courses, £14 3 courses. **Credit** MC, V.

The Palmerston goes from strength to strength, offering East Dulwich diners tantalising, inventive cooking. Its wood-panelled, bistro-like interior caters for all occasions, from casual lunches to smart parties. The finest produce – Loch Fyne scallops, Dorset crab, Herdwick Barnsley lamb – is now matched by an expanded wine list that takes in classier vintages than before, with prices to match. Timothy Taylor Landlord is the real ale on tap. Starters are outstanding; a salad of smoked sea trout looked like an exotic underwater creature, its flesh supported on spiky chicory leaves and studded with spring onions and quails' eggs. Chef Jamie Younger has a talent for reinvention. A tender slice of wild halibut, fried in the finest coating of batter and served with pea purée and crispy pancetta, was rendered delicious with a simple drizzle of mint oil (fried fish and mushy peas never tasted so good). The skilled, charming staff are clearly used to splitting portions for diners who can't bear to forgo a course. Though torn, we bypassed the prune and Armagnac mousse cake and shared a frisbee-sized pavlova with summer fruit compote and chantilly cream. Another attraction: the set lunch is a bargain.

Babies and children welcome: children's portions; high chairs; nappy-changing facilities. Booking advisable. Tables outdoors (6, pavement). **Map 23 C4.**

Hat & Feathers. See p117.

★ Rosendale NEW

2007 WINNER BEST GASTROPUB

65 Rosendale Road, SE21 8EZ (8670 0812/ www.therosendale.co.uk). East Dulwich or West Dulwich rail.

Bar **Open** noon-11pm Mon-Sat; noon-10.30pm Sun. **Meals served** noon-10pm daily. **Main courses** £9.50-£13.50.

Restaurant **Lunch served** noon-3pm Fri, Sat; noon-4pm Sun. **Dinner served** 7-10pm Mon-Sat. **Main courses** £14.50-£19.50.

Both **Credit** MC, V.

As soon as the butter arrives, you know you're in for something special at this sister to Battersea's Greyhound (*see p122*). Churned in-house by chef Matthew Foxon, it is flavoured differently as fancy strikes. On this occasion, it was coal-smoked: utterly delicious. From an alluring menu, we were wowed by terrifically tender Barbary duck with seared foie gras. Equally impressive was garlicky lamb rump atop puréed potato; an accompanying conker-sized lamb kofta was superfluous, but we forgave the show-off. Starters were also a pleasure. Smoked eel with anchovy mayonnaise might have had a bigger portion of the oily, flavourful fish, but delicacy was key to the dish; it was garnished with tiny, sweet cubes of apple jelly. Dessert maintained standards: three scoops of thick mousse, one of dark chocolate, one white, one toffee. The cavernous, echoey space (much shiny wood and leather banquettes) is divided in two: restaurant at the back, bar with its own shorter menu at the front. As we dithered over a vast wine list, our pleasant waitress suggested we consult the sommelier. He's co-owner Mark Van der Goot, but the very notion highlights the drastic gentrification of the gastropub. Still, with food of this quality, it's hard to complain.

Babies and children welcome: high chairs; nappy-changing facilities. Disabled: toilet. Separate rooms for parties, seating 20-100.

Herne Hill

★ Prince Regent

69 Dulwich Road, SE24 0NJ (7274 1567). Herne Hill rail/3, 196 bus. **Open** noon-11pm Mon-Wed; noon-midnight Thur-Fri; 11am-midnight Sat; noon-10.30pm Sun. **Lunch served** noon-3pm, **dinner served** 7-10pm Mon-Sat. **Meals served** noon-6pm Sun. **Main courses** £7-£15. **Credit** MC, V.

With its warm, honeyed-oak walls and furnishings, cut-glass windows and elegant wooden booths, the Prince Regent has a lived-in elegance that suits its dual purposes (drinking and dining) perfectly. Books, games and bric-a-brac line the window sills. Friendly staff welcome all comers, whether lone diners, lunching ladies, family groups or boozing workers (fans of the Black Sheep ale). The quality of food and generosity of portions also guarantee many return visits. A strong brunch menu and the usual pub staples are supplemented by daily-changing specials. Roast squash risotto came swimming in creamy liquid, with fat flakes of parmesan; coq au vin was served with a densely brown, meaty gravy and abundant fluffy mashed potato. Pan-roasted salmon, meanwhile, resembled a succulent Stonehenge slab, stacked on its mound of 'warm potato salad' in a peppery salsa. Chef Manu Lallier has spent time in Raymond Blanc's kitchens. His puddings reveal an exuberant creativity; rhubarb fool came in a thick, calorific swirl, topped with own-made hazelnut praline and two perfect shortbread biscuits. We left feeling stuffed and extremely satisfied, vowing to return.

Babies and children welcome (until 7pm): children's portions; high chairs. Disabled: toilet. Separate room for parties, seats 50. Tables outdoors (12, garden).

Map 22 E3.

Peckham

Old Nun's Head NEW

15 Nunhead Green, SE15 3QQ (7639 4007). Nunhead rail/78, P12 bus. **Open** noon-midnight Mon-Thur, Sun; noon-1am Fri, Sat. **Lunch served** noon-2.15pm, **dinner served** 6.30-10.15pm Mon-Fri. **Meals served** noon-10.15pm Sat; noon-9pm Sun. **Main courses** £6.50-£13. **Credit** AmEx, MC, V.

Once a shabby 1930s boozer, the Old Nun's Head has been commendably restored to prominence by folk who care about their beer and their food. Handsome furnishings of oak-panelled walls and abstract art provide the setting for proper, freshly cooked pub meals. The menu is a mixture of staples and specials, with meat dishes a forte: pork goulash served with boiled potatoes was thick and tangy; lamb cutlets with spinach and sweet-potato mash went down a treat. Pan-fried medallions of beef fillet were succulent, with a flavour slightly reminiscent of liver. But a starter of portobello mushrooms topped with mash and cheese had been taken from the grill too soon. There was nothing half-baked, however, about the service from personable staff or the management's evident commitment to making this a worthy local. There's only one regular dessert – a lush, warm chocolate brownie – but there are 'guest puddings' such as pecan pie or lemon polenta cake. Liquid attractions include Adnams ales and organic house wines.

Babies and children welcome (until 9pm): high chairs; nappy-changing facilities. Disabled: toilet. Entertainment: open mic, music Wed 8pm; jazz Sun 1-4pm. Separate room for parties, seats 30. Tables outdoors (4, garden).

East

Bow

Morgan Arms

43 Morgan Street, E3 5AA (8980 6389/ www.geronimo-inns.co.uk). Mile End tube. **Open** noon-11pm Mon-Thur, Sun; noon-midnight Fri, Sat. **Lunch served** noon-3pm Mon-Sat; noon-4pm Sun. **Dinner served** 7-10pm Mon-Sat. **Main courses** £10.50-£19. **Credit** AmEx, MC, V.

The light and airy Morgan Arms is a perfect local. As well as being a great venue to meet people (Friday night is branded 'Doctor and Dentist Central'), it also serves fabulous food. In a separate, quieter dining area we drooled over a menu on which starters included creamy goat's cheese topped with pesto on marinated artichoke and rocket, and a superb ham hock ravioli (slightly overpowered by an onion marmalade, with a watercress garnish that could have been punchier). A fellow diner described her oysters as some of the best she'd tasted. A main of steak and onion pudding was well rendered, but had a slightly oversweet flavour. The kale, mash and root veg julienne was perfectly cooked. Other main courses included crispy pork belly with thai lentils and pak choi, and confit of duck with buttered kale and toulouse sausage. We had no room for desserts, but they included rhubarb filo tart and a cheeseboard. Service was friendly and utterly professional. Prices are reasonable, and Adnams Bitter is on tap. If we lived in the area we'd certainly be regulars, especially on Fridays.

Bookings not accepted. Disabled: toilet. Tables outdoors (4, pavement; 3, terrace).

Docklands

Gun (100)

27 Coldharbour, E14 9NS (7515 5222/ www.thegundocklands.com). Canary Wharf tube/ DLR/South Quay DLR. **Open** 11am-midnight Mon-Fri; 11.30am-midnight Sat; 11.30am-11pm Sun. **Lunch served** noon-3pm Mon-Fri; 11.30am-4pm Sat; 12.30-4pm Sun. **Dinner served** 6-10.30pm Mon-Sat; 6-9.30pm Sun. **Main courses** £11.95-£18. **Credit** AmEx, MC, V.

Strictly speaking, this inordinately successful operation tucked away down a skinny Docklands street qualifies as a gastropub. However, it's hard to avoid the impression that the Gun is effectively a smartish British restaurant (white tablecloths, subtle cooking, modest service) attached to a likeable local boozer (heavy wooden furniture, Thames-side terrace, roaring fire, Young's Bitter and Adnams Broadside on tap). We've eaten very well here in the past, but our meal this year was a little underwhelming. It wasn't the fault of the starters: carefully sourced and beautifully steamed asparagus served with a deep-fried duck egg; and a similarly delicate if slightly over-elaborate trio of Devonshire crab, avocado mousse and cucumber gazpacho. However, the mains – poached halibut, and tender lamb rump with white bean purée and morel jus – were less memorable. Everything was at least decent, and delivered with pleasing efficiency. But at these not-exactly-pub prices (the halibut was £17, the lamb just 50p less, with a side of Jersey royals at four quid extra), we'd hoped to be blown away. There's a cheaper, more informal menu (roast beef sandwich £9.50, fat chips £2.75) available in the pub part of the operation. The White Swan and the Well (for both *see p117*) share the same owners.

Babies and children welcome: high chairs. Disabled: toilet. Separate rooms for parties, seating 14 and 22. Tables outdoors (11, terrace).

Map 24 C2.

Limehouse

★ The Narrow NEW

2007 RUNNER-UP BEST GASTROPUB

44 Narrow Street, E14 8DQ (7592 7950/ www.gordonramsay.com). Limehouse DLR.

Open noon-11pm Mon-Sat; noon-10.30pm Sun. **Lunch served** noon-3pm, **dinner served** 6-10pm daily. **Main courses** £8.50-£21.50. **Credit** AmEx, MC, V.

Professional food, professional service: the Narrow is Gordon to a T (or G). Yes, it's Gordon Ramsay Holding's first foray into gastropubs, heralded as the death knell of the genre or a welcome leap in its evolution, depending on who the pub bore is. We like the Narrow. In a show of commitment to the boozer origins of this riverside site, more than half the ground-floor space is still dedicated to drinkers. Table tops are sleek and stools are shiny, but there are six real ales, benches outside with fine river views, and a bar menu that lists proper pub snacks such as scotch eggs. The dining room is a smaller, sky-lit space, decorated with boating ephemera. It's the small number of dining tables, as much as the allure of brand Ramsay, that makes the Narrow so hard to get in to; even booking weeks ahead, we had to settle for a Monday lunchtime. Starters of gently spiced potted shrimp and pork pie were both classic dishes, reworked with first-rate ingredients. A main of pig's cheek in meaty jus, served generously with mashed swede, was terrific value at £10. Battered haddock and chips featured a zingy tartare sauce, and, on a previous visit, baked egg custard with shortbread was faultless. The wine list is extensive too.

Babies and children welcome: high chairs. Booking essential (several weeks ahead). Disabled: toilet. Separate room for parties, seats 16. Tables outdoors (36, riverside terrace).

Shoreditch

Fox

28 Paul Street, EC2A 4LB (7729 5708/ www.thefoxpublichouse.co.uk). Old Street tube/ rail. **Open** noon-11pm Mon-Thur; noon-midnight Fri, Sat; noon-6pm Sun. **Lunch served** noon-3pm Mon-Fri; noon-4pm Sun. **Dinner served** 6-10pm Mon-Sat. **Main courses** £11.50-£14.50. **Credit** MC, V.

Now under the same ownership as the Lansdowne (*see p128*) and recently refurbed, the Fox is a fine-looking establishment, but on a Friday night you might not notice. Getting to the dining room upstairs requires determination; the bar is packed with braying suits. Once settled at a chunky wooden table, you can admire your surroundings. Lighting is a mix of candelabras, fringed standard lamps and flickering candles that highlight a chocolatey aubergine ceiling and a lovely wooden dumbwaiter. Specials included squid on pea purée: slightly charred but delicious. Another was roast onglet (hanger steak) with chips and aïoli, but we opted for a perfectly seasoned guinea fowl, accompanied by a few interesting starters: pollack brandade (slightly undersalted) was served with soft-boiled duck egg; smoked herring salad with

beetroot and horseradish was moreish; broccoli in caper sauce was sharp and tasty (but more side dish than starter). The wine list is strong and reasonably priced, with a glass of malbec for £3.95, a Corbières for £4.20. Bombardier plus a regularly changing guest are on draught. Service was charming, attentive and professional. Our waiter didn't bat an eyelid when a group ordered 'sambucas all round' for aperitifs.
Babies and children admitted. Tables outdoors (6, terrace). Separate room for parties, seats 12. **Map 6 Q4**.

Princess

76-78 Paul Street, EC2A 4NE (7729 9270). Old Street tube/rail. **Open** noon-11pm Mon-Fri; 6.30-11pm Sat; 12.30-5pm Sun. **Lunch served** 12.30-3pm Mon-Fri; 1-4pm Sun. **Dinner served** 6.30-10.30pm Mon-Sat. **Main courses** £7-£15. **Credit** AmEx, MC, V.

Owned by the same folk who set up the fabulous Easton (*see p117*), the Princess is a winner. It has the same cool but comfortable feel, with statement wallpaper, dark wood and leather chairs. Candles and chandeliers add character. The pub's popularity can make it a tricky choice for dinner, however; to get to the dining area on a busy Friday night we had to cross a crowded bar and make our way up a narrow iron spiral staircase. The noise of the bar followed us up, but at least we got to sit down, and the waiting staff were courteous and efficient. The menu made a tempting read; a chosen starter of salt and pepper squid was perfectly adequate, yet could have done with more kick. The sole vegetarian dish was a rather lacklustre aubergine gratin that, though nicely creamy, had too much tarragon. Ribeye steak was a better order: beautifully cooked with a pat of tomatoey butter. A side dish of purple-sprouting broccoli was too garlicky. Ten wines by the glass include a lovely Pinot Reserve Agustinos (£6.75), while beer drinkers have London Pride and Timothy Taylor's Landlord.
Booking advisable. Restaurant available for hire. **Map 6 Q4**.

Royal Oak

73 Columbia Road, E2 7RG (7729 2220/ www.royaloaklondon.com). Bus 26, 48, 55. **Open** 6-11pm Mon; noon-11pm Tue-Thur; noon-midnight Fri, Sat; noon-10.30pm Sun. **Lunch served** noon-4pm Tue-Sun. **Dinner served** 6-10pm Mon-Sat; 6-9pm Sun. **Main courses** £9-£15. **Credit** AmEx, MC, V.

Located in Columbia Road (famous for its Sunday flower market), the Royal hardly needs to make an effort. Happily, it does. If you haven't booked into the first-floor dining room (all mismatched tables, linen cloths and soothing eau-de-nil paintwork), try to find a seat in the bustling bar below; it's worth it. On our visit, the chaotic crowd – funky 1940s land-girls, middle-aged couples (with dogs, flowers, aging relatives and children) – was served by a waitress as cool as a cucumber but friendly with it. Antipasti was a breadboard piled with chorizo, salami, cured ham, crumbly creamy feta, a spicy sauce and houmous. Half a dozen oysters served on ice with lemon and red wine vinegar were fresh and creamy. A simple main of warm mackerel and salad was delicious, but the prize went to the sunday roast: a mound of tender beef atop roast potatoes, savoy cabbage, roasted carrots and parsnips, covered in delicious gravy with a fluffy yorkshire pud on top. Beers change regularly; Adnams Bitter and London Pride are likely candidates. The wine list is well-rounded and reasonably priced; a house red Les Serres vin de pays (£12.50) was fine, but the recommended Syrah Reserve (L'Archet 2004, £24.50) was superb.
Babies and children welcome: high chairs. Booking advisable. Tables outdoors (4, yard). **Map 6 S3**.

William IV NEW

7 Shepherdess Walk, N1 7QE (3119 3012/ www.williamthefourth.co.uk). Old Street tube/ rail/55 bus. **Open** noon-11pm Mon-Wed; noon-1am Thur-Sat; noon-10.30pm Sun. **Lunch served** noon-3pm Mon-Sat; 1-6pm Sun. **Dinner served** 6-10pm Mon-Sat. **Main courses** £6.50-£10.50. Credit DC, MC, V.

Via swing doors at the back of this attractive Shoreditch pub (lacquered white furniture, a piano bedecked with board games in the corner), you'll reach the upstairs dining room. Photographs of school groups and cricket teams on the staircase make way for framed maps and cartographers' trinkets in the smart, high-ceilinged first-floor space (it's appropriately named the 'Geography Room'). A private room next door seats 12 around a big round table, and is great for parties. Food is carefully prepared and reliable; portions are large. We started with just-right asparagus – not too crunchy, not too soft. A main of lamb cutlets was the highlight: no less than six fleshy, tender pieces, accompanied by tomatoes roasted on the vine. A broad bean and parmesan linguine flavoured with mint was more pedestrian. For dessert, a brownie was moist and rich, improved by a dollop of mascarpone. Ten or so wines of each colour are all available by the glass. Back downstairs there's a separate bar menu (the likes of wild boar and apple sandwich) and three real ales on tap. If a pint of Black Sheep or Flowers IPA doesn't appeal, you can always pet the friendly pub cat, Harry.
Babies and children admitted. Booking advisable. Disabled: toilet. Separate rooms for parties, seating 12 and 40. Tables outdoors (4, pavement). **Map 5 P3**.

North East

Hackney

Cat & Mutton

76 Broadway Market, E8 4QJ (7254 5599). Bethnal Green tube/rail then 26, 48 or 55 bus/ London Fields rail. **Open** 6-11pm Mon; noon-11pm Tue-Thur, Sun; noon-midnight Fri, Sat. **Lunch served** noon-3pm Tue-Sat; noon-5pm Sun. **Dinner served** 6-10pm Mon; 6.30-10pm Tue-Sat. **Main courses** £11-£16. **Set meal** (Mon) £12.50 2 courses, £15 3 courses. **Credit** AmEx, MC, V.

More pub than gastropub (in spite of the quality food), the Cat & Mutton can be a disappointing dining venue. On a Tuesday night we sat at a busy, beer-stained table, ordered from the bar, and were charged prices not unusual for a mid-range restaurant where coats are taken and table service comes as standard. Our starter of admittedly very tasty scallops (four) on a pile of wild garlic and pickled lemon cost £7.50. A main course of tuna loin – perfectly seared – came on a pile of buttery spinach but without a carb in sight (£14); a well-cooked fillet steak on more rocket was better balanced with good chunky chips and aïoli. A cheese plate took the biscuit: two meagre slices of gruyère, a cube of blue cheese (more danish than stilton) and an unspecified goat's cheese served with a few water biscuits, slices of apple and celery sticks for £7. Attractive but distracted service meant that a glass of wine ordered at the bar was only half-full, and between the till and the bar our waitress forgot whom she was serving. At these prices we expect much more. House wines (from a decent list) start at £12. Beers include Shepherd Neame's Spitfire and Adnams Spindrift.
Babies and children welcome (until 8pm): high chairs. Disabled: toilet. Entertainment: DJs 7.30pm Sun. Separate room for parties, seats 50. Tables outdoors (5, pavement).

North

Archway

★ St John's

91 Junction Road, N19 5QU (7272 1587). Archway tube. **Open** 5-11pm Mon-Thur; noon-11pm Fri, Sat; noon-10.30pm Sun. **Lunch served** noon-3.30pm Fri; noon-4pm Sat, Sun. **Dinner served** 6.30-9.30pm Mon-Fri, Sun; 6.30-11pm Sat. **Main courses** £9.75-£18.50. **Credit** AmEx, MC, V.

Sister to the Ealing Park Tavern (*see p119*), in an earlier life St John's was the social hub of Irish Archway, with Guinness in the bar and dancing in the large back room that now serves as the restaurant. It's an impressive space, with a high

Interview

JAMIE PRUDOM

Who are you?
Co-owner of the **Brown Dog** (*see p121*), the **Pig's Ear** (*see p121*) and **As Greek As It Gets** (*see p135*).

Eating in London: what's good about it?
The diversity of food on your doorstep.

What's bad about it?
A two-hour sitting policy makes me furious: why should I be told how long I have to enjoy my dinner when I'm paying? It's often the case that in the stated two hours you don't get the best service anyway. And don't start me on the subject of the rise of the three-month waiting list...

Which are your favourite London restaurants?
After 15 years in London I'm rather fickle with my favourites. They tend to come and go and the best bit is discovering a new one. So right at this minute, if I was in north London, it would be the **Holly Bush** (*see p344*) for real ale and a brilliant homemade pie. Feeling adventurous and venturing East, it would be **Champor- Champor** (*see p179*) – it's a feast for the eyes and a rumbling belly, if a little eccentric. I would even take a No.49 bus for a pizza at **Eco** (*see p322*). And still right up there for many years is **Assaggi** (*see p187*): unbeatable service, food and atmosphere.

Who or what has had the biggest impact on London's restaurant scene in the past 25 years?
I'm secretly pleased that the pan-Asian trend seems to have passed and there is more demand for local produce cooked in British style. Undeniably, Gordon Ramsay and his entourage of chefs have made their mark, and his interest in pubs has to be good news.

Any hot tips for the coming year?
The rise and rise of the 'Great British Menu'. And we should all demand a better bowl of chips.

bronze ceiling, apple-green walls, scrubbed tables and a large collection of portraits, some of which are the work of the owner. Guinness is still on offer; other draughts may include Grand Union wheat beer, Brakspear and Abbot Ale. The wine list starts at a reasonable £12 a bottle, though the group next to us drank champagne all night. Dishes from the semi-open kitchen are cut-above renditions from the gastropub songbook: ox heart with pickled walnut and cauliflower salad for fans of British food; taleggio, artichoke and spinach tart for those with hearts in the Mediterranean. We loved the traditional beer-battered pollock that came with chips, pea purée and tartare sauce. Chargrilled squid with chorizo and piquillos featured tender seafood and the hoped-for tang of peppery flavours. Desserts, at a fiver, are worth ordering too – perhaps a seasonal concoction of ice-cream with matching biscuit. Experienced, confident staff make meals here a pleasure.
Babies and children welcome: high chairs. Booking essential. Tables outdoors (6, patio). **Map 26 B1**.

Camden Town & Chalk Farm

★ Engineer

65 Gloucester Avenue, NW1 8JH (7722 0950/ www.the-engineer.com). Chalk Farm tube/31, 168 bus. **Open** 9am-11pm Mon-Sat; 9am-10.30pm Sun. **Breakfast served** 9-11.30am daily. **Lunch served** noon-3pm Mon-Fri; 12.30-4pm Sat, Sun. **Dinner served** 7-11pm Mon-Sat; 7-10.30pm Sun. **Main courses** £12.50-£16.75. **Credit** MC, V.
It's thought that Brunel built this grade II-listed public house, and may even have kept offices here. As a gastropub, the Engineer (opened 1995) has achieved some fame in its own right as one of the genre's pioneers. Only the smallish front bar is for serious drinkers; the wine list, which starts at £13.50, is helpfully annotated and includes a choice of three good rosés – perfect for drinking in the convivial walled garden. Cheerful staff made every effort to secure us a table outside even though we'd have been as happy in one of the dishevelled interior dining rooms, decorated with bold floral wallpapers. The menu confidently ploughs its own global furrow, with starters featuring such opposing ideas as sweet potato samosas and salt beef with piccalilli. Salmon koulibiac with spinach and herb butter sauce came with a perfectly cooked poached egg, while miso-marinated cod with mash, pak choi and miso sauce was succulent and sweetly tangy. The puds list wasn't that tempting, so we were pleasantly surprised by the success of cinnamon-dusted chimichanga, filled with mascarpone and served with a quenelle of apple compote and blackberries. A lovely meal all round.
Babies and children welcome: children's menu; high chairs. Disabled: toilet. Separate rooms for parties, seating 20-32. Tables outdoors (15, garden). **Map 27 B2**.

Lansdowne

90 Gloucester Avenue, NW1 8HX (7483 0409/ www.thelansdownepub.co.uk). Chalk Farm tube/ 31, 168 bus.
Bar **Open** noon-11pm Mon-Fri; 9.30am-11pm Sat; 9.30am-10.30pm Sun. **Breakfast served** 9.30-11.30am Sat, Sun. **Lunch served** noon-3pm Mon-Fri; 12.30-3.30pm Sat; noon-4pm Sun. **Dinner served** 7-10pm Mon-Sat; 7-9.30pm Sun.
Restaurant **Lunch served** 1-3pm Sat, Sun. **Dinner served** 7-10pm daily.
Both **Main courses** £10-£16.50. **Credit** MC, V.
An enduringly popular, rather déshabillé establishment, where visitors battle with a loyal local following to secure tables. Many drop by for just a pint and a pizza; there's a list of 13 well-made options including a child's version, and specials such as white pizza with summer truffles and mushrooms. There's also a sizeable menu of bar snacks, including the likes of houmous and flatbread. The busy bar staff can be arrogant, but the electronic ordering system is typically efficient and the front-of-house people are friendly, doing their best to help amid the crowds. Draught beers on our visit included Jaipur IPA and Wells Bombardier. There are several wines by the glass, plus bloody marys and Pimm's, but very little to satisfy non-drinkers. With prices on the blackboard menu around £7-£8 for starters, and £14.50-£16.50 for mains, the Lansdowne begs comparison with restaurants and doesn't always deliver. We liked our grilled prawns with beetroot and orange salad, and creamy salmon rillettes with pickled cucumber, but both were let down by indigestibly wiry stems of rocket. Dessert options may include eton mess, plum and almond cake with greek yoghurt, or a plate of goat's cheeses. There's no background music, but you'll still have to shout. Did we mention this place was popular?
Babies and children admitted. Booking advisable. Disabled: toilet. Tables outdoors (5, pavement). **Map 27 B2**.

Crouch End

Queens Pub & Dining Room

26 Broadway Parade, N8 9DE (8340 2031). Finsbury Park tube/rail then W3, W7 bus. **Open** noon-midnight daily. **Meals served** noon-10pm Mon-Sat; noon-9pm Sun. **Main courses** £8.50-£13.50. **Credit** MC, V.
We made two visits to the gloriously Victorian Queens in the space of a few weeks and had two quite different culinary experiences – based, we suspect, on the presence (or not) of the head chef. Such is the benefit of an open-plan kitchen to the food critic. Let's focus on the good: fab, thick-cut chips, quick adoption of seasonal treats such as Jersey Royals, sides of asparagus and savoy cabbage, and an unusual range of salads and potatoes. Staff are chirpy and the decor – with its cosy alcoves, tiled fireplace and wrought ironwork – is a foreigner's English pub fantasy. But our modest lamb burger with beetroot and mozzarella was not good enough to compete with the gourmet burger chains. Grilled chicken breast with couscous and pesto dressing was very ordinary – not the juicy, pancetta-wrapped version we'd enjoyed on our earlier visit, along with spiced duck breast served with a stir-fry of pak choi, oyster mushrooms and beansprouts. On the plus side, the wine list is fairly priced and there's plenty of non-alcoholic presses, crushes and juices – though whether they're all in stock is another matter.
Babies and children welcome (until 6pm): children's menu; high chairs. Booking advisable. Disabled: toilet. Tables outdoors (10, garden).

Highgate

Bull

13 North Hill, N6 4AB (0845 456 5033/ www.inthebull.biz). Highgate tube. **Open** 5-11pm Mon; noon-11pm Tue-Sat; 11am-11pm Sat; 11am-10.30pm Sun. **Lunch served** noon-2.30pm Tue-Fri; 11am-3.30pm Sat; 11am-4pm Sun. **Dinner served** 6-10.30pm Mon-Sat; 6.30-9.30pm Sun. **Main courses** £12-£20. **Credit** AmEx, MC, V.
A pub where you're met on the patio by aproned staff who ask if you're joining them for dinner? Where all the tables are set? Where waiters invite you to select a piece of bread from a basket (50p per person)? This is not the sort of pub you'd stroll into and order a pint, even if the menu does highlight a weekly-changing guest ale (perhaps Eversham from Lincolnshire, or Harvest Down blonde beer from Scotland). A blackboard lists daily specials, but there's no bar menu and the prices and spiffy presentation are on par with a proper restaurant. Several dishes can be served as starters or mains and seafood options are plentiful. Suppliers such as Goosnargh and Elwy Valley are namechecked. Of the mains, lamb pot au feu featured hunks of root vegetables and a light broth with the roasted meat; roast chicken came with a vol-au-vent of tarragon-flavoured mushrooms; but the winner was grilled sea bass with delicious porcini mash and jammy caramelised onion sauce. Dessert portions were uneven, though we enjoyed

The Narrow. See p125.

buttermilk pudding with roast rhubarb, banana tarte tatin and chocolate orange cheesecake. Staff were mostly friendly and briskly efficient.
Babies and children welcome: children's menu; high chairs. Disabled: toilet. Separate room for parties, seats 70. Tables outdoors (16, terrace).

Islington

Charles Lamb

16 Elia Street, N1 8DE (7837 5040/www.the charleslambpub.com). Angel tube. **Open** 4-11pm Mon, Tue; noon-11pm Wed-Sat; noon-10.30pm-Sun. **Lunch served** noon-3pm Wed-Sat; noon-6pm Sun. **Dinner served** 6-9.30pm Mon-Sat. **Main courses** £8-£12. **Credit** MC, V.
Just about the only thing wrong with this gem is that the odds of scoring a table are low, thanks to the growing army of fans. The two small rooms are decorated in a down-home fashion, with fairy lights around the fireplace, framed maps and a notice saying 'Don't feed Mascha' (the cute, neckerchief-wearing pub dog). As a gastropub, the Charles Lamb is at the no-nonsense end of the spectrum. Food is hearty and there are plenty of bar snacks: from pork scratchings and cockles to sausage rolls. Blackboards list French and Spanish sharing plates, and fish and shepherd's pies – comfort food supreme – plus smaller dishes such as rollmops and salad, pork rillettes on toast, and brie with crackers. Occasional dishes disappoint (tomato and lentil soup was dull), but with no main costing more than £12, it's hard to feel cheated. A good selection of world beers (from the US and Belgium especially) is sold alongside ales such as Fuller's Honey Dew. Laudably, several wines are sold by the glass, carafe and bottle. What else? Well, the staff are lovely, the atmosphere relaxed and the clientele a nicely varied bunch. Oh – the loos are a cut above most pub facilities too.
Babies and children admitted. Bookings not accepted. Tables outdoors (6, pavement). **Map 5 O2**.

Drapers Arms

44 Barnsbury Street, N1 1ER (7619 0348/ www.thedrapersarms.co.uk). Angel tube/Highbury & Islington tube/rail. **Open** noon-11pm Mon-Sat; noon-10.30pm Sun. **Lunch served** noon-3pm daily. **Dinner served** 7-10pm Mon-Sat; 6.30-9.30pm Sun. **Main courses** £11-£15. **Credit** AmEx, MC, V.
On the phone and in person, it's rare to find a welcome as warm as that proffered by this spacious pub discreetly positioned in one of Islington's leafiest quarters. The barman immediately volunteered a taster of the guest ale, Wyre Piddle's Piddle in the Hole, which tasted like it too – how we all laughed as we ordered pints of London Pride instead. The wine list features several by the glass, plus 500ml carafes, while a blackboard advertises bin ends. Outside is a pretty heated garden with smart metal chairs; inside are grey-green walls lined with colour photographs loosely maintaining a drapers theme. The menu typically offers eight dishes for each course. Chilled white gazpacho with crayfish was well suited to the hot weather, though it didn't need a dollop of tsatsiki in addition to flaked almonds and grapes. Field mushrooms on tapenade toast with melted brie was surprisingly lacklustre: the cheese fine, the mushrooms strangely bland. A fine example of fish and chips came with breadcrumbed rather than battered fish, served with a crème fraîche variation of tartare sauce, but best was a rich confit of lamb shoulder with meltingly tender red onions and garlic potatoes – enough to feed a small army. The Drapers Arms is a great find.
Babies and children admitted (until 7pm unless dining). Tables outdoors (20, garden). **Map 5 N1**.

Duchess of Kent

441 Liverpool Road, N7 8PR (7609 7104/ www.geronimo-inns.co.uk). Highbury & Islington tube/rail. **Open** noon-11pm Mon-Thur, Sun; noon-midnight Fri, Sat. **Lunch served** noon-3pm Mon-Fri; noon-4pm Sat, Sun. **Dinner served** 7-10pm Mon-Thur, Sun; 7-10.30pm Fri, Sat. **Main courses** £8-£15. **Credit** MC, V.
Now boasting a lucky 13 pubs in London, the Geronimo Inns chain has become a quiet success story by concentrating on the simple things and not getting ideas above its station. There's no better example than the Duchess of Kent. Revived from obsolescence a few years ago and given a handsome, gastropub-standard wood-and-books refit, it's now a fixture at the far end of the Liverpool Road: a pleasing watering hole and ever-reliable eating option. A starter of crispy black pudding potato cake with soft-poached egg and horseradish dressing was blander than its description suggested. However, a special of roasted pork cutlet with braised savoy cabbage and cider sauce was rich in flavour, the excellence of the meat in particular suggesting that no corners are cut in sourcing ingredients. Prices are very fair, with most mains around a tenner. Service is tidy. The all-things-to-all-people soundtrack, carefully fading from reggae to nouveau-Britrock to vintage pop, felt like part of a grand corporate strategy, but this is otherwise a likeable spot.
Babies and children admitted (until 9pm). Disabled: toilet. Tables outdoors (13, pavement).

Duke of Cambridge

30 St Peter's Street, N1 8JT (7359 3066/ www.dukeorganic.co.uk). Angel tube. **Open** noon-11pm Mon-Sat; noon-10.30pm Sun. **Lunch served** 12.30-3pm Mon-Fri; 12.30-3.30pm Sat, Sun. **Dinner served** 6.30-10.30pm Mon-Sat; 6.30-10pm Sun. **Main courses** £10-£18. **Credit** AmEx, MC, V.
In the decade since the Duke of Cambridge opened, demand has soared both for organic food and for houses in these increasingly rarefied Islington backstreets. But aside from the 2005 conversion of the garden into a conservatory (a calm contrast to the loud and busy front room), this all-organic gastropub remains largely unchanged. Prices range from the acceptable to the stratospheric (five quid for Sam Smith's Organic Lager!). Likewise, the food persists in lurching from the excellent to the ordinary, perhaps as a result of the ever-changing menu. For starters, yellow split-pea, cauliflower and bacon soup was hearty but not overwhelming, while a slightly dry confit of duck leg came with an appetising salad of apple, beetroot, fennel and hazelnut. Though the rich shortcrust pastry exterior was a treat, the innards of the beef and gorgonzola pie were too ordinary for its £13.75 price tag. Considerably better was a substantial whole trout, roasted and then served with a perfectly pitched potato gratin. The ranges of beers and wines are very good. Service is generally efficient and friendly, though there's usually one member of staff who flunked out of charm school before the first semester was over.
Babies and children welcome: children's portions; high chairs. Tables outdoors (5, pavement). **Map 5 O2**.

House

63-69 Canonbury Road, N1 2DG (7704 7410/ www.inthehouse.biz). Highbury & Islington tube/ rail. **Open** 5-11pm Mon; noon-11pm Tue-Thur; 5pm-1.30am Fri, Sat; noon-10.30pm Sun. **Lunch served** noon-2.30pm Tue-Fri; noon-3.30pm Sat; noon-4pm Sun. **Dinner served** 6-10.30pm Mon-Sat; 6.30-9.30pm Sun. **Main courses** £13.95-£23. **Credit** AmEx, MC, V.
This delightful bar-restaurant looks perfect for a romantic dinner or celebration – unless the fire alarm goes off, as it did on our visit. The chic interior of dark woods, abundant floral displays and candlelight is enhanced by charming, solicitous waiting staff and an excellent menu that makes use of high-quality, often seasonal, ingredients. Own-made breads (including white chocolate and chilli) arrived with glasses of prosecco chosen from a broad wine list starting at £17.50 a bottle. Draught Adnams Bitter is the beer-drinkers' choice. A starter of Dorset crab on toast was fabulously fresh and moreish, but a pear and goat's cheese risotto (optional starter or main course) was bland. Much better was an enormous roasted Goosnargh Farm chicken – cooked to perfection – in a delectable gravy enhanced with capers, parsley and lemon. Other choices included sea trout, and Gloucester Old Spot pork chops. For afters, there might be warm Valhrona chocolate pudding with espresso ice-cream. Colston Bassett stilton, mull of kintyre cheddar and wensleydale feature on the tasty cheeseboard. The House is open for breakfast at weekends (using produce from Islington Farmers' Market) and hosts 'effervescent "lounge" nights' with DJs from Thursday to Saturday.
Babies and children welcome: children's portions; high chairs; nappy-changing facilities. Bar available for hire. Disabled: toilet. Entertainment: DJs 10pm Fri, Sat. Tables outdoors (24, terrace).

★ Marquess Tavern

32 Canonbury Street, N1 2TB (7354 2975/ www.themarquesstavern.co.uk). Angel tube/ Highbury & Islington tube/rail. **Open** 5-11pm Mon-Thur; 5pm-midnight Fri; noon-midnight Sat; noon-11pm Sun. **Lunch served** noon-4pm Sat; 12.30-5pm Sun. **Dinner served** 6.30-10pm Mon-Sat; 6.30-9pm Sun. **Main courses** £12-£17. **Credit** AmEx, MC, V.
A booking line open only during office hours had us worrying that pretension had taken hold at the Marquess, winner of Time Out's Best Gastropub award in 2006. But fears quickly dissipated on arrival. The front half remains a true, pubby bar, serving the entire Young's beer range. The glass-roofed dining room at the rear has a pared-back aesthetic of white and wood. Simple English cooking is the aim, with starters including devilled whitebait, smoked sprats with horseradish cream, and a seasonal salad of soft lettuce, radishes and young goat's cheese. Devon crab came whole, with tools for cracking and picking. Winningly restrained poached chicken sat in a clear broth with chunks of carrot, celery and potato; roast lamb was lovely too. You can also get roast rib of beef to share: available joints are listed on the blackboard by weight and size, and crossed off as each is ordered. For desserts, chocolate pudding was intensely flavoured, while gooseberry fool boasted a practised balance of tart, sweet and creamy ingredients. This is one of the few venues in London conscientious enough to note vintage changes on its wine list, a fact typical of the Marquess's attention to detail. We still like it.
Babies and children admitted (until 6pm). Tables outdoors (6, patio). Separate room for parties, seats 14.

Northgate

113 Southgate Road, N1 3JS (7359 7392). Essex Road rail/38, 73 bus. **Open** 5-11pm Mon; noon-11pm Tue-Thur; noon-midnight Fri, Sat; noon-10.30pm Sun. **Lunch served** noon-3pm Tue-Fri; noon-4pm Sat, Sun. **Dinner served** 6.30-10.30pm Mon-Sat; 6.30-9.30pm Sun. **Main courses** £9.50-£15. **Credit** MC, V.
Several others have followed suit, but the Northgate was the first pub in De Beauvoir to go gastro, and it remains the most popular. The large front room feels pubby, a mix of matey locals making themselves heard over the stereo. You can eat in this front area, but it's a bit quieter at the back, in a dining room overlooked by a small, open-plan kitchen. Chalked tidily on a couple of boards, the menu changes frequently, though the kitchen is careful to keep things simple. On the night we visited, three of the five starters were salads, supplemented by a subtle carrot and sweet potato soup, and a sizeable portion of grilled merguez sausages served with rocket and slightly herby yoghurt. Main courses are just as generous and similarly uncomplicated. 'Mushroom sauce' rather overwhelmed its conchiglie pasta – not what we had in mind, thanks to too much cream. Happily, a gently cooked cod fillet hit the spot. To drink, there are three real ales and several wines by the glass. A decent, reliable local.
Babies and children admitted (patio, restaurant). Booking advisable weekends. Tables outdoors (15, patio). **Map 6 Q1**.

Kentish Town

Junction Tavern

101 Fortess Road, NW5 1AG (7485 9400/ www.junctiontavern.co.uk). Tufnell Park tube/ Kentish Town tube/rail. **Open** noon-11pm

Mon-Sat; noon-10.30pm Sun. **Lunch served** noon-3pm Mon-Fri; noon-4pm Sat, Sun. **Dinner served** 6.30-10.30pm Mon-Sat; 6.30-9.30pm Sun. **Main courses** £10.50-£14.50. **Set lunch** (Sun) £15 2 courses. **Credit** MC, V.

With 13 beers on its weekly real ales list, drawn from Edinburgh to Cornwall, the Junction Tavern is a haven for those looking for a more characterful pint than lager to enjoy with their meal. Oxfordshire's fruity-tasting Old Hooky was well kept, clean and at the right temperature. The wine list starts at £13.50. Generously sized dishes range from homely to show-off cheffy. Two vegetarian options featured on the list of six main courses. Skate was fresh-tasting and moist, ribeye steak wonderfully tender. Poshest was pancetta-wrapped pork fillet served with teeny onions, clear rich gravy and a swoosh of lightly spiced pumpkin purée. Shame we had to wait around 45 minutes for the dishes, but waiters were friendly, efficient and worked purposefully throughout the busy evening. Two desserts – cream-laden rice pudding with chunks of spiced pineapple, and cardamon-scented plum crumble – were nice twists on traditional ideas. The dark wood interior is roomy yet cosy. At the back is a light but less atmospheric conservatory; if it's not raining, better to grab a table in the heated garden.

Babies and children admitted (if dining). Booking advisable. Tables outdoors (15, garden). **Map 26 B4**.

Oxford

256 Kentish Town Road, NW5 2AA (7485 3521/www.realpubs.co.uk). Kentish Town tube/rail. **Open** noon-11pm Mon-Thur; noon-midnight Fri, Sat; noon-10.30pm Sun. **Lunch served** noon-3.30pm Mon-Fri; noon-4.30pm Sat. **Dinner served** 6-10pm Mon-Sat. **Meals served** noon-9pm Sun. **Main courses** £9-£13. **Credit** MC, V.

Occupying a long corner site in the heart of Kentish Town, the Oxford stands out thanks to its matt black exterior and, on sunny evenings, large groups enjoying a drink outside. Inside, a bustling bar and dining room sit either side of a small open kitchen. Large flower arrangements, orange lampshades and old black and white photographs of the locality strike a formulaic but successful note; the loos, however, were shameful. On our visit, the blackboard menu was confusingly different from the printed one, but proffered a good spread of proteins: salmon, halibut, poussin, lamb and beef. Vegetarians could have a terrific timbale of spinach filled with sweet potato and mushrooms, served with tomato, rocket and courgette. Decent roast lamb came with grilled aubergine, red pesto and a potato cake. We liked the choice of cheeses, but old-school desserts were an opportunity fumbled. Sticky toffee pudding arrived piping hot with half the accompanying ice-cream melted over it; the fruit crumble's topping tasted like sickly sweet chalk. Where this member of the Realpubs mini-chain does satisfy, however, is in the choice of draught beers (Sharp's Doom Bar, Grand Union, Timothy Taylor Landlord and others) and wines by the glass.

Booking advisable. Children admitted. Entertainment: jazz 8.30pm Mon. Disabled: toilet. Separate room for parties, seats 70. Tables outdoors (6, pavement). **Map 26 B5**.

Tufnell Park

Lord Palmerston

33 Dartmouth Park Hill, NW5 1HU (7485 1578/www.geronimo-inns.co.uk). Tufnell Park tube. **Open** noon-11pm Mon-Sat; noon-10.30pm Sun. **Lunch served** noon-3pm, **dinner served** 7-10pm Mon-Sat. **Meals served** noon-9pm Sun. **Main courses** £9.50-£15. **Credit** AmEx, MC, V.

Trees decked with fairy lights make this Geronimo Inn an eye-catching venue. If the outdoor benches or lively front bar are full, don't panic – there are plenty more seating options out back, including a raised garden and a conservatory dining area. Decoration varies from Andy Warhol prints to black and white photographs of Kentish Town. Interesting draught beer options include Eden and Otter, though in our view Liefmans raspberry beer was steeply priced at £4.90 a bottle. A blackboard lists intriguing specials, including snails and scallops. Sadly, the food on our visit lacked finesse. We weren't impressed by ageing vegetables; seafood was perfectly fresh but a piece of cod that came with lentils and chorizo was slightly burnt. Roast lamb loin was served with 'pea and mint broth' – a bitter-tasting twist on mushy peas. At the other tables, high-rise salmon fish cakes with poached egg and hollandaise were very popular. Come dessert, a pretty sugar decoration featured on a proud square of sticky toffee pudding but, like our chocolate brownie, it lacked intensity. Our plum crumble (attractively presented in an enamel dish) was almost cold, but the complaint was handled swiftly and with charm.

Babies and children admitted. Bookings not accepted. Separate room for parties, seats 35. Tables outdoors (7, garden; 13, pavement). **Map 26 B3**.

North West

Hampstead

Horseshoe

28 Heath Street, NW3 6TE (7431 7206). Hampstead tube. **Open** 10am-11pm Mon-Sat; 10am-10.30pm Sun. **Lunch served** noon-3.30pm Mon-Sat; noon-4.30pm Sun. **Dinner served** 6.30-10pm Mon-Sat; 6.30-9.30pm Sun. **Main courses** £8-£15. **Set lunch** £7 1 course incl glass of wine. **Credit** MC, V.

With its large fold-back windows, fashionably aproned staff and relaxed bonhomie, the Horseshoe could easily be mistaken for a hip café, but its pub credentials are better than most. McLaughlin's beers – on our visit, floral spring and honeyed summer varieties – are brewed on the premises, while other draught options included Adnams and Rutterkin ale from Lincolnshire. The OJ is freshly squeezed. Plentiful staff are diligent and efficient, telling you where to sit and bringing drinks from the wood bar and its adjacent open kitchen promptly. A popular lunch special featured attractive plates of scrambled eggs and smoked salmon, including a glass of rosé or a pint of McLaughlin's, for £8.50. Fatty salmon fillet, which came with a cheery horseradish potato salad, was let down by too-thorough cooking and wilted, browning salad leaves. Much better was the crunchy-battered pollock and chips (the menu thoughtfully specified that animal fats are used in the fryer), and chewy hunks of bread. Desserts included a chocolate brownie and disappointingly tart summer fruit jelly. The serious consideration given to sourcing of ingredients and drinks here is to be commended, but while the Horseshoe ticks all the boxes for a contemporary English pub, it falls just short of A-plus.

Babies and children welcome: high chairs. Booking advisable. **Map 28 B2**.

Wells

30 Well Walk, NW3 1BX (7794 3785/ www.thewellshampstead.co.uk). Hampstead tube. **Open** noon-11pm Mon-Sat; noon-10.30pm Sun. **Lunch served** noon-3pm Mon-Fri; noon-4pm Sat, Sun. **Dinner served** 6-10pm Mon-Fri; 7-10pm Sat, Sun. **Main courses** £9.95-£16. **Credit** MC, V.

Bitter chocolate walls brightened with colour photos of pak choi and pandan leaves may suggest that here lies an oriental fusion menu, but the Wells' fare is mostly classic gastropub stuff. It's an appealing Georgian building within walking distance of the Heath, though most customers are local. Upstairs are three quite formal dining rooms; downstairs, though also dining-oriented, has sofas and a stack of board games for drinkers. Smokers tend to command the outdoor benches these days. Beers on tap include Black Sheep Bitter, but prominence is given to wines and cocktails. We chose a gloriously coloured Puglian rosé from Feudi San Marzano to accompany dishes of celeriac remoulade with bayonne ham, and a thick slab of chicken terrine large enough to serve as a main course. Salt marsh lamb was delicious and perfectly cooked, but the accompanying goat's cheese was superfluous. Crisp-fried confit duck was treated to one of the few fusion flourishes on the menu: a well-judged combination of rice noodles, pak choi and carrot ribbons. Desserts may include blueberry cheesecake or rice pudding with caramel sauce and pistachios. The Wells is a highly enjoyable local, but not worth a trek.

Babies and children welcome: children's menu; colouring books; high chairs. Disabled: toilet. Entertainment: guitarist 8.30pm alternate Mon (winter). Separate room for parties, seats 12. Tables outdoors (8, patio). **Map 28 C2**.

Kilburn

Salusbury

50-52 Salusbury Road, NW6 6NN (7328 3286). Queens Park tube/rail. **Open** 5-11pm Mon; 10am-11pm Tue-Thur; 10am-midnight Fri, Sat; noon-11pm Sun. **Lunch served** 12.30-3.30pm Tue-Sun. **Dinner served** 7-10.30pm daily. **Main courses** £11.50-£16. **Credit** MC, V.

Base of the social scene on trendified Salusbury Road, the Salusbury gets the gastropub formula spot on – and not just because of its archetypical stripped-down wood decor. Sunday-brunching families and drinkers don't bother each other, as the dining area and bar are separate: one is a comfortable restaurant, the other retains the feel of a proper bar. Service is friendly and obliging, the atmosphere pleasantly relaxed. Food doesn't have the refined ambitions of some gastropubs, but it's consistent and enjoyable. Parma ham with peaches in a balsamic and honey reduction made a lovely summer starter; king prawns sautéed with chilli and rocket was prepared with high-quality fresh seafood. Pan-frying is a feature of many main courses, as in duck breast with a well-blended fennel and orange salad; or a hefty slab of cod with roast tomatoes and spinach. The wine list contains no big surprises but is fairly priced. As you finish, there's no pressure to choose between lingering at your table, or heading to the bar to while away an afternoon – perhaps with a pint of Adnams (Broadside or Bitter), Grolsch Weissen, or Staropramen.

Babies and children welcome (until 7pm): high chairs. Tables outdoors (4, pavement).

Outer London

Kew, Surrey

Inn at Kew Gardens

292 Sandycombe Road, Kew, Surrey, TW9 3NG (8940 2220/www.theinnatkewgardens.com). Kew Gardens tube. **Open** 11am-11pm daily. **Lunch served** noon-3pm Mon-Fri; noon-4pm Sat, Sun. **Dinner served** 6-10pm daily. **Main courses** £9.95-£14. **Credit** AmEx, DC, MC, V.

Service started with a wobble at this usually flawless gastropub; it was early evening on a boiling hot summer Sunday, bar staff were tired, some dishes had run out. But once we were settled, nothing disappointed. The fish platter was plenty for two, with sardines, mussels, crayfish, smoked mackerel, shrimps and crab meat, plus a little salad and four triangles of brown bread. Mains followed promptly: beef-battered cod with minty mushy peas and thick chips; and chicken breast with sweetcorn potato cake and merguez sausages. Not that adventurous, then, but the latter was a notably delicious combination. The wine list is short but carefully chosen; an excellent sauvignon blanc from the respected Villard estate in Chile cost £15. Desserts weren't needed, but from a list that contained profiteroles, cheeses and chocolate mousse with sponge cake, we opted for what looked like the lightest option: lemon and lime soufflé. Not very light, as it turned out, and not tangy enough either. Any other cons? Well, the Heathrow air traffic is relentless, especially if you're out in the leafy beer garden, but that's unavoidable in this part of town.

Babies and children welcome: children's portions; high chairs; nappy-changing facilities. Disabled: toilet. Separate room for parties, seats 50. Tables outdoors (2, pavement; 8, terrace).

Global

If this is multiculturalism, give us second helpings. London's ethnic diversity is without equal and nowhere is the fact more apparent than in the range of national cooking styles to be found. The major cuisines are celebrated elsewhere in this guide, but here we list the enticing rarities: venues such as the marvellous **Mandalay**, the city's sole Burmese restaurant; or the equally alluring **Masa**, where top-notch Afghani cuisine brightens up a Harrow precinct. This year, we've noticed a resurgence in Mediterranean restaurants, with three new venues joining the esteemed **Eyre Brothers** – including **St Alban**, contender for Best New Restaurant in the 2007 Time Out Eating & Drinking Awards. But perhaps the best thing about visiting these restaurants is the chance to immerse yourself for a couple of hours in another, more exotic culture. It's like going on holiday – yet emerging with a carbon footprint no larger than a ballet shoe.

Afghan

North

Islington

★ Afghan Kitchen

35 Islington Green, N1 8DU (7359 8019). Angel tube. **Lunch served** noon-3.30pm, **dinner served** 5.30-11pm Tue-Sat. **Main courses** £5-£6.50. **No credit cards.**

Although lacking any obvious Afghani design influence, this tiny two-floored space is pleasant enough. Jade-green walls, shared pine tables and lots of light create a fresh and straight-up vibe. The menu is equally simple, consisting of four meat and four vegetarian dishes: all pre-prepared and generally fairly mild (and often featuring yoghurt). Lamb with spinach (qurma suhzi gosht) was flavourful and filling. Vegetarian dishes are tapas-like in terms of ingredients, yet portion sizes are reasonably large. Unless you're dining with someone who is willing to go halves on everything, you might have to get through a large plate of spiced pumpkin with yoghurt (borani kado) or dal – tasty, but rather repetitive, and better suited as side dishes. Still, bowls of rice are available, and the large portions of warm fresh bread are great for mopping up such food. Afghan Kitchen is no place for lingering (there's little space and the rather complacent staff are hard to engage), but it's a good bet for a quick, cheap bite, and makes a break from the norm.

Babies and children admitted: high chairs. Booking advisable. Takeaway service. **Map 5 O2.**

Outer London

Harrow, Middlesex

★ ★ Masa (100)

24-26 Headstone Drive, Harrow, Middx HA3 5QH (8861 6213). Harrow & Wealdstone tube/rail. **Meals served** noon-11pm daily. **Main courses** £4.50-£12. **Set meal** £19.95 (2 people) 2 courses; £47.95 (4-6 people) 2 courses. **Unlicensed. Corkage** no charge. **Credit** AmEx, MC, V.

Bewitchingly exotic, Masa is a glitzy beacon on an otherwise drab suburban precinct. Inside, below a substantial central chandelier, you'll find heavy wooden furniture, shiny tiled flooring, a satellite TV, maroon and wood-panelled walls, a cushion-bestrewn area at the back (for the taking of tea), and a shiny open kitchen. The food is fabulous. Picture a marriage between the best of Middle Eastern and Pakistani cuisine, with a few Balkan salads thrown in as bridesmaids. Hence the bread (resembling roti, hot from a tandoor) and the rice (fluffy pilaus) are sublime: the juicy seared kebabs likewise. Yet the enticing menu holds much more. Try the mantoo, pasta dumplings filled with minced lamb and sweetly flavoured onions, covered with a mince and split-pea sauce; or a starter of bourani-e-afghani (a tangy, moussaka-like dish of aubergine in a tomato sauce with quroot – reconstituted yoghurt); or a side dish of chickpeas and new potatoes in a minty relish. For dessert, there are ice-creams, baklava or fereeni (a rosewater-based pudding). Slinky, black-clad staff, low prices, a BYO policy and the almost entirely Afghani clientele add to the allure.

Babies and children welcome: high chairs. Takeaway service; delivery service (within 3-mile radius).

Belgian

North West

Camden Town & Chalk Farm

Belgo Noord

72 Chalk Farm Road, NW1 8AN (7267 0718/ www.belgo-restaurants.com). Chalk Farm tube. **Lunch served** noon-3pm Mon-Fri. **Dinner served** 5.30-11pm Mon-Thur; 5.30-11.30pm Fri. **Meals served** noon-11.30pm Sat; noon-10.30pm Sun. **Main courses** £9.25-£17.95. **Set lunch** £5.95 1 course incl drink. **Credit** AmEx, DC, JCB, MC, V.

Steaming tureens of mussels, excellent Belgian beers and generous special offers keep Belgo buzzing. On our Friday night visit there was a genial hum of conversation and a rapid turnover of tables. The decor in the subterranean dining room is utilitarian, with close-packed, sturdy wooden tables, and ochre walls somewhat inexplicably inscribed with scatological-sounding Flemish-English nonsense words ('shittail, tomturdy, crapbreech, poorfish'). Although the place is famed for its crustaceans, we were left underwhelmed by a half kilo of moules classiques, awash in a sea of salty but bland cream sauce and much in need of a garlic kick. A more adventurous smoked bacon, duck, black pudding and lentil salad was far better, its earthy flavours working beautifully together. Kilo pots of mussels aside, mains are robust, generally meaty affairs, in which beer often makes a star turn. Having manfully resisted the enormous haddock and chips with Hoegaarden batter, we opted for a beautifully tender lamb shank with red cabbage braised in raspberry beer, and a chunky pork cutlet in deliciously creamy apple beer and mustard sauce. It's good, hearty fare at fair prices – just don't come here for a quiet dinner for two.

Babies and children welcome: children's menu; colouring books; high chairs. Booking advisable. **Map 27 B1.**

For branches (Belgo Centraal, Bierodrome) see index.

Burmese

Central

Edgware Road

★ ★ Mandalay (100)

444 Edgware Road, W2 1EG (7258 3696/ www.mandalayway.com). Edgware Road tube. **Lunch served** noon-2.30pm, **dinner served** 6-10.30pm Mon-Sat. **Main courses** £3.90-£6.90. **Set lunch** £3.90 1 course, £5.90 3 courses. **Credit** AmEx, DC, MC, V.

One of our favourite London restaurants, Mandalay, astonishingly, has been untarnished by success for more than a decade. With laudable lack of greed, the solicitous, friendly Ali family (from Burma, via Norway) have refused to turn their business into a chain, to hike prices or to dilute recipes. They still operate from this cosy, 28-seater room on drab Edgware Road (wooden blinds protecting diners from traffic), where etchings and travel posters of Myanmar/Burma add decoration to the rudimentary furnishings. Young food-adventurers, some perhaps of Burmese origin, are attracted by the exciting menu. Burmese cuisine has influences from Thailand, India and China, with several dishes all its own. Nothing we sampled was mundane. Start with minced chicken samosas or one of several bhaji-like fritters – all freshly cooked. Cleanse your palate with a salad (strips of assorted veg coated in sesame oil and chilli flecks, say) or an equally refreshing soup (the bottle gourd is recommended). To follow, pickle-style lamb is a tangy dry curry, whereas adorably light omelette curry comes in ladles of tomato-based curry sauce. Sprinkle balachaung (intensely fishy dried prawns) over the lot, and tonight you'll dream you went to Mandalay again.

Babies and children welcome: high chairs. Booking essential. Takeaway service. **Map 2 D4.**

Mediterranean

Central

Clerkenwell & Farringdon

Zetter

86-88 Clerkenwell Road, EC1M 5RJ (7324 4455/www.thezetter.com). Farringdon tube/rail. **Breakfast served** 7-10.30am Mon-Fri; 7.30-11am Sat, Sun. **Brunch served** 11am-3pm Sat, Sun. **Lunch served** noon-2.30pm, **dinner served** 6-10.30pm daily. **Main courses** £15.50-£18.50. **Credit** AmEx, MC, V.

Clerkenwell's first hip hotel, refashioned – of course – from a former Victorian warehouse, declares itself to be a 'restaurant with rooms'. Head chef Diego Jacquet takes this statement of ambition in his stride, overseeing a creative monthly changing Italian-Mediterranean menu with international rovings and big flavours. On the whole, the results are impressive. Our starters were immaculate: creamy jerusalem artichoke soup with baby spinach empanada was set off

beautifully by a sprinkling of toasted nuts; and smoked salmon with pumpkin blini, quail's egg and citrus crème fraîche was impeccably balanced. Shame, then, that the kitchen took its eye momentarily off the ball when it came to our caramelised duck breast, which arrived a touch dry. The scale of the lofty, crescent-shaped dining space has been handled handsomely. Oversized retro disc lampshades and swirly red graphic devices provide design accents in an otherwise classically good-looking room inhabited by dark browns, whites and wraparound sash windows overlooking cobbled St John's Square. A fabulous pink chandelier in the lobby, inventive cocktails and the retro-styled Atrium Bar administer the Farringdon factor. But Zetter's care over the essentials (food, service, pricing) suggests that this particular brand of hip will last.
Babies and children welcome: children's portions; crayons; high chairs. Disabled: toilet. Separate rooms for parties, seating 10 and 40. Tables outdoors (14, pavement). **Map 5 O4**.

Piccadilly

★ St Alban NEW (100)

2007 RUNNER-UP LEFFE BEST NEW RESTAURANT

4-12 Regent Street, SW1Y 4PE (7499 8558/ www.stalban.net). Piccadilly Circus tube. **Lunch served** noon-3pm daily. **Dinner served** 5.30pm-midnight Mon-Sat; 5.30-11pm Sun. **Main courses** £9.25-£26. **Credit** AmEx, DC, MC, V.

At night this is a sleek, space-age restaurant, designed by architects Stiff + Trevillion, with big art by Michael Craig-Martin and lots of curvy white fittings. Owned by Chris Corbin and Jeremy King, who also run the Wolesley (and before that the Caprice, the Ivy and J Sheekey), St Alban marks a departure for them as the space is entirely modern, and the menu concentrates on modern Mediterranean dishes. It's a mouth-watering read. Sadly, there was no slow-roasted Norfolk Black pig with seared potatoes and lemon, though this was the only disappointment. We were treated to a procession of punchy flavours right from the start, beautifully demo-ed by Sardinian tomato and mozzarella salad, courgette flowers stuffed with salt cod, and broad beans with chorizo. Mains were equally impeccable: nicely spicy Sardinian fish stew, and juicy seared scallops with a big tangle of samphire. Dark chocolate tart with white chocolate mousse was a fine pudding, though we couldn't help but envy a neighbouring table their wild strawberry soufflé with chocolate sauce. Prices are very reasonable for this level of cooking. As with all Corbin-King venues, it's the attention to detail that counts: interesting breads and grissini come with glorious olive oil; beautifully chewy mini macaroons accompany the coffee; staff are ultra-attentive without being bothersome.
Babies and children admitted; high chairs. Booking advisable. Disabled: toilet. **Map 10 K7**.

South Kensington

Brompton Quarter Café NEW

225 Brompton Road, SW3 2EJ (7225 2107). Knightsbridge or South Kensington tube.
Meals served 7am-10.30pm Mon-Fri; 8am-10.30pm Sat, Sun. **Main courses** £9.75-£24.95. **Credit** AmEx, MC, V.

Café, pâtisserie, juice bar, restaurant – BQC tries to be all things to all people of Knightsbridge. And as long as you have deep pockets, it might just fit the bill. Certainly, the look is all you want in these parts, with goldfish-bowl glass and steel chic allowing diners to see and be seen on the ground floor. Stay here if a quick coffee, croissant, eggs florentine or full english breakfast is all you want. Likewise, a tapas menu and larger staples such as moussaka, fish pie or meatballs probably don't require great intimacy. Otherwise, you can hide in the basement restaurant amid soft colours and feminine fabrics on upholstered benches. The boldly seasoned, Mediterranean à la carte menu tempts with such starters as crispily seared scallops with pea purée, caramelised spring onions and fennel salad. Main courses satisfy most tastes by ranging from rack of lamb to seafood linguine – both suggesting the chef's weakness for the sweet and sticky. An enjoyable spot, but at £78 (including service) for one starter and two mains, plus one of the few bottles of wine for less than £20 on an uninspiring list, it's certainly pricey.
Babies and children welcome: high chairs. Takeaway service. **Map 14 E10**.

West

Hammersmith

Snow's on the Green

166 Shepherd's Bush Road, W6 7PB (7603 2142/ www.snowsonthegreen.co.uk). Hammersmith tube.
Lunch served noon-3pm Mon-Fri. **Dinner served** 6-11pm Mon-Sat. **Main courses** £11.25-£16. **Set meal** (lunch, 6-8pm) £13.25 2 courses, £16.50 3 courses. **Credit** AmEx, DC, MC, V.

The Green in question is Brook Green, and this W6 stalwart has been around for as long as the area has been coined in estate agent parlance. From the moment Snow's opened 15 years ago, its plum position on the posh bit of Shepherd's Bush Road (these things are relative) has made it a favourite neighbourhood eaterie with well-heeled locals. Sebastian Snow, the chef-proprietor and one-time sidekick of Antony Worrall Thompson, manages to attract a healthy crowd most nights with the promise of a relaxed, friendly vibe; hearty bistro dishes (belly of pork, calf's liver); and a reasonably priced) wine list, including plenty of by-the-glass options. Snow isn't scared to keep things simple. A main course of chargrilled Angus ribeye steak with fries and green salad was a beautifully tender cut, and showed the chef is as keen on the source as he is on the sauce. Decor is as straightforward as the dishes: all white linen and ochre walls. The set menu is a bargain in west London terms and might include dishes like zampone sausage with lentils and salsa verde, and red berry vacherin.
Babies and children welcome: high chair. Booking advisable. Separate room for parties, seats 28. Tables outdoors (2, pavement). **Map 20 C3**.

South

Balham

★ Fat Delicatessen NEW

7 Chestnut Grove, SW12 8JA (8675 6174/ www.fatdelicatessen.co.uk). Balham tube/rail.
Meals served 8am-8pm Mon-Wed; 8am-10pm Thur-Sat; 11am-6pm Sun. **Main courses** £3.50-£6.75. **Credit** MC, V.

The Fat Delicatessen uses a similar approach to the adjacent and slightly longer-established Trinity Stores, in that it's both a smart food shop and a café, but, in the Fat Deli's case, the balance is shifted in favour of the café. Even though there are only four tables, plus a few bar stools, it's very spacious and doesn't feel cramped. The menu offers Italian-accented Spanish tapas, with dishes of the day – such as puréed white bean soup topped with smoked butter – chalked on a blackboard. Colourful slivers of jamón ibérico were cut to order and dished up with a salad; little padrón peppers were grilled and served as a warm snack. Not everything is Mediterranean or Iberian, however; many of the cheeses are British. Some good wines by the glass or bottle are a bonus. If you're not eating in, Fat Deli is still a good place to browse; the chilled display cabinet near the till is packed with mouth-watering traiteur dishes to take away, and banks of shelves are loaded with oils, dried beans, Ortiz tuna, wines, walnuts and other southern European store-cupboard staples.
Babies and children welcome: high chairs. Disabled: toilet. Takeaway service.

South East

Gipsy Hill

Numidie

48 Westow Hill, SE19 1RX (8766 6166/ www.numidie.co.uk). Gipsy Hill rail. **Dinner served** 6-10.30pm Tue-Sat. **Meals served**

RESTAURANTS

Upper Glas. See p134.

noon-10.30pm Sun. **Main courses** £9.50-£15. **Set meal** (Tue-Thur; Sun) £13 2 courses. **Credit** MC, V.

Opt for a window seat and a glowering Woolworths sign across the road will keep you rooted in gritty Westow Hill. Sit facing inwards, however, and the continental clutter at Numidie will whisk you to one of Paris's more Algerian-flavoured arrondissements. It's an amicable marriage: a picture of Zizou seems utterly at ease alongside one of Jacques Brel; and North African drums gather dust between wooden tables set with salt and pepper shakers made from miniature Bonne Maman conserve jars, and cabinets filled with Armagnac bottles. But cultural compatibility is most prominent in the food itself. Algerian influences are evident in starters such as spicy merguez sausages with pepperade and harissa, while the melt-in-the-mouth courgette and roquefort fritter with cherry and ginger compote is a more consciously European offering. Ditto the mains: from the slow-cooked, Berber-style lamb shank capping a mountain of couscous to a generous fillet steak, rich with truffle butter and served alongside a gratin dauphinoise that would have pleased the Dauphin himself. Locals seem well aware of their good fortune. Several regularly prop up the cavernous basement wine bar or chat affectionately with owner Serge Ismail over dinner.
Babies and children welcome: booster seats.

East

Shoreditch

★ Eyre Brothers (100)

70 Leonard Street, EC2A 4QX (7613 5346/ www.eyrebrothers.co.uk). Old Street tube/rail. **Lunch served** noon-3pm Mon-Fri. **Dinner served** 6.30-10.45pm Mon-Sat. **Main courses** £13-£22. **Credit** AmEx, DC, MC, V.

From its heavy wooden reception desk to its sleek decor (dark wood panels, lots of leather and sophisticated deep-red hues), Eyre Brothers is a decidedly grown-up affair. Tables are well spaced, allowing romantic tête-à-têtes and boozy family reunions (which constituted most bookings on our visit) to coexist in comfort. Everything about this restaurant is carefully thought out and well executed. Service is knowledgeable and you get the distinct sense you're in very safe hands. Safe enough, we decided, to order the recommended medium-rare iberico pork – a superior taste sensation. Starters of morcilla blood sausage with plump seared scallops, and a boldly flavoured salt cod salad were equally fine. The menu's Spanish-Portuguese mix reflects the Mozambican upbringing of the owners (brothers David and Robert Eyre). The menu changes regularly yet some constants remain, such as the huge (and hugely popular) Mozambican tiger prawns served with pilau rice and cucumber salad. Accompany the food with one of the excellent (mostly) Iberian wines. For a more informal taste of what the Eyres have to offer, grab a table in the loungey bar area for top-notch tapas and a Rioja or two.
Babies and children admitted. Booking advisable. Disabled: toilet. No-smoking tables. **Map 6 Q4.**

Scandinavian

Central

Marylebone

Garbo's

42 Crawford Street, W1H 1JW (7262 6582). Baker Street or Edgware Road tube/Marylebone tube/rail. **Lunch served** noon-3pm Mon-Fri, Sun. **Dinner served** 6-11pm Mon-Sat. **Main courses** £6.50-£17. **Set lunch** £10.95 2 courses, £11.95 3 courses, £12.95 smörgåsbord. **Set buffet lunch** (Sun) £14.95. **Cover** £1 (à la carte only). **Credit** AmEx, MC, V.

The Dala horses in the window sum up the Garbo's experience; if you're looking for a taste of Sweden, you won't be disappointed. Alongside a patriotic

picture gallery including the Swedish royal family, Abba tribute band 'Fabba' and, of course, Greta Garbo, there's a plethora of Swedish memorabilia decorating the place. The mid-priced menu contains traditional favourites such as meatballs, gravadlax and elk. Swedish is spoken as much as English among staff and clientele. Our meal started with a chunky pea and ham soup and a pickled herring selection with plentiful accompaniments. Both proved simple and filling, as were the dishes that followed. Pyttipanna – diced, pan-fried meats, onion and potato, topped with an egg – required generous seasoning to bring out the individual flavours. Conversely, salmon steak came with an intensely rich white wine sauce. Staff were exceptionally welcoming and the food reflected the mood: this is home-style cooking in a homely environment – no pretensions here, on the menu or otherwise.
Babies and children welcome: high chair. Booking advisable. Separate room for parties, seats 35. **Map 8 F5**.

South Kensington

Lundum's

117-119 Old Brompton Road, SW7 3RN (7373 7774/www.lundums.com). Gloucester Road or South Kensington tube. **Brunch served** 9am-noon, **dinner served** 6-11pm Mon-Sat. **Lunch served** noon-4pm Mon-Sat; noon-1.30pm Sun. **Main courses** £13.50-£27.25. **Set lunch** (Mon-Sat) £14.50 2 courses, £18.50 3 courses; (Sun) £21.50 buffet. **Set dinner** £19.50 2 courses, £24.50 3 courses. **Credit** AmEx, DC, MC, V.
An air of relaxed elegance makes this Danish restaurant equally suitable for a romantic dinner or a corporate night out. Muted shades, abundant foliage and soft lighting create a peaceful haven away from London's bustle. Customers are well dressed, but the friendly, discreet service leaves you at ease. There's an impressively broad wine list; for a four-figure sum you can enjoy a Château Pétrus 1994, but prices cover the spectrum and the house merlot was both palatable and fairly priced. From a European menu with a Danish slant, we began with delicate slivers of smoked salmon, accompanied by a sweet dill tuile and stacked with a potato salad. Following this, a stroganoff of tender beef fillet with chunks of gherkin and crisp smoked bacon was delicately executed and deserved its 'speciality' status. Pork meatballs had a pleasantly light texture. Dessert ticked all the boxes too: a triumph of contrasts between a tender poached pear and crunchy brandy snap, cold vanilla parfait and warm chocolate sauce. Lundum's offers fine food and fine wine – expect a price tag to match.
Babies and children welcome: high chairs. Booking advisable. Separate room for parties, seats 18. Tables outdoors (11, patio). **Map 14 D11**.

North

Islington

Upper Glas NEW

The Mall, 359 Upper Street, N1 0PD (7359 1932/www.glasrestaurant.co.uk). Angel tube. **Lunch served** noon-3pm, **dinner served** 5.30-11pm Mon-Sat. **Main courses** £12-£17. **Credit** AmEx, MC, V.
Atop the Mall antiques arcade lies a bright and airy restaurant that encapsulates laid-back Swedish charm. Glas has moved from Borough Market to Islington and become Upper Glas. Its decor evokes a swathe of ripe lingonberries with accents of red, green and white throughout. Adhering closely to tradition, the menu includes meatballs, venison, salmon, and herring dishes aplenty. You can select a smörgåsbord of small plates or go for the standard course-by-course option. We chose the latter, and mustard herring made a pleasing starter of tender fish bathed in sweet, dill-laden sauce. Toast 'skagen' served with mayonnaise-bound prawns, roe and chives tasted strongly of onion, but was moreish nonetheless. The chefs clearly pride themselves on presentation, but overall the food is competently handled rather than grand. Slow-cooked beef brisket with crushed potatoes typified this, appearing as an impressive tower that belied the simplicity of its flavours. Pink-hued beetroot salmon made an equally attractive dish and a subtle yet agreeable change from gravadlax. Accommodating service and many long tables make Upper Glas a great venue for groups.
Babies and children welcome: high chairs. Booking essential weekends. **Map 5 O2**.

South African

South West

Putney

Chakalaka

136 Upper Richmond Road, SW15 2SP (8789 5696/www.chakalakarestaurant.co.uk). East Putney tube. **Dinner served** 6-10.45pm Mon-Fri. **Meals served** noon-10.45pm Sat, Sun. **Main courses** £9.95-£16.95. **Set meal** (dinner Mon-Fri; lunch Sat; lunch & dinner Sun) £15 2 courses. **Credit** AmEx, MC, V.
A haven for expatriate South Africans, Chakalaka makes a colourful spectacle with its zebra-striped frontage, red walls and tribal ethnic artefacts. It's an informal venue, popular with young, well-off professionals. The menu gives a modern spin to dressed-up Afrikaner dishes, grills sauced with peri-peri marinades, and occasional African specialities. These guys are big on game; should ostrich, crocodile or antelope be your thing, this spot's for you. We've had excellent meals here in the past, but more recently, cooking has fallen short of expectations. However, service remained as smiley and swift as ever. Highlights included fresh-from-the-sea oysters doused with red chilli and onion salsa: simple, unspoilt and delicious. Salmon and crab meat fish cakes scented with lemongrass were let down by their impenetrable breadcrumb crust. Main courses delivered better results, with a meaty hunk of succulent springbok loin served with crushed sweet potatoes and caramelised onion confit. Steak lovers have choice aplenty; there's even a whopping 650g Namibian T-bone steak. Vegetarians aren't top priority, their options limited to butternut soup and a couple of salads. Expect hearty rather than gourmet cooking – and lots of meat.
Babies and children welcome: children's portions; high chairs. Booking advisable. Separate room for parties, seats 60.
For branch (Boom Bar) see index.

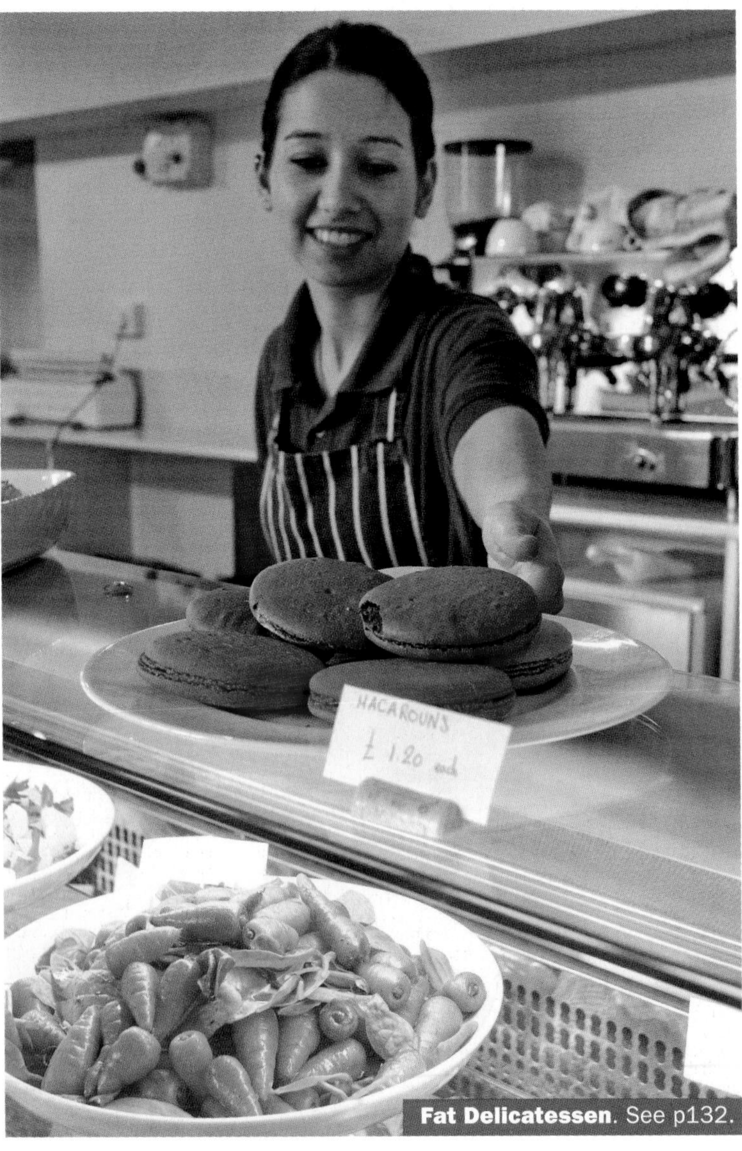

Fat Delicatessen. See p132.

Greek

We start this section with a Greek tragedy. The closure of the original Real Greek in Hoxton has dealt a cruel blow to Modern Hellenic dining in London. A destination restaurant, it had raised the bar to Olympian standards in recent years – but its sale to new owners in 2004 and the departure of chef Theodore Kyriakou eventually led to drastic dumbing down of the menu. As we went to press, all the branches of the much inferior Real Greek Souvlaki & Bar (the cheaper spin-off, under the same ownership) were, confusingly, changing their name to the **Real Greek**. The original Real Greek's wine bar neighbour, Mezedopolio, is also a goner: both spaces have now merged and become part of the newly renamed chain. In other words: same name, same location, but these two Hoxton landmarks are now a totally different dining experience.

For the most part, the city's other Greek restaurateurs have been moving in slow-mo. The cuisine hasn't witnessed any sort of evolution of late, with few tavernas offering creative twists to classic dishes. Nevertheless, dependable venues remain. You'll know a good Greek or Greek-Cypriot restaurant by the lengths it takes to source the most authentic ingredients. On this count, **Retsina** is our current pick of the bunch, though old-stagers such as **Lemonia**, **Limani**, **Andy's Taverna**, **Daphne** and **Vrisaki** all pass muster. And despite its name and quasi-diner furnishings, visit **As Greek As It Gets** if you're a kebab enthusiast.

Central

Clerkenwell & Farringdon

The Real Greek

140-142 St John Street, EC1V 4UA (7253 7234/ www.therealgreek.com). Farringdon tube/rail. **Meals served** noon-11pm Mon-Sat. **Main courses** £3.95-£6.25. **Credit** MC, V.

Formerly called the Real Greek Souvlaki & Bar, this chain was in the process of changing its name to the Real Greek as we went to press. The meze bar concept remains the same though, with innovative twists on Mediterranean bites designed to accompany drinks (the wine and spirit selection is excellent), rather than vice-versa. Hip and slick, this branch has a huge mahogany bar dominating the floor, surrounded by diner-style stools. A few small tables and a lower-floor banqueting room accommodate serious diners, who must pay handsomely for a hearty meal. Mezédes include fish and vegetarian choices. Dolmádes are packed with gloriously aromatic rice sprinkled with sultanas and pine nuts; their leaves tasted fresh from the vine. We needed extra flatbread for the creamy dips, which included an interesting tzatzíki garnished with mixed herbs. The mixed souvláki for two consisted of only three mini skewers of lamb, pork and chicken, but they were faultless: delicately chargrilled and tender. Unfortunately, the salad was limp and swimming in juices, the vegetables soft and tasteless. This is a great place to pick and mix your mezédes, but there are some serious lapses.

Babies and children welcome: high chairs. Booking advisable. Disabled: toilet. Separate room for parties, seats 40. Tables outdoors (2, pavement). Takeaway service. **Map 5 O4.**

For branches see index.

West

Bayswater

Aphrodite Taverna

15 Hereford Road, W2 4AB (7229 2206/ www.aphroditerestaurant.co.uk). Bayswater, Notting Hill Gate or Queensway tube. **Meals served** noon-midnight Mon-Sat. **Main courses** £8.50-£28.50. **Set mezédes** £17.50 vegetarian, £19.50 meat, £28.50 fish. **Cover** £1. **Credit** AmEx, DC, JCB, MC, V.

A visit here feels like a trip to see old family friends. Aphrodite is run by Brazilian Rosana and her Greek-Cypriot husband. If open to banter, you might get to meet three generations of the clan. The premises are charmingly haphazard; this is a red-cushioned, copper-potted, caricature-walled sort of place that feels unabashedly chintzy – in carefree contrast to the street's manicured environs. The menu is extensive and includes an excellent house French wine. Greek salad, huge juicy green olives, and fasólia made an impeccable start to our meal. Houmous and taramosaláta weren't exceptional, though the fluffy Paphitiko-style (from Paphos) pitta bread provided for hearty olive-oil dipping. Partnering a gently roasted golden-yellow Cyprus potato, sheftaliá were aromatic, though the cinnamon should have been less of a dominant flavour. The succulent skewered monkfish (a house speciality) had a slightly sweet flavour and pleasingly firm springy texture. The food is wholesome and attentively prepared, but best of all there's no pressure from the owners if you try nothing more than the occasional loukoúmi, sip coffee, and toss around backgammon pieces.

Babies and children welcome: high chairs. Booking advisable dinner. Tables outdoors (12, terrace). Takeaway service. **Map 7 B6.**

Notting Hill

★ Greek Affair

1 Hillgate Street, W8 7SP (7792 5226). Notting Hill Gate tube. **Lunch served** noon-3pm, **dinner served** 5.30-11pm Tue-Sun (Oct-Apr). **Meals served** noon-11pm daily (May-Sept). **Main courses** £7.40-£13.90. **Credit** MC, V.

This is probably just the right place for a Greek affair, as few Greek people actually go here. Don't get us wrong though: the restaurant, ideally located by the Gate cinema, is worth a visit. Its decor is simply lovely. By the entrance, a mahogany side table is home to a grandiose lamp and gold-framed mirror. Service is friendly, if a little sleepy. The problem lies in the food delivery. Dishes lacked consistency, and portions were meagre on our visit – a big faux pas for the Greek diner. Ordering from a vegetarian-friendly menu, we chose the grand mixed meze for two, but there were serious omissions: no kalamári, soúvla or souvláki. Instead, we were presented with dips and cold pitta bread; octopus, mussel and crab salad; lukewarm average-tasting keftédes; and an uninspiring salad. On the bright side, the tomato-based stifádo had a powerful kick, and the bland-looking kléftiko was succulent and unusually lemony. The fasólia and gígantes were tasty too: freshly dressed and well seasoned. Good coffee accompanying an exquisitely naughty nut- and honey-laced kataïfi dessert rounded off a hit and miss meal.

Babies and children welcome: high chairs. Booking advisable. Tables outdoors (10, roof garden). Vegetarian menu. **Map 19 C5.**

Shepherd's Bush

Vine Leaves

71 Uxbridge Road, W12 8NR (8749 0325/ www.vineleavestaverna.co.uk). Shepherd's Bush tube. **Lunch served** noon-3pm, **dinner served** 5pm-midnight Mon-Thur. **Meals served** noon-1am Fri, Sat; noon-11.30pm Sun. **Main courses** £6.95-£15.95. **Set meal** (Mon-Thur, Sun) £9.95 3 courses incl coffee. **Set mezédes** £9.95 mini, £13.95 mixed, £16.95 fish. **Set lunch** (Mon-Fri) £5.75 2 courses. **Credit** MC, V.

Vine Leaves provides the Uxbridge Road's multicultural rainbow of restaurants with its Greek hue. Complete with vine-ensconced bar, its design subscribes to the authentic village taverna look. Service is friendly, but the cooking needs refinement. The menu runs the breadth of Greek-Cypriot dishes, with a selection of hot and cold starters, oven-baked pastas and meat, and fish mezédes including a shellfish platter of deep-fried scampi, kalamári, prawns and crab claws. Oil-drenched olives, smoky loúntza and warm pitta bread arrived promptly. The melitzanosaláta was bland and had too much tahini and too little aubergine or lemon. The roast potatoes were actually chips, with a crisp and fluffy texture; these arrived with a bowl of comforting tomato rice garnished with coriander. A main course lamb soúvla was a let-down; it was actually lamb chops, and the meat was overcooked, unattractive and bland. The super-size king prawns in garlic and chilli were better, and arrived in generous portions. There may be better-quality dishes at Vine Leaves, but our choices proved the menu to be over-ambitious.

Babies and children welcome: children's menu. Booking advisable weekends. Takeaway service. Vegetarian menu. **Map 20 B2.**

South West

Earl's Court

★ As Greek As It Gets

233 Earl's Court Road, SW5 9AH (7244 7777). Earl's Court tube. **Meals served** noon-11pm Sat, Sun. **Main courses** £6-£9. **Credit** MC, V.

Luring in the neighbourhood's young Greeks, this souvláki restaurant is a little at odds with its design. The heavy chandelier, 1970s retro brown and orange walls, and LCD screens featuring

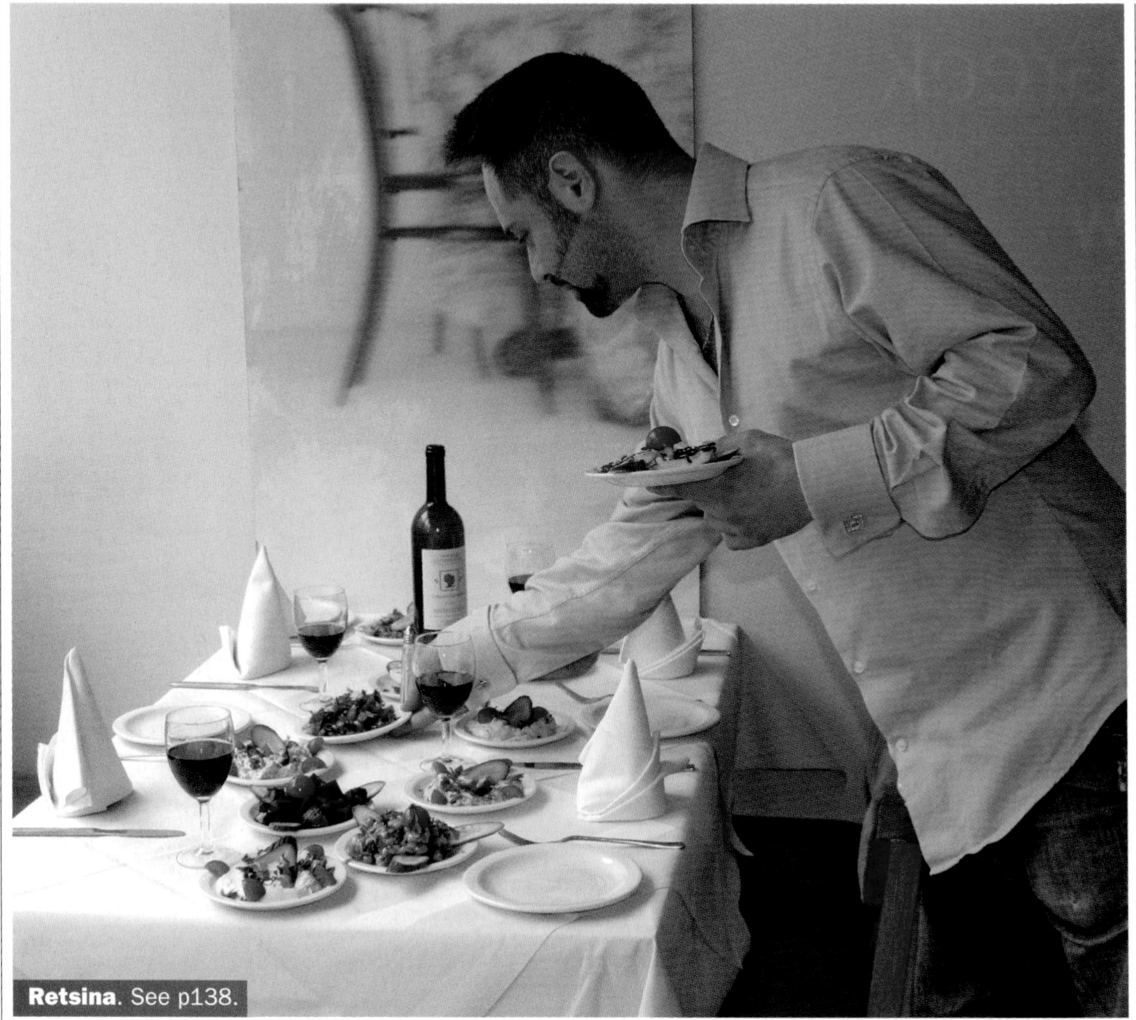

Retsina. See p138.

Hellenic popsters would never alert you that the place serves Greek takeaway food at its healthiest. Though why the owners chose to call souvláki 'wraps' with names like 'D-light' and 'Original-eaty' is anyone's guess. Vegetarians have a choice of just two or three token dishes, but there are also imported Greek and Cypriot drinks, a few 'mother's pride' dishes and an array of meaty 'D-lights'. Partnering authentic Greek flatbread and served with a chunky tzatziki, the pork gyro (doner kebab) was tasty and succulent, with a crisp salty coating. An oregano-sprinkled salad was fresh, if a little underdressed. The oven-baked pastítsio (rarely seen outside mother's kitchen) had plenty of hearty flavour; a clove and cinnamon béchamel sauce topped a parsley and tomato mince base, with macaroni in consort. Friendly staff, a reasonable bill and a dessert menu that included decent baklava and frappé (Greece's frothy answer to iced-coffee) all count in the establishment's favour.
Babies and children welcome: high chairs. Tables outdoors (4, pavement). Takeaway service.

North

Camden Town & Chalk Farm

Andy's Taverna

81-81A Bayham Street, NW1 0AG (7485 9718). Camden Town or Mornington Crescent tube.
Lunch served noon-2.30pm, **dinner served** 6pm-midnight Mon-Fri. **Meals served** noon-midnight Sat, Sun. **Main courses** £8.95-£14. **Set mezédes** £13.95 per person (minimum 2). **Credit** AmEx, DC, JCB, MC, V.
Mama's home cooking is a pillar of the cuisine, so it's not surprising that most Greek restaurants aspire to create a homely, intimate feel. Andy's Taverna is similar to several other venues in the vicinity, but it does have a refreshingly sedate atmosphere. The premises are set away from the cacophony of central Camden, so the cavernous low-key interior provides a haven for regulars who can while away hours here. Low wooden beams and the odd photo of the Greek islands provide a measure of nostalgia, but nothing overwhelming – in stark contrast to the in-house pianist who we were seated by, and who began with a race through *Zorba*. Our meal also proved oddly contrasting. Enticing fresh produce made up the artichoke, broad bean and village salads, but they were sparsely seasoned. Another starter, king prawns, was bland. Outstanding star of the meal was the stifádo. The beef in rich onion and red wine sauce struck the perfect balance between spiciness and tenderness. Grilled swordfish, delicately herbed, fresh and meaty, was also finely executed. Prices are quite high, though portions are generous. Traditional orange filo spirit is served gratis as a digestif.
Babies and children welcome: high chairs. Booking advisable Fri, Sat. Entertainment: pianist; phone for details Separate rooms for parties, seating 35 and 45. Tables outdoors (7, garden). Takeaway service. **Map 27 D2**.

Daphne

83 Bayham Street, NW1 0AG (7267 7322). Camden Town or Mornington Crescent tube.
Lunch served noon-2.30pm, **dinner served** 6-11.30pm Mon-Sat. **Main courses** £9-£13.50. **Set lunch** £7.75 2 courses, £9.25 3 courses. **Set mezédes** £15.50 meat or vegetarian, £19.50 fish. **Credit** MC, V.
Ambling here from the tube station you'll encounter several Greek-Cypriot restaurants; Camden was a hub for the community's early immigrants in the 1950s. Cheery and lovingly cared-for, Daphne attracts customers ranging from after-hours City workers to families, Greeks and non-Greeks. The menu is diverse. Our waiter volunteered to explain everything on the specials board, but ignoring his recommendation we opted for a koúpes starter (ground wheat-paste shell stuffed with spiced mince); it was crumbly on the outside and moist and flavourful inside. Tiger prawns wrapped in feta cheese and filo pastry proved an inventive twist on the usual prawn starter, but like the koúpes and Greek salad, they were disappointingly small. Lamb lemonado (oven-cooked lamb with lemon dressing) looked chunky on the plate, yet had a tenderness born of lengthy gentle cooking. It came with a lively, perfectly cooked spinach side dish. Our monkfish, salmon, swordfish, scallops and prawns grilled mezédes were fresh, but over-marinated and oily. The food is expensive, but service was good. Any setbacks were smoothed over by genial waiters who patiently left us to forget the passage of time.

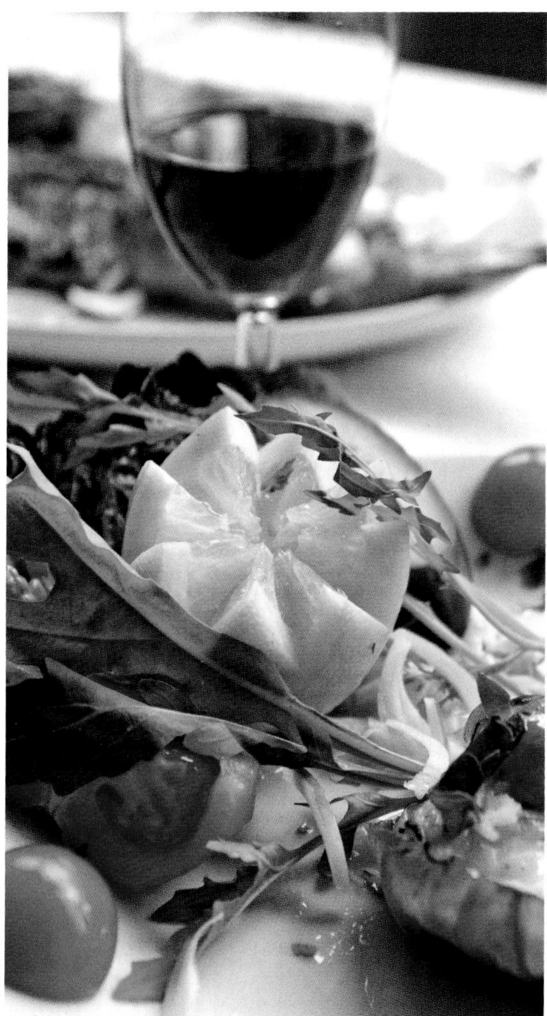

Babies and children welcome; high chairs. Booking essential Fri, Sat. Disabled: toilet. Separate room for parties, seats 50. Tables outdoors (8, roof terrace). **Map 27 D2**.

★ Lemonia

89 Regent's Park Road, NW1 8UY (7586 7454). Chalk Farm tube. **Lunch served** noon-3pm Mon-Fri; noon-3.30pm Sun. **Dinner served** 6-11.30pm Mon-Sat. **Main courses** £9-£15. **Set lunch** (Mon-Fri) £8.50 2 courses incl coffee, £9.75 3 courses. **Set mezédes** £17.75 per person (minimum 2). **Credit** MC, V.

Since 1979 Lemonia has remained one of London's most popular Greek-Cypriot restaurants. Situated halfway up Primrose Hill, it is patronised by well-heeled local couples, animated families, and on our visit, a 97-year-old actor's birthday troupe. At peak times, the place can get too popular for its own good, with service – usually self-assured yet convivial – left wanting. Like the food, the setting is traditional and simple. Clean white walls contrast with wooden taverna-style beams; a conservatory embellished with vines lends a fresh, earthy feel. The Cypriot food has long been lauded; the standard of cooking is high, though prices are moderate. Delicately battered kalamári and baked aubergine salad (mint-tinged and creamy) made perfectly light appetisers. Next, chargrilled sea bream was remarkably succulent and moist, dressed lightly in olive oil and lemon. Lemon is a favourite dressing of the cuisine, yet unlike many Cypriot restaurants, Lemonia (meaning lemon grove) uses condiments in subtle measure, as it should. No cloves or cinnamon were in the kléftiko (slow oven-roasted lamb in white wine stock), simply tender, delectable meat literally falling of the bone: just right.

Babies and children admitted. Booking advisable. Separate room for parties, seats 40. Tables outdoors (6, pavement). **Map 27 A1**.

Limani

154 Regent's Park Road, NW1 8XN (7483 4492). Chalk Farm tube. **Lunch served** noon-3pm Sat. **Dinner served** 6-11.30pm Tue-Sat; 3.30-10.30pm Sun. **Main courses** £8.75-£16.50. **Set mezédes** £16 meat or vegetarian, £18 fish, per person (minimum 2). **Credit** MC, V.

Just a skip over the road from its sister Lemonia, Limani (meaning little port) has been harbouring a crew of regulars for nearly 30 years. Despite its Primrose Hill environs and appealing setting, prices haven't become too licentious and the food is reliably good. The tiny tables packed into the rustic interior can feel a little cramped at peak times, but a prime table in the covered porch is ideal for watching the flow of Primrose Hill promenaders. Steer clear of the loukánika if you intend an amorous evening, as these sausages are for the connoisseur – assertively peppered, and heavy with garlic. Lightly battered crispy slices of aubergine were great for dipping into a smooth creamy skordaliá dip. Next, a simply-seasoned portion of kléftiko, served naked on the plate but for a healthy portion of lemony potatoes, was Greek-Cypriot cuisine at its simplest and best. The red mullet, gloriously fresh and gently fried, were tiny so we were wise to have ordered a side of fluffy own-baked bread and a crunchy village salad heaped with creamy chunks of feta. Service can be erratic, but Limani has a wealth of high-quality Greek-Cypriot food.

Babies and children admitted. Booking essential weekends. Separate room for parties, seats 30. Takeaway service. **Map 27 A1**.

Wood Green

Vrisaki

73 Myddleton Road, N22 8LZ (8889 8760). Bounds Green or Wood Green tube. **Lunch served** noon-4pm, **dinner served** 6-11.30pm Mon-Sat. **Meals served** noon-9pm Sun. **Main courses** £10-£18. **Set mezédes** £18 per person (minimum 2). **Credit** AmEx, MC, V.

This large suburban restaurant is accessed via a poky kebab shop that belies a dining room brimming with happy families – but the contrast only adds to the charm. Vrisaki's enduring popularity with north London's Greek-Cypriot community is testimony to its authenticity. Time seems to stand still here. Delightful, old-school moustachioed waiters, poised to dispense a joke or debate the abiding 'Cyprus problem', are a key feature of this vibrant venue. You might be in Cyprus. The food is standard, robust Greek-Cypriot fare. The appetisers, consisting of dips, tsakistés, Greek salad, loúntza, halloumi, kalamári and dolmádes, were superb, though arrived an hour into the meal and followed too many unnecessary 'fillers' such as prawns, scampi and tinned tuna. Field mushrooms drizzled in warm

olive oil and lemon were fleshy and succulent, and the tsípoura (grilled sea bream) was lovely. Chefs here clearly don't subscribe to the 'less is more' school of cuisine, and by the time the mains (sheftaliá, souvláki and quails) arrived, three hours into the meal, we were full. Yet what Vrisaki lacks in consistency of quality and timing, it makes up for in a wonderful atmosphere.
Babies and children admitted. Booking advisable; essential weekends. Takeaway service (8881 2920).

North West

Belsize Park

★ Retsina NEW

48-50 Belsize Lane, NW3 5AN (7431 5855). Belsize Park or Swiss Cottage tube. **Lunch served** noon-3pm Tue-Sun. **Dinner served** 6-11pm daily. **Main courses** £9-£22.50. **Set lunch** (Tue-Fri) £9 1 course; (Sat, Sun) £11 2 courses. **Set mezédes** £19.50 fish, £17 meat. **Credit** MC, V.

Retsina has moved from Regent's Park Road to the former site of Halepi. Everything about the new operation is spot on: the cream-walled and candlelit decor is relaxed and stylish; service is jovial; prices are great; and the cooking is effortlessly authentic. No wonder the restaurant gets packed to the rafters at night. The food exhibits the enthusiastic attention to ingredient-quality that some of London's established Greek restaurants have abandoned. Tzatzíki contained the creamiest yoghurt; taramosaláta was rich and punchy; and the Greek salad (simply fresh rocket, salty feta chunks and ripened tomatoes) was faultless. Mixed hot starters included crisp whitebait with a slice of lemon for extra zing, spicy loukánika, plump dolmádes, fresh mint gigantes and springy kaskavalli (a saltier alternative to grilled halloumi). There were interesting additions to the list of mains, such as stuffed kalamári, though the traditional version was lusciously light, fresh and moreish. The lamb soúvla really impressed, served with an ample side of honey-centred Cyprus potatoes, well-seasoned and cooked to perfection. Two Greek coffees and complimentary loukoúmi rounded off a meal that cost £56 for two; we'd happily have paid more.
Babies and children welcome: high chairs. Separate room for parties, seats 50. Tables outdoors (5, pavement). Takeaway service.
Map 28 B3.

Swiss Cottage

Hellenic Restaurant

291 Finchley Road, NW3 6ND (7431 1001/ www.gonumber.com/hellenic). Swiss Cottage tube. **Lunch served** noon-3pm, **dinner served** 5.30pm-midnight daily. **Main courses** £8.50-£12.50. **Set lunch** £7.95 2 courses. **Set mézedes** £15.50 per person (minimum 2). **Credit** AmEx, MC, V.

The most impressive thing about the Hellenic is its airy modern feel; refreshingly, the interior is uncluttered by the usual tributes to the motherland. Large windows, white walls and a deep-blue starlit ceiling create a calming coastal ambience. In contrast, the food would barely pass muster in Greece. Generous starters of warm pitta and creamy dips were good, but the loukánika were plain and lacklustre. To follow, the fatty soúvla cuts were way too pricey at £19, and left us with a little of that unpleasant aftertaste pork can have. As most mince and rice in Greek restaurants tend to appear in dolmádes, it was exciting to see gemistá (stuffed aubergines) on the menu. We were delighted when two plump aubergines arrived, their filling suffused with the aroma of cinnamon and clove, and tasting just as good. We finished with lovely Greek coffee and a honey-laced baklavá dessert. This place is apparently recommended by the Hellenic Centre, but we reckon it needs to refine its dishes and savvy-up its prices. On Fridays and Saturdays a bouzouki band plays.
Babies and children welcome: high chairs. Entertainment: band 8.30pm Fri, Sat. Separate room for parties, seats 65. Takeaway service.
Map 28 B3.

Menu

Dishes followed by (G) indicate a specifically Greek dish; those marked (GC) indicate a Greek-Cypriot speciality; those without an initial have no particular regional affiliation. Spellings often vary.

Afélia (GC): pork cubes, ideally from filleted leg or shoulder, stewed in wine, coriander and other herbs.
Avgolémono (G): a sauce made of lemon, egg yolks and chicken stock. Also a soup made with rice, chicken stock, lemon and whole eggs.
Baklavá: a pan-Middle Eastern sweet made from sheets of filo dough layered with nuts.
Dolmádes (G) or **koupépia (GC)**: young vine leaves stuffed with rice, spices and (usually) minced meat.
Fasólia plakí or **pilakí**: white beans in a tomato, oregano, bay, parsley and garlic sauce.
Garídes: prawns (usually king prawns in the UK), fried or grilled.
Gígantes or **gígandes**: white butter beans baked in tomato sauce; pronounced 'yígandes'.
Halloumi (GC) or **hallúmi**: a cheese traditionally made from sheep or goat's milk, but increasingly from cow's milk. Best served fried or grilled.
Horiátiki: Greek 'peasant' salad of tomato, cucumber, onion, feta and sometimes green pepper, dressed with ladolémono (oil and lemon).
Hórta: salad of cooked wild greens.
Houmous, hoúmmous or **húmmus (GC)**: a dip of puréed chickpeas, sesame seed paste, lemon juice and garlic, garnished with paprika. Originally an Arabic dish.
Htipití or **khtipití**: tangy purée of matured cheeses, flavoured with red peppers.
Kalamári, kalamarákia or **calamares**: small squid, usually sliced into rings, battered and fried.
Kataïfi or **katayfi**: syrup-soaked 'shredded-wheat' rolls.
Keftédes or **keftedákia (G)**: herby meatballs made with minced pork or lamb (rarely beef), egg, breadcrumbs and possibly grated potato.
Kléftiko (GC): slow-roasted lamb on the bone (often shoulder), flavoured with oregano and other herbs.
Kopanistí (G): a cheese dip with a tanginess that traditionally comes from natural fermentation, but is often boosted with chilli.
Koukiá: broad beans.
Loukánika or **lukánika**: spicy coarse-ground sausages, usually pork and heavily herbed.
Loukoumédes: tiny, spongy dough fritters, dipped in honey.
Loukoúmi or **lukúmi**: 'turkish delight' made with syrup, rosewater and pectin, often studded with nuts.
Loúntza (GC): smoked pork loin.
Marídes: picarel, often mistranslated as (or substituted by) 'whitebait' – small fish best coated in flour and flash-fried.
Melitzanosaláta: purée of grilled aubergines.
Meze (plural mezédes, pronounced 'mezédhes'): a selection of either hot or cold appetisers and main dishes.
Moussaká(s) (G): a baked dish of mince (usually lamb), aubergine and potato slices and herbs, topped with béchamel sauce.
Papoutsáki: aubergine 'shoes', slices stuffed with mince, topped with sauce, usually béchamel-like.
Pastourmá(s): dense, dark-tinted garlic sausage, traditionally made from camel meat, but nowadays from beef.
Pourgoúri or **bourgoúri (GC)**: a pilaf of cracked wheat, often prepared with stock, onions, crumbled vermicelli and spices.
Saganáki (G): fried cheese, usually kefalotyri; also means anything (mussels, spinach) made in a cheese-based red sauce.
Sheftaliá (GC): little pig-gut skins stuffed with minced pork and lamb, onion, parsley, breadcrumbs and spices, then grilled.
Skordaliá (G): a garlic and breadcrumb or potato-based dip, used as a side dish.
Soutzoukákia or **soutzoúki (G)**: baked meat rissoles, often topped with a tomato-based sauce.
Soúvla: large cuts of lamb or pork, slow-roasted on a rotary spit.
Souvláki: chunks of meat quick-grilled on a skewer (known in London takeaways as kebab or shish kebab).
Spanakópitta: small turnovers, traditionally triangular, stuffed with spinach, dill and often feta or some other crumbly tart cheese.
Stifádo: a rich meat stew (often beef or rabbit) with onions, red wine, tomatoes, cinnamon and bay.
Taboúlleh: generic Middle Eastern starter of pourgoúri (qv), chopped parsley, cucumber chunks, tomatoes and spring onions.
Taramá, properly **taramosaláta**: fish roe pâté, originally made of dried, salted grey mullet roe (avgotáraho or botárgo), but now more often smoked cod roe, plus olive oil, lemon juice and breadcrumbs.
Tavás (GC): lamb, onion, tomato and cumin, cooked in earthenware casseroles.
Tsakistés (GC): split green olives marinated in lemon, garlic, coriander seeds and other optional flavourings.
Tyrópitta (G): similar to spanakópitta (qv) but usually without spinach and with more feta.
Tzatzíki, dzadzíki (G) or **talatoúra (GC)**: a dip of shredded cucumber, yoghurt, garlic, lemon juice and mint.

Hotels & Haute Cuisine

Time waits for no man... even at lunchtime. Restaurants in this section of the guide may be among the classiest in London, but they are increasingly responding to the time-poor diner by offering 'menu rapides' or as **Sketch: The Lecture Room** describes it: 'Three courses delivered swiftly and elegantly for just £35 including our magnificent petits fours'. Sketch is joined in the midday race against time by the **Greenhouse**, **Jaan**, **Addendum**, **Bonds**, **Galvin at Windows** and even **Le Gavroche** – all of which can serve a fabulous meal in 60 minutes or less if time is not on your side. Several establishments voiced their concern to us this year about the lack of female diners at lunchtime. A tutorial from a great chef, with lunch included, makes an excellent present and is a good way of getting a girl and her friends back to the restaurant on a regular basis (blokes are welcome too, of course). The **Greenhouse**, **Tom Aikens** and the **Capital** are seeing their cookery classes and demonstrations sell out – cannily capitalising on the fashion for all things foodie and the skill of their resident chefs.

This year, we've also noticed a strong trend for novel ingredients, not merely for publicity's sake but to be used in truly wonderful, carefully considered combinations. **Jaan**, **Tom Aikens**, the **Capital**, **Pearl**, **Foliage**, **Maze**, the **Square**, **Gordon Ramsay at Claridge's** and even the **Ritz** have joined a growing band offering culinary curios. Notable creations include Foliage's gorgeous beef with oysters, smoked potato and red wine; Gordon Ramsay at Claridge's salt marsh lamb with crystallised walnuts, cumin and Umbrian lentils; and Jaan's scallop and oxtail wth laksa steam buns, trumpet salad and chestnut foam. Hiccups aren't unknown, though; may we add that braised lettuce, which turned up in a surprising number of meals, is as much a turn-off now as it was decades ago?

As we went to press, **Angela Hartnett at the Connaught** was closed as part of the Connaught's multi-million pound restoration; the hotel – and restaurant – should be reopening at the end of 2007.

Central

City

Addendum

Apex City of London Hotel, 1 Seething Lane, EC3N 4AX (7977 9500/www.addendum restaurant.co.uk). Tower Hill tube. **Lunch served** noon-2.30pm, **dinner served** 6-9.30pm Mon-Fri. **Main courses** £16.75-£19.50. **Set lunch** £21.95 2 courses, £27 3 courses. **Credit** AmEx, DC, MC, V.

As you'd expect from a hotel restaurant located smack bang in the City, most if not all of Addendum's clientele are business people. Brief, stylish lunches over which one debates the ebb and flow of the world's economies and politics are the order of the day. Staff are adept at making the logistics of serving food melt into the background with as few interruptions as possible. No expansive menu descriptions are recited and explanations on the menu are concisely written. Talented chef Tom Illic has departed, handing over the reins to his deputy Darren Thomas. The savoury side of things is now simpler, more conventional and hasn't necessarily been improved by the handover – although desserts are still on sparkling form. A starter of barbecued beef with mustard leaves and horseradish sauce was, unexpectedly, a fragile-tasting carpaccio skimming the bottom of the plate, with a confetti dusting of baby leaves and dash of indistinct sauce. A main course of tomato tarte tatin, also served with salad, made a barely discernible impression, resting unimaginatively on a pile of sliced tomatoes, while a faint balsamic glaze somewhere along the line lent scant flavour to a few salad leaves. Pudding really got the taste buds going, belying its simple description on the page. Lemon meringue pie was a truly delightful, tangy carnival of contrasting tastes, textures and temperatures, including chunky shreds of candied peel and a dab of shiveringly cold, tart lemon sorbet to counteract the sweet warm meringue – almost worth a visit on its own.

Disabled: lift; toilet (in hotel). Separate rooms for parties, seating 10-50. Tables outdoors (12, terrace). **Map 12 R7.**

Bonds

Threadneedles, 5 Threadneedle Street, EC2R 8AY (7657 8088/www.theetongroup.com). Bank tube/DLR. **Lunch served** noon-2.30pm, **dinner served** 6-10pm Mon-Fri. **Main courses** £15.95-£23. **Set lunch** £19.50 2 courses, £24.50 3 courses. **Credit** AmEx, MC, V.

Stowed away in the stylish heart of Threadneedles hotel, a fabulous 19th-century pile standing tall and stately amid the buzz and traffic of City life, Bonds offers a welcome escape from the working day. That said, many City workers continue slaving to the god of finance over lunch, so, depending on the company you keep, a midday visit here may not be such a departure from the desk job. Evenings provide a more relaxing backdrop to Barry Tonks' classy modern French menu. This is dotted throughout with British ingredients that are for the most part cooked and presented with great flair. In keeping with the needs of the regulars, a short lunch menu is served with relative speed, taxing the mind with fewer components than its à la carte sibling. From this lunch menu, rustic chestnut and mushroom soup had gorgeous depth, enhanced by a fragrant and creamily filled herb raviolo. Salmon and cod fish cake came in a generous portion, garnished with good tartare sauce. It was perfectly nice, albeit heavier on the potato side than the fish side, and pulverised into a homogeneous ball. Ideally, a fish cake should contain obvious flakes of fish lightly bound together with a touch of potato. Still, there's not much to complain about at Bonds. More complex dishes from the main menu might be roast duck with caramelised red onion tarte tatin and fondue of gem lettuce, or wild Scottish salmon with shimeji mushrooms, asparagus and Sauternes sauce. Desserts are hearty man-pleasers such as apple tart, crème brûlée or chocolate pudding.

Disabled: lift; toilet. Dress: smart casual. Separate rooms for parties, seating 9, 12 and 20. **Map 12 Q6.**

Embankment

★ Jaan

Swissôtel London, The Howard, 12 Temple Place, WC2R 2PR (7300 1700/www.swissotel.com). Temple tube. **Lunch served** noon-2.30pm Mon-Fri. **Dinner served** 5.45-10.30pm Mon-Sat. **Set lunch** £19.75 2 courses, £23.75 3 courses. **Set dinner** £33 2 courses, £38 3 courses, £42 4 courses, £46 tasting menu. **Credit** AmEx, DC, JCB, MC, V.

Why haven't you been to Jaan yet, when it so richly deserves your custom? Chef Simon Duff cooks modern French food, but, as you might guess, he isn't from across the Channel. He isn't even from this hemisphere, but from Australia. Hence he knows his gingko nuts as well as his onions. An intriguing larder-load of Asian ingredients crop up in Jaan's menu, which is markedly subtle, sophisticated and well priced. A daily changing business lunch, '47', promises to be light and delivered in 47 minutes to the frazzled worker. At less than £20 it is superb. From this menu, tuna carpaccio was faultlessly fresh, fine, tender and stunningly partnered by pistachios, spiced shredded duck, a few enlivening shreds of spring onion and coriander, a dash of wasabi foam and speckles of orange segment. It sounds overly involved, but the dish was beguilingly delicate and devilishly moreish. Main course assiette of kid goat was likewise an amazing feast of unexpected yet harmonious flavours. Dinky rib and sliced fillet were served hot, succulent and sweet on vivid terracotta-coloured harissa and fennel purée, while cold shredded kid came in a little heap topped with sweet cool yoghurt and tonka bean ice-cream: again a stunning

combination of flavours carefully thought through. Tasting menus are more complex to absorb on initial reading – grilled lamb rack, sichuan-crusted braised mutton shoulder, roasted fig, asparagus, smoked aubergine and basil cress to mention one; and honey caramel-coated duck breast with ginger confit leg, caramelised butternut squash, green tea noodles, foie gras parfait, wasabi and pepper sauce to mention another – but a few minutes of concentration on your part will be well rewarded.
Book dinner. Children welcome: high chairs. Disabled: toilet. Dress: smart casual. Restaurant available for hire. Tables outdoors (12, garden).
Map 10 M7.

Fitzrovia

★ Pied à Terre

34 Charlotte Street, W1T 2NH (7636 1178/ www.pied-a-terre.co.uk). Goodge Street or Tottenham Court Road tube. **Lunch served** 12.15-2.30pm Mon-Fri. **Dinner served** 6.15-11pm Mon-Sat. **Main courses** £29.50. **Set lunch** £24.50 2 courses, £30 3 courses. **Set dinner** £49.50 2 courses, £60 3 courses, £80 tasting menu (£132 incl wine). **Credit** AmEx, MC, V.

Although surrounded by broad, scruffy and busy shopping thoroughfares, Charlotte Street still has the ambience and charm of old Soho, plus the boggling array of restaurants that goes with such territory. Shoehorned in among them is one of London's best, Pied à Terre. Another refit since our last visit has updated the decor so that the long narrow room is now stylishly monochrome, moody and much more special. Space is tight, with staff zipping between the snugly packed tables in an unavoidably hectic manner. This isn't a sign of disorder, but the bustle does sometimes register. Given the food, the lack of space is a minor inconvenience. Also, booking is never a problem, despite the handful of tables. Chef Shane Osborne and manager David Collins have been here for years and clearly make good partners; staff hardly change from year to year and are clearly at the top of their game. Listening to them describe the all-French cheeseboard or extensive wine list is an education in itself. Prices are high but worth every penny. The luxurious tasting menu, as balanced as a tightrope walker, included vibrant, silky-smooth chilled pumpkin soup with toasted seeds and ice-cream; a second course of raw tuna wrapped in parma ham and accompanied by picked mooli; a dish of seared and poached foie gras served with its own gloriously intense broth; followed by fabulous john dory and then a tender, flavour-packed nugget of salt marsh lamb. Cheese, leading on to a shockingly good black treacle mousse, and the main dessert of molten, bitter-chocolate tart with stout ice-cream, were all complete heaven. Absolutely unmissable.
Babies and children admitted. Booking advisable; essential weekends. Dress: smart casual. Separate room for parties, seats 12. Vegetarian menu.
Map 17 B1.

Holborn

★ Pearl Bar & Restaurant

Chancery Court Hotel, 252 High Holborn, WC1V 7EN (7829 7000/www.pearl-restaurant.com). Holborn tube.
Bar **Open** 11am-11pm Mon-Fri; 6-11pm Sat. *Restaurant* **Lunch served** noon-2.30pm Mon-Fri. **Dinner served** 6-10pm Mon-Sat. **Set lunch** £25.50 2 courses, £28.50 3 courses. **Set dinner** £49 3 courses, £55 tasting menu (£100 incl wine). *Both* **Credit** AmEx, DC, MC, V.
Transforming the old banking hall of the former Pearl Assurance HQ into a restaurant was quite a feat, and in its formative years Pearl the restaurant struggled to inhabit this cavernous, marble-sheathed room. Now, with bags more confidence, bags more customers and some canny wall-positioning to break up the vast space and introduce some intimacy, Pearl is doing very well, thank you. So it should. Jun Tanaka's Japanese-American roots and classical French training have given him a fearless approach to pillaging the world's larders. Practice in pleasing London diners over the past five years has streamlined this approach, honing Tanaka's skill into a wonderful talent. A couple of pounds have been added to the lunch menu this year, but both lunch and dinner are superb value for a fine-dining experience with all the cutting-edge style and elegance you'd expect from a luxury hotel in London. Food is seasonal and simply stated, but beautifully, artistically presented (fabulous appetisers and petits fours included). A meal might begin with sardine tempura with an incisive caper, olive and tomato dressing. To follow, perhaps, there will be melt-in-the-mouth osso buco, shredded and sandwiched between silk-thin sheets of pasta to make a single bulging raviolo sitting on roasted artichokes and whole shallots – all surrounded by a rich pool of beefy consommé, vanilla foam and crispy wild mushrooms. Desserts are magical, oozing flavour, and almost gravity-defying in trembling, barely set lightness. A cracking restaurant.
Babies and children welcome (if dining). Disabled: toilet. Entertainment: pianist 7.30pm Wed-Sat.
Map 10 M5.

Knightsbridge

Boxwood Café

The Berkeley, Wilton Place, SW1X 7RL (7235 1010/www.gordonramsay.com). Hyde Park Corner or Knightsbridge tube. **Lunch served** noon-3pm Mon-Fri; noon-4pm Sat, Sun. **Dinner served** 6pm-12.45am Mon-Fri; 6-10.45pm Sat, Sun. **Main courses** £10.50-£28. **Set lunch** £25 3 courses. **Set meal** £55 tasting menu. **Credit** AmEx, MC, V.

Boxwood may have to close during 2008 as part of The Berkeley's renovations of that wing, but in the meantime, the socialising goes on like there's no tomorrow. A more casual branch of the Gordon Ramsay empire, Boxwood is hugely popular by day with the WAGs, no doubt due partly to the restaurant's tempting proximity to designer shopping heaven and partly to its flexible menu. For those whose primary reason for lunching is to natter, not nibble, such flexibility allows them to eat as little as possible while still appearing to join in the fun. Evening is when the men tear themselves away from whatever occupies them during daylight hours, and one and all heartily immerse themselves in Boxwood's easy-going menu of bistro favourites. Puddings reflect the whole attitude to food here; the list draws on effortlessly comforting classics such as vanilla and gingerbread cheesecake with summer berries, bakewell tart with seville orange marmalade and clotted cream, hot sugared doughnuts, or hot chocolate fondant with cappuccino ice-cream. Savoury dishes are equally affable, with strong leanings towards the Mediterranean, as in seared tuna with chilli and coriander, or creamy risotto with chunky tomato sauce and lobster. Our cold-smoked pork belly with watercress salad, and a pillow-soft potato gnocchi vegetarian dish were fresh and delicious, with subtle saucing and garnishes. True à la carte pricing means you can go as mad as you like, or not, as the whim and the crowd take you.

Babies and children welcome: children's menu; high chairs. Booking essential. Disabled: toilet (in hotel). Separate room for parties, seats 16. **Map 9 G9.**

Pied à Terre

★ The Capital

22-24 Basil Street, SW3 1AT (7589 5171/7591 1202/www.capitalhotel.co.uk). Knightsbridge tube. Bar **Open** noon-1am daily. **Tea served** 3-5.30pm daily. **Set tea** £18.50-£34.50 incl glass of champagne.
Restaurant **Breakfast served** 7-10.30am Mon-Sat; 7.30-10.30am Sun. **Lunch served** noon-2.30pm daily. **Dinner served** 7-11pm Mon-Sat; 7-10.30pm Sun. **Set breakfast** £14 continental, £18.50 full English. **Set lunch** £29.50 3 courses, £48 tasting menu. **Set dinner** £55 3 courses, £70 tasting menu.
Both **Credit** AmEx, DC, MC, V.

Tucked away behind Harrods and Pâtisserie Valerie (don't get waylaid en route), this intimate dining room exudes class and calm. Furnishings add to the feel, with smooth pale maple-wood walls, duck-egg blue silk drapes, little pencil sketches dotted about and etched-glass panels blurring the edges of the world outside. An inviting bar is the setting for conversation and nibbles, to wind the appetite up or down. The Capital doesn't shout about itself like most haute cuisine destinations. Chef Eric Chavot has been quietly making inroads on excellence here for years, so your fellow diners are likely to be locals, regulars and those in the know, rather than the followers of recommendations in weekend newspaper supplements. The whole experience is soothing and dignified, the staff kindly, the wine list tempting and the food luscious. Deftly presented and arranged with great skill, Chavot's style of cooking is difficult to pigeonhole. Fine British ingredients and a dash of pioneer spirit are brought to bear on classical French foundations, and the result is an intriguing and hugely appealing set of menus. These might include dishes as diverse as honey-roasted duck with macaroni gratin and pear jelly, and lamb served with cumin jus and spicy couscous. Our starters – white bean velouté with chorizo ravioli; and scallops, black pudding and featherweight onion bhajis – were superb, unusual and too good to share across the table. Main courses of sea bass and a platter of pork served four ways were succulent, faultless and subtly flavoured with interesting spices. The day's dessert of chocolate sponge, Baileys ice-cream and mascarpone was a more straightforward satisfaction. Be prepared to add the Capital to your list of favourites.

Booking advisable; essential weekends. Children over 12 years admitted. Dress: smart casual. Restaurant available for hire. Separate rooms for parties, seating 10, 12 and 24. **Map 8 F9.**

★ Foliage

Mandarin Oriental Hyde Park Hotel, 66 Knightsbridge, SW1X 7LA (7201 3723/www.mandarinoriental.com). Knightsbridge tube. **Lunch served** noon-2.30pm, **dinner served** 7-10.30pm daily. **Set lunch** £27 4 courses (£35 incl wine). **Set dinner** £55 4 courses, £75 tasting menu. **Credit** AmEx, DC, JCB, MC, V.

Kitchen supremo Chris Staines has stealthily slipped into Foliage restaurant the most radical change to London's fine dining arrangements for about 15 years. An entirely new set of menus tempts with the merest suggestion of an ingredients list, served you-don't-know-how until they arrive, and in portions that allow you to experiment to your heart's content, confident that every morsel will be up to Staines' usual amazing standard. Best of all, the new dishes are simply listed as savouries or desserts and you choose four of whatever you fancy – from the savoury selection that could be quail, artichoke, celery and hazelnuts; or scallops, tapioca, meyer lemon and lotus root. From the desserts: pear mousse, hibiscus and sea salt caramel; or guava sorbet, raspberry tuille and exotic fruits. The result: a whole meal of desserts, if pudding's your thing, or all savoury, or two of each, or extra courses if you're feeling particularly thin. This adorable flexibility flies free and fantastic in the face of every stuffy London restaurant and prima donna chef. And the food is so innovative, beautifully cooked and diverse that you could eat here every week for a year without getting bored. The flexi menu is available lunch and dinner along with excellent wine pairings, or you can pick a more traditional six-course tasting menu, again with wines by the glass, or not. Most adventurous is the Menu Surprise: six seasonal, market-fresh dishes that could be absolutely anything; not even ingredients are revealed, although you're advised to inform waiters of any likes or dislikes.

Babies and children welcome: high chairs. Booking advisable. Disabled: toilet. Dress: smart casual. **Map 8 F9.**

Mju

The Millennium Knightsbridge, 16-17 Sloane Street, SW1X 9NU (7201 6330/www.millenniumhotels.com). Knightsbridge tube. **Lunch served** noon-2.30pm Mon-Fri. **Dinner served** 6.30-10.30pm Mon-Sat. **Main courses** £18-£26. **Set lunch** £12 2 courses, £15 3 courses. **Set dinner** £34.50 3 courses, £50 tasting menu (£100 incl wine). **Credit** AmEx, DC, JCB, MC, V.

A few years without care and investment has left the first-floor restaurant at this Sloane Street hotel looking as shabby and soulless as an airport lounge. A ground-floor café caters for most residents' appetites at midday, leaving the cavernous upper dining rooms empty save for whichever disparate bunch happens to be attending a conference that day, plus an occasional unsuspecting tourist or two. Even the bosses seem to have given up on Mju; all but the manager looked like agency staff and bore the distinctive hallmark of the bored, unpolished and uninspired, who want to be anywhere but waiting on tables. Even the honcho served a long-opened bottle of Portuguese pinot noir with the words 'I never recommend Portuguese wine because it's all so tannic'. This is such a shame, since Mju's menu is one of the best French-Asian fusions we've come across. Many dishes are outstandingly creative and delicious: our venison with celeriac gateau and bitter chocolate and sharp raspberry sauces being a case in point. Apart from goat's milk panna cotta with lavender and almond emulsion, which sounds like something off a Dulux colour chart, you can look forward to a surprising medley of well-travelled, well-matched and well-cooked ingredients.

Babies and children welcome: high chairs. Disabled: lift; toilet. Restaurant available for hire. **Map 8 F9.**

La Noisette

164 Sloane Street, SW1X 9QB (7750 5000/www.gordonramsay.com). Knightsbridge or Sloane Square tube. **Lunch served** noon-2.30pm Mon-Fri. **Dinner served** 6-11pm Mon-Sat. **Set lunch** £21 3 courses. **Set dinner** £55 3 courses, £65 tasting menu. **Credit** AmEx, MC, V.

If you've been to the beautiful Greenhouse (*see p146*), where Bjorn van der Horst was chef a while back, his present residing place, La Noisette, might come as a shock. An obscure wooden door on Sloane Street and nondescript signage are the only clues at street level as to the restaurant's location; the tiny reception could belong to a dentist. Up the brown carpeted stairs you are led into a room decorated in dull tones of brown and black, clearly intentioned to be retro chic but bypassing the chic detail. Some staff have been seconded from the Greenhouse, including a sommelier of rather severe countenance who tries to sell wine blighted by huge mark-ups. Including service, a single glass here would buy you a bottle elsewhere. What of the food? We know van der Horst can cook brilliantly and a few touches of his genius remain scattered throughout the menu: notably in our favourite foie gras with espresso syrup and

RESTAURANTS

amaretto foam, plus other flashes of insight in a pea and bacon espuma appetiser and a weird but excitingly refreshing dessert of fragrant warm green tea soup, jelly-entombed lychee and granita. However, our main courses were little better than pub food. A fish pie was mostly double cream with a few fish bits and a crazy-eyed crayfish jumping out of the mashed potato, while seven-hour cooked shoulder of Somerset lamb disintegrated into a pile of wobbling fat and connective tissues (from which we picked scant edible meat), surrounded by more fat in the form of herb-infused oil. The ingredients for the entire meal must have cost the kitchen close to a tenner, but the bill to us was £128. We love Bjorn's food, but we don't feel that his partnership with Gordon Ramsay is doing him or us any favours.
Babies and children welcome: high chairs. Booking essential. Disabled: lift; toilet. Restaurant available for hire. **Map 14 F9.**

One-O-One
101 William Street, SW1X 7RN (7290 7101). Knightsbridge tube. **Lunch served** noon-2.30pm, **dinner served** 7-10.30pm daily. **Main courses** £22-£28. **Set lunch** £25 3 courses. **Set dinner** £48 5 courses, £79 tasting menu. **Credit** AmEx, DC, JCB, MC, V.
There have been significant improvements here since our last visit, but One-O-One still isn't exactly packed to the gills – surprising, given its constantly busy locale. Staff have a new-found confidence to match the friendliness of old, and seem to have gained the knack of working as a team. The whole performance is smoother and more relaxing for the diner. The food has always been good. Focusing on fish and shellfish (particularly from the chilly waters of the Barents Sea and Norwegian fjords), menus highlight the provenance of dishes such as red king crab, traditional Breton fish soup with all the trimmings, and wild sea bass baked under an impressively crusty blanket of Guérand sea salt. There are only two meat dishes on the à la carte menu, one being roasted duck with the awesome accompaniments of peach and spring onion fricassee, vanilla mash parmentier and ginger bigarade sauce. Do the chefs want anyone to try it or not? A short but fairly priced lunch menu featured some lovely dishes; grilled scallop had been barely flashed across the griddle but arrived sweet and delicious in a creamy, well-seasoned cappuccino of jerusalem artichokes, ceps and truffle. Although on paper this was dissimilar to a main course of roasted salmon with lemon-chervil nage, the sauces were almost identical, the latter being sweet, creamy and very unlike any nage we've had before. Desserts are light, sound and greatly improved from a year ago.
Babies and children welcome: high chairs. Booking advisable Thur-Sun. Disabled: toilet (in hotel). Dress: smart casual. **Map 8 F9.**

Pétrus
The Berkeley, Wilton Place, SW1X 7RL (7235 1200/www.petrus-restaurant.com). Hyde Park Corner or Knightsbridge tube. **Lunch served** noon-2.30pm Mon-Fri. **Dinner served** 6-10.45pm Mon-Sat. **Set lunch** £30 3 courses. **Set dinner** £65 3 courses, £80 tasting menu. **Credit** AmEx, MC, V.
The most daringly glamorous of all Gordon Ramsay's enterprises, with purple and black walls, lashings of silverware and crystal lights twinkling from every corner, Pétrus is the domain of GR's right-hand man, Marcus Wareing. Of late, dishes on the menu have become simpler, as is the current mode in the restaurant world, with the tricksiest assembly being tuna with spiced pineapple, marinated mooli, cardamom and mint. Starters from the set lunch (still at last year's prices and undeniably fine value) promised much but delivered rather less, with a bland duck confit and chargrilled watermelon salad, and a crab bisque with pretty garnishes that all but sank without trace into the soup. From then on, things picked up nicely. Poached monkfish tail was pale and lovely against a vivid palette of carrots, carrot purée, escabeche and coriander cress – although there was no mention of the powerful orange flavour steering the whole dish, which subsequently came as a surprise. Roasted loin of Tamworth pig was pronounced superb: tender, juicy and full of flavour, accompanied by heart-stoppingly buttery mashed potato, creamy morel sauce and slender wild asparagus spears. Yet it was in the desserts and extra little freebies that the food became glowingly exciting, reinforcing the view that Ramsay keeps close, centralised check on all the savoury dishes in his restaurants, leaving the brigades of perfectly competent staff freedom to express their own talents mostly in the bonus nibbles and afters. A special dessert of the day, apple tarte tatin, was the most gorgeous we've ever tasted: an unbeatable arrangement of crisp, buttery, flaky pastry, truly intense, caramelised apples and plenty of caramel-encrusted, chewy edges to work on, emphasised all the more by super-smooth vanilla ice-cream and clotted cream – the star of an impressive show.
Babies and children welcome: high chairs. Booking essential. Dress: smart; jacket preferred. Separate room for parties, seats 16. Vegetarian menu. **Map 9 G9.**

Marble Arch

★ Rhodes W1 NEW
The Cumberland, Great Cumberland Place, W1A 4RF (7479 3737/www.garyrhodes.co.uk). Marble Arch tube.
Bar **Open/snacks served** noon-11pm Tue-Sat.
Brasserie **Breakfast served** 6.30-10am Mon-Fri; 7-10am Sat, Sun. **Lunch served** noon-2.30pm, **dinner served** 6-10.30pm daily. **Main courses** £12-£22.50.
Restaurant **Lunch served** noon-2.30pm Tue-Fri. **Dinner served** 7-10.30pm Tue-Sat. **Main courses** £22.50. **Set lunch** £28 3 courses. **Set dinner** £45 3 courses.
All **Credit** AmEx, MC, V.
Nearly two years after its planned opening, a fine dining restaurant has joined the Rhodes W1 bar and brasserie. It's the restaurant Gary Rhodes 'always dreamed of' – and boy, is it good. Glamorously decorated by Kelly Hoppen, the room secreted behind a forbidding black wooden door that (if you have the courage to push it open) leads along a darkened cellar-cum-foyer and into a bright, sparkly world of fun for the monied and greedy. Every table has its own Swarovski crystal chandelier; a semi-private dining room with camply decorated antique French chairs is set behind a silky taupe curtain. Food is suitably stunning; while the menu's not quite as flag-waving as one might expect from the man who kick-started the British food renaissance, local, seasonal and traditional ingredients are treated with a light, inventive touch. Service is friendly, but also very formal. Seafood dishes stole the show on our visit. Deep-fried pieces of smoked eel served with horseradish cream; mackerel ravioli with steamed turbot and buttered baby leeks; and 'double oyster ragout' (poached oysters with 'oysters' of dark chicken meat and samphire) outclassed an underseasoned suckling pig ravioli with bramley apple sauce. A predominately French wine list starts at £18 and swiftly moves higher. The brasserie, as you'd expect, is more laid-back; a vast, lobby-like space where you can eat in jeans and T-shirt. And the food, while good, is simpler fare (grilled steaks, seafood pasta, white chocolate cheesecake), though the brasserie name is misleading – prices are restaurant-high.
Babies and children admitted (restaurant); children's portions (brasserie). Booking advisable. Disabled: toilet. Dress: smart casual (restaurant). **Map 9 G6.**

Mayfair

Brian Turner Mayfair
Millennium Hotel Mayfair, 44 Grosvenor Square, W1K 2HP (7596 3444/www.millenniumhotels.com). Bond Street tube.
Bar **Open** 8.30pm-midnight Mon-Fri; 6.30pm-midnight Sat.
Restaurant **Lunch served** 12.30-2.30pm Mon-Fri, Sun. **Dinner served** 6.30-10.30pm daily. **Main courses** £13.50-£42. **Set lunch** £24.50

Interview
JUN TANAKA

Who are you?
Executive chef of **Pearl Bar & Restaurant** (*see p140*).
Eating in London: what's good about it?
London restaurants have led the way in shattering traditional perceptions of particular types of cuisine. There was a time when food wouldn't really vary from one Indian restaurant to the next; now there is so much diversity. The same can be said for Chinese, Spanish and most types of cuisine.
What's bad about it?
London is a tough city for restaurants to survive in, which means that it can seem like restaurants are constantly coming and going. But at least you can be confident that the ones that do make it are generally very good.
Which are your favourite London restaurants?
My favourite Japanese restaurant is **Roka** (*see p197*). I love the decor, it has a fantastic buzz, a beautiful bar and the food is consistently delicious. **Zafferano** (*see p182*) is great for Italian food in warm, rustic surroundings. For sheer gastronomy, it has to be **Pied à Terre** (*see p140*). And when I finish work, I love going to **HK Diner** (*see p72*) with my chef friends.
Who or what has had the biggest impact on London's restaurant scene in the past 25 years?
Terence Conran transformed the industry by putting an emphasis on the design and concept of the restaurant, showing the importance of the overall experience. Marco Pierre White too. He made cooking glamorous and changed people's perception of chefs. And he was one of the first chefs to take over a hotel restaurant – now it's the norm for five-star hotels to install a top chef in their restaurant.
Any hot tips for the coming year?
Everyone is becoming very conscious of environmental issues.

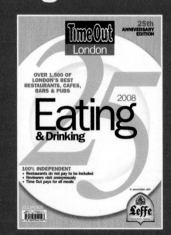

Main courses £13.50-£42. **Set lunch** £24.50 2 courses, £28.50 3 courses.
Both **Credit** AmEx, DC, MC, V.
This large ground-floor restaurant is bright, airy and inoffensively decorated, has a pleasant leafy view through the plane trees of Grosvenor Square (the opposite side to Maze, *see p146*), and together with a seductively lit bar is attached to a suitably glamorous hotel foyer. The wine list is slim but not too alarmingly priced; the daily changing and à la carte menus are similarly aimed at not excluding the average London diner. If, however, you frequent hotel restaurants on a regular basis, you'll find a few annoying devils in the detail. Water glasses are stored somewhere musty and MDF-smelling, so your water will taste the same. Staff need to call a manager over if you ask a question about anything. Spoons are too deep to eat from without slurping noisily; menu descriptions don't always accurately reflect the dish you are given; and you're asked to choose a wine nanoseconds after arriving, well before most people have decided what to eat. Paying £4 for an ordinary coffee without any chocolate nibbly bits on the side is also a bit mean – we like chocolate nibbly bits! But, details aside, Brian Turner's food is much as the man himself is portrayed: affable, upfront, unpretentious – all good things. Where it sometimes misses the mark is in the subtlety department. Casserole of Italian aubergines with poppy seed and garlic sauce and cardamom rice was good, but without sign of poppy seeds or mention of the Indian spices running through the dish: at odds with the Italian description. And pear tarte tatin with blackberry ice-cream was nicely flavoured but overly sweet and had none of the textural satisfaction that characterises ideal tarte tatin. Value is fair, though, and the place is popular with birthdaying family groups and suited business people talking shop over lunch.
Babies and children admitted. Booking advisable. Disabled: toilet (in hotel). Dress: smart casual. Separate room for parties, seats 45. Tables outdoors (5, terrace).
Map 9 G7.

Galvin at Windows

28th floor, The London Hilton, Park Lane, W1K 1BE (7208 4021/www.galvinatwindows.com). Green Park or Hyde Park Corner tube.
Lunch served noon-2.30pm Mon-Fri; noon-2.45pm Sun. **Dinner served** 6-10.45pm Mon-Sat. **Set lunch** £29-£58 3 courses. **Set dinner** £58 3 courses, £75 tasting menu. **Credit** AmEx, DC, MC, V.
Not before time, Windows has stepped out of the gastronomic dark ages and into the limelight with the aid of savvy duo Chris and Jeff Galvin. These brothers have stacks of inside knowledge from London's high-end restaurant scene, with fingers in such tasty pies as the Orrery, the Wolseley and Galvin Bistrot de Luxe on Baker Street. They have given Galvin at Windows a credible menu of relaxed French cuisine far more deserving of the wraparound cityscape views up here on the breezy 28th floor of the Hilton. Gone are the twin dinosaurs of entertainment stage and self-service buffet, replaced by restrained panels of hazy, space-blurring string curtains, crisp linen, acres of ubiquitous dark wood and comfortable leather chairs. Centrally, a section of floor has been raised to allow all to take in the view, not just those seated around the periphery – it's very stylish without trying too hard. The result is that the restaurant is busier than ever (booking is wise), with plenty of families taking advantage of a reasonably priced set lunch menu on the weekend of our visit. The food is also stylish, without overdoing things. Although advertised as French haute cuisine, it is in reality more casual, along the lines of creamy butternut risotto scattered with hazelnuts and rocket, or beautifully braised pork cheeks simply served on buttery mash with a subtly spiced gravy. Puddings, such as blood orange cheesecake or rice pudding with poached rhubarb, are competent and prettily presented.
Babies and children welcome: high chairs. Booking advisable. Disabled: toilet (in hotel). Dress: smart casual. **Map 9 G8.**

SHELF LIFE

Looking for some special chocolates for that special occasion? Try these. Chocolatier/café **William Curley** (*see p312*) is also worth a visit.

L'Artisan du Chocolat

89 Lower Sloane Street, SW1W 8DA (7824 8365/www.artisanduchocolat.com). Sloane Square tube. **Open** 10am-7pm Mon-Sat.
As chosen by prestige chefs including Gordon Ramsay and Heston Blumenthal, this company specialises in inventive flavour combinations and fun, glamorous seasonal gifts.

Paul A Young

33 Camden Passage, N1 8EA (7424 5750/www.payoung.net). Angel tube. **Open** 11am-6pm Wed, Thur, Sat; 11am-7pm Fri; noon-5pm Sun.
You no longer have to visit fine restaurants to enjoy the choc-fuelled output of this highly regarded pastry chef. Expect wonderful brownies and inspired curiosities such as Marmite Guinness ganache.

Melt

59 Ledbury Road, W11 2AA (7727 5030/www.meltchocolates.com). Notting Hill Gate tube. **Open** 9am-6pm Mon-Fri; 10am-6pm Sat, Sun.
Master chocolatier Keith Hurdman has hooked up with celeb chefs including Mark Hix, Skye Gyngell and the River Café owners to produce special-edition chocolates to complement his own carefully produced range.

Montezuma's

51 Brushfield Street, E1 6AA (7539 9208/www.montezumas.co.uk). Liverpool Street tube/rail. **Open** 10am-6pm daily.
The flavours listed on the jars and boxes of this Spitalfields shop may sound crazy – and they are. Try the air-dried mango strips dipped in white chocolate and flavoured with lime and chilli.

Theobroma Cacao

43 Turnham Green Terrace, W4 1RG (8996 0431/www.theobroma-cacao.co.uk). Turnham Green tube. **Open** 9am-6pm Mon-Sat; 9.30am-5.30pm Sun.
Good for novelty gifts (how about a Buddha-shaped chocolate?). The rich dark chocolate sticks – plain, or flavoured with cardamom or chilli – are almost a dessert in themselves.

★ Le Gavroche (100)

43 Upper Brook Street, W1K 7QR (7408 0881/www.le-gavroche.co.uk). Marble Arch tube.
Lunch served noon-2pm Mon-Fri. **Dinner served** 6.30-11pm Mon-Sat. **Main courses** £27-£40. **Minimum** (dinner) £60. **Set lunch** £48 3 courses incl half bottle of wine, mineral water, coffee. **Set dinner** £95 tasting menu (£150 incl wine). **Credit** AmEx, DC, JCB, MC, V.
Le Gavroche is so special (and pricey, let's be honest) that, unlike many restaurants in this section, it's not awash with people having business lunches. Some are, but there are usually as many women dining as men, and they might be mothers and daughters celebrating a birthday or friends catching up. So the talk isn't just about work, which completely changes the atmosphere and jollies things along enormously. The second factor is the dizzying quantity of front-of-house staff and the pace at which they work. Many restaurants achieve good service, but here it's amazing; every customer's moves are predicted and catered for in a fabulously mannerly fashion. Such professionalism is only achieved through the driving force of the business being constantly on hand; we've yet to visit and not see wonder-chef Michel Roux Jr and manager Silvano hard at work. Food is incredibly special too: complex, richly rewarding, outstandingly fresh and cooked to split-second perfection. The three-course set lunch at £48 with water, wine, coffee and petits fours is a must-have experience if you haven't been here before. The à la carte dishes are a little larger, a little more luxurious, perhaps, and contain a few more ingredients. From the set lunch, lobster salad tartlets and hot, deliciously crunchy turbot goujons with cool caper sauce and micro salad were paraded as canapés. Starters included classic fish soup with beautiful, traditional garnishes served from cherished Le Gavroche silverware, and seasonal asparagus with intensely smoky bacon lardons and fresh green herb sauce. Main courses ranged from classic braised guinea fowl to salt marsh lamb or a chunky wedge of salmon trout with pea purée, tomato coulis and the most perfect, handmade tagliatelle glossed with butter. What's not to love?
Children admitted. Booking essential. Dress: jacket; no jeans or trainers. Restaurant available for hire. **Map 9 G7.**

Gordon Ramsay at Claridge's

Claridge's, 55 Brook Street, W1K 4HR (7499 0099/www.gordonramsay.com). Bond Street tube.
Lunch served noon-2.45pm Mon-Fri; noon-3pm Sat, Sun. **Dinner served** 5.45-11pm Mon-Sat; 6-11pm Sun. **Set lunch** £30 3 courses. **Set dinner** £65 3 courses, £75 6 courses. **Credit** AmEx, DC, JCB, MC, V.
This plush and peachy dining room is a soft, feminine contrast to the reflective, art deco and marble crispness found in the public areas of Claridge's: a hotel that has remained an icon of the London hospitality industry since 1898. Staggeringly beautiful and opulent flower displays and rose petal-strewn tables laid for tea set the tone. Diners – well-heeled ladies who lunch, betrothed couples, business folk and families – continue past all this and into the main restaurant, possibly Gordon Ramsay's most relaxed venue in the capital. In the Ramsay manner to which we have become accustomed, expect an abundance of smartly uniformed staff, who in this instance looked the part more convincingly than they played it (our three-course meal took nearly three hours to serve). Take heed of the little tricks they have for increasing your spend and cutting their costs. You are asked to order dessert at the same time as starter and main course, for example, which means that a two-course meal isn't really an option; and the set lunch has fewer complimentary frills and nibbles attached. Nevertheless, food will be of the highest quality from start to finish, and you'll not begrudge a penny spent on the likes of chilled celery consommé poured over crab meat and a savoury granita, which melted into a delicious kind of grown-up slush puppy; or fat, fresh pea tortellini with mint sauce and tender shreds of slow-cooked pork knuckle. Fanciful presentation and real culinary skill also shone through mains of baby spring chicken roasted golden and served with tender young vegetables, and fantastic lemon sole with sweet-tart capers, tenderstem broccoli and lemon butter sauce.
Babies and children welcome: high chairs. Booking essential. Disabled: toilet. Dress: smart; jacket preferred; no jeans or trainers. Separate rooms for parties, seating 6, 10, 12 and 24.
Map 9 H6.

★ Greenhouse (100)

27A Hay's Mews, W1J 5NY (7499 3331/ www.greenhouserestaurant.co.uk). Green Park tube. **Lunch served** noon-2.30pm Mon-Fri. **Dinner served** 6.45-11pm Mon-Sat. **Set lunch** £25 2 courses, £29 3 courses. **Set meal** £60 3 courses, £65-£75 tasting menu. **Credit** AmEx, DC, MC, V.

Tucked at the end of a Mayfair mews, the Greenhouse is surrounded by one-way streets and restricted parking zones. Your best bet is to amble here from a few streets away and enjoy the select surroundings en route. A lush garden beckons you into the smart dining room. From the word go, staff exude welcome and expertise. With chef Antonin Bonnet you are also in safe hands, so relax and relish a perfectly prepared and served meal with nothing to challenge you unduly. The food is instantly likeable, and service is unhampered by the uncomfortable frills and flounces that some posh places lay on with a trowel. Culinary frills are included, of course, by way of seductive little appetisers, wonderful bread rolls, the finest olives (steeped in a hint of vanilla, just to make sure you're awake), and too-good petits fours to end. In between you'll be treated to a seasonal menu packed with lovely fresh vegetables and fruit, along with more unusual main course ingredients such as eel, sea bream sashimi and grade '00000' Cadoret oysters (of exceptional pedigree). Prices are high, as you might expect. Water and coffee are both a fiver plus service, but the set lunch is several pounds less than last year and is excellent value. Ours included delicately stuffed baby turnips with organic egg 'mimosa' and kalamata olives, and a sublime warm salad of mangetout and pea shoots with braised pork shank. Main courses of seared mackerel and Limousin veal were also faultless, the latter embellished with roasted cashews and subtle spicing. The wine list is notable too, and includes some 40 by-the-glass options. Exclusive, delicious and worth a far greater detour than is necessary.

Babies and children admitted. Booking essential. Dress: smart casual. Separate room for parties, seats 10. **Map 9 H7**.

The Grill

Brown's Hotel, 33-34 Albemarle Street, W1S 4BP (7493 6020/www.roccofortehotels.com). Green Park tube. **Lunch served** 12.30-2.30pm daily. **Tea served** 3-6pm Mon-Fri; 2-6pm Sat, Sun. **Dinner served** 6-10.30pm Mon-Sat; 7-10.30pm Sun. **Main courses** £16.50-£28.95. **Set meal** (lunch, 6-7pm Mon-Sat) £25 2 courses, £30 3 courses. **Set tea** £32.50 (£41 incl glass of champagne). **Credit** AmEx, DC, MC, V.

After a less than glowing performance on our last visit, it's a pleasure (and a bit of a surprise) to report that the Grill has pulled up its socks astoundingly this year. The gracious room with lofty Georgian proportions, capacious stone fireplace and original honeycombed ceilings (buffed to a sheen by recent big money) is now home to a vintage London dining experience. In fact, the beautiful moss-green decor, tall windows and fine oak panelling (wrapped around scores of crisply suited and nicely aging businessmen) reminds us of the Connaught before Gordon Ramsay and the tourists moved in. As for the food, again we witnessed a stunning transformation from the steakhouse mediocrity of last year. Roasted meat is still very much in favour, with two choices for each day of the week wheeled over and carved at table. In addition there's a huge à la carte menu where the quality is now top-notch: every morsel hot, delicious and tender, and served with an aplomb more appropriate to the glamorous surroundings. The cooking is traditional to the core. Expect saddle of lamb; roast sirloin or rib of beef with yorkshire pudding; pan-fried skate with capers; treacle tart with banana ice-cream; floating island with proper custard; or the very occasional wild departure into more fashionable territory, like Welsh goat's cheese panna cotta with beetroot and watercress. The set lunch is excellent value, but be sure to book since half of Piccadilly and Bond Street will be joining you.

Booking advisable. Children over 12 years admitted (lunch). Disabled: toilet (in hotel). **Map 9 J7**.

★ Maze (100)

13-15 Grosvenor Square, W1K 6JP (7107 0000/ www.gordonramsay.com). Bond Street tube.
Bar **Open** noon-5pm, 6pm-midnight daily.
Restaurant **Tapas** £3.50-£6. **Main courses** £16.50-£29.50.
Both **Lunch served** noon-2.30pm, **dinner served** 6-11pm daily. **Credit** AmEx, DC, MC, V.

Sitting lazily on a sunny afternoon, martini in hand, surrounded by grown-up buff leather, zebrano wood and lustrous glass panels, gazing out across Grosvenor Square's soft green canopy of plane trees – you might conclude that Maze enjoys one of London's loveliest locations. The proximity of the US Embassy ensures a constant flow of babbling office folk along with their food-savvy visitors, all eager to catch a glimpse of Britain's most talkative chef. Yet though the name on the door is Ramsay's, the kitchen belongs to Jason Atherton: a man with a similar god complex and eye for perfection. We were given some distinctly rancid butter, but chef relayed word back to us that it was supposed to taste so. Otherwise, we had difficulty faulting much from Maze's lengthy menu of tapas-sized dishes. Our small but perfectly formed portions of artichoke velouté with cep brioche, and crisp-skinned bass with lobster risotto and lemongrass glaze were spellbindingly sumptuous. So too was a combination of Berkshire pork loin and belly, enhanced by an apple and cardamom purée and a bittersweet jasmine reduction. Being free to order as much or as little of what you fancy is a real treat, since you can dine at lunchtime and still have energy to face the rest of the working (or shopping) day. Just one small thing: if the butter is unpasteurised, why wasn't the pregnant lady on the next table told?

Babies and children welcome: high chairs. Booking advisable. Disabled: toilet. Separate room for parties, seats 10. **Map 9 G6**.

★ Sketch: The Lecture Room

9 Conduit Street, W1S 2XZ (0870 777 4488/ www.sketch.uk.com). Oxford Circus tube. **Lunch served** noon-2.30pm Tue-Fri. **Dinner served** 7-10.30pm Tue-Sat. **Main courses** £45-£59. **Set lunch** (Tue-Fri) £30 2 courses; £35 3 courses. **Set dinner** £80-£140 3 courses. **Credit** AmEx, DC, MC, V.

Apologies if you can't relate to this, but a trip to Sketch is like the rush of joy you might experience in a fantastic shoe shop or jeweller's – an expensive one that's unashamedly fun and ridiculously pretty. The media headlines that accompanied the opening in 2002 of this 18th-century 'house' of many facets and eateries (once owned by Christian Dior) judged the place to be outrageously priced and too pretentious by half. But the past few years have softened the edginess, leaving a warmly inviting den of glamour with just a touch of madness in the spice-bright decor and innovative menus. Any waywardness is tempered by the impeccably mannered staff and prices that tend to go downwards if they move at all. A new 'gourmet rapide' lunch can be served in an hour. On our visit, it featured a combination of four starters (you get all four), a choice of two main courses and three desserts (again, you get all three). Portions are quite dinky, but bread is good and plentiful. Wine can confidently be chosen, courtesy of a helpful collaboration between sommelier Frederic Brugues and wine guru Andrew Jefford. Of the starters, we loved the sweet earthy contrast of beetroot purée against the intense sea-saltiness of smoked haddock and shavings of dried white tuna. Main-course roasted flank of beef was bravely rare, chewy and primordial – but lovely, especially when matched against mashed potato enriched with olives, olive oil and confit duck leg. Desserts are amazing and also available to take away from the Parlour downstairs. Many Japanese eat here, including apprentice pastry chefs from London's best cookery schools; Asian influences creep in to complement the light uplifting dishes. A spellbinding performance.

Babies and children admitted. Booking essential. Dress: smart casual. Restaurant available for hire. **Map 9 J6**.

★ The Square

6-10 Bruton Street, W1J 6PU (7495 7100/ www.squarerestaurant.com). Bond Street or Green Park tube. **Lunch served** noon-2.45pm Mon-Fri. **Dinner served** 6.30-10.45pm Mon-Sat; 6.30-9.45pm Sun. **Set lunch** £25 2 courses, £30 3 courses. **Set dinner** £65 3 courses, £80 tasting menu. **Credit** AmEx, DC, JCB, MC, V.

It's difficult to imagine what else you could want from a super-cool restaurant beyond what the Square already dishes up. A nicer looking building from outside, perhaps? A few more seats in the bar, maybe? Nothing too important, anyway. Discerning food lovers come here for Phil Howard's consummate cooking plus an inspiring wine list, excellent service and comfortable, stylishly metropolitan surroundings. The carte and tasting menus are where the food gets intensely serious (in a good way), but the modestly priced set lunch is still difficult to beat for quality, and the experience is pleasantly devoid of tedious celebrity cheffing and the annoying reservation procedures that go with it. Clean-flavoured, dill-infused risotto was perfect for a sunny day: nuttily al dente, packed with crisp asparagus and succulent salmon flakes, hidden under a cheeky asparagus foam and trimmed with a soft boiled gull's egg. Following on from this – on the set lunch menu there are just two starters, two mains courses and two desserts to choose from, plus cheese for a supplementary fiver – came new-season English lamb: pink, sliced and tasty in light jus with a fresh pea and broad bean cannelloni, another foamy sauce and refreshing little braised spring onion bulbs. The wine was lovely (an unusual, richly perfumed Austrian grüner veltliner) and laudably available by the glass. Staff were lovely too, treading that precarious line between attentiveness and interference. Desserts looked so good we could hardly bear to eat them; they are lessons in the art of pastry making and might include delicious mysteries such as truffled hydromel jelly and smoked chocolate.

Babies and children admitted. Booking advisable. Disabled: toilet. Dress: smart. Restaurant available for hire. Separate room for parties, seats 18. **Map 9 H7**.

★ Theo Randall at the InterContinental NEW

1 Hamilton Place, Park Lane, W1J 7QY (7409 3131/www.theorandall.com). Hyde Park Corner tube. **Lunch served** noon-3pm Mon-Fri; noon-3.30pm Sun. **Dinner served** 6-11pm Mon-Sat. **Main courses** £20-£28. **Set meal** (lunch, 6-7pm Mon-Fri) £18 2 courses, £23 3 courses; (Sun) £23 2 courses, £28 3 courses. **Credit** AmEx, DC, MC, V.

After nearly two years, the InterContinental is emerging in phases from a £60 million refit. Gone is the smoked glass and gilded naffness of the reception, supplanted by intimate areas of sweeping contemporary furniture and palm tree-sized flower displays far more befitting a behemoth hotel on Park Lane in 2008. Most astounding is the blinding transformation of the ground-floor restaurant, which as Le Soufflé featured rag-rolled turquoise walls. The decorators moved in, moved everything else out and stamped a totally chic new signature on the place. Sleek floorboards and wall panels run like melted chocolate into ice-green glass and snazzy backlit silhouettes. The result is a super-cool look that's a million years (or is that pounds?) away from the previous bolt-on hotel facility. Chef Theo Randall comes fresh from a food recce of Italy and 15 years at the River Café, where he was head chef and a major shareholder. In the celebrity smokescreen surrounding that restaurant you probably missed his name, but make note of it now. Randall aims to provide authentic Italian food in a relaxed yet luxury-tinged environment, and it seems to be working. Waiting staff hover ideally on the cusp of smartness and friendliness. Menus take seasonal and regional influence from Italy, concentrating on deep flavours, wood-roasted, slow-cooked meats and vegetables as primary elements. For instance, baby wood-roasted beetroots, celeriac and jerusalem artichokes played

Theo Randall at the InterContinental

a major role alongside sizzling, juicy lamb rack and herb salsa. Panna cotta was divine: innocently pale, tremblingly set, headily infused with vanilla and a whisper of lemon liqueur, served with champagne rhubarb. Charred bruschetta doused in single-estate olive oil, an Italianate wine list, luscious nibbles, chocolates and Illy coffee – all are ace. There is no earthly reason not to come here.
Babies and children welcome: high chairs. Booking advisable. Disabled: lift; toilet. Separate room for parties, seats 24. **Map 9 G8**.

Piccadilly

The Ritz

150 Piccadilly, W1J 9BR (7493 8181/ www.theritzhotel.co.uk). Green Park tube.
Bar **Open** 11.30am-11pm Mon-Sat; noon-10.30pm Sun.
Restaurant **Breakfast served** 7-10.30am Mon-Sat; 8-10.30am Sun. **Lunch served** 12.30-2.30pm daily. **Tea served** (reserved sittings) 11.30am, 1.30pm, 3.30pm, 5.30pm, 7.30pm daily.
Dinner served 6-10.30pm Mon-Sat; 7-10pm Sun. **Main courses** £25-£40. **Set lunch** £37 3 courses. **Set tea** £35. **Set dinner** (6-7pm, 10-10.30pm) £45 3 courses; (Mon-Thur) £65 4 courses; (Fri, Sat) £80 4 courses.
Both **Credit** AmEx, MC, V.
To get you in the mood for a bite to eat here, drop into the wildly outré Rivoli Bar with its faux leopard-skin chairs, seashell scalloped ceiling and gilded, mirrored, Lalique-embellished, orchid-strewn everything else. A cocktail or glass of bubbly at £18 will also give you a taste of what's to come, for a meal at the Ritz is really only comfortable for the comfortably well-off, and men who still wear red socks and women who say 'good-oh!' on a frequent basis. Food under executive chef John Williams has come a long way over the past few years and the lighter touch is far more befitting this century than the previous one – but the extraordinary prices are no joke for anyone on an average salary. No doubt that's the way regulars and the management prefer things to be, with nary a ripple on their gilded façade. 'Definitely, definitely no trainers or jeans,' said the man taking the bookings. Expect high-quality, attractively presented and extravagant dishes served with bling (except that the silver is very real and very antique), such as seared scallops with mooli and crab spring roll brought together with a hint of crystallised ginger, or main-course classics such as hand-carved smoked salmon and trimmings, or boiled brisket and tongue with baby spring vegetables and chive butter sauce. We asked if we could take our petits fours home with us and the manager was only too happy to oblige – as all the staff are. But the delicate little pastries came back to us bouncing around in a box big enough to stow away a wardrobe, which pretty much sums up the Ritz: it's big on appearances.
Babies and children welcome: children's menu; high chairs. Disabled: toilet. Booking advisable restaurant; essential afternoon tea. Dress: jacket and tie; no jeans or trainers. Entertainment: dinner dance Fri, Sat (restaurant); pianist daily. Separate rooms for parties, seating 22 and 55. Tables outdoors (8, terrace).
Map 9 J7.

St James's

L'Oranger

5 St James's Street, SW1A 1EF (7839 3774/ www.loranger.co.uk). Green Park tube. **Lunch served** noon-2.30pm Mon-Fri. **Dinner served** 6.30-10.30pm Mon-Sat. **Main courses** £24-£34. **Set lunch** £27 2 courses, £32 3 courses.
Set dinner £45 3 courses, £75 tasting menu.
Credit AmEx, DC, MC, V.
If you like a slice of vintage chic with your dinner, but can't quite picture yourself in the gilded splendour of the Ritz or similar ballroom-cum-restaurants, L'Oranger could be what you're looking for. Oozing intimate charm, it's tucked away at the end of posh St James's Street. Airs of modernism are introduced by bold jewel-coloured carpets and geometric canvases on the walls, plus a pretty atrium flooding the room with light – this is a lovely space in which to dine. There's room for minor improvements, though, as the premises are looking well worn this year. And though staff are plentiful, they don't always work seamlessly together. Food, from a French menu care of chef Laurent Michel, also didn't score on all fronts. A starter of salmon rillettes from the set lunch menu – not so different from the à la carte and significantly less costly – was overly rich and lazily served in a slack pile topped with greasy fried 'toast' and creamy sauce that lacked the zing to cut through the overt fishiness. In comparison, a main of roasted monkfish (mostly fried in butter rather than roasted) was delicious, tender, hot and bathed in oodles of sunny, roughly chopped herbs and presented with a tasty vegetable tian: roundels of slowly baked onion, courgette and cherry tomato with a dusting of garlicky provençale breadcrumbs. Classic dishes, all of them, described in crisply correct French ahead of the English translation, cooked and served by French men and women. Desserts shine with professionalism, and could include summery strawberry soup with passionfruit granita, or breton shortbread with roasted apples, ginger crème anglaise (there had to be a nod to England somewhere) and apple liquor sorbet. The wine list's a corker too.
Children over 7 years admitted. Booking essential. Dress: smart casual; no trainers. Separate room for parties, seats 32. Tables outdoors (6, courtyard). **Map 9 J8**.

South Kensington

★ Tom Aikens

43 Elystan Street, SW3 3NT (7584 2003/ www.tomaikens.co.uk). South Kensington tube.
Lunch served noon-2.30pm, **dinner served** 6.45-11pm Mon-Fri. **Set lunch** £29 3 courses.
Set meal £65 3 courses, £80-£100 tasting menu.
Credit AmEx, JCB, MC, V.
Things have taken on a lighter tone at Tom Aikens since our last review. The dining room's paler walls and brighter lights have brought an end to the semi-dark fumbling previously necessary in the evening. Staff too have lightened up and are far more friendly and responsive. There's still a nasty £55 charge per person for late cancellations, but at least they tell you about it with a cheerier tone. Food is incredibly refined: beautiful to eat and to look at. It is served on a playful array of mismatched tableware, which doubles as virtually the only decoration in a minimalist room set. Dozens of canapés emerging from the kitchen (on stalks, in scoops and shot glasses wrapped in burr walnut) looked like little enchanted forests on each table and tasted wonderful, as did an earthy pumpkin and rosemary appetiser. The cooking was without exception superb. Both our main courses – sea bass with small parsley gnocchi and caramelised celeriac; and dover sole with melting pork belly and ham hock ravioli – came with a glittering mix of vegetables, herbs, salad shoots, sauces, reductions and foams. In fact, Tom 'The Foam' Aikens rather likes a bit of fluff with everything. Surprisingly, though, these skilfully add to, rather than subtract from, each dish. Fun yet fabulous desserts and petits fours, served in more witty containers (sweet jars, glasses and test tubes) are the icing on the cake.
Children over 7 years admitted. Booking essential dinner. Disabled: toilet. Dress: smart.
Map 14 E11.

South West

Chelsea

Aubergine

11 Park Walk, SW10 0AJ (7352 3449/ www.auberginerestaurant.co.uk). Bus 14, 345, 414. **Lunch served** noon-2.15pm Mon-Fri. **Dinner served** 7-11pm Mon-Sat. **Set lunch** £34 3 courses incl half bottle of wine, mineral water, coffee. **Set dinner** £64 3 courses, £77 tasting menu (£130 incl wine). **Credit** AmEx, DC, JCB, MC, V.
Aubergine is a pretty restaurant, intimate without feeling cramped, welcoming by day, soothing and flatteringly low-lit by night. It's a firm hit with Chelsea locals and you'll need to book at popular times, especially since lunch remains one of the best-value haute cuisine deals in London. William Drabble has headed the kitchen for ten years and his sound grasp of classic French cooking is blended with tenacious sourcing of fine British ingredients. Offal is a passion. Expect cooking that is seasonal, varied and skilfully executed, but also eschews passing fads in favour of a studied and occasionally challenging style. This is food for food-lovers rather than restaurant-goers. Our meal started deliciously with a plate of tender snails in red wine, heartily garnished with frizzled bacon, truffle dust and boudin blanc. Different but equally lovely were sweet scallops on a tangy pool of gingered apple sauce. Though a main course fillet of dry aged beef with celeriac purée, seared foie gras and Madeira jus was perfect, things went badly wrong with our other choice, advertised as roast saddle and confit leg of rabbit with various trimmings. What actually arrived, after a good half an hour's wait, was something that could easily have been saddle of a somewhat tame rabbit – on pan-fried calf's liver. When we questioned this we were told that the rabbit legs hadn't been delivered that day. An apology was forthcoming, and a glass of dessert wine later on, but that's not enough. Did the staff simply serve the wrong meal and hope we wouldn't know the difference between rabbit legs and calf's liver? We weren't impressed. Service was on the panicky side too. New restaurant manager, Jean Kessler, has his work cut out.
Children over 5 years admitted. Booking advisable; essential weekends. Dress: smart casual.
Map 14 D12.

Gordon Ramsay

68 Royal Hospital Road, SW3 4HP (7352 4441/ www.gordonramsay.com). Sloane Square tube.
Lunch served noon-2pm, **dinner served** 6.30-11pm Mon-Fri. **Set lunch** £40 3 courses.
Set meal £85 3 courses, £110 tasting menu.
Credit AmEx, DC, JCB, MC, V.
Post-makeover, Gordon Ramsay's original restaurant is looking spick, span and modern with milky stretches of opalescent wall, mirrored corners, silk blinds and groovy sputnik lights, the edges softened and soundproofed with smart geometric carpet. A small but comfortable lounge area has at last replaced the diminutive perches to which you were made to 'retire' when tables were turned. Maybe table-turning is a lesser problem now that bookings are taken two months ahead instead of just one. In fact, there were a few empty tables: a sight impossible to imagine in the past. Booking is still a lengthy telephonic performance followed by an intimidating email on which to sign your life away. There's a truly staggering charge of £150 per person for no-shows (GR innocently calls this new form a 'booking confirmation', but make no mistake, it's a written contract between you and the restaurant). Lunch, à la carte, prestige and vegetarian menus all follow typical Ramsay form with a parade of perfectly sculpted proteins garnished with daisy-fresh, brightly coloured vegetables that to some extent match the seasons. Baby violet artichokes were flavour of the month and turned up in four or five dishes, including delectable pan-bronzed, line-caught sea bass. Cornish lamb was beautifully tender and beguilingly good-looking; ditto the precise oblong of chicken and foie gras terrine with port reduction. Desserts are equally winsome: toffee soufflé delightfully marrying banana ice-cream. Yet everything except appetisers and petits fours seems too careful, too prescriptive, too tame, as if all the ingredients have been somehow moulded into a corporate template. For the money (the three-course set meal costs £15 more than last year, and the four-course £20 more) we want thrills as well as shipshape discipline.
Booking essential. Children admitted. Dress: smart; jacket preferred; no jeans or trainers.
Map 14 F12.

Indian

We're very proud of London's South Asian restaurants. They are not only superior to the best we've visited in New York, Dubai and Singapore, but they also compare favourably with the many we've tried in India, Pakistan, Bangladesh and Sri Lanka. Part of the reason is that, for generations, 'good Indian food' has meant the rich, meaty Moghul-court cookery of the north. But in London, South Asian chefs – mostly Indian chefs, it must be said – are breaking away from the dishes of the international hotels and going back to their roots, introducing home-style regional Indian dishes to a new audience. They are also being more experimental, learning from European and other traditions about contemporary dish presentation, and creating health-conscious recipes using less ghee and other saturated fats. This new style of 'Modern Indian' food is demonstrated most successfully at restaurants such as **Amaya**, **Benares**, **Cinnamon Club**, **Moti Mahal**, **Rasoi Vineet Bhatia** and **Veeraswamy**, to name just a few.

All the above are top-notch, special-occasion venues, with correspondingly high prices. But you can eat out very well on a low budget; London is still teeming with good, affordable Indian restaurants. For the best, you might have to travel to Tooting, Wembley, Southall or Whitechapel, though there are outstanding examples even in the heart of London; the growing **Masala Zone** chain hits the spot for a fraction of the price charged by its more celebrated peers.

Like Nepali cooking, Bangladeshi cuisine has been conspicuous by its absence from London – extraordinary when you consider that most of London's 'Indian' restaurants are, in fact, run by Bangladeshis. But we're pleased to report the glimmer of a renaissance in Brick Lane, where, among the formula curry houses, you can find a few caffs offering proper Bangladeshi dishes. You need to know where to look, mind. The more modest places are all outshone by **Kolapata**, which is the ambassador for Bangladeshi food that we've all been waiting for.

Central

Covent Garden

Mela

152-156 Shaftesbury Avenue, WC2H 8HL (7836 8635/www.melarestaurant.co.uk). Leicester Square tube. **Meals served** noon-11.30pm Mon-Thur; noon-11.45pm Fri; 1.30-11.45pm Sat; noon-10.30pm Sun. **Main courses** £8.95-£14.95. **Set lunch** £2.95-£5.95 1 course. **Set dinner** (vegetarian) £14.98 (non-vegetarian) £18.47 (both minimum 2 people). **Set meal** (5.30-7pm, 10-11pm) £10.95 3 courses. **Credit** AmEx, MC, V.
Pan-Indian

Over the past year, Mela has found its niche and earned an enviable reputation for delivering authentic dishes at fair prices. The cream-themed interior is informal and inviting, vibrant murals adding colour while skewer-wielding chefs provide drama in a glass-fronted mini-kitchen. It's a popular spot, drawing office groups and theatre-goers, as well as nostalgic Indians yearning for a taste of home. Starters of plump mussels, steamed in a light tomato broth boosted by lemongrass and garlic, made a splendid beginning to the meal; portions are large and one helping will suffice for two people. Raj kachori (a wafer-thin hollow pastry globe crammed with chickpeas, yoghurt, mint relish, and tamarind chutney) provided a tantalising medley of sweet and tangy notes. Satiated by starters, we found main courses hard work – a shame because burrah kebab (chunky lamb pieces, steeped in chilli and garlic yoghurt, and cooked over charcoal) was succulent and deliciously smoky. Only prawn curry was disappointing, cloaked in a bland soupy tomato sauce. Service was swift and attentive: a definite improvement on previous visits.
Babies and children welcome: children's menu; high chairs. Booking advisable. Restaurant available for hire. Separate room for parties, seats 40. Takeaway service. Vegetarian menu. **Map 18 K6.**

★ Moti Mahal

45 Great Queen Street, WC2B 5AA (7240 9329/www.motimahal-uk.com). Covent Garden or Holborn tube. **Lunch served** noon-3pm, **dinner served** 5.30-11.30pm Mon-Sat. **Main courses** £14-£23.50. **Set lunch** £15 2 courses incl glass of wine. **Credit** AmEx, MC, V. Modern Indian

Moti Mahal ('Pearl Palace') is a branch of a long-established chain in India, but its London incarnation is quite unlike the original. This restaurant is at the cutting edge of contemporary Indian food. The canapés and petits fours mirror European haute cuisine, but the Indian flavours still ring true. Lotus seeds are often fried and used in Punjabi dishes; the speckled white seeds resemble popcorn, but here they are cooked with baby wild mushrooms and spinach to create a vegetarian main course resembling palak paneer. The dum pukht technique (slow-cooked in a sealed pot) has been all the raj in smart Indian restaurants for more than a decade, but this is the first time we've seen rabbit well and truly pukht (slow-cooked with morels and mint); the pink meat is served on the bone, and the creamy sauce is a delight. Expensive and unusual ingredients are strewn across the menu like rose petals at a Punjabi wedding: shiitake mushrooms, scallops, lobster, guinea fowl. White poppy seeds are usually used in Indian cooking to thicken and enrich masalas, but here they add gentle aroma to nan breads: one of many brilliant details. In contrast to the elaborate cooking, the dining room is white and simple. Service is solicitous and professional.
Babies and children welcome: children's portions; high chairs. Booking advisable dinner. Disabled: lift; toilet. Dress: smart casual. Restaurant available for hire. Vegetarian menu. **Map 18 E3.**

Sitaaray NEW

167 Drury Lane, WC2B 5PG (7269 6422/www.sitaaray.com). Covent Garden or Holborn tube. **Lunch served** noon-3pm, **dinner served** 5.30-11pm Mon-Sat. **Set lunch** £8 2 courses. **Set dinner** £18 buffet. **Credit** MC, V.
Pan-Indian

Autographed photos of Bollywood sex bombs and musclemen smile down from the walls of this dazzling new restaurant. A blaring flat-screen shows dance sequences. Sharing premises with the New London Theatre, Sitaaray ('Stars') is dedicated to Hindi cinema and to the chargrilled cuisine of the north-west frontier. The memorabilia spewed all over the interior is fun to gawk at, but it's the food that stars. The all-you-can-eat set price dinner allows a choice of kebabs accompanied by three well-executed dishes: khadai chicken (saucy boneless pieces cooked in an old-fashioned iron wok); vegetable miloni (courgettes, carrots and mushrooms sunk in spinach); and dal makhani (lentils at their most decadent). Ample portions of nan, raita, salad and popadoms top this off. Seafood lovers should try the malabar crab cakes (listed under 'extras to order'): delectable, but 'mirchi' (chilli-hot). The lunch menu includes South Indian idlis and dosais, as well as kebabs. Sitaaray has reincarnated the galouti kebab into a

BEST INDIAN

For vegetarian delights
Meat-free treats at **Dadima** (*see p173*), **Ram's** (*see p169*), **Rasa** (*see p166*), **Sagar** (*see p158*) and **Sanghamam** (*see p174*).

For cutting-edge creativity
Marvel at the Modern Indian trailblazing of **Amaya** (*see p151*), **Benares** (*see p151*), **Cinnamon Club** (*see p158*) and **Moti Mahal** (*see left*).

For a subcontinental grand tour
Sample the best of four countries at Gujarati **Dadima** (*see p173*), Punjabi **Papaji's Lounge** (*see p172*), Bangladeshi **Kolapata** (*see p166*), Goan **Ma Goa** (*see p161*), Pakistani **Nauroz** (*see p169*), Keralite **Rasa Samudra** (*see p151*) and Sri Lankan **Sekara** (*see p157*).

Radha Krishna Bhavan. See p163.

vegetarian's dream. This traditionally mutton-based mince is here made of mushrooms and laced with nutmeg. The friendly waiters tried to tempt us with kulfi and ice-cream for dessert, but we were full and content.
Babies and children admitted. Disabled: toilet. Takeaway service. **Map 18 E3.**

Fitzrovia

Rasa Samudra

5 Charlotte Street, W1T 1RE (7637 0222/ www.rasarestaurants.com). Goodge Street tube. **Lunch served** noon-3pm Mon-Sat. **Dinner served** 6-10.45pm daily. **Main courses** £6.25-£12.95. **Set meal** (vegetarian) £22.50, (seafood) £30. **Credit** AmEx, JCB, MC, V. South Indian

The flagship restaurant of a seven-strong chain (that includes Rasa, *see p166*), pink-fronted Rasa Samudra is famed for its authentic Keralite seafood dishes and is frequented by the West End's movers and shakers. Decor is homely: silk sari hangings, traditional wood carvings and religious artefacts. For a lighter, more modern vibe, head upstairs to the first floor. We began with crisp popadom-like snacks and a beguiling set of own-made pickles; perky lemony prawns is our current favourite. A first course of stir-fried prawns and tilapia strips honed the appetite with green chillies, golden-fried onions and a shower of curry leaves. An equally good prawn and green mango curry provided a soothing contrast, with a coconut milk-based sauce flecked through with sweet mango shreds. Sadly, varatha meen masala (fried king fish fillets doused in tomato masala) was let down by overcooked, leathery fish. Crab varuthathu (flash-fried crab pieces whooshed around a karahi with slit chillies, curry leaves and heaps of fried onions) was divine – ditch the cutlery for this one. Charming service tempers any culinary shortfalls. Despite occasional glitches, the cooking remains true to its Keralite roots.
Babies and children welcome. Booking advisable. Separate rooms for parties, seating 12, 15 and 25. Takeaway service. Vegetarian menu.
Map 9 J5.
For branches see index.

Knightsbridge

★ Amaya (100)

19 Motcomb Street, Halkin Arcade, SW1X 8JT (7823 1166/www.realindianfood.com). Knightsbridge tube. **Lunch served** 12.30-2.15pm Mon-Sat; 12.45-2.30pm Sun. **Dinner served** 6.30-11.15pm Mon-Sat; 6.30-10.15pm Sun. **Main courses** £8.50-£25. **Set lunch** £25. **Set dinner** £37.50 tasting menu. **Credit** AmEx, DC, JCB, MC, V. Modern Indian

Sleekly appointed, with striking terracotta statues, sparkly chandeliers, and darkly seductive decor, Amaya attracts a mix of expense-accounters, curious tourists and couples out on a special date. Watch chefs in action behind the open kitchen counter as they draw kebabs from clay ovens, glide sizzling patties across skillets, and spear meat on to skewers. The menu is flamboyant, offering a dressy Indian spin to the tapas formula. Alongside kebabs are soothing salads, vegetable grills, curries and excellent birianis – all created for sharing. Green mango and papaya ribbons, heaped into crisp lettuce cups, scored points for simplicity and clean-cut fruity flavours. The dori kebab (pounded lamb, trussed around a skewer, and cooked over coals) was de-threaded at the table with aplomb. Delicately scented with cardamom and mace, it had a velvety texture that marked it out as an authentic rendition of a dish from a maharajah's Lucknow kitchen. Also notable were some meltingly soft griddle cakes made from watercress and filled with chopped figs; and lightly seared broccoli florets, cloaked in a deliciously tart yoghurt and tamarind sauce. Enjoy the theatre of the open kitchen – unless you're spooning and romancing, when a more discreet table might be a better bet.
Babies and children admitted (until 8pm). Booking advisable. Disabled: toilet. Dress: smart casual. Separate room for parties, seats 14. **Map 9 G9.**

Haandi

7 Cheval Place, SW3 1HY (7823 7373/ www.haandi-restaurants.com). Knightsbridge tube. **Lunch served** noon-3pm daily. **Dinner served** 5.30-11pm Mon-Thur, Sun; 5.30-11.30pm Fri, Sat. **Main courses** £6-£16. **Set lunch** £8-£12 incl soft drink. **Credit** MC, V.
North Indian

The long interior at Haandi stretches out in a beige swathe of light-wooden floors and creamy walls. It is saved from blandness by potted palms and the glass-fronted kitchen, where the chefs are on full display. Food is feisty North Indian with a hint of an African influence. The business has branches in Nairobi and Kampala, and the jeera chicken we tried is a Kenyan favourite (as is the Tusker beer that went rather well with it). The dish was exemplary, based on a light yet intense tomato sauce laced with a judicious amount of cumin to give it a deep warmth. Tandoor-cooked lamb chops had a good gingery kick, but the creamy urad (black lentil) dal left a slightly bitter aftertaste, and the bhaturas (deep-fried puffy bread) were a touch greasier than they should have been. Starters showcased the expert spicing that underlines most dishes here: earthy potatoes nicely offset by tangy tamarind sauce, and bhajis based on a winning onion and okra combination. The food is certainly a cut above curry house fare, and prices remain as realistic as they can be in Knightsbridge.
Babies and children welcome: high chairs. Booking advisable weekends. Restaurant available for hire. Separate room for parties, seats 25. Takeaway service; delivery service (within 1-mile radius).
Map 14 E9.
For branch see index.

Salloos

62-64 Kinnerton Street, SW1X 8ER (7235 4444). Hyde Park Corner or Knightsbridge tube. **Lunch served** noon-2.15pm, **dinner served** 7-11pm Mon-Sat. **Main courses** £13.50-£16.50. **Credit** AmEx, DC, MC, V. Pakistani

Located on a genteel side street, this first-floor Pakistani restaurant has been serving pricey curries to wealthy Belgravia residents for more than three decades. Colonial-style decor – twinkling chandeliers, geometrical grilles on windows, and weighty table-linen – lends it a Raj vibe. Even the service team has a restrained, old-school feel. Salloos is renowned for its kebabs. Our succulent tandoori chops, well-steeped in garlicky yoghurt, were deliciously smoky and cooked to the right pinkness, but the hefty price tag left us blushing too. Tender chicken tikka morsels, interspersed with seared peppers on a long skewer, didn't match this, but they were reprieved by a pleasant tangy ginger coating. A fragrant pilau (basmati rice simmered in cardamom-scented lamb stock) scored top marks for subtle spicing and fluffy texture. Low points included a disappointing main course of oversized chicken koftas, surrounded by a lacklustre moat of tomato masala. Opt for meat grills as safe bets, and look elsewhere if you're vegetarian.
Booking advisable. Children over 8 years admitted. Dress: smart casual. Takeaway service.
Map 9 G9.

Mayfair

Benares

12A Berkeley Square House, Berkeley Square, W1J 6BS (7629 8886/www.benaresrestaurant.com). Green Park tube. **Lunch served** noon-2.30pm Mon-Fri, Sun. **Dinner served** 5.30-10.30pm Mon-Sat; 6-10pm Sun. **Main courses** £15-£40. **Set meal** (lunch, 5.30-7pm) £20 3 courses. **Credit** AmEx, DC, MC, V.
Modern Indian

Appearances on TV's *Great British Menu* have helped raise the profile of Benares' Atul Kochhar to that of celebrity chef; a pile of books sits ready for signing by the exit, but it's now much harder to book a table at a reasonable time – we were given an early two-hour slot then asked if we'd like to move to the bar with half an hour still to go. Such hype and pre-emptive haste can be irritating, but this is still a beautifully designed restaurant (dark and low-lit), with interesting cooking. Some dishes

Interview
RIAZ ALI

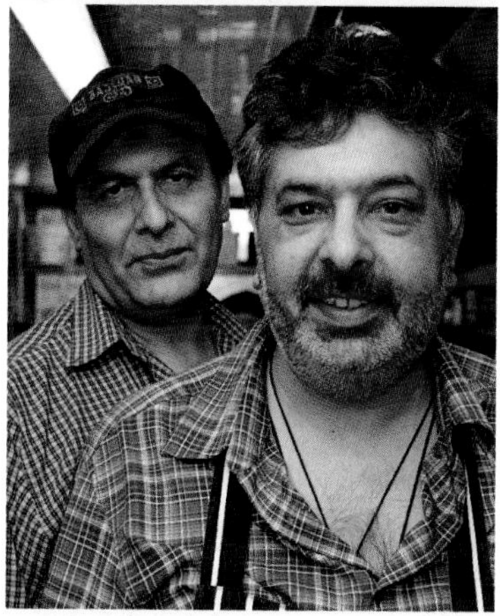

Who are you?
Co-owner of **Nauroz** (*see p169*), with brother Raza (bare-headed above). I was just a boy when we moved from Pakistan to England – I'm a chemical engineer, but running a restaurant is what I do best. Our restaurants have included Five Hot Chillies, Karahi King and Kabana, but when they became too busy, we sold them. Nauroz is for keeps, though.

Why did you get involved with restaurants?
When I was at university, local curry houses churned out standard English-style curries – dreadful stuff. I thought I could do a lot better and provide the real thing, not just for homesick Asians, but for everyone.

Eating in London: what's good about it?
The last decade or so has seen so many global cooking styles gain popularity – this is a city that caters to all people, all tastes, and all budgets.

What's bad about it?
Cowboy rookies, short cuts and big bucks. Invariably, the food quality suffers – many 'Indian-themed' places survive on a menu of frozen and ready-made food.

Who or what has had the biggest impact on London's restaurant scene in the past 25 years?
Local community caffs – it's us guys who have quietly gone about raising the profile of Indian cooking and not losing sight of what makes authentic preparations so great. We often get chefs from swish West End restaurants coming into our kitchen to learn our secrets.

Who do you most admire in the Asian catering scene?
My wife and my brother: they're brilliant at recreating homely meals for our customers. All our dishes are made in small quantities rather than in industrial-sized vats.

owe more to European tradition than Indian; a terrine of foie gras with a sliver of apple jelly was only orientalised by a garnish of chat masala containing black salt. Not all the flavour combinations are successful; one starter had bitter rocket, sweet and sour sauce and breaded soft-shell crab all on one plate. The most successful dishes were the traditional ones; the fresh-spice flavours sang in a rogan josh. But unless you don't mind paying a rajah's ransom to eat here – a tiny basket of mixed breads costs £4.95, a side dish of raita £4.50 – this is the sort of restaurant best left to the trust-fund managers who fill the place.
Booking advisable. Disabled: toilet. Dress: smart casual. Restaurant available for hire. Separate rooms for parties, seating 12, 22 and 28. **Map 9 H7**.

★ Tamarind

20-22 Queen Street, W1J 5PR (7629 3561/ www.tamarindrestaurant.com). Green Park tube. **Lunch served** noon-2.45pm Mon-Fri, Sun. **Dinner served** 6-11.30pm Mon-Sat; 6-10.30pm Sun. **Main courses** £16-£28. **Set lunch** £16.95 2 courses, £18.95 3 courses. **Set dinner** £49.50-£68 3 courses. **Credit** AmEx, DC, MC, V.
Pan-Indian
Tamarind's large basement interior (from 1995, with a gilding and bronzing refurb a few years ago that brought a distinctly nouveau riche feel) is now looking scuffed, but a lily still lies beneath. Chef Alfred Prasad produces North and South Indian dishes that are consistently excellent, and clearly play to the kitchen's strengths. A North Indian gosht dum biriani is topped with a pastry lid which releases the dish's aromas when lifted; the generous amounts of lamb within were tender, the rice distinct grains with fresh, clear spice flavours. The South Indian prawn chettinad had a thick, dark-brown gravy with intense flavours of toasted spices. Even something as simple as tarka dal is sublime. Not all dishes are as classic though; the tandoor oven is used creatively for dishes such as paneer tikka or grilled chunks of kingfish: both light dishes cooked with well-matched marinades. Although prices are high – this is Mayfair, after all – we didn't grudge paying for the excellent cooking and friendly, attentive service. Another refurb restoring the clean, simpler looks of the original Emily Todhunter design wouldn't go amiss, but otherwise we couldn't find fault with Tamarind.
Babies and children welcome (early evening only): high chair. Booking advisable. Dress: smart casual. Takeaway service; delivery service (within 1-mile radius). **Map 9 H7**.

★ Veeraswamy

Mezzanine, Victory House, 99-101 Regent Street, W1B 4RS (7734 1401/www.realindian food.com). Piccadilly Circus tube. **Lunch served** 12.30-2.15pm Mon-Fri; 12.30-2.30pm Sat, Sun. **Dinner served** 5.30-10.30pm Mon-Sat; 6-10.15pm Sun. **Main courses** £14-£27. **Set meal** (lunch, 5.30-6.30pm, after 10pm Mon-Sat) £16.50 2 courses, £19.50 3 courses; (Sun) £20 3 courses. **Credit** AmEx, DC, JCB, MC, V.
Pan-Indian
Now more than 80 years old, Veeraswamy has regained its former elegance after a stylish refurbishment. Owners Camellia and Namita Panjabi – of Amaya (*see p151*) and Chutney Mary (*see p160*) fame – oversee a classy restaurant where assorted memorabilia is displayed in a modern setting of coloured glass shades, candles, and glossy black granite flooring. On our evening weekday visit, the spacious dining area buzzed with the genteel conversation of smartly attired guests: business types, romantic couples, and the occasional celebrating family. Seafood lovers are in luck; succulent oysters, served on wooden skewers, were flash-seared over charcoal and delivered an explosion of smoky garlicky flavours. Our second starter was a triumph too: a glossy heap of plump on-the-shell mussels, steamed in soupy South Indian broth – a perfect balance of sea-fresh flavours infused in a ginger-flecked coconut broth. Keralite chicken stew showcased the very best of Syrian Christian cooking: tender chicken chunks, simmered with carrots and potatoes and scented with pounded peppercorns, curry leaves and creamy coconut milk. Side dishes are sublime; our current favourite is baby aubergines simmered in a velvety pounded peanut

Pan-Indian menu

Spellings of Indian dishes vary widely; dishes such as gosht may appear in several versions on different menus as the word is transliterated from (in this case) Hindi. There are umpteen languages and several scripts in the Indian subcontinent, the most commonly seen on London menus being Punjabi, Hindi, Bengali and Gujarati. For the sake of consistency, however, we have tried to adhere to uniform spellings. The following are common throughout the subcontinent.

Aloo: potato.
Ayre: a white fish much used in Bengali cuisine.
Baingan: aubergine.
Balti: West Midlands cooking term for karahi cooking (qv, North Indian menu), which became all the rage a decade ago. Unfortunately, many inferior curry houses now apply the name to dishes that bear little resemblance to real karahi-cooked dishes.
Bateira, batera or **bater**: quail.
Bengali: Bengal, before Partition in 1947, was a large province covering Calcutta (now in India's West Bengal) and modern-day Bangladesh. 'Bengali' and 'Bangladeshi' cooking is quite different, and the term 'Bengali' is often misused in London's Indian restaurants.
Bhajee: vegetables cooked with spices, usually 'dry' rather than sauced.
Bhajia or **bhaji**: vegetables dipped in chickpea-flour batter and deep-fried; also called pakoras.
Bhindi: okra.
Brinjal: aubergine.
Bulchao or **balchao**: a Goan vinegary pickle made with small dried prawns (with shells) and lots of garlic.
Chana or **channa**: chickpeas.
Chapati: a flat wholewheat griddle bread.
Chat or **chaat**: various savoury snacks featuring combinations of pooris (qv), diced onion and potato, chickpeas, crumbled samosas and pakoras, chutneys and spices.
Dahi: yoghurt.
Dahl or **dal**: a lentil curry similar to thick lentil soup. Countless regional variations exist.
Dhansak: a Parsi (qv) casserole of meat, lentils and vegetables, with a mix of hot and tangy flavours.
Dhaniya: coriander.
Ghee: clarified butter used for frying.
Gobi: cauliflower.
Gosht, josh or **ghosh**: meat, usually lamb.
Gram flour: chickpea flour.
Kachori: crisp pastry rounds with spiced mung dahl or pea filling.
Lassi: a yoghurt drink, ordered with salt or sugar, sometimes with fruit. Ideal to quench a fiery palate.
Machi or **machli**: fish.
Masala or **masaladar**: mixed spices.
Methi: fenugreek, either dried (seeds) or fresh (green leaves).
Murgh or **murg**: chicken.
Mutter, muter or **mattar**: peas.
Nan or **naan**: teardrop-shaped flatbread cooked in a tandoor (qv, North Indian menu).
Palak or **paalak**: spinach; also called saag.
Paan or **pan**: betel leaf stuffed with chopped 'betel nuts', coconut and spices such as fennel seeds, and folded into a triangle. Available sweet or salty, and eaten at the end of a meal as a digestive.
Paneer or **panir**: Indian cheese, a bit like tofu in texture and taste.
Paratha: a large griddle-fried bread that is sometimes stuffed (with spicy mashed potato or minced lamb, for instance).
Parsi or **Parsee**: a religious minority based in Mumbai, but originally from Persia, renowned for its cooking.
Pilau, pillau or **pullao**: flavoured rice cooked with meat or vegetables. In most British Indian restaurants, pilau rice is simply rice flavoured and coloured with turmeric or (rarely) saffron.
Poori or **puri**: a disc of deep-fried wholewheat bread; the frying makes it puff up like an air-filled cushion.
Popadom, poppadom, papadum or **papad**: large thin wafers made with lentil paste, and flavoured with pepper, garlic or chilli. Eaten in the UK with pickles and relishes as a starter while waiting for the meal to arrive.
Raita: a yoghurt mix, usually with cucumber.
Roti: a round, sometimes unleavened, bread, thicker than a chapati and cooked in a tandoor or griddle. Roomali roti is a very thin, soft disc of roti.
Saag or **sag**: spinach; also called palak.
Tamarind: the pods of this East African tree, grown in India, are made into a paste that imparts a sour, fruity taste – popular in some regional cuisines, including Gujarati and South Indian.
Thali: literally 'metal plate'. A large plate with rice, bread, containers of dahl and vegetable curries, pickles and yoghurt.
Vadai or **wada**: a spicy vegetable or lentil fritter; dahi wada are lentil fritters soaked in yoghurt, topped with tamarind and date chutneys.
Vindaloo: originally, a hot and spicy pork curry from Goa that should authentically be soured with vinegar and cooked with garlic. In London restaurants, the term is usually misused to signify simply very hot dishes.
Xacuti: a Goan dish made with lamb or chicken pieces, coconut and a complex mix of roasted then ground spices.

and tamarind sauce. But the desserts don't live up to expectations – unlike everything else.
Babies and children admitted (lunch). Booking advisable weekends. Disabled: lift. Dress: smart casual. Separate room for parties, seats 36.
Map 17 J7.

St James's

Quilon

41 Buckingham Gate, SW1E 6AF (7821 1899/ www.thequilonrestaurant.com). St James's Park tube. **Lunch served** noon-2.30pm Mon-Fri, Sun. **Dinner served** 6-11pm Mon-Sat; 6-10.30pm Sun. **Main courses** £8.50-£23. **Set lunch** £15.50 2 courses, £18 3 courses. **Credit** AmEx, DC, MC, V. South Indian

The Taj Hotel Group has tried, with limited success, to transform a dull corporate hotel restaurant into something a bit more stylish, by way of pot plants suspended in front of mirrors, a mural and judiciously placed spotlights. As indicated by the name (Quilon is a backwater town in Kerala), South Indian food is the forte and on the whole we couldn't fault it – though the typical chilli heat of South Indian cuisine is lacking, possibly in deference to Quilon's clientele of business people and western hotel guests. Ingredients in particular shone throughout, and were especially bright in the starters of Cochin mixed seafood broth (plump prawns, mussels and juicy chunks of fish), and delectably light fillets of breadcrumbed fish. Best main course was crispy fried stuffed squid, the tender sliced cephalopod curled around a minced prawn and crisp spinach filling. A side of mango curry had juicy chunks of fruit in yoghurt, though too few of the curry leaves and mustard seeds we'd relished on previous visits. Guinea fowl stew was soupy, but creamy and tasty. Staff were polite, but failed to explain what the set lunch entailed (main course plus bread and rice, but not side dishes). Breads, rice and beers all come in a number of interesting varieties, though à la carte prices are high.
Babies and children welcome: high chair. Booking advisable. Takeaway service. Vegetarian menu.
Map 15 J9.

Soho

★ Chowki

2-3 Denman Street, W1D 7HA (7439 1330/ www.chowki.com). Piccadilly Circus tube. **Meals served** noon-11.30pm Mon-Sat; noon-10.30pm Sun. **Main courses** £6.95-£11.95. **Set meal** (vegetarian) £15.95, 3 courses; (non-vegetarian) £18.95, 3 courses. **Credit** AmEx, DC, MC, V. Pan-Indian

Famed for its monthly changing regional menus, Chowki aims to showcase the diversity of Indian cooking styles with a selection of homely dishes. It's a brilliant idea and gives many enthusiasts their only taste of little-known regional cooking. Tourists and office groups aren't put off by the slightly gloomy interior: Formica-topped tables, red leatherette stools and industrial piping. In past visits, we've enjoyed excellent meals here, but this year have witnessed a drop in standards. On our most recent visit we had hoped to experience the fiery chilli heat of Rajasthani cooking, but our supposedly 'red hot' lamb curry was meek beyond redemption and had more in common with curry-house food. A Mangalorean coastal speciality of crisp-fried prawns, coated in crunchy rawa (semolina) made a pleasing snack, but needed strident spicing to make it memorable. Our spirits were lifted by a decent chicken curry made with a toasted peppercorn and fresh coconut masala (enlivened with astringent hits of pounded coriander seeds). Service is charming, and attempts to compensate for culinary shortcomings. Nevertheless, the experienced chef-proprietor Kuldeep Singh – who runs a string of restaurants including Mela (*see p149*) and 3 Monkeys (*see p163*) – needs to get Chowki's kitchen back on track. And quickly.
Babies and children welcome: high chairs. Booking advisable. Separate room for parties, seats 40.
Map 17 K7.

Nauroz. See p169.

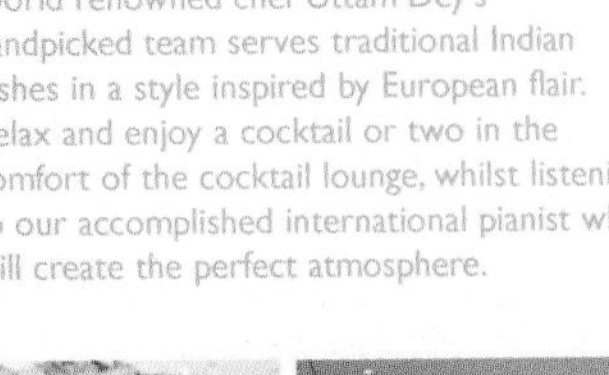

karma

karma

North Indian menu

Under the blanket term 'North Indian', we have included dishes originating in the Punjab (the region separating India and Pakistan), Kashmir and all points down to Hyderabad. Southall has some of London's best Punjabi restaurants, where breads cooked in the tandoor oven are often preferred to rice, marinated meat kebabs are popular, and dahls are thick and buttery.

Bhuna gosht: a dry, spicy dish of lamb.
Biriani or **biryani**: a royal Moghul (qv) version of pilau rice, in which meat or vegetables are cooked together with basmati rice, spices and saffron. It's difficult to find an authentic biriani in London restaurants.
Dopiaza or **do pyaza**: cooked with onions.
Dum: a Kashmiri cooking technique where food is simmered slowly in a casserole (typically a clay pot sealed with dough), allowing spices to permeate.
Gurda: kidneys.
Haandi: an earthenware or metal cooking pot, with handles on either side and a lid.
Jalfrezi: chicken or vegetable dishes cooked with fresh green chillies – a popular cooking style in Mumbai.
Jhingri, **jhinga** or **chingri**: prawns.
Kaleji or **kalezi**: liver.
Karahi or **karai**: a small iron or metal wok-like cooking dish. Similar to the 'balti' dish made famous in Birmingham.
Kheema or **keema**: minced lamb, as in kheema nan (stuffed nan).
Kofta: meatballs or vegetable dumplings.
Korma: braised in yoghurt and/or cream and nuts. Often mild, but rich.
Magaz: brain.
Makhani: cooked with butter (makhan) and sometimes tomatoes, as in murgh makhani.
Massalam: marinated, then casseroled chicken dish, originating in Muslim areas.
Moghul, **Mogul** or **Moglai**: from the Moghul period of Indian history, used in the culinary sense to describe typical North Indian Muslim dishes.
Nihari or **nehari**: there are many recipes on the subcontinent for this long-simmered meat stew, using goat, beef, mutton or sometimes chicken. Hyderabadi nihari is flavoured with sandalwood powder and rose petals. North Indian nihari uses nutmeg, cloves, dried ginger and tomato. In London, however, the dish is made with lamb shank (served on the bone).
Pasanda: thin fillets of lamb cut from the leg and flattened with a mallet. In British curry houses, the term usually applies to a creamy sauce virtually identical to a korma (qv).
Paya: lamb's feet, usually served on the bone as paya curry (long-cooked and with copious gravy); seldom found outside Southall.
Punjabi: Since Partition, the Punjab has been two adjoining states, one in India, one in Pakistan. Lahore is the main town on the Pakistani side, which is predominantly Muslim; Amritsar on the Indian side is the Sikh capital. Punjabi dishes tend to be thick stews or cooked in a tandoor (qv).
Roghan gosht or **rogan josh**: lamb cooked in spicy sauce, a Kashmiri speciality.
Seekh kebab: ground lamb, skewered and grilled.
Tak-a-tak: a cooking method – ingredients (usually meat or vegetables) are chopped and flipped as they cook on a griddle.
Tandoor: clay oven originating in north-west India in which food is cooked without oil.
Tarka: spices and flavourings are cooked separately, then added to dahl at a final stage.
Tikka: meat, fish or paneer cut into cubes, then marinated in spicy yoghurt and baked in a tandoor (qv).

★ Imli

167-169 Wardour Street, W1F 8WR (7287 4243/www.imli.co.uk). Tottenham Court Road tube. **Meals served** noon-11pm daily. **Tapas** £3.95-£6.95. **Set lunch** £5-£7.50 1 course. **Credit** MC, V. Pan-Indian

A branch of the fine-dining restaurant Tamarind (*see p152*), this Soho café makes much of its affordable selection of snacks and curries. It's a spacious venue, smartly furnished with Indian artefacts, splashes of orange-themed colour and chunky wooden furniture. Young office groups and tourists are attracted. The tapas-style menu aims for a sophisticated yet relaxed dining experience. But on our most recent visit, our lunch was one of hits and misses. A pleasing starter of crisp-fried wholewheat pastry discs, doused in yoghurt and streaked with sweet tamarind chutney, worked well with a nutty-tasting crunchy beansprout topping. In contrast, we struck unlucky with an apology for bhel poori; less-than-crisp puffed rice, soggy gram-flour sev, and scant drizzles of tamarind chutney did it no favours. An otherwise decent rendition of Punjabi-style fried lamb mince, flecked with peas, was let down by fibrous meat – a shame, as its masala of golden-fried onions, ginger and garlic was a winner. Homely chicken curry benefited from tender chicken morsels and a comforting herby masala. We've had much better meals here in the past; Imli needs to raise its standards if it's to regain lost ground.

Babies and children welcome: children's menu; high chairs. Disabled: toilet. Separate room for parties, seats 45. Takeaway service; delivery service (over £15 within W1). **Map 17 J6.**

★ ★ Masala Zone

9 Marshall Street, W1F 7ER (7287 9966). Oxford Circus tube. **Lunch served** noon-3.30pm Mon-Fri; 12.30-3.30pm Sun. **Dinner served** 5.30-11pm Mon-Fri; 5-10.30pm Sun. **Meals served** 12.30-11pm Sat. **Main courses** £6.95-£7.95. **Thalis** £7.40-£11.95. **Credit** MC, V. Pan-Indian

The Masala Zone chain is expanding rapidly, but we reckon the Soho original is still the most reliable branch. It's hugely popular too, with queues at busy times reminiscent of Wagamama's heyday. The queues move fast though, seating is comfortable, and the booths are secluded enough for private conversation. This is a chic-looking place, with murals by tribal artists, ochre walls, and clever partitions that make the best use of an awkward, low-ceilinged space. But the real draw is the menu. Many dishes are interpretations of regional Indian fast food that you don't often see in the UK, such as the gosht dabalroti: a rich lamb curry served with chunks of bread. Or there's the Gujarati combo called undhiyu and lentil khichdi, with an unusual mix of vegetables in a stew that includes raw banana and sweet potato. The thalis are good value, and even the ayurvedic thali had plenty of contrasts of flavour and texture. The only dishes we've found to underachieve are the noodle bowls and the masala burgers. The chefs are far better at traditional food than the modern, fusion-style recipes.

Babies and children welcome: high chairs. Bookings not accepted. Separate area for parties, seats 40. Takeaway service. **Map 17 A3.**
For branches see index.

★ Red Fort

77 Dean Street, W1D 3SH (7437 2115/ www.redfort.co.uk). Leicester Square or Tottenham Court Road tube. **Lunch served** noon-2pm Mon-Fri. **Dinner served** 5.45-11pm Mon-Sat; 5.30-10pm Sun. **Main courses** £12.50-£20. **Set lunch** £12 2 courses. **Set meal** (5.45-7pm) £16 3 courses incl tea or coffee. **Credit** AmEx, MC, V. North Indian

Seriously stylish, Red Fort has a fine dining menu that's a magnet for media moguls and moneyed tourists. Sandstone walls, a sleek water feature and antique artefacts lend elegant restraint to the feng shui ordered interior. The menu focuses on authentic North Indian classics and select dishes from the regal kitchens of and around Lucknow. Hara kebab starters – smooth patties coated with a crunchy poppy-seed crust – contained a delicious cumin-scented spinach purée sharpened with mustard greens. Equally satisfying, tender chicken chunks enrobed in a fresh mint, coriander and green chilli paste, had just the right level of astringency after being seared in the clay oven. An earthy Punjabi masala of garlicky onions, swished around in a karahi with sliced peppers and slit green chillies, made a fine complement to pristine cubes of paneer. Sadly, the lamb biriani, cooked in a sealed pot, had had its lid removed in the kitchen instead of at the table; although the tenderness of the Welsh lamb was creditable, the fragrance of the fluffy basmati rice and warming spices didn't equal that of previous visits. A small hiccup in an otherwise faultless meal.

Babies and children admitted. Booking advisable. Disabled: toilet. Dress: smart casual. Entertainment: DJ 8pm Thur-Sat (bar). Vegetarian menu. Vegan dishes. **Map 17 K6.**

Victoria

★ Sekara

3 Lower Grosvenor Place, SW1W 0EJ (7834 0722/www.sekara.co.uk). Victoria tube/rail. **Lunch served** noon-3pm, **dinner served** 6-10pm daily. **Main courses** £7.95-£14.95. **Set lunch** (Mon-Sat) £5 1 course. **Set buffet** (Sun) £12. **Credit** MC, V. Sri Lankan

A haven from the Victoria maelstrom, Sekara provides homely surroundings, friendly staff and interesting food. It's an unassuming place, with parquet flooring, elaborately framed paintings on the walls (above red wooden panelling) and a counter at the back. A happy crowd of regulars, mixed in age and ethnicity, adds to the appeal. The menu offers a wide selection from the Sri Lankan culinary canon, including a couple of pork dishes (indicating a Christian heritage). More commonplace Indian food is also served. We'd recommend skipping the Sri Lankan starters (a routine choice of fish patties and mutton rolls that were similar to packet ones) and feasting on main courses instead. Chicken lamprais is an excellent choice: a biriani of Dutch ancestry, singing with spices (peppercorns, cinnamon bark, cardamom), baked in a banana leaf. For £11.95 it came with a gorgeous on-bone chicken curry, seeni sambol (beautifully caramelised onions) and aubergine curry. Don't miss the dhal: a splendid aromatic version with lemongrass, curry leaves and coconut

milk. Less pleasing were the seer fish curry (excessively bony, in a tame, creamy sauce) and the slow service. But choose wisely here and joy will be yours.
Babies and children admitted. Booking advisable. Restaurant available for hire. Takeaway service. Vegetarian menu. **Map 15 H9**.

Westminster

★ Cinnamon Club

The Old Westminster Library, 30-32 Great Smith Street, SW1P 3BU (7222 2555/ www.cinnamonclub.com). St James's Park or Westminster tube. Restaurant **Breakfast served** 7.30-9.30am Mon-Fri. **Lunch served** noon-12.30pm, **dinner served** 6-10.45pm Mon-Sat. **Main courses** £11-£29. **Set meal** £19 2 courses, £22 3 courses. **Credit** AmEx, DC, MC, V. Modern Indian

Located in a former Victorian library, Cinnamon Club is the destination of choice for power brokers, politicians and big-business types. Its spacious dining hall has the feel of a grand colonial club: crisp white linen, a high ceiling, and a gallery of bookshelves adding to the sense of occasion. The menu embraces dressed-up rustic staples and regal stalwarts. A starter of hot yoghurt soup, garnished with meltingly soft gram-flour dumplings, whetted the appetite with a sizzling seasoning of fried curry leaves, popped mustard seeds, and zesty tamarind. Chef Vivek Singh opts for western-style presentation, but doesn't hold back on classic Indian spicing. Juicy tandoori swordfish steak, steeped in gingery yoghurt and crowned with a precariously balanced seared king prawn, delivered the catch of the day: a well-matched balance of tart yoghurt and sea-fresh flavours. We also relished a sizeable helping of fried lamb mince cooked with chicken livers – notable for its onion and green cardamom masala, spiked with chilli and toasted garlic. Regional food festivals keep the menu fresh and exciting while promoting the talents of in-house chefs. Try the Indian-themed breakfasts for a spicy beginning to the day.
Babies and children welcome: high chairs. Bars available for hire. Booking advisable. Disabled: toilet. Separate rooms for parties, seating 30 and 60. **Map 16 K9**.

West

Hammersmith

Green Chilli NEW

220 King Street, W6 0RA (8748 0111/ www.greenchilliltd.co.uk). Hammersmith or Ravenscourt Park tube. **Lunch served** 11.30am-3pm, **dinner served** 5.30-11.30pm daily. **Main courses** £8.50-£11.50. **Set meal** £17.95-£19.95 3 courses. **Credit** AmEx, DC, MC, V. Pan-Indian

Light, bright and airy, Green Chilli was rather empty on the Sunday lunchtime we visited. This belied its reputation as a popular venue for unfussy yet distinctive cooking (it's frequently packed in the evenings). Perhaps some of the gloss is wearing off (a chipped plate and a couple of smeary glasses took the shine off an otherwise sleek setting), but the food continues to attract locals. The menu is varied and enticing, including wine-matched vegetarian and non-veg set meals, and the likes of South Indian lobster kalimirch (with lime, curry leaves and a peppery onion and fennel masala) on the à la carte. A dish that shouldn't work – deep-fried mushrooms laced not just with spices but with strawberry jam – turned out to be delightful. Murg malai kebab was a triumph of garlicky succulence. The only disappointment was methi chicken: dry chunks of meat in a fenugreek sauce puréed to the texture of watery soup, with a bitter edge. Handkerchief-thin roomali roti made a good foil for rich, homely dhal makhani (black lentils). A truly excellent lime rice (with lime quarters and curry leaves) was quite good enough to eat without accompaniment.
Babies and children welcome: high chairs. Booking essential weekends. Disabled: toilet. Restaurant available for hire. Takeaway service; delivery service (over £15 within 3-mile radius). **Map 20 B4**.

★ ★ Sagar (100)

157 King Street, W6 9JT (8741 8563). Hammersmith tube. **Lunch served** noon-2.45pm Mon-Fri. **Dinner served** 5.30-10.45pm Mon-Thur; 5.30-11.30pm Fri. **Meals served** noon-11.30pm Sat; noon-10.45pm Sun. **Main courses** £5-£12. **Thalis** £8.95-£11.45. **Credit** AmEx, DC, JCB, MC, V. South Indian vegetarian

Our top choice for sampling the best of South Indian vegetarian cooking, Sagar enjoys the patronage of a wide range of customers: from well-heeled couples to students with a yen for tropical spices. The restaurant has an upmarket vibe with its glass-paned entrance, blond-wood fittings, and restrained display of elegant artefacts. It's a friendly spot where the menu celebrates home-style cooking at easy-on-the-pocket prices. Excellent, crisp dosais had a delectably soft underside: ideal for dipping into soupy sambar (made from lentils sharpened with perky tamarind and softened aubergine). The versatility of rice knows no bounds, witness the spongy idlis: pillowy steamed rice cakes, best dunked in sambar and enjoyed with a dab of coconut or red chilli chutney. Spicing tends to be mellow rather than fiery, seasoned with curry leaves and peppy mustard seeds. Even though the restaurant specialises in the cuisine of the southern states, its chef has quietly sneaked in a couple of classic Punjabi numbers, including puffed bhatura (fried yeasted bread) with gingery chickpea curry – seriously good. As good as the cooking back in Karnataka, in fact.
Babies and children welcome: high chairs. Booking advisable. Takeaway service. Vegetarian menu. **Map 20 B4**.
For branch see index.

Kensington

Zaika

1 Kensington High Street, W8 5NP (7795 6533/www.zaika-restaurant.co.uk). High Street Kensington tube. **Lunch served** noon-2.45pm Mon-Fri, Sun. **Dinner served** 6.30-10.45pm Mon-Sat; 6.30-9.45pm Sun. **Main courses** £14.50-£19.50. **Set lunch** £19.50 4 courses. **Set meal** £39-£89. **Credit** AmEx, DC, JCB, MC, V. Modern Indian

A former bank, this fine-dining restaurant capitalises on its exalted setting with sweeping drapes, a high ceiling and weighty antiques. The raised bar area has attractive low seating, which adds to the indulgent vibe. Zaika is popular with wealthy business folk on elastic expense accounts. It's also well-liked by well-off tourists who come here for social currency and a feast of adventurous pan-Indian dishes. A cheese-themed first course included tandoori paneer: notable for its fresh flavour, soft spongy texture, and smoky crust scented with toasted nigella seeds. Tandoori salmon was less pleasing, its overly sweet marinade overshadowing all other spicing. Spicy hariyali chicken curry (cooked in a masala of watercress, spinach and green chillies) may have been as verdant as a bowling green, but it cried out for more punchy chillies. A vegetarian thali rejuvenated our taste buds; choice morsels included a fiery whole-lentil dhal, and excellent spinach stir-fry tossed with toasted chillies and garlic. Breads are light and very moreish; there's even a nan flavoured with mushrooms and truffle oil. Service wasn't up to scratch on our visit. The team need to be more attentive and better acquainted with the well-chosen wine list.
Babies and children welcome: high chair. Booking advisable; essential weekends. Dress: smart casual. Restaurant available for hire. Vegetarian menu. **Map 7 C8**.

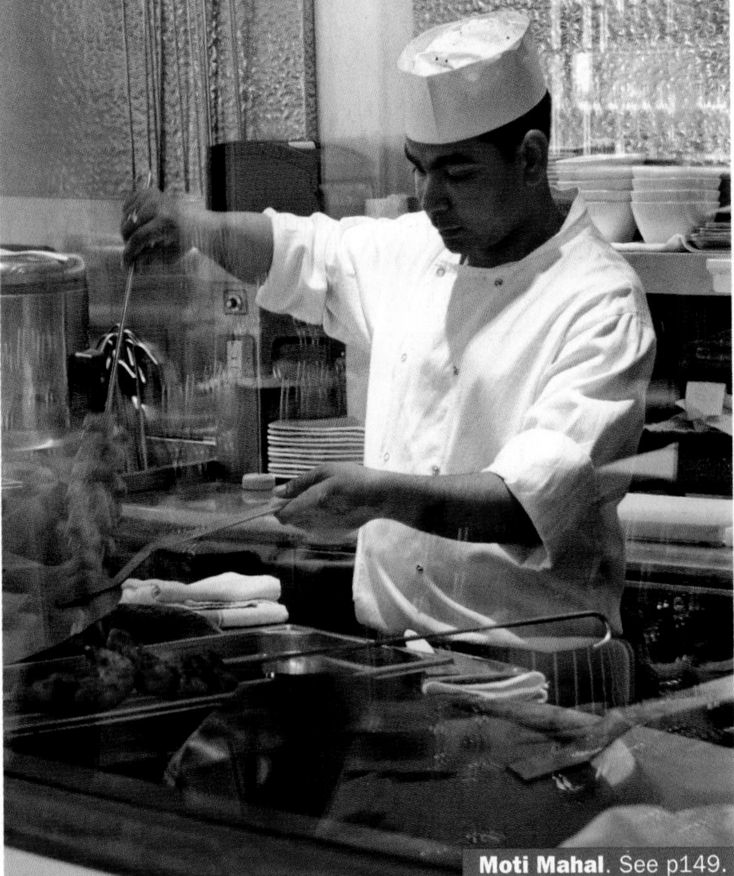

Moti Mahal. See p149.

South West

Chelsea

Chutney Mary

535 King's Road, SW10 0SZ (7351 3113/ www.realindianfood.com). Fulham Broadway tube/11, 22 bus. **Lunch served** 12.30-2.30pm Sat; 12.30-3pm Sun. **Dinner served** 6.30-11pm Mon-Sat; 6.30-10.30pm Sun. **Main courses** £14.50-£31. **Set lunch** £20.50 3 courses. **Credit** AmEx, DC, JCB, MC, V.
Pan-Indian

One of the first restaurants to celebrate pairing wine with Indian cuisine, Chutney Mary enjoys wide acclaim for its innovative style. This classy venue is run by the Panjabi sisters, who also oversee Amaya (*see p151*), Veeraswamy (*see p152*), and the Masala Zone group (*see p157*). Smartly attired Americans, well-off Chelsea diners, and youngish couples come here to eat. A ground-floor reception leads to a darkly seductive candlelit basement, spread over two levels. There's also an airy conservatory, framed by leafy green plants. Our meal began with the signature soup, nihari shorba: a sublime cardamom-scented meaty broth, sealed under a crisp lid of golden puff pastry. We also sampled duck galouti (a posh patty made from pounded meat spiced with cardamom and garam masala); although not as velvety in texture as we'd hoped for, it had succulence and was enlivened by perky blueberry chutney. Following this, our chicken curry was outstanding: tender morsels and gingery broth sharpened by zesty orange juice. Desserts were pale in comparison; we couldn't detect any garam masala in our spicy crème brûlée, and serving it with an overdose of custard did it no favours. Efficient service compensates for the occasional glitch.
Babies and children welcome: high chairs. Booking advisable dinner. Dress: smart casual. Entertainment: jazz 12.30pm Sun. Separate room for parties, seats 34. **Map 13 C13.**

Painted Heron

112 Cheyne Walk, SW10 0DJ (7351 5232/ www.thepaintedheron.com). Sloane Square tube/11, 19, 22, 319 bus. **Lunch served** noon-2.30pm Mon-Fri. **Dinner served** 6-11pm daily. **Main courses** £11-£16. **Thalis** £11-£15. **Credit** AmEx, JCB, MC, V.
Modern Indian

After the Kennington branch of Painted Heron closed, Yogesh Datta has had more time to concentrate on fine-tuning affairs at his flagship restaurant. Located within a stone's throw of the Thames, it's a tranquil place with soothing cream-coloured walls, skylights, candles and crisp table-linen. Affluent Chelsea residents dine here. The menu certainly contains some eyebrow-raisers: the likes of rhubarb-marinated seafood and rosemary-scented nan. Results are variable. Tender lamb strips, immersed in silky-smooth kashmiri rogan josh, were given a modern twist with a new-wave infusion of rose petals and a dab of red chilli jam: a superb sweet-sour match with its garlic and mild chilli flavours. Fish and seafood dishes weren't as impressive. Swordfish steaks were overcooked, and had been simmered in a tart tamarind and sweet pumpkin masala with a cloying texture. Seared scallops coated in dried red chilli flakes were succulent, yet let down by an incongruous chilled yoghurt and rice accompaniment. Excellent cardamom-scented rice pudding was weirdly showered with children's cake decorations; it didn't work. Service needed to be more attentive too.
Babies and children admitted. Booking advisable weekends. Separate room for parties, seats 25. Tables outdoors (5, garden). Vegetarian menu. **Map 14 D13.**

Rasoi Vineet Bhatia

10 Lincoln Street, SW3 2TS (7225 1881/ www.rasoirestaurant.co.uk). Sloane Square tube. **Lunch served** noon-2.30pm Mon-Fri. **Dinner served** 6-10.30pm Mon-Sat. **Main courses** £14-£36. **Set meal** £75 tasting menu. **Credit** AmEx, DC, MC, V. Modern Indian

Former head chef at highly rated Zaika (*see p158*), Vineet Bhatia runs his namesake restaurant at a discreet Chelsea townhouse furnished with antiques, wall-mounted ornaments and silk hangings. Attentive waiters usher guests from a chocolate-hued hallway into two intimate and elegant dining areas. The menu has fusion leanings, containing the likes of cocoa-dusted lobster and goat's cheese samosas. A more traditional first course of assorted kebabs got our meal off to a shaky start, the main culprits being tough lamb seekh kebabs and overcooked tandoori prawns. However, we relished the contrasting flavours of creamy, savoury semolina, topped with succulent scallops, surrounded by a lagoon of tabasco-spiked tomato juice. Unfortunately, our main courses failed to deliver. Two overcooked tandoori chops missed tangy, lemony notes and made a disappointing match with buttery black lentils. Even fish biriani, although studded with juicy prawns and scallops, didn't live up to expectations, exhibiting a lacklustre blend of aromatic spicing. Prices are astronomical, so there's no excuse for these basic shortfalls. Bhatia needs new recipes – it's time to move on from revamping his dated Zaika dishes.
Babies and children admitted. Booking advisable. Dress: smart casual. Separate rooms for parties, seating 8 and 15. Vegetarian menu.
Map 14 F11.

Vama

438 King's Road, SW10 0LJ (7351 4118/ www.vama.co.uk). Sloane Square tube then 11, 22 bus. **Lunch served** 12.30-3pm daily. **Dinner served** 6.30-11.30pm Mon-Sat; 6.30-10.30pm Sun. **Main courses** £9.50-£15.50. **Set buffet** (noon-3pm Sun) £14.99. **Credit** AmEx, DC, MC, V. North Indian

This acclaimed restaurant clearly doesn't skimp when it comes to ingredients. Our masala chaaps appetiser was tender and juicy, steeped in a divine ginger, garlic and yoghurt marinade. Think fine French dining meets the back alleys of Lahore. But

our second appetiser, mushrooms stuffed with pomegranate, cheese and masala, was a rather half-baked attempt at fusion. A main course of crab kofta curry was equally disappointing. When prepared well, this consists of scrumptious balls of minced crab rolled in chickpea flour, with a rich tomato sauce; Vama's version was more like a sloppy keema, mashed meat (if this was crab you couldn't tell) in a red sea of overpowering spices and oil. But we enjoyed the bhindi bhojpuri, a traditional dish (served in northern and eastern India) made up of batter-coated okra strips shallow-fried and sprinkled with salty mango powder; a convenient half-plate option was available. The ambrosial mango kulfi arrived smartly decorated and ended the meal on a tasty note. A trip to Vama won't leave you feeling heavy and sleepy, but grumpy service left us a little frustrated – especially at these prices.
Babies and children welcome: high chairs. Booking essential weekends. Separate room for parties, seats 35. Tables outdoors (2, patio). Takeaway service. **Map 14 D12**.

Putney

Ma Goa

242-244 Upper Richmond Road, SW15 6TG (8780 1767/www.ma-goa.com). East Putney tube/Putney rail/74, 337 bus. **Lunch served** noon-2.30pm Tue-Fri; 1-3.30pm Sun. **Dinner served** 6.30-11pm Mon-Sat; 6-10pm Sun. **Main courses** £7.50-£12. **Set dinner** (6.30-8pm) £10 2 courses. **Set buffet** (Sun lunch) £10. **Credit** AmEx, DC, MC, V. Goan

Family-run Ma Goa sets itself apart by showcasing Portuguese-influenced Goan specialities. There's a miniature deli by the entrance, which leads into two plain but neatly furnished dining areas. Although the menu acknowledges pan-Indian tandoori grills and street snacks, the emphasis is on homely Goan classics. We were impressed by the tang of pickled shrimps (balchao), warmed through with curry leaves and served with sanna: a sponge-like steamed rice cake fermented with toddy (palm wine). Curry-house vindaloo has nothing in common with the real thing; true vindaloo is made with pork and characterised by garlicky hits and vinegary sharpness. Ma Goa's rendition ticked almost all the boxes, but we wished the chef had upped the chilli quotient for true authenticity. Fish caldin, made with strips of escolar fillets, was too mild to impress and needed an extra dollop of a coconut and tamarind masala to deliver the goods. This restaurant is well-liked by Putney locals and the branch in Fulham seems just as popular.
Babies and children welcome: children's menu; high chairs. Booking advisable; essential weekends. Dress: smart casual. Restaurant available for hire. Separate room for parties, seats 35. Takeaway service; delivery service (within 3-mile radius).
For branch see index.

South

Tooting

Tooting remains a hotspot for interesting and affordable Indian restaurants, as it has been for the past 20 years. This is still the only area of London where you can find good East African Asian, Gujarati, South Indian, Pakistani and Sri Lankan restaurants within a ten-minute walk of one other. The closure of the Tooting branch of vegetarian Sakonis in 2007 has been partially offset by one new meat-free arrival: **Sarashwathy Bavans** (70 Tooting High Street, SW17 0RN, 8682 4242) and the promise of another (opening 'imminently'): **Dosa n Chutny** (68 Tooting High Street, SW17 0RN, 8682 5252).

Other long-established restaurants of note that didn't quite make our final cut (but are nonetheless worth exploring) include the Sri Lankan café **Suvai Aruvi** (96 High Street Colliers Wood, SW19 2BT, 8543

Eriki. See p167.

RESTAURANTS

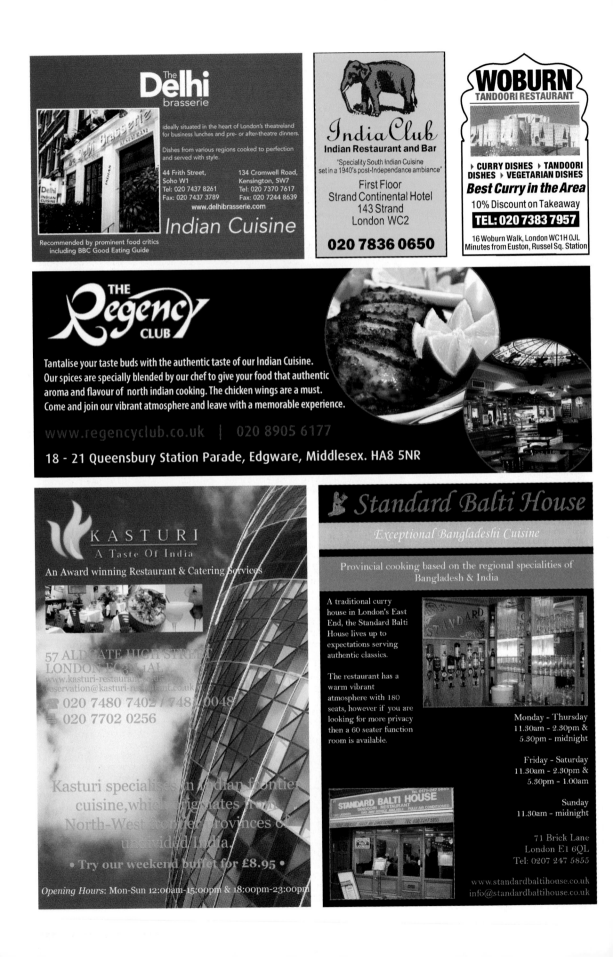

6266); Tanzanian Punjabi restaurant **Masaledar** (121 Upper Tooting Road, SW17 7TJ, 8767 7676); the Tooting branch of the Norbury original karahi joint, **Mirch Masala** (213 Upper Tooting Road, SW17 7TG, 8672 7500); and the oldest of them all (established 1973), the South Indian **Sree Krishna** (192-194 Tooting High Street, SW17 0SF, 8672 4250).

★ Apollo Banana Leaf

190 Tooting High Street, SW17 0SF (8696 1423). Tooting Broadway tube. **Meals served** noon-11pm daily. **Main courses** £3.50-£6.25. **Unlicensed. Corkage** no charge. **Credit** AmEx, MC, V. Sri Lankan

The peculiar name and the decor of mirrors and mismatched 'car boot sale' art do it few favours, but ignore such idiosyncrasies and discover why Apollo Banana Leaf is so popular with local Tamil families. The kitchen produces excellent renditions of classic Sri Lankan dishes, with the spicing just the way the locals like it. The mutton string-hopper fry is almost biriani-like, coloured the dark teak brown of roasted spices, with the vermicelli noodles (string hoppers) lightly chopped and not at all claggy; the mutton chunks were tender, the spice rush balanced. Food marked as hot really does scorch. Even a dish tagged with a single chilli symbol (such as a squid curry, the cut squares of squid immersed in a runny orange sauce) had us reaching for a quenching lassi. Lemon rice was slightly oily, but tasted fine and was beautifully garnished with fried curry leaves, mustard seeds and crimson-coloured chillies: amazing value at £2.25. In the past we've also enjoyed crab curry, and devilled mutton, but the more usual masala dosais and idlis pass muster too. With starters such as fish cutlets starting from 60p and few main courses costing more than £4, it's well worth putting up with the canned music and Sahara prints.

Babies and children welcome: high chairs. Booking advisable weekends. Takeaway service.

★ Kastoori

188 Upper Tooting Road, SW17 7EJ (8767 7027). Tooting Bec or Tooting Broadway tube. **Lunch served** 12.30-2.30pm Wed-Sun. **Dinner served** 6-10.30pm daily. **Main courses** £4.75-£6.25. **Thalis** £8.50-£16.25. **Minimum** £7. **Credit** MC, V. East African Gujarati vegetarian

This family-run stalwart has become something of a destination restaurant, and not just for vegetarians. The decor gets a lift from the bright-yellow tablecloths and spot-lit stone reliefs of temple dancers, and the well-executed Gujarati menu generally gets a fillip from East African influences and ingredients. Yet the cassava in our starter of mogo bhajia was over-blended to a cloying consistency, with spicing too subtle to counteract the sweetness of the patties, making a relentlessly dull dish. Pani poori – little crisp pastry shells (the pooris) filled with potato, chickpeas and sprouting lentils in a spicy, watery sauce (the pani) – should explode in the mouth with flavour and contrasting textures. These didn't, as the fillings were skimpy and the sauce too thick. However, main courses were a hit, with outstanding creamy cauliflower curry laced with cumin and fresh coriander, and tomato curry vibrant with mustard seeds and curry leaves. Matoki (green banana) curry was an exemplary East African Gujarati dish from the list of family specials (one available daily). Kofta curry was a let-down though, the vegetable dumplings swamped by diced vegetables in the oily sauce. In contrast, the bread (fluffy light bhatura) and rice (fried with onions) were perfect.

Babies and children admitted. Booking advisable. Takeaway service. Vegan dishes.

★ Radha Krishna Bhavan

86 Tooting High Street, SW17 0RN (8682 0969/ www.mcdosa.co.uk). Tooting Broadway tube. **Lunch served** noon-3pm daily. **Dinner served** 6-11pm Mon-Thur, Sun; 6pm-midnight Fri, Sat. **Main courses** £1.95-£6.95. **Thalis** (noon-3pm Sun) £5.95-£7.95. **Minimum** £5. **Credit** AmEx, MC, V. South Indian

The house (bhavan) of Krishna and his paramour Radha is a vision of high kitsch. The walls are papered with giant photos of sunsets and beach scenes; a dummy of a kathakali dancer in full costume stands in one corner. Temple elephant brass decorations and other Keralite knick-knacks are everywhere. But the reason that Radha Krishna Bhavan has very loyal customers is not the crazy decor, it's because the cooking of the South Indian dishes is consistently good, and prices are low. The several varieties of dosa are all tip-top, with thin, crisp batter and well-spiced sambar and fillings. The thorans (dry vegetable stir-fries) are excellent: enough to win over anyone who despised school boiled cabbage and vinegared beetroot. Dishes such as kappa (cassava root) and kadala (black chickpea curry) make a nice change once you've worked your way through the more usual Keralite seafood and vegetable curries. The only food we'd advise against ordering is the bog-standard curry house fare: to choose this is to miss the point.

Babies and children admitted. Booking advisable. Takeaway service; delivery service (within 3-mile radius). Vegetarian menu.

For branch see index.

South East

Herne Hill

3 Monkeys

136-140 Herne Hill, SE24 9QH (7738 5500/ www.3monkeysrestaurant.com). Herne Hill rail/ 3, 37, 68 bus. **Lunch served** noon-2.30pm, **dinner served** 6-11pm Mon-Sat. **Meals served** noon-10.30pm Sun. **Main courses** £6.95-£8.95. **Set lunch** £7.95 2 courses, £10.95 3 courses. **Buffet lunch** (Sun) £5.95. **Set dinner** £12.95 2 courses. **Credit** AmEx, DC, JCB, MC, V. Pan-Indian

Housed in a grand, red-brick corner building, this two-floor eaterie is large but crammed with tables and chairs. It is quiet, impersonal and formal: ideal for a business lunch. The open kitchen means that things can get smoky; ask a waiter to turn on the extractor fan (and hope he isn't as surly as ours). We sampled the set lunch menu, which offers an impressive selection of medium-sized dishes over three courses. Gilafi seekh kebab (lamb mince wrapped in seasoned peppers) was a colourful but unremarkable starter. Our other appetiser, murgh kalimirch, proved a better choice: tender pieces of delicately peppered chicken. To follow, macher jhal

South Indian menu

Much South Indian food consists of rice-, lentil- and semolina-based dishes (semolina being small grains of crushed wheat). Fish features strongly in non-vegetarian establishments, and coconut, mustard seeds, curry leaves and red chillies are widely used as flavourings.

If you want to try South Indian snacks like dosas, idlis or uppama, it's best to visit restaurants at lunchtime, which is when these dishes are traditionally eaten, and they're more likely to be cooked fresh to order. In the evening, we recommend you try the thalis and rice- and curry-based meals, including South Indian vegetable stir-fries like thorans and pachadis. For the tastiest Tamil food, try **Sanghamam** (*see p174*) in Wembley. **Satya** (*see p173*) in Uxbridge offers some of the liveliest, most colourful Keralite specialities. **Sagar** (*see p158*) in Hammersmith is best for Udupi vegetarian cooking from Karnataka.

Adai: fermented rice and lentil pancakes, with a nuttier flavour than dosais (qv).
Avial: a mixed vegetable curry from Kerala with a coconut and yoghurt sauce. Literally, 'mixture' in Malayalam (the language of Kerala).
Bonda: spiced mashed potatoes, dipped in chickpea-flour batter and deep-fried.
Dosai or **dosa**: thin, shallow-fried pancake, often sculpted into interesting shapes; the very thin ones are called **paper dosai**. Most dosais are made with fermented rice and lentil batter, but variants include **rava dosai**, made with 'cream of wheat' semolina. **Masala dosais** come with a spicy potato filling. All variations are traditionally served with sambar (qv) and coconut chutney.
Gobi 65: cauliflower marinated in spices, then dipped in chickpea-flour batter and deep-fried. It is usually lurid pink due to the addition of food colouring.
Idli: steamed sponges of ground rice and lentil batter. Eaten with sambar (qv) and coconut chutney.
Kadala: black chickpea curry.
Kalan: a thin curry from the southern states made from yoghurt, coconut and mangoes.
Kancheepuram idli: idli (qv) flavoured with whole black peppercorns and other spices.
Kappa: cassava root traditionally served with kadala (qv).
Kootu: mild vegetable curry in a creamy coconut and yoghurt sauce.
Kozhi varutha: usually consists of pieces of chicken served in a medium-hot curry sauce based on garlic and coconut; it is very rich.
Moilee: Keralite fish curry.
Pachadi: spicy vegetable side dish cooked with yoghurt.
Rasam: consommé made with lentils; it tastes both peppery-hot and tamarind-sour, but there are many regional variations.
Sambar or **sambhar**: a variation on dahl made with a specific hot blend of spices, plus coconut, tamarind and vegetables – particularly drumsticks (a pod-like vegetable, like a longer, woodier version of okra; you strip out the edible interior with your teeth).
Thoran: vegetables stir-fried with mustard seeds, curry leaves, chillies and fresh grated coconut.
Uppama: a popular breakfast dish in which onions, spices and, occasionally, vegetables are cooked with semolina using a risotto-like technique.
Uthappam: a spicy, crisp pancake/ pizza made with lentil- and rice-flour batter, usually topped with tomato, onions and chillies.
Vellappam: a bowl-shaped, crumpet-like rice pancake (same as appam or hoppers, qv, Sri Lankan menu).

deya, a Bengali tomato-based curry made of fish pieces marinated in mustard and fennel, was insipid and watery. More satisfying was the murgh kulka makhanwala, a creamy tomato concoction dotted with well-prepared pieces of chicken. The surprising delight of the meal, however, was dhal makhani, which along with nan and rice, comes gratis with the set menu. Indulgent, buttery and delicious, it's worth kissing any diet goodbye. Dessert was a simple scoop of chocolate ice-cream, but the set lunch leaves room for little else.
Babies and children welcome: high chairs. Booking advisable. Disabled: toilet. Separate rooms for parties, seating 16 and 40. Takeaway service; delivery service (7738 5550, over £10 within 3-mile radius). **Map 23 A5.**

East

The Bangladeshi presence is at last asserting itself on the menus of Whitechapel, especially at the southern-most end of Brick Lane where few non-Bangladeshi visitors tread. Several of the small cafés and restaurants on this stretch serve proper Bangladeshi food in addition to the usual formula curries and fried chicken. However, the difficulty is in finding these dishes; often, the menus are written only in Bengali script, if at all. During 2007 we've enjoyed the point-and-order dishes in the display cabinets of **Sabuj Bangla** (102 Brick Lane, E1 6RL, 7247 6222); and at **Ruchi** (303 Whitechapel Road, E1 1BY, 7247 6666), where the dining room is concealed up stairs at the back. Both these places are basic, but the food is the real deal. By far the best, most polished Bangladeshi restaurant – not just in Whitechapel, but the whole of London – is **Kolapata** (*see p166*), which is well worth the extra journey from Brick Lane (it's a brisk 20-minute walk from the Old Truman Brewery).

Brick Lane

You may be surprised that this guide doesn't carry reviews of any Brick Lane restaurants. The reason is simple: we have tried many, year after year, but in recent times none has been of a sufficient standard.

Despite this, Brick Lane touts still make claims to be recommended by *Time Out*. In 2006 Tower Hamlets Council introduced a byelaw that banned restaurateurs from touting for customers. Brick Lane touting waned for a while, but on our recent visits, it seemed to have returned to the previous level. The salesman's patter might offer a free bottle of wine, two-for-one pricing, or other special deals. The clincher, for many, seems to be 'recommended by *Time Out*'. Maybe their restaurant was – five, ten, or more years ago. Ask to see proof, as we did. The only evidence they could summon up was favourable reviews that were several years old, some with the dates conveniently removed. A review that old is, of course, no recommendation at all.

Whitechapel

Café Spice Namaste

16 Prescot Street, E1 8AZ (7488 9242/ www.cafespice.co.uk). Aldgate East or Tower Hill tube/Tower Gateway DLR. **Lunch served** noon-3pm Mon-Fri. **Dinner served** 6.15-10.30pm Mon-Fri; 6.30-10.30pm Sat. **Main courses** £11.25-£18.95. **Set meal** £30 3 courses, £60 tasting menu. **Credit** AmEx, DC, JCB, MC, V.
Pan-Indian

Cyrus Todiwala's upmarket restaurant is a colourful spectacle, with bold Bollywood hues and artfully draped swathes of fabric. Proximity to the City makes it a popular venue for business groups, who visit for smoky grills, pan-Indian curries and Parsi specialities. Todiwala celebrates his own Parsi heritage with dishes that can still be traced back to Persian roots. Expect sweet-sour flavours, mild spicing, and fruity notes in meat curries. High points included mashed potato patties encasing a filling of garlicky minced beef – a good match with cinnamon-infused tomato sauce. Patra ni machi (whole pomfret, slathered with herby coconut chutney, and steamed in a banana leaf) was unwrapped at the table; its refreshing lemony notes spiked with hits of chilli made for a delicious dish. Good news over: we were less than impressed

Gujarati menu

Most Gujarati restaurants are located in north-west London, mainly in Wembley, Sudbury, Kingsbury, Kenton, Harrow, Rayners Lane and Hendon, and they tend to be no-frills, family-run eateries.

Unlike North Indian food, Gujarati dishes are not normally cooked in a base sauce of onions, garlic, tomatoes and spices. Instead they're tempered; whole spices such as cumin, red chillies, mustard seeds, ajwain (carom) seeds, asafoetida powder and curry leaves are sizzled in hot oil for a few seconds. The tempering is added at the start or the end of cooking, depending on the dish. Commonplace items like grains, beans and flours – transformed into various shapes by boiling, steaming and frying – are the basis of many dishes. Coriander, coconut, yoghurt, jaggery (cane sugar), tamarind, sesame seeds, chickpea flour and cocum (a sun-dried, sour, plum-like fruit) are also widely used.

Each region has its own cooking style. Kathiyawad, a humid area in western Gujarat, and Kutch, a desert in the north-west, have spawned styles that are less reliant on fresh produce. Kathiyawadi food is rich with dairy products and grains such as dark millet, and is pepped up with chilli powder. Kutchis make liberal use of chickpea flour (as do Kathiyawadis) and their staple diet is based on khichadi. In central Gujarat towns such as Baroda and Ahmedabad, grains are widely used; they appear in snacks that are the backbone of menus in London's Gujarati restaurants.

The gourmet heartland, however, is Surat – one of the few regions with heavy rainfall and lush vegetation. Surat boasts an abundance of green vegetables like papadi (a type of broad bean) and ponk (fresh green millet). A must-try Surti speciality is undhiyu. Surti food uses 'green masala' (fresh coriander, coconut, green chillies and ginger), as opposed to the 'red masala' (red chilli powder, crushed coriander, cumin and turmeric) more commonly used in western and central regions.

The standard of Gujarati food available in restaurants has improved since the last edition of this guide. **Dadima** (*see p173*) serves excellent Ahmedabadi food; authentic Surti food is now available at **Ram's** (*see p169*); and **Sakonis** (*see p174*) offers good Kenyan-Gujarati versions of Mumbai street snacks. The best time to visit Gujarati restaurants is for Sunday lunch, which is when you'll find little-seen regional specialities on the menu – but you will almost certainly need to book.

Bhakarvadi: pastry spirals stuffed with whole spices and, occasionally, potatoes.
Bhel poori: a snack originating from street stalls in Mumbai, which contains crisp, deep-fried pooris, puffed rice, sev (qv), chopped onion, tomato, potato and more, plus chutneys (chilli, mint and tamarind).
Farsan: Gujarati snacks.
Ganthia: Gujarati name for crisply fried savoury confections made from chickpea flour; they come in all shapes.
Ghughara: sweet or savoury pasties.
Kadhi: yoghurt and chickpea flour curry, often cooked with dumplings or vegetables.
Khandvi: tight rolls of 'pasta' sheets (made from gram flour and curds) tempered with sesame and mustard seeds.
Khichadi or **khichdi**: rice and lentils mixed with ghee and spices.
Mithi roti: round griddle-cooked bread stuffed with a cardamom-and-saffron-flavoured lentil paste. Also called puran poli.
Mogo: deep-fried cassava, often served as chips together with a sweet and sour tamarind chutney. An East African Asian dish.
Pani poori: bite-sized pooris that are filled with sprouted beans, chickpeas, potato, onion, chutneys, sev (qv) and a thin, spiced watery sauce.
Patra: a savoury snack made of the arvi leaf (colocasia) stuffed with spiced chickpea-flour batter, steamed, then cut into slices in the style of a swiss roll. The slices are then shallow-fried with sesame and mustard seeds.
Pau bhajee: a robustly spiced dish of mashed potatoes and vegetables, served with a shallow-fried white bread roll.
Puran poli: see mithi roti.
Ragda pattice or **ragada patties**: mashed potato patties covered with a chickpea or dried-pea sauce, topped with onions, sev (qv) and spicy chutney.
Sev: deep-fried chickpea-flour vermicelli.
Thepla: savoury flatbread.
Tindora: ivy gourd, a vegetable resembling baby gherkins.
Undhiyu: a casserole of purple yam, sweet potatoes, ordinary potatoes, green beans, Indian broad beans, other vegetables and fenugreek-leaf dumplings cooked with fresh coconut, coriander and green chilli. A speciality of Surat.

Rooburoo

with the spicing in some classic masalas; they lacked distinctive character and needed to be pepped up with bolder flavours. Chicken curry and its foundation of pounded nuts, poppy seeds, and red chillies, was underwhelming and mundane. We've had marvellous meals here – let's hope our recent experience was a temporary glitch and normal service will soon be resumed.
Babies and children welcome: high chairs. Booking advisable. Disabled: toilet. Tables outdoors (8, garden). Takeaway service; delivery service (within 2-mile radius). **Map 12 S7**.

★ ★ Kolapata NEW

222 Whitechapel Road, E1 1BJ (7377 1200). Whitechapel tube. **Meals served** noon-11.30pm daily. **Main courses** £3.95-£8.95. **Set buffet** (12.30-3pm Mon-Fri) £4.95. **Unlicensed. Corkage** no charge. **No credit cards.** Bangladeshi

Whitechapel has long had little caffs serving a few home-style Bangladeshi dishes, but Kolapata is the area's first proper ambassador for the country's authentic cuisine. True, simple things are on the menu, but so are the complex dishes you might find in top restaurants in Dhaka. Lamb biriani is a Muslim classic, perfectly rendered with chunks of bone still in the dish; haleem is lamb and crushed wheat cooked with lentils and spices into a texture resembling thick lentil soup, but with much more intensity of flavour. More distinctively Bangladeshi are the fish dishes. Rupchanda (what we call pomfret) is served whole in a tangy curry sauce. We were particularly impressed by the bhortas: mixed vegetable dishes, pungent with mustard oil. Make sure you try the aloo chop, a perfectly cooked starter of potato cutlet filled with delicate shreds of beef; like all the cooking here, you wonder how the restaurant does it for such a low price. Booze isn't sold – Kolapata, for all its fine cooking and bright paint, still looks very much like a wipe-clean caff – but the yoghurt-based wedding drink called borhani is a good foil for the spice heat of the food.
Babies and children welcome: high chairs. Booking advisable. Takeaway service.

North East

Stoke Newington

Rasa

55 Stoke Newington Church Street, N16 0AR (7249 0344/www.rasarestaurants.com). Stoke Newington rail/73, 393, 476 bus. **Lunch served** noon-3pm Sat, Sun. **Dinner served** 6-10.45pm Mon-Thur, Sun; 6-11.30pm Fri, Sat. **Main courses** £3.95-£5.95. **Set meal** £16 4 courses. **Credit** AmEx, DC, MC, V. South Indian vegetarian

Hot pink walls, smouldering incense sticks, assorted South Indian artefacts and warm service complement the absolutely authentic Keralite menu here. Food is based on vegetarian dishes influenced by the home cooking of Kerala's Hindu Nair caste. Ambience and a fine pedigree don't guarantee consistency across the board, however. Our mains were superb: a light, crisp rava dosa (a South Indian pancake studded with onions and green chillies, which provided hot bursts of flavour against the smooth batter); and a kayi (green bean) curry, laced with ginger and full of tender beans, cauliflower and carrots, which went especially well with perfectly cooked lemon rice. But some of the starters and sides fell short of these high standards. The coconut chutney and sambar – key partners to many South Indian dishes – were insipid. This wouldn't have mattered as much if the accompanying idlis and masala vadai (deep-fried dumplings made with a lentil batter) had been as fluffy and light as they can be. But Rasa was full of happy chatter on the Tuesday night we visited, and on balance, deservedly so.
Babies and children welcome: high chairs. Booking essential weekends. Takeaway service. Vegetarian menu. Vegan dishes. **Map 25 B1.**
For branches see index.

North

Archway

The Parsee

34 Highgate Hill, N19 5NL (7272 909/www.theparsee.com). Archway tube. **Dinner served** 6-10.45pm Mon-Sat. **Main courses** £9.75-£12. **Set dinner** £25 3 courses, £30-£35 4 courses incl coffee. **Credit** AmEx, MC, V. Parsi

Cyrus Todiwala, of Café Spice Namaste fame (*see p164*) also runs this more modest enterprise dedicated to the food of his Parsi upbringing. It's an attractive little place, with bare wooden flooring and bright yellow and blue walls embellished with curly iron light fittings. On our Tuesday evening visit there were no other diners, which was a shame as we found the food carefully prepared and of a high standard. The Parsi platter provided a varied spread of starters, including appetising, freshly made renditions of such standards as vegetable samosas and onion bhajis, but also (the highlight of the meal) a strip of grilled venison, tenderised to almost pâté-like consistency and brimming with the flavour of star anise. Expertly presented main courses include a fair version of that Parsi signature dish lamb dhansak, and a more notable prawn patia featuring exquisitely textured shellfish in a tamarind-enhanced red masala, served with smooth dhal. The crunchy-fresh coconut and pistachio pancakes are worth ordering for pudding too. Service is avuncular.
Babies and children admitted. Booking advisable weekends. Separate rooms for parties, seating 18-35. Takeaway service. **Map 26 B1**.

Islington

★ Rooburoo NEW

21 Chapel Market, N1 9EZ (7278 8100/ www.rooburoo.com). Angel tube. **Meals served** 11am-11pm Tue-Sun. **Dinner served** 6-11pm Mon. **Main courses** £5.50-£9.95. **Set lunch** £5.95 2 courses. **Set meal** £10.95 3 courses. **Credit** AmEx, MC, V. Pan-Indian

Just off Islington's main drag, this new-look Indian was quiet on two separate visits; it shouldn't be. The service (from groovy young waiters) was attentive and welcoming, and the menu is appealing and well-priced. Yes, there are clichés such as chicken tikka masala, but the formula dishes are thankfully in the minority. Try the wraps instead, maybe the sea bass fillet, marinated in herbs and lemon juice, served in a banana-leaf pocket. Other wraps include paratha, chapati and stretchy roomali roti, with various curried fillings. Familiar dishes are given a new spin; lamb slivers were swirled around a karahi with onions and split green chillies, for a lighter take on the classic curry lamb dopiaza. There are many unusual side dishes such as fried bitter gourd crisps, as well as three children's meals, on the printed table mat menus: almost enough to spoil you with choice. Desserts include such toothsome delights as mishti doi (Bengali baked yoghurt pudding), or a sponge cake with cinnamon. With its reasonable prices and modern interpretations of home-style Brit-Indian dishes, Rooburoo stands out from some very averag competition on Chapel Market.
Babies and children welcome: high chairs. Booking advisable. Disabled: toilet. Takeaway service; delivery service (over £15 within 2-mile radius). **Map 5 N2**.

North West

Hampstead

★ Woodlands

102 Heath Street, NW3 1DR (7794 3080/ www.woodlandsrestaurant.co.uk). Hampstead tube. **Lunch served** noon-3pm Sat, Sun. **Dinner served** 6-11pm daily. **Main courses** £5-£6.50. **Thalis** (dinner) £9.95-£17.95. **Credit** MC, V. South Indian vegetarian

Settle yourself into one of Woodlands' cosy, burgundy booths. The decor is tasteful and simple: red organza curtains, exposed brick and a tidy bar at the back. Tenacious waiters are keen to suggest 'specialities' from the extensive menu, though these mainly consist of South Indian standards. We started with chaat, but were disappointed by the dahi bateta poori: yoghurt, potatoes and black salt lumped on top of deep-fried wheat discs that were stale and meagre. The soggy, bland dosais are avoidable too. The accompanying sambar had the right consistency – but was hot enough to burn even the most experienced Tamil tongue. Instead head for the Woodlands thali, consisting of rice, pooris or chapatis and three vegetarian choices from a selection of more than 12 dishes. We sampled the chanas, the malai paneer and the vegetable kootu (an authentic South Indian vegetable curry, in this case made with okra in coconut milk). All were worthy, if unambitious, renditions. A decent spot for a first date

Babies and children welcome: high chair. Booking advisable. Takeaway service. Vegetarian menu. Vegan dishes. **Map 28 C1.**

For branches see index.

St John's Wood

Eriki NEW

122 Boundary Road, NW8 0RH (7372 2255/ www.eriki.co.uk). St John's Wood tube. **Lunch served** noon-2.30pm Tue-Sun. **Dinner served** 6-11pm Mon-Sun. **Main courses** £8.95- £11.95. **Credit** AmEx, MC, V. Pan-Indian

There was something amiss on the midweek night we visited this new branch of Eriki – it was virtually empty. We've always loved the Swiss Cottage original for its unpretentious, well-priced and first-rate renditions of proper Indian food from across the subcontinent. Kokum (fish tamarind) is used in the Goan fish curry; deghi mirch chillies grace the lucknowi lamb chop masala. The same menu is available here, and standards are almost as high. Highlights of the 'vegetarian panorama' selection of five starters were a nicely packed little masala dosa and a crisp spinach and onion bhaji. Next, malabar seafood masala was a generous helping of succulent king prawns, squid rings and scallops in a mouthwateringly savoury masala. Khumb palak, from a long list of enticing vegetarian dishes (sadly not available as side dishes), featured juicy spinach, pepped up with mushrooms and fresh-tasting spices. So, the food was fine, as was the comforting little yellow and orange dining room (with seating at brown leather benches or on substantial wooden chairs). The problem was the service. The waiter seemed keen to leave, advising us not to order extra dishes, then, at 9.30pm stating 'we don't have any desserts'. Maybe that explains the lack of customers. Stick to the original branch.

Babies and children admitted. Booking advisable. Restaurant available for hire. Takeaway service. Delivery service (over £15 within 3-mile radius). Vegetarian menu. Vegan dishes.

For branch see index.

Swiss Cottage

Atma NEW

106C Finchley Road, NW3 5JJ (7431 9487). Finchley Road or Swiss Cottage tube. **Lunch served** noon-2.30pm, **dinner served** 6-11.30pm daily. **Main courses** £12.50-£14.50. **Set meal** £24.50 tasting menu. **Credit** AmEx, MC, V. Modern Indian

Oxblood-red walls, crisp white linen, black leather seating and outstanding service – Atma is upmarket, and sophisticated enough to take some risks with its stylised cooking. Generally, the results work beautifully. Even a dish with the dubious name 'a great drowned death' is delectable, consisting of crab koftas, all silky and softly spicy in a creamy coconut and cinnamon sauce. A dish that would be mere 'butter chicken' in an average curry house, showed the difference careful sourcing and a bit of soul (atma) makes to a simple recipe. Here the blend of tomatoes, pungent paprika and fenugreek was vibrantly fresh, and the dish came with a raita ice-cream that was a clever, perfectly complementary touch. Lamb chops dusted with crushed coriander seeds was another winner, marinated to total tenderness. A couple of dishes didn't quite come off: dull, forgettable spiced liver, and a dryish venison main course. The venison dish was a complex affair involving tandoori spicing, a truffle sauce, and rice noodle cakes that sat atop the plate like a trio of crazy black wigs (they were made from squid ink, and this was, finally, a flavour too far). Nevertheless Atma is almost there as a destination restaurant.

Babies and children admitted. Booking advisable weekends. Takeaway service. **Map 28 B3.**

Cumin

O_2 Centre, 255 Finchley Road, NW3 6LU (7794 5616/www.cumin.co.uk). Finchley Road tube. **Meals served** noon-11pm daily. **Main courses** £6-£9.95. **Credit** MC, V. Pan-Indian

There's a corporate tang to Cumin, due mostly to its shopping mall location (it's a three-sided space, opening on to the second floor of the O_2 Centre), but also to the waiting staff (amenable Euro-employees – no family-run concern this) and the menu design (reminiscent of Nando's). The place seems like a chain in the making, but it's not all bad. Funky beats combine with turquoise and purple ceiling lighting, colourful wall photos and

functional seating to produce an uptempo vibe. Food, an unsurprising batch of North Indian curries and tandoori dishes, outstrips curry house fare. The Indian-born chefs mix their own spice blends, as evidenced by the flavour-packed kashmiri roghan gosht (with kashmiri chillies) and the mustardy machi masala (with salmon). We preceded these main courses with a mixed sharing platter featuring dryish seekh and hara bhara (spinach and mixed veg) kebabs, but admirably fresh samosas and juicy chicken tikka. The children's menu (real Indian food, mildly spiced) is praiseworthy too, but the overall cost of a meal is higher than you might expect. Perhaps that explained all the empty seats.
Babies and children welcome: children's menu; crayons; high chairs. Booking advisable weekends. Disabled: toilet. Tables outdoors (2, balcony). Takeaway service; delivery service (over £10 within 1.5-mile radius). Vegetarian menu. Vegan dishes. **Map 28 A/B3.**

Outer London

Eastcote, Middlesex

★ ★ Nauroz (100)

219 Field End Road, Eastcote, Middx HA5 1QZ (8868 0900). Eastcote tube. **Meals served** noon-midnight Tue-Sat. **Main courses** £3-£9. **Set lunch** (vegetarian) £4 1 course, (meat) £5 1 course. **Unlicensed. Corkage** no charge. **Credit** MC, V. Pakistani

Eastcote residents have done well out of their neighbourhood local. Nauroz is an established family-run concern, with owners whose previous business interests include such popular haunts as Five Hot Chillies (*see p172*) and Karahi King (*see p173*). Easy-wipe tables and melamine plates lend it a functional feel – but the look is surprisingly light and airy, with occasional knick-knacks softening the decor. There's plenty of banter between family members as they exchange pleasantries. Reflecting the owners' Pakistani roots, cooking is robust and focuses on earthy fried onion masalas, tandoori kebabs, and top-notch breads. Robustly spiced deighi gosht (on-the-bone lamb chunks, simmered in a silken masala of browned onions with cardamom) was an outstanding rendition of mum's-own cooking. Just as endearing, slow-cooked black dhal (enriched with cream and dollops of butter) made a marvellous match with piping-hot nan. Feasting continued with smoky fish tikka, steeped in yoghurt scented with pungent thyme-like carom seeds. This is meat-eating heaven and vegetables are very much a side line. A meal here won't be gilded with gold leaf, but it will be cooked with passion, served with friendliness, and pegged at a reasonable price.
Babies and children welcome: high chairs. Booking advisable. Takeaway service. Vegetarian menu.

Harrow, Middlesex

Blue Ginger

383 Kenton Road, Harrow, Middx HA3 0XS (8909 0100/www.bgrestaurant.com). Kenton tube/rail. **Lunch served** noon-3pm Tue-Sat. **Dinner served** 6-11pm Mon-Sat. **Meals served** 1-10.30pm Sun. **Main courses** £5.25-£10.95. **Credit** AmEx, MC, V. North Indian

Imagine a sports bar with a penchant for all things Bollywood. Blue Ginger may not look like much from the outside, but it certainly taps into the tastes of well-to-do British Asians. Flat-screen TVs, low-slung sofas, and a glossy black granite bar draw the cool crowd, while a dining area is geared towards extended family feasting at weekends. The menu embraces Indo-oriental cookery: North Indian kebabs, Punjabified sichuan chicken with extra chilli hits, and even South Indian idlis (rice cakes) doused in black bean sauce. Our last visit wasn't Blue Ginger's finest hour. Well-meaning but chaotic service, confused orders and noisy families didn't impress. When the food finally arrived, we received salty gram-flour fritters and oily chicken curry; the meal was partially redeemed by battered chunks of tilapia fish flavoured with carom seeds, pounded peppercorns, and pleasantly astringent ginger. Best bet is to order a chilled beer, an assortment of tandoori kebabs, and the soy and chilli-speckled sichuan chicken bites. Drop by on weekend evenings, after the boisterous families have left.
Babies and children welcome: high chairs. Booking essential. Disabled: toilet. Dress: smart casual. Restaurant available for hire. Tables outdoors (7, terrace). Takeaway service.

★ ★ Ram's (100)

203 Kenton Road, Harrow, Middx HA3 0HD (8907 2022). Kenton tube/rail. **Lunch served** noon-3pm, **dinner served** 6-11pm daily. **Main courses** £4-£5. **Thalis** £4.99-£8.99. **Set meal** £16.50 (unlimited food and soft drinks). **Credit** AmEx, DC, MC, V. Gujarati vegetarian

Located on busy Kenton Road, Ram's commands a loyal following among the local Gujarati community. They regularly gather here to gossip and feed on an array of specialities from Surat, an industrial city in the heart of Gujarat. We began our meal with khandvi, a popular snack made of steamed gram flour flattened into a thin film then rolled into a delectable, taut spiral and garnished with vagar (a fried concoction of mustard seeds, grated coconut and coriander leaves). This palate-pleasing appetiser was enough to fill us, but there were more treats in store. Khichdi (steamed rice flour dumplings infused with chillies, oil and lemon) were soft and moist, almost melting in the mouth. Enjoyable too was the Mumbai favourite bhel (a melange of crunchy, savoury sev, finely chopped onions, potatoes and tamarind chutney), made with delightfully fresh ingredients, each suitably pronounced in flavour. Not much can be said for the cutlets, which on our visit resembled sorry-looking oily cakes and were as disappointing to taste. However, the meal soon got back on track with some ambrosial shrikhand, delicately made from hung curd with nuts, cardamom and silky strands of saffron.
Babies and children welcome: high chairs. Booking advisable weekends. Disabled: toilet. Restaurant available for hire (Mon-Thur). Takeaway service.

Rayners Lane, Middlesex

★ Eastern Fire

430 Alexandra Avenue, Rayners Lane, Middx HA2 9TW (8866 8386). Rayners Lane tube. **Meals served** 6-11pm Mon-Fri. **Main courses** £2.95-£6.50. **Corkage** £2. **Credit** MC, V. South Indian

Geared towards the local community, Eastern Fire is a family-oriented diner, attracting predominately Sri Lankan and South Indian custom. It's a brightly lit, modern, spick-and-span set-up. The menu embraces southern staples, but gives a nod to Indo-Malaysian choices, including spicy noodles and sambols. First-time customers can get lost in the lengthy menu. After several visits, we've concluded that the broth-like curries are consistent, and notable for distinctive spicing. Chicken curry scored highly for its tender morsels and sharp hits of green chilli, cutting through an onion and tomato masala. Hoppers – saucer-like ground-rice pancakes – make fine accompaniments. In contrast, vadai (fried lentil dumpling) was a serious let-down, marred by a dense, unyielding texture. Its partner, sambar, also got the thumbs-down, due to lacklustre spicing. Fiery relishes added verve to otherwise bland lentil-based dishes; shredded coconut with red chillies saved us from what would have been a timidly spiced meal. Service is keen and eager to please. The chef often meets and greets customers. However, Eastern Fire's staples need to improve if the restaurant is to win more custom.
Babies and children admitted. Booking advisable. Disabled: toilet. Restaurant available for hire. Takeaway service; delivery service (over £5 within 2-mile radius).

Southall, Middlesex

Southall's Broadway and surrounding streets boast all the fun of a bustling Indian bazaar. From wedding caterers to sari shops, wholesale grocers to pavement stalls, there's little you can't get here. Visit on the weekend and you'll be welcomed with colourful chaos, jostling crowds, maddening traffic, and earthy tones of Punjabi vernacular.

Known for their hard work and business savvy, the Punjabi community has improved its financial lot in recent years. Flashy cars, glitzy shop fronts and redecorated restaurants testify to newly acquired wealth. But in spite of gussied-up websites with online bookings and slick restaurant marketing, the cooking style remains resolutely Punjabi. It's the no-frills food and no-nonsense presentations that pull in the punters: hot samosas sold from street stalls, smoky kebabs cooking over coals, stacks of breads and hearty meaty curries.

Although there have been attempts to develop healthy menu choices at a few spots, it's not a trend that is bedded into Punjabi culture. We're talking stacks of buttery naans, black creamy dals, and deliciously smoky skewered meats: food to

SHELF LIFE

Asian corner shops often stock the basics, and the big supermarkets now sell once-rare ingredients such as curry leaves. But if you need something a bit more out of the ordinary – or just prefer the cheaper prices in Asian cash 'n' carrys – the following stores are all exemplary.

Deepak Cash & Carry
953-959 Garratt Lane, SW17 0PF (8767 7819). Tooting Broadway tube. **Open** 9am-7.30pm Mon-Sat; 10am-5pm Sun.
An astonishingly wide selection of spices, pulses and dried goods at rock-bottom prices. The staff are helpful and can find almost everything you might need.

Fruity Fresh
111-113 Ealing Road, Wembley, Middx HA0 4BP (8902 9797/ www.fruityfresh.com). Alperton tube/Wembley Central tube/rail. **Open** 9am-10.30pm daily.
This neat and spacious greengrocer is one of the best, with low prices, and fruit and veg delivered daily.

Ganapathy Cash & Carry
34-38 Ealing Road, Wembley, Middx HA0 4TL (8795 4627). Alperton tube/Wembley Central tube/rail. **Open** 6am-midnight Mon-Sat; 8am-midnight Sun.
An enticing array of fresh fruit and vegetables greets you at this Sri Lankan shop. Different shades of rice, a huge selection of fish, and spices aplenty.

Taj Stores
112 Brick Lane, E1 6RL (7247 3844). Shoreditch tube/Liverpool St tube/rail. **Open** 9am-9pm daily.
Brick Lane's biggest Bangladeshi supermarket, with a vast selection of frozen fish and unusual leaf and stem vegetables.

Sri Lankan menu

Sri Lanka has three main groups: Sinhalese, Tamil and Muslim. Although there are variations in the cooking styles of each community and every region, rice and curry form the basis of most meals, and curries are usually hot and spicy.

The cuisine has evolved by absorbing South Indian, Portuguese, Dutch, Arabic, Malaysian and Chinese flavours over the years. Aromatic herbs and spices like cinnamon, cloves, nutmeg, curry leaves and fresh coriander are combined with South-east Asian ingredients such as lemongrass, pandan leaves, sesame oil, dried fish and rice noodles. Fresh coconut, onions, green chillies and lime juice (or vinegar) are also used liberally, and there are around two dozen types of rice – from short-grained white varieties to several long-grained, burgundy-hued kinds.

Curries come in three main varieties: white (cooked in coconut milk), yellow (with turmeric and mild curry powder) and black (with roasted curry powder, normally used with meat). Hoppers (saucer-shaped pancakes) are generally eaten for breakfast with kithul palm syrup and buffalo-milk yoghurt, while string hoppers (steamed, rice-flour noodles formed into flat discs) usually accompany fiery curries and sambols (relishes).

Sri Lankan cafés in Tooting, Southall, Wembley and Harrow are becoming increasingly popular, and contemporary venues such as **Eastern Fire** (*see p169*) have also sprung up.

Ambul thiyal: sour fish curry cooked dry with spices.
Appam or **appa**: see hoppers.
Badun: black. 'Black' curries are fried; they're dry and usually very hot.
Devilled: meat, seafood or vegetable dishes fried with onions in a sweetish sauce; usually served as starters.
Godamba roti: flaky, thin Sri Lankan bread, sometimes wrapped around egg or potato.
Hoppers: confusingly, hoppers come in two forms, either as saucer-shaped, rice-flour pancakes (try the sweet and delectable milk hopper) or as string hoppers (qv). Hoppers are also known as appam.
Idiappa: see string hoppers.
Katta sambol: onion, lemon and chilli relish; fearsomely hot.
Kiri: white. 'White' curries are based on coconut milk and are usually mild.
Kiri hodi: coconut milk curry with onions and turmeric; a soothing gravy.
Kuttu roti, kottu or **kothu roti**: strips of thin bread (loosely resembling pasta), mixed with mutton, chicken, prawns or vegetables to form a 'bread biriani'; very filling.
Lamprais or **lumprice**: a biriani-style dish where meat and rice are cooked together, often by baking in banana leaves.
Lunnu miris: a relish of ground onion, chilli and maldives fish (qv).
Maldives fish: small, dried fish with a very intense flavour; an ingredient used in sambols (qv).
Pittu: rice flour and coconut steamed in bamboo to make a 'log'; an alternative to rice.
Pol: coconut.
Pol kiri: see kiri hodi.
Pol sambol: a mix of coconut, chilli, onions, maldives fish (qv) and lemon juice.
Sambols: strongly flavoured relishes, often served hot; they are usually chilli-hot too.
Seeni sambol: sweet and spicy, caramelised onion relish.
Sothy or **sothi**: another name for kiri hodi.
String hoppers: fine rice-flour noodles formed into flat discs. Usually served steamed (in which case they're dry, making them ideal partners for the gravy-like kiri hodi, qv).
Vellappam: appams (qv) served with vegetable curry.
Wattalappan or **vattilapan**: a version of crème caramel made with kithul palm syrup.

be shared with family and friends. For a taster of the best kebabs and yoghurt-based snacks, take a brisk walk away from The Broadway, down South Street, and head for **New Asian Tandoori Centre** (*see p172*). We recommend their butter chicken curry and parathas, all washed down with a tall and cooling glass of icy, cumin-scented lassi.

If you're driving, park the car at the main parking lot behind The Broadway's Himalaya Centre. Better still, take the train or bus; shops are close by and there's plenty to see on the way. Check out **Kwality Foods** (47-61 South Road, UB1 1SQ, 8917 9188) for groceries and fresh veggies pegged at rock bottom prices: gourds, leafy greens and a brilliant display of chillies.

For local residents going about their business, Old Southall still has its well-worn charm. **Glassy Junction** (97 South Road, UB1 1SQ, 8574 1626), a regular Punjabi pub, has a working-men's-club vibe with its patterned carpet, pints of beer and tandoori bar snacks. More upmarket, **Madhu's** (*see below*), located just down the road, is a dressy restaurant, with its black granite floors and stylish Indo-Kenyan menu: a world far removed from Southall's street life. For more down-to-earth munchies, grab a bag of samosas or box of sweetly spiced sweetmeats from **Ambala** (107 The Broadway, UB1 1LN, 8843 9049). If you'd rather chill out with an ice, or indulge in jalebis (crisp-fried batter whirls, drenched in syrup), cross the road and visit **Moti Mahal** (94 The Broadway, UB1 1QF, 8571 9443) for the very best in street snacks (don't confuse it with the identically named but unrelated restaurant in Covent Garden). Southall remains true to its colours: a fascinating outpost of Punjabi culture.

Brilliant

72-76 Western Road, Southall, Middx UB2 5DZ (8574 1928/www.brilliantrestaurant.com). Southall rail. **Lunch served** noon-2.30pm Tue-Fri. **Dinner served** 6-11.30pm Tue-Sun. **Main courses** £4.50-£13. **Credit** AmEx, DC, JCB, MC, V. East African Punjabi

The owner's daughter has stepped into Dad's shoes and is keen to energise Brilliant's Kenyan-influenced Punjabi menu, giving a healthy spin to selected dishes. A recent makeover has spruced up the interior with a shiny new bar, wooden and tiled flooring, and swish fittings. Only the imposing statues of Kenyan Masai tribes-people remain – a testament to the family's African background. A huge helping of papri chat (crisp discs of wholewheat pastry drenched in deliciously tart yoghurt and sweet tamarind chutney) was top-notch, and evocative of Indian street food. It was billed as a healthy dish, so we hoped the pastry discs were baked instead of being fried as usual. Tandoori tilapia chunks couldn't match this in quality, the dish being let down by overcooked fish and vivid artificial colouring. A home-style chicken curry, flecked with mustard greens and gingery masala, lost marks for oiliness. Service is polite, if a trifle distracted at times. Brilliant is a well-intentioned restaurant, but if it's to take healthy eating seriously, it will have to do much more than exercise artistic licence with the menu.

Babies and children welcome: high chairs. Booking advisable weekends. Separate room for parties, seats 120. Takeaway service. Vegetarian menu.

Delhi Wala

11 King Street, Southall, Middx UB2 4DG (8574 0873). Southall rail. **Meals served** 8.30am-10pm daily. **Main courses** £2-£4.50. **Unlicensed. Credit** MC, V. Punjabi vegetarian

It's hard to find fault with the inviting atmosphere at Delhi Wala. This bright, airy eaterie has smiling, efficient staff who seat you at clean, plastic-coated tables. Unfortunately, the food was not of a similar standard on our most recent visit. We started off with the dokhra (steamed gram-flour cakes infused with ginger, garlic and chilli and garnished with roasted mustard seeds); they were stale and dry, cracking at the slightest prod. The restaurant's Delhi staples such as mutter paneer were freshly prepared but ordinary (the paneer was lightly fried and flavourful, but the watery tomato sauce in which it arrived was uninspired). At least the bhindi dish had character; the okra (prepared with onions) contained excessive amounts of garam masala and red pepper and scorched our mouths. We gave up and ate only the tandoori roti. End with a comforting cup of masala chai (tea) and something from the tempting sweet counter, which contains a fantastic selection of pure ghee treats. They just might tempt you back for a second visit.

Babies and children welcome: high chairs. Separate room for parties, seats 70. Takeaway service. Vegetarian menu. Vegan dishes.

★ Madhu's (100)

39 South Road, Southall, Middx UB1 1SW (8574 1897/www.madhusonline.com). Southall rail. **Lunch served** 12.30-3pm Mon, Wed-Fri. **Dinner served** 6-11.30pm Mon, Wed-Sun. **Main courses** £6-£12. **Set meal** £17.50-£20 per person (minimum 6) 16 dishes incl tea or coffee. **Credit** AmEx, DC, MC, V. East African Punjabi

When Madhu's had a makeover in 2003, some regulars worried that style might take precedence over good food. The place may be sparklier now, all gleaming glass panels and granite tiles, but the cooking remains among Southall's best. Service is sleek, from the greeting by a charming sari-clad hostess, to waiting staff who remained attentive throughout a terrific early-evening rush. A side of mango chutney judiciously flecked with chilli was devoured by a three-year-old in our party; grown-up tasters found it just sweet enough, just feisty enough. Main dishes were similarly well-spiced. One of the most popular is lamb ribs cooked 'nyama choma-style' (roasted over an open fire; popular throughout Kenya, where Madhu's

RESTAURANTS

owners, the Anand family, originated); the ribs were superbly seasoned, lemony, salty and slightly smoky. A juicy chicken curry on the bone – machuzi kuku – is another Indian-African special and was rich in taste though thin in texture, with garlic and ginger notes ringing out through the tomato-based sauce. Aloo tikki (potato patties) were a triumph too: fluffy potato given a tang from pomegranate-seed powder and tamarind sauce, the spiciness offset by yoghurt. To conclude: there's as much substance as style here.
Babies and children welcome: high chairs. Booking advisable. Disabled: toilet. Dress: smart casual. Separate room for parties, seats 35. Takeaway service.

★ New Asian Tandoori Centre (Roxy)

114-118 The Green, Southall, Middx UB2 4BQ (8574 2597). Southall rail. **Meals served** 8am-11pm Mon-Thur; 8am-midnight Fri-Sun. **Main courses** £3-£7. **Credit** MC, V.
Punjabi
With elongated, crumb-covered tables, carelessly strewn chairs and grim-faced, efficient servers, the Roxy possesses the vibe of a school cafeteria. Thankfully, this boisterous canteen is more Jamie Oliver than soggy peas and gravy. Most Punjabi classics are here. Old favourites like rajmah (kidney beans in a rich stew of spices and tomato) and channa batura (a flavourful serving of chickpeas served with deep-fried puffed bread) would elicit a nod of approval from any North Indian granny. Our starter, aloo tikki chaat (fried potato patties) were smothered in a yoghurt sauce that was uncharacteristically warm. It was topped with too many chickpeas, too few onions and tamarind that was anything but silky. Another appetiser, meat samosa, was dripping in oil, but was a deep-fried indulgence that left us craving more. The same could be said for the oleaginous butter chicken, yet this was accompanied by a roomali roti that tasted like cardboard. A little salt saved the saag: steaming hot spinach exuding an alluring aroma of garlic, butter and ginger. Paired with maki di roti (thick maize-flour flatbread traditionally eaten in winter), this winning combination is enough to keep you returning here time and time again.
Babies and children welcome: high chairs. Booking advisable. Disabled: toilet. Separate room for parties, seats 60. Takeaway service. Vegetarian menu.

Stanmore, Middlesex

★ Papaji's Lounge NEW

865 Honeypot Lane, Stanmore, Middx HA7 1AR (8905 6966/www.papajis.com). Cannons Park tube. **Lunch served** noon-3pm daily. **Dinner served** 6-11pm Mon-Fri, Sun; 6pm-midnight Sat. **Main courses** £4.95-£12.95. **Credit** AmEx, DC, MC, V. Punjabi
We've tried more than 20 dishes at this north Indian restaurant, owned by Sikh musician Satwinder Singh ('Papaji' is a term of endearment that refers to elderly north Indian men). There's been only one dud. It was butter chicken, served in a lacklustre, tikka masala-style sauce; we sent it back, and it was swiftly replaced with another, incomparably more delicious chicken curry. There was much else to admire and enjoy, like lamb kebabs that let the spices embellish rather than mask the high quality of meat; perky potato, sweetcorn, cashew and tapioca patties; stridently flavoured mustard leaf, fresh fenugreek and spinach curry; and velvety yoghurt soup in which pakoras had been soaked for long enough to take on the pillowy, comforting texture of dumplings. It's not easy to make Punjabi food contemporary: the flavours are earthy and homely, textures tend to be mushy, and dishes lack the elegant razzle-dazzle of their sexier Awadhi and Mughlai cousins. But here, the talented Andhra-born head chef Mahesh Flora (from the Taj hotel in Mumbai) and his three-strong brigade from Delhi and Dubai have kept the dishes true to their peasant roots, while bringing them into the 21st century. We'll be back for 20 more, as long as Flora and team keep churning them out.
Babies and children welcome: high chairs. Booking advisable. Takeaway service; delivery service (within 3-mile radius).

Sudbury, Middlesex

★ ★ Five Hot Chillies

875 Harrow Road, Sudbury, Middx HA0 2RH (8908 5900). Sudbury Town or Sudbury Hill tube. **Meals served** noon-midnight daily. **Main courses** £3.50-£9. **Unlicensed. Corkage** no charge. **Credit** MC, V.
Punjabi
'Where great food is made better' is the motto of this popular Punjabi corner caff. Sit near the counter at one of the green easy-wipe tables, and you can judge for yourself; from here you can see the chefs at work in the back kitchen, reflected in the shiny stainless-steel panelling. The menu is full of unusual twists to the Punjabi theme: karahi butter bean methi (highly savoury, highly recommended), garlic mussels (six Pacific big boys, a bit chewy, but covered in mouth-watering fried garlic and coriander), and lamb with tinda (tender meat and marrow-like veg in a tangy tomato gravy). As is the Punjabi norm, karahi curries, tandoori meats and bread are the highlights, and are cooked to an extremely high standard (savour, for instance, the gorgeously marinated fish tikka). One tip though: order steamed rice or a plain roti or nan as accompaniment; the strong, rich flavours and oily consistency can be overwhelming without them. Bring your own alcohol, or do as we did and follow the recommendation of the waiter (a softly spoken chap in a baseball hat) and drink passion-fruit juice.
Babies and children welcome: high chairs. Booking advisable. Takeaway service. Vegetarian menu.

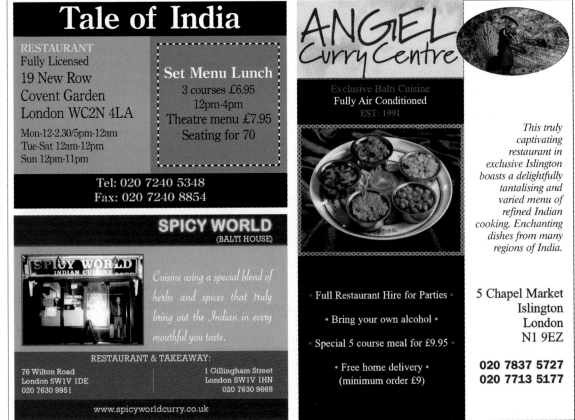

Twickenham, Middlesex

Tangawizi

406 Richmond Road, Richmond Bridge, East Twickenham, Middx TW1 2EB (8891 3737/ www.tangawizi.co.uk). St Margaret's rail. **Dinner served** 6.30-11pm Mon-Sat. **Main courses** £6.95-£12.95. **Credit** AmEx, MC, V.
North Indian

The contemporary decor at this busy local favourite is beguiling: deep aubergine and saffron walls, fretwork copper panels, tables inlaid with sari fabric – all beautifully lit. The charming Indian couple that own Tangawizi were born in Uganda and Tanzania, so there are one or two East African touches to the light and fresh North Indian cooking. Every item on our platter of mixed starters scored highly, with spicing ranging from subtle (paneer tikka with a hint of pickling spices) to searing (masala-marinated lamb chops). Lamb seekh kebabs were notable: tender, and with a strong suggestion of fresh green chilli. The methi chicken main course impressed too, with the fenugreek providing a base note to a vibrant tomato sauce, instead of being the main focus as it often is. Samaki choma (grilled fish) is a take on the African staple of chargrilled meat (nyama choma); here it came in the form of red snapper, cooked to an appropriate smoky intensity. Service was as polished as the surroundings.
Babies and children welcome: high chairs. Booking advisable Fri, Sat. Restaurant available for hire. Takeaway service; delivery service (over £15 within 3-mile radius). Vegetarian menu.

Uxbridge, Middlesex

★ Satya

33 Rockingham Road, Uxbridge, Middx UB8 2TZ (01895 274250). Uxbridge tube. **Lunch served** noon-3pm, **dinner served** 6-11pm daily. **Main courses** £5.50-£9.50. **Set buffet** (noon-3pm Mon-Fri) £6.50. **Credit** AmEx, MC, V.
South Indian

Good-looking Satya occupies three rooms, the first featuring bare floorboards and bar, the back room sporting tasteful gold and cranberry walls and South Indian carvings, the third providing a seemly spot for private parties. The warm welcome from the cohort of young waiters, who maintained top-notch service through our evening, got things off to a fine start, and the eclectic origins of the diners (romantic couples, well-behaved lads out for a curry, Indian families) suggested good things to come – and they did. The menu incorporates lamb and chicken favourites, but it's the South Indian dishes that entice. Star of our meal was a chat masala starter; crisp sev boosted by crunchy pickled veg, topped with thick yoghurt criss-crossed with sweet tamarind relish. We'd no complaints either about the masala dosa (packed with comforting mash), nor main course dishes of nutty cabbage thoran and tasty aloo cochin (potatoes pepped up with lime leaves and mustard seeds). Slightly more challenging were the strongly flavoured king fish steaks, tempered by coconut milk in the 'fish molly'. Manthanga erissery (pumpkin with black-eyed beans) was a touch bland, but overall, Satya makes for a gratifying night out, as you might expect from the people behind it; they also run Ram's (*see p169*).
Babies and children welcome: high chair. Booking advisable. Disabled: toilet. Separate room for parties, seats 10. Takeaway service.

Wembley, Middlesex

This bustling, atmospheric area of London is home to many of the capital's Gujarati, South Indian and Sri Lankan residents. The stretch of Ealing Road close to Wembley Central station is where you'll now find some of the city's best Tamil eateries, along with Sri Lankan grocers and butchers. Walk further down Ealing Road, towards Alperton tube station, and you'll come across family-run Gujarati cafés, grocery stores, greengrocers, aromatic shops selling sweets and snacks, pavement stalls displaying many varieties of Indian and Pakistani mangoes, and ice-cream vans that offer a range of kulfis and faloodas. At its busiest, Ealing Road looks like an Indian bazaar. Don't miss the fashionable vada pau (Indian-style vegetarian burgers, with a deep-fried, potato-based patty), the masala-corn-in-a-cup kiosk or the freshly pressed sugar cane and coconut juices. Budding chefs can find all the essential utensils for pan-Indian cooking here, from idli moulds to rolling pin and board sets (perfect for making fresh chapatis). In recent years, some of the action in the area seems to have moved further north-west, away from Wembley into outlying areas, where interesting new restaurants are also popping up.

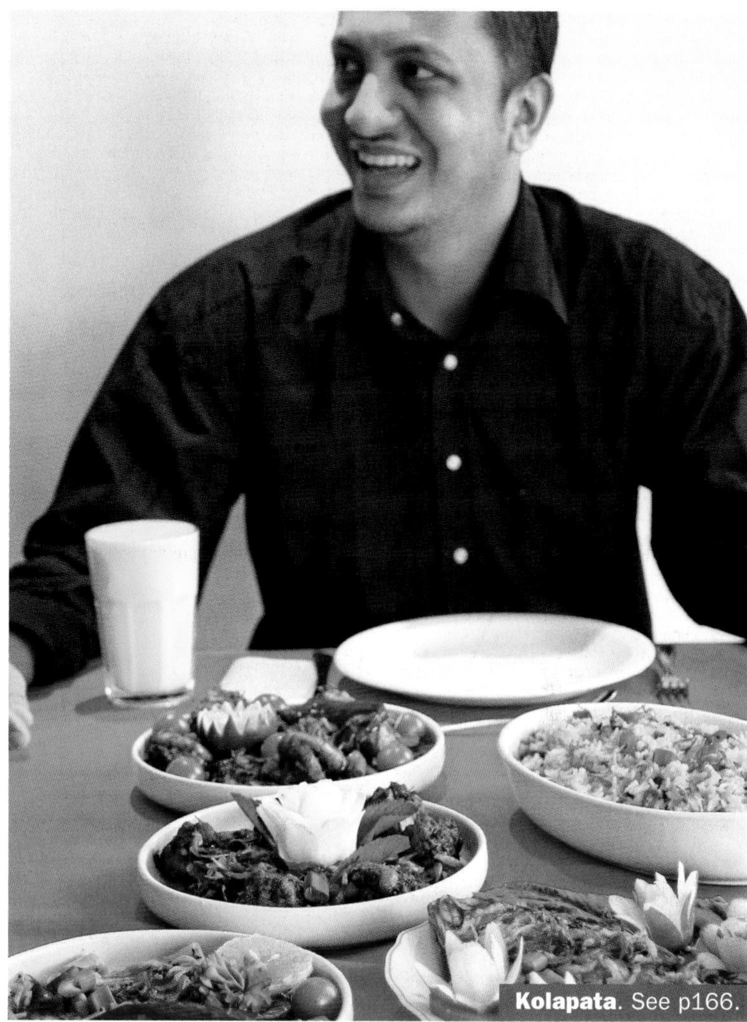
Kolapata. See p166.

★ ★ Dadima

228 Ealing Road, Wembley, Middx HA0 4QL (8902 1072). Alperton tube/79, 83, 297 bus. **Lunch served** noon-3pm, **dinner served** 5-10pm Mon, Wed-Fri; 5.30-10pm Tue. **Meals served** noon-10pm Sat, Sun. **Main courses** £3-£4.50. **Thalis** £4.99-£5.99. **Credit** MC, V.
Gujarati vegetarian

There's no mistaking the authenticity of this gem on lively Ealing Road. With its array of dishes, plastic flowers, a religious idol adorned in flashing lights, and an efficient but grim-faced waiter, Dadima could be in any city in Gujarat. From the snacks, we tried the saporous dahi wada (lentil cakes doused in yoghurt flavoured with cumin and tamarind) and the crispy bhajia (a simple plate of potato slices deep fried in gram flour batter). It's easy to gorge on the starters, but try and save room for the dadi ni special thali, which consists of four chapatis (or four pooris); spicy chickpeas; potato cubes in a sweetened tomato sauce; cauliflower steeped heavily in turmeric; khadi (a mouth-smacking melange of yoghurt, gram flour, garlic and bay leaves); a salty shash (a thinner version of lassi). The farsan (savoury snacks), such as the patra and kachoris, are also excellent. Traditionally, Gujaratis mix their sweets with their savouries, as expertly exemplified in the bona fide rotalla plate (listed under side orders). Made from black millet flour, hand-shaped, the rotalla is covered in ghee and served with sweet jaggery and savoury garlic chutney. Dadima also breaks the mould by offering an impressive selection of alcoholic drinks.
Babies and children welcome: high chairs. Booking essential weekends. Disabled: toilet. Takeaway service. Vegetarian menu. Vegan dishes.

Karahi King

213 East Lane, North Wembley, Middx HA0 3NG (8904 2760). North Wembley tube/245 bus. **Meals served** noon-midnight daily. **Main courses** £4-£12. **Unlicensed. Corkage** no charge. **Credit** AmEx, DC, MC, V. Punjabi

Despite being spruced up over the years and expanding into adjacent premises, Karahi King is still used principally as an early evening stop-off during the week. Local Asian families account for

RESTAURANTS

most customers, though there are plenty of others, as news has spread. The menu is split into vegetarian and non-veg choices, with the occasional sweetcorn dish indicating an East African influence. Tandoori breads and meat are the best option, closely followed by the karahis. Lamb tikka was a marvellous appetiser: juicy, well-marinated, tender and slightly pink inside, seared on its surface. Less impressive was a dry masala fish. To follow, thick, nourishing mixed dal (with moong and urad beans) had an appetising taste of ghee, jeera rice was a delicate blend of fried cumin, browned wisps of onion and free-flowing grains. Only the homogeneous mound of karahi keema failed to excite. Best was a karahi kebab: chunks of seekh kebab served in a tangy, tomato-based sauce. The amenable staff were happy to bring glasses for our perry; we were happy to sit at the easy-wipe tables, beneath pictures of flowers, and admire the chefs in their stainless-steel kitchen.
Babies and children welcome: high chairs. Separate room for parties, seats 60. Takeaway service. Vegetarian menu.

★ Sakonis (100)

129 Ealing Road, Wembley, Middx HA0 4BP (8903 9601). Alperton tube/183 bus. **Breakfast served** 9-11am Sat, Sun. **Meals served** noon-10pm daily. **Main courses** £3.50-£7. **Set buffet** (breakfast) £3.99; (noon-4pm) £6.99; (7-9.30pm) £9.99. **Credit** MC, V. Gujarati vegetarian

Situated between sprawling fruit and vegetable shops and colourful sari boutiques, Sakonis is an Ealing Road institution. This branch of the famous Gujarati vegetarian chain is packed at weekends, with queues falling out of the doors. It's easy to see why. Though the white-tiled interior is functional, the food remains vibrant and well-executed. A masala dosa was huge and crunchy, filled with spicy potatoes, served with delicious sambar and coconut chutney. Dahi wada (lentil dumplings with cool yoghurt, hot spices and sweet tamarind) hit all the right notes, and the pani poori (filled with a tamarind, green chilli and coriander sauce) brought an explosion of flavour. Only the idlis weren't as light and fluffy as they might have been. After the full-flavoured food, we enjoyed a refreshing passion-fruit juice from a drinks menu of fresh juices. Service was quiet and unassuming, but a firmer hand is seen in strict notices around the restaurant telling customers not to abuse the legendary buffets (these comprise Gujarati specialities and Chinese-Indian dishes). There's a large takeaway counter, should all the tables be full.
Babies and children welcome: high chairs. Takeaway service.
For branches see index.

★ ★ Sanghamam

531-533 High Road, Wembley, Middx HA0 2DJ (8900 0777/www.sanghamam.co.uk). Wembley Central tube. **Meals served** 8am-11pm daily. **Main courses** £4.25-£6.95. **Set lunch** (11am-4pm) £3.95 3 dishes. **Thalis** £4.95-£6.95. **Credit** MC, V. Pan-Indian vegetarian

'Gujarati, South Indian, North Indian, Chinese' ... the signs outside Sanghamam's large corner premises (on the busy Ealing Road, High Road junction) embrace with gusto the concept of choice. On a Sunday afternoon, there was barely space to queue within, as dozens of South Asian families waited eagerly to be seated. Entertainment is supplied by a juice counter (fresh-made apple juice £2.25), a sweets and snack counter, Bollywood classics on a flat-screen TV, the street-scene outside, and, on our visit, helium-filled balloons floating above the glass-topped tables. South Indian food certainly had the edge over our rather oily Gujarati dishes. Best was the plain dosa: an 18in (45cm) whopper accompanied by moreish coconut and coriander chutneys, a pot of sambar and a scrumptious vegetable curry, all for £2.50. The South Indian thali was equally great value (ten little bowls, including two puds, surrounding a mound of rice for £4.95), and the idli sambar will transport you back to breakfast in Kerala. Fennel seeds and asafoetida were in feisty evidence in several dishes. Food is remarkably good for the price, and while service verged on the chaotic, everyone remained impeccably polite and patient.
Babies and children welcome: high chairs. Separate room for parties, seats 80. Takeaway service.

Sweets menu

Even though there isn't a tradition of serving puddings at everyday meals in South Asia, there is much ceremony associated with distributing sweetmeats at auspicious events – especially weddings and religious festivals. Many of these delicacies are rarely found in the West: shahi tukra (nursery-like bread and butter pudding); nimesh (rose-scented creamy froth, scooped into clay pots); and misti dhoi (jaggery-flavoured set yoghurt from Bengal).

Desserts served at many Indian restaurants in London include the likes of gulab jamun (deep-fried dumplings in a rosewater-flavoured syrup), cardamom-scented rice pudding, creamy kulfi, and soft, syrup-drenched cheese dumplings. Home-style family meals don't often include a dessert; you're more likely to be treated to a platter of seasonal fruit. Even in Britain, thousands of miles away from mango groves, the onset of India's mango season in May is a date for the calendar. To appreciate this lush fruit at its best, look out for boxes of alfonso mangoes in Asian stores.

Winter warmers also have their place, including comforting, fudge-like carrot halwa, a Punjabi favourite and popular street snack. In Punjabi villages, a communal cauldron is often simmered for hours on end, sending out wafts of aromatic cardamom and caramelised carrots as the halwa cooks down into an indulgent treat. Winter is also the season for weddings, where other halwas, made with wholewheat flour, semolina, lentils and pumpkin might be served.

Most 'sweets' take a long time to make, which is why people prefer to visit sweetmeat shops, the best known of which is **Ambala**'s flagship store near Euston station (112 Drummond Street, NW1 2HN, 7387 3521). Here, an impressive array of eye candy for the seriously sweet-toothed includes soft cheese-based dumplings immersed in rose-scented syrup, cashew nut fudgy blocks, toasted gram-flour balls, and marzipan-like rolls. Expect floral flavours, shed-loads of sugar and a good whack of calorie-laden ghee (clarified butter). It's hard to believe that with all the varieties offered, specialist sweet-makers (known as halwais) cook with so few ingredients; milk products, dried fruit, sugar and ghee are the key constituents. We're also pleased to see a resurgence in Bangladeshi-accented Bengali sweets in the several sweet shops in Brick Lane; **Alauddin Sweetmeat** (72 Brick Lane, E1 6RL, 7377 0896) was the first to sell proper Bangladeshi sweets (they're in the lefthand counter) a decade ago.

Lighter, fresher flavours have made their mark on dessert menus too – **Amaya**'s fresh pomegranate granita and the rose-water jelly at **Benares** are a world away from calorie-laden options. Sweetly aromatic spices continue to get a look-in with western-style puds – white chocolate and cardamom mousse (**Tamarind**) and pistachio crème brûlée (**Zaika**). Traditional Asian classics aren't yesterday's news, but in the drive to be different, fine dining chefs are swayed by flashy plate presentations and untenable flavour combos – batter-fried rice pudding anyone? When it comes to kheer – Indian rice pudding – Eastcote's **Nauroz** hits the spot with their creamy rendition.

Barfi: sweetmeat usually made with reduced milk, and flavoured with nuts, fruit, sweet spices or coconut.
Bibenca or **bibinca**: soft, layered cake from Goa made with eggs, coconut milk and jaggery.
Falooda or **faluda**: thick milky drink (originally from the Middle East), resembling a cross between a milkshake and a sundae. It's flavoured with either rose syrup or saffron, and also contains agar-agar, vermicelli, nuts and ice-cream. Very popular with Gujarati families, faloodas make perfect partners to deep-fried snacks.
Gajar halwa: grated carrots, cooked in sweetened cardamom milk until soft, then fried in ghee until almost caramelised; usually served warm.
Gulab jamun: brown dumplings (made from dried milk and flour), deep-fried and served in rose-flavoured sugar syrup, best served warm. A traditional Bengali sweet, now ubiquitous in Indian restaurants.
Halwa: a fudge-like sweet, made with semolina, wholewheat flour or ground pulses cooked with syrup or reduced milk, and flavoured with nuts, saffron or sweet spices.
Jalebis: spirals of batter, deep-fried and dipped in syrup, best eaten warm.
Kheer: milky rice pudding, flavoured with cardamom and nuts. Popular throughout India (there are many regional variations).
Kulfi: ice-cream made from reduced milk, flavoured with nuts, saffron or fruit.
Payasam: a South Indian pudding made of reduced coconut or cow's milk with sago, nuts and cardamom. Semiya payasam is made with added vermicelli.
Rasgullas: soft paneer cheese balls, simmered and dipped in rose-scented syrup, served cold.
Ras malai: soft paneer cheese patties in sweet and thickened milk, served cold.
Shrikhand: hung (concentrated) sweet yoghurt with saffron, nuts and cardamom, sometimes with fruit added. A traditional Gujarati favourite, eaten with pooris.

International

Mixing cuisines in one dish or, more often, one menu, is a delicate and tricky affair, fraught with potential taste explosions that should never have seen the light of day. But the capital's restaurateurs continue to experiment like medieval alchemists, a handful creating gold in the process. South-east Asian spices and styles continue to mix well with Antipodean at Peter Gordon's **The Providores & Tapa Room**. Pierre Gagnaire, presiding over the Sketch spaces, opts for less obvious pairings at **Sketch: The Glade**, drawing inspiration for his dishes from wherever he fancies, including France and Japan. At **Palate**, a small but perfectly formed menu is drawn from the best of Mediterranean cuisine, and **Penk's** also successfully trawls the southern Med for its wide-ranging selection, offering inventive dishes from France, Spain and Italy. **Ottolenghi** goes further and manages to get everything right with its impressive worldwide mix of dishes and standout decor and service.

Central

Clerkenwell & Farringdon

Vic Naylor Restaurant & Bar

38-42 St John Street, EC1M 4AY (7608 2181/ www.vicnaylor.com). Barbican tube/Farringdon tube/rail. **Lunch served** noon-3pm Mon-Fri. **Dinner served** 5.30-11.30pm Mon-Wed; 5.30pm-1am Thur-Sat. **Main courses** £9-£17.50. **Credit** AmEx, MC, V.

Some of the old get up and go seems to have got up and left here. Weekday evenings have the whiff of convenience about them, with pubby grub casually presented to groups of jovial colleagues. The party only arrives come the weekend, when DJs crank it up with easy tunes (from the 1970s and onwards) and a clubbier crowd lets loose in the adjoining bar. Once a haunt of Tracey Emin and the Britart posse, Vic's still prides itself on a laid-back style. Service is informal, the burnished walls, high ceiling and torch-style uplighters are more characterful than much of the competition. Despite protestations to the contrary, however, the starchy tablecloths suggest that (like the Emins of this world) Vic's has become a little remote from the underground vibe. To eat well, stick to the sensible-sounding likes of ham, split pea and vegetable soup; venison steak with mash and braised shallots; or porcini ravioli with cream, rocket and parmesan. Occasionally, a pairing (such as duck breast with stir-fried vegetables) tastes a bit too 'student cookbook'. Fine up to a point, but Vic's needs to get its groove back.

Babies and children admitted. Booking advisable. Separate room for parties, seats 35. **Map 5 O5.**

Covent Garden

Asia de Cuba

St Martins Lane Hotel, 45 St Martin's Lane, WC2N 4HX (7300 5588/www.morganshotel group.com). Leicester Square tube. **Breakfast served** 6.30-11am Mon-Fri; 7-11am Sat, Sun. **Lunch served** noon-2.30pm daily. **Dinner served** 5pm-midnight Mon-Wed; 5pm-12.30am Thur-Sat; 5-10.30pm Sun. **Main courses** £16.50-£48. **Set meal** (noon-7pm daily) £22.50-£30 bento box. **Credit** AmEx, DC, MC, V.

From the row of Philippe Starck seats shaped like molars in the lobby, to the location inside chic St Martins Lane Hotel, this design-led restaurant piles on the modernist style, yet is never quite as cool as it thinks it is. Clubby music at busy sittings means conversation is not a priority – unless you include the charmtastic staff, who pause prettily at your elbow to elucidate on everything you wanted to know about the menu but were too distracted by the stylish clientele to ask. Hybrid dishes are inspired by the Chino-Latino cafés of Havana, Miami and New York. All are intended for sharing, which goes some way towards justifying the premier league pricing. Of particular note are the bountiful house salad of crispy calamares with sesame orange dressing, and the simple medium-rare wagyu beef with mash. Cocktails are engagingly inventive; the lychee and apple mojito just tops the signature 'ADC' of champagne, vanilla-infused rum, raspberries and lime juice. Keep a clear head for the bill, mind; a 15% service charge is included while the slip's left open.

Babies and children welcome: high chairs. Booking advisable. Disabled: toilet. Separate rooms for parties, seating 48 and 96. Vegetarian menu. **Map 18 D5.**

Le Deuxième

65A Long Acre, WC2E 9JH (7379 0033/ www.ledeuxieme.com). Covent Garden tube. **Lunch served** noon-3pm, **dinner served** 5pm-midnight Mon-Fri. **Meals served** noon-midnight Sat; noon-11pm Sun. **Main courses** £14-£25. **Set meal** (noon-3pm, 5-7pm, 10pm-midnight Mon-Fri; noon-11pm Sun) £11.95 2 courses, £15.50 3 courses. **Credit** AmEx, MC, V.

Pre-theatre dining is too often dictated by convenience rather than propelled by reputation. Not so at Le Deuxième, where chef Geoffrey Adams has pleasingly upped his game. There are no radical changes, it's just that dishes are a little less generic and executed with more panache than you'd expect from an otherwise anonymous restaurant that services a whistle-stop throng of theatregoers. A favourite starter is the velvety foie gras with mango tart tatin and madeira jus. Mains, such as duck breast scented with honey and thyme (and almost upstaged by cheeky potato beignets), and sesame-glazed rare tuna with wilted choi sum, arrive with an astutely judged whizziness geared to a 'doors open at 7pm' getaway. These 'understudies' could just as easily be the leading act of the evening in their own right. The tide of customers ebbs and flows with Shaftesbury Avenue's programme times; you'd do well to book in advance. Le Deuxième comes 'second' only in the sense that it is the more recently founded sibling of wine bar/brasserie Café des Amis around the corner. In terms of performance, it's first rate.

Babies and children admitted. Booking advisable. **Map 18 E3.**

Fitzrovia

Archipelago

110 Whitfield Street, W1T 5ED (7383 3346/ www.archipelago-restaurant.co.uk). Goodge Street or Warren Street tube. **Lunch served** noon-2.30pm Mon-Fri. **Dinner served** 6-10.30pm Mon-Sat. **Main courses** £13.50-£19.50. **Set lunch** (Mon-Fri) £12.50 per person (minimum 2). **Credit** AmEx, DC, JCB, MC, V.

Dining out with picky refuseniks is no one's idea of fun. And at Archipelago, it's a complete no-no, which has to be a blessing. The list of dishes here is more menagerie than menu, with crocodile, wildebeest, kangaroo and frogs' legs all appearing under the guise of such exotically named concoctions as 'Cayman Islands', 'Serengeti dusk', 'hot marsupial' and 'Jamaican mountain chicken'. Crocodile fillet is a house favourite: juicy hunks of seared flesh bundled into vine leaves with plum dipping sauce on the side. Sliced wildebeest (gnu) fillets taste like lamb, but have the close chewy texture of beef. Spicy vegetarian fare is available, but, tasty as it may be, nobody comes here expressly to try 'Durban bunny chow' (lentil curry) or 'Arabian parcels' (mixed bean Middle Eastern curry). Be warned: all sense of normality is lost the moment you step inside and hear the crunch of gravel underfoot (from a patch the size of a welcome mat). Tables are intimately arranged and presided over by fertility idols and African masks; the menu is coiled like a Dead Sea scroll; and your bill is presented between the elegant digits of a carved wooden hand.

Babies and children admitted. Booking advisable. Tables outdoors (2, patio). **Map 3 J4.**

Mash

19-21 Great Portland Street, W1W 8QB (7637 5555/www.mash-bar.co.uk). Oxford Circus tube. **Lunch served** noon-3pm Mon-Sat. **Dinner served** 6-10.30pm Mon-Sat. **Main courses** £11.50-£16.50. **Set meal** £24 3 courses. **Admission** £5 after 9pm Fri, Sat; £10 after 10pm Sat. **Credit** AmEx, MC, V.

It's not mash as in 'comforting mounds of creamy potato', it's mash as in 'hops' – as the gleaming vats of the upstairs microbrewery testify. And of late, it's also been about getting mashed, as wackily haired students from UCL troop into the street-level bar for beery, bleary club nights (when loud DJs and bouncers are in evidence, as is a post-watershed door fee). Draught own-brews are the main event, including the house tipple: a flavoursome wheat beer. Upstairs from the self-conscious cool of the plasticky ground floor (with its curvy sofas and lozenge-shaped lights) is a calmer space that proves to be a midweek find for an after-work bite. Food is pitched at mid-market prices and a simple palate. The Mash beefburger is a reliable monster of a main course, with red pepper and coriander relish, and chunky fries. Chops, steak, fish cakes and a good selection of pizzas (look out for the prosciutto di parma, tomato, radicchio and Colston Bassett stilton) amount to superior pub grub. Service is uneven, but at least the beer chills you out.

Babies and children admitted. Bar available for hire. Disabled: toilet. Dress: smart casual. Entertainment: DJs 9pm Wed-Sat. Separate room for parties, seats 28. Tables outdoors (4-8, pavement). **Map 9 J6.**

Marylebone

★ The Providores & Tapa Room

109 Marylebone High Street, W1U 4RX (7935 6175/www.theprovidores.co.uk). Baker Street or Bond Street tube.

The Providores **Lunch served** noon-2.45pm daily. **Dinner served** 6-10.30pm Mon-Sat;

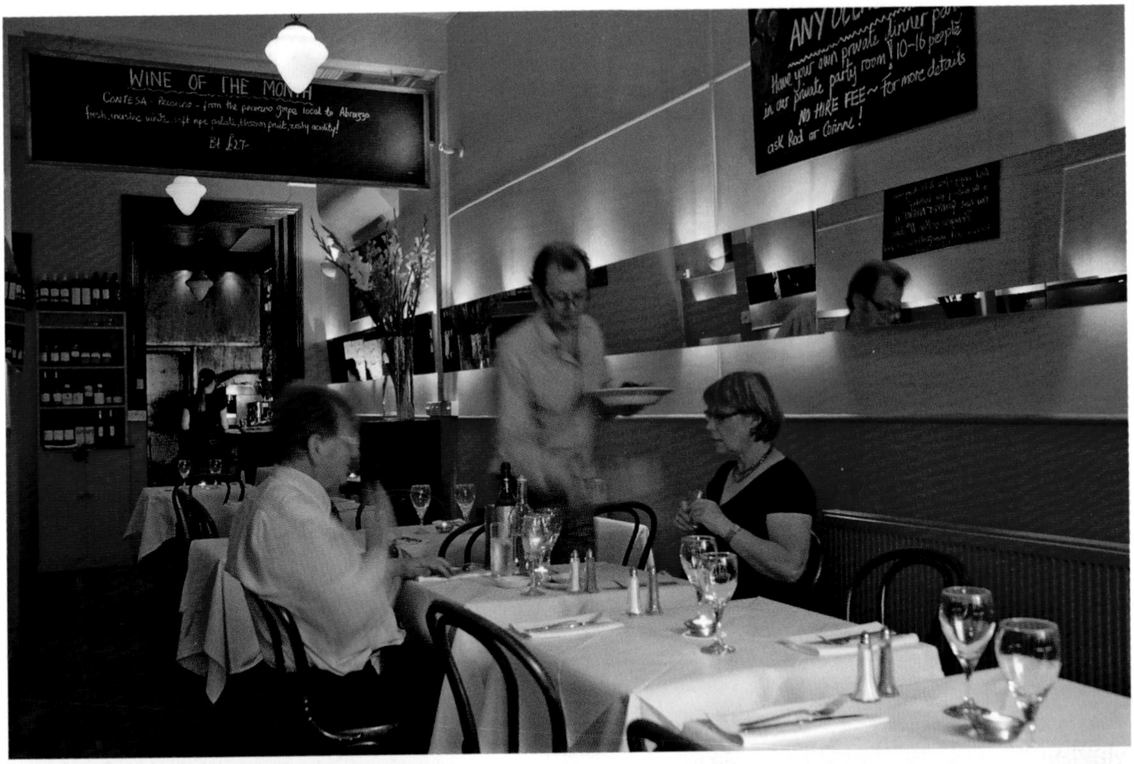

Penk's. See p180.

6-10pm Sun. **Main courses** £18-£24.50.
Cover (lunch Sat, Sun) £1.50.
Tapa Room **Breakfast served** 9-10.30am Mon-Fri; 10am-3pm Sat, Sun. **Meals served** noon-10.30pm Mon-Fri; 4-10.30pm Sat; 4-10pm Sun. **Tapas** £2-£14.40.
Both **Credit** AmEx, MC, V.
Over the past year the star of executive chef and co-owner Peter Gordon has risen, so the TV appearances multiply and his latest book *Vegetables: the New Food Heroes* is bang on trend (signed copies sold here). 'Face' status aside, Gordon, the man behind the Sugar Club, has what it takes in the kitchen. His fusion cooking (South-east Asia meets New Zealand) remains inspirational. At ground level the up-tempo Tapa Room is a buzzy drop-in for the pretty and privileged, by day and night. Here, you'll find everything from breakfasts to sparky cocktails, as well as refined tapas containing more ingredients than appear in many haute cuisine main courses. Upstairs at the grown-up Providores, the food is even more fiendishly complicated, with (sharp intake of breath) smoked aubergine, pine nut, coriander and spiced currant raviolo on roast butternut and barba di frate with fried manouri ewe's milk cheese, pickled beetroot and soy-truffled mushrooms – comprising a single main. Yet each dish uses first-rate produce so delicately balanced you taste only harmony, not over-complexity. Service is friendly and well judged, the New Zealand wine list an education. It's virtually impossible to eat badly here, but elbow room is a scant commodity.
Babies and children welcome: high chairs. Booking advisable (Providores); bookings not accepted (Tapa Room). Disabled: toilet. Tables outdoors (2, pavement). **Map 9 G5.**

Mayfair

Sketch: The Gallery (100)

9 Conduit Street, W1S 2XG (0870 777 4488/ www.sketch.uk.com). Oxford Circus tube. **Dinner served** 7-11pm Mon-Sat. **Main courses** £12-£32. **Credit** AmEx, DC, JCB, MC, V.
High-concept dining goes into overdrive at this extravagant destination restaurant that thinks it's an art gallery. In place of a dado rail, art stills are projected high on to the blackest of walls. At eye level, the spirited multinational crowd (many wearing avant-garde black) continues to consume, seemingly au courant with the changing imagery above. White padded sofas and ornate chairs are angled so as to break up what is a large and regular space; several screens decorated with pretty collages contribute to the effect. Pierre Gagnaire's dishes are modestly sized and immodestly priced, with little dairy produce or carbs in evidence, and plentiful variation. Hence shucked Irish rock oysters come with dainty sausage slices on a cocktail stick; cubes of wood-fired beetroot and a morsel of rye bread with pungent beaufort cheese. Saddle of lamb has a strongly seasoned herb crust and garlic leaf, but contrasts with, say, the organic chicken where almond cream and grapefruit juice are gently to the fore. Service is intrusive. Even first-timers can expect to be greeted warmly several times over – by reception, front desk, wine waiter and table staff. The Gallery is one of various eating places: there's also the cheaper Glade (*see below*), the (much) more expensive Lecture Room and café Parlour.
Booking essential. Entertainment: DJs 11pm-2am Thur-Sat. Restaurant available for hire. **Map 9 J6.**

★ Sketch: The Glade

9 Conduit Street, W1S 2XG (0870 777 4488/ www.sketch.uk.com). Oxford Circus tube. **Lunch served** noon-3pm Mon-Sat. **Main courses** £12-£20. **Set lunch** £19.50 2 courses, £24 3 courses. **Credit** AmEx, DC, JCB, MC, V.
Diners are ushered past theatrical drapes and a pitch-black hallway punctuated by art installations and an Ottoman-style couch. In comparison, this lunchtime brasserie (where staff wear jeans) threatens to jar with Sketch's finely honed artistic sensibilities. Quickly, though, you tune into the playful juxtapositions. Yes, the tables are melamine, but the salt and pepper pots are weighty silver. The handmade cream wallpaper borrows from the Victorian craft of paper relief, but hidden among the floral cut-outs are glinting rhinestones and the curves of naked dancers. Of the restaurants at Sketch – including the Gallery (*see above*) and the haute-cusine Lecture Room – the Glade is Pierre Gagnaire's most egalitarian. This is reflected in the choice of Market Menu, a set selection of straightforward dishes such as mushroom velouté and fish mousseline. Likewise the carte, which adds global interest at (relatively) purse-friendly prices. A Japanese element plays through in the 'Ryukisan' salad with its zesty grapefruit, grilled shiitake mushrooms and beansprouts, while even a simple-sounding roast breast of chicken defies expectation, arriving with a marmalade of madras curry. It's artfully done, as you'd expect, but nothing prepares you for the loos, each housed in a gleaming 'alien pod'.
Babies and children welcome: high chairs. Booking advisable. Disabled: ramp; toilet. Separate room for parties, seats 50. **Map 9 J6.**

Soho

Refuel

The Soho Hotel, 4 Richmond Mews, W1D 3DH (7559 3007/www.refuelsoho.com). Tottenham Court Road tube. **Meals served** 7am-11pm Mon-Sat; 7.30am-11pm Sun. **Main courses** £13.50-£30. **Set meal** (noon-11pm Mon-Sat) £19.95 3 courses; (noon-3pm Sun) £24.95 3 courses. **Credit** AmEx, JCB, MC, V.
When this hotel hideaway gets it right, it's very, very right. Set back from Dean Street, the Soho Hotel has its own little mews enclave that reeks of exclusivity. Inside is immaculate. Boldly coloured walls are unapologetically forthright, the modern style tempered by natural textures such as the pebbles disguising supporting columns, or the rustic amphoras separating bar from restaurant. Problem is, when so much is right, any oversight is startling. Dishes can be brave, or borderline foolhardy. Fish is done best, with a sizeable range (roast halibut, seared swordfish, crab salad, line-caught sea bass, chargrilled monkfish). A smoky fennel seed and coriander seared tuna loin starter would have been an unqualified success had the serving been more generous. Robust main courses seem decent: the likes of calf's liver with pecorino and wet polenta; or braised neck of lamb with cavolo nero and roast peppers. Yet given the W1 prices, you'd want more from a chicken than a potent pot roast involving a vinegary pool of artichoke, salsify and caramelised endive. The wine list is a strength, as is the lively, compact bar, where the limited space is given over to loungey seats. Such are priorities.
Babies and children welcome: high chairs. Booking advisable. Disabled: toilet. Separate room for parties, seats 45. **Map 17 B3.**

Westminster

The Atrium

4 Millbank, SW1P 3JA (7233 0032/www.atrium restaurant.com). Westminster tube. **Lunch served** noon-3pm, **dinner served** 6-9.45pm Mon-Fri. **Main courses** £8.50-£19.75. **Set meal** £17.95 2 courses. **Credit** AmEx, DC, MC, V.
Is the usual tableside small-talk irksome? If so, descend the sweeping staircase at Four Millbank and head for the back bar, where politicos adjourn for the obligatory lunchtime tipples that oil the wheels of Westminster. Diners will find more elbow room 'outside', which means planting yourself in a central courtyard bathed in light, producing an alfresco ambience. Despite possessing the benchmarks of restaurant status (an à la carte menu, a charge for bread and olives, tidy linen tablecloths), the Atrium retains a café vibe. Its menu contains simple staples that lack ambition: onion and artichoke tart; spaghetti with seafood, chilli and garlic; and roast chicken breast with mushroom and broad bean fricassee. Starters vary from heavy-handed tom yum chicken soup to the clean flavours of marinated salmon with crème fraîche, capers, olives and tempura mussels. Dishes aren't necessarily balanced, so pan-fried crab cakes come with a double whammy of sweet pepper relish and mango salsa, but no proper veg. Sadly, evenings here are all but deserted, conveying the sensation you've outstayed your welcome. Go, but go for lunch – and the chance to earwig something salacious about a miscreant MP.
Booking advisable lunch. Disabled: lift; toilet. Separate rooms for parties, seating 12 and 30. **Map 16 L10.**

The Vincent Rooms

Westminster Kingsway College, Vincent Square, SW1P 2PD (7802 8391/www.westking.ac.uk). St James's Park tube/Victoria tube/rail. **Lunch served** noon-1.15pm Mon-Fri. **Dinner served** 6-7.15pm Tue, Thur. Closed 2 wks Apr, July-Sept, 2 wks Dec-Jan. **Main courses** £7.25-£10.50. **Set meal** *Escoffier Room* £18 2 courses, £20 3 courses inc coffee. **Credit** MC, V.
This 1910 establishment promises a lot, stating that it gives you the chance to spot the culinary stars of tomorrow. How so? The Brasserie and Escoffier Room are both attached to Westminster Kingsway College, where fresh-faced novices cook up a storm in specialist training kitchens. The results are served to the public in a sweetly affected style – the product of students earnestly applying the rigorous industry standards they've learnt during the day. You can't fault the concept, or the affordable pricing. Brasserie selections might include the likes of leek and salmon fish cake with carefully coiffed carrots, or chicken with an underseasoned crumb topping. The haute aspirations of the Escoffier Room, where dishes boast up to ten separate components, are more akin to *Masterchef* grandstanding. Only advanced students cater to the public, learning to walk (albeit walk to the tune of the legendary Georges Escoffier) before they run free in the professional world of catering, alongside such famous alumni as Jamie Oliver and Ainsley Harriott. Note that the college is closed during holidays and half-term.
Babies and children welcome: high chair. Booking advisable. Disabled: toilet. Separate room for parties, seats 30. **Map 15 J10.**

West

Kensington

Abingdon

54 Abingdon Road, W8 6AP (7937 3339/ www.theabingdonrestaurant.com). High Street Kensington tube. **Lunch served** 12.30-2.30pm Mon-Fri; 12.30-3pm Sat, Sun. **Dinner served** 6.30-10.30pm Mon; 6.30-11pm Tue-Sat; 7-10pm Sun. **Main courses** £12.50-£18.25. **Set lunch** (Mon-Fri) £15.95 2 courses. **Credit** AmEx, MC, V.
There aren't quite as many eateries on Abingdon Road as there are shiny four-wheel drives, but it's a close call. In spite of newer openings, Abingdon's popularity seems undiminished. Outside, it resembles a regular gastropub, but the inside houses a drinking space and two distinct dining areas: one well-groomed in toning taupes, the other with high-backed red booths. The menu avoids the usual gastropub dishes, offering vignettes of Middle Eastern, Mediterranean and continental food, promising bold flavours. Most are successful. Beetroot gazpacho, with a swirl of olive oil and vivid-green avocado and apple floating in the centre looked psychedelic, but the flavours were just right. Also good was pan-seared yellow-fin tuna with grilled octopus, spiced lentil salad and yoghurt (the tuna rare, the octopus tender). Roast Devon lamb with aubergine and almond skordalia missed a beat or two, with slightly overcooked lamb, and a lack of garlic in the sauce. A starter of cumin-breaded goat's cheese with caramelised chicory was devoid of the advertised cumin and came with too many dull salad leaves. The wine list is short but has good selections, particularly from South Africa and France. Prices reflect the chi-chi neighbourhood.
Babies and children welcome: high chairs. Booking essential. Tables outdoors (4, pavement). **Map 13 A9.**

Ladbroke Grove

Palate

269 Portobello Road, W11 1LR (7229 4779). Ladbroke Grove tube. **Meals served** 8am-11pm Tue-Sun. **Main courses** £3.50-£9. **Credit** MC, V.
Palate is the new incarnation of Food@The Muse. The changeover hasn't involved any alteration in ownership, and many of the staff are the same. It's a typical Portobello café-gallery with white walls, tables and plastic chairs. The food, however, is not so conventional, revolving around a menu of just five main courses. All reasonably priced under a tenner, these include salmon with beetroot, squid with mushrooms, and prawn with chilli. An excellently matured sirloin steak was rendered light and fresh by herb butter, while melt-in-the-mouth pork belly was sweetened by glazed onions. Aside from these, there are satellite dishes, including some gorgeous mixed olives and other antipasti, a tomato, basil and mozzarella salad, a very crisp and herby salad, gazpacho and, of course, french fries. Apart from a tempting set of classic puds, that's your lot. But on the plate the cooking's as good as anywhere in these foodie parts, yet costs less than half the usual price. The decent wine list is also considerately priced. New ventures in Notting Hill are delicate flowers vulnerable to commercial winds and whimsy; long may this one last.
Babies and children welcome: high chairs. Disabled: toilet. Separate room for parties, seats 40. Takeaway service. **Map 19 B2**.

South

Clapham

The Sequel

75 Venn Street, SW4 0BD (7622 4222/www.thesequelclapham.com). Clapham Common tube/ 35, 37, 355 bus. **Brunch served** 10am-4pm Sat; 10am-6pm Sun. **Dinner served** 6-11pm Tue-Thur; 6pm-2.30am Fri, Sat; 6-10.30pm Sun. **Main courses** £9-£15.50. **Credit** MC, V.
This long-standing film buffs' haunt (it's next door to the Clapham Picturehouse) has become more serious on the foodie front recently, leaving sister Rapscallion on the other side of Venn Street to shake the cocktails. There's long been an Antipodean feel here, and the menu has a distinct hint of Down Under, with ingredient-loaded dishes, clever fruity elements and lots of fish. Now there's a footnote promising traceable, organic meats from local butcher Chadwick's too. Decor-wise, it's all shades of tobacco and caramel, split over a ground floor and mezzanine and overlooked by a large screen showing movies with the sound turned off. On a recent visit, there were no apparent duds on the menu. Seafood starter options were particularly impressive, running to oysters, razor clams, venus clams, crab and calamari. A beef carpaccio with roquefort, shallots, courgettes and beans came improbably thinly sliced and beautifully juicy, while a main-course seafood spaghetti was busy, tasty and generous. There's not much under £20 on the fairly extensive wine list, but staff are bright and friendly, and service is neat, so it's worth the premium.
Babies and children admitted. Booking advisable. Tables outdoors (5, pavement). **Map 22 A2**.

Waterloo

Laughing Gravy

154 Blackfriars Road, SE1 8EN (7721 7055/ www.thelaughinggravy.com). Southwark tube/ Waterloo tube/rail. **Food served** noon-10pm Mon-Fri; 7-10pm Sat. **Main courses** £10.50-£15.75. **Credit** MC, V.
A curate's egg, the Laughing Gravy. Before it fell into new hands in 2006, its USP was the unselfconsciously quirky decor, the carefully delineated spaces for drinking and eating, and the friendly service. It was one of London's most romantic restaurants, and the food wasn't the reason you returned. Now, much of the clutter has been cleared away – although the wooden figurines of Laurel and Hardy, whose short film *Laughing Gravy* inspired the name, remain – and the drinking and eating areas have morphed into one unmemorable space. What's more, the service on our visit was shocking (premature bills, incorrect orders and much else besides). However, the food was serious, finally doing justice to prices that have always been inflated. The signature bison tournedo was massively improved from previous incarnations, and the accompanying vodka raspberry and Tabasco sauce was surprisingly successful, neither overpowering the bison nor being cowed by it. Starters were similarly bold (Vietnamese crisp-fried frogs' legs, for instance). If you're wary of novelty, fear not: a regular fillet steak with brandy pepper sauce was just so. Bonus points for the excellent drinks: Barbar Honey Ale, St Peter's Organic Ale and Peroni on tap.
Babies and children admitted. Booking advisable. Disabled: toilet. Restaurant available for hire. Tables outdoors (2, pavement). Map 11 O9.

South East

London Bridge & Borough

Champor-Champor

62-64 Weston Street, SE1 3QJ (7403 4600/ www.champor-champor.com). London Bridge tube/rail. **Lunch served** by appointment Mon-Fri. **Dinner served** 6.15-10.15pm Mon-Sat. **Set meal** £23.50 2 courses, £27.90 3 courses, £42 tasting menu. **Credit** AmEx, JCB, MC, V.
From the moment you enter Champor-Champor, you really want to feel you've discovered a gem. The intimate space is filled with a jumble of conversation pieces sourced from around Asia: a medley that would be kitsch elsewhere, but somehow works here. True to the restaurant's name (it means 'mix and match' in Malay), the menu is cheerfully eclectic, offering an intriguing fusion of flavours and cuisines. Curiously, these don't quite include Malaysian. Perhaps the chef from Johor (just north of Singapore) should stick to what he knows best. Salmon roe dumplings made a splash, but came in a watery prawn bisque. Carpaccio of beetroot with chinese pear was a delight in taste and texture, despite lashings of bland pumpkin-seed oil. A palate-cleansing granita of oolong tea and honey – served between the starters and mains – did the job with subtlety. But the mains were disappointing: roast ostrich fillet was tough and its sweet potato mash more of a mush, while coriander-crusted veal chop was short on flavour, and its peanut sauce was short on, well, peanuts. The meal ended with a whimper – a dryish steamed chocolate and cardamom cake.
Babies and children welcome: high chair. Booking essential. Separate room for parties, seats 8. **Map 12 Q9**.

East

Shoreditch

Cantaloupe

35-42 Charlotte Road, EC2A 3PD (7613 4411/ www.cantaloupe.co.uk). Old Street tube/rail/55 bus. **Brunch served** noon-4pm Sun. **Lunch served**

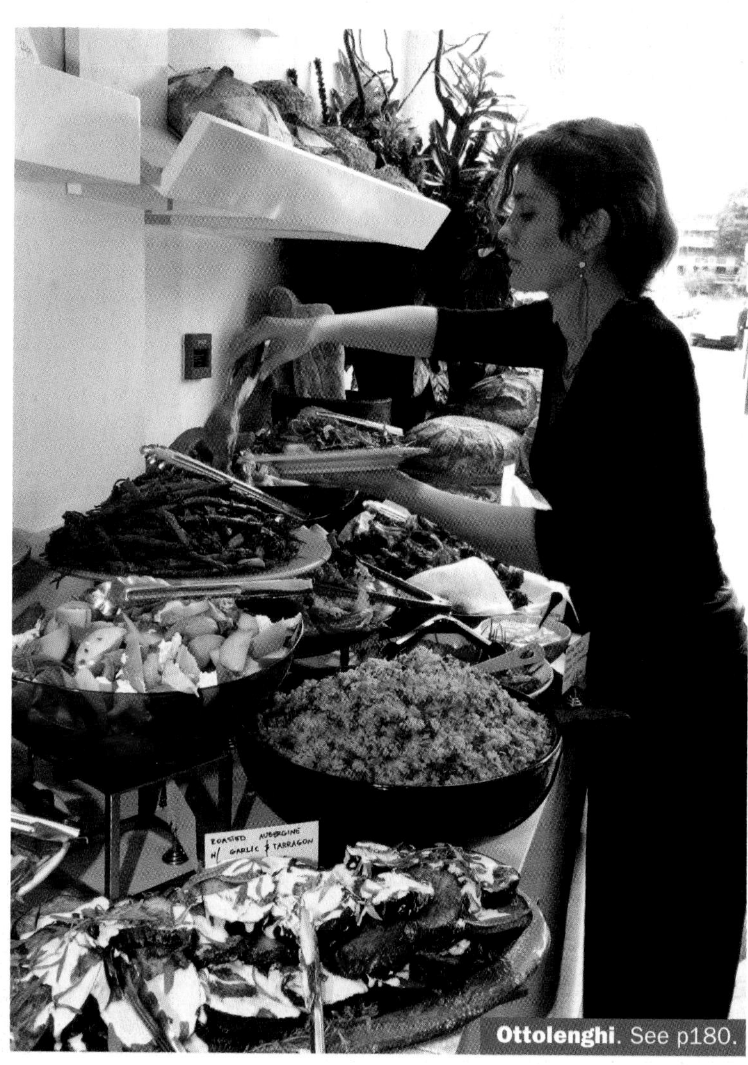

Ottolenghi. See p180.

RESTAURANTS

11am-3pm Thur, Fri. **Dinner served** 6-10pm Mon-Wed; 6pm-10.30pm Thur, Fri; 7-10.30pm Sat. **Main courses** £9.50-£19.75. **Set meal** (lunch Mon-Fri; 6-7pm Mon) £12 2 courses. **Credit** MC, V.

Cantaloupe (sold by its original owners to Alphabet Bars in late 2006) is better known for its DJ bar than its restaurant – and not without good reason. If you can ignore the din from the bar, the set-up is pleasant enough: neat rows of wooden tables in view of a busy open kitchen. Steaks and Latin American dishes (Brazilian moqueca stew, empaniditas and the like) are the mainstays, though the menu branches out with some unusual – some would say ill-advised – combinations. Our ham croquettes tasted more 'crispy pancakes' than the advertised salt-cured serrano ham and parsley cakes, while the seafood in the Colombian la bomba was unappetisingly chewy. Mains were similarly off-key. Chargrilled swordfish was undercooked and served with lumpen onion gravy (yes, swordfish and gravy) and the roast chicken (not bad) came with hard, watery new potatoes. Slow and indifferent service added little to the overall appeal. Although many diners seemed unconcerned by the standards (the steaks are perhaps a safer option), they all appeared to be on the kind of lairy office nights out only a corporate credit card and sky-high blood-alcohol levels can cheerfully sustain.

Bar available for hire. Disabled: toilet. Entertainment: DJ 8pm Fri-Sun. Restaurant available for hire. **Map 6 R4.**

Shish

313-319 Old Street, EC1V 9LE (7749 0990/ www.shish.com). Liverpool Street or Old Street tube/rail. **Meals served** 11.30am-11.30pm Mon-Fri; 10.30am-11.30pm Sat; 10.30am-10.30pm Sun. **Main courses** £4-£8.95. **Set meal** (until 7pm Mon-Fri) £6.95-£8.45 2 courses. **Credit** AmEx, DC, JCB, MC, V.

This bright, goldfish bowl of a restaurant (the big windows are great for keeping an eye on the Old Street bar queues) is best approached as a quick fix. While the swift efficient service and pick 'n' mix meze and kebabs work well for a swift refuel (lone diners can take a stool at the bar), the loud background noise, uncomfortable seating and hurried atmosphere make a leisurely meal more troublesome. The menu offers 'Silk Road' cuisine, with dishes hailing from Turkey, China, Japan and points in between, but kebabs served with rice, couscous, chips or salad are the mainstays. The place was deserted on our Sunday visit (in dramatic contrast to the usual buzz) and the meat lacked the freshness we've experienced on other, busier, occasions. Lamb kofta – served with a bland, oversized portion of couscous – proved lukewarm and unappetising, while a halloumi and vegetable option was better, if slightly undercooked. On a brighter note, the freshly squeezed juices are excellent (try the ludicrously virtuous vegetable blend) and the unusual meze (chinese beans, tzatziki made with courgette) make for great grazing while you await the main event.

Babies and children welcome: children's menu; high chairs. Bookings not accepted for parties of fewer than 8 (restaurant). Disabled: toilet. Entertainment: DJs 8pm Thur, Fri. Tables outdoors (6, pavement). Takeaway service. Vegetarian menu. Vegan dishes. **Map 6 R4.**

For branches see index.

Victoria Park

Frocks

95 Lauriston Road, E9 7HJ (8986 3161). Mile End tube then 277 bus. **Lunch served** noon-4pm Sat. **Dinner served** 6.30-10.30pm Mon-Sat. **Meals served** noon-9pm Sun. **Main courses** £11-£17. **Credit** MC, V.

There was something amiss at Frocks on our recent visit. For a restaurant known for its loyal local fans, and queues down the street on weekend mornings, it was eerily quiet at 9pm on a Saturday. The set-up is pleasantly laid-back, with friendly service and a down-to-earth feel (quirky quotes painted on walls; diners propping their feet up on chairs). However, the barely audible background music did little to detract from the clinking cutlery and whispered conversations of the nine other diners. Starters proved a mixed bag: our gnocchi was good, but the asparagus served with poached egg and hollandaise was tough and vinegary. Mains courses show strong bistro and gastropub influences. We tried the slow-cooked pork belly (meltingly tender but no crunch) and cod served with mussels (firm, flaky fish with a flavoursome sauce). By the time we tucked into our trio of crèmes brûlées, staff were tidying up around us (it was only 11pm), so we turned our attention to the lively Empress of India across the road. Could it be that Frocks is having trouble keeping up with the competition?

Babies and children welcome: high chair. Booking advisable weekends. Separate room for parties, seats 40. Tables outdoors (6, pavement; 6, walled garden).

North East

Wanstead

Hadley House

27 High Street, E11 2AA (8989 8855). Snaresbrook or Wanstead tube. **Breakfast served** 10-11.30am Mon-Fri; 10am-noon Sat, Sun. **Lunch served** noon-2.30pm Mon-Fri; noon-3pm Sat. **Dinner served** 6.30-9.30pm Mon-Sat. **Meals served** 12.30-9pm Sun. **Main courses** £9-£17.50. **Set dinner** (Mon-Thur) £19.95 2 courses, £24.95 3 courses. **Credit** MC, V.

Hadley House does impressive weekend trade with local families, catering to both extremes of the age scale. Indeed, there were evidently plenty of returning customers during our most recent visit. Bright yellow decor, pink drapes at the broad roadside windows, wall art and chandeliers keep the large single room appealingly bouncy, helped along by chatty waitresses. A large menu board of specials, plonked on the table when you arrive, is reinforced by a printed list of crowd-pleasers that covers all the bases: burgers and gastropub sausages, pancakes and omelettes, crab cakes and seared duck breast. The cooking is very eager to please, then, but on this showing excessively so. The retro dishes were generally less fun than they sounded: the raspberry coulis we hoped might enliven parma ham and gala melon failed to deliver the anticipated kick of sharpness, and half-lobster thermidor remained as ponderous an enterprise as ever. Chargrilled asparagus would have provided some welcome lightness had the dish not also been freighted with a sturdy portion of chips. Better were baked sardines with rosemary and tomato dressing, and Asian-spiced chargrilled pork on sautéed spinach with puy lentils.

Babies and children welcome (lunch; Sun): high chairs. Booking advisable. Tables outdoors (7, patio). Takeaway service (lunch).

North

Islington

★ Ottolenghi (100)

287 Upper Street, N1 2TZ (7288 1454/ www.ottolenghi.co.uk). Angel tube/Highbury & Islington tube/rail. **Meals served** 8am-10.30pm Mon-Sat; 9am-7pm Sun. **Main courses** £8.50-£13.50. **Meze** (dinner) £7-£9.50. **Credit** AmEx, MC, V.

Heaven! What a rare treat to go somewhere that gets everything so right, while making it seem so effortless. Nothing here feels laboured, from the cool, minimalistic white furniture (with a simple wire mesh sculpture running the length of the wall) to the stylish but relaxed and friendly staff – and food to die for. At lunchtime, choose from the selection of salads and other main courses, which abound with innovative flavour and texture combinations, and taste stunning. Simpler options might include broccolini with tofu, chilli, sesame oil and soy, or red rice and quinoa with orange zest, caramelised onion, pistachio and rocket. More involved dishes include sesame-crusted seared tuna with a thai fruit salsa, or baked fresh sardines with bulgur, 'Iranian berries', pistachio, lemon and pomegranate. Seating is mainly at long, shared tables, but there are some small, solitary tables against the wall if you yearn to be à deux. Ottolenghi doubles as a bakery and deli, so after your savoury courses, swoon over the enticing array of cakes and tarts on the front counter, then rejoice in an outrageously rich chocolate tart or a splendid chocolate meringue, accompanied by a strong, smooth espresso. We're smitten!

Babies and children welcome: high chairs. Booking advisable dinner; not accepted lunch. Takeaway service. **Map 5 O1.**

For branches see index.

North West

Queen's Park

Hugo's

21-25 Lonsdale Road, NW6 6RA (7372 1232). Queen's Park tube/rail. **Meals served** 9.30am-11pm daily. **Main courses** £11.50-£15.80. **Credit** MC, V.

Hugo's fits its location like the proverbial glove. It sits in a street of workshops, colonised by small craft and media operations, in the gentrified zone of Queen's Park. Food is available all day. The decor, with burgundy walls, cushions and wooden pews, creates a look somewhere between a farm, a Moroccan tea room and a boho church: a laid-back setting for the multi-generational clientele. Weekend brunch is a main event, when local couples, their children and their buggies linger into the afternoon. The menu covers every angle, from brunch favourites, generous sandwiches or coffee and own-made cakes to mains like roast chicken with mushrooms, spinach and a caramelised lemon sauce, or a nicely fresh vegetarian lasagne. Hugo's may no longer go by its original name of the Organic Café, but high-quality organic ingredients remain a forte; our Hugo's Burger (with bacon and cheese) featured first-rate meat. Fish stew with plenty of haddock, salmon, squid and herby flavours was satisfying too. Beers and organic wines are decently priced, and service is obliging. Classy jazz every Sunday (free for diners) completes the mellow feel.

Babies and children welcome: high chairs. Booking advisable dinner. Entertainment: musicians 8pm Mon, Thur, Sun. Tables outdoors (7, pavement). Takeaway service (lunch). **Map 1 A1.**

For branch see index.

★ Penk's

79 Salusbury Road, NW6 6NH (7604 4484/ www.penks.com). Queen's Park tube/rail. **Brunch served** 9.30am-3pm Sat. **Lunch served** 11am-3pm Mon-Fri. **Dinner served** 6-11pm Mon-Thur; 6-11.30pm Fri, Sat. **Meals served** 9.30am-10.30pm Sun. **Main courses** £9.95-£16.95. **Set meal** (noon-3pm, 6-7.30pm) £12 2 courses. **Credit** MC, V.

Perhaps the ideal modern London bistro, Penk's is also a strong candidate for the smallest restaurant façade. Its tiny ex-shopfront leads to a long bar facing one line of two-seater tables, which opens into a slightly bigger space and a conservatory at the back. Any thoughts of claustrophobia are dispelled by the unflustered, friendly atmosphere and excellent food. Dishes are imaginative, but with no cheap tricks; ingredients are first rate. A game terrine was rich and meaty, offset by tangy chutney and pecan and raisin toast. Roast red and golden beetroot with goat's cheese croutons and mixed leaves was a great variation on the salad norm. Being able to turn out standards with no hint of routine is a good test for a restaurant, and Penk's minute steak with red wine and shallots didn't disappoint: the meat just so, the sauce smooth and satisfying. Sea bream, the day's grilled fish, came with tunisian roast veg, couscous and a sparky dressing featuring anchovy, capers and caraway. The menu offers many alternatives, including sandwiches and brunch faves. Even the house wines are above average. A highly enjoyable asset to the area. As we went to press, a revamp of the decor and menu was on the cards.

Babies and children admitted (lunch). Booking advisable. Separate room for parties, seats 20. **Map 1 A2.**

Italian

Read on to find London's finest Italian restaurants; for budget Italian eateries, turn to **Pizza & Pasta**, starting on p319. That's why you'll find no bargain, green-starred restaurants in this chapter. Instead, a lot of the smarter Italian establishments charge around £100 for two for dinner, especially in the West End. But why so dear? Because there is demand. Italian is still the first choice of Londoners when they want a nice meal out; people feel safe spending money in an Italian restaurant, and expect convivial service, a pleasant atmosphere and food that they're used to. This familiarity factor has for years held back the capital's Italian chefs from introducing more authentic dishes, but in the past decade we've noticed a shift towards lesser-known regional dishes; for example, **2 Veneti** serves Venetian cuisine, while **Vasco & Piero's Pavilion** specialises in Umbrian food. **Sardo** is still the best choice for Sardinian, though Sardinian dishes seem to be everywhere nowadays. **Obika** – a small chain with outlets in Milan and Rome, as well as Selfridges – is unsurpassed for its selection of mozzarella and charcuterie one can usually only find locally in Italy. Also, small, family-run restaurants such as **Assaggi**, **La Collina** and **Sardo** aren't scared to offer proper regional Italian dishes that are less familiar to Londoners. *Buon appetito!*

Central

Belgravia

Il Convivio

143 Ebury Street, SW1W 9QN (7730 4099/ www.etruscagroup.co.uk). Sloane Square tube/ Victoria tube/rail. **Lunch served** noon-2.45pm, **dinner served** 7-10.45pm Mon-Sat. **Set lunch** £17.50 2 courses, £21.50 3 courses. **Set dinner** £27.50 2 courses, £33.50 3 courses, £39.50 4 courses. **Credit** AmEx, DC, JCB, MC, V.

The Etrusca Group own several Italian restaurants in London, but we think this one is the best of them (though Caravaggio, in the City, is good too). Even with rain beating down on the glass roof, the rear dining area of this comfortably upmarket Italian was a cheering place to be on our Monday night visit. Wealthy locals and businessmen formed a sizeable crowd, which the experienced staff handled with grace. The kitchen was in fine form, matching flavours with ingenuity and presenting them with a flourish. Superb creamy risotto was topped with a flower of grilled chicory that secreted a neat slab of suckling pig. Pork scratchings never looked so elegant as when pressed into a savoury croccante and balanced between rolls of moist veal-shank cannelloni. Attention to detail showed too in the sprigs of thyme laid under a fillet of caponata-crusted sea bream to subtly flavour the fish, and in the crisp-fried skin architecturally arranged on top. Desserts might be gianuja semifreddo with sbrisolona and blood oranges, or the 'white espresso' ice-cream. Wines are taken seriously here; when guests order by the glass, staff bring the bottle to the table for them to check and taste. We like Il Convivio very much; our only complaint is the irritating tendency of staff to push bottled water by constantly refilling glasses.

Babies and children admitted. Booking advisable dinner. Restaurant available for hire. Separate room for parties, seats 14. **Map 15 G10.**
For branch (Caravaggio) see index.

Olivo

21 Eccleston Street, SW1W 9LX (7730 2505). Sloane Square tube/Victoria tube/rail. **Lunch served** noon-2.30pm Mon-Fri. **Dinner served** 7-11pm Mon-Sat; 7-10.30pm Sun. **Main courses** £14.50-£18. **Set lunch** £18 2 courses, £20.50 3 courses. **Cover** £1.50. **Credit** AmEx, DC, JCB, MC, V.

Olivo's bold Mediterranean decor and rustic charm make it a popular choice for office workers keen to escape the hustle and bustle around nearby Victoria station. The fairly priced menu is skewed towards home-style Sardinian cooking, and is supplemented by daily specials that feature a promising array of seasonal ingredients. The actual dining experience, however, can be far from memorable. Spaghetti with bottarga, a typical Sardinian recipe, turned out to be the biggest disappointment, marred by a heavy, overly fishy sauce. A starter of chargrilled courgettes on a bed of rocket, topped with ungenerous shavings of bottarga, fared marginally better than bland roast rabbit with polenta. From a compact wine list, the Sardinian wines are the best bet in terms of value for money and quality. Allow plenty of time if you're planning to get back to work after lunch, as service can be extremely slow. We couldn't help feeling sorry for our seriously overworked waitress during a busy lunchtime. Perhaps standards here have slipped as more attention is being paid to the latest branch, a seafood restaurant called Olivomare.

Children admitted. Booking advisable.
Map 15 H10.
For branch (Olivetto) see index.

Volt

17 Hobart Place, SW1W 0HH (7235 9696/ www.voltlounge.com). Victoria tube/rail. **lunch served** noon-3pm Mon-Fri; **dinner served** 6-11pm Sat. **Main courses** £10-£16. **Credit** AmEx, DC, MC, V.

In these enlightened times of tasteful minimalism, Volt's decor can come as something of a shock; colour-shifting neon tubes, flamboyant pink lilies and a red velvet-clad pillar seem more brash lounge bar than upmarket Italian. A cocktail at the bar soon steadied our nerves, with charming bartenders offering a knowledgeable précis of the eye-wateringly expensive whiskies – and an impromptu vodka sampling. If the decor is slightly fussy, the elegantly simple, self-assured cooking is anything but. Splendid own-made bread, including crunchy Sardinian pane carasau, came with deliciously fruity olive oil and immense, garlicky olives. Equally good were the seared Cornish squid with potato salad and piquillo peppers, and the beef carpaccio with rocket and parmesan. Pan-fried sea bream, perched on chunky, tomatoey grilled courgette and aubergine, was crisp-skinned perfection, while the pink, flavoursome sirloin steak with gorgonzola sauce was marred only by slightly undercooked sauté potatoes. A banana panna cotta with liquorice sauce sounded odd but tasted heavenly, as did the complimentary own-made petits fours and glass of limoncello that rounded off proceedings.

Babies and children welcome: booster seat. Booking advisable. Separate rooms for parties, seating 14, 18 and 30. **Map 15 H9.**

City

Refettorio

Crowne Plaza Hotel, 19 New Bridge Street, EC4V 6DB (7438 8052/www.refettorio.com). Blackfriars tube/rail. **Lunch served** noon-2.30pm Mon-Fri. **Dinner served** 6-10.30pm Mon-Sat. **Main courses** £11.50-£22. **Credit** AmEx, MC, V.

Hotel restaurants can be soulless places, and in the evening Refettorio is sometimes quiet. But at lunchtime there's a buzz around the vast booth tables (practically the size of football pitches). With Giorgio Locatelli as the consultant, this place gives good, strong *cucina*. The menu offers all the conventional dishes such as bresaola with rocket and parmesan, but there's always a twist or a challenge – as with a starter of ox tongue with honey potato bread, served with a salad and marinated button onions. Nine pasta and risotto dishes are similarly classic concoctions, but even something as simple as mixed seafood pasta was pleasantly light and sticky. And when mains include john dory with shredded cucumber, martini and vanilla sauce, you know the subtly cooked pork with basil and peppers won't be as plain as it sounds. The specialist cheese selections merit exploration, although the elegantly presented desserts are hard to resist. With cheerfully professional service and a sommelier to provide an exegesis of the intercontinental wine list, Refettorio is a safe bet for City brokers – if not lesser mortals in search of intimacy.

Babies and children admitted. Booking advisable. Separate room for parties, seats 30. **Map 11 O6.**

Covent Garden

Orso

27 Wellington Street, WC2E 7DB (7240 5269/ www.orsorestaurant.co.uk). Covent Garden tube. **Meals served** noon-midnight daily. **Main courses** £8.50-£17. **Set meal** (5-6.45pm Mon-Sat) £16 2 courses, £18 3 courses incl coffee. **Credit** AmEx, MC, V.

For good, middle-range, sensibly priced Italian food, Orso is still a market leader. It also affords excellent thespian spotting opportunities, without the indignity of loitering outside the Ivy. The restaurant occupies a tiled, cavernous basement, where food, mostly with a Tuscan tilt, is served on hand-painted earthenware crockery. Traditional starters range from artichoke, bean and thyme soup, to deep-fried courgettes with ricotta, tomato and basil stuffing. Just as pleasing is the selection of pizzas (prawn, fennel, salami, vegetable, or goat's cheese), which shares the menu with an equally well-balanced list of own-made pasta (including a simple, enjoyable seafood linguine). All this is ideal for a quick pre- or post-theatre bite,

but main courses are worth lingering over, especially the likes of tuna and roast peppers with rocket and capers, or roast duck with white beans and apricots – or just a good old-fashioned grilled sirloin. There's also a notable choice of desserts, from fresh fruit to cheese, via sundry tarts. But perhaps best of all is an enticing wine list, accommodating 25cl carafes alongside fine Italian wines. With smart, cheerful service to boot, Orso is a West End stalwart.
Babies and children welcome: booster seats. Booking advisable. **Map 18 E4.**

Fitzrovia

Bertorelli

19-23 Charlotte Street, W1T 1RL (7636 4174/ www.santeonline.co.uk). Goodge Street tube.
Bar **Open** 3-11pm Mon-Sat.
Café **Meals served** noon-11pm Mon-Sat.
Main courses £7.50-£14.95.
Restaurant **Lunch served** noon-3pm Mon-Fri.
Dinner served 6-11pm Mon-Sat. **Main courses** £13.75-£24. **Set meals** £15.50 2 courses, £18.50 3 courses.
All **Credit** AmEx, DC, MC, V.
Bertorelli's experiment in 2006 with a ground-floor deli didn't last, and now they're back to doing what they do best: running restaurants. First a Charlotte Street institution and now part of a London chain, the Bertorelli HQ remains a respectable Italian. Both the ground-floor café and the restaurant upstairs are in the modern, clinical Italian style that is as standard now as raffia-wrapped Chianti bottles were in the 1970s. The menu shies away from the entirely obvious – although 'creamy baby buffalo mozzarella with thinly sliced plum tomato, rocket, and basil and pine nut dressing' is a tricolore pesto salad by any other name. Nonetheless, Bertorelli staples such as prawns with ginger and Marsala wine are distinctive, while a seasonal special of white asparagus with rocket and parmesan was a good simple opener, albeit not improved by a poached egg on top. There's enough variety among the pastas to meet all tastes; seafood spaghetti was a fine example of its kind. Salmon with poppy-seed crust served on a tomato and aubergine caponata with green pea sauce was also well-executed. Desserts caused no surprises, and the wine list is helpfully laid out by style.
Babies and children welcome: high chairs. Booking advisable. Restaurant available for hire. Separate rooms for parties, seating 22 and 44. Tables outdoors (5, terrace). **Map 17 B1.**
For branches see index.

Latium

21 Berners Street, W1T 3LP (7323 9123/ www.latiumrestaurant.com). Oxford Circus tube.
Lunch served noon-3pm Mon-Fri. **Dinner served** 6.30-10.30pm Mon-Fri; 6.30-11pm Sat.
Main courses £12.50-£16. **Set meal** £24.50 2 courses, £28.50 3 courses. **Credit** AmEx, JCB, MC, V.
Latium performs the difficult balancing act of suiting business lunches as readily as romantic dinners. Elegantly padded chairs and modern abstract art strike a relaxing note, though the spacious tables can also generate a bit of buzz. The main menu is supplemented by a special ravioli section offering several more choices. Portions, in general, are modest. Oxtail ravioli was tepid and chewy, but its silky celery sauce and sticky jus were a treat. A plate of crab tortelloni with rocket was pretty and delicious yet too much like a salad. Sea bass carpaccio with blood orange salad was a first-class contrast of tangy citrus, soft fish and crunchy greens. The wine list features a decent choice of half bottles and wines by the glass, and iced tap water was replenished throughout the meal. Desserts such as candied artichoke with ricotta are easy to skip when a plate of exquisite chocolate truffles is in the offing. Included extras such as these and the bodacious canapés and breads (which arrive soon after ordering), make the final bill more appealing – when you can get it. Service, although gracious and attentive during the meal, fell away at bill time.
Babies and children welcome: high chairs. Booking advisable weekends. **Map 17 A2.**

Passione

10 Charlotte Street, W1T 2LT (7636 2833/ www.passione.co.uk). Goodge Street tube. **Lunch served** 12.30-2.15pm Mon-Fri. **Dinner served** 7-10.15pm Mon-Sat. **Main courses** £14-£22. **Credit** AmEx, DC, JCB, MC, V.
Pastel-green walls, blond floorboards and displays of rustic preserve jars may lend Gennaro Contaldo's restaurant the look of a family-run establishment, but a cursory glance at the menu says otherwise. At Passione, expect to find starters priced above £10 and a special wine list including treasures such as a £550 bottle of 1987 Brunello di Montalcino. With Contaldo busying himself with writing cookery books, the restaurant's reputation for culinary finesse has been maintained by head chef Mario Magli, with a short but refined menu that features top-quality ingredients. Although primi piatti are limited to a choice of four pasta or risotto dishes, they feature inspired twists on tradition like the remarkable ravioli filled with pear and taleggio cheese, lightly dressed with a simple walnut sauce. At times, though, the kitchen's wizardry felt slightly contrived, especially in an over-rich main course of lamb loin filled with artichokes, pecorino cheese and mint. Unfortunately, desserts are no match for the inventiveness of the main menu, and service can become distracted as the restaurant gets busier.
Babies and children admitted. Booking advisable. Restaurant available for hire. Separate room for parties, seats 18. Tables outdoors (2, patio; 1, pavement). **Map 17 B1.**

Sardo

45 Grafton Way, W1T 5DQ (7387 2521/ www.sardo-restaurant.com). Warren Street tube.
Lunch served noon-3pm Mon-Fri. **Dinner served** 6-11pm Mon-Sat. **Main courses** £8.90-£18. **Credit** AmEx, MC, V.
One of the first restaurants to introduce an extensive Sardinian menu to London, Sardo remains the best place to sample this rustic yet elegant Mediterranean fare. An array of traditional Sardinian favourites – such as malloreddus pasta in an aromatic tomato and sausage sauce, and spaghetti with mullet roe – are complemented by a monthly changing menu featuring seasonal ingredients. The sausage used in the malloreddus sauce can also be sampled as a main course, chargrilled and served in a coil shape, accompanied by endive and roast potatoes. Sebadas, a traditional puff pastry filled with cheese and topped with honey, makes an unusual alternative to the own-made tiramisu and panna cotta. Moreish olives and scrumptious bread baskets, laden with crispy pane carasau and hand-rolled grissini, are placed on each table; you'll be charged extra for them. Wines are all Italian, but the best value is found in the bottles from Sardinia. Service lives up to the Sardinian reputation for brusqueness, especially at busy times.
Babies and children admitted. Booking advisable. Separate area for parties, seats 30. Tables outdoors (3, patio). **Map 3 J4.**
For branch (Sardo Canale) see index.

BEST ITALIAN

For corking Italian wine
You'll find great lists at **Alloro** (*see p184*), **Il Convivio** (*see p181*), **Enoteca Turi** (*see p190*), **Locanda Locatelli** (*see p184*), **Osteria dell'Arancio** (*see p190*), **Ristorante Semplice** (*see p184*), **Riva** (*see p190*), the **River Café** (*see p189*) and **Zafferano** (*see right*). Grappa lovers should head to **Al Duca** (*see p186*).

Dining alfresco
Plenty of outdoor seating at **La Collina** (*see p193*), **La Famiglia** (*see p190*), **Manicomio** (*see p190*) and the Canary Wharf branch of **Carluccio's Caffè** (*see p193*). **Marco Polo** (*see p191*) and the **River Café** (*see p189*) both have large riverside terraces.

To feel like you're in Italy
Alloro (*see p184*), **Cibo** (*see p189*), **Luciano** (*see p187*), **Osteria Antica Bologna** (*see p191*) and **Vasco & Piero's Pavilion** (*see p187*).

Family fun
Children are welcome at **La Famiglia** (*see p190*), **Manicomio** (*see p190*), **Marco Polo** (*see p191*) and **Philpott's Mezzaluna** (*see p195*).

Knightsbridge

San Lorenzo

22 Beauchamp Place, SW3 1NH (7584 1074). Knightsbridge tube. **Lunch served** 12.30-3pm, **dinner served** 7.30-11.30pm Mon-Sat. **Main courses** £15.50-£28.50. **Cover** £2.50. **No credit cards.**
This fashionable Knightsbridge restaurant remains enduringly popular, and to some extent it's possible to understand why. The rooms are attractive, and the welcome is friendly even if you're not a famous fashion designer (like the one seated a couple of tables away on our visit). Perhaps the fans don't care much about food, or simply don't know the difference between adequate and exceptional. For those with more demanding palates and/or less capacious wallets, San Lorenzo has little to offer. Our food wasn't terrible, but neither did it excite at any stage. Many ingredients were anaemic: a watery broth in stracciatella (Roman soup with whisked eggs and parmesan); bland chunks of fish in an otherwise creditable zuppa di pesce; the insipid oil; low-taste tomatoes; and low-voltage ham on a salad of rocket with prosciutto. With places such as nearby Zafferano (*see below*) putting extraordinary effort into every ingredient and every basic preparation, this lack of care grates – especially when prices are so high. Service was hesitant and slow. The wine list offers little hope if you can't spend at least £40 a bottle. San Lorenzo's regulars clearly can afford those prices. The rest of us can do better elsewhere.
Babies and children welcome: children's portions; high chairs. Booking advisable Fri, Sat. Dress: smart casual. Restaurant available for hire. Separate rooms for parties, seating 20 and 40. **Map 14 F9.**
For branch see index.

Zafferano

15 Lowndes Street, SW1X 9EY (7235 5800/ www.zafferanorestaurant.com). Knightsbridge tube. **Lunch served** noon-2.30pm Mon-Fri; 12.30-3pm Sat, Sun. **Dinner served** 7-11pm Mon-Sat; 7-10.30pm Sun. **Set lunch** £25.50 2 courses, £29.50 3 courses, £34.50 4 courses. **Set dinner** £29.50 2 courses, £39.50 3 courses, £49.50 4 courses. **Credit** AmEx, DC, MC, V.
The decor at this 12-year-old veteran, newly spruced up in earthy hues, looks sprightly; the crisply attired waiting staff are smart and (mostly) on the ball. And the cooking – based on ingredients of almost surreal excellence – is as good as it was under founding chef Giorgio Locatelli. Our lunch contained four dishes that were simple in approach yet complex in flavour. Delicate tomato and basil soup was given substance by a tartare of tuna. A generous portion of crab salad, topped with lovely salad leaves, exemplified the kitchen's belief in letting ingredients speak for themselves. Another salad of green beans with cuttlefish and improbably delicious olives used deeply caramelised red onions to add richness and succulence. Calf's liver, perfectly cooked, came with expertly prepared and subtly seasoned Swiss chard. Our only serious complaint: a long wait between courses. The wine list is exemplary, every bottle chosen with care from top-notch producers; you can get away with £20 or so, but the best value lies between £30 and £40. Prices are high, especially at dinner, and more especially if the dishes carrying a supplement prove irresistible. Warning: for dinner, book several weeks ahead.

Babies and children welcome: high chairs. Booking essential, at least 1 week in advance for lunch, 4-6 weeks in advance for dinner. Dress: smart casual; no shorts (dinner). Separate room for parties, seats 20. **Map 15 G9.**

Marble Arch

Arturo

23 Connaught Street, W2 2AY (7706 3388/ www.arturorestaurant.co.uk). Marble Arch tube. **Lunch served** noon-2.30pm Mon-Sat; 12.30-3.30pm Sun. **Dinner served** 6-10pm Mon-Sat; 6-9.30pm Sun. **Main courses** £12-£16. **Set meal** £13.95 2 courses, £16.95 3 courses. **Credit** AmEx, MC, V.

Arturo appears to have endeared itself to a crowd of locals, attracted by its modestly priced set menu and a bright conservatory that overlooks perfectly manicured gardens. But just like the stark, 1980s-style dark wood and metal decor, its food lacks pzazz (despite serious efforts with the peppermill by the pleasant but unobtrusive staff). We ordered a variety of dishes – including own-made gnocchi in a creamy herb and spinach sauce, and a starter of ricotta tortelli served with butter and sage – yet nothing really stood out. Instead of being redolent of tangy Mediterranean flavours, a parcel of red snapper with potatoes, tomatoes, capers and olives came close to the uniform blandness of microwaved ready meals. Even the bread, with its over-crumbly texture, was ungenerously served one slice at a time. The selection of Italian wines is appealing, but not especially good value. This is a passable neighbourhood restaurant, useful if you happen to live nearby, but we wouldn't recommend going out of your way to dine here.

Babies and children admitted. Tables outdoors (3, pavement). **Map 8 F6.**

Obika

2nd floor, Selfridges, 400 Oxford Street, W1A 1AB (7318 3620/www.obika.co.uk). Bond Street tube. **Meals served** 11.30am-7.30pm Mon-Wed, Fri, Sat; 11.30am-8.30pm Thur; noon-5.30pm Sun. **Main courses** £12-£18. **Credit** AmEx, DC, MC, V.

The concept of a dedicated mozzarella bar might have sounded unlikely at first, yet the slick Selfridges outpost of this Italian chain keeps improving. True, some of the price tags seem to match those of the high-fashion labels for sale upstairs, but they reflect the fact that the delicate cheese is flown in daily from Italy. Although the menu includes a small but pleasant batch of antipasti and pasta dishes, Obika's main draw is its platters, combining a choice of three mozzarella varieties with a changing selection of charcuterie rarely found outside Italy. If it's available, don't miss the prized prosciutto di cinta senese, which comes from a type of pig bred free-range in oak forests. Starting at £12 for three items degustation platters don't come cheap, but they attract hordes of shoppers. The crowds don't faze fast, competent Italian staff, who didn't miss a beat during a busy Saturday lunchtime. In a bid to attract homesick Italian expats (those with a generous pay package, we presume), Obika now offers aperitivo evenings on Thursdays, with food included in the cost of drinks.

Babies and children welcome: high chairs. Disabled: toilet (in Selfridges). Takeaway service. **Map 9 G6.**

Trenta NEW

30 Connaught Street, W2 2AF (7262 9623). Marble Arch tube. **Lunch served** 12.30-2.30pm Tue-Sat. **Dinner served** 6.30-10.30pm Mon-Sat. **Main courses** £13.50-£17.50. **Set lunch** £14.50 2 courses. **Set dinner** £19.50 2 courses. **Credit** AmEx, MC, V.

Open for just over a year, Trenta (Italian for '30') has established itself as a pleasant neighbourhood restaurant well worth a detour. The fixed-price menu is compact. Some dishes incur supplements, but the bill is generally fair. There's an appealing choice of classic and contemporary dishes from all over Italy. A moreish selection of ciabatta, focaccia and crisp Sardinian pane carasau (as well as savoury titbits including plump olives and pizza

The River Café. See p189.

RESTAURANTS

strips) accounts for the £2 cover charge. Well-chosen dishes featuring seasonal ingredients – like grilled baby squid with chilli, lemon and olive oil; and own-made pasta parcels generously filled with langoustine – were the highlights of our visit. The dessert list also deserves notice, with lush chocolate panna cotta and exquisite own-made hazelnut ice-cream standing out among an enticing and imaginative selection. Staff are unobtrusive and efficient. Well-heeled locals flock to both the basement and the minute, tastefully decorated dining room on the ground floor.
Babies and children admitted. Booking essential weekends, advisable weekdays. Separate room for parties, seats 12. **Map 8 E/F6**.

Marylebone

2 Veneti

10 Wigmore Street, W1U 2RD (7637 0789). Bond Street or Oxford Circus tube. **Lunch served** noon-3pm Mon-Fri. **Dinner served** 6.30-10.30pm Mon-Sat. **Main courses** £10.50-£28.50. **Credit** AmEx, MC, V.

The cuisine from Veneto doesn't rely heavily on olive oil and the pungent Mediterranean flavours usually associated with Italian food, and as a result it hasn't travelled well beyond Italian borders. With a Venetian-inspired menu particularly strong on seafood, 2 Veneti has been steadily garnering converts to this lesser-known regional cuisine. Starters can be hit or miss. Beef carpaccio with parmesan mayonnaise was a textbook example of the dish, while the creamed salt cod, served in a tiny portion with rubbery polenta croûtons, was not. Pasta and main courses proved much better. The own-made sedanini pasta with venison and Amarone wine ragout was rich and gutsy, but the highlight of our visit turned out to be a gargantuan dish of fritto misto: a selection of battered fried fish that's a speciality of Venetian cooking. It shouldn't be missed here. An all-Italian wine list, delectable bread basket and own-made sorbets and ice-creams in unusual flavours (pear, for instance) provide nice finishing touches. Service is solicitous without being obtrusive. The brick wall decor is somewhat dated, but customers, a mix of regulars and locals, don't seem to mind.
Babies and children welcome: high chairs. Booking advisable. Restaurant available for hire. Tables outdoors (2, pavement). **Map 9 H5**.

Caffè Caldesi

118 Marylebone Lane, W1U 2QF (7935 1144/ www.caffecaldesi.com). Bond Street tube.
Bar **Meals served** noon-10.30pm Mon-Sat. **Main courses** £9-£19.
Restaurant **Lunch served** noon-3pm Mon-Fri. **Dinner served** 6-10.30pm Mon-Sat. **Main courses** £15-£21.
Both **Credit** AmEx, JCB, MC, V.

The 'Caffè' part of the name is misleading. This is a fully-fledged Italian restaurant with prices to prove it – even if it isn't as fully-fledged as its mother, Caldesi, up the alley. Located over a bar in the heart of Marylebone, Caffè Caldesi attracts a younger cross-section of the continental yuppies who work, rest and play hereabouts. The restaurant itself is bright and airy, with many of the tables by windows festooned with exploding flower boxes. Staff speak Italian with little encouragement, as if to vouch for the authenticity of cooking drawn from all over the peninsula (though centred on Tuscany). Starters aren't just run of the mill Italian dishes; cuttlefish in tomato and chilli sauce was a good thick fishy pleasure, while imaginative pastas included ravioli with a nice sticky duck ragù. Three types of fish and five types of meat follow; we had no complaints about the veal, asparagus, mash and truffle oil – except its upper-end price of £19. The wine list is also confidently priced, but covers a wholly desirable Italian spectrum.
Babies and children welcome: high chairs; nappy-changing facilities. Booking advisable (restaurant). Disabled: toilet. Restaurant and bar available for hire. Tables outside (3, pavement). **Map 9 G5.**
For branch (Caldesi Tuscan) see index.

Locanda Locatelli

8 Seymour Street, W1H 7JZ (7935 9088/ www.locandalocatelli.com). Marble Arch tube. **Lunch served** noon-3pm Mon-Fri; noon-3.30pm Sat, Sun. **Dinner served** 6.45-11pm Mon-Thur; 6.45-11.30pm Fri, Sat; 6.45-10pm Sun. **Main courses** £19.50-£29.50. **Credit** AmEx, JCB, MC, V.

Georgio Locatelli has won numerous accolades for the impossibly high quality of his regional Italian food, and his kitchen team show no sign of compromising their flair. The 1970s lounge atmosphere of the dining room feels louche and glamorous, but the effect can easily be marred by rushed service that aims to squeeze in two sittings per evening. Starters are imaginative, such as fennel salad topped with mullet roe shavings and served on a bed of crisp Sardinian pane carasau. Pasta dishes remain Locatelli's strength, drawing inspiration from deceptively simple combinations of flavours and ingredients. There are times when they don't deliver as they should, however; a dish of red onion pasta parcels in Chianti sauce sprinkled with salted ricotta shavings felt contrived, despite being faultlessly executed. A main course of chargrilled pork involtini with herbs served with fried courgettes neared perfection, but felt somewhat clinical. The dessert list is impressive, featuring modern takes on traditional puddings, as well as lesser-known delicacies such as Sardinian sebadas (cheese-filled parcels drizzled with honey). The wine list is almost entirely Italian, with a good selection of outstanding wines by the glass.
Babies and children welcome: high chairs. Booking essential. Disabled: toilet (hotel). Dress: smart casual. **Map 9 G6**.

Mayfair

★ Alloro

19-20 Dover Street, W1S 4LU (7495 4768). Green Park tube.
Bar **Open** noon-11pm Mon-Fri; 7-11pm Sat. **Main courses** £8-£16.
Restaurant **Lunch served** noon-2.30pm Mon-Fri. **Dinner served** 7-10.30pm Mon-Sat. **Set lunch** £26 2 courses, £31 3 courses. **Set dinner** £28.50 2 courses, £34 3 courses, £39 4 courses.
Both **Credit** AmEx, DC, JCB, MC, V.

This elegant Mayfair veteran, with its tiled floor and small, nicely intimate bar, specialises in modernising classic Italian themes. In the kitchen, it never sets a foot wrong; our food ranged from excellent to sublime. Starters and pasta were uniformly excellent. One main, confit rabbit leg with pancetta, wild mushrooms and baby onion, was superb; another, duck breast with endive, pears, and a beautifully balanced red wine sauce, was world-class. And the best came at the end, in three beautifully presented puddings that were simply out of this world. Sadly, the food was let down by some sloppy, erratic service. We waited nearly half an hour for our starters. The wine list is outstanding, a concise catalogue of many of Italy's best producers, and the sommelier guided us wisely. But the selection is clearly designed for expense-accounters; our choices, though excellent, at £35 and £40 lay near the bottom of the price range. Towards the end of our meal, a powerful smell of disinfectant wafted up from the toilets in the basement. The problems we encountered could be cleared up with an hour's worth of staff training. That's why Alloro retains its red star this year.
Babies and children admitted. Booking advisable. Restaurant and bar available for hire. Separate room for parties, seats 16. Tables outdoors (2, pavement). **Map 9 J7**.

Giardinetto

39-40 Albemarle Street, W1S 4TE (7493 7091/ www.giardinetto.co.uk). Green Park tube. **Lunch served** 12.30-3pm Mon-Fri. **Dinner served** 6-10.30pm Mon-Sat. **Main courses** £9-£35. **Credit** AmEx, DC, JCB, MC, V.

Giardinetto's à la carte lunch menu offers amazing value. At our visit, the food (based on Ligurian cooking but with a light, modern touch) was blindingly good. Starters were wonderful: poached egg and asparagus with shaved parmesan, and an octopus carpaccio with a julienne of mixed vegetables. Mains were even better. A plate of grilled veal – three thick slices from an organic rare breed – was captivating in its simplicity. Scorpion fish on a bed of mashed potatoes with mushrooms was equally satisfying. With bread, water and coffee included in the price, the lunch, in this ultra-luxurious location, must be one of the best-value deals in London. The drawback: Giardinetto is probably better for dinner than for lunch, as the decor, though beautifully executed, may be darker than you'd want on a sunny day. And at dinner, prices rise considerably. The wine list is a magnificent monument to Italy's rich diversity, but there's almost nothing under £20 and little under £30. A generous selection of wines by the glass takes away some of the pain. Many of the customers here are Italian businessmen who take food seriously. It's easy to see why they choose Giardinetto.
Babies and children admitted. Booking advisable. Separate rooms for parties, seating 10 and 14. **Map 9 J7**.

Ristorante Semplice NEW

9-10 Blenheim Street, W1S 1LJ (7495 1509). Bond Street tube. **Lunch served** noon-2.30pm Mon-Fri. **Dinner served** 7-10.30pm Mon-Sat. **Main courses** £14-£19. **Set lunch** £14 2 courses, £18 3 courses. **Credit** AmEx, MC, V.

Mayfair may needs another grown-up Italian restaurant like an It Girl needs a new handbag, but the name of this one suggests an appreciation of the simple things in life. A bowl of minestra di sfarrata (a soup of pearl barley, chickpeas, lentils and buckwheat) might be testament to rustic Italian ambitions – but sits alongside less Italian dishes employing the trendy French sous-vide slow cooking technique, and ingredients such as Sarawak pepper. Nor were we convinced by the presentation of a dish of slightly overcooked calf's liver, which came with a pretentious little white bowl of steamed vegetables on the side. Best were a special of buffalo ricotta pasta parcels with hazelnut and sage butter, the own-made ice-creams, and a molten pudding of dark Domori chocolate (a high-quality Italian brand) with sophisticated sauces of bitter almond cream and puréed pear. The lengthy Italian wine list impresses too, with Sicily's Borgo Selenes starting at a fair-minded £12.50 per bottle, ten wines by the carafe, twelve by the glass. The overall mood is restrained and calm, with the service discreetly professional.
Babies and children admitted. Booking advisable. Disabled: toilet. Tables outdoors (4, pavement). **Map 9 H6**.

Sartoria

20 Savile Row, W1S 3PR (7534 7000/ www.danddlondon.com). Oxford Circus or Piccadilly Circus tube.
Bar **Open/snacks served** 9am-11pm Mon-Sat.
Restaurant **Lunch served** noon-3pm Mon-Fri. **Dinner served** 6-10.45pm Mon-Sat. **Main courses** £17-£25. **Set meal** £19.50 2 courses, £24.50 3 courses.
Both **Credit** AmEx, JCB, MC, V.

We can only hope that our unfortunate meal here was a blip in what is obviously a professionally run operation. Part of D&D, formerly the Conran group, Sartoria is a sleek and attractive restaurant if a bit sterile for some tastes. On a spring evening, the large, airy space lit with glowing lamps and ceiling spots looked great. But our meal was a disappointment, lacking sparkle. Potato soup, nicely judged sweetbreads and a main course of roasted rabbit were all good. Sadly, the most memorable occurrence was a pasta dish, own-made bigole with a veal ragù. The pasta was inedibly chewy when first brought out, though the sauce was wonderful; staff took it back graciously when asked to do so, but when the dish returned a few minutes later, further cooking had ruined the sauce. (And the other main course had been eaten.) The wine list is difficult to navigate for all but those with the deepest pockets. Other diners on our visit seemed to be expense-account visitors from local businesses. With all the competition in this area, Sartoria will have to raise its game.

GRANA PADANO
ITALY'S FINEST CHEESE

For over 1,000 years the stunning Padana Valley has been home to Italy's favourite cheese – Grana Padano.

First produced by Cistercian monks in the 12th century, this hard cheese with its distinctive flavour and grainy texture is a must-have for any London gourmet.

The name Grana Padano is derived both from its famously grainy texture ('grana') and its enchanting birthplace.

Each cheese is carefully matured, and though Grana Padano tastes good at any age, the foodstuffs that accompany it best change depending on the maturity of the cheese.

After ageing for nine months, Grana Padano is in its youthful prime and ideal in light gratins and sauces, or delicately flaked on carpaccio, or in artichoke, wild mushroom or chanterelle salads.

For connoisseurs Grana Padano, aged over 16 months can simply be served with balsamic vinegar from Modena or Reggio, or with rustic pickles, strong honeys, fresh figs, olives or a selection of nuts. It is equally enjoyable on its own.

After more than twenty months, and following further quality checks, Grana Padano reaches 'Riserva' status. Fully matured, it is now best enjoyed grated, to allow its enticingly fruity flavours to permeate pastas, stews and soups.

This uniquely versatile cheese complements white wines with enduring bouquets, as well as medium reds and those with greater tannin content; either a Brunello from Tuscany or a Piedmontese Bartelo. The piquant flavour of Grana Padano can also be twinned with the dried fruit aroma of a chilled Sicilian Marsala.

In short, Grana Padano is the essential choice for the discerning foodie!

The health-conscious should note that Grana Padano is a superb source of easily digestible protein. Only 25g provides over a quarter of the Recommended Daily Amount (RDA) of calcium, critical for strong bones and teeth.

It can be enjoyed by all ages.

Don't just take our word for it: here's a tantalising recipe for you to try.-

GRANA PADANO SLOW-ROASTED TOMATO & PEPPER TARTS

Try these delicious savoury vegetarian tarts as a main course or starter – they're perfect for summer entertaining or for a smart picnic.

8 small plum tomatoes, halved
1 red pepper, deseeded and thickly sliced
1 yellow pepper, deseeded and thickly sliced
2 tablespoons Italian olive oil
Salt and freshly ground black pepper
1 teaspoon dried oregano
1 x 500g pack puff pastry, thawed if frozen
8 teaspoons red and green pesto sauce
75g (3oz) Grana Padano cheese, finely grated
A few rocket leaves
Shavings of Grana Padano cheese

1. Preheat the oven to 180°C/ fan oven 160°C/ Gas Mark 4
2. Arrange the halved tomatoes, cut side up, in a roasting pan with peppers. Season with salt and pepper, sprinkle with dried oregano, then drizzle with the olive oil. Transfer to the oven and roast for 20 minutes.
3. Meanwhile, roll out the pastry on a lightly floured surface to a rectangle measuring approximately 30cm (12 inch) square. Cut out 8 rounds with a 10cm (4inch) cutter.

Lift them on to a lightly greased baking sheet. Spread 1 teaspoon of pesto sauce over each circle, then sprinkle with the grated Grana Padano.

4. Cool the roasted tomatoes and peppers for 10 minutes, then arrange them over the pastry circles. Increase the oven temperature to 2000C/fan oven 180oC/ Gas Mark 6. Bake for 12-15 minutes until well-risen and golden.

5. Cool for a few minutes, then top with the rocket and shavings of Grana Padano cheese. Serve whilst warm.

Makes 8

Cook's tip: *If you like, serve the tarts drizzled with extra virgin olive oil and a little balsamic vinegar.*

Why Not Try?

Babies and children welcome: high chairs. Booking advisable; essential lunch. Disabled: toilet. Entertainment: pianist 7-10pm Thur-Sat. Restaurant available for hire. Separate rooms for parties, seating 20 and 45. **Map 9 J7**.

★ Via Condotti

23 Conduit Street, W1S 2XS (7493 7050/ www.viacondotti.co.uk). Oxford Circus tube. **Lunch served** noon-3pm Mon-Fri; 12.30-3pm Sat. **Dinner served** 6.30-11pm Mon-Sat. **Main courses** £9.50-£18.50. **Credit** AmEx, MC, V.

Via Condotti lies opposite the Vivienne Westwood shop and right next to Rigby & Peller, but this lively restaurant is not the preserve of ladies who lunch. Our midday visit saw a buzzy mix of shoppers and businessmen enjoying the efficient, smiling service and fine cooking. The smart yet relaxing decor features vintage advertising posters and neat leather chairs reminiscent of the art deco period. Lovely chunks of crumbly parmigiano reggiano were quickly brought to the table. So too were fat, nutty-tasting olives that looked like dark green apples, and a generous, varied bread basket. Paper-thin slicing on the mandolin turned worthy carrot, celery and radish into an elegant topping for sea bass carpaccio. Delicate tubes of own-made wholemeal pasta served with spring vegetables and marjoram also demonstrated the kitchen's perfect judging of texture. Being picky? The red mullet was a tad too dry, though delicious served with a fennel-flavoured brodetto and clams. No complaints about roast rack of lamb with thin mild green peppers, a crisp side of sautéed escarole, the lovely petits fours or the macchiato coffee. Carefully practised attention to detail makes Via Condotti one of the West End's brightest jewels.
Babies and children admitted. Booking advisable. Separate room for parties, seats 18. **Map 9 J6.**

Tentazioni. See p193.

Piccadilly

Brumus NEW

Haymarket Hotel, 1 Suffolk Place, SW1Y 4BP (7470 4000/www.haymarkethotel.com). Piccadilly Circus tube. **Meals served** 7am-11.45pm Mon-Sat; 8am-11pm Sun. **Main courses** £8.50-£17.50. **Set dinner** (3-7pm daily; 10.45-11.45pm Mon-Sat; 10.45-11pm Sun) £15 2 courses, £20 3 courses. **Credit** AmEx, DC, MC, V.

The Haymarket Hotel is the latest from Firmdale Hotels, whose earlier ventures include Soho Hotel, Charlotte Street Hotel and Covent Garden Hotel – three of London's most stylish yet relaxed design hotels. Haymarket is colourful and has a distinctive Regency look, similar to Brighton's Royal Pavilion; the dining room, Brumus, is coloured a dusty, dark pink. The menu is broadly based around northern Italian classics, such as vitello tonnato, in this case garnished with baby shiso leaves. Impressive precision is evident in the construction of the dishes: a slab of Icelandic cod was given a crust of baccala (dried saltcod, ground up) and perfectly baked, served in a vegetable broth flavoured with baubles of fregola (giant couscous). The timing of the meat cookery was perfect, as judged by sections of pancetta-wrapped rabbit loin, served with a little pie of shredded rabbit meat in a shortcrust pastry made using a polenta mixture. The desserts are as enticing as the main courses, from chestnut-flour cake with espresso ice-cream to an almond-milk sorbet that tasted like marzipan. Service was attentive and knowledgeable on our visit, and the list of Italian wines by the glass was better (but pricier) than it needed to be.
Babies and children welcome: high chairs. Booking advisable. Disabled: toilet. Separate rooms for parties, seating 15-100. **Map 10 K7.**

St James's

Al Duca

4-5 Duke of York Street, SW1Y 6LA (7839 3090/ www.alduca-restaurant.co.uk). Piccadilly Circus tube. **Lunch served** noon-3pm Mon-Fri; 12.30-3pm Sat. **Dinner served** 6-11pm Mon-Sat. **Set lunch** £20.50 2 courses, £24.50 3 courses, £27.50 4 courses. **Set dinner** £23.50 2 courses, £26.50 3 courses, £31.50 4 courses. **Credit** AmEx, MC, V.

A profusion of blond wood, terracotta hues and crisp white linen lend Al Duca an air of understated elegance befitting its Mayfair location. Affluent locals and theatregoers are attracted. On our visit we couldn't help admiring the waiting staff, who kept their cool despite having to dodge several unruly children running amok in the busy dining room. The same admiration didn't extend to the kitchen, whose performance was uneven at best. We were looking forward to one of Al Duca's signature dishes, a salad of warm poached egg with parmesan wafer, bacon, asparagus and tomato, hoping it would turn out to be an inventive take on Italy's traditional dish of asparagus and eggs. It was – except for the rubbery texture of the egg. An enticing-sounding risotto of the day with radicchio and taleggio cheese arrived lukewarm and almost soup-like; a plateful of ravioli filled with pumpkin and amaretto, simply dressed with melted butter and sage, was much better. Also on the plus side, the all-Italian drinks list is extensive, featuring lesser-known wines from South Tyrol and an astonishing 17 varieties of grappa.
Babies and children welcomer. Dress: no shorts. Restaurant available for hire (Sun). **Map 9 J7.**

Franco's

61 Jermyn Street, SW1Y 6LX (7499 2211/ www.francoslondon.com). Green Park or Piccadilly Circus tube. **Breakfast served** 7.30-10.30am, **lunch served** noon-2.30pm Mon-Sat. **Tapas served** 2.30-11pm Mon-Thur; 2.30pm-midnight Fri, Sat. **Dinner served** 5.30-11pm Mon-Thur; 5.30pm-midnight Fri, Sat. **Tapas** £7.50-£14. **Main courses** £15-£25. **Set lunch** £25 2 courses, £30 3 courses. **Credit** AmEx, MC, V.

A continental-style café-bar and restaurant serving food all day, Franco's is a welcome concept. However, prices reflect rather too enthusiastically its St James's location. The 1940s art deco inspired interior is comfortably smart, and the alfresco tables look as though they could have been snapped up from a Florentine street. There's plenty of choice on the menu. In addition to the large number of mains, there's meat, poultry and fish from the charcoal grill. Interesting sides included a salad of fennel, orange and olives. Seafood salad begged for chilli heat and acidity, the herbs and lemon failing to provide the necessary kick. Portion sizes were strangely imbalanced: one main course being dainty, the second too generous; other diners were struck by this too, especially with steaks and fish coming from the grill. Our veal milanese, with bone extending from one end, looked like a large ping pong bat, but we enjoyed its buttery flavour. Service was prompt (we were in and out in an hour), though not all ran smoothly. Being told that certain dishes weren't available (after we'd ordered them), and other dishes arriving with different accompaniments to those listed on the menu, suggested a current of disorganisation that the waiters' bravura could not bridge.

Babies and children admitted. Disabled: toilet. Dress: smart casual. Separate rooms for parties, seating 18 and 50. Tables outdoors (4, pavement). **Map 9 J7.**

Luciano

72-73 St James's Street, SW1A 1PH (7408 1440/ www.lucianorestaurant.co.uk). Green Park tube. **Lunch served** noon-3pm, **dinner served** 6-11pm Mon-Sat. **Main courses** £16.50-£26. **Credit** MC, V.

Marco Pierre White's glamorous Italian dining room and bar occupies the original site of Madame Prunier's fish restaurant, one of London's most fashionable spots during the first half of the 20th century. The sumptuous art deco ambience, jazzed up with slick photography, could easily be mistaken for that of a gentleman's club. In line with the overall masculine feel, the menu features classic and contemporary Italian dishes in hearty portions. Starters range from a classic, yet elegantly executed mozzarella salad, to a traditional dish of moreish cold ox tongue dressed with mostarda: a northern Italian condiment made with candied fruit and mustard. Robust meat dishes are the kitchen's undisputed strength, with highlights like unctuous roast pork belly with jerusalem artichokes coming in oversized portions we couldn't possibly finish. Pasta and risotto dishes are less exciting, lacking the perfectionist streak that characterises main courses. Desserts can also be hit or miss. The superb wine list features choices from all over Italy, but also plenty from the New World and France. Service, at best indifferent and at worst surly and rushed, failed to match up to the lofty expectations set by the food.

Babies and children admitted. Booking advisable. Disabled: toilet. Separate room for parties, seats 22. **Map 9 J8.**

Soho

Quo Vadis

26-29 Dean Street, W1D 6LL (7437 9585/ www.whitestarline.org.uk). Leicester Square, Piccadilly Circus or Tottenham Court Road tube. **Lunch served** noon-2.30pm Mon-Fri. **Dinner served** 5.30-11pm Mon-Sat. **Main courses** £12-£17. **Set meal** (lunch, 5.30-6.30pm) £14.95 2 courses, £17.95 3 courses. **Credit** AmEx, DC, JCB, MC, V.

Elegant quirkiness sums up Quo Vadis, one of Marco Pierre White's stable of restaurants. Bizarre artwork, stained-glass windows and attentive service provide a buffer against the din of Soho. Media types (mostly male) dine here, keen on sampling the modern Italian cooking, which is jazzed up with a playful nouvelle-cuisine twist. The food looks as eccentric as the surrounding art pieces. It involves unusual ingredient combinations that often succeed, but can sometimes fail spectacularly. A morsel of buffalo mozzarella hidden in a delicate cocoon of tempura batter was one of the winners, yet was so dainty it could almost be classed as an amuse-bouche rather than a starter. The green, bland, sludge-like purée that smothered an otherwise pleasant dish of black ink tagliolini with prawns was, in contrast, a major turn-off. Dessert choices include rocket ice-cream, olive fondant and parsley macaroons, but diners with a more conventional sweet tooth can find solace in equally exquisite, if less daring, concoctions.

Children admitted. Booking advisable. Dress: smart casual. Separate rooms for parties, seating 12, 14, 30 and 80. **Map 17 B3.**

Vasco & Piero's Pavilion

15 Poland Street, W1F 8QE (7437 8774/ www.vascosfood.com). Oxford Circus or Piccadilly Circus tube. **Lunch served** noon-3pm Mon-Fri. **Dinner served** 6-11pm Mon-Sat. **Main courses** £9.50-£20. **Set dinner** £23 2 courses, £28 3 courses. **Credit** AmEx, DC, JCB, MC, V.

Despite its Soho location, Vasco & Piero's Pavilion has maintained the friendly and unpretentious atmosphere usually found in good neighbourhood restaurants. Yet the careful attention to detail and first-rate ingredients bear the hallmark of a top-notch establishment. The menu, which changes twice daily, is skewed towards earthy Umbrian dishes, using only two or three ingredients for each recipe. Extra-virgin olive oil, cured meats, cheeses and wild mushrooms are sourced from local producers in central Italy, while the celebrated Umbrian truffles also make an appearance when in season. On our visit, the list of own-made pasta dishes yielded a plate of delectable aubergine-filled tortelloni. From the main course menu, a juicy, butter-soft grilled chicken breast served with green beans was outstanding in its simplicity. A slice of moreish chocolate truffle cake with vanilla ice-cream helped us forgive the patchy service, which slowed down considerably as the restaurant became busier.

Booking advisable. Children over 6 years admitted. Separate room for parties, seats 36. **Map 17 A3.**

South Kensington

Daphne's

112 Draycott Avenue, SW3 3AE (7589 4257/ www.daphnes-restaurant.co.uk). South Kensington tube. **Lunch served** noon-3pm Mon-Fri; noon-3.30pm Sat; 12.30-4pm Sun. **Dinner served** 5.30-11.30pm Mon-Sat; 5.30-10.30pm Sun. **Main courses** £12.75-£26.50. **Set lunch** £16.75 2 courses, £18.75 3 courses. **Credit** AmEx, DC, JCB, MC, V.

We've had complaints about the quality of food at this Brompton Cross stalwart, but our most recent visit saw the kitchen in fine form. Veal milanese was tender yet crisp and perfectly grease-free. A good chunk of salt cod was glazed with an eggy topping and served with an inventive green bean sauce, the dish held together with a judicious kick of red chilli. Daphne's flies the flag for British produce (chef-director is Mark Hix), name-checking suppliers such as East Riding lamb, and using traditional ingredients such as cardoons and samphire. Dorset crab was flecked with tomato in a lovely dish of golden tagliatelle. We had no room for dessert, though were tempted by honeycomb ice-cream with caramel sauce, and apricot and almond tart with lime cream. The list of wines by the glass contains the usual collection of Tuscans, plus value-oriented Sicilian wines and a luscious merlot from Friuli. Despite the Porsches, Bentleys and Ferraris lining the road outside, and the seriously Sloaney regulars, Daphne's has five wines under £20 and an appealing set lunch menu. Staff are caring and generous, adding to the air of conviviality.

Babies and children welcome: high chairs. Booking advisable. Separate room for parties, seats 40. **Map 14 E10.**

Westminster

Quirinale

North Court, 1 Great Peter Street, SW1P 3LL (7222 7080/www.quirinale.co.uk). St James's Park or Westminster tube. **Lunch served** noon-2.30pm, **dinner served** 6-10.30pm Mon-Fri. **Main courses** £12.50-£19. **Credit** AmEx, DC, MC, V.

Within strolling distance of Parliament, Quirinale occupies an understated, elegant basement room with well-spaced tables that allow for discreet power-broking. Our evening here was a frustrating study in extreme contrasts of quality. Service was erratic, sometimes bordering on the dismissive. Food, from the seasonal menu and a list of specials, varied wildly and dispiritingly. Starters of culatello (a type of prosciutto) with thin discs of buffalo mozzarella, and a squid-ink risotto with two appetising slabs of squid, were dazzling; octopus salad and a salad with spelt (wheat-like grain) were merely adequate. Main courses, apart from a special of venison with a parsley crust and wild mushrooms, disappointed hugely. Mushy, clumsily sauced osso bucco was likened to 'school dinners'; this dish should never have left the kitchen. Another special of trofie (handmade pasta) with 'duck ragù' featured a gloopy, lacklustre sauce. Things picked up with good puddings and cheeses served with top-notch condiments. Excellent wines, fairly priced though not cheap, were supplied with expert guidance. Yet at these prices, the lapses in food and service were unforgivable. The kitchen is capable of great things. On our visit, too much of the other extreme was in evidence.

Babies and children admitted. Booking advisable. **Map 16 L10.**

West

Bayswater

★ Assaggi (100)

1st floor, 39 Chepstow Place, W2 4TS (7792 5501). Bayswater, Queensway or Notting Hill Gate tube. **Lunch served** 12.30-2.30pm Mon-Fri; 1-2.30pm Sat. **Dinner served** 7.30-11pm Mon-Sat. **Main courses** £18-£24. **Credit** MC, V.

Given that Assaggi is renowned for celebrity custom and premium prices, you may be surprised how relaxed and informal this discreetly positioned restaurant is. Upstairs from a pub, with furniture on a par with that found in gastropubs and brasseries, it is decorated simply in bright colours, with the only extravagant gesture being a spectacular triffid-like flower arrangement that threatens to engulf the room. Normally we sigh when a wine list starts at above £20, but the nuragus at £21.95 is an interesting old Sardinian grape variety and a highly satisfying choice. Other Sardinian touches include the use of pane carasau, fregola pasta and bottarga on a menu that sticks to what it knows best. Tuna tartare included tiny cubes of radish, cucumber, capers and a topping of sesame seeds. It was good, but outclassed by a glamorous plate of pan-fried tagliolini patties with lobster pieces and a good thick fish-stock sauce. Truffle was generously scattered over a main course of tender pork fillet like a ticker-tape parade. Assaggi's tiramisu features a strong, juicy layer of black coffee. Flourless chocolate cake with ice-cream is another classic dessert produced with textbook precision. Service is efficient and confident, the manageress ebullient and jokey. Saturday lunch is in our experience the best time to visit.

Babies and children welcome: high chairs. Booking advisable. **Map 7 B6.**

ZERO QUATTRO

28 Ridgeway Wimbledon | London | SW19 4QW
Tel. +44 (0)20 8946 4840 | Fax. +44 (0)20 8879 3595
Email info@zeroquattro.co.uk

Opened in the summer of 2005, Zero Quattro has quickly gained a reputation for serving authentic, regional Italian food; prepared daily from the freshest, organic ingredients, that has their clientele returning time after time. Situated on The Ridgway in the heart of Wimbledon Village, the restaurant is owned and managed by Giovanni Agozzino; a genial host who ensures that the atmosphere is always welcoming and warm. Everyone is always welcome, including families.

The superb menu is complimented by an extensive and well selected wine list, featuring classic Italian wines, as well as some regional wines for you to choose from. Zero Quattro opens for luncheon from Monday to Friday from 12 to 3pm and dinner from 6 to 11.30pm. Saturday from 12 to 12am and Sundays from 12 to 10.30pm. A private dining area is available for functions.

'Authentic, regional Italian food, prepared daily from the freshest, organic ingredients & guaranteeing a very warm Sicilian welcome'

To Go Magazine

Hammersmith

★ The River Café (100)

Thames Wharf, Rainville Road, W6 9HA (7386 4200/www.rivercafe.co.uk). Hammersmith tube. **Lunch served** 12.30-3pm daily. **Dinner served** 7-9.30pm Mon-Sat. **Main courses** £23-£32. **Credit** AmEx, DC, MC, V.

Paper tablecloths, utilitarian glasses and a full view of the kitchen live up to the café name, but that's where similarities with humble workers' canteens end. Prices at this famous establishment are steep, but match the freshness and seasonality of perfectly cooked Mediterranean food that never fails to impress. Starters are imaginative yet uncontrived, letting the gleamingly fresh ingredients (baby broad beans, creamy buffalo mozzarella, fresh anchovies) speak for themselves. A few dishes are rooted in Italian tradition, such as linguine with sardines and fennel: clearly inspired by a typical Sicilian recipe. But the chefs generally play with flavour blending, which culminated in a zingy combination of pan-fried pork drizzled with olive oil and basil on our last visit. While the celebrated chocolate nemesis is a must-try for chocoholics, other desserts – such as grilled nespole (apricot-like fruits) accompanied by a delicate custard – are no less tempting. The mostly Italian wine list is far from daunting, because the wines are handily listed according to their regional provenance. Service is friendly and informal, yet knowledgeable and impeccable. The riverside setting and outside tables, when available, are the ultimate treat for leisurely weekend lunches.

Babies and children welcome: high chairs. Booking essential. Disabled: toilet. Dress: smart casual. Tables outdoors (15, terrace). **Map 20 C5.**

Holland Park

Edera

148 Holland Park Avenue, W11 4UE (7221 6090). Holland Park tube. **Coffee served** 10am-noon, **lunch served** noon-2.30pm, **dinner served** 6.30-11pm Mon-Sat. **Meals served** noon-10pm Sun. **Main courses** £11-£18. **Credit** AmEx, MC, V.

Edera has a highly appealing interior, modern yet soothing, but dare we suggest the restaurant is suffering from a touch of arrogance? There was no bargain lunch menu, yet in this wealthy part of town only four or five tables were occupied on our visit. Starters comprise mainly deli items and salads, and there's a long list of pastas. Sardinian flourishes can be found in the use of malloreddus and fregola pastas, and bottarga. Risotto of the day was a creamy broad bean version. Tuna carpaccio, slightly overpowered by a strong-tasting olive oil, contained very fresh, succulent fish served with squeaky green beans and semi-dried tomatoes. Monkfish strips came in a tomato sauce with crunchy nuggets of celery (nicer than it sounds) though the jury is out on the success of green olive mash. Best not to dally with creativity when the basics aren't right; our sea bass was cooked over too high a heat, resulting in an almost charred skin and underdone centre – and the accompanying pinwheel of dry courgettes needed their pesto sauce garnish for moistness. We left half of a thick, woolly, berry panna cotta dessert. And we had trouble attracting the staff. More consistency is needed.

Babies and children admitted. Booking advisable dinner. Restaurant available for hire. Separate room for parties, seats 15. Tables outdoors (4, pavement). **Map 19 B5.**

Kensington

Timo

343 Kensington High Street, W8 6NW (7603 3888/www.timorestaurant.net). High Street Kensington tube. **Lunch served** noon-2.30pm Mon-Sat. **Dinner served** 7-11pm Mon-Sat. **Main courses** £14.90-£21.95. **Credit** AmEx, JCB, MC, V.

No one at Timo appeared to have bothered checking the weather forecast on our visit; the menu was full of comforting dishes that seemed more suited to a chilly winter evening than lunch on a sunny spring afternoon. A succulent, if a touch undercooked, roast pork belly with potato and celeriac purée was pleasantly executed, but felt overly rich given the balmy temperature outside. More seasonal – and far more welcome – was a starter of caponata, a Sicilian dish featuring tomatoes and aubergines, in this case chopped into confetti-like shapes and served on a piece of crispy, paper-thin Sardinian pane carasau bread. A quick glance at the dessert list uncovered more unseasonal offerings in the guise of chocolate and hazelnut cake and chestnut semifreddo. The smiling and efficient service made up for the disappointingly heavy meal. Timo's pleasantly airy, pale-cream decor and value-for-money menu make it a popular spot at lunchtime.

Babies and children admitted. Booking advisable. Restaurant available for hire. Separate room for parties, seats 18. **Map 13 A9.**

Ladbroke Grove

Essenza

210 Kensington Park Road, W11 1NR (7792 1066/www.essenza.co.uk). Ladbroke Grove tube. **Meals served** 12.30-11.30pm daily. **Main courses** £15.50-£17.50. **Set lunch** £11 2 courses. **Credit** AmEx, MC, V.

Once Notting Hillbillies become yummy parents, they tend to decamp to relaxed, family-friendly Essenza: an upmarket sister trattoria to the livelier Osteria Basilico and Mediterraneo down the road. The ambience is understated chic, with mandarin-coloured banquettes and dark-wood panelling. In contrast, the extensive menu focuses on huge portions of home-cooking stalwarts such as amatriciana, pesto and carbonara pasta, as well as classic dishes from most regions of Italy. A selection of chargrilled scallops, prawns, squid and langoustine stood out among a remarkable batch of seafood dishes. The small dessert list cannot compete with the rest of the menu, but offers nice touches like a voluptuous chocolate soufflé with crème anglaise. The all-Italian wine list is, for the most part, fairly priced. Service is crisply efficient, but friendly and extremely accommodating with children, who have a special menu and are lavished with charming Italian attention. There's an express business lunch menu for grown-ups who have to rush back to work.

Babies and children welcome: children's menu; high chairs. Booking essential Fri, Sat. Tables outdoors (2, pavement). **Map 19 B3.**

For branches (Osteria Basilico, Mediterraneo) see index.

Olympia

Cibo

3 Russell Gardens, W14 8EZ (7371 6271/2085/ www.ciborestaurant.co.uk). Shepherd's Bush tube/Kensington (Olympia) tube/rail. **Lunch served** noon-2.30pm Mon-Fri, Sun. **Dinner served** 7-11pm Mon-Sat. **Main courses** £10.50-£23.50. **Set lunch** (Mon-Fri) £16.50 2 courses; (Sun) £18.95 2 courses, £24.95 3 courses. **Credit** AmEx, DC, JCB, MC, V.

Tucked away in a quiet enclave off a busy road near Olympia, Cibo attracts a crowd of monied locals, keen to soak up its unpretentious and relaxed atmosphere. The decor is cosy and Mediterranean, enlivened by artwork and mirrors on the walls. Smaller rooms off the main dining area provide a more intimate setting. The food, if not revelatory, is reliably traditional Italian fare that pays little heed to trendiness. Seafood dishes are Cibo's main strength, with such highlights as fregola (a type of Sardinian pasta, similar to couscous) served with grilled scallops and herbed breadcrumbs. Meat dishes – the likes of lamb with radicchio, or duck ravioli with mushrooms – come in huge portions, yet they lack bite and feel far less exciting. The Italian wine list is good value, and offers a fair selection of wines by the glass. Desserts include crowd-pleasing puddings like affogato, semifreddo and zabaglione. The friendly service can be a little too unrushed at times.

Interview
ROSE GRAY

Who are you?

Chef-owner, with Ruth Rogers, of the **River Café** (*see left*) – about to celebrate its 20th anniversary. Author of ten River Café cookbooks, most recently the River Café Pocket Books series.

Eating in London: what's good about it?

The extraordinary variety of ethnic restaurants and the fact that their ambition, quality and style genuinely reflect the traditions of their countries of origin. And, in many cases, prices are incredibly reasonable.

What's bad about it?

There are still too many fast-food restaurants with no nod to the growing awareness of the importance of healthy eating and a care for the environment.

Which are your favourite London restaurants?

Zuma (*see p198*), for the sushi, after meeting Endo Kazutoshi, who helped me to gain an understanding of the history and development of Japanese food. Also **Chutney Mary** (*see p160*) because it has a changing menu devised by chefs from all regions of India, so one can experience genuine curries without having to travel.

Who or what has had the biggest impact on London's restaurant scene in the past 25 years?

The opening of the gateways to Europe, and the development of niche suppliers, has meant that access to fresh, quality ingredients has become much easier. Also, the interest of the media has had a huge impact, opening up the London restaurant scene to more people and encouraging restaurants to strive for higher standards.

Any hot tips for the coming year?

An emphasis on real food sourced locally, in a modern environment, with educated staff who are proud to represent the industry, and understand – and talk confidently about – the food they are serving.

Babies and children welcome: high chair. Booking advisable dinner. Dress: smart casual. Restaurant available for hire. Separate rooms for parties, seating 12 and 16. Tables outdoors (4, pavement).

South West

Barnes

★ Riva (100)

169 Church Road, SW13 9HR (8748 0434). Barnes or Barnes Bridge rail/33, 209, 283 bus. **Lunch served** 12.15-2.15pm Mon-Fri, Sun. **Dinner served** 7-10.30pm Mon-Sat; 7-9pm Sun. **Main courses** £12-£21. **Credit** AmEx, MC, V.

Riva continues to attract crowds of vaguely famous locals, and visitors from across town, to its classy and understated (if slightly cramped) dining room. The food is simple fare from north-eastern Italy, prepared with fastidious attention to detail and superb ingredients. Sublime seafood – in the guise of tender grilled baby squid simply dressed in an olive oil and herb sauce, or an equally simple octopus salad – was just one of the highlights of our meal. Meat-eaters are catered for with appealing choices that include butter-soft roast suckling pig or melt-in-the-mouth lamb. Service is unfussy and competent, and staff are happy to help diners navigate the outstanding all-Italian wine list, which (like the menu) is skewed towards the north-east of Italy. Even the best Italian establishments can at times fall flat with an unimaginative dessert list, but not Riva. Fregolotta (a wonderfully crumbly cake from Veneto) served with mascarpone cheese was an exciting surprise. Moreish chocolate budino or zingy blood-orange sorbet provided lighter alternatives to round off our perfect meal.

Babies and children welcome (lunch): high chairs. Booking essential dinner. Tables outdoors (3, pavement).

Chelsea

Manicomio

85 Duke of York Square, SW3 4LY (7730 3366/ www.manicomio.co.uk). Sloane Square tube.
Deli **Open** 8am-7pm Mon-Fri; 10am-7pm Sat; 10am-6pm Sun.
Restaurant **Lunch served** noon-3pm Mon-Fri; noon-5pm Sat, Sun. **Dinner served** 6.30-10.30pm Mon-Sat; 6.30-10pm Sun. **Main courses** £12-£55.
Both **Credit** AmEx, JCB, MC, V.

Set in the Duke of York shopping precinct off King's Road, Manicomio is well-liked for its outdoor tables, which are discreetly shielded by tastefully manicured potted trees. The restaurant is highly popular with affluent locals, keen on dining alfresco at weekends while indulging in a spot of people watching. Unfortunately, the attention lavished on the decor doesn't always extend to the modern Italian food or the service, which became increasingly distracted as the place got busier. A starter described as vitello tonnato (paper-thin slices of cold roast veal served in a creamy tuna sauce) was a disappointing modern take on the original classic, the rocket leaves and tuna flakes a pointless exercise in trying to improve on a classic recipe. The own-made pasta dishes, such as pleasantly punchy black-ink seafood tagliolini, are far more preferable to the main courses. The dessert list veers away from the tried-and-tested Italian puddings, yielding interesting finds such as blood-orange sorbet. Despite the relaxed atmosphere, prices can be on the steep side.

Babies and children welcome: booster seats. Booking advisable. Separate room for parties, seats 30. Tables outdoors (30, terrace). **Map 14 F11.**

Osteria dell'Arancio

383 King's Road, SW10 0LP (7349 8111/ www.osteriadellarancio.co.uk). Fulham Broadway or Sloane Square tube. **Lunch served** noon-2.30pm Mon-Fri; noon-3pm Sat; noon-4pm Sun. **Dinner served** 6.30-11pm Mon-Sat; 6.30-10pm Sun. **Main courses** £12-£18. **Set dinner** £40 tasting menu. **Credit** AmEx, DC, MC, V.

The crowds of Chelsea-dwelling Italians that flock to Osteria dell'Arancio at weekends would appear to be a sure-fire indicator of authenticity and value for money. At first glance, the informal ambience and a compact menu strong on traditional Italian home cooking (just like mamma's) also look very promising. But our initial impressions were quickly let down by variable food and amateurish service. The food order was taken first, followed by water and then, at last, the wine. An even longer time-lag followed a pleasant starter of fresh buffalo mozzarella and tomato, before the main courses materialised. Most disappointing was a bland dish of linguine dressed with a rather forgettable courgette, artichoke and cheese sauce, while the signature tagliata (tuscan-style steak) was far from tender. On the plus side, there's an outstanding list of unusual fine Italian wines by the glass, with a special selection of bins from the Marche region. However, such quality comes at a steep price.

Babies and children welcome: high chairs; nappy-changing facilities. Disabled: toilet. Separate room for parties, seats 35. Tables outdoors (14, terrace). **Map 14 D12.**

Fulham

La Famiglia

7 Langton Street, SW10 0JL (7351 0761/7352 6095/www.lafamiglia.co.uk). Sloane Square tube then 11, 22 bus/31 bus. **Lunch served** noon-2.45pm, **dinner served** 7-11.30pm daily. **Main courses** £8.50-£22.50. **Cover** £1.75. **Minimum** £18.50 dinner. **Credit** AmEx, DC, JCB, MC, V.

Alvaro Maccioni's Fulham stalwart has been feeding the famous and not-so-famous since the mid-1960s, with black-and-white pictures of youthful Swinging London celebrities attesting to its pedigree status. Four decades later, the place remains much loved by locals, who flock here at the weekend to enjoy unfussy Italian food with a Tuscan bent, and old-style service complete with fawning waiters. The menu doesn't make a single concession to fashion, featuring seasonal food strictly entrenched in tradition. Fagioli al fiasco, a Florentine speciality where beans are slow-cooked inside a flask, is a must-try starter, along with delicately crispy deep-fried courgette flowers, if in season. Other highlights include spaghetti with mussels and shrimp, and a homey combination of juicy pan-fried leg of lamb with roast potatoes. Diners with a taste for retro will look forward to the appearance at the end of the meal of the dessert trolley, laden with a bedazzling assortment of cakes. Being able to choose your table – the garden is very popular in summer – is another welcome, old-fashioned touch.

Babies and children welcome: high chairs. Booking advisable dinner and Sun. Tables outdoors (30, garden). **Map 13 C13.**

Putney

Enoteca Turi

28 Putney High Street, SW15 1SQ (8785 4449/ www.enotecaturi.com). Putney Bridge tube/Putney rail/14, 74, 270 bus. **Lunch served** noon-2.30pm, **dinner served** 7-11pm Mon-Sat. **Main courses** £10.50-£19.50. **Set lunch** £14.50 2 courses, £17.50 3 courses. **Credit** AmEx, DC, MC, V.

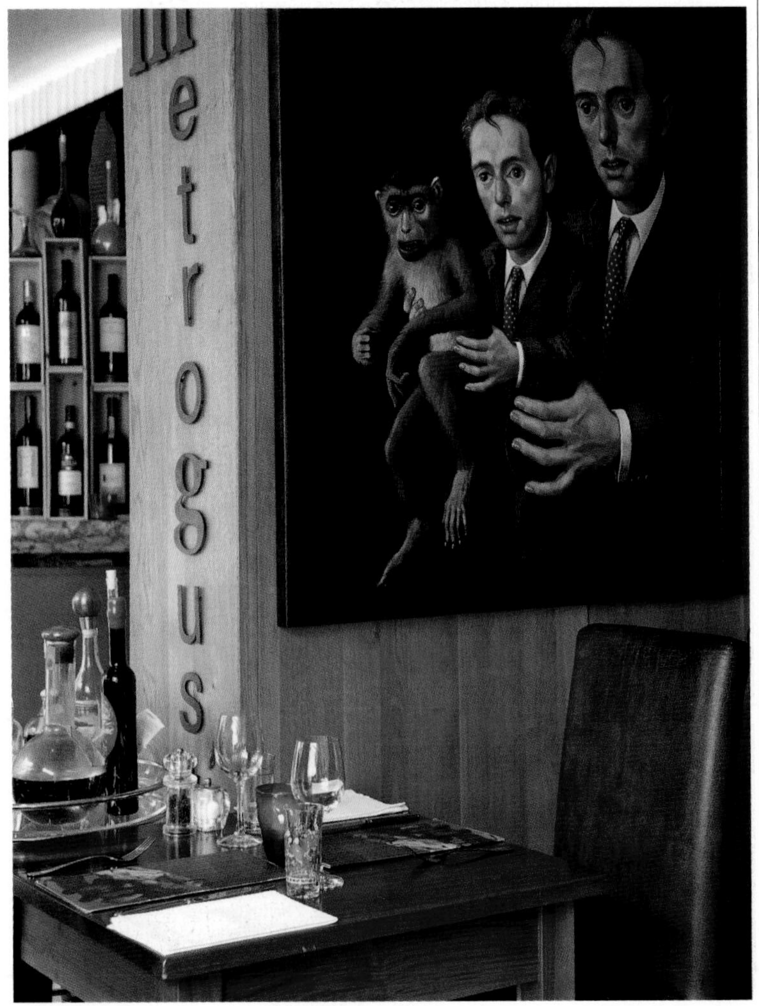

On a sunny Monday lunchtime we had Enoteca Turi almost to ourselves. The room looked lovely, and the warmth of the welcome showed no hint of the gloom sometimes found in a nearly empty restaurant. We were equally pleased by the accomplished cooking. Apart from a slightly undercooked risotto, everything we sampled was of near-perfect quality. A starter of deep-fried buffalo mozzarella with roasted butternut squash showed that the kitchen has a light hand, even with potentially rich dishes. But the star here, as the name suggests, is the wine. If you took the 13 pages of the 'Rest of the World' section, the list would rank among London's best. Add the 36 pages devoted to Italy and you know you're dealing with something special; the country is covered from top to toe, with ample choice at around £20. Mark-ups are low, especially for pricier wines; one fancy claret was selling for little more than retail price. Each dish is marked with a number indicating a wine – available by the glass – that will suit it. At most restaurants, you decide what to eat and then choose something to drink. At Enoteca Turi, you might consider reversing those steps.
Babies and children admitted. Booking advisable. Disabled: toilet. Separate room for parties, seats 30.

Marco Polo

6-7 Riverside Quarter, Eastfields Avenue, SW18 1LP (8874 6800/www.marcopoloriverside.co.uk). East Putney tube. **Meals served** noon-11pm Mon-Sat; noon-10pm Sun. **Main courses** £11.95-£16.95. **Set lunch** £8.95 2 courses, £9.95 3 courses. **Credit** MC, V.

Bringing life and character to another shiny glass and steel development of plush goldfish-bowl flats can't be easy, but Marco Polo has a good go, boosted by its verdant river views. By day, the adjoining nursery that spills on to the new-sown grass of this Thames-side site must lend a touch of chaotic humanity. Yet although the restaurant may be austere in design, the staff are anything but stiffs. The three waiters who came and went from our table joked readily, sang along to canned music and absent-mindedly misplaced orders. So if you're out to impress the boss, beware. But if the boss is a three-year-old child, you'll find the place pleasingly informal. Although said child's pizza came late, not as ordered and then burnt, forgiveness came as easily as reparation. Abundant antipasti included a good salmon carpaccio, while a fine spread of pasta ranged from excellent seafood variations to good ol' spag bol. Veal with lemon and capers is among the main courses. Desserts are mostly of the typical Italian kind, although banoffi pie was a dependable kid-pleaser. Being given wine to taste before ordering made the service charge easier to pay.
Babies and children welcome: high chairs. Booking advisable. Disabled: toilet. Separate room for parties, seats 30. Tables outdoors (60, riverside terrace).

South

Battersea

Osteria Antica Bologna

23 Northcote Road, SW11 1NG (7978 4771/ www.osteria.co.uk). Clapham Junction rail/35, 37, 319 bus. **Lunch served** noon-3pm Mon-Fri. **Dinner served** 6-11pm Mon-Thur; 6-11.30pm Fri. **Meals served** noon-11.30pm Sat; noon-10.30pm Sun. **Main courses** £8.90-£16.90. **Set lunch** (Mon-Sat) £11.50 2 courses, £14 3 courses. **Cover** 90p. **Credit** AmEx, MC, V.
In Italy, osterias are basic, family-run outfits serving satisfying, good-value food with a homely feel. Unfortunately this doesn't apply to Osteria Antica Bologna. While the 1970s dark-wood, cellar-like decor may have its charms, sullen staff and carelessly prepared food do not. This is rather unfortunate, since the large menu includes enticing little-known specialities from Bologna and its surrounds, such as eel and gutsy meat dishes served with mostarda, a classic northern Italian fruit condiment. The own-made saffron tagliolini with red mullet ragù would have been pleasant if it hadn't been slightly undercooked, and if the olives used in the sauce hadn't been of similar quality to those found in supermarket jars. The dessert list looked promising, but more disappointment followed when we discovered that the two most appealing choices weren't available. The all-Italian wine list is basic, yet represents reasonable value. Outside tables overlooking the hustle and bustle of Northcote Road made some amends for the lacklustre culinary experience.
Babies and children admitted: high chairs. Booking essential dinner Fri, Sat. Restaurant available for hire. Tables outdoors (6, pavement). **Map 21 C4.**

Clapham

Mooli

36A Old Town, SW4 0LB (7627 1166/www.moolirestaurant.com). Clapham Common tube. **Lunch served** noon-3.30pm, **dinner served** 6.30-11pm Mon-Fri. **Tea served** 3-6pm Mon-Sat. **Meals served** noon-11pm Sat; 1-11pm Sun. **Main courses** £12.95-£14.50. **Credit** AmEx, MC, V.
Now in its second year, Mooli has hit its stride with exceptional confidence. The restaurant is small, with subdued lighting at dinner; some diners won't like the cushioned benches that provide seating at a few tables, but no one in our group complained. Mooli's key to success is keeping things short and focused. The cocktail list, menu and wine list are all models of brevity, and that makes choosing easy – though vegetarians will have a restricted choice of mains. The cooking adds unexpected modernising tweaks to stalwarts of the Italian kitchen; a chutney served with a traditional veal scaloppine alla milanese exemplifies the approach. Our food ranged from good to excellent, with special prizes going to a main course of calf's liver with pancetta and heavenly mash. Portions are, if anything, too big; that scaloppine must have weighed 250g (9oz) at least. We're not griping, especially when it's possible to eat three courses for under £20. The wine list, all Italian, is also sensibly priced; best value comes at around £25. Service was wonderful (though none of our waiting staff was Italian): attentive when needed and hands-off when not. A great local. Claphamites should flock here.
Babies and children welcome: high chairs. Booking advisable. **Map 22 A1.**

South East

Bermondsey

Arancia

52 Southwark Park Road, SE16 3RS (7394 1751). Bermondsey tube/Elephant & Castle tube/ rail then 1, 53 bus. **Lunch served** 12.30-2.30pm, **dinner served** 7-11pm Tue-Sat. **Main courses** £9-£11.75. **Set lunch** £7.50 2 courses, £10.50 3 courses. **Credit** AmEx, MC, V.
If you were picking a site for a local restaurant, a glass fronted former shop with an unforgiving view of the A2206 and its unlovely flanks of brown brick new-builds might not tickle your fancy. But that's where Arancia settled and, location aside, it has a great deal to recommend it with an excellent short menu of high quality home cooking. Identifying itself by an orange exterior

Metrogusto. See p193.

RESTAURANTS

rossodisera

RESTAURANT & COFFEE SHOP

5 Monmouth Street
Covent Garden
London
WC2H 9DA

020 7240 3683

Truffles, parmigiano, olive oil, speck, cheeses and salumi...the finest and freshest ingredients from Italy's Marches region, served to you in a setting of a rustic marchigiana country house. Accompanied by over 60 hand-picked wines, enjoy he reassuring simplicity of good food with powerful flavours, evocative of this little known region with its long culinary history.

"Notable for yummy retro Italian food and restrained prices."
THE GUARDIAN

"At last! Simple but top quality Italian food at real prices. One visit and you're well and truly hooked."
TIMEOUT

To find your local restaurant visit
www.strada.co.uk

Fratelli la Bufala

If you have been brought up and taught right, the benefits will always shine through. There's no better example of this than Mimo Rimoli, owner of South End Green's popular Fratelli la Bufala. Born in Pozzuoli, Naples (birthplace of Sofia Loren), the Italian was destined to make his mark in the restaurant world. While Mimo was growing into the man he is today, his family restaurant business was continuing to grow.

Fratelli la Bufala is a brand that showcases the gastronomic heritage of Naples, using bufalo meat and mozzarella cheese. The bufalo meat is healthy, low in fat and beautifully tender. Whilst the acclaimed Fratelli la Bufala were springing up all over Italy, the rest of the world was taking notice; Mimo decided he would be the first to bring the family business to England.

Showing the same passion he has had for art and motorcycles, Mimo threw himself into creating a menu that showcased what Fratelli la Bufala was all about. Lip-smacking bufalo fillets, sausages, mozzarella and authentic pizzas, all cooked in a traditional rural Italian way, with the emaphasis on quality and freshness.

Northwest London has some fantastic restaurants and it is places, like Fratelli la Bufala, that bring something different.

'Best Italian'

Ham & High food & drink awards

ARCHANT LONDON

45a South End Road, NW3
www.fratellilabufala.com

020 7435 7814

in keeping with its name, inside it is bare bricks and stripped floors, with paper cloths clipped to the tables. Foodwise, starters includedchickpea and mussel soup or crabmeat and chilli linguine, and a gorgeous chicken liver salad – all for about a fiver. Mains meanwhile remain under £12 and aside from fishcakes, roast poussin and porcini risotto, they included a fine mutton and vegetable stew and an excellent juicy pork fillet with beetroot and lentil salad. Among desserts, undistinguished figs did not benefit from roasting, but there's little cause for complaint about the food here – it's too appetising and too favourably priced. The same goes for a wine list that includes good quality house numbers for £12-£13. A serious orange.
Babies and children welcome: high chair. Booking advisable evenings. Separate room for parties, seats 8.

Tower Bridge

Cantina del Ponte

Butlers Wharf Building, 36C Shad Thames, SE1 2YE (7403 5403/www.danddlondon.com). Tower Hill tube/Tower Gateway DLR/London Bridge tube/rail/47, 78 bus. **Lunch served** noon-3pm daily. **Dinner served** 6-11pm Mon-Sat; 6-10pm Sun. **Main courses** £9.50-£16. **Credit** AmEx, DC, JCB, MC, V.
A few yards downriver from Le Pont de la Tour, Cantina del Ponte remains a respectable, if businesslike restaurant, not noticeably altered since its change of ownership from Conran Restaurants to D&D London. The food isn't fussy, but the views of Tower Bridge are distracting. Inside, a Tuscan market mural and terracotta floors seek to transform a featureless four-square riverside room into a little piece of *campagna*. The menu describes serious Italian cooking, but the food smacks of standardisation on the plate: like Habitat is to Heal's – mass market copies of something more sophisticated. So, following diverting starters (including quail and radicchio, tuscan summer salad and a couple of soups), pappardelle with porcini and rabbit ragù was as plain and simple as the tagliatelle with prawns and salsa cruda. At £11.50 and £13 these were pricey for primi piatti, especially when fish and meat courses range from £12.50 to £15.50. Slow-roast pork was a good sticky dish, but spring lamb was ordinary and chewy. It would be easy to write off this place as an upmarket canteen for local offices, but service is breezily efficient and Cantina, like its wine list, is not without charm.
Babies and children welcome: children's portions; high chairs. Booking advisable. Dress: smart casual. Restaurant available for hire. Tables outdoors (20, terrace). Takeaway service (pizza only, noon-3pm, 6-10pm daily). **Map 12 S8**.

★ Tentazioni

2 Mill Street, SE1 2BD (7237 1100/www.tentazioni.co.uk). Bermondsey tube/London Bridge tube/rail. **Lunch served** noon-2.45pm Tue-Fri. **Dinner served** 6.30-10.45pm Mon-Sat. **Main courses** £17-£20. **Set dinner** £29 4 courses, £38 tasting menu (£60 incl wine). **Credit** AmEx, MC, V.
Tentazioni has been operating in an out-of-the-way street near Tower Bridge since 1997. The main room on the ground floor, lovely and subdued in the evening, showed that maturity has not dimmed the boldness of the kitchen. The approach can be gauged from two of our dishes: risotto with foie gras topped with a leg of confit duck and bathed in a rich port sauce; and roast fillet of pork with black ravioli, scampi, and a sauce of peas and prosciutto di cinghiale (wild boar). Ambitious stuff – but every single dish was a complete success, in both the individual components and the assembled whole. If there is a complaint, it's that portions are too large; both our starters were generous enough to serve as mains. We barely had room for a shared dessert of ambrosial panna cotta with wild berries and berry sorbet. Consider sharing a starter if you're determined to eat pudding. The wine list is a pleasure, chosen with unusual imagination, and posing no problems for those whose budget stops at around £25. Ask for advice and you'll get it with undiluted joy; the people at Tentazioni love what they're doing, and it shows.
Babies and children admitted. Booking advisable dinner Fri, Sat. Restaurant available for hire. Separate room for parties, seats 24. **Map 12 S9**.

East

Docklands

Carluccio's Caffè

Reuters Plaza, E14 5AJ (7719 1749/www.carluccios.com). Canary Wharf tube/DLR. **Meals served** 7am-11pm Mon-Fri; 9am-11pm Sat; 10am-10.30pm Sun. **Main courses** £8.75-£12.75. **Credit** AmEx, DC, MC, V.
The original Covent Garden restaurant that spawned the idea for Antonio Carluccio's successful café chain may have closed for good, but the concept of providing simple, traditional Italian food served in unassuming surroundings, goes from strength to strength. More outlets are planned beyond London. The utilitarian-looking deli-cum-cafés are blessed with generously long opening hours, making them perfect places for breakfast, or for lingering in after a late dinner. They do, however, get busier and deafeningly noisy at lunchtime. Large antipasti to share and textbook pasta dishes remain the fortes, with a surprisingly good selection of vegetarian-friendly food. Penne with courgette, chilli and deep-fried spinach balls stood out among more traditional gnocchi and filled-pasta dishes. Don't expect to find top-notch authentic regional cooking. The fegato alla veneziana (calf's liver with onions) was a poor relation of the original recipe, and betrayed the disappointing quality of the ingredients. Nevertheless, even at the busiest times, staff are charming and accommodating.
Babies and children welcome: children's menu; high chairs; toys. Disabled: toilet. Tables outdoors (30, pavement). Takeaway service. **Map 24 B2**.
For branches see index.

Shoreditch

★ Fifteen

15 Westland Place, N1 7LP (0871 330 1515/www.fifteenrestaurant.com). Old Street tube/rail. Trattoria **Breakfast served** 7.30-11am Mon-Sat; 9-11am Sun. **Lunch served** noon-3pm Mon-Sat; noon-3.30pm Sun. **Dinner served** 6-10pm Mon-Sat. **Main courses** £11-£18. *Restaurant* **Lunch served** noon-2.30pm, **dinner served** 6.30-9.15pm daily. **Main courses** £12-£24. **Set lunch** £22 2 courses, £25 3 courses. **Set meal** £50-£60 tasting menu. *Both* **Credit** AmEx, DC, JCB, MC, V.
Despite celebrating its fifth anniversary in 2007 and sprouting offshoots as far as Melbourne, standards haven't slipped at Jamie Oliver's Fifteen. The modern Italian food remains nigh-on flawless, while service is unpretentious yet consummately professional. Whether you opt for the informal ground-floor trattoria, now open for breakfast, or the funky, retro-style basement restaurant, expect to find produce sourced from top-notch suppliers and a daily changing seasonal menu offering quirky regional specialities. One of the highlights of our lunchtime visit was outstanding pizzoccheri, a wintry dish of buckwheat tagliatelle with cheese and greens that originates from Valtellina, a valley near the Swiss border. Still, Fifteen's forte lies in creative dishes that are less rooted in authenticity, like an impressive starter of roasted beets, blood orange and fresh goat's cheese salad with a mint and pomegranate dressing was remarkable. When we realised that the only dessert available on the set lunch menu was unsuitable for vegetarians, our waiter promptly substituted it with another from the à la carte without additional charge. The involvement of Matt Skinner as wine buyer and occasional sommelier ensures that the compact wine list remains fairly priced and diverse.
Babies and children welcome: high chairs. Booking essential. Disabled: toilet (trattoria). Dress: smart casual. **Map 6 Q3**.

North

Camden Town & Chalk Farm

La Collina

17 Princess Road, NW1 8JR (7483 0192). Camden Town or Chalk Farm tube. **Lunch served** noon-3pm Fri-Sun. **Dinner served** 6.30-11pm daily. **Set meal** £19.50 2 courses, £23.50 3 courses. **Credit** MC, V.
Staff need to be skinny to bob and weave through the cramped tables in the basement of this otherwise pleasant local; the problems come when customers try to move. One couple left after just a few minutes, such was the difficulty of being squeezed into the tiny space. Upstairs is a little more serene without the open kitchen, but only slightly more spacious. The sensible wine list starts at £13.50 a bottle, glasses at £4; we found the white better than the red. Herb risotto with scallops had a good buttery finish, with just the right degree of camphoric rosemary flavour. Rolls of savoy cabbage were stuffed with sausage meat and served with wedges of caramelised apple and a coulis-style pepper sauce – surprisingly tasty. Desserts disappointed. There was a pretty panna cotta flavoured with grappa and set with raspberries, but we ordered bonet (chocolate and amaretti pudding), which had the texture of a wet jumper, and a truly stingy portion (a small scoop and a half) of zabaione and gianduja ice-creams served with the tiniest cat's tongue biscuits. Staff were very pleasant. Working harder isn't the issue here, it's the need to work smarter.
Babies and children welcome: high chair. Booking advisable. Separate room for parties, seats 16. Tables outdoors (14, garden). **Map 27 B2**.

Islington

Casale Franco

Rear of 134-137 Upper Street, N1 1QP (7226 8994). Angel tube/Highbury & Islington tube/rail. **Lunch served** noon-2.30pm Sat. **Dinner served** 6-11.30pm Tue-Sat. **Meals served** noon-10pm Sun. **Main courses** £8.50-£17.50. **Cover** £1. **Credit** AmEx, JCB, MC, V.
Still one of Islington's more charming cellar-like, stone-floored Italians, Casale Franco is falling behind in its cooking. The kitchen needs to raise its game if it's to keep up with the other Italian restaurants around town. Down a little side alley, the venue has bags of atmosphere but too many empty seats. Cold marinated sardines with sweet and sour onions, pine nuts and sultanas made an uninspiring start to our meal. Seared scallops swam in a sea of cream and puréed spinach, on which bobbed the odd buoy of pancetta. Pastas are satisfactory, with wild boar spaghetti and an ample seafood risotto providing good solid sustenance. Belly of pork, however, was thick, chewy and dry. Perhaps you'll fare better if you stick to less ambitious dishes, such as one of the seven standard pizzas. The wine list is lacklustre, but staff are considerate, justifying both cover and service charges. If you want atmosphere and intimacy, this remains a likeable retreat. For serious cooking, try elsewhere.
Restaurant available for hire (Tue-Thur, Sun). Separate room for parties, seats 50. Tables outdoors (32, courtyard). **Map 5 O1**.

Metrogusto

13 Theberton Street, N1 0QY (7226 9400/www.metrogusto.co.uk). Angel tube. **Lunch served** noon-2.30pm Fri, Sat; noon-3pm Sun. **Dinner served** 6.30-10.30pm Mon-Thur; 6.30-11pm Fri, Sat; 6-10pm Sun. **Main courses** £11.50-£17.50. **Set meal** (6-9pm Mon-Thur; 12.30-2.30pm Sat; 12.30-2.30pm, 6-9pm Sun) £14.50 two courses, £19.50 3 courses. **Credit** AmEx, JCB, MC, V.
This is a star of the crowded Islington restaurant scene. Prices are reasonable, especially in the set-price pre-cinema menu, which makes it possible to eat three courses for less than £20. The decor is charming: rustic wood and odd but intriguing modern paintings. But it's the service that shines

RESTAURANTS

brightest, combining precision with true warmth. The owner presides with straight-backed dignity yet makes jokes and has a permanent twinkle in his eye. Our waiter was no less precise; when he spilled a single droplet of wine down the side of the glass, he poured the wine into a clean glass. The menu combines tradition with well-judged innovation ('progressive cooking'), and we ate nothing that was less than good. Starters of stuffed baby squid and a lovely, light caponata could not have been better. Mains of roasted guinea fowl and a vast bowl of penne all'arrabbiata (pancetta, tomato, chilli) kept up the pace. The wine list offers some of Italy's best bottles at fair prices, while giving ample satisfaction under £20. If you're in the area, give it a try. If you live locally, you can make regular visits without breaking the bank.
Babies and children welcome: high chairs. Booking advisable; essential weekends. Separate room for parties, seats 24. Tables outdoors (4, pavement). **Map 5 O1.**

Kentish Town

Pane Vino

323 Kentish Town Road, NW5 2TJ (7267 3879). Kentish Town tube/rail. **Lunch served** noon-3pm Mon-Sat. **Dinner served** 6.30-11pm Mon-Sat. **Main courses** £10.80-£16.90. **Credit** MC, V.
Hidden away in the gastronomic wasteland of Kentish Town, unassuming Pane Vino keeps quietly serving pleasant Mediterranean food with a Sardinian flavour to a crowd of faithful regulars. During our visit service was so unfriendly it verged on the robotic, and not all dishes were available, but the food offered was of remarkable quality and reasonable value, making up for the disappointments. As well as pizza (unavailable on our visit), the menu specialises in the cornerstones of Sardinian cuisine: moreish linguine with bottarga (dried grey mullet roe) and parsley; and satisfying malloreddus (like little gnocchi but made from semolina) dressed in a pork-sausage sauce. A starter of grilled sardines on a bed of rocket and pane carasau (the traditional bread of Sardinian shepherds) was so fresh and zingy it made us forgive the lengthy wait for it to be served. The dessert list somewhat surprisingly forsakes traditional Sardinian sweets, but features timeless classics such as a suitably wobbly panna cotta with red fruit compote.
Babies and children admitted. Tables outdoors (2, pavement). Takeaway service. **Map 26 B5.**

North West

Golders Green

Philpott's Mezzaluna

424 Finchley Road, NW2 2HY (7794 0455/ www.philpotts-mezzaluna.com). Golders Green tube. **Lunch served** noon-2.30pm Tue-Fri; noon-3pm Sun. **Dinner served** 7-11pm Tue-Sun. **Set lunch** £12 1 course, £17 2 courses, £20 3 courses, £25 4 courses. **Set dinner** £19.50 1 course, £24.50 2 courses, £29.50 3 courses, £34.50 4 courses, £39.50 5 courses. **Credit** MC, V.
New, boldly coloured portraits of Marlon Brando, Dean Martin and Madonna contrast with this reliable local's otherwise traditional decor of blowsy pink tea roses and double-layered tablecloths. Spaghetti and meatballs seemed the appropriate order, but Don Philpott's kitchen also turns out more refined fare such as a tender chicken and foie gras sausage on lemon-flavoured barley risotto. What united these dishes was the use of finger-licking stocks. Of the mains, guinea fowl came with chestnuts, lentils and spinach, while steak was nicely seasoned with pepper before being chargrilled and served with a cushion of oxtail cottage pie. Staff impressed us by offering to bring a jug of iced tap water. The wine list contains nearly 70 bottles under £20 (there's a fine-wine collection too). Chile, Australia, Bulgaria, even Switzerland make it into the cellar; our Spanish Grenacha X was among the cheapest at £14. The menu is similarly kind to wallets. Portions are generous for the good-value Sunday lunch, where extras include coffee and an own-made petit four (featuring wonderful soft amaretti). A well-balanced dolce di cioccolata had a coffee liqueur kick; a slice of passion fruit semifreddo (with fresh fruit) was less impressive, but still tasty – and at just £3 extra, why say no?
Babies and children welcome: high chairs. Booking advisable dinner Sat. Restaurant available for hire. Tables outdoors (3, terrace).

Maida Vale

Green Olive

5 Warwick Place, W9 2PX (7289 2469). Warwick Avenue tube/6 bus. **Lunch served** noon-3pm Fri; Sat. **Dinner served** 6-10.30pm Mon-Fri; 6.30-11pm Sat. **Main courses** £14-£19. **Credit** AmEx, JCB, MC, V.
Hidden in a leafy street off Warwick Avenue, Green Olive looks every bit as polished as the patrician Victorian mansions that surround it. A serene interior with pale wood and cream walls, adequate – if not overwhelming – modern Italian food, and reasonable prices attract an affluent local clientele. Service, however, can be stand-offish and awkward at first. Although the restaurant was initially empty, staff disappeared without proffering the menu or drinks. Nonetheless, they managed to turn on the Italian charm as the evening got busier. Daily specials liven up the rather short menu, which includes tried-and-tested crowd-pleasers like buffalo mozzarella salad and risotto. A main course of pork cheeks on potato and leek purée was pleasant and well-executed, but failed to excite. An earthy dish of lasagnette with mushrooms provided a flavoursome alternative for vegetarians. The dessert menu sticks to old favourites such as tiramisu and panna cotta, while the small all-Italian wine list is pretty good value.
Babies and children admitted. Booking advisable. Restaurant available for hire. **Map 1 C4.**

St John's Wood

★ Rosmarino

1 Blenheim Terrace, NW8 0EH (7328 5014/ www.rosmarino.co.uk). St John's Wood tube. **Lunch served** noon-3pm Fri, Sat; 12.30-3pm Sun. **Dinner served** 6.30-10.30pm Tue-Thur; 6.30-11pm Fri, Sat; 7-10pm Sun. **Main courses** £12.50-£18.50. **Credit** AmEx, JCB, MC, V.
The people of St John's Wood are lucky – though they sometimes don't seem to realise it. This local gem, with its quietly elegant modern interior and lovely conservatory (best place to sit), serves terrific food with a winning combination of professionalism and friendliness. Everything we ate was simply sensational: inventive, but judged with unfailing mastery of flavour and texture. Own-made fettuccine with shellfish sauce featured noodles deep-yellow from the intense colour of the egg yolks. Grilled baby squid with a piquant sauce was accompanied by exceptional bruschetta. Mains were even better. The gorgonzola sauce on a perfectly cooked ribeye managed to be powerful but not overwhelming, and sea bass with saffron potatoes and grilled red peppers had marvellous perfume and exquisite, complementary flavours. We received expert and enthusiastic wine advice, which steered us to two glasses from a fine list with interesting and unusual 'wines of the week'. The downbeat moment in our memorable meal was hearing that Rosmarino is plagued by no-shows, sometimes as high as 50% of covers. Those affluent St John's Woodmen should show more appreciation.
Babies and children welcome: high chairs. Booking advisable dinner Thur-Sun. Restaurant available for hire. Separate room for parties, seats 35. Tables outdoors (7, terrace). **Map 1 C2.**

Outer London

Twickenham, Middlesex

A Cena

418 Richmond Road, Twickenham, Middx TW1 2EB (8288 0108). Richmond tube/rail. **Lunch served** noon-3pm Tue-Sun. **Dinner served** 7-10.30pm Tue-Sat. **Main courses** £13.75-£19. **Set lunch** (Sun) £22 3 courses. **Credit** AmEx, MC, V.
Just over Richmond Bridge, you're hit by the shock of the suburbs after the Georgian elegance of Richmond proper. Thankfully, A Cena raises the tone with its bistro-like design of wooden bar, stripped floors, pew seats, bare tables and dripping candles. Although getting hard to book, it remains a middle-ranking restaurant providing muscular cuisine. Food has a tendency towards the rich, even in a starter as seemingly light as gem salad with cream, shallot and parmesan. Otherwise, starters might include bresaola with truffle oil and parmesan, or slow-roast rabbit with pancetta, parmesan and bruschetta. Among just three fresh pastas, fusilli with tomato sauce was a large, lush dish. Mains too are solid – more in tune with Anglo-Saxon meat and two veg, than typical Italian secondi piatti. So, leg of lamb with salsa verde (resembling mint sauce) and fried courgette arrived on a mattress of olive oil mash: just like the veal rump with broad beans and ham. After such robust pleasures, desserts like cheesecake and panna cotta were desirable yet not physiologically feasible. The red-blooded Italian wine list fits well with the wholesome cooking. Service isn't over-indulgent.
Babies and children welcome: high chairs. Booking advisable. Restaurant available for hire.

SHELF LIFE

Restaurants **Caffè Caldesi** (*see p184*), **Carluccio's Caffè** (*see p193*), **Manicomio** (*see p190*) and **Zafferano** (*see p182*) also have attached delis.

Giacobazzi's

150 Fleet Road, NW3 2QX (7267 7222/www.giacobazzis.co.uk). Belsize Park tube/Hampstead Heath rail. **Open** 9.30am-7pm Mon-Fri; 9am-6pm Sat.
The Giacobazzis hail from Emilia-Romagna, but you'll also find carefully chosen food and wines from the rest of Italy. Fresh filled pasta is a speciality and the own-made lasagne (frozen in handy oven trays) is superb.

Lina Stores

18 Brewer Street, W1F 0SH (7437 6482). Piccadilly Circus tube. **Open** 8am-6.30pm Mon-Fri; 8am-5.30pm Sat.
This Soho deli is a slice of old Italia. Despite all the mass-market groceries, you'll also find gourmet lines, including fresh truffles in season.

Luigi's

349 Fulham Road, SW10 9TW (7352 7739). South Kensington tube then 14 bus. **Open** 9am-9.30pm Mon-Fri; 9am-7pm Sat.
Opened in 1973, this cheerful red shop with panettone boxes hanging from the ceiling, is crammed with dried pastas, olive oil, salamis and hams, olives, cheese and sweets. The occasional item from Switzerland or Spain is added to the mix.

Olga Stores

30 Penton Street, N1 9PS (7837 5467). Angel tube. **Open** 9am-8pm Mon-Fri; 9am-7pm Sat; 10am-2pm Sun. **Credit** MC, V.
Long-established neighbourhood deli selling all the pecorino, parma ham and panettone you could want, plus ready-made dishes.

Japanese

Japanese food grows in popularity year on year: it seems that Londoners can't get enough of sushi, sashimi, noodles, tempura and teppanyaki or their fusion cousins. Maybe the reason is because it's a highly aesthetic, low-calorie, omega-rich cuisine; or perhaps because there is now such a variety of Japanese restaurants in the capital, from ultra-glamorous venues for that special occasion to bargain-priced noodle joints. The capital's restaurateurs have been happy to feed the need with a slew of openings in 2007, the most significant being **Dinings** in Marylebone, ex-Nobu alumnus Tomonari Chiba's compact den of 'Japanese tapas'. At the more basic end of the spectrum, Hanover Square's Café Plaza has reopened as **@Japan** to provide a cheap and cheerful respite from the consumer vortex of Oxford and Regent Streets.

Other newcomers include smart **Atami** in Westminster, kaiten-zushi bar **Sushi Hiroba** in Holborn, yakitori specialist **Bincho** on the South Bank, and a bunch of neighbourhood restaurants: **Kushi-Tei** (Wimbledon), **Sa Sa Sushi** (Islington), **Yumenoki** (Fulham) and **Wow Simply Japanese** (Crouch End). Meanwhile, the the capital's high-end Japanese restaurants, including **Zuma** and offspring **Roka**, **Nobu** and siblings **Nobu Berkeley Street** and **Ubon**, remain as impressive and popular as ever. Old-school, new-wave, high-end, low-cost... London has it all.

Central

Bloomsbury

Kobe Jones NEW

111A Great Russell Street, WC1B 3NQ (7300 3250/www.kobejones.co.uk). Tottenham Court Road tube.
Bar **Open** noon-3pm, 5.30-11pm Mon-Wed; noon-3pm, 5.30pm-midnight Thur; noon-3pm, 6pm-1am Fri, Sat; 6-10.30pm Sun.
Restaurant **Lunch served** noon-2.30pm Mon-Fri. **Dinner served** 6-10pm Mon-Wed; 6-10.30pm Thur-Sat; 6-9.30pm Sun. **Main courses** £13.50-£24. **Set lunch** £22. **Set dinner** £35 per person (minimum 2).
Both **Credit** MC, V.

If you're hankering after the East-West fusion food of yesteryear, Kobe Jones may just be your thing. With branches in Sydney, Melbourne and Bangkok, and claiming a 'Californian' influence, it seems to have ridden into Bloomsbury on the coat tails of Nobu (*see p199*) and others. The decor is lovely, in a dramatic, magazine-photo-shoot way, with dark, dark wood and low, low lighting. Prices might make you wince, though, as several main courses cruise easily past the £20 barrier. Starters, including agedashidofu and various sashimi, tend to be more traditional than main courses. 'Kobe rolls' such as our spider roll (deep-fried soft-shell crab with smelt roe, crab salad, avocado and cucumber) are California-style – fat rolls with many fillings. A 'signature dish' of tuna tataki (slices of peppered, seared tuna with sliced mushrooms and asparagus spears, bound together with a creamy, sharp sauce) left us underwhelmed. Grilled Chilean sea bass was more impressive: two thick slices of succulent, crisp-skinned fish, served with rice and miso soup. The loungey music does its best to create a trendy vibe, but Kobe Jones seems more a follower than a setter of trends.
Babies and children admitted. Bar available for hire. Takeaway service. **Map 17 C2.**

City

Miyabi

Great Eastern Hotel, Liverpool Street, EC2M 7QN (7618 7100/www.great-eastern-hotel.co.uk). Liverpool Street tube/rail. **Lunch served** noon-2.30pm Mon-Fri. **Dinner served** 6-10.30pm Mon-Fri; 6-10pm Sat. **Main courses** £6.50-£23. **Set lunch** £18-£25. **Credit** AmEx, DC, MC, V.

Since changing hands from Conran to Hyatt in 2006, Miyabi has retained its sleek looks, but the food appears less refined. Perhaps the lunch hour is too hectic to allow much time and care to be spent on presentation (brown paper bags of orders stacked on the sushi counter stools testify to a brisk takeaway trade), but the sushi and trimmings sometimes look a little thrown together. And toppings, though fresh enough, aren't generous. With its heart-of-the-City location, this little, wood-panelled bento-box of a restaurant in the Great Eastern Hotel naturally fills up with suits at lunchtime, when the menu is a streamlined selection of staples (chicken or pork katsu, chicken or salmon teriyaki, mixed tempura and so on) in bento arrangements for £19, plus a couple of grander spreads for £25. Desserts (such as 'cremeux lychee') sound more interesting than they taste. In the evening, the menu is more varied. Food here is not of great finesse, but is good value on the takeaway menu, making Miyabi a decent option 'to go'.
Babies and children admitted. Booking advisable. Disabled: toilet. Takeaway service. **Map 12 R6.**

Moshi Moshi Sushi

24 Upper Level, Liverpool Street Station, EC2M 7QH (7247 3227/www.moshimoshi.co.uk). Liverpool Street tube/rail. **Meals served** 11.30am-10pm Mon-Fri. **Dishes** £1.70-£3.50. **Main courses** £8-£11. **Credit** MC, V.

Clever design and better-than-average sushi make this branch of Moshi Moshi a peaceful refuge from the commuter madness of Liverpool Street Station. The look is part Japanese sci-fi, with industrial metal trappings softened by quirkier features such as bamboo plants and a fun Zen garden under a perspex stair. There's the usual salmon and tuna nigiri and maki, but novelty-seekers can opt for sushi of cheshire cheese with red onion and lettuce, while the more hardcore might prefer chilli cod roe. A 'platter' of small dishes is a good way to graze through the menu. Highlights of our 'seasonal platter' were a light, tender pollack tempura and a gently spicy fish ceviche. Less successful was dry tori kara-age (deep-fried chicken). All the fish in our 'gourmet' sushi and sashimi set was commendably fresh and well prepared. Salmon sashimi (from Loch Duart) was firm and flavourful, but the rice in our nigiri was too hard and cold. Better was an à la carte hot dish of seared tuna tataki with chilli sauce. Service is sweet, but can be erratic.
Babies and children admitted. Disabled: toilet. Takeaway service; delivery service. Vegetarian menu. **Map 12 R5.**
For branch see index.

Clerkenwell & Farringdon

★ Saki

4 West Smithfield, EC1A 9JX (7489 7033/www.saki-food.com). Barbican tube/Farringdon tube/rail.
Bar **Open** noon-11pm Mon-Wed; noon-midnight Thur, Fri; 6pm-midnight Sat.
Deli **Open** noon-7.30pm Mon-Fri.
Restaurant **Lunch served** noon-2.30pm, **tea served** 2.30-6pm Mon-Fri. **Dinner served** 6-10.30pm Mon-Sat. **Main courses** £8.50-£29.50. **Set lunch** £9.90-£14.90. **Set dinner** £38-£80.
All **Credit** JCB, MC, V.

Presumably to compensate for the absence of windows in its basement dining room, Saki has an expansive centrepiece of white stalagmite-like candles rising up from a sea of white gravel. Striking, if a little pointless. The food is also striking, but definitely purposeful. Having received a restrained thumbs-up from us when it opened in spring 2006, Saki seems to have sharpened its culinary skills in 2007 – this may have something to do with acquiring an ex-head chef of Nobu to helm its adventurous kitchen. The high quality of

BEST JAPANESE

Niche nosh

Visit **Abeno Too** (*see p202* **Bargain central**) for okonomiyaki, **Benihana** (*see p210*) for teppanyaki, **Bincho** for yakitori (*see p205*), **Kushi-Tei** (*see p203*) for kushiyaki and **Sushi-Hiro** (*see p202*) for sushi.

Mixed blessings

For fusion fare, try **Chisou** (*see p199*), **Dinings** (*see p198*), **Kobe Jones** (*see left*), **Nobu** (*see p199*) – and siblings **Nobu Berkeley Street** (*see p199*) and **Ubon** (*see p206*) – **Saki** (*see above*), **Tsunami** (*see p205*) and **Yakitoria** (*see p203*).

Moveable feast

Watch your food glide by on the conveyer belts at **Kulu Kulu**, **Yo! Sushi** (for both, *see p202* **Bargain central**), **Moshi Moshi Sushi** (*see left*) and **Sushi Hiroba** (*see p197*).

Celebrating in style

Flash some cash at **Nobu** (*see p199*), **Nobu Berkeley Street** (*see p199*), **Roka** (*see p197*), **Tsunami** (*see p205*), **Ubon** (*see p206*), **Umu** (*see p199*), **Yakitoria** (*see p203*) and **Zuma** (*see p198*).

A room with a view

Get a window on the world at **Bincho** (*see p205*) **Nobu** (*see p199*), **Ozu** (*see p206*) and **Ubon** (*see p206*).

ingredients is exemplified by the lobster used in the first dish of our yanagi course, and the king crab sashimi that was recommended by our charmingly attentive waiter. Both crustacea were ultra-fresh and visually impressive – and, most importantly, not overcooked. First-time visitors would do well to build an extra 20 minutes into their estimated dining time, as the length and interest of the monthly changing food menu is surpassed only by the marathon read that is the drinks list: an emphasis reflected in the adjoining, music-filled bar. And perhaps another ten minutes to explore the high-tech loos. Great food, thoroughly drilled service and never a dull moment.
Babies and children admitted. Booking advisable. Disabled: lift; toilet. Separate room for parties, seats 12. Takeaway service. Vegetarian menu. **Map 11 O5**.

Fitzrovia

★ Roka

37 Charlotte Street, W1T 1RR (7580 6464/ www.rokarestaurant.com). Goodge Street or Tottenham Court Road tube.
Bar **Open** 6pm-midnight Mon, Sat, Sun; noon-midnight Tue-Fri.
Restaurant **Lunch served** noon-3.30pm Mon-Fri; 12.30-3.30pm Sat. **Dinner served** 5.30-11.30pm Mon-Sat; 5.30-10.30pm Sun. **Main courses** £3.60-£21. **Set lunch** £25 tasting menu. **Set dinner** £50-£75 per person (minimum 2) tasting menu.
Both **Credit** AmEx, DC, MC, V.
Where to begin? Everything about Roka is enticing: from the soft honey-coloured walls to the aroma of wood burning at the centrepiece robata grill and, above all, the food – a modern take on traditional Japanese cuisine. Roka is the younger sibling of runaway success Zuma (*see 198*), but is more than able to hold its own. Wraparound floor-to-ceiling windows and a spacious interior exude a relaxed confidence that's reflected in the customers: media types in big shades, suited bankers and the odd celebrity. The exquisitely presented food is divided into à la carte and taster menus. Vegetable tempura was feather-light and crisp; aubergine coated in ginger, mirin and shoyu, and charred on the grill, was beautifully smoky; velvety sashimi of tuna, sea bass and salmon arrived on a block of ice as clear as glass – all delivered by knowledgeable and attentive staff. The only off-note was some tear-inducingly salty kimchi. Roka is a prime venue for sampling shochu, which can be fully (un)focused on in the basement Shochu Lounge. The drinks menu also includes an extensive choice of high-quality saké. Roka might rock your budget, but it will rock your taste buds too.
Babies and children welcome: high chairs. Booking advisable. Disabled: toilet. Tables outdoors (10, pavement). **Map 17 B1**.

Holborn

★ Aki

182 Gray's Inn Road, WC1X 8EW (7837 9281/ www.akidemae.com). Chancery Lane tube.
Lunch served noon-2.30pm Mon-Fri.
Dinner served 6-11pm Mon-Fri; 6-10.30pm Sat.
Main courses £4.50-£11.50. **Set lunch** £5.10-£17. **Set dinner** £18-£40.50. **Credit** AmEx, JCB, MC, V.
First impressions are less than auspicious here. The interior is awash with knick-knacks, faded posters and scuffed furniture. Yet any initial foreboding is laid to rest with the arrival of the menu: a broad and well-considered list, from sushi and sashimi to tempting hotpot dishes designed for four or five people to share. Sea-scented, delectably fresh razor clam sashimi came simply served with shiso leaves. Ebi and mackerel nigiri were marked by well-textured and slightly warm rice with just the right amount of vinegar. The many small dishes are made with drinking in mind (there's a small but well-formed list of sakés and shochus). We were impressed with our moist, savoury mackerel cooked in sweet miso, and with a bowl of agedashidofu. Next, konnyaku dengaku, chewy squares made from the root of the amorphophallus konjac (devil's tongue) plant, were

Sushi Hiroba

flavoured with miso and sesame. Less exotic was marinated tuna kushiage: skewers of tuna coated in panko (breadcrumbs), deep-fried and served with a punchy tonkatsu sauce. This great-value establishment demands repeat visits.
Babies and children admitted. Booking advisable. Separate room for parties, seats 30. Takeaway service. **Map 4 M4**.

★ Matsuri

71 High Holborn, WC1V 6EA (7430 1970). Chancery Lane or Holborn tube. **Lunch served** noon-2.30pm, **dinner served** 6-10pm Mon-Sat. **Main courses** £16-£23 lunch; £17-£35 dinner. **Set lunch** £8.50-£45. **Set dinner** (6-7pm) £20; £35-£70. **Credit** AmEx, DC, JCB, MC, V.
This is the newer, trendier sister of the original St James's Matsuri. The family resemblance isn't obvious; here, sleekness and minimalism prevails, with wood-slatted walls separating the teppanyaki room and the sushi counter from the main restaurant. It takes a while to peruse the menus – one for sushi, an à la carte and a seasonal list of chef's specials. Read carefully, though; the teishoku aren't the most imaginative nor are they particularly good value. We put together a far more interesting feast for a similar outlay. There's a 'fusion' edge to the chef's specials. Octopus was marinated in olive oil, served on marinated seaweed and vegetables and topped with a light tomato sauce and tiny cubes of gelatine flavoured with balsamic vinegar. Back in traditional territory, yaki nasu (pieces of grilled aubergine topped with bonito shavings) was smoky and succulent. Tender rare-grilled ox tongue was served with two dipping sauces: soy and mustard, and sesame oil. Japanese pickles provided piquancy and crunch. The only let-down was a rather heavy tempura. Service is sweet, polite and well-informed.
Babies and children admitted. Booking advisable. Disabled: toilet. Separate rooms for parties, seating 10 and 30. **Map 10 M5**.
For branch see index.

Sushi Hiroba NEW

50-54 Kingsway, WC2B 6EP (7430 1888/ www.sushihiroba.co.uk). Holborn tube. **Lunch served** noon-3pm Mon-Fri. **Dinner served** 6-11pm Mon-Sat; 5-10pm Sun. **Main courses** £7.50-£9. **Set lunch** £13-£15. **Set meal** £50. **Credit** MC, V.
This Korean-run sushi bar serves daringly experimental dishes in a modern, well-decorated setting. The interior is evocative of the East, with its clever use of black marble and bamboo trompe l'oeil. A conveyor-belt sushi counter dominates the centre of the dining room. Perch here to admire wild-looking creations such as inside-out salmon maki in a panko (breadcrumb) crust, or banana, avocado and cucumber maki. Drizzles of mayonnaise or wine sauce, garnishes of brightly coloured flying-fish roe or matt black sesame seeds jazz up already busy combinations. Sushi purists might prefer to stick to the classics; grilled eel and tuna nigiri were both good, bettering the specimens

found in some well-known kaiten-zushi chains. If you're tempted by tempura or other dishes such as takoyaki (diced octopus fried in little balls of batter), take heed of the sign that 'hot dishes can be reheated on request'. How prawn tempura is reheated, we're not sure. There's also a good selection of katsu curry, noodle and Korean-style bulgogi dishes, which are best enjoyed at the spacious booth seating.
Babies and children admitted. Takeaway service.
Map 18 F2.

Knightsbridge

★ Zuma (100)

5 Raphael Street, SW7 1DL (7584 1010/ www.zumarestaurant.com). Knightsbridge tube.
Bar **Open** noon-11pm Mon-Fri; 12.30-11pm Sat; noon-10pm Sun.
Restaurant **Lunch served** noon-2.15pm Mon-Fri; 12.30-3.15pm Sat; 12.30-2.45pm Sun. **Dinner served** 6-10.45pm Mon-Sat; 6-10.15pm Sun. **Main courses** £14.80-£70.
Both **Credit** AmEx, DC, MC, V.
Zuma is still one of the most exciting spots in town in which to dine and schmooze. The crowd is Knightsbridge and City meets *Sex and the City*, where model types and their swains wear designer gear and expect others to notice. Don't let the 'modern izakaya' tag fool you – this is high-end dining. The lengthy menu features the likes of umami-rich sautéed Japanese mushrooms with akadashi miso, or cubes of fried tofu with a spicy crust served with avocado salad and tiny sprouted herbs. From the robata grill, barbecued tuna with umeboshi (salt-pickled plum) sauce and grilled vegetables is typical of Zuma's innovation. Baby chicken marinated in barley miso and roasted on cedar wood was tender, succulent and smoky. There's an equally deft hand at work with classics: turbot nigiri were tiny fingers of rice draped with translucent turbot; sashimi of chu-toro was an exemplary cut of tuna. Zuma has one of the best saké lists in town, with a knowledgeable saké sommelier to guide you around it. Drawbacks? A meal here doesn't come cheap, and the two-hour sittings are strictly enforced.
Babies and children welcome: high chairs. Booking advisable. Disabled: toilet. Separate rooms for parties, seating 12 and 14. Tables outdoors (4, garden). **Map 8 F9.**

Marylebone

CoCoRo NEW

31 Marylebone Lane, W1U 2NH (7935 2931). Bond Street tube. **Lunch served** noon-2.30pm Mon-Fri. **Dinner served** 6-10.30pm Mon-Fri; 6-10pm Sat, Sun. **Main courses** £7-£12. **Set lunch** £8. **Set dinner** £19. **Credit** AmEx, DC, MC, V.
These modest beige and brown premises used to be nondescript Nakamura, but appear to be enjoying more success now. On our Saturday evening visit, every table was occupied, and some customers seemed quite familiar with the staff. The relaxed atmosphere was aided by modern upholstered chairs that had us feeling settled in for the night – which our neighbouring diners may well have been, judging by the earnest saké comparisons going on at their table. A refreshing Iki beer (similar to Hoegaarden in taste, but with a dash of green tea) is also recommended. The sushi, sashimi, tempura and noodles are rendered proficiently, but it's the more obscure offerings that shine, such as buta kimchi gyoza (minced pork and chilli-pickled chinese leaf dumplings), iwashi bainiku age (sardine fillets and salt-pickled plum in batter) and mochi agedashi (deep-fried, nori-wrapped rice cakes). On the other hand, yaki tarako (grilled cod's roe) was almost too dry to eat; and the pleasant decor ends abruptly at the stairs that lead up to the first-floor toilet, featuring a ghastly green carpet ingrained with grime.
Babies and children admitted. Separate rooms for parties, seating 10 and 12. Takeaway service; delivery service (within 2-mile radius).
Map 9 G6.
For branch (CoCoRo Sushi) see index.

★ Dinings NEW

22 Harcourt Street, W1H 4HH (7723 0666). Marylebone tube/rail. **Lunch served** noon-3pm Mon-Fri. **Dinner served** 6-11pm Mon-Sat. **Main courses** £6.50-£16. **Set lunch** £10-£15. **Credit** AmEx, MC, V.
Outside: traditional brick terraced house. Inside: brutalist grey concrete. The decor at Dinings is a jarring exercise in juxtaposition. But the food of chef-owner (and Nobu alumnus) Tomonari Chiba is about cuisines complementing each other. While the sushi remains faithful to its origins, his 'Japanese tapas' feature sashimi of white fish beneath a 'small bomb' of coriander and red onion, dressed in oil enlivened by chilli and fish sauce; or scallop on asparagus with a piquant yuzu (Japanese citrus) garlic sauce. While the 'tapas' are Japanese at heart, for pudding, the tables are turned and Western classics receive Eastern input, resulting in jasmine tea panna cotta, or black sesame crème caramel, or even matcha crème brûlée – a great result in the case of custard blended with green tea. Squeezing past the angular sushi counter on the ground floor to get down the narrow stairs to the bunker-like basement, those with an aversion to brutalist architecture may feel like they're dining in a fallout shelter. Thankfully, the unfailingly helpful staff manage to make customers feel snug and welcome rather than hemmed in.
Babies and children admitted. Takeaway service.
Map 8 F5.

Mayfair

★ @Japan NEW

7A Hanover Street, W1S 1YS (7629 8801). Oxford Circus tube. **Lunch served** noon-3.30pm, **dinner served** 5-10pm Tue-Sun. **Main courses** £5-£14. **Set meal** £7-£12. **Credit** MC, V.
After a 'grand opening' in February 2007, what used to be Café Plaza next to souvenir store Igirisuya became sushi bar Sen and an izakaya called Kai (next to a Whittard café rubbing shoulders with Japanese jewellery and handicrafts concessions) – all within a corner complex that includes a sizeable Mini J-Mart on the side. Mostly decent renditions of staples, some 'kobachi' specials (£2 apiece) on a blackboard, 'harakiri price!' Red Stripe and eager-to-please waitresses aren't sufficient to make Kai a dinner-date destination. The narrow choice of dishes, functional bench seating and shopping-mall

RESTAURANTS

ambience prevent it being anything more than a cheap pitstop. However, the more self-contained Sen, with its softer furnishings, is a slightly cosier proposition. Here, the nigiri come draped in high-quality toppings bearing low price tags (the sushi and sashimi are also available in Kai). Situated so close to the Oxford Circus shops, Sen makes an excellent lunch-break bolthole.
Babies and children admitted. Takeaway service. **Map 9 J6**.

★ Chisou

4 Princes Street, W1B 2LE (7629 3931/ www.chisou.co.uk). Oxford Circus tube. **Lunch served** noon-2.30pm, **dinner served** 6-10.15pm Mon-Sat. **Main courses** £3.50-£22. **Set lunch** £10-£18. **Credit** AmEx, JCB, MC, V.
This bright and orderly establishment just off Regent Street is deservedly full most nights, abuzz with mainly Western diners and the diligent ministrations of many chefs and servers. You don't have to wait long for service when the staff-to-customer ratio is so high. Plain cream walls, black slate accents and stylish air-con ovoids suspended from the ceiling don't fit the description of a typical Japanese tavern, but the menu explains Chisou's hybrid identity: 'traditional dishes with a modern twist, served izakaya style'. From various salt-grilled fish, superior sushi, tempura and noodles to lesser-spotted zensai such as buta bara kimuchi (stir-fried pork belly with garlic and chilli-pickled chinese leaves) and intriguing specials like asari no sakémushi (saké-steamed clams) – the choices here are plentiful and delicious, but watch out for sizeable price tags. Some are understandable; a special of tarabagani yaki (grilled giant crab leg, £14) is always going to be expensive. But why does simple inaniwa udon (thin white noodles served with wasabi, ginger, spring onion and tempura crumbs) cost so much over the odds at £12.50?
Babies and children welcome: high chairs. Booking advisable. Separate room for parties, seats 12. Takeaway service. **Map 9 J6**.

★ Nobu (100)

1st floor, The Metropolitan, 19 Old Park Lane, W1K 1LB (7447 4747/www.noburestaurants.com). Hyde Park Corner tube. **Lunch served** noon-2.15pm Mon-Fri; 12.30-2.30pm Sat, Sun. **Dinner served** 6-10.15pm Mon-Thur; 6-11pm Fri, Sat; 6-9.30pm Sun. **Main courses** £3.50-£29.50. **Set lunch** £25 bento box; £50, £60. **Set dinner** £70, £90. **Credit** AmEx, DC, JCB, MC, V.

Zuma

London's first Nobu has two siblings in town, Nobu Berkeley Street (*see below*) and Ubon (*see p206*), as well as a host of cousins around the globe. The panoramic views over Hyde Park give you something to gaze at when there's a lack of famous people to ogle. Nobu is no longer the celeb-magnet it used to be, but we were pleased to see food presentation is as artful as ever and, for the most part, the modern Japanese dishes still dazzle. Tiradito Nobu-style (raw sea bass dressed with yuzu and dabs of chilli) was a good palate-primer. Our star dish was sea bass sashimi with red miso and yuzu; the dried miso had a rich savoury flavour complemented by slivers of deep-fried garlic and a fresh squeeze of the Japanese citrus fruit – fabulous. But not every innovative dish was a success. Soft-shell crab harumaki (spring rolls) exhibited a confusion of flavours in which the crab was overwhelmed. 'Field greens' with signature Matsuhisa dressing were ordinary salad leaves. Service (charged at 15%) was charming on our visit and Nobu is quite child-friendly in the day.
Babies and children welcome: high chairs. Booking essential. Disabled: toilet. Dress: smart casual. Separate room for parties, seats 14-40.
Map 9 H8.

★ Nobu Berkeley Street

15 Berkeley Street, W1J 8DY (7290 9222/ www.noburestaurants.com). Green Park tube.
Bar **Open** noon-1am Mon-Wed; 1pm-2am Thur, Fri; 6pm-2am Sat; 6-9pm Sun.
Restaurant **Lunch served** noon-2.15pm Mon-Fri. **Dinner served** 6-11pm Mon-Wed; 6pm-midnight Thur-Sat; 6-9pm Sun. **Main courses** £8.50-£26.60.
Both **Credit** AmEx, MC, V.
If you can drag yourself away from the sumptuous ground-floor cocktail bar, you'll sashay up the sweeping staircase feeling like Scarlett O'Hara. The dining room lacks the glamour of the bar, but the left-hand seating area, with its bustling sushi counter and a ceiling that resembles the underside of a squid, is the more appealing. The menu is broadly similar to that at the original Nobu (*see above*), with the addition of dishes cooked in a wood-fired oven. The Latin American influence is evident in Nobu classics such as 'tacos' (cute little pastry shells) filled with raw tuna and red onion, served with a spiky tomato salsa. Our 'new style' beef was flash-seared, served with citrus-sharpened sesame oil, chives and sesame seeds. From the oven came tender roast aubergine, simply served with shavings of bonito that waved in the heat. Sashimi of razor clam played it straight, as did a maki of soft-shell crab. The only disappointment was an oven-roasted baby squid with ginger, saké and shoyu; it was soupy, with too much onion and questionable use of broccoli. Desserts such as green tea flan or nashi pear tatin sound tempting. Black-clad waiting staff are professionalism personified. Thankfully, the no-bookings policy has been dumped.
Babies and children welcome: high chairs. Booking advisable. Disabled: toilet. Dress: smart casual. Entertainment: DJ 9pm Wed-Sat. Vegan dishes.
Map 9 H7.

★ Umu

14-16 Bruton Place, W1J 6LX (7499 8881/ www.umurestaurant.com). Bond Street or Green Park tube. **Lunch served** noon-2.30pm Mon-Fri. **Dinner served** 6-11pm Mon-Sat. **Main courses** £11-£55. **Set lunch** £21-£45. **Set dinner** £60-£135. **Credit** AmEx, DC, JCB, MC, V.
Michelin-starred, Kyoto-centric Umu allows its (no doubt wealthy or expense-endowed) customers through an enigmatic sliding portal at the touch of a pad. Within the low-lit, dark-timbered, mirror-lined cocoon of a dining room, carefully choreographed staff proffer drinks, explain ingredients and hover with trays when necessary to ensure perfectly synchronised dish delivery. Choosing your beverage could take some time, as the list covers more than 80 saké labels and 300 wines; orientally inclined cocktails include a Nihon Colada, Sakerinha and Wasabi Mary. The classic kaiseki course (£60, rather than £90 or £135) tickled our taste buds at every turn, with green tea tofu, garlic-spiked amberjack and pungent kinome bud-

studded rice. This is the kind of place where you'll find sea urchin roe and pine nuts folded into deep-fried scorpion fish, where you can choose between grade six and grade nine wagyu beef. It's not so much eating, as an epicurean entertainment, even if some of the surprises might not be pleasant (we weren't taken with a rather strong red miso soup that packed a startling citrus tang). Exceptional food, yes, though you may take exception to the prices.
Babies and children welcome: high chairs. Booking advisable dinner. Disabled: toilet. Dress: no shorts. **Map 9 H7**.

Piccadilly

★ Yoshino (100)

3 Piccadilly Place, W1J 0DB (7287 6622/ www.yoshino.net). Piccadilly Circus tube.
Meals served noon-9pm Mon-Sat. **Set meal** £5.80-£19.80 bento box. **Credit** AmEx, MC, V.
Maybe it's the waitresses' long, white, starched aprons; maybe it's the clean, cool design inside (it's certainly not the ugly mishmash of styles outside); or maybe it's just the careful preparation that evidently goes into the food – somehow Yoshino manages to feel posher than its prices suggest. Five or six years ago the menu was varied and full of kanji script, to the point of mystification for some non-Japanese customers. Now, the fully explained dinner list mainly comprises bentos and some à la carte sushi. Sets vary in complexity from the Mini Yoshino to the Yuki no Zen, which deserves to be called the 'Maxi'. The latter is a double-decker affair; lacquer compartments are stacked in order to accommodate sashimi, tempura, eel teriyaki, grilled mackerel, deep-fried tuna, pickles, spinach goma-ae (with a sesame dressing), potato salad, fried tofu and the dish of the day – green-lipped mussels and a jumbo prawn on our visit. All this is unarguably value for money at £19.80, but if your appetite isn't huge, go for the bargain £7.80 Mini. You can also get Yoshino's food to take away from the Japan Centre (*see p202* **Bargain central**) just down the road.
Babies and children admitted. **Map 17 A5**.

Soho

Donzoko

15 Kingly Street, W1B 5PS (7734 1974). Oxford Circus or Piccadilly Circus tube. **Lunch served** noon-2.30pm Mon-Fri. **Dinner served** 6-10.15pm Mon-Sat. **Main courses** £6.50-£28. **Set lunch** £6.50-£30. **Credit** AmEx, DC, JCB, MC, V.
If the red lantern hanging outside the entrance doesn't signal clearly enough that this is an izakaya – a tavern, Japanese-style – the homely surroundings and often loud groups of diners soon will. Donzoko is popular with Japanese salarymen, tourists and students, as well as Londoners keen to experience a Japanese drinking den. Staff are happy to guide customers through the dishes on offer, from the raw (sushi and sashimi) to the grilled (yakitori). If you're sampling the great saké list or the subtle-but-strong shochu cocktails, don't miss out on the garlic dishes, made with drinking in mind. Sushi's a good choice as well; uni gunkan maki, a daily special, was superbly fresh. Grilled eel maki and the grilled salmon-skin sunomono were enjoyable too. In contrast, some grilled dishes, including ox tongue yakitori and grilled spicy cod's roe, suffered from overcooking. Natto salad, with sliced iceberg lettuce, was no more than workmanlike, but our spirits were lifted by juicy grilled tsukune (balls of minced chicken). Donzoko has its ups and downs, yet remains popular: you'd do well to book.
Babies and children admitted. Booking advisable. Takeaway service. **Map 17 A4**.

So Japanese NEW

3-4 Warwick Street, W1B 5LS (7292 0760/ www.sorestaurant.com). Piccadilly Circus tube. **Lunch served** noon-3pm Mon-Sat. **Dinner served** 6-10.30pm Mon-Thur; 6-11pm Fri, Sat. **Main courses** £12-£36. **Set lunch** £7-£14. **Set dinner** £28-£50. **Credit** AmEx, MC, V.
So's USP is the grilling of food over 'volcanic rocks from Mount Fuji'. Any added flavour from this process wasn't discernible in the wagyu beef that topped off our pricey Yukimi dinner course (£50). Still, most diners are tempted to try one of the half-dozen enticing choices from the vulcan section of the menu – a menu that's not so Japanese, with foie gras, lamb shank and black truffle scattered among the tuna, tempura and tofu. The seasonal and calorie-counting kenkouna ('healthy') course was better value at £20 for seaweed salad (tasty), sea bass and cucumber sushi (fresh), lamb shank oden (tender, excellent) and a matcha snowball (amusing) of green tea ice-cream encased in meringue. The restaurant is also big on cha, offering 'exclusive tea from Kyoto by one of the most respected tea houses in Japan', as well as displaying tea-drinking accoutrements for sale on shelves around the sencha-hued ground-floor dining room-bar. Although our dinner was facilitated by pleasant and prompt staff, the quality of dishes was erratic and the tea shop sideline blurs So's identity.
Babies and children welcome: high chairs. Separate room for parties, seats 4. Takeaway service. **Map 17 A5**.

Dinings. See p198.

Bargain central

Kyoto

For a cheap and cheerful meal in the centre of town – around the West End and Fitzrovia – try the following.

THE ALL-ROUNDERS

Centrepoint Sushi

20-21 St Giles High Street, WC2H 8JE (7240 6147/www.cpfs.co.uk). Tottenham Court Road tube. **Meals served** noon-10.30pm Mon-Sat. **Main courses** £8.50-£15.50. **Set lunch** £8-£14.50. **Credit** MC, V.
Situated above a Japanese-Korean food shop, Hana is an oasis of oriental calm amid the West End's bustle. Brisk, friendly staff serve deliciously fresh sushi, noodle and rice dishes.
Best for A relaxed vibe – the booth seating is a world away from the usual pack-'em-in ethos.
Babies and children welcome. Booking advisable. Takeaway service. Vegetarian menu. **Map 17 C2.**

Japan Centre

212 Piccadilly, W1J 9HG (7255 8255/www.japancentre.com). Piccadilly Circus tube.
Shops **Open** 10am-7pm Mon-Fri; 10.30am-8pm Sat; 11am-7pm Sun.
Restaurant **Meals served** noon-10pm Mon-Sat; noon-8pm Sun. **Main courses** £5-£14. **Set meal** £9.60-£27.80. **Credit** JCB, MC, V.
Slightly pricier than the other bargain outlets, but worth it. The vast menu has all the traditional favourites, and a good choice of teas.
Best for Miso soup – suffused with a subtle lemony flavour, it's a one-off.
Babies and children welcome: booster seat. Booking advisable. Vegetarian menu. **Map 17 B5.**

Kyoto

27 Romilly Street, W1D 5AL (7437 2262). Leicester Square or Piccadilly Circus tube. **Lunch served** noon-3pm, **dinner served** 5-11pm Mon-Sat. **Main courses** £6-£12. **Set lunch** £8-£11 bento box. **Credit** JCB, MC, V.
The kitsch mix of calligraphy hangings and Ultramen models lining the walls are straight from a Tokyo izakaya. Sushi, noodles and fried rice dishes all hit the spot, but some are too salty.
Best for Sashimi: the seared tuna and cracked pepper is a treat.
Babies and children admitted. Booking advisable. Tables outdoors (2, pavement). Takeaway service. **Map 17 C4.**

Ramen Seto

19 Kingly Street, W1B 5PY (7434 0309). Oxford Circus tube. **Meals served** noon-9.30pm Mon, Tue; noon-10pm Wed-Sat; 1-8pm Sun. **Main courses** £5.70-£8. **Set meal** £6-£9.60. **Credit** JCB, MC, V.
A no-frills noodle bar that's popular with Japanese students. The bowls of ramen are huge and steaming, but the noodles were mushy on our last visit.
Best for Rice dishes and gyoza, which count among the best in town.
Babies and children welcome: high chairs. Booking advisable weekends. Takeaway service. **Map 17 A4.**

Satsuma

56 Wardour Street, W1D 3HN (7437 8338/www.osatsuma.com). Piccadilly Circus tube. **Meals served** noon-11pm Mon, Tue; noon-11.30pm Wed, Thur; noon-midnight Fri, Sat; noon-10.30pm Sun. **Main courses** £5.50-£15.90. **Credit** AmEx, DC, JCB, MC, V.
This favourite with the Soho media brigade produces decent versions of trad dishes, although the gyoza can be chewy.
Best for Bentos, such as the smoky unadon (grilled eel over rice).
Babies and children welcome: high chairs. Bookings not accepted. Disabled: toilet. Takeaway service. **Map 17 B4.**

Soho Japan

52 Wells Street, W1T 3PR (7323 4661/www.sohojapan.co.uk). Oxford Circus tube. **Lunch served** noon-2.30pm Mon-Fri. **Dinner served** 6-10.30pm Mon-Sat. **Main courses** £6.50-£14 lunch; £9-£10 dinner. **Set lunch** £6-£14. **Set dinner** £9-£38. **Credit** AmEx, JCB, MC, V.
An intimate spot with an all-round menu. Grilled fish and chicken dominate the lunch sets, but there's also a fine choice of side dishes.
Best for Hard-to-find appetisers such as mentaiko oroshi (cod's roe with grated radish).
Babies and children admitted. Booking advisable. Tables outdoors (3, pavement). Takeaway service. **Map 17 A2.**

Taro

10 Old Compton Street, W1D 4TF (7439 2275). Leicester Square or Tottenham Court Road tube. **Lunch served** noon-2.50pm Mon-Fri; 12.30-3.15pm Sat, Sun. **Dinner served** 5.30-10.30pm Mon-Sat; 5.30-9.30pm Sun. **Main courses** £5.90-£8.80. **Set meal** £8.50-£14. **Credit** JCB, MC, V.
Food at this airy, double-height basement restaurant includes noodles, sushi and rice dishes – good, if not spectacular.
Best for Teriyaki chicken: perfectly crisp outside and moist inside.
Booking advisable. Separate room for parties, seats 30. Takeaway service. **Map 17 C3.**
For branch see index.

Tokyo Diner

2 Newport Place, WC2H 7JP (7287 8777/www.tokyodiner.com). Leicester Square tube. **Meals served** noon-midnight daily. **Main courses** £4.40-£12.90. **Set lunch** (noon-5pm Mon-Fri) £4.40-£9.80. **Credit** JCB, MC, V.

Westminster

Atami NEW

37 Monck Street, SW1P 2BL (7222 2218/www.atamirestaurant.co.uk). St James's Park tube. **Lunch served** 12.30-3pm Mon-Fri, Sun. **Dinner served** 6-10.30pm Sat. **Main courses** £8.50-£19.50. **Set lunch** £8.50-£12.50. **Credit** MC, V.
The decor is good enough to eat at this glass-sided corner site in the heart of Westminster. Amid acres of full-height glazing (through which you might spot the odd MP or minister scurrying by) and black polished concrete flooring, there is nori backlit behind the front desk, laid beneath the sushi counter top and running along the two glass sides of the restaurant. Original head chef Anthony Sousa Tam (ex of Nobu, Hakkasan and Tsunami) left a long time ago, but much of his innovative menu remains; it's a suitably sophisticated carte to match these stylish surroundings. Regrettably, the cooking no longer evinces Tam's delicate touch, but a cosmopolitan crowd still appreciates rare marble beef with super-skinny green bean tempura, and marinated lamb chops with miso-coated aubergine – despite steep prices. In addition to old-school sushi and sashimi, more adventurous raw creations include ultra-soft razor clam sliced into ribbons and served on its own shell under a piquant ginger dressing. We've heard some negative comments about service, but on our latest visit food arrived in an orderly fashion and the smiling staff paid us ample attention.
Babies and children welcome: high chairs. Takeaway service. **Map 16 K10.**

West

Ealing

★ ★ Sushi-Hiro (100)

1 Station Parade, Uxbridge Road, W5 3LD (8896 3175). Ealing Common tube. **Lunch served** 11am-1.30pm, **dinner served** 4.30-9pm Tue-Sun. **Sushi** 60p-£2.20. **Set meal** £5-£14. **No credit cards.**
The sushi here is of such high quality, the restaurant might just as well be called 'Sushi Hero'. The decor has a kind of municipal feel – wipe-clean tiled walls and bright strip lighting – with the half-dozen or so utilitarian tables packed tightly together. Most customers seem to be from Ealing's Japanese community, stopping in for a quick bite or a takeaway. Service can be amateurish, but that's our only gripe. Nigiri sets go beyond the usual salmon and tuna standards; the chef puts together a selection of what's best on the day: sea bass, scallop and organic salmon on our visit. A la carte sushi is pricier, but the selection, including many off-the-beaten-track offerings, is excellent. Maki (squid and shiso, eel and cucumber) are imaginative. To drink, there's green tea, Japanese beer or saké, the latter served in hefty measures in glass tumblers (a bargain at £5). Sushi-Hiro is excellent value, but credit cards aren't accepted. And it's wise to book ahead, as it gets busy and shuts early.
Babies and children welcome: high chair. Booking advisable. Disabled: toilet. Takeaway service.

Hammersmith

Tosa

332 King Street, W6 0RR (8748 0002/www.tosatosa.net). Ravenscourt Park or Stamford Brook tube. **Lunch served** 12.30-2.30pm daily. **Dinner served** 6-11pm Mon-Sat; 6-10.30pm Sun. **Main courses** £5.30-£12. **Set meal** £20-£25. **Credit** MC, V.
The smell of smoke from the robata grill greets you as you arrive at this small, friendly, neighbourhood place. Grab a seat at the front and watch the action, as skewers of tasty morsels are

A homely little restaurant serving decent food most of the time. The teriyaki fish dishes are better options than the katsu variations.
Best for A strong environmental policy, eschewing tuna and using renewable energy sources.
Babies and children admitted. Bookings not accepted Fri, Sat. Takeaway service. **Map 17 C4.**

Zipangu
8 Little Newport Street, WC2H 7JJ (7437 5042). Leicester Square tube. **Meals served** noon-11pm Mon-Sat; noon-10.30pm Sun. **Main courses** £4.50-£14. **Set lunch** (noon-5.30pm) £6.50-£12.50. **Set dinner** £8.50 bento box; £14 5 dishes. **Credit** AmEx, MC, V.
A modest, slightly scruffy restaurant offering bargain set meals – but the salmon teriyaki isn't recommended.
Best for Some of the cheapest Japanese food in town.
Bookings not accepted Fri, Sat. Separate room for parties, seats 6. Takeaway service. **Map 17 C4.**

THE SPECIALISTS

Abeno Too
17-18 Great Newport Street, WC2H 7JE (7379 1160/www.abeno.co.uk). Leicester Square tube. **Meals served** noon-11pm Mon-Sat; noon-10.30pm Sun. **Main courses** £7.50-£19.50. **Set lunch** £7.95-£12.80. **Credit** AmEx, DC, JCB, MC, V.
Okonomiyaki is wonderful comfort food. Choose from an extensive menu of fillings; there's also teppanyaki, noodle dishes and desserts.
Best for Vegetarian variety; you can customise fillings to suit yourself.
Babies and children admitted. Bookings not accepted. Disabled: toilet. Takeaway service. **Map 18 C4.**
For branch (Abeno) see index.

Kulu Kulu
51-53 Shelton Street, WC2H 9HE (7240 5687). Covent Garden tube. **Lunch served** noon-2.30pm Mon-Fri; noon-3.30pm Sat. **Dinner served** 5-10pm Mon-Sat. **Dishes** £1.20-£3.60. **Credit** JCB, MC, V.
Come here for some fine old-school kaiten-zushi. Arrive early as the sushi and sashimi selection quickly dwindles, but the colour-coded plate tariff easily beats other conveyor-belt chains.
Best for Superb prawn tempura temaki.
Babies and children admitted. Bookings not accepted. Takeaway service. **Map 18 D3.**
For branches see index.

Ryo
84 Brewer Street, W1F 9UB (7287 1318). Leicester Square or Piccadilly Circus tube. **Meals served** 11.30am-midnight Mon-Wed, Sun; 11.30am-1am Thur-Sat. **Main courses** £5-£14. **Set meal** £5.50-£10. **No credit cards.**
Formerly Hamine, this noodle bar is the real thing, serving ramen as it should be: hot but slightly springy and swimming in a tasty stock.
Best for A late-night noodle pitstop.
Babies and children admitted. Separate rooms for parties, seating 25 and 40. Takeaway service. **Map 17 A4/5.**

Yo! Sushi
Myhotel, 11-13 Bayley Street, Bedford Square, WC1B 3HD (7636 0076/ www.yosushi.com). Tottenham Court Road tube. **Meals served** noon-11pm Mon-Sat; noon-10.30pm Sun. **Dishes** £1.50-£5. **Credit** AmEx, DC, JCB, MC, V.
Perhaps not the best sushi joint in town, but the most fun. Raw and cooked delicacies glide around on the conveyor-belt. Look out for tofu salads and desserts too. There's a cheeky £1 charge for water that comes from a pump at your table.
Best for Funky concoctions such as crispy duck and miso futomaki.
Babies and children welcome: high chairs. Bookings not accepted. Disabled: adapted tables; toilet. Tables outdoors (3, terrace). Takeaway service (0870 190 8040). Vegetarian menu. **Map 17 C1.**
For branches see index.

put to the heat and cooked to perfection. A set robata selection is a good way to sample the offerings; we munched through skewers of velvety chicken liver, crisp wings and succulent breast, as well as slightly rubbery quails' eggs. We also chose a couple of à la carte skewers of chicken skin, plus pork belly with asparagus. From the daily specials list, ox tongue with ponzu was a great combination of tender textures and sharp flavours. Sushi – such as oshinko (pickle) maki and luscious hamachi sashimi – doesn't disappoint either. Tosa is a small place and popular with locals, so it's wise to book.
Babies and children admitted. Booking advisable. Tables outdoors (3, terrace). Takeaway service. Vegetarian menu. **Map 20 A4.**

Paddington

★ Yakitoria *(100)*
25 Sheldon Square, W2 6EY (3214 3000/ www.yakitoria.co.uk). Paddington tube/rail. **Lunch served** noon-3pm Mon-Fri. **Dinner served** 6-11pm Mon-Sat. **Meals served** noon-10pm Sun. **Main courses** £13.50-£39. **Set lunch** £12.50-£17. **Credit** AmEx, DC, JCB, MC, V.
Yakitoria oozes post-industrial chic: it's all concrete and shiny-black with eau-de-nil chairs and a gorgeous shocking-pink backlit sushi bar. Little wonder it won the Best Design category at the 2006 Time Out Eating & Drinking Awards. Modernity extends to the menu, with 'fusion' dishes (such as miso 'cappuccino', tofu with Japanese pesto, and pizza sushi) appearing alongside traditional sushi, sashimi and tempura. A standout dish was a daily special of oysters with red saké jelly (made with saké from red rice). Simple-sounding silken tofu with three dressings was spectacularly presented: a trio of tofu cubes on a black rectangular plate, each with a different subtle but flavourful dressing. Our selection of chicken skewers included the heart, liver, skin, wings and minced breast, served with two dipping sauces: simple but well done. Also exemplary was a maki roll with eel, crab, avocado and tobiko (flying fish roe), wrapped in slices of salmon then lightly battered and fried – sounds odd but it worked. Service has improved since the opening, and Yakitoria is popular with glamorous young things. The basement bar has a great saké selection; let the French sommelier talk you through the tipples.
Babies and children welcome: high chairs. Booking advisable. Disabled: lift; toilet. Dress: smart casual. Tables outdoors (15, terrace). Takeaway service. Vegetarian menu. **Map 7 C6.**

South West

Fulham

Yumenoki NEW
204 Fulham Road, SW10 9PJ (7351 2777/ www.yumenoki.co.uk). Fulham Broadway or South Kensington tube then 14 bus. **Lunch served** noon-3pm, **dinner served** 5.30-10.30pm daily. **Main courses** £7.80-£28. **Set lunch** £8-£15 bento box. **Credit** AmEx, MC, V.
Much effort has gone into prettifying Yumenoki – from pseudo-shoji (wood and paper screens), wagasa (bamboo and paper umbrellas) and a babbling stone fountain on the ground floor to delicate plywood dragonflies flitting over pale wooden partitions in the basement. There's also a two-table patio at the rear, with whitewashed walls and flower-filled tubs: a plus for summer months. Service is provided with a smile by an attentive, pan-oriental crew. The menu includes a few curve balls (such as lamb steak and tofu in a coconut red curry), but sashimi, gyoza, tori kara-age and noodles are more the order of the day. We were greeted by the delicious aroma of dashi (stock) when we walked in. Despite this, our miso soup was mediocre. In addition, the sauce used in a huge helping of chicken yakisoba was off-puttingly strong, and the green tea ice-cream was disappointingly weak. So the decor couldn't be fresher and the staff couldn't be nicer, but the cooking doesn't quite make Yumenoki (Dream Tree) a dream meal ticket.
Babies and children admitted. Separate room for parties, seats 25. Takeaway service; delivery service (within 2-mile radius). **Map 13 C12.**

Putney

Chosan
292 Upper Richmond Road, SW15 6TH (8788 9626). East Putney tube. **Lunch served** noon-2.30pm Sat, Sun. **Dinner served** 6.30-10.30pm Tue-Sat; 6.30-10pm Sun. **Main courses** £3.30-£25. **Set lunch** £7.90-£13.90. **Set dinner** £18.90-£20.90; £19.90-£24.90 bento box. **Credit** MC, V.
This homely, long-standing restaurant is a magnet for locals. Take time to look at the multiple menus to find delights such as baigai (a kind of whelk) simmered in saké, sliced thinly and served with lemon; or burdock and carrot simmered in dashi, with a pleasantly smoky flavour. Also good was a small dish of cooked angler-fish liver, served cold in a vinegar-based sauce with grated radish and sliced spring onion. Uni sushi was ultra-fresh, wrapped in crisp nori. Less impressive was our zenmai shirataki (royal fern with devil's tongue noodles), served without the shirataki, and an odd 'scallop and kidney bean' tempura: green beans and a tiny amount of scallop in a heavy jacket of batter. The rather kitsch decor is looking a bit dated. Service, though friendly, could also do with a spruce-up. We dined off cheap blue and white plastic plates, which weren't changed at all during the course of our meal. We were also disappointed to be charged £4 for a single shot glass of fairly low-grade saké.
Babies and children admitted. Separate area for parties, seats 25. Takeaway service.

Wimbledon

Kushi-Tei NEW
264 The Broadway, SW19 1SB (8543 1188/ www.kushi-tei.com). Wimbledon tube/rail. **Meals served** 6-10.30pm daily. **Main courses** £2.80-£8.65. **Set meal** £9.95-£26.95. **Credit** MC, V.
Kushiyaki (literally, 'skewer grilling') specialists serve an array of animal, vegetable and seafood parts, the best-known in the West being yakitori: bite-sized pieces of chicken grilled over charcoal on bamboo skewers. In Japan, kushiyaki dishes are popular accompaniments to a drinking session. At this new restaurant you'll find a clinical and sanitised London version of a kushiyaki-ya: not over-designed or rowdy, simply functional and understated. The menu contains enough of interest to attract a large number of Japanese customers. Takoyaki is a snack of chopped octopus, grilled in

a metal mould that forms small mushy balls when filled with batter. The version here is topped with katsuobushi (thin shavings of smoked and dried bonito fish). Chicken skin yakitori was correctly salty and crisp, if a little too dried out. Shiokara is squid preserved using salt (in this case), which creates a challenging dish with the strong savoury flavour typifying umami. If you want to drink saké, try the Tamano-Hikari (a Junmai Daiginjo): excellent quality and decent value, even at £13.50 for a 300ml bottle.
Babies and children welcome: high chairs.

South

Battersea

Tokiya

74 Battersea Rise, SW11 1EH (7223 5989/ www.tokiya.co.uk). Clapham Junction rail. **Lunch served** 12.30-3pm Sat, Sun. **Dinner served** 6.30-10.30pm Tue-Sun. **Main courses** £7-£15. **Set dinner** £16-£28. **Credit** AmEx, JCB, MC, V.
This good, solid, neighbourhood all-rounder – with its homely noren fabrics, chipped paint on the floorboards and haphazard knick-knackery on the walls – serves good, solid, neighbourhood food (well, it would do if its neighbourhood was a Tokyo suburb). The main menu competently covers sushi, sashimi and the three Ts (tempura, teriyaki and tonkatsu), while the specials board springs no surprises; black cod in miso, and grilled squid was as rarefied as it got on our most recent visit. However, salmon sashimi elicited an 'ooh' when it arrived nestled next to a crystal-clear iceberg – like a family of orange, polar-dwelling seals. Chicken gyoza, perfectly formed and seared-steamed, ranked with the best in London. Sedate at lunchtime, bustling on weekend evenings, Tokiya opened in 2000 but doesn't look a day under 20. However, the fish is fresh, the noodle stock just right and the service welcoming. What decor lacks in quality it makes up for in quirkiness; look out for the giant plastic ebi nigiri inside the front door.
Babies and children admitted. Booking essential weekends. Takeaway service; delivery service (over £20). **Map 21 C4**.

Clapham

★ Tsunami

5-7 Voltaire Road, SW4 6DQ (7978 1610/ www.tsunamirestaurant.co.uk). Clapham North tube. **Dinner served** 6-11pm Mon-Fri. **Meals served** noon-11.30pm Sat; 1-4pm, 6-9.30pm Sun. **Main courses** £7.50-£16.50. **Set meal** (12.30-4pm Sat; Sun) £6.50-£10.50. **Credit** AmEx, MC, V.
Tsunami, like its unfortunate name, is something of a surprise. Located off a grey Clapham side street, its airy, clean-lined space, mirrors and white walls would look more at home on a swanky West End stretch. The food gives a nod to major central London players such as Nobu (*see p199*) and Zuma (*see p198*), but thankfully doesn't follow suit with its prices. Well-executed Asian-themed cocktails include the tiny but delectable oyster shooter: a glass containing an oyster immersed in saké and a quail's egg yolk. We ordered from the extensive menu of sushi, sashimi, tempura and rice dishes. Meltingly soft yellowtail sashimi came with a taste bud-tingling ponzu sauce; black cod in miso was succulent and smoky; and soft-shell crab rolls burst with freshness. Plump, sticky rice and a fine miso soup proved Tsunami can cut the mustard on the basics too. Our desserts were pleasant if not spectacular. Service was unfailingly courteous and discreet. During the evening, a young crowd trickled in and the atmosphere livened up, but the room can get seriously noisy thanks to its bare concrete floor.
Babies and children welcome: booster chairs. Booking advisable weekends. Takeaway service (before 7pm). **Map 22 B1**.

Waterloo

Bincho NEW

Second floor, Oxo Tower Wharf, Barge House Street, SE1 9PH (7803 0858/www.bincho.co.uk). Blackfriars or Waterloo tube/rail. **Lunch served** noon-3pm, **dinner served** 5-11.30pm Mon-Fri. **Meals served** noon-11.30pm Sat; noon-10.30pm Sun. **Dishes** £1.20-£11. **Credit** AmEx, DC, MC, V.
The latest aspiring modern Japanese starlet is an interpretation of a yakitori-ya: a restaurant serving yakitori. In Japan these are casual places where office workers gather for a tapas-style meal and a beer/saké or two. Bincho looks the part. The long dining room is done out in a mini-forest of wood and bamboo, the large windows giving jaw-dropping views over the Thames. An enticingly smoky aroma drew us from the bar to chairs at a counter in front of hibachi-style grills, from where we watched chefs dip skewers into earthenware pots of taré and baste them over the grills. We

Atami. See p202.

RESTAURANTS

sampled kawa (chicken skin), negima (chicken and spring onion), sunazuri (chicken gizzard) – all pretty good – and aigamo (duck with spring onion) – succulent and juicy. Other bits on sticks (kushiyaki) were less successful. From the selection of salads, pickles and soups we were looking forward to the earthy flavours promised by motsu nikomi (daikon and pig's tripe soup), but its insipid flavours disappointed. So we didn't fall in love with Bincho. It lacks the experimentation of Zuma (*see p198*) and the sense of innovation obvious at Yakitoria (*see p203*); and its dishes are competent rather than exciting.
Babies and children welcome: high chairs. Booking advisable. Disabled: toilet. **Map 11 N7**.

Ozu
County Hall, Westminster Bridge Road, SE1 7PB (7928 7766/www.ozulondon.com). Embankment tube/Charing Cross or Waterloo tube/rail. **Lunch served** noon-2.30pm, **dinner served** 6-10.30pm daily. **Main courses** £12-£17. **Set lunch** £14-£19.50. **Credit** MC, V.
Big Ben to the left, the London Eye to the right, assorted river traffic cruising by in between – a sure-fire location for any restaurant, you'd think. Unfortunately, in spite of a large banner on Queen's Walk, Ozu is tricky to spot; and once you have made it inside, great chunks of grade II-listed masonry break up what should be a glorious panorama. The interior is a handsome mix of lightened original wood panelling, corniced ceiling and curvaceous white ventilation ducts; the latter efficiently remove smoke and vapour from the central charcoal grill and hotplate. However, the restaurant has shrunk since its move (in 2006) from the back to the front of County Hall, and so has the menu. This is now a modest collection of kobachi (starters, from which okra with pickled plum paste and fish flakes stood out), sushi, sashimi, sumibiyaki grills (charcoal-grilled dishes including great lamb and so-so squid) and teppanyaki. There's no faulting the ingredients used here, and they are handled competently, but this dining room – with an admittedly stunning view – is a little high on prices and low on atmosphere.
Babies and children welcome: high chair. Booking advisable. Disabled: toilet (in County Hall). Vegetarian menu. **Map 10 M9**.

East

Docklands

★ Ubon
34 Westferry Circus, Canary Wharf, E14 8RR (7719 7800/www.noburestaurants.com). Canary Wharf tube/DLR/Westferry DLR. **Lunch served** noon-2.30pm Mon-Fri. **Dinner served** 6-10.30pm Mon-Sat. **Main courses** £3.75-£29.50. **Set lunch** £45-£60. **Set dinner** £45-£90. **Credit** AmEx, DC, MC, V.
The original Nobu (*see p199*) has magnificent views over Hyde Park, but we reckon the views at Ubon (that's 'Nobu' backwards) are more staggering. The gracious curve of the Thames at Limehouse Reach is so impressive, particularly at dusk, that you may have difficulty concentrating on the menu, which includes such Nobu classics as black cod with miso and Peruvian-style anti-cucho skewers. There's a range of more conservative dishes like grilled rib-eye steak or grilled lobster with spicy lemon-garlic dressing, but we stuck to the more characteristic choices. Beautifully presented ceviche combined mackerel, tuna, white fish, prawn and octopus with red onion and coriander and a (slightly too sharp) citrus dressing. Snow crab with creamy spicy sauce came gratinated in a shallow dish, looking like a pink-tinged Mac 'n' cheese but tasting richly of shellfish and roe. In a nod to East-West fusion, asparagus egg sauce and salmon roe looked and tasted quite like asparagus with a frothy hollandaise. Classic o-toro sashimi (the highest-grade fat-marbled cut of tuna) was pristine. Ubon is very business-oriented at lunch, more relaxed come the evening.
Babies and children welcome: high chairs. Booking advisable. Disabled: lift; toilet. Dress: smart casual. Takeaway service. Vegetarian menu. **Map 24 A2**.

North

Camden Town & Chalk Farm

★ Asakusa
265 Eversholt Street, NW1 1BA (7388 8533/8399). Camden Town or Mornington Crescent tube. **Dinner served** 6-11.30pm Mon-Fri; 6-11pm Sat. **Main courses** £5.50-£13. **Set dinner** £5.20-£9.80. **Credit** MC, V.
The red leatherette banquettes in the rather dingy basement might have been 're-purposed' from a 1970s steak house, and the smell of the stairs hints at a feline resident. Fortunately, first impressions don't last at this Camden institution. The food is great and the prices are a steal. Despite the decor, Asakusa is perennially jammed with student types who can spot quality (at a good price) when they see it. Teishoku tend to feature fried things, but there's plenty of choice for the fry-shy. The menu's huge and includes a selection of small dishes such as maguro nuta (neat squares of raw tuna in a savoury miso sauce topped with spring onion and nori flakes) and unagi kabayaki (fillets of barbecued eel basted in a thick, sweet-savoury sauce). There are some imaginative takes on maki; shiitake rolls and mackerel and ginger rolls were both impressive and moreish. We also relished some melt-in-the-mouth hamachi sashimi – perfectly tender. Service is on the ball and copes well, even during the busiest times. We recommend asking for a table upstairs when you book – it's nicer than the basement.
Babies and children admitted. Booking advisable Fri, Sat. Separate room for parties, seats 22. Takeaway service. Vegetarian menu. **Map 27 D3**.

Menu

For further reference, Richard Hosking's *A Dictionary of Japanese Food: Ingredients & Culture* (Tuttle) is highly recommended.

Agedashidofu: tofu (qv) coated with katakuriko (potato starch), deep-fried, sprinkled with dried fish and served in a broth based on shoyu (qv), with grated ginger and daikon (qv).
Amaebi: sweet shrimps.
Anago: saltwater conger eel.
Bento: a meal served in a compartmentalised box.
Chawan mushi: savoury egg custard served in a tea tumbler (chawan).
Daikon: a long, white radish (aka mooli), often grated or cut into fine strips.
Dashi: the basic stock for Japanese soups and simmered dishes. It's often made from flakes of dried bonito (a type of tuna) and konbu (kelp).
Dobin mushi: a variety of morsels (prawn, fish, chicken, shiitake, ginkgo nuts) in a gently flavoured dashi-based soup, steamed (mushi) and served in a clay teapot (dobin).
Donburi: a bowl of boiled rice with various toppings, such as beef, chicken or egg.
Dorayaki: mini pancakes sandwiched around azuki bean paste.
Edamame: fresh soy beans boiled in their pods and sprinkled with salt.
Gari: pickled ginger, usually pink and thinly sliced; served with sushi to cleanse the palate between courses.
Gohan: rice.
Gyoza: soft rice pastry cases stuffed with minced pork and herbs; northern Chinese in origin, cooked by a combination of frying and steaming.
Hamachi: young yellowtail or Japanese amberjack fish, commonly used for sashimi (qv) and also very good grilled.
Hashi: chopsticks.
Hiyashi chuka: Chinese-style (chuka means Chinese) ramen (qv noodles) served cold (hiyashi) in tsuyu (qv) with a mixed topping that usually includes shredded ham, chicken, cucumber, egg and sweetcorn.
Ikura: salmon roe.
Izakaya: 'a place where there is saké'; an after-work drinking den frequented by Japanese businessmen, usually serving a wide range of reasonably priced food.
Kaiseki ryori: a multi-course meal of Japanese haute cuisine, first developed to accompany the tea ceremony.
Kaiten-zushi: 'revolving sushi' (on a conveyor belt).
Katsu: breaded and deep-fried meat, hence **tonkatsu** (pork katsu) and **katsu curry** (tonkatsu or chicken katsu with mild vegetable curry).
Maki: the word means 'roll' and this is a style of sushi (qv) where the rice and filling are rolled inside a sheet of nori (qv).
Mirin: a sweetened rice spirit used in many Japanese sauces and dressings.
Miso: a thick paste of fermented soy beans, used in miso soup and some dressings. Miso comes in a wide variety of styles, ranging from 'white' to 'red', slightly sweet to very salty and earthy, crunchy or smooth.
Miso shiru: classic miso soup, most often containing tofu and wakame (qv).
Nabemono: a class of dishes cooked at the table and served directly from the earthenware pot or metal pan.
Natto: fermented soy beans of stringy, mucous consistency.
Nimono: food simmered in a stock, often presented 'dry'.
Noodles: second only to rice as Japan's favourite staple. Served hot or cold, dry or in soup, and sometimes fried. There are many types, but the most common are **ramen** (Chinese-style egg noodles), **udon** (thick white wheat-flour noodles), **soba** (buckwheat noodles), and **somen** (thin white wheat-flour noodles, usually served cold as a summer dish – hiyashi somen – with a chilled dipping broth).
Nori: sheets of dried seaweed.
Okonomiyaki: the Japanese equivalent of filled pancakes or a Spanish omelette, whereby various ingredients are added to a batter mix and cooked on a hotplate, usually in front of diners.
Ponzu: usually short for ponzu joyu, a mixture of the juice of a Japanese citrus fruit (ponzu) and soy sauce. Used as a dip, especially with seafood and chicken or fish nabemono (qv).
Robatayaki: a kind of grilled food, generally cooked in front of customers, who make their selection from a large counter display.
Saké: rice wine, around 15% alcohol. Usually served hot, but may be chilled.
Sashimi: raw sliced fish.
Shabu shabu: a pan of stock is heated at the table and plates of thinly sliced raw beef and vegetables are cooked in it piece by piece ('shabu-shabu' is onomatopoeic for the sound of washing a cloth in water). The broth is then portioned out and drunk.
Shiso: perilla or beefsteak plant. A nettle-like leaf of the mint family that is often served with sashimi (qv).
Shochu: Japan's colourless answer to vodka is distilled from raw materials such as wheat, rice and potatoes.
Shoyu: Japanese soy sauce.
Sukiyaki: pieces of thinly sliced beef and vegetables are simmered in a sweet shoyu-based sauce at the table on a portable stove. Then they are taken out and dipped in raw egg (which semi-cooks on the hot food) to cool them for eating.
Sunomono: seafood or vegetables marinated (but not pickled) in rice vinegar.
Sushi: a combination of raw fish, shellfish or vegetables with rice – usually with a touch of wasabi (qv). Vinegar mixed with sugar and salt is added to the rice, which is then cooled before use. There are different sushi formats: **nigiri** (lozenge-shaped), **hosomaki** (thin-rolled), **futomaki** (thick-rolled), **temaki** (hand-rolled), **gunkan maki** (nigiri with a nori wrap), **chirashi** (scattered on top of a bowl of rice), and **uramaki** or **ISO maki** (more recently coined terms for inside-out rolls).
Tare: a general term for shoyu-based cooking marinades, typically on yakitori (qv) and unagi (qv).
Tatami: a heavy straw mat – traditional Japanese flooring. A tatami room in a restaurant is usually a private room where you remove your shoes and sit on the floor to eat.
Tea: black tea is fermented, while green tea (**ocha**) is heat-treated by steam to prevent the leaves fermenting. **Matcha** is powdered green tea, and has a high caffeine content. **Bancha** is the coarsest grade of green tea, which has been roasted; it contains the stems or twigs of the plant as well as the leaves, and is usually served free of charge with a meal. **Hojicha** is lightly roasted bancha. **Mugicha** is roast barley tea, served iced in summer.
Teishoku: set meal.
Tempura: fish, shellfish or vegetables dipped in a light batter and deep-fried. Served with tsuyu (qv) to which you add finely grated daikon (qv) and fresh ginger.
Teppanyaki: 'grilled on an iron plate' or, originally, 'grilled on a ploughshare'. In modern Japanese restaurants, a chef standing at a hotplate (teppan) is surrounded by several diners. Slivers of beef, fish and vegetables are cooked with a dazzling display of knifework and deposited on your plate.
Teriyaki: cooking method by which meat or fish – often marinated in shoyu (qv) and rice wine – is grilled and served in a tare (qv) made of a thick reduction of shoyu (qv), saké (qv), sugar and spice.
Tofu or **dofu**: soy beancurd used fresh in simmered or grilled dishes, or deep-fried (agedashidofu), or eaten cold (hiyayakko).
Tokkuri: saké flask – usually ceramic, but sometimes made of bamboo.
Tonkatsu: see above katsu.
Tsuyu: a general term for shoyu/mirin-based dips, served both warm and cold with various dishes ranging from tempura (qv) to cold noodles.
Umami: the nearest word in English is tastiness. After sweet, sour, salty and bitter, umami is considered the fifth primary taste in Japan, but not all food scientists in the West accept its existence as a basic flavour.
Unagi: freshwater eel.
Uni: sea urchin roe.
Wafu: Japanese style.
Wakame: a type of young seaweed most commonly used in miso (qv) soup and kaiso (seaweed) salad.
Wasabi: a fiery green paste made from the root of an aquatic plant that belongs to the same family as horseradish. It is eaten in minute quantities (tucked inside sushi, qv), or diluted into shoyu (qv) for dipping sashimi (qv).
Yakimono: literally 'grilled things'.
Yakitori: grilled chicken (breast, wings, liver, gizzard, heart) served on skewers.
Zarusoba: soba noodles served cold, usually on a bamboo draining mat, with a dipping broth.
Zensai: appetisers.

Feng Sushi

1 Adelaide Road, NW3 3QE (7483 2929/ www.fengsushi.co.uk). Chalk Farm tube. **Meals served** 11.30am-10pm Mon-Wed; 11.30am-11pm Thur-Sat; noon-10pm Sun. **Main courses** £6-£15. **Credit** AmEx, MC, V.

There are six branches of Feng Sushi across London. All combine a busy takeaway and delivery service with eat-in dining. The Chalk Farm branch is light and airy (other branches can feel cramped); service is relaxed and helpful. The menu contains a wide range of maki and some interesting nigiri, such as line-caught mackerel or gravadlax with pesto, as well as 'value boxes' (nigiri selections and bentos), plus a few cooked dishes. Of these, baby squid tempura was hot and crisp, served with piquant pickled cucumber slices. The range of sashimi is limited, but our 'new style' sea bass, dressed with chilli, sesame oil, coriander and sesame seeds, broke the tuna-salmon mould. The flavours were well judged and the presentation lovely, but the sea bass was thickly sliced and a bit tough. Nevertheless, it was hard to fault the seasonal special of 'rearranged yellowtail upside down': discs of cucumber topped with succulent raw yellowtail, avocado, wakame (seaweed) salad, chopped jalapeño and coriander, zapped with chilli sauce. Vegetarians and vegans aren't forgotten here. There are a few tempting meat- and fish-free maki and salads; brown rice avocado maki were fine.

Babies and children admitted. Takeaway service; delivery service (over £10). **Map 27 B1.**

For branches see index.

Crouch End

Wow Simply Japanese NEW

18 Crouch End Hill, N8 8AA (8340 4539). Finsbury Park tube/rail then W3 bus/Crouch Hill rail. **Lunch served** noon-2.30pm Wed-Sun. **Dinner served** 6-10.30pm Mon-Sat; 6-10pm Sun. **Main courses** £7.80-£40. **Set lunch** £5.90-£8.80. **Credit** MC, V.

It took an exceedingly long time, but culinarily cosmopolitan Crouch End finally got a Japanese restaurant in 2006. Despite the name, food here isn't all simply Japanese. Standard udon, tempura, teriyaki and sushi rub shoulders with, for example, a generous portion of tender Gressingham duck in a citrusy tare (on the regularly changing specials blackboard) and a thoroughly modern-looking seared tuna and asparagus salad (on the main menu). If steamed rice seems too plain an option, a tasty bowl of garlic egg fried rice is recommended. Most dishes are executed well, though you may hit the occasional dud; our chirashi sushi bore an impressive ten toppings but was a slightly tired affair of thin-cut slices. At busy times (the latter half of the week) staff are noticeably overstretched. Maybe this neat, cream-walled, wooden-floored, brightly lit little restaurant doesn't quite merit a 'wow!' but it's a definite asset to the area.

Babies and children welcome: high chairs. Takeaway service.

Islington

Sa Sa Sushi NEW

422 St John Street, EC1V 4NJ (7837 1155). Angel tube. **Lunch served** noon-2.30pm daily. **Dinner served** 5.30-10pm Mon-Thur; 5.30-11pm Fri, Sat. **Main courses** £3.50-£18. **Sushi** £1.20-£2.50. **Set meal** £15.50 per person (minimum 2). **Set dinner** £22.50-£45 3 courses. **Credit** AmEx, MC, V.

It may sound like a sushi bar, but Sa Sa is an all-rounder with a varied choice of hot dishes, including, on the pricier side, black cod with miso and foie gras teriyaki (both £18). At the cheaper end of the menu, we devoured our gyoza (minced pork and chive dumplings), which were full of flavour and nicely browned – even if we expected more than four for £4.50. Our à la carte sushi pickings yielded such an appetising collection of nigiri that we couldn't resist ordering seconds of toro (fatty tuna) and foie gras, though we could have just as happily relished more of the juicy, fresh yellowtail, succulent eel or translucent squid on shiso (perilla leaf). The smiling, courteous, Vietnamese chef rustling up these gems clearly cares about his craft; without seeming at all intrusive, he popped out from behind his counter a couple of times to check diners were happy with their choices. You might as well fully indulge any sushi cravings as the drinks and dessert lists are minimal, with ice-cream tempura the only choice beyond the usual trio of Japanese ice-cream flavours; mind you, it's worth noting that the beer is fairly priced at £2.80 a bottle.

Babies and children admitted. Booking advisable. Disabled: toilet. Takeaway service; delivery service (over £15 within 2-mile radius). **Map 5 N3.**

North West

Golders Green

Café Japan

626 Finchley Road, NW11 7RR (8455 6854). Golders Green tube/13, 82 bus. **Lunch served** noon-2pm Sat, Sun. **Dinner served** 6-10pm Wed-Sat; 6-9.30pm Sun. **Main courses** £8-£9. **Set lunch** £8.50. **Set dinner** £12-£17. **Credit** MC, V.

This patch of Golders Green must have reached saturation point for Japanese food. Café Japan is now neighbours with Hi Sushi, while Eat Tokyo (*see p209*) sits around the corner, just a couple of doors down from grocery-cum-takeaway store Unohana. Sashimi and sushi dominate proceedings here, with the itamae (chef) slicing and splicing behind the front counter to please customers who regularly fill the yellow-walled dining room. Oyako chirashi – bearing cucumber, kanpyo (dried gourd), tamago (sweet omelette) and crabstick – was so well endowed that the salmon and ikura (salmon roe) had to be served on a separate plate. The specials list is always worth a read to catch rarities like yakigani ('grilled Japanese giant crab') or good deals such as six ebi tempura for £9. This well-worn North London favourite has changed hands twice since winning a Time Out gong in 1996, but still seems to be the king of the Golders Hill. However, it failed to wow on our last visit. While portions were healthy, prices trim and the waitresses as welcoming as ever, the sauces contained too much sugar and the sashimi looked a tad tired.

Babies and children admitted. Booking advisable. Takeaway service.

Eat Tokyo

14 North End Road, NW11 7PH (8209 0079). Golders Green tube. **Lunch served** 11.30am-3pm Tue-Fri; 11.30am-4pm Sun. **Dinner served** 5.30-10.30pm Mon-Fri; 5.30-11.30pm Sat; 5.30-10pm Sun. **Main courses** £2.50-£10 lunch; £7-£18 dinner. **Set lunch** £5.80-£13. **Set dinner** £7-£25. **Credit** MC, V.

Had enough of the minimalist aesthetic favoured by so many Japanese restaurants? Eat Tokyo could be the antidote you're looking for. The clutter starts on the pavement, with billboards plastered in colour printouts of dishes. The entrance is home to boxes of biscuits and Japanese groceries for sale on a trolley. Then you reach a long room with an awful lot going on: florid kimono and haori pinned to the walls; camellia-pink upholstered chairs; and a large TV screen on one wall (showing a Chelsea-Tottenham match during our Sunday afternoon visit). Like the billboards, the weighty menu is decked out in pictures. As well as aiding adult novices, this is a boon to pre-schoolers, allowing them to participate fully in ordering. The casual atmosphere, the straightforward cooking and the matter-of-fact Japanese staff make for a homely, family-friendly vibe. Best of all – with five pieces of salmon sashimi for £3.60, geso kara (battered squid tentacles) for £1.80, five gyoza for £2.80 and kake udon for £2.50 – a meal here really is phenomenally good value.

Babies and children welcome: high chairs. Booking advisable dinner. Takeaway service.

Hampstead

Jin Kichi

73 Heath Street, NW3 6UG (7794 6158/ www.jinkichi.com). Hampstead tube. **Lunch served** 12.30-2pm Sat, Sun. **Dinner served** 6-11pm Tue-Sat; 6-10pm Sun. **Main courses** £4.90-£14.80. **Set lunch** £7.70-£14.90. **Credit** AmEx, DC, JCB, MC, V.

Hung with noren screens and paper lanterns, this homely restaurant feels as if it could have been airlifted from a Tokyo side street. Diners sit elbow to elbow around the sushi bar and charcoal grill, or squeeze around tables on the ground floor and in the basement. Yes, it can get cramped, but don't let that put you off. The food is spot-on and the atmosphere convivial – aided by a good selection of saké, shochu and Japanese beers. Izakaya fare rules here, including a long yakitori menu. Skewered asparagus and chicken livers were suffused with flavour from the charcoal grill. Adventurous diners might like to sample the ox tongue and chicken gizzards. Then there are broths and hotpots, noodles, sushi, grilled fish… the list goes on and on. Customers (couples and groups, some Japanese) may radiate a certain Hampstead smugness, but staff are friendly – although service can be slow. On leaving, we noted the display of letters from satisfied celebrity customers, but you don't have to be famous to come away happy from a meal here.

Babies and children welcome: booster seats. Booking advisable Fri-Sun. Takeaway service. **Map 28 B2.**

SHELF LIFE

Japanese foodstuffs are also for sale at **Saki** (*see p196*) and at the **Japan Centre** (*see p202* **Bargain central**).

Arigato Japanese Supermarket

48-50 Brewer Street, W1R 3HN (7287 1722). Leicester Square or Piccadilly Circus tube. **Open** 10am-9pm Mon-Sat; 11am-8pm Sun.

Everything from wasabi peas to wakame, crammed into a handy little Soho supermarket.

Atari-ya

7 Station Parade, Noel Road, W3 0DS (8896 1552/www.atariya.co.uk). West Acton tube. **Open** 11am-6.30pm Tue; 10am-6.30pm Wed-Fri; 9am-7pm Sat; 11am-7pm Sun.

Miso-marinated cod to rival Nobu's, a sushi party platter service and all the packaged groceries you could wish for. Branches include Finchley, Kingston and Selfridges.

Japanese Kitchen

9 Lower Richmond Road, SW15 1EJ (8788 9014/www.japanese kitchen.co.uk). Putney Bridge tube. **Open** noon-7pm Mon-Sat.

A smart grocery for Japanese expats and culinary explorers, with a range that includes frozen edamame, furikake and soft drinks, plus kitchen equipment and cookbooks.

Minamoto Kitchoan

44 Piccadilly, W1J 0DS (7437 3135/ www.kitchoan.com). Piccadilly Circus tube. **Open** 10am-7pm Mon-Fri, Sun; 10am-8pm Sat.

Rice flour and aduki beans may not be your first thought when it comes to delicious sweets, but this authentic confectioner could change all that.

Swiss Cottage

Benihana

100 Avenue Road, NW3 3HF (7586 9508/ www.benihana.co.uk). Swiss Cottage tube.
Lunch served noon-3pm daily. **Dinner served** 5.30-10.30pm Mon-Sat; 5-10pm Sun. **Set lunch** £11.50-£33.75. **Set dinner** £17-£58. **Credit** AmEx, DC, JCB, MC, V.

This is the oldest of three branches in London (opened in 1984), and part of a global chain founded in the 1960s in New York by former Olympic wrestler Rocky Aoki. Benihana offers an international interpretation of Japanese teppanyaki dining infused with a heavy dose of showmanship: great for parties and even better for kids. Customers sit at large tables while red-toqued chefs cook, tell jokes, show off their skills with razor-sharp knives and set things alight 'for the fun of it' (Benihana's 1970s catchphrase). At its worst, the showmanship can seem hackneyed; we heard the same jokes in a different branch a few years ago. The quality of ingredients, such as beef and prawns, is decent, but the food can seem beside the point – and not terribly Japanese. Our teriyaki beef and 'hibachi' prawns were fine if unexciting; a side salad of iceberg lettuce and under-ripe tomato fell firmly into the 'could do better' category. This is a fun, 'Japanese-lite' place to come with young ones (Benihana won the Best Family Restaurant category in the 2006 Time Out Eating & Drinking Awards), but beware the prices, which aren't so likely to put a smile on your face.

Babies and children welcome: children's menu (Sun); high chairs. Booking advisable; essential weekends. Tables outdoors (4, garden). Takeaway service. **Map 28 B4.**

For branches see index.

Wakaba

122A Finchley Road, NW3 5HT (7586 7960). Finchley Road tube. **Lunch served** noon-2.30pm, **dinner served** 6.30-1.30pm Mon-Sat. **Main courses** £4.50-£19.80. **Set lunch** £7.30 (buffet). **Set dinner** £22.50-£34. **Credit** AmEx, DC, JCB, MC, V.

Radically whited out but reassuringly old-school, Wakaba has improved its visibility. The formerly enigmatic curved façade of frosted glass now has a strip of clear squares at shoulder height, which allows passers-by to peek in. On view is a square room filled with broad tables and sagging wood-and-weave chairs. Behind a low wall at the rear, sushi chefs craft a greater variety than usual of traditional nigiri and maki. Toro and scallops were exemplary. This is one of the few restaurants in London to serve engawa natto ae – a moreish mix of enjoyably chewy turbot fringe and fermented soy beans. Our cooked dishes didn't always hit such highs. Hamachi kamayaki (grilled yellowtail head) had plenty of succulent gobbets to tease out with diligent chopstick work, but ika geso kara age (battered squid tentacles) were alarmingly orange and not the most tender specimens. Except for okonomiyaki and kaiseki ryori, the regular menu covers every aspect of Japanese cuisine, while the specials list adds interest without straying from tradition. A minimalist restaurant with a maximalist menu.

Babies and children admitted. Booking advisable Fri, Sat. Restaurant available for hire. Takeaway service. **Map 28 B3.**

Kushi-Tei. See p203.

Willesden

★ Sushi-Say

33B Walm Lane, NW2 5SH (8459 2971). Willesden Green tube. **Lunch served** noon-2.30pm Tue-Fri; 1-3.30pm Sat, Sun. **Dinner served** 6.30-10.30pm Tue-Fri; 6-11pm Sat; 6-10pm Sun. **Main courses** £6.30-£19.50. **Set dinner** £21-£35. **Credit** JCB, MC, V.

Sushi-Say has had a makeover. Gone is the drab utilitarian look, replaced with brown suede banquette seating, Japanese screens and pale wood fittings. It's as friendly and busy as ever and the quality of the food remains just as high. Try the seasonal specials, or the ponzu-dressed dishes (a particular forte). From the former, kabocha no nitsuke (pumpkin simmered in mirin, shoyu and saké) was firm, tender and soothing. The quality of fish here is outstanding; turbot sashimi, served on a glass plate with spring onion, a dash of cayenne pepper and ponzu dipping sauce, was superb. So too was maguro natto, squares of firm red tuna with stringy natto and just the right balance of shoyu, spring onion and wasabi. The only dish that didn't quite pass muster was a too-oily, too-sweet nasu dengaku (aubergine topped with sweet miso, then grilled). There's a lot to choose from, but staff are happy to help. The well-composed teishoku make a good starting point. Just don't miss out on the raw gems.

Babies and children welcome: high chairs. Booking advisable dinner. Takeaway service.

Outer London

Richmond, Surrey

Matsuba

10 Red Lion Street, Richmond, Surrey TW9 1RW (8605 3513). Richmond tube/rail. **Lunch served** noon-3pm, **dinner served** 6-11pm Mon-Sat. **Main courses** £10-£30. **Set lunch** £5.50-£16.50. **Set dinner** £35-£45.90. **Credit** AmEx, JCB, MC, V.

Matsuba has the good looks of a well-brought-up Richmond restaurant. There's much designer detail here, from slate floors to dark wood-grained wall panels and photogenic red gerbera, set just-so on each table. Pity about the rather naff warbling on the easy-listening soundtrack. This is a Korean-run establishment, so you'll find the likes of bulgogi (grilled meat), bibimbap (rice with mixed toppings) and kimchi on the menu, as well as trendy offerings such as aburi nigiri, in which the raw fish is burnished with a blow torch to cook it lightly. The food is generally good; our vegetable gyoza, served pan-hot, had a thin elastic skin that contained savoury, finely cut vegetables. Crisp-skinned salt-grilled mackerel was juicy and tender, served with wok-fried beansprouts and red-dyed pickled ginger. The sushi and sashimi can be pricey, so choose carefully. Sea bass nigiri was fine, but more adventurous was the inside-out florida maki; a dusting of crumbled seaweed over the rice gave it an interesting flavour reminiscent of green tea. Matsuba is small, so booking is a good idea.

Babies and children admitted. Booking advisable. Takeaway service.

Jewish

The kosher restaurant scene in London is in constant flux, with new establishments opening and closing each year. Those who want supervised food used to be happy to eat lockshen soup and a beef sandwich, but long-haul travel and more elaborate catering at parties have led to a desire for sushi, fresh pasta and Indian dishes. All but one of the restaurants below follow the laws regarding permitted animals and fish and the rules about the separation of meat and dairy products. Yet the menus only partly reflect what you would eat in a Jewish home. There's only one place selling the superlative slow-cooked Sabbath stew, cholent (a vegetarian version at the new **Garden Sandwich Bar**). And festival foods such as latkes and matzah balls made in a commercial kitchen are rarely as good as grandma's.

So how do you choose where to go? The restaurants are either meat or dairy – except for the non-kosher **Harry Morgan's**, which offers chicken soup like mamma makes, followed by cheesecake. So for char-grilled steak or chicken, go to **Dizengoff's** or **Bloom's**, or **Reuben's** for traditional salt beef and chips. **Novellino** scores with an excellent menu of fish and vegetable dishes and newcomer **Armando** specialises in own-made pasta as well as a wide range of well-executed sushi.

There are two venues offering a more elegant dining experience, where you'll find both style and inventive cooking: **Bevis Marks Restaurant** with its enchanting location beside an 18th-century synagogue, and **Six-13**, the business diner's West End favourite. Unlike most of the other meat restaurants, where desserts are limited and often include pale imitations of cream, the chefs at both these establishments have managed to conjure up non-dairy sweets that are nigh-on perfect.

Central

City

★ Bevis Marks Restaurant

Bevis Marks, EC3A 5DQ (7283 2220/ www.bevismarkstherestaurant.com). Aldgate tube/Liverpool Street tube/rail. **Lunch served** noon-2.15pm Mon-Fri. **Dinner served** 5.30-8pm Mon-Thur. **Main courses** £11.50-£18.90. **Credit** AmEx, MC, V.

Through Bevis Marks' windows you can see the brass chandeliers and candles of the adjoining 18th-century synagogue. It's a stark contrast to the restaurant's minimalist modern surrounds, full of City suits looking for that rare combination of stylish kosher food and quality wines. Chef Jason Prangnell brings an inventive touch to a well-balanced menu, strong on seasonal ingredients and presentation. While the food has been inconsistent in the past, our last visit suggested that the kitchen has now hit its stride. A trio of summer soups – beetroot, green pea, red pepper – offered a light, colourful prelude to succulent roast salmon, served on spiced cabbage with asparagus. Traditional ingredients were given a twist in dishes such as chopped liver with fig compote or crispy thai salt beef, while main courses also reflected a global array of influences, from a classical, perfectly cooked rack of lamb with cassis sauce to moroccan duck confit with lemon couscous. Ambitious desserts cater for the Jewish sweet tooth; parev ingredients are well disguised, leaving non-Jewish customers oblivious to the constraints of kashrut. Gooseberry crumble with rich crème anglaise, frangipane tart and a host of subtly flavoured ices completed a superb meal.

Babies and children admitted. Booking advisable lunch. Disabled: toilet. Kosher supervised (Sephardi). Restaurant available for hire. Tables outdoors (4, courtyard). Takeaway service. Vegetarian menu. **Map 12 R6.**

★ Garden Sandwich Bar NEW

32 Hatton Garden, EC1N 8DL (7831 1022). Farringdon tube/rail. **Meals served** *Summer* 9.30am-4.30pm Mon-Fri. *Winter* 9.30am-4.30pm Mon-Thur; 9.30pm-2.30pm Fri. **Main courses** £2.25-£6. **No credit cards.**

Hidden in the basement of a jewellery centre in the heart of the diamond district, this dairy café is a gem. It's nothing fancy – just a dozen metallic tables and café chairs, and a counter offering hot and cold dishes. A treat for vegetarians, it serves a mean breakfast of scrambled egg, baked beans and toast, and also provides passing tourists and the many orthodox Jews who work nearby with fresh, appetising-looking bagels and rolls for lunch (the vegetarian sausages and burgers look less appealing). For afters, there's a superb fruit salad, with passion fruit and mango replacing the usual apple and grapes. If you go on Thursday or Friday you can enjoy a bowl of hot and spicy cholent: the slow-cooked dish usually only found in Jewish homes on the Sabbath. This version has no meat, but is a hearty, deeply satisfying blend of pulses (kidney, butter and white beans), potato and onion. The Garden isn't a place to linger, but as a quick stop-off for a warming meal it offers great value.

Kosher supervised (Kedassia). Takeaway service. Vegetarian menu. **Map 11 N5.**

Marylebone

Reuben's

79 Baker Street, W1U 6RG (7486 0035/ www.reubensrestaurant.co.uk). Baker Street tube. Deli/café **Open** 11.30am-4pm, 5.30-10pm Mon-Thur; 11.30am-3pm Fri; 11.30am-10pm Sun. *Restaurant* **Meals served** 11.30am-4pm, 5.30-10pm Mon-Thur; 11.30am-3pm Fri; 11.30am-10pm Sun. **Main courses** £9-£23. **Minimum** £10. **Credit** MC, V.

One of only two kosher restaurants in the West End, Reuben's does a bustling trade at lunchtime. The ground-floor cafeteria serves a full range of Ashkenazi dishes: barley soup, liver, egg and onion, stuffed cabbage and fried fish. The speciality sandwich is salt beef, with a side order of coleslaw. Downstairs sits a smarter, turquoise-walled restaurant; equally popular, it was packed on our last visit. Service was attentive and our starters arrived without delay. Chicken soup was richly flavoured, with a good dark colour; leek and potato soup also had a meaty base and tasted smooth and satisfying. Main courses tend to be simple (chicken schnitzel, grilled lamb chops, entrecôte steak and the like), with the occasional French dish such as grilled magret of duck (unavailable on our visit). You can't do better than order the incredibly tender salt beef; even a small portion is a generous seven slices. Chips and a large, thin latke were both crisp and well-fried. Desserts are unexceptional: a spicy apple strudel (reheated to make the pastry less soggy), and an alarmingly brightly coloured lockshen pudding. Reuben's can also provide meals to order for Shabbat, with wine and challah.

Babies and children welcome: high chairs. Booking advisable (restaurant). Kosher supervised (Sephardi). Tables outdoors (3, pavement). Takeaway service. **Map 3 G5.**

Six-13

19 Wigmore Street, W1U 1PH (7629 6133/ www.six13.com). Bond Street or Oxford Circus tube. **Lunch served** noon-2.30pm Mon-Fri. **Dinner served** 6-10.30pm Mon-Thur. **Main courses** £15-£27. **Set meal** £42.50 3 courses. **Credit** AmEx, MC, V.

The restaurant's name comes from 613, the number of religious commandments. Its menu has been compiled with equal devotion. Dishes are beautifully presented, although the nondescript interior – dimly lit French art deco – does little to create much atmosphere. Standards are high and service is seamless. Elaborate meat and fish dishes occupy most of the menu, with vegetarian main course options limited to two pasta dishes on our visit. Duck breast and steak were both competently grilled, though there was a touch too much seasoning in the latter's red wine sauce. Vegetables were attractively al dente. The desserts are inspired, though perhaps unlikely to tempt the time-constrained business clientele. If deciding between the likes of chilled coconut rice pudding, triple chocolate parfait, and lemon meringue pie with blueberry coulis, is all too much, a platter of mini desserts provides the obvious solution. A warm chocolate, date and walnut cake with coffee ice-cream made a pleasant end to a good (if highly priced) meal.

Babies and children welcome: high chairs. Kosher supervised (Sephardi). Separate room for parties, seats 22. Takeaway service; delivery service (within W1). **Map 9 H6.**

North

Finchley

The Burger Bar

110 Regents Park Road, N3 3JG (8371 1555). Finchley Central tube. **Meals served** noon-midnight Mon-Thur; noon-11pm Sun. **Main courses** £5.40-£6.95. **No credit cards.**

This unpretentious space is filled with hungry diners of all ages. It is under the same Israeli ownership as the dairy Orli café next door. The format is simple: a hefty round of choice beef, sandwiched in a sesame bun, with an array of extras to choose from. These include sauces (barbecue, pesto or chilli), mango, slices of avocado, or grilled aubergine and peppers. To start, there's houmous and crisp chargrilled pitta, though it's probably advisable to save your appetite for the main event. Burgers are cooked to order, so expect a fairly long wait; you may end up devouring most of the chips (which sometimes arrive a good five minutes before the main plates) before you tuck in to a chunk of beef that will leave you full for hours. There's also a portobello mushroom version; a veggie burger with fried eggs; and wraps with chicken or beetroot and mayo. Children are offered chicken wings or smaller burgers with fried onion rings. Desserts include an unexceptional apple or pear pie, parev ice-creams and vividly hued shakes, but it might be better to quit while you're ahead and go home for some fresh fruit instead.
Babies and children welcome: children's menu. Booking advisable. Kosher supervised (Federation). Tables outdoors (8, pavement). Takeaway service.

Olive Restaurant

224 Regents Park Road, N3 3HP (8343 3188/ www.olivekosherrestaurant.co.uk). Finchley Central tube. **Meals served** 10am-11pm Mon-Thur, Sun; 10am-5pm Fri. **Main courses** £10-£18. **Set meal** £37 2 courses (minimum 2). **Credit** AmEx, MC, V.

Offering Persian kosher cuisine, Olive has carved its own niche in London's dining scene. Barely a year after it opening, the bright white dining area, with dots of colour provided by red carnations, is being enlarged. The food, brought by smiling Iranian waitresses, exhibits the authentic, slightly sour flavours that predominate in Persian cuisine. In terms of both quantity and texture, it is lighter than better-known types of Jewish cooking. Herbs play an important role, with sabzi (parsley, coriander and other fresh greens) appearing both as a starter salad and in ghormeh sabzi (lamb cooked in a spring onion and herb sauce). More substantial was the salad olivieh, a pleasing blend of finely diced chicken, gherkins, egg and mayonnaise. Aubergines (said to originate in Persia) played a starring role in mirza ghasemi, a smooth, garlic-infused dip, and in various lamb dishes. Those who prefer a slightly sweeter flavour might enjoy ghoresht eh fezenjoon, chicken in a subtly blended sauce of puréed walnuts and pomegranate. To complete the Persian experience, try the rose-scented pistachio baklava – less sweet than the Turkish version.
Babies and children welcome: children's menu; high chairs. Booking advisable. Disabled: toilet. Kosher supervised (Sephardi). Restaurant available for hire. Tables outdoors (3, pavement). Takeaway service.

North West

Golders Green

Armando NEW

252 Golders Green Road, NW11 9NN (8455 8159). Brent Cross tube. **Lunch served** noon-3pm, **dinner served** 6-11pm Mon-Thur, Sun. **Main courses** £8-£16. **Sushi** £2-£8. **Set lunch** £15 3 courses. **No credit cards**.

Situated at the quieter end of bustling Golders Green Road, Armando declares itself to be a Japanese and Italian fusion restaurant. Born of the Italian owner's passion for sushi, it actually – and wisely – addresses the two cuisines separately, rather than attempting to merge them. Behind an unimposing entrance lies a small dining area, its dark wood tables set with stylish white crockery. The menu offers a complete selection of lush, velvety sushi and sashimi, with perfectly executed maki rolls plus tempura, miso soup and marinated fish in the Japanese style. The idea is that a group of friends with different tastes can dine together, so while one chooses toro or yellowtail, another can have fried fish. A thick piece of cod with snow-white flakes was delicious, covered in crunchy batter and topped with delicate strands of fried potato. The food is cooked to order and tastes immaculately fresh, with own-made Italian pasta anointed with much olive oil and intensely flavoured sauces. Service was friendly and obliging; an overcooked chocolate pudding was promptly whisked away and replaced by a fresh one. Let's hope that word gets around and the crowds start arriving.
Babies and children welcome: children's menu. Booking advisable. Kosher supervised (Beth Din). Tables outdoors (2, pavement). Takeaway service.

Bloom's

130 Golders Green Road, NW11 8HB (8455 1338/www.blooms-restaurant.co.uk). Golders Green tube. **Lunch served** noon-3pm Fri. **Meals served** noon-10.30pm Mon-Thur, Sun. **Main courses** £15-£25. **Credit** AmEx, MC, V.

Bloom's is still a bastion of old-fashioned east European cooking, though the decor has changed. The layout is the same, yet brighter, with a mural depicting Moses leading the children of Israel. The Ashkenazi food is, thankfully, unaltered – but prices have crept upwards and booking is essential. Our waiter, on the staff at Blooms for 40 years, was charmingly cheery, offering extra matzah crackers to our companion as he delivered a hefty plate of chopped liver, egg and onion, telling us, 'Give her some of your starter – you won't eat it all'. Chicken soup proved equally substantial, with enough meat-filled kreplach to make you think twice about ordering a main course. But how can you leave without sampling the signature salt beef, served with chips or in sandwiches? Beef used to come with more fat, but these days customers prefer a less succulent, lower-cholesterol version. The curries or chargrilled chicken with fresh vegetables on the expanded menu are another nod to change. But looking around the room, it's the same old clientele, happy to tuck into generous portions of the old familiar food.
Babies and children welcome: children's menu; high chairs. Kosher supervised (Beth Din). Tables outdoors (2, pavement). Takeaway service.
For branch see index.

★ Dizengoff's

118 Golders Green Road, NW11 8HB (8458 7003/www.dizengoffkosherrestaurant.co.uk). Golders Green tube. **Meals served** *Summer* 11am-11.30pm Mon-Thur, Sun; noon-3.30pm Fri. *Winter* 11am-11.30pm Mon-Thur, Sun; noon-3.30pm Fri; 7pm-1am Sat. **Main courses** £12-£18. **Credit** AmEx, MC, V.

With pictures of Tel Aviv on the wall, generous portions and a bustling ambience, this is a convivial spot for dinner. Previous problems with service and a lack of attention to detail have been ironed out, and Dizengoff's is producing some great meals. Our waiter brought olives and spicy pickled carrots and cauliflower, followed by excellent starters: freshly made and deliciously smooth houmous, along with creamy (although not deeply meaty) chopped liver. For the seriously hungry, there are hearty Yemenite or kooba soups, tandoori chicken laffa, moussaka and the odd more inventive dish, such as stuffed artichoke. A medium-rare steak was served as ordered, while lamb kebabs and chicken livers with fried onions were judged 'just right'. Chips were nicely crisp on the outside and soft inside, and the fluffy rice was equally good. Both are included with main courses, along with a salad. Dizengoff's welcomes children, offering them multicoloured straws with their drinks, and half portions. To finish there are syrupy sweet filo pastries with nuts, or gently spiced warm apple strudel.
Babies and children welcome: children's menu; high chairs. Book weekends. Kosher supervised (Sephardi). Tables outdoors (3, pavement). Takeaway service.

La Fiesta

235 Golders Green Road, NW11 9PN (8458 0444). Brent Cross tube. **Meals served** noon-11pm Mon-Thur, Sun. **Main courses** £8.75-£26.50. **Set lunch** £15.50 3 courses. **Credit** AmEx, MC, V.

After a fire destroyed the old restaurant in spring 2007, La Fiesta moved a few doors along Golders Green Road. The new premises are less inviting, with the air of an unappealing café. At the front is a takeaway area, furnished with green plastic chairs and serving burgers or baguettes stuffed with beef. Argentinian specialities are dished up in a windowless area at the back that's kitted out with chunky, gaucho-style furniture. Though there are a couple of fish choices, this is a place for serious meat eaters. Only a nod is given to tradition; there's chicken soup, but it's slightly peppery. You'd do well to start with a mushroom empanada, saving your appetite for a steak grilled over hot coals. For rare meat, the best choice is a thick cut shared between two. Just remember it continues to cook on the sizzling brazier at the table. Lamb cutlets, chorizo and asado ribs were all chargrilled and succulent, and chips, green salad and little pots of ketchup and mustard were brought swiftly. Nevertheless, the experience is sadly lacking – maybe a move back to the old space and some white tablecloths would do the trick.
Babies and children admitted. Booking advisable dinner. Kosher supervised (Beth Din). Takeaway service.

Mattancherry NEW

109A Golders Green Road, NW11 8HR (8209 3060/www.mattancherry.net). Golders Green tube. **Lunch served** noon-2.30pm Mon-Fri, Sun. **Dinner served** 6-10.45pm Mon-Fri, Sun. **Main courses** £10.90-£17.95. **Set buffet** (lunch) £12.95. **Credit** MC, V.

The second kosher Indian restaurant to open in London (after Kavanna, *see p215*), Mattancherry takes its name from a town in the southern state of Kerala – though the style of food is mainly from the north. Its orange tablecloths and walls aren't exactly relaxing, and you'll strain to make out the background music over the busy hum of conversation, but charming waitresses soon bring chilled beer. Geared towards a clientele that may not have tasted Indian food before, the menu starts by describing the basic flavours and techniques (tandoori, biriani and so on). We found the ingredients and spicing authentic, if a little mild. Starters of deep-fried chicken wings and spherical lamb patties were more successful than vegetable pakoras and ghosht baigan (deep-fried aubergine stuffed with minced lamb). Vegetarian main courses are limited, and tend to need bolder and more adventurous spicing. In contrast, the beef and lamb curries were robust, with rich sauces that could be soaked up with a nan or kashmiri rice. If you're not a fan of parev ice-cream, round off the evening with exotic fruit salad, mango sorbet or saffron-infused kulfi.
Babies and children welcome: high chairs. Booking advisable: dinner. Kosher supervised (Kedassia). Takeaway service. Vegetarian menu.

Met Su Yan

134 Golders Green Road, NW11 8HB (8458 8088/www.metsuyan.co.uk). Golders Green tube. **Lunch served** noon-2.30pm, **dinner served** 6-11pm Mon-Thur, Sun. **Main courses** £12.95-£15.95. **Set lunch** £12.95 2 courses. **Set meal** £25 3 courses, £30 4 courses. **Credit** AmEx, MC, V.

This kosher oriental restaurant, now under new management, takes its name from the Hebrew word for 'excellent' – and the airy, modern interior and elegant china promise high standards. On a quiet day we found the service friendly and efficient, though our table could have done with a wipe between courses. Dishes from the sizeable menu follow well-trodden paths (chicken in black bean sauce, beef with ginger and spring onion), but proved slightly variable. The 'imperial' hors d'oeuvres comprised a tasty, if predictable, collection of dishes (sesame-encrusted tofu, fried seaweed, chicken satay and spring rolls), although the spare ribs were marred by an overpowering barbecue sauce. Flavours were balanced far more successfully in chicken and sweetcorn soup, and duck with ginger. Lamb in peking sauce, while pleasantly spicy, was a touch too sweet for our

Dizengoff's

Menu

There are two main strands of cooking: Ashkenazi from Russia and eastern Europe; and Sephardi, originating in Spain and Portugal. After the Inquisition, Sephardi Jews settled throughout the Mediterranean, in Iraq and further east. London used to contain mainly Ashkenazi restaurants, but now Hendon and Golders Green are full of Sephardi bakeries and cafés, specialising in the Middle Eastern food you might find in Jerusalem. You can still get traditional chicken soup and knaidlach or fried latkes, but these are never as good as you'll find in the home. Nor will you find the succulent, slow-cooked Sabbath dishes that are made in many homes every Friday. The Israeli-type restaurants are strong on grilled meats and offer a range of fried or vegetable starters.

Since most kosher restaurants serve meat (and therefore can't serve dairy products), desserts are not a strong point. Rather than non-dairy ice-cream, it's better to choose baklava or chocolate pudding. Though, by the time you've got through the generous portions served in most places, you may not have room for anything more than a glass of mint or lemon tea.

Bagels or **beigels**: heavy, ring-shaped rolls. The dough is first boiled then glazed and baked. The classic filling is smoked salmon and cream cheese.
Baklava: filo pastry layered with almonds or pistachios and soaked in scented syrup.
Blintzes: pancakes, most commonly filled with cream cheese, but also with sweet or savoury fillings.
Borekas: triangles of filo pastry with savoury fillings like cheese or spinach.
Borscht: a classic beetroot soup served either hot or cold, often with sour cream.
Challah or **cholla**: egg-rich, slightly sweet plaited bread for the Sabbath.
Chicken soup: a clear, golden broth made from chicken and vegetables.
Chopped liver: chicken or calf's liver fried with onions, finely chopped and mixed with hard-boiled egg and chicken fat. Served cold, often with extra egg and onions.
Chrane or **chrain**: a pungent sauce made from grated horseradish and beetroot, served with cold fish.
Cigars: rolls of filo pastry with a sweet or savoury filling.
Falafel: spicy, deep-fried balls of ground chickpeas, served with houmous and tahina (sesame paste).
Gefilte fish: white fish minced with onions and seasoning, made into balls and poached or fried; served cold. The sweetened version is Polish.
Houmous: chickpeas puréed with sesame paste, lemon juice, garlic and oil, served cold.
Kataifi or **konafa**: shredded filo pastry wrapped around a nut or cheese filling, soaked in syrup.
Kibbe, **kuba**, **kooba**, **kubbeh** or **kobeiba**: oval patties, handmade from a shell of crushed wheat (bulgar) filled with minced meat, pine nuts and spices. Shaping and filling the shells before frying is the skill.
Knaidlach or **kneidlach**: dumplings made from matzo (qv) meal and eggs, poached until they float 'like clouds' in chicken soup. Also called matzo balls.
Kreplach: pockets of noodle dough filled with meat and served in soup, or filled with sweet fillings and eaten with sour cream.
Laffa: large puffy pitta bread used to enclose falafel or shwarma (qv).
Latkes: grated potato mixed with egg and fried into crisp pancakes.
Lockshen: egg noodles boiled and served in soup. When cold, they can be mixed with egg, sugar and cinnamon and baked into a pudding.
Matzo or **matzah**: flat squares of unleavened bread. When ground into meal, it is used to make a crisp coating for fish or schnitzel.
Parev or **parve**: a term describing food that is neither meat nor dairy.
Rugelach: crescent-shaped biscuits made from a rich, cream cheese pastry, filled with nuts, jam or chocolate. Popular in Israel and the US.
Salt beef: pickled brisket, with a layer of fat, poached and served in slices.
Schnitzel: thin slices of chicken, turkey or veal, dipped in egg and matzo meal and fried.
Shwarma: layers of lamb or turkey, cooked on a spit, served with pitta.
Strudel: wafer-thin pastry wrapped around an apple or soft cheese filling.
Tabouleh: cracked wheat (bulgar) mixed with ample amounts of fresh herbs, tomato and lemon juice, served as a starter or salad.
Viennas: boiled frankfurter sausages, served with chips and salt beef.
Worsht: beef salami, sliced thinly to eat raw, but usually cut in thick pieces and fried when served with eggs or chips.

liking. Fragrant rice and fried noodles were good but expensive, and a cup of jasmine tea (made from a tea bag) added a further £2 to an already costly meal. There's a set lunch for just under £13, but à la carte costs about £40 a head for two courses – a high price for what isn't quite up to 'excellent' standards.
Babies and children welcome: high chairs. Booking advisable. Kosher supervised (Federation). Takeaway service; delivery service (over £30 within 2-mile radius).

★ Novellino

103 Golders Green Road, NW11 8EN (8458 7273). Golders Green tube. **Meals served** 8.30am-11.30pm Mon-Thur, Sun; 8.30am-4pm Fri. **Main courses** £9-£18. **Credit** MC, V.
From the welcoming dish of black olives to the scrumptious desserts, attention to detail is much in evidence at Novellino. The most professional of north-west London's kosher restaurants, this place is a haven for vegetarians. Roasted beetroot and goat's cheese salad, aubergine parmigiana and risotto with saffron were all substantial enough for a main course, while artichoke and carrot soup arrived with a basket of fresh bread (nut and raisin was the best). Pasta dishes were equally fresh and inviting, dressed with pesto, garlicky oil, a creamy tomato and tuna sauce or flakes of fresh cod with vegetables. Fish features heavily, with starters of tuna carpaccio, gravlax or a puff pastry case of marinated salmon and scrambled egg, along with mains of sea bass and grilled salmon. Staff were charming and attentive; this is a pleasant place to linger over a leisurely meal. You may need a separate visit to do justice to the coffee and pastries, however. We opted for cheesecake with a glossy, dark-chocolate top, and a perfect lemon tart, but vowed to return to sample the chocolate concoctions: melting fondant with ice-cream, truffle cake, florentines and a decadent three-layer mousse.
Babies and children welcome: children's menu; high chairs. Booking advisable. Disabled: toilet. Kosher supervised (Beth Din). Tables outdoors (5, pavement). Takeaway service.

Solly's

148A Golders Green Road, NW11 8HE (ground floor & takeaway 8455 2121/first floor 8455 0004). Golders Green tube.
Ground floor **Lunch served** 11.30am-5pm Fri. **Meals served** 11.30am-11pm Mon-Thur, Sun. *Winter* 1hr after Sabbath-1am Sat.
First floor **Lunch served** 12.30-4.30pm Sun. **Dinner served** 6.30-11pm Mon-Thur, Sun. *Winter* 1hr after Sabbath-midnight Sat.
Both **Main courses** £10-£15. **Set dinner** £24 3 courses. **Credit** MC, V.
At the ground-floor café and takeaway you can watch a cook tending the pitta oven, deftly turning out hot, puffy breads. Upstairs is the 'Exclusive' restaurant, with its slightly faded Moroccan-style decor. The menu is similar on both floors, with starters undoubtedly being the kitchen's strong point. Houmous was soft and creamy with melting chickpeas, while smoky aubergine and tomato dip was well-spiced; vegetarian cigars were crisp, if slightly oily. In fact, it wouldn't be a bad idea to make a whole meal of the meat or mushroom kooba, falafel, aubergine with tahina or herby tabouleh (the bread was delicious too), as the mains we sampled proved to be less accomplished. Lamb shish kebabs could have been more tender, while our steak was thin, rather than thick and juicy. Chips and rice were faultless, but charged as extras rather than being included with the mains. Service was on the languid side; the apparently inexperienced waitresses struggled to cope with the large number of customers. One new departure is that Solly's now offers salt beef – it might do better to stick to the Israeli specialities, but beef up the service.
Babies and children welcome: high chairs. Booking advisable (first floor). Disabled: toilet. Kosher supervised (Beth Din). Separate room for parties, seats 100. Takeaway service.

Hendon

La Dorada NEW

134 Brent Street, NW4 2DR (8202 1339). Hendon Central tube. **Meals served** noon-10pm Mon-Thur, Sun. **Main courses** £10.95-£18.95. **Set meal** (until 6.30pm) £11.95 2 courses; (6.30-10pm) £15.95 2 courses. **Credit** MC, V.
Refurbished and under new management, La Dorada is a big hit among locals, with a bustling takeaway section. Most customers ignore the pizzas, jacket potatoes and pastas and make a beeline for the fried fish: plaice on the bone, crispy cod fillet or a more expensive tranche of halibut or dover sole. While the fish is fresh and perfectly cooked and the chips enjoyable enough, starters of egg mayonnaise or cold borscht were unexceptional, and many of the advertised desserts are not always available. To make up for the lack of fruit salad, apple pie or warm chocolate cake, we sampled the rather oddly named 'Delicatessen Individual': a moreish concoction featuring layers of sponge, chocolate mousse and cream, drizzled with chocolate sauce.

The decor is slightly stark, and the service, though smiling, was amateurish at best; our cold starters arrived a good five minutes apart, with bread and butter taking another eight minutes to make an appearance. At these prices, you'd expect better – although we'd certainly go back for a takeaway.
Babies and children welcome: children's menu; high chairs. Kosher supervised (Beth Din). Takeaway service.

Eighty-Six Bistro Bar

86 Brent Street, NW4 2ES (8202 5575). Hendon Central tube. **Lunch served** noon-3pm Sun. **Dinner served** 5.30-11pm Mon-Thur, Sun; **Main courses** £9.95-£22.95. **Credit** MC, V.
You need to book at Eighty-Six, as tables fill up early with families and later with more leisurely diners. The adventurous menu is certainly appealing. Cold starters include gravlax with brandy and honey marinade, aubergine grilled with tahina, and two delicious slices of rare roast beef. Less usual meats such as veal also feature, along with a sumptuous calvados foie gras (sadly, often unavailable as kosher goose liver is hard to source). Main courses include grilled poussin or chicken breast stuffed with mushrooms, courgette and smoked goose breast; duck, however, was disappointing, served with an oversweet sauce. Vegetables (sweet pepper, garlicky mushrooms or grilled tomatoes) may arrive cold on the plate, but the chips are perfect. Main course prices can be on the high side, although less expensive options abound, from spaghetti bolognese to gourmet burgers. There's not much for vegetarians, but fish eaters should check if the salmon or sea bass is available. Portions are large; if you don't have room for a slab of chocolate cake or pear tart for afters, linger instead over a glass of wine, served by a charming French waiter.
Babies and children welcome: children's portions; high chairs. Booking advisable. Kosher supervised (Federation). Takeaway service.

Kavanna

60 Vivian Avenue, NW4 3XH (8202 9449/ www.kavanna.co.uk). Hendon Central tube. **Dinner served** 5.30-11pm Mon-Thur, Sun. **Main courses** £9.50-£15.50. **Set meal** £22 per person (minimum 2); £20 per person (minimum 4). **Credit** MC, V.
A year after its launch, Kavanna's combination of authentic Indian spicing and kosher meat is still very much in demand. On a weekday evening the waiters were relaxed enough to stop and chat, explaining how the creamy dishes are created using soya milk and yoghurt instead of cow's milk and cream. Crisp white linen tablecloths add an elegant note and the cooking (by an Indian chef) is competent, with a well-judged balance of garlic, turmeric and chilli and thick, slowly simmered sauces. Onion bhajis were crisp and nicely spiced, while a starter of red tandoori chicken was almost big enough to serve as a main course. There's a good array of baltis, sizzling grills and birianis, with plenty of vegetarian options. Chicken jalfrezi with green peppers, served with pilau rice, was rich and full of flavour, although the lamb in a smooth, creamy almond sauce could have been more tender. Sweet peshwari nan, stuffed with almonds, coconut and sultanas, provided some consolation. End with mango sorbet or, in winter, a warm bowl of kheer (saffron-tinged rice pudding).
Babies and children welcome: children's portions; high chairs. Booking advisable. Kosher supervised (Beth Din and Kedassia). Takeaway service. Vegetarian menu.

Orli NEW

96 Brent Street, NW4 2HH (8203 7555). Hendon Central tube. **Meals served** *Summer* 7am-11pm Mon-Fri, Sun. *Winter* 7am-11pm Mon-Fri, Sun; 7am-5pm, 7pm-midnight Sat. **Main courses** £4.95-£13.95. **Set lunch** £10 2 courses. **No credit cards.**
Under the same ownership as Eighty-Six (*see above*), the Burger Bar (*see p211*), an excellent bakery and two other Orli outlets, this café offers an extensive all-day menu. For breakfast there are omelettes, borekas and danish pastries. Lunch options include pizzas, jacket potatoes, salads and toasted bagels, but there are more substantial grilled fish and pasta dishes to be had too, served with a generous scoop of side salad. Soups are fresh and gutsy, with toasted challah rolls or pitta on the side. Deep-fried mushrooms were filled with slightly oily tuna and coated with a thick layer of batter, while savoury blintzes were accompanied by a thinnish, bland cream sauce. A plate of penne with tomato was splendid, with perfectly al dente pasta and a sauce that packed a flavoursome punch. There's also a small but inviting selection of cakes, with apple pie, white or dark chocolate cake and an excellent crumble-topped cheesecake. Our visit was marred by slightly amateurish service, with a surly waitress bringing the main courses before we'd even finished our starters.
Babies and children welcome: high chairs. Booking advisable. Kosher supervised (Federation). Vegetarian menu.
For branches see index.

Sami's Kosher Restaurant

157 Brent Street, NW4 4DJ (8203 8088). Hendon Central tube. **Meals served** noon-11pm Mon-Thur, Sun. **Main courses** £11.95-£14.50. **Set lunch** (Mon-Thur) £9.95-£12.95 2 courses. **Credit** MC, V.
With its charming (if occasionally absent-minded) Israeli waitresses, Sami's feels like a family-run affair. Dark wood tables contrast with bright walls of windows or mirrors. The menu offers several types of cuisine: simple grills, spicy Indian dishes (tandoori chicken and lamb tikka) and, most appealingly, Iraqi home cooking. Start with chicken soup, or a plate of houmous and shwarma that's big enough for a main course. Sticking to the Iraqi specialities, there's sambousek (pastry with meat filling), cracked wheat kubbeh or cigars of filo pastry with beef or chicken. Dishes such as kubah shwandar (rice and semolina dough enclosing minced meat) with sweet and sour beetroot sauce; meuleh (stuffed pepper or cabbage); and t'bit (dark chicken slow-cooked with red rice and tender white beans) – were distinctive and richly flavoursome. This is the kind of food you'd find in an Iraqi home on a Friday evening. Many customers stick to the shwarma in pitta. Given the size of the portions, few will have room for a dessert of lockshen pudding, strudel or cinnamony baklava.
Babies and children welcome: children's menu; high chairs. Kosher supervised (Federation). Takeaway service.

St John's Wood

Harry Morgan's

31 St John's Wood High Street, NW8 7NH (7722 1869/www.harryms.co.uk). St John's Wood tube. **Breakfast served** 8.30-10.30am Mon-Fri. **Meals served** 11.30am-10pm Mon-Fri; noon-10pm Sat, Sun. **Main courses** £9.95-£12.95. **Credit** AmEx, MC, V. Not kosher
Despite the competition, with ten eateries within a few hundred yards, this long-established 'Jewish style' restaurant still packs 'em in. The decor is plain (granite tables, metallic chairs), but it's the food that attracts the lunchtime shoppers and loyal local following. Harry's proudly trumpets its excellent reputation, with a collage of reviews and comments on one wall ('Best chicken soup in town,' claims one). This is the place for nostalgia without the strict rules of kashrut: hot borscht with potato, deep-flavoured chopped liver and stuffed cabbage, followed by creamy cheesecake or lockshen pudding. Service is casual and offers little finesse, but the food is closer to homemade than you might expect. Lockshen soup was superb, tongue was full of flavour and the fried haddock tasted crisp and fresh, with tender flakes. The menu caters to all appetites, with lighter options of bagels, bean and barley soup and salads (mozzarella, houmous or sautéed chicken) alongside more hefty meat dishes and sandwiches. We sampled an apple strudel and a warm cherry and almond tart with crème fraîche from the famed dessert menu; both were pâtisserie standard. It's just a shame you can't try everything. A new mini concession (mainly a takeaway) has recently opened in Harrods.
Babies and children welcome: children's portions; high chairs. Booking advisable (not accepted Sat, Sun). Tables outdoors (5, pavement). Takeaway service. **Map 2 E2.**
For branch see index.

Outer London

Edgware, Middlesex

Aviv

87-89 High Street, Edgware, Middx HA8 7DB (8952 2484/www.avivrestaurant.com). Edgware tube. **Lunch served** noon-2.30pm Mon-Thur, Sun. **Dinner served** *Summer* 5.30-11pm Mon-Thur, Sun. *Winter* 5.30-11pm Mon-Thur, Sat, Sun. **Main courses** £10.95-£14.95. **Set lunch** (noon-2.30pm Mon-Thur) £9.95 2 courses. **Set meal** £15.95-£19.95 3 courses. **Credit** AmEx, MC, V.
Competitive pricing and generous portions ensure that Aviv retains a loyal following, and you'll need to book in the evening. On our visit service was efficient, and complimentary crudités with pink mayonnaise arrived as soon as we sat down. Starters of meaty chopped liver, minced meat cigars and duck pancakes were cleared away fast (slightly too hastily, in fact); the first two were spot-on, but the thinly filled pancakes were a bit short on sauce. The set menus offer a variety of dishes, for three generous courses. Quantity is never an issue, whether you opt for half a barbecued chicken, the hefty kevas batanur (lamb on the bone) or perfectly grilled rib steak. With chips, rice, vegetables and salad arriving in abundance, plates soon jostle for space on the unadorned tables. The meat was inconsistent, however, even on one plate, with a mix of tender and chewy pieces. Sauces lacked finesse; an oversweet barbecue sauce was heavy with chilli, while the goulash lacked paprika and a mushroom sauce was over-salted. Dairy-free versions of classic desserts such as tiramisu aren't the best choice; instead, go for sticky toffee pudding or fresh fruit salad. Overall, great value if you choose wisely.
Babies and children welcome: children's portions; high chairs. Booking essential. Kosher supervised (Federation). Tables outdoors (14, patio). Takeaway service.

Ralphy's New York Grill NEW

32-34 Station Road, Edgware, Middx HA8 7AB (8952 6036/www.ralphys.com). Edgware tube. **Lunch served** noon-3pm, **dinner served** 6-11pm Mon-Thur, Sun. **Main courses** £5.95-£15.95. **Set lunch** £8.50 1 course and soft drink. **Credit** AmEx, MC, V.
'Bringing the Big Apple to Edgware' is the lofty claim of this new grill restaurant. Dishes are named after New York landmarks, with Madison Avenue lamb cutlets or Broadway beef cubes; for vegetarians, there's a Staten Island vegetable burger, Central Park portobello mushrooms or an Empire State salad – chargrilled veg, presumably piled into a suitably towering stack. But is the food authentic? On our visit the kitchen was finding it hard to deliver orders together, but produced a succulent corned beef sandwich (layers of thin slices instead of the thicker salt beef) and hot and crispy fried chicken. Ralphy's is a good place for families with children; there's something for everyone (with the possible exception of those watching their waistlines). You could have a juicy steak salad with capers and mixed leaves, or a hot dog with corn cobs and chips. The chefs also do a mean chocolate pudding, with gooey sauce oozing out. Ice-cream and milkshakes are, of course, parev – so expect colour rather than flavour. Ralphy's is a stone's throw from the long-established, non-kosher B&K Salt Beef Bar. In this area, which has a growing observant community, it should do well.
Babies and children welcome: children's menu; high chairs. Booking advisable. Kosher supervised (Beth Din). Takeaway service.

Korean

Korean food is defined by simplicity. Rather than drowning ingredients in spices and sauces, the cuisine brings together inspired combinations of natural flavours that complement each other perfectly. The building blocks of Korean cookery are barbecued meats, toenjang (fermented bean paste), soy sauce, sesame (both the oil and the seeds), fish and eggs, noodles and tofu, and kimchi (pickled vegetables, usually chinese cabbage, with chilli and garlic). From these simple materials, Korean cooks create an astounding array of textures and flavours, some spicy, some subtle, but all famously clean on the palate.

Korean dining in London is led by the Korean expat community. The West End is dotted with Korean barbecue houses, serving authentic Korean food to a mixed clientele of expat workers and London foodies. Soho has by far the largest concentration of restaurants, but Korean eateries are also found in Piccadilly, Mayfair and Holborn. There's another excellent cluster in New Malden in Surrey (on the south-west edge of London), where the capital's main Korean community is based.

New Malden is still the place for blisteringly authentic Korean food. **Jee Cee Neh** and **You-Me**, new-arrival **Su La**, and **Cah Chi** in nearby Raynes Park, are little pieces of Seoul, transported to the London suburbs. In the West End, restaurants such as **Myung Ga**, **Jindalle**, **Dong San** and **Asadal** are finding a new clientele among theatre-goers and City workers, while cafés like **Bi Won**, **Nara** and **Woo Jung** do a brisk trade serving inexpensive set lunches to crowds of Korean students.

If this is your first experience of Korean food, try a set lunch of chigae (stew with bean paste and chill), bulgogi (barbecued beef) or bibimbap (rice stirred with meat and vegetables in a hot stone bowl). We promise you'll come back for more.

Central

Bloomsbury

★ Bi Won

24 Coptic Street, WC1A 1NT (7580 2660). Tottenham Court Road or Russell Square tube. **Meals served** noon-11pm daily. **Main courses** £5-£8. **Set lunch** £6.50. **Set meal** £17-£25 per person (minimum 2). **Credit** MC, V.

You could easily walk past Bi Won and assume it was a West End sandwich shop. Think again – this bright, café-like restaurant serves some of the best Korean food in town, in double-quick time to an eager clientele of Korean students and office workers. It specialises in set meals, but the menu also runs to barbecues and huge jeongols. Lunch is a bargain at £5-£8 for a barbecue, soup or stew with rice on the side and a dish of well-spiced kimchi. We hit the jackpot with the kimchi chigae, a flavoursome broth of fermented cabbage, silken tofu, belly pork, leeks and onions with a searing chilli heat that got stronger towards the bottom of the bowl. The daeji bulgogi was also inspired: strips of pork barbecued in a sweet chilli sauce, served on a sizzling platter. Bi Won's decor is refreshingly simple: pine barbecue tables, cream paint and a line of cutesy Korean dolls lined along one wall. Factor in rapid service and reasonable prices and it's easy to see why so many people lunch here.

Babies and children welcome: high chairs. Separate room for parties, seats 30. Tables outdoors (2, pavement). **Map 18 D2.**

Chinatown

Corean Chilli

51 Charing Cross Road, WC2H 0NE (7734 6737). Leicester Square tube. **Meals served** noon-midnight Mon-Sat; noon-11pm Sun. **Main courses** £6.50-£15. **Set lunch** £4.50-£5. **Credit** JCB, MC, V.

A rare Korean choice in an area dominated by Cantonese food, Corean Chilli woos a younger east Asian crowd with a futuristic charcoal-coloured interior and a broad menu of Korean favourites served café-style with minimum fuss. There are rooms on several levels, all lined with concrete and grey slate tiles. It feels a little like dining in a multistorey car park, but service is fast, the vibe upbeat and the location handy for theatre-goers. CC's menu reveals a slight Japanese bent, so as well as bibimbap and bulgogi you'll find ramen and udon noodles. Our cabbage kimchi was suitably fiery and we also enjoyed the mini pork pancakes (dim sum-like pork balls served with shredded cabbage and a delicious tangy relish). Tteokpokki (rice sticks in chilli sauce) was more hit and miss; the flavour of the dish was swamped by too much chilli and rather overpowering Korean fish cakes. We were more impressed by jjambong, an incendiary seafood noodle soup often referred to as 'Chinese food' in Korea. Our conclusion? Not bad, but probably better for a swift bite on the go than a lingering supper.

Babies and children welcome: high chairs. Booking advisable Fri, Sat. Restaurant available for hire. Takeaway service. **Map 17 C4.**

Covent Garden

★ Woo Jung

59 St Giles High Street, WC2H 8LH (7836 3103). Tottenham Court Road tube. **Meals served** noon-1am Mon-Sat; 5pm-midnight Sun. **Main courses** £6-£8. **Set lunch** £6-£8. **Set meal** £17-£23. **Credit** MC, V.

When most people look for Korean cuisine in the West End, they head to the barbecue houses in central Soho, but there's another cluster of cheap Korean cafés squeezed shoulder to jowl on St Giles High Street, behind Centrepoint. Woo Jung is the liveliest of these laid-back caffs, attracting student diners from lunch till late. The faded mock-Tudor interior seems to belong to a different kind of restaurant, but paper-screen trim around the serving counter adds a Korean feel to the ground-floor dining area (a second room upstairs feels a bit disconnected). Service is rapid, but food can be a mixed bag. We found the mandu soup a little plain, though the dish was redeemed by flavoursome meaty dumplings and some tangy, almost effervescent kimchi on the side. Our main course wasn't a big hit; deep-fried shredded beef arrived in a gloopy batter with an overpowering syrupy sauce. Woo Jung is a decent choice for an inexpensive lunch, but it might be worth following regular diners and sticking to fail-safe options like chigae, bibimbap and bulgogi.

Babies and children admitted. Takeaway service. **Map 18 C2.**

Holborn

★ Asadal

227 High Holborn, WC1V 7DA (7430 9006). Holborn tube. **Lunch served** noon-3pm Mon-Sat. **Dinner served** 6-11pm Mon-Sat; 5-10.30pm Sun. **Main courses** £6-£20. **Set lunch** £10.50-£14. **Set dinner** £17.50-£30. **Credit** MC, V.

Blink and you could miss Asadal. This sophisticated Korean hides behind a modest doorway next to Holborn tube. We strongly recommend descending into the basement dining room; the ambience and food here put most other West End Korean restaurants to shame. Wooden partitions and mood lighting give the place an intimate, sophisticated feel – equally suited to a date or a business lunch. This operation is a branch of the well-regarded Asadal in New Malden and authentic Korean flavours shine through in the food. The menu strays well beyond the London Korean norm, but we opted for the classics and weren't disappointed. The house chapch'ae was one of the best we've tasted: tender beef, fried separately with ear mushrooms and spring onions, then tossed with a huge mound of glassy sweet-potato starch noodles. In comparison, battered tofu cheon was slightly plain on the palate, but the spicy dak galbi (spicy chicken barbecue) was a delight, served sizzling in a stone pan with oodles of chilli and sweet potato. Service is snappy, and there's even a lift for customers with disabilities.

Babies and children welcome: high chairs. Booking advisable. Disabled: toilet. Separate rooms for parties, seating 6 and 10. Takeaway service. **Map 18 E2.**

For branch see index.

Leicester Square

Jindalle

6 Panton Street, SW1Y 4DL (7930 8881). Piccadilly Circus tube. **Meals served** noon-11pm daily. **Main courses** £6.90-£25. **Set lunch** £4.50. **Set dinner** £19.90-£25. **Credit** AmEx, MC, V.

Edging into theatreland on a side street off Haymarket, Jindalle looks like a 1950s vision of the future. Perhaps it's the brushed-steel extractor fans

that hover over each table, sucking away the curls of smoke from sizzling Korean barbecues. Exposed brickwork, wooden panels and a giant frieze in Mondrian colours on the back wall add more visual interest – a refreshing change from the unimaginative black and white colour scheme employed by most West End Korean restaurants. Food is good too, and the menu runs to regional specialities like neng myun (cold buckwheat noodles) and trumpet shells in rich seafood stews. We decided to put the extractor fan to use with a well-marinated kalbi (beef rib) barbecue, which arrived rolled up on the bone (the meat was chopped up with shears during the cooking process). Melting squares of battered cod cheon were decorated with faces made from red and green pepper, and seafood chigae had oodles of flavour, though there was rather more silken tofu than clams or prawns. Overall, Jindalle is a great choice for a pre-show dinner.
Babies and children welcome: high chairs. Booking advisable. Takeaway service.
Map 17 C5.

Mayfair

★ Kaya

42 Albemarle Street, W1S 4JH (7499 0622/ 0633/www.kayarestaurant.co.uk). Green Park tube. **Lunch served** noon-3pm, **dinner served** 5-11pm Mon-Sat. **Main courses** £9-£20. **Set lunch** £10-£15. **Credit** JCB, MC, V.
Elegant, tidy and calm, Kaya fits perfectly into posh Mayfair. The interior is a subtle nod to Korean temple architecture, with canopies of blue-green roof tiles and swirling landscape murals. At the back, a screen window conceals a private banquet room; in the basement, Korean office workers sip soju and sing along to Korean pop in a convincing re-creation of a Seoul karaoke bar. Despite the swish location and the diligent service, prices are on a par with other West End Koreans, and the food is worth every penny. The menu includes interesting specials to share, but we went for old favourites. Bindaedok was light and fluffy, and miyeokguk soup had a deep sesame flavour, with tender strips of beef and long ribbons of seaweed. Kalbi (beef ribs) were slow-cooked on the barbecue in a sublime marinade, and the tolsot bibimbap was exemplary: egg, beef shreds, mushrooms, green leaves, chilli sauce and rice, folded together and cooked on the spot in a hot stone bowl. We can still remember the roasted flavour of the rice.
Booking advisable. Separate rooms for parties, seating 8 and 12. **Map 9 J7.**

Soho

Dong San

47 Poland Street, W1F 7NB (7287 0997). Oxford Circus tube. **Meals served** 11.30am-11.30pm daily. **Main courses** £6-£12. **Set lunch** £6-£10. **Set dinner** £15-£20. **Credit** AmEx, DC, MC, V.
Dong San is as Korean as they come. Expats flock here for authentic food and the temporary illusion of dining in a barbecue house in downtown Busan. There are two dining spaces: a small café-like front room and a massive back room with tables divided by venetian blinds. The sense of stepping out of London is reinforced by the giant karaoke machine in the corner; lyrics to Korean pop hits scroll over a video of tacky tourist scenes. For dinner, we chose a well-prepared tolsot bibimbap (rice with meat, egg, chilli and vegetables in a stone bowl) for its filling starch quotient, and cheyuk pokkeum (stir-fried belly pork slices) for the complex flavours and robust chilli kick. Both dishes surpassed our expectations. We also enjoyed Korean dumpling soup; the broth was delicately seasoned and the mince and vegetable dumplings melted with each bite. In contrast, veg tempura was a let-down, with a soft, doughy batter that failed to set off the crispness of the vegetables. Every so often, the karaoke microphones are handed around: be warned.
Babies and children admitted. Booking advisable. Takeaway service. **Map 17 A3.**

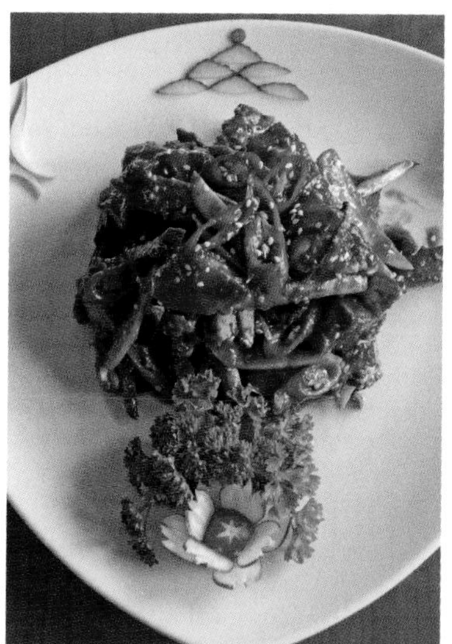

Su La. See p219.

SHELF LIFE

You can also find everyday Korean foodstuffs in many Chinese, Japanese and other oriental stores.

Centre Point Food Store
20-21 St Giles High Street, WC2H 8LN (7836 9860/www.cpfs.co.uk). Tottenham Court Road tube. **Open** 10am-10.30pm Mon-Sat; noon-10pm Sun.
Centrally located shop with all the Korean essentials.

Korea Foods
Unit 5, Wyvern Industrial Estate, Beverley Way, New Malden, Surrey KT3 4PH (8949 2238/www.koreafoods.co.uk). New Malden or Raynes Park rail. **Open** 9am-8pm Mon-Sat; noon-6pm Sun.
London's largest and best-stocked Korean supermarket.

Seoul Plaza
136 Golders Green Road, NW11 8HB (8731 7999/www.koreafoods.co.uk). Golders Green tube. **Open** 9am-9pm daily.
North London branch of a chain run by Korea Foods.

Jin

16 Bateman Street, W1D 3AH (7734 0908). Leicester Square or Tottenham Court Road tube. **Lunch served** noon-3pm, **dinner served** 6-10.30pm Mon-Sat. **Main courses** £8-£15. **Set lunch** £7.50-£10. **Set dinner** £30-£35. **Credit** AmEx, MC, V.
Young, cheerful staff raise Jin above the pack. Outwardly, the place looks like your typical Soho Korean – off-white walls, black modernist furniture and granite-topped barbecue tables – but what a difference a smile can make. At lunchtime, young Koreans crowd into the small dining room for inexpensive set lunches and filling box sets like cheyuk pokkeum (spicy fried pork) with fried glass noodles, cheon (Korean pancake), miso soup, kimchi and namul. In our opinion the boxes are better value than the set meals. We enjoyed the crisp onion and satisfying crunch of deep-fried noodles in our vegetable noodle set lunch, but the miso soup was small and namul was restricted to sesame-scented beansprouts. Bibimbap was nicely presented, but arrived in a bowl so we missed the ritual of folding it together in a sizzling hot stone pot. For a more substantial meal, try the barbecues; as well as beef, pork and chicken, you can feast on mussels, prawns or squid, and there are vegetable and mushroom barbecues for vegetarians.
Babies and children admitted. Booking advisable weekends. Separate room for parties, seats 10. Takeaway service. **Map 17 C3.**

★ Myung Ga

1 Kingly Street, W1B 5PA (7734 8220/www.myungga.co.uk). Oxford Circus or Piccadilly Circus tube. **Lunch served** noon-3pm Mon-Sat. **Dinner served** 5.30-11pm Mon-Sat; 5-10.30pm Sun. **Set lunch** £9.50-£12.50. **Set dinner** £25-£35. **Credit** AmEx, DC, MC, V.
We were lucky to get a seat at Myung Ga on a busy Friday night, but the food was well worth the wait. This is one of the more accessible Soho Korean restaurants, attracting plenty of theatre diners among the Korean and Japanese regulars. Inside, it's bright and busy, with staff in red bow ties zipping around with platters of chapch'ae and stone bowls of bubbling chigae and bibimbap. Tables are separated by etched glass partitions, but the atmosphere is animated rather than intimate. The menu is built around Korean favourites rather than rare delicacies. Battered deep-fried vegetables (pepper, carrot and potato) were assembled into bird's nest-like bundles with a zingy soy dip, providing a clean, starchy counterpoint to the meaty flavours of the barbecues – lean strips of rib beef and punchy daeji (spicy pork) with rich flavours of caramel and chilli. A set of mixed kimchi on the side ticked all the boxes: well-steeped pickled cabbage, radish and cucumber with a generous chilli heat. Don't be put off by the bustle and the smoke from the barbecues; food here is better than it needs to be.
Babies and children welcome: high chair. Booking advisable. Separate room for parties, seats 12. **Map 17 A4.**

Nara

9 D'Arblay Street, W1F 8DR (7287 2224). Oxford Circus or Tottenham Court Road tube. **Lunch served** noon-3.30pm Mon-Sat. **Dinner served** 5-11pm daily. **Main courses** £6.50-£30. **Set lunch** £6.50. **Set dinner** £7.50. **Credit** AmEx, MC, V.
There's something about Nara that harks back to the 1980s. It could be the coloured uplighting, recalling old Duran Duran videos, or the fact that the Korean students who flock here for cheap lunches are enthusiastic fans of the *Desperately Seeking Susan* school of fashion. Nevertheless, the fitted black barbecue tables lend Nara a degree of sophistication and the set lunches with rice, soup, kimchi and namul are a bargain. The menu includes several Japanese dishes, but it's the Korean food that steals the show. We visited on a busy weekday and, once seated, were presented with full-flavoured kimchi, spinach and beansprouts with sesame and translucent cubes of mung bean jelly. Mains weren't far behind; the satisfying beef bulgogi was served on a sizzling iron platter with lots of onion and vegetables (table-top barbecues are mainly used in the evenings). Seafood tang was also impressive: whole shrimps, mussels and white fish in a rich, chilli-infused, bouillabaisse-like soup. However, the evening service can fall short; diners have complained about being rushed from their tables by overzealous staff.
Babies and children admitted. Booking not accepted Fri, Sat. Takeaway service. **Map 17 B3.**

Ran

58-59 Great Marlborough Street, W1F 7JY (7434 1650/www.ranrestaurant.com). Oxford Circus tube. **Lunch served** noon-3pm Mon-Sat. **Dinner served** 6-11pm daily. **Main courses** £5.90-£12. **Set lunch** £7-£10. **Set dinner** £23-£69. **Credit** JCB, MC, V.
Some Korean restaurants try to rush you out the door, but Ran encourages you to linger. There's a bar at the front where you can sip an OB beer while waiting for a table. Diners take their time over meals, ordering extra dishes as they go. The decor is everything you'd expect from a Soho Korean: black and white photos, etched-glass partitions, fitted barbecue tables and wisps of smoke curling up to spotlights in the ceiling. The menu features barbecues, bibimbap, chigae stews and jeongol hotpots, plus a scattering of Japanese noodle and teriyaki dishes. We kicked off with deliciously light and crisp vegetable tempura, served with a delicate soy dipping sauce. Chicken in chorim (Korean pepper) sauce was full of rich, smoky flavours, and the spicy barbecued pork ticked all the right boxes – particularly when wrapped in lettuce leaves with shredded spring onion and a dollop of fermented bean paste. Energetic waiters are on hand to tend the barbecues, but it pays to watch the meat as they sometimes leave it to singe. This niggle aside, the food is generally excellent. We've been coming for years and haven't had a duff meal yet.
Babies and children welcome: high chairs. Booking advisable. Separate room for parties, seats 14. Takeaway service. **Map 17 A3.**

South West

Raynes Park

★ Cah Chi (100)

34 Durham Road, SW20 0TW (8947 1081). Raynes Park rail/57, 131 bus. **Lunch served** noon-3pm, **dinner served** 5-11pm Tue-Fri. **Meals served** noon-11pm Sat; noon-10.30pm Sun. **Main courses** £6-£14. **Set dinner** £18. **Corkage** 10% of bill. **No credit cards.**
Restaurants don't come any friendlier than Cah Chi. Just around the corner from Raynes Park station, this welcoming canteen looks more like a kindergarten than a restaurant, with children's drawings on the walls and a noticeboard of family photos. Signs of loving care abound; the blue-green frontage always looks freshly painted and the pine-filled interior is spotless. The menu has the full range of stews, soups, noodles and barbecues – including two-person specials like bosam (pork with mixed vegetables and Korean condiments). Staff are delightfully attentive. Cah Chi's yukkaejang (spicy beef soup) could well be the best in London: a tangle of tender beef shreds and spring onion in a fiery, chilli-rich broth that tingled on the palate. We also enjoyed the bulgogi, lean slivers of barbecued beef that we wrapped into parcels with lettuce leaves, denjang (fermented soy bean paste) and pa'muchin (zesty marinated shreds of spring onion). Food is usually cooked in the kitchen for solo diners, but groups can use the table-top barbecues. Namul and kimchi come free with most meals, but it's best to order some nutty red rice as well.
Babies and children welcome: high chairs. Booking essential. Separate room for parties, seats 18. Takeaway service.

North West

Golders Green

Kimchee

887 Finchley Road, NW11 8RR (8455 1035). Golders Green tube. **Lunch served** noon-3pm Tue-Fri; noon-4pm Sat, Sun. **Dinner served** 6-11pm Tue-Sun. **Main courses** £5.90-£8.50. **Set lunch** £5.90-£6.90. **Credit** JCB, MC, V.
Looking out towards the clocktower in the middle of Golders Green, Kimchee is a touch classier than your average Korean canteen. The interior is styled like a traditional yeogwan (Korean inn), with faux screen windows, dangling lanterns, dark wood furniture and funky wallpaper with a repeating pattern of woodcut village scenes. The cash booth by the entrance and waitresses in Korean frocks add a certain authenticity to the scene. North London is poorly served by Korean restaurants, but Kimchee fills the gap well; meals run the circuit from grills, rice and fried noodles to chigaes, hotpots and barbecues. On our latest visit, a first course of shigumchi soup (Korean-style miso with spinach and tofu) was adequate but uninspiring, held back by overzealous use of fermented bean paste. We also found the house kimchi a little short on oomph. However, grilled mackerel with sweet soy dressing was a hit, with a light, crisp batter and crispy skin adding bite to the delicious softness of the fish. Dishes are simply served, but barbecues are grilled at the table and bibimbaps come in authentic stone pots.
Babies and children admitted: high chairs. Booking essential Fri, Sat. Takeaway service.

Outer London

New Malden, Surrey

Han Kook

Ground floor, Falcon House, 257 Burlington Road, New Malden, Surrey KT3 4NE (8942 1188). Motspur Park rail. **Lunch served** noon-3pm Mon, Tue, Thur, Fri. **Dinner served** 6-11pm Mon-Fri. **Meals served** noon-11pm Sat, Sun. **Main courses** £6.50-£50. **Credit** MC, V.
Burlington Road has a reputation for authentic Korean food, but Han Kook is still an unexpected find amid the builders' merchants and furniture shops. Inside, a former industrial space has been reinvented as a mock-up of dynastic Korea, with fretwork partitions, paper screens and a raised stage with low tables and truncated, legless chairs. There are also conventional tables for those who haven't mastered the art of eating cross-legged. An aquarium houses live lobsters, abalones and turbot, used for fresh sashimi and spicy seafood

stews. Barbecues are prepared on portable hotplates; lettuce and denjang (bean paste) for wrapping are included in the price. The menu gives dish names only in Korean, with brief descriptions in English. Service was prompt on our visit. Neng myun (cold buckwheat noodles) arrived within seconds, rolled into grey nests with a chilled soy-based soup for dipping and a dollop of fiery wasabi paste on the side. The fish cheon was one of the best we've tasted: cubes of fish with marvellous flavour and texture, and a delicious soy and chilli dip. Things are quiet at lunchtimes, but get busier in the evenings.
Babies and children welcome: high chairs. Booking essential dinner Fri-Sun.

★ Jee Cee Neh

74 Burlington Road, New Malden, Surrey KT3 4NU (8942 0682). New Malden rail.
Lunch served noon-3pm, **dinner served** 6-11pm Mon-Fri. **Meals served** 11.30am-10.30pm Sat, Sun. **Main courses** £6.50-£8.50. **Credit** (over £20) MC, V.
New Malden's Burlington Road is lined with Korean eateries, and Jee Cee Neh is the pick of the bunch. It's every inch the Korean canteen, but this canteen has class. The immaculate, tiled interior is filled with pot plants and colourful striped panels; it's a firm favourite with Korean ladies who lunch. As well as table-top barbecues and hearty stews, the extensive menu has plenty of intriguing specials for two, including slow-cooked jeongol casseroles, yuk hwe (raw beef with pear) and bosam (boiled pork with vegetables and garnishes). It also contains lots of photos to pique your interest. We plumped for a pile of lightly steamed mandu dumplings with an inspired tangy soy dip and cabbage kimchi with white onion as a secret ingredient and a searing, dry chilli heat. A main course of kimchi chigae was also a delight: full-flavoured, spicy and loaded with kimchi, leeks and tender slices of pork. Waiting staff were tirelessly attentive and service was zippy, despite the lunchtime crowd. This is one of our favourite Korean restaurants.
Babies and children welcome: high chair. Takeaway service.

★ Su La NEW

79-81 Kingston Road, New Malden, Surrey KT3 3PB (8336 0121). New Malden rail.
Lunch served noon-3pm, **dinner served** 6-11pm Mon-Fri. **Meals served** noon-11pm Sat. **Main courses** £7.50-£11. **Set lunch** £5-£7. **Set dinner** £12.50 per person (minimum 2). **Credit** MC, V.
One of New Malden's more sophisticated dining establishments, Su La has been styled with panache. The main room is fairly typical for a Korean barbecue restaurant – red barbecue tables, potted bamboo and Heath Robinson chrome extractor vents dangling from the roof – but the private banquet rooms are gorgeous. Separated by sliding shoji (wood and paper) screens, these intimate spaces have floor cushions and low wooden tables where you can faithfully recreate the feel of a banquet dinner in a traditional Korean kalbi house. The menu is primarily in Korean, and the English descriptions aren't always revealing; 'bulgogi' appears as 'roasted beef', for instance. Ask if you're not sure. We stopped by for a set lunch. For £5.90 we received a huge mound of sweet-marinated bulgogi beef and rice, a bowl of beancurd soup and a spread of namul and panch'an, including apple and potato in mayonnaise, tingly cabbage kimchi and sesame-seasoned beansprouts. A side order of mandu soup was also expertly prepared, with soft dumplings and plenty of meat shreds, egg and onions in a fresh, clear broth. Speedy service also made eating here a pleasure. Highly recommended.
Babies and children welcome: high chair. Booking essential weekends. Takeaway service.

You-Me

96 Burlington Road, New Malden, Surrey KT3 4NT (8715 1079). New Malden rail.
Meals served noon-10.30pm Mon, Wed-Sun; 6-10.30pm Tue. **Main courses** £4.90-£20. **Set meal** £17.90-£19.90. **Credit** MC, V.
Pleasingly informal, dining at You-Me is like eating at a friend's house. The eclectically decorated dining room seems to morph into a family living room the further back you go. In the corner, a TV cheerfully babbles with Korean soaps and dramas. As soon as you sit down, a metal pot of Chinese tea appears on the table. There's a full Korean menu here, with all the anticipated barbecues, soups and stews, but the moderate prices attract younger customers looking for the comforts of home cooking. There were just a few late lunchtime diners when we visited, so service was lightning fast. A tasty bindaedok (mung bean pancake with pork and vegetables) arrived before we had finished unwrapping the cutlery. Next came a huge bowl of galbitang: a warming broth of beef ribs, egg and spring onions that fills the same niche in Korean society as chicken soup does for Jewish families. The free namul on the side was superb; sprouting soy beans with chilli paste were positively on fire. You won't find many more laid-back Korean venues in London – and the food's good too.
Babies and children welcome: high chairs. Separate room for parties, seats 10. Takeaway service.

Menu

Chilli appears at every opportunity on Korean menus. Other common ingredients include soy sauce (different to both the Chinese and Japanese varieties), sesame oil, sugar, sesame seeds, garlic, ginger and various fermented soy bean pastes. Until the late 1970s eating meat was a luxury in Korea, so the quality of vegetarian dishes is high.

Given the spicy nature and overall flavour of Korean food, drinks such as chilled lager or vodka-like soju/shoju are the best matches. A wonderful non-alcoholic alternative that's always available, although not always listed on the menu, is barley tea (porich'a). Often served free of charge, it has a light dry taste that works perfectly with the food. Korean restaurants don't usually offer desserts (some serve orange or some watermelon with the bill). Spellings on menus vary hugely; we have given the most common.

Bibimbap or **pibimbap**: rice, vegetables and meat with a raw/fried egg dropped on top, often served on a hot stone.
Bindaedok, bindaedoek or **pindaetteok**: a mung bean pancake.
Bokum: a stir-fried dish, usually including chilli.
Bulgogi or **pulgogi**: thin slices of beef marinated in pear sap (or a similar sweet dressing) and barbecued at the table; often eaten rolled in a lettuce leaf with shredded spring onion and fermented bean paste.
Chang, jang or **denjang**: various fermented soy bean pastes.
Chapch'ae or **chap chee**: mixed vegetables and beef cooked with transparent vermicelli or noodles.
Cheon, jeon or **jon**: the literal meaning is 'something flat'; this can range from a pancake containing vegetables, meat or seafood, to thinly sliced vegetables, beancurd and so on, in a light batter.
Cheyuk: pork.
Chigae or **jigae**: a hot stew containing fermented bean paste and chillies.
Gim or **kim**: dried seaweed, toasted and seasoned with salt and sesame oil.
Gu shul pan: a traditional lacquered tray with nine compartments containing individual appetisers.
Hobak chun or **hobak jun**: sliced marrow in a light egg batter.
Japch'ae or **jap chee**: alternative spellings for chapch'ae (qv).
Jjim: fish or meat stewed for a long time in soy sauce, sugar and garlic.
Jeongol: casserole.
Kalbi, galbi or **kalbee**: beef spare ribs, marinated and barbecued.
Kimchi, kim chee or **kimch'i**: pickled vegetables, usually chinese cabbage, white radishes, cucumber or greens, served in a small bowl with a spicy chilli sauce.
Kkaktugi or **kkakttugi**: pickled radish.
Koch'ujang: a hot, red bean paste.
Kook, gook, kuk or **guk**: soup. Koreans have an enormous variety of soups, from consommé-like liquid to meaty broths of noodles, dumplings, meat or fish.
Ko sari na mool or **gosari namul**: cooked bracken stalks dressed with sesame seeds.
Mandu kuk or **man doo kook**: clear soup with steamed meat dumplings.
Namul or **na mool**: vegetable side dishes.
Ojingeo: squid.
P'ajeon or **pa jun**: flour pancake with spring onions and (usually) seafood.
Panch'an: side dishes; they usually include pickled vegetables, but possibly also tofu, fish, seaweed or beans.
Pap, bap, bab or **pahb**: cooked rice.
Pokkeum or **pokkm**: stir-fry; for example, **cheyuk pokkeum** (pork), **ojingeo pokkeum** (squid) **yach'ae pokkeum** (vegetable).
Porich'a: barley tea.
Shinseollo, shinsonro, shinsulro or **sin sollo**: 'royal casserole'; a meat soup with seaweed, seafood, eggs and vegetables, all cooked at the table.
Soju or **shoju**: a strong Korean vodka, often drunk as an aperitif.
Teoppap or **toppap**: 'on top of rice'; for example, **ojingeo teoppap** is squid served on rice.
Toenjang: seasoned (usually with chilli) soy bean paste.
Tolsot bibimbap: tolsot is a sizzling hot stone bowl that makes the bibimbap (qv) a little crunchy on the sides.
Tteokpokki: bars of compressed rice (tteok is a rice cake) fried on a hotplate with veg and sausages, in a chilli sauce.
Twaeji gogi: pork.
T'wigim, twigim or **tuigim**: fish, prawns or vegetables dipped in batter and deep-fried until golden brown.
Yach'ae: vegetables.
Yuk hwe, yukhoe or **yukhwoe**: shredded raw beef, strips of pear and egg yolk, served chilled.
Yukkaejang: spicy beef soup.

Malaysian, Indonesian & Singaporean

Although some restaurants in this chapter have a smattering of Indonesian and Singaporean dishes, most are Malaysian – or more specifically, Chinese-Malaysian. The food of Malaysia itself is far more diverse than anything you'll find in London, and reflects the multiracial country; it can be broadly subdivided into Malay, Chinese-Malaysian and Indian-Malaysian, three distinct styles. Which means that Malaysians really are spoilt for choice. If there's any common thread to 'Malaysian food' at all, it's the emphasis on freshness of local ingredients.

Although Malaysian food is not that well represented in London, you can find the dishes prepared properly if you know where to look. The newly redesigned **Satay House** continues to work wonders, as it has since 1973. For something more upmarket (and more expensive), try **Awana**. New this year is **Kiasu**, winner of Best Cheap Eats in the 2007 Time Out Eating & Drinking Awards, and the closest you'll get to authentic Singaporean hawker food in London. **New Fook Lam Moon**, once an average Chinatown haunt, now offers a short (and excellent) menu of Chinese-Malaysian dishes. During the life of this guide we'll shed a tear for the loss of **Oriental City**, the shopping mall in Colindale, which is due to close in summer 2008; the food court currently offers a number of authentic hawker dishes, including freshly made roti canai – it's the best version of this dish in town.

Central

Soho

New Fook Lam Moon NEW

10 Gerrard Street, W1D 5PW (7734 7615/ www.newfooklammoon.com). Leicester Square tube. **Meals served** noon-11.30pm Mon-Sat; noon-10.30pm Sun. **Main courses** £6.90-£11. **Set meal** £11.50-£18.50 per person (minimum 2). **Credit** AmEx, MC, V.

New Fook Lam Moon looks much like its neighbours in Chinatown: Cantonese barbecued meats, offal and bright orange cuttlefish hang in the window, tables are cramped, and the interior is tidy and serviceable. But choose carefully from the gargantuan menu (or ask the friendly staff for help) and you can experience the best Chinese-Malaysian cooking in town. Butter prawn (on the menu here as 'deep-fried prawn with planta margarine') requires skill to cook and the rendition here took us right back to Kuala Lumpur: firm but juicy king prawns in the shell were topped with a gorgeous, buttery floss. The bak kut teh, another Chinese-Malaysian classic, is worth trying too – pork ribs, belly pork, offal and tofu arrived in a rich blackish-brown broth of herbs and spices that had an appropriately medicinal flavour. Served in the traditional manner, with complimentary steamed rice and pieces of deep-fried dough for dipping, it's a lunchtime meal on its own. Other highlights included a wonderfully authentic turbot curry hotpot. Less adventurous diners may wish to give the otherwise expertly stir-fried sator (petai) beans a miss. An acquired taste, Malaysians call them smelly beans – and for good reason.

Babies and children welcome: high chairs. Booking advisable. Takeaway service. **Map 17 C4.**

South Kensington

Awana

85 Sloane Avenue, SW3 3DX (7584 8880/ www.awana.co.uk). South Kensington tube.
Bar **Open** noon-11pm Mon-Fri; noon-11.30pm Sat; noon-10.30pm Sun.
Restaurant **Lunch served** noon-3pm daily. **Dinner served** 6-11pm Mon-Fri, Sun; 6-11.30pm Sat. **Main courses** £9.50-£25. **Set lunch** £12.50 2 courses, £15 3 courses. **Set dinner** £36 tasting menu.
Both **Credit** AmEx, DC, MC, V.

It's not easy for Malaysian food to find a following in London, overshadowed as it is by its crowd-pleasing cousins from India and China. Smart, handsome, expensive Awana in Brompton Cross makes a valiant attempt to promote the cuisine. Starters such as tender and plump chicken satay elicit love at first bite; peppered soft-shell crab with stir-fried greens and chilli jam (ketam lembut lada hitam) seduces with its fragile textures and intense flavours. Not unlike the wary lover playing it safe, main courses lose the momentum: stir-fried aubergine with sambal chilli (sambal jerong) was bland, its sauce diluted to insipidness. A speciality of braised rib of beef with coconut milk (rendang daging awana) was unobjectionable yet unremarkable, its house-blended spices providing little distinction. Malaysian flatbread (roti canai) was adequately fluffy and chewy, but let down by anaemic accompaniments including a drab dal and a subdued chilli dip. For the fussy Sloane Rangers that frequent the place, Awana is a polite, palatable introduction to Malaysian cooking. If you're more au fait with this cuisine, however, you may be left feeling mildly frustrated.

Babies and children welcome: high chairs. Booking advisable Fri, Sat. Takeaway service. **Map 14 E10.**

West

Bayswater

★ ★ Kiasu NEW

2007 WINNER BEST CHEAP EATS

48 Queensway, W2 3RY (7727 8810). Bayswater or Queensway tube. **Meals served** noon-11pm daily. **Main courses** £4.90-£7.50. **Set meal** (noon-3pm) £8.90 2 courses. **Credit** (minimum £10) MC, V.

'Kiasu' is a Hokkien Chinese word that roughly means 'fear of being second best'. But it's not just for literary convenience that the restaurant won the Best Cheap Eats category in the 2007 Time Out Eating & Drinking Awards. What's more, the reasonable prices are merely a bonus to the exceptional Peranakan cooking. If you ignore the few concessions to Thai and Vietnamese cuisine (as you should when ordering), the menu could be straight out of a Singaporean food court – as could the astonishingly authentic dishes. Hainanese chicken rice and laksa are two of Singapore's most obsessively loved dishes. At Kiasu, both were as good as any we've ever tried. The former consisted of a single piece of boneless white chicken bathed in a sublime, rich stock and correctly served with three extra dips of ginger, chilli and soy. The laksa was a giant bowl of noodles and prawns in a rich, thick chilli and coconut soup. Just as perfect were starters of otak otak (fish cake) and roti pratha (the Singaporean variant of roti canai). A fairly informal café atmosphere prevails, but proper wooden furniture and a snazzy blue decor mean Kiasu is, thankfully, a more civilised venue than the bare-bones food courts from which it borrows. So stop and savour.

Babies and children welcome: high chairs. Booking advisable dinner. Separate room for parties, seats 60. Takeaway service. **Map 7 C6.**

Notting Hill

★ Nyonya

2A Kensington Park Road, W11 3BU (7243 1800/www.nyonya.co.uk). Notting Hill Gate tube. **Lunch served** 11.30am-2.45pm, **dinner served** 6-10.30pm Mon-Fri. **Meals served** 11.30am-10.30pm Sat, Sun. **Main courses** £5.50-£8.50. **Set lunch** (Mon-Fri) £8 2 courses. **Credit** AmEx, DC, MC, V.

We can't help comparing this tiny family-run restaurant to the culinary juggernaut Wagamama. There's a minimalist interior; diners share communal tables; a shortish menu offers no appetisers, just 'side dishes'; and everything leaves the kitchen at a rapid pace. The food, however, is very different. Nyonya means 'lady', but also refers to a unique cuisine that originated with Straits-born Peranakan families; it marries Chinese and Malaysian cooking. Traditionally the food is spicy with robust flavours, but at Nyonya we found some of the dishes had been toned down. Laksa, a speciality of the Peranakan people, had nice, firm ramen noodles but was dominated by coconut and lacked chilli heat. Crisp, deep-fried 'blachan' chicken needed a little more of the fearsome shrimp paste. On the plus side, a chef's special of mixed vegetable achar (crisp cucumber, carrot, mooli and cauliflower dressed in peanut sauce) emphasised the kitchen's commitment to fresh ingredients. The

tiny multicoloured, coconut-rich steamed cakes (kueh) were also enjoyable. Fast, home-style cooking at a fair price.
Babies and children welcome: high chairs. Booking advisable. Separate room for parties, seats 40. Takeaway service. **Map 7 A7**.

Paddington

★ Satay House (100)

13 Sale Place, W2 1PX (7723 6763/www.satay-house.co.uk). Edgware Road tube/Paddington tube/rail. **Lunch served** noon-3pm, **dinner served** 6-11pm daily. **Main courses** £5-£18.50. **Set meal** £13.50, £18, £25 per person (minimum 2). **Credit** AmEx, MC, V.

In 2006 this tiny 34-year-old veteran received a sleek makeover from the designers of Wagamama and Gourmet Burger Kitchen. Prices may have increased as a result, but Satay House remains popular with Malaysians, including the royal family, who appear to regard it as a home from home. The new design, led by stencil cuts of the country's national flower (the hibiscus), supports rather than detracts from the food – which remains exemplary. The satay, served in the traditional way with cucumber, onion, rice cubes and a fantastic peanut sauce, continues to be a treat. The nasi lemak (coconut rice), with its fiery prawn sambal and crisp accompaniments (roasted peanuts, deep-fried anchovies), also remains the best in town. We loved the golden squares of roti telur (Malaysian bread with egg and onion) and adored the richly flavoured rendang daging, where large cubes of beef had seemingly melted into the accompanying spices. Bursting at the seams, we finished with a comforting glass of es kacang: a pleasingly sweet and refreshing mix of shaved ice, rose syrup, red beans, evaporated milk and jelly. Tucked down a residential side street, this is one of London's culinary wonders.
Babies and children welcome: high chairs. Booking advisable Fri, Sat. Separate room for parties, seats 35. Takeaway service. Vegetarian menu. **Map 8 E5**.

Westbourne Grove

C&R Restaurant

52 Westbourne Grove, W2 5SH (7221 7979). Bayswater or Queensway tube. **Meals served** noon-11pm daily. **Main courses** £6-£15. **Set meal** (vegetarian) £14.50, (meat) £17 per person (minimum 2). **Credit** MC, V.

C&R Café, the Soho sister to this plainly decorated restaurant, has a high reputation among Malaysian

RESTAURANTS

Kiasu

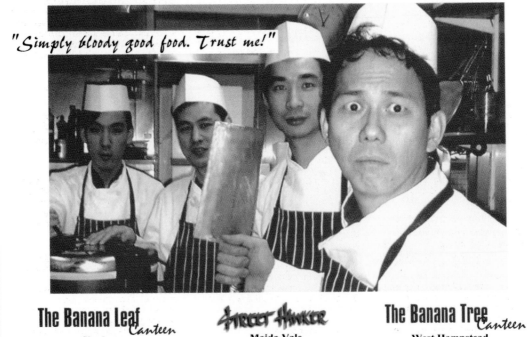

students for providing simple nourishment, so we were looking forward to our meal here. Unfortunately, things got off to an uncomfortable start. Sitting on the long banquette that stretches the length of the dining room, we found ourselves sandwiched between two other tables only a few centimetres away. Any sense of privacy was gone. Dodging the ubiquitous Chinese and Thai favourites that make up the bulk of the menu, we sought salvation in the Malaysian street dishes. Nasi lemak, regarded by many as the unofficial national dish of Malaysia, was generously portioned with plenty of tiny extras (pickled veg, roast peanuts, deep-fried anchovies, mild chicken curry, sambal), but the key serving of coconut rice was dry and lukewarm. This set the tone for the rest of our meal: char kway teow (flat rice noodles with egg, prawn, fish cake and beansprouts) was overcooked; pak choi with salted fish arrived limp; and a signature dish, C&R chilli king prawn, was overwhelmed by the taste of lemongrass. Disappointing.

Babies and children welcome: high chairs. Takeaway service. **Map 7 B6.**
For branch (C&R Café) see index.

North West

Swiss Cottage

Singapore Garden

83A Fairfax Road, NW6 4DY (7624 8233/ www.singaporegarden.co.uk). Swiss Cottage tube. **Lunch served** noon-3pm Mon-Sat; noon-4pm Sun. **Dinner served** 6-10pm Mon-Thur, Sun; 6-11pm Fri, Sat. **Main courses** £6-£29. **Set meal** £23.50-£38.50 per person (minimum 2). **Minimum charge** £15 per person. **Credit** AmEx, MC, V.

There's no disputing the popularity of this 23-year-old veteran. Early on a Saturday night it was full, while other restaurants nearby lay empty. Glammed up under new ownership in 2006, Singapore Garden is now a classy, bright, modern place where waitresses beautifully attired in patterned cheongsams and bold batik prints speedily serve mainly Anglo-Chinese favourites such as prawn toast and crispy shredded beef to equally well-dressed locals. Even so, there are still some Singaporean delights to try, particularly if you're willing to overlook a few culinary shortcuts on the part of the kitchen. Hainanese chicken rice, for example, is traditionally accompanied by the broth the chicken was poached in. Here, the stock was similar to that of wun tun soup. A crisp circle of roti canai was paired with laksa sauce rather than the traditional curry. More impressive was the hawker-style ho jien; golden brown and crisp at the edges, the thin omelette was generously studded with tiny oysters. The best dish, however, was rojak – the mere sight of the fresh fruit, cucumber and beansprouts dressed in a chunky peanut sauce was enough to encourage two neighbouring diners to order it.

Babies and children admitted. Booking advisable. Takeaway service; delivery service (within 1-mile radius). **Map 28 A4.**

Menu

Here are some common terms and dishes. Spellings can vary.

Acar: assorted pickled vegetables such as carrots, beans and onions, which are often spiced with turmeric and pepper.
Assam: tamarind.
Ayam: chicken.
Bergedel: a spiced potato cake.
Blachan, belacan or **blacan**: dried fermented shrimp paste; it adds a piquant fishy taste to dishes.
Char kway teow or **char kwai teow**: a stir-fry of rice noodles with meat and/or seafood with dark soy sauce and beansprouts. A Hakka Chinese-derived speciality of Singapore.
Chilli crab: fresh crab, stir-fried in a sweet, mild chilli sauce.
Daging: meat.
Ebi: shrimps.
Gado gado: a salad of blanched vegetables with a peanut-based sauce on top.
Galangal: also called yellow ginger, Laos root or blue ginger, this spice gives a distinctive flavour to many South-east Asian dishes.
Goreng: wok-fried.
Hainanese chicken rice: poached chicken served with rice cooked in chicken stock, a bowl of light chicken broth and a chilli-ginger dipping sauce.
Ho jien: oyster omelette, flavoured with garlic and chilli.
Ikan: fish.
Ikan bilis or **ikan teri**: tiny whitebait-like fish, often fried and made into a dry sambal (qv) with peanuts.
Kambing: actually goat, but in practice lamb is the usual substitute.
Kangkong or **kangkung**: water convolvulus, often called water spinach or swamp cabbage – an aquatic plant often steamed and used in salads with a spicy sauce.
Kecap manis: sweet dark soy sauce.
Kelapa: coconut.
Kemiri: waxy-textured candlenuts, used to enrich Indonesian and Malaysian curry pastes.
Keropok or **kerupuk**: prawn crackers.
Laksa: a noodle dish with either coconut milk or (as with penang laksa) tamarind as the stock base; it's now popular in many South-east Asian cities.
Lemang: sticky Indonesian rice that is cooked in bamboo segments.
Lengkuas or **lenkuas**: Malaysian name for galangal (qv).
Lumpia: deep-fried spring rolls filled with meat or vegetables.
Masak lemak: anything cooked in a rich, red spice paste with coconut milk.
Mee: noodles.
Mee goreng: fried egg noodles with meat, prawns and vegetables.
Mee hoon: rice vermicelli noodles.
Murtabak: an Indian-Malaysian pancake fried on a griddle and served with a savoury filling.
Nasi ayam: rice cooked in chicken broth, served with roast or steamed chicken and a light soup.
Nasi goreng: fried rice with shrimp paste, garlic, onions, chillies and soy sauce.
Nasi lemak: coconut rice on a plate with a selection of curries and fish dishes topped with ikan bilis (qv).
Nonya or **Nyonya**: the name referring to both the women and the dishes of the Straits Chinese community. *See below* Peranakan.
Otak otak: a Nonya (qv) speciality made from eggs, fish and coconut milk.
Pandan leaves: a variety of the screwpine plant; used to add colour and fragrance to both savoury and sweet dishes.
Panggang: grilled or barbecued.
Peranakan: refers to the descendants of Chinese settlers who first came to Malacca (now Melaka), a seaport on the Malaysian west coast, in the 17th century. It is generally applied to those born of Sino-Malay extraction who adopted Malay customs, costume and cuisine, the community being known as 'Straits Chinese'. The cuisine is also known as Nonya (qv).
Petai: a pungent, flat green bean used in Malaysian cooking.
Poh pia or **popiah**: spring rolls. Nonya or Penang popiah are not deep-fried and consist of egg or rice paper wrappers filled with a vegetable and prawn medley.
Rempah: generic term for the fresh curry pastes used in Malaysian cookery.
Rendang: meat cooked in coconut milk, a 'dry' curry.
Rojak: raw fruit and vegetables in a sweet spicy sauce.
Roti canai: a South Indian/Malaysian breakfast dish of fried unleavened bread served with a dip of either chicken curry or dal.
Sambal: there are several types of sambal, often made of fiery chilli sauce, onions and coconut oil; it can be served as a side dish or used as a relish. The suffix 'sambal' means 'cooked with chilli'.
Satay: there are two types – terkan (minced and moulded to the skewer) and chochok ('shish', more common in London). Beef or chicken are the traditional choices, though prawn is now often available too. Satay is served with a rich spicy sauce made from onions, lemongrass, galangal (qv), and chillies in tamarind sauce; it is sweetened and thickened with ground peanuts.
Sayur: vegetables.
Soto ayam: a classic spicy chicken soup, often with noodles.
Sotong: squid.
Tauhu goreng: deep-fried beancurd topped with beansprouts tossed in a spicy peanut sauce, served cold.
Udang: prawns.

DESSERTS

Ais or **es**: ice; a prefix for the multitude of desserts made with combinations of fruit salad, agar jelly cubes, palm syrup, condensed milk and crushed ice.
Ais (or **es**) **kacang**: shaved ice and syrup mixed with jellies, red beans and sweetcorn.
Bubur pulut hitam: black glutinous rice served in coconut milk and palm sugar.
Cendol or **chendol**: mung bean flour pasta, coloured and perfumed with essence of pandan leaf (qv) and served in a chilled coconut milk and palm sugar syrup.
Gula melaka: palm sugar, an important ingredient with a distinctive, caramel flavour added to a sago and coconut-milk pudding of the same name.
Kueh or **kuih**: literally, 'cakes', but used as a general term for many desserts.
Pisang goreng: banana fritters.

Middle Eastern

As a long-standing beacon for economic migrants, political refugees, students and shoppers from all over the Middle East, London has been blessed with a far greater variety of Middle Eastern restaurants than you'd find anywhere in the Arabic-speaking world itself. Here you'll discover dishes from the kitchens of Aleppo, Cairo, Baghdad, Damascus and Beirut. According to respected food writer and Middle Eastern expert Claudia Roden, the origin of all these cuisines lies in the Zahle Valley in central Lebanon, but over the centuries every valley, village, town and city, let alone nation, has developed its own cooking traditions and specialities. All share a predilection for the small 'starter' dishes known as meze, and for grilled meat, but the variations are enticing. Dine one night at **Mesopotamia** (Iraqi), another at **Ali Baba** (Egyptian), another at **Abu Zaad** (Syrian), and yet another at **Noura** (Lebanese) to experience some of the differences for yourself.

Then there's the Persian kitchen, which is something altogether apart, involving subtle marinades in which the meat is soaked before grilling, mounds of fluffy, saffron-stained long-grain rice, and vast discs of taftun (a chapati-like bread). As with much else concerning the Middle East, there's more to the cuisine than first meets the eye – especially in London.

Central

Belgravia

Noura

16 Hobart Place, SW1W 0HH (7235 9444/ www.noura.co.uk). Hyde Park Corner tube/ Victoria tube/rail. **Meals served** 11.30am-11.30pm daily. **Main courses** £10-£23. **Set lunch** (noon-6pm) £16.50 2 courses incl coffee. **Set meal** £29-£38 per person (minimum 2) 3 courses. **Credit** AmEx, DC, MC, V. Lebanese

Sweeping, rather swanky decor in cream and brown hues lends an air of modernity and class to this spacious branch of Noura: the first of a well-respected chain that brought a new sense of style to London's Lebanese dining. Appealing to a monied international clientele, the place engenders a real sense of occasion. This was tempered on our recent visit by a few let-downs with the food. First off, we weren't given the plate of salad vegetables that comes along with olives at the beginning of a high-end Lebanese meal (other diners had them). Then there were a couple of duff dishes: a vinegary tabouleh and a rather sad spinach fatayer that managed to be both soggy and burnt. Otherwise, we enjoyed moujadarra (an earthy mix of onions and lentils, topped with caramelised onions), thick and luscious houmous, moussaka (the Lebanese kind, with aubergine, tomato and onions only) and sfeeha (minced lamb in pastry, this time well flavoured, with perfect pastry). A bottle of Ksara gris de gris made a refined accompaniment. Service was black-suited and formal, but not unhelpful.

Babies and children welcome: high chairs. Booking advisable; essential dinner. Disabled: toilet. Takeaway service; delivery service (over £20 within 2-mile radius). **Map 15 H9.**

For branches (Noura Central, Volt Lounge) see index.

BEST MIDDLE EASTERN

Street life

Superior fast food in a casual atmosphere at **Abu Zaad** (*see p228*), **Ali Baba** (*see right*), **Fresco** (*see p227*), **Patogh** (*see right*) and **Ranoush Juice** (*see right*).

For a real flavour of Iran

For authenticity in spades – in both food and decor – try **Mahdi** (*see p227*), **Alounak** (*see p228*) or **Mohsen** (*see p228*).

For more than food

For fancy design, a party atmosphere and belly dancing, visit **Levant** (*see p225*) or **Maroush** (*see right*).

Edgware Road

★ Maroush

21 Edgware Road, W2 2JE (7723 0773/ www.maroush.com). Marble Arch tube. **Meals served** noon-2am daily. **Main courses** £14-£22. **Set meal** £21-£35 per person (minimum 2). **Cover** (after 7pm) £3. **Minimum** (after 8.30pm Fri, Sat) £41 set meal incl £6 cover. **Credit** AmEx, DC, MC, V. Lebanese

The Maroush empire's flagship branch pulls out all the stops. Over 50 meze dishes, plus main courses, are offered in the dark-red basement dining area; there's a café upstairs that's good for lunch; and entertainment now takes place nightly. Maroush is a traditional but upmarket spot. It doesn't shy away from hard-line dishes such as beid ghanem (lambs' testicles) cooked in a light lemony sauce, or hlaywat (sweetbreads, fried or chargrilled). Presentation is a highlight: a silky smooth houmous arrived swirled into its bowl, dotted with red peppers; an indentation is left in the middle, which is filled with olive oil. Service is male, besuited and formal. We could find little fault with the food on a recent visit, also enjoying meltingly tender chicken livers in lemon sauce, falafels that were crisp and grease-free on the outside, soft within, a zesty tabouleh and a butter-soft chicken shish. At 9.30pm it's on with the singers (Arabic songs and western standards) and belly dancers (high-quality ones). The atmosphere heats up and a good time is had by all. Note there's a minimum £41 spend on Friday and Saturday – so it's not a cheap night out.

Babies and children admitted (lunch). Booking essential after 10pm Fri, Sat. Dress: smart casual. Entertainment: musicians and singer 9.30pm-2am nightly; belly dancers (phone for details). Separate room for parties, seats 100. Takeaway service. **Map 8 F6.**

For branches (Beirut Express, Maroush) see index.

★ Patogh (100)

8 Crawford Place, W1H 5NE (7262 4015). Edgware Road tube. **Meals served** 12.30-11pm daily. **Main courses** £6-£12. **Unlicensed. Corkage** no charge. **No credit cards.** Iranian

The Iranian equivalent of a chip shop – but for deep-fried fish and chipped potatoes substitute grilled meat and rice. But this is fast food of the highest order, with immaculately fresh, leafy salads, thick own-made aubergine and yoghurt dips (with chopped cucumber or shallots), and huge wheels of flatbread, delivered too-hot-to-touch from the oven. The handful of lamb and chicken kebabs that make up the menu (supplemented, in season, by sea bream and sea bass) are prepared over a smoky charcoal grill in an open kitchen that takes up half the tiny ground-floor room. The meat, which is marinated for several hours before cooking, is sensational, particularly the lamb fillet and the boneless chicken, yellowed with saffron. No alcohol is served, but you can bring your own. Competition is fierce for Patogh's half dozen or so cramped tables, and you may well have to resign yourself to queuing outside or settling for a takeaway.

Book weekends. Takeaway service. **Map 8 E5.**

★ Ranoush Juice (100)

43 Edgware Road, W2 2JR (7723 5929/ www.maroush.com). Marble Arch tube. **Meals served** 8am-3am daily. **Main courses** £3-£10. **No credit cards.** Lebanese

A café-style outpost of the successful Maroush chain, Ranoush Juice does a roaring trade in Lebanese meze, shawarma sandwiches, and – of course – juices, to eat in or take away. Furnishings are of black marble and wood. There are only a few tables, plus a line of stools at the mirrored wall counters. Meze dishes (including the likes of sujuk sausages and chicken livers, as well as vegetarian snacks) are displayed behind a glass counter. Juices are prepared at one end; the other is given over to frenetic shawarma preparation. Tomatoes and gherkins are diced, lamb or chicken is sliced; everything is placed on waiting discs of thin shami bread, garlic sauce is added, the bread is rolled up and the whole thing is wrapped in paper. Quality is high. Our shawarma, with lashings of sloppy garlicky sauce that oozed out with every bite, was satisfying, especially when matched with a dense, garlic-laden houmous. Juices are good too; there's a wide range, but other places (like Fresco, *see p227*) serve them in bigger glasses. A great, cash-only pit-stop, but not somewhere to linger.

Babies and children admitted. Takeaway service. **Map 8 F6.**

For branches see index.

Marylebone

★ Ali Baba

32 Ivor Place, NW1 6DA (7723 7474/5805). Baker Street tube/Marylebone tube/rail. **Meals served** noon-midnight daily. **Main courses** £6-£8. **Unlicensed. Corkage** no charge. **No credit cards.** Egyptian

London's low-key monument to the Egyptian culinary repertoire, Ali Baba serves a gamut of dishes, from street-food staples such as fuul and

falafel to adopted favourites such as macarona (as Egyptians call macaroni in béchamel sauce) and escalope panée, via 'only in Egypt' recipes like molokhia (a stew made with meat and a green leaf that lends a distinctive slithery texture). Customers are, in the main, an appreciative audience of nostalgists (Egyptians and others). They know this food's never going to be fashionable, and often it's not even that good. On a recent visit, our molokhia was somewhat watery and not well seasoned. But we hit the jackpot with another trad choice: a comforting om ali, a piping-hot bread and butter pudding with sugar, nutmeg, raisins and coconut; we loved its sweet crispy crust. Lunchtimes can be quiet here, but things often get lively in the evenings. The interior recently had a makeover: gone is the old dark decor; walls are now cream, lights are halogen. Only the kitsch paintings of medieval Cairo remain, along with the pleasant people who run the place.
Babies and children welcome: high chairs. Booking advisable. Takeaway service; delivery service. **Map 2 F4.**

★ Fairuz

3 Blandford Street, W1U 3DA (7486 8108/ 8182/www.fairuz.uk.com). Baker Street or Bond Street tube. **Meals served** noon-11.30pm Mon-Sat; noon-11pm Sun. **Main courses** £10.95-£18.95. **Set meze** £18.95. **Set meal** £26.95 3 courses. **Cover** £1.50. **Credit** AmEx, MC, V. Lebanese

Fairuz distinguishes itself from London's other top-tier Lebanese restaurants with a very different vibe. Instead of the usual smart-international look, this little place resembles a generic Med-taverna, with rough-plastered white walls, wicker chairs and fold-back frontage for fine weather. It's a relaxed, pleasant spot, although tables are packed quite tightly and it can get loud. Food is consistently excellent. Take falafel: someone had worked wonders, transforming the workaday chickpea ball into a crispy shell with a soft, almost fluffy filling. It's the best we've tasted for a while. Fuul moukala was a little unusual, but satisfying; the green broad beans were more oniony and spicy than usual. Other hits included a subtly spiced batata hara; and shankleesh or 'aged cheese', as the menu put it. Shankleesh is sometimes served as a salad with crumblings of the powerful cheese, but in this version the cheese was crumbled wholesale on to a plate, and dressed with black pepper, lashings of olive oil and a generous topping of walnuts – wonderful. Jawaneh (chicken wings), with a garlicky mayonnaise, packed in even more flavour. A selection of complimentary pastries with our Turkish coffee brought a fine meal to a fine end.
Babies and children welcome: high chairs. Booking essential dinner. Separate room for parties, seats 25. Takeaway service; delivery service (within 3-mile radius). **Map 9 G5.**

Levant

Jason Court, 76 Wigmore Street, W1U 2SJ (7224 1111/www.levant.co.uk). Bond Street tube. *Bar* **Open** noon-12.30am Mon-Wed, Sun; noon-2.30am Thur-Sat.
Restaurant **Meals served** noon-11.30pm daily. **Main courses** (Mon, Tue, Sun) £12.50-£26. **Set lunch** (noon-5.30pm Mon-Fri) £8-£15 2 courses. **Set dinner** (Wed-Sat) £35.50-£50 per person (minimum 2) 3 courses; £60 per person (minimum 8) kharuf feast.
Both **Credit** AmEx, DC, JCB, MC, V. Lebanese

Taken in the right spirit and company, a night at Levant could be hugely enjoyable. Diners head down a candlelit, rose petal-strewn staircase, and pull open a heavy wooden door to reveal an oriental wonderland. There's an attractive bar area with low tables and, beyond, the restaurant with brass-topped tables, beaded lamps and walls with tadelakt (lime plaster)-effect walls. You can bet your bottom lira that a belly dancer will appear during the evening. Unfortunately, the menu is equally staged. Diners are presented with prix-fixe options only. Starting at £29 for three meze plus a main, and peaking with the 'kharuf feast' of a whole roasted lamb (minimum of eight people) at £60 a head, these aren't cheap. So it's especially unwelcome when staff try to bump you up to a higher priced meal by explaining that meze are 'small and not very filling'. Quality is variable. Our goat's cheese roundels studded with sesame seeds were lovely; fried cauliflower had a lemony zest; but the pastry parcels, sambousek and fatayer were doughy. Mains attempt to make up for in volume what they lack in finesse. 'Are you having a fantastic Lebanese experience?' asked our waiter. 'Keep enjoying it,' he said, without really listening to our answer.
Booking advisable. Entertainment: belly dancer 8.30pm, 11.30pm nightly. Separate area for parties, seats 12-14. **Map 9 G6.**
For branch (Levantine) see index.

Mayfair

★ Al Hamra

31-33 Shepherd Market, W1J 7PT (7493 1954/ www.alhamrarestaurant.co.uk). Green Park or Hyde Park Corner tube. **Meals served** noon-11.30pm daily. **Main courses** £14-£22.50. **Cover** £2.50. **Minimum** £20. **Credit** AmEx, DC, JCB, MC, V. Lebanese

Al Hamra is to Lebanese restaurants what Rules is to British ones: iconic, stuffy and especially beloved of fat men in straining suits and women who've overdressed for the occasion. It's a strangely claustrophobic place; the low ceiling, strip-like windows and tables set out banquet-fashion give it the appearance of a dining room on board ship. The restaurant is packed out every night – and despite the air of formality, everybody seems to be having a bloody good (and boozy) time. Food, although possibly secondary to the Al Hamra experience, is nonetheless tip-top, comprising a bewildering array of hot and cold meze and a handful of French classics. It's hard to go wrong, although if we were to venture any criticism it would be that a few dishes lack bite and delicacy. Order sparingly, because even the meze are incredibly rich and filling, and make sure you sample the lamb; the meat is fabulous. There is a £20 minimum spend per head (drinks not included), but given the upper-end pricing, even grazing diners will have no trouble breaching it.
Babies and children welcome: high chairs. Book dinner. Tables outdoors (24, terrace). Takeaway service; delivery service. **Map 9 H8.**

Al Sultan

51-52 Hertford Street, W1J 7ST (7408 1155/ 1166/www.alsultan.co.uk). Green Park or Hyde Park Corner tube. **Meals served** noon-midnight daily. **Main courses** £12-£14. **Minimum** £20. **Cover** £2. **Credit** AmEx, DC, MC, V. Lebanese

In recent years Al Sultan has shrugged off a reputation for chilliness to become a comfortable – though still traditional and pastel-shaded – place to dine. Heavily starched tablecloths, suedette-covered chairs and sparkling glassware are still very much the order of the day, but we found efficient, relaxed and friendly staff on a recent visit, engendering a relaxed conviviality among diners – the perfect mode for enjoying some top-class Lebanese food. We liked everything we tried. Fatayer had lovely soft pastry and fresh-tasting, lemony spinach. Classic fuul, mashed up in its pool of olive oil, was mellow and filling (add a swirl of smooth, smoky houmous for a denser, different flavour). Chicken livers (sawda djaj) were soft and zesty (thanks to just the right balance of lemon and pomegranate juice in their thin sauce), and halloumi cheese was grilled to perfection. Green dishes, like tabouleh (tangy, tasty and meticulously chopped into tiny pieces) and a fresh fuul moukala, complemented other dishes beautifully. We finished our meal with Turkish coffee, served with a selection of complimentary, fresh Arabic pastries.
Babies and children welcome: high chairs. Book dinner. Tables outdoors (4, pavement). Takeaway service; delivery service (over £35 within 4-mile radius). Vegetarian menu. **Map 9 H8.**

Piccadilly

Fakhreldine

85 Piccadilly, W1J 7NB (7493 3424/www. fakhreldine.co.uk). Green Park tube. **Meals served** noon-midnight Mon-Sat; noon-11pm Sun. **Main courses** £13-£23. **Set lunch** £17 2 courses, £22 3 courses. **Credit** AmEx, DC, JCB, MC, V. Lebanese

Alounak. See p228.

RESTAURANTS

The Dervish
Café / Bistro

Alounak
Restaurant
Alounak Restaurant for a real taste of Persian cooking served by charming staff in Persian ambience
10 Russell Gardens, London W14 8EZ
Telephone: 020 7603 1130

restaurant
fairuz
finest lebanese cuisine

özer

GABY'S
DELI

ADULIS
ERITREAN RESTAURANT AND BAR
Little Eritrea
TRADITIONAL ERITREAN DISHES
ADULIS
RESTAURANT
44-46 Brixton Road
London
SW9 6BT
020 7587 0055
info@adulis.co.uk
www.adulis.co.uk
Nearest Tube: Oval
Open 7 days a week
Mon-Thu 5pm-12am
Fri-Sat 1pm-2am
Sun 1pm-1am

Mangal 1 OCAKBASI RESTAURANT
• STARTERS RANGE FROM £1.50-£5.00 •
• KEBABS START FROM £6.50-£9.00 •
10 Arcola Street • London • E8 2DJ
(off Stoke Newington Road)
Tel: 020 7275 8981 • www.mangal1.com

Maison Touaregue
Moroccan & Lebanese Restaurant

The modern face of Lebanese, this is a head-turning, good-looker of a restaurant that is part hip bar/lounge, part smart eaterie. It also boasts some of the best views of any London restaurant – whatever the cuisine – thanks to windows overlooking Green Park. However, you take your chances with the food. Our meze ranged from poor to inspired: the former represented by houmous (which at £5.50 is perhaps the most expensive of its kind in London) that had a slurryish, porridge-like quality; the latter by an exquisite twist on kibbeh that replaced the traditional minced lamb with a filling of pumpkin, walnuts and pine nuts. Main courses look terrific, but in a lamb dish the meat had been out of the oven far too long and was consequently dry and had to be wrestled off the bone. Worse, an aubergine mash that accompanied three tiles of deep-fried sea bream was so thoroughly drenched in pomegranate juice that it was inedible. 'Did you enjoy the meal?' asked our waitress confronted with two abandoned, near-untouched plates. 'No,' we answered. She smiled and left us with our very expensive bill.
Babies and children welcome: high chairs. Booking advisable. Takeaway service; delivery service (within 4-mile radius). **Map 9 H8.**

West

Bayswater

★ Al Waha

75 Westbourne Grove, W2 4UL (7229 0806/ www.waha-uk.com). Bayswater or Queensway tube. **Meals served** noon-midnight daily. **Main courses** £9.50-£18.50. **Set lunch** £12.50 2 courses. **Set dinner** £21 per person (minimum 2) 3 courses, £25 per person (minimum 2) 4 courses. **Cover** £1.50. **Minimum** £12.50 (dinner Fri, Sat). **Credit** MC, V. Lebanese
There are other Lebanese restaurants in London that are more glamorous, many that attract a more ritzy and high-powered crowd, and a handful with more enticing menus. But when it comes down to consistent culinary excellence, Al Waha has few serious challengers. A refit some 18 months ago smartened up the paintwork and reorganised the furniture to maximise the limited space; while it's neat and pleasant, nothing really hints at the superlative quality of the food. Meze choices run to 50 or more: over the year we've probably sampled more than half, and have yet to be disappointed. Creamy houmous was spiced up with diamonds of crisp red pepper; labneh included half slices of cucumber and was sprinkled with diced mint; falafel took the form of crisp mini doughnuts, studded with sesame seeds and delivered with a small pot of tahina for dipping. Best of all was the skinkleesh, a salad of finely chopped tomato, onion and parsley, mixed with sharp and tangy crumbled cheese and doused with vinaigrette. Even the mains, a let-down in most Lebanese restaurants, were excellent here. Leave room for the baklava too, freshly made in-house each morning – one kind, in particular, a triangular pastry filled with cream, is bite-sized bliss – and enough on its own to guarantee a return visit.
Babies and children welcome (until 7pm): high chairs. Booking advisable; essential dinner. Tables outdoors (4, patio). Takeaway service; delivery service (over £20 within 3-mile radius).
Map 7 B6.

Beity

92 Queensway, W2 3RR (7221 8782/www.beity.co.uk). Bayswater tube. **Meals served** 9am-1.30am Mon-Sat; 9am-midnight Sun. **Main courses** £9.75-£15.75. **Set lunch** £12.75 2 courses. **Set dinner** £16.50-£23.50 3 courses. **Credit** MC, V. Lebanese
Beity hovers midway between a café and restaurant, aiming squarely at the middle of the market. A few tables have been placed near the glass takeaway counter at the front; at the back, the space opens into a square restaurant (with waitress service), where a roster of Lebanese meze and main courses is served in slightly antiseptic surroundings. Decor is standard for this kind of place: black marble tables, brown marble floor, orangey wood. Our meze dishes varied from excellent (a gorgeously lumpy-yet-smooth moutabal, with a smoky trace of the charcoal grill), through supremely ordinary (kallaj: a version of grilled halloumi in pitta bread that had the charisma of a slightly warm cheese sandwich), to below-par (tabouleh that was too heavy on the parsley and coarsely chopped). We were impressed with the basturma; the Beity version wasn't sliced as thinly as you'd find in more refined places, but the smoked beef and its herb crust were a deep beetroot colour and it was wonderfully chewy and salty. Juices and sandwiches are also available.
Babies and children welcome: high chairs. Restaurant available for hire. Tables outdoors (5, pavement). Takeaway service; delivery service (over £20 within 2-mile radius). **Map 7 C6.**

★ Fresco

25 Westbourne Grove, W2 4UA (7221 2355/ www.frescojuices.co.uk). Bayswater or Royal Oak tube. **Meals served** 8am-11pm daily. **Main courses** £5.95-£7.95. **Set meze** £11.95. **Credit** MC, V. Lebanese
A modest little café and juice bar, Fresco does a roaring lunchtime trade in takeaways. Between the hours of 12 and two, it's almost impossible to get in the door. The draw is a long glass counter filled with heaped bowls of enticing-looking Lebanese meze such as mashi (stuffed vine leaves), tabouleh, falafel and dozens of salads. Everything can be served in a pitta sandwich or a plastic container to go, or on a plate to eat in. It's almost all vegetarian, except for some chicken kebabs and escalopes, and an occasional lamb-based hot dish of the day. For such a basic operation, the food is exceptional – the thick creamy houmous and smoky moutabal (puréed chargrilled aubergine) set the standards as far as these dishes go, and are as good as we've ever had. The juices are also terrific; not just fruit, but also greens such as parsley and broccoli, and even beets. Choose your ingredients and they're blended to order (£2.50-£2.95 for a tall, sundae-style glass). A set lunch with juice is a bargain at under a fiver. The wonder is that there isn't a Fresco on every street in town.
Babies and children welcome: high chairs. Bookings not accepted. Takeaway service; delivery service (within 3-mile radius). Vegetarian menu.
Map 7 B6.
For branches see index.

Hafez

5 Hereford Road, W2 4AB (7221 3167/7229 9398/www.hafez.com). Bayswater tube/328 bus. **Meals served** noon-midnight daily. **Main courses** £6-£14.50. **No credit cards.** Iranian
Hafez displays few of the flashy embellishments that characterise the neighbourhood's more self-consciously Persian restaurants. Its white and bare brick walls forgo elaborate tapestries in favour of calligraphic Farsi prints, its handful of wooden tables are dotted around the small space with workmanlike regularity, and ornately tiled clay ovens are notable by their absence. All of which might hint at an authenticity refusing to bow to orientalist stereotypes, were it not for the fact that our meals at Hafez have been so hit and miss over the past few years. Bread comes hot from the oven to accompany starters that almost always do the business – masto khiar, for example, a cucumber, mint and yoghurt dip, or aash, a bitter soup thick with herbs and mung beans – but mains are less reliable. The kebab-e makhsous (one skewer of filleted lamb and one of minced) was tender, but surprisingly diminutive for £13.50, and we've found the jujeh kebab (marinated chunks of chicken) unpleasantly dry in the past. Various stews are also delivered in less than gut-busting portions, including a decent khoresht-e bademjan (lamb with tomatoes and aubergines) and a disappointingly meagre ghorm-e sabzi (lamb with greens, dried lemons and kidney beans).
Babies and children welcome: high chairs. Tables outdoors (4, pavement). Takeaway service.
Map 7 B6.
For branch see index.

SHELF LIFE

Damas Gate
81-85 Uxbridge Road, W12 7NR (8743 5116). Shepherd's Bush tube. **Open** 9am-10pm daily.
Shepherds Bush's first stop for big bunches of sparkling fresh herbs and exotic vegetables, plus Middle Eastern cheeses, pastries, nuts, olives and freshly made falafel.

Green Valley
36-37 Upper Berkeley Street, W1H 5QF (7402 7385). Marble Arch tube. **Open** 8am-midnight daily.
The intricate stacks of baklava in the window tempt you in; once inside, you'll find everything from fresh fruit and veg to spit-roast chickens and take-home meze.

Phoenicia Mediterranean Food Hall
186-188 Kentish Town Road, NW5 2AE (7267 1267). Kentish Town tube/rail. **Open** 9am-8pm Mon-Sat; 10am-4pm Sun.
A spacious store with a good range of Middle Eastern breads, grains (including freekeh), halal meat, inexpensive meze and baklava. Plus a few tables for coffee.

Reza Pâtisserie
345 Kensington High Street, W8 6NW (7603 0924). Kensington (Olympia) tube/rail. **Open** 9am-9pm daily.
Despite the name – a reference to the wonderful Iranian pastries made on-site – this long-established favourite sells all manner of Middle Eastern foods, including eye-catching speciality vegetables.

Hammersmith

★ Mahdi NEW

217 King Street, W6 9JT (8563 7007). Hammersmith or Ravenscourt Park tube. **Meals served** noon-11pm daily. **Main courses** £5-£12. **Set lunch** (noon-6pm Mon-Fri) £4.90 1 course. **Unlicensed.** No alcohol allowed. **Credit** MC, V. Iranian
Many of the capital's Iranian restaurants have spent decades slaving over hot clay ovens, yet it's taken newcomer Mahdi just four years to endear itself so deeply to London's Iranian expats that few would be happy letting anyone else cater at their daughter's wedding. The reason is simple: Mahdi's dishes are the most authentic, generously portioned and jaw-droppingly delicious you'll find anywhere in the city. That's not to say the place will appeal to everyone: the ten-minute walk from Hammersmith tube and absence of alcohol (BYO or otherwise) may deter lazybones and booze-hounds – but it's all part of what makes Mahdi so irrefutably Iranian. The same is true of the cheerfully functional aesthetics (bright lighting, plastic tablecloths, a smattering of Persian posters on the walls) and fleet of polite, white-shirted waiters. An extensive menu lists plenty of unusual dishes – a starter of tah chin, for example, with oblongs of crispy rice bound with eggs and sweetened with barberries – while standards were cooked to perfection: lamb and chicken kebabs were richly flavoursome, stews packed with ingredients that others tend to skimp. Giant portions mean almost everyone can be seen scooping leftovers into plastic tubs at the end of the evening, smiling at the thought of tucking in for a second time.
Booking advisable. Disabled: toilet. Takeaway service. **Map 20 B4.**

Kensington

Randa

23 Kensington Church Street, W8 4LF (7937 5363). High Street Kensington tube. **Meals served** noon-midnight daily. **Main courses** £11.95-£16. **Set lunch** £12 2 courses. **Set dinner** £45 per person (minimum 2) 3 courses. **Credit** MC, V. Lebanese

The relentless expansion of the Maroush empire – which includes the Maroush restaurants, Ranoush juice bars and newcomer Sidi Maarouf (a departure from the Middle East to North Africa) – continues apace. This former corner-pub site just up from Kensington High Street is where it ditches the jacket and tie and slips into something a little more casual. Service remains formal and smiles are tightly rationed, but there's a modish open kitchen, a mezzanine with smoked-glass floor that speaks of a fat cheque to a design agency, and chairs upholstered in primary colours. It's a pleasant, non-Middle Eastern setting for a familiar Maroush menu. The food is as reliably good as at the company's long-established businesses on the Edgware Road. Highlights of a recent visit included melt-in-the-mouth cheese sambousek with lovely light pastry, dense falafel with a good crunch to the outside (served with a light tahina sauce), and smooth houmous. Knuckle of lamb was generous and tender and shouldn't be attempted by anyone who has overindulged in meze.

Separate room for parties, seats 40. Takeaway service; delivery service (over £25 within 1-mile radius). **Map 7 B8.**

Olympia

Homely, good-value **Chez Marcelle** (34 Blythe Road, W14 0HA, 7603 3241, map 20 C3) was closed at time of writing, but should have reopened by autumn 2007.

★ ★ Alounak

10 Russell Gardens, W14 8EZ (7603 7645). Kensington (Olympia) tube/rail. **Meals served** noon-midnight daily. **Main courses** £6.30-£12.30. **Unlicensed. Corkage** no charge. **Credit** MC, V. Iranian

It's not the most accessible place (a ten-minute slog even from geographically anomalous Kensington Olympia tube station), but Alounak is worth the extra effort. Its interior is perhaps the most inspired of all London's Iranian outposts – the artful clutter of Persian teapots, painted ashtrays and ornamental light fittings is like a sanitised snapshot of Tehran's bustling bazaar – but there's also authenticity in spades, from the small fridge packed with unlabelled plastic bottles of home-made doogh (a salty yoghurt drink) to the dusty Nescafé jars filled with tea leaves and cardamom pods. Then there's the food, which leaves many of its competitors at the starting gates. The clay oven dispenses proper taftoon bread for mopping up starters like borani (yoghurt and spinach dip) and torshi makhloot (a sour vegetable pickle), while adeptly cooked lamb and chicken kebabs are served with perfectly fluffy Persian rice; a knob of butter and a sprinkle of bitter sumak and you're away. Dishes of the day are also excellent; if possible, visit on a Thursday to try the other-worldly loobia polo, an enormous portion of saffron rice with lamb and green beans – easily one of the best Iranian dishes we've eaten in London.

Babies and children welcome: high chairs. Booking advisable. Takeaway service.
For branch see index.

★ Mohsen

152 Warwick Road, W14 8PS (7602 9888). Earl's Court tube/Kensington (Olympia) tube/rail. **Meals served** noon-midnight daily. **Main courses** £12-£15. **Unlicensed. Corkage** no charge. **No credit cards.** Iranian

An authentic little eaterie, with an atmosphere more akin to one of Tehran's uptown dinner parties than its downtown chelo kebab houses. The effusively cheerful Mrs Mohsen is usually on hand to meet you at the door with a smiling 'salaam', before whisking you to a table and popping open your bottle of BYO wine. Dangerously moreish fresh bread was on hand for scooping up a range of first-class starters, including halim bademjan (aubergine dip) masto musir (zingy shallot-infused yoghurt) and plates piled high with bitter sabzi greens. Leave room for mains, though: the kebabs – joojeh (chicken marinated in saffron, lemon and onion) and koubideh (minced lamb) – were cooked to perfection, and accompanied by an Alborz mountain range of pillowy rice. Then there are the daily specials, from baghali polo ba mahiche (lamb shank on a bed of rice with dill and lima beans) to ghorm-e sabzi (lamb stew with greens, kidney beans and dried lemons), the latter often watery and short on meat in Iranian restaurants, but here as hearty and delicious as you could desire. For afters, most settle for black tea and a dish of sugary zoolbia and bamieh sweets.

Babies and children admitted. Takeaway service.
Map 13 A10.

Yas

7 Hammersmith Road, W14 8XJ (7603 9148/ www.yasrestaurant.co.uk). Kensington (Olympia) tube/rail. **Meals served** noon-4.30am daily. **Main courses** £7-£12. **Credit** MC, V. Iranian

A short walk from the sterilised grandeur of the Olympia Exhibition Centre lies this understated haven of Iranian home cooking, small enough to feel intimate, but lent a cavernous air by its low lighting and mirrored walls. It's not the cheapest Persian restaurant in town (needless to say, it's hardly bank-breaking either), but remains perennially popular with both Iranian expats and locals, thanks to its flavoursome take on traditional Persian favourites. The generous starters were uniformly delicious – the heaped bowl of mirza ghasemi (a regional Caspian delicacy made with aubergines, garlic, tomatoes and eggs) was especially hard to resist – and made the perfect partner to the fresh bread seen being beaten into shape at the clay oven by the door. Kebabs were similarly excellent. Boneless joojeh chicken was wonderfully tender, its bitter sweetness suggesting a long, leisurely marinade in saffron and lemon – although we've occasionally been overwhelmed by overuse of the latter in the house ghorm-e sabzi (lamb stew with greens and beans). Save room for the stunning desserts, including traditional Persian pistachio ice-cream and faloudeh – an unlikely concoction of rosewater and frozen rice noodles that's both exotic and eminently satisfying.

Babies and children welcome: high chairs. Booking advisable. Takeaway service.

Shepherd's Bush

★ Abu Zaad

29 Uxbridge Road, W12 8LH (8749 5107/ www.abuzaad.co.uk). Shepherd's Bush tube. **Meals served** 11am-11pm daily. **Main courses** £4.50-£11. **Credit** MC, V. Syrian

Despite doing away with the deli counter, Abu Zaad is still very much geared up to takeaways and quick snacking. No amount of brass pots, lanterns and views of Damascus in oils can soften the hard edges of tiled floors and marble-topped tables. The food is canteen cuisine; it arrives quickly having been prepared beforehand and it lacks finesse. That's not to say it's bad. This is superior fast food , with lots of fresh Mediterranean salads and meze including standards such as tabouleh, fattoush and stuffed vine leaves. A good-value set option gets you any three cold dishes for just £3.90. Mains are similarly well priced, many at £4-£5. The menu includes plenty of dishes not commonly seen in London's Middle Eastern restaurants: specialities of the Syrian kitchen. Unlike most businesses run by fellow Syrian nationals, Abu Zaad doesn't feel the need to masquerade as Lebanese. Hence the odd spicy kebab and lots of oven-baking in yoghurt. Though you wouldn't cross town for the food, you'd be here most lunchtimes if you lived or worked in the neighbourhood.

Babies and children welcome: high chairs. Book weekends. Separate room for parties, seats 30. Takeaway service. **Map 20 B2.**

★ Sufi NEW

2007 RUNNER-UP BEST CHEAP EATS

70 Askew Road, W12 9BJ (8834 4888/ www.sufirestaurant.com). Hammersmith tube then bus 266. **Meals served** noon-11pm daily. **Main courses** £5.50-£11. **Credit** MC, V. Iranian

Sufism is an ancient school of Islamic mysticism that aims to nurture spiritual contentment – but a speedier route to satisfaction is to dine at this excellent Persian restaurant. Like the road it sits on, Sufi is an unprepossessing little place. Its plain,

Sufi

RESTAURANTS

muted decor is perked up by a few pictures of modern Iran on the walls and sundry ethnic trinkets. At the front, a miniature clay kiln for baking taftoon (flatbread) is the first hint of quality. A wafer-thin disc of the dough is rolled out and fired as soon as you take your seat. Best consume it with a selection of terrific starters such as a rich, earthy dip of kashk-e bademjan, or salad olivieh. Freshness and quality of ingredients distinguished both these dishes, and main courses followed suit. On a mixed-meat skewer, chunks of lamb were, surprisingly, not as moist and tender as the soft pieces of chicken (which tasted of a mild but deliciously complex marinade). Luckily, the lamb in khoresht fessenjan (stewed with walnut and pomegranate sauce) more than made amends, the meat falling apart under the influence of the sweet, rich gravy. We're happy to report that, on repeat visits, high standards were maintained.
Babies and children welcome: high chair. Separate room for parties, seats 40. Takeaway service.
Map 20 A2.

East

Brick Lane

Lebanese Lounge

50-52 Hanbury Street, E1 5JL (7539 9200/ www.lebaneselounge.com). Aldgate East tube/ Liverpool Street tube/rail. **Meals served** noon-11pm daily. **Main courses** £9-£15. **Set lunch** (noon-5pm Mon-Fri) £9.90 2 courses. **Set dinner** £18 3 courses. **Credit** MC, V.
Lebanese

Hidden at the end of a small courtyard, Lebanese Lounge is an unusual Middle Eastern incursion into the Brick Lane area. Its spacious premises comprise two distinct sections. On one side is an ethnic-look lounge with colourful walls, cushions, low-slung seating and tables (for drinks and, formerly, sheesha). On the other side is a large, formal, sparsely decorated restaurant that gives the impression of being a windowless basement (but isn't). Maybe the vibe isn't quite spot-on, but there's someone in the kitchen with the patience and precision to produce the best Lebanese food – who knows, for example, the correct proportion of finely chopped parsley and mint and the exact amount of lemon juice and olive oil that go into the perfect tabouleh. Other fine dishes included a mellow kibbeh, lemony spinach fatayer, spicy arayes (minced lamb in strips of pitta bread) and an excellent mixed grill. Wine policy is unusual: on our visit there was just one red and one white on offer. The latter, from Massaya in the Bekaa Valley, was a good, fruity accompaniment. There are quirks here, but the atmosphere thawed as more diners arrived – and service was helpful, and the food good.
Babies and children admitted. Booking advisable Fri, Sat. Disabled: toilet. Separate room for parties, seats 20. Takeaway service.
Map 12 S5.

North

Camden Town & Chalk Farm

Le Mignon

98 Arlington Road, NW1 7HD (7387 0600). Camden Town tube. **Lunch served** noon-3pm, **dinner served** 6pm-midnight daily. **Main courses** £9.50-£18.50. **Credit** MC, V.
Lebanese

Le Mignon's business card features cheerleading quotes from various luminaries of the foodie scene and from BBC journo Robert Elms – who happens to live just around the corner. It's impressive for such a modest corner eaterie in the backstreets of north London. If this suggests an extraordinary find, well, no, but Le Mignon is a very good little Lebanese restaurant, delivering a lengthy menu of well-executed dishes in relaxed surroundings. Chefs make the most of fresh ingredients: fattoush (a green salad with shards of crisp pitta bread) was given zing with lots of garlic and lemon juice, and there was a similar zest to the fatayer (pastry triangles stuffed with lemon-drenched spinach). Of the grilled meat and fish mains, the stuffed lamb (actually strips of lamb on rice, topped with sliced almonds, cashews and pine nuts) was lovely. The charcoal-grilled chicken was also terrifically tender, and beautifully flavoured with spices and marinade. The only downside is the gauntlet of winos and teenage substance abusers you have to run on the way back to the bus stops on Camden High Street.
Babies and children admitted (daytime). Booking advisable. Tables outdoors (4, pavement). Takeaway service. **Map 27 D3.**

Menu

See also the menu boxes in **North African** and **Turkish**. Note that spellings can vary. For more information, consult *The Legendary Cuisine of Persia*, by Margaret Shaida (Grub Street).

MEZE

Baba ganoush: Egyptian name for moutabal (qv).
Basturma: smoked beef.
Batata hara: potatoes fried with peppers and chilli.
Falafel: a mixture of spicy chickpeas or broad beans ground, rolled into balls and deep fried.
Fatayer: a soft pastry, filled with cheese, onions, spinach and pine kernels.
Fattoush: fresh vegetable salad containing shards of toasted pitta bread and sumac (qv).
Fuul or **fuul medames**: brown broad beans that are mashed and seasoned with olive oil, lemon juice and garlic.
Kalaj: halloumi cheese on pastry.
Kibbeh: highly seasoned mixture of minced lamb, cracked wheat and onion, deep-fried in balls. For meze it is often served raw (**kibbeh nayeh**) like steak tartare.
Labneh: Middle Eastern cream cheese made from yoghurt.
Moujadara: lentils, rice and caramelised onions mixed together.
Moutabal: a purée of chargrilled aubergines mixed with sesame sauce, garlic and lemon juice.
Muhamara: spiced and crushed mixed nuts.
Sambousek: small pastries filled with mince, onion and pine kernels.
Sujuk: spicy Lebanese sausages.
Sumac: an astringent and fruity-tasting spice made from dried sumac seeds.
Tabouleh: a salad of chopped parsley, tomatoes, crushed wheat, onions, olive oil and lemon juice.
Torshi: pickled vegetables.
Warak einab: rice-stuffed vine leaves.

MAINS

Shawarma: meat (usually lamb) marinated then grilled on a spit and sliced kebab-style.
Shish kebab: cubes of marinated lamb grilled on a skewer, often with tomatoes, onions and sweet peppers.
Shish taouk: like shish kebab, but with chicken rather than lamb.

DESSERTS

Baklava: filo pastry interleaved with pistachio nuts, almonds or walnuts, and covered in syrup.
Konafa or **kadayif**: cake made from shredded pastry dough, filled with syrup and nuts, or cream.
Ma'amoul: pastries filled with nuts or dates.
Muhallabia or **mohalabia**: a milky ground-rice pudding with almonds and pistachios, flavoured with rosewater or orange blossom.
Om ali: bread pudding, often made with filo pastry, also includes nuts and raisins.

IRANIAN DISHES

Ash-e reshteh: a soup with noodles, spinach, pulses and dried herbs.
Halim bademjan: mashed chargrilled aubergine with onions and walnuts.
Joojeh or **jujeh**: chicken marinated in saffron, lemon and onion.
Kashk-e bademjan: baked aubergines mixed with herbs.
Kuku-ye sabzi: finely chopped fresh herbs with eggs, baked in the oven.
Masto khiar: yoghurt mixed with finely chopped cucumber and mint.
Masto musir: shallot-flavoured yoghurt.
Mirza ghasemi: crushed baked aubergines, tomatoes, garlic and herbs mixed with egg.
Sabzi: a plate of fresh herb leaves (usually mint and dill) often served with a cube of feta.
Salad olivieh: like a russian salad, with chopped potatoes, chicken, eggs, peas, gherkins, olive oil and mayonnaise.

Outer London

Wembley, Middlesex

Mesopotamia

115 Wembley Park Drive, Wembley, Middx HA9 8HG (8453 5555/www.mesopotamia.ltd.uk). Wembley Park tube. **Dinner served** 6pm-midnight Mon-Sat. **Main courses** £11-£14.50. **Set dinner** £23 3 courses. **Credit** AmEx, DC, MC, V. Iraqi

We're usually very distrustful of any restaurant that overdoes on the ethnic decor, but Iraqi restaurant Mesopotamia – which exhibits all the restraint of a national pavilion at a world's fair – is a delight. The walls are gussied up like a Babylonian palace, with parades of stylised lions trotting along the rough plaster walls, and a turquoise-tiled frieze with other regal creatures picked out in gold. If so inclined, you could turn your back on all of this and bag the table at the front of the restaurant with its views of the arch of Wembley Stadium, just over the road. The menu combines the houmous, fattoush and tabouleh typical of Lebanese cuisine with Turkish dolma and Iranian fesanjun (chicken stew with a sauce of pomegranate juice and walnuts). Iraqi specialities include dhob, a lean prime cut of beef braised in a rich gravy spiced with cloves, black peppercorns and cardamom – a dish, so the menu claims, served nowhere else in the UK. Dates also feature heavily (Iraq being a prolific producer of the fruit). On a Friday and a Saturday, the short dessert list is supplemented by a chocolate fountain, or the 'Babylon Tower!!' as the menu has it.
Babies and children admitted. Booking advisable. Restaurant available for hire. Vegetarian menu.

Modern European

Welcome to Zone One for food as fashion. The restaurants listed in this section include some of the most talked-about venues in town: those that attract food fashionistas like WAGs to a Bond Street dress sale. Yet along with a little of the flummery associated with the 'see and be seen' scene, you'll find much creative flair. The professional kitchens of London have been crucial in forging Modern European cookery over the past 25 years. In this time the cuisine has evolved tremendously, becoming increasingly eclectic (and in so doing changing its name from the earlier 'Modern British' to 'Modern European'), absorbing influences from Asia, the Pacific Rim and, especially, the Mediterranean. In Australia and the US, a very similar cuisine is more commonly termed 'Contemporary', and the new generation of mix-and-match has certainly become a worldwide phenomenon: a palatable manifestation of postmodern culture.

After flirtations with garish fusion cookery in the 1990s, the combinations of ingredients are generally more considered these days, the cuisine more anchored in the European idiom. This doesn't preclude exciting experimentation, however, and London's Modern European restaurants are still among the most innovative in the land. Like the cooking style itself, the Modern European restaurant scene is constantly changing; this year has brought a crop of notable new venues – including **Skylon**, **L'Atelier de Joël Robuchon** and the winner of the Best New Restaurant gong in the 2007 Time Out Eating & Drinking Awards, **Wild Honey**.

Central

City

The Don

The Courtyard, 20 St Swithin's Lane, EC4N 8AD (7626 2606/www.thedonrestaurant.com). Bank tube/DLR.
Bistro **Lunch served** noon-3pm, **dinner served** 6-10pm Mon-Fri. **Main courses** £8.95-£14.95. *Restaurant* **Lunch served** noon-2.30pm, **dinner served** 6-10pm Mon-Fri. **Main courses** £12.95-£23.95.
Both **Credit** AmEx, DC, MC, V.

Offering 32 wines by the glass, the Don is a great friend to sherry and port lovers. It is owned by Sandeman and occupies the firm's 200-year-old former cellars. We were disappointed, then, that the engaging French sommelier seemed better versed in his own country's wines. Food aims to complement the excellent wine list, but sometimes, what sounds good on paper turns out to be overly sweet and rich. Our meal started well. A foie gras and duck confit terrine was rich and earthy, perfectly punctuating its sauternes jelly. Roasted quail on a mushroom gateau was delicious too. But a main of expertly seared sea bass served with a crunchy potato galette and spinach was unforgivably marred by too-sweet sherried aubergine. Staff are supremely solicitous, yet can seem omnipresent. Order forms on each table for the company's New Zealand wine range added an unpleasant commercial note to proceedings. Eat in the basement bistro with its vaulted brick walls to appreciate the building's history; here the menu is enticing, but simpler and cheaper. The ground-floor restaurant is cluttered with garish abstract art, distracting customers from the beautiful high ceilings. Friday evening wine promotions are worth considering, including a half-price offer on bottles over £50.
Children over 10 years admitted. Booking essential. Dress: smart casual. Separate room for parties, seats 24. **Map 12 Q7**.

Prism

147 Leadenhall Street, EC3V 4QT (7256 3875/www.harveynichols.com). Monument tube/Bank tube/DLR.
Bar **Open** 11am-11pm, **lunch served** 11.30am-3pm Mon-Fri. **Main courses** £10-£12.50. *Restaurant* **Breakfast served** 8-10am, **lunch served** noon-3pm, **dinner served** 6-10pm Mon-Fri. **Main courses** £18-£24.
Both **Credit** AmEx, DC, MC, V.

Prism's main room is a beauty – grand and high-ceilinged, with artworks dotted around the walls. For our same-day booking, however, we were offered the 'conservatory', which is little more than a glass-roofed corridor of tables. Prices and clientele are as you'd expect for a restaurant almost opposite the Lloyd's building. The food combines pretty, picky, ladies-who-lunch presentation with hearty, by-the-balls City-boy components. Thus canon of salt marsh lamb with fondant potatoes was accompanied by a basil mousse topped with a flash-fried basil leaf; and monkfish with fennel choucroute and smoked bacon was exquisitely presented with a swirl of celeriac purée mottled with shavings of black truffle and pea shoots. The dishes weren't faultless; the choucroute's vinegariness did the fennel few favours in the monkfish dish, while a swordfish carpaccio's show-off oyster tempura was sullen and soggy rather than crisp and light. The cheerfully self-possessed service was exemplified by our waiter opening a bottle of Galician albariño specially to pour us a single glass; otherwise, the wine list is for City gents, but manageable if you're willing to spend up to £35.
Babies and children welcome: high chairs. Booking advisable. Disabled: toilet. Separate rooms for parties, seating 20 and 40. Vegetarian menu. **Map 12 Q6**.

Clerkenwell & Farringdon

★ Ambassador (100)

55 Exmouth Market, EC1R 4QL (7837 0009/www.theambassadorcafe.co.uk). Farringdon tube/rail/19, 38, 341 bus. **Breakfast served** 8.30am-noon, **lunch served** noon-3pm Mon-Fri. **Brunch served** 11am-4pm Sat, Sun. **Dinner served** 6.30-10.15pm Mon-Sat. **Main courses** £9.50-£17. **Set lunch** £12.50 2 courses, £16 3 courses. **Credit** AmEx, MC, V.

As a day-long café-style operation the Ambassador – runner-up for Best New Restaurant in the 2006 Time Out Eating & Drinking Awards – aims to please all the people all the time. That it succeeds, and impressively, is down to skill, commitment and an eye for detail. The various menus include breakfast waffles and pastries, a weekend brunch, dinner, and small sharing dishes for those primarily here to enjoy the beautifully crafted wine list. The room and furnishings are simple. Tables spill seamlessly out on to the street when weather allows. Everything that matters is made to count: tap water arriving unprompted on a hot day, linen napkins, perfectly judged service. And of course the food. We've not had a dud dish here. From the terrine-and-omelette style of the good-value set lunch to the more cheffy, complex à la carte (pollock, for example, with soft celeriac, crispy fennel and a ghosting of foam) – everything has impressed. Desserts deserve special mention: no afterthought, these, but exquisite riffs on a theme; blood orange three ways is a lesson in texture. Enjoy the casual atmosphere and reasonable prices, but don't be deceived by them: this is a fine restaurant indeed.
Babies and children welcome: children's menu; high chairs; toys. Booking advisable. Disabled: toilet. Tables outdoors (5, pavement). **Map 5 N4**.

Clerkenwell Dining Room

69-73 St John Street, EC1M 4AN (7253 9000/www.theclerkenwell.com). Barbican tube/Farringdon tube/rail. **Lunch served** noon-2.30pm Mon-Fri. **Dinner served** 6-11pm Mon-Fri; 7-11pm Sat. **Main courses** £15-£17. **Set meal** £15 2 courses, £19.50 3 courses. **Credit** AmEx, DC, JCB, MC, V.

A smart restaurant, with bold flowers and white linen, the CDR makes a good first impression. Even the slightly fussy service (a tong-wielding waiter proffering minute wedges of lemon for your water, for example) has initial appeal. Multi-tasking, however, is not a strong point. We found almost every request (wine orders, menu queries) involved a frustratingly lengthy redirection to an alternative waiter. That said, the menu is enticing, with lots of inventive meat and fish dishes. In a primarily Modern European menu, however, the occasional Asian-fusion dish struck us as misplaced; chewy smoked duck breast served with so-so pak choi and noodles unfortunately proved us right. Swordfish with ratte potatoes and excellent anchovies was much more successful. Starters (salmon gravadlax, oxtail ravioli, baby artichoke salad) are well proportioned – as they should be for £8-£10. Still, the prices are unlikely to raise an eyebrow among the boomingly loud suits that make up much of the clientele. An unexpected but (we were told) long-running discount offer took our bill down to reasonable levels; without it, we'd have been unimpressed by the value for money.
Babies and children welcome: high chairs. Booking advisable. Separate room for parties, seats 40. **Map 5 O4**.

L'Atelier de Joël Robuchon. See p232.

Smiths of Smithfield (100)

67-77 Charterhouse Street, EC1M 6HJ (7251 7950/www.smithsofsmithfield.co.uk). Barbican tube/Farringdon tube/rail.
Wine Rooms **Open/dinner served** 5.30-10.30pm Mon-Wed; 5.30pm-1.30am Thur-Sat. **Main courses** £10-£28.
Dining Room **Lunch served** noon-2.45pm Mon-Fri. **Dinner served** 6-10.45 pm Mon-Sat. **Main courses** £11-£12.50.
Ground-floor bar/café **Open/meals served** 7am-4.30pm Mon-Fri; 9.30am-5pm Sat, Sun. **Main courses** £4-£7.50.
All **Credit** AmEx, DC, MC, V.
The extraordinary popularity of John Torode's four-floor warehouse is testament to its reliability. No matter how busy it gets, standards remain constant. The ground floor holds a bar perpetually packed with a democratic mix of City workers and night owls, its fever-pitch vibe at odds with the more demure British restaurant, Top Floor. The first floor has recently been converted into 'Wine Rooms', offering small and big plates and wines, but the hub of the operation remains the second-floor Dining Room, its bare-brick walls and raucous acoustics offering an ad-agency approximation of kinetic urban style. Repeated visits have taught us a few fail-safe lessons, not least that eating fresh pays dividends. For starters, simple but beautiful asparagus was more successful than uninspiring Portuguese saltcod fritters. For mains, the excellent burgers remain better bets than the cheap-tasting steaks. We also enjoyed a characterful risotto made with truffled leeks and jerusalem artichokes. The wine list contains a few cheapies, but you'll need to spend at least £20 to get anything of substance. Table service, as usual, was excellent; on a packed Saturday night, our waitress made a very difficult job look easy.
Babies and children welcome (restaurant): high chairs. Disabled: toilet. Entertainment: DJs 7pm Thur-Sat ground floor. Separate room for parties, seats 26. Tables outdoors (4, pavement; 6, terrace). **Map 11 O5.**

Covent Garden

L'Atelier de Joël Robuchon NEW

2007 RUNNER-UP BEST DESIGN

13-15 West Street, WC2H 9NE (7010 8600/ www.joel-robuchon.com). Leicester Square tube.
Bar **Open** 2pm-2am Mon-Sat; 2-10.30pm Sun.
Restaurant **Lunch served** noon-2.30pm, **dinner served** 5.30-10.30pm daily. **Main courses** £15-£55. **Set lunch** £35 3 courses incl tea or coffee. **Set dinner** (5.30-6.30pm) £29 2 courses, £35 3 courses. **Set meal** £75-£85 9 courses.
Both **Credit** AmEx, DC, MC, V.
The London branch of French chef Joël Robuchon's international chain of high-concept brasseries is a three-floor extravaganza. At ground level, granite-black pools of darkness are illuminated by bright spots of colour in the otherwise all-black open kitchen, which is as well ordered as any Zen monastery. The Japanese style is no coincidence; the first L'Atelier opened in Tokyo, and Robuchon liked it so much he copied the Japanese look at his second branch, in Paris, and subsequent openings. You can't book after 7pm for the ground level, but you can for the first-floor dining room (called La Cuisine), which is lighter and brighter. The menu in both is broadly similar. Dishes tend to be a little whimsical, but without too much stacking and primping going on; you won't see the chefs trying to make balloon animals out of your boudin noir. Two baby burgers consisted of buns the size of eggshells, filled with a slab of seared foie gras as well as tiny patties. A kind of oeufs en cocotte was served in martini glasses; 1970s-retro crinkle-cut chips accompanied the steak tartare. There are plenty of ingredients to titillate gourmets: intensely flavoured sweetbreads, for example, or pig's trotter on little toasts, minced to maximise the gelatinous burst of fatty textures that explode in the mouth. L'Atelier is an excellent restaurant, but the pricing (expect to pay at least £150 for two people for dinner) makes it best suited to special-occasion splurges.
Babies and children admitted. Booking advisable. Disabled: access; toilet. Dress: smart, casual. Restaurant available for hire. **Map 17 C3.**

Axis

One Aldwych, 1 Aldwych, WC2B 4RH (7300 0300/www.onealdwych.com). Covent Garden or Embankment tube/Charing Cross tube/rail.
Lunch served noon-2.30pm Mon-Fri. **Dinner served** 5.45-10.30pm Mon-Fri; 5.45-11.30pm Sat. **Main courses** £15.50-£23. **Set meal** £17.50 2 courses, £20.50 3 courses. **Credit** AmEx, DC, JCB, MC, V.
There's a distinctly masculine, monied feel to the elegant dining room at Axis, located beneath the chic One Aldwych hotel. Its black leather chairs and linen-clad tables are, for the most part, occupied by sleekly besuited businessmen. A vast, Vorticist-style mural of New York's skyscrapers overlooks proceedings. Thankfully, well-spaced tables mean that any talk of stocks and shares remains a lulling background buzz. Dim lighting and opulent displays of pink orchids soften the room's contours and add a pleasingly intimate note. The menu, like the decor, is classic without being stuffy. Attention to detail is immaculate. Take the freshly cut fig and tiny cube of honeycomb that accompanied a smooth chicken liver parfait (which looked lovely and tasted even better). Tender lamb rump, served with unexpectedly delicious green tomatoes atop a garlicky, mint-infused pile of bulgar wheat, demonstrated the same flair. Sea bass from the menu's extensive grill section was pleasant, if unremarkable – though wonderfully smooth mash and perfectly cooked green beans were beyond reproach. Service was attentive and consummately professional, without being chilly. Chocolate truffles and supremely light lemon petits fours ended the meal on a suitably indulgent note.
Babies and children welcome: high chairs. Booking advisable. Disabled: toilet. Entertainment: jazz 8pm Tue, Wed. Restaurant available for hire. Vegetarian menu (book in advance). **Map 18 F4.**

The Ivy

1 West Street, WC2H 9NQ (7836 4751/www.the-ivy.co.uk). Leicester Square tube. **Lunch served** noon-3pm Mon-Sat; noon-3.30pm Sun. **Dinner served** 5.30pm-midnight daily. **Main courses** £9.75-£26.75. **Set lunch** (Sat, Sun) £24.75 3 courses. **Cover** £2. **Credit** AmEx, DC, MC, V.
It's possible to book for dinner less than a month ahead at this legendary thespians' rendezvous, as long as you're prepared to eat at 6pm or 10.30pm. The glamour may be diluted by tourists, but a meal in the Ivy's old-school dining room, with its diamond-paned stained-glass windows and green leather banquettes, is still an occasion. Upright staff make a fuss of everyone, pulling out chairs and (ironically, given the booking situation) urging you to 'come back soon' upon departure. The eclectic menu caters to most cravings, from welsh rarebit to grilled lobster. You can splash out on Beluga caviar at £95 for 30g, but also get a hamburger for under a tenner and a decent bottle of wine for less than £20 (with plenty of choice for under £30). Our grilled squid starter was a little rubbery, while mains – a plump salmon fish cake, and a goat's cheese tortelloni with slivers of artichoke – were nice, but nothing special. No matter. Everyone (except a sulky Tracey Emin) was too busy sneaking glances at everyone else to pay much attention to the food. Baked alaska, set alight at the table with flaming kirsch, made a suitably theatrical finale.
Babies and children welcome: high chairs. Booking essential, several weeks in advance. Separate room for parties, seats 60. Vegetarian menu. Vegan dishes. **Map 18 D4.**

Fitzrovia

Villandry

170 Great Portland Street, W1W 5QB (7631 3131/www.villandry.com). Great Portland Street tube.
Bar **Open** 8am-11pm Mon-Fri; 9am-11pm Sat. **Breakfast served** 8-11.45am Mon-Sat. **Lunch served** noon-3.30pm Mon-Fri; noon-3pm Sat. **Dinner served** 5-10pm Mon-Fri; 7-10pm Sat. **Main courses** £11.50-£22.50. **Set dinner** (7-10pm Sat) £20 3 courses.
Restaurant **Lunch served** noon-3pm Mon-Fri; 11.30am-4pm Sat, Sun. **Dinner served** 6-10.30pm Mon-Sat. **Main courses** £11.50-£32.50.
Both **Credit** AmEx, MC, V.
There's a lot going on at Villandry. It's a deli and catering company as well as an all-day bar and restaurant, and is so large it has entrances on both sides of the block. The restaurant is a pleasing modern space, decorated in a restrained way, with only the odd flourish. Diners sit at solid wooden tables and choose from a crowd-pleasing, monthly-changing set of European dishes. Typical starters include the house salad (a splendid medley, with polenta croutons), crudités with an anchovy dip (finger-lickingly good) and beef carpaccio with wild rocket. Mains might be fettuccine with roast aubergine and sun-dried tomato sauce (our only poor dish – just a notch above a student supper), seared tuna niçoise, steak tartare, or salt and pepper squid (a decent, not too greasy version). As well as Villandry's famed cheeses, there are desserts such as baked alaska and eton mess. An attractive wine list and charming service add to the sense of well-being. The bar looks and feels much like the restaurant, but tends to get packed. This is where breakfast is served, and once again the menu presses all the right buttons; porridge, bacon sandwich, and french toast with maple syrup all make an appearance. An on-form operation.
Babies and children welcome: children's menu; high chairs. Bar and restaurant available for hire. Booking advisable. Entertainment: jazz 7.30pm Sat (bar). Tables outdoors (13, pavement). Takeaway service. **Map 3 H5.**

Gloucester Road

L'Etranger

36 Gloucester Road, SW7 4QT (7584 1118/ www.etranger.co.uk). Gloucester Road tube.
Lunch served noon-3pm Mon-Fri. **Dinner served** 6-11pm Mon-Sat. **Main courses** £16.40-£49. **Set meal** (lunch, 6-6.45pm Mon-Fri) £14.50 2 courses, £16.50 3 courses. **Credit** AmEx, MC, V.
The streets surrounding Gloucester Road are chock-full of neighbourhood eateries, but judging by the glam crowd dining here on a midweek night, L'Etranger is a different kind of animal. From the moment you walk through the door, service is sublime. So it should be at these prices. The great draw is Jerome Tauvron's wonderfully slick East-West menu, which stretches from magret de canard to wagyu beef teppanyaki (a snip at £49 a go). This is serious designer-dining territory. Shades of lilac and pale grey create a cool backdrop to the main event. A starter of squid with chilli and coriander was crisp and flavoursome, but the sublime quality of the ingredients shone through in the main courses: melt-in-the-mouth Pyrenean shoulder of lamb with grilled aubergines; and scallops, beef and prawn shabu shabu (a bowl of sumptuous raw ingredients presented fondue-style to cook in boiling water at the table). The wine list is encyclopaedic to the point of burden; a basic but drinkable Chianti starts things off at £28 and a Montrachet comes in at £1,400 – but the sommelier is able to size you up quickly enough.
Babies and children welcome: high chairs. Booking advisable. Restaurant available for hire. Vegetarian menu. **Map 13 C9.**

Holborn

The Terrace

Lincoln's Inn Fields, WC2A 3LJ (7430 1234/ www.theterrace.info). Holborn tube. **Breakfast served** 8-11am, **lunch served** noon-3pm Mon-Fri. **Brunch served** 11am-5.30pm Sat. **Dinner served** 5.30-8.30pm Mon-Sat. **Main courses** £10.50-£17.95. **Set lunch** £13.50 2 courses, £15.50 3 courses. **Credit** AmEx, MC, V.
Give the High Holborn mayhem the slip and escape into leafy Lincoln's Inn Fields, where you'll find this relaxed, light-filled restaurant. Everything

about the Terrace, from its garden-shed-cum-greenhouse design to the outdoor tables overlooking the tennis courts, exudes summertime easy living. Indeed, the venue is best suited to long, balmy evenings and lazy afternoons in the sunshine (our visit saw it packed with local workers making valiant attempts to redefine the concept of 'lunch hour'). The inventive menu combines crisp, fresh flavours (caesar salad) with a touch of the Caribbean (jerk chicken, curried goat) to interesting effect. Haddock with pea purée came topped with a perfect poached egg and zesty hollandaise, while beetroot-cured salmon and crayfish cocktail – a modern take on the 1970s classic – packed a boldly flavoured punch. Pan-fried pollock with cucumber salad was less successful, let down by watery veg and an odd-tasting watermelon-coloured sauce. Service was friendly and faultless. Book ahead at the first sign of sun (note: it's first-come, first-served for the terrace tables) and give the great-value set lunch a try.
Babies and children welcome: high chairs. Booking advisable. Disabled: toilet. Tables outdoors (15, terrace). **Map 10 M6.**

Knightsbridge

Fifth Floor

Harvey Nichols, Knightsbridge, SW1X 7RJ (7235 5250/www.harveynichols.com). Knightsbridge tube.
Café **Breakfast served** 8am-noon, **lunch served** noon-3.30pm, **dinner served** 6-10.30pm Mon-Sat. **Brunch served** 11am-5pm Sun. **Tea served** 3.30-6pm Mon-Sat; 3.30-5pm Sun. **Main courses** £9.50-£15.
Restaurant **Brunch served** noon-4pm Sat, Sun. **Lunch served** noon-3pm Mon-Fri. **Dinner served** 6-11pm Mon-Sat. **Main courses** £15-£24. **Set dinner** £34.50 2 courses, £39.50 3 courses incl unlimited house wine.
Both **Credit** AmEx, DC, JCB, MC, V.
Fifth Floor's new chef Jonas Karlsson has stuck to the concept of ladylike food to fit the feminine decor (sky-blue walls, cream leather seating, unusual tube lighting casting a glamorous glow). On a recent visit, though, we felt the subtle line between imaginative delicacy and fussiness – or even silliness – was occasionally breached. Was a rocket salad, tossed in vinaigrette by the waiter at the table, in a hollowed-out stilton, a clever modern homage to the spirit of flambé showmanship, or just plain daft? Scallops were melt-in-the-mouth tender, but apricot purée added little to the dish, and some creamy foam even less. Things were much more sensible for main courses. Beautifully cooked lamb was served in succulent slices on a small but densely flavoured patty of some of the best couscous ever: warmly spiced, with tart little morsels of apricot and veg. Rounded off with a piece of lamb's tongue and a little roll of spinach, this was a great complete dish. Service was awry, however, with repeated enquiries into our well-being, food served too quickly, and wine kept in a cooler out of arm's length and seldom refilled. The Harvey Nichols own-label wines are of sound quality, but diners who go further are in for a treat: the globe-hopping wine list is long and excellent.
Babies and children welcome: children's menu; high chairs; nappy-changing facilities. Disabled: lift; toilet. Tables outdoors (15, café terrace). **Map 8 F9.**

Marylebone

Orrery

55 Marylebone High Street, W1U 5RB (7616 8000/www.danddlondon.com). Baker Street tube.
Bar **Open** 11am-11pm daily.
Restaurant **Lunch served** noon-2.30pm daily. **Dinner served** 6.30-10.30pm Mon-Wed, Sun; 6.30-11pm Thur-Sat. **Main courses** £16-£28. **Set lunch** £23.50 3 courses, £38 3 courses incl wine. **Set meal** (noon-1.30pm, 6.30-9.30pm) £58 6 courses (£96 incl wine). **Credit** AmEx, DC, JCB, MC, V.
Flooded with light by day, Orrery's long first-floor room is generous with the space between tables. Other luxuries such as the champagne trolley, unintimidating sommelier and well-drilled French service suggest this is a place for celebrations. The menu du jour seems a steal, though wines by the glass recommended with each course certainly aren't. The wine list is majestic in scope, fearlessly globe-trotting, and organised principally by grape variety or wine style. The 'sommelier's selection' simplifies matters greatly. A chaser tasse of carrot, cardamom and orange mousse was too sweet to sharpen the palate. Though undoubtedly refined, cooking suffered from reticent flavours. Chorizo with a sprinkling of chickpeas (no peasanty plateful this), fennel and squiggles of squid lacked punch. Cucumber velouté poured over crab and ribbons of salted cucumber tasted wan. Horseradish crème fraîche offered with mackerel was dabbed on the plate; Jersey Royals were cold and undercooked. Our most successful dish of sweet, tender braised pork cheek matched with tart lamb's lettuce and apple salad wasn't enough to allay the sense that ordering the cheapest option here is a false economy. The menu gourmand pulls out the stops, and might be worth saving up for. Along with other ex-Conran restaurants, Orrery is now owned by restaurant giant D&D London.
Babies and children welcome: high chairs. Booking essential. Disabled: toilet. Tables outside (12, bar roof terrace). Vegetarian menu. **Map 3 G4.**

Mayfair

Embassy

29 Old Burlington Street, W1S 3AN (7851 0956/ www.embassylondon.com). Green Park or Piccadilly Circus tube. **Dinner served** 6-11.30pm Tue-Sat. **Main courses** £14-£25. **Set dinner** £20 3 courses. **Credit** AmEx, MC, V.
Dining at the super-successful restaurant and private members' club Embassy is an odd affair. We began our evening in the 1970s-looking bar before moving to a dining area that's reminiscent of 18th-century France: an unexpected shift. The fact the food was brilliant was another oddity. These days, head chef Garry Hollihead spends time at new souped-up fish and chip restaurant Geales, leaving the obviously capable Mladen Vidakovic in charge. A beef tartare starter was deeply flavoured with spices and capers, on slim discs of plain beetroot: flawless. Salmon sashimi was subtle, with notes of fennel and dill, served with sweet pickled ginger. Chicken breast sat on a round of dauphinoise potatoes, surrounded by aubergine spears, broad beans and tiny, long-stemmed mushrooms: great ingredients presented without fuss, allowing their flavours to shine. Service, in contrast, was a shambles. Starters appeared before wine; we had to ask three times for tap water; and, worst of all, we were told there were no chips, only to see platefuls being delivered to other tables. Perhaps those diners had ordered from the £20 set menu, the one we weren't shown until the pudding stage. We emerged mentally bruised and a bit bemused; food this good – and pricey – deserves more respect.
Booking advisable. Dress: smart casual. Restaurant available for hire. Tables outdoors (6, terrace). **Map 9 J7.**

Langan's Brasserie

Stratton Street, W1J 8LB (7491 8822/ www.langansrestaurants.co.uk). Green Park tube.
Meals served 12.15-11pm Mon-Thur; 12.15-11.30pm Fri; 12.30-11pm Sat. **Main courses** £13.50-£18.50. **Cover** £1.50. **Credit** AmEx, DC, JCB, MC, V.
One glance at Langan's menu and you half expect a school dinner lady to serve lunch, rather than the smartly turned-out waiters. Sausage and mash, fish and chips, liver and bacon – the choice is cunningly designed to lead your taste buds down memory lane. It's not all canteen classics (a main course of monkfish kebab with couscous was light and fresh), but the old faves are still the big sellers. Just witness the traditional nosh weighing down the tables occupied by City suits. Judging by the clean plates, business here is most definitely a pleasure. Liver and bacon was a refreshingly thin cut of tender calf's liver and a couple of strips of crisp bacon. Unlike school, though, extras are, well,

Interview
BRYN WILLIAMS

Who are you?
Head chef at **Odette's** (*see p246*) and ex-star of BBC2's *Great British Menu*.
Eating in London: what's good about it?
The choices are fantastic. I can eat practically every cuisine under the sun; I love it all. Also, though we have some of the most expensive fine-dining restaurants in the world, there are also masses of great-value local restaurants to choose from. Near where I live in Camden there's a fantastic Japanese place, **Sushi Waka** (75 Parkway, NW1 7PP, 7482 2036), that serves incredible sushi at very reasonable prices.
What's bad about it?
There are a lot of large, characterless restaurants. I like small, intimate places where the staff can really look after you – we pride ourselves on that at Odette's. Also, I think it's too easy to source produce from all over the world, so some restaurants have become lazy about buying seasonal ingredients, without thinking about the cost to the environment.
Which are your favourite London restaurants?
Trinity (*see p112*) in Clapham is great, I also love Ian Pengelley's food at **Gilgamesh** (*see p255*). Both serve quite small dishes, so you can try lots of different flavours and techniques in one evening out.
Who or what has had the biggest impact on London's restaurant scene in the past 25 years?
The Roux brothers, for me, have had the greatest impact. Most top chefs worked under one or both of them in their heyday and they've given a brilliant grounding in classic cookery to many of our best chefs.
Any hot tips for the coming year?
Wild food should really hit mainstream this year, particular wild herbs such as wood sorrel and sea beet.

extra. You want mash? It costs £2.50, as do vegetables. In such an institutionalised venue as Langan's, a poor pudding would be an expellable offence, but all was well; a slightly stodgy treacle tart was saved by a boule of vanilla ice-cream, while strawberry pavlova was every schoolboy's dream. If you want innovation, head elsewhere, but if you're after food so comfortable it almost leaps off the plate and gives you a hug, then form an orderly queue at Langan's.
Babies and children welcome: booster seats. Booking advisable; essential dinner. Entertainment: jazz 10.30pm Thur-Sat. Separate room for parties, seats 50. **Map 9 H7**.

Nicole's

158 New Bond Street, W1F 2UB (7499 8408/ www.nicolefarhi.com). Bond Street or Green Park tube.
Bar **Open** 10am-6pm Mon-Sat. **Meals served** 11.30am-5.30pm Mon-Sat. **Main courses** £9-£13.50.
Restaurant **Breakfast served** 10-11am Mon-Fri; 10-11.30am Sat. **Lunch served** noon-3.30pm Mon-Fri; noon-4pm Sat. **Tea served** 3.30-6pm Mon-Sat. **Main courses** £15.50-£25. **Cover** (noon-4pm Mon-Sat) £1.
Both **Credit** AmEx, DC, JCB, MC, V.
It takes a few beats to adjust to the idea of a restaurant and bar in the basement of a designer clothes shop, but once its calming beige curves enfold you, Nicole's (as in Farhi) feels very natural indeed. So natural that the place is full through its daytime-only opening hours, not only with refuelling shoppers but also fond regulars who come specifically to dine. They can choose from a bar menu of mainly Mod-Med classics, a modest afternoon tea menu or the à la carte. The starters are largely unshowy dishes whose success depends on ingredient quality and perfect rendition. Ours failed to pass muster on both counts: warm tiger prawns were of unpleasant consistency; apple and celeriac soup, served with neither soup spoon nor bread, was sub-homemade. Mains are generally a piece of fish or meat plus seasonal veg, with the occasional flourish (such as asparagus tempura). Excepting a piece of garlic-crusted cod scarcely larger than a fish finger, they were better, but still not as good as we've had in the past. We suspect an off-day, but that's not something you want at these prices. Nor is the plate-plonking service.
Babies and children admitted. Booking advisable. Restaurant available for hire. **Map 9 H7**.

Patterson's

4 Mill Street, W1S 2AX (7499 1308/www.pattersonsrestaurant.co.uk). Bond Street or Oxford Circus tube. **Lunch served** noon-3pm Mon-Fri. **Dinner served** 6-11pm Mon-Fri; 5-11pm Sat. **Main courses** £13-£17. **Set lunch** £15 2 courses, £20 3 courses. **Credit** AmEx, MC, V.
The sleek but intimate decor at Patterson's goes perfectly with the Mayfair location, and its tables seem to be full of affluent diners every night. Raymond Patterson's cooking also matches the upscale neighbourhood in its luxuriousness and intricacy – at times a touch overwhelmingly. Our first courses were both hugely impressive: a magnificently rich shellfish vol-au-vent (cooked on a scallop shell) with a densely smooth paysanne of leeks and tarragon crème fraîche, and a delicate carpaccio of beef with avocado and parmesan. To follow, though, pork belly with scallops, black pudding, red onion confit, carrot purée and pork jus (that's one dish), and rack and canon of lamb with fondant potato with thyme and garlic, lamb jus with pesto and a timbale of tomato fondue, mozzarella and aubergine (that's the other), seemed to have just too much going on. The individual elements, while exquisitely presented and often delicious, sometimes had little to do with each other. Lovers of the simple and straightforward, look elsewhere. Desserts continue in the same opulent, no-holding-back vein, and there's a grand but not over-long wine list. Certainly a restaurant with its own style.
Babies and children welcome: high chairs. Booking advisable. Separate room for parties, seats 20. **Map 9 H/J6**.

Sotheby's Café

Sotheby's, 34-35 New Bond Street, W1A 2AA (7293 5077). Bond Street or Oxford Circus tube. **Breakfast served** 9.30-11.30am, **lunch served** noon-3pm, **tea served** 3-4.45pm Mon-Fri. **Main courses** £12.50-£17. **Set tea** £5.75. **Credit** AmEx, DC, MC, V.
Were Holly Golightly ever to tire of breakfasting at Tiffany's, her unfailing panacea for the blues, she'd do well to consider lunch at Sotheby's (dinner's not an option). There's something wonderfully calming about its elegant wood and mirror-panelled café, where bouffant-haired ladies in pearls gossip over afternoon teas and twinkly old gents (known by name to the staff) meditatively savour the lobster club sandwich – a constant on the otherwise weekly-changing menu. From the short, well-conceived selection of bistro classics, a starter of squid was sautéed and seasoned to perfection, accompanied by artichoke, rocket and fiery dabs of chilli jam. Guinea fowl with mashed potato and deliciously creamy broad bean sauce was simple and deeply satisfying. It was more successful, perhaps, than the fish plate, which, despite having top-notch ingredients (tiger prawns with baby gem lettuce; Dumfries-smoked salmon on toast with sour cream and chives; and tuna loin with lentils, fennel and salsa verde) was slightly too elaborate. To finish, a rosewater yoghurt panna cotta with red berries and shortbread was delightfully subtle and deliciously yielding: far too good to share.
Babies and children admitted. Booking essential lunch. Disabled: toilet. **Map 9 H6**.

★ Wild Honey NEW

2007 WINNER LEFFE BEST NEW RESTAURANT

12 St George Street, W1S 2FB (7758 9160). Oxford Circus or Bond Street tube. **Lunch served** noon-2.30pm Mon-Sat; 12.30-3.30pm Sun. **Dinner served** 5.30-10.30pm Mon-Sat; 5.30-9.30pm Sun. **Set lunch** £15.50 3 courses. **Set dinner** (5.30-7pm) £17.50 3 courses. **Credit** AmEx, MC, V.
Anthony Demetre and Will Smith, owners of Arbutus (*see p236*) – which won Best New Restaurant in the 2006 Time Out Eating & Drinking Awards – certainly have the magic touch. Though Wild Honey is very different from that Soho original in feel and decor (this is an oak-panelled but subtly modern space that's deeply convivial and made for lingering), the alluring combination of exceptionally good food at fair prices and a user-friendly wine list are the same. We wish more restaurants would start to copy their genius policy of making wines available in 250ml carafes as well as by the bottle, and keeping mark-ups low. The menu changes daily; we hope belly of pork with carrot and cumin purée and borlotti beans becomes a staple dish – deeply savoury, with melt-in-the-mouth meat and glorious crackling, it was a triumph, and cost just £14.95. Fillet of halibut with Cornish razor clams, langoustines, ratte potatoes and parsley, though good, couldn't compete. Starters also garnered plaudits: a flavoursome Mediterranean fish soup with all the trimmings made a nice contrast with a delicate, summery fresh sheep's ricotta served with watermelon, peas and pancetta. Pick of the puddings was vanilla waffles with crushed warm strawberries and chantilly cream, though the La Fromagerie cheese board (which takes centre stage in the dining room) is hard to resist. Service is unstuffy but mostly on the ball; tables are nicely spaced; and, as at Arbutus, you can eat at the bar. Pay them a visit as soon as you can; the set lunch, in particular, is astounding value for money.
Babies and children admitted. Booking essential. **Map 9 H6**.

Piccadilly

The Wolseley (100)

160 Piccadilly, W1J 9EB (7499 6996/www.thewolseley.com). Green Park tube. **Breakfast served** 7-11.30am Mon-Fri; 8-11.30am Sat, Sun. **Lunch served** noon-2.30pm daily. **Tea served** 3.30-5.30pm Mon-Sat; 3.30-6.30pm Sun. **Dinner served** 5.30pm-midnight Mon-Sat; 5.30-11pm Sun. **Main courses** £6.75-£29.50. **Set tea** £8.25-£19.50. **Cover** £2. **Credit** AmEx, DC, JCB, MC, V.
The Wolseley has always had that one commodity that money can't buy: glamour. It emanates from the grand and gorgeous 1920s room, the battalions of beautifully turned-out waiters, the clink and shine of the table-settings, and the sense that everyone in here, yourself included, could be in a 1950s film. On this year's visit, though, the illusion was punctured by a 20-minute wait for a (booked) table, no apology given. Part of the Wolseley's European grand-café schtick is to offer a variety of eating and drinking options: crustacea and caviar, cocktails and coffees, breakfast and afternoon tea, sandwiches and sundaes. On the more casual offerings, it succeeds brilliantly. On the lunch and dinner menu, however, the Euro eclecticism (a classic from every cuisine) can be unappealing to the adventurous, and the cooking doesn't always compensate. A chicken salad was merely so-so, roast pork belly dreary, and pea risotto actively disappointing: only the pre-prepared foie gras and chicken liver parfait was good. No one comes for the food alone, of course; in fact, our guess is that most people are here for an occasion of some kind. That said, at its best the Wolseley can elevate even a solo cup of coffee to the status of an occasion. It just needs to make sure that it doesn't get lazy.
Babies and children welcome: crayons; high chairs; nappy-changing facilities. Booking advisable. Disabled: toilet. **Map 9 J7**.

Pimlico

Rex Whistler Restaurant at Tate Britain

Tate Britain, Millbank, SW1P 4RG (7887 8825/ www.tate.org.uk). Pimlico tube/87 bus. **Breakfast served** 10-11.30am Sat, Sun. **Lunch served** 11.30am-3pm, **tea served** 3.15-5pm daily. **Main courses** £14.95-£19.95. **Credit** AmEx, DC, MC, V.
Despite Rex Whistler's wonderful 1927 mural, *The Expedition In Pursuit of Rare Meats*, which winds itself around the walls, Tate Britain's restaurant lacks atmosphere – maybe it's the big white pillars that divide the space or the ugly false ceiling. The lunchtime crowd (it's not open in the evening), mainly gallery-goers of a certain age, are a sober lot too. You can also visit for breakfast (pastries, a couple of cooked dishes) or tea (cakes, traditional afternoon tea, savoury snacks). No praise could overstate the excellence or reasonable pricing of the wine list; it's one of the few in London where the under-£25 bracket is taken just as seriously as fancy claret and Bordeaux. The food is a different matter. It's a fixed price per course (with five or six choices in each), so you pay £14.95 for a main, regardless of whether you opt for Gressingham duck breast with braised lettuce and broad bean velouté or the vegetarian dish of cauliflower and goat's cheese gratin with tomato and lentil sauce (much cheaper ingredients, surely?). The food is pleasant if unadventurous – though the puds (elderflower sorbet with fennel crisp, say, or chocolate truffle with cherry compote) are always worth trying – but now that the National Gallery has revamped its eating outlets to great success, isn't it time Tate followed suit?
Babies and children welcome: high chairs. Booking advisable. Disabled: toilet. Tables outdoors (8, terrace). **Map 16 L11**.

St James's

★ The Avenue

7-9 St James's Street, SW1A 1EE (7321 2111/ www.danddlondon.co.uk). Green Park tube.
Bar **Open** noon-11pm Mon-Fri; 6-11pm Sat.
Restaurant **Lunch served** noon-3pm Mon-Fri. **Dinner served** 5.45pm-11.30pm Mon-Thur; 5.45pm-12.30am Fri, Sat. **Main courses** £12.50-£18. **Set meal** £19.95 2 courses, £21.95 3 courses.
Both **Credit** AmEx, DC, MC, V.
Everything about the Avenue (even its name) suggests you could be in Manhattan. A vast glass outer window leads past a bar glittering with

exotic spirits to a large and very white room hung with black and white photos. The only splash of colour is in the low, red banquettes; even the other diners on our visit were in dark suits and white shirts. Given the standard of cooking and location, the food offers great value. Pick of our starters were delicate crab cakes with a saffron mayonnaise and tomato coulis; potted salmon with cornbread was almost as good. Main courses were more robust: lambs' kidneys with bacon were pink and plump and came with a lovely mustard mash; chicken breasts were slightly overcooked, but a spicy sauce came to their rescue. Puddings, though, were a disappointment: a raspberry pavlova was uninspiring, while a custard tart was marred by way too much cinnamon. Still, service shimmered efficiently in true NYC style. Wines are well chosen, humanely priced and there's plenty by the glass – an ethos entirely in keeping with the cooking. The Avenue is a happy place in which to dream of your next transatlantic trip.
Babies and children welcome: high chairs. Booking advisable. Disabled: toilet. **Map 9 J8**.

Le Caprice

Arlington House, Arlington Street, SW1A 1RJ (7629 2239/www.caprice-holdings.co.uk). Green Park tube. **Lunch served** noon-3pm Mon-Sat; noon-5pm Sun. **Dinner served** 5.30pm-midnight Mon-Sat; 6-11pm Sun. **Main courses** £14.25-£26.50. **Cover** £2. **Credit** AmEx, DC, MC, V.
Le Caprice gets a long way on its celebrity reputation, dating back a quarter of a century now to when that appellation meant something. These days, the Jagger, Depp and friends that gaze down on the black and white art deco room from their years-old black and white photos look improbably fresh-faced. The place still has some rich and powerful friends, but most people seem to come here to bask dressily in its perceived glamour. Is it any good? Yes, is the qualified answer – if you like this kind of thing, and these kind of prices. The menu ranges from international classics – eggs benedict, steak tartare, grilled calf's liver, thai-baked sea bass – to the more imaginative and seasonal likes of pork chop with pickled gooseberries, monkfish tail with surf clams and broad beans, and jellied beetroot soup with horseradish and salmon. Everything we tried was flavoursome, colourfully presented and generous, except a rather dry 'chopped steak Americaine' burger, which was well beyond medium rare. The solicitous staff take an enormous pride in their establishment, instantly knocking off the cost of the offending item.
Babies and children welcome: high chairs. Booking essential, several weeks in advance. Entertainment: pianist 6.30pm-midnight daily. Vegetarian menu. **Map 9 J8**.

Quaglino's

16 Bury Street, SW1Y 6AJ (7930 6767/www.danddlondon.co.uk). Green Park tube.
Bar **Open** 11.30am-1am Mon-Thur; 11.30am-2am Fri, Sat; noon-11pm Sun.
Restaurant **Lunch served** noon-3pm daily. **Dinner served** 5.30-11.30pm Mon-Thur; 5.30pm-12.30am Fri, Sat; 5.30-10.30pm Sun. **Main courses** £10.50-£32. **Set meal** (noon-3pm, 5.30-6.30pm, 10.30-11.30pm) £16.50 2 courses, £19 3 courses.
Both **Credit** AmEx, DC, JCB, MC, V.
When it launched in 1993, Quaglino's was the hottest ticket in town, cementing Sir Terence Conran's name as a man with a golden touch – and a nice line in ashtrays. Now, like the sexy cigarette girls who once patrolled its tables, there's a sense that Quag's has had its day. A touch of the old glamour endures nonetheless; the piano tinkles in the bar, and there's still a frisson to be found in descending the grand sweeping staircase. The cavernous dining room is buzzing, even if the hip crowd has moved on. Frequent special offers attract groups with an eye for a deal. The carte offers an unchallenging but wide-ranging array of brasserie food, from caesar salad and fish cakes to fillet steak with foie gras, or crustacea from the gleaming oyster counter. Whole roast sea bream with fennel was perfectly cooked, yet the accompanying chunky tomato sauce tasted woefully insipid. Rump of salt marsh lamb was flavoursome but slightly chewy; we wished the waiter had told us it came with spinach, which we'd ordered as a side dish. Puddings, by contrast, were faultless: molten chocolate fondant with nutty pistachio ice-cream, and a luscious crème brûlée, big enough for two.
Babies and children welcome: children's menu; high chairs. Booking advisable. Disabled: toilet. Entertainment: musicians 7pm daily. Separate room for parties, seats 44. **Map 9 J7**.

Soho

Alastair Little

49 Frith Street, W1D 4SG (7734 5183). Leicester Square or Tottenham Court Road tube. **Lunch served** noon-3pm Mon-Fri. **Dinner served** 6-11.30pm Mon-Sat. **Main courses** £22 (lunch); £23 (dinner). **Set lunch** £38 3 courses. **Set dinner** £40 3 courses. **Credit** AmEx, JCB, MC, V.
The reputation of this Soho stalwart rests on its pioneering role in the 'invention' of Modern European cooking some 20 years ago, and on its ability to handle high-quality, seasonal ingredients with aplomb. But Alastair Little hasn't been involved with the place for several years, so perhaps our disappointment on a recent visit was inevitable. Our meal began well; the set dinner menu was enticing, and the garnet-red juice of blood orange, rhubarb and cranberries made a delicious aperitif. Next, an earthy soup of jerusalem artichokes was enhanced by truffles and an accompanying wild mushroom tart. But nothing else really sang. The sizzling prawns were oversalted, and fillet steak was served with a too runny béarnaise and indifferent chips. Duck breast 'schnitzel' was also too salty, while its garnishes of cucumber and beetroot were insipid. For dessert, vanilla panna cotta came with stewed rhubarb and pistachio praline; each element was lovely, but the tastes and textures sat awkwardly together. Ricotta and lemon zest pancakes were tasty, yet seemed more suitable for a hefty breakfast. On the plus side, service was friendly, and we enjoyed the quiet, unassuming atmosphere of the dining room, with its pale colours and abstract paintings.
Babies and children admitted. Booking advisable. Separate room for parties, seats 25. Tables outdoors (2, pavement). **Map 17 C3**.

Andrew Edmunds

46 Lexington Street, W1F 0LW (7437 5708). Leicester Square, Oxford Circus or Piccadilly Circus tube. **Lunch served** 12.30-3pm Mon-Fri; 1-3pm Sat; 1-3.30pm Sun. **Dinner served** 6-10.45pm Mon-Sat; 6-10.30pm Sun. **Main courses** £8.95-£15. **Credit** MC, V.
Would it be déclassé to suggest that the restaurant ever-popular Andrew Edmunds most reminds us of is the cheap and cheerful Stockpot on Old Compton Street? There's the same cosy (bordering on cramped) basement dining room, the handwritten menu, favourable prices and comfort food – although the kitchen here operates at a much higher standard, of course. This Soho mainstay is often dubbed one of London's most romantic restaurants. We find the tables in the basement are much too close together for that sort of thing, but it's certainly a good bet for a classy yet not stupidly expensive second date – especially if you can grab a table on the marginally more spacious ground floor. Start with a classic (in-season asparagus, pressed ox tongue or chicken liver parfait), then move on to more of the same: wild halibut; free-range chicken on artichoke, broad bean and pea salad; or ribeye steak. Nothing mind-blowing, but all quietly satisfying. Drinks-wise, the speciality is sherry, though the well-sourced wine list remains good value: champagne at £6.50 a glass, a veritable bargain by West End standards. A classic.
Babies and children admitted. Booking essential. Tables outdoors (2, pavement). **Map 17 A4**.

★ Arbutus (100)

63-64 Frith Street, W1D 3JW (7734 4545/www.arbutusrestaurant.co.uk). Tottenham Court Road tube. **Lunch served** noon-2.30pm Mon-Sat; 12.30-3.30pm Sun. **Dinner served** 5-11pm Mon-Sat; 5.30-9.30pm Sun. **Main courses** £12-£15.50.

Set meal (lunch daily, 5-7pm Mon-Sat) £13.50 2 courses, £15.50-£17.50 3 courses. **Credit** AmEx, MC, V.
Time Out's Best New Restaurant of 2006 has sailed through that potentially tricky consolidation period. It remains permanently full (though not to that irritating book-months-ahead extent), but the service and kitchen cope well, and the menu is still instinctively alluring. Dishes are primarily British and Mediterranean in influence, precise but unfussy in execution. Braised pig's head with potato purée and caramelised onions has become a trademark; the porchetta pork, fatty yet delicate, is a worthy alternative. We've also had a good pollock with tomato and capers, simple but flavoursome tallegio risotto, and mention-worthy rice pudding mousse. The room is fresh and pleasant with Japanese notes to the decor, the diners a mixed bunch (and not too businessy at lunch) and the staff friendly and prescient. Wines are aimed at ordinary wine lovers rather than millionaires and are available by the carafe, showing a respect for the customers' pockets that is echoed in the excellent-value set meal. We have visited often and only at one dinner did we have adverse criticisms – it was noisy and the staff were untypically flustered, perhaps because there was

Arbutus

a queue for tables. Wild Honey (*see p235*), the new restaurant from owners Anthony Demetre and Will Smith, looks set to be just as big a hit.
Babies and children welcome: children's portions; high chairs. Booking advisable. **Map 17 B3**.

South Kensington

Bibendum

Michelin House, 81 Fulham Road, SW3 6RD (7581 5817/www.bibendum.co.uk). South Kensington tube. **Lunch served** noon-2.30pm Mon-Fri; 12.30-3pm Sat, Sun. **Dinner served** 7-11pm Mon-Fri; 7-11.30pm Sat; 7-10.30pm Sun. **Main courses** £19-£42. **Set lunch** £28 3 courses. **Credit** AmEx, DC, MC, V.

Set up by three chums – Terence Conran, chef Simon Hopkinson and the late Paul Hamlyn – Bibendum remains one of Terence Conran's better investments. The location in the Michelin building, with its original tiles and loopy art deco stained-glass windows of bicycling Michelin men, gives it a real sense of occasion; the atmosphere is buzzy yet relaxed. Service by the mostly French staff is very smooth: professional yet welcoming. And the French-based food of current chef Matthew Harris is refined, luxurious, varied and enjoyable. Grilled scallops were delicately but richly combined with wild garlic and thyme risotto; a more classic French soup with rouille was nicely subtle. Mains include some English standards in line with Conran tradition (posh fish and chips), but Bibendum's style seems to sit better with intricately flavoured fare such as roast pigeon with broad beans, mint and foie gras, or lamb with puy lentils and morcilla. The justly famous wine list is huge and imposing, but includes excellent bottles at £30 and under among the grand labels. Yet even without wine, you'll find eating here comes at a hefty, and sometimes exaggerated, price.
Babies and children welcome: high chair. Booking essential; 1 week in advance for dinner. Bookings not accepted for more than 10. **Map 14 E10**.

Westminster

Bank Westminster

45 Buckingham Gate, SW1E 6BS (7379 9797/ www.bankrestaurants.com). St James's Park tube.
Bar **Open** 11am-11pm Mon-Wed; 11am-1am Thur-Fri; 5pm-1am Sat.
Restaurant **Lunch served** noon-3pm Mon-Fri. **Dinner served** 5.30-10.30pm Mon-Sat. **Main courses** £10.95-£25.
Both **Credit** AmEx, MC, V.

Expect an upmarket, business clientele (lots of older men on not-so-hot dates with their laptops) and swift, efficient service to match. Bank Westminster has a fabulous setting. Tables – set in a huge conservatory lit by dramatic overhead sphere lights – look out over a grand courtyard complete with fountain, an impressive backdrop for alfresco dining. The menu is a varied, lengthy roster of crowd-pleasers: risottos, pasta dishes, steaks, oysters, fish and salads. While ideal for meeting the varied dietary requirements of a large business lunch, Bank's 'something for everyone' approach doesn't leave much room for specialism. We started with perfectly cooked asparagus with hollandaise (served with a slightly cold poached egg) and delicately spiced thai fish cakes; both were very good, if unspectacular. Mains received more praise. A huge chunk of tuna was cooked exactly as requested and served with a mound of greens, while haddock and leek risotto proved deliciously creamy. Despite its contemporary styling and constant buzz (things get busy on weekday evenings from 8.30pm), Bank isn't the edgiest venue in town, but it's a reliable choice.
Babies and children welcome: children's menu; high chairs. Booking advisable. Disabled: toilet. Separate room for parties, seats 40. Tables outdoors (15, courtyard). **Map 15 J9**.

West

Bayswater

Island Restaurant & Bar

Royal Lancaster Hotel, Lancaster Terrace, W2 2TY (7551 6070/www.islandrestaurant.co.uk). Lancaster Gate tube.
Bar/Restaurant **Open/meals served** noon-11pm daily. **Main courses** £8.50-£22.50. **Set meal** (noon-5pm) £12.50 1 course incl glass of wine.
Both **Credit** AmEx, DC, MC, V.

The magenta light bathing the smart dark wood and white restaurant on the raised bottom floor of the Royal Lancaster Hotel didn't add to the atmosphere. Nor did the lobbyish music. But the Island was far from deserted. Little local competition, fair prices and a view of Hyde Park must account for the number of hotel guests and locals eating here after work. The friendly waiting staff were somewhat overstretched. The kitchen, visible through a widescreen hatch, acquits itself well, turning out greatest contemporary British hits – but again distinguishing features are few. A pea and broad bean soup was a beautiful colour, but the truffle oil and wild mushroom cream conspired against the freshness of the spring vegetables and made it needlessly lavish. A main course of grilled calf's liver with pancetta and creamy cauliflower and spinach also erred on the rich side. Fish in an exceptionally light crisp batter with chips was a respectable rendition, but didn't set the Thames on fire. So far, good enough. Cheesecake stuck to the bottom of a bowl and, topped with undercooked rhubarb, did make a lasting impression. It remained almost untouched.
Babies and children welcome: children's menu; high chairs. Bar/restaurant available for hire. Booking advisable. Disabled: toilet. **Map 8 D6**.

Chiswick

Sam's Brasserie & Bar

11 Barley Mow Passage, W4 4PH (8987 0555/ www.samsbrasserie.co.uk). Chiswick Park or Turnham Green tube.
Bar **Open** 9am-midnight Mon-Wed, Sun; 9am-1am Thur-Sat. **Brunch served** 9am-noon, **lunch served** noon-3pm, **dinner served** 6.30-10.30pm daily. **Main courses** £4.75-£9.50.
Restaurant **Brunch served** 9am-4pm Sat, Sun. **Lunch served** noon-3pm Mon-Fri; 9am-4pm Sat, Sun. **Dinner served** 6.30-10.30pm Mon-Sat; 6.30-10pm Sun. **Main courses** £8.75-£17.50. **Set lunch** (Mon-Fri) £11.50 2 courses, £15 3 courses; (Sun) £19.50 3 courses.
Both **Credit** AmEx, MC, V.

Set in a stunning converted Victorian industrial space behind Chiswick Green, Sam's has a slightly corporate feel. There's real potential here – it won Best Local Restaurant in our 2006 Eating &

Drinking Awards – but on our lunchtime visit the place lacked atmosphere. Although the restaurant incorporates an open kitchen, the buzz of the chefs at work just didn't translate into the rest of the space. Food was well prepared, but uninspiring. Twice-baked blue cheese soufflé had a melt-in-the-mouth texture, yet the ceps vinaigrette that came with it was overpowering and vinegary. Also, we were coaxed into ordering a tomato and onion salad, which was both unnecessary and dull. Own-made fish fingers from the children's menu were crunchy and full of flavour – worth including on the adult list. For dessert, chocolate torte had just the right texture, halfway between a cake and a mousse; ice-cream (good but not great) arrived with fruits and sauce. The meal was good value, but lacked the wow factor the impressive interior leads you to expect – though it's buzzier at night. The bar by the entrance is friendly and relaxed, with a substantial wine list and extensive brunch menu.
Babies and children welcome: children's menu; high chairs; toys. Booking advisable Thur-Sat. Disabled: toilet.

Kensington

★ 11 Abingdon Road

11 Abingdon Road, W8 6AH (7937 0120/ www.abingdonroad.co.uk). High Street Kensington tube. **Lunch served** noon-2.30pm Mon-Sat; noon-3pm Sun. **Dinner served** 6.30-10.45pm Mon-Sat; 6.30-10.30pm Sun. **Main courses** £11.95-£17.50. **Set lunch** £13.50 2 courses. **Set dinner** £17.50 2 courses. **Credit** MC, V.
There are plenty of London restaurants with a cool, minimalist look, but few manage to carry it off with as much charm as this excellent local (sister to Sonny's, *see below*, and the Phoenix, *see p241*). White or ultra-pale green walls are offset by flowers, modern paintings and some rather glitzy armchairs in the bar. The atmosphere is bright but not brittle, mellow but not dull, stylish but genuinely child-friendly. Service is excellent, unfussily welcoming and obliging. And the food is as refreshing as the overall style. The largely Mediterranean menu is strongly seasonal, with plenty of fresh, vivid flavours. Gnocchi of ricotta, peas, speck, mint and parmesan threatened creamy overkill, but turned out to be beautifully light. There was also culinary flair on show in the mains, such as succulent rack of lamb with aubergine, borlotti beans and a pepper sauce, or a nicely smoky sea bream with a sauce vierge. A Laroche Provence rosé at just the right temperature went deliciously with our food on a warm day, and was one of several fairly priced wines on an attractive list. No.11 could easily become a habit.
Babies and children welcome: children's portions; high chairs. Booking advisable. Disabled: toilet. Separate rooms for parties, seating 20-60. **Map 7 A9**.

Babylon

7th floor, The Roof Gardens, 99 Kensington High Street, W8 5SA (7368 3993/www.roofgardens.com). High Street Kensington tube. **Lunch served** noon-3pm daily. **Dinner served** 7-11pm Mon-Sat. **Main courses** £18.50-£24. **Set lunch** (Mon-Fri) £16 2 courses, £18 3 courses; (Sat) £16.50 2 courses, £19.50 3 courses; (Sun) £18.50 2 courses, £21.50 3 courses. **Credit** AmEx, DC, JCB, MC, V.
Pleasant as Babylon's sleek, glass-walled dining room may be, it's not a patch on the wooden-decked terrace outside. Hence, on balmy evenings, the latter's no-bookings rule can occasion the odd temper tantrum from the well-heeled clientele. The seventh-floor vantage point offers magnificent views, with the city lights glimmering beyond the lush tree-tops of the roof gardens below (where resident pink flamingos add a wonderfully surreal touch). The menu combines a seasonal focus with quietly luxurious ingredients. A starter of Kent asparagus, dandelion leaves and jerusalem artichoke shavings, topped with truffles, was lovely in its simplicity. Alas, the same couldn't be said for the bread; slightly stale, it was served with rapeseed oil: definitely an acquired taste. Truffles and artichoke appeared again in a beautifully fresh, light pasta dish, accompanied by peppery wild rocket and parmesan. Lemon sole was served with splendid buttered samphire and fennel, braised celeriac and tiny clams; unfortunately, the fish was a touch overcooked. A bottle of Spanish rosé from the extensive, New World-dominated wine list was suitably summery. As dusk fell, even City slickers bickering over a wine bill couldn't dispel the romance.
Babies and children welcome: children's menu; entertainer (Sun); high chairs. Booking advisable. Disabled: lift; toilet. Entertainment: musicians dinner Thur. Separate room for parties, seats 12. Tables outdoors (15, terrace). **Map 7 B9**.

Clarke's (100)

124 Kensington Church Street, W8 4BH (7221 9225/www.sallyclarke.com). Notting Hill Gate tube. **Brunch served** 11am-2pm Sat. **Lunch served** 12.30-2pm Mon-Fri. **Dinner served** 7-10pm Tue-Sat. **Main courses** (lunch) £14-£16. **Set dinner** £43.25 3 courses, £49.50 4 courses, incl coffee. **Credit** AmEx, JCB, MC, V.
Sally Clarke worked in California (and was inspired by Alice Waters' Chez Panisse) before bringing Cal-Ital cooking back to the UK in the mid 1980s. Her approach to food is still uncompromising. A lunchtime burger looks unpromising until you factor in Clarke's chargrilling skill and free hand with herbs. Fragrant, herby, juicy and beefy, it was exceptional – as it should be for £16. The equally understated wine list (reasonable mark-ups) is notable for its New World emphasis, with some rare California wines. But the crisp white tablecloths with bowls of roses, and the cut-glass-accented clientele are frightfully English, making the place a tad chilly. Sourcing is impeccable, preparation deceptively simple, and everything tastes just-so: from terrific raisin and walnut bread to the deepest, darkest chocolate truffles (which can be purchased in the next-door shop). A generous starter of Jersey Royal frittata with wild Irish smoked salmon and a salad of pea shoots and shelled peas was a typically inspired, seasonal assembly of fab ingredients. Dinner promises equally good things, and after 21 years of famously being no-choice, the set-price menu now has three options for each course. If only this slightly 1980s-looking place engendered the sense of occasion you'd expect for the prices.
Babies and children welcome: high chair. Booking advisable; essential weekends. Restaurant available for hire. **Map 7 B7**.

Kensington Place

201-209 Kensington Church Street, W8 7LX (7727 3184/www.danddlondon.co.uk). Notting Hill Gate tube. **Lunch served** noon-3.30pm daily. **Dinner served** 6.30-11.15pm Mon-Thur; 6.30-11.45pm Fri, Sat; 6.30-10.15pm Sun. **Main courses** £14-£25. **Set lunch** (Mon-Fri) £19.50 3 courses; (Sun) £24.50 3 courses. **Set dinner** £24.50 3 courses (£39.50 incl wine). **Credit** AmEx, DC, JCB, MC, V.
Liner-like Kensington Place has steered a steady course for more than 20 years. The glass-sided room is as bright and ship-shape as ever, and has aged better than the clientele: an older crowd representing what passes for bohemia in Kensington. The long and varied menu is a Modern European archetype. A warm salmon mousse was a well-behaved starter; asparagus, simple and seasonal, couldn't fail. But mains were slipshod. Red mullet with a couple of dried-up slices of chorizo came with fennel so undercooked the fish knife couldn't cut it. Pot roast poussin, on the other hand, was cooked to a mush, making a knife redundant. Everything was underseasoned. Service goes through the professional paces well enough, and the notorious acoustics may explain a misunderstood wine order – from a lively and well-ordered list – but not the shoulder-shrugging reaction. Though never a dull place to be, Kensington Place needs to put some lustre back into the food. Could the December 2006 departure of Rowley Leigh, chef of KP since it opened in 1987, explain the kitchen's inconsistency? The acquisition of the restaurant in summer 2007 by D&D (owners of the former Conran stable) had yet to have an effect as we went to press.
Babies and children welcome: high chairs. Booking advisable; essential weekends. Disabled: toilet. Separate room for parties, seats 45. **Map 7 B7**.

Launceston Place

1A Launceston Place, W8 5RL (7937 6912/ www.danddlondon.co.uk). Gloucester Road or High Street Kensington tube. **Lunch served** 12.30-2.30pm Mon-Fri, Sun. **Dinner served** 6-11pm Mon-Sat; 6-10pm Sun. **Main courses** £14.50-£20.50. **Set lunch** (Sun) £24.50 3 courses. **Set meal** (Mon-Sat) £16.50 2 courses, £18.50 3 courses. **Credit** AmEx, DC, JCB, MC, V.
The world may be collapsing around us, but all is well inside Launceston Place, the older, more refined but considerably less funky sister to Kensington Place. The sign in the window boasts that the finest Sunday lunches have been produced here for 21 years, but it could easily have been two centuries. Set in a charming Kensington backwater, the place has the feel of a civilised gentlemen's club, with red banquettes in little nooks, and Victorian landscape paintings adorning the walls. The Sunday set lunch has at least ten choices for each course. A simple starter of asparagus, balsamic and parmesan was an ideal pre-roast amuse-gueule, the trio of intense flavours limbering up the palate for the main event. Roast beef came out on the rare side of 'medium', but was all the better for it. The only let-down was the rather dowdy selection of vegetables, including broccoli florets smothered in an overpowering white sauce. For pudding, a well-crafted version of eton mess seemed entirely appropriate for W8. Service is unobtrusive but highly professional. Let's hope LP's summer 2007 acquisition by D&D London does it no harm.
Babies and children welcome: high chair. Booking advisable. Separate room for parties, seating 12. **Map 7 C9**.

The Terrace

33C Holland Street, W8 4LX (7937 3224/ www.theterracerestaurant.co.uk). High Street Kensington tube. **Brunch served** noon-3pm Sat; noon-3.30pm Sun. **Lunch served** noon-2.30pm Mon-Fri. **Dinner served** 6.30-11pm Mon-Sat.

BEST MODERN EUROPEAN

For location

Sights for sore eyes (whether the view or the surroundings) at **L'Atelier de Joël Robuchon** (*see p232*), **Blueprint Café** (*see p245*), **Petersham Nurseries** (*see p247*), **Plateau** (*see p245*), **Skylon** (*see p243*) and **Wapping Food** (*see p246*).

For the buzz

The crowd is often a feast for the eyes at **L'Atelier de Joël Robuchon** (*see p232*), **Bumpkin** (*see right*), **Embassy** (*see p233*), **Fifth Floor** (*see p233*), **The Ivy** (*see p232*) and **Smiths of Smithfield** (*see p232*).

For wine

Corking lists at **Ambassador** (*see p230*), **Arbutus** (*see p236*), **The Avenue** (*see p235*), **Bibendum** (*see p237*), **Blueprint Café** (*see p245*), **The Don** (*see p230*), **Orrery** (*see p233*), **Ransome's Dock** (*see p242*), **Redmond's** (*see p241*) and **Wild Honey** (*see p235*).

For business

Expect things to run like clockwork at **Axis** (*see p232*), **Bibendum** (*see p237*), **Glasshouse** (*see p247*), **Oxo Tower Restaurant, Bar & Brasserie** (*see p243*), **Plateau** (*see p245*) and **Prism** (*see p230*).

Main courses £11-£19. **Set brunch** (Sat, Sun) £17.50 2 courses, £21.50 3 courses. **Set lunch** £14.50 2 courses. **Credit** AmEx, JCB, MC, V.
The small, low-key Terrace is tucked neatly away in the heart of conservative W8. Its prime attraction, especially on a sunny day, is the chance to munch alfresco on the pretty outdoor terrace. Surrounded by tall box-hedges to fend off the traffic noise of Holland Street, this makes a fine spot to sip a glass or two of rosé and soak up the gossip of the well-heeled clientele (a mix of Stateside bankers with their smartly dressed offspring and old-school Kensington couples). The food is less alluring. A crab cake starter was subtle to the point of blandness, while a main course of pork chop was tough; a handful of tasty green beans cost an extra £3.50. Sea bass on a bed of lentils was a more successful combination, but showed a lack of adventure in both cooking and presentation. With mains hovering around £18, we expected better. Puddings were an improvement, yet the overall taste was soured by an £80 bill for a rather mediocre lunch for two (including a couple of glasses of wine). The saving grace is the wildly friendly hostess/waitress, whose presence almost made up for the unexciting cuisine… almost.
Babies and children welcome: children's portions; high chairs. Booking advisable. Restaurant available for hire. Tables outdoors (8, terrace). **Map 7 B8**.

Whits

21 Abingdon Road, W8 6AH (7938 1122/ www.whits.co.uk). High Street Kensington tube. *Bar* **Open** 5.30-11pm Tue-Sat; 5-11pm Sun. *Restaurant* **Lunch served** 12.30-3pm Sun. **Dinner served** 6.30-10.30pm Tue-Sat. **Main courses** £13.50-£19.50. **Set lunch** £18.50 3 courses. **Set dinner** £23.50 3 courses. **Credit** AmEx, MC, V.
Abingdon Road has become a restaurant row over the past few years, easing the shortage of decent eating options in Kensington. Whits was one of the first on the scene and it now has a loyal following. It's that kind of place; from the genuine greeting on arrival to the generous portions served in the narrow, whitewashed, wood-floored room, this is cosy cuisine done to a T. A starter of foie gras was a smooth slab of terrine, offset neatly by a side of confit and brioche. A towering cheese soufflé was too heavy for an opener, though, and hinted at chef-patron Steve Whitney's training under Swiss chef Anton Mosimann. Main courses of belly of pork and beef chop with ratatouille and pommes dauphinoise were fittingly rich for the surroundings (heavy portions, heavy sauces), and meant the trio of chocolate puds for dessert was more than enough for two. Service was impeccable. Just one word of warning: don't book much past 9pm. Whereas turning up early often jeopardises the atmosphere of a place, here staying too late has a similar effect, with most of the well-heeled, well-aged locals having put away three courses and a bottle of Vacqueyras well before the watershed.
Babies and children admitted. Booking advisable. Restaurant available for hire. **Map 7 A9**.

Notting Hill

Notting Hill Brasserie

92 Kensington Park Road, W11 2PN (7229 4481). Notting Hill Gate tube. **Lunch served** noon-3pm daily. **Dinner served** 7-11pm Mon-Sat. **Main courses** £18.50-£23.50. **Set lunch** (Mon-Sat) £17.50 2 courses, £22.50 3 courses; (Sun) £25 2 courses, £30 3 courses. **Credit** AmEx, MC, V.
Corniced ceilings, pale furnishings, soft lighting, intimate alcoves, starched table linen, jazz duos and manicured customers create serene environs in this select townhouse. Flurries of expert waiters (including a famously gruff elder statesman) add seasoning. This is Notting Hill's brasserie for the haute bourgeoisie: except it doesn't keep brasserie hours, and the food transcends the genre. Sea bass is paired with crispy frogs' legs; even a humble pea soup comes with morels. The menu makes a thrilling read: exciting combinations of luxury ingredients at scary prices. To start, a whisper-light cannelloni of juicy lobster segments was covered in foamy shellfish velouté and bordered by a rectangle of intense cep purée. The food looks prim on the plate: beautiful yet excessively well ordered. Logs of chips were stacked like children's building blocks next to a tender chateaubriand, with a bowl of béarnaise (heavy on the tarragon) as a dip. Some portions verge on nouvelle nonsense – another second course, pan-fried halibut with jerusalem artichoke purée, peas, broad beans and morels, left us wanting more. Yet chef Karl Burdock's flavours are as precise and interlocking as a master carpenter's dovetail joint. Wine and puddings (sublime vanilla cheesecake with raspberry and cocoa tuile) are notable too.
Babies and children welcome: entertainer (Sun lunch); high chairs. Booking advisable. Entertainment: jazz/blues musicians 7pm daily. Separate rooms for parties, seating 12 and 32. **Map 7 A6**.

Shepherd's Bush

Brackenbury

129-131 Brackenbury Road, W6 0BQ (8748 0107/www.thebrackenbury.co.uk). Goldhawk Road or Hammersmith tube. **Brunch served** 10am-3.30pm Sat, Sun. **Lunch served** 12-2.45pm Mon-Fri. **Dinner served** 7-10.45pm Mon-Sat. **Main courses** £9-£18. **Set lunch** (Mon-Fri) £12.50 2 courses, £14.50 3 courses. **Credit** AmEx, MC, V.
The manicured little terraces around here create a sense of community that feeds into the Brackenbury. Mind you, the community is posh (think Ralph Lauren shirts or pearl necklaces), as reflected in the prices at this cosy little split-level restaurant. Most nights the taupe-hued interior is full of folk who think nothing of spending £10 on a diminutive starter of crab salad. Food on the daily-changing carte combines British ingredients and Med touches with a French sensibility. A starter of lamb sweetbreads came in an appetising creamy sauce with not-quite seasonal fresh peas (a little hard), unadvertised french beans and barely discernible mint. To follow, sea bass fillet with courgette fritters, watercress and aïoli was a perfectly cooked, well-balanced dish, though a side order of Jersey Royals took its cost up to £20. The set lunch seems great value in comparison. Sautéed rabbit (with spring vegetables and grain-mustard sauce) was a mite tough. Puddings (creamy citrus tart, say) are a highlight, as is a wine list that starts at £12 for a decent merlot and rises to £190 for a St-Émilion. Service is low-key and polite, but can slow as the evening progresses.
Babies and children welcome: children's portions; high chairs. Booking advisable. Separate rooms for parties, seating 30-40. Tables outdoors (8, patio). **Map 20 B3**.

Westbourne Park

Bumpkin NEW

209 Westbourne Park Road, W11 1EA (7243 9818/www.bumpkinuk.com). Westbourne Park tube.
Brasserie **Lunch served** noon-3.30pm Tue-Fri; 12.15-4pm Sun. **Brunch served** 11am-4pm Sat. **Dinner served** 6pm-midnight daily.
Restaurant **Lunch served** 12.15pm-4pm Sun. **Dinner served** 6pm-midnight Tue-Sat.
Both **Main courses** £8-£20. **Credit** AmEx, MC, V.
Only in David Cameron's Notting Hill fantasy world could a restaurant pretend to be a country 'brasserie', while closing between mealtimes and not serving drinks unless you're eating. But despite contrived concept and aesthetic – pretty, if you like mock-rustic decor and waiters with beards – there's some serious intent behind the menus. British-leaning but with occasional excursions into Italian or French produce and cooking, we could find no fault with the 'charter pie', a mix of leek, shredded chicken and fragments of ham, topped with a flaky pastry lid: scrumptious. You can tell you're not up-country, though, when you have to pay extra for vegetables: £3 for peas and bacon, £4 for a firm gratin dauphinois. We also liked a starter salad of Fine Fettle cheese (a British-made feta) with mint, radishes and proper lettuce leaves from Secretts Farm. Meats are also top-quality, from Ginger Pig or Frank Godfrey. The best thing about Bumpkin is the charming staff and generally friendly atmosphere; the worst thing is that no bookings are taken for the ground-floor brasserie, so you either have to queue, or book for the first-floor dining room (which offers a very similar menu, but is more formal).
Babies and children welcome: children's portions; crayons; high chairs. Bookings not accepted (brasserie). Separate rooms for parties, seats 20-30. **Map 7 A5**.

South West

Barnes

Sonny's

94 Church Road, SW13 0DQ (8748 0393/ www.sonnys.co.uk). Barnes or Barnes Bridge rail/33, 209, 283 bus.
Café **Open** 10.30am-5pm Mon, Tue; 10.30am-5.30pm Wed; 10.30am-6pm Thur-Sat. **Lunch served** noon-4pm Mon-Sat. **Main courses** £4.50-£10.25.
Restaurant **Lunch served** 12.30-2.30pm Mon-Sat; 12.30-3pm Sun. **Dinner served** 7.30-10.45pm Mon-Thur; 7-11pm Fri, Sat. **Main courses** £10.25-£19.95. **Set lunch** (Mon-Sat) £15.50 2 courses, £17.50 3 courses; (Sun) £21.50 3 courses. **Set dinner** (Mon-Thur) £18.50 2 courses, £21.50 3 courses.
Both **Credit** AmEx, MC, V.
The decor and convivial vibe remain unchanged at this ever-popular Barnes stalwart. An eclectic array of modern art still adorns the white walls; the low-lit back room is more soothing than the brighter front area; well-mannered staff continue to attend assiduously to the wealthy clientele. The cooking is now more straightforward, though; oysters and a half pint of prawns were among the starters, and steak tartare was offered as both a first course and main (maybe not such a good idea, when the menu isn't long). Rump of lamb – a generous main course, cooked medium rare as requested – was excellent, served with a tasty thyme and red wine jus and broad beans (peeled: a sign of a kitchen that cares). However, risotto of girolles and butternut squash was insipid, the squash adding colour but no flavour. A starter salad of stilton, endive and walnuts was no better than a home-assembled version, but tarte tatin with Calvados ice-cream was worth the 15-minute wait; the pears had a delightfully chewy, caramelised edge (desserts are a high point here). The wine list is enterprising and imaginative; although there's no reason to spend over £30, the higher-priced bins represent the best value for money. Siblings the Phoenix (*see p241*) and 11 Abingdon Road (*see above*) are commended too.
Babies and children welcome: high chairs. Booking advisable (restaurant). Restaurant available for hire. Separate room for parties, seats 20.

Chelsea

Bluebird

350 King's Road, SW3 5UU (7559 1000/ www.danddlondon.com). Sloane Square tube then 11, 19, 22, 49, 319 bus.
Bar **Open** noon-midnight Mon-Thur; noon-1am Fri, Sat; noon-11.30pm Sun.
Restaurant **Brunch served** noon-3.30pm Sat, Sun. **Lunch served** 12.30-2.30pm Mon-Fri. **Dinner served** 6-11pm Mon-Sat; 6-10pm Sun. **Main courses** £13.50-£25. **Set meal** (lunch, 6-7pm Mon-Fri) £18 2 courses £22 3 courses. **Credit** AmEx, DC, JCB, MC, V.
After ten years serving the lunching ladies of the King's Road, Bluebird unveiled a new look (and new menu) in spring 2007. The restaurant and bar occupy the single, glorious upper room (not to be confused with the less formal café on the ground floor) and it is looking grander than ever. Several vast chandeliers have been hoisted high up to the light-filled ceiling; sofas and armchairs now mingle with the formal white tables; and a glittering bar dominates the far end. The user-friendly menu has also been given a boost by executive chef Mark Broadbent and there's an emphasis on local

Lunch Monday to Friday
12 noon to 3.30pm

Dinner Monday to Friday
5.30pm to 11.30pm

Saturday, open all day
12 noon to 11.30 pm

Sunday, 12 noon to 6pm

"One of the finest river views in London ... tamesa@oxo is the ideal pit stop on a weekend walk along the South Bank"

FAY MASCHLER, THE EVENING STANDARD

Waterside dining, ideal for romantic 2's to celebrating 20's. Enjoy a meal in the retro chic surroundings of our brasserie or simply relax in an oasis of cocktail cool.

tamesa @ oxo
bar and brasserie

second floor
oxo tower
bargehouse street
london SE1 9PH

Reservations 020 7633 0088
http://www.oxotower.co.uk/tamesa.html

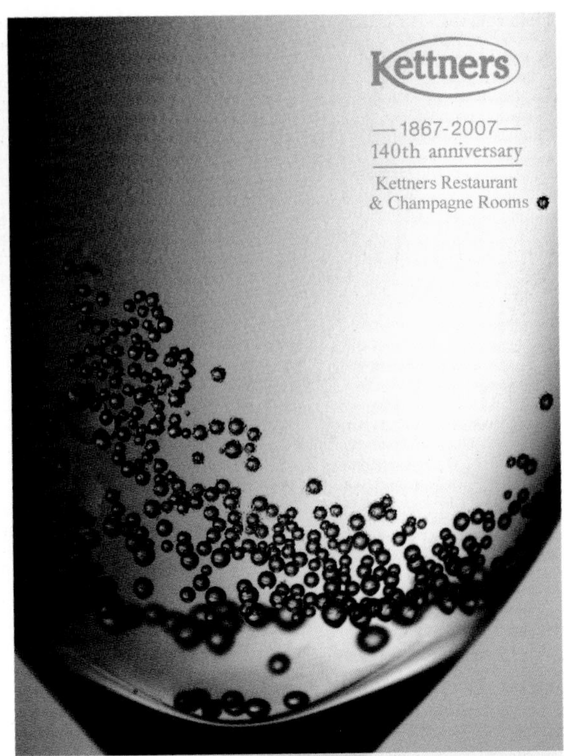

29 Romilly Street, Soho, London, W1D 5HP, 020 7734 6112
www.kettners.com

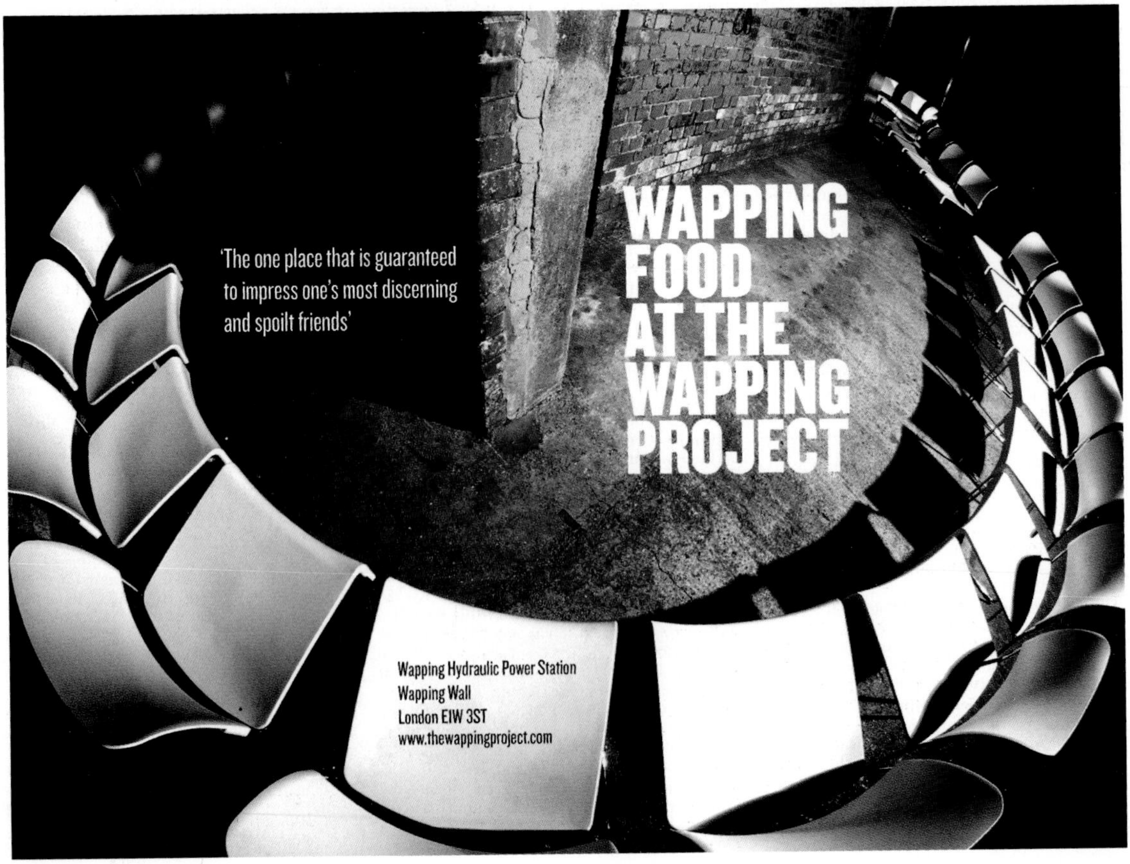

'The one place that is guaranteed to impress one's most discerning and spoilt friends'

WAPPING FOOD AT THE WAPPING PROJECT

Wapping Hydraulic Power Station
Wapping Wall
London EIW 3ST
www.thewappingproject.com

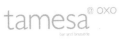

producers. On our visit, minestrone soup was filled with fresh seasonal flavours. Crab salad was surf-fresh and came with splendid, own-made mayo. Their burger (with big glossy chips) is done to a turn and served in a brioche. The one less perfect note was the fish pie, which was slightly featureless, despite being advertised as 'day boat fish with crustacea sauce and potato crust'. Service, as you'd expect from a revitalised venture, was bouncy. In all, a relaxing and pampering place to be (we saw a civilised hen party, several families and loitering couples on a Saturday lunchtime), with prices that won't shock the locals.
Babies and children welcome: high chairs; nappy-changing facilities. Disabled: lift; toilet. Dress: smart casual. Separate rooms for parties, both seating 30. **Map 14 D12**.

East Sheen

Redmond's

170 Upper Richmond Road West, SW14 8AW (8878 1922/www.redmonds.org.uk). Hammersmith tube then 33 bus/Mortlake rail. **Dinner served** 7-10pm Mon-Sat. **Set dinner** (Mon-Thur) £24 2 courses, £27 3 courses; (Fri, Sat) £27.50 2 courses, £32 3 courses. **Credit** MC, V.

Behind a nondescript shopfront on the traffic-heavy main road through East Sheen, long-lived Redmond's is a hidden gem. The decor is modern and anonymous, well lit but bland. The popularity, and atmosphere, can vary. We tried to visit three weekends running (it's open only for dinner) and found the place booked out, then on the Friday night of our visit the place was virtually empty. The service and food, however – by a husband-and-wife team – is first-rate. The wine list is extraordinary, expertly chosen, beautifully written, full of detail (and there are wine tasting courses too). You pay for this – the cheapest bottle is £15.25 – but it's worth it. The set menu has a half dozen choices per course. To start, a salad of English asparagus and broad beans with a lemon dressing was fresh and zinging with flavour. Seared mackerel fillet with celeriac and lime purée was melt-in-the-mouth stunning. The main courses were no less brilliant. Roast halibut with red onion and potato rosti, sautéed sugar snaps and salsa verde was spot-on: just-so fish, crisp veg. And corn-fed chicken breast with rosemary and truffle sauce was the ultimate in buttery, French-style comfort food. Desserts (perhaps pear and almond tart with Marsala ice-cream or sorbets of pineapple, charentais melon and blood orange) are equally memorable. An excellent local restaurant.
Babies and children welcome: booster seat; children's menu. Booking advisable. Restaurant available for hire.

★ Victoria

10 West Temple Sheen, SW14 7RT (8876 4238/www.thevictoria.net). Hammersmith tube then 33 bus/Mortlake rail. **Open** 8am-11pm Mon-Sat; 8am-10.30pm Sun **Lunch served** noon-2.30pm Mon-Fri; noon-3pm Sat; noon-4pm Sun. **Dinner served** 7-10pm Mon-Sat; 7-9pm Sun. **Main courses** £9.95-£21.95. **Credit** AmEx, MC, V.

One notch up from a gastropub but without a restaurant's formality, the Victoria is tucked away in the leafy suburbs. Wealthy locals expecting first-rate produce and zero pretension dine here; it's also a real find for families, as the airy dining room looks out on a private playground. There's a separate, cosy bar with a (good, but limited) menu. The cooking in the main dining area is sublime. Ingredients are locally sourced wherever possible. Pan-fried scallops on a bed of rocket is a typical dish: simple, unfussy, allowing flavours to speak for themselves. Roasted asparagus with balsamic vinegar and parmesan was another great example. A generous Sunday roast of lamb was tender, the veg and potatoes gloriously traditional, while the fish and chips is to die for; almost tempura-like coley came balanced on a bed of pea purée. Desserts are tempting if not spectacular: chocolate nemesis was rich but had a lightness to it; the own-made ice-cream was great. Impeccable service, a good wine list and relaxed surroundings further boost the Victoria's standing. It's also a hotel, with seven double bedrooms.
Babies and children welcome: children's menu; high chairs; play area (garden). Booking essential. Restaurant available for hire. Separate area for parties, seats 40. Tables outdoors (10, garden).

Fulham

The Farm

18 Farm Lane, SW6 1PP (7381 3331/www.thefarmfulham.co.uk). Fulham Broadway tube/11, 14, 211 bus.
Bar **Open** noon-midnight Mon-Fri; 10am-midnight Sat; 10am-11.30pm Sun. **Meals served** noon-11pm Mon-Fri; 10am-11pm Sat, Sun. **Main courses** £3.95-£9.95.
Restaurant **Brunch served** 10am-4pm Sat; 10am-4.30pm Sun. **Meals served** noon-11pm Mon-Fri; 10am-11pm Sat, Sun. **Main courses** £9.95-£18.95.
Both **Credit** AmEx, MC, V.

In an unprepossessing side street off North End Road sits the unprepossessing-looking Farm. But step through the doors of this converted pub and things improve dramatically, with a cosy front section featuring plenty of stretch-out sofas gathered around a large, square bar. The restaurant area is perched at the back of the building, and comes complete with a pianist to aid digestion. The look is all dark wood and velvet panelling, but the mood is brightened by floor-to-ceiling windows looking out on to a white-painted brick wall (nicer than it sounds, especially when the fairy lights come on after dark). Service is young, but eager to please, with a surfeit of smiling faces; one of the waitresses moonlights as in-house chanteuse at weekends. The menu is well thought out, with plenty of emphasis on sourcing. Succulent loin of Elwy Valley spring lamb with roast cherry tomatoes, baked aubergine and spiced couscous was a tender, well-balanced combination. Puds are the usual roll-call (tarte tatin, crème brûlée). An intense chocolate tart made the sofas in the bar all the more welcoming afterwards.
Babies and children welcome: high chairs. Booking advisable. Disabled: toilet. Tables outdoors (8, pavement; 4, terrace).
Map 13 A13.

Putney

Phoenix Bar & Grill

162-164 Lower Richmond Road, SW15 1LY (8780 3131/www.sonnys.co.uk). Putney Bridge tube/22, 265 bus. **Lunch served** 12.30-2.30pm Mon-Sat; 12.30-3pm Sun. **Dinner served** 7-11pm Mon-Sat; 7-10pm Sun. **Main courses** £9.50-£16.50. **Set lunch** (Mon-Sat) £13.50 2 courses, £15.50 3 courses; (Sun) £19.50 3 courses. **Set dinner** (Mon-Thur, Sun) £15.50 2 courses, £17.50 3 courses. **Credit** AmEx, MC, V.

Rebecca Mascarenhas is queen of the local restaurant; as well as this Putney favourite, she oversees long-established Sonny's (*see p239*) and more recent arrival 11 Abingdon Road (*see p238*) – all attractive, welcoming, well-run operations, with imaginative menus and good-value set meals. The highlight here is the bamboo-surrounded front terrace, complete with fairy lights and heaters, but the capacious interior, all blond wood and colourful artworks, is appealing too. Staff were exemplary: all smiles when we turned up without a booking, and happy to accommodate dietary needs and a wheelchair. The menu has Italian touches, from the signature dish of vincisgrassi maceratesi (a rich lasagne from an 18th-century recipe), to vin santo and cantuccini biscotti for afters. It was hard to fault our dishes: perfectly cooked roast halibut (fish is a forte), partnered by crisp green beans and sauce vierge; linguine with a tasty crab, tomato, garlic and chilli sauce; and desserts of intensely flavoured sorbets (mango, lemon, blackcurrant), and chocolate espresso cake (dense but not overly rich) with latte cream.
Babies and children welcome: children's menu (Sun); crayons; high chairs. Booking essential summer; advisable winter. Disabled: toilet. Tables outdoors (19, terrace).

South

Balham

Lamberts

2 Station Parade, Balham High Road, SW12 9AZ (8675 2233/www.lambertsrestaurant.com). Balham tube/rail. **Lunch served** noon-3pm Sat. **Dinner served** 7-10.30pm Tue-Sat. **Meals served** noon-9pm Sun. **Main courses** £14-£18. **Set meal** (Tue-Thur) £15 2 courses, £18 3 courses. **Credit** MC, V.

This is a great neighbourhood restaurant, and still Balham's finest. The muted taupe tones set the right mood; banquettes and booths provide some privacy for those that want it. The Aussie waiting staff are on the ball. And, most importantly, the kitchen uses good-quality local ingredients, turning them into Anglo-French-oriented dishes that look beautiful on the plate. A starter of Red Poll beef and Guinness pudding was perfect in every detail, from the suet pastry to the poached oyster on top. A whole squid was stuffed with black pudding, the richness of the filling contrasting with the firm texture of the squid. This year, the main courses were not quite as faultess as we've come to expect. A slice of crisp pork belly had crackling that was so tough it was barely edible – but the meat below was perfect, and the pretty flower of julienned salsify and crubeens-like

SHELF LIFE

There's also a walk-in cheese room at Marylebone food shop/café **La Fromagerie** (*see p307*).

Cheese@Leadenhall

4-5 Leadenhall Market, EC3 1LR (7929 1697/www.cheeseatleadenhall.co.uk). Bank or Monument tube. **Open** 9am-5pm Mon, Tue; 9am-7pm Wed-Fri.
Former Harvey Nichols cheese buyer Sue Cloke has fused a cheese shop and wine bar to create a delightful spot for a light meal or to pick up some supplies on the way home.

Hamish Johnson

48 Northcote Road, SW11 1PA (7738 0741). Clapham Junction rail. **Open** 9am-6pm Mon-Sat.
An extensive array of cheese from all regions of Europe, plus olive wood products to serve them with, and some carefully selected gourmet groceries.

Jeroboams

96 Holland Park Avenue, W11 3RB (7727 9359/www.jeroboams.co.uk). Holland Park tube. **Open** 8am-8pm Mon-Fri; 8am-7pm Sat; 10am-6pm Sun.
This long-established shop, selling cheese, wine and deli goods, specialises in artisan-made French cheeses, in particular the carefully nurtured pave d'affinois.

Neal's Yard Dairy

17 Shorts Gardens, WC2H 9UP (7240 5700/www.nealsyarddairy.co.uk). Covent Garden tube. **Open** 11am-6.30pm Mon-Thur; 10.30am-6.30pm Fri, Sat.
You'll find feta and parmigiano reggiano, but it's the range of British cheeses for which Neal's Yard is renowned, plus quirky regional lines such as Shropshire oatcakes. There's another shop at Borough Market.

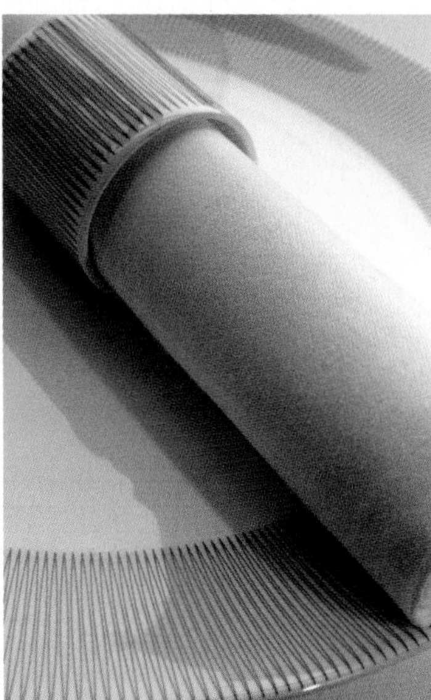

Skylon

discs of stuffed fried trotter were a good match. Wood pigeon was perfectly dissected, cooked and presented, with a tangy watercress salad, but we're not sure it needed the addition of dessert: a dollop of juniper ice-cream and a drizzle of raspberry reduction. But these are minor quibbles; we don't hesitate in recommending Lambert's.
Babies and children welcome: children's menu (weekends); high chairs. Booking advisable. Restaurant available for hire.

Battersea

Louvaine

110 St John's Hill, SW11 1SJ (7223 8708/ www.louvaine.co.uk). Clapham Junction rail.
Brunch served 12.30-4pm Sat, Sun. **Dinner served** 6-10.30pm Tue-Sat. **Main courses** £9-£16.50. **Set dinner** (Tue-Thur) £15.50 2 courses, £19.50 3 courses. **Credit** AmEx, MC, V.

The big front windows, burgundy and eau de nil colour scheme, and eccentric decorations (vintage kitchen moulds arranged in patterns on the walls) give Louvaine the air of a quirky Parisian bistro. The look seems equally popular with romantic diners and group get-togethers. A menu of no-nonsense meat dishes (ribeye steak with herb butter and chips) and seasonal dishes (asparagus risotto) is supplemented by daily fish specials. While chicken liver mixed with foie gras keeps the cost down (£6), the resulting parfait was a little bland. In fact, all the dishes we sampled, although well presented and perfectly palatable, seemed muted in flavour. Pan-fried silver mullet with roasted pepper, caper and olive dressing wasn't as vibrant as it had seemed on the blackboard; roast cod with saffron risotto was tastier but failed to excite. Even the own-made ice-cream was on the mild side of sweet. Service is admirable; the tireless staff regularly tramped up to the rather cramped gallery level to check on the few tables there. With good-value mains (most £13 or under), this is undoubtedly a local asset, but not worth a long trip.
Babies and children welcome: high chair. Booking advisable. Tables outdoors (5, pavement).
Map 21 B4.

Niksons

172-174 Northcote Road, SW11 6RE (7228 2285/www.niksons.co.uk). Clapham Junction rail.
Bar **Open** 5pm-midnight Mon; noon-midnight Tue-Sat; noon-11pm Sun.
Restaurant **Meals served** noon-11pm Tue-Sun. **Main courses** £10-£20. **Set lunch** £10.50 2 courses, £12.50 3 courses.
Both **Credit** AmEx, MC, V.

When customers could still smoke inside, Niksons used at times to feel more like a bar than a restaurant. Now (at least in summer) the balance has shifted, and the affluent, loud, hard-puffing crowd is as much on the pavement as at the dark wood, circular bar. The small, civilised white room at the back has always been quieter, but there's also a restaurant space on the other side of the bar, where you can enjoy some competent cooking. Service is relaxed but very attentive. We were steered towards decent yet unspectacular starters of linguine with chilli and garlic, and smoked halibut with lime and coriander. For mains, fillet steak was overwhelmed by peppercorns, but medallions of pork with crushed potatoes, apple and spring onions was far better: beautifully tender, well flavoured and faultlessly presented. Puddings manage to hit the heights (especially the sorbet selection), as well as covering more familiar ground with a workaday crème brûlée. The best thing about Niksons is its easy atmosphere: pleasant staff, enjoyable cooking, music on Sundays and a loyal, local crowd.
Babies and children welcome: high chairs. Booking advisable. Disabled: toilet. Separate room for parties, seats 30. Tables outdoors (3, pavement).
Map 21 C5.

Ransome's Dock

35-37 Parkgate Road, SW11 4NP (7223 1611/www.ransomesdock.co.uk/restaurant). Battersea Park rail/19, 49, 319, 345 bus.

Brunch served noon-3.30pm Sun. **Meals served** noon-11pm Mon-Fri; noon-midnight Sat. **Main courses** £10.50-£21.50. **Set meal** (noon-5pm Mon-Fri) £15 2 courses. **Credit** AmEx, DC, JCB, MC, V.
Despite its location in a modern development, the smoothly efficient Ransome's Dock is the epitome of a relaxed local restaurant. An S-shaped room, decorated in a lovely deep blue, curls around the gleaming central bar. Natural light streams in through the conservatory-style windows. Tables are well spaced and usually packed with a contentedly chuntering, slightly older Battersea crowd. Perky staff serve a nicely executed array of food. From a starter menu that included gently spiced Morecambe Bay potted shrimps we loved a brace of minty courgette fritters served with gorgeous, plump, orange-stuffed olives. Less successful was a special of pork terrine that lacked punch. Best of the mains, surprisingly, was the only vegetarian dish: six lovely spinach and ricotta gnocchi came dosed with a velvet-smooth beurre blanc and fried sage. English rose-veal saltimbocca had great flavour, but was overwhelmed by the accompanying orange, chicory and green bean salad. The massive wine list is a treasure, offering abundant scope for budget drinkers – and mark-ups are not just reasonable but low, especially for the more expensive wines. Staff are eager to help customers navigate their way through it.
Babies and children welcome: high chairs. Booking advisable. Disabled: toilet. Tables outdoors (12, terrace). **Map 21 C1**.

Brixton

Upstairs

89B Acre Lane, entrance on Branksome Road, SW2 5TN (7733 8855/www.upstairslondon.com). Clapham Common tube/Brixton tube/rail.
Dinner served 6.30-9.30pm Tue-Thur; 6.30-10.30pm Fri, Sat. **Set dinner** £20 2 courses, £25 3 courses. **Credit** MC, V.
There's a whiff of the speakeasy about Upstairs. You need to ring a bell to be let in, then it's up the winding stairs to a small, sleek, chilled-out bar area that feels a little like someone's front room. The dining room is up more stairs; there are just a few small tables, giving the place an unusual level of intimacy. Upstairs has found an appreciative clientele and in 2006 was a runner-up in the Best Local Restaurant category of the Time Out Eating & Drinking Awards. There are just three choices on the fixed-price menu. Seasonality is important, and there's always a vegetarian starter and main. Cured salmon, firm-textured, sliced thinly and served with neatly trimmed fingers of asparagus, was difficult to fault. A main of sea bream with braised little gem lettuce was cooked à point, served with new potatoes and tiny balls of cucumber, all wrapped in a creamy sauce flavoured with fresh dill – very continental. In contrast was the very English apple crumble: a chunky, buttery version with no 'restauranty' frou-frous. The wine list is chosen with a buff's eye, but is fairly priced. Service is charming and French-accented.
Babies and children welcome: high chair. Booking advisable weekends. **Map 22 C2**.

Clapham

Fouronine NEW

409 Clapham Road, SW9 9BT (7737 0722/ www.fouronine.co.uk). Clapham North tube.
Dinner served 6-10.30pm daily. **Main courses** £13-£19. **Credit** MC, V.
First, find the locked alley door in Landor Road, just to the side of the noisy Clapham North pub. Ring the buzzer to gain admission, then head up a whiffy fire escape to a smart, separate restaurant above the pub, where the windows give a grandstand view of the constant commotion around Clapham North tube station. Chef Iain Smart's background at acclaimed French restaurant Chez Bruce shows in the precision timing and presentation of dishes, such as a summery plate of grilled plaice with peas, broad beans and brown shrimps with a light dill velouté, or a scoop of crabmeat and shredded mango served with baby spinach leaves. The standard of cooking is very high – though we didn't see the point of adding coriander to the broth that accompanied a roll of tender pork belly and bean salad. And a dark, correctly sour gazpacho would have been better without a scattering of almond flakes, and with a bit more garlic instead. For sophisticated food at such high prices (starters around £7, mains around £17, desserts £6), the service was oddly amateurish on our visit. Our booking was lost; wrong orders plonked on our table; a waitress couldn't pronounce the 'semillon' of our wine order. But around us, the well-to-do Clapham crowd seemed very pleased to have found this newcomer.
Babies and children admitted. Booking advisable. **Map 22 C1**.

Morel

14 Clapham Park Road, SW4 7BB (7627 2468/ www.morelrestaurant.co.uk). Clapham Common tube. **Dinner served** 6-10.30pm Tue-Sat. **Meals served** noon-4pm Sun. **Main courses** £11-£17. **Set dinner** (Tue-Fri) £17 2 courses. **Credit** MC, V.
I'm sorry it's so quiet tonight... no rhyme or reason to it,' trilled our Antipodean waiter. Actually, it's nice having a restaurant to yourself when every other Clapham venue is bursting on Friday night. All the better to take in the softly lit magnolia interior, with splashes of colour confined to the artworks on the walls. The menu is quite sophisticated, with a starter of rabbit confit served with morel gnocchi, and a carefully prepared risotto of morels and parmesan with a strong aroma of truffle oil. Little details, such as a spinach soup appetiser, and a mango sorbet palate-cleanser before the main course, also suggest there's serious intent here. 'The chef's not happy with the turbot. Would you like the same dish but with monkfish?' We would, and we did: the flesh roasted just-so, still juicy. Some desserts take an extra 15 minutes to prepare, but we opted for the quicker trio of crème brûlées, which may not have been wise; while the tops were warm, the underneaths were fridge- cold, and the banana version contained grey banana that went uneaten. Otherwise, they tasted fine. 'No rhyme or reason to it,' the waiter trilled, as new diners arrived when we were leaving.
Babies and children welcome: high chairs. Booking advisable. **Map 22 B2**.

Tooting

Rick's Café

122 Mitcham Road, SW17 9NH (8767 5219). Tooting Broadway tube. **Lunch served** noon-3pm Mon-Sat; 1-4pm Sun. **Dinner served** 6.30-11pm Mon-Sat; 6-10pm Sun. **Main courses** £6-£12. **Credit** MC, V.
In the past, we've sometimes thought Tooting's only Modern European restaurant – a casual place, with small tables and canned-music radio in the background – suffered from complacency, and was only as good as it needed to be. But on our most recent visit, we were pleasantly surprised. A gazpacho was as fresh and flavoursome as you'd find in Spain, and a whole crab (from West Sussex) was packed with both dark and white meat, served in the shell with new potatoes and decent aïoli. There's a Spanish accent to many of the dishes, though others are more offbeat; feta cheese with watermelon worked very well with fresh mint leaves (this combo was popularised by Nigella Lawson, but is now found everywhere). Our only disappointment was the ratatouille under a fillet of halibut, which was sodden and slightly bitter. Puds included the three waist-thickeners of the apocalypse (chocolate nemesis, sticky toffee pudding and panna cotta), though there was also a lighter fruit pavlova for Dame Edna fans. The wine list has some decent wines at reasonable prices. At this rate, Rick's will be giving Balham (an area well supplied with good, mid-range places to eat) a run for its money.
Babies and children welcome: children's portions; high chairs. Booking advisable dinner and weekends. Disabled: toilet.

Waterloo

Skylon NEW (100)

2007 WINNER BEST DESIGN

Royal Festival Hall, Belvedere Road, SE1 8XX (7654 7800/www.danddlondon.com). Waterloo tube/rail.
Bar **Open/snacks served** 11am-1am daily.
Brasserie **Meals served** noon-11.45pm daily. **Main courses** £9.50-£18.50. **Set dinner** (5.30-6.30pm, after 10pm) £19.50 2 courses, £23.50 3 courses.
Restaurant **Lunch served** noon-2.30pm, **dinner served** 5.30-10.45pm daily. **Set lunch** £19.50 2 courses, £24.50 3 courses. **Set dinner** (5.30-6.30pm, after 10pm) £24.50 2 courses, £29.50 3 courses.
All **Credit** MC, V.
Set at the front of the refurbished Royal Festival Hall (in what used to be the People's Palace), this lofty space – with a fantastic view of the Thames – is divided into three separate destinations: a raised bar in the centre separates the formal restaurant area from the more casual brasserie. The room is dominated by five enormous bespoke bronze chandeliers, their lozenge shape and ring of fins one of many subtle references to design details around the recently refurbished main building. Chef Helena Puolakka's menus contain the likes of Swedish classic jansson's temptation, and the Finnish-style hot-smoked-to-order fish dishes; there's even a hamburger on the brasserie menu, though no meatballs. Well-judged flavour combinations were a hallmark of our meal in the brasserie area. A good rendition of gazpacho was judiciously spiked with sherry vinegar, but the show-stopper was a risotto of crab, cream and pearled spelt. Disappointments included a gritty side dish of spinach and fried onions, a dull coconut tart, and the wine list (which offers little under £5 per 175ml glass). The brasserie is expensive, but the restaurant's even dearer – for dishes such as fricassee of morels and young vegetables, or sea bass en papillote with Spanish ham, fennel, olives and puy lentils. Staff are friendly – and their *Star Trek* uniforms are a fashion sensation.
Babies and children welcome: children's menu; high chairs. Disabled: lift; toilet.
Map 10 M8.

Oxo Tower Restaurant, Bar & Brasserie

8th floor, Oxo Tower Wharf, Barge House Street, SE1 9PH (7803 3888/www.harveynichols.com). Blackfriars or Waterloo tube/rail.
Bar **Open** 11am-11pm Mon-Wed; 11am-midnight Thur-Sat; noon-10.30pm Sun.
Brasserie **Lunch served** noon-3.15pm Mon-Sat; noon-3.45pm Sun. **Dinner served** 5.30-11pm Mon-Sat; 6-10.15pm Sun. **Main courses** £11.75-£22. **Set meal** (lunch, 5.30-6.45pm Mon-Fri) £17.50 2 courses, £21.50 3 courses.
Restaurant **Lunch served** noon-2.30pm Mon-Sat; noon-3pm Sun. **Dinner served** 6-11pm Mon-Sat; 6.30-10pm Sun. **Main courses** £17.50-£26. **Set lunch** £31.50 3 courses.
All **Credit** AmEx, DC, JCB, MC, V.
The trio of Harvey Nichols-owned venues occupying the eighth floor of the Oxo Tower (restaurant, brasserie, bar) are renowned for one thing: fantastic views. Stylish summer terraces and huge windows make the most of the setting, while the fresh, international vibe (think plenty of light and a lively, upwardly mobile clientele) might transport you to Sydney Harbour – until you take in the London sights below. Food is also part of the draw. The cooking may not stand out for originality, but everything we sampled from the brasserie menu was fresh and well executed. Dishes sway towards Italy: typical starters include buffalo mozzarella with green beans, roasted tomatoes and black olive tapenade; mains feature the likes of chicken breast with caponata, taleggio cheese and fried polenta; or porcini and ricotta tortellini. There are also clear nods towards the East (thai pork and coconut patties) and North Africa (chermoula spiced lamb rack with a chorizo and chickpea tagine), and vegetarians get their own menu (on request). The long wine list doesn't

L-RESTAURANT & BAR

2 Abingdon Road London W8 6AF

Opening Times:

Tues - Sun: 12:00 - 14:30
18:00 - 22:30 last orders

Mon: 18:00 - 22:30
last orders

www.l-restaurant.co.uk
E-mail: info@l-restaurant.co.uk

020 7795 6969

L Restaurant and Bar has replaced one of London's landmark restaurants, Trattoo, created originally some forty years ago by the famous theatrical designer Sean Kenny.

Now the site has been brought into the modern age, making full use of the long glass roof, and the gallery area, to create the sort of space that a trendy diner is looking for.

Service is friendly and the food is interesting, described as Modern Iberian, with plenty of tempting dishes - Tuna & Veal Carpaccio with Minted Truffle Dressing, Hand Carved Iberico De Bellota Ham Served with Grilled Chicory, Zarzuela de Pescado (Monkfish & Shellfish Catalonian Stew), Roasted Pork Belly with Sautéed Ginger Kai Lan. Not forgetting the twice weekly live jazz performances that provide the perfect accompaniment to your meal.

The menu is constantly changing so check the website for up to date news.

Set lunch available:
£12.75 for two courses or £15 for three.

BELGRAVIA MAYFAIR PICCADILLY

NOURA
BRASSERIES LONDON
WWW.NOURA.CO.UK

Lebanese cuisine

BELGRAVIA, 16 HOBART PLACE, SW1W 0HH, TEL. 020 7235 9444

PICCADILLY, 122 JERMYN STREET, SW1Y 4UJ, TEL. 020 7839 2020

MAYFAIR, 16 CURZON STREET, W1J 5HP, TEL. 020 7495 1050

Open 7 Days a Week
Non-stop Service Midday to Midnight

really entice unless you've at least £35 to spend, but a decent selection of half bottles and wines by the glass helps. Professional service rounds off the experience nicely.
Babies and children welcome: children's menu; high chair. Booking advisable. Disabled: lift; toilet. Entertainment: jazz 7.30pm daily (brasserie). Restaurant and brasserie available for hire. Tables outdoors (34, brasserie terrace; 27, restaurant terrace). Vegetarian menu. **Map 11 N7.**

South East

Blackheath

Chapter Two

43-45 Montpelier Vale, SE3 0TJ (8333 2666/ www.chaptersrestaurants.co.uk). Blackheath rail. **Lunch served** noon-2.30pm Mon-Sat; noon-3pm Sun. **Dinner served** 6.30-10.30pm Mon-Thur; 6.30-11pm Fri, Sat; 6.30-9pm Sun. **Set lunch** (Mon-Sat) £15.95 2 courses, £19.95 3 courses; (Sun) £14.50 2 courses, £16.50 3 courses. **Set dinner** (Mon-Thur, Sun) £18.45 2 courses, £23.95 3 courses; (Fri, Sat) £24.50 3 courses. **Credit** AmEx, DC, JCB, MC, V.

With its hardwood flooring, block-colour design scheme and spiralling metal staircase (linking the ground and first-floor dining rooms), Chapter Two can feel slightly like the restaurant of a 1980s cruise ship, but Londoners have been swearing by the place since it opened in 1998 as a sister to Kentish gastro-goldmine Chapter One. Their affection hangs partly on the attentive service and fair prices, yet the biggest draw is in gazing at, then gobbling-up, head chef Trevor Torbin's inimitable 'food-as-art'. His starter of skate and brown shrimp raviolo came veiled in an airy ginger velouté that casual observers might mistake for a bowl of cappuccino froth. Main courses exhibited similar creative prowess. Pork belly arrived as a round tower surrounded by a smoky moat of lentils and cider jus; one touch with a fork and 24 hours of slow roasting caused it to collapse in a pile of sublimely tender meat. Certain dishes seemed overly conceptual. A ball of shoulder lamb in cabbage leaves on a bed of white bean purée looked rather like a floating green brain – but such gripes are merely aesthetic, and the results are seldom less than delicious.
Babies and children welcome: high chairs. Booking advisable. Disabled: toilet. Restaurant available for hire.

Greenwich

Inside

19 Greenwich South Street, SE10 8NW (8265 5060/www.insiderestaurant.co.uk). Greenwich rail/DLR. **Lunch served** noon-2.30pm Tue-Fri; noon-3pm Sun. **Dinner served** 6.30-11pm Tue-Sat. **Main courses** £10.95-£16. **Set lunch** £11.95 2 courses, £15.95 3 courses. **Set dinner** (6.30-8pm) £15.95 2 courses, £19.95 3 courses. **Credit** AmEx, MC, V.

Given the gentrified neighbourhood, it's a bit surprising that Greenwich is so lacking in decent eateries. Aside from a seemingly flourishing batch of overstyled bars and bistros, Inside is pretty much all there is. As if to flaunt the contrast, the decor is deliberately understated in a minimalist art gallery sort of way. The food is a rigorous representation of chef-patron Guy Awford's skills; the choice and flavour combinations at every course arouse much pained deliberation among diners. It was impossible to fault our starters, some just-crunchy, buttery English asparagus, and pappardelle of Cornish crab coated in a creamy basil and broad bean sauce. Mains were also impeccable: a Welsh lamb chump with a perfect pink interior served with a mouth-watering mint jus; and pan-fried sea bass, with moist shards of fish that worked beautifully against velvet-textured and strangely smoky aubergine, fresh green beans and a flavoursome tomato sauce. Our only quibble arose over a slightly sloppy crème brûlée that was otherwise nicely flavoured with cardamom and served with ginger shortbread. Service was unobtrusive and efficient, the crowd a lively mix of grateful gourmet locals and incomers looking for a good night out.
Babies and children admitted. Booking advisable. Disabled: toilet.

London Bridge & Borough

Bermondsey Kitchen

194 Bermondsey Street, SE1 3TQ (7407 5719/ www.bermondseykitchen.co.uk). Borough tube/ London Bridge tube/rail. **Brunch served** 9.30am-3.30pm Sat, Sun. **Lunch served** noon-3pm Mon-Fri. **Dinner served** 6.30-10.30pm Mon-Sat. **Main courses** £10.25-£16. **Credit** AmEx, DC, MC, V.

A case study in the transformation of once-grimy old London. Bermondsey Kitchen sits opposite a 1907 pile called the Time and Talents Settlement, which presumably strived to keep local urchins on the straight and narrow. Nowadays, modern urchins and urchinettes can pop across the street to lounge on leather sofas or at plain wooden tables, around an open range that produces interesting, eclectic food. The menu is as much gastropub as restaurant in style, with strong Spanish influences. Superior organic and/or rare-breed meats are a feature, mostly sourced from the Ginger Pig farm in Yorkshire. Juxtapositions of meat and fruit, savoury and sweet, are a recurring theme – as in pan-fried scallops with pomme purée (yes, scallops and apple sauce, which turned out to be delicious), or a great, hefty grilled white pudding with pearl barley and prunes wrapped in pancetta. However, these combos aren't compulsory, and simpler constructions include grilled sea bass with sorrel mash. Staff are laid-back yet attentive, and the imaginative, well-priced wine list goes swimmingly with the easy-going atmosphere. There's a pan-Mediterranean range of tapas for lighter eating and at weekends the Kitchen serves a very popular, high-quality brunch.
Babies and children welcome: high chairs. Booking advisable. Disabled: toilet. Restaurant available for hire. **Map 12 Q9.**

Delfina

50 Bermondsey Street, SE1 3UD (7357 0244/ www.thedelfina.co.uk). London Bridge tube/rail. **Lunch served** noon-3pm Mon-Fri. **Dinner served** 7-10pm Fri. **Main courses** £9.95-£12.95. **Credit** AmEx, DC, MC, V.

Part of a smart studio and gallery space in a converted warehouse typical of 'the new Bankside', Delfina still looks and feels like a gallery café. There's plain wooden flooring, avenues of space between the tables, lofty white walls displaying striking artwork, and a mellow feel throughout. Yet the place now has a separate existence as a restaurant, and the cooking of chef Maria Elia is well above any café norm. There are no routine dishes on the menu; just interesting, imaginative, yet not over-flashy creations. Some are carried off better than others. Pan-fried spiced pears with goat's cheese, pine nuts and coriander was a lovely mix of sweet and savoury, warming and refreshing. Confit of chicken came unusually wrapped in spinach leaves; the meat was a touch overcooked, but still satisfying. Chargrilled varieties of Australian fish are another speciality. Staff are friendly, obliging and on the ball, with none of the brittleness found in some venues nearby. A glass of rosé from the short but wide-ranging list, served at perfect temperature, rapidly put us at ease. A likeable place for a relaxing lunch.
Babies and children admitted. Booking advisable. Disabled: toilet. Separate rooms for parties, seating 12, 30 and 260 (7564 2400). **Map 12 Q9.**

Tower Bridge

Blueprint Café

Design Museum, 28 Shad Thames, SE1 2YD (7378 7031/www.danddlondon.com). Tower Hill tube/Tower Gateway DLR/London Bridge tube/ rail/47, 78 bus. **Lunch served** noon-3pm Mon-Sat; noon-4pm Sun. **Dinner served** 6-11pm Mon-Sat. **Main courses** £12.50-£22. **Credit** AmEx, DC, MC, V.

The view's the thing at the Blueprint Café. Raised up on the first floor of the Design Museum, you're treated to a giant panorama of the modern Thames, from the Gherkin round to Canary Wharf. Enclosed in a floor-to-ceiling glass box, you can continue your reverie over the river even when black walls of cloud are rising and the open-air terraces nearby are having to shut. Be sure to enjoy the vista, as the restaurant has little else that is memorable. As often in mid-range ex-Conran restaurants (now part of D&D London), it's the finer points, or rather lack of them, that lets the food down. A starter of goat's cheese with young garlic and tapenade was pleasant, but an unusually hefty, flavour-lite portion of skate came with a butter and horseradish sauce that had little trace of the latter and was heavy and indigestible. Prices are high for this standard of food, but the wine list, at any rate, is a pleasure: concise, quality-led and offering house wines (three each of champagne, white and red) that will cover most needs. Service was keen, in a corporate kind of way. And there's always that view.
Babies and children welcome: high chairs. Booking advisable dinner. Disabled: lift; toilet (in Design Museum). Restaurant available for hire. Tables outdoors (4, terrace). **Map 12 S9.**

Le Pont de la Tour

Butlers Wharf Building, 36D Shad Thames, SE1 2YE (7403 8403/www.danddlondon.com). Tower Hill tube/Tower Gateway DLR/London Bridge tube/rail/47, 78 bus.
Bar & grill **Lunch served** noon-3pm, **dinner served** 6-11pm daily. **Main courses** £11.50-£22. **Set lunch** £12.50 2 courses, £14.95 3 courses.
Restaurant **Lunch served** noon-3pm, **dinner served** 6-11pm daily. **Main courses** £11.50-£35.50.
Both **Credit** AmEx, DC, JCB, MC, V.

Now part of D&D London, Le Pont doesn't have to try too hard to impress. With a riverside terrace for warm evenings, and huge windows through which to view the sparkling cityscape and floodlit Tower Bridge, it's already on to a winner even before you open the menu. We prefer the grill, with its slightly art deco vibe, red leather banquettes and understated jazz trio, to the sometimes starchy formality of the restaurant. In both, the highlights are seafood platters and strikingly fresh fish dishes. We savoured rich, saffron-infused fish soup and velvety gravadlax with dill, before mains of delicate, plain grilled lemon sole and a skewer of rollickingly robust, juicy grilled scallops wrapped in parma ham – delicious, but not altogether sustaining given the small portions and lack of carbs. We certainly had room for creamy rice pudding and waffles with chocolate sauce. The wine list is vast but pricey, so if you're sticking to a budget your choice will be limited. That said, we reckon Le Pont delivers on its promise of a glam, top-end evening out. Location, location, location!
Babies and children welcome: high chairs. Booking advisable. Entertainment: pianist 7pm daily (bar & grill). Separate room for parties, seats 20. Tables outdoors (22, terrace). **Map 12 S8.**

East

Docklands

Plateau (100)

Canada Place, Canada Square, E14 5ER (7715 7100/www.danddlondon.com). Canary Wharf tube/DLR.
Bar & grill **Meals served** noon-11pm Mon-Sat; noon-4pm Sun. **Main courses** £10-£18.75.
Restaurant **Lunch served** noon-3pm Mon-Fri. **Dinner served** 6-10.30pm Mon-Sat. **Main courses** £17.50-£27.50. **Set dinner** £26.50 3 courses, £32 4 courses.
Both **Credit** AmEx, DC, MC, V.

Plateau absorbs the length of Canada Place's fourth floor (take the lift to the right of Waitrose), huge windows affording unparalleled views of the area's dazzling modernity. It's a vast place, stretching from the buzzing bar (with its own menu) to the private dining rooms. The restaurant comes with the easy combination of formality and unstuffiness that characterise most operations

RESTAURANTS

opened by the Conran group (now D&D London). It is sleek, if sterile. The white and beige decor mixes with the formal office attire worn by the diners (at least during the week) to create a vision in monochrome. Happily, the food, which is at least as expensive as you'd expect, comes with more colour. A dressed crab starter was subtle, even mild, topped with strands of green apple and a little rye crisp; Loch Fyne smoked salmon arrived with a gentle if superfluous brioche. For mains, a gastropubby rotisserie poussin was served on a bed of spinach and garlic mash; it was decent, but the real treat was barbary duck with candied almonds, an unexpected but successful combination that more than made up for the accompanying cubes of slightly fibrous swede. One of Docklands' destination restaurants.
Babies and children welcome: high chairs; nappy-changing facilities. Booking advisable. Disabled: toilet. Dress: smart casual. Separate rooms for parties, seating 15 and 24. Tables outdoors (17, terrace). Vegetarian menu.

Shoreditch

Hoxton Apprentice

16 Hoxton Square, N1 6NT (7739 6022/ www.hoxtonapprentice.com). Old Street tube/rail. *Bar* **Open** noon-11pm Mon-Sat; noon-10pm Sun. *Restaurant* **Lunch served** noon-3pm daily. **Dinner served** 6-11pm Mon-Sat; 6-10pm Sun. **Main courses** £9.90-£16.75. **Set lunch** (Mon-Fri) £6.99 1 courses, £9.99 2 courses, £12.99 3 courses.
Both **Credit** AmEx, MC, V.
Housed in a former school at the back of Hoxton Square, this noble eaterie bills itself as a 'training restaurant', employing 'apprentices' from disadvantaged backgrounds to help the professionals create and serve a lively, varied menu. All profits are reinvested in Training for Life, the charity that opened the restaurant in 2004 with the help of Prue Leith. It's a handsome, cultured space, a world or two away from some of its more demonstrative neighbours – as was the rather surprising Friday-evening soundtrack of Dire Straits' Brothers in Arms. That said, the cooking is a little uneven. A starter of seared scallops and pork belly was a dish of two halves, the seafood excellent but the meat rather rougher; grilled mackerel served over virtually raw vegetables was unappetising; and a £15 bottle of viognier was poor. We had considerably better luck elsewhere on the menu, most notably with a beautifully tender rabbit entrée (baked, stuffed with black pudding and served with apple and parsnip), and a moreish celeriac soup with parmesan and a perfect lovage scone. Prices are very fair and service was faultless. We wish it well.
Babies and children welcome: children's menu; high chairs. Disabled: toilet. Separate room for parties, seats 40. Tables outdoors (9, pavement). **Map 6 R3.**

Wapping

★ Wapping Food (100)

Wapping Hydraulic Power Station, Wapping Wall, E1W 3ST (7680 2080/www.thewappingproject.com). Wapping tube/Shadwell DLR. **Brunch served** 10am-12.30pm Sat, Sun. **Lunch served** noon-3.30pm Mon-Fri; 1-4pm Sat, Sun. **Dinner served** 6.30-11pm Mon-Fri; 7-11pm Sat. **Main courses** £11-£19. **Credit** AmEx, MC, V.
Conceived as an arts centre, the Wapping Project – housed in a former hydraulic power station – is best known for its restaurant, Wapping Food. There are few more unusual spots to dine. Stylish black tables and plastic chairs are arranged around the mint-coloured machinery that's still in place in the old turbine hall. With soaring ceilings, original brickwork and metal piping, 'industrial chic' is the watchword. The food is equally remarkable. A dish of watermelon, feta, olives, mint, basil and pine nuts made for a refreshing start. Mains of salmon with green papaya and chilli lime, and potato and nettle gnocchi, were equally faultless, though we were very tempted by alternatives of braised lamb and rosemary pie, and goat's cheese with courgette flowers, lentils and chicory. The treats continue for pudding, featuring such delights as plum custard tart with lavender ice-cream. Also worthy of note is the 100-strong all-Australian wine list (a nod to the founder's roots), the highly professional staff and the tempting brunch menu. Art exhibitions, held in the basement space, often spill into the restaurant, contributing to its unique atmosphere.
Babies and children welcome: high chairs. Disabled: toilet. Entertainment: performances and exhibitions; phone for details. Tables outdoors (20, garden).

North

Camden Town & Chalk Farm

★ Odette's NEW

2007 RUNNER-UP LEFFE BEST NEW RESTAURANT

130 Regent's Park Road, NW1 8XL (7586 8569/ www.vpmg.net). Chalk Farm tube/31, 168, 274 bus. **Lunch served** 12.30-2.30pm Tue-Sun. **Dinner served** 7-11pm Mon-Sat. **Main courses** £15-£23. **Set lunch** £16.50 2 courses, £20 3 courses. **Credit** AmEx, JCB, MC, V.
The reinvention of Odette's under the ownership of impresario Vince Power has brought some striking changes to this NW1 old-timer. The interior, by Shaun Clarkson, is one example. You'll either like the egg-yolk yellow leather chairs and banquettes against white painted brick walls (in the back room), the statement wallpaper (in the front room) and the dark, moody bar area (in the basement), or you'll pine for the old-fashioned romance of yesteryear. You will like the food, though; Bryn Williams cooks like a dream, from delicate amuses-bouche to utterly delicious petits fours (most notably the whiter-than-white, lighter-than-air marshmallows). Best dishes from a memorable meal were seared and ceviched hand-dived scallops with fennel and basil salad (a starter), and ice strawberry parfait with poached strawberries and strawberry jam doughnuts. There are some quibbles: the tables are really close together, so it's hard to avoid hearing other people's conversation (a gastric bypass on one side, the charms of Dubai on the other); and the prices (£3.50 for an espresso) are at odds with the fact that Odette's still feels like a local restaurant despite the haute nature of the food and service. Even so, well worth visiting.
Babies and children admitted. Booking advisable. Restaurant available for hire. Separate rooms for parties, seating 8 and 30. Tables outdoors (7, conservatory). **Map 27 A2.**

Islington

Frederick's

Camden Passage, N1 8EG (7359 2888/ www.fredericks.co.uk). Angel tube. **Lunch served** noon-2.30pm, **dinner served** 5.45-11pm Mon-Sat. **Main courses** £12-£21. **Set meal** (lunch, 5.45-7pm) £14 2 courses, £17 3 courses. **Credit** MC, V.
Frederick's certainly looks a class act. Behind the traditional frontage lies a series of surprises, as you pass from the plush bar down into the glass-vaulted Garden Room. Here, stylish artwork decorates the walls, and doors open on to a pretty terrace, producing one of the most striking dining spaces in town. The problem on our visit was with the food. The menu is fairly traditional French, with a few Brit touches. Chicken liver and foie gras terrine turned out to be an over-liverish pâté, totally out of kilter with the too-sweet grape chutney that came with it. A salad featured quite pleasant roast peppers amid a pile of rocket, but also mozzarella that was distinctly rubbery. Mains were just plain bland: fillet of sea bream with dull mushrooms and (yes!) tasty smoked garlic mash; and côte de boeuf that was ordered rare but arrived with burnt edges, accompanied by nearly flavourless béarnaise sauce. Service began disorganised, though it got better; the wine list is pricey, yet ambitious. Our impression on this occasion was of a place that's all fancy packaging with nothing special inside.
Babies and children welcome: children's menu; high chairs. Booking advisable weekends. Separate rooms for parties, seating 18 and 32. Tables outdoors (12, garden). **Map 5 O2.**

North West

West Hampstead

Walnut

280 West End Lane, NW6 1LJ (7794 7772/ www.walnutwalnut.com). West Hampstead tube/rail. **Dinner served** 6.30-11pm Tue-Sun. **Main courses** £9.50-£15. **Credit** AmEx, DC, JCB, MC, V.
It's not just the unusual angle of Walnut's roadside façade that makes it stand out from its surroundings on chain-dominated West End Lane. With its stylish interior (including raised open kitchen), and cooking that uses fresh, quality ingredients, Walnut pitches itself as a superior alternative – and mostly succeeds. Beautifully presented starters included juicy seared scallops, and a wild mushroom filo parcel with crisp, delicate pastry and a rich filling. To follow, crispy pork (a daily special), was quite delicious, with cracking crackling, tender belly meat and vibrant apricot compote. Venison sausages were less impressive: intensely but overpoweringly meaty, and the accompanying mashed potato was dry, smothering the palate and obscuring the more subtle red wine and myrtle jus. A side order of garlic mash was similarly stodgy, and the chips delivered to our neighbours looked overcooked. On the plus side, there's a decent if unspectacular wine list (we enjoyed a bottle of Picpoul de Pinet, an increasingly fashionable Languedoc white), and the enthusiastic staff were able to identify the provenance of ingredients when asked. The menu claims all food is locally sourced and organic 'where appropriate'; considering the prices (side dishes cost £3-£4), it's a surprise they don't make more of this fact.
Babies and children welcome: children's portions; high chairs; nappy-changing facilities. Booking advisable weekends. Restaurant available for hire. Tables outdoors (4, pavement). **Map 28 A2.**

Outer London

Barnet, Hertfordshire

Dylan's Restaurant

21 Station Parade, Cockfosters Road, Barnet, Herts EN4 0DW (8275 1551/www.dylans restaurant.com). Cockfosters tube. **Lunch served** noon-2.30pm Mon-Sat; noon-3pm Sun. **Dinner served** 6-10pm Mon-Sat; 6-9pm Sun. **Main courses** £13.50-£17.75. **Set lunch** (Sun) £18.95 2 courses, £22.95 3 courses. **Set meal** (lunch Mon-Sat, 6-7pm daily) £12.95 2 courses, £15.95 3 courses. **Credit** AmEx, JCB, MC, V.
With its block creams and deep reds, plus a smattering of hot pink cushions, there's something very grown up about Dylan's. It's a bit reminiscent of an early 1990s airport club lounge. Located right at the end of the Piccadilly line, this two-tiered Cockfosters restaurant has proved popular with both champagne-quaffing businessmen and couples. In keeping with the just-retro decor, the menu harks back to a time when fusion was the last word in sophistication: delicious crispy thai salmon; silky sweet-potato and coconut soup; barely overdone trout with olive gnocchi, stir-fried asian vegetables and artichokes. It was good enough to keep us deliberating despite being ravenous. The bread (olive, sun-dried tomato, cheese and onion) was frequently offered, thanks to faultless service from owner Dylan Murray and his black-clad staff – one of the qualities that earned Dylan's the accolade of runner-up in the Best Local Restaurant category of the 2006 Time Out Eating & Drinking Awards. Sundays feature jazz musicians alongside traditional roasts or set menus. Enthusiastic home cooks can sign up for one of the restaurant's cookery demonstrations.
Babies and children admitted: children's menu; high chairs. Booking essential Fri, Sat lunch. Entertainment: jazz 1-4pm Sun.

Kew, Surrey

★ The Glasshouse

14 Station Parade, Kew, Surrey TW9 3PZ (8940 6777/www.glasshouserestaurant.co.uk). Kew Gardens tube/rail. **Lunch served** noon-2.30pm Mon-Sat; 12.30-2.45pm Sun. **Dinner served** 7-10.30pm Mon-Thur; 6.30-10.30pm Fri, Sat; 7.30-10pm Sun. **Set lunch** (Mon-Fri) £23.50 3 courses; (Sat) £25 3 courses; (Sun) £29.50 3 courses. **Set dinner** (6.30-7.30pm Mon-Thur, Sun) £17.50 3 courses; £35 3 courses, £50 tasting menu. **Credit** AmEx, MC, V.

Kew's connection with lovely perennials bred from fine root-stock extends to this member of the small, well-rounded group that includes haute cuisine's the Square, and French restaurants Chez Bruce and La Trompette. The glass-fronted room has a subtle, classy comfort (leather-upholstered chairs help), the pace is perfectly calibrated and the wine list worth reading. Assured since the restaurant opened, the cooking rarely falters. It's not fussy, but there's much happening on the plate. Roast halibut with pea purée, bubble and squeak, a soft poached egg and bayonne ham was typical of how many elements can be kept in balance. Favourites such as anjou pigeon with ingenious, deep-fried truffled egg (crisp breadcrumbs without, soft yolk within – brilliant) inspired anticipation. Rump of lamb, barely pink, with a jus flavoured with mediterranean vegetables, potatoes steeped in olive oil, and rosemary-spiked haricot beans also felt well practised. Ingredients including, on our visit, shoots, sprouts and miniature leaves, are ahead of the game. Sprouted peanut in a perfectly perky salad of leaves, beetroot, mozzarella and spring onions was new to us. The Glasshouse is as good for a long, daylit lunch as for an unrushed evening over a tasting menu. Prices are high, mind.

Babies and children welcome (lunch): children's menu; high chairs. Booking essential dinner and Sun lunch.

Richmond, Surrey

Petersham Nurseries Café

Church Lane, off Petersham Road, Petersham, nr Richmond, Surrey TW10 7AG (8605 3627/ www.petershamnurseries.com). Richmond tube/ rail then 30min walk or 65 bus.
Café **Lunch served** 12.30-3pm Tue-Sun. **Main courses** £14-£22. **Credit** AmEx, MC, V.
Tea house **Tea served** 11am-4.30pm Mon, Sun; 10am-4.30pm Tue-Sat. **No credit cards**.

Skye Gyngell's restaurant may be under threat of closure from Richmond Council, but it clearly has the backing of the many well-heeled diners who book weeks ahead to dine here. The appeal is obvious: Petersham Nurseries must be the prettiest garden centre in the UK, with its carefully styled faux-ramshackle look of old greenhouses, tangled flowers and potting shed knick-knacks. The Indian antiques and furniture are for sale (our wobbly dining table for two: £650). Dish prices are also very expensive for what is – let's face it – a garden centre café run by eager but amateurish posh girls. A starter of fresh crab meat, pink grapefruit and salad leaves (£18) was an excellent mix, showing Gyngell's flair for flavour combinations, but was sloppy in execution: it contained lemon pips and shards of crab shell as well as a lovely verjuice and olive oil dressing. A vegetarian tomato curry (the cheapest main course at £16) was heavy on the coconut milk; although pleasant, it wasn't too far off something a home cook could turn out. A slice of hazelnut tart was another highlight, though the accompanying raspberries were bland. A lovely spot maybe, but lunch for one with no booze came to a staggering £46. Living proof that an excellent cookery book and prominent newspaper column will do wonders for your restaurant's business.

Babies and children welcome: high chairs; nappy-changing facilities. Booking essential (several weeks in advance at weekends). Disabled: toilet. Tables outdoors (15, garden).

Odette's

North African

While all things Moroccan are no longer quite as fashionable as they were just a few years ago, London's North African restaurants are doing very nicely, thank you. Since the last edition of this guide, there has been just one notable new opening – **Sidi Maarouf** on the Edgware Road – but most of the old favourites remain consistently good. **Momo** still manages to be one of the most exciting restaurants in the metropolis: not so much for the food, but because, on form, it feels like the most glamorous, sexy venue in town, while **Pasha** offers both sophisticated surroundings and great cooking. At the other end of the scale, bargain-priced **Adam's Café** just gets better and better.

Central

Covent Garden

Souk Medina

1A Short's Gardens, WC2H 9AT (7240 1796/ www.soukrestaurant.co.uk). Covent Garden tube. **Meals served** noon-midnight daily. **Main courses** £8.50-£12.95. **Set lunch** £16.95 4 courses. **Set dinner** £19.50 4 courses. **Credit** AmEx, DC, MC, V.

Souk Medina in the flesh is not quite as sumptuous as the artfully lit promotional photos might lead you to imagine. It has the usual kasbah look, with terracotta walls, ample tiling and well-stuffed divans – but there's plenty more going for it. Even on a hectic Saturday night when several big groups were eating, the acoustics and general vibe seemed to work equally well for those dining à deux. Service was professional and attentive, if at times a little harried. Maghrebi music played at just the right volume, giving a party feel without being overwhelming. There's even equal-opportunity belly dancing here; our rather conservative North African companion was definitely fazed by the transvestite performer. For central London, prices are fair, and the food is decent. From a wide range of not very Maghrebi starters, we tried traditional merguez and chicken briouats. As well as the usual couscous and tagine options, there are several vegetarian dishes. Finish with a creamy rice pudding with almonds and honey. A good-time venue that won't dent your wallet too much.

Babies and children welcome: high chairs. Booking advisable Fri, Sat. Disabled: toilet. Entertainment: belly dancer, DJ 9pm Fri, Sat. Separate rooms available for parties, seating 45 and 100. Takeaway service; delivery service (within 2-mile radius). Vegetarian menu. Vegan dishes. **Map 18 D3.**

For branch (Souk Bazaar) see index.

Edgware Road

★ Sidi Maarouf NEW

56-58 Edgware Road, W2 2JE (7724 0525). Marble Arch tube. **Meals served** noon-12.30pm Mon-Sat; noon-midnight Sun. **Main courses** £14-£18. **Credit** AmEx, DC, MC, V.

Lebanese restaurateur Marouf Abouzaki's stealthy colonisation of the Edgware Road continues, but instead of adding this latest property to his Maroush chain (see the Middle Eastern chapter, starting on p224), he has left behind the Levant and headed for North Africa. It's a highly successful change of direction. We loved Sidi Maarouf's take on the little pastries known as briouats. The kitchen makes them beautifully, in five varieties including feta with mint, crab and shrimp, and chicken and lemon. Two people can share a platter consisting of one of each for £8.50. The tagine and couscous main dishes were less inventive, but more than competently rendered. Vegetables in a Berber-style couscous retained their crispness, while prunes in a lamb tagine were reduced to bubbling molasses, with flakes of burnt almond for unexpected crunch (you need a side order of plain couscous to soak up this wonderfully tangy gloop). The restaurant is a bit of a looker, formal but softened by sophisticated design: the ceiling billows with loops of golden cloth, and red ethnic rugs fill the floorspace between tables. The serving staff aren't Moroccan, hence the overheard exchange: Lebanese waiter to Lebanese customer, 'Yeah, it looks funny to me too, but the chef says that's how it's supposed to be.' Trust us, the chef knows what he's doing.

Babies and children admitted. Booking advisable. Tables outdoors (6, pavement). **Map 8 F6.**

Gloucester Road

★ Pasha

1 Gloucester Road, SW7 4PP (7589 7969/ www.pasha-restaurant.co.uk). Gloucester Road tube/49 bus. **Meals served** noon-11.30pm Mon-Wed, Sun; noon-midnight Thur-Sat. **Main courses** £13-£20. **Set lunch** (noon-5pm) £6 4 dishes, £8-£15 6 dishes. **Set dinner** £30-£50 per person (minimum 2) tasting menu. **Credit** AmEx, DC, MC, V.

If you're looking for glamour and oriental opulence, Pasha is likely to fulfil all your fantasies. The restaurant glisters like no other. Diners pass through the heavy wooden door into a rich red and copper-hued wonderland, full of beguiling, kitsch-free artisanship. It's so sexy, we'd defy any date not to smoulder here. The place does get noisy, though, once larger groups arrive and the belly dancers get going, so save sweet nothings for later. There's a slightly bewildering variety of set meals, even the most modest of which is substantial – two meze and a main course each. Elegantly spiced minced scallop and red pepper briouat and feather-light courgette fritters really set the taste buds singing, but beware the viciously vinegary beetroot salad. Main courses were absolute stunners: seafood tagine full of voluptuous prawns, scallops and mussels (but, strangely, served with neither bread nor couscous to mop up the juices); and chargrilled chicken breast couscous, artfully presented with separate bowls of vegetable broth, harissa and sweet sultanas. Mint tea arrived with a delicately wrought, towering cake stand full of sweetmeats and pastries. It's all pretty pricey, but when did gorgeousness ever come cheap?

Book weekends. Dress: smart casual. Separate room for parties, seats 18. Vegetarian menu. **Map 7 C9.**

Leicester Square

Saharaween

3 Panton Street, SW1Y 4DL (7930 2777). Leicester Square or Piccadilly Circus tube. **Meals served** noon-midnight daily. **Main courses** £8-£14. **Set lunch** (noon-3pm) £17 2 courses. **Credit** MC, V.

Menu

North African food has similarities with other cuisines; see the menu boxes in **Middle Eastern** and **Turkish**.

Bastilla or **pastilla**: an ouarka (qv) envelope with a traditional filling of sliced or minced pigeon, almonds, spices and egg, baked then dusted with cinnamon and powdered sugar. In the UK chicken is often substituted for pigeon.
Brik: minced lamb or tuna and a raw egg bound together in paper-thin pastry, then fried.
Briouats, briouettes or **briwat**: little envelopes of deep-fried, paper-thin ouarka (qv) pastry; these can have a savoury filling of ground meat, rice or cheese, or be served as a sweet, flavoured with almond paste, nuts or honey.
Chermoula: a dry marinade of fragrant herbs and spices.
Chicken kedra: chicken stewed in a stock of onions, lemon juice and spices (ginger, cinnamon), sometimes with raisins and chickpeas.
Couscous: granules of processed durum wheat. The name is also given to a dish where the slow-cooked grains are topped with a meat or vegetable stew like a tagine (qv); couscous royale usually involves a stew of lamb, chicken and merguez (qv).
Djeja: chicken.
Harira: thick lamb, lentil and chickpea soup.
Harissa: very hot chilli pepper paste flavoured with garlic and spices.
Maakouda: spicy potato fried in breadcrumbs.
Merguez: spicy, paprika-rich lamb sausages.
Ouarka: filo-like pastry.
Tagine or **tajine**: a shallow earthenware dish with a conical lid; it gives its name to a slow-simmered stew of meat (usually lamb or chicken) and vegetables, often cooked with olives, preserved lemon, almonds or prunes.
Zaalouk or **zalouk**: a cold spicy aubergine, tomato and garlic dip.

Sidi Maarouf

Saharaween remains something of an enigma. With its chilly ground-floor tea lounge, and slightly gloomy basement restaurant, it can be rather cheerless. Indeed, we've always found it pretty quiet. As the location is right near Leicester Square, you get the feeling the place should be doing better. It has no licence (you're encouraged to pop to the offie round the corner for booze), so the profits aren't coming from wine mark-ups. The menu is very short and to the point – usually encouraging in a small place like this. We chose mixed meze, all of which were excellent: falafel, chicken with ground peanuts and honey, zaalouk and a rich tomatoey salsa. The couscous always comes smothered in smen (butter fat); even for the butter-lover, it's too pungent, so the delicate spicing of the chicken and its broth was overwhelmed. Tagine mhama (a rather daunting chunk of lamb with apple and prunes) was tasty enough, but came in a watery sauce that we couldn't soak up with the pitta bread provided. Saharaween is a peaceful, relaxing venue and the owner seems keen to please, but it's not quite getting things right.
Babies and children admitted. Separate rooms for parties, seats 35 and 40. Tables outdoors (2, pavement). Takeaway service. **Map 17 B5.**

Marylebone

Occo

58 Crawford Street, W1H 4NA (7724 4991/ www.occo.co.uk). Edgware Road tube. **Lunch served** noon-3pm Mon-Fri. **Dinner served** 6.30-11pm Mon-Fri; 6.30-10pm Sat. **Credit** AmEx, MC, V.
A converted corner pub just off the Edgware Road, Occo (as in Mor-occo) is a stylish bar-restaurant run by a young guy from Tangier. Proud of his heritage, he has imported some eye-catching North African elements, not least the 12ft slab of bone-inlaid marble that forms the bar counter. The food also loosely takes its inspiration from Morocco, although recipes are subject to lots of tinkering – the menu calls it 'modern Moroccan'. So instead of the traditional potatoes, courgette, carrots and cabbage, a vegetable tajine includes sugar snaps, baby sweetcorn and baby aubergines. Chicken d'wida sits on a mound of vermicelli rather than the expected couscous. It's all very agreeable. If gastropubs existed in Casablanca, this is what they'd serve. We do take issue though with having to pay £2.70 each for bread and olives, when in most places charging these kind of prices they are complimentary. Note too that you need to navigate the wine list with care, as some of the Moroccan bottles are poor.
Babies and children admitted. Separate rooms for parties, seating 20 and 50. Tables outdoors (6, pavement). **Map 8 F5.**

Original Tagines

7A Dorset Street, W1U 6QN (7935 1545). Baker Street tube. **Lunch served** noon-3pm Mon-Fri. **Dinner served** 6-11pm daily. **Main courses** £9.50-£11.95. **Set lunch** £8.50 2 courses. **Credit** MC, V.
The area around Baker Street station isn't blessed with fine dining options, so Original Tagines stands out for being a good little local restaurant. It is pleasingly free of the ethnic knick-knacks that pass for decor in other North African venues and instead favours a minimal aesthetic. There are perhaps one or two too many mosaic-topped tables for true comfort, but this is an otherwise laid-back place. Over the years the food has always been excellent: a selection of beautifully prepared couscous dishes and tagines offering intriguing combinations of meat and fruit (lamb with prunes, chicken with apricots), prefaced by an enticing array of starters. This time, however, the cooking was poor. We won't dwell on the faults (dishes underspiced and undercooked), but just hope the kitchen resumes normal service as quickly as possible. Desserts are still good, particularly a rice pudding prepared with essence of orange blossom. There's a fair selection of Moroccan wines by the glass, from which we favour the rosé. Also worthy of note is the pub next door, the 18th-century Barley Mow.
Babies and children welcome: high chairs. Booking advisable. Tables outdoors (5, pavement). Takeaway service. **Map 3 G5.**

Mayfair

★ Momo (100)

25 Heddon Street, W1B 4BH (7434 4040/ www.momoresto.com). Piccadilly Circus tube. **Lunch served** noon-2.30pm Mon-Sat. **Dinner served** 6.30-11pm Mon-Sat; 6.30-10.30pm Sun. **Main courses** £13-£22.50. **Set lunch** £11 1 course, £14 2 courses, £18 3 courses. **Credit** AmEx, DC, MC, V.
London's most high-profile Moroccan restaurant celebrated its tenth anniversary in 2007, and one hell of a party was thrown by owner Mourad 'Momo' Mazouz. But then, most nights at Momo feel like a party thanks to a terrific mix of sexy decor, even sexier staff and excellent music. The food's not bad either. Moroccan isn't the most sophisticated of cuisines, but at least here it seems exotic and fun. The wood pigeon pastilla is dusted with a star-and-crescent design in icing sugar; main courses are served on plates especially designed by Laurent Guimoi. Although the food is pricey, certain dishes (notably the couscous options) are enormous and could almost feed two. Leave room for desserts, though, which are possibly the best thing on the menu, especially the incredible milk pastilla (a cream-filled flaky pastry) served with crème brûlée ice-cream. For tea and pastries, visit Mô Tea Room next door, filled with jewellery, carpets, lanterns and suchlike, many of which are for sale.
Babies and children admitted. Booking advisable weekends. Disabled: toilet. Tables outdoors (5, terrace). Takeaway service. Vegetarian menu. **Map 17 A4.**
For branch (Mô Tea Room) see index.

RESTAURANTS

Moroccan Tagine

West

Bayswater

Couscous Café

7 Porchester Gardens, W2 4DB (7727 6597). Bayswater tube. **Meals served** noon-11pm Mon-Thur, Sun; noon-midnight Fri, Sat. **Main courses** £9.95-£15.95. **Licensed. Corkage** no charge. **Credit** AmEx, MC, V.

Queensway is a bastion of Lebanese fast food, with more shawarma joints per block than a Beirut snack street. As the name suggests, this little place peddles an altogether different kind of Arab cuisine. Tucked alongside the massive bulk of Whiteleys, Couscous Café is a lower-ground-floor bolt-hole made homely with terracotta-tiled floors, mosaic-tiled tables and a low bamboo ceiling. It's all quite charming and obviously well liked by the many regulars who probably consider the place a bit of a find – you can tell they're regulars because they know to bring their own wine and beer. The food is, to be honest, a bit hit and miss. The harira, which should be a thick, spicy soup, was a watery, bland affair. But the dish for which the café is named was far better. Generally, couscous is served in one dish with vegetables and meat all piled on top: not here. Waitresses deliver it as a DIY kit of six items (couscous, vegetables, meat, sauce, chickpeas and spicy harissa sauce). Diners assemble the ingredients to taste. It's a fun way of eating and portions are extremely generous. Service was friendly and attentive.

Babies and children admitted. Booking essential. Tables outdoors (2, pavement). Vegetarian menu. **Map 7 C6**.

Ladbroke Grove

★ Moroccan Tagine

95 Golborne Road, W10 5NL (8968 8055). Ladbroke Grove or Westbourne Park tube/23 bus. **Meals served** 11am-11pm daily. **Main courses** £5.50-£6.92. **Unlicensed**. No alcohol allowed. **Credit** MC, V.

Having heard glowing reports of Moroccan Tagine's authentic home-style cooking and its wide range of tagines, we were disappointed on our recent visit – was it just an off night? This no-nonsense café is right in the middle of London's old Moroccan quarter. It's popular with locals and well-heeled types doing a spot of shopping at Portobello Market and around. Even early on a Saturday evening the place was busy. Alcohol isn't served, so we looked forward to one of the enticing-sounding fresh fruit cocktails – but none was available that night. Beetroot salad was very under-dressed (just cold sliced beetroot), though salata mechouia (grilled peppers, tomatoes, chillies, garlic and olive oil) was fresh and nicely smoky. Orika tagine (lamb with green peas and artichoke) was fine, but the very delicate spicing didn't bring out the essence of the vegetables: the factor that distinguishes great Moroccan cooking. Chicken couscous was very dry indeed and came with a stingily inadequate bowl of vegetable broth. Even the bread seemed in short supply, and when we pleaded for more, it took an age to appear. Maybe there's too much resting on laurels here.

Babies and children welcome: high chairs. Book weekends. Tables outdoors (4, pavement). Takeaway service. **Map 19 B1**.

Shepherd's Bush

★ ★ Adam's Café (100)

77 Askew Road, W12 9AH (8743 0572). Hammersmith tube then 266 bus. **Dinner served** 7-11pm Mon-Sat. **Set dinner** £11.50 1 course, £14.50 2 courses, £16.95 3 courses. **Licensed. Corkage** £3. **Credit** AmEx, MC, V.

Adam's just keeps getting better. It has always been a favoured local for its laid-back atmosphere and low prices, but recently the friendly owners – he hails from the Tunisian island of Djerba, she's British – seem to have raised their game a notch. Once you've ordered, spicy little meatballs and fiery harissa with olive oil appear. That most traditional of Tunisian starters, the brik au thon, was a beauty: the lightest, crispiest fan of ouarka pastry stuffed with egg, tuna and herbs. Grilled merguez were some of the best we've had in London: coarsely ground meat, well spiced, without that terrifying bright red hue. Moroccan-style tagine of lamb with prunes and almonds came with a slightly too watery sauce, but the absolute pièce de résistance was a perfect, moist, lightly charred whole sea bass with a coating of zingy herbs and spices, served with rice, green salad and another Tunisian classic, ojja (eggs lightly scrambled with tomato and harissa). Food aside, the amiable, efficient service, crisp linen tablecloths and soundtrack of 1950s-style French *chansons* all add up to a first-class experience at bargain prices.

Babies and children admitted. Booking advisable weekends. Separate room for parties, seats 24. Vegetarian menu. **Map 20 A1**.

North

Islington

Maghreb

189 Upper Street, N1 1RQ (7226 2305/www.maghrebrestaurant.co.uk). Highbury & Islington tube/rail. **Meals served** 6-11.30pm daily. **Main courses** £8.50-£13.50. **Set dinner** (Mon-Thur, Sun) £9.95 2 courses. **Credit** AmEx, JCB, MC, V.

We like Maghreb for its attempts to break away from the North African norm. This starts with the decor, which eschews the stereotypical souk aesthetic for a simple but striking pairing of mustard-yellow walls against burgundy and blue upholstery. Although the bulk of the menu is made up of Moroccan staples, the ingredients are far from standard. For instance: a tabouleh salad, traditionally made with parsley, onions and tomatoes, is prepared here with crab and prawns; and pastilla has a goat's cheese filling rather than chicken or pigeon. This must also be the only London restaurant to offer tajines of duck, rabbit, and lentil and pumpkin. Not everything comes off: a chakchouka (usually a spicy tomato and pepper stew to which eggs are added), made with prawns instead of the customary red peppers, resembled reheated leftovers; and pears turned out not to be a good accompaniment to rabbit – but we do applaud the ambition. Desserts include yeasty pancakes with an irresistible honey and butter sauce. Service is extremely friendly. We get the impression that Maghreb is very much a labour of love for its owners.

Babies and children welcome: high chairs. Booking advisable. Restaurant available for hire. Separate areas available for parties, seating 38 and 44. Takeaway service. Vegetarian menu. **Map 5 O1**.

North West

Hampstead

Safir

116 Heath Street, NW3 1DR (7431 9888/www.safir-restaurant.co.uk). Hampstead tube. **Dinner served** 6-11.30pm Mon-Thur. **Meals served** 1.30-11.30pm Fri-Sun. **Main courses** £10.25-£31.95. **Set meal** £13.95 2 courses, £14.95-£17.95 3 courses. **Credit** MC, V.

Our Saturday night here was quieter than usual, though things picked up when a typically well-heeled, middle-aged Hampstead crowd arrived. With traditional green and yellow tenting, and chairs and comfy divans upholstered in brightly striped satin, Safir looks a tad old-fashioned. And the service is a touch too formal, though by no means unfriendly. What keeps us returning is the quality of the traditional cuisine. Simplicity is key, no over-complex flavours or wacky ingredients; try, for example, the chicken livers and juicy grilled prawns in a vibrant chermoula. Couscous royale came without the promised merguez, but was an otherwise perfect rendition, served with a supremely flavoursome broth, vegetables and excellent home-style harissa. Nevertheless, the highlight is the tagine of lamb with prunes. The chef should offer a masterclass to his London-based compatriots, demonstrating how to get that perfectly reduced, sweet but not sickly, gloopy sauce that elsewhere tends to be too watery. Even the end-of-meal pastries were fresh and delicious, served with good fresh mint tea. If you're shy and retiring, beware the belly dancer who appears at the end of the week.

Babies and children welcome: high chairs. Booking essential Fri, Sat, dinner Sun. Entertainment: belly dancer 8pm Sat. Restaurant available for hire. Separate room for parties, seats 25. Takeaway service. **Map 28 C1**.

BEST NORTH AFRICAN

For Arabian Nights-style glamour

Opulence rules at **Pasha** (*see p248*), where rich colours and warm copper hues make a sumptuous setting for a special date.

For Moroccan with a twist

Both decor and dishes offer a touch of the unexpected at **Maghreb** (*see left*), where staple dishes come unstapled with adventurous ingredients, and the souk look is ditched in favour of a sophisticated interior.

For new and notable

Lebanese resturauratеur Marouf Abouzaki spreads his culinary wings with **Sidi Maarouf** (*see 248*), a bold venture into Moroccan cuisine that's worked a treat.

RESTAURANTS

Oriental

London's oriental restaurants are divided between fashionable, designled venues and what are essentially simple noodle bars serving up big bowls of pick-and-mix Asian. At best, you can enjoy a modern blend of individual South-east Asian cuisines in a glamorous environment; at worst, you get the same old 'greatest hits' guaranteed not to rock any westerner's boat. Menus too often hold a disproportionate amount of what can only be called 'deep-fried food in a sweet sauce'. Some places – you know who you are – now deep-fry dishes that are not traditionally deep-fried. Others distort tradition by turning pad thai noodles into Chinese sweet-and-sour, or by putting curry spices into char kway teow as if it were singapore fried noodles. In researching this chapter, we tried to discover the origins of the chef or owner – Thai, Malay, and so on – and advise accordingly. We did this to point to the possible strengths of a restaurant, and to encourage the owners to concentrate on what they do best.

There were highlights: the modest **Mangosteen** stole our hearts with its charm and surprisingly good wine list; and we also relished the slightly mad **Gilgamesh**, where chef Ian Pengelley (who flew too close to the sun with the ill-fated Pengelley's) is cooking like a star. The **Great Eastern Dining Room** stood out as the best kitchen in the Will Ricker empire, with a real handle on Thai food. Of the few newcomers this year, **Haiku** at least deserves credit for having four separate kitchens to cope with its massive pan-Asian menu; **Suka** at the Sanderson was disappointing.

To discover the main ingredients of some of the dishes mentioned here, refer to the menus in **Chinese**, **Japanese**, **Malaysian**, **Thai** and **Vietnamese**.

Central

Bloomsbury

Wagamama (100)

4A Streatham Street, WC1A 1JB (7323 9223/ www.wagamama.com). Holborn or Tottenham Court Road tube. **Meals served** noon-11pm Mon-Sat; noon-10pm Sun. **Main courses** £5.95-£9.95. **Credit** AmEx, DC, MC, V.

Wagamama is still the mother of all noodle bars. Since starting life in this Bloomsbury basement in 1992, it has grown to a network of more than 80 restaurants around the globe with its clever concept of no bookings, wooden communal tables, bench seating, electronic ordering, and a menu of japan-easy noodle soups and 'side dishes' that come in no particular order. These days, the Streatham Street branch lacks the smartness of newer siblings, but it's still sardine-packed with local workers and shoppers who give it the look and feel of a bustling office canteen. The food is an easygoing mixed bag of fill-'em-up, get-'em-out fare running from the ubiquitous edamame to the popular laksa-like kare noodle dishes. Our Wagamama ramen (egg noodles, chicken, prawns and fish in soup) came in a generous portion, but the chicken was bland and the single prawn overcooked. Chicken yakitori had more punch, thanks mainly to the feisty sauce, while a special of grilled sea bass on rice worked well in spite of the aggressively pickled vegetables. Thrill-seekers should finish on the tamarind and chilli pavlova.

Babies and children welcome: high chairs. Takeaway service. Vegan dishes. **Map 18 D2.**

For branches see index.

Fitzrovia

Bam-Bou

1 Percy Street, W1T 1DB (7323 9130/www. bam-bou.co.uk). Goodge Street or Tottenham Court Road tube.
Bar **Open** 6pm-midnight Mon-Sat.
Restaurant **Lunch served** noon-3pm Mon-Fri. **Dinner served** 6-11pm Mon-Sat. **Main courses** £8.50-£14.
Both **Credit** AmEx, JCB, MC, V.

Caprice Holdings (the Ivy, Scott's, Le Caprice and so on) approach oriental food with typical style and attention to detail, and Bam-Bou is no exception. A delightful Georgian townhouse with more than a hint of Indochinese elegance comes complete with wooden tables, oversized mirrors, potted ferns and oriental pop art. The crowd at Bam-Bou is young, the atmosphere loud and chatty, and the food loosely based on refined Vietnamese, with forays into Thai-style curries and Chinese stir-fries. Most people start with prawn crackers or edamame. The kitchen is keen on deep-frying even those dishes not normally fried; we found the deep-fried tamarind-glazed frogs' legs tasted of little more than their batter. A peanutty chicken salad with lime and chilli was lively and fresh-tasting, while herb-baked Chilean sea bass was sensitively cooked. Massaman curried tiger prawns starred fresh bamboo shoots and pea aubergines, but the sauce was overpoweringly thick and sweet. Finish with a civilised pot from the range of 14 infusions, from pai mu silver needle tea to nettle and mistletoe.

Babies and children admitted. Booking advisable. Separate rooms for parties, seating 9, 12, 14 and 20. Tables outdoors (4, terrace). **Map 10 K5.**

Crazy Bear

26-28 Whitfield Street, W1T 2RG (7631 0088/ www.crazybeargroup.co.uk). Goodge Street or Tottenham Court Road tube.
Bar **Open** noon-10.45pm Mon-Fri; 6-10.45pm Sat. *Restaurant* **Meals/dim sum served** noon-10.45pm Mon-Fri. **Dinner served** 6-10.45pm Sat. **Dim sum** £2.50-£3.50. **Main courses** £10-£28. **Set meal** £30-£40 tasting menu.
Both **Credit** AmEx, DC, MC, V.

An offshoot of an Oxfordshire gastropub-hotel, Crazy Bear doesn't look like an oriental restaurant. It more closely resembles the belle époque Orient Express train with its long, narrow, moodily lit dining rooms lined with parquetry, leather banquettes and romantic lamps. In the basement, the bar scene is heaving, while upstairs, girls-on-the-town, family gatherings and first-daters happily munch their way through a mix of glamorously presented Thai curries, wok-fried noodles, and Cantonese dim sum. We particularly liked the delicate prawn har gau, meaty siu mai, and subtle garlic chive dumplings. Also good were crisp, golden peking duck spring rolls, and a meaty fillet of steamed red snapper bathed in quite a sweet chilli sauce. Pad thai noodles were dry, and made less thrilling by the addition of tasteless prawns. Most dishes, however, are capably sourced and cooked, service is sleek and intelligent, and the wine list has plenty of interest. Make time to view the over-the-top loos – even if you don't have to go.

Babies and children admitted. Booking advisable. Vegetarian menu. **Map 4 K5.**

Suka NEW

The Sanderson, 50 Berners Street, W1P 4AD (7300 1444/www.morganshotelgroup.com). Oxford Circus or Tottenham Court Road tube. **Breakfast served** 6.30-11.30am, **lunch served** noon-2.30pm daily. **Dinner served** 5pm-midnight Mon-Wed; 5pm-12.30am Thur-Sat; 5-10.30pm Sun. **Main courses** £11-£32. **Set lunch** £30 3 courses. **Credit** AmEx, JCB, MC, V.

What used to be the critically slammed Spoon+ restaurant inside the über-trendy Sanderson hotel has metamorphosed into Suka, which claims to offer 'modern authentic Malaysian cuisine'. In reality, food consists of the vaguely oriental, elaborately presented plate garnishes that are popular with people who've never made it further east than Walthamstow. Dishes are a visual feast; the Sanderson is the kind of hotel where looks are everything. But who is going to relish canapé-sized 'Malaysian' burgers at £13 a pop? Or long for a curried crab 'laksa' that wasn't (a laksa, that is) and costs £15 for a tiny starter portion? Prices are heavy (even rice costs £6); you're likely to fork out £60 or more per head for a dinner with a modest bottle of wine. Our dishes arrived willy-nilly; one person at our table was left empty-plated for 15 minutes, waiting for their order to arrive. Still, Suka must appeal to someone: someone more interested in style than substance; who doesn't care about paying through the nose for it; and who doesn't mind a 15% service charge when it's clear that customers must fit into the kitchen's timetable not vice versa.

Babies and children welcome: high chairs. Booking advisable Wed-Sat. Tables outdoors (20, garden). **Map 9 J5.**

Mayfair

Haiku NEW

15 New Burlington Place, W1S 2HX (7494 4777/www.bukhara.com). Oxford Circus or Piccadilly Circus tube. **Lunch served** noon-3pm, **dinner served** 6-11pm Mon-Sat. **Main courses** £4-£24. **Set meal** £30-£50; £60 tasting menu. **Credit** AmEx, DC, MC, V.

One of the latest 'Modern Oriental' restaurants to open in London, Haiku clearly has ambitions to be among the best. The dark interior looks alluring, with lots of black wooden screens, glass, open kitchens and clever lighting on three levels. Well-chosen chill-out music and beautiful Japanese-style tableware suggest an eye for detail. Food is far

from the haphazard collision of techniques and flavours often found in pan-oriental cuisine. The menu is separated into distinct dish types: sushi, sashimi, dim sum, grilled dishes, curries, wok-fried dishes. Each category has its own section in the kitchen: a Japanese chef in charge of the sushi and the robata (grill) dishes; Hong Kong chefs in the wok section and preparing dim sum; Indian chefs creating the tandoor dishes; and so on. Haiku's sushi was certainly up to Chinatown standards; a spicy prawn version of siu mai was our pick. Scallops with lashings of spicy XO sauce provided some kick. Not all dishes were tip-top; coconut rice was stolid, and the (Chinese) cheung fun featured rather indelicate rolls of rice pasta. Excellent ice-creams made a simple but satisfying finish.
Children admitted. Booking advisable. Disabled: toilet. Separate rooms for parties, seating 35 and 40. **Map 9 J6.**

Piccadilly

Cocoon

65 Regent Street, W1B 4EA (7494 7609/ www.cocoon-restaurants.com). Piccadilly Circus tube. **Lunch served** noon-3pm Mon-Fri. **Dinner served** 5.30pm-midnight Mon-Sat. **Main courses** £7.50-£45. **Credit** AmEx, MC, V.

Much money has been spent on what is still a highly fashionable dining experience at Cocoon – witness the Riedel wine glasses, the *American Beauty* tables of clear perspex encasing faux rose petals, the celebrity wine list, and the swivelling leather chairs. Designer Stephane Dupoux has created pod-like rooms divided by sheer net curtains that tend to kill the atmosphere, but not the noise from the loud groups of Euro-corporates and property developers. While much of the high-born menu borrows from the likes of Zuma, Hakkasan and Nobu, it is classily put together by chef Andrew Lasseter and his team. A starter of scallop and salmon nigiri sushi positively beamed with freshness; and a three-seaweed salad tossed with tofu, baby leaves, edamame and pumpkin seeds was a textural treat, if a little heavy with sesame oil. Silky flaps of seared tuna served with miso aïoli were both lush and light, and Korean 'bulgogi' of rare beef ribeye with wild mushrooms spoke volumes for the quality of Lasseter's suppliers.
Babies and children welcome: high chairs. Booking advisable. Disabled: toilet. Dress: smart casual. Entertainment: DJs 11pm Thur-Sat. Separate room for parties, seats 14. **Map 17 A5.**

West

Ladbroke Grove

E&O

14 Blenheim Crescent, W11 1NN (7229 5454/ www.rickerrestaurants.com). Ladbroke Grove or Notting Hill Gate tube.
Bar **Open** noon-midnight Mon-Sat; 12.30pm-11.30pm Sun. **Dim sum served** noon-10.30pm Mon-Sat; noon-10pm Sun. **Dim sum** £2.50-£6.50.
Restaurant **Lunch served** noon-3pm Mon-Fri; noon-4pm Sat; 12.30-4pm Sun. **Dinner served** 6-11pm Mon-Sat; 6-10.30pm Sun. **Main courses** £9.50-£32.
Both **Credit** AmEx, DC, MC, V.

Aussie restaurant whiz, Will Ricker, opened this Notting Hill celebrity magnet in 2001. Minimalist and mirror-edged, with atmospheric brown slatted walls, it's a warm, dark and cosy space, full of likely lads with Hugh Grant hair and blondes with designer sunglasses perched on their heads. At night, Perrier Jouët ice buckets cling to table-tops covered with stylish plates and bowls of edamame, tempura and futomaki rolls. There is more than a passing nod to Nobu in a menu that includes both rock shrimp tempura and black cod in miso, both of which seem to pop up on every table. Fat prawn and chive dumplings were well-made but overly sticky, while a salad of duck, watermelon and cashew nut felt wet and lacked punch. Far better were the refreshing tuna tartare (dramatically presented on iced seaweed and topped with wasabi flying fish roe) and a platter of perfectly seared rare beef paired with delectable soy-cooked aubergine. Service can be a bit scatty, as evidenced by one waiter who described our sauvignon blanc as 'crispy'.
Babies and children welcome: high chair. Booking essential. Separate room for parties, seats 10-18. Tables outdoors (5, pavement). Vegan dishes.
Map 19 B3.
For branch (XO) see index.

South West

Chelsea

Itsu

118 Draycott Avenue, SW3 3AE (7590 2400/ www.itsu.com). South Kensington tube. **Meals served** 11am-10.30pm Mon-Sat; 11am-9.30pm Sun. **Main courses** £3.75-£6.45. **Credit** MC, V.

Waiting for a seat at the sushi counter or a booth at the back to become free is no hardship here, thanks to the chic, dimly lit first-floor bar: a sort of Bouji's club for those who eat. You almost don't want to leave when your electronic beeper buzzes and flashes, telling you it's time to reach for your chopsticks. As with all conveyor belt sushi, the simpler items work best. New-style salmon sashimi (cut thinly and dressed with lemon and oil) had a real spring in its step; and an omelette and chive sushi roll was bright and bouncy. In contrast, gyoza dumplings had a ready-meal anonymity; thai-style coconut soup had overdosed on sugar and fish sauce; and the rice paper skin of the vietnamese duck and hoi sin roll was so chewy the filling kept popping out. But dining at Itsu is still fun, with everything you need in front of you from napkins to spoons, soy, wasabi and a service button. Warning: staff clear away your colour-coded plates as you progress, so you could lose count of how much you've eaten – and spent.
Babies and children welcome: booster seats. Booking not accepted. Takeaway service; delivery service (over £50 within 3-mile radius).
Map 14 E10.
For branches see index.

South

Battersea

★ Banana Leaf Canteen

75-79 Battersea Rise, SW11 1HN (7228 2828). Clapham Junction rail. **Lunch served** noon-3pm, **dinner served** 6-11pm Mon-Fri. **Meals served** noon-11pm Sat, Sun. **Main courses** £5.95-£9.20. **Credit** MC, V.

There's no doubting the popularity of this buzzy Battersea hotspot. Even midweek, the queues are forming at the door by 7.30pm, and the place is as rowdy as a pub on football night. BLC feels like a low-tech Wagamama (*see p252*) with its wooden floors, dark brown shared tables, wooden stools and steamy on-view kitchen. The cooking is mainly Malaysian, with occasional forays into Vietnamese, Indonesian and Thai. Not everything works: kau chi steamed pork and prawn

Suka

RESTAURANTS

Haiku. See p252.

dumplings felt wet and floppy; Thai sweetcorn cakes were bland and oily; and a sesame glass noodle salad was seriously lacking in the noodle department. However, chargrilled chicken baka jawar (marinated in Balinese spices) was tender and brightly flavoured, and a Vietnamese pork stew with lemongrass and cinnamon had a nice spicy, tangy uplift. Most regulars just settle for a big post-gym, pre-clubbing bowl of noodles (laksa, kway teow mee, pad thai) and a glass of wine or a beer, which would seem to be the best bet here.
Babies and children welcome: children's menu; high chairs. Booking advisable. Disabled: toilet.
Map 21 C4.

South East

Gipsy Hill

★ Mangosteen

246 Gipsy Road, SE27 9RB (8670 0333). Gipsy Hill rail/322 bus. **Lunch served** 11am-3pm Fri-Sun. **Dinner served** 6-11pm Mon-Sun. **Main courses** £8.50-£10.50. **Credit** MC, V.

This modern, well-run little restaurant is an unexpected find in an area not exactly renowned for culinary fireworks. For a start, the place looks a treat with its smart banquettes, rust-coloured walls and atmospheric black and white photographs of rural Vietnam. There's even a small terrace for sunny days. Essentially a Vietnamese restaurant with Thai options, Mangosteen doesn't mind going out of its way to please customers, offering scrambled eggs on toast at lunchtimes as well as a bargain-priced, spiced-up burger and chips. Far better, however, to stick to what the Vietnamese chef does best: from the fat, fresh, rice paper spring rolls, to what must rate among the best pho ga (chicken noodle) soups in London. Laced with tender strips of chicken and slippery rice noodles and served correctly with fresh asian basil, beansprouts and chilli on the side, the soup is a complex, long-flavoured stunner. As a bonus, there's even a special reserve wine list featuring, among other choice bottles, two different Puligny-Montrachets.
Babies and children welcome: high chairs. Booking advisable weekends. Tables outdoors (5, terrace). Takeaway service.

Herne Hill

Lombok

17 Half Moon Lane, SE24 9JU (7733 7131). Herne Hill rail/37 bus. **Lunch served** noon-3pm Tue-Sun. **Dinner served** 6-10.30pm Tue-Thur, Sun; 6-11pm Fri, Sat. **Main courses** £6-£8. **Set lunch** £7.95. **Credit** MC, V.

There is something endearingly colonial about this well-presented dining room, with its ceiling fans, art nouveau dressers and reclining Buddhas. In essence a Thai restaurant, Lombok ventures further afield with dishes such as Vietnamese sugar cane prawns, Japanese tempura, Malaysian satay and Singapore chilli crab. Most of our fellow diners stuck to Thai standards such as a nicely intense and fiery tom yam prawn soup, and a good pungent red chicken curry. We also liked the chicken with thai basil and chilli: a simple no fuss stir-fry that leaves you with a nice mouth-filling chilli afterglow. Vietnamese lettuce wraps turned out to be cold, stodgy rice paper rolls served with nowhere near enough lettuce for wrapping – which rather spoilt the general idea of the dish.
Babies and children welcome: high chairs. Booking essential weekends. Takeaway service.
Map 23 A5.

East

Shoreditch

★ Great Eastern Dining Room

54-56 Great Eastern Street, EC2A 3QR (7613 4545/www.greateasterndining.co.uk). Old Street tube/rail/55 bus.
Below 54 bar **Open/meals served** 7.30pm-1am Fri, Sat. **Main courses** £9-£15.

Ground-floor bar **Open/dim sum served** noon-midnight Mon-Fri; 6pm-midnight Sat. **Dim sum** £5-£6.50.
Restaurant **Lunch served** 12.30-3pm Mon-Fri. **Dinner served** 6.30-10.45pm Mon-Sat. **Main courses** £9-£17.50.
All **Credit** AmEx, DC, MC, V.
You have to like the way owner Will Ricker puts a room together. Here is a man fully aware of our base tribal needs. GEDR is relaxed, good-looking and people-friendly, with squishy banquettes, paper-over-cloth tables, rich dark wooden floors and a chandelier conspiring to create a space you camp in as much as eat in. The menu pushes all the right buttons too, with its tour of South-east Asia: from dim sum, maki rolls and tempura, to curries and wok-fries. A starter plate of mixed sashimi and sushi produced flappingly fresh fish, generously cut and attractively arranged. Great Eastern's real strength, however, is in its Thai food. An enormous pile of pad thai noodles came generously endowed with chicken and properly garnished with chilli, peanuts, shallots and lime for squeezing. Som tum green papaya salad was authentically raw, wild and fresh tasting. A pepped-up spicy-sweet-sour nam jim sauce boosted a well-cooked crisp-skinned, whole farmed sea bass. This is the most together restaurant in the ever-swelling Ricker stable; we had inferior food at the latest branch, XO in Belsize Park.
Babies and children admitted (restaurant). Bar available for hire. Booking advisable; essential Fri, Sat. Entertainment: DJs 9pm Fri, Sat.
Map 6 R4.
For branch (XO) see index.

North East

Stoke Newington

★ Itto

226 Stoke Newington High Street, N16 7HU (7275 8827). Stoke Newington rail/67, 73, 76, 149, 243 bus. **Meals served** noon-11pm daily. **Main courses** £3.90-£6.20. **Credit** MC, V.
Itto has the temporary look of somewhere just about to close – or just about to open. Decor has been whittled down to off-purple walls, a framed Chinese art print and a free-standing heater. Tables are laminated wood, seating is on wooden stools, and only the dining room to the rear is softened by tea lights and place mats. Yet this easygoing pan-Asian noodle caff is considered something of a godsend by Stoke Newington folk, pulling in a good weekend crowd and steady takeaway trade. Staff are agreeably helpful, the menu a pleasant ramble through Thai curries, Chinese stir-fries, noodle soups and fried rice five ways. Vietnamese seems to be the strength, judging by a commendable, clean-tasting chicken pho (rice noodle soup with poached chicken, fresh herbs and chilli), and golden vietnamese spring rolls with a nuoc cham dipping sauce. For some reason, the kitchen gave vegetable pad thai noodles a cloyingly sweet, thick sauce reminiscent of an old-style Chinese sweet and sour.
Babies and children welcome: high chairs. Takeaway service; delivery service (over £10 within 2-mile radius). **Map 25 C1.**

North

Camden Town & Chalk Farm

★ Gilgamesh (100)

Camden Stables Market, Chalk Farm Road, NW1 8AH (7482 5757/www.gilgameshbar.com). Chalk Farm tube.
Bar **Open/snacks served** 6pm-2.30am Mon-Thur; noon-2.30am Fri-Sun.
Tea house **Open/snacks served** noon-6pm Sat; noon-7pm Sun. **Lunch served** noon-3pm Fri-Sun. **Dinner served** 6pm-midnight Mon-Thur; noon-12.30am Fri, Sat; noon-midnight Sun. **Set dim sum** £16. **Set lunch** (Mon-Fri; Sun) £18 2 courses, £22 3 courses. **Main courses** £10-£25.80.
All **Credit** AmEx, MC, V.
When it first opened in a futuristic new building in Camden Stables market, we thought Gilgamesh would be tagged for its hubris rather than for its food. After all, with a 50ft (15m) long lapis lazuli bar, epic Babylonian film set decor, miked-up DJs and a jazzy retractable glass roof, there's an awful lot to distract. Nevertheless, Ian Pengelley (ex-E&O, *see p253*) and his kitchen team have really found their feet and are cooking some of the most consistent, assured – and occasionally inspired – pan-Asian food in the country. Long elegant platters of sushi (salmon and tuna nigiri) sparkled with freshness and vitality. The scallop siu mai and the crisp, dry, duck spring rolls wouldn't have been out of place in Yauatcha. Thai son-in-law eggs, deep-fried under a shower of coriander, shallots and chilli, were a spicy revelation. Marvellous too was a coconut-rich talapia fish curry that contained baby pea aubergines, fragrant kaffir lime leaves and some stunning smoked trout dumplings. Gilgamesh is often compared to Paris's famous Buddha Bar – but you'll eat better here.
Babies and children admitted: high chairs. Booking essential. Disabled: lift; toilet. Dress: smart casual; no flip-flops or shorts. Vegetarian menu. **Map 27 C1.**

★ Lemongrass

243 Royal College Street, NW1 9LT (7284 1116). Camden Town tube. **Dinner served** 5.30-11pm daily. **Main courses** £5.40-£8.60. **Set dinner** £16.60-£18.80 per person (minimum 2). **Credit** JCB, MC, V.
What you see is what you get at this little Camden hole-in-the-wall. With its bare tile floors, paper tablecloths and semi-open kitchen (where the chef can be seen wrestling with his giant woks), Lemongrass doesn't pretend to be anything more than a neighbourhood caff that happens to do pan-Asian food. At the next table, a large family group with toddlers in tow was tucking into a predominantly deep-fried 'Treats' platter of prawn toasties, golden triangles, mini spring rolls and chicken satays. The food here is hard to place, with no noodle dishes or recognisably Thai curries, but with Vietnamese, Thai, Cambodian and Chinese influences throughout. Vegetarian spring rolls were oily, tom yum style prawn soup was murky and coarsely chilli-hot, and something called phnom penh chicken was a right puzzle. Billed as chicken, basil, onion and carrot with sweet chilli sauce, it tasted like just another sweet-and-sour chicken topped with chunks of pineapple. We think Lemongrass could try quite a lot harder.
Babies and children welcome: high chairs. Booking advisable weekends. Restaurant available for hire. Takeaway service. Vegetarian menu.
Map 27 D1.

North West

Hampstead

★ dim T café

3 Heath Street, NW3 6TP (7435 0024/www.dimt.co.uk). Hampstead tube. **Meals served** noon-11pm Mon-Thur, Sun; noon-11.30pm Fri, Sat. **Main courses** £5.95-£8.95. **Credit** AmEx, MC, V.
From the prawn crackers at the start to the fortune cookies finale, this friendly, welcoming noodle bar seems determined to give the public what they want. Certainly, there's better dim sum to be had in London. And the noodles-by-numbers routine (Step 1: choose your main ingredient; Step 2: the noodle; Step 3: the topping; Step 4: soup or stir-fry) is a bit naff. Yet rarely has good, fresh, pan-Asian cooking and dim sum been so accessible. This branch has a comfortable, easygoing dining room with dark wood tables, cosy chairs and disco pink ball lights, with (wow!) a real dim sum trolley in action. Adventurous dumpling fillings such as lemongrass and prawn, and wasabi chicken, tasted better than they sounded, while the dumplings themselves were well-formed and freshly cooked. Singapore noodles were light and clean-tasting with a nice undercurrent of curry, and Malaysian yellow chicken curry with star anise had an authentic, earthy presence. We'd like to have seen more fresh herbs and fewer sweet sauces, but for the money, you can't complain too loudly.
Babies and children welcome: children's menu; high chairs. Booking advisable; not accepted 7.30-9.30pm. Separate room for parties, seats 35. Tables outdoors (2, pavement). Takeaway service. **Map 28 B2.**
For branches see index.

Outer London

Barnet, Hertfordshire

Emchai

78 High Street, Barnet, Herts EN5 5SN (8364 9993/www.emchai.co.uk). High Barnet tube.
Lunch served noon-2.30pm daily. **Dinner served** 6-11pm Mon-Thur; 6pm-midnight Fri, Sat; 5-10pm Sun. **Main courses** £4.20-£7.90. **Set meal** £14.50-£18.50 per person (minimum 2). **Credit** AmEx, MC, V.
'Understated' is the word for this vast 80-seater with its bare floorboards, bare wooden tables and bare walls devoid of decoration. But you can always look at the chefs at work in the open kitchen (which runs down one wall) and pretend you're at home watching *Iron Chef* on the telly. While South-east Asian dishes such as beef rendang, singapore laksa and chicken satay dominate, there's some pretty adventurous Chinese cooking to be sampled as well, including an unexpected nod to Hakkasan (sea bass with champagne sauce). Traditionalists tend to stick with the likes of aromatic crispy duck, or sweet and sour chicken. We particularly liked the verdant, lightly crunchy gai lan (chinese broccoli) in ginger sauce, and the scorchy, character-laden char kway teow (rice noodles with chicken and prawns), although a little crisped lup cheong sausage wouldn't have gone astray. Gado gado (beansprout salad with sweet peanut sauce) was a bit grim, with a hard-boiled egg showing a distinct grey ring from overcooking.
Babies and children welcome: high chairs. Disabled: toilet. Restaurant available for hire. Takeaway service.

Kingston, Surrey

Cammasan

8 Charter Quay, High Street, Kingston upon Thames, Surrey KT1 1NB (8549 3510/www.cammasan.com). Kingston rail.
Meinton noodle bar **Lunch served** noon-3pm, **dinner served** 5.30-11pm Mon-Fri. **Meals served** noon-11pm Sat, Sun. **Main courses** £5.50-£8.90.
Chaitan restaurant **Lunch served** noon-3pm, **dinner served** 5.30-11pm Mon-Fri. **Meals served** noon-11pm Sat, Sun. **Main courses** £5.50-£30. **Set meal** £14.90-£20.90 per person (minimum 2). **Minimum** £15.
Both **Credit** AmEx, MC, V.
Charter Quay is what town planners charmingly refer to as a 'Mixed Use Development', meaning that it's a modern mix of apartments, shops, restaurants, canals and paddling ducks. As well as bringing new life to a derelict area, it has also attracted what many locals regard as Kingston's best oriental restaurant, or rather, two best oriental restaurants. On the first floor is a plush, intimate dining room, decked out with fine table linen and serving a huge variety of Chinese specialities, from good old sweet and sour pork to peking duck with the works. Downstairs is a modern noodle bar where freshly cooked Malay, Thai and Chinese dishes pull in a mix of Asian students, residents and local businessmen to sit at long communal benches. From a menu divided into little plates, big plates and big bowls, we particularly liked our big bowl of roast duck and egg noodles served in a delightfully aromatic chicken stock. Also good was a selection of daily dim sum. The only jarring note was the unwanted (and inauthentic) curry powder in an otherwise terrific char kway teow (rice noodles with seafood).
Babies and children welcome: high chairs. Booking advisable. Disabled: toilet. Tables outdoors (12, terrace). Takeaway service.
For branch (China Royal) see index.

Portuguese

Authentic Portuguese dining is far from being a rushed affair. If you're heading to the handful of informal, expat restaurants in Vauxhall or Stockwell, perhaps you should leave your watch at home. In all these eateries, beer and seafood dominate, with dishes relying on the freshest of marine life rather than any fancy sauces. Meat usually comes marinated and grilled, or in robust stews. No Portuguese diet is complete without football, so expect at least one mounted television in every venue, often with an attendant horde of fans gathered around it. A faster-paced experience can be found in Ladbroke Grove, London's second Portuguese hub. Here, on either side of Golborne Road, you'll discover two of London's best Portuguese pâtisseries – **Café Oporto** and **Lisboa Pâtisserie** – which have a friendly rivalry mimicking that of Portugal's two greatest cities.

For most of these restaurants, food fashions are not an important concern; they prefer instead to recreate the flavours and the feel of a traditional Portuguese hostelry. There used to be two exceptions, but with the closure of Tugga in summer 2007, that leaves only **Portal** to prove that Portuguese flavours can mix it with London's finest in in a modern, glamorous, upmarket setting.

PASTELARIA

West

Ladbroke Grove

★ Café Oporto

62A Golborne Road, W10 5PS (8968 8839). Ladbroke Grove or Westbourne Park tube/23, 52 bus. **Open** 8am-7pm daily. **No credit cards.**

The rivalry between the cities of Oporto and Lisbon goes beyond football. Fierce allegiance to these cities is played out on Golborne Road, a decades-old centre of London's Portuguese community. Opposite Lisboa Pâtisserie (*see below*), Oporto is a place where locals meet to chat over espressos and pastries. With more seating than its competitor, this café also has a friendlier vibe as customers relax around tables to enjoy their homeland treats – from classic savoury pastries filled with salt cod, chicken or cheese, to lighter sweeter versions with almond, egg yolks, cinnamon, orange or lemon. We heard Brazilian Portuguese spoken on our visit, and spotted stacks of Guaraná Antarctica (a popular Brazilian soft drink) in the fridge. Oporto has long been in Lisboa's shadow, but this year has taken the lead.

Babies and children admitted. Tables outdoors (3, pavement). Takeaway service. **Map 19 B1.**

★ Lisboa Pâtisserie

57 Golborne Road, W10 5NR (8968 5242). Ladbroke Grove or Westbourne Park tube/ 23, 52 bus. **Open** 8am-7.30pm daily. **Credit** AmEx, MC, V.

Saturday mornings see Portobello Road's market-goers queue down the street for this café's famed pastéis de nata (custard tarts) and bicas (espressos). High-quality coffee is a Portuguese staple, and Lisboa's bica holds the Ladbroke Grove crown. With limited seating, this cultural hotspot is used predominantly as a takeaway, but it's a shame not to linger here and take in the well-aged charm (including a grand blue and white tiled mural of Lisbon). An imposing glass counter fills much of the interior, stacked high with fresh sandwiches and pastries, along with sweets made mostly from egg yolks and sugar. In summer, outdoor seating is in great demand, but if you're lucky enough to bag a chair, soak up the noisy Portuguese chatter, close your eyes and bite into a creamy custard tart. You might be in Belem.

Babies and children admitted. Tables outdoors (3, pavement). Takeaway service. **Map 19 B1.**
For branches see index.

South

Vauxhall

★ Café Madeira

46A-46B Albert Embankment, SE1 7TN (7820 1117). Vauxhall tube/rail. **Open** 6am-9pm daily. **Credit** (over £10) MC, V.

The converted arches of Albert Embankment bear an uncanny resemblance to those in *EastEnders*, and produce a similarly dodgy atmosphere. Four lanes of unrelenting traffic further make this an odd choice of location for the Madeira delicatessen, bakery and café. The café is the most popular arm of the operation and much bigger than expected, its interior enhanced by white tiles and walls and upstairs seating. A huge mounted TV holds the attention of many customers: mostly middle-aged businessmen. Regrettably, Madeira's Portuguese specialities have recently taken second place to an array of sandwiches for the business types. Nevertheless, on our visit there was a traditional feijão com grão (beans with chickpeas and pork), packed with chunks of succulent chorizo and costing only £5. Pity that it's usually served only at weekends. Thankfully, the drinks menu is more reminiscent of the old country, boasting Super Bock and Sagres beers along with a wealth of Portuguese soft drinks. A good-value pit-stop only a short walk from the train station.

Babies and children admitted. Disabled: toilet. Internet access. Tables outdoors (10, pavement). Takeaway service. **Map 16 L11.**

RESTAURANTS

Central

Clerkenwell & Farringdon

★ Portal

88 St John Street, EC1M 4EH (7253 6950/ www.portalrestaurant.com). Barbican tube/ Farringdon tube/rail. **Lunch served** noon-3pm Mon-Fri. **Dinner served** 6-10.15pm Mon-Sat. **Main courses** £13-£20. **Credit** AmEx, MC, V.

Portal deserves to be known not just as the scene of an attempt to bug Jose Mourinho's table (the restaurant is a favourite of the Chelsea manager, apparently). Beyond a modishly penumbral and bare bar (for an interesting selection of Portuguese wines and and a lengthy and appetising range of petiscos, aka tapas) it opens up into a glamorous, glass-sided room that feels as close to eating outdoors as possible. Here premier division food put together with panache by head chef Ricardo Janco is served at premier division prices, and the space between tables explains the need for a listening device. The clientele are appropriately sharp-suited. Of the half-dozen dishes we sampled, the best stayed closest to traditional Portuguese cooking. Take the arroz de pollo, for example: a soupy stew of rice and octopus, luxuriously topped with extra fried tentacles. But with a 'harmony', 'cornucopia' and 'symphony' on the menu – as in a Portuguese crab salad in cornucopia and ginger pesto, for example – and stabs at Iberian-style experiments with foams, it pays to be cautious. Octopus carpaccio had slivers of cephalopod covering the plate like large scales, but was surprisingly successfully accessorised with squid ink and potato foam and red pepper sauce. But oxtail stuffed with carrots and spinach, with sticky-sweet slicks of pumpkin and tomato jam, was oversalted and unenjoyable. A board of terrific cheeses was let down by stale biscuits. Commendably, gluten-free, vegan and vegetarian dishes are always available. For that extra-special occasion, you can order a whole Portuguese roast suckling pig at £420.

Babies and children welcome: high chairs. Disabled: toilet. Separate room for parties, seats 14. **Map 5 O4.**

Knightsbridge

★ O Fado

49-50 Beauchamp Place, SW3 1NY (7589 3002/ www.restauranteofado.co.uk). Knightsbridge or South Kensington tube. **Lunch served** noon-3pm daily. **Dinner served** 6.30pm-1am Mon-Sat; 6.30pm-midnight Sun. **Main courses** £10.95-£17.50. **Credit** AmEx, MC, V.

Walk past the showy eateries of Knightsbridge and into the homely basement that is O Fado. London's oldest Portuguese restaurant is probably also its best. The look is authentic rather than tacky, with paintings and tiles of Portuguese landmarks providing the decoration. During our visit, authenticity was maintained with olives and bread arriving at table only fractionally after we did. Staff were friendly and informative – handy, given the lengthy menu and even longer wine list. We opted for the recommended starter of pastéis de bacalhau: light, salty salt cod fritters. Prices may seem steep for this cuisine, but mammoth portions for main courses and sides soften the blow. Both garlic-crusted trout, and veal in madeira sauce were rich and rewarding. We found space for a chocolate mousse that was noticeably own-made as it had a slightly gritty texture. A couple of the waiters double as fado musicians, and played intermittently through the evening. Our only niggle was with the dim lighting, which was lowered through the evening until it was hard to see the next table, let alone the way out.

Babies and children admitted. Booking advisable; essential dinner weekends. Entertainment: guitarists 8pm Wed-Sun. Separate room for parties, seats 35. Takeaway service. **Map 14 F9.**

South

Brixton

The Gallery

256A Brixton Hill, SW2 1HF (8671 8311). Brixton tube/rail/45, 109, 118, 250 bus. **Dinner served** 7-10pm Fri, Sat. **Main courses** £7-£14. **Credit** MC, V.

Waiting to be buzzed through a door at the back of a takeaway chicken shop keeps expectations low. But prepare to be enchanted by a courtyard-style restaurant with kitsch, mural-lined walls, terracotta floor tiles and a gallery tier above. At the time of our visit, the restaurant opened only on Friday and Saturday, but almost every table was occupied by relaxed, laughing customers being served with efficient skill by just two waiters who were kept perpetually out of breath, yet were still eager to practise their English chat-up lines. We opted for the flaming chorizo starter after spotting that our neighbours' 'fisherman's catch' was decidedly small fry. Fisherman's rice (arroz de marisco) and pork alentejana-style arrived a good while later, though both were worth the wait. The soupy arroz contained a more than generous amount of seafood, and the pork came richly marinated, teamed with clams and a handful of fresh coriander. We took a risk with dessert and chose the own-made Molotov, which, thankfully, contained nothing more explosive than fluffy sugared egg whites, swimming in toffee sauce.

Babies and children welcome: high chairs. Booking advisable. Takeaway service. **Map 22 D3.**

Stockwell

Bar Estrela

111-115 South Lambeth Road, SW8 1UZ (7793 1051). Stockwell tube/Vauxhall tube/rail. **Meals served** 8am-11pm Mon-Sat; 10am-11pm Sun. **Main courses** £7-£13. **Tapas** £3.90-£5. **Credit** AmEx, MC, V.

An FC Porto match had star billing on the TV the night we visited Bar Estrela. Portuguese men filled both the restaurant and bar, spilling out on to the pavement to watch the match through the french windows. We didn't fancy our luck, yet there was one table nobody wanted – directly underneath one of the mounted TVs. Under such demanding circumstances the staff were on fire, moving quickly through the heaving throng. Customers snacked on steamed clams and supped Super Bock beer. We divided an uninspiring cheese-heavy version of garlic bread to start, followed by a piece of scabbard – a truly delicious fish (a Madeiran favourite), easily enough for two to share. During our pudding of flawless custard tarts, FC Porto won the match and we spent the rest of the evening swept up in an authentic Portuguese party.

Babies and children admitted. Tables outdoors (10, pavement). **Map 16 L13.**

Grelha D'Ouro

151 South Lambeth Road, SW8 1XN (7735 9764). Stockwell tube/Vauxhall tube/rail. **Meals served** 7am-11pm daily. **Main courses** £4.50-£12. **Credit** MC, V.

The hordes of beer-swigging, football-crazed men filling the tables at Grelha D'Ouro on our visit were clearly not put off by the rustic whitewashed decor and worn-out floor tiles of this café-restaurant. No one else seemed to mind the kerfuffle (or the sharp smell of aftershave); groups of men tucked into colossal portions of grilled sea bass and chilli squid, stopping only to glance up occasionally at the footie on the TV. Daily specials are written solely in Portuguese, so the waitress had to look up the English word for 'cordeiro' (lamb). Said lamb was roasted to falling-apart perfection. It came well seasoned, and served with the traditional carb-combo of rice and potatoes. A seafood feijoada was large enough for two, packed with mussels, clams, squid and prawns of all sizes, but it had few similarities to its famous Brazilian counterpart, using creamy soft cannellini beans instead of the more traditional black beans. The dining room and basement games room are both off-limits during the day, but the waitress assured us that some rowdy table football takes place downstairs in the evening.

Babies and children welcome: children's portions. Booking advisable weekends. Separate room for parties, seats 60. Takeaway service. **Map 16 L13.**

O Moinho

355A Wandsworth Road, SW8 2JH (7498 6333). Stockwell tube/Vauxhall tube/rail/77, 77A bus. **Meals served** 10am-11pm daily. **Main courses** £6.50-£9.50. **Credit** MC, V.

Standing out among a row of shabby shops, O Moinho is a well-maintained family-run restaurant. On a sunny afternoon, wind-protected pavement seating had tempted many punters outside, but we were enticed by the Portuguese kitsch interior. A traditional white and blue tiled mural of a windmill (moinho) is teamed with football shirts, signed photos of Portuguese singers and a sparkling marble bar. We skipped starters, taking advantage of the complimentary crusty bread, cheese, mixed olives and fish pâté. There's a variety of main courses, including pizzas and pastas, as well as the expected fish, seafood and meat dishes. We kept our meal traditional, ordering salt cod with ham and port (bacalhau à transmontana), which arrived with a sad piece of crispy ham sandwiched inside a chunk of overcooked cod. A mixed fish and vegetable kebab was far more impressive, featuring king prawns nearly as big as lobsters, and salmon, squid and cod which were all tender and flavoursome. The wine list is extensive, but the 'sommelier's choice' section seems out of place, with bottles costing around £100. Otherwise, this is a thoroughly reasonable restaurant.

Babies and children admitted. Booking advisable. Separate area for parties, seats 50. Tables outdoors (5, pavement). Takeaway service.

Menu

If you think the cooking of Portugal is just a poor man's version of Spanish cuisine, you haven't eaten enough Portuguese food. It's true that many of Portugal's dishes share the Spanish love for chorizo-style sausages (chouriço), dry cured ham (presunto) and salt cod (bacalhau), but the Portuguese have developed a cooking style that has a character, a culture and a cachet all its own. Take the famous arroz (rice) dishes that appear on practically every Portuguese menu. While they are often compared to paella, they are, in fact, far soupier, with the rice used almost as a thickening agent.

Portuguese cooking is in essence a peasant cuisine: the food of farmers and fishermen. Pork, sausages and charcuterie figure prominently, as does an abundance of fresh fish, seafood and olive oil (azeite). There's a strong tradition of charcoal-grilled fish and meats. The hearty bean stews from the north and the thick bready soups (açordas) are also worth trying, as is the coastal speciality of caldeirada, Portugal's answer to bouillabaisse. Garlic, lemon juice, wine and wine vinegar are much used in marinades, with favoured spices being piri-piri (hot peppers, often used to flavour oil in which chicken is basted) and, for the cakes, cinnamon – the latter showing the culinary influence of Portugal's colonial past.

To finish, there is always a lush arroz doce (rice pudding), a wobbly pudim flan (crème caramel) or the world's most loved custard tart, the deliciously scorched pastel de nata.

Açorda: a bread stew, using bread that's soaked in stock, then cooked with olive oil, garlic, coriander and an egg. Often combined with shellfish or bacalhau (qv).
Amêijoas à bulhão pato: clams with olive oil, garlic, coriander and lemon.
Arroz de marisco: soupy seafood rice.
Arroz de tamboril: soupy rice with monkfish.
Arroz doce: rice pudding.
Bacalhau: salt cod; soaked before cooking, then boiled, grilled, stewed or baked, and served in myriad variations – Portugal's national dish.
Bifana: pork steak, marinated in garlic, fried and served in a bread roll.
Caldeirada: fish stew, made with potatoes, tomatoes and onions.
Caldo verde: the classic green soup of finely sliced spring cabbage in a potato stock, always served with a slice of chouriço (qv).
Canela: cinnamon; a favourite spice, used in sweet and savoury dishes.
Caracois: boiled snails, eaten as a snack with a Super Bock or Sagres beer.
Carne de porco alentejana: an Alentejo dish of fried pork, clams and potato.
Cataplana: a special copper cooking pan with a curved, rounded bottom and lid; it gives its name to several southern Portuguese lightly simmered seafood dishes.
Chouriço assado: a paprika-flavoured smoked pork sausage cooked on a terracotta dish over burning alcohol.
Cozido à portuguesa: the traditional Sunday lunch of Portugal – various meats plus three types of sausage, cabbage, carrots, potatoes and sometimes white beans, all boiled together.
Dobrada: tripe stew.
Espadarte: swordfish.
Feijoada: bean stew, cooked with pork and sausages.
Molotov: a fluffy white pudding made from egg whites combined with caramelised sugar, often covered in custard.
Pastel de bacalhau (plural **pasteis**): salt cod fish cake.
Pastel de nata: a rich egg custard tart made with crisp, thin, filo pastry.
Piri-piri or **peri-peri**: Angolan hot red pepper.
Pudim flan: crème caramel.
Queijo: cheese.
Sardinhas assadas: fresh sardines, roasted or char-grilled.

Spanish

Modern innovations in Spanish cooking have been widely publicised in the press, but slow to exert a definite influence in the kitchens of restaurants abroad. In London, unreconstructed tapas bars are still the norm, many of them turning out mediocre, measly approximations of Spanish classics in a yawnfully clichéd setting. Fortunately, we've no cause to list those here, as there's a good crop of places which do the old favourites with panache – and without a Gipsy Kings soundtrack. Among the best, and most authentic, are **Barrafina** (contender for Best New Restaurant in the 2007 Time Out Eating & Drinking Awards), **Rebato's**, **Galicia**, **Los Molinos** and Walthamstow newcomer the **Orford Saloon**. Meanwhile, veterans **El Parador** and **Moro**, and more recent arrivals **L Restaurant & Bar** and **Tapas y Vino** (nominated for Best Local Restaurant), put Spanish ingredients and recipes at the heart of a more inclusive menu that borrows from elsewhere in Europe or North Africa with great success. And some of the more ambitious kitchens are finally starting to follow their mentors on the Peninsula, taking tentative steps into the territory of *nueva cocina*. **Cambio de Tercio** was among the first; of late it's been joined by the brilliant **Salt Yard** in Fitzrovia, stylish **El Faro** in Docklands and funky **Lola Rojo** in Battersea (also a contender for Best Local Restaurant).

Central

Bloomsbury

Cigala

54 Lamb's Conduit Street, WC1N 3LW (7405 1717/www.cigala.co.uk). Holborn or Russell Square tube.
Bar **Open/tapas served** 5.30-10.45pm Mon-Sat. *Restaurant* **Meals served** noon-10.45pm Mon-Fri; 12.30-10.45pm Sat; noon-9.45pm Sun. **Main courses** £11-£19.50. **Set lunch** (noon-3pm Mon-Fri) £15 2 courses, £18 3 courses. **Set meal** (Sun) £10.50 1 course. *Both* **Credit** AmEx, DC, MC, V.
Properly laid tables and a clean, refined design incorporating whites and woods lend Cigala a sophistication that is lacking in an average neighbourhood Spanish bar. That's not to say classic Hispanic comfort food is absent from the menu; the list of tapas offers plenty of homely sharing food. This was the route we chose on our latest visit. Diligently prepared dishes included gambas al ajillo: three giant, fleshy prawns in a piquant sauce ideal for subsequent bread-dunking. Chicken livers had been seared for just one merciful moment – leaving them deliciously creamy, to be served with a sticky-sweet jus. A separate menu of starters and main courses caters for diners wanting a little more formality, with dishes such as fillet of sea bream or slow-roasted pork belly, accompanied by simple vegetables. A very grown-up, all-Spanish wine list is also pitched at the more formal diner, yet includes something to please most budgets; excellent sherries and brandies add to the range.
Babies and children welcome: high chairs. Bar available for hire. Booking advisable. Tables outdoors (11, pavement). **Map 4 M4.**

Clerkenwell & Farringdon

★ Moro (100)

34-36 Exmouth Market, EC1R 4QE (7833 8336/ www.moro.co.uk). Farringdon tube/rail/19, 38 bus.
Bar **Open/tapas served** 12.30-11.45pm Mon-Sat (last entry 10.30pm). **Tapas** £2.50-£12. *Restaurant* **Lunch served** 12.30-2.30pm, **dinner served** 7-10.30pm Mon-Sat. **Main courses** £13.50-£17.50. *Both* **Credit** AmEx, DC, MC, V.
It took us three attempts to reserve a table, with 48 hours' notice: not bad for a restaurant that celebrated its tenth birthday in 2007. Moro owes such popularity to several factors. Exmouth Market is an unrivalled setting, coming into its own in summer when tables are placed outside. The restaurant is no less pleasant indoors; the softly lit open-plan dining room is restrained in decor, yet cosy and romantic in atmosphere. Food is the primary draw. The menu is a daily-changing Modern Mediterranean ensemble (starters and mains, not tapas) with heavy Spanish and North African accents. Slow-roasted kid was an extraordinarily tender and succulent cut of rare meat on the bone, paired with a fino sauce and vegetables. A roasted skate wing came with a light beetroot pilaf and a herby yoghurt dressing. We also enjoyed great sherries, a bottle from the well-chosen wine list, and olives and bread that were as good as any we've tasted. Naturally, there's a price for such excellence; Moro is one of the more expensive restaurants in this chapter. We consider it to be worth every penny – just remember to book a few days ahead.
Babies and children welcome: high chairs. Booking essential. Disabled: toilet. Tables outdoors (6, pavement). **Map 5 N4.**

Fitzrovia

Fino

33 Charlotte Street, entrance on Rathbone Street, W1T 1RR (7813 8010/www.finorestaurant.com). Goodge Street or Tottenham Court Road tube.
Lunch served noon-2.30pm Mon-Fri; 12.30-2.30pm Sat. **Dinner served** 6-10.30pm Mon-Sat. **Tapas** £4-£15.50. **Credit** AmEx, MC, V.
As a well-known couple brushed by our table on their way out of this smart, if slightly austere, subterranean restaurant, the lady, clearly well satisfied by her dinner, turned to us. With a knowing wink, she declared 'it's rather good here, isn't it?' then vanished into the night. She's right; the food is very good indeed. It's classic, unembellished Spanish tapas. The ingredients are first-rate, the cooking is precise. Pulpo a la gallega was delicious, super-soft octopus dressed in olive oil and paprika. Clams with bacon and sherry was no more, no less, but very moreish. Meat was tasty and succulent; vegetables perfectly al dente. The catch is the prices, which are just too bloated for such unerringly simple food. There's no alchemy in this kind of cooking, and you can eat tapas just as good for half the price elsewhere. The cheapest Rioja is £24. So, Fino is one for expense accounts – something most people have already figured out, judging by the number of suits in attendance. Buoyed by Fino's success, owners (and brothers) Sam and Eddie Hart have opened a new tapas bar in Soho, Barrafina (*see p261*).
Babies and children welcome: high chair. Booking advisable. Disabled: lift; toilet.
Map 9 J5.

★ Salt Yard

54 Goodge Street, W1T 4NA (7637 0657/ www.saltyard.co.uk). Goodge Street tube. **Open** noon-11pm Mon-Fri; 5-11pm Sat. **Tapas served** noon-3pm, 6-11pm Mon-Fri; 5-11pm Sat. **Tapas** £2.75-£8.50. **Credit** AmEx, DC, MC, V.
The hybrid Spanish-Italian cooking at this classy restaurant is unique in London. In spirit, the seasonal menu resembles a traditional list of tapas, relying on unfussy recipes that allow the flavours of top-quality ingredients to tell; yet in its detail, the choice is fascinating. Signature dishes include deep-fried courgette flowers stuffed with Spanish cheese and drizzled with honey, and confit of Old Spot pork belly with cannellini beans. On a recent visit, new additions included a delectable tapa of pan-fried polenta with salsa verde, baby beetroot and grana padano cheese, and a smoked tuna carpaccio with vinaigrette – a worthy rival to the exemplary range of charcuterie offered. The clean, sophisticated decor is a perfect match for such careful cooking, making the restaurant ideal for a date, but not too formal for a relaxed meal with friends. You'll also find excellent sherries, wines and desserts to accompany the great food. The only problem? Getting a table – Salt Yard is a little diminutive and certainly no secret.
Babies and children admitted. Booking advisable. Tables outdoors (3, pavement).
Map 9 J5.

BEST SPANISH

Nueva cocina

To experience the new school of Spanish cooking, head to **Cambio de Tercio** (*see p262*), **El Faro** (*see p267*), **Lola Rojo** (*see p265*) and **Salt Yard** (*see above*).

Tapas with a buzz

Meza (*see p261*) and **Barrafina** (*see p261*) please the media types of Soho with their excellent tapas. **Camino** (*see p261*) and **Pinchito Tapas** (*see p267*) are jumpier and more bar-like, but both boast quality kitchens.

Outdoor eating

Goya (*see p261*) and **Moro** (*see left*) offer pavement tables, **El Parador** (*see p267*) has a pleasant garden, and the courtyard at **Camino** (*see p261*) is gorgeous.

For a real Spanish feel

Head to Spanish-owned, Spanish-run joints such as **El Pirata** (*see p261*), **Cambio de Tercio** (*see p262*), **Galicia** (*see p263*), **Lola Rojo** (*see p265*) and **Rebato's** (*see p265*).

Barrafina. See p261.

King's Cross

★ Camino NEW

3 Varnishers Yard, Regents Quarter, N1 9FD (7841 7331/www.barcamino.com). King's Cross tube/rail.
Bar **Open/tapas served** noon-midnight Mon-Wed; noon-1am Thur-Sat. **Tapas** £3-£6.
Restaurant **Breakfast served** 8-11.30am, **dinner served** 6.30-11pm Mon-Sat. **Lunch served** noon-3pm Mon-Fri. **Main courses** £10.50-£20.
Both **Credit** AmEx, MC, V.

After years of talk about the regeneration of King's Cross, we're finally starting to see some interesting developments. One of the most exciting so far has been the opening of this bar-restaurant, a new venture from the owners of Shoreditch's Cargo and W1's Market Place. Rustic materials such as stripped wood and cork have been used to create a clean, contemporary aesthetic that is equal parts London and Spain. In the spacious bar area and its outdoor courtyard, simple tapas are available. The restaurant, round the other side, offers an expanded menu including fish and steaks from the parrilla (charcoal grill). Ingredients and cooking are top-notch. We enjoyed a delicate fillet of red mullet with shallots and tomato, as well as a chunky, tender ribeye steak. The drinks list alone distinguishes Camino; all the wines from a great, compact list are available by the glass, as are three sherries and three cavas. Lesser-known Spanish beers include the magnificent Àmbar from Zaragoza. Spanish travellers stepping off the new Eurostar at St Pancras will feel like they've never left home.
Babies and children welcome: high chairs; nappy-changing facilities. Disabled: toilet. Booking advisable. Tables outdoors (5, garden).
Map 4 L3.

Mayfair

El Pirata

5-6 Down Street, W1J 7AQ (7491 3810/ www.elpirata.co.uk). Green Park or Hyde Park Corner tube. **Meals served** noon-11.30pm Mon-Fri. **Dinner served** 6-11.30pm Sat. **Main courses** £10.50-£16. **Tapas** £3.95-£9. **Set lunch** (noon-3pm) £9 2 dishes incl glass of wine. **Set meal** £13.95-£17.75 per person (minimum 2) 8 dishes. **Credit** (over £10) AmEx, JCB, MC, V.

True to its name, El Pirata feels like a trespasser amid the high seas of Mayfair's super-restaurants. But its continuing popularity – the place was busy when we visited on a Monday lunchtime – shows that even round here there's a need for honest, good-quality comfort food. We quickly filled up on wholesome dishes like fabada asturiana (made correctly with pork shoulder, chorizo and morcilla) and arroz negro (squid with squid-ink-coloured rice), and balanced them with a lovely salad made with spinach, rocket, pine nuts and shaved manchego cheese. The decor is rustic in monochrome (white paint, black wood, black tablecloths) and the walls are crammed with Spanish repro art – a bit of a cliché, but quite charming. Charming also are the attentive Spanish waiters, who come properly uniformed in the classic way: a little gesture of formality that's rarely unwelcome. Two other strengths are the budget set lunch menu (two tapas and a drink) and a large, informed choice of regional Spanish wines, including some excellent reserve Riojas.
Babies and children admitted. Booking advisable dinner. Separate room for parties, seats 65. Tables outdoors (4, pavement). Takeaway service.
Map 9 H8.

Pimlico

Goya

34 Lupus Street, SW1V 3EB (7976 5309/ www.goyarestaurant.co.uk). Pimlico tube.
Lunch served noon-3pm, **dinner served** 6-11.30pm daily. **Main courses** £10.90-£16.95. **Tapas** £1.80-£6.85. **Credit** AmEx, MC, V.

Location is the main thing at this little neighbourhood restaurant, which brings a dash of Hispanic colour to the whitewashed austerity of Pimlico's calm backstreets. The wide pavements and corner position allow for plenty of outdoor seating in clement weather – when, picking at olives and sipping manzanilla, you just about feel like you're on holiday. Big windows mean it's nice and bright inside too, but space is limited on the ground floor and you don't really want to be shoved in the basement. The menu is a relatively unchallenging list of tapas classics, plus a handful of straightforward meat and fish mains. Still, freshness and careful cooking is all this food needs to succeed, and both requirements were met in our selection of Galician octopus, garlic prawns (bathed in a delicious piquant white wine gravy), and pan-fried chistorra sausage, followed by a whole grilled sea bass that we couldn't fault. Service was jolly and the dishes arrived in just the right procession. Estrella beer accompanied our feast, but there's also a range of reasonably priced Spanish wines in the £10-£40 bracket, plus sherries and cavas.
Babies and children admitted. Booking advisable. Restaurant available for hire. Tables outdoors (6, pavement). **Map 15 J11.**
For branch see index.

Soho

★ Barrafina NEW (100)

2007 RUNNER-UP LEFFE BEST NEW RESTAURANT

54 Frith Street, W1D 4SL (7813 8016/ www.barrafina.co.uk). Tottenham Court Road tube. **Lunch served** noon-3pm, **dinner served** 5-11pm Mon-Sat. **Tapas** £1.90-£16.50. **Credit** AmEx, MC, V.

There's an agreeable slickness and bustle about Sam and Eddie Hart's sleek new tapas bar. Unless you eat here outside regular mealtimes, there will be a queue (check it out on the webcam!), but staff work hard at keeping waiting diners happy, giving them updates on length of wait and plying them with drinks. Once you're seated at the L-shaped bar (which, apart from the kitchen and grill area behind it, pretty much constitutes the whole shebang), the fun really starts. Everything we tried was a masterclass in quality ingredients simply prepared to maximum effect – except a batch of strangely flavoured clams. Staff disagreed with us about the unpleasantness of the flavour, but didn't hesitate to take the dish off the bill. All other choices from a very appealing menu were hoovered up with enthusiasm. Standouts were a flavour-packed chickpea, spinach and bacon dish, and a light-as-air crema catalana. All tapas favourites are present and correct: pimientos de padrón, pan con tomate, various tortillas and glorious sliced meats (chorizo ibérico, jamón de jabugo, salchichón). Far more fun than the Hart brothers' previous venture, Fino (*see p258*), though prices are similarly eye-widening; the meats on the £10.50 cold meat platter, for example, were top-notch but very thinly sliced indeed.
Babies and children admitted. Booking not accepted. Tables outdoors (4, pavement).
Map 17 C3.

Meza

100 Wardour Street, W1F 0TN (7314 4002/ www.danddlondon.com). Leicester Square tube or Tottenham Court Road. **Open** noon-2am Mon-Wed; noon-3am Thur-Sat. **Tapas served** 5pm-12.30am Mon-Sat. **Tapas** £3.50-£10. **Set lunch** (noon-2.30pm Mon-Sat) £8 2 courses, £10 3 courses. **Credit** AmEx, DC, MC, V.

You wouldn't think old-school Spanish tapas had a place among all the sushi and dim sum of medialand, but that is what's for dinner now at the former home of Conran's Mezzo on Wardour Street. Dishes such as peppers stuffed with crab, pan-fried chicken livers, or morcilla with quail's egg and white beans are virtually unreconstructed Spanish classics, although the presentation here is meticulous. There's the odd new-school touch too – such as the velvety pea purée that came with some deliciously juicy scallops, each one topped with a slice of slightly crisp fried chorizo. A slice of tarta de santiago (the famous almond cake) was jazzed up with a scoop of cinnamon ice-cream.

Interview

SIMON MULLINS & SANJA MORRIS

Who are you?
Co-owners of **Salt Yard** (*see p258*).

Eating in London: what's good about it?
London is recognised internationally as a city buzzing with diversity – just near Salt Yard we have an amazing array of restaurants, from two-star Michelin establishments to Korean barbecue to classic French.

What's bad about it?
Compared to New York or, say, Valencia and Genoa, it is still relatively hard to eat good food in stylish surroundings without spending a lot of money. Also, service can range from bad to lacklustre as waitstaff suffer from a combination of bad training and low pay.

Which are your favourite London restaurants?
Roka (*see p197*) for its buzzy, stylish surroundings and delicious, inventive food. In Chiswick, **La Trompette** (*see p108*) is a favourite for excellent, considered food at good prices, served in an unstuffy and relaxed atmosphere. And the wine list is superb. **Uli** (16 All Saints Road, W11 1HH, 7727 7511) is our local Asian restaurant, where the food is fantastic and service absolutely charming.

Who or what has had the biggest impact on London's restaurant scene in the past 25 years?
Cheap air travel has made more people more knowledgeable and experimental with other cuisines, and more demanding when it comes to quality.

Any hot tips for the coming year?
The popularity of Spanish food is still growing, reflecting people's attitudes towards good, ingredient-led food and casual dining. People want to be able to eat great food in a relaxed and friendly environment. Hopefully, the amount of independent restaurants providing just that will continue to grow.

There's nothing Spanish about the spacious dining room, which is divided into a hotchpotch of sections in various contemporary styles. Apart from the food, a large bar and a great drinks list are the draws for the evening Soho crowds. A good tip is to come here for lunch, when Meza tends to be much quieter, in contrast to many of its busier, oversubscribed neighbours.
Babies and children admitted (lunch). Booking advisable weekend. Disabled: lift; toilet. Separate room for parties, seats 38. **Map 17 B3**.

South Kensington

★ Cambio de Tercio

163 Old Brompton Road, SW5 0LJ (7244 8970/ www.cambiodetercio.co.uk). Gloucester Road or South Kensington tube. **Lunch served** 12.30-2.30pm Mon-Fri; 12.30-3pm Sat, Sun. **Dinner served** 7-11.30pm Mon-Sat; 7-11pm Sun. **Main courses** £13.90-£15.50. **Credit** AmEx, DC, MC, V.
To most Londoners, Spanish cooking means simple, rustic fare like meatballs, croquettes and paella. But there's a new school of cuisine in Spain that takes the top-quality ingredients of Spanish tradition and combines them in more flamboyant ways. Cambio de Tercio is one of the few British restaurants that embraces this *nueva cocina*. It offers some of the best, most original Spanish food in London. Typical dishes are gazpacho, made exciting with a chunk of lobster and a scoop of cherry sorbet, or sea bream with courgette purée and a manchego cheese foam. There are some concessions to tradition too, such as king prawns in garlic and olive oil. On our visit, 12-hour slow-roasted oxtail in a red wine jus was a highlight, but nothing failed to delight. The restaurant has a rich, romantic decor set off by a sexy black tiled floor and red ceiling; it's a place for special occasions. Sister restaurant Tendido Cero across the road (*see below*) serves more conventional tapas for everyday consumption. The all-Spanish wine list is an impressive tome, though prices start at a rather hefty £20.
Babies and children admitted. Booking advisable dinner. Restaurant available for hire. Separate room for parties, seats 22. Tables outdoors (4, pavement). **Map 13 C11**.

Tendido Cero

174 Old Brompton Road, SW5 0BA (7370 3685/www.cambiodetercio.co.uk). Gloucester Road or South Kensington tube. **Tapas served** noon-11pm daily. **Tapas** £4-£14. **Credit** AmEx, MC, V.
Opening two Spanish restaurants directly opposite each other, in London, might sound daft, but try telling that to the owners of Tendido Cero and partner restaurant Cambio de Tercio (*see above*), both of which seem to be full of customers most nights. Key to this double success is the restaurants' contrasting remits: Cambio de Tercio is for fine dining, while Tendido Cero, on the whole, specialises in more traditional tapas. Though more casual than its big brother, it's designed along the same smart lines, with a colour scheme of black, dark red and mustard yellow. The menu runs to standards like patatas bravas and padrón peppers, as well as more unusual options. The undisputed highlight of our recent selection was baby eels on toast with aïoli. Each square of bread had vanished beneath a tangle of delicious meat; these had been crowned by a dollop of fresh, garlicky mayonnaise, then briefly set under the grill. In comparison, a couple of other choices (bland strips of chicken breast in oil and paprika, dry pork medallions) were underwhelming. However, other favourable elements – a buzzy and convivial atmosphere, knowledgeable service, a good wine list – helped make up for the little disappointments.
Babies and children admitted. Booking advisable dinner Tue-Sat. Restaurant available for hire. Tables outdoors (5, pavement). **Map 13 C11**.

West

Hammersmith

Los Molinos

127 Shepherd's Bush Road, W6 7LP (7603 2229/www.losmolinosuk.com). Hammersmith tube. **Lunch served** noon-3pm Mon-Fri. **Dinner served** 6-10.45pm Mon-Sat. **Tapas** £3.50-£6.50. **Credit** AmEx, DC, MC, V.
What this diminutive restaurant lacks in floor space, it more than makes up for in other ways. Los Molinos has charm in abundance, with pretty wooden furniture and salmon-pink walls bedecked with dainty collectibles. Also ample is the long menu, which must list nearly 60 dishes – something we might have cause to frown upon elsewhere, but it's not a problem here. There are no fillers; lovingly rendered favourites from across Spain sit alongside less familiar offerings. There are even a couple of Mexican dishes. Most importantly, food is fresh, properly cooked and quite delicious. Extra-length ham croquettes had chunks of red pepper inside: a nice twist on the standard. A bowl of chickpeas and spinach came in a hearty, cumin-scented broth. Gambas al ajillo were plump, succulent prawns in a rich, garlicky sauce. Best of all was a revuelto of baby eels, artichokes, red peppers and mushrooms: one of the best tapas we've tried in a while. If anything, cooking at Los Molinos has improved recently, and the restaurant remains, as ever, one of the area's better dining spots.
Babies and children welcome: high chairs. Booking advisable dinner Fri, Sat. Separate room for parties, seats 50. **Map 20 C3**.

Kensington

★ L Restaurant & Bar NEW

2 Abingdon Road, W8 6AF (7795 6969/www.l-restaurant.co.uk). High Street Kensington tube. **Lunch served** noon-3pm Tue-Sat. **Dinner**

Meza. See p261.

served 6-11pm Mon-Sat. **Meals/tapas served** 12.30-8.30pm Sun. **Main courses** £9.50-£17.50. **Tapas** £3.25-£4.95. **Credit** AmEx, MC, V.
A recent addition to W8's ample dining options, L Restaurant stands out from the crowd in several ways. The design, for a start, is unconventional – though this is probably through necessity not choice. The narrow, glass-roofed dining room seems to have been constructed to fill a former back garden; the result is curious, but nevertheless classy and amenable. Cooking is outstanding. Though Spanish ingredients and techniques feature heavily, the menu is cosmopolitan in scope. If visiting for the first time, eschew the tapas and go for exquisite starters such as seared scallops with apple and dandelion leaves, or tuna and veal carpaccio (you can hardly tell which is which) with a minted truffle dressing. Then on to magnificent mains like roast rump of lamb with spinach, leek and sun-dried tomatoes; or, a particular highlight, a rich, irresistible bowl of zarzuela (fish stew). Best of all, perhaps, was a very grown-up crème brûlée, the custard bursting with vanilla but, unusually, not too sweet in itself (leaving that to the caramel on top). As L demonstrates, sometimes it's good to be different.
Babies and children admitted. Booking advisable. Separate room for parties, seats 14. Tables outdoors (2, pavement). **Map 13 A9**.

Ladbroke Grove

★ Café García

246 Portobello Road, W11 1LL (7221 6119/ www.cafegarcia.co.uk). Ladbroke Grove tube.
Tapas served 9am-5pm daily. **Tapas** £1.50-£5. **Credit** AmEx, MC, V.
Shrewd shoppers at Portobello Market nip into García for a lunch break. The café arm of the Spanish groceries importer (supermarket adjacent) is hard to beat for a filling snack or quick coffee. The bright, modern eaterie is often peaceful and quiet, even when the market outside is bustling – surprising, given the high standard of hot and cold tapas, coffees, drinks and pastries here. All the food available on a given day is displayed in a counter at the front. The selection of tortillas, empanadas and salads is often accompanied by a paella or, as on our most recent visit, a fideuá (a similar pan-cooked dish that uses a kind of noodle instead of rice). None of the food is complicated, and some of it may be heated upon order in the microwave (as it often is in Spain), but it's all fresh and invariably tasty. The variety of cakes, pastries and biscuits is first-rate. Spanish coffees, soft drinks, beer and even the much-loved hot chocolate Cola Cao are among the liquid offerings.
Babies and children admitted. Disabled: toilet. Takeaway service. **Map 19 B2**.

Galicia

323 Portobello Road, W10 5SY (8969 3539). Ladbroke Grove tube. **Lunch served** noon-3pm Tue-Sun. **Dinner served** 7-11.30pm Tue-Sat; 7-10.30pm Sun. **Main courses** £7.90-£13.95. **Tapas** £2.95-£6.50. **Set lunch** £7.50 3 courses; (Sun) £8.50 3 courses. **Credit** AmEx, DC, MC, V.
Even the glitzy folk of Portobello Road sometimes need a place to eat, drink and be merry in familiar, homely comfort – and this vintage, unassuming Spanish venue does them proud. It's not fashionable to stay the same round these parts, but Galicia defiantly continues to do what it does best: serve consistent, rustic food, year after year. Few places this side of the Bay of Biscay are more authentic; the Spanish owners, clientele, decor and sibilant chit-chat make for a great facsimile of a peninsular taberna. The menu reads like a list of summer-holiday favourites: albóndigas, calamares, boquerones, chipirones, croquetas. Everything is cooked competently and without unnecessary flourish, which is just what you'd want in this setting. There's plenty of Spanish beer, wine and sherry to accompany your repast too. The staff are generally convivial and welcoming, even if you're not part of the expat mob; best of all, Galicia is pretty cheap for a restaurant in this neck of the woods.
Babies and children admitted. Booking essential weekends. **Map 19 B1**.

Maida Vale

★ Mesón Bilbao

33 Malvern Road, NW6 5PS (7328 1744/ www.mesonbilbao.com). Maida Vale tube.
Lunch served noon-3pm Mon-Fri. **Dinner served** 6-11pm Mon-Thur; 7-11.30pm Fri; 6-11.30pm Sat. **Main courses** £9.95-£12.95. **Tapas** £3.50-£6.95. **Credit** MC, V.
Look on a map and you'll see how, just west of Maida Vale, the unreconstructed borough of Brent stubs its thumb into the upmarket pie of W9. But if you're brave enough to cross the frontier into bedraggled Malvern Road, you'll discover one of London's best-value Spanish restaurants. It's worth booking ahead, as the tiny, romantic ground-floor room can't fit more than about 20 diners, and you don't want to be relegated underground. A tapas list covers the various regions of Spanish cooking. We would recommend, among other things, a hearty fabada asturiana (white bean stew with chorizo and morcilla) and moreish chipirones (squid in its own ink). The Basque emphasis suggested by the restaurant's name is most obvious in the selection of fish main courses, which are well worth ordering to share if you still have room. Our merluza a la vasca was a perfectly cooked fillet of hake in a buttery broth with peas, asparagus and potatoes. Low prices, including a decent selection of wines for under £20 a bottle, means you can get out of here for less than £50 for two.
Babies and children welcome: high chairs. Booking advisable. Tables outdoors (2, pavement). **Map 1 A3**.

South West

Putney

Olé

240 Upper Richmond Road, SW15 6TG (8788 8009/www.olerestaurants.com). East Putney tube/Putney rail.

CAMINO
SPANISH BAR RESTAURANT
Regent Quarter King's Cross N1
Reservations 020 7841 7330
"Inspired, meticulously crafted... simple top-notch food. Camino puts King's Cross on the map." ★★★★★ Time Out
"Unapologetically, unpretentiously Spanish." Evening Standard
"Charming service, gutsy food." The Independent
www.camino.uk.com

Bar **Open/tapas served** noon-midnight Mon-Thur; noon-1am Fri, Sat; noon-11pm Sun. *Restaurant* **Meals served** noon-11pm Mon-Thur; noon-11.30pm Fri, Sat; noon-10pm Sun. **Main courses** £11.95-£15.50. **Set lunch** (noon-6pm) £8.95 2 tapas; £9.95 2 tapas and glass of wine. **Set meal** (Sun) £12.50 2 courses. *Both* **Tapas** £2.95-£6.50. **Credit** AmEx, DC, JCB, MC, V.

A blackboard greeting our entry informed us that Olé had been 'Voted best Spanish restaurant in London' – by *Time Out*. That was news to us as no such vote took place, and we would not grant Olé that accolade even if it did. The dishes here are certainly not the best in the capital, but, to be fair, they're not bad either. Two hard-to-perfect choices from the large menu – calf's liver with onions and red wine sauce, and a dish called 'mar y tierra', a sauté of octopus, prawns and wild mushrooms – came off very well. The tender, fleshy textures of each dish were treated with care, and the sauces were complementary, not camouflaging. But the undisputed highlight of our meal was a shared main-course fillet of sea bass with courgette and salsify and a smattering of romesco sauce. The biggest let-down is the sterile decor; white walls and tablecloths do not go well with blond wood floors and furniture, especially during the day when so much light floods in through the glass walls. Still, this doesn't seem to deter the punters – they're too busy enjoying what's on their plates.

Babies and children welcome: high chairs. Booking advisable weekends. Disabled: toilet. Restaurant/bar available for hire.

South

Clapham

★ Lola Rojo NEW (100)

2007 RUNNER-UP BEST LOCAL RESTAURANT

78 Northcote Road, SW11 6QL (7350 2262). Clapham Junction rail. **Meals served** noon-10.30pm Mon-Fri; 10am-10.30pm Sat; noon-5pm Sun. **Main courses** £7.50-£11. **Credit** AmEx, DC, MC, V.

Forget earthenware crockery and colourful tiles: there's nothing old-fashioned about Lola Rojo. The two-room space is modern and bright (white and scarlet, with monochrome patterned wallpaper); the staff (all Spanish) are young and upbeat; and the food is contemporary and inventive. The menu – in English – is divided into different tapas: hot, cold, meat, fish, cured meats, paellas and rices. There's even an 'entertainment' section, including manchego 'lolly pops': crisp discs of melted cheese on a stick. Almost all the dozen dishes we tried were excellent. Ingredients are top-quality: witness the cécina (dried cured beef from Leon) and the mojama (paper-thin slices of smoked dried tuna). Black rice was vibrantly flavoured, with chunks of squid and a big dollop of allioli – you'd be pushed to find better in Spain. Ditto the confit of suckling pig with vanilla apple purée. Only the 'brava potato' was a bit insipid; a clever take on patatas bravas, with hollowed-out roast spuds containing a foamy tomato sauce, but we'd have preferred the more rough-and-ready original. The *nueva cocina* approach is most evident in the desserts: mango ice-cream sat in a bowl of white chocolate 'soup', with a smear of thyme-flavoured toffee. The all-Spanish wine list is an eclectic treat, including the much-heralded Petalos del Bierzo (£21.50).

Babies and children admitted. Booking advisable Thur-Sat. Separate room for parties, seats 15. Tables outdoors (16, terrace). Takeaway service. **Map 21 C5**.

Vauxhall

Rebato's

169 South Lambeth Road, SW8 1XW (7735 6388/www.rebatos.com). Stockwell tube. *Tapas bar* **Open** 5.30-10.45pm Mon-Fri; 7-11pm Sat. **Tapas** £3.25-£5.50. *Restaurant* **Lunch served** noon-2.30pm Mon-Fri. **Dinner served** 7-10.45pm Mon-Sat. **Main courses** £11.95. **Set lunch** £11.50 2 courses incl glass of wine. *Both* **Credit** AmEx, MC, V.

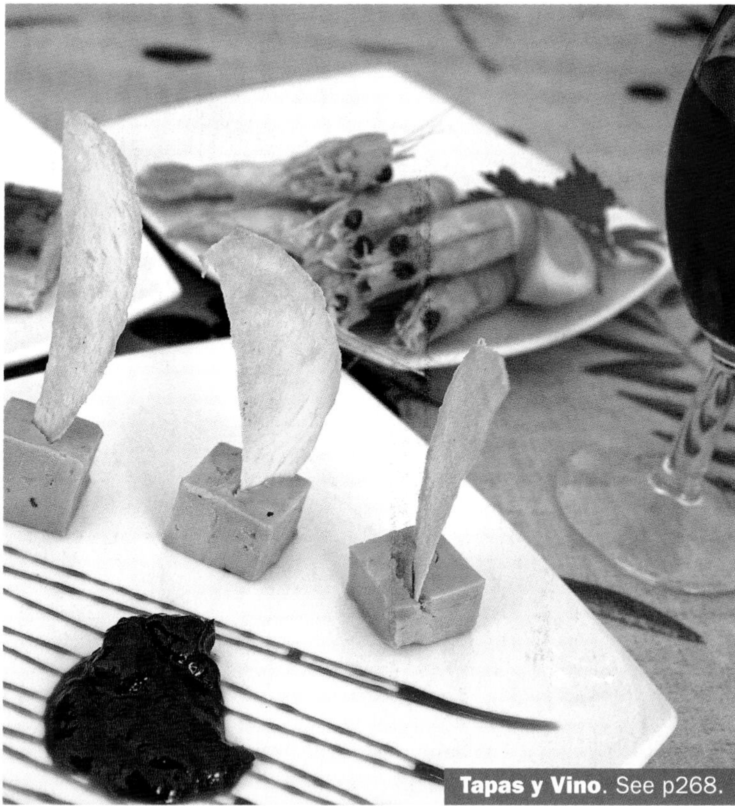

Tapas y Vino. See p268.

It's a fair hike from the nearest tube to Rebato's: a pilgrimage beset by the temptation of South Lambeth Road's many enticing Portuguese cafés. Those who go the distance will be rewarded handsomely by the romantic atmosphere and accomplished cooking of one of London's most authentic Spanish dining establishments. You can eat formally in the 'restaurant' section at the back, but we've always preferred the cosier front-of-house bar, with plush sofa seating and separate tapas menu. Here, waiters in classic white-shirt, dark-trouser attire will read you the day's specials in emphatic, evocative Castilian accents, then efficiently deliver plate after plate of hot and tasty comestibles. Specials this time included baby squid in garlic and chilli, which was perfectly tender and bathed in a rich, salty broth; and slices of suckling pig's liver, which could not have been improved (seared on the outside to give bite, the cuts were dreamily soft and creamy within). Rebato's remains defiantly old school, so don't expect any of the surprises of Spain's culinary new wave. But in its genre, as a cosy neighbourhood tapas restaurant, it has few peers.

Babies and children admitted: high chairs. Booking essential. **Map 16 L13**.

Waterloo

Mar i Terra

14 Gambia Street, SE1 0XH (7928 7628/www.mariterra.co.uk). Southwark tube/Waterloo tube/rail. **Tapas served** noon-3pm, 6-11pm Mon-Fri; 5-11pm Sat. **Tapas** £3.50-£7.95. **Credit** AmEx, MC, V.

Though the fledgling branch at Victoria Park proved ill-fated (it has now closed), the original Mar i Terra survives for business as usual. It occupies a cosy converted pub betwixt the railway arches of Southwark. Sanded-down dark wood is the key aesthetic within, and the original, mirror-backed bar has been mercifully retained – just two of the draws that have earned the place a loyal following among local workers. On the menu, there are no real surprises among the chorizo and calamares, except for a couple of regional niceties such as espinacas a la catalana (spinach sautéed with pine nuts and raisins) and chipirones a la vizcaina (baby squid in a tomato sauce). Most dishes we tried were properly cooked, hearty and tasty; we forgave the rather parched meat in a tapa of rabbit casserole. Prices are refreshingly modest, especially given the proximity of costlier dining hotspots at Borough Market and the South Bank. Not one to cross town for, perhaps, but as somewhere for a good-value meal in relaxing surrounds, Mar i Terra is a well-kept secret well worth sharing.

Babies and children welcome: high chairs. Booking advisable. Separate room for parties, seats 50. Tables outdoors (15, garden). **Map 11 O8**.
For branch see index.

South East

Herne Hill

Number 22

22 Half Moon Lane, SE24 9HU (7095 9922/www.number-22.com). Herne Hill rail/3, 37, 68 bus. **Tapas served** noon-4pm, 6-11pm Mon-Sat; noon-11pm Sun. **Tapas** £3-£8. **Credit** MC, V.

Dark wood, lots of chocolate-brown leather and flickering candlelight give this contemporary establishment a sleek and cosy feel. Tables are tightly packed but the intimate atmosphere is relaxed and friendly, as are the staff. Cruzcampo on draught and a good house tempranillo set the mood. Tapas options make up the bulk of the menu, which has the odd non-Spanish influence, although some larger dishes are available to satisfy hungrier stomachs. Clams with chilli and jamón serrano were delicately steamed and came with a white wine broth ideal for dunking. Typical of the chef's light-handed approach, pollo al ajillo was subtly garlicky and not greasy. Presentation got top marks: sharp spears of salty manchego on chargrilled toast married beautifully with sweet cubes of membrillo (quince jam). An uncharacteristic disappointment was the dry-tasting chorizo served among a plate of

Mediterranean sausages, but fortunately the accompanying merguez and morcilla were up to scratch. The highlight, though, was an exquisite pan perdido with crisp, toffee-laden bread that yielded to the bite. Bijou it may be, but Number 22 proves good things do come in small packages.
Babies and children admitted. Restaurant available for hire. Tables outdoors (16, patio). **Map 23 A5.**

London Bridge & Borough

★ Tapas Brindisa (100)

18-20 Southwark Street, SE1 1TJ (7357 8880/ www.brindisa.com). London Bridge tube/rail. **Breakfast served** 9-11am Fri, Sat. **Lunch served** noon-3pm Mon-Thur; noon-4pm Fri, Sat. **Dinner served** 5.30-11pm Mon-Sat. **Tapas** £3.25-£9. **Credit** AmEx, MC, V.

It's no surprise that the restaurant arm of the renowned Spanish delicatessen turns out first-rate tapas, which make the best of Brindisa's fine imports. These are married with fresh, seasonal produce from closer to home, in a frequently changing menu. Dishes such as asparagus with duck egg, serrano ham and romesco sauce, or battered hake with morcilla and red-pepper coulis, perfectly illustrate the unfussy cooking that lets the ingredients do the talking. There's also a superb list of Spanish wines to please every taste as well as most budgets. The only problem is that, despite its auspicious Borough Market location and stylish design, the restaurant lacks space; it gets rammed very quickly, and you may have to wait at length for a table (bookings aren't taken). Service, it must be said, is also sometimes compromised as a result. Still, you can make do by sipping sherries at the bar and working up an appetite as you watch the glorious plates pour forth from the open kitchen.
Babies and children admitted. Booking not accepted. Disabled: toilet. Tables outdoors (4, pavement). **Map 11 P8.**

East

Docklands

★ El Faro NEW

3 Turnberry Quay, Pepper Street, E14 9RD (7987 5511/www.el-faro.co.uk). Crossharbour DLR. **Meals served** noon-3.30pm, 5-11pm Mon-Fri; 1-11pm Sat; 1-5pm Sun. **Main courses** £14-£19. **Tapas** £3.50-£14. **Credit** AmEx, MC, V.

This recent Docklands opening cheekily styles itself 'the best Spanish restaurant in the City'. As it happens, we'd be hard pressed to disagree, overlooking the detail that it's outside the boundaries of the Square Mile. In fact, El Faro benefits from a great position, overlooking the serene waters of the old Millwall Docks. Though the building is part of a dull modern development, the interior has been converted into an elegant, stylish dining room, populated by properly laid, chunky dark-wood tables and slick black leather chairs. The cooking leans towards traditional Spanish styles, but has some *nueva cocina* flourishes, especially in its exemplary dish presentation. We found nothing to criticise in starters of battered squid with romesco sauce or marinated suckling pig with honey, and shared an outstanding main course of pork medallions with a cream and ceps sauce. There's a first-rate selection of Riojas on the all-Spanish wine list. For those who live and work in the area, this is a must; for others, it might be too much of a hike – though if you're prepared to make the trip, you're unlikely to be disappointed.
Babies and children admitted (until 8.30pm). Booking advisable. Disabled: toilet. Separate room for parties, seats 70. Tables outdoors (16, terrace). **Map 24 B3.**

Shoreditch

Laxeiro

93 Columbia Road, E2 7RG (7729 1147/ www.laxeiro.co.uk). Bus 26, 48, 55. **Meals served** noon-3pm, 7-11pm Tue-Sat; 9am-3pm Sun. **Main courses** £3.50-£8.95. **Credit** AmEx, DC, MC, V.

Romantic Columbia Road makes a perfect home for this diminutive but charming tapas restaurant. A welcoming decor of burnt orange walls, ornamental tiling, and unusually tasteful artwork has earned Laxeiro a loyal following among locals. It's a winning formula that the owners are rightly reluctant to mess with, so little changes here from one year to the next. That includes the menu; though chalked up on a blackboard, suggesting flux, it rarely alters. Occasionally, such an unseasonal approach (meaning everything has to be in stock all the time) throws up a lacklustre dish. On a recent visit, octopus in paprika was rather bland and a bit chewy. Yet this was the anomaly in an accomplished selection that included tender, fleshy cuts of cochinillo (suckling pig) with crackling, some above-average patatas bravas, rich and gooey salt-cod croquettes, and a carefully cooked slab of calf's liver in a sherry and onion gravy. Food is supplemented by a good, sub-£30 all-Spanish wine list.
Babies and children welcome: high chairs. Booking advisable; not accepted Sun. Tables outdoors (4, pavement). Takeaway service. **Map 6 S3.**

Pinchito Tapas NEW

32 Featherstone Street, EC1Y 8QX (7490 0121/ www.pinchito.co.uk). Old Street tube/rail. **Tapas served** 8am-midnight Mon-Fri; 6pm-midnight Sat. **Tapas** £3.50-£12. **Credit** AmEx, MC, V.

The new London outpost of Brighton's excellent Pintxo People is, as the diminutive in the name implies, only a pared-down version of the original. That's a shame in some ways, because there's still nowhere in London offering sophisticated Catalan nueva cocina (as found at Pintxo People's upstairs restaurant). Never mind: the simple Spanish tapas here are still pretty good. The best things are on the 'cazuela' (casserole) section of the menu. Squid with chickpeas and spinach, and spiced pork with garlic, both consisted of little pots of tender meat in a piquant, complex gravy. Also enjoyable was a mug of tangy, ice-cold gazpacho and a satisfyingly deep tortilla with chorizo and mango. The large three-sided bar, not to mention the Old Street location, suggests this is intended to be as much a drinking venue as an eatery. So it's gratifying that the drinks list is excellent – it includes seven sherries, as many bubblies, and a very grown-up list of all-Spanish wines. A laudable addition to the local options, even if it does lack some of the ambition of its Brighton sibling.
Babies and children admitted. Takeaway service. **Map 6 Q4.**

North East

Walthamstow

Orford Saloon NEW

32 Orford Road, E17 9NJ (8503 6542). Walthamstow Central tube/rail. **Tapas served** 6-11.30pm Tue-Fri; noon-3pm, 6-11.30pm Sat; noon-5pm, 6-10.30pm Sun. **Tapas** £3.50-£10.50. **Set paella** £8 per person (minimum 2). **Credit** MC, V.

Evidently this was just what the residents of Walthamstow Village were waiting for: a decent, laid-back neighbourhood tapas bar to bolster the area's still-limited dining options. A year after it opened, the Orford Saloon is packed most nights of the week; booking ahead is highly advisable. A vaguely rustic decor avoids the decorative clichés often encountered in more textbook tapas bars; the exceptionally authentic cooking, overseen by a Spanish head chef, means they aren't needed. Well-known classics populate the menu and, familiar though they are, they're cooked with uncommon precision. Bacalao a la roteña was plump, glistening chunks of salt cod in a tomato and pepper sauce. Slivers of tender fillet steak came with chunks of sweet, sautéed potato. Chicken livers in white wine had a perfect creamy texture and offally-rich flavour. To lubricate, there's a short but intelligent round-up of about a dozen Spanish wines and four sherries; the beers include Cruzcampo on tap and Estrella in bottles. This is a lesson in how to do traditional tapas abroad; the Orford's popularity is entirely deserved.
Babies and children admitted. Booking advisable. Disabled: toilet.

North

Camden Town & Chalk Farm

★ El Parador

245 Eversholt Street, NW1 1BA (7387 2789). Mornington Crescent tube. **Lunch served** noon-3pm Mon-Fri. **Dinner served** 6-11pm Mon-Thur; 6-11.30pm Fri, Sat; 6.30-9.30pm Sun. **Tapas** £3.90-£7. **Credit** MC, V.

To look at, El Parador is just your average neighbourhood tapas joint, sandwiched into a forgettable row of shops round the back of Mornington Crescent tube. It's cosy enough, with neat, homely decor, but not the kind of setting you'd hike across town for. Not so with the cooking, which is well worth a detour. The Spanish, North African-tinged menu demonstrates a passion and skill that make this one of the best tapas restaurants in town. There are some classic dishes (calamares, chorizo) to appease the unadventurous, but wise diners will opt for the more creative recipes. Dishes we've loved recently include pan-fried monkfish with samphire and garlic; artichoke hearts with flageolet beans and harissa; and

SHELF LIFE

The most popular Spanish exports like jamón serrano can be found in delis across the city, but a clutch of strictly Hispanic retailers stock a much broader and more esoteric range of goods.

Brindisa
31 Exmouth Market, EC1R 4QE (7713 1666/www.brindisa.com). Farringdon tube/rail. **Open** 9am-6pm Mon-Sat.
This Exmouth Market mainstay is as popular as ever, selling a wide range of charcuterie, cheeses and fresh produce alongside store-cupboard items, confectionery and even kitchenware. A branch, and the associated tapas bar (*see left*), are in Borough Market.

R García and Son
248-250 Portobello Road, W11 1LL (7221 6119). Ladbroke Grove tube. **Open** 9am-6pm Mon-Fri; 9am-7pm Sat; 10am-6pm Sun.
Soaring rents forced the closure of Portobello's other Spanish deli, P de la Fuente, in 2007, but the blow was softened by the continued brilliance of this veteran upermarket, which sells a bounteous range of Spanish imports both fresh and processed. Next door is the associated café (*see p263*).

Rias Altas
97 Frampton Street, NW8 8NA (7262 4340) Edgware Road tube. **Open** 9.30am-6.30pm Mon-Sat.
Thirty years in the same premises and still going strong, Rias Altas sells good-quality Spanish jamón, plus other charcuterie and cheeses, canned foods, biscuits, cakes, and more.

Lola Rojo. See p265.

sautéed duck breast with quince and spring onions. Another – unlikely – highlight was a salad of cabbage, swiss chard and chicory, lightly pan-fried with caraway seeds, which demonstrated perfectly the chef's mastery of his territory. The food is matched by a decent, moderately priced wine list, and efficient, knowledgeable service.
Babies and children admitted. Bookings accepted for 3 or more only. Separate room for parties, seats 30. Tables outdoors (10, garden). Vegetarian menu. **Map 27 D3**.

Crouch End

La Bota

31 Broadway Parade, Tottenham Lane, N8 9DB (8340 3082). Finsbury Park tube/rail then 91, W7 bus. **Lunch served** noon-2.30pm Mon-Fri; noon-3pm Sat. **Dinner served** 6-11pm Mon-Thur; 6-11.30pm Fri, Sat. **Meals served** noon-11pm Sun. **Main courses** £7.95-£12.50. **Tapas** £2.50-£4.50. **Credit** MC, V.

Only a few tapas bars in the capital can claim to be the real deal and not a London pastiche – this ever-popular spot in Crouch End is one of them. La Bota's expat owners preside over an authentic slice of the peninsula where the waiters are Spanish, the art's Spanish, the food's most assuredly Spanish (in the old-school, comfort-cooking way) and the prices are almost, almost Spanish. The bulk of the tapas dishes weigh in at around £3, yet portions are ample. There were some disappointments on a recent visit: stuffed mushrooms with cheese and tomato was a bit of a limp mess (and the mushrooms had no stuffing); and the baby squid could have been fresher. But we forgot these minor mishaps as we tucked into a delicious main course of lemon sole with capers, almonds, peas and white wine sauce. Our fellow diners – of whom there were plenty on our week-night visit, as usual – all seemed more than happy. Neither too romantic for a knees-up, nor too scruffy for a date, La Bota is an asset to its neighbourhood.
Babies and children welcome: high chairs. Booking advisable dinner Fri, Sat. Takeaway service.

Outer London

Twickenham, Middlesex

★ Tapas y Vino NEW

2007 RUNNER-UP BEST LOCAL RESTAURANT

111 London Road, Twickenham, Middx, TW1 1EE (8892 5417/www.elvinotapas.co.uk). Twickenham rail. **Tapas served** noon-2.30pm, 6-10.30pm Mon-Sat. **Tapas** £2-£5. **Credit** MC, V.

To look at, this recent addition to Twickenham's dining scene has nothing to distinguish it from any local tapas restaurant: the decor is a Mediterranean synthesis of white walls, terracotta-tiled floor, wooden chairs and oilcloths on the tables, but hardly striking. Good thing chef-restaurateur John McClements (who also owns adjoining French restaurants La Brasserie and Ma Cuisine) is a better cook than interior designer, for the menu surpasses such forgettable surrounds. The remit is wider than just Spain, with the likes of halloumi, houmous and chicken tagine on the menu. The selection of hot and cold tapas is not as interesting as the 'speciality' list, which includes Moroccan pigeon bastilla, snails with jabugo ham in a dinky pastry case, and zarzuela (the Basque shellfish stew – here an impressively overflowing bowlful). Clams with chickpeas and chorizo was earthy and hearty; gazpacho was suitably thick and tangy. The quality of meat and its preparation was excellent; the use of herbs and spices expert. Yet the tapas cost only £4 each or thereabout – even a small plate of jabugo ham, which routinely sells for £12 or more in lesser venues. Service was charming, though staff could perhaps be better informed. And the wine list is no more than decent: ironic, given the restaurant's name.
Babies and children admitted. Booking advisable weekends. Disabled: toilet. Restaurant available for hire. Tables outdoors (2, pavement).
For branch see index.

Thai

The 1990s were the boom years of expansion for London's Thai restaurants, but this explosion is now well and truly over. Not only has the number of new openings slowed, but we have also seen no improvement in the standards of cooking in recent years. Too many high-street Thais could try harder, while the same good restaurants have remained virtually unchanged for the last few years; places such as plush hotel restaurant **Nahm** and the more convivial, canteen-style mini-chain **Busaba Eathai** still have no real challengers to their culinary crowns. Instead, newcomers have tended to focus on creating opulent interiors, such as the startling Thai architecture of **Saran Rom**, modelled after Bangkok's Vimanmek Palace.

So what happened? Why has the Thai restaurant boom run out of steam? The answer may lie in changing culinary fashion, but it might also lie in the growth of Thai ready meals and also the home-cooking of Thai food. Now that anyone can pick up a green curry on the way home for a fraction of the price you'd pay in a restaurant, it's little wonder that diners are questioning why Thai restaurants are still so expensive when compared to Chinese or Indian restaurants of comparable quality. We've had a shake-down of the restaurants included in the chapter in this edition, and are confident those listed below are London's best, and offer something far superior to the usual high-street Thai.

Central

Belgravia

★ Nahm (100)

The Halkin, Halkin Street, SW1X 7DJ (7333 1234/www.nahm.como.bz). Hyde Park Corner tube. **Lunch served** noon-2.30pm Mon-Fri. **Dinner served** 7-10.45pm Mon-Sat; 7-9.45pm Sun. **Main courses** £11-£16.50. **Set lunch** £26 3 courses. **Set dinner** £55 3 courses. **Credit** AmEx, DC, JCB, MC, V.

David Thompson may not always be in the kitchen (he spends much time in Thailand), but the influence of the master of Thai cooking at this quiet, understated hotel dining room is as strong as ever. This year Thompson has given the lunch menu a revamp to include more 'street food' – not that we've ever had street food like this before. Appetisers of ma hor (minced prawns and chicken simmered in palm sugar) on fruit slices were a foretaste of his distinctive style. Starters included a crisp rice pancake rolled around a filling of fresh herbs, fresh longan (like little lychees) and shreds of salted chicken: unexpected, and tantalising. Among the main dishes was a recipe similar to Burmese khow suey: that is, a bowl of kanom jim noodles (rice-flour spaghetti) with a coconut-rich slurry of slow-cooked fish; this had a surprising sour-sweet tang. Unusual ingredients appear in unexpected places, such as shards of banana flower deep-fried as a massive garnish, or guava in the accompanying herb-laced salad. Puds hit the 'refresh' button even more assertively: a bowl of slush flavoured with jasmine and shreds of dried tropical fruit, served with a soft brittle of peanut, sesame and puffed rice. Why can't all Thai food be this thrilling?

Babies and children welcome; high chairs. Booking advisable. Disabled: toilet. Dress: smart casual. **Map 9 G9.**

Marylebone

★ Busaba Eathai (100)

8-13 Bird Street, W1U 1BU (7518 8080). Bond Street tube. **Meals served** noon-11pm Mon-Thur; noon-11.30pm Fri, Sat; noon-10pm Sun. **Main courses** £5.50-£10.90. **Credit** AmEx, MC, V.

More branches of Alan Yau's Thai fast-food canteen are planned, but as we went to press, this was still the latest. Having created a winning formula, there has been little reason to tamper with Busaba's shared tables and bench seating, or the oriental mystique created by clever design, dark wood, incense and low lighting. The dishes are consistently interesting, as you might expect of a menu initially created by chef David Thompson of Nahm (*see above*), though the menu does evolve and changes regularly. Current dishes worth seeking out are the rice served with a generous amount of crab meat, or the delicately textured tofu, lightly fried then served with a spicy yellow bean sauce. Salads, such as the pomelo with water chestnut and chilli, are a strong point; so are the hot drinks (lemongrass and honey). Occasionally the noodle dishes can disappoint: our vegetarian pad thai had flaccid noodles, and had a gloopy sauce coating the baby sweetcorn and shiitake mushrooms. But the disappointments are easily outnumbered by the hits at this popular joint, and the dishes are never dull in either flavour or ingredients.

Babies and children admitted. Bookings not accepted. Disabled: toilet. Takeaway service. **Map 9 G6.**
For branches see index.

Eat-Thai.net

22 St Christopher's Place, W1U 1NP (7486 0777/www.eatthai.net). Bond Street tube. **Meals served** noon-10.30pm daily. **Main courses** £10.50-£23.95. **Set lunch** £12.95 3 courses. **Set dinner** £25-£35 per person (minimum 2) 3 courses. **Credit** AmEx, MC, V.

The name may not just grate; it may also mislead. Because instead of geeks clustered around monitors in a cyber-café, this is the sort of restaurant favoured by older couples who like its spotless napery and hushed yet welcoming atmosphere. There's an oriental fusion section on the menu, but we suggest skipping this and sticking to the so-called 'royal Thai' dishes. In fact, these aren't courtly dishes at all, they're just the usual fish cake/tom yum/green curry dishes – but they're rendered to a high standard. The pad thai, for example, is garnished with a delicate egg lace omelette, like a doily draped over the top; and the titbits and garnishes in this noodle dish were all of top-quality, present, and correct. Mussaman curry ran the full range of flavours we'd hope for in this dish: sour, sweet, salty and hot, underscored by the rich coconut cream and unctuous texture of the braising beef used. With charming service and an intimate, relaxed feel, it's a very different experience to the conveyor-belt approach of the nearby Busaba Eathai (*see above*).

Babies and children welcome: high chairs. Takeaway service. **Map 9 G6.**

Mayfair

Patara

3&7 Maddox Street, W1S 2QB (7499 6008). Oxford Circus tube. **Lunch served** noon-2.30pm, **dinner served** 6.30-10.30pm daily. **Main courses** £6.50-£15.50. **Set lunch** £11.95-£14.95 2 courses. **Credit** AmEx, DC, JCB, MC, V.

The four branches of Patara are all in prime sites, and consequently attract customers more gilded than a reclining buddha. But standards can be variable; we've found this Oxford Circus branch to be the best, and fellow diners seem to agree because booking is essential. It has a friendly, relaxed vibe, decent chill-out music, great service and very appealing design, from the clever lighting, Indian sculptures and expensive-looking partitions to the lovely brown crockery. Our waitress seemed to know every dish off by heart, and could describe the ingredients and heat levels without hesitation. A dish of stewed beef cheek had been cut into thin slices, then sautéed with thai basil and whole black peppercorns; the coconut curry sauce was salty, but good. Black cod was the best dish, but brown jasmine rice was nothing special. There are plenty of offbeat pairings and ingredients, from 'tacos' you fill with a fry-up of beansprouts, chicken and prawn, to wild boar meat or a Thai-style tuna tartare. The set lunches seem good value, but corners are cut; our dish of crabmeat in an aromatic yellow curry contained a lot more onion and celery than crab.

Babies and children admitted. Booking advisable. Disabled: toilet. Separate room for parties, seats 30. **Map 9 J6.**
For branches see index.

West

Bayswater

★ Nipa

Royal Lancaster Hotel, Lancaster Terrace, W2 2TY (7262 6737/www.niparestaurant.co.uk). Lancaster Gate tube.
Bar **Open** 11am-11pm Mon-Sat; 11am-10.30pm Sun.
Restaurant **Lunch served** noon-2pm Mon-Fri. **Dinner served** 6.30-10.30pm Mon-Sat. **Main courses** £7.85-£14. **Set meal** £27-£32 4 courses.
Both **Credit** AmEx, DC, MC, V.

The Royal Lancaster Hotel at Lancaster Gate has a Thai owner, which explains this homage to a teak-panelled Thai palace lovingly constructed inside a concrete high-rise. And Nipa does faithfully recreate a 'traditional' tourist hotel restaurant in Thailand, right down to the tinkling background muzak, comfy furnishings and the clientele composed entirely of affluent foreign tourists. Chef (Ms) Nongyao Thoopchoi has been

here since Nipa opened in 1995 and uses only first-class produce – evident in dishes such as the 'prawn cake' (fried breaded minced prawn), which had resilient bite and fresh, clean aromas. The chilli heat seems toned down a lot for the benefit of *farang* diners; larb, for example, had a citrus tang and the sharpness of raw onion, but little discernible capsaicin. Roasted duck in red curry was also very mild and included whole seedless grapes and cherry tomatoes, but this sweetness was nearly balanced out by the inclusion of slightly bitter pea aubergines. A very polished operation with brilliantly executed cooking and smooth service; but if you're after full-on Thai flavours that assault your palate, look elsewhere.
Babies and children welcome: high chairs. Booking essential Fri, Sat. Disabled: toilet (hotel). Dress: smart casual. Restaurant for hire. Takeaway service. Vegetarian menu. **Map 8 D6**.

Tawana

3 Westbourne Grove, W2 4UA (7229 3785/ www.tawana.co.uk). Bayswater tube. **Lunch served** noon-3pm, **dinner served** 6-11pm Mon-Sat. **Meals served** noon-10pm Sun. **Main courses** £5.75-£17.95. **Set meal** £15.95 2 courses. **Minimum** £10 per person (food only). **Credit** MC, V.
Traditionally decorated with heavy dark wood and gilded paintings, Tawana remains light and airy thanks to a window that spans the entire front façade. If you like people-watching, window tables offer a view of bustling Westbourne Grove. Looking inward, warm smiles and attentive service make for a charming dining experience. The menu contains a broad range of typical dishes and includes a page dedicated to vegetarian fare. Crisp corn fritters were lightly battered and beautifully sweetened by syrupy plum dipping sauce. A fresh and crunchy satay sauce accompanied skewers of pork, chicken and our choice of succulent grilled shiitake mushrooms. Mains were equally successful. Green curry with tender chicken strips and pea aubergines was not at all heavy, its sauce balancing coconut cream with fragrant stock. The fried tofu retained a silky centre and flavours of fresh ginger, chilli and spring onion could easily be discerned in a light oyster sauce. Exotic fruits and pumpkin custard were delivered to the table for our perusal. Rambutans, prettily decorated with orchids, were sufficient to finish a well-proportioned meal.
Babies and children admitted. Booking advisable. Separate room for parties, seats 50. Takeaway service; delivery service (over £20 within 2-mile radius). Vegetarian menu. **Map 7 B6**.
For branches (Thai Hut, Thai Kitchen) see index.

Shepherd's Bush

★ ★ Esarn Kheaw

314 Uxbridge Road, W12 7LJ (8743 8930/ www.esarnkheaw.com). Shepherd's Bush tube/ 207, 260, 283 bus. **Lunch served** noon-3pm Mon-Fri. **Dinner served** 6-11pm daily. **Main courses** £5.50-£9.85. **Credit** MC, V.
Most of London's Thai restaurants have expunged all bitter and 'off' flavours and aromas from their menus, but Esarn Kheaw is proud to offer the true flavours of north-eastern Thailand (Esarn). A chicken dish is laced with 'pickled' bamboo shoots, a fermented condiment with a distinctive 'off' smell which adds complex and appealing sour flavours. Similarly, the own-made sausages have the distinctive sour tang of the cured pork sausages from the region bordering Laos. Esarn being landlocked, catfish are popular; the spiced north-east-style catfish has full-strength chilli heat (take note if you have a sensitive palate). Of course, not all the dishes are so extreme. Mainstream Thai classics from the length of the country are also on the menu, and the version of som tam here is peerless, although on a recent visit ours had no chilli at all; we suspect the chef forgot to add it. The best way to get the most out of Esarn Kheaw is to take a few risks: even simple-sounding dishes such as black sticky rice wrapped in pandanus leaf

Menu

We've tried to give the most useful Thai food terms here, including variant spellings. However, these are no more than English transliterations of the original Thai script, and so are subject to considerable variation. Word divisions vary as well: thus, kwaitiew, kwai teo and guey teow are all acceptable spellings for noodles.

Thailand abandoned chopsticks in the 19th century in favour of chunky steel spoons and forks. Using your fingers is usually fine, and essential if you order satay sticks or spare ribs.

USEFUL TERMS

Khantoke: originally a north-eastern banquet conducted around a low table while seated on traditional triangular cushions – some restaurants have khantoke seating.
Khing: with ginger.
Op or **ob**: baked.
Pad, pat or **phad**: stir-fried.
Pet or **ped**: hot (spicy).
Prik: chilli.
Tod, tort, tord or **taud**: deep-fried.
Tom: boiled.

STARTERS

Khanom jeep or **ka nom geeb**: dim sum. Little dumplings of minced pork, bamboo shoots and water chestnuts, wrapped in an egg and rice (wun tun) pastry, then steamed.
Khanom pang na koong: prawn sesame toast.
Kratong thong: tiny crispy batter cups ('top hats') filled with mixed vegetables and/or minced meat.
Miang: savoury appetisers with a variety of constituents (mince, ginger, peanuts, roasted coconut, for instance), wrapped in betel leaves.
Popia or **porpia**: spring rolls.
Tod mun pla or **tauk manpla**: small fried fish cakes (should be lightly rubbery in consistency) with virtually no 'fishy' smell or taste.

SOUPS

Poh tak or **tom yam potag**: hot and sour mixed seafood soup.
Tom kha gai or **gai tom kar**: hot and sour chicken soup with coconut milk.
Tom yam or **tom yum**: a hot and sour soup, smelling of lemongrass. **Tom yam koong** is with prawns; **tom yam gai** with chicken; **tom yam hed** with mushrooms.

RICE

Khao, kow or **khow**: rice.
Khao nao: sticky rice.
Khao pat: fried rice.
Khao suay: steamed rice.
Pat khai: egg-fried rice.

SALADS

Laab or **larb**: minced and cooked meat incorporating lime juice and other ingredients like ground rice and herbs.
Som tam: a popular cold salad of grated green papaya.
Yam or **yum**: refers to any tossed salad, hot or cold, but it is often hot and sour, flavoured with lemon and chilli. This type of yam is originally from the north-east of Thailand, where the Laotian influence is greatest.
Yam nua: hot and sour beef salad.
Yam talay: hot and sour seafood salad (served cold).

NOODLES

Generally speaking, noodles are eaten in greater quantities in the north of Thailand. There are many types of **kwaitiew** or **guey teow** noodles. Common ones include **sen mee**: rice vermicelli; **sen yai** (river rice noodles): a broad, flat, rice noodle; **sen lek**: a medium flat noodle, used to make pad Thai; **ba mee**: egg noodles; and **woon sen** (cellophane noodle): transparent vermicelli made from soy beans or other pulses. These are often prepared as stir-fries.

The names of the numerous noodle dishes depend on the combination of other ingredients. Common dishes are:
Khao soi: chicken curry soup with egg noodles; a Burmese/Thai dish, referred to as the national dish of Burma.
Mee krob or **mee grob**: sweet crispy fried vermicelli.
Pad si-ewe or **cee eaw**: noodles fried with mixed meat in soy sauce.
Pad Thai: stir-fried noodles with shrimps (or chicken and pork), beansprouts and salted turnips, garnished with ground peanuts.

CURRIES

Thai curries differ quite markedly from the Indian varieties. Thais cook them for a shorter time, and use thinner sauces. Flavours and ingredients are different too. There are several common types of curry paste; these are used to name the curry, with the principal ingredients listed thereafter.
Gaeng, kaeng or **gang**: the generic name for curry. Yellow curry is the mildest; green curry (**gaeng keaw wan** or **kiew warn**) is medium hot and uses green chillies; red curry (**gaeng pet**) is similar, but uses red chillies.
Jungle curry: often the hottest of the curries, made with red curry paste, bamboo shoots and just about anything else to hand, but no coconut cream.
Massaman or **mussaman**: also known as Muslim curry, because it originates from the area along the border with Malaysia where many Thais are Muslims. For this reason, pork is never used. It's a rich but mild concoction, with coconut, potato and some peanuts.
Penang, panaeng or **panang**: a dry, aromatic curry made with 'Penang' curry paste, coconut cream and holy basil.

FISH & SEAFOOD

Hoi: shellfish.
Hor mok talay or **haw mog talay**: steamed egg mousse with seafood.
Koong, goong or **kung**: prawns.
Maw: dried fish belly.
Pla meuk: squid.

are a flavour revelation. Don't expect high style, though: the interior is standard high-street Thai circa 1993, and surely overdue a refurb.
Babies and children welcome: high chairs. Booking advisable. Takeaway service. **Map 20 B1**.

South West

Fulham

Blue Elephant

4-6 Fulham Broadway, SW6 1AA (7385 6595/ www.blueelephant.com). Fulham Broadway tube. **Lunch served** noon-2.30pm Mon-Fri; noon-3pm Sun. **Dinner served** 7-11.30pm Mon-Thur; 6.30-11.30pm Fri, Sat; 7-10.30pm Sun. **Main courses** £10.60-£28. **Set meal** £33-£39 3/4 courses. **Set buffet** (lunch Sun) £25. **Credit** AmEx, DC, MC, V.

This restaurant is so extravagantly verdant and over-orientalised (a waterfall, carp pools and hanging tendrils of creeping vines) that it could be a Hollywood film set. The menu follows suit: ginger lobster, according to the menu, 'swims in a sea of vegetables, ginger and perfumed mushroom': obtuse dish names such as Koh Samui and Chiang Mai disguise the fact that many are well-known Thai dishes. The cooking can lack the fiery, fermented authenticity of the 'real thing', but isn't as ersatz as the stage-set venue suggests. Grilled aubergine salad had a smoky flavour sharpened with lime juice, fish sauce and red chilli. Artfully presented som tam featured crunchy green papaya, but needed more chilli kick. Bangkok fish, pieces of fried cod in a tamarind and chilli sauce, was also short on chilli and was too sweet for our tastes. A lamb stir-fry hit the right notes, however, spiked with a fistful of green peppercorns and tart little pea aubergines – Blue Elephant, an international chain, air-freights huge quantities of fresh ingredients from Thailand every week. Order with care to avoid the blander and more boring dishes (plus the bottled water at £4.90) and you'll be in for some good food – and a retreat from reality.
Babies and children welcome: colouring books; face painting (Sun); high chairs. Booking advisable. Disabled: toilet. Dress: smart casual; no shorts. Takeaway service; delivery service (over £30 within SW6). Vegetarian menu. **Map 13 B13**.

Saran Rom

Waterside Tower, The Boulevard, Imperial Wharf, Townmead Road, SW6 2UB (7751 3111/www.saranrom.com). Fulham Broadway tube then 391, C3 bus. **Meals served** noon-11.30pm daily. **Main courses** £6.50-£18.95. **Set lunch** £12 2 courses. **Set dinner** £30 per person (minimum 2) 2 courses. **Credit** AmEx, MC, V.

Located in an obscure and soulless residential riverside development, this luxurious three-level restaurant – modelled after Bangkok's Vimanmek Palace – aims high in order to lure customers from far and wide. Ornate teak carvings, splendid silks, fragrant orchids and sweeping river views promise a sumptuous dining experience, while a heated outdoor terrace offers the rare opportunity to dine alfresco by the water. The food tries hard to live up to the surroundings; dishes appear crafted with pride, and are beautifully presented on elegant earthenware. The quality of the cooking, however, is mixed. A starter of garlic- and pepper-fried soft shell crab with chilli sauce was well executed, but the dish lacked the herbal bouquet that distinguishes authentic Thai cuisine. A bigger disappointment was sab nok nuea (curry of ribeye beef). The meat was chewy, the sauce watery and insipid, more like a broth than a curry. Service, while efficient, lacked the warmth of genuine Thai hospitality. Given the lofty prices and the remote location, there is little temptation to rush back – even if the restaurant's resident tuk tuk can fetch us at the tube station.
Babies and children welcome: high chairs. Disabled: lift; toilet. Separate rooms for parties, seating 8, 25, 35 and 110. Tables outdoors (28, riverside patio). Takeaway service. **Map 21 A2**.

Parsons Green

★ Sukho

855 Fulham Road, SW6 5HJ (7371 7600). Parsons Green tube. **Lunch served** noon-3pm, **dinner served** 6.30-11pm daily. **Main courses** £8.95-£12.95. **Set lunch** £7.95 1 course, £10.95 2 courses. **Credit** AmEx, MC, V.

Sukho offers one of London's more creative takes on Thai cuisine; come here for a romantic and sophisticated meal. Pots of bamboo separate the bustle of Fulham Road from the intimate dining room, which is dominated by serene neutral tones and an impressive traditional wood carving. The room's beauty is echoed by the dishes, which are wonderful medleys of complex, contrasting flavours arranged elegantly on the plate along with flowers and elaborately carved root vegetables. The chefs, who boast impressive Bangkok pedigrees, deliver intriguing combinations. Forget fatty deep-fried spring rolls. At Sukho, rice paper encases smoky tofu, cucumber, spring onion and just enough sharp mustard to cut through the honeyed dipping sauce. Fried soft-shell crab was excellent, accompanied by a chutney of shredded papaya, chilli and tamarind. Whole deep-fried sea bass – 'creative, not traditional' according to the friendly server – was spectacularly presented with a sweet chilli and spring onion sauce poured on top at the table. Confit of duck leg was infused with cinnamon, covered in toasted garlic, and served with grilled pineapple slices. Sweetness dominates the flavour wheel in Sukho's kitchen, but with such delicate spicing, it works. Have the excellent coconut ice-cream for dessert.
Babies and children admitted. Booking advisable. Takeaway service.
For branch see index.

Sukho

Busaba Eathai
Wardour Street
Phone 020-7255-8686
106–110 Wardour Street
London W1T 0TR
Store Street
Phone 020-7299-7900
22 Store Street
London WC1E 7DF
Pre-booking available
for groups of 12+
Take away available
Bird Street
Phone 020-7518-808
8–13 Bird Street
London W1U 1BU
Take away available

Putney

Thai Square

Embankment, 2-4 Lower Richmond Road, SW15 1LB (8780 1811/www.thaisq.com). Putney Bridge tube/14, 22 bus.
Bar **Open/snacks served** noon-midnight Mon-Thur; noon-2am Fri, Sat; noon-10.30pm Sun. *Restaurant* **Lunch served** noon-3pm daily. **Dinner served** 6-11pm Mon-Sat; 6-10.30pm Sun. **Main courses** £7.95-£23. **Set dinner** £35 per person (minimum 2) 3 courses, £40 per person (minimum 2) 4 courses.
Both **Credit** AmEx, MC, V.
Thai Square enjoys one of the most serene and affordable riverside views going in the capital – and the food isn't bad either. Starters of kratong thong filled with garlicky minced prawns and chicken served with plum sauce offered a pleasant crunch, while tod mun pla were perfectly spongy and springy. It was a grand shame, however, that the side salads served with both dishes were drowned in thousand island dressing, which has no place on the Thai table. Som tam (papaya salad) was spicy and tart, and was served with fragrant and tender baked chicken thigh on the side. Jungle curry with beef had a good assortment of vegetables, all of which were perfectly cooked to maintain their bite. Thai Square is far more elegant and singular – in its bright but restrained design and in its spectacular view over Putney Bridge – than its chain status might imply. It's well worth making a reservation to be guaranteed a prime position in the first-floor dining room, which has the best views.
Babies and children welcome: high chairs. Bar available for hire. Disabled: lift; toilet. Takeaway service; delivery service (over £15 within 3-mile radius). Vegetarian menu.
For branches (Thai Pot, Thai Square) see index.

South East

Blackheath

Laicram

1 Blackheath Grove, SE3 0DD (8852 4710). Blackheath rail. **Lunch served** noon-2.30pm, **dinner served** 6-11pm Tue-Sun. **Main courses** £4-£13.90. **Credit** MC, V.
Tucked away as it is down a leafy side street near Blackheath station, this small, low-ceilinged restaurant can be hard to find without an *A-Z*. But with its typically Thai decor (carved wooden panels, dark beams and portraits of the Thai royal family in prime position) and authentic menu, it's a much-loved local that's well worth seeking out. Our tom yum was a full-flavoured and delightfully sour starter, and while the pla lard prik (crispy fried fish) was just a slab of salmon, rather than a whole fish, the sauce was so sweet, sticky and moreish that we used our rice to clean the serving plate. The dessert trolley proved our undoing with its delicious, coconut cream-based desserts. It wasn't a perfect meal, though: a disappointing jungle curry lacked the fiery and robust kick it needs, while a mysterious, anonymous figure on the bill turned out not to be the soft drinks but the service charge. Still, the small queue waiting patiently outside in the rain was a clear testament to this restaurant's deserved popularity.
Babies and children admitted. Booking essential Fri, Sat. Takeaway service. Vegetarian menu.

London Bridge & Borough

Kwan Thai

The Riverfront, Hay's Galleria, Tooley Street, SE1 2HD (7403 7373/www.kwanthairestaurant.co.uk). London Bridge tube/rail. **Lunch served** 11.30am-3pm Mon-Fri. **Dinner served** 6-10.30pm Mon-Sat. **Main courses** £9.50-£15. **Set lunch** £7.95-£8.95 2 courses. **Set dinner** £21-£30 per person (minimum 2) 3 courses.
Credit AmEx, DC, MC, V.
If you find yourself near London Bridge in need of some good food, you could do far worse than Kwan Thai. Friendly staff steer you through a predictable menu of well-executed classics while you gaze out at St Paul's. The simple richness of tom kha gai, a coconut broth with tender chicken and a subtle lemongrass undertone, paved the way for bolder flavours in spicy Thai salads. A classic som tam had plenty of heat, with peanuts adding crunch, and dried shrimps enriching the flavour, while the beef salad (yam nua) was not bashful: with three varieties of onion (white, red and spring), it was difficult to detect too much flavour from the slightly overcooked strips of meat, but chillies and coriander kept the dish alive. Pad thai featured delicate rice noodles and a soothing honeyed flavour pervaded the succulent prawns and crunchy bean sprouts and peanuts, making it the perfect foil to the spicier salads. The split-level dining room is unlikely to win any design awards, but it is clean, functional and provides an excellent vantage point from which to watch the world bustle by.
Babies and children welcome: high chairs. Booking advisable. Tables outdoors (40, riverside terrace). Takeaway service. Vegetarian menu.
Map 12 Q8.

New Cross

Thailand

15 Lewisham Way, SE14 6PP (8691 4040). New Cross or New Cross Gate tube/rail. **Lunch served** noon-2.30pm Mon-Fri. **Dinner served** 5-11.30pm daily. **Main courses** £4.95-£10. **Set meal** (lunch, 5-7pm) £3.95 2 courses. **Credit** MC, V.
The unimaginative name and nondescript decor may hint at a similar laziness in the kitchen, but in this case, appearances could not be more deceptive. This canteen-like eaterie serves authentic, first-rate Thai and Laotian food at fair prices. The menu, like the surroundings, does not pretend to offer anything highbrow; yet the staples it serves are faultlessly rendered. A well-balanced tom yum came with a generous portion of prawns that were not overcooked – a refreshing rarity. Chargrilled marinated beef wrapped in betel leaves was fragrant, tender and juicy, while the red duck curry was among the best we've tried in London: daringly rich, creamy and sweet without being cloying. Most impressive was the pork laab: the minced meat was roughly chopped and flash boiled, giving each tender bite extra heft. Its marinade boasted a perfect balance of sour, salty and sweet flavours, enhanced by the unmistakeable perfumes of fresh galangal, coriander and thai basil. Two minor complaints: dishes were given liberal lashings of MSG and tossed with red onions rather than shallots. Still, that won't stop us heading back for more.
Babies and children admitted. Booking essential Fri, Sat. Takeaway service; delivery service (over £10 within 3-mile radius). Vegetarian menu.

South Norwood

★ ★ Mantanah

2 Orton Building, Portland Road, SE25 4UD (8771 1148/www.mantanah.co.uk). Norwood Junction rail. **Lunch served** noon-3pm Sat, Sun. **Dinner served** 6-11pm Tue-Sun. **Main courses** £5.75-£8.50. **Set dinner** £16 per person (minimum 2) 3 courses, £22 per person (minimum 2) 4 courses. **Set buffet** (lunch Sun) £7.95 adults. **Credit** AmEx, DC, MC, V.
Sunshine-yellow walls and pearly pink damask tablecloths greet your arrival to the hyperreally colourful and flavoursome world of this excellent Thai outpost – the genuine article in an otherwise drab and uninspiring suburban setting. An impressive array of dish names are winningly translated from the Thai, including 'Cinderella's Best Friend' (pumpkin deep fried in coconut batter, served with plum sauce) or 'Treasure Bag' (a rice pastry parcel of crab and sweet potato). Though staple Thai dishes (green curry, tom yum gai) are all present and correct, you're best advised to go off-piste and sample taste explosions such as the lemon, chilli and garlic-drenched 'yum lanna' salad of shredded chicken, roasted coconut and banana blossom, or chicken and pumpkin stewed in coconut milk and chilli ('Midnight Chicken'). Vegetarians will delight at the many meat-free options, which make creative use of ingredients such as aubergine, pumpkin, nuts and tofu. On a rainy Wednesday night, a couple of the more exotic dishes were off the menu due to lack of ingredients, but the quality of food and service was otherwise very high. It's a crying shame the place isn't better patronised (or perhaps located).
Babies and children admitted. Booking advisable. Takeaway service. Vegetarian menu.
For branch (Chon Thong) see index.

North

Archway

Charuwan

110 Junction Road, N19 5LB (7263 1410). Archway or Tufnell Park tube. **Lunch served** noon-3pm Mon-Fri. **Dinner served** 6-11pm daily. **Main courses** £4.95-£8.95. **Set dinner** £18-£20 per person (minimum 2) 3 courses.
Credit AmEx, MC, V.
Reasonable, reliable cooking keeps the locals coming back to this neighbourhood favourite, but the real draw is the delightful interior, crowned by a Lanna-style peaked teak roof typical of the

SHELF LIFE

Thai groceries are stocked by many neighbourhood Thai and oriental supermarkets, but the following are among the best.

Amaranth
527 Garratt Lane, SW18 4SR (8871 3466/8879 7360). Earlsfield rail. **Open** 11.30am-8.30pm Mon-Sat.
Helpful staff, and a good range of Thai vegetables, curry pastes, and cooking utensils such as giant mortars and pestles.

Sri Thai
56 Shepherd's Bush Road, W6 7PH (7602 0621). Goldhawk Road or Shepherd's Bush tube. **Open** 9.30am-7pm daily.
Compact shop selling Thai groceries and goods on Shepherd's Bush Road. Look for the lurid pink sign.

Talad Thai
326 Upper Richmond Road, SW15 6TL (8789 8084/www.taladthai.co.uk). Putney rail/East Putney tube. **Open** 9am-8pm Mon-Sat; 10am-8pm Sun.
Talad Thai may not look very big, but it's a major supplier of Thai produce to London's restaurants.

Tawana
16-18 Chepstow Road, W2 5BD (7221 6316/www.tawana.co.uk). Notting Hill Gate tube. **Open** 9.30am-8pm daily.
The surprisingly extensive range of Thai ingredients includes fresh vegetables, fruit and herbs flown in from Thailand twice a week.

Thai Smile
283-287 King Street, W6 9NH (8846 9960/www.thaismile.com). Ravenscourt Park tube. **Open** 9.30am-8pm daily.
A large supermarket with a wide range of fresh and frozen foods, snacks, canned and bottled goods. Friendly service too.

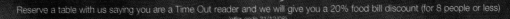

traditional architecture of northern Thailand. The resulting ambience is calm and civilised. Gaps in conversation are filled by mouthfuls of familiar Thai dishes (the usual range of starter nibbles, curries and stir-fries), plus some less commonly seen dishes, such as baby squid stuffed with minced prawns, which was disappointingly dry and a bit chewy on this occasion. But for the most part the cooking was as crisp and fresh as authenticity demands. Salads were a highlight, particularly a beef 'tiger cry' with, unusually – for a lower-budget Thai restaurant – tender and juicy steak. The tom yum soup was also notable, its chilli, lemongrass, galangal and citrus flavours perfectly balanced. While not every dish is up to the same high standard, the exceptional surroundings and deferential service more than make up for any minor lapses in the kitchen.
Booking advisable. Children over 5 years admitted. Takeaway service. Vegetarian menu. **Map 26 B2.**

Islington

Isarn

119 Upper Street, N1 1QP (7424 5153). Angel tube/Highbury & Islington tube/rail. **Lunch served** noon-3pm, **dinner served** 6-11pm Mon-Fri. **Meals served** noon-11pm Sat; noon-10.30pm Sun. **Main courses** £6.50-£14.50. **Set lunch** £5.90 3 courses. **Credit** AmEx, MC, V.
The canopied roof gives Isarn a sense of space, despite its actual, diminutive size and long, narrow shape, while the butterfly-themed lighting adds style. The menu combines creative selections such as crispy duck and pomelo on betel leaf or soft shell crab with mango dressing with traditional fare such as tom yum koong or massaman curry. The duck and pomelo was crunchy and sweet, with the texture of betel leaf offering a pleasing contrast to the crispy meat. A main course of steamed mussels, though fresh, was bland, despite the kaffir lime, chilli and basil sauce, and a prawn pad thai was too sweet. Overall, while the presentation of dishes was enticing, they tended to lack variety of flavour. The restaurant is co-owned by Tina Juengsoongneum, sister of Alan Yau (Hakkasan, Busaba Eathai), and earned accolades when it opened in 2005. But visits from our reviewers during 2006 and 2007 have yielded very mixed reports, which suggests Isarn is at best unreliable. On our visit, an annoying Kenny G elevator soundtrack was on loop; we can only hope that by now it's been retired.
Babies and children admitted. Tables outdoors (2, garden). Takeaway service. **Map 5 O1.**

North West

Kensal

★ Tong Ka Nom Thai NEW

833 Harrow Road, NW10 5NH (8964 5373). Kensal Rise tube. **Lunch served** noon-3pm Mon-Fri. **Dinner served** 6-10pm Mon-Sat. **Main courses** £4.20-£5.70. **No credit cards.**
Turquoise walls, ornate fabrics and shimmering wall hangings make a welcoming contrast to the grey urban landscape of the Harrow Road outside. The menu here is typical Thai restaurant fare, with most dishes competitively priced at around the £5 mark. Tender skewers of chicken satay came with a sweet, coconutty sauce. Prawns in rice pastry 'blankets' were pleasingly spiced, although the ratio could have been more in favour of the prawn. A main course of red curry with succulent tiger prawns had a hot, sweet-savoury sauce that encapsulated the distinctive contrasts of Thai cuisine. Less impressively, spare ribs with a promised garlic and lemongrass sauce seemed bereft of the latter ingredient. Desserts are periodically changing specials: on our visit an offering of sticky coconut rice with juicy alphonso mangoes was a triumph that deserves to be a permanent fixture. The restaurant was busy but relaxed, the service laid-back but not inefficient. For the price, this restaurant undoubtedly punches above its weight.
Babies and children admitted. Takeaway service. Vegetarian menu.

Esarn Kheaw. See p271.

Turkish

The spread of authentic Turkish food around London continues, though new restaurants often launch themselves as Mediterranean rather than Turkish, and established places are adding generic Med dishes to their menus. There's no real harm in this, especially given the failure of new Turkish restaurants to continue trading at the top end of the market; Shoreditch's Savarona was a casualty since the last edition. The range of 'night-out' restaurants is becoming impressive, spreading from **Escale** in Richmond to **Mez** on the Isle of Dogs. Most of these newcomers haven't fallen into the bad habit of adding a charge for bread (a practice that blights several otherwise excellent eateries). But the heartland of Turkish eating remains the areas with the largest Turkish and Kurdish communities, notably Dalston, Stoke Newington and Harringay. This is where you'll find the greatest concentration of good cheap cafés and restaurants, including such reliable stalwarts as **19 Numara Bos Cirrik**, **Mangal Ocakbaşi**, **Mangal II** and **Antepliler**.

Slowly but surely, Londoners are coming to realise that Turkish is one of the world's great cuisines, and doesn't deserve its unhealthy reputation, gained from the greasy late-night döner kebab. Many of the capital's Turkish restaurants and cafés have an ocakbaşı: a large open grill usually placed in the main part of the restaurant, so it's possible to see how fresh the ingredients are as you watch the food prepared.

Central

Bloomsbury

Tas

22 Bloomsbury Street, WC1B 3QJ (7637 4555/ www.tasrestaurant.com). Holborn or Tottenham Court Road tube. **Meals served** noon-11.30pm Mon-Sat; noon-10.30pm Sun. **Main courses** £5.95-£14.45. **Set meal** £18.50 3 courses (minimum 2 people). **Set meze** £8.95. **Credit** AmEx, MC, V.

All the restaurants in the Tas group are similar in character, despite being variously called Tas, Tas Pide and EV. This branch, just by the British Museum, benefits from its corner location, big windows and a light ground floor, though there's also a basement with additional seating. Quirky chairs shaped like giant hands form a conversation piece in the waiting area by the entrance. Walls are painted in pastel shades or decorated with tiny tiles. Our meal began with complimentary olives and yoghurt. First courses, houmous kavurma and mussel soup, were both straightforward and boasted first-rate ingredients. A main course of lamb böbrek was superb, the meat almost dissolving on the tongue. Mackerel was fresh and succulent. Dishes were brought to the table on enormous trays, accompanied by folding stands, and mixed meze were served on neat rows of little oblong white plates. Rather against the Turkish tradition of mixing simple flavours, Tas chefs always seem to prefer combining intense flavours, rather than risk blandness. In general, though, the inventiveness of the menu pays off.

Babies and children welcome: high chairs. Booking advisable Fri, Sat. Disabled: toilet. Separate room for parties, seats 80. Tables outdoors (12, pavement). Takeaway service. **Map 18 D1.**

For branches (EV, Tas, Tas Café, Tas Pide) see index.

City

Haz

9 Cutler Street, E1 7DJ (7929 7923/www.haz restaurant.co.uk). Liverpool Street tube/rail. **Meals served** 11.30am-11.30pm daily. **Main courses** £7-£13. **Set meal** £8.45 2 courses, £18.45 3 courses incl coffee. **Set meze** £5.95. **Credit** AmEx, MC, V.

The atmosphere at Haz is remarkably impersonal, with diners seated at long tables as if in a well-fitted-out canteen. The restaurant is usually busy and noisy; unsurprisingly, given the location, most of the customers are City workers. The wine list is extensive, but Haz relies on the quality of its food (from a large and relatively adventurous menu). However, on a recent visit our starters weren't quite up to scratch for such an upmarket venue. Ciğer tava (liver sautéed with red onion) was slightly overcooked and dry, while patlıcan biber kizartma, fried aubergine with tomato and yoghurt, was pleasant but bland. Pitta rather than pide accompanied the meal, though previous experience suggests this can vary during the course of an evening. Main courses were much more assured. Erikli tavuk (chicken and prune with cinnamon and lime) was an interesting choice, if too sweet for our taste. But cevizli kaşarli köfte (grilled minced lamb with walnuts, cheddar cheese, roast vegetables and rice) was appetising and faultless. As is common with Turkish food, the vegetable accompaniments were outstanding. It was occasionally difficult to attract attention, but in general service was reasonably efficient.

Babies and children welcome: high chair. Booking advisable Mon-Fri. Restaurant available for hire. Takeaway service. **Map 12 R6.**

For branch see index.

Covent Garden

Sofra

36 Tavistock Street, WC2E 7PB (7240 3773/ www.sofra.co.uk). Covent Garden tube. **Meals served** noon-11pm daily. **Main courses** £6.95-£21.95. **Set meal** £9.95-£11.95 2 courses. **Set meze** £8.95-£10.95. **Credit** AmEx, MC, V.

This branch of the upmarket chain is a little lost in the space between Covent Garden and the Strand, but don't miss it, as Sofra serves top-quality food. The compact interior is long, thin, intimate and civilised. The wood floor is paired with a wooden bar, behind which rises a scarlet wall reminiscent of Özer (*see below*), the flagship of the chain. On the first floor is another dining area, and there's also a roof garden. On our visit, complimentary houmous and queen olives were of the highest quality. We followed these with mixed meze – memorably fresh broad beans, tarator, falafel and börek – presented on individual plates for each diner. Recently, Sofra has started to promote fish on its menus; we plumped for a commendable fillet of sea bream, which arrived atop mashed potato with a leek and rocket salad. The chain has also joined the recent fashion for serving steak, but we chose lamb külbastı, large squares of tender lamb fillet. Sofra also serves pideler (Turkish pizzas) and a range of daily specials. Service during our stay was good and very, very fast.

Babies and children welcome: children's portions; high chairs. Booking advisable. Separate area for parties, seats 80. Takeaway service.
Map 18 E4.

For branches see index.

Fitzrovia

★ Istanbul Meze

100 Cleveland Street, W1T 6NS (7387 0785/ www.istanbulmeze.co.uk). Great Portland Street or Warren Street tube. **Meals served** noon-11pm Mon-Thur; noon-midnight Fri, Sat. **Dinner served** 5-11pm Sun. **Main courses** £7-£12. **Set lunch** £8.90 2 courses incl coffee. **Set dinner** £11.90 2 courses. **Set meze** £20. **Credit** AmEx, MC, V.

With the atmosphere of a local restaurant, despite its location near the West End, Istanbul Meze is always worth a visit. An enormous portion of arnavut ciğeri (lamb's liver) made a first-rate starter, sautéed and served with parsley and onion. So did grilled halloumi cheese with tomato and lettuce, though you should only order it if you like salty food. Starters came with a fresh tray of warm pitta; pide bread would be an improvement. For mains, karni yarik (diced, stewed lamb on a bed of aubergine, served with rice and very thick yoghurt) was beautifully flavoursome, if not artistically presented. Charmingly, the waiters still tour the tables spooning the lovely fresh chilli sauce from a saucepan. İskender was a mixture of chicken, köfte and lamb on pitta in a rich tomatoey sauce. As is traditional with iskender there were no vegetables, but unusually the same thick yoghurt was on the side rather than mixed in. Service was good and the welcome warm. The restaurant is popular with Turks; musicians frequently play downstairs, especially at weekends, though you might need to book to be sure of seeing them.

Babies and children admitted. Booking essential weekends. Separate room for parties, seats 50. Tables outdoors (3, pavement). Takeaway service. Vegetarian menu. **Map 3 J4.**

★ Özer

5 Langham Place, W1B 3DG (7323 0505/ www.sofra.co.uk). Oxford Circus tube.
Bar **Open** noon-11pm daily.
Restaurant **Meals served** noon-midnight daily. **Main courses** £8.70-£15.70. **Set lunch** (noon-6pm) £8.95 2 courses. **Set dinner** (6-11pm) £10.95-£16.45 2 courses.
Both **Credit** AmEx, DC, MC, V.

The restaurant proper is reached through a busy bar area. Its large size comes as a surprise, as do an odd metallic sculpture hanging from the ceiling

RESTAURANTS

and the striking scarlet wall. The ambience is professional and efficient rather than laid-back. As cards on the table inform diners, speed of service is one of Özer's boasts; so diners are quickly seated and dealt with. The menu is wide-ranging, with a recently extended choice of beef steaks; there's also a sizeable wine list. Börek had been stuffed with a particularly tasty feta and was perfectly textured, while kalamar marinated in vodka also had a pleasing texture and was a success. Next, salmon stew on a bed of potato was very nice, if too salty for some tastes. But the house special of köfte with sauce, yoghurt and pide was beyond reproach. Özer is perhaps the leading Turkish restaurant in the West End, and confident enough to experiment. We're not complaining.
Babies and children welcome: children's menu; high chairs. Disabled: toilet. Tables outdoors (5, pavement). Takeaway service. **Map 9 H5**.

Holborn

Turquoise NEW

25-26 Red Lion Street, WC1R 4PS (7242 7900/ www.turquoiserestaurant.co.uk). Holborn tube. **Meals served** noon-11.30pm Mon-Sat. **Main courses** £7.85-£12.25. **Set meal** £8.85 2 courses, £14.95 3 courses incl coffee. **Credit** AmEx, MC, V.
The large interior of this new restaurant – popular with a business crowd – has a vaguely 1970s feel, perhaps because of all the turquoise lighting and fittings. We visited for dinner; as we chose from the extensive menu, some enormous olives, a couple of dips and lovely hot pide were provided. The list includes fish, Turkish pizzas and pasta dishes, as well as all the standard grills and stews. For starters, balık çorbası soup was brimming with mussels and huge prawns, and garnished with coriander. We also enjoyed a sizeable portion of slightly chewy kalamar, partly redeemed by a very good walnut tarator sauce. All dishes were tastefully presented on oblong white plates. A main course of patlıcanli köfte was rather bland, involving a slightly too salty lamb köfte on a slightly too oily aubergine and tomato base. At least the accompanying couscous was tasty. Fildişili tavuk, an unusual chicken and cashew nut casserole, was also most agreeable. Turquoise is full of promise and merits a visit, but we reckon it should concentrate its efforts on a smaller menu – rather than risk erratic quality.
Babies and children welcome: high chairs. Booking advisable. Restaurant available for hire. Takeaway service. **Map 10 M5**.

Marylebone

Grand Bazaar

42 James Street, W1N 5HS (7224 1544/ www.grand-bazaar.co.uk). Bond Street tube. **Meals served** noon-11pm Mon-Thur, Sun; noon-midnight Fri, Sat. **Main courses** £9-£11. **Set lunch** £6.95 2 courses. **Set meze** £9.45. **Credit** AmEx, MC, V.
Grand Bazaar remains a popular choice in central London. The atmosphere is young and hectic, buzzing and noisy, though service can be erratic. Notably small tables are clustered together, both inside and on the pavement, and a sea of lanterns overhangs the cluttered, dark interior. Both our starters came in big portions: houmous kavurma was a very sweet chickpea blend containing tasty nibbles of good lamb; triangular börek were also satisfying. These were accompanied by an unusual inflated bread that seemed more Iranian than Turkish. For mains, külbastı was oddly presented: a fillet of lamb with rice, carrots and peas, garnished with three (count 'em) chips. It was OK, but not especially authentic. Kaburga kept to its Turkish roots, but was a disappointment: the lamb ribs were not very meaty and a tad overcooked, with a charcoal taste. The large portion of pide bread on which they sat also made the dish a rather heavy choice. One final gripe: two toilet cubicles are really not enough for a restaurant this busy.
Babies and children admitted. Booking advisable. Tables outdoors (16, pavement). Takeaway service. **Map 9 G6**.

Ishtar

10-12 Crawford Street, W1U 6AZ (7224 2446/ www.ishtarrestaurant.com). Baker Street tube. **Meals served** noon-11pm Mon-Thur, Sun; noon-11.30am Fri, Sat. **Main courses** £7.95-£13.50. **Set lunch** (noon-6pm) £6.95 2 courses. **Set meal** £16.95 3 courses. **Set meze** £9.95. **Credit** MC, V.
With wooden flooring and ceiling, and a staircase that sweeps down from the main ground floor to a cellar with an arched roof, Ishtar has a modern look. The ground floor contains a long curved bar and an ocakbaşı grill; part of it is on a raised level. On the walls, shelves display preserved fruit in jars. Heavy white tablecloths cover the tables and help to contain the noise level. A starter of houmous kavurma was very pleasing, though unusual in being topped with minced lamb rather than small cubes or strips. The pide bread that came with it was outstanding. Rocket salad with orange, pear and walnut was highly appetising too, though perhaps relied too much on the pear. As a main course, chicken iskender was brilliant, with wonderful thick yoghurt and an exceptional sauce. The wine list is a highlight too. Our waitress was noticeably efficient and enthusiastic, though on previous visits service has been erratic. In all, though, Ishtar has become an established destination and deserves to be visited.
Babies and children welcome: high chairs. Booking advisable Thur-Sat. Entertainment: musicians Tue-Sat; belly dancer Thur-Sat. Separate room for parties, seats 120. Tables outdoors (6, pavement). Takeaway service. Vegetarian menu. **Map 2 F5**.

Pimlico

Kazan

93-94 Wilton Road, SW1V 1DW (7233 7100/ www.kazan-restaurant.com). Victoria tube/rail. **Meals served** noon-11pm daily. **Main courses** £9.95-£17. **Set meal** (noon-6pm) £9.99-£14.95 2 courses. **Credit** AmEx, MC, V.
Just around the corner from Victoria station, Kazan combines a bright modern bar with a Turkish restaurant. The interior is divided in two, the bar on one side and the restaurant proper on the other. Food consists of variations on traditional Turkish cuisine. Presentation was immaculate; food was served on stylish plates, many dishes covered by metal covers shaped like Ottoman domes, rising to a point. For starters, börülce was a tasty black-eyed bean salad, while börek were raised above the norm by virtue of the outstanding filo pastry. A main course of sultan lamb kebab was in essence a well-prepared şiş with vegetables, served with rice and a salad. The vegetarian moussaka was excellent, featuring layers of nicely cooked vegetables and a good green salad. The Turkish desserts here, particularly the baklava, are first-rate too. Kazan's very Turkish take on a modern restaurant remains popular, and the enterprise deserves its continued success.
Babies and children welcome: high chairs. Booking advisable dinner. Disabled: toilet. Entertainment: belly dancers; phone for details. Separate rooms for parties, seating 30 and 50. Tables outdoors (3, pavement). Takeaway service. **Map 15 J11**.

West

Notting Hill

Manzara

24 Pembridge Road, W11 3HL (7727 3062). Notting Hill Gate tube. **Meals served** 8am-1am Mon-Sat; 8am-11.30pm Sun. **Main courses** £6.75-£9.95. **Set meze** £5.95. **No credit cards**.
Advertised as Mediterranean, Manzara is indeed anything but a standard Turkish restaurant. It opens early, offering breakfast (including cereals), and stays open late. During the day, staff rustle up sandwiches and provide a range of cakes and gateaux at the takeaway counter by the front. Customers eating in can choose organic beefburgers and organic wine, but Turkish food is the mainstay of the menu. A mixed meze included

Ishtar

RESTAURANTS

a good spread of starters: börek, houmous, cacik and dolma. To follow, 'spicy lamb with yoghurt' was deceptively named, as it wasn't very spicy. This was served on diced pitta, accompanied by a dollop of thick yoghurt and rice. A lamb kebab offered slices of aubergine interspersed with slightly heavy köfte, decent rice, and tomato. Pitta is the only bread option, but you can order pide pizzas. Blue tablecloths cover tables that aren't unlike those of a fast-food café, but the overall emphasis is on takeaways rather than the restaurant – a pity, as Manzara remains the only serious Turkish eaterie for miles around.
Babies and children welcome. Booking advisable. Tables outside (2, pavement). Takeaway service. **Map 7 A7**.

West Kensington

★ Best Mangal

104 North End Road, W14 9EX (7610 1050). West Kensington tube. **Meals served** noon-midnight Mon-Thur; noon-1am Fri, Sat. **Main courses** £8.50-£17.50. **Set meal** £17 2 courses, £19 3 courses, incl soft drink. **Credit** MC, V.

This West Ken stalwart has been redecorated; paintings of modern Istanbul now adorn the walls, and the room is brightened up by yellow tablecloths. The interior is still pretty small, with room for perhaps 30 diners behind a buzzing takeaway. Staff on our visit were attentive and happy to offer advice on what to order, and service during the meal was amazingly quick. A starter of patlıcan esme was a remarkably creamy white aubergine purée with a smoky flavour garnished with a black olive. It came with very good saç and warm pide bread. For mains, karburga (succulent grilled lamb spare ribs) was served with a sparklingly fresh salad of lettuce, sliced red cabbage and shredded carrot. All portions were enormous and in danger of spilling from the plate. The range of desserts is limited, but of a high quality. Best Mangal deserves its local reputation and continues to go from strength to strength. The former branch at No.66 is now called H&H and no longer connected.
Babies and children welcome: high chairs. Booking advisable. Takeaway service. Vegetarian menu.

South West

Earlsfield

Kazans

607-609 Garratt Lane, SW18 4SU (8739 0055/ www.kazans.com). Earlsfield rail/44, 77, 270 bus. **Dinner served** 6-11pm Mon-Fri. **Meals served** 11am-11pm Sat, Sun. **Main courses** £7.50-£14.95. **Credit** AmEx, MC, V.

The front of Kazans is divided into a restaurant and a separate bar, both looking on to the street. Its walls are stencilled with patterns and decorated with fascinating family photos from 1960s Turkey. Further back, there's less light, so tables are decorated with coloured glass lanterns. Starters come in big portions. Fava bean (broad bean) purée tasted fresh and flavoursome, though the texture was a little rough, but patlıcan salata (smoky aubergine purée with lemon) was exemplary. More adventurous daily specials have started to crop up on the menu recently, such as shashlik, or lamb wrapped in pastrami. We ordered izgara tavuk, translated here as piri-piri chicken. A whole small chicken marinated in white wine and chilli arrived; it was marvellously spicy. Meanwhile, loin of lamb came accompanied by an interesting combination of rocket and mashed sweet potato. Kazans was formerly reticent about its Turkishness. Having 'come out' and built a solid menu, it seems to feel the need to go further, but we reckon the new options aren't as accomplished as the core menu.
Babies and children welcome: high chairs. Booking advisable weekends. Disabled: toilet. Separate rooms for parties, seating 30 and 50. Tables outdoors (4, decking). Takeaway service.

South

Waterloo

Troia

3F Belvedere Road, SE1 7GQ (7633 9309). Waterloo tube/rail. **Meals served** noon-midnight daily. **Main courses** £8.25-£12.95. **Set lunch** (noon-4pm) £7.95 2 courses. **Set meze** £9.95 per person (minimum 2). **Credit** AmEx, MC, V.

A large relief showing the Trojan horse, with the Greeks riding inside like passengers on a bus, dominates the bright yellow and red walls of Troia, and the ceiling is adorned with a great wagon wheel of lamps. In the past the restaurant has seemed a little troubled by its location, tucked away behind the London Eye. Yet when we visited recently it was full, suggesting the earlier difficulties have been overcome. A starter of kalamar, fried with walnut sauce, was fresh and piquant. Just as good was patlıcan biber kizartma, fried aubergine with tomato sauce. These were followed by interesting and slightly unusual main courses. Kuskonmazli tavuk was grilled chicken with lightly grilled seasonal vegetables, including asparagus; it was exceptionally tasty, even if the asparagus was overdone. Armutlu kuzu tandir stew was a delight: melt-in-the-mouth lamb accompanied by spiced pear. The small designer chairs round the tables may be very Ottoman, but they're are a little hard to rise from after a big meal. Small gripes aside, Troia is now established as a very respectable restaurant.
Babies and children welcome: children's menu; high chairs. Booking advisable. Disabled: toilet. Tables outdoors (14, pavement). Takeaway service. Vegetarian menu. **Map 10 M9.**

South East

Lewisham

★ Meze Mangal

245 Lewisham Way, SE4 1XF (8694 8099/ www.meze-mangal.co.uk). St John's rail/Lewisham rail/DLR. **Meals served** noon-2am Mon-Thur; noon-3am Fri, Sat; noon-1am Sun. **Main courses** £7-£14. **Set meze** £11 per person (minimum 2), £16 per person (minimum 4). **Credit** MC, V.

Notwithstanding its situation on an increasingly shabby parade, Meze Mangal is an excellent, no-nonsense restaurant serving all the basic grills along with Turkish pizzas and vegetarian dishes. Inside, the decor is hardly upmarket, but it's welcoming in comparison to the exterior, and in any case, the dubious location doesn't put off the loyal regulars. On the Sunday evening of a recent visit, the place was full to bursting with a mixed local crowd occupying most of the closely packed tables. A starter of kısır came in a hearty portion with good bread; the texture was unusually rough, but the flavour was fresh and nutty. Çop şiş was simply excellent, perfectly tender, and served with a large salad dominated by shredded carrot and red cabbage. Meze Mangal is also popular for takeaways. It's surprising that such a well-loved eaterie doesn't entice other Turkish restaurants to open in the area. But perhaps others are afraid they wouldn't be able to compete.
Babies and children welcome: high chair. Booking advisable. Takeaway service. Vegetarian menu.

East

Docklands

Mez NEW

571 Manchester Road, E14 3NZ (7005 0421/ www.mezrestaurant.com). South Quay DLR. **Meals served** noon-midnight daily. **Main courses** £8.95-£12.45. **Set meal** £10.95 2 courses. **Set meze** (noon-3pm) £7.45. **Credit** MC, V.

Kazans

Windows running the length of this new restaurant provide a long thin view of the council estate across the road, which obscures the river and, on the opposite bank, the Dome. Mez is in an odd position for an upmarket restaurant on the Isle of Dogs: in the hinterland between the financial area and the surrounding run-down estates. Understandably, it makes an effort to be refined. A map on the wall shows the birth of civilisation in the Fertile Crescent of Mesopotamia, and depicts Assyrian warriors riding across the desert. On our recent visit, service was generally efficient, despite of one waiter's sternness. Things seemed more relaxed for a family across the aisle with a five-year-old child. While we scrutinised the menu, saç bread was brought, along with olive purée. Plenty of thought goes into dish presentation. Starters – zeytinyağli bakla (lightly simmered broad beans) and vezir cigiri (delicately fried chicken livers): both gorgeous – were accompanied by whole mini pides. To follow, the köfte in an iskender kebab was exceptional; and kuzu tandir (oven-cooked lamb) was subtly flavoured and served with couscous and some very nice steamed vegetables. With such excellent food, Mez deserves to do well.
Babies and children welcome: high chairs. Booking advisable. Disabled: toilet. Separate room for parties, seats 100. Takeaway service. Vegetarian menu. **Map 24 C3**.

North East

From Dalston Kingsland station up the A10 to Stoke Newington Church Street, you are in the Turkish and Kurdish heart of Hackney. The food available along this strip is more authentic and varied than anywhere else in London. The intense competition means that restaurants and cafés come and go at a dizzying rate, and there's a constant race to provide different services and dishes.

None of the following establishments gets a full review, but each one would stand out were it anywhere else in London: **Bodrum Café** (61 Stoke Newington High Street); **Dervish Bistro** (15 Stoke Newington Church Street); **Evin** (115 Kingsland High Street); **Istanbul Iskembecisi** (9 Stoke Newington Road) – no longer the leader of the pack, but still good; **Sölen** (84 Stoke Newington High Street); **Somine** (131 Kingsland High Street); **Tava** (17 Stoke Newington Road), good for stews; **Testi** (36 Stoke Newington High Street); and **Café Z Bar** (58 Stoke Newington Road).

Dalston

★ ★ 19 Numara Bos Cirrik

34 Stoke Newington Road, N16 7XJ (7249 0400). Dalston Kingsland rail/76, 149, 243 bus. **Meals served** noon-midnight Mon-Thur, Sun; noon-1am Fri, Sat. **Main courses** £6.50-£9.50. **Set meal** £6.95 2 courses incl soft drink. **Unlicensed. Corkage** £4. **Credit** AmEx, MC, V.

Perfect grills continue to garner much adulation for 19 Numara, but the quality is less obviously outstanding now that other establishments are catching up with the techniques. Izgara soğan (grilled onion with pomegranate and turnip sauce) is served as a complimentary starter; its sweet and sour glory remains another reason for recommending this place, although to be fair the dish is now served in many restaurants in the area. A plate of onion with chilli also appeared. There's a range of perfectly serviceable starters on the menu, but few people need to go beyond what is provided gratis. On our latest visit, the small restaurant was, as usual, very crowded. Kaburga (lamb spare ribs) were faultlessly cooked and very succulent. The böbrek (kidneys) were slightly overdone, but were still sensational. Service was friendly and efficient. The restaurant's popularity means there are now two other branches: one in Stoke Newington, the other near Hackney Central station. These are popular, but not as good as the original – spreading the 19 Numara effect seems to weaken it. So, the magic may not last, but make the most of it in the meantime.
Babies and children admitted. Booking advisable. Takeaway service. **Map 25 C4**.
For branches see index.

★ Mangal II

4 Stoke Newington Road, N16 8BH (7254 7888/ www.mangal2.com). Dalston Kingsland rail/76, 149, 243 bus. **Meals served** 3pm-1am Mon-Fri; 2pm-1am Sat, Sun. **Main courses** £7.95-£12.95. **Set meal** £16.25 3 courses (minimum 2). **Credit** MC, V.

Decorated in a cheery yellow and blue, Mangal II is highly popular with Turkish families, but also attracts a wide range of other locals – and deservedly so. It is one of three connected Mangals in the area, the first being the original, legendary grill shop in a nearby side street (*see below*), and the third a café specialising in Turkish pizza (Mangals elsewhere are unrelated, as the name simply refers to a type of grill). Ispanak manca – spinach with yoghurt and garlic – made a refreshingly fresh starter, yet was surprisingly heavy. No complaints, though, about our great main course: uskumru veya alabalik (in this case, grilled mackerel, though it's also available as rainbow trout), served with a salad containing gherkins and shredded carrot. Lokma kebab was fatty, but had the melting fat of high-quality lamb, and came with fine rice. We also enjoyed decent warm pide, including paper-thin saç. The skill with the ocakbaşı that made the original Mangal famous is also evident here. Though the place is bustling and busy, the atmosphere is relaxed.
Babies and children welcome: high chairs. Booking essential weekends. Takeaway service. **Map 25 C4**.

★ Mangal Ocakbaşi (100)

10 Arcola Street, E8 2DJ (7275 8981/ www.mangal1.com). Dalston Kingsland rail/ 73 bus. **Meals served** noon-midnight daily. **Main courses** £7-£13. **Unlicensed. Corkage** no charge. **No credit cards**.

In recent years, the side street on which Mangal is located has significantly improved, mainly due to the opening of the Arcola Theatre. What keeps Mangal abuzz, however, is its legendary and quite specific reputation. There are no frills in decor or service, staff are curt, and starters and desserts in short supply. There are no menus. The thrills are in the grills. Diners arrive and queue with the takeaway crowd in the small entrance. Having chosen a kebab from the raw meat on display, they sit in the cramped, tiled interior while it's cooked. All the standard Turkish grills are usually available. A çop şiş came in an enormous portion: small cubes of beautifully grilled meat served on fine saç bread, with a side order of pide. The salad contained a lot of freshly shredded carrot and red cabbage, with a good deal of pickled gherkin. Though prices here are no longer ridiculously cheap, and the competition is now much fiercer, it's still worth visiting Mangal at least once to see why this remains a cult restaurant.
Booking essential weekends. Takeaway service. **Map 25 C4**.

Newington Green

★ Sariyer Balik

56 Green Lanes, N16 9NH (7275 7681). Manor House tube then 141, 341 bus. **Meals served** 5pm-1am daily. **Main courses** £6.50-£10. **No credit cards**.

Little has changed in this cosy fish restaurant over the past few years, though the nets that hang from the ceiling as part of the eccentric decoration have acquired more dried fish with babies' dummies in their mouths. The interior is dark and intimate, certainly not a place to discuss matters you'd rather diners at the next table didn't hear. Three starters are available: prawns in spicy tomato

RESTAURANTS

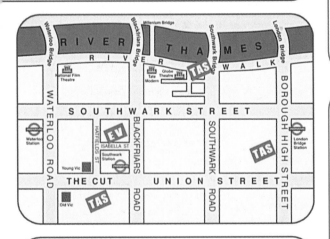

sauce, battered mussels marinated in beer, and kalamar marinated in vodka. Each is excellent, so it's worth ordering the mixed starter that includes them all. Recently, steamed fish has been added to the menu alongside the traditional chargrilled dishes, though it wasn't available on a recent visit. The restaurant is highly dependent on what fish it can source fresh, so chances are not everything on the printed menu will be available. We ate hamsi, small sardine-like fish that melt in the mouth, and large, tender swordfish steaks, grilled to perfection. Yes, Sariyer Balik is still outstanding. The part-open kitchen at the back, which allows you to see the chef at work close up, gives the place an untypical but welcome intimacy. Service is excellent: friendly and fast.
Babies and children welcome: high chairs. Booking advisable. Separate rooms for parties, seating 30 and 40. Takeaway service.
Map 25 A3.

North

Finchley

The Ottomans

118 Ballards Lane, N3 2DN (8349 9968/ www.theottomans.co.uk). Finchley Central tube. **Meals served** noon-11pm daily. **Main courses** £5.90-£12.50. **Set lunch** £5.95 2 courses. **Set dinner** £14.50-£15.90 3 courses incl coffee. **Credit** JCB, MC, V.

A cheerful local venue, the Ottomans offers light snacks and lunch deals as well as more hearty evening meals. Fresh flowers on every table help create a light, sunny atmosphere whatever the season. A mirror's frame is painted with small whirling dervishes, while a mural takes up an entire wall, showing boats being rowed languidly across the Bosphorus. Paintings and a glass front conspire to make the restaurant appear more spacious than it really is. On our visit, staff were very helpful and friendly. For starters, mixed meze – with a good selection of falafel, muska böreği, houmous, patlıcan esme, tabouleh, cacik and kısır – were noticeably fresh and moist, and came with warm pide bread. Basic grills are another forte, and both the unusually long beyti mince kebabs and the inegöl köfte (spiced patties with cheese) were exceptional. Successful as both a café and a restaurant, the Ottomans is the best among a pretty decent batch of Turkish eateries in the area.
Babies and children welcome: children's portions; high chairs. Booking essential weekends. Takeaway service. Vegetarian menu.

Finsbury Park

Petek NEW

96 Stroud Green Road, N4 3EN (7619 3933). Finsbury Park tube/rail. **Lunch served** noon-6pm, **dinner served** 6pm-midnight daily. **Main courses** £6.45-£13.85. **Set lunch** £5.85 2 courses. **Set dinner** £6.65 2 courses. **Set meze** £6.85-£8.95 per person (minimum 2). **Credit** AmEx, MC, V.

This new restaurant has enthusiastic staff who flit between the wooden tables and rush to open the door for people as they come and go. The lights are dim and the atmosphere favours dating couples, though a blackboard lists lunch specials along with daily changing dishes and wine offers. The menu and the look tend towards the Mediterranean, but the room displays the lamps, ephemera and photos that seem compulsory in most modern Turkish dining establishments. Food, though, goes beyond the standard Turkish grills. Good, own-marinated olives and a spicy tomato dip with yellow pepper were supplied to start our meal, along with plentiful hot, fresh pide. We followed this with a very large Petek tantuni: thin strips of fried beef mingling with strips of pitta. Dishes were presented elegantly on oblong white plates, and our meal was accompanied by a good, dressed salad. Petek is trying hard to establish itself, and its efforts seem to be paying off.
Babies and children welcome: high chairs. Booking advisable. Tables outdoors (2, pavement). Takeaway service.

★ Yildiz

163 Blackstock Road, N4 2JS (7354 3899). Arsenal tube. **Meals served** noon-midnight daily. **Main courses** £6.50-£11. **Set lunch** £7 2 courses incl soft drink. **Credit** MC, V.

After passing through the busy takeaway section, dodging the copper hood on the ocakbaşı grill along the way, we found ourselves in a long, dark room that can seat perhaps 40 people. Here, the walls are burnt orange, the tablecloths heavy and red. Yildiz's menu isn't exclusively Turkish; it happily borrows from other Mediterranean cuisines. Starters of yaprak dolma (rice and pine nuts wrapped in vine leaves) were freshly made, but a bit heavy, and seven of them was a lot for an appetiser; a more successful choice was hellim (slices of halloumi cheese grilled to bring out the flavour). But you may care to skip starters, as the complimentary dishes of grilled onion in turnip and pomegranate sauce, and lightly fried chopped onion with chilli powder are reasonably filling in themselves. Tasty, thin pide bread was also replenished without us needing to ask. For mains, a basic adana kebab (an eastern Turkish dish made of mince and cayenne pepper) was flavoursome though slightly stringy, but halep kebab (an adana served over bread with a buttery tomato sauce and mushrooms) was excellent. Currently, Yildiz is on pretty good form; we recommend it for a cheap night out if you're in the area.
Babies and children welcome: high chair. Takeaway service.

Harringay

With some 20 cafés and restaurants along the strip, Harringay's Green Lanes offers the most intense concentration of Turkish food in London. It is also home to several Turkish grocers, pâtisseries, greengrocers and butchers. The restaurants may lack the variety of the cluster around Dalston and Stoke Newington in Hackney, but many of the ocakbaşı cafés are well worth a visit. Few are licensed for alcohol, but most will let you bring your own. The menu rarely strays from the standard grills, güveç and pide (both bread and pizza), but the food is good, fresh and very cheap. The following is a non-exhaustive selection of some of the better choices (street numbers are given in brackets, numbers under 100 are technically on Green Lanes Grand Parade): **Ari** (7 Salisbury Promenade), a Turkish café and pâtisserie; **Gaziantep** (No.52); **Gökyüzü** (No.27); **Harran** (No.399); **Mizgin** (No.485); **Selale** (2 Salisbury Promenade); **Tara** (No.6), which has a more Middle Eastern feel; **Yayla** (No.429); and **Zigzag** (No.64), which is licensed.

★ Antepliler

46 Grand Parade, Green Lanes, N4 1AG (8802 5588). Manor House tube/29 bus. **Meals served** 11.30am-11.30pm daily. **Main courses** £5-£8.50. **Credit** AmEx, MC, V.

Antepliler was absurdly busy on the evening we visited. By the door, people queued for takeaways, while potential diners were asked to wait in the pâtisserie next door ('antepliler' means pâtisserie). This says something about the restaurant's reputation on a strip so crammed with alternatives; it stands out on Green Lanes as a restaurant rather than a café, and one with a more adventurous menu than some of the competition. It specialises in food from Gaziantep in the Kurdish east of Turkey (that city is also home to a leading football team, which explains the signed strip on the wall). But departures from the usual Turkish fare available in London are subtle rather than radical. A main dish of soğan kebab (grilled minced lamb) gained extra piquancy by being cooked with shallots. Urfa were long kebabs made from finely minced lamb, like a less spicy version of adana. As well as the pâtisserie and the restaurant, Antepliler now has a new juice bar a couple of doors down.
Babies and children welcome: high chairs. Takeaway service.

Öz Sofra NEW

421 Green Lanes, N4 1EY (8347 7587). Harringay rail/141, 341 bus. **Meals served** 6am-2am daily. **Main courses** £1-£6. **Unlicensed.** No alcohol allowed. **No credit cards.**

On a street lined with Turkish eateries, Öz Sofra always seems to be full. It has an inviting, brightly lit café feel. A jug of water is on each table; yoghurt, good pide bread and salad are then brought as a matter of course. Though we found nothing exceptional about the starter of lahmacun, it was hearty and tasty, spread with spicy minced lamb and served with a salad. To follow, minced lamb beyti kebab was equally competent; it could have been spicier, but that's a matter of taste. As is typical on this stretch of road, Öz Sofra serves soups and stews in addition to the grills; the exact selection varies from day to day. The strength of these cafés is in the freshness of the food rather than the originality of the menu – but it's a towering strength and explains why so many of them prosper.
Babies and children welcome: high chairs.

Highbury

★ İznik

19 Highbury Park, N5 1QJ (7354 5697). Highbury & Islington tube/rail/4, 19, 236 bus. **Meals served** 10am-midnight daily. **Main courses** £7.50-£12.50. **Credit** MC, V.

Named after a city famous for its intricately patterned tiles, İznik has been redecorated in pink. The interior is more ordered yet still filled with glorious Ottoman clutter, including not only lamps and incense burners, but also wooden screens and even a jacket on the wall. It also has new menus, though the variety of dishes is now diminished. We ordered a mixed vegetable meze platter to start. The portion was small, but we appreciated the subtle flavours of the excellent selection: dolma, patasea köftesi (lightly textured potato balls), houmous, cacik and börek. Unfortunately, İznik still serves pitta rather than pide and has joined the objectionable trend of charging for bread. The restaurant built its reputation on supplying Ottoman stews and baked dishes (rather than the grills more commonly found in London). These are still a highlight. For mains, a vegetable stew was thoroughly satisfying. Karni yarik, aubergine stuffed with minced lamb and baked in a tomato sauce served with rice and salad, was first-rate too.

SHELF LIFE

Middle Eastern and Greek-Cypriot supermarkets also stock produce that's suitable for Turkish cooking.

Tas EV
97-99 Isabella Street, SE1 8DA (7620 6191). Waterloo tube/rail. **Open** 8am-10pm daily.
Chic deli and organic store in a railway arch, attached to one of the Tas chain of restaurants (*see p278*).

Turkish Food Centre
89 Ridley Road, E8 2NH (7254 6754). Dalston Kingsland rail. **Open** 8am-10pm Mon-Sat; 8.30am-9pm Sun.
Large, excellent and well-priced supermarket on the edge of Ridley Road Market.

Turkish Food Market
385-387 Green Lanes, N4 1EU (8340 4547). Manor House tube. **Open** 24hrs daily.
A big shop – open non-stop – packed with fresh produce and dried goods.

Petek. See p283.

And a freshly squeezed fruit juice was superb. The dessert menu has been trimmed, but still includes decadent delights such as kayısı tatlısı: spiced apricot with cream and pistachios.
Babies and children admitted. Booking essential weekends. Takeaway service.

Islington

Bavo NEW

105-107 Southgate Road, N1 3JS (7226 0334/ www.bavo-restaurant.co.uk). Essex Road rail/ 141, 271 bus. **Meals served** noon-11pm daily. **Main courses** £9.50-£16.50. **Set meal** £18 per person (minimum 2) 4 courses. **Credit** MC, V.
With a modern, light interior and an owner who flits about asking how diners' meals are going, Bavo aims to be stylish. Wine comes in very tall, long-stemmed glasses; staff place napkins on your lap. Furnishings include polished wooden floorboards and big windows; massive flowers provide the decoration. However, olive-green tables and chairs jar somewhat with the ambience, looking more like café furniture. Complimentary green olives and plenty of warm pide bread were brought to our table, and the bread was replenished during the meal. A fresh, hearty mixed meze consisted of cacik, kısır, dolma, a lovely own-made houmous and içli köfte. The patlıcan kebab was admirable, with plenty of grilled aubergine. Pirzola (lamb chops) were done to perfection too. Service was polite and efficient. Bavo sells itself as Mediterranean, yet serves excellent Turkish food and is part of a general drift upmarket for the cuisine across London. An undoubted success.
Babies and children welcome: high chairs. Booking essential weekends. Disabled: toilet. Takeaway service.

Gallipoli Again

120 Upper Street, N1 1QP (7359 1578/ www.gallipolicafe.com). Angel tube. **Meals served** 10.30am-11pm Mon-Thur, Sun; 10.30am-midnight Fri, Sat. **Main courses** £6.50-£10. **Set lunch** £11.95 3 courses. **Set dinner** £14.95 3 courses incl coffee. **Credit** MC, V.
The three Gallipoli restaurants on Upper Street – Gallipoli at No.102, Gallipoli Bazaar at No.107 and this one – remain enormously popular with young Islingtonians. The food in the first two is identical, though Gallipoli Bazaar has a North African decor. Gallipoli Again, meanwhile, has red and green striped walls and a great chandelier. The place is always lively, but we find it more pleasant sitting near the front rather than at the back. Mixed meze provided an enjoyable selection of starters, including potato salad, a fine börek and falafel. A nominal 60p-per-head charge is made for rather chewy pide bread (this hardly seems worth levying, in defiance of the convention of serving complimentary bread with Turkish food). After this, imam bayıldı tasted wonderful, but was presented in an unusual fashion, with the 'stuffing' displayed on top of a slice of aubergine, rather than inside the cooked vegetable. Also, a daily special of moussaka was leaden, with heavy layers of cheese, potato and döner. The Gallipoli restaurants will undoubtedly maintain their popularity as punters like the atmosphere, but it's a pity the food can't be a little more consistent.
Babies and children welcome: high chairs. Booking advisable. Tables outdoors (5, pavement). Takeaway service. **Map 5 O1.**
For branches see index.

Gem

265 Upper Street, N1 2UQ (7359 0405/ www.gemrestaurantbar.co.uk). Angel tube/ Highbury & Islington tube/rail. **Meals served** noon-midnight Mon-Sat; noon-10.30pm Sun. **Main courses** £6.45-£8.95. **Set lunch** £5.95 3 courses, £7.95 4 courses. **Set dinner** £8.95 3 courses, £11.95 4 courses, £22.95 5 courses incl house wine or beer. **Credit** MC, V.
Although it's further from Angel than many Islington diners are prepared to travel, this little Kurdish restaurant shouldn't be missed. It was one of the first to station a woman in the window making qatme (Kurdish flatbread stuffed with cheese or spinach); this has since become quite a fashion in Hackney. The whole atmosphere of the place is pleasingly unpretentious – closer to what you expect in Green Lanes or Dalston than Upper Street. The deep-orange walls are decorated with real farm implements; the peasant feel is emphasised with heavy wooden furniture. Mücver fritters showed the reliable quality of the cooking, neither heavy nor oily, as did arnavut ciğeri (delicately sautéed lamb's liver with red pepper). These were followed by an outstanding iskender, made with lamb şiş rather than the more common döner. Grilled bıldırcın (quail) were exceptionally tender and meaty. A selection of vegetarian dishes is also available. A single complimentary baklava, served with ice-cream, appeared for dessert. Gem should attract a larger crowd, though we're not complaining; those of us who appreciate it can easily get a table.
Babies and children admitted: high chairs. Booking advisable weekends. Separate room for parties, seats 100. Takeaway service. Vegetarian menu. **Map 5 O1.**

★ Pasha

301 Upper Street, N1 2TU (7226 1454/www. thepasharestaurant.co.uk). Angel tube/Highbury & Islington tube/rail. **Meals served** 11am-11.30pm Mon-Sat; 11am-11pm Sun. **Main courses** £7.95-£13.95. **Set meal** £16.95 2 courses, £19.95 3 courses. **Credit** AmEx, MC, V.
A refit has given Pasha a slight change of emphasis. The look is modern rather than traditional, with muted pale-khaki colouring and a mirror at the back to increase the sense of space. The front still opens out on to the street. The menu has now been extended to include separate breakfast and lunch menus; on Sunday, roast beef with yorkshire pudding is offered alongside the traditional Turkish fare. Mixed meze were very fresh, with houmous and a mackerel-like fish particularly notable. Main courses didn't disappoint either; outstanding choices included lamb stew, which boasted chunks of melt-in-the-mouth meat, and duck kapama (stewed in a covered pot), served with sweet pomegranate sauce, potato and cabbage. Service was attentive, even if the staff were, as ever, slightly manic. Though it's made a few changes, Pasha's position as Islington's top Turkish restaurant is not under threat. The food is still excellent, and the more adventurous flourishes on the new menu are more than welcome.
Babies and children admitted. Booking advisable weekends. Restaurant available for hire. Separate room for parties, seats 18. Tables outdoors (3, pavement). Takeaway service. **Map 5 O1.**

Sedir

4 Theberton Street, N1 0QX (7226 5489). Angel tube/Highbury & Islington tube/rail. **Meals served** 11.30am-11.30pm Mon-Thur, Sun; 11.30am-midnight Fri, Sat. **Main courses** £6.95-£11.95. **Set lunch** (11.30am-5.30pm) £6.95-£7.95 2 courses. **Set meal** £16.50 per person (minimum 2) 3 courses. **Credit** AmEx, JCB, MC, V.
There are two dining rooms, on different floors, at Sedir, and in fine weather a few tables are placed outside on the quiet street. The interior is often noisier, on account of the wooden floors and lots of clinking glass. Staff were friendly on our recent visit and, if anything, a little over-attentive. A small plate of olives and carrot was brought for nibbling while we awaited our order. For starters, triangular börek were pleasant, though the cheese was a bit too molten. Next, we enjoyed a notably well-flavoured adana kebab, served on bread with rice and salad. Imam bayıldı was marvellously spiced and tasty, even if it wasn't especially attractive, its vegetable stuffing spilling out across the plate. Of late, the menu has moved away from being exclusively Turkish; many dishes are now served with chips or mash, and there are some generic Mediterranean pasta choices. But for dessert, we tried the very Turkish sütlaç rice pudding flavoured with cinnamon, and an authentic Turkish coffee: both were excellent. Standards are being maintained here, but widening the menu has marginally compromised the restaurant's attention to detail.
Babies and children welcome: children's menu; high chairs. Booking essential dinner. Separate room for parties, seats 50. Tables outdoors (4, pavement). Takeaway service. **Map 5 O1.**

Muswell Hill

Bakko

172-174 Muswell Hill Broadway, N10 3SA (8883 1111/www.bakko.co.uk). Highgate tube then 43, 134 bus. **Meals served** 11.30am-10.30pm daily. **Main courses** £8.90-£16.90. **Set lunch** (11.30am-4pm Mon-Fri) £7.90 3 courses. **Set meal** £16.90 per person (minimum 2) 4 courses. **Credit** MC, V.
The glass front at Bakko opens up on to noisy Muswell Hill Broadway in warm weather. Of late, new 'Mediterranean' dishes have appeared on the clearly explained menu, and most customers now seem to be older, non-Turkish diners. A starter of patlıcan salad was pleasant but bland, lacking the smoky heartiness that characterises this dish at its best – an odd slip for a restaurant that continually announces its peasant origins. Photos of Kurdish peasants at work still adorn the walls, along with Kurdish artefacts ('bakko' is a Kurdish term for 'village elder'). A main course of incik came with a good chunk of lamb knuckle, the meat almost falling off the bone. The accompanying vegetables (carrots, peppers and new potatoes) were beautifully cooked too. Unfortunately the rice, served with traditional pasta strands, was slightly overdone. The pudding menu features standard Turkish desserts and such European favourites as gateaux. Staff were helpful and attentive. Bakko remains popular and worth visiting, but appears to have lost its culinary direction somewhat.
Babies and children welcome: high chairs. Booking essential weekends. Vegetarian menu.

North West

Belsize Park

★ Zara

11 South End Road, NW3 2PT (7794 5498). Belsize Park tube/Hampstead Heath rail. **Meals served** noon-11.30pm daily. **Main courses** £7.50-£12. **Credit** MC, V.
With its relaxed atmosphere, Zara is an ideal place to stop after a walk on Hampstead Heath. In summer the glass front opens on to the wide pavement, and customers sometimes play board games on outside tables. Inside, cushioned benches run along the walls, and a pastel colour scheme is complemented by colourful lanterns. There's nothing relaxed about Zara's standards, though. The menu isn't extensive, but the quality is high. A starter of mixed hot and cold meze included sigara börek, falafel, halloumi, cacik, kısır and houmous: each distinct and flavoursome. Crisply toasted and plentiful pide bread was supplied. To follow, a Zara special, elsewhere known as lokma kebab, was tremendous: tender morsels of grilled lamb rolled around a skewer, while Islim kebab (lamb wrapped in aubergine) brought out the flavours of both ingredients. For dessert, there are rich Turkish puddings such as the glorious armut tatlısı (poached pears). With its efficient and cheerful staff, Zara remains deservedly popular.
Babies and children welcome: high chairs. Booking essential weekends. Tables outdoors (4, pavement). Takeaway service. Vegetarian menu. **Map 28 C3.**

Golders Green

Beyoglu

1031 Finchley Road, NW11 7ES (8455 4884). Golders Green tube/82, 160, 260 bus. **Meals served** noon-midnight daily. **Main courses** £6.50-£10. **Set dinner** £12-£13.75 3 courses incl coffee. **Credit** MC, V.
Spacious Beyoglu has always been a good local restaurant, and its cooking has continued to improve. Typical Turkish restaurant fittings, patterned cloths, well-matched red tablecloths and

incense burners define the relaxed ambience. The cooking benefits from attention to fine detail, amply demonstrated by the fava bean salad and light kısır in an exceptional mixed meze. Main dishes of chicken iskender with yoghurt and pide, and inegöl köfte (gently spiced patties of minced lamb) were both excellent and well presented. Again, the little things were remembered: the accompanying salad was unusually fresh, the rice perfectly cooked. The menu also features seafood, stews and vegetarian dishes. Service was friendly and attentive, and Beyoglu remains the best of the Turkish restaurants in Temple Fortune. In fact, it compares favourably with many Turkish venues elsewhere in town.
Babies and children welcome: high chairs. Booking advisable weekends. Tables outdoors (2, pavement). Takeaway service. Vegetarian menu.

Outer London

Richmond, Surrey

Escale NEW

94 Kew Road, Richmond, Surrey TW9 2PQ (8940 0033/www.escale.co.uk). Richmond tube/rail. **Meals served** 11am-10.30pm daily. **Main courses** £8.95-£14.50. **Set meal** £7.50 1 course, £9.50 2 courses, incl soft drink. **Set meze** £11.95-£13.95 per person (minimum 2). **No credit cards.**

Occupying a corner site, with large windows looking out over Kew Road, Escale is a pleasingly relaxed spot. There's a terrace outside on two sides of the restaurant, with just enough room for a single row of tables, surrounded by a low hedge. Inside, framed prints of ancient ruins decorate the pale walls, and diners sit at wooden tables with distinctive, high-backed wooden chairs. It was mostly couples on a recent evening visit. Good olives and excellent pide were brought to our table. Starters of sardines were extremely tasty in their tangy lemon marinade. Mücver courgette fritters were faultless, exceedingly light in texture. A main course of fish güveç was also a winner, with plenty of swordfish and prawns, yet lacking the promised mussels. Izgara köfte was delicately flavoured, and served with bulgur and a green salad, plus cherry tomatoes. The atmosphere was relaxed, although that sometimes meant it was hard to get the staff's attention. Escale is well worth visiting, but could keep a closer eye on the details.
Babies and children admitted. Booking essential weekends. Disabled: toilet. Tables outdoors (20, garden). Takeaway service.

Menu

It's useful to know that in Turkish 'ç' and 'ş' are pronounced 'ch' and 'sh'. So şiş is correct Turkish, shish is English and sis is common on menus. Menu spelling is rarely consistent, so expect wild variations on everything given here. See also the menu boxes in **Middle Eastern** and **North African**.

COOKING EQUIPMENT

Mangal: brazier.
Ocakbaşı: an open grill under an extractor hood. A metal dome is put over the charcoal for making paper-thin bread.

SOUPS

işkembe: finely chopped tripe soup, an infallible hangover cure.
Mercimek çorbar: red lentil soup.
Yayla: yoghurt and rice soup (usually) with a chicken stock base.

MEZE DISHES

Arnavut ciğeri: 'albanian liver' – cubed or sliced lamb's liver, fried then baked.
Barbunya: spicy kidney bean stew.
Börek or **böreği**: fried or baked filo pastry parcels with a savoury filling, usually cheese, spinach or meat. Commonest are **muska** or **peynirli** (cheese) and **sigara** ('cigarette', so long and thin).
Cacik: diced cucumber with garlic in yoghurt.
Çoban salatası: 'shepherd's' salad of finely diced tomatoes, cucumbers, onions, perhaps green peppers and parsley, sometimes with a little feta cheese.
Dolma: stuffed vegetables (usually with rice and pine kernels).
Enginar: artichokes, usually with vegetables in olive oil.
Haydari: yoghurt, infused with garlic and mixed with finely chopped mint leaves.
Hellim: Cypriot halloumi cheese.
Houmous: creamy paste of chickpeas, crushed sesame seeds, oil, garlic and lemon juice.
Houmous kavurma: houmous topped with strips of lamb and pine nuts.
Imam bayıldı: literally 'the imam fainted'; aubergine stuffed with onions, tomatoes and garlic in olive oil.
Ispanak: spinach.
Kalamar: fried squid.
Karides: prawns.
Kısır: usually a mix of chopped parsley, tomatoes, onions, crushed wheat, olive oil and lemon juice.
Kizartma: lightly fried vegetables.
Köy ekmeği: literally 'village bread'; another term for saç (qv).
Lahmacun: 'pizza' of minced lamb on thin pide (qv).
Midye tava: mussels in batter, in a garlic sauce.
Mücver: courgette and feta fritters.
Patlıcan: aubergine, variously served.
Patlıcan esme: grilled aubergine puréed with garlic and olive oil.
Pide: a term encompassing many varieties of Turkish flatbread. It also refers to Turkish pizzas (heavier and more filling than lahmacun, qv).
Pilaki: usually haricot beans in olive oil, but the name refers to the method of cooking not the content.
Piyaz: white bean salad with onions.
Saç: paper-thin, chewy bread prepared on a metal dome (also called saç) over a charcoal grill.
Sucuk: spicy sausage, usually beef.
Tarama: cod's roe paste.
Tarator: a bread, garlic and walnut mixture; **havuç tarator** adds carrot; **ıspanak tarator** adds spinach.
Yaprak dolması: stuffed vine leaves.
Zeytin: olive.

MAIN COURSES

Alabalık: trout.
Balik: fish.
Güveç: stew, which is traditionally cooked in an earthenware pot.
Hünkar beğendi: cubes of lamb, braised with onions and tomatoes, served on an aubergine and cheese purée.
İçli köfte: balls of cracked bulgar wheat filled with spicy mince.
İncik: knuckle of lamb, slow-roasted in its own juices. Also called kléftico.
Karni yarik: aubergine stuffed with minced lamb and vegetables.
Kléftico: see íncik.
Mitite köfte: chilli meatballs.
Sote: meat (usually), sautéed in tomato, onion and pepper (and sometimes wine).
Uskumru: mackerel.

KEBABS

Usually made with grilled lamb (those labelled **tavuk** or **piliç** are chicken), served with bread or rice and salad. Common varieties include:
Adana: spicy mince.
Beyti: usually spicy mince and garlic, but sometimes best-end fillet.
Bıldırcın: quail.
Böbrek: kidneys.
Çöp şiş: small cubes of lamb.
Döner: slices of marinated lamb (sometimes mince) packed tightly with pieces of fat on a vertical rotisserie.
Halep: usually döner (qv) served over bread with a buttery tomato sauce.
İskender: a combination of döner (qv), tomato sauce, yoghurt and melted butter on bread.
Kaburga: spare ribs.
Kanat: chicken wings.
Köfte: mince mixed with spices, eggs and onions.
Külbastı: char-grilled fillet.
Lokma: 'mouthful' (beware, there's a dessert that has a similar name!) – boned fillet of lamb.
Patlıcan: mince and sliced aubergine.
Pirzola: lamb chops.
Şeftali: seasoned mince, wrapped in caul fat.
Şiş: cubes of marinated lamb.
Uykuluk: sweetbread.
Yoğhurtlu: meat over bread and yoghurt.

DESSERTS

Armut tatlısı: baked pears.
Ayva tatlısı: quince in syrup.
Baklava: filo pastry interleaved with minced pistachio nuts, almonds or walnuts, and covered in sugary syrup.
Kadayıf: cake made from shredded pastry dough, filled with syrup and nuts or cream.
Kazandibi: milk pudding, traditionally with very finely chopped chicken breast.
Kemel pasha: small round cakes soaked in honey.
Keşkül: milk pudding with almonds and coconut, topped with pistachios.
Lokum: turkish delight.
Sütlaç: rice pudding.

DRINKS

Ayran: refreshing drink made with yoghurt.
Çay: tea.
Kahve (aka Turkish coffee): a tiny cup half full of sediment, half full of strong, rich, bitter coffee. Offered without sugar, medium or sweet.
Rakı: a spirit with an aniseed flavour.

Vegetarian

Gone are the days when red-blooded alpha-male chefs refused to stuff a mushroom; changing attitudes towards health and the provenance and welfare of livestock mean that more of us are incorporating vegetarian dishes into our diet, which means wider choice for vegetarians at 'regular' restaurants, but more competition for dedicated vegetarian restaurants with tighter purse strings. Many of London's vegetarian outlets are bargain-priced, daytime-only cafés catering to the lunchtime crowd – such as **Food for Thought**, which has been feeding Covent Garden workers since the 1970s – but plenty are full-blown restaurants serving into the evening, including **Carnevale**, **Blah Blah Blah**, **Eat & Two Veg** and **Manna**. And the long-running **Gate** remains London's most impressive vegetarian specialist. For more restaurants that make a special effort for vegetarians and vegans, look under 'vegetarian food' in the **Subject Index**, starting on p392.

Central

Barbican

Carnevale

135 Whitecross Street, EC1Y 8JL (7250 3452/ www.carnevalerestaurant.co.uk). Barbican tube/ Old Street tube/rail/55 bus. **Lunch served** noon-3.30pm Mon-Fri. **Dinner served** 5.30-10.30pm Mon-Sat. **Main courses** £11.50. **Minimum** (noon-2.30pm Mon-Fri) £5.50. **Set meal** (lunch Mon-Fri, 5.30-7pm Mon-Sat) £13.50 3 courses. **Credit** MC, V.

Fronted by a delicatessen ideally placed for City lunch hours, Carnevale offers inspiring vegetarian sandwiches such as baba ganoush, manchego or halloumi, alongside an array of store-cupboard deli items. The compact restaurant, with skylit extension prettified by hanging flowers, is much quieter in the evenings and attracts young couples and suits from nearby offices. From a broadly Mediterranean menu, a starter of artichokes stuffed with walnuts, lemon and parsley proved a delectable combination of flavours. The waitress was working her second day on our visit and couldn't answer questions about the menu, but was perfectly polite; she helped us warm to the place by bringing a bread basket with fragrantly grassy olive oil for dipping. Main courses seem slightly overpriced at £11.50. Fennel potato cakes sat incongruously on a portion of provençal vegetable casserole, but a wild mushroom risotto with chestnut purée was satisfyingly savoury. The wine list (excepting the dessert wines) is organic and includes Sedlescombe from Sussex. Unusual aperitifs and digestifs (Isle of Skye single malt, Basque pacharán) provide added interest.

Babies and children welcome: high chairs. Booking advisable. Tables outdoors (3, conservatory). Takeaway service. Vegan dishes. **Map 5 P4.**

City

★ The Place Below

St Mary-le-Bow, Cheapside, EC2V 6AU (7329 0789/www.theplacebelow.co.uk). St Paul's tube/Bank tube/DLR. **Breakfast served** 7.30-11am, **lunch served** 11.30am-2.15pm, **snacks served** 2.30-3pm Mon-Fri. **Main courses** £5.25-£7.75. **Unlicensed. Corkage** no charge. **Credit** MC, V.

Located in the cool crypt of St Mary-le-Bow, the Place consists of a canteen-like serving area and a larger, more obviously church-like space. A newspaper-strewn communal table set with a white linen tablecloth is surrounded by individual tables with solid pews for seats. Slightly upmarket versions of vegetarian classics are the order of the day. Quiches are made with crumbly shortcrust and filled with the likes of sweet potato surrounded by rich but not stodgy egginess. A substantial salad of minted new potatoes and asparagus gave us spring on a plate. Some dishes, like a coconut and cauliflower soup, were underseasoned (we spotted several customers shaking salt cellars). A different hot meal (thai green curry, moroccan casserole) is served each day, alongside salads, sandwiches, puddings and a lip-smackingly sweet and sour own-made lemonade. The clientele is largely made up of Cityworkers from nearby offices, plus a few tourists who've had a lucky find after sightseeing around St Paul's. The Place is only open weekdays until early afternoon and makes a lovely retreat from the rat race going on above ground.

Babies and children admitted. Tables outdoors (16, churchyard). Takeaway service. Vegan dishes. **Map 11 P6.**

Covent Garden

★ Food for Thought (100)

31 Neal Street, WC2H 9PR (7836 9072). Covent Garden tube. **Meals served** noon-8.30pm Mon-Sat; noon-5pm Sun. **Main courses**

RESTAURANTS

Mildred's. See p289.

£4.20-£6.90. **Minimum** (noon-3pm, 6-7.30pm) £2.50. **Unlicensed. Corkage** no charge. **No credit cards.**
The customers patiently queuing down the street for a takeaway at peak hours attest to the perennial popularity of this veggie hotspot. The space inside is scarcely less cramped. Heavy wooden tables line the whitewashed brick wall at the back – good for people-watching if you're one of the many lone lunchers. Vegetarian staples are served in rustic bowls from a central counter manned by laid-back yet efficient staff. The Indian masala soup had us hooked with its hearty texture and punchy, addictive spicing. Mains range from that old favourite quiche to seasonal stews or daily changing options like pasticcio: a Greek pasta bake layered with flavoursome béchamel and tons of vegetables (spinach, button mushrooms, sweet cherry tomatoes, chunks of aubergine, courgette roundels and fresh parsley). Many praise the desserts, but our coconut flapjack was cloying, smelled horribly of oil, and had indiscernible coconut. Old-school rainbow hippie trousers can still be spotted at Food for Thought, but this being Covent Garden, you get all types: couples, middle-aged women, and shop workers grabbing lunch. An unpretentious, reliable stalwart.
Babies and children admitted. Bookings not accepted. Takeaway service. Vegan dishes. **Map 18 D3.**

★ World Food Café

First floor, 14 Neal's Yard, WC2H 9DP (7379 0298/www.worldfoodcafe.net). Covent Garden tube. **Meals served** 11.30am-4.30pm Mon-Fri; 11.30am-5pm Sat. **Main courses** £5.95-£8.45. **Minimum** (noon-2pm Mon-Fri; 11.30am-5pm Sat) £6. **Credit** MC, V.
Climb up a flight of stairs from Neal's Yard, and you'll enter this light, airy room overlooking the health food/natural remedy centre of Covent Garden. On a fine day sunshine pours in, highlighting the photographs of idyllic vistas that adorn the walls – mementoes from owners Chris and Carolyn Caldicott's trips around the world. The menu reflects their distant travels and features thali-style platters dotted with West African spiced sweet potato, Indian vegetable masala with coconut chutney, Middle Eastern meze or Mexican refried beans with guacamole. The masala with brown rice was just fine, but included the horror that is undercooked potatoes. Wholesome oat pancakes stuffed with fresh spinach and unspecified cheese were perked up by the sourness of fresh salsa. Most diners sit at a central counter where you can watch food being prepared, but there are a few window tables with chunky, sunshine-coloured plastic chairs. The café exudes good vibes, only slightly mitigated by staff who can be in their own little world. The food might not be ground-breaking, but this is a cheery venue for a leisurely lunch.
Babies and children welcome: children's portions; high chairs. No alcohol allowed. Takeaway service. Vegan dishes. **Map 18 D3.**

Euston

★ Greens & Beans NEW

31 Drummond Street, NW1 2HL (7380 0857/ www.greensandbeans.biz). Euston Square tube/ Euston tube/rail. **Meals served** 9am-3pm Mon-Fri. **Main courses** £4.25-£6.95. **Set lunch** £5.95 buffet. **Credit** AmEx, MC, V.
Opened in 2006, this little place in the veggie enclave of Drummond Street (there are plenty of vegetarian Indian restaurants on the same stretch) does a brisk business in takeaway lunches for nearby office workers and Euston Station employees. At the front of the ground floor is a shop (open until 6pm), with the takeaway counter at the back. The hot and cold buffet is a notch above the norm, featuring such dishes as egg flan with artichoke, roasted butternut squash, rice noodles with tofu, and mixed peppers with feta. You can also get freshly made smoothies with faddy ingredients such as gogi berries and barley grass – which are good but could do with some ice (warm smoothies aren't very appetising). In the basement is a low-ceilinged but bright café serving the likes of vegetarian bangers and mash, sun-dried tomato and spinach pizza, and gluten-free, superfood vegan salads. Just to make sure all bases are covered, there's a decent selection of organic grocery items and bodycare products to buy. Staff are pleasant and unhurried, and the loyalty card is handy if you're local.
Babies and children admitted. Separate room for parties, seats 22. Tables outdoors (1, terrace). Takeaway service. Vegan dishes. **Map 3 J3.**

Marylebone

Eat & Two Veg

50 Marylebone High Street, W1U 5HN (7258 8595/www.eatandtwoveg.com). Baker Street tube. **Meals served** 9am-11pm Mon-Sat; 10am-10pm Sun. **Main courses** £8-£10.25. **Credit** AmEx, MC, V.
In a salubrious location on Marylebone High Street, this diner-like establishment is a slick operation populated by equally well-turned-out customers. The design may be all exposed brick and steel pipes, but it's done in a decidedly upmarket way. The wood is polished, the scarlet banquettes complemented by turquoise table-tops. Artfully angled mirrors line the walls, and a skylight lifts the whole room. A central row of tables-for-two is a little closely packed for complete comfort, but booths offer more privacy. The shopfront bar is useful for awaiting your date, and the open kitchen lends a sense of action to the room. To start, broccoli soup was light and came with excellent crusty bread. The rest of the menu is heavy on meat substitutes. The burgers are everything you'd hope for in a faux-meat meal: savoury, flavoursome and not a bean in sight. A marinated artichoke salad came with an intensely coloured and satisfying boiled egg. Staff were over-eager, but we prefer that to indifferent any day. A stylish choice for a retro-chic dinner.
Babies and children welcome: high chairs; nappy-changing facilities. Booking advisable. Disabled: toilet. Tables outdoors (3, pavement). Takeaway service. Vegan dishes. **Map 3 G4.**

Soho

★ Beatroot

92 Berwick Street, W1F 0QD (7437 8591). Oxford Circus, Piccadilly Circus or Tottenham Court Road tube. **Meals served** 9.15am-9pm Mon-Sat. **Main courses** £3.70-£5.70. **No credit cards.**
The clamorous street market outside Beatroot sets the tone for this bustling, on-the-go lunch spot. A constant stream of Soho's stylish and stylishly dishevelled lines up for takeaways (Beatroot's stock in trade), but there's also a handful of tables in nursery-bright colours. Choose a container size (small, medium or large, priced £3.70-£5.70), and the staff of international hipsters will cram it full of healthy fast food. Hot choices include lentil shepherd's pie topped with creamy mash; chunky moussaka; vegan sausage rolls; and stir-fry with brown rice. These can be a little bland, but the salads are much better: try citrus-dressed carrot batons with pumpkin seeds; beansprouts jazzed up with tahini vinaigrette; or beetroot with toasted sesame seeds. Labels on the counter would be helpful, so that staff don't have to repeat the food descriptions to each customer. Vegan desserts include an earnestly hippyish hemp-seed flapjack, and there's even a crop of wheatgrass behind the till (though, thankfully, the smoothie list features plenty of virtuous recipes that don't include it).
Babies and children admitted. No alcohol allowed. Tables outdoors (4, pavement). Takeaway service. Vegan dishes. **Map 17 B3.**

Mildred's

45 Lexington Street, W1F 9AN (7494 1634/ www.mildreds.co.uk). Oxford Circus or Piccadilly Circus tube. **Meals served** noon-11pm Mon-Sat. **Main courses** £6-£7.95. **No credit cards.**
Choosing Mildred's means you won't be wanting for company – the place is usually overflowing. You can't book, but staff do a good business keeping customers in drinks at the bar. The effervescent atmosphere and dense table spacing suggest you wouldn't want to come here for an intimate rendezvous, but as a venue for a boisterous group dinner it fits the bill. Vivid photos adorn the walls around a long narrow space, brightened by a central skylight. The menu incorporates ingredients and cooking styles from around the world; pear and blue cheese salad, artichoke crostini, and gyoza with mirin all feature as starters. Our red pepper and sweetcorn burrito was lifted by the addition of smoked cheddar, but we were less taken with a chickpea tagine overpowered by roasted fennel. The flatbread was

SHELF LIFE

As the consumer appetite for organic and ethically produced groceries booms, well-stocked wholefood shops are springing up thick and fast across the capital. The biggest news in 2007 was the opening of the UK's first branch of US giant Whole Foods Market.

Earth Natural Foods

200 Kentish Town Road, NW5 2AE (7482 2211/www.earthnatural foods.co.uk). Kentish Town tube. **Open** 9am-7pm Mon-Sat.
Fruit and vegetables, fresh bread, cheese, and all kinds of store-cupboard supplies.

Farm W5

19 The Green, W5 5DA (8566 1965/ www.farmw5.com). Ealing Broadway tube/rail. **Open** 8am-7.30pm Mon-Fri; 10am-7.30pm Sat; 10am-6pm Sun.
This shop buys much of its meat, fish, dairy products, fresh fruit and veg, and other goods direct from small UK suppliers. There's also cakes, cereals, biscuits, coffees, teas, juice, ice-cream…

Natural Kitchen

77-78 Marylebone High Street, W1U 5JX (7486 8065/www.the naturalkitchen.com). Baker Street tube. **Open** 8am-8pm Mon-Fri; 8am-6pm Sat; 11am-5pm Sun.
A mini supermarket stocking artisan-produced, locally sourced, ethical foods, including a wide range of fruit and vegetables, meat, fish and packaged goods.

Nuts About Life

44 Hampstead High Street, NW3 1QG (7431 6866/www.nutsaboutlife.com). Hampstead tube. **Open** 10am-7pm Mon-Sat; 11am-5pm Sun.
Nuts in all shapes and forms are the speciality at this new mini chain, along with dried fruits, preserves, oils, pastries, teas and biscuits. There are also branches in Chiswick and Kensington.

Whole Foods Market

63-97 Kensington High Street, W8 5SE (7368 4500/www.wholefoods market.com). Kensington High Street tube. **Open** 8am-10pm Mon-Sat; noon-6pm Sun.
It's big, it's bold and now it's over here – in the former Barkers building. Imagine a cross between Harrods Food Hall and the biggest Waitrose you can imagine.

great, though, especially when dipped in a side of chargrilled chilli aubergine. This being the Carnaby Street side of Soho, customers are mostly bright young things, marking Mildred's out as somewhere to go before a night on the tiles.
Babies and children admitted. Bookings not accepted. Separate room for parties, seats 24. Tables outdoors (2, pavement). Takeaway service. Vegan dishes. **Map 17 A4**.

West

Hammersmith

★ The Gate

51 Queen Caroline Street, W6 9QL (8748 6932/ www.thegate.tv). Hammersmith tube. **Lunch served** noon-2.45pm Mon-Fri. **Dinner served** 6-10.45pm Mon-Sat. **Main courses** £8.50-£13.50. **Credit** AmEx, MC, V.
For a little while, London's grande dame of quality vegetarian cuisine lost its balance, but we're pleased to report the Gate is back to its best. The elevated, airy attic above a picturesque courtyard is a joy in daylight, and the atmosphere transforms to cosiness when staff come round with gem-coloured candles for each table. All our food was brimming with interesting textures, tastes and touches. A courgette flower stuffed with sweet potato and pine nuts had been coated in a fragile, crispy beer batter and was complemented by a silky lemon aïoli. Sweet, crunchy, thai salad was a riot of green mango, paw-paw, mouli, baby corn and crushed peanuts. Root vegetable rotolo featured a variety of seasonal veg, each retaining its distinctiveness. The show-stealer, however, was an artfully presented aubergine balanced vertically and stuffed with okra soldiers; it came with a guacamole and chipotle salsa that didn't scrimp on the heat or garlic. To follow, hazelnut crème brûlée was too cloying, and more praline than crème. Staff are attentive. The smart-casual customers, from silver foxes to young sophisticates, filled the Gate to near capacity – not bad for a Monday night.
Babies and children welcome: high chairs. Booking essential. Tables outdoors (15, courtyard). Vegan dishes. **Map 20 B4**.

Shepherd's Bush

Blah Blah Blah

78 Goldhawk Road, W12 8HA (8746 1337/ www.gonumber.com/2524). Goldhawk Road tube/94 bus. **Lunch served** 12.30-2.30pm, **dinner served** 6.30-10.30pm Mon-Sat. **Main courses** £9.95. **Unlicensed. Corkage** £1.45 per person. **No credit cards**.
It may not have the world's best location, but this eccentrically named restaurant turns out some of the best food of its kind. The interior is furnished with a mishmash of high-backed, 1980s power-dining chairs, battered gold backrests, sparkly disco balls, dainty mirrors and ecclesiastical-design finds – all set against deep burgundy walls. A lone waitress coped cheerfully and competently with a full midweek house consisting mostly of groups of women out for a chatty evening. Halloumi fried in breadcrumbs with red pepper and pesto started our meal nicely, helped by luscious fresh mango salsa. Asparagus, perched atop a puff pastry tart with béarnaise sauce, was overcooked, but we soon forgot this when the mains arrived (remarkably quickly). An impressively balanced sweetcorn tostada stack with black beans and jalapeño cream gave an original and thoroughly enjoyable twist to a Mexican dish often found on vegetarian menus. Fantastic own-made houmous and a moreish salad of loubia (Middle Eastern green beans) came with an artfully layered filo pie. The menu changes every few weeks, so there's always something new to try at this great neighbourhood restaurant.
Babies and children admitted. Booking advisable. Separate room for parties, seats 35. Takeaway service. Vegan dishes. **Map 20 B2**.

West Kensington

222 Veggie Vegan

222 North End Road, W14 9NU (7381 2322/ www.222veggievegan.com). West Kensington tube/ 28, 391 bus. **Lunch served** noon-3.30pm, **dinner served** 5.30-10.30pm daily. **Main courses** £7.50-£10.50. **Set buffet** (lunch) £5.95. **Credit** MC, V.
The idea of a vegan restaurant may induce a certain wariness, especially if the establishment happens to occupy a rather dreary stretch of road like this. Run by chef Ben Asamani, 222 is also big on avoiding refined carbohydrates. This results in dishes that verge towards stodginess: witness the seitan (wheat gluten) stroganoff in cashew cream served with brown rice; and the heavy wholemeal pasta with unremarkable mushrooms in a similar sauce that a touch of lime failed to leaven. We can see how the proliferation of creaminess would be a draw for those avoiding dairy products, and clearly it was – despite the pedestrian decor and tightly spaced tables, the place was nearly full on the weekend of our visit. The menu also contains a Middle Eastern/Afro-Caribbean platter (offering the chance to sample baked plantain, okra and falafel), and for afters, tofu cheesecake and vegan ice-cream. The latter emphasise why, while not thrilling for lacto-ovo vegetarians, 222 is probably a godsend for vegans. At lunchtime a buffet is laid out, with the option to eat in or take away.
Babies and children welcome: high chairs. Booking advisable. Takeaway service. Vegan dishes. **Map 13 A12**.

East

Bethnal Green

★ Wild Cherry

241-245 Globe Road, E2 0JD (8980 6678). Bethnal Green tube/8 bus. **Meals served** 10.30am-7pm Tue-Fri; 10.30am-4.30pm Sat.

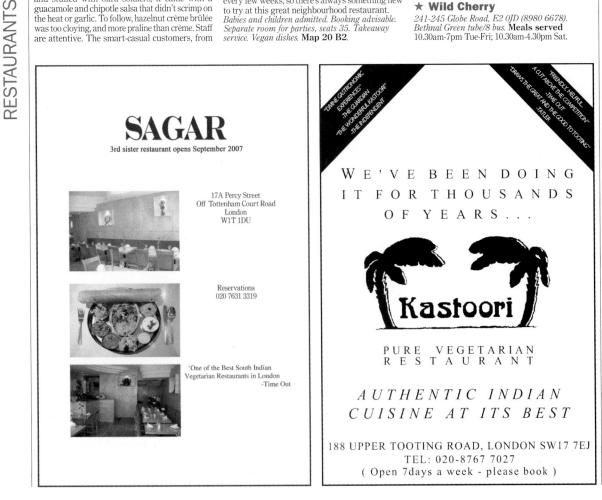

Main courses £3.25-£5.95. **Unlicensed. Corkage** £1. **Credit** MC, V.
This laid-back café is deservedly packed on Saturdays, when all-day breakfasts that are worth dragging yourself out of a warm bed are dished up to the Bethnal Green bourgeoisie. Couples recover from the night before, over the papers; families with young rugrats liven up the atmosphere; and the occasional sandal-wearer keeps the vegetarian stereotype alive. The decor features changing contemporary art, while there's a cute flower-sprinkled courtyard for the sunnier months. The star of a veggie take on the full english were some crushed, intensely flavoured tomatoes. The sausage was so meaty it made us do a double-take, but the eggs were a little so-what (no fear, tabasco sauce is at hand for peppering). If you're hankering after a sugar rush, plump for the US-style pancakes drenched in maple syrup; a cinnamon-infused fruit salad of dates, apricots and figs added a semblance of virtue to our indulgent stack, which was magnificently topped with scoops of vanilla-flecked mascarpone. Portions are vast, and the Buddhist staff are serenely smiley – as you will be once you've imbibed the goodness of Wild Cherry.
Babies and children welcome: high chairs. Tables outdoors (9, garden). Takeaway service. Vegan dishes.

North

Camden Town & Chalk Farm

Manna

4 Erskine Road, NW3 3AJ (7722 8028/ www.manna-veg.com). Chalk Farm tube/31, 168 bus. **Brunch served** 12.30-3pm Sun. **Dinner served** 6.30-11pm daily. **Main courses** £9.50-£13.25. **Credit** MC, V.
Taking its cue from the quiet, elegant Primrose Hill location, Manna emits an easy composure and attracts a similarly relaxed clientele. The atmosphere is set by low lighting and light wood. We've had fabulous meals here in the past, but were disappointed on our latest foray. A sushi starter was let down by gummy rice and chewy seaweed. Moroccan briouat triangles were wrapped in good filo, but the filling of kasha (roasted buckwheat) and tempeh (similar to beancurd) was offputtingly bitter. The least successful dishes were the ones trying to emulate meaty textures: for instance, a smoky tofu pâté accompanying an aubergine main course that went largely uneaten. The well-executed tempura batter and highly savoury white miso sauce were better. Chef Matthew Kay is planning a Manna cookbook, so perhaps these blips on the regularly changing menu are the result of experimentation. Certain details, such as a deeply luscious red wine reduction and the intricate presentation of dishes, prove there is real skill at work. Safer dishes to try include tortillas and salads, which come piled high.
Babies and children welcome: children's portions; high chairs. Booking essential. Tables outdoors (2, pavement; 2, conservatory). Takeaway service. Vegan dishes. **Map 27 A1.**

Outer London

Kingston, Surrey

Riverside Vegetaria

64 High Street, Kingston upon Thames, Surrey KT1 1HN (8546 0609/www.rsvegplus.com). Kingston or Surbiton rail. **Meals served** noon-11pm Mon-Sat; noon-10.30pm Sun. **Main courses** £6.95-£8.50. **Credit** MC, V.
The location by the Thames in Kingston is idyllic. In the warmer months you can sit on the terrace overlooking the river as swans glide past, or take a window seat to watch the world stroll by this unaffectedly cosy restaurant. The globetrotting menu runs to two dozen main dishes, and there's an equal number on a blackboard. Alongside the vegetarian dishes, vegan, gluten-free and wheat-free options are available, with some unusual choices like string-hopper biriani (made with rice noodles); red lentil and avocado kedgeree, spiced with cinnamon and cardamom; and tofu teriyaki. Mushroom, sage and olive pâté with crudités was an appetising starter; gazpacho, however, lacked pep and character. Tofu tandoori with potato curry had a slightly mushy texture, but the confident spicing was a definite plus. Our verdict on the mixed bean, sweet potato and coconut stew: wholesome, hearty and hunger-defeating. Staff are competent and unobtrusive, the clientele a mix of suburban ladies who lunch and weary shoppers. We left in a bit of a carb coma, but perhaps it was the calming effect of the waterside.
Babies and children welcome: children's portions; high chairs. Book weekends. Separate room for parties, seats 25. Tables outdoors (7, riverside terrace). Takeaway service. Vegan dishes.

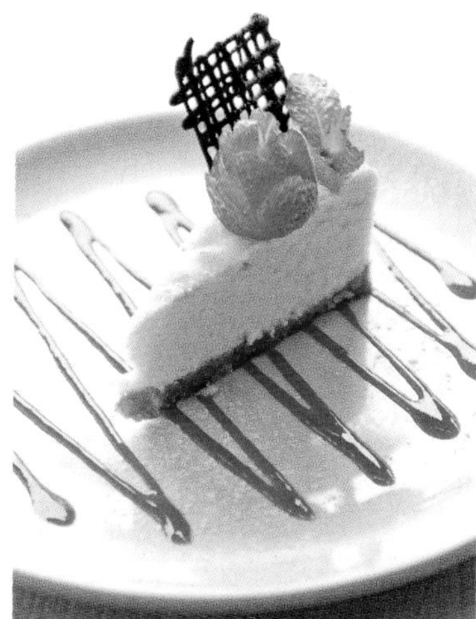

Blah Blah Blah

RESTAURANTS

Vietnamese

Most of London's Vietnamese community is based in Hackney (around 4,000 people) and, over the past decade or so, a culinary enclave has grown up in this district. We first listed one of the pioneers, **Viet Hoa**, in our 1996 guide. Today, the main concentration of budget restaurants is at the southern end of Kingsland Road, clustering around Viet Hoa. Yet despite the rising number of venues, finding authentic Vietnamese food is still tricky: you often have to sift through scores of Chinese-influenced dishes before discovering truly Vietnamese recipes. It is the prolific use of fresh, aromatic herbs that differentiates the cuisine from Chinese food and oriental cooking in general, making a Vietnamese meal a nuanced, multifaceted culinary experience. In the UK, fresh Vietnamese herbs are rare and expensive, so far fewer are used. Herbs such as rau ram ('Vietnamese coriander'), ngo om ('rice paddy herb'), ngo gai ('sawleaf') and kinh zoi ('green perilla leaves') are still so rare that even the English translations are either misleading or meaningless. Yet some restaurants do make the effort to use the correct ingredients. **Tre Viet** is one of the best, offering excellent and authentic dishes that attract many Vietnamese locals. Also notable are **Song Que** and **Tay Do Café**, which not only manage to get hold of many of the fresh herbs, but also offer specialities from all three culinary regions of Vietnam (north, south and central).

Central

Clerkenwell & Farringdon

★ Pho

86 St John Street, EC1M 4EH (7253 7624/ www.phocafe.co.uk). Barbican tube/Farringdon tube/rail. **Lunch served** noon-3pm, **dinner served** 6-10pm Mon-Fri. **Main courses** £5.95-£7.95. **Credit** MC, V.

Unlike the many other Vietnamese restaurants in town, this chic little café is run by English owners, who, after a culinary excursion to Vietnam, felt the need to import 'Vietnam in a bowl' to the Big Smoke. We had to try the restaurant's trademark dish, pho bo dac biet (literally 'special beef noodle pho'). Though the own-made beef balls were so delicate they almost disintegrated in the mouth, the flavour was rather unexciting and had lost the characteristic rich anise and cinnamon flavours on the journey across the continents. The Vietnamese-style baguette, a pâté- and mayonnaise-filled French import from colonial times (made Vietnamese by the use of coriander, pickled carrots and kohlrabi, slices of chilli and Vietnamese sausage), had also undergone an English transformation; something resembling a chicken beansprout stir-fry was spread across the neatly presented baguette. Goi tom salad, though promising in description, was a big bowl of lettuce with a few succulent prawns and fewer strips of papaya, drenched in what tasted like bland nuoc cham. Altogether a rather tame version of Vietnam.

Babies and children admitted. Bookings not accepted. Takeaway service. **Map 5 O4.**

King's Cross

★ Pho @ King's Cross NEW

126 King's Cross Road, WC1X 9DS (7833 9088/www.eatpho.co.uk). King's Cross tube/rail. **Lunch served** noon-3pm Mon-Sat; 12.30-3pm Sun. **Dinner served** 5.30-11.30pm Mon-Sat; 5-11pm Sun. **Main courses** £5-£6. **Set lunch** £4.50. **Set dinner** £9 per person (minimum 2). **Credit** MC, V.

No relation to the Pho in Clerkenwell (*see above*), this newcomer is a budget caff that hedges its bets by offering both Chinese and Vietnamese dishes. We tried the pho soup with beef tendon, tripe and beef balls. The stock was on the watery side, with no discernible spice aromas, and the tripe was bland. Banh cuon was filled with minced beef; it was a decent, slithery version of this rice-pasta 'texture food'. But our final dish was quite disappointing: a bun (salad of vermicelli rice noodles) topped with grilled pork that was slightly burnt. Some fresh and verdant Vietnamese herbs could have made up for this slip, but instead a meagre and slightly droopy selection accompanied the dish. Pho is a handy place to pop into if you fancy eating something a bit different near King's Cross; but if you're seeking Vietnamese culinary finesse, you'll need to venture further.

Babies and children admitted. Takeaway service; delivery service (over £8 within 2-mile radius). **Map 4 M3.**

West

Hammersmith

Saigon Saigon

313-317 King Street, W6 9NH (0870 220 1398/ www.saigon-saigon.co.uk). Ravenscourt Park or Stamford Brook tube.
Bar **Open/snacks served** 6pm-midnight Fri, Sat.
Restaurant **Lunch served** noon-3pm Tue-Sun. **Dinner served** 6-11pm Mon-Thur, Sun; 6-11.30pm Fri, Sat. **Main courses** £5.50-£12.95.
Both **Credit** MC, V.

Evocative of old Indochina, Saigon Saigon has a nostalgic look produced by furnishings of dark wooden furniture, bamboo screens and carved wooden artworks. The menu is similarly traditional, with specialities ranging from fragrant pho soup, through sour hotpot lau, to lean little frogs' legs. Goi bo tai chanh (thinly sliced raw beef) came saturated in a lime-spiked sweet sauce; combined with fresh coriander, crunchy slivers of celery and peppers, and sprinkles of peanuts, it made for a divine mishmash of textures. We also relished some joyfully tender little morsels of bo nuong la lot: bite-sized beef wrapped in la lot (a relative of betel leaf). Bo xao xa ot (beef stir-fried with chopped lemongrass and onions) was a chewy treat, if a bit sweet by Vietnamese standards. The highlight was steamed sea bass chung tuong, covered in an assembly of tomato chunks, glass noodles, black beans, wood-ear mushroom, dried lily flower and tiny pickled onions – again, a touch too sweet, though the combination of authentic ingredients made up for it. Prices are high, but Saigon Saigon delivers great food in classy surroundings.

Babies and children welcome: high chairs. Bar available for hire. Booking advisable. Tables outdoors (4, pavement). **Map 20 A4.**

East

Shoreditch

Au Lac

104 Kingsland Road, E2 8DP (7033 0588). Old Street tube/rail/26, 48, 55, 67, 149, 242, 243 bus. **Lunch served** noon-3pm Mon-Fri. **Dinner served** 5.30-11pm Mon-Thur; 5.30pm-midnight Fri. **Meals served** noon-midnight Sat; noon-11pm Sun. **Main courses** £4.50-£8.50. **Set dinner** £12-£15.50 per person (minimum 2). **Credit** MC, V.

Dimmed lighting and dark wooden furniture give Au Lac a more relaxing atmosphere than other restaurants in this frantic stretch of Kingsland Road. The menu contains one major highlight, the seldom-seen 'fire pot' – a Vietnamese hotpot where diners can see their little pieces of squid and prawns boiling in the sweet and sour stock. Apart from this dish, the food we tried was not particularly authentic. Canh chua dau hu (sweet and sour tamarind soup with tofu) was a little too tame by Vietnamese standards, and could have been improved with more dill, tamarind and vegetables. Bun hue dac biet, translated as 'special noodle soup from Hue', wasn't as special as it claimed to be. The broth tasted no better than a stock cube, yet the various cuts of beef – flank, beef balls and rare-sliced steak – partially made up for it. The best dish was stewed goat in hotpot; a sweet and salty dish made with a dark and thick soy sauce, it contained lots of coriander and tender chunks of goat meat. All in all, though, the food here is less fancy than the decor.

Babies and children welcome: high chairs. Booking advisable weekends. Takeaway service. **Map 6 R3.**

★ Hanoi Café

98 Kingsland Road, E2 8DP (7729 5610/ www.hanoicafe.co.uk). Old Street tube/rail/26, 48, 55, 67, 149, 242, 243 bus. **Meals served** noon-11.30pm daily. **Main courses** £3.50-£6.90. **Set lunch** £3.80. **Credit** (over £10) AmEx, MC, V.

A cosy, understated little place, Hanoi Café has its white walls decorated with black and white photographs of Vietnam. According to the menu, the food offers the visual excitement of the Japanese, the quick cooking techniques of the Chinese, the spiciness of the Thai and the complex seasonings of the French. Starters lived up to the promise. Nom ga xe phay (shredded chicken salad) was a tangy, hot, sweet and sour mix of cabbage, carrots, and nuts; mint and coriander gave it the nuances typical of Vietnamese cookery. A side dish of cha nem thit (triangular-shaped deep-fried imperial spring rolls) was similarly scrumptious, and so hot that we hastily downed our Vietnamese iced coffees (made with condensed milk and strong black coffee) after only a few bites. The main dish, com vit quay (roast duck with steamed rice), was disappointing. Drenched in something resembling

Huong-Viet. See p295.

hoi sin sauce, the red lacquered skin had lost its crispness and no longer resembled anything from Vietnamese cuisine.
Babies and children welcome: high chair. Restaurant available for hire. Takeaway service. **Map 6 R3**.

★ ★ Song Que (100)

134 Kingsland Road, E2 8DY (7613 3222). Old Street tube/rail/26, 48, 55, 67, 149, 242, 243 bus. **Lunch served** noon-3pm, **dinner served** 5.30-11pm Mon-Sat. **Meals served** noon-11pm Sun. **Main courses** £4.70-£7.10. **Credit** MC, V.
Hailed by critics and always crammed with hungry Hoxtonites, Song Que still sits on the culinary throne of Kingsland Road's Little Vietnam. Spartan decor and brusque waiters are certainly not the reason for this popularity; it's the wonderfully mastered northern and southern Vietnamese specialities. Don't order willy-nilly though: quite a few Chinese dishes lurk amid those 170 listed on the menu; some of the stir-fries, clothed in thick sauces, are nothing like the light meat and veg stir-fries you find in Vietnam. So here are a few recommendations. Bo tai chanh, a Vietnamese equivalent to the Italian raw beef carpaccio, is a light appetiser that combines a variety of textures. Cua lot ('peeled crab'), a deep-fried salty delight, has chillies spicing up the little shellfish. The massive king prawns (tom sot me), still in their crunchy shells, are served in a bright orange sauce that, though a little sweet, has a distinct tamarind taste authentic to Vietnamese cuisine. Rightly beloved of its many fans, Song Que is one of London's best Vietnamese restaurants.
Babies and children welcome: high chairs. Booking advisable. Takeaway service. **Map 6 R3**.

★ ★ Tay Do Café

65 Kingsland Road, E2 8AG (7729 7223). Old Street tube/rail/26, 48, 55, 67, 149, 242, 243 bus. **Lunch served** 11.30am-3pm, **dinner served** 5-11.30pm daily. **Main courses** £4-£8.50. **Set lunch** £3.30. **Unlicensed. Corkage** £1. **Credit** (over £10) AmEx, MC, V.
Tiny Tay Do Café may not be the most comfortable place to grab some Vietnamese food, as it's often so packed you'll have to share tables; young Hoxton folk crowd into this canteen-like place almost every evening of the week. The popularity is well earned, as the kitchen produces an extensive variety of Vietnamese dishes, with specialities from all regions, plus a couple of ice-cold bean and jelly pudding desserts. Bo bia summer rolls (a southern Vietnamese street snack filled with fried shredded radish, carrots and dried shrimp) was a much lighter variation of the more common rice paper rolls; the combination of sweet crunchy vegetables with the salty shrimp was sublime. Mekong fish braised in caramel sauce came still sizzling in a clay pot; it contained three round chunks of tender catfish soaked in delicately sweet, thick sauce. If you ask for chao tom (prawn paste on sugar cane sticks) to be served with rice paper, the prawn can be taken off the sugar cane and put into DIY summer rolls with fresh coriander, thin rice noodles and nuoc cham – just the way families do in Vietnam.
Babies and children admitted. Takeaway service. **Map 6 R3**.
For branch (Tay Do Restaurant) see index.

★ Thang Loi NEW

122 Kingsland Road, E2 8DP (7729 3074). Old Street tube/rail/26, 48, 55, 67, 149, 242, 243 bus. **Meals served** noon-11pm Mon-Fri, Sun; noon-midnight Sat. **Main courses** £4-£7. **Unlicensed. Corkage** no charge. **Credit** MC, V.
Thang Loi is London's first specialist in northern Vietnamese cuisine, centred on Hanoi. One of that city's best-loved dishes is cha ca, and you'll find a credible version here; the chunks of fish are served sizzling-hot in a cast-iron dish, soaking up the turmeric colour, the flavours still delicate yet the pieces made slithery by the oil. Bun cha is another classic dish, originating from the Bun Cha Dac Kim restaurant in Hanoi's Old Quarter. It's a big bowl of cold vermicelli served with a bowl of char-grilled pork patties suspended in a broth that has a perfect balance of flavours: fish sauce, lime juice, sugar, black pepper. The traditional accompaniment is hanoi spring rolls – fat spring rolls cut into sections. These are just a few of the northern dishes from a menu listing scores, including mekong catfish cooked in a clay pot (tasty, but very bony), shredded kohlrabi salad, sizzling eel dishes, flash-fried goat, rabbit in wine, stir-fried frog with betel leaves. The execution might not always be up to Hanoi standards, but at least Thang Loi makes the effort to produce something different.
Babies and children welcome: high chairs. Restaurant available for hire. Takeaway service. **Map 6 R3**.

Viet Grill NEW

53 Kingsland Road, E2 8DP (7739 6686/ www.vietnamesekitchen.co.uk). Old Street tube/ rail/26, 48, 55, 67, 149, 242, 243 bus. **Lunch served** noon-3pm, **dinner served** 5.30-11.30pm daily. **Main courses** £5.50-£7. **Set dinner** £15-£20. **Credit** MC, V.
This more recent branch of the popular Cay Tre (around the corner on Old Street) does a busy trade with non-Vietnamese diners. Its accessible name and clean-cut interior help, as do the poetic food descriptions on the English menu ('gently simmered' duck, 'lacquered' pork). The restaurant claims to serve authentic cuisine, but our meal didn't live up to the promise. Braised citronella prawn curry was unlike anything we'd seen in Vietnamese cookery, the shellfish arriving with finely diced peppers and lemon slices in an oily orange-coloured curry sauce (of passable flavour). The 'fragrant' piper la lot (the la lot leaf, a relative of betel, wrapped around deep-fried minced beef) had its characteristic aroma almost entirely overwhelmed by that of cooking oil, and the beef

Thang Loi

was chewy. Mussel soup was an improvement. It tasted of sour tamarind and the citrous flavour of rau ram ('Vietnamese coriander', sprinkled on top of the dish), which worked well with the earthy flavour of the mussels. In all, though, Viet Grill merely skims the surface of Vietnamese cuisine.
Babies and children welcome: high chairs. Booking advisable weekends. Takeaway service. **Map 6 R3.**
For branch (Cay Tre) see index.

★ Viet Hoa

70-72 Kingsland Road, E2 8DP (7729 8293). Old Street tube/rail/26, 48, 55, 67, 149, 242, 243 bus. **Lunch served** noon-3.30pm, **dinner served** 5.30-11pm Mon-Fri. **Meals served** 12.30-11.30pm Sat, Sun. **Main courses** £3.50-£8.50. **Credit** AmEx, MC, V.
As one of London's first restaurants to introduce non-Vietnamese people to Vietnamese cuisine, Viet Hoa is a landmark around these parts. In recent years, though, it has been upstaged by nearby competitors. Our latest meal was not a success. Rice flour 'pancakes' (banh cuon) were flabby and devoid of stuffing, instead being served with a pile of sliced cha lua (Vietnamese sausage) – a poor variation. Bun bi cha gio (a layered dish with lettuce on the bottom, rice vermicelli in the middle and shredded pork and cut-up spring rolls on top) was also a let-down; the shredded pork was bland, but at least the spring rolls (with a bean, wood-ear mushroom, carrot and glass noodle stuffing) gave the rice vermicelli a crunchy contrast. Only the sea bass raised our spirits. The fish had been wrapped in a banana leaf then grilled to precision: crunchy on the outside, soft inside. Viet Hoa seems to be struggling to live up to its former reputation.
Babies and children welcome: high chairs. Booking advisable; essential dinner. Takeaway service. **Map 6 R3.**

Victoria Park

★ Namo

178 Victoria Park Road, E9 7HD (8533 0639/ www.namo.co.uk). Mile End tube then 277 bus. **Lunch served** noon-3.30pm Thur-Sun. **Dinner served** 5.30-11pm Tue-Sun. **Main courses** £5.70-£8.50. **Credit** MC, V.
Nestled in a cluster of cute gift shops and smart restaurants near Victoria Park, the little café Namo provides the finishing touch to what is already a picture-perfect neighbourhood with its chic and bohemian look. Everything seems idyllic: the owner chats with her customers about the weather as a bronze Buddha statue beams at the customers on the summer terrace outside. The menu contains a limited choice of classic dishes – cha ca (grilled fish), water mimosa, rau muong (morning glory), pho – and occasional Chinese ingredients (black bean sauce, a duck and hoi sin starter). Tamarind-flavoured canh chua soup was the best we've had in London, with fresh chunks of pineapple, bamboo shoots, tender pieces of fish, shiitake and cup mushrooms, and mangetouts floating atop. Fresh sweet basil gave the broth a nice sharp contrast to the sweet pineapple flavour. Ca ri do bien, a sweet seafood curry, was a piquant and scrumptious assembly of squid, prawns, mushrooms and onions. The only problem was that few of the ingredients in this Thai-inspired curry were specifically Vietnamese. Still, Namo is a highly congenial spot with good food.
Babies and children welcome: children's menu; high chairs. Booking essential weekends. Tables outdoors (5, garden). Takeaway service.

North East

Dalston

★ ★ Huong-Viet

An Viet House, 12-14 Englefield Road, N1 4LS (7249 0877). Bus 67, 149, 236, 242, 243. **Lunch served** noon-3.30pm Mon-Fri; noon-4pm Sat. **Dinner served** 5.30-11pm Mon-Sat. **Main courses** £4.20-£6.90. **Set lunch** £6. **Set dinner** £13 per person (minimum 4). **Credit** MC, V.
Situated within the building of the An Viet Foundation, a charity devoted to helping Vietnamese refugees settle in London, this historic café occupies a site that has long been a Vietnamese dining establishment (though the management and name have changed over time). On first impressions, Huong-Viet looks more like a meeting room than a restaurant, with its neatly arranged folding tables and folding chairs. We tried the benchmark dish beef pho, and were impressed. This little bowl of broth, rice noodles, chopped spring onions, thinly sliced sweet onions and fresh coriander was brimful of aromas: a subtle blend of cinnamon, star anise and cloves. The banh xeo, a bright yellow pancake dyed with turmeric and filled with fried onions, beansprouts, chicken and prawns, was a crisp delight to be rolled into pert lettuce leaves. Ca ri ga (chicken curry with onions, carrots, aubergine and mushrooms) had the distinct sweet and piquant flavour of Vietnamese curry powder – no bad thing. Yes, this old stager has still got what it takes.
Babies and children welcome: high chairs. Booking advisable; essential weekends. Disabled: toilet. Separate room for parties, seats 25. Takeaway service. Vegetarian menu.

Hackney

★ Green Papaya

191 Mare Street, E8 3QE (8985 5486/ www.greenpapaya.co.uk). Bus 48, 55, 253, 277, D6. **Dinner served** 5-11pm Tue-Sun. **Main courses** £5-£8. **Credit** DC, MC, V.
Green Papaya, with its Bordeaux-red walls and neat wooden furniture, keeps both the decor and menu minimal. Besides a batch of Vietnamese standards such as pho and bun, the menu (dinner only) contains a few treasures that utilise the produce from next door's London Star Night Supermarket. Thinly sliced banana flowers were flavoured with an intensely sour, spicy and lip-smacking dressing. The vegetarian banh xeo, a classic yellow pancake filled with fried beansprouts and onions, contained a nice surprise: smoked tofu (hard to make and even harder to find, with the taste and texture of ham yet completely meatless). One of the best finds on the menu, however, was the braised pork with king prawns and a hard-boiled egg. This Vietnamese stew (with a barely detectable hint of ginger and sweet soy sauce) contained succulent prawns and cubes of pork meat, striped with thin layers of juicy fat. Green Papaya sticks to just a few dishes, but it does them well.
Babies and children welcome: high chairs. Booking advisable. Tables outdoors (5, garden). Takeaway service.

★ ★ Tre Viet (100)

251 Mare Street, E8 3NS (8533 7390). Hackney Central rail/26, 48, 55, 253, 277, D6 bus. **Meals served** 11.30am-11pm Mon-Thur; 11.30am-11.30pm Fri, Sat; 11.30am-10.30pm Sun. **Main courses** £4.70-£13. **Unlicensed. Corkage** no charge. **No credit cards.**
With London's largest Vietnamese community residing in the area, and quality fresh foods sold in Vietnamese supermarkets around the corner, it's no wonder that Tre Viet serves some of the most authentic Vietnamese food in town to an appreciative mixed crowd of families and urban Hackneyites. We tried many dishes and none failed to impress. The fiery noodle soup, bun bo hue, is

SHELF LIFE

Hackney is the centre of London's Vietnamese community, and its shops. On Mare Street alone you'll find **Le-Mi Supermarket** (No.257A), **Vietnam Supermarket** (No.193A) and **Huong-Nam** (Nos.185-187) – though London Star Night Supermarket is the biggest.

Ha-Noi Supermarket
84 Deptford High Street, SE8 4RG (8692 5676). Deptford rail. **Open** 9am-9pm daily.
Small store in south-east London.

London Star Night Supermarket
213 Mare Street, E8 3QE (8985 2949). Hackney Central or London Fields rail/48, 55, 253 bus. **Open** 10am-9pm daily.
An excellent selection of fish and shellfish, condiments and pastes, fresh Vietnamese herbs and Vietnamese cooking utensils.

See Woo Hong
18-20 Lisle Street, WC2H 7BA (7439 8325). Leicester Square tube. **Open** 10am-8pm daily.
This Chinese supermarket also has a good range of Vietnamese fish sauces, pickles, vegetables and ricepapers.

Menu

Although most Vietnamese restaurants in London offer a range of Chinese dishes, it's best to ignore these and head for the Vietnamese specialities. These contain fresh, piquant seasonings and raw vegetables that create entirely different flavours from Chinese cuisine. Vietnamese cookery makes abundant use of fresh, fragrant herbs such as mint and sweet basil; it also utilises refreshing, sweet-sour dipping sauces known generically as nuoc cham. Look out for spices such as chilli, ginger and lemongrass, and crisp root vegetables pickled in sweetened vinegar.

Some dishes are assembled at the table in a way that is distinctively Vietnamese. Order a steaming bowl of pho (rice noodles and beef or chicken in an aromatic broth) and you'll be invited to add raw herbs, chilli and citrus juice as you eat. Crisp pancakes and grilled meats are served with herb sprigs, lettuce leaf wraps and piquant dipping sauces. Toss cold rice vermicelli with salad leaves, herbs and hot meat or seafood fresh from the grill. All these dishes offer an intriguing mix of tastes, temperatures and textures.

Aside from the pronounced Chinese influence on Vietnamese culinary culture, there are hints of the French colonial era (in sweet iced coffee, for example, and the use of beef), along with echoes of neighbouring South-east Asian cuisines. Within Vietnamese cooking itself there are several regional styles; the mix of immigrants in London means you can sample some of the styles here. The food of Hanoi and the north – try **Thang Loi** (*see p294*) – is known for its street snacks and plain, no-nonsense flavours and presentation. The former imperial capital Hue and its surrounding region are famed for a royal cuisine and robustly spicy soups; look out for Hue noodle soups (bun bo hue) on some menus. The food of the south and what used to be called Saigon (now Ho Chi Minh City) is more elegant and colourful, and makes much greater use of fresh herbs (many of these unique to Vietnam), vegetables and fruit.

Below are some specialities and culinary terms; spellings can vary. For recipes and info about Vietnamese food culture, look for *Pleasures of the Vietnamese Table* by Mai Pham. It's published in the US by HarperCollins, but is available in the UK.

Banh cuon: pancake-like steamed rolls of translucent fresh rice pasta, sometimes stuffed with minced pork or shrimp (reminiscent in style of Chinese cheung fun, a dim sum speciality).
Banh pho: flat rice noodles used in soups and stir-fries, usually with beef.
Banh xeo: a large pancake made from a batter of rice flour and coconut milk, coloured bright yellow with turmeric and traditionally filled with prawns, pork, beansprouts and onion. To eat it, tear the pancake apart with your chopsticks, roll the pieces with sprigs of herbs in a lettuce leaf, and dip in nuoc cham (qv).
Bun: rice vermicelli, served in soups and stir-fries. They are also eaten cold, with raw salad vegetables and herbs, with a nuoc cham (qv) sauce poured over, and a topping such as grilled beef or pork – all of which are tossed together at the table.
Cha ca: North Vietnamese dish of fish served sizzling in an iron pan with lashings of dill.
Cha gio: deep-fried spring rolls. Unlike their Chinese counterparts, the wrappers are made from rice paper rather than sheets of wheat pastry, and pucker up deliciously after cooking.
Chao tom: grilled minced prawn on a baton of sugar cane.
Goi: salad; there are many types in Vietnam, but they often contain raw, crunchy vegetables and herbs, perhaps accompanied by chicken or prawns, with a sharp, perky dressing.
Goi cuon (literally 'rolled salad', often translated as 'fresh rolls' or 'salad rolls'): cool, soft, rice-paper rolls usually containing prawns, pork, fresh herbs and rice vermicelli, served with a thick sauce similar to satay sauce but made from hoi sin mixed with peanut butter, scattered with roasted peanuts.
Nem: north Vietnamese name for cha gio (qv).
Nom: north Vietnamese name for goi (qv).
Nuoc cham: the generic name for a wide range of dipping sauces, based on a paste of fresh chillies, sugar and garlic that is diluted with water, lime juice and the ubiquitous fish sauce, nuoc mam (qv).
Nuoc mam: a brown or pale liquid derived from fish that have been salted and left to ferment. It's the essential Vietnamese seasoning, used in dips and as a cooking ingredient.
Pho: the most famous and best-loved of all Vietnamese dishes, a soup of rice noodles and beef or chicken in a rich, clear broth flavoured with aromatics. It is served with a dish of fresh beansprouts, red chilli and herbs, and a squeeze of lime; these are added to the soup at the table. Though now regarded as quintessentially Vietnamese, pho seems to have developed as late as the 19th century in northern Vietnam, and may owe its origins to French or Chinese influences. Some restaurants, such as **Song Que** (*see p294*), offer many versions of this delicious, substantial dish.
Rau thom: aromatic herbs, which might include Asian basil (rau que), mint (rau hung), red or purple perilla (rau tia to), lemony Vietnamese balm (rau kinh gioi) or saw-leaf herb (ngo gai).
Tuong: a general term for a thick sauce. One common tuong is a dipping sauce based on fermented soy beans, with hints of sweet and sour, often garnished with crushed roasted peanuts.

served with the herb purple perilla on the side. Floating in the soup were various tender sliced meats, including cha lua sausages, with a consistency like frankfurters. Raw rau muong (morning glory) was a sweet and sour crunchy salad sprinkled with salty balls of dried, shredded meat and sharp-tasting fragments of mint. The frogs' legs had a saline crust and were served with onions and fried stems of rau ram (Vietnamese coriander), which gave the soft meat a subtle aromatic note. Mekong fish, braised with a thick, sweet soy sauce, arrived in a clay pot and rounded off the meal nicely. The rare ingredients at Tre Viet (fresh herbs, meats and vegetables) make it a must for anyone looking for authentic Vietnamese cuisine.
Babies and children welcome: high chairs. Booking advisable weekends. Disabled: toilet. Separate room for parties, seats 30. Takeaway service.
For branch (Laing Huong) see index.

North

Camden Town & Chalk Farm

★ Viet Anh

41 Parkway, NW1 7PN (7284 4082). Camden Town tube. **Lunch served** noon-4pm, **dinner served** 5.30-11pm daily. **Main courses** £4.50-£7.95. **Credit** MC, V.
Come here to dine under a sky painted on to the ceiling, surrounded by turquoise walls that give Viet Anh an airy and spacious feel. The list of 250 or so dishes can be overwhelming; all sound like rather unexciting variations of each other. The trick is to order dishes labelled 'Vietnamese' or 'authentic'. Bun rieu, for instance – a soup so red you can almost see how spicy it is – is a seldom-seen northern Vietnamese crabmeat soup with a sweet seafood undertone that's combined with the sourness of tomatoes and the saltiness of fish sauce. Viet Anh's version with thin strips of poached egg and prawn cake (similar in texture to fish cake) was sublime, though it could have done with a few more fresh herbs and fewer processed crab sticks. The fried tilapia fish, swimming in nuoc cham and topped with ripe mango, was equally delightful, the sweet and sour flavour of both the sauce and fruit harmonising well with the crunchy fish. Viet Anh has minor flaws, but when its menu says 'Vietnamese', Vietnamese is what you get.
Babies and children admitted. Booking advisable. Tables outdoors (2, pavement). Takeaway service.
Map 27 C2.

Crouch End

★ Khoai Café

6 Topsfield Parade, N8 8PR (8341 2120). Finsbury Park tube/rail then W3, W7 bus or Archway tube then 41, W5 bus. **Lunch served** noon-3.30pm, **dinner served** 5.30-11.30pm daily. **Main courses** £3.60-£8.50. **Set lunch** £7.45. **Credit** MC, V.
Khoai Café fits perfectly into Topsfield Parade, a street full of charming shops and chic restaurants. A green interior, plastic foliage and a large mirror wall give this busy place a relaxing atmosphere. The food is fresh and luscious. Canh cai be xanh (choi sum soup with a delicate clear broth containing little pieces of tofu) was a refreshing treat. Goi xoai xanh, shredded unripe mango drenched in a sweet and sour dressing, was just as light; the fruit's citrous flavour, the aromatic mint and coriander, and the crunchy nuts and fried onions made a harmonious mixture. Our friendly waitress recommended two mouth-watering main dishes. Plump, succulent prawns, still in their shell but bursting open, had been speckled with crushed peanuts and were served with strips of unripe mango and rice vermicelli. Tender hanoi grilled fish (cha ca) arrived still sizzling in a cast-iron dish; it came with the delectable accompaniment of chopped fresh dill. Lovely service, lovely location and most importantly great, fresh food.
Babies and children welcome: high chairs. Booking not accepted Fri, Sat. Restaurant available for hire. Takeaway service.

Cheap Eats

Budget

Time and again, well-travelled diners complain about prices in London's restaurants. True, this is generally an expensive city for dining, but there are many bargains to be had. Trouble is, the best-value venues need winkling out. You'll have to look beyond the trashy cheapness of most burger and pizza chains; further, even, than local curry-house clones and greasy kebab shops. Here we list our favourite budget venues, concentrating on those inhabiting otherwise expensive districts of the city. We've included sections on London's pride and joy – traditional pie and mash shops – and on the new wave of gourmet burger grills (where the beef tastes of beef, rather than the production line). Most of the places listed below open into the evening; for daytime venues, see **Cafés**, starting on p305. And for low-priced meals connected to the cuisine of a particular country, consult the relevant chapter elsewhere in this guide (Chinese, Indian, Korean, Thai, Turkish...), where you'll find inexpensive venues indicated by a ★.

For the most extensive choice of budget eateries, grab a copy of Time Out's *Cheap Eats in London* (£6.99), which covers more than 500 eating places across the city where you can dine for less than £20 a head.

Central

Bloomsbury

Square Pie

Brunswick Centre, WC1N 1BS (7837 6207/ www.squarepie.com). Russell Square tube. **Open** 11.30am-10.30pm Mon-Sat; 11.30am-10pm Sun. **Main courses** £4.25-£6.96. **Credit** MC, V.

Square Pie has gone from being a little takeaway in Spitalfields Market (closed for a refurb as we went to press and reopening at the end of 2007) to stardom, with smart new premises popping up everywhere and Square Pies even served on Virgin Upper Class flights. This branch is right at home among the chain restaurants of the redeveloped Brunswick Centre. Outside, it shares alfresco seating space with Strada and Giraffe; the compact, bright interior has another handful of seats, but is dominated by a counter displaying the day's glorious pies. The secret of SP's success? Top pies, made with top-quality ingredients. The steak versions are as generously filled as Jordan's swimsuit, with crusts firmer than Peter Andre's abs. Besides the usual beefcakes are varieties such as chicken, leek and ham, lamb and rosemary, and 'Friday fish pie'. Vegetarians will be satisfied with mushroom and asparagus pie with vegetarian onion gravy. Our favourite detail is that the maris piper potatoes are mashed skin-on. To drink, there's scrummy Chegworth Valley apple juices – and this branch even has an alcohol licence.

Babies and children welcome: high chairs. Disabled: toilet. Tables outdoors (10, patio). Takeaway service. **Map 4 L4.**

For branches see index.

City

Grazing NEW

19-21 Great Tower Street, EC3R 5AR (7283 2932/www.grazingfood.com). Monument or Tower Hill tube/Fenchurch Street rail. **Meals served** 7am-4pm Mon-Fri. **Main courses** £3.95-£5.50. **No credit cards.**

You don't often find a café in London where suits and site workers, tourists and bus drivers happily mingle, but such is the unifying power of the bacon sarnie. Grazing is a part-caff, part-sandwich shop in the heart of the City that takes its meat very seriously. Order from a blackboard before taking a seat at the bench tables at the rear, which offer sufficient space to spread out your newspaper. The fried egg and black pudding sandwich served on white was a touch above the greasy-spoon norm, but satisfyingly unfussy, while dry-cured back bacon butty featured thick-cut slices. All meat is free-range and sourced from small farms. Bread comes from the Bread Factory and condiments from Tracklements. A lunchtime menu focuses on hot meat rolls – beef, pork or lamb – but there are also soups, salads and cold sandwiches, including a splendid straightforward ham, cheese and pickle doorstep. Daily specials keep things nice and varied.

Babies and children admitted. Tables outdoors (2, pavement). Takeaway service; delivery service (over £25 within the City). **Map 12 R7.**

Leon

3 Crispin Place, E1 6DW (7247 4369/www.leon restaurants.co.uk). Liverpool Street tube/rail. **Meals served** 8am-10.30pm Mon, Tue; 8am-11pm Wed-Fri; 9am-11.30pm Sat; 10am-9.30pm Sun. **Main courses** £4.20-£11. **Credit** MC, V.

Set up in 2003 by racy celebrity chef Allegra McEvedy, Leon (now with eight branches in London) emphasises careful sourcing and seasonal produce in its fast food. For a late breakfast we ignored outdoor tables under Spitalfields Market's permanent canopy and headed inside, where standard modern café furniture on one side of the central counter gives way to a spacious loungey zone on the other. Sofas, a cowskin armchair and red diner-style seating combine with pinned-up foodie cuttings and gherkin-tin lampshades to hit the right note between café and bar (some booze is served alongside impressive smoothies and a short list of teas and coffees). Lunch and evening menus are mostly Mediterranean (salads, wraps and hot and cold meze), but for breakfast there's fruit, porridge and baked goods. The sole remaining bap was a filling wholemeal bun of slender, dense, delicious sausages, but the bacon and goat's cheese muffin – new for summer according to the menu's cheery 'join our club' spiel – was claggy, despite the addition of spring onion. A gooseberry and white chocolate version was also heavy in texture, but summer-light in taste.

Babies and children welcome: high chairs. Disabled: toilet. Tables outdoors (30, market). Takeaway service. **Map 12 R5.**

For branches see index.

Clerkenwell & Farringdon

Little Bay

171 Farringdon Road, EC1R 3AL (7278 1234/ www.little-bay.co.uk). Farringdon tube/rail. **Meals served** noon-midnight Mon-Sat; noon-11pm Sun. **Main courses** £6.45-£8.45. **Credit** MC, V.

It looks like Laurence Llewelyn-Bowen ran riot in here. There's a huge golden face of Zeus on the wall, the ceilings are clad in turquoise velvet, and the lampshades are made of gaudy beads and twisted wire. Fortunately, the bouffant-haired designer hasn't been let loose on the food, which is considerably more straightforward. Wild boar sausages and mash was a dream of gloopy gravy and piquant meat, and braised beef fell off the bone – notable achievements, considering they cost less than a tenner (and are cheaper still before 7pm). The crowning glory was an apple cake smothered in dollops of both cream and custard. And the decor grows on you; it's better than another identikit Ikea refit. On our visit, the place was packed with a trendy, youngish crowd, having a ball. Staff were attentive, but their highlighting of the tip on the bill was unnecessary: probably the only sour note at an otherwise delightful restaurant. There are branches in Battersea, Fulham, Kilburn and Croydon.

Babies and children admitted. Booking advisable. Disabled: toilet. Separate room for parties, seats 120. **Map 5 N4.**

For branches see index.

Covent Garden

Canela

33 Earlham Street, WC2H 9LS (7240 6926/ www.canelacafe.com). Covent Garden tube. **Meals served** 9.30am-10pm Mon-Thur; 9.30am-11pm Fri, Sat; 10am-8pm Sun. **Main courses** £5.90-£8.90. **Credit** MC, V.

Wedged rather awkwardly into the corner of the Thomas Neal Centre, Canela ('cinnamon' in Portuguese) is unusual among Covent Garden cafés in that it stays open for dinner. It is busiest during lunch, however, turning out a mix of Brazilian and Portuguese specialities for local workers with hollow stomachs. From the weighty cheese breads (try the chorizo version) to the brigadeiros (fudgy Brazilian chocolate balls, served as part of a tempting dessert list), cooking here is unapologetically hearty. Happily, much of the food is worth the effort. The feijoada (black bean and pork stew served with rice) is fine, but a better option is bacalhau à brás (salt-cod combined with fried potatoes, onions and eggs). The room itself is plain and simple, with high ceilings adding a little drama. Staff mix a capable caipirinha, but beer hounds should make a beeline for the Super Bock stout – a mellow, easy-drinking Portuguese beer that's seen only rarely over here.

Babies and children admitted. Tables outdoors (4, pavement). Takeaway service. **Map 18 D3.**

Fitzrovia

★ Ooze NEW

2007 RUNNER-UP BEST CHEAP EATS

62 Goodge Street, W1T 4NE (7436 9444/ www.ooze.biz). Goodge Street tube. **Meals served** noon-11pm Mon-Sat. **Main courses** £5.25-£9.95. **Credit** AmEx, MC, V.

Risotto is one of the simple yet infinitely flexible dishes that have made Italian cuisine so globally popular. Given the grossly over-saturated market

for the other major exports in that category – pizza and pasta – it's a wonder that Ooze is the first venture to concentrate solely on different permutations of gooey rice. You'll soon forget the dubiously anatomical name once you're seated in the clean, contemporary dining room: bright and white with the odd dash of colour. More colourful still are the risottos, over a dozen of which are available at any time (specials add to that number). It would usually be too difficult for a restaurant to have so many different pots of risotto ready-to-serve simultaneously, but a clever method, involving part-cooking batches in advance, is employed to great success. On a recent visit, a mixed seafood risotto with tomato and courgette chunks was a delectable highlight. Bland, rather homogeneous cubes of chicken breast let down an otherwise tasty dish with tarragon and red peppers. These risottos aren't the finest in the world, but they're undeniably tasty, cooked in the correct way with just the right amount of bite, and supplemented by some fantastic salads and desserts. Ooze is an attractive – and reasonably priced – addition to the West End's eating options.
Babies and children welcome: children's menu; high chairs. Tables outdoors (2, pavement). Takeaway service. **Map 17 A1**.

Squat & Gobble

69 Charlotte Street, W1T 4RJ (7580 5338/ www.squatandgobble.co.uk). Goodge Street or Warren Street tube. **Meals served** 7am-5pm Mon-Fri; 9am-5pm Sat. **Main courses** £3.50-£5.25. **No credit cards.**
Squat & Gobble could teach London's mediocre sandwich bars a few lessons in tasty budget eating. It's a small place, with barely room for a size-zero model to squeeze between the tightly packed tables (chunky wood inside, metal outside on the pavement), but customers tend to be so delighted they've nabbed a seat they don't mind. Efficient staff cope admirably. The place is hugely popular at lunch with both eat-in and takeaway trade (avoid the 1pm rush if you're able), but you can also come here for a hearty breakfast (porridge with fruit; full english; steak and eggs), or just a slice of cake in the afternoon. The long menu offers the works: soup, salads, sandwiches, jacket potatoes with superior fillings (tarragon chicken, prawn mayo with smoked salmon, mexican veg chilli), sausages (cumberland pork or vegetarian), daily specials and old-school puds. Portions are never less than generous, and prices absurdly low for the quality and quantity. Alcohol isn't available, but teas, coffees, juices, smoothies and a wicked hot chocolate should suffice.
Babies and children admitted. Tables outdoors (9, pavement). Takeaway service. **Map 3 J5**.

Leicester Square

Gaby's

30 Charing Cross Road, WC2H 0DB (7836 4233). Leicester Square tube. **Meals served** 11am-midnight Mon-Sat; noon-10pm Sun. **Main courses** £3.80-£9. **No credit cards.**
Almost as legendary as the theatres that surround it, Gaby's has been serving home-style eastern European and New York Jewish food since 1965. Signed posters from the West End point to sporadic celebrity patronage; Matt Damon's visit is documented in more than one photograph. Ignoring the occasional thesp, this is a popular meeting place for London Jews, despite the fact that food is non-kosher. Seating is at close-packed tables at the rear; at the front is a glass counter showcasing the café's range of salads (mushrooms in tomato sauce, chopped beetroot, ladies' fingers, potato salad with chopped pickles). Our plump salt beef sandwich was not quite as vast as NYC counterparts, but it was well packed with moist, tender meat, and prepared with fresh-tasting rye bread. Soups are straightforward (lentil, bean and barley); there are kebab dishes served with rice for those with a taste for the Med. Cheesecake was rich and filling: a thin biscuit base not distracting from a cheesy filling flecked with sultanas.
Babies and children admitted. Takeaway service. **Map 18 D5**.

Marylebone

★ Quiet Revolution

1st floor, Inn 1888, 21A Devonshire Street, W1G 6PG (7486 7420). Baker Street or Regent's Park tube. **Meals served** 11am-10pm daily. **Main courses** £5.95-£12.95. **Credit** MC, V.
Formerly housed in Aveda on Marylebone High Street, this organic café has moved round the corner to the first floor of a restored Victorian boozer. Proudly overseen by bubbly, welcoming chef/proprietor Jenny Wilson, the classic pub dining room (dusky-pink wallpaper, black leather chairs, restored fireplaces) seems oddly juxtaposed with the wholesome health food, but the new premises have resulted in an expansion of the menu. As well as freshly squeezed juices, hearty soups and bountiful salads, there is now a wider repertoire of cooked dishes, from British stalwarts such as shepherd's pie and sausage and chips to more exotic fare like a tender, flavour-packed pumpkin and tomato bake laced with fresh rosemary. Breakfasts are for late risers (it doesn't open until 11am), but the immaculate full english would put even the poshest farmhouse B&B to shame. Wine, beer and (mediocre) coffee are brought up from the bar downstairs. Tucked away as it is, the place seemed worryingly quiet on a Saturday lunchtime, but hopefully word of this reasonably priced gem will spread.
Babies and children admitted: children's menu. Tables outdoors (3, pavement). Takeaway service. Vegan dishes. Vegetarian menu. **Map 3 G5**.

Soho

★ Hummus Bros (100)

88 Wardour Street, W1F 0TJ (7734 1311/ www.hbros.co.uk). Oxford Circus or Tottenham Court Road tube. **Meals served** 11am-10pm Mon-Wed; 11am-11pm Thur, Fri; noon-11pm Sat; noon-10pm Sun. **Main courses** £2.50-£6. **Credit** AmEx, MC, V.
Like many a successful venture, Hummus Bros has a formula that is simple and focused, centred as it is on one key dish. Guessed what yet? Here, the dip comes shaped around the edges of a bowl, which is then filled with vibrant toppings (stewed beef, fava beans, chicken, guacamole). Those in the know put themselves in the hands of the kitchen and order one of two daily-changing (and often excellent) specials. In the past we've had coconut dal, spinach in sesame sauce, tomatoes with pesto, and char siu pork. You wouldn't think these global flavours would work with houmous, but they do. Bowls come with a generous portion of white or brown warmed pitta; side dishes of tabouleh or smoked aubergine appease the very hungry. HB's team of young, cosmopolitan staff are absurdly friendly, often offering customers complimentary mint teas after the meal. If dining in, be prepared to sit elbow-to-elbow with fellow diners in the rather cramped space (ruby-red walls, long wooden benches). It's not an ideal place to linger or talk intimately, but for a nutritious lunch or pre-cinema meal, the Bros are hard to beat.
Babies and children admitted. Bookings not accepted. Takeaway service. Vegan dishes.
Map 17 B3.
For branch see index.

★ Mother Mash NEW

2007 RUNNER-UP BEST CHEAP EATS

26 Ganton Street, W1F 7QZ (7494 9644/ www.mothermash.co.uk). Oxford Circus tube. **Meals served** 8.30am-10pm Mon-Fri; noon-10pm Sat; noon-5pm Sun. **Main courses** £6.95-£7.95. **Credit** AmEx, MC, V.
This isn't the first café-restaurant to reinterpret a British classic, but others – S&M (*see p303*), Square Pie (*see p298*) – have followed convention by making the meaty bit (sausages, pies) their focus. At Mother Mash you can get sausages and pies, but it's the spud that takes the limelight – and why not? Who doesn't love a heap of expertly mashed potato? A standard butter-and-milk mash is offered alongside a handful of variants, including irish champ (with spring onions and cheese). We had no reason to doubt the 'mashed to order' promise as we tucked into the piping-hot, fluffy mounds. Pies were very respectable: one bursting with tender Angus steak, another with chunks of haddock and hard-boiled egg. There's also a choice of gravies, including the 'liquor' (parsley sauce) served in MM's pie and mash shop forebears. These pie shops are the inspiration for the restaurant's

Ooze

Gourmet burger bars

The rise of London's upmarket hamburger chains started with the Kiwi-run **Gourmet Burger Kitchen** in Battersea. This enterprise sprouted from an idea borrowed and adapted from New Zealand, where gourmet burger bars are about as common as sheep. Three years after GBK flipped its first patty and topped it with beetroot (to make a kiwiburger, of course), several other restaurateurs were doing the same.

While this new wave is superior to the traditional fast-food chains, the various ventures also tend to share a certain uniformity of appearance – dark wood interiors, counter ordering, wipe-clean tables – that can make it difficult to tell the different brands apart. But tread carefully, for while the burgers are never bad, they don't always live up to expectations. We reckon you can't go far wrong at the original and (still) the best, GBK.

Burger Shack

17 Irving Street, WC2H 7AU (7839 3737/ www.smollenskys.com). Leicester Square tube. **Meals served** 11am-midnight Mon-Sat; noon-midnight Sun. **Main courses** £5.95-£15.95. **Credit** AmEx, MC, V.

By some distance the poorest of the new burger wave, Burger Shack is an offshoot of Smollensky's, which has rebranded its own Metro mini-chain, looking to take advantage of some pretty decent West End locations and the current vogue for posh meat patties. The outlets are dressed in the uniform of classics like the Hard Rock Café, with images of 1950s Americana adorning the walls, but that US diner is head and shoulders above the limp fare offered here – aimed squarely at tourists and, in all honesty, little better than what is served at the fast-food chains across Leicester Square. Our burger was greasy, the bun insubstantial and the chips anaemic. A seemingly reasonable meal-deal (which offered burger, chips and drinks at a discount) didn't make clear that the chips would be a handful-sized portion and the burger seemingly little bigger than a ten-pence piece.

BS has some interesting sides (including old-school chips with gravy!), but real burger fans should look elsewhere.

Babies and children welcome: children's menu. Disabled: toilet. Tables outdoors (5, pavement). Takeaway service.
Map 17 C5.
For branches see index.

Fine Burger Company

50 James Street, W1U 1HB (7224 1890/ www.fineburger.co.uk). Bond Street tube. **Meals served** noon-11pm Mon-Sat; noon-10pm Sun. **Main courses** £5.45-£7.75. **Credit** AmEx, MC, V.

Fairly anodyne in appearance, FBC was one of the first of the chains to start offering more unusual burger options. The Hawaiian is a burger with pineapple, bacon and cheddar, plus the usual toppings (mayo, lettuce, tomato and red onion are pretty standard across the genre). There's also a fish finger sandwich that's nearly as good as the one you loved at uni, while tempura onion rings – practically the size of Saturn's hoops – are deliciously spicy and moreish. FBC's bog-standard burger is a well-made thing: decently stacked, pleasantly juicy and housed in a good, firm bun. Chips are chunky and tasty; shakes slightly above average. The menu's insistence that its beef is happy beef may come as news to the cows.

Babies and children welcome: children's menu; high chairs; toys. Separate room for parties, seats 26. Tables outdoors (4, pavement). Takeaway service.
Map 9 G6.
For branches see index.

★ Gourmet Burger Kitchen (100)

44 Northcote Road, SW11 1NZ (7228 3309/www.gbkinfo.com). Clapham Junction rail/49, 77, 219, 345 bus. **Meals served** noon-11pm Mon-Fri; 11am-11pm Sat; 11am-10pm Sun. **Main courses** £5.55-£7.65. **Credit** MC, V.

Branches of GBK continue to open across London: there are now 19, one of which, sadly, has taken over the former premises of classic Cockney pie and mash shop Goddard's in Greenwich. Still, that's not GBK's fault; for our money, this outfit can do little wrong.

It all began on Northcote Road, and that first small restaurant still has crowds queuing out the door at weekends, for massive portions of interesting, well-cooked burgers. There are classic varieties alongside some that stay just the right side of novelty: like the Jamaican with mango and ginger sauce.

Started by Kiwis, GBK is now owned by the Clapham House chain; the cheerily Antipodean atmosphere is retained, partly accounting for the friendlier-than-usual service and the braver selections on the menu (produced with the help of noted NZ chef Peter Gordon). Excellent.

Babies and children welcome: children's portions; high chairs. Tables outdoors (4, pavement). Takeaway service.
Map 21 C4.
For branches see index.

Ground NEW

217-221 Chiswick High Road, W4 2DW (8747 9113/www.groundrestaurants.com). Turnham Green tube. **Meals served** noon-10pm Mon, Tue; noon-10.30pm Wed, Thur; noon-11pm Fri; 11am-11pm Sat; 11am-10pm Sun. **Main courses** £5.35-£8.95. **Credit** AmEx, MC, V.

A huge skylight channels plenty of light into the ground-floor dining room at this burger newcomer – all exposed brick and wooden floors, overlooked by tables on a mezzanine level. A couple of diners braved unseasonable July winds to sit at pavement tables on Chiswick High Street. Another perched on one of the diner-style stools at the counter inside. It's the quality of the hamburgers that makes Ground a contender: meat is plump and juicy (though we weren't asked how we would like it cooked), salad crisp and colourful, the bun firm yet not too heavy. The usual variations are offered on the standard burger (with cheese, with bacon, with guacamole), plus oddities such as a version served with parma ham and sour cream. Deep-fried courgette strips made a nice change from the usual sides and shakes.

Babies and children welcome: children's menu; high chairs. Disabled: toilet. Separate room for parties, seats 52. Tables outdoors (4, pavement). Takeaway service.

★ Haché

24 Inverness Street, NW1 7HJ (7485 9100/www.hacheburgers.com). Camden Town tube. **Meals served** noon-10.30pm Mon-Sat; noon-10pm Sun. **Main courses** £5.95-£11.95. **Credit** AmEx, MC, V.

Not a chain, Haché is a bistro-style restaurant that specialises in burgers. They're good-quality Ayrshire steaks, chopped, grilled and served in ciabatta-like buns; the superiority of the meat compared to most rivals is undeniable. Sides too are a cut above – fruit smoothies were delicious, chips (fat or skinny) disappeared quickly, and onion rings were among the best we've sampled. Given the deadly combination of comfort food and cosy surroundings (fairy lights, Hopper prints and muted colours), it can be very easy to over-indulge here (did we really need the chocolate brownie for dessert?) and the resulting bill might remind you that this is a restaurant, not a chain. Still, a great spot for a superior meat feast.

Babies and children welcome: high chairs. Tables outdoors (4, pavement). Takeaway service. **Map 27 C2.**

Hamburger Union

64 Tottenham Court Road, W1C 2ET (7636 0011/www.hamburgerunion.com). Goodge Street or Tottenham Court Road tube. **Meals served** 11.30am-9.30pm Mon; 11.30am-10.30pm Tue-Sat; 11.30am-8pm Sun. **Main courses** £5-£8. **Credit** AmEx, MC, V.

As well as spreading quickly through the usual haunts – Islington and Hampstead – Hamburger Union has also developed quite a footprint in central London, with four branches boasting WC or W1 postcodes. The Tottenham Court Road restaurant has a prominent corner site on Goodge Street and packs in the lunchtime customers with its promise of quick, easy but low-guilt meat (cows are 'grass-reared'). Red meat options are relatively straightforward. Only the chorizo, paying homage to the Brindisa stall in Borough Market, breaks new ground. Beef is succulent, and the encasing ciabatta-like buns are sturdy; chips are fat, but we found them lacking in flavour. Vegetarian burgers include an excellent citrus-marinated halloumi with beetroot. In all, a satisfactory operation – although extra marks are garnered for a drinks menu that includes Hook Norton Best Bitter, Fentimans Ginger Beer and Chegworth juices.

Babies and children welcome: children's menu. Takeaway service. **Map 10 K5.**
For branches see index.

★ Natural Burger Company NEW

12 Blenheim Terrace, NW8 0EB (7372 9065). St John's Wood tube. **Meals served** noon-11pm Mon-Sat; noon-10.30pm Sun. **Main courses** £8.75-£12. **Credit** MC, V.

Well located, just off Abbey Road between the competing plushness of Maida Vale and St John's Wood, the compact and stylish NBC is a mini-chain waiting to be rolled out. Don't hang around long before checking it out. Burgers here are outstanding: giant, juicy hunks of ground meat. Toppings might be familiar to any connoisseur of the gourmet burger scene (avocado and bacon, chorizo and rocket); ingredients are well sourced and combined. The NBC has proved popular with the area's American population – proof, if it were needed, that it's working to the right blueprint. The small interior is frequently packed; on sunny evenings the outside space really comes into its own. Courgette chips were an enjoyable alternative to the usual variety, and the American-style cheesecake for pud was delicious.

Babies and children welcome: children's menu; high chairs. Separate room for parties, seats 35. Tables outdoors (6, pavement). Takeaway service. **Map 1 C2.**

Ultimate Burger

34 New Oxford Street, WC1A 1AP (7436 6641/www.ultimateburger.co.uk). Tottenham Court Road tube. **Meals served** noon-11.30pm daily. **Main courses** £5.55-£6.95. **Credit** MC, V.

With a name like that, Ultimate Burger can't be accused of selling itself short. And while it doesn't quite live up to the description, it's certainly not the worst of the new burger crowd. Owned by the people who run the quietly expanding (and rather good) pizza chain Prezzo, Ultimate has just two branches, both in the centre of town. Ultimate serves big sesame buns, medium-cooked beef and excellent chips that tread the fine line between crispy and crisps. A smoky mountainburger came smothered in a sweet and spicy barbecue sauce, with real cheese and what seemed like half a tomato. Four chicken and a couple of lamb variants are also on the menu. A worthy option.

Babies and children welcome: high chairs. Disabled: toilet. Takeaway service. **Map 18 D2.**

For branch see index.

Natural Burger Company

design: customers sit in booths on high-backed wooden banquettes; white ceramic tiles glisten on the walls. Breakfast and salad options broaden the appeal, as does a list of wines and beers. It adds up to a simple, successful, easily expandable formula; surely it won't be long before this Mother spawns another.

Babies and children admitted. Tables outdoors (6, pavement). Takeaway service. **Map 17 A4.**

Stockpot

18 Old Compton Street, W1D 4TN (7287 1066). Leicester Square or Tottenham Court Road tube. **Meals served** 11.30am-11.30pm Mon, Tue; 11.30am-midnight Wed-Sat; noon-11.30pm Sun. **Main courses** £3.40-£5.50. **Set meal** (Mon-Sat) £4.95-£6.50 2 courses; (Sun) £6.50 2 courses. **No credit cards.**

The Old Compton Street location and low prices ensure the Stockpot is always busy. But low prices don't mean low standards; dish quality is consistently high, and portions are large. How does the 'Pot do it? Possibly by keeping to pretty much the same menu since opening its first branch in 1958. So, you'll still find classics such as avocado vinaigrette (£1.60) and penne carbonara (£4.10). These 1960s dinner-party favourites are joined by dishes of the school dinner ilk. How about banana sponge pudding with custard, apple crumble with custard, or jelly and cream? Such treats are all produced with aplomb, and cost a mere £1.50. Stockpot is one of the few remaining places in Soho where you can eat a decent, satisfying meal for under a fiver. It also has the bonus of a continental atmosphere, with french windows opening on to Old Compton Street. Service is prompt too. Just the place to refuel before tackling central London.

Babies and children admitted. Tables outdoors (2, pavement). Takeaway service. **Map 17 C3.**

South

Battersea

Fish in a Tie

105 Falcon Road, SW11 2PF (7924 1913). Clapham Junction rail. **Lunch served** noon-3pm, **dinner served** 6pm-midnight Mon-Sat. **Meals served** noon-11pm Sun. **Main courses** £5.95-£10.50. **Set meal** (lunch; dinner Mon-Thur, Sun) £7 3 courses. **Credit** MC, V.

Walking into this endearingly entitled, eccentrically decorated little bistro in Battersea is like entering a friend's living room: except there's a few more chairs and tables. A lot more chairs and tables, in fact – so many that getting back to your seat can present a problem if you've overindulged, which you could be forgiven for doing, as the food is great. From tricolore chicken (with mozzarella, tomatoes and pesto) to the OTT black tulip pudding (a pancake concoction with pears and chocolate), Fish in a Tie provides good bistro staples at low prices. This isn't fancy cuisine, but judging from the cheerful faces all around, that's not what people want from this long-established, well-loved local. Add a homely, welcoming atmosphere, complete with beaming staff who provide prompt service (and can also hold a tune and bake a mean cake; a nearby table was celebrating a birthday), and you're on to a winner. Well worth a visit.

Babies and children welcome: children's portions; high chairs. Booking advisable. Separate rooms for parties, seating 25 and 40. **Map 21 C3.**

South East

Bankside

★ The Table (100)

83 Southwark Street, SE1 0HX (7401 2760/ www.thetablecafe.com). Southwark tube/London Bridge tube/rail. **Meals served** 7.30am-8.30pm Mon-Thur; 7.30am-11pm Fri; 9am-4pm Sat. **Main courses** £3.50-£8. **Credit** MC, V.

Based in the ground floor of Bankside architecture company Allies and Morrison, the Table – winner of the Best Cheap Eats award (and runner-up for

Best Design) in our 2006 Eating & Drinking Awards – is a cut above your regular office canteen. The first sight is of an enormous, richly varied and fresh-as-a-daisy salad bar – reclaiming the genre from the pizza restaurants and buffet bars that have so devalued it – which dominates one side of the room, while another long wooden counter groans under the weight of artisan breads, soups and other treats. Mix and match your salad or choose from a selection of hot meals that includes numerous flans, a daily risotto, sardines (recommended) and pasta dishes, then hope to find a seat at the solid wood tables with shared bench seating. Although the place is usually buzzing at lunchtime, it's an equally good – and slightly quieter – walk-by spot for breakfast, when you can get granola, porridge, bacon sarnies and excellent pastries as well as tea and coffee. The Table is also open into the evening for cocktails: something much in demand since the mammoth Bankside 1-2-3 development opened in 2007. Multifunctional, cheap and rather stylish.
Babies and children admitted. Disabled: toilet. Tables outdoors (8, terrace). Takeaway service.
Map 11 O8.

East

Bethnal Green

E Pellicci (100)

332 Bethnal Green Road, E2 0AG (7739 4873). Bethnal Green tube/rail/8, 253 bus. **Meals served** 6.15am-5pm Mon-Sat. **Main courses** £5-£8. **Unlicensed**. **Corkage** no charge. **No credit cards**.
Where to start? This much-loved primrose-coloured caff, owned by the Pellicci family for over a century, has played an integral role in the social history of the East End, providing a home-from-home for gangsters (the Krays), artists (Gilbert & George), taxi drivers, local workers and families. Customers are welcomed warmly by Nevio and family; if Nevio Junior is about, then good-natured ribbing of customers is par for the course. The art deco interior is grade II-listed (it was remodelled in 1946): think marquetry panelling, laminate wood tables, framed family portraits and bottles of traditional condiments. Pellicci has welcomed a fair few celebs over the years (David Schwimmer, Dizzy Rascal, Noel Gallagher), but the place remains a proper, good-value caff, serving quality fry-ups, traditional English and Italian dishes, sarnies and classic puddings. To many, indeed, this is more than a greasy spoon. As Eric 'Monster' Hall – like many customers, a regular since childhood, and our recent table companion – put it, Pellicci is as much a social club as anything. London would be a sadder place without it.
Babies and children welcome: children's menu.

Nando's

366 Bethnal Green Road, E2 0AH (7729 5783/ www.nandos.co.uk). Bethnal Green tube/rail/8, 253 bus. **Meals served** noon-11pm Mon-Thur, Sun; noon-11.30pm Fri, Sat. **Main courses** £4.70-£8.40. **Credit** AmEx, DC, MC, V.
Portuguese-style piri-piri (chilli-spiced) chicken is the stock-in-trade of this international chain. The interior of the Bethnal Green branch – warm yellow and orange walls, terracotta tiled floors, sturdy dark wooden furniture – has a cosy, friendly atmosphere. The bonhomie is aided by such slogans as 'wipe that smile off your face' and 'our chicks rule', displayed on employee uniforms, walls and napkins. Upbeat staff guide customers through the not-so-tricky process of ordering at the counter, before escorting them to a table. The menu includes salads, steak and vegetarian choices, though most punters plump for the finger-licking option. Choose the piri-piri spice level for your chicken, which is added to the pre-marinated, pre-cooked birds. These are then briefly flame grilled. Fast food it is, but not as you know it. Many ingredients are fresh, there's a good selection of Portuguese wine and beer, and you'll even get proper crockery. This branch sells halal chicken too. With such attention to detail, the Nando's chain is set to grow still further.
Babies and children welcome: high chairs. Takeaway service.
For branches see index.

Brick Lane

Story Deli (100)

3 Dray Walk, The Old Truman Brewery, 91 Brick Lane, E1 6QL (7247 3137). Liverpool Street tube/rail. **Meals served** noon-4pm Mon-Fri; noon-6pm Sat, Sun. **Main courses** £6-£10. **Unlicensed**. **Corkage** no charge. **Credit** AmEx, MC, V.
Amid the achingly cool environs of Brick Lane, this no-nonsense, 100%-organic pizzeria and café makes a welcome break from all the nu-rave neon. All distressed floorboards, bags of flour and wooden slabs (instead of plates), it offers a great, chilled-out lunch option. The menu currently focuses on pizza, which is a shame as the other dishes were good, but the range of fresh, innovative toppings is vast. Featuring ingredients from prawns to pumpkin, on paper-thin, crisp bases, these pizzas are brilliant, and about as far from the generic, grease-laden takeaway examples as you can get. Add the deli's special 'hot pepper sauce' and you can see why Story attracts punters from all walks of life. On a busy Saturday lunchtime, most people chose a cool juice to accompany their food, but the café now has a licence and offers wine, as well as coffees and teas. There are ice-creams for afters – if you've room.
Babies and children welcome: children's portions; high chairs; toys. Tables outdoors (10, pavement). Takeaway service. Vegan dishes.
Map 6 S5.

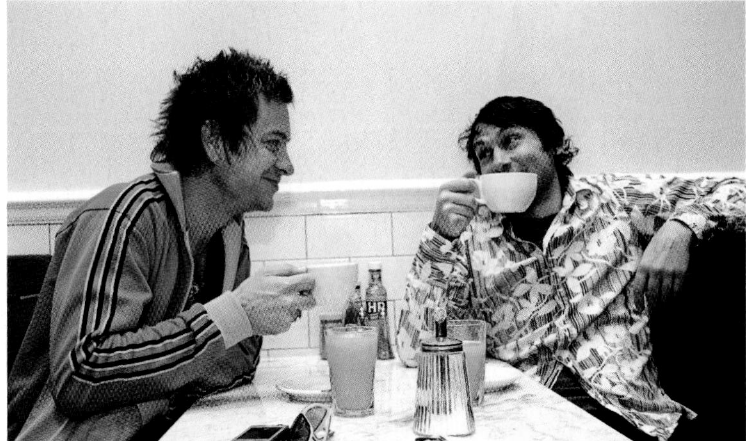

Mother Mash. See p299.

North East

Hackney

LMNT

316 Queensbridge Road, E8 3NH (7249 6727/ www.lmnt.co.uk). Dalston Kingsland rail/236 bus. **Meals served** noon-11pm Mon-Sat; noon-10.30pm Sun. **Main courses** £8.95. **Credit** MC, V.

This place hasn't changed much during its seven years in business – but you'd be hard-pressed to know how to update such a distinctive, over-the-top venue. LMNT's USP is its bizarre interior decoration: figures from Greek and Roman drama meet those from ancient Egypt; kitsch statues of Cleopatra, a sphinx and a Greek god stand around; the ceiling is covered in drapes; a mural depicts a medieval Tuscan landscape; and there are tables in unusual spaces (in a giant urn, for instance). With so much to look at, you almost forget you're here to eat. The Mediterranean menu seems rather ordinary in comparison to the decor. Pricing is simple. Starters such as tomato tarte tatin or salmon fish cake all cost £3.45; mains like lamb chops with potato gratin, or fillet of salmon with sautéed potatoes, are £8.95; side dishes go for £2.35; and desserts (perhaps banoffi shortbread) are £3.45. Prices are lower still at lunchtime. Dishes can be hit or miss, but overall this is a good-value spot. Clientele – a diverse mix of locals, plus birthday groups attracted by the novelty factor – seem right in their LMNT.

Babies and children admitted. Entertainment: opera 8pm Sun. Tables outdoors (6, garden). **Map 25 C5.**

For branch see index.

Stoke Newington

Blue Legume

101 Stoke Newington Church Street, N16 0UD (7923 1303). Stoke Newington rail/73 bus. **Meals served** 9.30am-11pm Mon-Sat; 9.30am-6.30pm Sun. **Main courses** £4.95-£8.95. **Credit** (after 6pm) MC, V.

Consistently delicious food, obliging staff and myriad reasonably priced vegetarian, fish and carnivorous choices on the menu make this a justified Stokey hotspot. Reserve yourself a seat in the cosy front bar, with its mosaic tables, quirkily painted ceiling and singular artworks, to absorb the best atmosphere – though the airy conservatory at the back is ideal for larger parties, and those with kids in tow. The brunch menu (served until 6pm) brims with rich smoothies and juices, eggs cooked multiple ways, and special delights such as organic waffles accompanied by a fruit platter and maple syrup. Night-time sees a change in ambience, with candles and a soundtrack of soft jazz complementing a decent wine list and Turkish-inspired food – such as the trademark Blue Legume, a delicious aubergine parcel of roasted vegetables crowned with goat's cheese. Make sure you leave room for one of the fresh, own-made desserts on show at the front counter; the lemon cheesecake is legendary.

Babies and children welcome: high chairs. Booking advisable dinner. Tables outdoors (5, pavement). Takeaway service. **Map 25 B1.**

North

Camden Town & Chalk Farm

Marine Ices

8 Haverstock Hill, NW3 2BL (7482 9003/ www.marineices.co.uk). Chalk Farm tube. **Lunch served** noon-3pm, **dinner served** 6-11pm Tue-Fri. **Meals served** noon-11pm Sat; noon-10pm Sun. **Main courses** £6.10-£13.75. **Credit** MC, V.

Though the name Marine Ices harks back to an original nautical design, this has been long abandoned; the two back rooms are painted white and populated by standard caff furniture. However, the steady trade this family company has done on Haverstock Hill since 1947 suggests customer loyalty is not built on aesthetics alone. From large family troupes to father-son outings, the theme here is delighted, sugar-fuelled kids. The surprisingly full savoury menu concentrates on salads, pastas and pizzas, but the main event is the extensive ice-cream menu. A Copa Gino sundae had too many roasted almonds, but the chocolate and vanilla ice-creams tasted authentic (if not quite as rich as their Roman or Florentine equivalents). Laced with Baileys, the hazelnut, coffee and vanilla Copa Rita is one of several concoctions to include a splash of spirits – presumably to help you deal with cacophonous children. Service was slightly frantic, and two drinks failed to materialise. However, neither did they appear on the bill, and the staff graciously obliged when our 11-year-old expert's order changed at the last minute.

Babies and children welcome: children's portions; high chairs. Takeaway service. **Map 27 B1.**

Islington

Candid Arts Café

Candid Arts Trust, 3 Torrens Street, EC1V 1NQ (7837 4237/www.candidarts.com). Angel tube. **Meals served** noon-10pm Mon-Sat; noon-5pm Sun. **Main courses** £4-£12. **Credit** AmEx, MC, V.

Attached to the Candid Arts Trust theatre and gallery, this second-floor café is popular with Islington's arty types. They lounge in its atmospheric, attic-like room, on red velvet chairs or at the stately communal table. Come nightfall the space gets absurdly dark, lit mainly by candles with aeons of wax dripping down their metal holders. It all adds to the louche vibe – Candid is bohemian to a T. Indeed, the only thing missing from the fit is bohemian-friendly prices. Homely meals of lasagne, pies, quiches, stews and curries are fine for what they are (own-made earlier, then heated to order and served with salad or rice), but are very expensive; expect to pay between £8 and £12 for a dish that should really cost half as much. Cakes with coffee or tea represent slightly better value. Staff are scatty yet not unfriendly. In warm weather a downstairs courtyard holds a cluster of tables.

Babies and children admitted. Booking advisable. Separate room for parties, seats 30. Tables outdoors (8, courtyard). **Map 5 O2.**

Le Mercury

140A Upper Street, N1 1QY (7354 4088/ www.lemercury.co.uk). Angel tube/Highbury & Islington tube/rail. **Meals served** noon-1am Mon-Sat; noon-11.30pm Sun. **Main courses** £6.45. **Credit** AmEx, JCB, MC, V.

This friendly French local eaterie, perched on the corner of Upper Street and Almeida Street, manages to holds its own against hordes of nearby competitors. A charmingly lackadaisical attitude probably helps, and the bargain basement prices can't hurt (£3.95 starters, £6.45 mains), particularly in a notoriously pricey area. The food isn't bad either. A starter of gnocchi with butternut squash was light and delicious; steak and chips ticked all the right boxes; and a frankly sinful banana shortcake with strawberries for pud was scrumptious. As long as you don't want to impress with your wealth, Le Mercury would make quite a good first-date restaurant, with its tables for two, pictures of Paris on the walls, and candles stuck artfully in bottles. If you run out of things to talk about, there's sure to be plenty of other customers enjoying their dinner and providing eavesdropping opportunities – both theatre-goers heading for curtain-up at the nearby Almeida theatre, and locals enjoying a wallet-friendly evening à deux.

Babies and children admitted. Booking advisable weekends. Separate room for parties, seats 50. **Map 5 O1.**

S&M Café (100)

4-6 Essex Road, N1 8LN (7359 5361/www.sandmcafe.co.uk). Angel tube. **Meals served** 7.30am-11pm Mon-Fri; 8.30am-11pm Sat; 8.30am-10.30pm Sun. **Main courses** £5.75-£7.95. **Credit** MC, V.

Interview

KEVIN FINCH

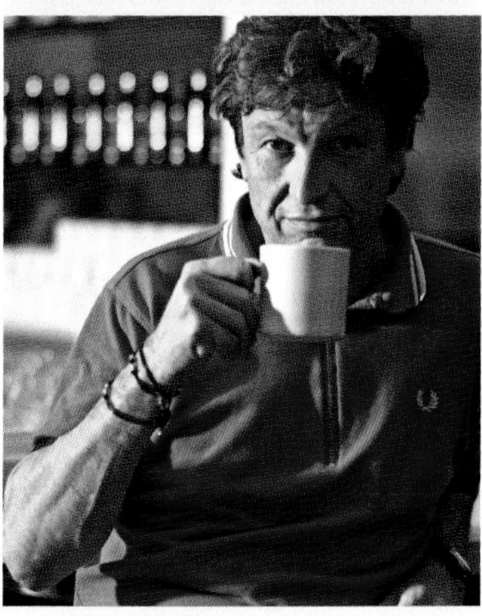

Who are you?

Owner of the **S&M Café** group (*see left*), which celebrates the quintessentially British caff. We've also recently launched an event catering division – S&M Live! – which has been in action at various music festivals, including Glastonbury, Lovebox and Secret Garden.

Eating in London: what's good about it?

The variety, quality and range of ethnicity.

What's bad about it?

It's often expensive – too expensive – with variable quality and inadequately trained service and kitchen staff.

Which are your favourite London restaurants?

At steak restaurant **Le Relais de Venise l'entrecôte** (*see p106*), you get *absolutely* the same thing every time you eat there. **The Ledbury** (*see p111*) is one of the few restaurants to offer real fine dining outside the West End. **Haché** (*see p300*) is head and shoulders above other like-minded burger joints. And I like the **Holly Bush** pub (*see p344*), which is my local.

Who or what has had the biggest impact on London's restaurant scene in the past 25 years?

Oliver Peyton. He created grand spaces and celebrated high design. He was in tandem with the emerging and exciting Britpop and Britart scenes, and put food on the same level as either of those cultural experiences. Also Marco Pierre White, because he set the standards for excellence in London and was the first to have two three-star Michelin restaurants.

Any hot tips for the coming year?

A significant rise in the quality of food at airports, partly because people are spending more time there. Also the quality of fare at music gigs is changing rapidly – people now go to eat and drink, not just to see a band.

A good balance between caff and trendy diner, S&M (that's sausage and mash) flies the flag for traditional British cuisine. It might have been surpassed in terms of meat-and-spud quality by the likes of Mother Mash (*see p299*), but it still draws a hugely diverse clientele: everyone from brickies to celebrities. Bangers and mash is the focus. You can 'mix & mash' from a selection of ten sausages (including pork, lamb, chicken, vegetarian and gluten-free varieties, plus daily specials), four types of mash, and three of gravy. Shepherd's pie, steak and kidney pie, smoked haddock fish cakes, all-day breakfasts and a nostalgic range of puddings also appear; there's a reasonable choice of wines and beers. This branch has preserved features of the original Alfredo's café (featured in *Quadrophenia*); the shopfront is an art deco classic. Inside are Formica tables and chrome-trimmed fittings. Staff are friendly, music is eclectic, and ethical considerations are made (free-range pork, Fairtrade coffee).
Babies and children welcome: children's menu; high chair. Booking advisable; not accepted before 4pm weekends. Tables outdoors (5, pavement). Takeaway service. **Map 5 O1.**
For branches see index.

Outer London

Richmond, Surrey

Stein's

55 Richmond Towpath, west of Richmond Bridge, Richmond, Surrey, TW10 6UX (8948 8189/ www.stein-s.com). Richmond tube/rail then 20-min walk or 65 bus. **Meals served** noon-10pm Mon-Fri; 10am-10pm Sat, Sun (call to check winter times). **Main courses** £2.90-£16.90. **Credit** MC, V.

Opened on Richmond's riverside walkway in 2004, Stein's is a Bavarian-themed beer garden. It's a good-value alfresco spot, set up by a German couple who wanted somewhere relaxed to take their children. The menu contains a variety of huge, sausage-based dishes, along with hot and cold sharing platters, side orders (of sauerkraut, potato salad and suchlike), breakfasts, and puddings of the cake or strudel variety. The daily stew, which comes complete with a pretzel and is priced at under a fiver, is a highlight. It's a slightly odd dining experience; you order at the counter, where a helpful waitress will translate the German titles into English. The restaurant licence means you must order food if you want to drink – and it would be a shame to miss out on the likes of draught Erdinger wheat beer, imported from Bavaria, or a bottle of Trollinger Löwenstein from the German-dominated wine list. The only problem with Stein's is the inclement British climate, as it's entirely outdoors (though parasols might keep off a brief shower). Check the weather before you go.
Babies and children welcome: high chairs. Tables outdoors (28, towpath). Takeaway service.

Pie & mash shops

Pie and mash – the traditional foodstuff of London's working classes – is fast disappearing. Its detractors probably think that's no bad thing, but along with the food go the pie and mash shops, and these *are* worth mourning, whatever your culinary bent. A choice bunch of these establishments remains – all are listed below – resplendent with tiled interiors, marble-topped tables and worn wooden benches. Most are located in the traditional working-class areas of east London (Bethnal Green, Hackney, Bow, Walthamstow) or across the river in Deptford and Peckham, but there's the occasional lone outpost in the west (**Cockneys**) and north (**Castle's**). The oldest and most beautiful is **M Manze** on Tower Bridge Road, established in 1902, though **F Cooke** of Broadway Market, the **Kellys**' and the **Harrington's** shops all date from the early 20th century. Visit these friendly, family-run businesses while you can, for each year another one closes (Bert's in Peckham since the last edition), and with it vanishes a slice of old London.

The food has altered little since the middle of the 19th century: a wedge of glutinous mashed potatoes, pies (minced beef and gravy in a watertight crust), liquor (loosely based on parsley sauce) and eels (jellied and cold, or warm and stewed) – though escalating eel prices mean that many places only serve pie and mash. Vinegar and pepper are the preferred condiments, a fork and spoon the tools of choice. Relish the food, the surroundings, the prices (you'll rarely pay more than a fiver) and also your dining companions: Londoners to the core, not yet seduced by the trashy allure of the international burger chains. Note that none of the shops serves alcohol; all offer takeaways.

Hardcore enthusiasts should consider joining the **Pie & Mash Club** (www.pie-n-mash.com), formed in 1994. It offers social history with a competitive eating element; members meet in different pie shops over the course of the season (September to May) to see who can eat the most pie and mash. If you leave anything on the plate, points are docked.

WJ Arment

7 & 9 Westmoreland Road, SE17 2AX (7703 4974). Elephant & Castle tube/ rail/12, 35, 40, 45, 68A, 171, 176, 468 bus. **Open** 10.30am-5pm Tue, Wed; 10.30am-4.30pm Thur; 10.30am-5.30pm Fri; 10.30-6pm Sat. **No credit cards.**

Castle's

229 Royal College Street, NW1 9LT (7485 2196). Camden Town tube/Camden Road rail. **Open** 10.30am-3.30pm Tue-Fri; 10.30am-4pm Sat. **No credit cards. Map 27 D1.**

Clark's

46 Exmouth Market, EC1R 4QE (7837 1974). Farringdon tube/rail/19, 38, 341 bus. **Open** 10.30am-4pm Mon-Thur; 10.30am-5pm Fri, Sat. **No credit cards. Map 5 N4.**

Cockneys Pie & Mash

314 Portobello Road, W10 5RU (8960 9409). Ladbroke Grove tube. **Open** 11.30am-5.30pm Tue-Thur, Sat; 11.30am-7pm Fri. **No credit cards. Map 19 B1.**

F Cooke

150 Hoxton Street, N1 6SH (7729 7718). Old Street or Liverpool Street tube/rail/ 48, 55, 149, 242, 243 bus. **Open** 10am-7pm Mon-Thur; 9.30am-8pm Fri, Sat. **No credit cards. Map 6 R2.**

F Cooke

9 Broadway Market, E8 4PH (7254 6458). Liverpool Street tube/rail then 26, 48 or 55 bus/London Fields rail. **Open** 10am-7pm Mon-Thur; 10am-8pm Fri, Sat. **No credit cards.**

AJ Goddard

203 Deptford High Street, SE8 3NT (8692 3601). Deptford rail/Deptford Bridge DLR/ 1, 47 bus. **Open** 9.30am-3pm Mon-Fri; 9am-3pm Sat. **No credit cards.**

Harrington's

3 Selkirk Road, SW17 0ER (8672 1877). Tooting Broadway tube. **Open** 11am-9pm Tue, Thur, Fri; 11am-2pm Wed; 11am-7.30pm Sat. **No credit cards.**

G Kelly

526 Roman Road, E3 5ES (8980 3165). Bow Road or Mile End tube/Bow Church DLR/8, 339 bus. **Open** 11am-3pm Mon; 10am-3pm Tue-Thur; 10am-7pm Fri; 10am-5.30pm Sat. **No credit cards.**

G Kelly

600 Roman Road, E3 2RW (8983 3552/www.gkellypieandmash.co.uk). Bow Road or Mile End tube/Bow Church DLR/8, 339 bus. **Open** 10am-2.30pm Thur, Fri; 10am-5pm Sat. **No credit cards.**

G Kelly

414 Bethnal Green Road, E2 0DJ (7739 3603). Bethnal Green tube/ rail/8 bus. **Open** 10am-3pm Mon-Thur; 10am-6.30pm Fri; 9.30am-4.30pm Sat. **No credit cards.**

S&R Kelly

284 Bethnal Green Road, E2 0AG (7739 8676). Bethnal Green tube/rail/ 8 bus. **Open** 9am-2.30pm Mon-Thur; 9am-5.30pm Fri; 10am-3.30pm Sat. **No credit cards. Map 6 S4.**

Manze's

204 Deptford High Street, SE8 3PR (8692 2375). Deptford rail/Deptford Bridge DLR/1, 47 bus. **Open** 9.30am-1.30pm Mon, Thur; 9.30am-3pm Tue, Wed, Fri, Sat. **No credit cards.**

L Manze

76 Walthamstow High Street, E17 7LD (8520 2855). Walthamstow Central tube/rail. **Open** 10am-4pm Mon-Wed; 10am-5pm Thur-Sat. **No credit cards.**

L Manze

74 Chapel Market, N1 9ER (7837 5270). Angel tube. **Open** 11am-5pm Tue-Sat. **No credit cards. Map 5 N2.**

M Manze (100)

87 Tower Bridge Road, SE1 4TW (7407 2985/www.manze.co.uk). Bus 1, 42, 188. **Open** 11am-2pm Mon; 10.30am-2pm Tue-Thur; 10am-2.15pm Fri; 10am-2.45pm Sat. **No credit cards.**

M Manze

105 Peckham High Street, SE15 5RS (7277 6181/www.manze.co.uk). Peckham Rye rail. **Open** 11am-2pm Mon; 10.30am-2pm Tue-Thur; 10am-2.15pm Fri; 10am-2.45pm Sun. **No credit cards.**

M Manze

226 High Street, Sutton, Surrey SM1 1NT (8286 8787/www.manze.co.uk). Sutton rail. **Open** 11am-2.45pm Mon; 11am-5pm Tue-Fri; 10.30-5pm Sat. **No credit cards.**

Cafés

The past year has seen a grand spread of new cafés in London. For a start, there's a brace from Oliver 'Café King' Peyton: the jauntily styled **Meals** at Heal's department store (contender for Best Design in the 2007 Time Out Eating & Drinking Awards) and the equally stylish **Peyton & Byrne** inside the Wellcome Collection. Among other new inclusions, **Shipp's Tea Rooms** in Borough Market and **Orange Pekoe** in Barnes are destinations for tea connoisseurs, while award-winning pâtisserie is to be found at **William Curley** in Richmond. Welcome also to **Bullet**, **Fernandez & Wells**, **Flat White**, **Nordic Bakery** and **Sacred** – all of which made the shortlist for Best Coffee Bar in the 2007 Eating & Drinking Awards. They help broaden still further the staggering array of cafés to be found in London: a range that encompasses supremely elegant afternoon teas, adventurous pâtisserie, the alfresco delights of park cafés and the child-friendly charms of neighbourhood venues. Fancy a cuppa?

Central

Clerkenwell & Farringdon

Kipferl

70 Long Lane, EC1A 9EJ (7796 2229/ www.kipferl.co.uk). Barbican tube. **Open** 8am-5pm Mon-Fri; 9am-5pm Sat. **Main courses** £3-£6.50. **No credit cards.**

The cakes alone are worth a trip to London's only Austrian café. The selection changes, but usually includes sachertorte, linzer torte, baked cheesecake and deliciously moist apple strudel; have a slice with one of the excellent coffees (melange is the one with hot milk). If your tastes are more savoury, then the choice gets even wider. Daily-changing soups and salads, and hot sausages such as wiener and käsekrainer (like many other foodstuffs here, imported from Austria) sit alongside a range of super-tasty open sandwiches. Kipferl also sells deli items (lots of chocolates, pickles and preserves), Austrian wines and beers, and a selection of breads. Food aside, the main reason we like this place so much is the attitude of the staff – always welcoming – and the sweet touches, such as a cookie or chocolate with every coffee, even takeaway. As for the decor, they've made the most of a small, boxy modern space, with every inch crammed with comestibles (on shelves or in the big cold cabinet), tables and chairs.

Babies and children admitted. Takeaway service. **Map 11 O5.**

Covent Garden

★ Bullet NEW

2007 RUNNER-UP BEST COFFEE BAR

3rd floor, Snow & Rock, 4 Mercer Street, WC2H 9QA (7836 4922/www.bullet-coffee.com). Covent Garden tube/Charing Cross tube/rail. **Open** 10am-6pm daily. **Main courses** £2.80-£6. **Credit** MC, V.

To reach Bullet, you have to climb three flights of stairs in one of the most unexpected venues imaginable: the Covent Garden branch of the Snow & Rock sporting equipment chain. It's worth the climb, even if you don't have rock shoes or belays. This little jewel of a café, carved out of selling-space on the top floor by a roaster from New Zealand, serves coffee and food of exemplary quality. The espresso is textbook stuff, expertly made using Fairtrade organic beans roasted by the company (and available for sale). There are also the usual milky variants, including flat whites, made by Kiwi baristas. Snacks are a cut above: a pissaladière (thin onion tart on flaky pastry) was wonderfully crisp and nicely seasoned with fresh rosemary, and a chocolate brownie was dense, damp and totally dreamy. There are also more substantial dishes such as savoury pies, all made in the small kitchen out back. The perfect place to rest weary legs after a shopping session on nearby Long Acre – and there's internet access too.

Babies and children admitted: nappy-changing facilities. Disabled: toilet. **Map 18 D4.**

Kastner & Ovens

52 Floral Street, WC2E 9DA (7836 2700). Covent Garden tube. **Open** 8am-5pm Mon-Fri. **Main courses** £4.25-£4.75. **No credit cards.**

Owners Sue Ovens and Ann-Marie Kastner have created a Covent Garden gem relied on by many working Londoners, who queue every weekday to see what's on the lunch menu. And, whatever it is, it's fresh and tasty. A filling lunch will set you back just over a fiver and there's a good selection: salads might be chickpea and roasted vegetable, pea and feta, or tabouleh; hot mains range from caponata packed with juicy aubergines to beef lasagne or fish pie. The quiches and tartlets are stunning, with fresh and imaginative fillings and perfect crumbly pastry. One counter is packed with tempting cakes, biscuits and treats, such as lemon meringue pie and bakewell tart. Seating is limited (just one round table at the back), so most people take their food away – but don't be put off by the queue, it moves quickly and it's worth it.

Babies and children admitted. Takeaway service. **Map 18 E3.**

Paul

29 Bedford Street, WC2E 9ED (7836 5321/ www.paul-uk.com). Covent Garden tube. **Open** 7.30am-9pm Mon-Fri; 9am-9pm Sat; 9am-8pm Sun. **Main courses** £4-£8. **Credit** MC, V.

London's first outpost of this French bakery chain opened at this branch just seven years ago in 2000 – more than 100 years after the business was established. Pass through the shop selling traditionally made breads, pastries and cakes to the airy tea room, and the grandeur suggested by white panelled walls, historical murals and red velvet banquettes is beginning to look distinctly grubby round the edges – which isn't surprising considering the steady traffic of tourists and office workers. Breakfast concentrates on baskets of Paul's deliciously dense breads and croissants, or hot, savoury filled versions of the latter. Lunch options are equally Gallic: omelettes, quiche, paillassons (grated potato pancakes with various toppings) and sweet crêpes, as well as substantial, impeccably fresh salads. Not everything is an unqualified success: a quiche from the specials board, made with tomato, tuna and crème fraîche, was a flavoursome but slightly soggy choice, although a coffee and eclair (not too sweet, with proper custard filling) couldn't be faulted. Service is authentically pouty, but efficient.

Babies and children welcome: high chair. Disabled: toilet. Takeaway service. **Map 18 D5.**

For branches see index.

Euston

★ Peyton & Byrne NEW

Wellcome Collection, 183 Euston Road, NW1 2BE (7611 2142/www.peytonandbyrne.co.uk). Euston Square tube/Euston tube/rail. **Open** 10am-6pm Mon-Wed, Fri-Sun; 10am-10pm Thur. **Lunch served** 11am-3pm daily. **Main courses** £3.50-£9. **Credit** MC, V.

You may have your bags checked by security, but the Wellcome Collection is free to enter and its new cafeteria – an offshoot of the teeny Peyton & Byrne shop in Heal's on Tottenham Court Road – is easily accessible, bang in the centre of the foyer. As usual with Oliver Peyton venues, the design has been carefully considered: neat chairs with square cushions in taupe, lime and hot pink, and low, sharply cut sofas. The menu offers a choice of hot sandwiches, pies, terrines and hearty salads that are more of a meal than a snack. Our hot-smoked salmon sandwich was stupendous: properly ripe avocado, fresh baby spinach leaves and juicy slabs of fish layered in a noticeably high-quality bloomer-style white roll, served with boiled and buttered Jersey Royals and a fashionably cress-flecked salad. At £8.75 it was terrific value too.

BEST CAFÉS

Tea treasures

You can sample numerous different brews – and buy loose leaf teas – at **Orange Pekoe** (*see p310*) and the **Tea Palace** (*see p309*). For East-West flavours, try the tea room at **Yauatcha** (*see p308*).

Posh pâtisserie

Cakes to die for at **Ladurée** (*see p306*), **Macaron** (*see p310*), **Sketch: The Parlour** (*see p307*), **William Curley** (*see p312*), the **Wolseley** (*see p307*) and **Yauatcha** (*see p308*).

Global gateaux

For US-style treats, pop into **Hummingbird Bakery** (*see p308*). **Kipferl** (*see left*) offers a taste of Austria, newcomer **Nordic Bakery** (*see p308*) has little-seen Finnish foodstuffs.

Family favourites

Crumpet (*see p310*), **Brilliant Kids Café** (*see p312*), **Bush Garden Café** (*see p309*), **Gracelands** (*see p312*) and **Munchkin Lane** (*see p310*) all make an extra effort to accommodate kids. With their farmyard settings, **Frizzante@City Farm** (*see p311*) and **Mudchute Kitchen** (*see p311*) also provide plenty of distractions. Cafés in parks are another surefire bet (*see pp313-314*).

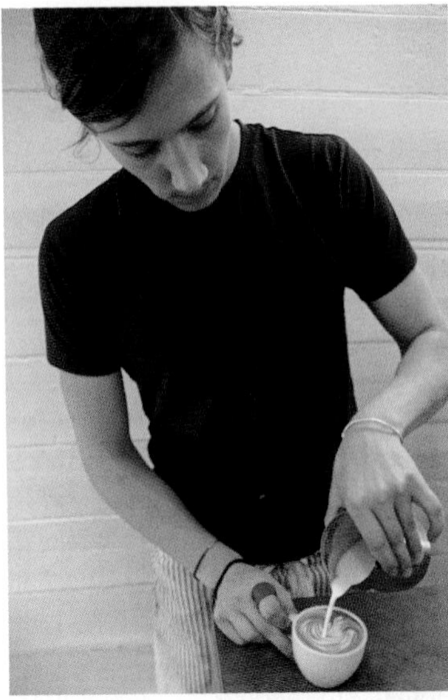

Fernandez & Wells

Also fab-a-roony was the generous jaffa cake with dark chocolate cover and luscious layers of orange jelly and chocolate mousse. Interesting drinks include New Forest Cider, Luscombe lemonade and St Clements refreshers, Chegworth Valley juices, well-made coffee served in elegant crockery or takeaway cups, and a good variety of teas.
Babies and children admitted. Disabled: toilet. **Map 4 K4**.

Fitzrovia

Meals NEW

2007 RUNNER-UP BEST DESIGN

1st floor, Heal's, 196 Tottenham Court Road, W1T 7LQ (7580 2522/www.heals.co.uk). Goodge Street or Warren Street tube. **Open** 10am-6pm Mon-Wed, Fri; 10am-7.30pm Thur; 9.30am-6.30pm Sat; noon-6pm Sun. **Afternoon tea served** 3-6pm daily. **Main courses** £9-£10.50. **Set lunch** £12.50 2 courses. **Credit** AmEx, DC, MC, V.

After walking past the crisp furniture and elegant accessories of Heal's, Oliver Peyton's Meals comes as something of a surprise. Done out (by architectural practice FAT) like a cross between an alpine lodge and a toddler's bedroom, the cut-out cupboards suggest a fairy tale landscape of foliage and stars, while fake wooden 'tablecloths' and marshmallow pink chairs are the ironic side of twee. It's a surprisingly jaunty space, with a playfulness quite at odds with the carefully cultivated serenity elsewhere in the shop. The food doesn't quite taste as well as it reads, but it's enjoyable, cultured and surprisingly generous: witness the splendid, sizeable fish cake topped with a perfectly poached egg (a better bet than the hearty steak sandwich served with average chips). Starters were also decent; a gentle blend of wild rice and smoked salmon came out ahead of a slightly clumsy asparagus and avocado salad. If you're still hungry after two courses, choose dessert from the incomparable selection of sweet treats at the Peyton & Byrne franchise on the ground floor. The 'squillionaire's shortbread', in particular, is not far short of sensational.
Babies and children welcome: children's menu; high chairs. Booking advisable. Disabled: toilet. Restaurant available for hire. **Map 4 K5**.

Knightsbridge

Ladurée

Harrods, entrance on Hans Road, SW1X 7XL (7893 8293/www.laduree.com). Knightsbridge tube. **Open** *Shop* 9am-9pm Mon-Sat; noon-6pm Sun. **Lunch served** 11.30am-3.30pm Mon-Sat; noon-3.30pm Sun. **Tea served** 3.30-6.30pm Mon-Sat; 3.30-6pm Sun. **Dinner served** 6.30-8pm Mon-Sat; 6-8pm Sun. **Main courses** £15-£27.50. **Set meal** £29 2 courses, £34 3 courses. **Set tea** £21. **Credit** AmEx, DC, JCB, MC, V.

Decked out in pretty pastel shades, the Harrods branch of this upmarket French chain of tea salons is popular with big spenders and tourists. Although the high ceiling and weighty chandeliers lend grandeur, it's the display of beautifully executed Parisian-style pâtisserie that is the main draw. Alongside classic favourites, Ladurée also boasts new-wave dainties that include 'Bollywood' fancies with exotic coconut custardy fillings, and meringues filled with lime blossom cream. Choosing to stick with convention, we opted for the millefeuille praline, which was marred by burnt layers of puff pastry. A billowy St Honoré was more enticing: the small choux pastry ring, filled with a mountain of vanilla cream, was as decadent as it was delicious. The macaroons remain as marvellous as ever; rose petal, liquorice and grenadine varieties, the current raves, didn't disappoint. Our biggest gripe was teabags in teapots – hardly a sumptuous statement of style. And the service was harried and at times chaotic, with a single waiter tending crowded tables while the manager looked on.
Babies and children welcome: high chairs. Bookings not accepted (tea). Disabled: toilet. Separate room for parties, seats 20. Tables outdoors (6, pavement). Takeaway service. **Map 14 E10**.

Marylebone

★ La Fromagerie (100)

2-6 Moxon Street, W1U 4EW (7935 0341/ www.lafromagerie.co.uk). Baker Street or Bond Street tube. **Open** 10.30am-7.30pm Mon; 8am-7.30pm Tue-Fri; 9am-7pm Sat; 10am-6pm Sun. **Main courses** £6-£12.40. **Credit** AmEx, MC, V.

It's all about the ingredients in the 'tasting café' at the rear of this Marylebone gourmet shop. The space, though attractively skylit, can get packed at weekends, when local foodies and shoppers cram the central communal table; some couples prefer to wait for one of the three two-person tables. The cheese plate understandably predominates on the daily-changing menu and features selections from the shop's walk-in cheese room (with detailed descriptions, should you want to buy some to take home), while the house ploughman's features a pork and veal pie from equally discerning neighbouring butcher, the Ginger Pig. Other plates are geared towards charcuterie and fish, and there are hearty cooked dishes such as, on a recent visit, a delectable gruyère and onion tart. Salads are bursting with individual flavours; a medley of asparagus and peas with lemon, mint and aged feta was suitably robust. Breakfast options range from simple brioche and jam to a full Spanish charcuterie, cheese and bread blow-out. The Florentine coffee is a potent hit and there's an extensive wine list with advice on pairing. On the whole, staff remain remarkably unflappable and accommodating, even in busy periods.

Babies and children admitted. Bookings not accepted. Café available for hire (evenings). Takeaway service. **Map 3 G3.**

For branch see index.

Le Pain Quotidien

72-75 Marylebone High Street, W1U 5JW (7486 6154/www.lepainquotidien.com). Baker Street or Bond Street tube. **Open** 7am-9pm Mon-Fri; 8am-9pm Sat; 8am-8pm Sun. **Main courses** £5.75-£7.95. **Credit** AmEx, MC, V.

Launched by a bread-loving chef in Brussels in 1990, LPQ has rapidly expanded in Europe, the US and Canada. So far, the quality of the food or the experience remains unaffected by the speedy roll-out. The spacious Marylebone branch has a laid-back, rustic feel, dominated by a farmhouse-style communal table, but there are enough smaller tables if you shy away from sharing. The menu revolves around the excellent organic loaves. There's a wide choice of sourdoughs and others for breakfast baskets, and the lunch speciality is the tartine – an open sandwich with various toppings, such as smoked salmon or salami, ricotta, tomato and rocket. Generous salads (mixed leaves with avocado, mango and jumbo prawns was fresh and tangy) and platters of charcuterie, cheeses, dips and antipasti also come with bread. There's a small range of wine, beer and cider. The other branches (except Aveda) serve more substantial cooked dishes in the evening.

Babies and children welcome: high chairs. Disabled: toilet. Tables outdoors (7, pavement). Takeaway service. **Map 9 G5.**

For branches see index.

Mayfair

Sketch: The Parlour

9 Conduit Street, W1S 2XJ (0870 777 4488/ www.sketch.uk.com). Oxford Circus or Piccadilly Circus tube. **Open** 8am-9pm Mon-Fri; 10am-9pm Sat. **Tea served** 3-7.30pm Mon-Sat. **Main courses** £3.50-£8.50. **Set tea** £7.50-£18.50; £30 incl glass of champagne. **Credit** AmEx, DC, MC, V.

There's been a change of atmosphere at Parlour – it's more edgy, the crowd has become younger, and there's more wine-sipping and cork-popping than in previous years. But it remains a swish place in which to indulge your French fancies, and the comfy sofas help shut out the real world. Although the exquisite range of pâtisserie has been cut back, signature delicacies remain. We were particularly impressed by the simple clean flavours of a tangy, cream-enriched lemon tart. A raspberry tart was almost as good: sweet pastry, a tiny spoonful of red pepper jelly, almond sponge and a tidy pile of berries providing a tease of spicy rich flavours. Tonka bean cream tart (the beans taste similar to vanilla) didn't make the grade, however, let down by a seriously tough pastry case and discordant dab of apple compote. Other bites (meringues, eclairs, chocolate slices) are good, but we've tasted better in the past. The service team, beautifully attired in flowing silk outfits, are utterly charming, but could definitely speed up their act.

Babies and children admitted. Bookings not accepted. Café available for hire. Takeaway service. **Map 9 J6.**

Piccadilly

★ The Wolseley

160 Piccadilly, W1J 9EB (7499 6996/www. thewolseley.com). Green Park tube. **Breakfast served** 7-11.30am Mon-Fri; 8-11.30am Sat, Sun. **Lunch served** noon-2.30pm daily. **Tea served** 3.30-5.30pm Mon-Sat; 3.30-6.30pm Sun. **Dinner served** 5.30pm-midnight Mon-Sat; 5.30-11pm Sun. **Main courses** £6.75-£29.50. **Set tea** £8.25-£19.50. **Cover** £2. **Credit** AmEx, DC, JCB, MC, V.

Embodying all that's good and great about afternoon tea, the Wolseley is the destination of choice for those who like to highlight their day with cream teas, fresh sandwiches and elegant pâtisserie. It's no surprise that this beautifully appointed art deco hall is as popular with business types and media bigwigs as it is with champagne-sipping ladies and privileged young families. Staff are as attentive as they are friendly. After several visits, we've been impressed by the consistency of service and quality of preparations. Standouts include sharply cut finger sandwiches with not a crumb out of place; light scones with all the trimmings; and excellent sponges, tarts and mini mousse cakes. Our top choices included an orange-scented madeline sponge crowned with a ruff of cream, and a darkly seductive viennese 'opera cake' made of coffee-steeped almond sponge layers, filled with coffee buttercream and chocolate ganache. We can't recommend the excellent loose leaf teas highly enough, particularly the darjeeling for its fragrance and delicacy.

Babies and children welcome: crayons; high chairs. nappy-changing facilities; Booking advisable. Disabled: toilet. **Map 9 J7.**

St James's

5th View NEW

5th floor, Waterstone's, 203-206 Piccadilly, W1J 9HA (7851 2468/www.5thview.co.uk). Piccadilly Circus tube. **Lunch served** noon-3pm Mon-Fri; noon-4pm Sat, Sun. **Tapas served** 5-9pm Mon-Sat. **Main courses** £9.50-£14. **Tapas** £3.50-£9.50. **Credit** MC, V.

The buzzy, refurbished café topping Waterstone's art deco flagship store may specialise in freshly cooked tarts (asparagus or crab, lemon and chive), but these had run out by the time we arrived at 1.30pm. Instead, there was a brash rocket salad with focaccia croutons, brie, chorizo and smoked chicken, and a pleasant platter of serrano ham that was unexpectedly pale in hue and flavour. From the dessert table, a nicely sharp berry tart nudged ahead of a somewhat flaccid rhubarb version, but both were rather institutional (catering is courtesy of Digby Trout, which works at a score of London venues, including Southwark Cathedral and the British Museum). Things get livelier on the drinks menu; two dozen interesting bottled beers (Dos Equis and Negra Modello alongside the tediously familiar Corona) and an impressive list of cocktails make this a good spot for an after-work drink or a pre-theatre pit-stop. The view offers more rooftops than sights, although the top of the London Eye and the Houses of Parliament are easily discerned – perfectly diverting, but hardly the 'sweeping view... towards Big Ben' promised by the website.

Babies and children welcome (until 5pm): high chairs. Disabled: lift; toilet. Separate room for parties, seats 60. **Map 17 A5.**

Soho

Amato

14 Old Compton Street, W1D 4TH (7734 5733/ www.amato.co.uk). Leicester Square, Piccadilly Circus or Tottenham Court Road tube. **Open** 8am-10pm Mon-Sat; 10am-8pm Sun. **Main courses** £3.95-£8.25. **Credit** MC, V.

Although it's long been overshadowed by Maison Bertaux and Pâtisserie Valerie (for both, *see p308*), its rather more charismatic neighbours in Soho café society, this established caffè and pasticceria nonetheless retains a devoted following. The coffee is generally good and strong, and the fuller-than-you'd-expect menu offers some nice options (including a confident rendition of eggs benedict, served from the breakfast menu until noon). But it's the cakes that really catch the eye, with the colourful window displays tempting all but the most miserable Soho stroller. The choice is immense; we particularly liked the giotto, a light yet immersive number soaked in mascarpone cheese that comes with a distinctly alcoholic tang, though the guiltiest pleasures are almost certainly the preposterously good doughnuts. The tidy seating area isn't very attractive, but it is pretty large, and the friendly, efficient staff generally don't mind if you linger for a while.

Babies and children welcome: high chairs. Takeaway service. **Map 17 C3.**

★ Fernandez & Wells NEW

2007 WINNER BEST COFFEE BAR

73 Beak Street, W1F 9RS (7287 8124). Oxford Circus or Piccadilly Circus tube. **Open** 8am-7pm Mon-Fri; 9am-7pm Sat. **Main courses** £3.50-£5. **Credit** (over £5) MC, V.

Fernandez & Wells runs an interesting pair of operations round the corner from one another: a takeaway/delicatessen in Lexington Street, specialising in highest-quality Spanish products and cooked dishes; and this café, offering a smaller and slightly different range. Here the emphasis is on sandwiches (made at the other store) and baked goods that are mostly bought in from first-class suppliers such as Melrose & Morgan and the Flour Station. There's no slouching on the coffee either, made using the espresso blend from the Monmouth Coffee Company, and with textbook crema (foam) on top. The baked goods are wonderful: grab some Valrhona chocolate mousse tart with raspberries if you can. The light, bright, simply decorated room has ample seating at tables and benches, and service is smiling and attentive; everyone working here seems to be genuinely enjoying what they do. And they bring you, unasked, a glass of water to go with your espresso – always a sign of extra care. A delightful establishment in every respect.

Babies and children admitted. **Map 17 A4.**

For branch see index.

Flat White NEW

2007 RUNNER-UP BEST COFFEE BAR

17 Berwick Street, W1F 0PT (7734 0370/ www.flat-white.co.uk). Leicester Square, Oxford Circus or Tottenham Court Road tube. **Open** 8am-8pm Mon-Wed; 8am-9pm Thur, Fri; 9am-7pm Sat; 10am-6pm Sun. **Main courses** £3.50-£4. **No credit cards.**

In Australia and New Zealand, a 'flat white' is a coffee made with a large shot of espresso and a hefty dose of milk that's frothed a little less than a cappuccino's. That drink has given its name to this buzzy coffeeshop, the result of an Antipodean partnership between an Australian and Kiwi who wanted to be able to drink the kind of coffee they liked back home. The tiny, dark space in Berwick Street seems to be constantly crowded, with customers spilling out on to the pavement even when the weather's less than Sydney-sunny. Most people order milky drinks, and they're probably better off with those than with an espresso. Though expertly made, using beans from the Monmouth Coffee Company, on our visit our espresso was just too intense for palates used to the softer Italian-style version. There are simple snacks (mainly baked goodies and sandwiches) to

go with the coffees – nothing special, but just fine. On a warm day the room was hot, and its narrow confines can be a little too tight for comfort. But no one seems to mind. Flat White is white hot.
Babies and children admitted. Takeaway service. **Map 17 B3**.

Konditor & Cook

Curzon Soho, 99 Shaftesbury Avenue, W1D 5DY (7292 1684/www.konditorandcook.com). Leicester Square tube. **Open** 9.30am-11pm Mon-Sat; 10.30am-10.30pm Sun. **Main courses** £1.90-£5.75. **Credit** MC, V.
The union of the Curzon cinema and Konditor & Cook is a happy marriage indeed. The stylish café space at the front of the ground floor is furnished with tall stools at long counters, a few seats around a coffee table, plus a bar from which food and drink are dispensed. There's a more limited selection of eats at this branch (soup is the only hot dish served; on our visit, it was creamed spinach with a cheese scone accompaniment), but the big plus is that the café is licensed, so alongside good coffee and interesting soft drinks is a range of wines and cocktails. Accompany these with a slice of quiche, a sandwich (smoked salmon with beetroot and cucumber, say) or a sausage roll. Or jump straight into the sweet stuff – a lip-smacking array of cakes, pastries, flapjacks and brownies, plus prettily packaged bags of biscuits (lemon moon, kipferl, gruyère), baby meringues, provençal-style nougat, chocolates and turkish delight. Have a look at the website to see the full glory of the company's wedding- and party-cake range.
Babies and children admitted. Tables outdoors (3, pavement). **Map 17 C4**.
For branches see index.

Maison Bertaux

28 Greek Street, W1D 5DQ (7437 6007). Leicester Square, Piccadilly Circus or Tottenham Court Road tube. **Open** 8.30am-11pm Mon-Sat; 8.30am-7pm Sun. **Main courses** £1.50-£4.50. **No credit cards**.
Despite a fashion boutique opening in its basement, Maison Bertaux remains an essential stop for café nostalgics and connoisseurs of lost afternoon melancholy. Behind a couple of pavement tables, display cases proffer mainly cream-based pastries: ours was a choux pastry of cream, kiwi fruit, strawberries, even a hidden grape and nectarine slice. Of the few savouries on offer, 'Dijon slice' is a kind of cold croque monsieur, with mustard trying to cut through the greasy cheese; broccoli quiche was also pretty stolid, although the veg was snappily fresh. Place your order with the swift-speaking and charmingly fierce matriarch at the counter, then find a seat – perhaps up the tight staircase where soothing jazz plays amid temporary exhibitions of modern art. The ground floor is smaller and quite lovely, with a piano almost disappearing beneath flowers. At the foot of the stairs we spied two wonderful-looking cakes, high out of reach on their cooling racks, just the kind of detail appreciated by a clientele of suited gents and a growing fanbase of fashionable Japanese kids young enough to know exactly what they like.
Babies and children admitted. Tables outdoors (5, pavement). Takeaway service. **Map 17 C4**.

★ Nordic Bakery NEW

2007 RUNNER-UP BEST COFFEE BAR

14 Golden Square, W1F 9JF (3230 1077/ www.nordicbakery.com). Oxford Circus or Piccadilly Circus tube. **Open** 8am-8pm Mon-Fri; noon-7pm Sat. **Main courses** £2.80-£4. **Credit** MC, V.
The simplicity of the Nordic Bakery formula takes a lot of beating: a small range of food; a high-ceilinged, exceptionally lovely room decorated with impeccable Scandinavian good taste; and good coffee. It's a winning combination that makes for a quiet and contemplative experience, something that's all too rare in bustling Soho. Order from the counter and you'll be brought a tray at the table, by notably charming staff. The open sandwiches (ask for the 'lid', the top half of the bread) feature a lot of cured salmon, but the boiled egg and anchovy version – the egg perfectly cooked, faintly moist at the centre of the yolk – was something to treasure. Sweet options include cinnamon buns, chocolate cake and Swedish classic Tosca cake (a buttery sponge cake with almond and vanilla topping). The espresso is good though not perfect, but perhaps it's made in a style that Finns (the world's largest consumers of coffee per capita) especially like. And Londoners should like it too. Indeed, they should like everything about this place. Design junkies, note: the black tables and chairs are by Alvar Aalto, crockery is by Iittala, and the wall-hanging is a re-creation of a 100-year-old design by a Finnish artist.
Babies and children admitted. Takeway service. **Map 17 A4**.

Pâtisserie Valerie

44 Old Compton Street, W1D 5JX (7437 3466/ www.patisserie-valerie.co.uk). Leicester Square, Piccadilly Circus or Tottenham Court Road tube. **Open** 7.30am-8.30pm Mon, Tue; 7.30am-11pm Wed-Sat; 8am-8pm Sun. **Main courses** £3.75-£8.25. **Credit** (over £5) AmEx, DC, MC, V.
This Soho fixture began life in 1926 in Frith Street; when a Luftwaffe bomb destroyed the building, the café simply moved around the corner to Old Compton Street, where it's been ever since. The 1950s decor has many fans, but we find the ground floor gloomy and the tables too cramped; head upstairs to the lighter first floor for a quieter meal and a better vantage point for people-watching. The menu is simple, but does the trick with soup, omelettes, pasta and salads; there are toasted ciabatta and club sandwiches for lighter lunches. Breakfast runs from a full english or eggs benedict to brioche french toast with maple syrup. The coffee's Illy and customarily good, but the croissants, while enormous, aren't always as fresh and fluffy as we'd like, and the biscuits and truffles (sold by weight in ribboned takeaway boxes) have also proved disappointingly dry in the past. Usually, though, the French pastries and gateaux fulfil the promise of their attractive window displays. We'd happily eat the tarte aux pommes every day to keep the doctor away, and dearly wish it could count as one of the recommended five-a-day portions.
Babies and children welcome: high chairs. Takeaway service. **Map 17 C4**.
For branches (Chelsea Left Wing Café, Chelsea Gelateria Valerie, Pâtisserie Valerie) see index.

Sacred NEW

2007 RUNNER-UP BEST COFFEE BAR

13 Ganton Street, W1F 9BL (7734 1415/ www.sacredcafe.co.uk). Oxford Circus tube. **Open** 7.30am-8.30pm Mon-Wed, Fri; 7.30am-9pm Thur; 10am-8pm Sat; 10am-6pm Sun. **Main courses** £4-£5.50. **Credit** (over £5) AmEx, MC, V.
Sacred, indeed: the espresso machine stands on a 19th-century Welsh wooden pulpit. And that's just one of the religious motifs in this friendly place. But then, coffee does seem to be something of a religion in New Zealand, where the owners hail from. Sacred occupies two levels, a small ground-floor room and a dark, attractive basement with plenty of seating and artworks for sale. If the espresso is anything to judge by (and it usually is), this is a place for coffee worship. The beans are Fairtrade, and our espresso was perfect: lovely crema (foam), beautifully balanced; it needed no sugar. Tea-drinkers are well catered for too, with green, fruit and ayurvedic offerings as well as classic black teas. Food was good, but not exceptional. A smoked salmon sandwich with mascarpone was excellent, but tasty lemon tart and cheesecake were ill-served by soggy bases. There are also generously portioned salads, and some hot dishes. A good choice for lunch or a snack in a crowded part of Soho; the main room is light and airy in warm weather and the basement a cosy snug in winter.
Babies and children admitted: nappy-changing facilities. Separate room for parties, seats 35. Tables outside (2, pavement). Takeaway service. **Map 17 A4**.

Yauatcha

15 Broadwick Street, W1F 0DL (7494 8888). Leicester Square, Oxford Circus, Piccadilly Circus or Tottenham Court Road tube.
Tea house **Tea/snacks served** 11am-11.45pm Mon-Sat; 11am-10.45pm Sun. **Dim sum served** noon-11.45pm Mon-Sat; noon-10.45pm Sun. **Set tea** £19-£26.50. **Dim sum** £3-£14.50. **Credit** AmEx, JCB, MC, V.
Light and airy, Yauatcha's chic ground-floor tea house and pâtisserie offers a fusion spin on tea and cakes. It's modern in looks, but the ever-shrinking dedicated café space means there are now just three tables; bag one of these or you'll be offered a seat in the restaurant area and find yourself being unceremoniously shifted around at mealtimes. In the café, regimentally aligned sweet treats provide a colourful spectacle of decorative moulded creams and mousses, many enclosed in wisps of sponge or chocolate. What distinguishes them from regular offerings is the East-meets-West flavour combos. We're talking tea infusions, floral flavours, spiced macaroons and wasabi chocolates. Delicately fragrant melon tiramisu wrapped in white chocolate delivered a sweet yet pleasingly astringent note, offset by its crisp chocolate case. Equally distinctive were a pat of blackberry confit in a blue tea cream, and chocolate ganache spiked with chillies. Flavours are more mellow than in previous years – a big plus. But staff need to become a lot more efficient and friendly; we've sat here for as long as an hour in the past without being served.
Babies and children admitted. Booking advisable (restaurant). Disabled: lift; toilet. Takeaway service (tea house). **Map 17 B3**.

South Kensington

Hummingbird Bakery

47 Old Brompton Road, SW7 3JP (7584 0055/ www.hummingbirdbakery.com). South Kensington tube. **Open** 10am-7pm daily. **Main courses** £1.55-£3.45. **Credit** AmEx, MC, V.
Following the success of Hummingbird's flagship bakery on Portobello Road, this new South Kensington branch is a dream place for cake lovers looking for a cosy, glass-fronted café and shop in which to sink into an armchair and indulge in guilty trysts with frostings, cheesecakes and softly seductive sponges. All-American cup cakes, topped with showers of sparkles and silver balls, are lined up in the display case, while the heavyweights – new york cheesecake, nutty pies, devil's food cake – command centre-stage on the sideboard. But there's more than just lemon meringue and mom's-own apple pies for the taking. Classy movers and shakers now include lavender-scented cup cakes and even a healthy token – the granola bar. On our visit, around teatime, this was the only plate that remained piled high; the lemon meringue had been wiped clean. Our only gripe was the chaotic service behind the counter.
Babies and children welcome. Tables outdoors (4, pavement). Takeaway service; delivery service (2.30-6pm Mon-Fri, over £12.95 within 3-mile radius). **Map 14 D10**.
For branch see index.

West

Ladbroke Grove

Books for Cooks

4 Blenheim Crescent, W11 1NN (7221 1992/ www.booksforcooks.com). Ladbroke Grove tube. **Open** 10am-6pm, **lunch served** noon-1.30pm Tue-Sat. Closed 3wks Aug, 10 days Christmas. **Set lunch** £5 2 courses, £7 3 courses. **Credit** MC, V.
There's not much point turning up after 12.30pm if you want to partake of the lunch served at the back of this bijou culinary bookshop. All six small tin tables in the bright, glass-covered back room will be taken, and the daily quota of food already allotted. That's because Books for Cooks is such a hit with Notting Hill's army of domestic goddesses. The set menu of three dishes – all made using recipes from the shop's cookery books – isn't

ground-breaking, but does supply imaginatively selected tasters of dishes you can try at home. On our visit, that meant a spread of stuffed peppers, thai fish cakes and a selection of gorgeous cakes. The four cakes, including a classic blackberry tart and a lovely, rich yoghurt cake with walnuts, was worth going for alone. What's more, it's very good value: we racked up only £13 for two, including excellent coffees. A modest selection of quality wine is available, but this isn't a place to tarry. And you can't book – another reason to arrive early. Regular cookery classes are held upstairs in the demonstration room.
Bookings not accepted. Disabled: toilet. Tables outdoors (1, pavement). **Map 19 B3**.

Shepherd's Bush

Bush Garden Café

59 Goldhawk Road, W12 8EG (8743 6372). Goldhawk Road tube. **Open** 7.30am-7pm Mon-Fri; 9am-5pm Sat. **Main courses** £4-£5. **Credit** (over £5) AmEx, MC, V.
Shepherd's Bush may be in the process of transforming itself from an area of urban blight to family territory, but the main artery of Goldhawk Road is still a far from child-friendly place, with plenty of pubs, plenty of traffic and not much else. So this Tardis-like organic café tucked next door to the tube station is a great refuge, with a warren of rooms and the added bonus of a back garden, complete with sloping lawn and a selection of toys to keep the kids amused while you enjoy your coffee. The look is French rustic (pale wood panelling, old mirrors, blackboard menus), but the fare is mostly standard café basics, from smoothies and lattes to builders' fry-ups – although the only builders we spotted were a couple of five-year-olds putting the finishing touches to a Lego skyscraper in the garden. Service is slow, but, in a haven like this, no one seems in a rush to leave.
Babies and children welcome: children's menu; high chairs; toys. Tables outdoors (8, garden). Takeaway service. Vegetarian menu. **Map 20 B2**.

Westbourne Grove

Raoul's Café

105-107 Talbot Road, W11 2AT (7229 2400/ www.raoulsgourmet.com). Westbourne Park or Ladbroke Grove tube. **Open** 8.30am-10.15pm daily. **Main courses** £8.50-£16. **Credit** AmEx, MC, V.
This younger sister to the ever-popular Maida Vale original is louder, flasher and shinier than its sedate sibling. Stylish retro light fittings, white leather banquettes, metallic textured wallpaper and a mirrored bar make this a fashionable haunt for the area's wealthy international crowd. The outside tables are busy as soon as the sun comes out, especially at weekends. The menu is the same as the Maida Vale branch, and rarely changes; there's a wide choice of breakfast dishes, spanning everything from kippers to eggs florentine, plus plenty of salads, sandwiches, pasta and steaks, as well as a few daily specials. On a recent visit we sampled a new fish meze selection, which was excellent; eggs benedict was as flawless as usual, with perfectly poached eggs and tasty hollandaise. The huge, fruity, frothy smoothies are highly recommended, and the cakes are fresh and tasty. Service is swift and professional. All in all, a stylish and reliable outfit.
Babies and children welcome: high chairs. Disabled: toilet. Separate room for parties, seats 30. Takeaway service. **Map 19 C3**.
For branches see index.

Tea Palace

175 Westbourne Grove, W11 2SB (7727 2600/ www.teapalace.co.uk). Bayswater or Notting Hill Gate tube. **Open** 10am-7pm daily. **Tea served** 3-7pm daily. **Main courses** £8-£13. **Set tea** £17-£23.50. **Credit** AmEx, MC, V.
The Tea Palace is pitched firmly at Notting Hill princesses shopping and pampering themselves at the boutiques and spas of Westbourne Grove. Tastefully swirly purple carpet covers the floor, starched linen stretches pristinely across the tables, and soft leather upholstery completes the languorous look and feel. On entering, you're greeted with shelves of tea for sale, in purple tea caddies: three types of assam, and even greater choice in other varieties, including darjeeling, ceylon, unheard-of herbals and many Far Eastern infusions. So proud is Tea Palace of its leaves that waiters bring a sample of your choice in a tiny dish for your inspection. Even the sugar is unrefined lest it cloud your cuppa – so don't even think of asking for coffee. Light three-course meals (juicily grilled lamb and tzatziki, or squid and prawn salad) are of a high standard and there's a decent selection of wine too. But afternoon tea is almost a blessed sacrament, and should be at these prices – £17 with finger sandwiches, scones and sundry cakes or £23.50 with champagne. You won't get a more sophisticated brew in London.
Babies and children welcome: high chairs; nappy-changing facilities. Booking advisable. Disabled: toilet. **Map 19 C3**.

Tom's Delicatessen

226 Westbourne Grove, W11 2RH (7221 8818). Notting Hill Gate tube. **Open** 8am-7.30pm Mon-Fri; 8am-6.30pm Sat; 8.30am-6.30pm Sun. **Main courses** £6.95-£11.95. **Credit** MC, V.
Join the queue at weekends for this ever-popular bohemian brunch spot. If your stomach rumbles while you wait, avert your eyes from the tempting cakes (carrot and pineapple, and coffee and walnut, among others) in the shop and gaze instead at the display cupboards full of vintage Vim and Rinso packaging. Upon reaching the hallowed café at the back, you'll find that seating has been crammed into every available space, including a tiny terrace and a charmingly ramshackle patio garden. Breakfast – served all day at weekends, until noon during the week – runs the gamut from the healthy (own-made granola with berries and Neal's Yard yoghurt) to the artery-challenging (full english with superior British meats, or a satisfyingly virtuous veggie version). A changing menu of mains is offered from midday, including salads, pizza and pleasingly chunky smoked haddock and salmon fish cakes with fresh tartare sauce. You can also

Tea Palace

buy ready-prepared dishes in the deli downstairs and generously filled sandwiches at ground level. *Babies and children welcome: high chairs. Tables outdoors (6, garden; 2, terrace). Takeaway service.* **Map 7 A6**.

South West

Barnes

★ Orange Pekoe NEW

3 White Hart Lane, SW13 0PX (8876 6070/ www.orangepekoeteas.com). Barnes Bridge rail/ 209 bus. **Open** 7.30am-5.30pm Mon-Fri; 9am-5.30pm Sat, Sun. **Main courses** £4.50-£8. **Credit** AmEx, DC, MC, V.

Tea lovers should make a beeline for this cute café, where you can sample (and buy) over 70 loose-leaf varieties – black, green, white, oolong, rooibos, herbal and fruit. The teas are stacked in black caddies on shelves near the entrance. All can be tasted for £3.50 a pot: a bargain (and a great way to experiment) when you realise that some, such as premium Japanese green tea gyokuro asahi, retails at over £20 per 100g. A blackboard menu lists the food, from breakfast (own-made muesli and granola) to platters (pâté, cheese, vegetarian), assorted pies and salads. Sandwiches, fat scones and luscious cakes (we recommend the lemon polenta) sit atop the front counter. It's fresh, tasty fare; a muffin came piled high with top-quality smoked salmon and proper cream cheese, while a 'golden vegetable' soup was a light, delicious broth studded with celery, courgette, carrot and tomato chunks and parsley. Wooden tables dot the trio of small rooms, simply decorated with white walls and pretty tea cups on cherub plinths, though many customers head for the old-fashioned (and rickety) cast-iron tables on the sunny front pavement. Staff are as charming as the setting.
Babies and children welcome: crayons; high chairs; nappy-changing facilities. Tables outdoors (4, pavement). Takeaway service.

South

Balham

Munchkin Lane NEW

2007 RUNNER-UP BEST FAMILY RESTAURANT

83 Nightingale Lane, SW12 8NX (8772 6800). Clapham South tube/Wandsworth Common rail. **Meals served** 8am-6pm Mon-Fri; 9am-5pm Sat. **Main courses** £2.50-£5.70. **Credit** MC, V.

The cutesy-pie name might conjure up images of Ikea plasticware and screeching toddlers, but, in fact, this child-friendly café displays admirable restraint. You don't have to be toting a tot to come here; the smart upstairs area is great for coffees, smoothies and light lunches whatever your age. It's good to know, however, that the basement – with its toys, blackboards, on-screen Disney classics and sweet little play den – is especially for young kids. There are plenty of tables below stairs, so families can eat in the playroom if they wish. Three times a week there are morning activities for youngsters (rhyme time, story time or a puppet show). Food is a happy fusion of sweet treats and wholesome organics. The children's menu is big on nursery favourites: shepherd's pie, organic fish pie, macaroni cheese or sandwiches. We enjoyed a fresh spinach, feta and walnut salad, accompanied by a thick mango smoothie, while the children tucked into scrambled egg on toast. To follow, chocolate fudge cake and excellent cappuccino, plus own-made gingerbread men and 'kiddieccino'.
Babies and children welcome: children's menu; high chairs; nappy-changing facilities; toys. Separate room for parties, seats 25. Tables outdoors (2, pavement).

Battersea

Crumpet

66 Northcote Road, SW11 6QL (7924 1117/ www.crumpet.biz). Clapham Junction rail. **Open** 9am-5.30pm Mon-Sat; 10am-5.30pm Sun. **Set tea** £4.95 (2-4pm). **Main courses** £3.95-£6.95. **Credit** AmEx, MC, V.

An enclosed play den, numerous high chairs, spacious, buggy-friendly hall and nursery-style menu make Crumpet a haven for harassed parents. The menu is extensive, ranging from salads, sandwiches and a set high tea served on a tiered stand with optional champagne, to a list of kids' portions that includes finger sandwiches and mini hot meals served with dainty thimblefuls of vegetables. Unstoppable Crumpet also does party catering and stocks own-brand teas, coffee and jams, as well as preparing lunchboxes and takeaways. Among the abundant selection of cakes are some 'baked by local mums who bake like mad when the children are asleep' – so says the menu, which is full of comic asides. There's a long list of teas and smoothies – and even 'smooteas', which combine the two – as well as organic fruit juices and good-quality coffee. The airy, white space creates a sense of calm that defies the toddler territory, and the loo even comes equipped with nappies to relieve parents of planning.
Babies and children welcome: children's menu; high chairs; nappy-changing facilities; toys. Tables outdoors (2, pavement). Takeaway service. **Map 21 C5**.

Clapham

Breads Etcetera NEW

127 Clapham High Street, SW4 7SS (7720 3601/ www.breadsetcetera.com). Clapham Common or Clapham North tube. **Open** 10am-10pm Tue-Sat; 10am-4pm Sun. **Main courses** £5-£8.95. **Credit** MC, V.

Breads Etcetera is an artisanal bakery based in Stockwell that makes award-winning, organic sourdough breads – six-seed (the bestseller), walnut, dark rye and others – all with outstanding taste and texture. This Clapham shop and café opened in 2006, but it has taken a whole year for an awning to be fitted, which makes its presence more obvious. Inside you'll find an unremarkable-looking space with Dualit toasters on every table – you can make your own toast after choosing from the extensive bread bar, where there's also a selection of spreads from tahini to Tiptree jams. The cooked breakfasts are fabulous. Top-quality ingredients include Moen's excellent cumberland sausages and bacon from free-range Plantation Pigs. Alternatively, there are sandwiches such as Forman's smoked salmon with cucumber, cream cheese, capers, dill and lemon, Breads Etcetera's own muffins, and fresh fruit salads. Lunch dishes include greek salad and beef brisket (both £5), but breakfast and brunch is the main event here.
Babies and children admitted. Tables outdoors (2, pavement). Takeaway service. **Map 22 B2**.

★ Macaron (100)

22 The Pavement, SW4 0HY (7498 2636). Clapham Common tube. **Open** 7.30am-8pm Mon-Fri; 9am-8pm Sat, Sun. **Main courses** £2.75-£4.10. **No credit cards.**

A blast from the past, Macaron recreates the atmosphere of a 1930s-style tea room with flowery crockery and a glass showcase crammed with cream-laden cakes, pastries and tarts. Winner of the Best Pâtisserie gong in the 2006 Time Out Eating & Drinking Awards, it's big on French pâtisserie, fancy teas and great breads. Besides the stalwarts – eclairs, pretty lemon tarts, dainty macaroons – there's also a nod to tropical flavours. Le lingot has to be our all-time favourite: a perfectly proportioned apricot mousse cake, punctuated with hints of toasted coconut and almond, and topped with a scrumptious slick of glossy apricot glaze. Not everything is as good: the custardy chocolate filling in an eclair was too sweet for our liking, and the lemon tarts were let down by a virtually impenetrable sweet pastry shell. A sizeable communal table is tailor-made for friendly exchanges, and there's also a window into the kitchen where chefs can be seen whipping up meringues and piping out rosettes of cream. Service was a trifle dour on our visit, but that didn't detract from the sweet seduction of the cakes and frothy coffees.
Babies and children admitted. Tables outdoors (4, pavement). Takeaway service. **Map 22 A2**.

Ice-cream shops

The Italians have a firm grip on London's premier ice-cream parlours, but the array of flavours – from Madagascan vanilla to plum and yoghurt – leap across national boundaries. And don't miss **Marine Ices** (*see p303*), the gelateria/caff that has been fattening up Chalk Farm residents since the 1930s.

Caffè Deli Paradiso

109 Highgate West Hill, N6 6AP (8340 7818). Bus C2, C11, 214. **Open** 8.30am-10.30pm Mon-Sat; 8.30am-9pm Sun.

Handy for Hampstead Heath, and with open french windows in summer, this Sicilian-style caffè and gelateria offers delicious renditions of flavours such as tartufo, sicilian lemon, stracciatella and zuppa inglese.

Gelateria Danieli

16 Brewers Lane, Richmond, Surrey TW9 1HH (8439 9807). Richmond tube/rail. **Open** 10am-6pm Mon; 10am-10pm Tue-Sun.

The queues stretch out of the door for Richmond's finest ices. Space is limited, so you might want to wander down to the Green to enjoy tubs of chocolate sorbet, or rum and raisin, plum and yoghurt, panna cotta, and pistachio ice-creams. The company also has a foothold on Oxford Street, with a kiosk on the pavement between John Lewis and House of Fraser.

Gelateria Valerie

Duke of York Square, SW3 4LY (7730 7978). Sloane Square tube. **Open** 8am-8.30pm Mon-Sat; 10am-6.30pm Sun.

It's as though easyJet has picked up a gelateria from Rome and plonked it in the middle of Chelsea. Glass walls and extensive alfresco seating add to the see-and-be-seen element. Diet options are provided for ladies who lunch.

Oddono's

14 Bute Street, SW7 3EX (7052 0732/ www.oddonos.co.uk). South Kensington tube. **Open** 11am-11pm Mon-Thur, Sun; 11am-midnight Fri, Sat.

Valrhona chocolate, Sicilian pistachios and Madagascan vanilla are the type of premium ingredients favoured by this artisanal producer. Co-founder Christian Oddono was inspired by the ice-cream of his Italian granny. We like the generous servings. There's also an Oddono's counter in Selfridges food hall.

Scoop

40 Shorts Gardens, WC2H 9AB (7240 7086/www.scoopgelato.com). Covent Garden tube. **Open** 9am-11.30pm daily.

We love the heady amaretto, made with ground amaretti biscuits and almond liqueur; and pinolo, made with pine kernels from Pisa. Hell, we like it all. Good sorbets and dairy-free ices using rice and berries also make Scoop a boon for anyone on a special diet.

South East

Dulwich

Blue Mountain Café NEW

18 North Cross Road, SE22 9EU (8299 6953/ www.bluemo.co.uk). East Dulwich rail. **Open** 9am-5pm Mon-Sat; 10am-5pm Sun. **Main courses** £3.90-£7.95. **Set breakfast** £6.95 incl tea or coffee. **Credit** AmEx, MC, V.

They say competition is good for you, and so it has proved for this East Dulwich stalwart. Now that SE22 has morphed into Nappy Valley, it's bristling with purveyors of croissants and cappuccinos, most of them serviceable. So this funky old grand dame, with its mosaic-tiled patio and wooden interior, has raised its game accordingly. Its 'full monty' breakfast and mouth-watering lunches – great hot stews in winter, good salads and meze in summer, and for a calorific blast, roast vegetable ciabatta with melted cheese – are generously sized and freshly cooked by a kitchen that gives a damn. And a wide selection of superlative cakes and pastries keeps it high in the 'nipping in for a treat' stakes. The place has been remodelled from the cave-like original, and is now open-plan and welcoming, with a rainbow-coloured mosaic in the back garden to match the one out front. Service has also improved, thanks to a central bar counter around which the charming young staff gravitate. A new wine list is being introduced, along with evening opening, in autumn 2007.

Babies and children welcome: children's menu; high chairs; nappy-changing facilities. Separate room for parties, seats 10. Tables outdoors (5, garden; 5, terrace). **Map 23 C4.**

Jack's Tea & Coffee House NEW

85 Pellatt Road, SE22 9JD (8693 0011). North Dulwich rail. **Open** 10am-5pm Mon-Fri; 10am-3pm Sat. **Main courses** £1.95-£5.95. **No credit cards.**

Tucked down a quiet side street, Jack's is one of Dulwich's best-kept secrets. Presided over by chef James Hoffman and his loyal deputy and baking queen Fi Sweeney, its counters are piled with warm-from-the-oven delicacies, from the superb caramelised french onion tart to the daily-changing cakes sinking under the weight of their frostings. Chalkboards display variations on own-made soups, salads and sandwiches to add to the staple offer of hot drinks, fresh juices, milkshakes, Criterion ice-creams and sundaes. With its genuine, friendly service, unfussy interior and tiny open kitchen, Jack's has the heart and soul of a classic British caff, but with infinitely superior food values. In place of bacon butties are the likes of toasted ciabatta with chargrilled chorizo, tomato salsa and rocket, swedish meatball sandwiches with beetroot mayo, own-made chicken pâté, or broad bean and pea salad with spinach and parma ham. Fresh, seasonal produce is also sold at the counter to supplement the larders of local foodies.

Babies and children welcome: high chairs; nappy-changing facilities; toys. Tables outdoors (4, garden; 4, pavement). Takeaway service. **Map 23 C5.**

London Bridge & Borough

★ Shipp's Tea Rooms NEW

4 Park Street, SE1 9AB (7407 2692). London Bridge tube/rail. **Open** 9.30am-5.30pm Mon-Fri; 10am-7pm Sat; 11am-5pm Sun. **Main courses** £2.25-£3.45. **Set tea** £17.50. **No credit cards.**

This new tea room (founded summer 2007) caters perfectly for Borough shoppers with its retro look and nostalgic feel. Owners Margaret Willis and partner John Rich have turned their former electrical contractor's premises (right next to Neal's Yard Cheeses) into a shrine to last-century tea sets, scones and victoria sponge cake. Other moist confections include chocolate sandwich cake, lemon drizzle cake and the daringly modern carrot cake, all trapped under giant glass cloches. Sandwiches are available too. Quality leaf teas are used, supplied by Postcard Teas and East Teas: ceylon and golden assam are the bestsellers, but there's also a couple each of green and herb teas. The afternoon tea costs a whopping £17.50 – but it's really a full meal, and still cheaper (and considerably more fun) than a fancy hotel tea. Although the food and drink are excellent, the thing we like most about Shipp's is that it successfully evokes a bygone era, when shoppers were less caffeine-fuelled and had time to nibble cakes over a cuppa in the afternoon.

Babies and children welcome: children's portions. Restaurant available for hire. Takeaway service. **Map 11 P8.**

Peckham

Petitou

63 Choumert Road, SE15 4AR (7639 2613). Peckham Rye rail. **Open** 9am-5.30pm Tue-Sat; 10am-5.30pm Sun. **Main courses** £5.95-£6.45. **Credit** AmEx, DC, MC, V.

There's an almost 1940s charm to Petitou, from the brown earthenware teapots to the delicate, mismatched china on which scrumptious chunks of moist, own-made cakes are served. Luckily, there's nothing post-war about the portions: slabs of granary toast groan under the weight of smoked salmon and scrambled eggs; fresh-cooked, daily-changing quiche platters arrive laden with assorted salads; large, sugar-dusted croissants ooze with delicious almond paste. A wide range of Indian and herbal teas, freshly pressed juices, organic wines and beers and fine Fairtrade coffee keep the place buzzing from dawn to dusk. Solitary, bookish types and lunching mums with or without toddlers are accommodated equally well. The excellent, mostly organic food and picturesque, tree-shaded location add up to more than the sum of their parts, thanks to the unfailing courtesy of Petitou's owners and staff; and the feeling (enhanced by local paintings, prints, textiles and flyers on the walls and shelves) that this is truly a community café for Peckham's bohemian fraternity. A real gem.

Babies and children welcome: children's portions; high chairs. Tables outdoors (6, patio). Takeaway service. **Map 23 C3.**

East

Docklands

Mudchute Kitchen NEW

2007 RUNNER-UP BEST FAMILY RESTAURANT

Mudchute Park & Farm, Pier Street, Isle of Dogs, E14 3HP (7515 5901/www.mudchute.org). Mudchute DLR. **Meals served** 9am-5pm Tue-Sun. **Main courses** £3-£8. **No credit cards.**

Mudchute Farm is a green and pleasant spot on the skyscraper-heavy Isle of Dogs; for family groups, the appeal is obvious. Across the yard from the squealing Gloucester Old Spot pigs and clucking Polish White Crest chickens sits the kitchen. Inside, you'll find farmhouse kitchen tables and settles, a big futon for babies, a book and toy corner and information boards outlining the Isle's history. Outside, picnic tables look out over riding stables. The bucolic location has its disadvantages – flies, for one. But such irritations are soon forgotten when you taste the food. The tireless young chefs certainly know about wholesome seasonal grub and can make lashings of sparkling ginger beer. There are usually four or five hot options (also available in child portions), such as penne with courgette and tomato sauce and goat's cheese, or fried polenta topped with wild mushrooms, herbs and cream cheese. Plain eaters can have the farm's own eggs, own-made jam or beans on toast. The own-made cakes are brilliant – brownies, cupcakes, flapjacks, victoria sponges – and Mudchute does the best cream teas this side of Totnes.

Babies and children welcome: children's menu; high chair; nappy-changing facilities (farm); toys. Tables outdoors (12, courtyard). **Map 24 C4.**

Shoreditch

Frizzante@City Farm

Hackney City Farm, 1A Goldsmith's Row, E2 8QA (7739 2266/www.frizzanteltd.co.uk). Bus 26, 48, 55. **Open** 10am-4.30pm Tue-Sun. **Main courses** £5-£7.45. **Credit** AmEx, MC, V.

Frizzante is such an unusual and pleasant spot for a traditional full english breakfast that we'd recommend it as a hangover cure – if it weren't for the noisy kids. It's so popular with families (and their buggies) that the atmosphere can be crèche-like. Order at the deli counter, where you'll be a given a number, then collect your cutlery and condiments and find a table in the indoor space, the conservatory or outdoors. Your food will then be brought to you. The Big Farm Breakfast (the full works) and the vegetarian equivalent are popular choices, and not too greasy, but there's plenty more to choose from, including soup, pasta with grilled vegetables and goat's cheese, jacket potatoes and sausage or bacon sandwiches (also available to take away). Children's choices are available, as is a full range of coffees, teas and juices. Ingredients are high-quality, service efficient and friendly, and there's always the calming prospect of a walk around the adjoining farmyard afterwards. We overheard neighbouring diners complaining about high prices; from our perspective, you get what you pay for.

Babies and children welcome: children's menu; high chairs. Bookings not accepted weekends. Disabled: toilet. Separate room for parties, seats 40. Tables outdoors (12, garden). Takeaway service. Vegan dishes. **Map 6 S3.**

For branch (Frizzante@Unicorn Theatre) see index.

Jones Dairy Café

23 Ezra Street, E2 7RH (7739 5372/www.jones dairy.co.uk). Bus 26, 48, 55. **Open** 9am-3pm Fri, Sat; 8am-3pm Sun. **Main courses** £2-£6.50. **No credit cards.**

You'll be lucky to get a seat here on a Sunday, when the popularity of Columbia Road Flower Market makes this small space – tucked into a lovely little alley – a better bet for a tasty takeaway bagel. On Fridays and Saturdays, however, the atmosphere is positively tranquil, with the rustling of newspapers and the quiet click of chess pieces the defining sounds. The homely vibe of the interior (kitchen supplies are messily arranged on shelves behind a high red counter) carries over into the selection of food, with eggs, muesli, porridge, own-made bread and cakes complemented by specials that might include kippers or delicious own-made baked beans. Freshly squeezed orange juice and basic but high-quality coffee are good drinks options, best enjoyed in the sun at one of the battered metal tables outside. Staff can be a bit standoffish and you might be left waiting ages for your order (as we were), but, for many, it's all part of the non-chainlike charm.

Babies and children welcome: high chair. Tables outdoors (2, pavement). Takeaway service. **Map 6 S3.**

North East

Clapton

Venetia NEW

55 Chatsworth Road, E5 0LH (8986 1642). Homerton rail/242, 308 bus. **Open** 8.30am-5pm Tue-Fri; 9am-5pm Sat; 9.30am-3.30pm Sun. **Main courses** £2.20-£3.50. **No credit cards.**

Hackney's regeneration has been slow, and nowhere slower than in Clapton, but Venetia's is one of the trendsetting pioneers at last bringing a bit of class to a scabby stretch of Chatsworth Road. The coffee puts the pitiful offerings of chain competitors to shame, as does the range of food. Lovely glass cake-stands display copious sweets and pastries, among them chocolate and fruitcakes, own-made victoria sponge crammed with jam and cream, and assorted croissants, brownies and cookies. If untempted by such sweet-toothed fare, there are delicious sandwiches too

SHELF LIFE

London has some fantastic bakers. Also try **Baker & Spice** (*see right*), **Breads Etcetera** (*see p310*), **St John Bread & Wine** (*see p61*) and Sally Clarke's bakery **& Clarke's** (122 Kensington Church Street, W8 4BU, 7229 2190, www.sallyclarke.com).

Blackbird Bakery
208 Railton Road, SE24 0JT (7095 8800). Herne Hill rail. **Open** 7am-7pm Mon-Fri; 7am-6pm Sat.
Eamon Sweeney's American-influenced bakery-pâtisserie sells top-notch cheesecake, sourdough loaves, honey-pecan sticky buns, muffins and packs of buckwheat pancake mix and five-grain granola. There's now a second branch at 73 Westow Street, SE19 3RW (8768 0357).

Carmelli Bakery
128 Golders Green Road, NW11 8HB (8455 2074/www.carmelli.co.uk). Golders Green tube. **Open** 7am-midnight Mon-Thur; 11.30pm Sat-midnight Sun.
You don't have to be Jewish to enjoy the chewy bagels, soft rye and sweet black breads produced at this long-established parev bakery. Great quiches and rugelach too.

Flour Power City
Stoney Street entrance, Borough Market, SE1 1TL (8691 2288/ www.flourpowercity.com) London Bridge tube/rail. **Open** 9am-5pm Mon-Fri; 9am-4pm Sat.
The Borough Market bakery is open six days a week, but you can also find this company's excellent loaves at leading delis and farmers' markets around London.

Old Post Office Bakery
76 Landor Road, SW9 9PH (7326 4408/www.oldpostofficebakery.co.uk). Clapham North tube. **Open** 7am-6pm Mon-Sat; 9am-1pm Sun.
Peace, love and sunflower seeds at this local favourite, where the 1970s-style wholemeal loaves and other delicious breads are certified organic. Hot savouries include spinach rolls and pizza.

Poilâne
46 Elizabeth Street, SW1W 9PA (7808 4910/www.poilane.fr). Sloane Square tube/Victoria tube/rail. **Open** 7.30am-7.30pm Mon-Fri; 7.30am-6pm Sat.
The trademark French sourdough loaves, available in wheat, rye and walnut varieties, are the choice of many a good gastropub and a great adjunct to any cheeseboard or smoked fish.

(toasted if you fancy), on organic white, brown or rye bread, or baguettes. Specials on our visit included dolcelatte and rocket, and halloumi and turkish sausage. Beyond the counter is a small area with bare brick walls, a low table, leather seats and some toys, where a family with small kids was happily chomping through brownies. A few more youngsters were out back playing games on the computer. Service is exceptionally friendly and, before 9am, a coffee and croissant combo is just £1.50. Come on, Clapton, this is more like it!
Babies and children welcome: high chair; nappy-changing facilities; toys. Tables outdoors (2, pavement). Takeaway service.

North West

Hampstead

Maison Blanc
62 Hampstead High Street, NW3 1QH (7431 8338/www.maisonblanc.co.uk). Hampstead tube.
Open 8am-7pm Mon-Sat; 9am-7pm Sun. **Main courses** £2.50-£6. **Credit** MC, V.
Last year's refurbishment (extra seating, a more efficient layout) certainly increased the appeal of the Hampstead branch of this growing French café chain. But Maison Blanc still struggles to stand out amid the crowd of competitors spread around the village; the fact the kitchen ceases to produce food after 4pm, even on a busy weekend, does it no favours. On the upside, surroundings are pleasant, with smiling staff, fresh flowers, tantalising smells and the firm's trademark pink colouring and elaborate lettering edging the decor. Authentic influences thread throughout the menu. Breads use French flour, and the freshly made salads, sandwiches and savouries are peppered with ingredients from across the Channel, such as rosette pork saucisson from Lyon. Blanc's expertise really shines in its chocolaterie. Cakes are rich and seductive, and the individual chocolates are enticing and innovative; try the coriander pralines for something different. Personalised cakes can be made to order.
Babies and children admitted. Disabled: toilet. Takeaway service. **Map 28 B2.**
For branches see index.

Kensal Green

Brilliant Kids Café
8 Station Terrace, NW10 5RT (8964 4120/ www.brilliantkids.co.uk). Kensal Green tube/ Kensal Rise rail. **Open** 8am-6pm Mon-Fri; 9am-5pm Sat. **Main courses** £5.50-£6.50. **Credit** MC, V.
Aptly named, this place offers a host of brilliant ideas for local parents. Stuck for childcare? Use the drop-in. Can't bear to supervise a painting session? Pick up the programme and sign your kids up for a workshop. The café works on the principle of providing nutritious, healthy and appealing food, all prepared with maternal devotion, to suit all ages. A list of daily specials (£6.50 for adults, £3 for kids) includes comforting favourites such as fish pie, shepherd's pie and lamb curry alongside a wide range of vegetables and salads. Breakfast options are extensive, as is the list of smoothies, while the enthusiastic kitchen really excels in the cake department. Trays of warm muffins, sticky carrot cake, almond slices and various chocolaty offerings are on show, devised for a predominately female (and largely breastfeeding) clientele, but equally tempting for anyone – though child-free visitors may feel slightly out of place. Children can play in a toy zone at the back of the space or in the pretty garden.
Babies and children welcome: children's portions; crèche; high chairs; play area; supervised activities. Disabled: toilet. Restaurant available for hire. Tables outdoors (2, pavement; 6, garden). Takeaway service.

Gracelands
118 College Road, NW10 5HD (8964 9161/ www.gracelandscafe.com). Kensal Green tube.
Open 8am-6pm Mon-Fri; 9am-5pm Sat; 9.30am-3pm Sun. **Main courses** £5.50-£7.50. **Credit** AmEx, MC, V.
With its designated toy corner, nutritious kiddie menu and community feel, Gracelands could quite easily alienate the childless newcomer, but, thanks to its friendly and relaxed vibe, it doesn't. It's a large space, frequented by local parents who bring their laptops and take advantage of the free internet access while their kids mingle. Local services are advertised, and the Gracelands Yard next door offers activities ranging from yoga and acupuncture to strange-sounding, romantic fiction-writing workshops. Blackboards list daily specials, with excellent quiches (the caramelised onion, olive and gruyère is recommended) and salads as perennial favourites. Salad selections are creative, featuring nuts, fruit and pulses as well as more usual options, and the soups are always hearty and made with seasonal vegetables. Children's choices include pasta, risotto and sausages; and there are plenty of cakes, pastries, sandwiches and breakfasts (finishing on the dot of 11am) and the odd meatier option. It may feel out of the way if you don't live nearby, but Gracelands' catchment area is wide and its popularity unstoppable.
Babies and children welcome: children's menu; high chairs; nappy-changing facilities; toys. Tables outdoors (4, pavement; 3, garden). Takeaway service.

Queen's Park

Baker & Spice (100)
75 Salusbury Road, NW6 6NH (7604 3636/ www.bakerandspice.com). Queen's Park tube.
Open 7am-7pm Mon-Sat; 8am-5pm Sun.
Main courses £4.25-£12. **Credit** MC, V.
If you've ever wondered what a £5 sausage roll tastes like, this is the place to find out (prices vary daily, but that's what we paid). Likewise a £7.50 portion of fruit salad, a £7.25 croque monsieur, a £6.50 bowl of granola and yogurt, or a £5.25 sliver of cheesecake. Yes, Baker & Spice is fantastically expensive, but we've got to concede it also bakes exceedingly good cakes – and breads and pastries, and has a knockout selection of colourful salads at lunchtime. It's as much bakery and traiteur as café. Bag a seat at the large shared table in the centre before perusing the chiller cabinet, which is stacked with enticing combinations of beetroot, mozzarella, roast aubergine, pine nuts, cherry tomato, wild rice and much more besides. Hot dishes might include two turkey meat fritters with a piquant dressing. The cakes (many are fruit- or chocolate-based) never fail to impress. This is a lovely place to sit and read the papers or chat with friends, but be warned that a simple lunch can easily top £15 per head.
Babies and children admitted. Tables outdoors (1, pavement). Takeaway service. **Map 1 A2.**
For branches see index.

Outer London

Richmond, Surrey

★ William Curley NEW
10 Paved Court, Richmond, Surrey TW9 1LZ (8332 3002/www.williamcurley.co.uk). Richmond tube/rail. **Open** 10am-6.30pm Tue, Sun; 9.30am-6.30pm Wed-Sat. **Main courses** £3-£3.75.
Credit MC, V.
This picture-perfect pastry shop and café is best known as a retailer, but it's also a dream location for romantic dalliances. You'll find it hard to resist the lure of award-winning pâtisserie – the French cakes, chocolates and own-made ices are lovingly crafted by William Curley and his Japanese wife, the pair combining to act as the culinary equivalent of haute couture designers. For added sparkle, there are oriental notes, such as red bean ice-cream, cakes made with green tea, and spiced truffles. We fell in love with a mound of whipped chocolate mousse, its nursery-like flavour tastefully offset by tangy raspberries and crunchy hazelnut praline. Equally good was a glossy, chocolate-glazed mousse cake, its crème brûlée filling laced with boozy rum-drenched raisins – a very grown-up indulgence. From tartlets piled high with fruit to single-estate chocolate truffles, puff pastry tarts and mini choux buns crowned with ruffs of cream, we're talking world-class everything. Early birds would do well to bag one of the two outdoor tables while sipping speciality brews (there's also a table inside). Service is friendly and knowledgeable.
Babies and children admitted. Tables outdoors (2, pavement). Takeaway service.

PARK CAFÉS

Central

Marylebone

Garden Café

Inner Circle, Regents Park, NW1 4NU (7935 5729/www.thegardencafe.co.uk). Baker Street or Regents Park tube. **Open** 9am-dusk daily. **Breakfast served** 9-11am, **lunch served** noon-4pm, **dinner served** 5-8pm (summer) daily. **Set lunch/dinner** £13 2 courses, £16 3 courses. **Main courses** £7.50-£12.95. **Credit** MC, V.

A lovely spot to linger on a sunny afternoon or balmy evening, this revamped 1960s park café offers monthly-changing menus based on seasonal ingredients. Orange and yellow curvy-backed chairs play up the retro feel, which you'll either love or hate – if the latter, the large garden with its landscaped flower beds is universally appealing, though you can be neglected by the well-meaning staff if you sit at the further-flung tables. The dishes are as unfussy as the surroundings, many with a retro bent: prawn cocktail, ribeye with 'respectable chips', sherry trifle. Ratatouille with chunky mixed peppers, aubergine and courgette was a flavour-packed, filling vegetarian option, but the slim tomato and gruyère tart left us wanting more. Ice-cream comes courtesy of Chalk Farm institution Marine Ices. Prices are pleasingly democratic: there are inflation-busting fixed-price menus and carafes of wine for under a tenner. It's handy for the Open Air Theatre, and to the left of the restaurant is a self-serve bar area for drinks, sandwiches and cakes at tables inside or out.

Babies and children welcome: children's menu; high chairs. Booking advisable. Disabled: toilet. Restaurant available for hire (autumn and winter only). Tables outdoors (38, garden). Takeaway service. **Map 3 G3.**

West

Kensington

Kensington Palace Orangery

The Orangery, Kensington Palace, Kensington Gardens, W8 4PX (7376 0239/www.digbytrout.co.uk). High Street Kensington or Queensway tube. **Open** *Mar-Oct* 10am-6pm daily. *Nov-Feb* 10am-5pm daily. **Main courses** £8.50-£15.95. **Set tea** £11.95-£44.95. **Credit** DC, MC, V.

With its white walls, Corinthian columns and views of manicured lawns through large picture windows, this airy café is the perfect setting in which to sample afternoon tea the way the Queen might do it. Formal but friendly service adds to the feeling of indulgence as you tuck into cakes and scones served on satisfyingly traditional tiered cake-stands. There are a few light lunch dishes on offer – soup, sandwiches or a sharing plate of English produce – but most people opt for tea and cakes. Chocolate cake was moist and rich, and a warm scone with Cornish clotted cream and jam was top-quality. To sample a variety of treats, go for a set tea; if you're pushing the boat out, try the Tregothnan Estate Tea – cakes served with tea plucked from the UK's first tea plantation. Tourists flock here, and it's not surprising – this is a great spot for an old-fashioned, very English indulgence.

Babies and children welcome: children's menu; high chairs; nappy-changing facilities. Disabled: toilet. Separate room available for hire, seats 30. Tables outdoors (12, terrace). **Map 7 C8.**

South West

Wandsworth

Common Ground

Wandsworth Common, off Dorlcote Road, SW18 3RT (8874 9386). Wandsworth Common rail. **Open** 9am-5.30pm Mon-Fri; 10am-5.30pm Sat, Sun. **Main courses** £3.95-£9. **Credit** MC, V.

Located in the rural heart of Nappy Valley, this popular park café is inevitably family-oriented, but offers enough culinary appeal and idyllic views to draw in a wider audience. The spacious terrace overlooks a bowling green and green expanse, while the interior of the country-house-style building is adorned with fresh flowers, leather sofas, quirky artworks and posters of local events, giving it a welcoming community feel. Early-risers benefit from a tempting breakfast menu: boiled egg and soldiers, perhaps, or the more refined own-made pancakes with greek yoghurt, honey and fresh berries. The seasonal lunch menu (available from noon) features all the popular favourites – generous jacket potatoes, fresh sandwiches, tasty burgers – but it's worth leaving room for dessert, as the own-made cakes are delicious. There's a varied children's menu too; doubtless the meal will end with a treat from the little ice-cream counter.

Babies and children welcome: children's menu; high chairs; nappy-changing facilities. Café available for hire. Tables outside (15, patio). Takeaway service.

Hummingbird Bakery. See p308.

South East

Dulwich

Pavilion Café

Dulwich Park, SE21 7BQ (8299 1383/ www.pavilioncafedulwich.co.uk). West Dulwich rail/P4 bus. **Open** *Summer* 9am-5.30pm Mon-Thur; 9am-6.30pm Fri-Sun. *Winter* 8.30am-3.30pm Mon-Fri; 9am-3.30pm Sat, Sun. **Main courses** £1.90-£6.95. **No credit cards.**

On summer weekends of old, the stressed demeanour of the Pavilion Cafe's staff used to suggest they'd rather there weren't quite so many customers in one of London's best park eateries. But a back-room boost (of staff and electricity) now ensures the operation glides effortlessly through from breakfast to high tea. Though staff are still slow at dishing up just what the aspiring foodie locals order, whether it's healthy kids' meals (there's always an own-made pasta dish plus

CHEAP EATS

carefully sourced sausage or fish fingers served with vegetables and deliciously crunchy chips), soups, French-inspired salads and sandwiches, or an assortment of fresh cakes, including wheat- and dairy-free, all baked on the premises. With such an emphasis on organic, own-made, free range and fresh-baked, plus wine or beer by the glass, there's an increasing lunchtime fanbase of grown-ups who even have their own 'kid-free' area. But it's the quieter breakfast sitting (before the hordes descend) that show off this café – and the park – to their best advantage.
Babies and children welcome: children's menu; high chairs; toys. Disabled: toilet. Tables outdoors (12, park). Takeaway service.

Greenwich

Pavilion Tea House

Greenwich Park, Blackheath Gate, SE10 8QY (8858 9695/www.capergreen.co.uk). Blackheath rail/Greenwich rail/DLR. **Open** *Summer* 9am-6pm daily. *Winter* 9am-4pm daily. **Main courses** £2.50-£7.50. **Credit** MC, V.

Tip-top food in large portions, served by helpful staff in pleasant surroundings – what more could you ask from a park café? Well, breakfast served beyond 11am at weekends for a start: if you turn up any later, the only cooked food you can order until noon is a round of toast. We weren't in the mood for the excellent sandwiches or cakes (not even the giant rock cakes) or salads (tuna niçoise, chicken and asparagus, goat's cheese), so settled down with a slightly too milky cappuccino to wait for noon. Welsh rarebit (delightfully rich) and smoked salmon and scrambled egg (lots of fish, fluffy eggs) didn't disappoint. Other hot options included steak baguette or salmon and dill fish cake. It's a real pleasure to eat outside at the chunky wooden tables under the chestnut trees, and a mixed bag of locals was taking full advantage. If only the menu was a little more flexible.
Babies and children welcome: high chairs; nappy-changing facilities. Disabled: toilet. Tables outdoors (20, garden). Takeaway service.

North

Highgate

Pavilion Café

Highgate Woods, Muswell Hill Road, N10 3JN (8444 4777). Highgate tube. **Open** *Summer* 9am-9pm daily. *Winter* 9am-4pm daily. **Main courses** £5.50-£10. **Credit** AmEx, JCB, MC, V.

The Pavilion Café, slap-bang in the middle of Highgate Woods, is surrounded by trees (peak through for a glimpse of the picturesque cricket pitch). The large patio has the vibe of a pub garden: people enjoying glasses of wine, bottled beer or cups of tea at wooden tables shaded by green umbrellas. Unfortunately, the food we tried didn't do the setting justice; a burger was ordinary and not a patch on the imaginative versions served at London's many gourmet burger joints (and at £8.95 the price is comparable). And it came with golden-coloured but soggy chips. A goat's cheese salad was also disappointing, with tasty grilled cheese undone by a salad of radicchio and nothing else – just a few tomatoes would have lifted it to a good standard. Better to plump for one of the meze dishes, perhaps garlicky houmous or grilled halloumi with warm flatbread. There's also pasta, soups, some fish dishes and a decent kids' menu.
Babies and children welcome: children's menu; high chairs; nappy-changing facilities. Entertainment: jazz 6-9pm, Fri (June-July). Tables outdoors (27, terrace; 8, veranda). Takeaway service.

Stamford Hill

Springfield Park Café

White Lodge Mansion, Springfield Park, E5 9EF (8806 0444/www.sparkcafe.co.uk). Stamford Hill or Stoke Newington rail/253, 254, 393. **Open** *Apr-Oct* 10am-6pm daily. *Nov-Mar* 10am-4pm daily. **Main courses** £3.90-£5.90. **No credit cards.**

Housed in the beautiful grade II-listed White Lodge Mansion, with a serene outlook across acres of grassy parkland, ancient trees and Walthamstow Marshes, this is a lovely spot. Bag yourself one of the sought-after plastic tables on the gated lawn to make the most of the view while you sample the healthy and diverse menu – the seasonal food is freshly cooked and Mediterranean in style (greasy chips and burgers have no place here). Thirst-quenchers include fruit teas, milkshakes, vitamin-packed smoothies and organic juices, while the hearty breakfasts, paninis and tasty meze keep everyone happy; our 'Absolute Mediterranean Platter' was a wholesome pleasure. There are also child-friendly choices, as well as vegetarian options and soya milk alternatives. For a change from the wide open spaces, check out the pictures on the walls and upcoming events list; the café always has an art or photography show and runs regular events and activities, children's music classes among them.
Babies and children welcome: children's menu; high chairs. Disabled: toilet. Tables outdoors (20, garden; 6, pavement). Takeaway service.

North West

Hampstead

Brew House

Kenwood, Hampstead Lane, NW3 7JR (8341 5384/www.companyofcooks.com). Archway or Golders Green tube then 210 bus. **Open** *Apr-Sept* 9am-6pm (9pm on concert nights) daily. *Oct-Mar* 9am-dusk daily. **Main courses** £4.25-£8.95. **Credit** MC, V.

It's hard to imagine a more idyllic position for a London park café than this: inside an old stable block of stunning neo-classical Kenwood House, surrounded by the beautiful expanses of Hampstead Heath. The outdoor tables (loads of 'em) give the best vantage point, and are usually filled with an atmospheric hubbub of visitors and dogs. There's no table service; a shame (though understandable, given the number of visitors) as this would greatly add to the Brew House's charm – instead you have queue, with precariously balanced tray, along the self-service counters. Food is organic and free-range where possible, and always homely and delicious. Breakfasts are highly praised by locals, with choices varying from yogurt with fresh fruit to a hearty full english, while the afternoon cake selection never fails to excite: the moist and flavoursome berry cheesecake is recommended. Lunchtimes can verge on chaos, so be prepared to jostle, or visit the smaller offshoot, the Steward's Room.
Babies and children welcome: children's menu; high chairs; nappy-changing facilities. Disabled: toilet. Restaurant available for hire (evenings only). Separate room for parties, seats 120. Tables outdoors (200, garden and terrace). Takeaway service. Vegetarian menu. **Map 28 C1.**

Hotel teas

Afternoon tea at a smart hotel is largely the preserve of tourists, but it's a quintessentially English ritual that Londoners should experience too, at least once. You'll have to dress up, of course, and book well in advance.

The Bentley

27-33 Harrington Gardens, SW7 4JX (7244 5555/www.thebentley-hotel.com). Gloucester Road tube. **Tea served** 3-6pm daily. **Set tea** £24-£30. **Credit** AmEx, DC, JCB, MC, V.
Babies and children welcome: children's menu; high chairs. Booking advisable. Dress: smart casual. **Map 13 C10.**

The Berkeley

Wilton Place, SW1X 7RL (7235 6000/ www.the-berkeley.co.uk). Knightsbridge tube. **Tea served** 2-6pm daily. **Set tea** £34; £42-£49 incl glass of champagne. **Credit** AmEx, DC, MC, V.
Babies and children welcome: high chairs. Booking essential. Disabled: toilet. Dress: smart casual. **Map 9 G9.**

The Capital

22-24 Basil Street, SW3 1AT (7589 5171/ 7591 1202/www.capitalhotel.co.uk). Knightsbridge tube. **Tea served** 3-5.30pm daily. **Set tea** £18.50-£34.50 incl glass of champagne. **Credit** AmEx, DC, MC, V.
Booking advisable; essential weekends. Children over 12 years admitted. Dress: smart casual. **Map 8 F9.**

Claridge's

55 Brook Street, W1K 4HA (7409 6307/ www.claridges.co.uk). Bond Street tube. **Tea served** 3.30-5.30pm daily. **Set tea** £31; £39 incl glass of champagne. **Cover** (except for set tea) £3.50. **Credit** AmEx, DC, MC, V.
Babies and children welcome: high chairs. Booking essential. Disabled: toilet. Dress: smart casual. Entertainment: musicians 3-6pm daily. **Map 9 H6.**

The Connaught

16 Carlos Place, W1K 2AL (7499 7070/ www.theconnaught.com). Bond Street or Green Park tube. **Tea served** 3-5.30pm daily. **Set tea** £18-£24. **Credit** AmEx, DC, JCB, MC, V.
Babies and children welcome: high chairs. Disabled: toilet. **Map 9 H7.**

The Dorchester

53 Park Lane, W1K 1QA (7629 8888/ www.thedorchester.com). Hyde Park Corner tube. **Tea served** 2.30pm, 4.45pm daily. **Set tea** £29.50; £38.50 incl glass of champagne; £43 high tea. **Credit** AmEx, DC, JCB, MC, V.
Babies and children welcome: high chairs. Booking essential. Disabled: toilet. Dress: smart casual. Entertainment: pianist 2.30-11pm daily. **Map 9 G7.**

The Lanesborough

1 Lanesborough Place, Hyde Park Corner, SW1X 7TA (7259 5599/www.lanesborough.com). Hyde Park Corner tube. **Tea served** 3.30-6pm Mon-Sat; 4-6pm Sun. **Set tea** £31-£39. **Minimum** £9.50. **Credit** AmEx, DC, MC, V.
Babies and children welcome: high chairs. Booking essential. Disabled: toilet. Dress: smart casual. Entertainment: pianist 3.30-6pm Mon-Sat; 4-6pm Sun. **Map 9 G8.**

The Ritz

150 Piccadilly, W1J 9BR (7493 8181/ www.theritzhotel.co.uk). Green Park tube. **Tea served** (reserved sittings) 11.30am, 1.30pm, 3.30pm, 5.30pm, 7.30pm daily. **Set tea** £36. **Credit** AmEx, MC, V.
Babies and children welcome: children's menu; high chairs. Disabled: toilet. Booking advisable restaurant; essential afternoon tea. Dress: jacket and tie; no jeans or trainers. **Map 9 J7.**

The Soho Hotel

4 Richmond Mews, W1D 3DH (7559 3007/www.firmdale.com). Tottenham Court Road tube. **Tea served** 3-5pm daily. **Set tea** £15. **Credit** AmEx, DC, JCB, MC, V.
Babies and children welcome: high chairs. Booking advisable. Disabled: toilet. Dress: smart casual. **Map 17 B3.**

Fish & Chips

Recent research posits the notion that the humble fish and chip supper, a stalwart of British cuisine, is anything but, emerging during the 19th century as a combination of French frites and Jewish fish dishes. Whatever its provenance, this once cheap, filling meal for the urban masses has become a dish served with ethical dilemmas; how to justify eating much-depleted sea stock while simultaneously risking the depletion of health service funds with deep-fried fish in batter accompanied by deep-fried chunks of potato? By species-swapping and not indulging too often, would be our advice. And choose your chippie wisely; only a tiny portion of the capital's practitioners get it right. The fish should be flaky and moist, wrapped in thin, crispy batter, the thick-cut chips golden brown and crunchy on the outside, deliciously fluffy rather than soggy on the inside. For a change, fish fried in matzo meal is also worth ordering if it's offered. For restaurants specialising in a wider range of fish dishes, see p94 **Fish**.

Central

Barbican

Fish Central

149-155 Central Street, EC1V 8AP (7253 4970). Old Street tube/rail/55 bus. **Lunch served** 11am-2.30pm Mon-Sat. **Dinner served** 5-10.30pm Mon-Thur; 5-11pm Fri, Sat. **Main courses** £7.95-£14.50. **Credit** AmEx, MC, V.

With its smart awning, big windows, abstract black and white photos and pastel colour scheme, Fish Central (est. 1968) is a step up from the average chippie. But bottles of malt vinegar atop the melamine tables show where its heart still lies, and you can't escape the smell of the fryer from the popular takeaway section next door. Fish and chips remain the core of a yard-long menu: cod, haddock, plaice, rock salmon or skate can be grilled, deep-fried or cooked in matzo meal; lobster and oysters are sometimes available, and there's a handful of meat dishes (cumberland sausages, lamb chops, steak) if you really must. Grilled haddock was faultless, mushy peas up to par, but the chips a bit tough. Most impressive was a starter of pan-fried scallops (despite the accompanying 'salsa verde', which was oily and odd-tasting); almost a dozen plump scallops is astonishing value for £5.95. It's popular with a noisy local crowd, and staff are an ebullient lot.

Babies and children welcome: children's portions; high chairs. Booking advisable. Separate room for parties, seats 60. Takeaway service. **Map 5 P3.**

Bloomsbury

North Sea Fish Restaurant

7-8 Leigh Street, WC1H 9EW (7387 5892). Russell Square tube/King's Cross tube/rail/ 68, 168 bus. **Lunch served** noon-2.30pm, **dinner served** 5.30-10.30pm Mon-Sat. **Main courses** £8.90-£18.95. **Credit** AmEx, MC, V.

Although the gussied-up Brunswick Centre marks out this quarter of Bloomsbury as an area on the move, one local institution remains steadfastly unchanged, lodged in a decade long past. Inside the North Sea you'll find worn carpets, velvet-padded chairs, net curtains – and a charm that can't be faked, no matter how pricey the refurb. The restaurant's chummy, seaside-chippie feel is a key draw, however, as the food is far from perfect. While we were impressed by the scale of a roasted sea bass (enormous, as were most of the portions), the fish itself was overcooked and dry. Same with a main of trout in parsley sauce; despite the pleasant sense of nostalgia, brought about by its near-comical lack of aesthetic finesse, the delicate fish wasn't prepared with enough attention. Starters were better: generous smoked salmon and a rich, salty fish soup were equally pleasing. Tartare sauce is own-made; we devoured it with a sizeable basket of not-too-oily chips. Proximity to the British Library means this a popular lunch stop for academics; many enjoy their meal with one of four bottled ales, St Peter's among them.

Babies and children welcome: high chairs. Booking essential weekends. Separate room for parties, seats 40. Takeaway service (until 11pm). **Map 4 L4.**

Covent Garden

Rock & Sole Plaice

47 Endell Street, WC2H 9AJ (7836 3785/ www.rockandsoleplaice.com). Covent Garden tube. **Meals served** 11.30am-11pm Mon-Sat; noon-10pm Sun. **Main courses** £8-£14. **Credit** MC, V.

The painted sign in the window reads 'established 1874'; on the menu it says '1871'. 'Est. 1949' says the contradictory receipt. In fact, owner Hassan Ziyaeddin moved to London in 1960, and we could find nothing to substantiate his claim to be London's oldest surviving fish and chip restaurant. Whatever, it's a sociable and busy little chippie in a handy Covent Garden location, with the mainstay of the menu – the fish and chips – done well (though with batter sometimes on the tough side) and coming in generous quantities. It's only when you stray from the main event that dishes might disappoint. We were unimpressed by our mushy peas (too much mush, not enough 'peas') and the fish cakes (we could have played hockey with them). The meal ended on a high with a very satisfying spotted dick and custard. This used to be a great spot for alfresco dining in summer, below the big ash tree and geranium baskets lit by fairy lights, but in May 2007 Westminster Council temporarily withdrew its licence for pavement tables. Rock & Soul Plaice has also applied to extend the premises next door.

Babies and children welcome. Booking advisable weekends. Separate room for parties, seats 36. Tables outdoors (45, pavement). Takeaway service. **Map 18 D3.**

Fitzrovia

★ Fish Bone

82 Cleveland Street, W1T 6NF (7580 2672). Great Portland Street or Warren Street tube. **Meals served** 11am-11pm Mon-Fri; 5-11pm Sat. **Main courses** £6-£9. **Credit** MC, V.

Inside this unassuming chippie a steady queue waits at the counter, while numbers at the tables at the rear grow as lunchtime progresses. The whole place is as bright and brisk as the wipe-clean, pink, white and green floral tablecloths. Diners are more mixed than you might expect, the usual preponderance of men in suits offset by skinny young Greeks and a pair of shopping ladies, hungover and summoning saveloys. The sausages arrived sooner than our halloumi, implying the relative level of care taken in preparation by the effusive Greek proprietors – certainly the cheese was perfectly textured. A main-course haddock was also firm, tasty and big enough to overwhelm the plate, its chips straight-from-the-fryer hot. There are more adventurous options (grilled bream, perhaps), and Fish Bone has an alcohol licence: at £2.50 a glass, you get the house wine you pay for, so Hoegaarden or a half-litre of Whitstable organic beer might be wiser choices. There's a dimmer switch on the wall, possibly for romantic evening fish-and-trysts.

Babies and children admitted. Bookings advisable. Tables outdoors (3, pavement). Takeaway service. **Map 3 J4.**

Holborn

★ Fryer's Delight

19 Theobald's Road, WC1X 8SL (7405 4114). Holborn tube/19, 38, 55 bus. **Meals served** noon-10pm Mon-Sat. **Main courses** £5.40-£6.70. **Minimum** £2.10. **Unlicensed. Corkage** no charge. **No credit cards.**

Unpretentious food, honest prices and retro, 1950s canteen-style decor continue to entice customers into this no-frills Holborn caff. The menu is limited (no mushy peas was a particular bugbear for us) and the greasy smell may linger on you long after you've left, but Fryer's Delight is everything a chippie should be. It's perfect for a greedy after-work dinner or lunchtime guilty pleasure, with resolutely rock-bottom prices; cod and chips currently stands at a respectable £6, Peter's pies are on offer for £3.70, and a battered sausage will set you back a measly £2.80. Orders come with a generous portion of chunky, if slightly soggy, chips, and the fish – double-fried in beef dripping – tasted fresh and crispy. Add a truly English mug of tea (you can also bring in your own booze) and a doorstop-thick slice of bread and butter into the equation, and you've got a classic fish supper from any post-war decade.

Babies and children admitted. Takeaway service (until 11pm). **Map 4 M5.**

Marylebone

★ Golden Hind (100)

73 Marylebone Lane, W1U 2PN (7486 3644). Bond Street tube. **Lunch served** noon-3pm Mon-Fri. **Dinner served** 6-10pm Mon-Sat. **Main courses** £5-£10.70. **Minimum** (lunch) £4, (dinner) £5. **Unlicensed. Corkage** no charge. **Credit** AmEx, JCB, MC, V.

Run by a group of Greek guys, this café-style chippie – established in 1914 – still has the feel of a traditional English gaff, despite a couple of Greek flourishes on the menu (greek salad and deep-fried feta cheese). The small, no-frills dining room has art deco touches including a disused 1950s fish fryer; it gets packed out by Marylebone locals, thanks to the reliably tasty grub and fantastic prices. There are no saveloys here; the short menu sticks to fish. Starters include scampi, calamari and fish cakes, mains cod, haddock and skate wing. All the fish we tried was fresh-tasting and skilfully cooked, either steamed or fried in light, crispy batter. Chips were slightly anaemic and could have been crunchier, but they were

cooked through and served in satisfying quantities. Time-honoured English puds include spotted dick, apple crumble and raspberry jam sponge, all served with a generous dollop of custard.
Babies and children welcome: children's portions. Booking advisable. Separate room for parties, seats 28. Takeaway service. **Map 9 G5**.

★ Sea Shell

49-51 Lisson Grove, NW1 6UH (7224 9000/ www.seashellrestaurant.co.uk). Marylebone tube/rail. **Lunch served** noon-2.30pm, **dinner served** 5-10.30pm Mon-Fri. **Meals served** noon-10.30pm Sat. **Main courses** £9.50-£18.95. **Set meal** (lunch, 5-7pm Mon-Sat) £12 2 courses, £14 3 courses. **Credit** AmEx, DC, JCB, MC, V.

This is no run-of-the-mill chippie: staff are professional, decor tasteful and food fantastic. Prices are on the high side too, but the little extra spent is well worth it: fish is top-quality (bought fresh and so occasionally subject to availability) and perfectly cooked. The menu caters to both those seeking full-on fried fare or more calorie-conscious customers: fish is served either fried or grilled, and you have the option of mash, chips or baked potato as sides. A few large salads are also available. Simple starters of garlic prawns and calamari with a spicy dip were packed with flavour and nicely presented. Mains were even better: lemon sole goujons and haddock fried in delectable, crunchy batter, both served with golden chips and a pot of delicious, own-made tartare sauce. Portions are massive, but it's still worth ordering a side of fine mushy peas. For dessert, try some apple cake or traditional bread and butter pudding. Locals can also enjoy takeaways from the shop at the front of the restaurant – lucky them.
Babies and children welcome: children's menu; high chairs. Booking advisable Thur-Sat. Disabled: toilet. Separate room for parties, seats 25. Takeaway service. **Map 2 F4**.

Victoria

Seafresh Fish Restaurant

80-81 Wilton Road, SW1V 1DL (7828 0747). Victoria tube/rail/24 bus. **Lunch served** noon-3pm, **dinner served** 5-10.30pm Mon-Fri. **Meals served** noon-10.30pm Sat. **Main courses** £5.50-£19.95. **Set lunch** £10 2 courses. **Credit** AmEx, DC, MC, V.

It has an attached takeaway shop, but Seafresh is very much a restaurant. The contemporary design of the brightly lit room includes a glass wall emblazoned with the restaurant's logo and long brown leather benches. These are filled with well-heeled families and elderly gents in pin-striped suits. The menu leans towards more high-end fish fare, with rope-grown mussels and dover sole nudging the £20 mark. Even the more basic options come at a mark-up of around £5 more than the takeaway next door. Still, there's no skimping on portions: salmon fillet was a brick-sized hunk of fish; a seafood platter contained so much smoky-flavoured grilled skate wing, haddock, cod, lemon sole, calamares and meaty king prawns that it spilled over the edges of the plate. Sure, it ain't 'cheap as chips' – but if you're willing to pay the prices, you'll be rewarded in terms of both quality and quantity.
Babies and children welcome: high chairs. Booking advisable. Restaurant available for hire. Takeaway service. **Map 15 J10**.

West

Bayswater

★ Mr Fish

9 Porchester Road, W2 5DP (7229 4161/ www.mrfish.uk.com). Bayswater, Queensway or Royal Oak tube. **Meals served** 11am-11pm daily. **Main courses** £5.95-£11.95. **Set lunch** (11am-3pm) £4.99 cod & chips incl soft drink, tea or coffee. **Credit** AmEx, MC, V.

Slap on your shades and tighten your pigtails in preparation for a visit to this kitsch restaurant. Decked out in the style of a 1950s ice-cream parlour on Miami Beach, with a chequered floor, neon sign and candy-coloured chairs, it's a surreal experience to be eating anything other than sundaes here. The retro theme continues through the menu, with prawn cocktail and breaded mushrooms to start, and jam sponge pudding and spotted dick for dessert – all at impressively low prices. The choice of mains is much wider than the name suggests, spanning pies, hamburgers, chicken, bean burgers and wraps, as well a wide selection of fish, available in everything from breadcrumbs to matzo meal. Our battered halibut steak was on the dry side, and we were not pleasantly surprised to discover some lurking fish roe inside, but a generous portion of fantastically crispy, fluffy and chunky chips on the side rescued the dish. Side orders include thick mushy peas and pickled onions. The extensive wine list features half bottles and champagne (£29.90).
Babies and children welcome: children's menu; high chair. Takeaway service (until midnight). **Map 7 C5**.

Notting Hill

★ Costas Fish Restaurant

18 Hillgate Street, W8 7SR (7727 4310). Notting Hill Gate tube. **Lunch served** noon-2.30pm, **dinner served** 5.30-10.30pm Tue-Sat. **Main courses** £5.20-£7.90. **No credit cards**.

Despite the recent, well-publicised upgrade of nearby Geales (now in the Fish chapter), an aesthetic revamp doesn't seem to be on the cards at Costas. The sparsely decorated, conservatory-like restaurant area might have had a recent coat of magnolia, but your route there still takes you past the takeaway counter and staff dunking fish into batter mix. It's an old-school establishment, with all the chippie-standard fried fish options on offer, but the menu is also scattered with dishes that belie the venue's Greek-Cypriot ownership; there's a selection of dips, pitta bread and greek salad, plus greek coffee and baklava for dessert. It's worth steering towards the Mediterranean dishes; a starter portion of refreshingly creamy taramasalata bore a pleasant resemblance to the typical Cypriot way of preparation (unlike most commercial efforts). Our chips were on the soggy side, though, and the mushy peas were a real disappointment: hard, overcooked peas sitting in a pool of thin green liquid. Our Friday night visit saw the restaurant half-empty. Might it be time for Costas to think about modernisation?
Babies and children admitted. Booking advisable dinner. Tables outdoors (2, pavement). Takeaway service. **Map 7 A7**.

Sea Shell

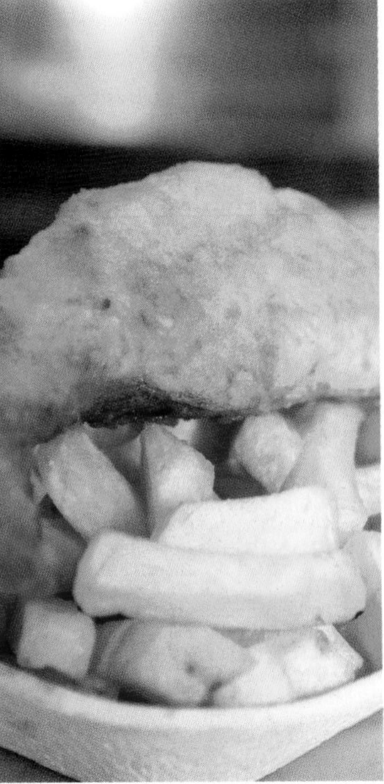

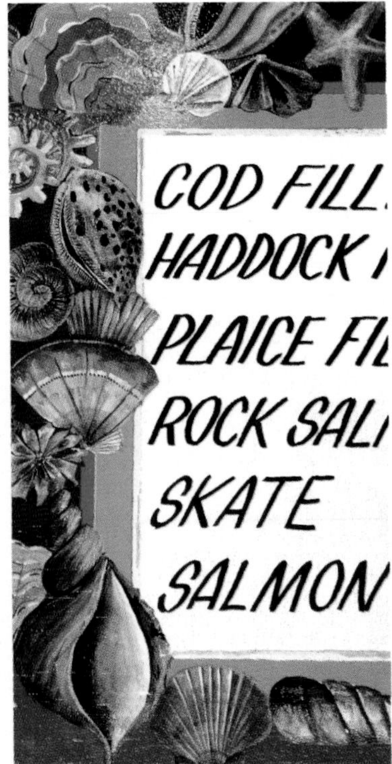

COD FILL
HADDOCK
PLAICE FI
ROCK SAL
SKATE
SALMON

South West

Wandsworth

Brady's

513 Old York Road, SW18 1TF (8877 9599). Wandsworth Town rail/28, 44 bus. **Lunch served** 12.30-2.30pm Tue-Fri; 12.30-3pm Sat. **Dinner served** 6.30-10pm Mon; 6.30-10.30pm Tue-Fri; 6-10pm Sat. **Main courses** £7.55-£10.25. **Credit** MC, V.

Better than a standard chippie but not quite a fish restaurant, Brady's is pitched firmly mid-market. The paintings of mermaids, fish charts and plenty of natural (and artificial) light give it a slightly seaside feel. Fish portion sizes are not as hearty as you can find in some more basic chippies: this is the middle-class end of Wandsworth, after all, where appetites seem to be more delicate. But the fish (from a wide selection) was nicely cooked, and the chips properly crisp and dry; the mushy peas were the real thing too. Just a few details disappointed on our visit. The half pint of prawns weren't freshly boiled and appeared to have been kept in the fridge for too long, being both cold and soggy, and the salad could have consisted of something more appealing than a pile of iceberg lettuce with bitter radicchio. But our charming waitress redeemed Brady's – as did the excellent apple crumble, with lashings of hot custard.

Babies and children welcome: children's portions. Bookings not accepted. Takeaway service. **Map 21 A4.**

South

Battersea

★ Fish Club (100)

189 St John's Hill, SW11 1TH (7978 7115/ www.thefishclub.com). Clapham Junction rail. **Meals served** noon-10pm Tue-Sat; noon-9pm Sun. **Main courses** £5.95-£12. **Credit** AmEx, MC, V.

When it opened in summer 2004, Fish Club brought the fish and chip shop right up to date by using only top-quality ingredients in contemporary interpretations of classic dishes. High standards have been maintained, even with the pressure of a second branch, opened in autumn 2007 on Clapham High Street. The selection of fish and seafood is still top-notch, with razor clams, smoked sprats, and prawn and chorizo kebab among the more unexpected offerings. A prawn cocktail starter resembled something Heston Blumenthal might recreate on his TV show *In Search of Perfection*: the lettuce not shredded, but assembled whole like a caesar salad, and super-tasty crevettes gris replacing the more usual, bland prawn varieties. Coley is a firm, meaty fish, perfect as a substitute for cod when fried in a tempura-light batter, as ours was – sublime. Even the greek salad used cucumbers that had been cored to deseed them. Despite the wonderful food and highish prices, Fish Club remains a simple place: you order from the glass display cabinet, then sit at a simple wipe-clean table, or – as a great many do – take your choice away.

Babies and children welcome: children's menu; high chair. Bookings not accepted. Disabled: toilet. Tables outdoors (3, courtyard; 2, pavement). Takeaway service. **Map 21 B4.**

For branch see index.

Waterloo

Masters Super Fish

191 Waterloo Road, SE1 8UX (7928 6924). Waterloo tube/rail. **Lunch served** noon-3pm Tue-Sat. **Dinner served** 5.30-10.30pm Mon; 4.30-10.30pm Tue-Sat. **Main courses** £6.75-£12.50. **Set lunch** (noon-3pm Tue-Sun) £6.50 1 course incl soft drink, tea or coffee. **Credit** MC, V.

With fish delivered daily from Billingsgate Market, this no-frills chippie has a small but solid takeaway menu; it's not unusual to see a queue out of the door on a Friday night. If you eat in, there's a larger menu offering extra choices such as dover sole and salmon fillet, plus the opportunity to have your fish grilled rather than fried (an extra wait is required). Rugged brick walls and withered hanging plants bespeak a long-gone era; and the ambience on our Saturday lunchtime visit wasn't enhanced by an absence of customers. Mustard-battered cod was prepared with a one-sided coating of light, crispy batter, which allowed the fish's flavour to come through. Things weren't so successful with more exotic choices: grilled swordfish was overcooked and tough, and the squid rings in our calamari starter were so tiny they were overpowered by their batter coating. Still, stick to the classics and Masters shouldn't disappoint.

Babies and children welcome: high chair. Booking advisable Fri, Sat. Takeaway service. **Map 11 N9.**

South East

East Dulwich

Sea Cow

37 Lordship Lane, SE22 8EW (8693 3111). East Dulwich rail/176, 196 bus. **Meals served** noon-11pm Tue-Sat; noon-8.30pm Sun. **Main courses** £7-£10. **Credit** MC, V.

Sea Cow's interior isn't a million miles away from traditional chippies, although chunky wooden tables encourage eating-in, and a large icebox at one end of the counter boasts fish brought daily from the coast or Billingsgate Market. No dejected-looking cod cuts or rubbery soles akin to those on a Londoner's shoe; the menu instead offers the likes of whole sea bass, red snapper and gilthead bream, all cooked to order and with a wine list tailored to accompany the day's catch. It's no wonder the place is now packed with the neighbourhood's well-heeled liberals, though perhaps the occasional slide in standards can be attributed to this surge in demand. House cod still comes piping hot and coated in impossibly thin crispy batter, but portions seem smaller than when it first opened. Staff are also less attentive, and we've had some surprisingly average chip portions in the past year or so. Elsewhere on the menu, though, it's business as usual: a starter of deep-fried whitebait was really a meal in itself, while coriander fish cakes were sublime. Seasonal specials such as mahi mahi help steer the Sea Cow into the waters of 21st-century dining. There's also an outlet in Stoke Newington, but the Clapham branch is now an outlet of Fish Club (*see above*).

Babies and children welcome: children's menu; high chairs. Takeaway service. **Map 23 C4.**

For branch see index.

Herne Hill

★ Olley's

65-69 Norwood Road, SE24 9AA (8671 8259/ www.olleys.info). Herne Hill rail/3, 68, 196 bus. **Dinner served** 5-10.30pm Mon. **Meals served** noon-10.30pm Tue-Sun. **Set lunch** £5 1 course. **Main courses** £10.95-£22.20. **Credit** AmEx, MC, V.

Olley's sets out to provide a breath of ocean air in a city where fish and chips is all too often an insipid takeaway option. Granted, there's something rather Harvester-like about the family-friendly interior – wooden beams and artfully rustic brick walls – and eating off a plate isn't quite as spiritual an experience as spearing tabloid-wrapped chips with a wooden fork, but otherwise this is as reverent a temple to the national dish of old as you'll find in the capital. The menu boasts a number of personified 'fish experiences': the cod supper, for example, is cheekily referred to as the Lord Archer ('tart not included'), and features crisp batter, proper thick-cut chips and a hearty portion of mushy peas – these rival 'Mandelson's avocado dip' as side order of choice. Those seeking less stereotypical sustenance can also order fried, grilled or steamed fillets of everything from haddock and hake to salmon, swordfish and whole sea bass. There's also grilled vegetables for the health-conscious, paella for the Spanish-inclined and pickled eggs for nostalgia freaks.

Babies and children welcome: children's menu; high chairs; nappy-changing facilities. Disabled: toilet. Separate room for parties, seats 25. Tables outdoors (6, pavement). Takeaway service. **Map 23 A5.**

Lewisham

★ Something Fishy

117-119 Lewisham High Street, SE13 6AT (8852 7075). Lewisham rail/DLR. **Meals served**

9am-6pm Mon-Sat. **Main courses** £5.55-£7.70. **No credit cards.**
Its one-piece plastic chairs and weathered Formica tables might seem cute as kittens to lovers of retro kitsch, but there's nothing ironic about Something Fishy. Despite the punny name, this is as earnest an eaterie as you could hope for – something that is reflected in the list of comforting if coronary-inducing mains (battered saveloys, hearty pies with generous helpings of buttery mash) and similarly traditional puds (jam roly-poly, knickerbocker glory). It's cod and chips, however, that keeps the place packed with everyone from leathery traders lunch-breaking from the nearby market to fresh-faced families and nostalgic old couples. Fish is wonderfully flaky and coated with crisp batter, while fluffy chips are served in portions big enough to satisfy even the most famished south Londoner. This isn't a place for a romantic lunch for two, nor are staff the type to waste time on pleasantries, but as a restaurant founded on tradition, it remains safely at the top of its game.
Babies and children welcome: children's menu; high chairs. Tables outdoors (5, pavement). Takeaway service.

East

Victoria Park

★ Fish House NEW

126-128 Lauriston Road, E9 7LH (8533 3327). Mile End tube then 277 bus. **Meals served** noon-10pm daily. **Main courses** £6.50-£10.50. **Credit** AmEx, MC, V.
This new addition to the eating options along south Hackney's Lauriston Road (run by the landlords of the Approach Tavern in Bethnal Green) is a poshed-up chippie, housed in an airy room that's handsomely tiled in white and black, and filled with neat little tables, chairs and benches. Assuming you don't order from the specials board, from which we enjoyed chunky, buttery prawns as a shared starter, your main decision will be which fish to have with your chips and mushy peas. While generous, a portion of rock was a little too greasy. But the haddock was perfect: crisp, golden batter cloaking a melt-in-the-mouth tender fillet. The chips were very fine too, fluffy within but firmer on the outside. Don't be surprised if you've got no room for dessert: if you do, gelati was supplemented on our visit by Eaton (sic) mess. You can also order from a slightly cheaper takeaway counter – an appealing picnic option since Victoria Park is a pickled onion's throw from the front door.
Babies and children welcome: children's menu; high chairs; toys. Booking advisable weekends. Takeaway service.

North East

Dalston

★ Faulkner's

424-426 Kingsland Road, E8 4AA (7254 6152). Dalston Kingsland rail/67, 76, 149, 242, 243 bus. **Lunch served** noon-2.30pm Mon-Fri. **Dinner served** 5-10pm Mon-Thur; 4.30-10pm Fri. **Meals served** 11.30am-10pm Sat; noon-9pm Sun. **Main courses** £10.50-£18. **Set meal** £15.90-£19.90 4 courses (minimum 2). **Credit** MC, V.
Really, really good fish and chips are a rare thing, and worth waiting for. At Faulkner's, a cheery East End chippie, you'll find them. Our cod was crisp, dazzling white and not too oily; chips were glistening yellow and perfectly cooked. Mushy peas, a worthwhile extra, were equally tasty, even if their luminous green colouring was slightly alarmingly. And while fried fish is the big draw here, the site itself is pretty charming too – a bonus on a somewhat charmless stretch of Kingsland Road. A hand-painted sign, mauve shutters on the windows and a definite smell of vinegar wafting from the takeaway section combine to give the feel of being at the seaside. If you can resist getting your chips wrapped for home, eat in – it's a riot of nostalgia, all laminated menus, lacy tablecloths and smiling waitresses in pinnies. Faulkner's has been going for years, and with good reason.
Babies and children welcome: children's menu; high chairs. Bookings advisable weekends. Disabled: toilet. Separate room for parties, seats 25. Takeaway service. **Map 6 R1.**

North

Finchley

★ Two Brothers Fish Restaurant

297-303 Regent's Park Road, N3 1DP (8346 0469/ www.twobrothers.co.uk). Finchley Central tube. **Lunch served** noon-2.30pm, **dinner served** 5.30-10.15pm Tue-Sat. **Main courses** £9-£21.50. **Minimum** £10.95. **Credit** AmEx, MC, V.
The brothers are Leon and Tony Manzi, and their smart, friendly restaurant has been a Finchley institution for years. The top-notch fish comes fresh from Billingsgate Market: firm, flavourful cod and haddock, as well as jellied eels, rock eel, cod's roe in batter, yummy salmon fish cakes, skate wing, oysters and mussels from Ireland, fresh Canadian lobster, and seasonal choices such as plaice on the bone. All frying is done in groundnut oil, and you can have your fish battered or coated in matzo, or steamed. They use real vinegar (no nasty non-brewed condiment), make their own sauces, and the chips – made 'with only the best Maris Piper potatoes' – are first-class. If you don't have time for a sit-down meal (or the money – there's a minimum charge of £10.95 a head, though if you vacate your table by 7pm you qualify for a 15% discount), you can get the classics in paper wrappers for half the price from the adjoining takeaway counter.
Babies and children welcome: high chairs. Bookings accepted lunch only. Takeaway service (until 10pm).

Muswell Hill

Toff's

38 Muswell Hill Broadway, N10 3RT (8883 8656). Highgate tube then 43, 134 bus. **Meals served** 11.30am-10pm Mon-Sat. **Main courses** £7.95-£18.50. **Set meal** (11.30am-5pm) £5.95-£7.95 1 course incl tea or coffee. **Credit** AmEx, DC, JCB, MC, V.
There is a mixed cocktail of influences at work in Toff's. Behind the counter, the staff wear branded T-shirts; the word 'Fish' is spelled out in the tiling of the takeaway area. Yet Toff's isn't all modern touches: a dark-wooden interior at the rear has more in common with a Victorian boozer, and there are signed photos of Les Dennis, Norman Wisdom and Iron Maiden hanging on the walls. Catering to the chattering classes of Muswell Hill – an ever-health-conscious clientele – fish is served grilled or coated with egg and matzo, in addition to the standard batter option; there are also parsley-flecked boiled potatoes as an alternative to chips. Own-made fish cakes were covered in a pleasantly crisp breadcrumb coating, but we found the interior a little damp; a main of rock salmon was slightly soggy too. But the humungous portions – followed by a moist, glistening treacle pudding from the range of trad Brit desserts on offer – provided ample reason for a return visit.
Babies and children welcome: children's menu; colouring books; high chairs; party bag. Separate room for parties, seats 24. Takeaway service.

North West

Golders Green

★ Sam's

68-70 Golders Green Road, NW11 8LM (8455 9898/7171). Golders Green tube. **Meals served** noon-10pm daily. **Main courses** £6.60-£12.50. **Set lunch** (noon-4pm) £6.95 2 courses incl tea or coffee. **Credit** MC, V.
With unfailingly cheerful staff and reliably good, well-priced grub, it's little wonder this Golders Green chippie should have made itself so popular since its launch in 2000. The long dining room can seat over 130, but its somewhat institutional dimensions are nicely offset by a decor of wood panels, fishing nets and framed scenes of a nautical nature. Sam's is usually busy, especially at lunchtime, when it fills with an older bunch of diners drawn by a £6.95 meal deal that dishes up fried cod and chips, a drink and dessert. A la carte, the essential dishes are the fried, grilled or steamed fish – the catch includes cod, halibut, haddock, sea bass and salmon – but there's also falafel, houmous and a small pick of veggie options such as spring rolls. Every main course comes with a generous if unexciting salad of lettuce, cucumber and tomato. The takeaway counter does bustling business.
Babies and children welcome: children's menu; high chairs. Booking advisable. Disabled: toilet. Restaurant available for hire. Takeaway service.

West Hampstead

★ Nautilus

27-29 Fortune Green Road, NW6 1DT (7435 2532). West Hampstead tube/rail then 328 bus. **Lunch served** 11.30am-2.30pm, **dinner served** 4.30-10pm Mon-Sat. **Main courses** £9.50-£19.50. **Credit** JCB, MC, V.
This nondescript-looking, family-run, traditional fish and chip shop is deserving of its near-cult following. Unpretentious, unreconstructed decor consists of Formica tables and minimal adornment (other than various certificates of quality on the walls) and there's a classic (and extremely busy) takeaway bar next door. The secret's in the batter – which isn't batter at all, but matzo meal. It coats the fish in perfect, light crispness without any of the gloopy lining that accompanies regular deep-fried fare. The menu is simple, albeit with a wider than average selection of fish, ranging from cod and haddock to skate and dover sole. All are offered grilled or fried. We loved fried skate and haddock cutlet, crispy on the outside and buttery inside; the chips were real and potatoey, though could have been a touch browner. It's not cheap, with fish costing up to £19.50, though portions are vast and the house wine comes in bargain-priced £6 carafes. The mushy peas were almost tasteless, but a tomato and red onion salad compensated. Friendly service adds to the likeable vibe.
Babies and children welcome: high chairs. Bookings advisable. Takeaway service. **Map 28 A1.**

Outer London

Kingston, Surrey

fish! kitchen

58 Coombe Road, Kingston, Surrey KT2 7AF (8546 2886/www.fishkitchen.com). Norbiton rail/57, 85, 213 bus. **Meals served** noon-10pm Tue-Sat. **Main courses** £8.95-£22.95. **Credit** AmEx, MC, V.
Attached to veteran fishmonger Jarvis, this smart chippie is decorated with black and white photographs depicting the shop as it was in the 1940s. Back then, a chippie would serve you fish deep-fried or not at all. There's more choice these days: fish! kitchen offers the likes of swordfish club sandwiches, tuna burgers or king prawn kebabs alongside its battered haddock, cod, plaice and halibut. There's also a daily specials board of grilled options, featuring, for example, dover sole, trout and scallops. In the past we've been impressed by the kitchen's fried offerings – crisp, thin batter and fleshy, moist fish – and so opted for an alternative this time: tuna steak, grilled. Seasoned simply and cooked just right, it flaked apart at the touch of a fork – perfect. Chips were golden and chunky, ideal for dipping in own-made tartare sauce. Ice-cream is the only offered pud; a compact wine list offers just three reds and four whites. The choice of starters is wider, Jarvis's own smoked salmon a highlight. Uniformed and friendly staff patrol the sleek, black-tiled interior, which was empty on a warm day, thanks to the array of tables on the front decking.
Babies and children welcome: children's menu; high chairs. Disabled: toilet. Tables outdoors (15, terrace). Takeaway service.

Pizza & Pasta

For a quick, cheap, cheerful meal, London's pizza and pasta joints make an obvious port of call. The scene is invariably dominated by the popular chain operations (which we've reviewed together, to make comparison easier – *see p326* **Chain gang**), but there are plenty of independent outfits too, offering a less standardised and more individual approach, with inventive toppings, a friendly vibe and value for money. For more restaurants serving pizza and pasta, see **Italian**, starting on p181, and **The Americas**, starting on p42.

Central

Clerkenwell & Farringdon

Santoré NEW

59-61 Exmouth Market, EC1R 4QL (7812 1488). Farringdon tube/rail/19, 38, 341 bus. **Meals served** noon-11pm Mon-Sat. **Main courses** £6.95-£13.95. **Set lunch** noon-4pm £8.95 2 courses. **Credit** AmEx, MC, V.

Competition's tough on Exmouth Market, with superlative Spanish restaurant Moro mere paces away and worthy Modern European restaurant the Ambassador bang next door. But Santoré draws a good crowd, surviving thanks to its excellent pizzas. Spun in an open kitchen at the rear, the pizza bases are so springy you feel they might bounce if dropped. The usual combinations are joined by interesting Naples-inspired specials such as spaccanapoli: goat's cheese and mortadella on a base that's already had a blast in the oven. Sharers can combine pizzas to create half- or full-metre monsters; results are served on wooden platforms. Supplementing all this are eight or so pasta dishes, plus a few meaty options; we enjoyed a perfectly thin and crisp veal milanese. A starter of marinated baby octopus chunks was too big to finish, though the dressing was nicely tangy. The spacious site is wide but not very deep; when the glass front is open to the elements (as it is throughout the summer), most tables have an alfresco feel. Wine bottles line a high shelf that skirts the room; a well-sourced list of a dozen reds and whites should please most tastes.

Babies and children admitted. Takeway and delivery service (£8 minimum). Tables outdoors (5, pavement). **Map 5 N4**.

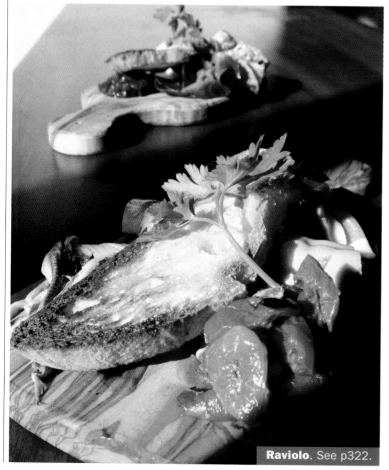

Raviolo. See p322.

Euston

Pasta Plus

62 Eversholt Street, NW1 1DA (7383 4943/ www.pastaplus.co.uk). Euston tube/rail. **Lunch served** noon-2.30pm Mon-Fri. **Dinner served** 5.30-10.30pm Mon-Sat. **Main courses** £6.50-£15.50. **Credit** AmEx, DC, MC, V.

This is a light and cheery refuge from the noise, grime and 'saunas' of Euston's seedy streets. The same Italian family has run Pasta Plus for more than 30 years; populated by faithful regulars, it has a cosy, local feel. A good-value menu makes it a decent pre-train meal option: an alternative to fast food from the station concourse. Pasta dishes and Italian classics (there's no pizza) are on offer. A tegamino starter – two eggs baked in cream, with a flavoursome tomato sauce – was an example of simple ingredients, simply cooked, and was delicious. Gorgonzola-filled tortelloni with pine nuts was also good, but ultimately too heavy, especially in its parmesan cream sauce. Penne rustiche had fresh-tasting spring onion, broccoli and good chicken fillets, lightly dressed in extra-virgin olive oil. If pushed to complain, we'd say that the presentation could be better, but fancy food isn't what PP is about. The wine list is concise but decent enough, with Italian labels (of course) taking centre stage. Tables in the conservatory area overlook a pretty garden; a pity that it's private and diners can't get in.

Babies and children welcome: high chairs. Tables outdoors (26, conservatory). Takeaway service. **Map 4 K3**.

Fitzrovia

Cleveland Kitchen

145 Cleveland Street, W1T 6QH (7387 5966). Great Portland Street or Warren Street tube. **Lunch served** noon-3pm Mon-Fri. **Dinner served** 6-10.30pm Mon-Sat. **Main courses** £9.50-£16. **Set lunch** £6-£7 1 course incl drink, £11.50 2 courses incl drink and coffee. **Set dinner** £16.50 2 courses. **Credit** AmEx, MC, V.

CK's great-value lunch deals pack in the locals: £6-£6.50 for any pizza or pasta, £7 for specials such as pan-roasted cod, £11.50 for two courses and coffee. Also thrown in is a glass of house wine, beer or a soft drink. Come evening, tablecloths and tea-lights are laid out, pizzas dropped and prices raised. Seven pasta and risotto choices balance out meatier mains such as calf's liver, veal escalope or swordfish (all pan-fried and served with vegetables). The food is fresh, nicely presented and competently cooked, and the small details that matter are not forgotten – such as a serrated knife for your pizza (with its just-right thin base). The restaurant layout is sweet and intimate, especially the basement tables reached via a fairy-lit spiral staircase. Popular as this place is at midday, the evening-menu price hikes are offputting, especially as several dishes also feature at lunch at half the cost – the reason, perhaps, that on our visit, only one other table was occupied by after-work diners. A shame; this little place has a lovely, relaxed vibe and service is friendly.

Babies and children admitted. Booking advisable lunch. Tables outdoors (2, pavement). Takeaway service. **Map 3 J4**.

Knightsbridge

Frankie's Italian Bar & Grill

3 Yeomans Row, off Brompton Road, SW3 2AL (7590 9999/www.frankiesitalianbarandgrill.com). Knightsbridge or South Kensington tube.

Rossopomodoro. See p322.

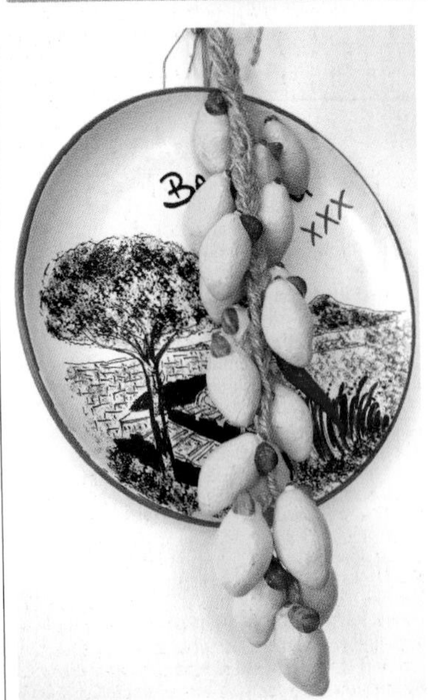

Lunch served noon-2.30pm, **dinner served** 5.30-10.30pm Mon-Fri. **Meals served** noon-11pm Sat; noon-10pm Sun. **Main courses** £7.50-£14.40. **Credit** AmEx, MC, V.
The branch of Frankie's within the neo-Byzantine Criterion at Piccadilly Circus didn't last long (the site is a French restaurant once more), but fans of the family-friendly chain still have four stylish restaurants to choose from. This branch's cavernous basement setting impresses: sparkling with reflections from mirrored walls and glitterballs, the dining area, like the lounge, features modern leather seats and well-spaced tables. It's a classy place for cocktails; equally, you could bring your kids – if they fingerpaint the table linen with pizza sauce, the waiters just smile. The food is less dramatic than the setting: efficiently produced, nicely presented Italian fare (gnocchi, pasta) plus burgers, ribeyes and the likes of veal milanese. Our salami pizza, chosen from the half-dozen offered, was very good. Grilled salmon steak with fennel was wonderfully flavoursome, but the fries were a little oversalted for our taste. Children get their own two-course menu for £7.50 (pasta, gnocchi, breaded chicken breast with fries), but order carefully across the menu – portions are huge. Service was as charming as Frankie Dettori himself, the flamboyant jockey who gave his name to this chain in collaboration with Marco Pierre White.
Babies and children welcome: children's menu, high chairs. Takeaway service (pizza only). **Map 14 E10.**
For branches see index.

Mayfair

★ Rocket

4-6 Lancashire Court, off New Bond Street, W1Y 9AD (7629 2889/www.rocketrestaurants.co.uk). Bond Street or Oxford Circus tube.
Bar **Open** noon-11pm, **meals served** noon-6pm Mon-Sat. **Main courses** £9-£12.
Restaurant **Lunch served** noon-3pm, **dinner served** 6-11pm Mon-Sat. **Main courses** £9-£15.
Both **Credit** AmEx, MC, V.
Hidden away in a tiny courtyard, Rocket is a popular spot with Mayfair shoppers. On fine evenings, drinkers in the ground-floor bar spill out on to the cobbled alley. The upstairs restaurant is an airy space with a huge skylight and windows that brighten the main dining area; several alcoves allow for more intimate dining. Relaxed yet lively, smart but not snobby, it would suit an after-work party as well as a weekend lunch with your mum. Pizzas are reliably good, with thin crusts and unusual toppings (spicy mediterranean sausage with pesto aubergine; black pudding and king prawns with chilli), but we are particularly taken with the fantastic, enormous salads. Intriguing combinations include coconut-coated crispy squid with mango and a peanut chilli dressing, for example, or a fish and chip salad with green mustard sauce. Alternative mains might include maple-glazed pork fillet with fried plantain and peppers. Don't miss the glorious date pudding with butterscotch sauce; the mango sorbet is also one of best we've had. The global wine list is divided into helpful categories such as as 'light aromatic' and 'medium-bodied fruity'. Service is commendably attentive and friendly.
Babies and children welcome: high chairs. Booking advisable. Separate rooms for parties, seating 10 and 28. **Map 9 H6.**
For branches (Rocket, Rocket Riverside) see index.

Soho

★ Italian Graffiti

163-165 Wardour Street, W1F 8WN (7439 4668/www.italiangraffiti.co.uk). Oxford Circus tube. **Lunch served** noon-3pm, **dinner served** 5.30-11.30pm Mon-Fri. **Meals served** noon-11.30pm Sat. **Main courses** £7-£14. **Credit** AmEx, DC, MC, V.
The antithesis of affected Soho dining, this family-run trattoria has served up reasonably priced, decent Italian fare for more than 20 years. Eschewing current interior design trends and sticking to what works best – simple decor, old Italian movie posters, cosy fires or air-con for year-round comfort – has earned it many fans. Wood-fired pizzas are the main draw: good vegetarian or seafood toppings balance out the ham and salami options, and bases are reliably thin and crispy (we've never had a soggy-bottomed pizza here). Pasta rates equally well: visiting in asparagus season, our tortelloni featured a baby asparagus cream sauce so fresh and flavoursome we wished the little pasta parcels had been stuffed with that instead of spinach and ricotta. The spag bol is always spot-on; heartier dishes such as steak, calf's liver or spinach-stuffed chicken breast also satisfy. For seafood fans, swordfish comes as two meaty slabs, grilled simply with olive oil, herbs and garlic. Desserts, rather less impressively, include tiramisu and banoffi pie; we always go for the panna cotta. At peak times, book.
Babies and children welcome: booster seat; children's portions. Booking advisable. Takeaway service. **Map 17 B3.**

Kettners

29 Romilly Street, W1D 5HP (7734 6112/www.kettners.com). Leicester Square or Piccadilly Circus tube. **Meals served** noon-midnight Mon-Wed, Sun; noon-1am Thur-Sat. **Main courses** £9.15-£19.90. **Credit** AmEx, DC, MC, V.
Founded in 1867 as a fancy French restaurant by Napoleon III's chef, Kettners was taken over by Pizza Express in the 1970s. A refurb a few years back spruced things up considerably, but the dusty-pink suites, private dining rooms and pianist retain a charmingly Edwardian atmosphere, making this a remarkably civilized venue for a slice of pizza. A modernised and expanded menu features grills, pasta, salads, even fish and chips (with fantastic crisp batter), but pizzas remain the main draw. Perfect, thin crusts are loaded with tasty, good-quality toppings – we always return for the reliably good boscaiola (wild mushrooms, parsley, spring onions) and salmone (smoked salmon, mascarpone, dill, and lemon juice added at the last minute). The adjoining champagne bars are ideal for swish celebrations or after-work drinks at respectable prices (cocktails from £7.75, half-bottle of Moët £25).
Babies and children welcome: high chairs. Music (pianist 1-3.30pm, 7-10.30pm Mon-Wed, Sun; 1-3.30pm, 6pm-midnight Thur-Sat). Separate rooms for parties, seating 12-85. **Map 17 C4.**

★ Spiga

84-86 Wardour Street, W1V 3LF (7734 3444/www.vpmg.net). Leicester Square, Piccadilly Circus or Tottenham Court Road tube. **Meals served** noon-11pm Mon, Tue; noon-midnight Wed-Sat. **Main courses** £8.50-£17.50. **Set meal** £17.95 2 courses, £21.95 3 courses. **Credit** AmEx, MC, V.
Spiga's stablemates in the Vince Power Music Group include a clutch of style bars and music venues. While there's no live music or DJs at this classy pizzeria, a light jazz soundtrack accompanies casual daytime dining and picks up when the buzzier evening crowd arrives. Modern decor, booth seating, a small bar and smart, black-clad Italian staff provide the good looks; food is similarly well presented and competently put together. Thin-crust pizzas are decked with reliably tasty toppings: funghi marinati, capricciosa, aubergine and salami, and a 'white pizza' with mozzarella, pecorino, taleggio and goat's cheese. Pasta dishes include egg-free strozzapreti with duck confit; own-made penne with hazelnut cream and pecorino cheese shavings; and linguine with lobster. The latter was excellent – the crustacea very fresh-tasting – though we had to ask for both a finger bowl and a dish for the empty shells. There are also hearty, meaty mains (pan-fried duck breast with white truffle honey) and seafood options such as chargrilled tuna steak. For a sweet finish, try raspberry and rum panna cotta or coconut sorbet with bitter chocolate sauce.
Babies and children welcome: high chairs. Booking advisable. Disabled: toilet. Restaurant available for hire. Takeaway service. **Map 17 B4.**

West

Maida Vale

★ ★ Red Pepper

8 Formosa Street, W9 1EE (7266 2708). Warwick Avenue tube. **Dinner served** 6.30-11pm Mon-Fri. **Meals served** noon-11pm Sat; noon-10.30pm Sun. **Main courses** £7.50-£10.50. **Credit** MC, V.
Packed more or less every night since it opened in 1994, this smartish Little Venice fixture could now coast along on reputation alone. Happily, though, it retains a palpable enthusiasm for its own cooking, and still ranks among the city's best pizzerias. Spirited if slightly scatty waiters serve dishes from an all-Italian menu and wine list, with pizzas supplemented by an appetising array of pastas (fettuccine with wild rabbit and olives was tasty, if slightly watery) and a list of daily specials. The pick of the starters is probably the flavourful crab salad with cucumber; the various components of the mixed antipasti were all very nice, but we'd have preferred more variety than just a few olives and a cluster of meats. But you're really here for the pizzas: our crisp primavera came drenched with san daniele ham and carefully dotted with black olive paste, while the spinaci was topped with an impeccable egg. The tight space and deafening acoustics mean it's not a place for a romantic dinner *per due*. But if you're in the mood, you'll leave smiling.
Babies and children admitted. Booking advisable. Separate room for parties, seats 25. Tables outdoors (5, pavement). Takeaway service. **Map 1 C4.**

Westbourne Grove

★ Mulberry Street NEW

84 Westbourne Grove , W2 5RT (7313 6789/www.mulberrystreet.co.uk). Bayswater or Queensway tube. **Breakfast served** 8am-noon Fri, Sat. **Meals served** noon-midnight daily. **Main courses** £7.50-£10. **Credit** AmEx, MC, V.
New York took the Neapolitan pizza and reinvented it as something slightly different. It's the same with much Italian-American food: it's not what you find in Italy, but it's great when done well. Unashamedly Italian-American, Mulberry Street gets most things right. The 20in pizzas (big enough for two) can have their toppings split 'half-and-half', just as they often are in New York. Our base was thin and elastic, though very slightly burnt. We stuck to the classic US toppings, which included good meatballs. The 'eggplant' parmesan was exactly as it's served in Italian-American homes, the moist and well-seasoned aubergine coated in breadcrumbs and fried, a flavoursome tomato sauce topping the dish and then spaghetti on the side. Perfect. Puddings include tempting fairy cakes and an unapologetically calorific hot-fudge sundae. What was least pleasing about Mulberry Street is that the New York theme extends to American pop culture. Three big TV screens dominate one end of the narrow dining area, so time your visit carefully.
Babies and children welcome: high chairs. Booking advisable. Separate room for parties, seats 30. Takeaway service; delivery service (within 5-mile radius). **Map 7 B6.**

South West

Fulham

Napulé

585 Fulham Road, SW6 5UA (7381 1122/www.madeinitalygroup.co.uk). Fulham Broadway tube. **Lunch served** noon-3.30pm Sat, Sun. **Dinner served** 6-11.30pm Mon-Sat; 6-10.30pm Sun. **Main courses** £6.95-£14.50. **Credit** MC, V.
Displays of tempting antipasti and own-made breads, welcoming staff, a long dining area leading to a lovely airy conservatory (partly open-air in summer) and lively guests create a fantastic first impression at Napulé. Neither does the menu

disappoint, with an interesting selection of starters and wood-fired pizzas served by the metre (whose toppings diners are strongly advised not to alter), plus a lengthy selection of specials and many seafood dishes. Unfortunately, the positive vibe isn't quite matched by the cooking. An underwhelming plate of antipasti to share consisted of an ordinary selection of hams, olives and mozzarella garnished with raw carrot and sprigs of rocket. Mains were better, though: pizza regina vittoria (like a posh margherita with balls of buffalo mozzarella, basil leaves and cherry tomatoes) was tasty enough, and the steak special came rare as ordered, though it was served with an overpowering red wine and onion sauce. There's no doubt that Napulé has a great atmosphere and lovely setting; if only it could raise the standard of its food a notch to match.
Babies and children welcome: high chairs. Booking advisable. Separate room for parties, seats 20. Takeaway service. **Map 13 A13.**
For branches (Luna Rossa, Made in Italy, Santa Lucia) see index.

Rossopomodoro

214 Fulham Road, SW10 9NB (7352 7677). South Kensington tube then 14 bus. **Meals served** noon-midnight daily. **Main courses** £5-£16. **Set lunch** £10 2 courses. **Credit** AmEx, MC, V.
A bland exterior on the Fulham Road hides a riotous gastronomic experience within the walls of Rossopomodoro, the London outpost of a thriving Italian chain. The decor is trendy and modern, brightened by bold paintings and red tiles. The open kitchen is staffed by theatrical Italian chefs, preparing dishes from a menu that is so long it unfolds off the table and into your lap. A meat-based antipasti was served, as were most starters, with a huge ball of juicy mozzarella in the centre of the plate. Pizzas are inventive (try the vesuvius, a spicy pizza folded up in twee but endearing fashion to resemble a volcano), as are mains such as a luxurious dish of beef strips scattered with truffle flakes. Fried pizza, a speciality, looked heart attack-inducing but enticing nonetheless. Clientele varied from families to dates to groups, and all seemed to be enjoying the ride. Service was a mite slow, but otherwise Rossopomodoro provided a most satisfactory experience. This is the sort of chain we'd like to see expand.
Babies and children welcome: high chairs. Booking advisable. Separate room for parties, seats 50. Takeaway service. **Map 13 C12.**

South

Balham

Ciullo's

31 Balham High Road, SW12 9AL (8675 3072). Clapham South tube/Balham tube/rail. **Dinner served** 6-11pm Mon-Thur; 6-11.30pm **Fri, Sat;** 5-10.30pm Sun. **Main courses** £5.50-£12.50. **Credit** MC, V.
Every night of the week, this family-run trat is packed with Balham folk who know just what to expect: welcoming, cheerful service and generous portions of cheap, no-nonsense Italian food. The pizzas are one of the main attractions. There are few trendy ingredients here; instead, just reliable toppings and combos we've all heard of, such as napoletana, margherita and fiorentina – all on thin, crisp bases. We've always found the pasta properly al dente too, and sauces such as the penne al'arrabiatta have just the right amount of kick, flavour and texture. The wine list is modestly priced, but this is one area in which Ciullo's needs to improve: with lots of exciting new Italian producers making great affordable wines, Ciullo's has a lot of plonk concealing the odd decent bottle. It isn't exactly Milanese in its approach to design and fashion either: although established in 2004, it's straight out of the 1980s. Newcomers such as nearby Raviolo (*see p322*) are now making Ciullo's look like a much loved but rusty old Fiat in comparison to a polished Alfa Romeo.
Babies and children welcome: high chairs. Booking advisable. Tables outdoors (3, terrace).

★ ★ Raviolo NEW

2007 RUNNER-UP BEST FAMILY RESTAURANT
1 Balham Station Road, SW12 9SG (8772 0433/ www.raviolo.co.uk). Balham tube/rail. **Meals served** 11am-11pm daily. **Main courses** £6.50-£9.50. **Credit** AmEx, MC, V.
Keeping up chic appearances from its handy position opposite Balham station, Raviolo is not just a lovely local; the quality of the food and service make it worth a train ride. The menu is a paean to quintessentially Italian ingredients and flavours, with cured meats, carefully concocted sauces, and olive-oil roasted vegetables, served in various bruschetta, panini and pasta variations. A starter of rocket-filled pasta bathed in pesto, with tiny new potatoes and french beans, was a jolly green delight. Also a hit was the sampling plate: a line-up of diminutive dishes featuring an excellent wild mushroom risotto, delicious meatballs and a pile of creamy mozzarella with sage, all served with grilled bread chips. Despite its rather sophisticated looks, Raviolo is a fine spot for families. Children have boxes of toys and high chairs at their disposal, and a menu that contains comfort dishes (spag bol, penne with tomato sauce, meat lasagne) as well as more adventurous suggestions, such as a sampling plate like the adult one, or baked mushroom crêpes. It's good food, served small – which is what every kids' menu should be.
Babies and children welcome: children's menu; high chairs; nappy-changing facilities; toys. Booking advisable Fri, Sat. Disabled: toilet. Separate room for parties, seats 40. Tables outdoors (4, terrace; 3 pavement). Takeaway service.

Battersea

★ Donna Margherita

183 Lavender Hill, SW11 5TE (7228 2660/ www.donna-margherita.com). Clapham Junction rail. **Lunch served** noon-3pm Fri, Sat. **Dinner served** 6-10.30pm Mon-Thur; 6-11pm Fri, Sat. **Meals served** 12.30-10.30pm Sun. **Main courses** £6.90-£17. **Credit** AmEx, DC, JCB, MC, V.
Budget airline companies beware: as far as many south Londoners are concerned, trips to Naples became less desirable when this slice of the Italian heartland opened on their doorsteps. A gleeful tweeness abounds: prints of provincial harbour life adorn the walls, while the miniature mezzanine has been converted into a Disneyesque Neapolitan balcony complete with cloves of garlic. The same cannot be said of the food, which is as studiously Italian as you'll find anywhere. Antipasti comes from both a hot and cold buffet (three dishes for £6.50) or an à la carte menu offering baked calamari and beef carpaccio. The wood-fired pizzas are heavenly, the bases soft and sublimely flavoured with virgin olive oil, the topping combinations subtle. Ingredients are regularly flown in from Naples. Pasta is perfectly al dente; penne al siciliana, with aubergine, basil and mozzarella, made for hearty eating. There's also a range of grilled fish and meat mains for those thinking outside the P&P box. Desserts include panna cotta; a selection of proseccos tops an expansive wine list.
Babies and children welcome: high chairs. Booking advisable. Separate room for parties, seats 18. Tables outdoors (18, terrace). Takeaway service; delivery service (over £10 within 1-mile radius). **Map 21 C3.**

Pizza Metro

64 Battersea Rise, SW11 1EQ (7228 3812). Clapham Junction rail. **Dinner served** 6-11pm Tue-Thur. **Meals served** noon-11pm Fri-Sun. **Main courses** £7-£15. **Set meal** £14 2 courses. **Credit** MC, V.
Neapolitan gusto is so prevalent at Pizza Metro that it can feel more like a holiday destination than a dining hotspot. Waiters seem constantly on the verge of bursting into song, the walls feature murals of provincial life in the shadow of Vesuvius, and there's even a gleaming Vespa parked between the tables. Food is similarly boisterous: regional starters such as calamari con fagioli (squid and cannelloni bean salad) are offered before fish and meat mains and a range of own-made pasta (including a mighty scialatielli pesciosa packed with pretty much every edible underwater creature). But it's the pizzas that have hungry punters hovering outside on busy weekend evenings. The olive oil-infused bases are as sublime as the combinations of fresh toppings, from baked aubergine and ricotta (somehow the consistency of melted marshmallow) to the patented Pizza Metro meatball pizza. All come in rectangular shapes and are served on towering metal trays that rise to eye level. This might intrude on conversation, if most customers weren't too busy stuffing their faces to talk.
Babies and children welcome: high chairs. Booking advisable. Tables outdoors (10, pavement). Takeaway service, delivery service (over £15 within 1-mile radius). **Map 21 C4.**

Clapham

Eco

162 Clapham High Street, SW4 7UG (7978 1108/ www.ecorestaurants.com). Clapham Common tube. **Lunch served** noon-4pm, **dinner served** 6.30-11pm Mon-Fri. **Meals served** noon-11.30pm Sat; noon-11pm Sun. **Main courses** £5.90-£13.50. **Credit** AmEx, MC, V.
Eco has seen little reason to change the decor or dishes on its menu for the last decade or more. But the mid 1990s trend for hard surfaces (in this case created from wavy plywood, solid-looking walls and wooden flooring) still creates terrible acoustics, not helped by the choice of music barely having changed in that time either (slightly too much 1980s R&B on our 2007 visit). The pizzas are still fine, though, with a 12-incher costing between £5.90 and £9.90. Eco's real problem is that since it opened in 1993, standards have soared elsewhere; its pizzas now seem little better than a supermarket's 'classy' range. Calzone tradizionale was a whopper, but the ingredients in both this and a napoletana were just so-so. Other dishes cover the expected bases: antipasti, bread, pasta, folded pizza-bread sandwiches, oven-baked or grilled dishes, side salads and some desserts including tiramisu, which seemed so cutting edge when we reviewed Eco in 1993. It's still on the menu (£4.75 instead of £2.10), and we still think it's a bit too light.
Babies and children welcome: high chairs. Booking advisable; essential weekends. Tables outdoors (3, pavement). Takeaway service.
Map 22 B2.
For branch (Eco Brixton) see index.

Verso

84 Clapham Park Road, SW4 7BX (7720 1515). Clapham Common tube. **Dinner served** 6-11pm Mon-Thur; 6-11.30pm Fri. **Meals served** 12.30-11.30pm Sat, Sun. **Main courses** £7.50-£15.90. **Set meal** (Mon-Thur; 12.30-7pm Sat, Sun) £10 2 courses. **Credit** AmEx, DC, MC, V.
Situated five minutes' walk from Clapham's main drag, Verso appears to play second fiddle to the busier, better-located and better-known Eco (*see above*). But pizza-lovers take note: we think both the ingredients and cooking at Verso are palpably better. It's true that this shop unit of a room lacks atmosphere (other than that generated by annoying radio muzak), but staff are cheerful and food arrives quickly. Pizza bases are foot-wide discs of thin and crisp dough, baked at searing temperatures and topped with either classic or more unusual topping combos. We savoured the speck (smoked 'prosciutto') with artichoke hearts, mozzarella and gorgonzola cheese. There are plenty more interesting dishes to choose from too: big bicycle inner-tubes of pasta served with a robustly textured ragu of duck, for example. The standard size of wine glass is a mighty 250ml (that's a third of a bottle), but they're not just serving plonk; an appealing nero d'avola from Sicily costs a very reasonable £4.90.
Babies and children welcome: high chairs. Booking advisable Fri, Sat. Disabled: toilet. Restaurant available for hire. Tables outdoors (8, pavement). Takeaway service; delivery service (within 2-mile radius). **Map 22 B2.**

South East

Peckham

★ The Gowlett

62 Gowlett Road, SE15 4HY (7635 7048/ www.thegowlett.com). East Dulwich or Peckham Rye rail/12, 37, 40, 63, 176, 185, 484 bus. **Open** noon-midnight Mon-Thur; noon-1am Fri, Sat; noon-11.30pm Sun. **Lunch served** 12.30-2.30pm Tue-Fri. **Dinner served** 6.30-10.30pm Mon-Fri. **Meals served** 12.30-10.30pm Sat; 12.30-9pm Sun. **Main courses** £7-£8. **Credit** AmEx, DC, MC, V.

Truth be told, people don't go to the Gowlett for pizza alone. Though the kitchen's stone-baked, crisp-based, densely topped pizzas are mouth-watering, the Gowlett is first and foremost a pub – a CAMRA award winner at that. Locals love it, helping pizzas down with pints of Adnams, guest ales such as Summer Lightning and Gale's HSB, or one of the well-priced organic wines. Best-selling pizzas are the Gowlettini (goat's cheese, pine nuts, prosciutto and rocket) and the american hot (pepperoni, pickled green chillies and lots of spicy chilli oil); there's also a roaring trade in the enormous discs of garlic bread or tuscan anchovy bread (there's a special reduction if you order both). The no-frills interior features battered leather sofas and expansive tables; a soul and funk soundtrack sets the mood, and a decked patio allows for alfresco dining in warm weather. It's easy to eat and drink too much here – leaving no room for puds like chocolate brownie with ice-cream – but a good time is always had in the process.

Babies and children admitted (until 9pm). Disabled: toilet. Entertainment: DJs 6.30pm Sun; jazz band first Wed of mth 8.30pm; quiz 8.30pm Mon. Tables outdoors (3, heated terrace; 4, pavement).

Camberwell

Mozzarella e Pomodoro

21-22 Camberwell Green, SE5 7AA (7277 2020). Elephant & Castle tube/rail then 12, 35, 45, 68, 176, 185 bus. **Lunch served** noon-3pm Mon-Fri. **Dinner served** 6-11.30pm Mon-Sat; 5-11pm Sun. **Main courses** £5.95-£28. **Set lunch** (Mon-Fri) £7.50 2 courses incl coffee. **Credit** AmEx, JCB, MC, V.

Those willing to look beyond the rather uninviting windows of Mozzarella e Pomodoro will find one of the most unexpectedly excellent Italian eateries south of the river. Aesthetically, it's unlikely to inspire: the framed prints are faded and the collection of plastic sea creatures more suited to a downmarket chippie. Nor has the piped samba music done anything particularly Italian to the atmosphere on previous visits. But such concerns pale into unimportance when it comes to the food – which is authentic, simple and good. A wide-ranging antipasti starter included caprini fritti, a fist-sized chunk of tender goat's cheese fried in breadcrumbs and artfully served on a bed of poached pears and cranberry sauce. Pizzas and pastas seldom break the £7 barrier, despite an abundance of fresh ingredients and formidable flavours. Fish dishes are well worth a look too – try the tonno al ferri, a sizeable tuna steak cooked as requested and served alongside a mountain of creamy caesar salad. Proof, were it needed, that restaurants shouldn't be judged by their covers.

Babies and children welcome: high chairs. Booking advisable Fri, Sat. Separate room for parties, seats 120. Takeaway service. **Map 23 A2.**

East

Shoreditch

Furnace

1 Rufus Street, N1 6PE (7613 0598/www.shoreditchlife.com). Old Street tube/rail. **Lunch served** noon-3pm Mon-Fri. **Dinner served** 6-11pm Mon-Sat. **Main courses** £6.75-£13. **Credit** MC, JCB, V.

Unenthusiastic service and tinny background music on our most recent visit did little to detract from our enjoyment of Furnace's main USP – good-quality, thin-crusted and generously sized pizzas. The 16-strong list (most priced well under a tenner) offers classics alongside more creative combos such as wild mushroom with truffle paste or sausage with spinach and salsa verde. We found gorgonzola and pear a delicious and well-balanced partnership; a classic fiorentina proved even better, with its perfectly runny egg yolk and mounds of fresh spinach. Daily pasta, meat and fish specials (king prawn tagliatelle or sea bass with prawn and dill pancakes) sounded enticing, but were largely ignored in favour of pizza by an artily scruffy clientele. While we wouldn't book a table here for the last party on earth, Furnace's exposed brickwork, blond wood and huge windows make it a stylish venue for a low-key date, birthday dinner or a swift mid-bar-crawl refuel.

Babies and children admitted. Takeaway service. Separate room for parties, seats 40. **Map 6 R4.**

★ StringRay Globe Café Bar & Pizzeria

109 Columbia Road, E2 7RL (7613 1141/ www.stringraycafe.co.uk). Bus 26, 48, 55. **Meals served** 11am-11pm daily. **Main courses** £5-£11. **Credit** MC, V.

A local favourite, StringRay Globe Café strives to convey a multitude of influences simultaneously: colourful orange, blue and yellow walls suggest Latin American leanings (heightened on our visit by background music from Gotan Project); a bar serving draught beer and wooden pub tables outside nod to its former incarnation as a pub; and the menu, despite dishes from an english breakfast to a lentil moussaka, is Italian in origin. Pizza is the speciality: there are 19 varieties available. Deliciously thin-crusted, these include classics (margherita, fiorentina, calzone), as well as more unusual varieties (a mexicana comes with jalapeño chillies, minced beef and sweetcorn). All are excellent value, especially when you consider that a single pizza is likely to be enough for two people. Classic pasta dishes (nine in total) are also served, though the desserts seem something of an afterthought. Service can be rather erratic, but nobody seems to mind too much.

Babies and children welcome: children's menu; high chairs. Booking essential. Tables outdoors (7, pavement). Takeaway service. **Map 6 S3.**
For branches see index.

Wapping

Il Bordello

81 Wapping High Street, E1W 2YN (7481 9950). Wapping tube/100 bus. **Lunch served** noon-3pm Mon-Fri. **Dinner served** 6-11pm Mon-Sat. **Meals served** 1-10.30pm Sun. **Main courses** £7.75-£22.95. **Credit** AmEx, DC, MC, V.

A neighbourhood Italian that's a cut above the average – mercifully free of phoney accents, greasy pizzas or pictures of the leaning tower of Pisa. Instead, there's a central brushed-copper bar, exposed brickwork and bustling, knowledgeable staff serving plates of chic and tasty food. Il Bordello does all the classics well, its simple bruschetta starter with rocket and fresh tomatoes a particular star. More adventurous options, such as monkfish in a spiced sauce, also tend to be successful, though portion sizes can be too large for such rich fare. A good wine list and a selection of fresh desserts, which are displayed in a glass cabinet, round off a perfectly pleasant restaurant experience. Unfortunately, prices are a cut above the average too: mains can pass the £20 mark and pizzas hover around a tenner. But this doesn't seem to put off the good people of Wapping, who regularly pack the place out.

Babies and children welcome: high chairs. Booking advisable. Disabled: toilet. Takeaway service.
For branch (La Figa) see index.

North East

Dalston

★ Il Bacio

Vortex Jazz Club, 11 Gillett Street, N16 8JH (7923 9532/www.vortexjazz.co.uk). Dalston Kingsland rail/38, 149, 242 bus. **Dinner served** 5-11pm daily. **Main courses** £5-£8.50. **No credit cards.**

Roughly 18 months after the Vortex Jazz Club relocated to Dalston having been forced from its N16 premises, Il Bacio followed it down the road. The family-run operation now supplements its two Stoke Newington and one Highbury eateries with a plainer café-restaurant directly under the Vortex, in the renovated but not quite regenerated Gillett Street. The newcomer has yet to engender the sort of raucous bonhomie that characterises its siblings. The food, however, is every bit as likeable and straightforward, served in portions that range from generous to gigantic. We were almost full after a starter of caprino alle perre: a sizeable poached pear (drizzled with honey) and a hunk of baked goat's cheese as big as a fist. Above-par pizzas are similarly large; 15 on the main menu are joined by three or four specials. We also enjoyed culurgiones al pomodoro, a main of own-made, potato-packed ravioli. A nice addition to the area, all told, although we hope the soundtrack of melodramatic 1980s Italia-pop isn't beamed upstairs between sets.

Babies and children welcome: high chairs. Booking advisable. Tables outdoors (8, pavement). Takeaway service; delivery (over £10 within 2-mile radius). **Map 25 B4.**
For branches see index.

Mozzarella e Pomodoro

Chain gang

Think that one pizza chain is much like any other? Think again. Here's the lowdown on the strengths and weaknesses of the main London chains.

★ ASK

160-162 Victoria Street, SW1E 5LB (7630 8228/www.askcentral.co.uk). Victoria tube/rail. **Meals served** noon-11pm Mon-Sat; noon-10.30pm Sun. **Main courses** £5.60-£8.45. **Credit** AmEx, DC, JCB, MC, V.

This branch is a big ASK (the name comes from the combined initials of founders Adam and Samuel Kaye), a 14-year-old pizza dynasty, which also has the more upmarket Zizzi (*see p327*) under its aegis. Once hailed as a serious rival to the mighty Pizza Express, it doesn't come close enough in our book. This branch – ideally placed opposite Victoria station, so not short of a punter or two – impresses initially with its reproduction Renaissance artwork, elaborate cornicing and spiral staircase leading to a prodigiously windowed first-floor space. On our visit, however, it was chilly and the staff displayed a general lassitude. This, combined with smudgy glassware and a tepid pizza, curbed our enthusiasm for the ASK experience. The salad, though, was good and fresh, and the ice-cream delicious.

What's available? 19 pizzas, 18 pastas, 8 salads.

How does the pizza rate? Ours was cold and the dough had a yeasty aftertaste.

Total number of branches 25.

Best for Boozy works lunches.

What's in it for the kids? The £4.95 children's menu (with colouring-in and wax crayons) is good value, giving sprogs a choice of six pastas and pizzas (ham and pineapple is in there), a soft drink and a scoop of top-quality ice-cream.

Babies and children welcome: high chairs. Booking advisable. **Map 15 H10.**

For branches see index.

★ Pizza Express

Benbow House, 24 New Globe Walk, SE1 9DS (7401 3977/www.pizzaexpress.com). London Bridge tube/rail. **Meals served** noon-11pm Mon-Sat; noon-10.30pm Sun. **Main courses** £5.45-£8.95. **Credit** AmEx, DC, MC, V.

They're both household names, but Pizza Express has always been the extra-virgin olive oil to the more lardy Pizza Hut. Its habitat is gentrified London: if a high street has a Pret and a Costa, it will have a Pizza Express. The chain also colonises heavily touristed environs, such as the new and improved South Bank. This branch, a symphony in glass and chrome, gives you Thameside seating and views. The menu currently vaunts a Rome theme, so two thinner-crusted Romana pizzas join the uniformly good regular pizzas. Children and youths go bonkers for the comforting dough balls and their accompanying excessive butter pot, but some starters, such as marinated olives and rustica tomatoes lack flavour. Branches are often absurdly busy.

What's available 21 pizzas, 5 pastas, 6 salads.

How does the pizza rate? Perfectly reliable, with pleasant-tasting crusts and an especially good line in vegetable-heavy toppings. The new-recipe giardiniera is splendid.

Total number of branches 98.

Best for Pleasing all of the family, all of the time – assuming they like pizza.

What's in it for the kids? The new Piccolo menu is a triumph, and must be responsible for the huge numbers of extended family groups we always find in this branch. For £5.25, the children can have their favourite – dough balls – followed by a choice of meaty or vegetarian pizza or pasta, with a mini side salad if they want it. Then comes toffee fudge sundae, chocolate sundae or chocolate fudge cake, rounded off with a bambinoccino (that's foamed milk and chocolate powder – no coffee). Terrific.

Babies and children welcome: high chairs; nappy-changing facilities. Disabled: toilet. Tables outdoors (10, pavement). Takeaway service. **Map 11 P7.**

For branches see index.

Pizza Paradiso

61 The Cut, SE1 8LL (7261 1221/ www.pizzaparadiso.co.uk). Southwark tube/Waterloo tube/rail. **Meals served** noon-midnight Mon-Sat; noon-11pm Sun. **Main courses** £6.10-£16.45. **Credit** AmEx, DC, MC, V.

A 1934-established, determinedly Sicilian and very mini chain, Paradiso started life as the Ristorante Olivelli and still keeps this alternate name in its official title. It isn't anything like its bigger chain rivals, though, and feels more like a neighbourhood trattoria. This branch is plainly decorated, with a few strategically placed signed photos of satisfied celebrity diners. The food is consistently well presented, with the taste of quality Italian produce very evident. Dough balls (nine to a portion) are fantastic, pasta is as good as the pizza, and salads are perky, with good use of dark, peppery rocket. The Sicilian profiterole dessert merits special mention.

What's available 13 pizzas, 13 pastas, 7 salads.

How does the pizza rate? Generously topped, with an excellent, fresh dough base and a straight-from-the-oven bite.

Total number of branches 5.

Best for A small party, or a couple who fancy lingering over a simple Italian meal.

What's in it for the kids? A weekend promotion gives children in a family group a free pizza margherita or spaghetti pomodoro; staff will knock a quid or two off some pasta dishes sold in child sizes.

Babies and children welcome: high chairs. Booking advisable Wed-Fri. Tables outdoors (4, pavement). Takeaway service.

Map 11 N8.

For branches (Pizza Paradiso, Ristorante Olivelli Paradiso) see index.

★ La Porchetta

33 Boswell Street, WC1N 3BP (7242 2434). Holborn or Russell Square tube. **Lunch served** 10am-3pm Mon-Fri. **Dinner served** 5-11pm Mon-Fri; 6-11pm Sat. **Main courses** £5.20-£10.70. **Credit** MC, V.

The pigs are everywhere, which is fitting, as this is undoubtedly the best pizza place for a big blowout. Pizzas are extremely large and the choice wide, including both porky and vegetarian options. We made the mistake of ordering two salads, not realising that these would also be gargantuan (if pedestrian). Tables are small and tightly packed together – we had to commandeer a neighbouring table to find space for all our meal for two – so don't come for an intimate evening. Harsh lighting, brash music and hurried

CHEAP EATS

North West

Hampstead

Fratelli la Bufala

45A South End Road, NW3 2QB (7435 7814/ www.fratellilabufala.com). Belsize Park tube/ Hampstead Heath rail. **Lunch served** noon-3pm Tue-Fri. **Dinner served** 6-11pm Mon-Fri. **Meals served** noon-11pm Sat, Sun. **Main courses** £7.90-£16. **Set lunch** (Mon-Fri) £10 2 courses. **Credit** MC, V.

Nestling on the edge of Hampstead Heath, this inviting pizzeria makes an attractive option for locals on a night out. All dishes incorporate buffalo products: the restaurant's celebration of the beast extends far beyond mozzarella. There are buffalo burgers, steaks and spicy sausages. A simple caprese salad showed off the quality of buffalo mozzarella: mouthwateringly creamy, its richness complemented perfectly by a dash of basil oil. Buffalo meatballs were light and interestingly textured. For mains, we found buffalo steak pretty ordinary for its price (£16.90); perhaps the gimmick was wearing thin. Pizza and pasta – all the classics – would have made a better bet: the couple next to us seemed to enjoy sharing a big, tasty-looking vegetarian pizza. Even the dessert menu doesn't escape the charge of the buffalo: there's a selection of buffalo ricotta cheesecakes, although we opted for a hefty and satisfying chocolate and ricotta fondue. Though surprisingly quiet on a Saturday night visit, Fratelli la Buffala's vibe remained jolly thanks to the chirpy staff; large, bright paintings on the walls helped too. A good casual-supper choice – especially for those with a liking for the ol' Prairie Cow.

Babies and children welcome: high chairs. Booking advisable evenings. Separate room for parties, seats 20. Tables outdoors (2, pavement). Takeaway service. **Map 28 C3.**

Kilburn

Osteria del Ponte

77 Kilburn High Road, NW6 6HY (7624 5793). Kilburn Park tube. **Open** 4-11pm Mon-Fri; noon-11pm Sat, Sun. **Lunch served** noon-3.30pm Sat, Sun. **Dinner served** 5.30-10.30pm daily. **Main courses** £5-£12. **Credit** MC, V.

Something seems awry at Osteria del Ponte. With pizzas this good (at for only a fiver a pop!), where is everyone? The restaurant was empty on a Saturday night. Perhaps passers-by mistake it for a pub; formerly the Bridge Tavern, a spacious bar area remains at the front, still enjoyed by regulars

service should in any case put off romantic couples, but party groups love it. Food is generally good, but forget about the fridge-tasting puddings – they're cheap, but not worth ordering.
What's available 26 pizzas, 35 pastas, 5 salads.
How does the pizza rate? Generously proportioned, with a fine thin crust. Toppings aren't that generous, but the flavours are well rounded – just like you would be if you ate here every night. Our spaghetti bolognese was delightfully tangy.
Total number of branches 5.
Best for A big hungry family, or a party of students on a budget.
What's in it for the kids? More adult in orientation than most chains. Kids can comfortably share one of the huge pizzas, or enjoy a half-portion of pasta at a reduced price.
Babies and children welcome: high chairs. Booking advisable (5 or more people). Takeaway service. **Map 10 L5.**
For branches see index.

★ Prezzo

17 Hertford Street, W1J 7RS (7499 4690/www.prezzoplc.co.uk). Green Park or Hyde Park Corner tube. **Meals served** noon-11.30pm Mon-Sat; noon-11pm Sun. **Main courses** £5.75-£8.95. **Credit** AmEx, DC, JCB, MC, V.
This Mayfair branch of a famously sophisticated seven-year-old chain is a treat. It's oddly reminiscent of a convent dining room, with dark oak panelling and votive candles, but that image might have been prompted by our sitting next to the massive oil painting of tonsured monks enjoying a pasta dinner. The atmosphere is classy, and the menu surprisingly good value for such a swish location. Tables are sensitively spaced, so couples trysting and business people brainstorming can relax a bit. Its location amid various top-end hotels makes it popular with wealthy American families too. Food is high quality, with some tempting flame-roasted chicken dishes for dough-avoiders, although our stale ice-cream let the side down.
What's available 15 pizzas, 19 pastas, 6 salads.
How does the pizza rate? Satisfying indeed. We plumped for one from the daily specials menu: vaguely Middle Eastern, with houmous on the crust and chillies, peppers, aubergine and courgette amid a thick coating of cheese – fantastic. All pizzas have a golden, crisp-crunchy lip, unlike the wood-fired/stone-baked standard, which makes a nice change.
Total number of branches 16.
Best for Informal meetings, or hungry folk relaxing after a day's shopping.
What's in it for the kids? They love the antique atmosphere and the young, Euro-poppy staff. Children's pasta dishes are half price: delicious spag bol rings in at £3.75.
Babies and children welcome: high chairs. Booking advisable. Takeaway service.
Map 9 H8.
For branches see index.

Strada

Riverside, Royal Festival Hall, Belvedere Road, SE1 8XX (7401 9126/www.strada.co.uk). Embankment tube/Waterloo tube/rail. **Meals served** noon-11pm Mon-Fri; 11am-11pm Sat; 11am-10.30pm Sun. **Main courses** £6.50-£16.50. **Credit** AmEx, MC, V.
Pizzaphiles continue to disagree on the subject of Strada. When the brand first came on the scene, the contemporary, hand-stretched, wood-burning schtick earned the burgeoning chain many fans. Detractors, however, see a case of the emperor's new clothes about the concept, allying it with Strada's wholehearted embracing of trendy areas such as Islington, Marylebone and Exmouth Market. We've had some disappointments in the past, but our last Strada meal was excellent: fresh and flavoursome Italian ingredients enhanced by perfectly cooked spaghetti and splendid breads and pizzas. There's a buzz in this Festival Hall branch that's missing from some of the quieter venues, but the staff were unruffled by a busy Sunday lunch influx. We continue to applaud Strada for its free chilled, bottled and filtered water on every table.
What's available 10 pizzas, 5 pastas, 4 salads.
How does the pizza rate? The caprino and piccante versions were excellent: hot, crisp and very fresh, with the flavours of goat's cheese, basil, rocket and tomato undampened.
Total number of branches 26.
Best for The health-conscious pizza lover, and family groups trying to keep the drinks bill down (that chilled free water means no second Cokes, kids).
What's in it for the kids? They can have a reduced-price pasta dish – say, a small bowl of spag bol for £4.25. Other pasta accompaniments for children include mozzarella and tomato or ham.
Babies and children welcome: high chairs. Disabled: toilet. Tables outdoors (22, terrace). Takeaway service (pizza).
Map 10 M8.
For branches see index.

★ Zizzi

73-75 Strand, WC2R 0DE (7240 1717/ www.zizzi.co.uk). Covent Garden or Embankment tube/Charing Cross tube/rail. **Meals served** noon-11.30pm Mon-Sat; noon-11pm Sun. **Main courses** £8-£10. **Credit** AmEx, DC, JCB, MC, V.
Part of the same family as ASK, but this swish basement branch of Zizzi exuded more warmth (literally) than its sister could muster, and seemed to be run on more professional lines. The warmth might have been illusory – after all, a huge wood-burning stove dominates the room and hundreds of cut logs are set into the walls, each sawn end bearing a message from jolly tourists. Our pizzas were good, a goat's cheese bruschetta yummy and the salads fresh and well presented. We were also happy to polish off a fantastic pistachio ice-cream for pudding; the chocolate version was gorgeous too. Service was patchy.
What's available 16 pizzas, 19 pastas, 7 salads.
How does the pizza rate? Thin-crusted and large, with pleasant, tasty toppings.
Total number of branches 21.
Best for Groups and families with older children. Couples can enjoy the secluded, shadowy side tables with velvety banquettes.
What's in it for the kids? Cheaper pasta portions, but no special menu. Zizzi tries to be a more sophisticated elder sister to the more workaday ASK.
Babies and children welcome: high chairs; nappy-changing facilities. Disabled: toilet. Takeaway service. **Map 15 E5.**
For branches see index.

watching the footie. Osteria's restaurant area is at the back, served by an open pizza kitchen and filled with candlelit wooden tables. Not utterly Italian, then, but you could've fooled us with the quality of the pizzas. They were excellent: perfectly crisp, near-wafer-thin bases supplied with abundant fresh toppings. A range of simple pasta dishes are also served, while a few meaty main courses command slightly higher prices, and desserts range from apple pie with custard to an own-made tiramisu. The atmosphere is admittedly a little drab, but that's nothing a few punters wouldn't fix. This is simple food, done well, at great prices. Perhaps Osteria needs to shed its pub past once and for all.
Babies and children welcome: high chairs. Booking advisable. Restaurant available for hire. Tables outdoors (5, pavement).
Map 1 B1.

West Hampstead

La Brocca

273 West End Lane, NW6 1QS (7433 1989). West Hampstead tube/rail/139, C11 bus.
Bar **Open** noon-11pm Mon-Thur; noon-1am Fri, Sat; noon-midnight Sun. **Lunch served** noon-4pm Mon-Fri; noon-4.30pm Sat, Sun. **Main courses** £5.95-£14.
Restaurant **Dinner served** 6.30-10.30pm Mon-Thur; 6.30-11pm Fri-Sun. **Main courses** £6.95-£14.50.
Both **Credit** AmEx, JCB, MC, V.
Head past noisy ground-floor Bar Brocca and downstairs to eat in the cosy dining room at this buzzy neighbourhood pizzeria. It's a dimly lit space, characterised by exposed brickwork and gingham tablecloths; if it's still light outside, try to get a table in the brighter conservatory. To start, we ignored the choice of bruschetta and opted for antipasti nostre – a tasty selection of meats served on a crisp pizza base. For mains, there are the predictable pizza and pasta choices, enlivened by more unusual variants like black crab ravioli. We've enjoyed La Brocca's pizzas in the past: crisp, huge (they spill over the edge of the plate) and with a good choice of toppings. This year we opted for pasta – served in equally generous portions, but too often unremarkable, as with our bland spaghetti carbonara. Ricotta and tomato ravioli didn't earn its £14 price tag; it was too salty. Next time we'll check out the specials – duck and mango salad, sea bream pappardelle, and artichoke ravioli all looked tempting. La Brocca is pleasant and homely, but prices are a little high for its adequate but unexceptional food.
Babies and children welcome: high chairs. Booking advisable. **Map 28 A2.**

Drinking

Bars

Here we list a few of our favourites from London's ever-growing, ever-changing bar scene, from louche cocktail lounges to swanky hotel bars, some attached to restaurants. The scene changes rapidly, as evidenced by the expensively refurbished Brazilian bar Mocotó, which opened and closed within the year. For pubs serving good food, see **Gastropubs**, starting on p115. For the best boozers, see **Pubs**, starting on p339. And for hundreds and hundreds of drinking options across the capital, consult the annual *Time Out Bars, Pubs & Clubs* guide (£9.99).

Central

Aldwych

★ Lobby Bar (100)

One Aldwych, WC2B 4RH (7300 1070/www.onealdwych.com). Covent Garden or Embankment tube/Charing Cross tube/rail. **Open** 8am-11.30pm Mon-Sat; 8am-10.30pm Sun. **Lunch served** noon-5pm daily. **Dinner served** 5.30-11.30pm Mon-Sat; 5.30-10.30pm Sun. **Main courses** £6.95-£13.75. **Credit** AmEx, DC, MC, V.

The Lobby Bar of One Aldwych innovates as much as it sparkles. It offers 30 kinds of martini (£9.40-£20), based on original mixes (Snow Cat with Snow Leopard vodka, strawberry purée and limoncello) or brand (Junipero, Ciroc, Kauffman Vintage 2003). The six-strong house selection allows the use of crushed fresh chilli (with Agavero tequila liqueur) in a Chilli del Toro, and fresh tamarillo (with Wyborowa) in a tamarillo martini. De Venoge is the base for the champagne cocktails, prosecco for the bellinis. Fresh cantaloupe melons flavour the cantaloupe daiquiri, fresh passionfruit pulp the Mexican Passion. Bar snacks (organic gravadlax, mini wagyu steak burgers) maintain quality control. The entire proceedings are overseen by impeccable staff.

Babies and children admitted. Disabled: lift; toilet. Separate rooms for parties, seating 8-50. **Map 18 F4.**

City

Hawksmoor (100)

157 Commercial Street, E1 6BJ (7247 7392/www.thehawksmoor.com). Liverpool Street tube/rail. **Lunch served** noon-2.30pm Mon-Fri. **Dinner served** 6-10.30pm Mon-Sat. **Main courses** £14.50-£25.50. **Credit** AmEx, MC, V.

Yes, there's a worthy selection of wines (six of each colour by the glass, 30 or so by the bottle) and assorted transatlantic bar snacks (macaroni cheese, grilled 'shrimp' – for which read 'prawns'), but this American-inspired venture exists primarily for its meat and its mixology. The former is taken care of by the restaurant half of the operation (*see p42*). The latter is performed with excellence. The highlights of our last visit were a Tobacco Old Fashioned (£7.50), stirred to marry its flavours of sugar, bitter orange and 'tobacco infusion' with a bourbon base; and the bar's own invention, R&R Sour (£6.50), made with Aperol, redcurrants and egg white. As a stand-alone bar, Hawksmoor is limited by space; much of the room is given over to dining tables. But there's a secluded mini-lounge at the back, and the barmen are loud and characterful enough to make plonking yourself on a stool at the counter worthwhile too.

Babies and children admitted. Disabled: toilet. **Map 6 R5.**

Fitzrovia

Crazy Bear

26-28 Whitfield Street, W1T 2RG (7631 0088/www.crazybeargroup.co.uk). Goodge Street or Tottenham Court Road tube.
Bar **Open** noon-10.45pm Mon-Fri; 6-10.45pm Sat.
Restaurant **Meals/dim sum served** noon-10.45pm Mon-Fri. **Dinner served** 6-10.45pm Sat. **Dim sum** £2.50-£3.50. **Main courses** £10-£28. **Set meal** £30-£40 tasting menu.
Both **Credit** AmEx, DC, MC, V.

Stylish, decadent yet supremely comfortable, the London outpost of the Oxfordshire-based hotel and pub group comprises a ground-floor oriental restaurant (*see p252*) and opulent bar below. You may have trouble finding it; the building is almost entirely unmarked (as are the toilets within, hidden behind a fake wall and signposted only by a spotlight). But you'll have no problem finding the swivel cowhide bar stools, red padded alcoves or low leather armchairs in the basement bar; a charming hostess will escort you down the ornate staircase. Once settled, choose from classic bellinis (£9.50) or house creations such as Thai Sunset (a twist on the tequila sunrise, £8.50) – all are mixed with high-end brands, exotic fruits and inventive purées. Fine dim sum keeps hunger pangs at bay.

Babies and children admitted. Booking advisable. Vegetarian menu. **Map 17 B1.**

★ Hakkasan (100)

8 Hanway Place, W1T 1HD (7907 1888). Tottenham Court Road tube.
Bar **Open** noon-12.30am Mon-Wed; noon-1.30am Thur-Sat; noon-midnight Sun.
Restaurant **Lunch/dim sum served** noon-3pm Mon-Fri; noon-4pm Sat, Sun. **Dinner served** 6-11pm Mon-Wed, Sun; 6pm-midnight Thur-Sat. **Dim sum** £3-£20. **Main courses** £9.50-£58.
Both **Credit** AmEx, MC, V.

Clearly aware of the importance of making an entrance, upmarket Chinese restaurant Hakkasan (*see p76*) whisks customers off a dingy alley and plunges them into a hidden Narnia of oriental other-worldliness. A cavernous descent opens into a stone-cut cloakroom peppered with purple blossoms and flickering candles, which in turn leads to the dining room: a three-dimensional Chinese woodcut of interlocking, intimate little booths. Along one side runs the bar, where aquamarine backlighting and flickering water patterns projected on to grey slate walls create a dreamy liquidity. Cocktails (£8.50-£10) are the stuff of Asian-influenced fantasy: Purple Emperor is sharp with a mix of Matusalem ten-year-old rum, saké and jasmine tea, and comes topped with a clipped purple pansy; Long Dragon is a blend of lime saké, Noilly Prat and ginger ale.

Babies and children admitted (until 7.30pm). Disabled: lift; toilet. Entertainment: DJs 9pm daily. Restaurant available for hire. Separate area for parties, seats 65. **Map 17 C2.**

Long Bar (100)

The Sanderson, 50 Berners Street, W1T 3NG (7300 1400). Oxford Circus or Tottenham Court Road tube. **Open** 11.30am-12.30am Mon; 11am-1am Tue, Wed; 11am-3am Thur-Sat; 11.30am-10.30pm Sun. **Snacks served** noon-midnight Mon-Wed; noon-2am Thur-Sat; noon-10pm Sun. **Snacks** £7-£15. **Credit** AmEx, DC, MC, V.

There's an Italian touch these days to the Long Bar at the high-design Sanderson hotel – not only in the nationality of the neat, able staff working the long bar in question (a thin onyx affair lined with eyeball-backed bar stools). Limoncello has crept in to the mix, slowly stirred with Ketel One and elderflower water in the Citroen martini (£12), one of a dozen offered. Quality spirits monopolize the menu: Wyborowa lemon and Polstar cucumber in the Sanderson martini; Kurant Absolut in the Long Bar Hi Ball (£11); Sauza Gold tequila in the Apassionata martini. Fresh fruit – grapes, Scottish raspberries, passionfruit – is used as flavouring throughout. Four pricey wines of each colour come by the bottle and glass, a Rizzardi pinot grigio weighing in at £7.50/£27.

Babies and children admitted (terrace). Disabled: toilet (in hotel). Tables outdoors (15, terrace). **Map 17 A2.**

Match Bar

37-38 Margaret Street, W1G 0JF (7499 3443/www.matchbar.com). Oxford Circus tube. **Open/meals served** 11am-midnight Mon-Fri; noon-midnight Sat; 4-10.30pm Sun. **Main courses** £5-£8.50. **Credit** AmEx, DC, MC, V.

As original as ever, even though they're now into a second decade, London's Match bars (including Match EC1 and Sosho) celebrate the craft of the bartender. Dale DeGroff oversees the annual drinks menu: a selection ranging from his authentic concoctions (£6.50-£8), such as a grapefruit julep (Wyborowa, pomegranate, lime and grapefruit, drizzled with honey), to those conceived by his counterparts here in recent years (Tom Ward's Kamomilla Fizz, perhaps, made from Wyborowa and camomile syrup with fresh lemon and cucumber). As well as a branch in Geneva, the Match group still runs three London bars, this West End outlet being a narrow but not squeezed space. Two rows of seating, one raised, connect a convivial front area to the bar, suiting the sharing of bowls of punch (£12), noodles and curries that Match encourages.

Disabled: toilet. Entertainment: DJs 7.30pm Fri, Sat. Tables outdoors (2, pavement). **Map 9 J5/6.**

Shochu Lounge

Basement, Roka, 37 Charlotte Street, W1T 1RR (7580 9666/www.shochulounge.com). Goodge Street or Tottenham Court Road tube. **Open/meals served** noon-midnight Mon-Fri; 5pm-midnight Sat; 6pm-midnight Sun. **Main courses** £3.60-£8.60. **Credit** AmEx, DC, MC, V.

The wooden vats and rustic bar counter, low tables and plush, boxy red seats in enclaves produce a setting that's half 21st-century style bar, half feudal Japan. Dim lighting and a low ceiling confer a louche yet sociable mood. And as befits a bar in the basement of trendsetting Japanese restaurant Roka (*see p197*), there's a pioneering focus on shochu. Here, this vodka-like spirit is tinctured with the likes of cinnamon (for joy of life) or lemon (for virility) and served neat or in cocktails by Tony Conigliaro. Try a Hello Kitty (shochu, rose, raspberries, lemon and sparkling water, £8.60) or a Plum Plum (shochu and plum vodka, £8.30). And to push the boat out, note that anything on Roka's tempting food menu can be ordered in the bar.

Entertainment: DJs 8.30pm Thur-Sat. **Map 17 B1.**

Social

5 Little Portland Street, W1W 7JD (7636 4992/www.thesocial.com). Oxford Circus tube. **Open/meals served** noon-midnight Mon-Wed; noon-1am Thur, Fri; 1pm-1am Sat; 7pm-midnight Sun. **Main courses** £3.50-£7. **Credit** AmEx, MC, V.

Fine beers, wines and cocktails; Dad food (even Twiglets!); great music, including quality weekend DJs in an evening-only basement bar; intimate ambience, sparky bar staff and just the right crowd – it's business as usual at Social. Daytime unfolds in the street-level diner, whose walls are decked out in rotating exhibitions of black and white photography with punky themes. Five tables bearing ketchup and HP sauce await a fish-finger sarnie or Square Pie. A long bar bookended by a Heavenly Jukebox begs your backside for company. Beers include San Miguel and Beck's on tap, plus bottled Tsingtao from China, Red Stripe and Pilsner Urquell. The eponymous house cocktail features Teichenné, a butterscotch schnapps mixed with Frangelico hazelnut liqueur.
Babies and children admitted (until 5pm). Entertainment: bands/DJs 7pm daily. **Map 9 J5**.

Holborn

Pearl Bar & Restaurant

Chancery Court Hotel, 252 High Holborn, WC1V 7EN (7829 7000/www.pearl-restaurant.com). Holborn tube.
Bar **Open** 11am-11pm Mon-Fri; 6-11pm Sat. *Restaurant* **Lunch served** noon-2.30pm Mon-Fri. **Dinner served** 6-10pm Mon-Sat. **Set lunch** £25.50 2 courses, £28.50 3 courses. **Set dinner** £49 3 courses, £55 tasting menu (£100 incl wine). *Both* **Credit** AmEx, DC, MC, V.
Like the accompanying haute-cuisine restaurant (*see p140*), Pearl is an expansively glamorous place. Tiled floors, walnut wood alcoves and leather banquette seating all contribute to a tonal neutrality that accentuates the little touches (strings of real pearls hanging from the ornamental light fixtures, for example). Much thought has gone into the drinks menu, which offers almost 500 wines by the bottle, glass, or as part of a £25 'wine flight' tasting tour. Premium spirit cocktails (including a tobacco-infused, seven-year-old rum Nicotini) are similarly intriguing. A shame, then, that public attendance remains so erratic. When the Pearl Bar is almost empty – as often seems to be the case – its sheer size is its atmospheric undoing.
Babies and children welcome (if dining): high chairs. Disabled: toilet. Entertainment: pianist 7.30pm Wed-Sat. **Map 10 M5**.

King's Cross

Big Chill House NEW

2007 RUNNER-UP BEST BAR

257-259 Pentonville Road, N1 9NL (7427 2540/ www.bigchill.net/house.html). King's Cross tube.
Open noon-midnight Mon-Wed, Sun; noon-1am Thur; noon-4am Fri, Sat. **Lunch served** noon-4pm, **dinner served** 5-11pm Mon-Sat. **Meals served** 1-11pm Sun. **Main courses** £7.95-£18.50. **Admission** £5-£10 after 9pm Fri, Sat. **Credit** MC, V.
On our visit to this branch of Brick Lane's Big Chill bar, all the action was taking place on the lively roof terrace. When the sun's out, this kooky and somewhat knocked-together eyrie is the perfect retreat from the smoky chaos of Pentonville Road. The pervading atmosphere inside is of a club, this 'House' being just that – a multi-levelled place with plenty of character within its nooks and crannies. The ground-floor bar is a simple open space with tables and chairs and appealing dark corners. Draught offerings aren't special – run-of-the-mill lager and cider prevails – though the spirits selection is rather more innovative. Often noisy and busy (it's a DJ bar, after all), waiting times at the bar can be long, but the Big Chill House has undeniable appeal. Food (hamburgers, fried snacks) is also served.
Babies and children admitted (until 6pm). Disabled: ramp; toilet. Entertainment: DJs/bands 8pm Wed-Sat. Tables outdoors (50, terrace). Venue available for hire. **Map 4 L3**.

Knightsbridge

Blue Bar (100)

The Berkeley, Wilton Place, SW1X 7RL (7235 6000/www.the-berkeley.co.uk). Hyde Park Corner tube. **Open/snacks served** 4pm-1am Mon-Fri; 3pm-1am Sat; 4-11pm Sun. **Snacks** £7-£11. **Credit** AmEx, DC, MC, V.
Walking into the David Collins-designed Blue Bar, with its glass walls and watery blue interior, feels akin to being immersed in an aquarium teeming with some of the most exotic and expensive fish on earth. Seating is limited to just 50, so each new entry halts conversation as heads crane to rate celebrity status on a sliding scale. Displays of wealth can border on the vulgar (rappers with supermodels draped over their arms like size-zero fur pieces), but the glamour tones are pitched to such a surreal sheen that it all feels strangely normal. Cocktails are seriously well crafted – the Spicy Queen blends 12-year-old Chivas whisky, fresh figs and lime juice with own-made caramel and chilli – but there's only one reason people come here, and it ain't the drinks. In terms of social statements, the Blue Bar is a great, glittering exclamation mark.
Disabled: toilet (in hotel). Dress: no shorts or caps. **Map 9 G9**.

Mandarin Bar

Mandarin Oriental Hyde Park, 66 Knightsbridge, SW1X 7LA (7235 2000/www.mandarinoriental.com). Knightsbridge tube. **Open/meals served** 10.30am-1.30am Mon-Sat; 10.30am-11.30pm Sun. **Main courses** £10-£15. **Admission** £5 after 11pm Mon-Sat. **Credit** AmEx, DC, MC, V.
Even if you can't quite stretch to the cost of a suite upstairs, it's worth popping into the bar at the Mandarin Oriental hotel in Knightsbridge for an evening of decadent escapism. Stroll past the immaculately attired doormen and through the glossy marble lobby to find the softly lit bar – luxuriously kitted out in teak and marble – with leather sofas to lounge on (with due elegance and decorum, of course). As well as catering for whisky aficionados (the 16-year-old Lagavulin is a choice option), the drinks menu offers a fine selection of well-prepared cocktails; our frothy french martini (£12.50) was vast and delicious. Attentive table service and nightly jazz round off a sophisticated but unstuffy experience.
Disabled: toilet (in hotel). Entertainment: jazz trio 9pm Mon-Sat, 8pm Sun. **Map 8 F9**.

Zuma

5 Raphael Street, SW7 1DL (7584 1010/ www.zumarestaurant.com). Knightsbridge tube.
Bar **Open** noon-11pm Mon-Fri; 12.30-11pm Sat; noon-10pm Sun. *Restaurant* **Lunch served** noon-2.15pm Mon-Fri; 12.30-3.15pm Sat; 12.30-2.45pm Sun. **Dinner served** 6-10.45pm Mon-Sat; 6-10.15pm Sun. **Main courses** £14.80-£70. *Both* **Credit** AmEx, DC, MC, V.

Big Chill House

DRINKING

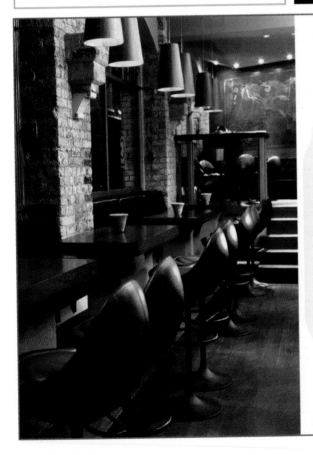

Notoriously fickle as London's A-listers may be, their affection for hip Japanese eaterie Zuma remains undiminished – which means excellent people-watching potential. Situated at the front of the restaurant (*see p198*), the sleekly minimalist bar area combines understated decor with a buzzing, vibrant atmosphere. Don't be surprised if you have to stand, as this place is invariably busy. There's an enticing array of saké, shochu and cocktails, many made from fresh fruit infusions and Japanese spirits. The sparkling Nigori saké Junmai Daiginjo (£18.75 a glass) was crisp and fresh, while a Zuma bellini (£12.50) was a fruity concoction that mixed saké, apricots, strawberry liqueur, champagne and a dash of Campari to inimitable effect.
Babies and children welcome: high chairs. Booking advisable. Disabled: toilet. Separate rooms for parties, seating 12 and 14. Tables outdoors (4, garden). **Map 8 F9.**

Marble Arch

Carbon NEW

Old Quebec Street, W1C 1LZ (7479 5050/ www.carbonbar.co.uk). Marble Arch tube. **Open** 4pm-1am Mon-Thur; 4pm-3am Fri, Sat. **Snacks served** 4pm-midnight Mon-Thur; 4pm-2am Fri, Sat. **Snacks** £6-£7. **Credit** AmEx, MC, V.
Rather than going for the contemporary clichés of chandeliers, wit and whimsy, this bar in the Cumberland Hotel is dark and high-tech industrial. Heavy iron chains form huge screens, and a mezzanine floor appears to be suspended in mid-air over the main bar. Sadly, it was roped off. 'It's only for people who buy at least one bottle of spirits,' we were told by staff (the cheapest spirit bottles cost about £100, and prices rise steeply – the mezzanine floor remained empty all evening). Still, the leather seats in cattle class are nice enough. Cocktails are well crafted; there's a good selection of premium spirit brands to mix with an equally impressive array of fresh fruits and juices. Service was attentive and friendly, despite the abundance of bouncers on our visit. Funky house from a DJ makes the room throb, but not so loud as to prevent conversation.
Disabled: toilet. Entertainment: DJ 9pm Mon-Sat. **Map 8 F6.**

Marylebone

★ Artesian NEW

2007 RUNNER-UP BEST BAR

Langham Hotel, 1C Portland Place, W1B 1JA (7636 1000/www.artesian-bar.co.uk). Oxford Circus tube. **Open/food served** 7.30am-2am Mon-Fri; 8am-2am Sat; 8am-midnight Sun. **Main courses** £8.50-£16.50. **Credit** AmEx, DC, MC, V.
Rum's the thing at the Langham Hotel's Artesian, where a 50-strong list is growing steadily as the staff are trained in each new variety (the sign of a classy bar). Prices are serious (£11-£14.50), but our classic champagne cocktail, made with rum, of course, was irresistible – fizzing with fruit flavours and boasting a lovely molasses finish. Staff are professional and forthcoming, ready with recommendations; drinks are served in remarkably beautiful glassware. A hugely elaborate (and hugely expensive) makeover, courtesy of David Collins, divides opinion. We find it sails nervously close to OTT and is somewhat schizophrenic, confused between sleek minimalism and opulent old-fashioned luxury. But for excellent cocktails with all the trappings, Artesian is hard to fault.
Babies and children admitted (until 6pm). Disabled: toilet (in hotel). **Map 9 H5.**

Mayfair

Donovan Bar

Brown's Hotel, 33-34 Albemarle Street, W1S 4BP (7493 6020/www.roccofortehotels.com). Green Park tube. **Open/meals served** 11am-midnight Mon-Sat; noon-midnight Sun. **Main courses** £10.50-£17.50. **Credit** AmEx, MC, V.
The polarised black and whiteness of the diminutive Donovan bar is a fitting testament to its muse, Stepney-born photographer Terence Donovan. His monochrome prints of the international celebrities and semi-clad women who characterised swinging 1960s London are liberally peppered over the walls. Black leather upholsters the chairs and the bar. Music on our last visit came courtesy of a laconic jazz guitarist bearing a passing resemblance to Johnny Depp. All this is the epitome of nostalgia-chic, but the cocktail list is surprisingly forward-thinking, with an eclectic range of manhattans, mojitos and martinis (the latter including saffron, pomegranate and apple variations) alongside the award-winning Space Race, a patented mix of Sputnik rose vodka, lychee liquor and Cointreau. The perfect spot to raise a glass to a more glamorous and reckless generation.
Disabled: toilet (in hotel). Entertainment: jazz 9pm Mon-Sat; bossa nova duo 9pm 2nd Tue of mth. **Map 9 J7.**

★ Library

The Lanesborough, 1 Lanesborough Place, Hyde Park Corner, SW1X 7TA (7259 5599/ www.lanesborough.com). Hyde Park Corner tube. **Open** 11am-1am Mon-Sat; noon-10.30pm Sun. **Meals served** 11am-midnight Mon-Sat; noon-10.30pm Sun. **Main courses** £10-£22. **Credit** AmEx, DC, MC, V.
Saunter through the lobby of the Lanesborough hotel to the Library and you're handed a book by staff in *Casablanca* attire. Within it you'll find (as you survey the elegant surroundings with roaring fire and towering fresh flowers) magic spells. In the house champagne cocktail (£13.50), Aperol mixes with orange juice and limoncello. Garlic, cognac and ginger beer combine in a Garlic Affair; and Wokka saké, fresh mint and strawberry purée mingle in the house martini (both £12.50). The choice of vintage armagnacs and cognacs is legendary. Of the dozen wines, all, including a Puligny-Montrachet La Garenne Larue (£19/£76), come by the glass. It's magic at a price – food includes spicy lobster nachos at £21 – but magic all the same.
Disabled: lift; toilet. Entertainment: pianist 6.30pm daily. **Map 9 G8.**

Mahiki NEW

1 Dover Street, W1S 4LD (7493 9529/ www.mahiki.com). Green Park tube. **Open** 5.30pm-3am, **tapas served** 5.30-10.30pm Mon-Sat. **Tapas** £5.95-£8.95. **Admission** £10 after 9.30pm Wed, Thur; £15 after 9.30pm Fri, Sat. **Credit** MC, V.
Informed by style mags and gossip pages that this is The Place To Be, yodelling trustafarians fight to get into Mahiki every night of the week. We find the underground venue cramped and rather tacky – a Hawaiian theme means wall-to-wall bamboo – but the cocktails are first-rate. Some of the best mixologists in London have been lured in, despite an obligation to wear an open Hawaiian shirt and a garland of flowers; they stir up 31 mixes from the standard menu alone, leisurely and at their own pace, but with undoubted aplomb. Our Zombie (£12) was sublime: four types of premium rum, maraschino, lime and grapefruit juices, finished with a slug of flaming absinthe. Unless armed with daddy's credit card, you might feel out of place among the children of rock stars and minor royals, but cocktail devotees should certainly take a look.
Bar available for hire. **Map 9 J7.**

Moose NEW

31 Duke Street, W1U 1LG (7224 3452/ www.vpmg.net). Bond Street tube. **Open** 4pm-2am Mon-Thur; 4pm-3am Fri, Sat. **Snacks served** 4-10pm Mon-Sat. **Snacks** £2-£7. **Credit** AmEx, MC, V.
We can't imagine anyone not liking Moose. The latest venture from the Vince Power Music Group is a rarity in the West End: cosy, reasonably priced and with decor that's simultaneously eccentric and inviting. There are two spaces: a small ground-floor bar and a much larger basement bar with DJs six nights a week. The decorative motif is that of a ski lodge in the Canadian Rockies, big pictures of which grace the walls. Antlers adorning the ceiling lights, and cowhide seating downstairs complete the rugged, rustic look. A daiquiri made with three-year-old Havana Club was excellent; a Beefeater martini seemed excessively vermouthy, but was quickly replaced by a charming bartender when told of the fault. Prices are fair: £6.50 for a cocktail (from an extensive list), £8.50 for a champagne cocktail. A very long happy hour (6-9pm) offers ordinary cocktails for just £3.75.
Booking advisable weekends. Entertainment: DJs 9pm Mon-Wed; 6pm Thur, Fri; 8pm Sat. Tables outdoors (6, pavement). **Map 9 G6.**

Polo Bar

Westbury Hotel, New Bond Street, W1S 2YF (7629 7755/www.westburymayfair.com). Bond Street or Oxford Circus tube. **Open** 11am-1am Mon-Sat; noon-midnight Sun. **Meals served** 11am-10.30pm Mon-Sat; noon-10.30pm Sun. **Main courses** £11.50-£22.50. **Credit** AmEx, DC, MC, V.
Polo succeeds where so many other hotel bars fail: it's an exceptionally good bar in its own right. Maybe this is because the entrance is independent of the hotel, or perhaps it's the sophisticated aura of quality, but Polo manages to tick every box as the perfect post-work wind-down venue. The interior is understated and luxurious, and the staff are among the politest and most attentive in London – yet the drinks are allowed to speak for themselves. Signature cocktails clock in at a pricey £18, but you get what you pay for. The beguiling black cherry and lavender martini (Ultimat cherry vodka, fresh lavender syrup) was pure sensuality: intense and fragrant rather than overwhelmingly perfumed. Standard martinis, such as the chilli raspberry (chilli vodka, framboise liqueur, raspberry syrup, £11) are anything but, and there's a wine list to match. The crowd is refreshingly unpretentious for a venue of this calibre: definitely one for the grown-ups.
Babies and children admitted (until 6pm). Bar available for hire. Disabled: toilet (in hotel). **Map 9 H7.**

Piccadilly

Cocoon

65 Regent Street, W1B 4EA (7494 7609/ www.cocoon-restaurants.com). Piccadilly Circus tube. **Lunch served** noon-3pm Mon-Fri. **Dinner served** 5.30pm-midnight Mon-Sat. **Main courses** £7.50-£45. **Credit** AmEx, MC, V.
Professional and imaginative, Cocoon is attached to the space-age first-floor oriental restaurant of the same name (*see p253*). Dinky stools revolve around a circular bar counter at the far end. There are plenty of Japanese drinks on the sumptuous menu: eight types of shochu and a dozen sakés. Beer is bottled Asahi and Kirin Ichiban. The two-dozen cocktails (£8-£9) are either contemporary or classic, or have an oriental twist, such as the Akari of fresh jonagold apple and fragrant lychee, shaken with saké and grapes; or the Japanese Mule of fresh ginger, coriander and Imo-shochu. Fresh ingredients (berries, rhubarb, watermelon) and high-end spirit bases are used throughout.
Babies and children welcome: high chairs. Booking advisable. Disabled: toilet. Dress: smart casual. Entertainment: DJs 11pm Thur-Sat. Separate room for parties, seats 14. **Map 17 A5.**

Pimlico

Millbank Lounge

City Inn Hotel, 30 John Islip Street, SW1P 4DD (7932 4700). Pimlico or Westminster tube. **Open** 11am-11pm Mon-Sat; noon-10.30pm Sun. **Meals served** noon-11pm Mon-Sat; noon-9.30pm Sun. **Main courses** £6-£11.50. **Credit** AmEx, DC, MC, V.
This quality hotel bar is criminally underused, hidden away down a Pimlico backstreet on the first floor of a city hotel. You'll have no trouble finding a relaxing low chair in the expansive bar area, but you'll need to take your time over the impressive drinks menu. 'Lounge Selective' is the core choice: mojitos, daiquiris and other classics made with standard (Mount Gay Eclipse, £8.25), superior (Havana 7 or Matusalem, £10.50) or deluxe (Mount Gay XO, Appleton 21, £15-£19) brands. 'Lounging Nostalgia' offers a more eclectic mix: perhaps

Plymouth gin mixed with elderflower in the elderflower collins, or Absolut Vanilla smashed with raspberries and strawberries in the Cascade. *Babies and children admitted (until 6pm). Disabled: toilet (in hotel).* **Map 16 K10**.

St James's

Dukes Hotel

Dukes Hotel, 35 St James's Place, SW1A 1NY (7491 4840/www.dukeshotel.co.uk). Green Park tube. **Open** noon-11pm Mon-Sat; noon-10.30pm Sun. **Snacks served** noon-3.30pm daily. **Snacks** £15-£20. **Credit** AmEx, DC, MC, V.

Tucked next to the lobby of the Dukes Hotel, this discreet cocktail bar offers four seating areas of striped walls and stately portraits. Settle into your leather chair with complimentary nuts and nibbles to peruse the famed martini menu (£14.50). House versions use Plymouth gin or Potocki vodka, frozen for 24 hours; eight Modern Classics also involve U'Luvka and Królewska vodkas, with Iranian saffron, fresh passionfruit juice or 'copious' olive juice. These quality brands are also used in the 25 Classics (£13-£16). Vintage malts (McPhail's 1948, £50) and cognacs are another speciality. Some 20 wines include a Châteauneuf-du-Pape Domaine du Grand Tinel (£9.50/£40) and a merlot Faucon Bleu (£6.50/£23).

Dress: smart casual. Tables outdoors (3, garden). **Map 9 J8**.

Soho

Floridita

100 Wardour Street, W1F 0TN (7314 4000/www.floriditalondon.com). Tottenham Court Road tube. Bar **Open** 5.30pm-2am Mon-Wed; 5.30pm-3am Thur-Sat.
Restaurant **Dinner served** 5.30pm-1am Mon-Wed; 5.30pm-1.30am Thur-Sat. **Main courses** £11-£35. **Admission** (after 7pm Thur-Sat) £15. **Credit** AmEx, DC, MC, V.

This large, Cuban-themed nightspot (located on the former Mezzo site, halfway down Wardour Street) is at pains to live up to its Havana namesake of Hemingway lore. The cocktail menu begins with a Hemingway quote before launching into a selection of five daiquiris (£7.50), all with Havana Club Anejo, some with a dash of maraschino or Curaçao. Also worth investigating is the New Cuban range (£8-£8.50), featuring the likes of a Santiago Blazer with ignited chocolate-infused rum, fresh blackberries and raspberries. Daiquiris come in plum, vanilla, melon and pineapple varieties. The glam restaurant (*see p51*) attached to the bar is a glitzy spot for Latino food, and musicians and dancers provide nightly entertainment.

Booking advisable. Disabled: toilet. Entertainment: Cuban band, DJ 8pm Mon-Sat. Dress: funky/glam. Separate room for parties, seats 40-60. **Map 17 B3**.

Lab (100)

12 Old Compton Street, W1D 4TQ (7437 7820/www.lab-townhouse.com). Leicester Square or Tottenham Court Road tube. **Open** 4pm-midnight Mon-Sat; 4-10.30pm Sun. **Meals served** 6-11pm Mon-Sat; 6-10.30pm Sun. **Main courses** £6.50-£10.50. **Credit** AmEx, MC, V.

Founded by Douglas Ankrah, Lab has long been at the forefront of London's cocktail scene. Some see it as the most innovative and exciting bar in the capital, others find it distinctly unenjoyable. We've been forced to side with the latter on occasion – affronted by overzealous doormen, drowned in a crush of intoxicated trendies and dying of thirst by the time we'd been served – but then you'd be a fool to come here for a quiet drink, especially at weekends. What Lab does is exuberance with panache, its intimate two-floor interior decked out with colourful retro aesthetics, its music euphoric and its (fairly priced) cocktail list among the finest in town – and handled by some of the world's best mixologists. Try a Kool Hand Luke (Myer's rum, fresh limes muddled with dark brown sugar and Angostura bitters, £7); or a Red Hot Chilli Pepper (lemongrass-flavoured tequila with ginger beer and champagne, £7).

Bar available for hire. Dress: no ties. Entertainment: DJs 8pm Mon-Sat. **Map 17 C3**.

★ Milk & Honey (100)

61 Poland Street, W1F 7NU (7292 9949/www.mlkhny.com). Oxford Circus tube. **Open** *Non-members* 6-11pm Mon-Fri; 7-11pm Sat. *Members* 6pm-3am Mon-Fri; 7pm-3am Sat. **Snacks served** 6pm-2am Mon-Sat. **Snacks** £3-£7. **Credit** AmEx, DC, MC, V.

Hiding behind unmarked black doors that seem straight out of the Prohibition era, this jazz-tinged speakeasy from the people behind the Player (*see below*) is a charming mix of semi-exclusivity and unprecedented friendliness. Non-members will need to book in advance (and leave by 11pm), but are treated like old friends by the staff – assuming they follow the House Rules (Rule No.1: 'No name dropping, no star fucking'). Diminutive light fixtures struggle to illuminate a spread of intimate leather booths and art deco tin tiles on the walls, but semi-blindness is a small price to pay for cocktails of this calibre (the sours embodying a perfect balance of lemon, sugar and egg-white; the swizzles and cobblers deliciously refreshing). The members-only Red Room boasts a reserve list of fine wines, but you don't need to spend like a celeb to feel like a celeb in this fantastic little hideaway.

Booking essential for non-members. Dress: smart casual; no sportswear. Separate rooms for parties, seats 12. **Map 17 A3**.

Player

8 Broadwick Street, W1F 8HN (7292 9945/www.thplyr.com). Oxford Circus or Tottenham Court Road tube. **Open** 5.30pm-midnight Mon-Wed; 5.30pm-1am Thur, Fri; 7pm-1am Sat. **Snacks served** 6-11pm Mon-Fri; 7-11pm Sat. **Snacks** £3-£7. **Admission** £5 after 9pm Thur-Sat. **Credit** AmEx, MC, V.

Few places hit the mark as meticulously as this subterranean cocktail lounge (open to non-members before 11pm, best to phone ahead), where the retroactively glamorous 1970s decor extends from turquoise, Player-branded carpet and sculpted wall panelling to the cluster of disco balls dangling behind the DJ. Not that there's anything faddish about this bar, which continues to slake the thirst of in-the-know lounge lizards. The vibe is intimate, aided by comfortable leather booths and fine service. On our visit, the barman conjured up a fiery tequila bloody mary while shooting the breeze like an old friend. Unpretentious and positively charged with cinematic elegance, it's the sort of place where even humble accountants can act like movie stars for the night.
Bar available for hire. Disabled: toilet. Entertainment: DJs 8pm Thur-Sat. **Map 17 B3.**

South Kensington

★ 190 Queensgate

The Gore Hotel, 190 Queensgate, SW7 5EX (7584 6601/www.gorehotel.co.uk). Gloucester Road or South Kensington tube. **Open/meals served** noon-1am Mon-Wed, Sun; noon-2am Thur-Sat. **Main courses** £9.95-£15. **Credit** AmEx, DC, MC, V.
The perfect pub, cocktail bar and destination lounge, this annex of the Gore Hotel hides between the Albert Hall and the Bulgarian Embassy. Upholstered seating and carved dark wood surround a sturdy bar. Table service frees you of the transactional bullshit of the metal change tray. Bar food of the charcuterie-plate variety and an ambient soundtrack also feature. Underpinning it all is a 20-strong list of cocktails (£8.50): mules and martinis made with Ketel One, Belvedere and Absolut, mixed with fresh raspberries, lychees and other fruit. The high-end brands can be ordered singly too: a shot of Matusalem Clasico rum is £7. Four quality champagnes (£9.95-£17) also come by the glass, including Veuve Clicquot.
Entertainment: DJs 10pm Fri, Sat. Separate room for parties, seats 60. **Map 8 D9.**

Artesian. See p333.

West

Ladbroke Grove

Montgomery Place NEW

2007 RUNNER-UP BEST BAR

31 Kensington Park Road, W11 2EU (7792 3921/www.montgomeryplace.co.uk). Ladbroke Grove tube. **Open** 5pm-midnight Mon-Fri, Sun; 2pm-midnight Sat. **Snacks served** 6-11pm daily. **Snacks** £5-£12. **Credit** AmEx, MC, V.
Despite the rather tired vision ('the drinks take their inspiration from Hemingway and the rebirth of cool, which was all about the Rat Pack and the Ritz'), Montgomery Place is a pleasingly intimate cocktail bar on a busy stretch of Ladbroke Grove. Alex Fitzsimmons and Matt Perovetz from sister bar Dusk (and other London and NYC mixers) have consulted on a cracking cocktail selection. Inspiration for the list comes from great bars of the 20th century and the classic drinks created therein. Concoctions start at £8.50; you might fancy the Montgomery-style martini (Tanqueray, Noilly Prat, named after Field Marshall Montgomery). Dark walnut tables and low lighting set the tone and though the place is small, it has a lovely array of seating options: on the street, at the bar, at one of the slide-in diner-style booths, or tucked at the back on a curved banquette. Tap water was provided without asking and the staff seemed to enjoy chatting with customers.
Bar available for hire. Booking advisable. Tables outdoors (2, pavement). **Map 19 B3.**

Ladbroke Grove

Trailer Happiness

177 Portobello Road, W11 2DY (7727 2700/ www.trailerhappiness.com). Ladbroke Grove or Notting Hill Gate tube. **Open** 5-11.30pm Tue-Fri; 6-11.30pm Sat; 6-10.30pm Sun. **Snacks served** 6-10.30pm Tue-Sat. **Snacks** £4-£8. **Credit** AmEx, MC, V.
Ah, a proper bar, no messing. This basement might look trashy (part bordello, part South Pacific), but the drinking is serious and the enterprise is darned professional and bags of fun. Along with a homage to great contemporary mixologists – Vincenzo Errico's Red Hook (rye whiskey, dry cherry, sweet vermouth) from New York's Milk & Honey circa 2003, for example – Trailer Happiness does its own grapefruit julep (with Finlandia, grapefruit and pomegranate juices, and a drizzle of honey) and a Hedgerow sling (Plymouth and sloe gins, lemon, mure, soda). Fifties-style tiki drinks are mixed with reverence for their Californian roots. Note that, sensibly, you're limited to two Zombies (five rums, absinthe, 'bitters and trepidation'). Most cocktails cost £6.50, while tikis go up to £12. Snacks are available, and DJs take to the decks in a corner hatch towards the end of the week.
Entertainment: DJs 8pm Thur-Sat. Tables outdoors (5, pavement). **Map 19 B3.**

Westbourne Grove

Lonsdale

44-48 Lonsdale Road, W11 2DE (7727 4080/ www.thelonsdale.co.uk). Ladbroke Grove or Notting Hill Gate tube. **Open** 6pm-midnight Mon-Thur; 6pm-1am Fri, Sat; 6-11.30pm Sun. **Dinner served** 6-10.30pm Mon-Sat. **Main courses** £12.20-£19. **Credit** AmEx, MC, V.
Dick Bradsell's old establishment is back in contention with the launch of a fabulously original cocktail menu in spring 2007. Simple in concept, it traces the history of the London cocktail, from the mojito conceived in Cuba in 1586, to the sours of the 1700s, the sangarees of the Antilles, the flips of the 1860s, the bucks of the 1920s and contemporary classics. It's a labour of love, a work of art, and it provides meticulously sourced concoctions at fair prices (£6-£7.50). In truth, Lonsdale was getting as jaded as the Prague Metro-style decor around its bar counter, and the expansive back area was often quiet. A Westbourne Sour (Miller's Westbourne Strength gin, fresh raspberry, gently frothed) should put the whizz back in W11.
Babies and children admitted (until 8.30pm). Disabled: toilet. Entertainment: DJs 9pm Fri, Sat. Separate room for parties, seats 22. Tables outdoors (5, terrace). **Map 19 C3.**

South West

Chelsea

Apartment 195

195 King's Road, SW3 5ED (7351 5195). Sloane Square tube then 11, 19, 22 bus. **Open** 5-11pm, **dinner served** 5-10.30pm Mon-Sat. **Main courses** £11-£14. **Credit** AmEx, MC, V.
You need to press a buzzer to get into this discreet little number. But despite such trappings of highfalutin exclusivity, a warm welcome awaits at the top of the stairs. There's a Vivienne Westwood meets laid-back gentleman's club feel to the decor, with sumptuous leather sofas, a garish pop hologram and royally purple walls adorned with artwork and an enormous, kitsch Penny Black stamp. The drinking is all about cocktails, especially mojitos; the delicious and surprisingly potent lulo mojito (containing Havana Club 7) costs £8. To celebrate its fourth anniversary, the bar has launched a special London-themed cocktail menu, featuring various fruity offerings. The star turn is the aptly named Crown Jewels: a glass of honey-sweetened rare cognac topped with vintage champagne that'll set you back a staggering £350.
Bar available for hire. Separate room for parties, seats 50. **Map 14 E12.**

Fulham

Mokssh NEW

222-224 Fulham Road, SW10 9NB (7352 6548/www.mokssh.com). Fulham Broadway tube. **Open** noon-midnight Tue-Thur; noon-1am Fri,

Sat; noon-10pm Sun. **Lunch served** noon-3pm Tue-Sun. **Dinner served** 6-11pm Tue-Thur; 6pm-midnight Fri, Sat; 6-9pm Sun. **Main courses** £6.75-£14.75. **Credit** AmEx, DC, MC, V.
This carefully styled Indian bar-cum-restaurant looks like the inside of a gigantic boiled sweet. The cocktails are similarly sugary, with classic recipes given candied, spicy overtones by serious-looking bartenders. The menu emphasises the staff's dedication to perfection; whisky isn't mixed with mint leaves, it's 'rambunctiously muddled', while cognac is 'reworked' with vanilla liqueur. Instead of nuts, you're served exquisite popadoms that hint at the quality of food the kitchen provides. A handful of reds and whites and a couple of Indian lagers (Kingfisher, Cobra) add variety to the drinks list, but it's the Rosebud martinis and fiery Gingeranis that keep pulling in the punters.
Bar available for hire. **Map 13 C12**.

South

Balham

Balham Bowls Club NEW

7-9 Ramsden Road, SW12 8QX (8673 4700). Balham tube/rail. **Open** 4-11pm Tue-Thur; 4pm-midnight Fri; noon-midnight Sat; noon-11pm Sun. **Dinner served** 7-9pm Wed-Sun. **Credit** MC, V.
A crusty bowls club goes into receivership, the old score cards, wall plaques ('Timber Traders Benevolence Society'!) and furniture are saved, and the place is opened to the public. What a treasure the result is. The front half could be Sir John Mortimer's living room, replete with Victorian dressing-screens, leather sofas and bookcases, while the space at the back could be a Labour Club in Barrow circa 1971 (we love the plastic bingo hall seats). This area also doubles as the dining room. Dishes on the daily changing menu come in sizes meant for sharing; the fish pie was a treat, overflowing with prawns – but expensive at £14. Draught beers include Bitburger and Cruzcampo. Overall, a genuine London peculiar.
Babies and children admitted (until 7pm). Disabled: toilet. Entertainment: quiz 8pm Tue. Tables outdoors (10, garden; 4, terrace).

Battersea

Dusk

339 Battersea Park Road, SW11 4LF (7622 2112/www.duskbar.co.uk). Battersea Park rail. **Open** 6pm-12.30am Tue, Wed; 6pm-1.30am Thur; 6pm-2am Fri, Sat. **Snacks served** 6-10.30pm Tue-Sat. **Snacks** £4-£9. **Credit** AmEx, MC, V.
The absurdly friendly (without being pushy) waiting staff clearly love working at this long-standing Battersea hotspot. And we love drinking here. A classic cosmopolitan was a delicate and masterful creation, while a Honey Berry Smash (Polish vodka smashed up with fresh berries, mint leaves, honey and lemon) was sensational – and a steal at £6.50. The bar snacks menu is worth exploring; shared bites include top-quality feta parcels stuffed with spinach (Filo Phil, £6.50). The Mr Scruff soundtrack sums up the place perfectly: fun, clever and not willing to take itself too seriously. The crowd of crepuscular hedonists know, as do we, that Dusk is still way ahead of the pack in this part of town.
Dress: smart casual. Entertainment: DJs 9pm Wed-Sat. Tables outdoors (10, terrace).

Frieda B

46 Battersea Rise, SW11 1EE (7228 7676/www.frieda-b.co.uk). Clapham Junction rail/35, 37 bus. **Open** 5pm-midnight Mon-Thur, Sun; 5pm-2am Fri, Sat. **Credit** AmEx, MC, V.
The display boxes in the basement showcasing pairs of sumptuous Jimmy Choo's say a lot about this extremely assured venture. The exterior has the air of a bespoke furniture shop of the kind you might find tucked away in a Mayfair backstreet. The tiny front bar branches out into a couple of nooks perfect for canoodling, and there's a downstairs space filled with brown leather sofas and scatter cushions that certainly haven't come from Ikea. The mint walls, portraits of pouting chanteuses and a cocktail list that mixes brevity with imagination (try the 180 Biflora, with Mount Gay rum, Falernum, lime juice and bitters) are fast proving popular with raffish couples looking to avoid the more corporate drinking dens nearby.
Bar available for hire. **Map 21 C4**.

Clapham

Lost Society

697 Wandsworth Road, SW8 3JF (7652 6526/ www.lostsociety.co.uk). Clapham Common tube/ Wandsworth Road rail/77, 77A bus. **Open** noon-midnight Tue, Wed; noon-1am Thur, Sun; noon-2am Fri, Sat. **Dinner served** 5-10pm Tue-Sun. **Main courses** £10-£12. **Admission** £5 after 9pm Fri, Sat. **Credit** AmEx, MC, V.
The winner of the Best Bar category in the 2006 Time Out Eating & Drinking Awards has sure become popular. Once you're past the queues and door staff, this is still the superbly crafted, fantasy country-house party that you wish you were invited to every night. Flat cap-clad barmen make knockout cocktails, both classic and modern (we fell head over heels for the Lost Sailor Berry, with Chambord, blackberries, rum and cabernet sauvignon). The interesting world beer menu includes Goose Island IPA from the USA, and Sleeman Honey Brown from Canada. The chaise longues and hidden garden make for an intimate, classy and wonderfully original space that will convert anyone who thinks south London bars follow the rules rather than make them.
Entertainment: DJs 9pm Thur-Sat; musicians 4pm Sun; burlesque show 9pm 2nd and last Wed of mth. Tables outdoors (20, garden). **Map 22 A1**.

South East

Blackheath

Zerodegrees

29-31 Montpelier Vale, SE3 0TJ (8852 5619/ www.zerodegrees.co.uk). Blackheath rail. **Open** noon-midnight Mon-Sat; noon-11.30pm Sun. **Meals served** noon-11.30pm Mon-Sat; noon-11pm Sun. **Main courses** £6.95-£12.25. **Credit** AmEx, MC, V.
Blackheath's microbrewery, bar and pizzeria has expanded from its base (at zero degrees longitude) between the village and the heath, and now has outlets in Reading and Bristol. The name is also a nod to the brewing process taking place in the vast vats by the entrance, producing four categories of beer for a buzzy young clientele. Black and pilsner lagers are made to Czech specifications, pale ale is of American provenance, while the wheat ale has German and Belgian influences. All are tasty and cost £2.60 a pint, with prices dropping to £1.90 during happy hour (4-7pm weekdays). Many customers also partake of the thin-crust pizzas of intriguing variety, or one of the kilo pots of mussels served in the adjoining sunken dining area.
Babies and children admitted.

London Bridge & Borough

Hide Bar NEW

39-45 Bermondsey Street, SE1 3XF (7403 6655). London Bridge tube/rail. **Open** 10am-midnight Mon, Tue; 10am-1am Wed, Thur; 10am-2am Fri; noon-2am Sat. **Meals served** noon-9.30pm Mon-Sat. **Main courses** £6-£13. **Credit** AmEx, MC, V.
'We really like drink' is the boast of this cocktail bar. A good start, and a promise it lives up to – Hide has a drinks list made in bar heaven. It stocks all the premium spirits you've ever heard of, plus quite a few you haven't. And the staff are happy to make anything; they even have a library of historic cocktail books which you can leaf through then pick what you fancy. There's also a decent selection of wine, draught beers from the Meantime Brewery in Greenwich, and bottled beers from Belgium and beyond. A few gripes: some of the staff seemed inexperienced, and the slightly gloomy interior lacks liveliness and a sense of fun. Hide is the only good cocktail bar for miles, and is worth a special journey if you care about what you drink – but it also illustrates the fact that it takes more than just a great drinks list to make a truly great bar experience.
Bar available for hire. Separate rooms for parties, seating 30-50. **Map 12 Q9**.

★ Rake NEW

2007 WINNER BEST BAR
14 Winchester Walk, SE1 9AG (7407 0557). London Bridge tube/rail. **Open/snacks served** noon-11pm Mon-Fri; 10am-11pm Sat. **Snacks** £1-£6. **Credit** AmEx, MC, V.
Small isn't the word. Like a licensed Tardis relocated to the streets around Borough Market, the Rake is a minature haven for lovers of exotic beer – just one tiny room (less than 100sq ft) and a canopied, heated patio adjunct. It's run by the knowledgable folks behind the Utobeer stall in the market; we sampled draught pints of German Veltins (a fine pilsner) and Belgian Kriek (a lip-smacking cheery beer) before plunging into the selection of more than 100 bottled beers with a glass of toothsome Power Station Porter, specially imported all the way from Battersea. There are also ciders, perrys, jenevers and schnapps; pork pies and crisps make up the uncomplicated snack list. Bringing the best of the worlds of bar and pub together, the Rake is a pint-sized gem.
Babies and children admitted. Tables outdoors (7, deck). Disabled: toilet. **Map 11 P8**.

East

Bethnal Green

Bistrotheque Napoleon Bar (100)

23-27 Wadeson Street, E2 9DR (8983 7900/ www.bistrotheque.com). Bethnal Green tube/ rail/Cambridge Heath rail/55 bus. **Open** 6pm-midnight Mon-Sat; 1pm-midnight Sun. **Credit** AmEx, MC, V.
The path that leads to this bar and French bistro (*see p113*) – an unlit and rather forbidding side street off Cambridge Heath Road – makes it clear you're heading for somewhere out of the ordinary, even before you enter the (unsigned) building. The dimly lit ground-floor bar (so-named because of its association with Courvoisier cognac, allegedly the Petit Corporal's favourite), with its grey-blue walls and retro carpet, has an industrial feel that echoes the building's previous incarnation as a clothing factory. Classic cocktails are expertly mixed by white-shirted staff and served to groups of arty thirtysomethings who appreciate the 1970s and 1980s music. If you time your visit correctly, you can catch a performance in the cabaret room.
Disabled: toilet. Entertainment: cabaret (check website or phone for details); pianist noon-4pm Sun. Separate room for parties, seats 50.

Shoreditch

Green & Red

51 Bethnal Green Road, E1 6LA (7749 9670/ www.greenred.co.uk). Liverpool Street tube/rail. **Open** 5.30pm-midnight Mon-Thur; 5.30pm-1am Fri, Sat; 5.30pm-10.30pm Sun. **Dinner served** 6-11pm Mon-Sat; 6-10.30pm Sun. **Main courses** £10.50-£14.50. **Credit** AmEx, MC, V.
Well conceived and well run, Green & Red has an almost evangelical commitment to fine tequila. Only 100% agave tequila is stocked, and the huge selection includes a large range of exceptional 'private reserve' tequilas for sipping neat. Latin bottled beers and cocktails round off the menu. We enjoyed a delicious watermelon margarita (£6.70), made with Jose Cuervo tequila, fresh watermelon and lime. DJs play upbeat music in the basement area at weekends, but with a restaurant (*see p53*) that serves great Mexican grazing food, G&R works equally well whether you're boozing, dancing, eating or just killing time with the papers.
Babies and children welcome: high chairs. Disabled: toilet. Entertainment: DJs 9pm-1am Fri, Sat. Tables outdoors (1, terrace). **Map 6 S4**.

Loungelover (100)

1 Whitby Street, E2 7DP (7012 1234/ www.loungelover.co.uk). Liverpool Street tube/rail. **Open** 6pm-midnight Mon-Thur, Sun; 6pm-1am Fri; 7pm-1am Sat. **Snacks served** 6-11.30pm Mon-Fri, Sun; 7-11.30pm Sat. **Snacks** £4.50-£7.50. **Credit** AmEx, DC, MC, V.

Loungeloving is a popular pastime in these parts. Shoreditch loves this bar's OTT approach to glamorous, cocktail-swilling bonhomie. The luxe junk-shop decor does much to impress: giant champagne glasses filled with flowers, palm-tree chandeliers, huge stage lights and glittering stag's horns cover every inch of available space. The cocktails (£7.50-£11) are utterly fabulous. But there's something about the neat, ordered service that makes it hard to relax. For a venue that looks as if it was made for chandelier-swinging excess, there isn't much scope for spontaneity (you need to book tables in advance, for a start). Still, it's well worth joining the upmarket in-crowd for a blowout drink and a gawp.

Booking advisable. Disabled: toilet. Entertainment: DJs 9pm Sat. **Map 6 S4.**

North East

Hackney

Dalston Jazz Bar

4 Bradbury Street, N16 8JN (7254 9728). Dalston Kingsland rail/67, 76, 149, 243 bus. **Open** 5pm-3am Mon-Thur; 5pm-5am Fri, Sat; 5pm-2am Sun. **No credit cards.**

It's been around for a while, but the Dalston Jazz Bar still has a temporary, 'put up overnight' feel. Glass-walled on three sides, and plonked in the middle of a car park in a Dalston side street, it might not seem to have much going for it. But something about the place – maybe it's the cocktails, maybe the up-for-it crowd – works. The interior is dotted with battered sofas and low tables, interspersed with eclectic tat (an old dentist's lamp, a cycling road sign), while at the makeshift-like bar there are five beers on tap (Erdinger the highlight), plus plenty of bottles in the fridge. Come Saturday and Sunday, you can sample some of the cheapest cocktails in London (£4.50 before midnight, £5 after). The place packs out as the wee hours approach, and is often the better for it.

Entertainment: DJs 10pm daily. Tables outdoors (3, pavement). **Map 25 B4.**

North

Camden Town & Chalk Farm

Gilgamesh (100)

Camden Stables Market, Chalk Farm Road, NW1 8AH (7482 5757/www.gilgameshbar.com). Chalk Farm tube.

Bar **Open/snacks served** 6pm-2.30am Mon-Thur; noon-2.30am Fri-Sun.

Tea house **Open/snacks served** noon-6pm Sat; noon-7pm Sun. **Lunch served** noon-3pm Fri-Sun. **Dinner served** 6pm-midnight Mon-Thur; noon-12.30am Fri, Sat; noon-midnight Sun. **Set dim sum** £16. **Set lunch** (Mon-Fri; Sun) £18 2 courses, £22 3 courses. **Main courses** £10-£25.80.

All **Credit** AmEx, MC, V.

Inspired by the Babylonian epic of King Gilgamesh, this is an opulent, theatrical temple to excess. The scale is breathtaking, from the splendid mosaic-inlaid bar to the huge sphinxes that stare implacably out of the embossed or embellished surfaces. Intricate hand-carved wall panels depict ancient battles, pillars are inset with polished stones, and the immense carved tree that stretches around the sweeping entrance staircase has to be seen to be believed. The adjoining oriental restaurant (*see p255*) is equally extravagant, with a retractable glass ceiling for open-air dining in summer. It all feels a world away from Camden Stables market below; grab a table by the floor-to-ceiling windows to enjoy the surreal contrast. Eye-wateringly expensive cocktails are blended with consummate skill, and taste as divine as they look.

Babies and children admitted: high chairs. Booking esssential. Disabled: lift; toilet. Dress: smart casual; no flip-flops or shorts. Vegetarian menu. **Map 27 C1.**

Islington

25 Canonbury Lane

25 Canonbury Lane, N1 2AS (7226 0955/ www.25canonburylane.co.uk). Highbury & Islington tube/rail. **Open** 5pm-midnight Mon-Thur; 5pm-2am Fri; noon-2am Sat; noon-midnight Sun. **Meals served** 7-10pm Mon-Thur. **Main courses** £5.95-£8.50. **Credit** MC, V.

Just off Upper Street, this supremely trendy bar claims to have 'redefined Islington bar culture with its eclectic combination of old and new', while offering an 'understated atmosphere of decadent chic'. It all sounds a bit try-hard to us, but this is an undeniably elegant, intimate little spot for a drink and a few tapas. The cocktails and shooters menu is extensive, although draught offerings are more limited (Stella, Grolsch, Hoegaarden). With its opulent decor (gilded mirrors, extravagant flower arrangements and crystal chandeliers) and beautiful clientele, the bar can seem a bit intimidating – and please, someone tell these people that wearing sunglasses inside is a faux pas.

Babies and children admitted (until 6pm). Tables outdoors (5, conservatory).

Warwick

45 Essex Road, N1 2SF (7688 2882/www.the warwickbar.com). Angel tube. **Open** 5pm-midnight Mon-Thur; 5pm-1am Fri; 3pm-1am Sat; 3pm-midnight Sun. **Credit** MC, V.

Purely because it doesn't have pale green walls and stripped leather furniture (as does seemingly every other destination on Essex Road), the Warwick is arguably the best bar on the strip. There's a certain charm to the retro interior, which has movie ironica on the walls, along with chairs, tables and sofas that look as if they've been lovingly saved from the dump. There's also a 'world famous' pop quiz and a jukebox that doesn't merely rotate the same two Kasabian and Killers albums. The beer selection is fairly standard, though Baltika, Paulaner and San Miguel stand out, but an adventurous cocktail list offers some consolation. At the rear is a great space with its own bar: perfect to hire for private parties.

Disabled: toilet. Entertainment: DJs 7pm Thur-Sun. Separate area for parties, seats 40. Tables outdoors (2, pavement). **Map 5 O1.**

North West

Hampstead

Roebuck

15 Pond Street, NW3 2PN (7433 6871). Belsize Park tube. **Open** noon-11pm Mon-Thur; noon-midnight Fri, Sat; noon-10.30pm Sun. **Lunch served** noon-3pm, **dinner served** 5-10pm Mon-Fri. **Meals served** noon-10pm Sat; noon-9pm Sun. **Main courses** £6.50-£12. **Credit** AmEx, DC, MC, V.

Never judge a book by its cover. From the outside, the Roebuck looks like an utilitarian drinking hole, as ugly as the monstrous Royal Free Hospital across the road. Inside, it's rather fabulous. Classic 1960s seats vie for attention with a huge pale sofa and old brown armchairs. Vintage lamps and globe lights illuminate a space wrapped in the sort of geometric wallpaper you might have seen in Biba. A pretty conservatory offers diners a view of the beer garden. There's decent food (burgers and the like) and a good choice of wine. An equally lovely downstairs lounge (tiled floor, exposed brickwork) is there to soak up overspill from the main room. What impresses us most, though, is the beer choice: an incredible 17 on tap on our visit. These included lagers Kirin and Paulaner, fruit beer Früli and three rotating ales (Greene King IPA, Timothy Taylor Landlord and Old Speckled Hen).

Babies and children admitted (until 7pm). Separate room for parties, seats 30. Tables outdoors (16, garden). **Map 28 C3.**

Balham Bowls Club. See p337.

Pubs

The relocation of the Young's brewery from Wandsworth to Hertfordshire in 2006 has left only one large brewery operating in London – Fuller's. But has this meant Londoners have lost their taste for real ale? Far from it. These days you'll find weird and wonderful brews served in more and more of the capital's pubs. Below is a choice selection of some of the capital's boozers; for more, consult the latest edition of the annual *Time Out Bars, Pubs & Clubs* guide (£9.99).

The **Gowlett** (listed under **Pizza & Pasta**) is also a very decent boozer. For pubs that specialise in food, see **Gastropubs**, starting on p115.

Central

Bloomsbury

★ Lamb

94 Lamb's Conduit Street, WC1N 3LZ (7405 0713). Holborn or Russell Square tube. **Open** 11am-midnight Mon-Sat; noon-10.30pm Sun. **Meals served** noon-9pm daily. **Credit** AmEx, MC, V.

Founded in 1729, this beautifully restored etched glass and mahogany masterpiece is class itself. Today the snob screens have a decorative role above the horseshoe island bar, but back in the days when music hall stars were regulars here, they were used to deflect unwanted attention. The stage stars are remembered with two rows of small, gilt-framed portraits running around the walls. Other vintage theatrical touches are provided by a polyphon (the old mechanical musical instrument in the corner), dinky brass balustrades around the bar tables, and the Pit, a sunken back area that gives access to a summer patio. The beer is Young's (and always served with correctly branded glass and beer mat), the wines a well-chosen half-dozen of each colour, and the menu seasonal, with most mains costing under a tenner: try the steak and mushroom pie.

Function room. No piped music or jukebox. Tables outdoors (3, patio; 3, pavement). **Map 4 M4.**

City

Black Friar

174 Queen Victoria Street, EC4V 4EG (7236 5474). Blackfriars tube/rail. **Open** 10am-11pm Mon-Wed, Sat; 10am-11.30pm Thur, Fri; noon-10.30pm Sun. **Meals served** 10am-10pm daily. **Credit** AmEx, MC, V.

Sir John Betjeman justifiably and successfully led the campaign to save this remarkable venue, now a Nicholson's pub. Built in the 1880s on the site of a medieval Dominican friary, the Black Friar had its interior completely remodelled by H Fuller Clark and Henry Poole of the Arts and Crafts movement. Bright panes, intricate friezes and carved slogans ('Industry is Ale', 'Haste is Slow') make a work of art out of the main saloon. This is adjoined by a prosaic second space, linked by a doorway and marble-topped bar. Upon the bar stand taps of Timothy Taylor Landlord, Adnams, London Pride and, on our visit, guest beer Robinsons Unicorn. Standard Nicholson's wines (none costing over £12 a bottle), may also accompany the range of pies.

Tables outdoors (10, pavement). **Map 11 O6.**

Lamb & Flag

Golden Heart

110 Commercial Street, E1 6LZ (7247 2158). Liverpool Street tube/rail. **Open** 11am-midnight Mon-Sat; 11am-10.30pm Sun. **Credit** DC, MC, V.

'Stand still and rot' flashes a sign in the Golden Heart, a motto for the East End arty types who see it as a home from home. Sandra Esquilant's famed corner boozer has stood still since the 1970s, which is precisely why they like it. The mounted evidence mounts: the moustache worn by one half of 'Mr and Mrs Dennis Esquilant' centrepiecing a Truman Pub of the Year 1983 poster, the Eagle Stout advertising, the neon Americana of the fluoro jukebox. And everyone seems to know the words to the Carpenters. This is retro at its most indulgent – and it's all marvellous fun. A big tap of Grolsch gets a daily caning, bottled choices include Peroni, Becks and Budvar, and unspecified wine flows like billy-o.

Babies and children welcome. Function room. Tables outdoors (4, pavement). **Map 12 S5.**

Clerkenwell & Farringdon

Jerusalem Tavern (100)

55 Britton Street, EC1M 5UQ (7490 4281/ www.stpetersbrewery.co.uk). Farringdon tube/rail. **Open** 11am-11pm Mon-Fri. **Lunch served** noon-3pm Mon-Fri. **Dinner served** 5.30-9pm Tue-Thur. **Credit** AmEx, MC, V.

So faithful are the devotees regularly massing for the Jerusalem's yeasty concoctions that some of them seem to think this may well be the promised land itself, an absurd theory given slight credence by the fact that St Peter's (the brewery, not the bloke) runs the place. Inside you'll find a range of interesting beers chalked up behind the small bar, from the always-popular Honey Porter and Golden Ale to seasonal favourites and fruit brews. But it's not a beer bores' establishment: with its wooden interior painted green and its clutter of tucked-away tables in countless nooks and crannies, the Jerusalem is like something straight out of Tolkien's Shire, and justly popular with punters of all ages and occupations. Certainly worth a trip.

Babies and children admitted. Bar available for hire (Sat, Sun). No piped music or jukebox. Tables outdoors (2, pavement). **Map 5 O4.**

Ye Old Mitre

1 Ely Court, Ely Place, at the side of 8 Hatton Gardens, EC1N 6SJ (7405 4751). Chancery Lane tube/Farringdon tube/rail. **Open** 11am-11pm Mon-Fri. **Meals served** 11am-9.30pm Mon-Fri. **Credit** AmEx, MC, V.

This oldie (established 1546) is only accessible through a narrow passage – incongruously described as 25m long. Still, the Mitre needs no yard conversion or 'ye olde' embellishment to prove its worth. Walk into its venerable, cramped three-room space, see what's on as the guest ale (Orkney Dark Island on our visit), then settle down amid the portraits of Henry VIII and sundry beruffed luminaries. The taps of Adnams Bitter and Broadside, Deuchars and Guinness will be easier to pick out than the extended history in small type lining the hatch of the bar counter. The handful of wines – Caliterra cabernet sauvignon, New Zealand pinot noir – are fairly priced at under £15. There are stand-up tables in the courtyard too.

No piped music or jukebox. Tables outdoors (10 barrels, pavement). **Map 11 N5.**

Covent Garden

Lamb & Flag

33 Rose Street, WC2E 9EB (7497 9504). Covent Garden tube. **Open** 11am-11pm Mon-Sat; noon-10.30pm Sun. **Lunch served** noon-3pm Mon-Fri, Sun; noon-4.30pm Sat. **Credit** MC, V.

A glance up Rose Street from Garrick Street after dark reveals a black streetlight throwing its light on to the frontage of the shamelessly traditional Lamb & Flag, Covent Garden's best pub. Also accessed by a tiny ancient passageway, this pub wears its history on its sleeve, proudly displaying its classic boozer credentials of real ale and, on the walls, local memorabilia. In summer, the upstairs

Prince Alfred & Formosa

windows allow air into a space that can be stifling due to the pub's popularity, but it's worth pitching up on the cobbles outside to soak up the atmosphere. Beers aren't bad either; there's an excellent line-up of mainly Young's ales, supplemented by guests that typically include the likes of Bombardier, Courage Best and Ridley's IPA. Pub grub and doorstep sandwiches are also available.
Babies and children admitted (lunch). Entertainment: jazz 7.30pm Sun. No piped music or jukebox. **Map 18 D4**.

Holborn

Cittie of Yorke

22 High Holborn, WC1V 6BN (7242 7670). Chancery Lane or Holborn tube. **Open** 11.30am-11pm Mon-Sat. **Lunch served** noon-3pm, **dinner served** 5-9pm Mon-Sat. **Credit** (over £10) AmEx, MC, V.
One of many historic taverns hereabouts, the Cittie of Yorke comprises a quite remarkable market-sized back room fit for a Hogarth scene, and an unremarkable front bar lined with some of the worst likenesses of historic figures in portrait form you'll ever laugh at. Ignore them and walk right through to the back. A row of soon-snagged snugs, upturned beer-barrel tables and powerful stand-up heaters are arranged around the crowded floor space, and a long, long bar counter dispenses the usual brews from the Samuel Smith stable.
Babies and children admitted (downstairs, until 5pm). Function rooms. **Map 10 M5**.

★ Seven Stars

53 Carey Street, WC2A 2JB (7242 8521). Chancery Lane, Holborn or Temple tube. **Open** 11am-11pm Mon-Fri; noon-11pm Sat; noon-10.30pm Sun. **Lunch served** noon-3pm, **dinner served** 5-10pm Mon-Fri. **Meals served** 1-9pm Sat, Sun. **Credit** AmEx, MC, V.
By the Royal Courts of Justice, Roxy Beaujolais' magic little pub-cum-bar-cum-eaterie fulfils its (admittedly complex) brief to near perfection while keeping a healthy tongue in cheek. Posters for courtroom dramas – *Action for Slander, Trial and Error*, Tracy and Hepburn on opposing toilet doors upstairs – overlook the legal fraternity tucking into well-chosen (and well-priced) merlots and malbecs. Craftily conceived daily dishes chalked up by the bar (Napoli sausages and mash, dill-cured herring) are devoured on green and white checked tablecloths in one side room; the other, purple in hue, copes with the inevitable bar overflow. A bar counter offers draught Bitburger, Adnams Bitter and Broadside and Licher Weizen, and guests such as London Pride and Crouch Vale's Brewers Gold.
No piped music or jukebox. **Map 10 M6**.

Knightsbridge

Nag's Head

53 Kinnerton Street, SW1X 8ED (7235 1135). Hyde Park Corner or Knightsbridge tube. **Open** 11am-11pm Mon-Sat; noon-10.30pm Sun. **Meals served** noon-9pm daily. **No credit cards**.
No mobiles and no credit cards at this charming time warp of a pub – it's a wonder they accept decimal coinage. The Nag's Head echoes a time when National Service was a given (note the cravats and regimental heraldry), James Mason was a sex bomb (note the line drawings) and glamorous destinations (Paris, New York) could only be glimpsed in crank-up machines, such as the one stood here beside a wireless-era Spangles sweets dispenser. The beer, served from behind a sunken counter in the main bar (and sold with sandwiches in the basement), includes draught Adnams and Bitburger. Handle the steps in between the two spaces with care.
No mobile phones. Tables outdoors (1, pavement). **Map 9 G9**.

Marylebone

Windsor Castle

29 Crawford Place, W1H 4LJ (7723 4371). Edgware Road tube. **Open** 11am-11pm Mon-Thur; 11am-midnight Fri, Sat; noon-10.30pm Sun. **Lunch served** noon-3pm Mon-Fri, Sun. **Dinner served** 6-10pm daily. **Credit** MC, V.
Not to be confused with the Windsor Castle near Regent's Park, this delightful brewhouse is the pub version of the houses covered in Cross of St George flags that you see on England match days. Inside, every free inch of wall space is plastered with patriotic memorabilia: a ceiling of royal family plates, royal tea tins, souvenir mugs, portraits of royals past and present, a photo of the Queen Mum pulling a pint. There's even a life-size mannequin of a Scots Guard, propped up in a sentry box by the door. It should be awful, but it's actually rather charming. A loyal troop of local drinkers helps – beer includes Adnams, Bombardier and 6X – and the kitchen serves pub-Thai favourites.
Babies and children admitted. Function room. Tables outdoors (5, pavement). **Map 8 F5**.

South Kensington

Anglesea Arms

15 Selwood Terrace, SW7 3QG (7373 7960/ www.capitalpubcompany.com). South Kensington tube. **Open** 11am-11pm Mon-Sat; noon-10.30pm Sun. **Lunch served** noon-3pm Mon-Fri; noon-5pm Sat, Sun. **Dinner served** 6.30-10pm Mon-Fri; 6-10pm Sat; 6-9.30pm Sun. **Credit** AmEx, MC, V.
Dickens and DH Lawrence both frequented this splendid free house, and both would probably still enjoy it today. There's a sympathetically dated feel to the sturdy wood interior – the large erotic painting, the sign saying 'To the loos' – but the drinks selection is bang up to date. With Kirin Ichiban and San Miguel on draught and Erdinger Weissbier, Tiger, Budvar and Peroni by the bottle, global lager drinkers are well catered for. Ales, though, are the speciality: Rand Bitter, Hogs Back, Brakspear Special, Adnams Broadside and London Pride all currently feature. The 20 wines, 19 by the glass, include a Bertrand Ambroise pinot noir (£8.25 a glass/£24.50 a bottle) and a Montmains Chablis 2005 (£9.50/£29.90). The front terrace overlooks a quiet residential corner.
No piped music or jukebox. Function room. Tables outdoors (10, terrace). **Map 14 D11**.

West

Hammersmith

★ Dove

19 Upper Mall, W6 9TA (8748 9474). Hammersmith or Ravenscourt Park tube. **Open** 11am-11pm daily. **Lunch served** noon-2.45pm Mon-Fri; noon-3.45pm Sat. **Dinner served** 6-8.45pm Mon-Fri; 5-9.15pm Sat. **Meals served** noon-5pm Sun. **Credit** AmEx, DC, MC, V.
British to its bones, the Dove is a 17th-century riverside inn with all the trimmings: low-beamed ceilings, dark panelled walls and historical gravitas. 'Rule Britannia' was penned in an upstairs room, and the manuscript hangs in a display case. Charles II and Nell Gwynne caroused here. The list of former regulars, posted above the roaring fire in the front bar, includes Tommy Cooper and Graham Greene. It's even had an entry in the *Guinness Book of Records* for the tiny front bar – although there are four sections, including a conservatory opening out on to a waterside terrace. It's a Fuller's pub, so ESB, Discovery and London Pride stand alongside standard lagers, and there are no surprises on the 25-strong wine list.
No piped music or jukebox. Tables outdoors (15, riverside terrace). **Map 20 A4**.

Holland Park

Ladbroke Arms

54 Ladbroke Road, W11 3NW (7727 6648/ www.capitalpubcompany.com). Holland Park tube. **Open** 11am-11pm Mon-Sat; noon-10.30pm Sun. **Lunch served** noon-2.30pm Mon-Fri; 12.30-3pm Sat, Sun. **Dinner served** 7-9.30pm daily. **Credit** AmEx, MC, V.
Gorgeous within and without. The tree-shrouded front garden is packed in summer, with drinkers

spilling out on to one of those majestic runs of lofty mini mansions that west London does so well. A perch here, adjacent to the cobbled mews and the pub's trailing ivy, is about as soothing as London boozing gets. Inside, a petite counter serves a small room beautified by a lovely etched mirror, framed pictures and some original Victorian stained-glass detailing. To the rear is a small eating area, where diners enjoy a Gallic-accented menu, and burrowed still further away is a bunker-like benched area. It's all very snug, and very popular. The clientele is an equal mix of under- and over-thirties, prim and poised the way W11 breeds 'em. Real ales – London Pride, Greene King IPA, Doom Bar – appease the rugger chaps, a well-chosen wine list the rest.
Bar available for hire. Babies and children admitted (dining only). No piped music or jukebox. Tables outdoors (12, terrace). **Map 7 A7**.

Maida Vale

★ Prince Alfred & Formosa Dining Rooms

5A Formosa Street, W9 1EE (7286 3287). Warwick Avenue tube. **Open** noon-11pm Mon-Sat; noon-10.30pm Sun. **Lunch served** noon-3pm Mon-Sat; noon-4pm Sun. **Dinner served** 6.30-11pm Mon-Sat; 6.30-10.30pm Sun. **Credit** MC, V.
Built in 1863, this magnificent old pub is visual testament to the divisions of Victorian society. Its five snugs are separated by ornately carved mahogany partitions, each with its own miniature door, designed to keep the classes and sexes apart. The beautiful, curved, etched plate-glass window at the front is another example of the 19th-century craftsmanship that went into creating the place. The rear dining room, in contrast, is a spacious and modern addition, with mosaic artwork, an open kitchen, views of the street whose name it borrowed and a menu of modern British/European fare. At the bar – another majestic piece of carved artistry, with an old clock on top – you can sup ale from the Young's stable, alongside Erdinger, Leffe, Staropramen Bombardier and Affligem, with Cruzcampo in bottles.
Babies and children admitted. Disabled: toilet. Restaurant available for hire. Tables outdoors (3, pavement). **Map 1 C4**.

South West

Barons Court

Colton Arms

187 Greyhound Road, W14 9SD (7385 6956). Barons Court tube. **Open** noon-3pm, 5.30-11.30pm Mon-Fri; noon-4pm, 6.30pm-midnight Sat; noon-4pm, 6.30pm-11pm Sun. **Snacks served** noon-2pm Mon-Fri. **No credit cards**.
This wonderful old boozer could be the only reason to visit the barren streets of Barons Court (unless you're a devoted *Grange Hill* fan – Fulham Prep, real-life location of the show for 25 years, is just across the road). Dark oak throughout gives the Colton's tiny front bar and back-room seating area a rural feel; completing the picture, toilets are labelled 'wenches' and 'sires'. A hidey-hole garden is ideal in summer; time it right and you can hear the thwacks, plonks and grunts from nearby Queen's tennis club, site of the annual Stella Artois Championship. Real ale fans have a choice of London Pride, Harveys, Deuchars IPA and Old Speckled Hen, and all pints come in dimpled beer mugs by firm order of landlord Jonathan. He's run the place for 37 years and is on first-name terms with most of the warhorses and wellies who gather here. Note that they don't take credit cards.
Tables outdoors (3, garden).

Colliers Wood

★ Sultan

78 Norman Road, SW19 1BT (8542 4532). Colliers Wood or South Wimbledon tube. **Open** noon-11pm Mon-Thur, Sun; noon-midnight Fri, Sat. **Credit** MC, V.
In south Wimbledon's backstreets lies an ale drinker's nirvana, and it's called the Sultan (named after the famous racehorse from the 1830s). Deserved winner of Time Out's Best Pub award in 2005, it's still an absolute gem – and the Wiltshire-based Hop Back Brewery's only London pub. The 1930s suburban architecture may not be particularly striking, but inside it's a delightful den, characterised by its colourful locals, two bars (the Ted Higgins bar is named after a beer-loving actor who once starred in Radio 4's *The Archers*) and Hop Back's lovely ales. There's GFB, Entire Stout and the much-acclaimed Summer Lightning, priced from £2.40 a pint (carryouts are also available), along with various bottled ales. Darts and dominoes are the only sports allowed – unless you count beer-swilling, or the quiz that takes place here on a Tuesday night.
Disabled: toilet. Entertainment: quiz 8.30pm Tue (Sept-June). Tables outdoors (8, garden).

Parsons Green

White Horse (100)

1-3 Parsons Green, SW6 4UL (7736 2115/ www.whitehorsesw6.com). Parsons Green tube. **Open** 11am-midnight Mon-Thur, Sun; 11am-1am Fri, Sat. **Meals served** noon-10.30pm Mon-Fri; 11am-10.30pm Sat, Sun. **Credit** AmEx, DC, MC, V.
Referring to this pub as the 'Sloaney Pony' has become a cliché; in fact, it should be recognised primarily for its sumptuous, globetrotting range of bottled beers, especially Belgian ones, from bruins and krieks to delicious Saison Dupont. The clientele is evenly split between hooraying poshos, bearded CAMRA members and lager-drinking Londoners wondering what on earth's going on. Aside from a well-appointed restaurant area, the pub is nothing flash; there are tables and benches rather than sofas and coffee tables, and the toilets are labelled 'Pistols' and 'Dolls'. A worthy pilgrimage for anyone even remotely interested in Belgian or British brews (draught offerings too).
Babies and children admitted. Disabled: toilet. Function room. No piped music or jukebox. Tables outdoors (30, garden).

South

Balham

Bedford

77 Bedford Hill, SW12 9HD (8682 8940/ www.thebedford.co.uk). Balham tube/rail. **Open** 11am-midnight Mon-Thur; 11am-2am Fri, Sat; noon-midnight Sun. **Lunch served** noon-3pm Mon-Sat; noon-5pm Sun. **Dinner served** 7-10.30pm Mon-Sat; 7-10pm Sun. **Credit** MC, V.
An institution that steadfastly refuses to rest on its laurels. This gigantic corner boozer is best known for its weekend Banana Cabaret comedy nights, held in the balconied back room called the Shakespearean Globe Theatre, and drawing top circuit names such as Brendan Burns and Milton Jones. The rest of the multitude of rooms in this

Colton Arms

hardy Victorian survivor are well used too. Classes in salsa, Argentine tango, pole-dancing and more all jostle for space in the schedule, alongside televised footie. The Bedford is no slouch in the beer and food stakes either, offering a decent line in real ale (Courage, Fuller's and 6X), plus a very popular menu that includes the frankly intimidating Homemade Balhamburger.
Babies and children admitted (until 7pm). Entertainment: comedy Fri-Sat; dance classes Mon-Thur, Sun; musicians Mon-Thur; nightclub Fri, Sat. Function rooms.

Clapham

Bread & Roses

68 Clapham Manor Street, SW4 6DZ (7498 1779/www.breadandrosespub.com). Clapham Common or Clapham North tube. **Open** noon-11pm Mon-Thur; noon-midnight Fri, Sat; noon-10.30pm Sun. **Lunch served** noon-3pm Mon-Fri; noon-4pm Sat. **Dinner served** 6-9.30pm Mon-Fri; 6-9.30pm Sat. **Meals served** noon-6pm Sun. **Credit** MC, V.
Run by the Workers' Beer Company, a funding organisation for trade unions and left-wing campaigns, this pub is named after a song sung by female textile workers during a 1912 strike over better working conditions (the lyric itself is daubed above the bar). They pride themselves on treating the staff well – and if friendliness is any indicator, they're doing a good job. There's a rotating selection of CAMRA medal-winning ales; Doom Bar, JHB Oakham and Woodford Wherry were available on our visit, along with draught lagers Erdinger, Budvar, Budvar Dark, Piretti, San Miguel and Leffe, and Aspall Suffolk Cyder. Those in the know shun the raucous venues of Clapham High Street and come here for a sophisticated, politically right-on pint.
Babies and children admitted (until 9pm). Disabled: toilet. Entertainment: musicians and burlesque monthly; check website for details. Function room. Tables outdoors (15, garden; 8, conservatory; 8, patio). **Map 22 B1**.

Stockwell

Priory Arms

83 Lansdowne Way, SW8 2PB (7622 1884). Stockwell tube. **Open** 11am-11pm Mon-Sat; noon-10.30pm Sun. **Meals served** noon-9pm Mon-Sat; 12.30-5pm Sun. **Credit** MC, V.
The Priory Arms is one of the most overtly proud bastions of old-fashioned pub culture that London has to offer. The lights are bright, the decor is set staunchly in the old-school red carpet mould, the fruit machine occupies pride of place by the door and there's even a Young's brewery clock. In keeping with the pub's pride in its craft, the beer selection is the stuff of CAMRA members' wet dreams. Harveys Sussex Best, Hop Back Summer Lightning and Adnams are permanent fixtures; there are also three guest ales, three kinds of Belgian fruit beer and 14 or so types of fruit wine. Above the bar are more than 200 pump labels from guest beers served in the past. The most impressive range of drinks in this part of London, no question.
Children admitted (Sun lunch only). Tables outdoors (4, patio).

South East

Deptford

Dog & Bell

116 Prince Street, SE8 3JD (8692 5664/ www.thedogandbell.com). New Cross tube/rail/ Deptford rail. **Open** noon-11pm Mon-Sat; noon-10.30pm Sun. **Lunch served** noon-2pm, **dinner served** 6-10pm Mon-Fri. **Meals served** noon-10pm Sat; noon-7pm Sun. **Credit** AmEx, MC, V.
This CAMRA-favoured landmark has come on leaps and bounds since the arrival of chef Adam and his wife Anmolia in 2005. There's still a reasonably priced and carefully sourced selection of ales, illustrated by the mosaic of beer mats over the bar; Dark Star Old Ale, Hop Back Elf & Hoppiness and Sharp's Atlantic IPA featured on this visit. There are 50 bottled Belgian beers too. But this place is far more than a real-ale retreat tucked down a dark street beyond the Greenwich end of Deptford High Street. The daily changing menu attracts a lunchtime and less blokey crowd, a favoured starter being the speciality salad of beetroot, horseradish and own-smoked mackerel. Wine sales have boomed, but without any loss in character: artists and artisans still gather in the side room, bookended by a pre-war bar billiards table and embellished by regular exhibitions.
Disabled: toilet. Tables outdoors (4, garden).

Greenwich

Greenwich Union

56 Royal Hill, SE10 8RT (8692 6258). Greenwich rail/DLR. **Open** noon-11pm Mon-Fri; 11am-11pm Sat; 11.30am-10.30pm Sun. **Meals served** noon-4pm, 5.30-10pm Mon-Thur; noon-10pm Fri, Sun; 11am-9pm Sat. **Credit** MC, V.
Success itself, Alastair Hook's bright Meantime Brewery flagship offers traditional house brews to a loyal and lively thirtysomething clientele. They create a buzz in the functional front and arty back areas, and around a narrow bar counter bearing the beer names. The result of Hook's specialist training in age-old techniques in Munich, the Pilsener, the Kolner, the Raspberry, the Helles, the Pale Ale, the Wheat and former seasonal beers Union and Dunkles (now served all year round) are produced in small batches, matured for long periods and never pasteurised. In addition, there's an enthusiastically sourced range of bottled brews: American Flying Dog, Australian Coopers and Belgian Trappist. Rwandan Fairtrade and Union's own coffees, 11 wines and a range of food from sandwiches to fish pie (plus Ray Richardson's artwork) complete the picture.
Babies and children admitted (until 9pm). Tables outdoors (12, garden).

Herne Hill

Commercial

210-212 Railton Road, SE24 0JT (7501 9051). Brixton tube/rail then 3, 196 bus/Herne Hill rail. **Open** noon-midnight daily. **Lunch served** noon-3pm, **dinner served** 5-10pm Mon-Fri. **Meals served** noon-10pm Sat; noon-9pm Sun. **Credit** AmEx, MC, V.
Formerly a down-at-heel railway boozer, the Commercial is proof that an extensive chain makeover (by Mitchells & Butler, in this case) doesn't have to mean loss of all character. This is by far the best and most popular pub hereabouts. Both bars are blessed with snug little micro living rooms complete with comfortable household furniture around open fires. Thought has gone into the detail: customised lighting, unusual artwork, restored old tiling. Even better is the selection on tap: Bombardier, Greene King IPA, Black Sheep and Marston's Pedigree, with Küppers Kölsch and Leffe nestling beside an excellent wheat beer selection (Paulaner, Franziskaner, Schneider and Hoegaarden). A mixed clientele and friendly staff are part of the appealing picture.
Babies and children admitted. Disabled: toilet. Tables outdoors (5, garden). **Map 23 A5**.

London Bridge & Borough

Charles Dickens

160 Union Street, SE1 0LH (7401 3744/ www.thecharlesdickens.co.uk). Southwark tube. **Open** noon-11pm Mon-Fri; noon-6pm Sun. **Lunch served** noon-3pm, **dinner served** 6-9pm Mon-Fri. **Meals served** noon-6pm Sun. **Credit** AmEx, MC, V.
Although the Inimitable drank at a handful of still-extant pubs in London, his connection with this one doesn't appear to extend much further than the wall-mounted prints of Dick Swiveller, the two Wellers and various other Dickensian creations. Happily, the theming isn't overwhelming, leaving this recently regenerated pub free to go about its business as a tidy, likeable local with a fabulously esoteric range of beers. On our visit, the six ales

Holly Bush. See p344.

from independent breweries included the easy-drinking Hair of the Hog from Surrey's Hogs Back brewery and the considerably richer Old Growler from Nethergate. The food menu contains a concomitantly stomach-lining array of old English favourites.
Bar available for hire. Entertainment: quiz 8pm Wed. Tables outdoors (3, pavement). **Map 11 O8.**

Market Porter

9 Stoney Street, SE1 9AA (7407 2495/ www.markettaverns.co.uk). London Bridge tube/rail. **Open** 6-8.30am, 11am-11pm Mon-Fri; noon-11pm Sat; noon-10.30pm Sun. **Lunch served** noon-3pm Mon-Fri; noon-5pm Sat, Sun. **Credit** AmEx, MC, V.
In terms of beer, the Porter is peerless: on our most recent visit, there were 11 ales on tap, and those we tried were in excellent shape. So why is it that we're often underwhelmed by this revered marketside boozer? It could be the lack of seats – necessary to enlarge capacity in the bustling S-shaped room, but hardly comfortable. It could be the fact that the quick, friendly staff appear slightly clueless as to what they're serving, a shame given both the huge variety and the lack of a board detailing what's on offer (desirable given the bar's layout). Or it could be the table that's permanently, frustratingly wedged in front of the dartboard. Don't get us wrong: we like it here. But a few minor changes would be a major improvement.
Babies and children admitted (restaurant). Disabled: toilet. Function room. **Map 11 P8.**

★ Royal Oak (100)

44 Tabard Street, SE1 4JU (7357 7173). Borough tube. **Open** 11am-11pm Mon-Fri; 6-11pm Sat; noon-6pm Sun. **Meals served** noon-3pm, 5-9.30pm Mon-Fri; 6-9.30pm Sat; noon-5pm Sun. **Credit** MC, V.
Tucked away around the back of Borough tube station, this Victorian corner pub is the only London outpost of the long-serving Harveys brewery in Sussex. As you'd hope, the ales (four to six of 'em) are all in splendid nick; there's always an extremely drinkable mild among the choice. The straightforward pub grub is very decent and priced extremely keenly: a towering, two-deck roast beef sandwich goes for £4.25. And it's a very handsome place, immaculately and unshowily maintained across its two bars. But the atmosphere is the thing. Less blokey and beardy than you might imagine, the Royal Oak remains a thriving cradle for a chatty community that usually includes local residents, after-work drinkers and interloping beer tourists. Perfect, essentially.
Function room. No piped music or jukebox. **Map 11 P9.**

East

Brick Lane

Pride of Spitalfields

3 Heneage Street, E1 5LJ (7247 8933). Aldgate East tube. **Open** 11am-midnight Mon-Thur, Sun; 11am-2am Fri, Sat. **Lunch served** noon-2.30pm Mon-Fri; 1-5pm Sun. **Credit** MC, V.
A reminder of what the area was like before the creative media types moved in, this homely Fuller's pub, tucked away behind Brick Lane's curry restaurants, attracts an interesting mix of customers, from older locals to younger trendy types. The inclusive atmosphere is due largely to the friendly staff – even the in-house cat is sociable – and a simple, cosy interior that's barely changed in years. Ancient bottles sit atop musty red curtains, and old photographs of Regent's Canal look down on the comfortable, old-fashioned sofas. On tap there's Fuller's ESB and London Pride, plus a couple of guest ales (Crouch Vale's Brewers Gold and Sharp's Doom Bar on our visit), while the lagers are standard stuff (Stella, Kronenbourg). A large pull-down screen features in the main room, and a TV in the smaller side room. The background of familiar pop tunes is a constant delight. A good 'un.
Babies and children admitted. Tables outdoors (4, pavement). **Map 12 S5.**

Limehouse

Grapes

76 Narrow Street, E14 8BP (7987 4396). Westferry DLR. **Open** noon-3pm, 5.30-11pm Mon-Thur; noon-11pm Fri, Sat; noon-10.30pm Sun. **Lunch served** noon-2pm Mon-Fri; noon-2.30pm Sat; noon-3.30pm Sun. **Dinner served** 7-9pm Mon-Sat. **Credit** AmEx, MC, V.
The Grapes isn't large, but it is lovely. The roadside front is all greenery and etched glass, the interior has the requisite dark wood, beams and open fire, and there's a sweet, rickety balcony overhanging the Thames. The current premises date from 1720 and there's a pretty solid Dickens connection (the pub was the model for the Six Jolly Fellowship Porters of *Our Mutual Friend*). But the Grapes isn't about plastic heritage: lively (if not always youthful) locals enjoy pints of Marston's Pedigree, Timothy Taylor Landlord and Adnams on draught, or snifters of wine, alongside grandad-style Sunday roasts and trimmings. Follow the narrow stairs up to an equally cosy dining room. The Grapes may have to contend with heavyweight newcomers such as Gordon Ramsay's Narrow gastropub, but it seems ready for battle.
Booking advisable (restaurant). No piped music or jukebox.

Mile End

Palm Tree

127 Grove Road, E3 5BH (8980 2918). Mile End tube/8, 277, D6 bus. **Open** noon-midnight Mon-Thur; noon-2am Fri, Sat; noon-1am Sun (last admission 10.45pm). **No credit cards.**
Isolated beside the canal in Mile End Park, this is a classic East End boozer. There is gorgeous old bronze-patterned wallpaper and, above the bar, publicity pics of forgotten crooners, while drums and a covered piano wait in the corner for the evening's trad jazz session. A second room, complete with a rare London Fives dartboard, can be entered only via the external doors. The landlady looks a little severe in her specs, but is thoroughly charming, pulling great pints of changing guest ales (Timothy Taylor Landlord and Hop Back Spring Zing on our last visit). Handwritten signs barring large bags after 8pm indicate the place's popularity with suit-and-sovereign East End oldies and younger incomers.
Entertainment: jazz 9.45pm Fri-Sun. Tables outdoors (4, park).

Shoreditch

Wenlock Arms

26 Wenlock Road, N1 7TA (7608 3406/ www.wenlock-arms.co.uk). Old Street tube/rail/ 55 bus. **Open** noon-midnight Mon-Thur, Sun; noon-1am Fri, Sat. **Meals served** noon-9pm daily. **No credit cards.**
Despite its no man's land location, the Wenlock packs 'em in for fine ales, doorstep sarnies and good-natured banter at the bar (if you prefix your drinks order with the words 'Can I get…' you'll be accused of bastardising the English language – and quite right too). This is a pub of the old school: gaudy carpet, friendly mutts and a rough-around-the-edges vibe. There's a cricket team, a football team, a Thursday night quiz, bands at the weekend and a hotchpotch crowd of fiercely loyal regulars. But real ales are the Wenlock's main USP. You'll find a changing menu of up to eight speciality brews: the fantastically named Oakham Asylum and Northern Soul Time were among the options on a recent visit; to check up-to-date incumbents, vist the the website.
Babies and children admitted (until 9pm). Entertainment: blues/jazz 9pm Fri, Sat; 3pm Sun; quiz 9pm Thur. Function room. **Map 5 P3.**

Stratford

King Eddie's

47 Broadway, E15 4BQ (8534 2313/www.king eddie.co.uk). Stratford tube/rail/DLR. **Open** noon-11pm Mon-Wed; noon-midnight Thur-Sat; noon-11.30pm Sun. **Meals served** noon-10pm daily. **Credit** MC, V.
Still the King of Prussia to regulars, this has been King Eddie's (or the Edward VII) since a fit of patriotism overtook the owner in World War I. It's now grade II-listed, with all the dark wood, open fires, etched glass and low ceilings that implies. There's a fine selection of beer (highlights include Skinner's Betty Stogs and Hook Norton Old Hooky on draught, Innis & Gunn Edinburgh ale and Nethergate Old Growler by the bottle), half a dozen each of red and white, and high-end spirits. As far as we're aware, it's the only gastropub in Stratford – though it could do with raising its game a bit. The same food is served in each of three rooms, and most meals are under a tenner. Roast chicken breast with chorizo and crispy potatoes (rather than asparagus, as advertised) wasn't bad, and other diners seemed happy with the breaded haddock and chips. Colchester rock oysters cost a bargain £1 each and are probably a better bet than the cloyingly sweet crab mayonnaise. In the saloon bar, grizzled, garrulous and tatted-up blokes sup with young professionals under the gaze of a mounted motorbike-riding stoat.
Babies & children admitted. Entertainment: acoustic/open mic 9pm Thur. Function room. Tables outdoors (7, yard).

Victoria Park

Royal Inn on the Park

111 Lauriston Road, E9 7HJ (8985 3321). Mile End tube then 277 bus. **Open** noon-11pm Mon-Sat; noon-10.30pm Sun. **Lunch served** 12.30-3.30pm Tue-Sat; 12.30-4pm Sun. **Dinner served** 6.30-10pm Tue-Sat. **Credit** MC, V.
There is little to fault at this wonderfully located old boozer on the edge of Victoria Park. With its high ceilings, original central bar, heavy drapes and muted lighting, it's a perfect place for meeting mates, having a meal or enjoying the jukebox offerings (Lou Reed, Nina Simone, Stevie Wonder). The fine selection of draught beers includes Fuller's Organic Honeydew, London Pride, Porter and Adnams, as well as Litovel, Hoegaarden, Leffe, Früli, Paulaner and Scrumpy Jack. There's a decent list of red and white wines from £11. Food is a big draw, especially at Sunday lunch, when you can have slow-roasted pork with crackling and all the trimmings or baked stuffed aubergine, chickpea and pepper stew. A large outdoor area offers heat lamps and summer barbecues.
Babies and children admitted (until 8pm). Disabled: toilet. Entertainment: quiz 8.30pm Tue. Function room. Restaurant. Tables outdoors (30, garden).

North East

Dalston

Prince George

40 Parkholme Road, E8 3AG (7254 6060). Dalston Kingsland rail/30, 38, 56, 242, 277 bus. **Open** 5pm-midnight Mon-Thur; 5pm-1am Fri; 2pm-1am Sat; 2-11.30pm Sun. **Credit** MC, V.
The George has always prided itself on the fact that it doesn't do food. It's a pub. And a much-loved one at that, drawing a loyal local following years before the latest Hackney upstarts arrived. The drinks selection is perfectly respectable, with well-kept London Pride, Flowers Original and Litovel on tap and a decent wine range (from £11.50 a bottle), plus the usual spirits. On Monday, friendly but focused locals pack in for the long-running pub quiz, and the jukebox offers an excellent range of tunes from the likes of Neil Simon and Nina Simone. The decor is strictly period Victorian: stuffed birds and fish, a bust of Brunel above the bar, and one of those old-school wall maps where England is the same size as France (and almost a quarter the size of India). In winter the fires blaze, but the welcome is warm year-round. And if you're hungry? Well, there's posh biltong or crisps.
Babies and children admitted (until 8.30pm). Entertainment: quiz 9pm Mon. Tables outdoors (24, heated forecourt). **Map 25 C5.**

North

Archway

Swimmer at the Grafton Arms

13 Eburne Road, N7 6AR (7281 4632). Holloway Road tube/Finsbury Park tube/rail. **Open** noon-3pm, 5-11pm Mon-Thur; noon-11pm Fri, Sat; noon-10.30pm Sun. **Lunch served** 1-3pm Thur, Fri; noon-4pm Sat, Sun. **Dinner served** 6-9pm Mon-Sat. **Credit** MC, V.

Sometimes it feels as if the Holloway Road, like the Great Wall of China, is so vast it must be visible from space. Thank goodness, then, for cosy havens like the Swimmer, where the weary can take the weight off. Free Wi-Fi is evidence that this refurbished Victorian gastropub is servicing a very different crowd to the neighbouring Hercules; fortunately, there's far too much fun stuff here for anyone to bother with their emails for long. There's the legendary, lucrative quiz on Mondays, a jukebox, board games and an open kitchen serving the best chips in the area (and there are lots of chips in the area). A well-heated outdoor space means you can enjoy an alfresco Litovel Premium (£3.20 a pint) or one of three Fuller's ales even after the sun goes down.

Entertainment: quiz 9pm Mon. Tables outdoors (14, garden).

Camden Town & Chalk Farm

Lord Stanley

51 Camden Park Road, NW1 9BH (7428 9488). Camden Town tube/Camden Road rail then 29, 253 bus. **Open** 10am-11pm Mon-Thur; 10am-midnight Fri, Sat; 10am-10.30pm Sun. **Lunch served** noon-3pm Mon-Sat; noon-4pm Sun. **Dinner served** 6.30-10pm Mon-Thur; 6.30-10.30pm Fri, Sat; 6.30-9.30pm Sun. **Credit** MC, V.

Once you're ensconced at a ramshackle wooden table – or better still, on one of the tatty but much coveted leather sofas – this is the kind of place where day segues into evening with dangerous ease. There's a convivial buzz: beardy intellectuals rub shoulders with vintage-chic girls and louche youths in skinny cords, while regulars hold court at the gleaming, horseshoe-shaped bar over a wordlessly replenished pint. Despite a plethora of good shoes and directional haircuts among the trendier clientele, this remains an unpretentious neighbourhood boozer, so there's minimal posing and preening. Draught offerings range from Adnams to Staropramen and the wine list is nicely chosen; the food is great, if pricey. Get here early if you can: latecomers invariably end up at the tiny table by the gents.

Babies and children admitted. Function room. Tables outdoors (10, garden; 5, pavement).

Harringay

Salisbury Hotel

1 Grand Parade, Green Lanes, N4 1JX (8800 9617). Manor House tube then 29 bus. **Open** 5pm-midnight Mon-Wed; 5pm-1am Thur; 5pm-2am Fri; noon-2am Sat; noon-11.30am Sun. **Meals served** 6-10pm Mon-Fri; noon-10pm Sat; noon-6pm Sun. **Credit** MC, V.

Once upon a time the Salisbury was a fairly rough and ready affair, but a makeover has enabled this majestic Victorian boozer to realise finally its potential. Worn carpets and tired fittings have been replaced with black and white floor tiles, stripped wood, potted plants and plush drapes, which nicely complement the period frescoes and cut-glass mirrors. At the back, the marble-clad exposed kitchen affirms the pub's newfound gastro credentials, dishing out upmarket pub grub along the lines of bangers and mash and own-made beefburgers (£7.50 upwards). Here too are black leather sofas to lounge on (on Sundays this area is sometimes given over to jazz musicians). There's ESB, London Pride and Discovery on tap at the handsome bar, alongside Litovel Czech lager and Fuller's Organic Honey Dew. Long may it continue.

Babies and children admitted (until 8pm). Disabled: toilet. Entertainment: jazz 8.30pm Sun mthly; phone to check; quiz 8.45pm Mon. Function room (seats, 80).

Islington

Island Queen

87 Noel Road, N1 8HD (7704 7631). Angel tube. **Open** noon-11pm Mon, Sun; noon-11.30pm Tue, Wed; noon-midnight Thur-Sat. **Lunch served** noon-3pm, **dinner served** 6-10.30pm Mon-Thur. **Meals served** noon-10.30pm Fri, Sat; noon-10pm Sun. **Credit** MC, V.

An absolute gem of a pub, buried in an anonymous row of terraced houses near the canal. Huge front windows showcase the welcoming, high-ceilinged Victorian saloon, complete with delicately etched glass and heavy velvet drapes. Comfy sofas occupy the back room, and an upstairs section can accommodate larger parties. With its hum of indie rock and cheery buzz of conversation, the Island Queen is a supremely relaxing spot. Staff are super-attentive and knowledgeable, and there's a fine selection of speciality beers (Früli, Leffe, Deuchars) and well-kept guest beers on draught. The food menu isn't vast, but what there is tends to be above-average pub grub – roasts, fish and chips and the like. Tuesday's quiz night is a hotly contested but genial affair.

Babies and children admitted (until 7pm). Entertainment: quiz 8.30pm Tue. Function room. Tables outdoors (4, pavement). **Map 5 O2.**

North West

Hampstead

Holly Bush

22 Holly Mount, NW3 6SG (7435 2892/ www.hollybushpub.com). Hampstead tube/ Hampstead Heath rail. **Open** noon-11pm Mon-Sat; noon-10.30pm Sun. **Meals served** noon-10pm Mon-Sat; noon-9pm Sun. **Credit** AmEx, MC, V.

Tucked away on a tiny lane amid some gorgeous NW3 piles, the Holly Bush is a gem of a place. It's a warren of little rooms, each offering their own distinctive historic patina alongside shared elements (burnished wood panels, low ceilings, sepia lighting). Only the rear dining room bucks the trend: it feels distinctly modern with its white painted walls and brighter lights. Adnams, Harveys and London Pride do the business on the pumps, though a lot of people check in for the food: quality nosh such as quails' eggs, smoked duck with fig and mint salad or a substantial organic rump steak. A few benches beckon from out front in summer, though keep the noise down if you don't want to gain the ire of local residents, who keep a wary eye on the place.

Babies and children admitted. Function room. Restaurant. **Map 28 B2.**

Spaniards Inn

Spaniards Road, NW3 7JJ (8731 6571). Hampstead tube/210 bus. **Open** 11am-11pm Mon-Fri; 10am-11pm Sat, Sun. **Meals served** 11.30am-10pm Mon-Fri; noon-10pm Sat, Sun. **Credit** AmEx, MC, V.

Perched on one of Hampstead's highest points, the Spaniards is one of the capital's most bona fide historic pubs, outside the Square Mile at least (it's the reputed birthplace of highwayman Dick Turpin). There's been a pub here since the 1580s, a fact that's particularly easy to believe in the fascinating upstairs room with its wonky floorboards and misshapen doors. The downstairs bar is surprisingly small given the number of punters, though in summer most just order then scuttle out to the huge courtyard, spread beneath an expansive centrepiece tree. In winter, the back room is a dim, cosy hideaway, as is a tiny private snug beneath the stairs. The draught options are good – Adnams, Harveys, Marston's Pedigree and Deuchars – with a decent complement of bottled Belgian beers. Keats reputedly composed 'Ode to a Nightingale' in the courtyard; maintaining tradition, the pub hosts weekly poetry readings.

Babies and children admitted. Entertainment: poetry readings 8pm Tue. Function room. Tables outdoors (90, garden).

St John's Wood

Clifton

96 Clifton Hill, NW8 0JT (7372 3427). St John's Wood tube. **Open** noon-11pm Mon-Sat; noon-10.30pm Sun. **Lunch served** noon-3pm Mon-Sat; noon-4pm Sun. **Dinner served** 6-9pm Mon-Sat; 6.30-9pm Sun. **Credit** MC, V.

A pub in a Georgian villa – just what you'd expect around these parts. Tucked away down a residential side street off Abbey Road, the Clifton is a bucolic hangout with a collection of distinctive rooms that appeal to a broad demographic. A century ago, it was even good enough for royalty: Edward VII conducted trysts with Lillie Langtry here. These days, a large rear room adorned with classical murals and other traditional touches suits posher locals, while the more down-to-earth customers convene by the old fireplace in a snug, red-trimmed section. Beer lovers are blessed with Adnams Explorer, Hogs Back ales, Greene King or London Pride; Hendrick's gin used as the base in G&Ts shows similar thoughtfulness. A lovely, leafy front terrace beckons in summer; borrow a board game from the bar and while the day away.

Babies and children admitted (until 7pm). Tables outdoors (12, garden). **Map 2 D1.**

Outer London

Richmond, Surrey

Cricketers

The Green, Richmond, Surrey TW9 1LX (8940 4372). Richmond tube/rail. **Open** noon-11pm Mon-Sat; noon-10.30pm Sun. **Meals served** noon-9pm Mon-Thur; noon-7pm Fri, Sat; noon-5pm Sun. **Credit** AmEx, MC, V.

The Cricketers' location, perched on the edge of genteel Richmond Green, is utterly idyllic – and not many pubs can boast their own cricket team, playing on their own doorstep. Inside, comfortable leather sofas and an intricately carved oak bench play host to a mixed clientele, ranging from sedate elderly locals to tipsy teenagers, who on our visit were discussing the merits of toenail scent (lovely). Far more salubrious are the wide range of globally slanted burgers (18 in all) and excellent draught ales (Greene King IPA, Abbot, Old Speckled Hen). The upstairs room, with its creaking floorboards and quaint window seats overlooking the green, is a gem – but spoiled by a TV permanently tuned to Sky.

Babies and children admitted (until 7pm, restaurant). Function room. Tables outdoors (3, pavement).

Twickenham, Middlesex

Eel Pie

9-11 Church Street, Twickenham, Middx TW1 3NJ (8891 1717). Twickenham rail. **Open** 11am-11pm Mon-Wed; 11am-midnight Thur-Sat; noon-10.30pm Sun. **Lunch served** noon-3.30pm daily. **Main courses** £4.95-£7.95. **Credit** MC, V.

Fear not, ye faint of stomach – the pub's name comes not from its fare but from nearby Eel Pie Island, where the cream of the emerging British rock 'n' roll aristocracy (the Rolling Stones, Eric Clapton, Jeff Beck) famously jammed in the 1960s. Situated on a quiet, pretty street leading to the river, this lovely little pub shuns any kind of freewheeling decadence (unless there's a rugby match on – then things can get a bit more hectic) and is much more akin to the aforementioned Rock Gods as they are now – comfortable and countrified. There's a wide range of Hall & Woodhouse Badger cask beers (King and Barnes Sussex, Tanglefoot), along with bottles of the deliciously gingery Blandford Fly. Decent pub grub is served, and there's a quiz every Thursday. We think Sir Mick would be impressed.

Babies and children admitted (until 7pm). Entertainment: quiz 9pm Thur.

Wine Bars

London's wine bar scene has improved dramatically in the past couple of years. One of the newer arrivals, East Dulwich's **Green & Blue**, has doubled in size of late, with a greatly expanded wine bar area and shop. Another success story is **Vinoteca**, the bar and shop in Smithfield owned by a couple of former wine merchants, which has built a private party room on profits from its first 18 months of trading.

So much development is afoot that even **Willie Gunn** in Earlsfield and Soho's **Shampers** have upped their game in response, rejigging their food menus and interior design. New this year are **1707** at Fortnum & Mason and the **Wonder Bar** at Selfridges; other major stores are likely to alter their wine departments along similar lines. Look out too for bars springing up in high-end wine merchants.

Two things lie behind the new wine bar phenomenon: first, the generally poor standard of gastropub wine lists; second, the increasingly dull wine found in supermarkets. Drinkers have been thirsting for more 'boutique' wines: bottles produced in lower quantities, often by smaller companies, around the world. Hence, entrepreneurs such as Kate Thal at Green & Blue and Trevor Gulliver at **Wine Wharf** stepped into the breach. The newer venues are modelled on the Italian enoteca, where shop and bar are combined. With the exception of **Bedford & Strand**, they don't try to replicate the old wine bar drinking dens. So far, larger operators have shied away from new enotecas because such venues lay bare the huge mark-ups that can be imposed on wine. Nevertheless, enterprises that are honest in their intentions are making the new format pay.

Central

Belgravia

Ebury Wine Bar & Restaurant

139 Ebury Street, SW1W 9QU (7730 5447/ www.eburywinebars.co.uk). Sloane Square tube/ Victoria tube/rail.
Bar **Open** 11am-11pm Mon-Sat; 6-10pm Sun. *Restaurant* **Lunch served** noon-2.45pm Mon-Sat. **Dinner served** 6-10.15pm Mon-Sat; 6-9.45pm Sun. **Main courses** £10-£19.50. **Set meal** (noon-2.45pm, 6-8pm) £14.50 2 courses, £17.50 3 courses. *Both* **House wine** £12.80 bottle, £3.40 glass. **Credit** AmEx, MC, V.

At first glance the Ebury seems like yet another stuffy old wine bar, the dark wood panels and staff who talk like Prince Charles leading you away from a drink. Don't be deterred. There are bright, sparky waiters also on hand, an accessible drinking area, and dining room walls covered in colourful painted scenes. Cherubs clamber over plants, and the names of famous books (look out for Jordan's autobiography – no kidding) are hidden among the temples and fauna. The approach to wine has also been updated. An admirable choice of 38 by the glass takes in plenty from the New World, although the dominance of sauvignon blanc has thankfully been reduced. A 2004 blend from Chilean winery Tamaya adds the sour cherry flavours of Italian grape sangiovese to the soft tannins of merlot, a variety rarely any good on its own. Four pieces of red, paprika-soaked lamb kebab gave the wine an extra lift. With its consistent food, grown-up service and no nasty surprises, the Ebury could be just the place to visit with your parents.

Babies and children admitted. Booking advisable. **Map 15 H10**.

Bloomsbury

Vats Wine Bar & Restaurant

51 Lamb's Conduit Street, WC1N 3NB (7242 8963). Holborn or Russell Square tube. **Open** noon-11pm Mon-Fri. **Lunch served** noon-2.30pm, **dinner served** 6-9.30pm Mon-Fri. **Main courses** £11.50-£17. **House wine** £13.95 bottle, £3.95 glass. **Credit** AmEx, DC, MC, V.

This is the kind of old-fashioned place that attracts regulars: men in pinstriped suits served by long-standing staff amid etchings and wood panels. Although the front area has been lightened up considerably, the wine list is rather in the dark ages, relying on the competent if not wildly exciting Louis Latour for basic Burgundy. Latour's logo appears on the wine list just to confirm he won't be shifted for a while. A glass of 2003 Rioja from Cune had decent acidity, with redcurrant flavours, but the fruit wasn't bright enough, suggesting the bottle had been open a while. Standing out from the list are Trimbach, with a 2003 gewurztraminer from Alsace, and the South African winery Vergelegen, its 2003 blend of cabernet sauvignon and merlot (first popularised in Bordeaux) being an excellent choice. Food ranges from the likes of salmon and tapenade in filo with green beans, to the occasional late 1990s recipe (a Jamie Oliver-style duck leg, borlotti bean and thyme ragoût, for example). Not a culinary destination this, but as a venue for a lunchtime business meeting, it's perfect.

Babies and children admitted. Separate room for parties, seats 50. Tables outdoors (4, pavement). **Map 4 M5**.

City

La Grande Marque

47 Ludgate Hill, EC4M 7JU (7329 6709/ www.lagrandemarque.com). St Paul's tube/ Blackfriars tube/rail. **Open/snacks served** 11.30am-11pm Mon-Fri. **Snacks** £3-£6.50. **House wine** £14.50 bottle, £4.25 glass. **Credit** AmEx, DC, MC, V.

The dark wood-panelled walls, intricately traced ceiling and large windows of this former bank make La Grande Marque an elegant place for an after-work drink (there's also a branch in Middle Temple Lane). Lawyers and financial consultants from nearby firms fill the tables in large groups. Service is fine, if a little anodyne. The champagne list is the forte, though you'll need to spend almost £50 for real quality; Taittinger comes in at £40, and Billecart-Salmon Brut and Pol Roger White Foil at £49.50. A half bottle of R de Ruinart at £21 might be a good budget option. Otherwise, the lengthy wine list makes an impressive attempt to tour the world. JM Brocard's Chablis is a better bet than a rather unyielding Domaine Daulny 2005 Sancerre by the glass, if you're after a white with your food (although in the evening only bar snacks are served). At lunch, the short menu includes smoked salmon and bread, and chicken tikka.

Off-licence. Separate room for parties, seats 25. Wi-Fi. **Map 11 O6**.
For branch see index.

El Vino

47 Fleet Street, EC4Y 1BJ (7353 6786/ www.elvino.co.uk). Chancery Lane or Temple tube/Blackfriars tube/rail. **Open** 8.30am-9pm Mon; 8.30am-10pm Tue-Fri. **Breakfast served** 8-11.30am, **meals served** noon-9pm Mon-Fri. **Main courses** £8.75-£12.95. **House wine** £14.70 bottle, £3.70 glass. **Credit** AmEx, DC, MC, V.

El Vino epitomises what some think a wine bar should be like: dark wood-panelled interior, lots of wines from the traditional regions of Bordeaux and Burgundy, and middle-aged men sounding off in posh voices. Founded in 1879, the firm delivers to anywhere in the UK, offering mixed cases and plenty of Cru Bourgeois wines: the appellation of choice for those who don't want to spend a fortune in Bordeaux. The owners certainly know their topic of choice, but this specialism hasn't been passed on to staff. Scrawled on a blackboard by the bar was a list of ten wines by the glass, but '2005 Mâcon-Villages' gave only an approximate idea of what the wine might taste like, as the name of the winemaker was missing. This El Vino own-brand Burgundy turned out to be crisp, citrous and refreshing. Head to the basement for safer ground – for comfort food such as Aberdeen Angus beef mixed with kidney, a tasty version of the well-known pie. If you like hanging out with *Rumpole*-style lawyers, you'll love El Vino.

Booking advisable. Separate room for parties, seats 50. Tables outdoors (4, courtyard). Wi-Fi. **Map 11 N6**.
For branches see index.

Clerkenwell & Farringdon

Bleeding Heart Tavern

Bleeding Heart Yard, 19 Greville Street, EC1N 8SJ (7404 0333/www.bleedingheart.co.uk). Farringdon tube/rail.
Tavern **Open** 7.30am-11pm Mon-Fri. **Lunch served** noon-3pm, **snacks served** 3-6pm, **dinner served** 6-10.30pm Mon-Fri. **Main courses** £7.95-£12.95. **House wine** £11.75-£14.45 bottle, £3.60 glass.
Bistro **Lunch served** noon-3pm, **dinner served** 6-10.30pm Mon-Fri. **Main courses** £7.45-£14.95. **House wine** £13.50-£14.25 bottle, £3.10-£3.65 glass.

Restaurant **Lunch served** noon-2.30pm, **dinner served** 6-10.30pm Mon-Fri. **Main courses** £11.95-£21.50. **House wine** £16.45-£19.95 bottle, £4.15-£4.95 glass.
All **Credit** AmEx, DC, MC, V.
This is where you'll find scrubbed-up history: a new version of the traditional tavern, from the owners of the Bleeding Heart restaurant next door. The ancient brickwork has been given a blast to clear the dirt, and a large glass panel by the stairs is etched with ancient street networks. The all-French staff are knowledgeable about the French wines that fill much of the list, but are also au fait with the draught English ale from Adnams. The menu follows a similar French-English line: suckling pig from Broadside Farm in Suffolk is served with black pudding and apple stuffing; guinea fowl terrine comes with roasted shallots, pink peppercorns and red onion jam. Owner Robert Wilson also part-runs a winery in Hawkes Bay, New Zealand, so there's plenty from the land of the Kiwi. His basic 2005 sauvignon blanc, £4.50 a glass, shies away from the big tropical fruit flavours found in some NZ wines, going instead for lean and mean, with lively citrus and gooseberry aromas.
Booking advisable. Dress: smart; no shorts, jeans or trainers (restaurant). Separate rooms for parties, seating 30-40. Tables outdoors (10, terrace). **Map 11 N5.**

★ Cellar Gascon

59 West Smithfield, EC1A 9DS (7600 7561/ 7796 0600/www.cellargascon.com). Barbican tube/Farringdon tube/rail. **Open** noon-midnight Mon-Fri; 7pm-midnight Sat. **Tapas served** noon-11.30pm Mon-Fri; 7pm-midnight Sat. **Tapas** £3.50-£6. **House wine** £15 bottle, £4.50 glass. **Credit** AmEx, MC, V.
Attached to the much-feted Club Gascon restaurant, this bar opened to take advantage of the clamour for foie gras next door. Owner Vincent Labeyrie has built a room with City workers in mind. Leather-style banquettes line a cool blue wall giving a clubby vibe – perhaps an odd evocation for Gascony, a region that's known for primitively stuffing corn down goose necks. Well-dressed bankers and lawyers come here to guzzle pre-dinner drinks from the south-west of France, and are rewarded with a large selection of expertly chosen bottles, such as Pacherenc du Vic Bilh, Château Montus 2002, and a barrel-fermented Petit Corbu with full, honeyed flavours. The delicious range of nibbles includes slices of fatty, rich Gascon black ham at £3.50, carved from a leg at the bar. Most unusually, the tasting notes are as good as the wines themselves: 'mountain fresh, bristling with pithy, lemon-edged fruit' being a great description of the 2004 Xuri d'Ansa Cave de St Etienne de Baïgorry. Some might find this place a bit 'too cool for school', but the restrained, competent service and an outstanding wine list are enough for us.
Babies and children admitted. Bar available for hire. Tables outdoors (3, pavement). Wi-Fi.
Map 11 O5.

★ Vinoteca (100)

7 St John Street, EC1M 4AA (7253 8786/ www.vinoteca.co.uk). Farringdon tube/rail.
Open 11am-11pm Mon-Sat. **Lunch served** noon-2.45pm Mon-Fri. **Dinner served** 6.30-10pm Mon-Sat. **Main courses** £8.50-£13. **House wine** £12.95 bottle, £2.95 glass. **Credit** MC, V.
The owners of Vinoteca were inspired by the overseas trend of attaching a wine shop to a bar, where the same bottles can be enjoyed with food. Sure enough, the formula has been a success; the compact main room gets packed like a tapas bar in Spain, a young crowd sitting down to sample the wine along with the Simon Hopkinson-inspired food. Perhaps bravely, takeaway wine prices are listed alongside the cost of drinking in; it generally works out at two-and-a-half times more if you stick around. Luckily, the choice is outstanding, ranging from one of the world's best whites – 1981 Viña Tondonia Rioja – to a new entry, 2004 cabernet sauvignon from Miolo in Brazil (top of no one's list, but with a pleasant chocolatey and ripe tannin edge). The latter went well with some melting rump of lamb, sourced from adjoining Smithfield market and served with pommes dauphinoise. There's a new private room in the basement for larger parties, but this busy bar is worth savouring in its entirety.
Babies and children admitted. Bookings not accepted dinner. Off-licence. Separate room for parties, seats 36. Tables outdoors (4, pavement).
Map 5 O5.

Vivat Bacchus

47 Farringdon Street, EC4A 4LL (7353 2648/ www.vivatbacchus.co.uk). Chancery Lane tube/ Farringdon tube/rail.
Bar **Open/snacks served** noon-10.30pm Mon-Fri. **Snacks** £4-£12.
Restaurant **Lunch served** noon-2.30pm, **dinner served** 6.30-9.30pm Mon-Fri. **Main courses** £13.50-£18. **Set meal** £15.50 2 courses, £17.50 3 courses.
Both **House wine** £15.50-£19.95 bottle, £4.90-£6.90 glass. **Credit** AmEx, DC, MC, V.
Despite the exposed air-vent ducts and bare brick walls, Vivat Bacchus is welcoming as well as lively. It has a high-quality Modern European restaurant in the basement, and there's another branch in South Africa, the land of its owners. The importance of wine is shouted from every wall – whether it's a map of Burgundy's main producing region, the Côte d'Or, or blackboards full of forthcoming events. South African wine is a highlight. Sure enough, Kevin Arnold's 2004 shiraz from Stellenbosch was showing beautifully, with lots of spice, dark fruit and leather aromas; VB's storage areas must be doing a good job of ageing. Manager Neleen Strauss has been broadening the range into expensive Burgundy and Bordeaux, but it's worth trying the higher-priced South African examples first. To eat, there's an array of tapas given national designation, including a Spanish Platter, Greek Platter and, probably the best bet if you like cold cuts, an Italian Platter with parma ham, wild boar salami and bresaola. An ideal venue in which to sample some outstanding South African wines.
Bar available for hire. Booking advisable. Disabled: toilet. Off-licence. Wine club (7pm Mon; £15).
Map 11 N5.

Covent Garden

Bedford & Strand

1A Bedford Street, WC2E 9HH (7836 3033/ www.bedford-strand.com). Covent Garden tube/ Charing Cross tube/rail. **Open** noon-midnight Mon-Fri; 5pm-midnight Sat. **Lunch served** noon-3pm Mon-Fri. **Dinner served** 5.30-11pm Mon-Sat. **Main courses** £8.50-£16.95. **Set meal** £12.95 2 courses, £15.50 3 courses. **House wine** £12.50 bottle, £3.15 glass. **Credit** AmEx, MC, V.
An ironic take on the 1970s wine bar, this basement hideaway resembles a curious blend of Yates's wine lodge (see the wooden 'window' panels in the eating section) and Havana chic (witness the dark wood back bar). Confused? Plenty of people are happy enough, the bar often packed with men in suits as well as spiky-haired youngsters who work for record companies. So, a chance is presented to educate the Covent Garden masses in matters vinous – but the opportunity has been squandered. True, the range has improved since the 2006 opening. A 2004 petit verdot from Trentham Estate in Australia, bursting with juicy fruit, had a lightness that went well with our food: chicken breast and porcini mushrooms; and a spicy, vinegary steak tartare. But the prevalence of brands such as Fetzer, d'Arenberg and Knappstein makes the shelves behind the bar resemble those of an Oddbins shop. Full marks for showing that aspects of the old-style wine bar can be brought back to life, but a big cross should be put against some choices on the wine list.

Babies and children admitted. Bar available for hire. Wine club (5.30pm 1st Mon of mth; £10-£15). Wi-Fi. **Map 18 E5**.

Café des Amis

11-14 Hanover Place, WC2E 9JP (7379 3444/ www.cafedesamis.co.uk). Covent Garden tube.
Bar **Open** 11.30am-1am Mon-Sat. **Meals served** 11.30am-11.30pm Mon-Sat. **Main courses** £12-£20.50.
Restaurant **Meals served** noon-3pm, 5-11.30pm Mon-Sat. **Main courses** £12.50-£21.50. **Set meal** (noon-3pm, 5-7pm, 10-11.30pm Mon-Sat) £14.50 2 courses, £16.50 3 courses.
Both **House wine** £15.75 bottle, £4.50 glass.
Both **Credit** AmEx, DC, MC, V.

A watering station for Opera House audiences, Café des Amis is either very busy or extremely quiet, so pick the time that suits you. A revamp has made it look more fashionable, with mini chandeliers and monochrome prints of dancers in painful-looking poses. In contrast, the wine list is traditional and French-dominated, taking in popular white Burgundy producer Oliver Leflaive, with his mouth-watering 2005 Montagny Bonnevaux, alongside acceptable versions of the classic regions of Sancerre and Pouilly-Fuissé. To be fair, the 'Vins Etrangers' section – a slightly cursory way of referring to anything produced outside France – has been increasing. Hence drinkers are now able to experience the lovely three-way blend of viognier, chardonnay and sauvignon blanc from Tamaya in Chile (2006). To eat, you can sample a plate of French cheeses (epoisses, comté or morbier), or for more serious dining, head upstairs to the ground-floor brasserie. Small wonder that so many choose this place in preference to the ROH's bars.
Bar available for hire. Separate room for parties, seats 80. Tables outdoors (20, terrace). Wi-Fi. **Map 18 E4**.

King's Cross

Smithy's

15-17 Leeke Street, WC1X 9HY (7278 5949/ www.smithyslondon.com). King's Cross tube/rail.
Open 11am-11pm Mon-Wed; 11am-midnight Thur; 11am-1am Fri, Sat; 11am-6pm Sun. **Lunch served** noon-3pm, **dinner served** 6-10.30pm Mon-Sat. **Meals served** 11am-5pm Sun. **Main courses** £7.75-£14.50. **House wine** £11.50 bottle, £2.95 glass. **Credit** AmEx, MC, V.

Now that the area around King's Cross is finally getting a much-needed spruce-up, this wine bar tucked down a narrow side street should become frequented by locals from trendy penthouse flats as well as the after-work crowd it has always attracted. Smithy's offers excellent lager on tap, from Czech brewery Budvar (a rarity indeed), though it also sells the inevitable big-name lager brands. Wines are equally patchy, the pick of them being Framingham's elegant 2005 New Zealand sauvignon blanc (flinty as well as the classic tropical fruit), and 2005 Chablis from accomplished producer Gérard Tremblay (mineral, smoked bacon-infused with a rich and buttery edge). Tremblay's wine made a great match with six rock oysters (£7.50). Our follow-up choice was also an excellent fit: 2005 cabernet sauvignon from Casa Azul in Chile, with rump of lamb and puréed potatoes. Despite a lack of creature comforts – the floor is cobbled and slopes alarmingly, with a very real danger that women in heels will get stuck – Smithy's gets packed after 5.30pm. It's an ideal place to bring a large group of friends who like a few drinks.
Babies and children admitted. Booking advisable. Bar areas available for parties, seating 60 and 120. **Map 4 M3**.

Leicester Square

Cork & Bottle

44-46 Cranbourn Street, WC2H 7AN (7734 7807/www.donhewitson.com). Leicester Square tube. **Meals served** 11am-11.30pm Mon-Sat; noon-10.30pm Sun. **Main courses** £11-£13.50. **House wine** £14.95 bottle, £3.75 glass. **Credit** AmEx, DC, MC, V.

Opened in 1971, this basement bar sits oddly amid the tacky chain restaurants around Leicester Square. Spiral stairs take you down to a room that seems to have been in existence forever. Art nouveau Perrier Jouët prints rub shoulders with adverts for Beaujolais Nouveau. The old arched vaults have room for a couple of cosy tables at one end. Alternatively, you can slide into a slim bar that's often full of American tourists about to see a show. Bottles from top producers in Australia, New Zealand and the Rhône are clearly on view. Stick to owner Don Hewitson's specialisms and sample the power and elegance of Jim Barry's 2003 McCrae Wood Shiraz, or wines from Domaine du Grand Montmirail. Hewitson has also added a few bottles from new regions, such as the 2000 Campus Viñas Viejas Toro (power oozing from some 100-year-old vines). The food has also improved a little, a sirloin sandwich providing a slab of juicy meat, served with fat chips. Come here to impress a group of friends from out of town.
Babies and children admitted. Booking advisable. Disabled: toilet. **Map 18 C5**.

Marble Arch

★ Wonder Bar NEW

Selfridges, 400 Oxford Street, W1A 2LR (0800 123400/www.selfridges.com). Bond Street or Marble Arch tube. **Open/meals served** 9.30am-8pm Mon-Wed, Fri, Sat; 9.30am-9pm Thur; noon-6pm Sun. **Main courses** £7.50-£19.95. **House wine** £18.50-£37.99 bottle, £4.65-£18.50 glass. **Credit** AmEx, DC, MC, V.

Comparisons with Fortnum & Mason's new outlet 1707 (*see below*) are inevitable, but while Selfridges could be accused of clambering on to the fashionable wine bar bandwagon, the concept here was a truly original one – until it fell foul of the law. Squeezed around the store's newly located wine department, the Wonder Bar still makes a dependable choice for an excellent selection of wines (if a predictable-looking one, given the ubiquitous Swedish sauna feel to the place). But the showpiece 'wine jukebox' that gave wine fans the chance to sample up to 52 fine wines in three small measures – 25ml, 75ml and 125ml – has gone, its departure forced by trading standards officials. Now just 125ml and 175ml servings are offered. Nevertheless, the bar still provides an excellent chance to taste the department's top wines, ranging from the likes of Bonny Doon riesling (£3.35) to 2003 Vieux Telegraph Châteauneuf-du-Pape (£8.25). Yellow-fin tuna plus niçoise salad is a typical food offering.
Bar available for hire. Disabled: lift; toilet. **Map 9 G6**.

Piccadilly

★ 1707 NEW

Lower ground floor, Fortnum & Mason, 181 Piccadilly, W1A 1ER (7734 8040/www. fortnumandmason.com). Piccadilly Circus tube.
Bar **Open** 11am-8.30pm Mon-Sat; noon-5.30pm Sun. **Corkage** £5 half bottle, £10 bottle.
Restaurant **Meals served** noon-8pm Mon-Sat; noon-5pm Sun. **Main courses** £6-£26.
Both **House wine** £19.75-£22.50 bottle, £5-£5.25 glass. **Credit** MC, V.

At the heart of the new basement at Fortnum & Mason's famous food emporium, 1707 is a stylish take on the traditional wine bar. Unpolished wood slats line the walls, propping up cream-painted arches – all courtesy of 'restaurant designer to the celebrity chef', David Collins. The wine list outdoes even these surroundings, encompassing options from Clare Valley in Australia and fortifieds from Jerez, plus a pre-selected range of wines from a particular region, or made from the same grape (known as a 'flight'). 'Red Austrian', for example,

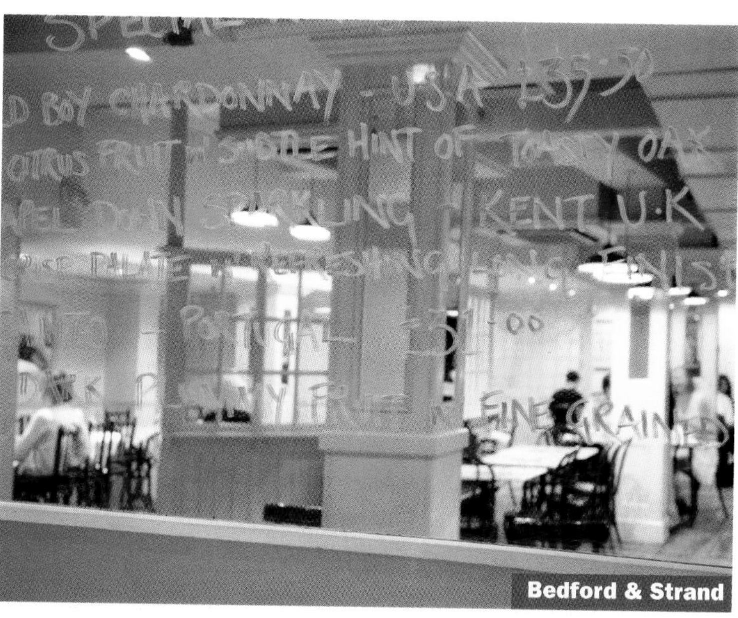

Bedford & Strand

BEST WINE BARS

Drink in or bottle out?

Sample at the bar or buy wine to take home, courtesy of the enoteca format at **Green & Blue** (*see p349*), **Negozio Classica** (*see right*), **1707** (*see p347*) and **Vinoteca** (*see p346*).

Vintage selection

The classic wine bar vibe emanates from old-stagers **Albertine** (*see right*), **Cork & Bottle** (*see p347*), **Gordon's** (*see right*) and **El Vino** (*see p345*) .

Bubbling over

For a lively time of it, try **Amuse Bouche** (*see p349*), **Bedford & Strand** (*see p346*), **Gordon's** (*see right*), **Smithy's** (*see p347*) and **Vinoteca** (*see p346*).

Suck it and see

For regular tastings, contact **Green & Blue** (*see p349*), **Vinoteca** (*see p346*), **Vivat Bacchus** (*see p346*) and **Wine Wharf** (*see p349*).

Good with...

Eat excellent food with your wine at **Cellar Gascon** (*see p346*), **Ebury Wine Bar & Restaurant** (*see p345*), **Negozio Classica** (*see right*), the **Oratory** (*see right*), **Putney Station** (*see p349*), **1707** (*see p347*) and **Vinoteca** (*see p346*).

Late harvest

For fortified and dessert wines, try **Cellar Gascon** (*see p346*), **Gordon's** (*see right*) and **1707** (*see p347*).

was good value at under a tenner for three wines from that country. It's doubtful whether customers will always appreciate such efforts; one middle-aged woman wanted something 'dry and light' rather than the glass of Krug bought by her wealthy partner. If nothing on the list appeals, grab a bottle you fancy from the shop; corkage is an additional £10 per bottle. Decent plates of food soak all this up. Fortnum pork pie with scotch egg, deliciously crumbly montgomery cheddar and a pot of chutney matched an unctuous Alsace pinot gris 2004 from Bruno Sorg. Fortnum's has an outstanding collection of wine, and 1707 shows it off in fine style.

Babies and children admitted. Disabled: toilet. Off-licence. **Map 9 J7**.

Soho

Shampers

4 Kingly Street, W1B 5PE (7437 1692/ www.shampers.net). Oxford Circus or Piccadilly Circus tube. **Open** 11am-11pm Mon-Sat (Aug closed Sat). **Meals served** noon-11pm Mon-Sat. **Main courses** £8.75-£15. **House wine** £11.95 bottle, £3.50 glass. **Credit** AmEx, DC, MC, V.

A long-overdue new carpet has given Shampers a cleaner edge, though the place still looks a world away from the minimalist modernity of two neighbouring bars. No matter: it has remained popular for two decades. Indeed, the crowds seem to have increased in the past few years, perhaps attracted by the lack of boys in shirts swigging bottled lager. Nine new wines on the Shampers list include the tasty 2003 Prado del Rey Ribera del Duero from Spain, though we'll sketch over the rather dull Latour chardonnay from the Ardèche. These join a list of around 150, with an impressive 28 by the glass at reasonable prices (below a fiver), such as Yalumba's 2006 'Y' series viognier. On the meat-dominated food menu there's a flavourful combination of lamb fillet with arrocina beans (small, white beans from Spain) and spinach. An ideal place for taking your mother after a hard day hitting the shops.

Babies and children admitted. Bar available for hire. Separate room for parties, seats 45. Tables outdoors (3, courtyard). **Map 17 A4**.

South Kensington

The Oratory

234 Brompton Road, SW3 2BB (7584 3493/ www.brinkleys.com). South Kensington tube. *Bar* **Open** noon-11pm Mon-Sun. **Meals served** noon-4pm; 6-11pm Mon-Sat; noon-4pm, 6-10.30pm Sun. *Restaurant* **Meals served** noon-11pm Mon-Sat; noon-10.30pm Sun. **Main courses** £7-£16. *Both* **House wine** £10.50 bottle, £3 glass. **Credit** AmEx, MC, V.

The age limit rarely dips below 40 and there are enough blazers, polo necks and pearls on display to make it seem as if you've landed at the Wimbledon tennis championships. To its credit, the Oratory has solicitous, friendly, able staff, and a look that's just the right side of kitsch: gold swirly fern patterns on eggshell-blue walls. The food appears to have dropped a notch in quality, with a rare beefburger lacking in size, meaty juices and flavour, and the bun missing its top half. In contrast, the wine list put out by owners Brinkley's (*see also p349* Putney Station) is excellent and fairly priced, with riesling from Clare Valley in Australia (2005, Skillogalee) at £15.50 and Hamilton Russell's 2003 pinot noir from South Africa at £28.50 – both examples of difficult grapes well handled. Some of the quality rubs off on the half-bottle list too, which is a much better proposition at lunch than the inadequate by-the-glass choice that satiates only the thirst for dull, flavourless pinot grigio. The view from the bar allows customers to see 4x4s sailing by on the road outside. Minor quibbles apart, though, the Oratory is a well-run place that deserves its popularity.

Babies and children admitted (restaurant). Booking advisable. Tables outdoors (6, pavement). **Map 14 E10**.

For branches (Brinkley's, Joe's Brasserie, Mortimer's, Wine Factory, Wine Gallery) see index.

Strand

Gordon's

47 Villiers Street, WC2N 6NE (7930 1408/ www.gordonswinebar.com). Embankment tube/ Charing Cross tube/rail. **Open** 11am-11pm Mon-Sat; noon-10pm Sun. **Meals served** noon-10pm Mon-Sat; noon-9pm Sun. **Main courses** £7.25-£9.75. **House wine** £12.95 bottle, £3.50 glass. **Credit** AmEx, MC, V.

Dripping with sweat, full of people and oozing charm, Gordon's is the classic wine bar with knobs on. Most of it is tucked under the low vaults by the Embankment. Here you can sit in semi-darkness with a date and a dripping candle. Watch your best suit, mind, as the brickwork is mouldy. If you want to come up for air, head for the bar: a high-ceilinged area full of old badminton racquets and pictures of Victorian nudes. Staff are loud and generally funny, serving lots of fortified stuff: fino or amontillado sherry (well-balanced sweet and acid, with burnished, fruit flavours) straight from barrels behind the bar, or a whole range of ports (white, LBV, tawny and 1985 vintage, many from the Messias stable). These come in what they call 'beakers', a 150ml serving, or, if you want to stay steady on your feet, 'schooners' (120ml, six to a bottle). A huge array of salads is displayed at a nearby counter (choose between smoked and poached salmon), all costing around £8. A taste of old London without the heritage naffness.

Babies and children admitted. Bookings not accepted dinner. Tables outdoors (20, terrace). Wi-Fi. **Map 10 L7**.

West

Shepherd's Bush

Albertine

1 Wood Lane, W12 7DP (8743 9593/ www.gonumber.com/albertine). Shepherd's Bush tube. **Open** 10am-11pm Mon-Thur; 10am-midnight Fri; 6.30pm-midnight Sat. **Meals served** noon-10.30pm Mon-Fri; 6.30-10.30pm Sat. **Main courses** £5.90-£9.50. **House wine** £11.40 bottle, £2.95 glass. **Credit** MC, V.

Despite a look that is best described as Oxbridge student bar circa 1980 – drippy candles, dark church pews, wines chalked on a large board – this long-standing venue has kept up with trends in the wine world. Australia forms a major part of the list, with posh versions of normally rather dull branded wines the highlight. Wynns 1996 John Riddoch cabernet sauvignon from Coonawarra, and Lindemans 1998 Pyrus from the same region, offer a chance to taste what these companies can really do. From an impressively long list of 38 wines by the glass, 2002 Redbank Fighting Flat shiraz from Victoria offered great chunks of wood and chocolate flavours, stained with blackcurrant and mint. Beef sausage with Guinness gravy was the only dish capable of standing up to such a wine, even though the accompanying mash tasted as if had been thinned out with milk. Albertine is a warm, convivial place with people chatting loudly and at length – a pleasant respite from much of Shepherd's Bush.

Bar available for hire. Bookings not accepted evenings. Off-licence. Separate room for parties, seats 25. Wi-Fi. **Map 20 B2**.

Westbourne Grove

Negozio Classica

283 Westbourne Grove, W11 2QA (7034 0005/ www.negozioclassica.co.uk). Ladbroke Grove or Notting Hill Gate tube. **Open** 11am-11pm Mon-Thur, Sun; 11am-midnight Fri, Sat. **Meals served** noon-10.30pm Mon-Thur, Sun; noon-11.30pm Fri, Sat. **Main courses** £6.95-£15.75. **House wine** £5.99 bottle, £3.50 glass. **Corkage** £5.50. **Credit** AmEx, MC, V.

With its modern lights, red walls and tiny dimensions, this bar has airport lounge coffee shop written all over it. Nevertheless, the quality of food and wine is top drawer. We enjoyed scouring the shelving of bottles filling one wall; all wines can be bought to take home, or drunk on site alongside the occasional posh local or shaggy-haired Euro student. The usual classic regions dominate, plus a smattering of hefty southern Italians: Altesino's 1998 Brunello di Montalcino 'Montosoli', and Li Veli 2004 'Orion' Primitivo from Puglia. There's also some very drinkable whites from ever-improving Slovenia; and white port from Churchill's, a commendable inclusion for its rarity. A good mid-priced option is the 2001 Barbera d'Asti from Spinetta, offering lovely violet and tar aromas, and a light texture that makes it suitable for lunchtime quaffing. Order it with a snack of beef carpaccio (striated with fat, dark and fully-flavoured) plus rocket and parmesan. Plenty of other delis offer more change from a £20 note, but none in Notting Hill is quite up to this standard.

Babies and children admitted. Off-licence. Tables outdoors (3, pavement). **Map 7 A6**.

South West

Earlsfield

Willie Gunn

422 Garratt Lane, SW18 4HW (8946 7773/ www.williegunn.co.uk). Earlsfield rail. **Open** 11am-11pm Mon-Sat; 11am-10.30pm Sun. **Meals served** 11am-10.30pm Mon-Sat; 11am-10pm Sun. **Main courses** £9.50-£15. **Set lunch** £7.50 1 course. **House wine** £12.50 bottle, £3.25 glass. **Credit** AmEx, MC, V.

In response to the new array of London wine bars, Willie Gunn has given the bar a smart new lick of paint and upped the quality in the restaurant at the back. Awnings loom over the slick black façade. Inside, there's a small bar where toned-down WAGs meet and middle-aged gents in specs read the paper alone. You can sit at the bar and chat to the friendly staff while sampling the wine list: impressive compared to Garratt Lane competition. The three rosés show how it should be done: one

rich and dark (Geoff Merrill, Oz), one more acidic and minerally (2005 Costières de Nîmes, France) and one lightly fruity (2005 Fortius Navarra, Spain). Elsewhere you need to spend a bit to get past the French country wine, 2005 Billaud-Simon Chablis being the real deal. The restaurant, all beiges and creams, offers a pricey but pleasing array of fashionable dishes such as roast halibut with spring onions and tiger prawns.
Babies and children welcome (until 6pm): high chairs. Booking advisable dinner. Tables outdoors (3, pavement).

Parsons Green

Amuse Bouche

51 Parsons Green Lane, SW6 4JA (7371 8517/ www.abcb.co.uk). Parsons Green tube. **Open** noon-11pm Mon, Sun; noon-midnight Tue-Thur; noon-12.30am Fri, Sat. **Lunch served** noon-3.30pm daily. **Dinner served** 6-10.30pm Mon-Sat; 4-9.30pm Sun. **Main courses** £4-£8.25. **House wine** £15 bottle, £5.50 glass. **Credit** AmEx, DC, MC, V.

Champagne bars are usually found in swanky town centre hotels, yet this busy place dedicated to high-quality fizz is located in Parsons Green. Wealthy banker types and women in hair bands splash out at will in calm, modern surroundings. Amuse Bouche has an advantage over central London hotel bars forced to list wines from one sponsoring champagne house only. It stocks 30 champagnes, from the crisply dry Laurent Perrier Ultra Brut to the sweet Louis Roederer Rich. A frequent mistake is to believe that different brands mean a variety of flavours, when a range of styles is needed too. It would be nice if some smaller growers were included in the list here, along with Lamandier-Bernier; and it's a shame that a medium-sized house, Ruinart, has been dropped. Never mind: the champagne comes at the right temperature, cold but not freezing, with plenty of bubbles and acidity – plus elegance in the case of Pol Roger White Label, with its characteristic touch of fruit. Some will be repelled by the braying customers who drink here, but this remains one of the best places in London dedicated to champagne.
Babies and children admitted. Booking advisable. Off-licence. Separate room for parties, seats 40. Tables outdoors (6, courtyard).

Putney

Putney Station

94-98 Upper Richmond Road, SW15 2SP (8780 0242/www.brinkleys.com). East Putney tube.
Bar **Open** 11.30am-midnight Mon-Sat; 11am-11pm Sun.
Restaurant **Meals served** noon-11.30pm Mon-Fri; 11am-11.30pm Sat, Sun. **Main courses** £4.50-£12.50 lunch; £7-£16 dinner.
Both **House wine** £10 bottle, £3.30 glass. **Credit** AmEx, MC, V.

Owned by Brinkley's, as is the Oratory (*see p348*), Putney Station is at opposite ends of the scale to that temple to bohemia. Here you'll find large plate-glass windows with metal frames, pot plants and venetian blinds. The look may be different from its sibling, but the food is up to the same high standard. A large plate of fish cakes made of potato, smoked haddock and tiny prawns arrived fried without breadcrumbs, and all the better for it. Chunks of tomato and red onion, with sorrel and lovely, earthy spinach made fine accompaniments. The wine list mirrors that of the Oratory too: good by the bottle, but poor by the glass. An exception to this rule was a glass of Rioja Marqués de Càceres 2002, which was showing delicious, fresh, raspberry-tinted flavours. Sure, you can find this wine in most off-licences, but the example we tried was in such good condition after five years of life, we reckon Brinkley's cellaring facilities make it worth a try even given the added mark-up. We also reckon this bar is ideal for a quick spot of lunch without the crowds.
Babies and children welcome: high chairs. Disabled: toilet. Separate room for parties, seats 40. Tables outdoors (3, pavement; 12, garden). Wi-Fi.

South East

Dulwich

★ Green & Blue

36-38 Lordship Lane, SE22 8HJ (8693 9250/ www.greenandbluewines.com). East Dulwich rail/ 37, 40, 176, 185 bus. **Open/tapas served** 9am-11pm Tue-Fri; 11am-11pm Sat, Sun. **Tapas** £6-£6.50. **House wine** £11.50 bottle, £3.20 glass. **Credit** MC, V.

There have been big changes at this outstanding wine bar – one of a wave of new places in London to combine a sit-down area and shop. Next door has been knocked through to form a deli counter and shelving for more wines, while the expanded bar is now packed, even on a lazy Sunday afternoon; and a new branch has opened in Clapham (on the former site of Vinifera). Green & Blue deserves the increase in business, the shabby-chic look being a backdrop for 150 carefully chosen wines, each accompanied by intelligent tasting notes and divided according to flavour. Staff suggested we try a 2004 Langhe Favorita 'Sarvai' (which offered weight and green pepper hints as well as expected citrus notes) to go with the 'fish plate' of rich gravadlax, organic bread plus rather poor, supermarket-style smoked mackerel. Few wines cost under £10, but this is no rip-off joint. Just £1 will buy you a litre bottle of filtered water, and for £3 you can take in your own food; staff will provide the plates and cutlery. These remarkable concessions, added to what is the most imaginative wine list of any shop or bar in London, more than earn G&B its red star.
Bar available for hire. Babies and children admitted (until 7pm). Off-licence. Wi-Fi. **Map 23 C4.**
For branch see index.

London Bridge & Borough

Wine Wharf

Stoney Street, SE1 9AD (7940 8335/www. winewharf.com). London Bridge tube/rail. **Open** 11.30am-11pm Mon-Sat. **Meals served** noon-10pm Mon-Sat. **Main courses** £4.50-£9. **House wine** £14 bottle, £3 glass. **Credit** AmEx, DC, MC, V.

A major overhaul of the Wine Wharf wine list, the first since it opened in 2000, has seen all but five bins receiving the chop – other wine bars take note. Most to benefit are Italian whites, with exciting new production reflected in a glass of 2005 La

1707. See p347.

DRINKING

Giustiniana, an apricot and almond-flavoured white from the Gavi di Gavi region. If you must have pinot grigio, sample the wares of expert winemaker Franz Haas, who offers his trademark zippy acidity but with white peach and complexity too. The US apart, the rest of the world is covered in expert style too, highlights including bottles from Western Australia winery Cullen and Chile's Leyda. Wine Wharf's casual brasserie food is less imaginative, with the inevitable fish-cakes paired with chilli sauce and chips, and a tasty warm duck leg confit coming with a beetroot dressing. The nooks and crannies of this warehouse space fill up quickly at night, but are eerily quiet during the day; probably the ideal time, then, to sneak in and sample some of the 100 wines by the glass. Wine Wharf's staff know their trade, as befits a venue sited so close to the Vinopolis wine museum.

Babies and children welcome (before 8pm): high chairs. Bar available for hire. Booking advisable. Disabled: toilet. Entertainment: jazz 7.30pm Mon. Off-licence. **Map 11 P8.**

North West

West Hampstead

No.77 Wine Bar

77 Mill Lane, NW6 1NB (7435 7787). West Hampstead tube/rail. **Open** 6-11pm Mon; noon-11pm Tue; noon-midnight Wed-Sat; noon-10.30pm Sun. **Meals served** 6-10.30pm Mon; noon-10.30pm Tue-Sat; noon-10pm Sun. **Main courses** £9.45-£15. **House wine** £12.50 bottle, £3 glass. **Credit** MC, V.

The classic 1980s wine bar lives on through the scrubbed wooden doors, spiral metal staircase and Monet prints of No.77. An array of rugby shirts in frames shows where the owners' sporting affections lie, and come Six Nations time the widescreen TV blares out games for a crowd of regulars. Although No.77 is off the West Hampstead main drag, it is surrounded by on-the-up Victorian terraced housing, and draws plenty of locals. Back to the mozzarella balls: these are part of a large choice of tapas costing about £3. Frankly, you're better off forking out a tenner or so for roast squash risotto, or sausage and mash. To drink, seven new whites have been added to the list – a praiseworthy move. There's a nod to the growing importance of coastal regions in Chile for aromatic grapes; Estampa's 2005 viognier-chardonnay 'Vo5' is a lovely, unctuous drop.

Babies and children admitted. Bar available for hire. Booking advisable. Tables outdoors (20, pavement). Wi-Fi. **Map 28 A1.**

The big four

There are four main wine bar chains in London, together responsible for around 100 outlets, many in the City. For venue details, check each chain's website; we also list all branches in the indexes at the back of this guide.

Balls Brothers

www.ballsbrothers.co.uk

It's easy to criticise places that look so old-fashioned, but many Balls Bros outlets are brim-full with women as well as men, and serve far better wine than most gastropubs. The firm also owns lighter, brighter venues in Victoria and near St Paul's, and has recently taken over a swish selection of seven Lewis & Clarke bars. Founded by Henry Balls in the middle of the 19th century, the company is still run by the same family (currently Richard Balls). There's no corporate air to the bars, and the wine selection isn't brand-dominated. A series of Balls Bros wine dinners has been instigated, many with a sporting flavour; Aussie cricketer Justin Langer was a recent attraction, if you're into that sort of thing.

How many? 15 bars, two restaurants, seven Lewis & Clarke bars (the Assembly, Cellar, Gable, Gallery, Last, Prophet, Sterling).

Best branches Any of the trendy and attractive new Lewis & Clarke bars in the City, but particularly the Assembly (Seething Lane, EC3), which has a slick new outdoor seating area. A more old-fashioned feel is found at Balls Brothers' Hay's Galleria branch, SE1, where there's a new British Grazing Platter, containing the likes of beef, Guinness and stilton meatballs.

Wines to try At last the wine list has been given an overhaul at the restaurant branches, reflecting the changing trends. Spain's progress has been recognised on lists such as Gow's in Old Broad Street, EC2; there's a new white from Castile-León. At the new Lewis & Clarke bars, New World choice is still minimal, but they have good drinking from provincial France. Burgundy and Bordeaux selections are excellent, as you'd expect of this long-trading firm. Try the 1988 Gruaud-Larose.

Corney & Barrow

www.corney-barrow.co.uk

Offering respite from the 'ye olde worlde' fare of most City wine bars, these concrete and glass edifices also provide good drinking. The range benefits from the link with the Corney & Barrow wine merchant business (founded 1780), with the New World being plundered as much as the classic regions of Bordeaux and Burgundy. Bars in the group target a business crowd, so quick lunches with unobtrusive service, and even champagne breakfasts, are the norm. Having experimented with fine-dining restaurants, then pulled back into a bars-only format, the group is now consolidating.

How many? 11 bars.

Best branches The branch at Paternoster Square, EC4 has great views of St Paul's Cathedral.

Wines to try There's a good spread here; you're in the unusual position of being able to down Gevrey-Chambertin from Domaine Trapet, Cuvée Ostréa, as well as good-value Aussie chardonnay from Heywood Estate. Too much dreary Sancerre, Chablis and Pouilly-Fumé let the side down a little, and the fine wine section could do with an overhaul. In contrast, there's some decent bottles from Spain, especially 2005 Pétalos del Bierzo from J Palacios, and a commendable 70 of the wines are available by the glass.

Davy's

www.davy.co.uk

The classic London wine bar look is served up by Davy's – so you won't find any style-bar zebra-patterned rugs. The dark wooden floors and sawdust (plus manacles and chains at the London Bridge branch) cater for City customers who like sipping their Bordeaux and Burgundy in traditional surroundings. Bars can be found as far afield as Barking in Essex.

How many? 39.

Best branches Don't be put off by some of the names. The Bung Hole Cellars on High Holborn, WC1 has a selection of fine wines that includes excellent-value Bordeaux, especially 1997 Gruaud-Larose at £58, plus 1963 Cockburn vintage port.

Wines to try Davy's list doesn't vary from place to place, but it excels in fortified wines. Two kinds of Madeira, sherry and a lovely Fonseca Guimaraens 1995 vintage port are among the highlights. If you want to drink New World chardonnay you should head elsewhere; the own-brand Davy's versions are drinkable, but no more. On the fine wine list, only Château Cantemerle from 1999 and Cockburn's vintage port stand out.

Jamies

www.jamiesbars.co.uk

In style, Jamies bars lie somewhere between the old-fashioned decor of Davy's and Balls Brothers, and the stark modernism of Corney & Barrow. The firm's PR bumf calls the look 'classic yet contemporary', a common fudge that refers to the stark walls but also the brass fittings. These venues are popular among City workers hankering after straightforward service and not too much design. The bars, which also include Hodgsons in Chancery Lane, WC2 and Number 25 in Birchin Lane, EC3 are owned by the Food & Drink Group, which also runs the Henry J Beans chain of American restaurants.

How many? 20, of which six are Jamies.

Best branches Jamies Bishopsgate, EC2 (by the Broadgate terrace), has floor-to-ceiling windows, comfortable leather banquettes and a buzzy but not overwhelmingly busy main room. There's also a pleasant outdoor terrace.

Wines to try 'We reject anonymous, blended industrial juice in favour of wines created by individuals', says the company. Well, there are no real boutique wines on the Jamies lists, and the Australian winemakers d'Arenberg aren't exactly tiny, but, to be fair, the presence of Stonier and Babich shows a commitment to less usual, premium-quality New World wine. 'National Treasures' is a nice way of showcasing grapes in which certain countries specialise, but overall Jamies has a lack of great drinking in classic French areas. Wine lists in Jamies' City branches are more thorough than those elsewhere.

Eating & Entertainment

Comedy

It's difficult to find a comedy venue that serves food and laughs of equal standard. There are, however, a few places in the capital that offer dishes of a higher quality than standard old-style pub grub. In south-east London, **Up the Creek** (302 Creek Road, SE10 9SW, 8858 4581, www.up-the-creek.com) is well worth a visit. Over in Maida Vale there's the **Canal Café Theatre** (first floor, The Bridge House, on the corner of Westbourne Terrace Road and Delamere Terrace, W2 6ND, 7289 6056, www.canalcafetheatre.com; map 1 C5), while in Shoreditch there's the **Comedy Café** (66-68 Rivington Street, EC2A 3AY, 7739 5706, www.comedycafe.co.uk; map 6 R4).

The best-known comedy club in London is probably Leicester Square's **Comedy Store** (1A Oxendon Street, SW1 4EE, bookings Ticketmaster 0870 060 2340, www.thecomedystore.co.uk; map 17 B5). Another favourite is **Jongleurs Camden Lock** (11 East Yard, Camden Lock, Chalk Farm Road, NW1 8AD, 0870 787 0707, www.jongleurs.com; map 27 C1) – which has two other London branches, in Battersea and Bow.

For up-to-date information on the capital's comedy clubs, see the Comedy section in the weekly *Time Out London* magazine.

Dining afloat

Vessels for hire include canal cruisers from the **Floating Boater** (Waterside, Little Venice, Warwick Crescent, W2 6NE, 7266 1066, www.floatingboater.co.uk; map 1 C5); the **Leven is Strijd** (West India Quay, Hertsmere Road, West India Docks, E14 6AL, 7987 4002, www.theleven.co.uk), a classic Dutch barge, for views of Canary Wharf; and the **Elizabethan** (8780 1562, www.thamesluxurycharters.co.uk), which is a replica of a 19th-century Mississippi paddle steamer that cruises from Putney to beyond the Thames Barrier.

The **Sunborn Yacht Hotel ExCeL** (Royal Victoria Dock, E16 1SL, 0870 040 4100, www.sunbornhotels.com) has good food, but a conference-centre vibe, while the **RS Hispaniola** next to Hungerford Bridge (Victoria Embankment, WC2N 5DJ, 7839 3011, www.hispaniola.co.uk; map 10 L8) is a popular party venue with tapas bar, cocktail lounge and a large restaurant.

DIY

Blue Hawaii

2 Richmond Road, Kingston upon Thames, Surrey KT2 5EB (8549 6989/www.bluehawaii.co.uk). Kingston rail. **Dinner served** 6pm-1am Mon-Sat. **Meals served** noon-1am Sun. **Set meal** £8.95-£11.95 unlimited barbecue. **Set dinner** £15 2 courses; (Fri, Sun) £19.50 3 courses; (8pm-1am Sat) £21.50 3 courses. **Credit** AmEx, DC, MC, V.

Every night is party night at Blue Hawaii. Surrey's own slice of the Big Island sees flowery-garbed waiting staff serve cocktails to bolshy birthday groups and after-work parties in a restaurant-cum-beach-hut setting. Ingredients are cooked to order on a big teppanyaki grill at the front; choose from a selection of vegetables, meat and seafood, mix in own-made Hawaiian sauces, select some spices and you're away. Cocktails are reasonably priced at around £4. Saturday nights play host to resident Elvis impersonator Matt King, while Sundays are more family-oriented.

Babies and children welcome: children's menu; high chairs; nappy-changing facilities; supervised play area (noon-5pm Sun). Booking essential weekends. Entertainment: musicians 10pm Fri, Sat.

Mongolian Barbeque

12 Maiden Lane, WC2E 7NA (7379 7722/www.themongolianbarbeque.co.uk). Covent Garden tube. **Meals served** noon-11pm Mon-Fri, Sun; noon-11.30pm Sat. **Set meal** £7.95 1 bowl, £9.95 starter & 1 bowl, £14.95 unlimited buffet. **Credit** AmEx, MC, V.

Genghis Khan and his warriors may have been a fearsome bunch, but after a hard day's fighting, they knew how to knock up a mean stir-fry. This venue takes inspiration from their ancient techniques, which seem to have involved throwing whatever ingredients are to hand into a metal 'shield' to create an impromptu meal. Diners pick the ingredients, sauces and spices, and chefs fry it in front of them on a metal hot plate. A wide range of ingredients includes Indian, Thai and Chinese flavours. Recipes on the wall help to guide combinations. As you'd expect, it's a popular venue with party groups and families.

Babies and children welcome: children's menu; high chairs. Booking advisable. Tables outdoors (8, patio). **Map 18 E5.**

Dogs' dinners

Walthamstow Stadium

Chingford Road, E4 8SJ (8531 4255/www.wsgreyhound.co.uk). Walthamstow Central tube/rail then 97, 97A, 215, 357 bus. **Meals served** 6.30-9.30pm Tue, Thur, Sat. **Set meal** £19 3 courses incl admission. **Admission** *Popular enclosure* £1 Tue, Thur; £3 Sat. *Main enclosure* £6 Tue, Thur, Sat. Free under-15s. **Credit** MC, V.

It's been north-east London's dog racing mecca since 1933, so you'll need to book three or four weeks in advance to get into Walthamstow Stadium's main restaurants on a Saturday. The Paddock Grill offers à la carte dining; the Stowaway Grill does a three-course set menu for £19. At both restaurants views of the track are good, and you can lay bets from your table. If you want a cheaper option, there's also the Classic Diner, offering burgers, chicken and chips.

Volupté. See p356.

Babies and children welcome: high chairs; nappy-changing facilities. Booking essential (Sat). Disabled: toilet. Private boxes for parties, seating 25-200.

Wimbledon Stadium

Plough Lane, SW17 0BL (8946 8000/www.lovethedogs.co.uk). Tooting Broadway tube/ Earlsfield rail/44, 270, 272 bus. **Dinner served** 7-9.30pm Tue, Fri, Sat. **Set meal** £20-£25 3 courses; £25-£30 3 courses incl half bottle of wine and racecard. **Admission** £5.50 grandstand. **Credit** MC, V.

With a choice of two restaurants, you can chow down at the dogs in style and comfort without missing any of the action. Star Attraction offers long rows of benches overlooking the finish line; Broadway, with its more intimate layout, shows all the races on TVs. Both eateries serve a range of internationally inspired dishes. Regular famous faces include Vinnie Jones and Jimmy White, who races his own greyhounds on the track.

Babies and children welcome: high chairs; nappy-changing facilities. Booking essential. Disabled: lift; toilet. Separate rooms for parties, seating 28-120.

Jazz & soul

Dover Street

8-10 Dover Street, W1S 4LQ (7629 9813/ www.doverstreet.co.uk). Green Park or Piccadilly Circus tube. **Open** noon-3.30pm, 5.30pm-3am Mon-Sat. **Lunch served** noon-3.30pm Mon-Fri. **Dinner served** 7pm-2am Mon-Sat. **Music** *Bands* 9.30pm Mon; 7.30pm Tue-Sat. *DJs* until 3am Mon-Sat. **Main courses** £13.95-£21.95. **Set lunch** £7-£12 1 course incl drink, £21.95 2 courses incl drink. **Set dinner** £24.95-£45 3 courses. **Admission** £6 after 10pm Mon; £7 after 10pm Tue; £8 after 10pm Wed; £12 after 10pm Thur; diners only until 10pm, then £15 Fri, Sat. **Credit** AmEx, DC, MC, V.

Is it a music venue or a restaurant? Well, it's a bit of both. Enjoy early evening cocktails at one of two bars, admiring the black-and-white fashion and jazz prints that adorn the walls. Then dine from a Modern European menu created by ex-L'Aventure chef Laurent Pichaureaux while a lounge jazz trio tootle away. After dinner, jazz bands invite diners on to the dancefloor to work off their desserts.

Booking advisable, essential weekends. Dress: smart casual. Separate rooms for parties, seating 20-100. **Map 9 J7.**

Green Note

106 Parkway, NW1 7AN (7485 9899/ www.greennote.co.uk). Camden Town tube. **Dinner served** 6-9.30pm Wed, Thur; 6-10pm Fri. **Meals served** noon-10pm Sat; noon-9.30pm Sun. **Music** 9-11pm daily. **Tapas** £2.25-£4.95. **Main courses** £7.95-£9.95. **Admission** £4-£8. **Credit** MC, V.

Paintings of folk icons Joni Mitchell and Bob Dylan adorn the walls of this Greenwich Village-style hangout for Camden's beatniks. Dine in the café/restaurant area out front, or the music venue in the back. Acts on the bill range from folk and blues to jazz and world music. The fully vegetarian menu offers a wide selection of tapas, fresh salads, and main course specials that change daily. Puddings include a vegan tofu cheesecake. Check website for gig listings and prices.

Babies and children admitted: high chair. Booking advisable. Vegan dishes. **Map 27 C3.**

Jazz After Dark

9 Greek Street, W1D 4DQ (7734 0545/ www.jazzafterdark.co.uk). Leicester Square or Tottenham Court Road tube. **Open** 2pm-2am Mon-Thur; 2pm-3am Fri, Sat. **Meals served** 2pm-midnight Mon-Sat. **Music** 9pm Mon-Thur; 10.30pm Fri, Sat. **Main courses** £5-£10. **Set menu** £10.95 3 courses. **Admission** £5 Mon-Thur; £10 Fri, Sat, £15 for non-diners. **Credit** AmEx, DC, JCB, MC, V.

Jazz After Dark is a jazz club of the old school: small, low-lit and laid-back. A young, after-work crowd take in unsigned bands and seasoned professionals, playing a range of jazz, blues, funk and Latin; some nights see impromptu sets from regular Pete Doherty. The cuisine is international, ranging from tapas to Tex-Mex, and an extensive cocktail list includes the 'ultimate mojito'.

Booking essential Fri, Sat. Dress: smart casual; no trainers. Restaurant available for hire. Tables outdoors (2, pavement). **Map 17 C3.**

Jazz Café

5-7 Parkway, NW1 7PG (7916 6060/www.meanfiddler.com). Camden Town tube. **Open** 7pm-1am Mon-Thur; 7pm-2am Fri, Sat; 7pm-midnight Sun. **Meals served** 7.30-9.30pm daily. **Music** 8.30pm daily. *Club nights* 11pm-2am Fri, Sat. **Main courses** £16.50. **Set meal** £26.50 3 courses. **Admission** £15-£45. **Credit** MC, V.

The balcony restaurant at this well-established venue has tables overlooking the stage, where a classy mix of soul, R&B, jazz and acoustic rock acts strut their stuff. The line-up often attracts a slightly more mature music fan, though things liven up on weekend club nights when diners descend on to the dancefloor. Check the website to see who's playing when.

Booking advisable. Disabled: toilet. **Map 27 D2.**

Pizza Express Jazz Club

10 Dean Street, W1D 3RW (7439 8722/ www.pizzaexpresslive.com). Tottenham Court Road tube.

Restaurant **Meals served** noon-midnight daily. *Club* **Meals served** 7.30-11.15pm daily. **Music** 9-11.15pm daily. **Admission** £15-£20. *Both* **Main courses** £4.95-£8.25. **Credit** AmEx, DC, MC, V.

Crowds have been loyally flocking to the basement club of this pizzeria since it opened in 1965. Acts have varied from Van Morrison to Amy Winehouse; up-and-coming stars often make the line-up. Pizza Express standards make the eating part of the equation perfectly pleasant, and the atmosphere is always friendly. Musicians play seven nights a week; check the website for details.

Babies and children welcome: high chairs. Booking advisable. Disabled: toilet. Takeaway service. **Map 17 B3.**

Ronnie Scott's

47 Frith Street, W1D 4HT (7439 0747/ www.ronniescotts.co.uk). Leicester Square or Tottenham Court Road tube. **Open/music** 6pm-3am Mon-Sat; 6pm-midnight Sun. **Meals served** 6pm-1am Mon-Sat; 6-11pm Sun. **Main courses** £9-£29.50. **Set meal** £23 2 courses. **Admission** (non-members) £25-£100. **Membership** £165/yr. **Credit** AmEx, DC, MC, V.

Opened in 1959, Ronnie Scott's is one of the UK's oldest and best-known jazz venues. The likes of Tony Bennett still occasionally perform in this intimate setting; on Tuesday nights, young musicians rip it up at a past-midnight jam session. The menu features internationally styled dishes ranging from seared yellowfin tuna to organic burgers. The website offers details of forthcoming acts, online booking and a jazz podcast.

Booking advisable. Disabled: toilet. Dress: no shorts. Members bar available for hire. **Map 17 C3.**

606 Club

90 Lots Road, SW10 0QD (7352 5953/ www.606club.co.uk). Earl's Court tube. **Open/ meals served** 7.30-11.45pm Mon; 7pm-12.30am Tue, Wed; 7pm-midnight Thur; 8pm-1.30am Fri, Sat; 7-11.30pm Sun. **Music** 9pm Mon; 7.30pm Tue, Wed; 8pm Thur; 9.30pm Fri, Sat; 8.30pm Sun. **Main courses** £8.95-£18.45. **Admission** (non-members) £8 Mon-Thur; £12 Fri, Sat; £10 Sun. **Membership** £95 first yr; £60 subsequent yrs. **Credit** AmEx, MC, V.

This candle-lit, Parisian-style basement jazz club has been chilling out Chelsea jazz aficionados both here on Lots Road and at its former location (606 King's Road) for over 30 years. There's music every night; the number of musicians that hang out after work give it some serious muso credibility. Diners can choose from a contemporary European menu that changes each month. Note that if you're not a member, you have to dine.

Babies and children admitted. Booking advisable weekends. **Map 13 C13.**

Latin

Nueva Costa Dorada

47-55 Hanway Street, W1T 1UX (7631 5117/ www.costadoradarestaurant.co.uk). Tottenham Court Road tube. **Open** noon-3am Tue-Fri; 5pm-3am Sat. **Lunch served** noon-3pm Tue-Fri. **Dinner served** 5pm-3am Tue-Sat. **Main courses** £13-£21. **Set lunch** (Tue-Fri) £8.95 2 courses. **Credit** AmEx, DC, MC, V.

Revamped under new management, Costa Dorada is no longer a tiled flophouse for post-midnight fun. It's still a popular choice for office parties, with dining tables set around a stage where nightly flamenco shows are performed (Tue-Sat). Decor has been refreshed, and the emphasis is now on a cosy cocktail bar feel. An expanded (still Spanish) menu offers tapas as well as à la carte options such as sea bream with basil crushed potatoes (£15.50), or paella to share (£21). Cocktails are £6.50; happy hour (5-7pm Tue-Sat) brings the price of most classics down to £4.

Babies and children admitted (until 11pm). Entertainment: DJ 11pm Thur-Sat; flamenco shows 9.30pm Tue-Thur, 10pm Fri, Sat. Restaurant available for hire. **Map 17 B2.**

Salsa!

96 Charing Cross Road, WC2H 0JG (7379 3277/www.barsalsa.info). Leicester Square or Tottenham Court Road tube.

Bar **Open** 5.30pm-2am Mon-Sat; 6pm-1am Sun. *Café* **Open** 9am-5.30pm Mon-Sat. **Snacks served** noon-5.30pm Mon-Sat. **Set buffet** (noon-6pm Mon-Sat) 99p per kilo. *Restaurant* **Meals served** 5.30-11pm daily. **Main courses** £4.75-£11.50. *Bar & Restaurant* **Admission** £4 after 9pm Mon-Thur; £2 after 7pm, £4 after 8pm, £8 after 9pm, £10 after 11pm Fri, Sat; £3 after 7pm, £4 after 8pm Sun. *All* **Credit** AmEx, MC, V.

Dance classes are held in the bar here on most evenings, followed by bands and DJs spinning commercial Latin hits – so you can practise your newly acquired moves into the night. Classes are £5 an hour, suitable for beginners as well as the more experienced. Free sessions are offered on Fri (6.30-8.30pm) and Sun (7-8pm). The cocktail list is substantial; check in at happy hour (5.30-7.30pm daily) for price reductions, or on Tuesday when caipirinhas are cost just £2 all night. During the week the café offers an authentic Brazilian buffet, charged by weight.

Booking advisable, essential weekends. Dress: smart casual. Entertainment: DJs 9.30pm daily; dance classes 7pm Mon, Wed-Sun; bands 9.30pm Tue, Thur, Fri, Sat. Tables outdoors (10, pavement). Takeaway service (café). **Map 17 C3.**

Music & dancing

The much-loved **Spitz** music venue is due to leave its Spitalfields home in October, and at the time of writing is still looking for new premises. Visit www.spitz.co.uk for more details.

Pigalle Club

215-217 Piccadilly, W1J 9HN (7734 8142/ www.thepigalleclub.com). Piccadilly Circus tube. **Open** 7pm-2am Mon-Wed; 7pm-3am Thur-Sat. **Dinner served** 7-11.30pm Mon-Sat. **Admission** £10 after 10pm Mon-Thur; £15 after 10.30pm Fri, Sat. **Credit** AmEx, DC, MC, V.

Part of the Vince Power stable, this 1940s-style supper club is a great music venue, with retro-swanky furnishings (the design is by interiors guru Shaun Clarkson), low lighting and tables with good views of the stage. Food is not as quite successful as the decor – it's pricey, and service can be wildly inconsistent. Still, a decent house band and headline acts (Van Morrison and Marianne Faithfull have played in the past) help to ease any disappointment. Thursday sees the popular Kitsch Lounge Riot. Cocktails are reasonable, and the expansive wine list offers house wine from £16.

Entertainment: band 8.30pm, 9.45pm, 10.45pm daily. **Map 17 B5.**

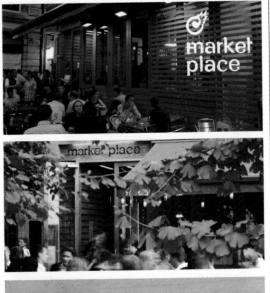

Roadhouse

35 The Piazza, WC2E 8BE (7240 6001/ www.roadhouse.co.uk). Covent Garden tube. **Open** 5.30pm-3am Mon-Sat; 3-11pm last Sun of mth. **Meals served** 5.30pm-1.30am Mon-Sat. **Main courses** £6.50-£13.90. **Admission** £3 after 10.30pm Mon-Wed; £5 after 10pm Thur; £10 after 9pm Fri; £5 after 7pm, £12 after 9pm Sat; £5 after 7pm Sun. **Credit** AmEx, MC, V.

The Roadhouse is a prime target for beery lads and riotous hen bashes (stag parties, however, are now banned), attracted by the happy-hour cocktails, DJs and rock/pop cover bands playing party anthems. You'll find comfort food such as chicken wings, steaks and nachos on the American diner menu.

Booking advisable. Dress: smart casual. Entertainment: bands/DJs 7pm Mon-Sat. **Map 18 E4.**

Tiroler Hut (100)

27 Westbourne Grove, W2 4UA (7727 3981/ www.tirolerhut.co.uk). Bayswater or Queensway tube. **Open** 6.30pm-1am Tue-Sat; 6.30pm-midnight Sun. **Dinner served** 6.30pm-midnight Tue-Sat; 6.30-11pm Sun. **Main courses** £10.90-£16.90. **Set meal** (Fri, Sat) £21.50 3 courses. **Credit** AmEx, DC, MC, V.

This kitsch, family-run basement restaurant is a breath of fresh air in otherwise staid Bayswater. It's utterly bizarre. The interior is decorated to resemble a traditional alpine ski lodge, and the waiting staff are all clad in lederhosen. More serious is the good selection of German and Austrian beers and wines. Tirolean music performances (Wed-Sun), ranging from accordions to cowbells, often get diners on their feet; the occasional sing-a-long means this is not a place for the easily embarrassed. In terms of food, expect sausages, sauerkraut, and strudel. Vegetarians are well catered for too.

Babies and children admitted. Booking essential. Entertainment: cowbell show 9pm Wed-Sun. Restaurant available for hire. Vegan dishes. **Map 7 B6.**

One-offs

Dans Le Noir

30-31 Clerkenwell Green, EC1R 0DU (7253 1100/www.danslenoir.com/london). Farringdon tube/rail. **Lunch served** by appointment. **Dinner served** (fixed sittings) 7-7.30pm, 9-9.30pm Mon-Thur; 7-7.30pm, 9.15-9.45pm Fri, Sat. **Set dinner** £29 2 courses, £37 3 courses. **Credit** AmEx, MC, V.

Launched in Paris in 2004, Dans Le Noir's pitch black interior has diners, quite literally, left in the dark – it's pitch black, and food is served by blind staff. An à la carte menu is eschewed in favour of a rather disconcerting 'surprise menu' concept – you order one of four different options (including a vegetarian choice) and then guess what you are eating. The competent Modern European menu is changed on a monthly basis. It's a little expensive, but the 'sensory culinary experience' gimmick is remarkable and educative. Napkin up; you'll drop plenty of food down your front.

Booking essential. Disabled: toilet. Separate room for parties, seats 60. **Map 5 N4.**

Lucky Voice

52 Poland Street, W1F 7NH (7439 3660/www. luckyvoice.co.uk). Oxford Circus tube. **Open/ snacks served** 6pm-1am Mon-Thur; 3pm-1am Fri, Sat; 3-10.30pm Sun. **Credit** AmEx, MC, V.

This small, stylish karaoke bar, decorated in contemporary red and black Japanese design motifs, offers reasonably priced (£7) oriental-themed cocktails such as a Lucky Destiny (vodka, cucumber, mint, kiwi, pressed apple juice) or an Otzu Spice (saké and apple schnapps mixed with sticky ginger apple jam and ginger). Saké and shochu are sold by the bottle. The karaoke pods have no stage and are very cramped, but there's an extensive playlist; friendly staff bring the drinks to you. The oriental snacks (bento boxes, vegetable gyoza) are not sensational, but work well enough.

Entertainment: karaoke pods for hire; £5-£10 per hr. Over-21s only. **Map 17 A3.**

Rainforest Café

20 Shaftesbury Avenue, W1D 7EU (7434 3111/ www.therainforestcafe.co.uk). Leicester Square or Piccadilly Circus tube. **Meals served** noon-10pm Mon-Thur, Sun; noon-7.30pm Fri, Sat. **Main courses** £10.25-£16. **Credit** AmEx, DC, MC, V.

The ultimate themed restaurant. This tropical hideaway in the heart of the West End, designed to thrill children with its animatronic animals, fishtanks, cascading waterfalls and jungle sound effects, cuts few aesthetic corners. The menu has plenty of family-friendly fare, from pizza and sausages for the kids to a host of amusingly named dishes for the grown-ups – 'Major Mojo Bones' (ribs) and 'Rasta Pasta' (with chicken and peppers), for instance. Try to steer them away from the shop full of stuffed toys the way out.

Babies and children welcome: bottle-warmers; children's menu; crayons; high chairs; nappy-changing facilities. Separate rooms for parties, seating 11-100. **Map 17 B5.**

Troubadour

263-267 Old Brompton Road, SW5 9JA (7370 1434/www.troubadour.co.uk). West Brompton tube/rail.

Café **Open** 9am-midnight daily. **Meals served** 9-11pm daily.

Deli **Meals served** noon-10pm Mon-Fri; 10am-10pm Sat, Sun.

Club **Open** 8pm-midnight Mon-Wed, Sun; 8pm-2am Thur-Sat. **Main courses** £8.25-£16.50. **Credit** MC, V.

This café-bar, part folk club, part tearoom, has a long and distinguished history. Part of London's 1950s bohemian café movement, it's had a lot of

Tiroler Hut

DRINKING

famous faces through its doors: this is where Dylan played his first London gig, *Private Eye* was first produced, and Ken Russell became mates with Oliver Reed. The café offers made-to-order sandwiches and bistro-style dishes (omelettes, burgers, fish cakes). The basement club hosts music, poetry readings and stand-up comedy (check the website for details). The deli offers gourmet, made-to-order sandwiches, a selection of charcuterie, cheeses and dry goods; there is also a traiteur counter selling prepared dishes from the café kitchen. The art gallery above the deli is available to hire for exhibitions or private parties.
Babies and children welcome: children's portions; high chairs. Tables outdoors (8, garden).
Map 13 B11.

Twelfth House

35 Pembridge Road, W11 3HG (7727 9620/ www.twelfth-house.co.uk). Notting Hill Gate tube. *Bar* **Open/snacks served** noon-11pm Mon-Fri; 10am-11pm Sat; 10am-10.30pm Sun. *Restaurant* **Meals served** noon-10pm Mon-Fri; 10am-10pm Sat, Sun. **Set menu** £14.50 2 courses, £19.50 3 courses.
Both **Credit** MC, V.
Reviving the 18th-century tradition of coffeeshop fortune-telling, this mystical, magical-themed café/ restaurant offers 'astrological chart sessions' with owner Priscilla for £30. You can also have your basic chart printed for £5, or select a 'tarot card of the day' for £3. The restaurant on the ground floor serves an international set menu, which changes every few months. Happy hour in the bar (6-8pm Mon-Thur) sees drink reductions; there's also a new range of astrologically-themed tipples.
Babies and children admitted (restaurant). Booking advisable. Restaurant available for hire, seats 25. Tables outdoors (4, garden).
Map 7 A7.

Volupté

7-9 Norwich Street, EC4A 1EJ (7831 1622/ www.volupte-lounge.com). Chancery Lane tube. **Open** 11.30am-1am Tue-Thur; 11.30am-3am Fri; 7.30pm-3am Sat. **Lunch served** 11.30am-4pm Tue-Fri. **Dinner served** 6-10pm Tue-Fri; 7.30-10.30pm Sat. **Main courses** £10.50-£21.
Credit MC, V.
As London's latest neo-burlesque bar, Volupté offers everything from jazz/rock bands and cabaret crooners to 1920s flapper dancers and table magicians. Food is international and organic; the menu changes on a monthly basis. Decently priced retro cocktails are served in the upstairs bar, warming up a louche crowd before they move downstairs for a glittery show in the fabulous Moulin Rouge-style stage room.
Booking advisable. Dress: smart casual. Entertainment: cabaret 8pm Tue-Sat. Restaurant available for hire. **Map 11 N5.**

Opera

Claiming 'the perfect acoustics for live opera', oriental restaurant **Gilgamesh** (*see p255*) holds opera nights on a Tuesday. Performances last for 20 minutes, and start at 8.30pm and 9.30pm.

Bella Italia

45 The Mall, W5 3TJ (8840 5888/www.bella italia.co.uk). Ealing Broadway tube/rail. **Meals served** 9.30am-11pm Mon-Thur, Sun; 9.30am-11.30pm Sat, Sun. **Main courses** £5.50-£15.
Credit AmEx, MC, V.
Sunday night is opera night at this rustic-themed family-friendly trattoria, and it gets packed. Against the backdrop of a traditional Italian kitchen and courtyard, complete with hanging washing and garlic, the singer walks among diners performing well-known works. Formerly Mamma Amalfi's, it's now part of the Bella Italia stable, so the menu includes a competent selection of pizzas, pastas and salads.
Babies and children welcome: children's menu; high chairs. Booking advisable Sun evening. Entertainment: opera 8pm Sun. Separate rooms available for parties, seating 15-25. Tables outdoors (8, pavement). Takeaway service.

Sarastro

126 Drury Lane, WC2B 5QG (7836 0101/ www.sarastro-restaurant.com). Covent Garden or Holborn tube. **Meals served** noon-11.30pm daily. **Main courses** £7.50-£15.50. **Set lunch** (noon-6.30pm Mon-Sat) £12.50 2 courses. **Set meal** £23.50 3 courses incl coffee. **Credit** AmEx, DC, MC, V.
Named after a character from Mozart's *The Magic Flute*, this flamboyant restaurant continues the operatic theme with individually styled boxes, velvet drapes, theatrical props and other colourful frippery. Established singers and up-and-coming stars from the nearby opera houses provide the entertainment, while the food is Mediterranean/ Turkish. Sister outfit Papageno is similarly showy.
Babies and children welcome: high chairs. Booking advisable. Disabled: toilet. Entertainment: opera, string quartet 1.30pm, 8.30pm Mon, 8.30pm Sun. **Map 18 F3.**
For branch (Papageno) see index.

Sports bars

All Star Lanes

Victoria House, Bloomsbury Place, WC1B 4DA (7025 2676/www.allstarlanes.co.uk). Holborn tube. **Open** 5-11.30pm Mon-Wed; 5pm-midnight Thur; noon-2am Fri, Sat; noon-11pm Sun. **Meals served** 6-11.30pm Mon-Wed; 6pm-midnight Thur; noon-2am Fri, Sat; noon-11pm Sun. **Bowling** (per person per game) £7.50 before 5pm; £8.50 after 5pm. **Credit** AmEx, MC, V.
A sleeker, more adult alternative to retail park bowling alleys that are filled with children's parties, All Star Lanes styles itself on Stateside 'boutique' bowling alleys. There are four lanes (plus two private lanes upstairs) and diner-style booths at which to enjoy burgers, steaks and the spectacle of players bowling gutterballs. Loosen up your bowling arm with a 1920s style cocktail (£6.90-£7.90) at the bar, or choose from a wide selection of bourbons. Branches in Bayswater and Shoreditch are set to open by 2008.
Babies and children admitted (until 6pm). Booking advisable. Disabled: toilet. Separate room for parties, seats 30. **Map 18 E1.**

Bloomsbury Bowling Lanes

Basement, Tavistock Hotel, Bedford Way, WC1H 9EU (7691 2610/www.bloomsburylive.com). Russell Square tube. **Open** noon-2am Mon-Wed; noon-3am Thur-Sat; noon-midnight Sun. **Meals served** noon-11.30pm daily. **Main courses** £6.95-£12.95. **Bowling** from £36/hr 1 lane (maximum 6 people); £3 (per person per game) Mon-Wed until 4pm. **Credit** AmEx, MC, V.
More than just a venue to throw down a few strikes, this 1950s-styled slice of Americana also offers three karaoke rooms (seating 8-20), a film-screening room for hire, and regular club nights and bands within earshot of the lanes. The Kingpin suite, with private lanes for hire, is set to open in November 2007. Burgers from the diner start at £6.95; lane-side snacks cost £6.50.
Booking essential. Disabled: toilet. No under-18s after 4pm. **Map 4 K4.**

Elbow Room

89-91 Chapel Market, N1 9EX (7278 3244/ www.theelbowroom.co.uk). Angel tube. **Open** 5pm-2am Mon; noon-2am Tue-Thur; noon-3am Fri, Sat; noon-1am Sun. **Meals served** 5-10pm Mon; noon-10pm Tue-Sun. **Main courses** £5-£8. **Admission** £5 9pm Sat. **Pool** £6-£10 per hr. **Credit** MC, V.
This popular, retro-chic bar has 11 pool tables on which to rack up some frames. Evenings and weekends are lively; there can be a long wait for a table. Regular DJs play a mixture of indie, funk and house, and a dancefloor provides leg room for the trendy, clubby crowd. Drinks include some fluorescent cocktails alongside the regulation lagers; dine at leather upholstered booths from a menu of burgers and wraps. Club and band nights are posted on the website.
Booking advisable weekends. Disabled: toilet. Entertainment: DJs 7pm Thur-Fri, 9pm Sat, Sun. Separate room for parties, seats 30. **Map 5 N2.**
For branches see index.

Sports Café

80 Haymarket, SW1Y 4TE (7839 8300/ www.thesportscafe.com). Piccadilly Circus tube/Charing Cross tube/rail. **Open** 11.30am-4am Mon, Tue, Fri; 11.30am-3am Wed, Thur; 11am-4am Sat; 11am-3am Sun. **Meals served** noon-11pm daily. **Main courses** £7.95-£16.95. **Admission** £5 after 10pm Mon, Tue, Fri, Sat. **Credit** AmEx, MC, V.
More brand than bar, the Sports Café's flagship London operation offers beer, burgers and non-stop TV sports. More than 100 screens beam out anything sport-related from football and rugby league to Formula One and tennis, as well as American sports for the noticeable US contingent. It's cramped and noisy for the big games, buy you can escape to shoot some pool (there are 11 tables), or grab a bite (buffalo wings, burgers, ribs, steaks) in the dining areas. DJs play chart hits from 10pm most nights.
Children admitted (until 9pm, dining only). Disabled: toilet. Music (DJs 10pm Mon, Tue, Fri, Sat). Restaurant available for hire.
Map 10 K7.

24-hour eats

Tinseltown

44-46 St John Street, EC1M 4DT (7689 2424/ www.tinseltown.co.uk). Farringdon tube/rail. **Open** 24hrs daily. **Main courses** £6-£13. **Set lunch** (noon-5pm Mon-Fri) £5.50 2 courses incl soft drink. **Unlicensed.** No alcohol allowed. **Credit** AmEx, DC, MC, V.
Late-night clubbers refreshing themselves on thick peanut butter milkshakes, cabbies and insomniacs frequent this Hollywood-themed basement diner and milkshake bar near Smithfield Market. Slide into a booth and munch on halal burgers, watch music videos and admire the photos of stars such as Travolta and De Niro lining the walls. Some settle in to wait for the first tube home. A sister restaurant in Hampstead is open until 3am on Friday and Saturday nights.
Babies and children welcome: children's menu; high chair. Takeaway service. **Map 5 O5.**
For branches see index.

Vingt-Quatre

325 Fulham Road, SW10 9QL (7376 7224/ www.vingtquatre.co.uk). South Kensington tube. **Open** 24hrs daily. **Main courses** £7.25-£14.75. **Credit** AmEx, MC, V.
Not your average 24-hour greasy spoon, this. V-Q caters for a posh post-club Kensington & Chelsea crowd, fresh out of high-class hotspots like nearby Boujis, and thirsty for more champers (a half-bottle of Krug will set you back £69). The more reserved look to wind down with a range of therapeutic teas (£3.50). Smart, uniformed staff serve classy versions of late-night fare. A full english starts at £7.25; the menu also features fish and chips, steak, club sandwiches with fries, and more adventurous options such as miso-glazed baby back ribs.
Babies and children admitted. Tables outdoors (2, pavement). **Map 14 D12.**

Views & victuals

Vertigo 42 Champagne Bar

Tower 42, 25 Old Broad Street, EC2N 1HQ (7877 7842/www.vertigo42.co.uk). Bank tube/ DLR/Liverpool Street tube/rail. **Open** noon-3pm, 5-11pm Mon-Fri. **Lunch served** noon-2.15pm, **dinner served** 5-9.30pm Mon-Fri. **Main courses** £5.50-£19. **Credit** AmEx, DC, MC, V.
Situated on the 42nd floor of Tower 42 (right at the top!), this bar offers truly breathtaking views. Seats are arranged so everyone can enjoy the panorama. Recently redecorated in a soothing purple colour-scheme, it now offers a selection of dishes from the menu of British restaurant Rhodes Twenty Four, some 18 floors down. Security arrangements mean that prior booking is essential for both bar and restaurant; diners must obtain a pass and walk through an X-ray machine. Be punctual: the last admission time (9.45pm) is strictly enforced.
Bar available for hire. Booking essential. Disabled toilet; lift. Dress: smart casual. **Map 12 Q6.**

Maps

The following maps highlight London's key restaurant areas – the districts with the highest density of good places to eat and drink. The maps show precisely where each restaurant is located, as well as major landmarks and underground stations. For an overview of every area, see Key to Maps **below; this shows which areas are covered, and places them in context.**

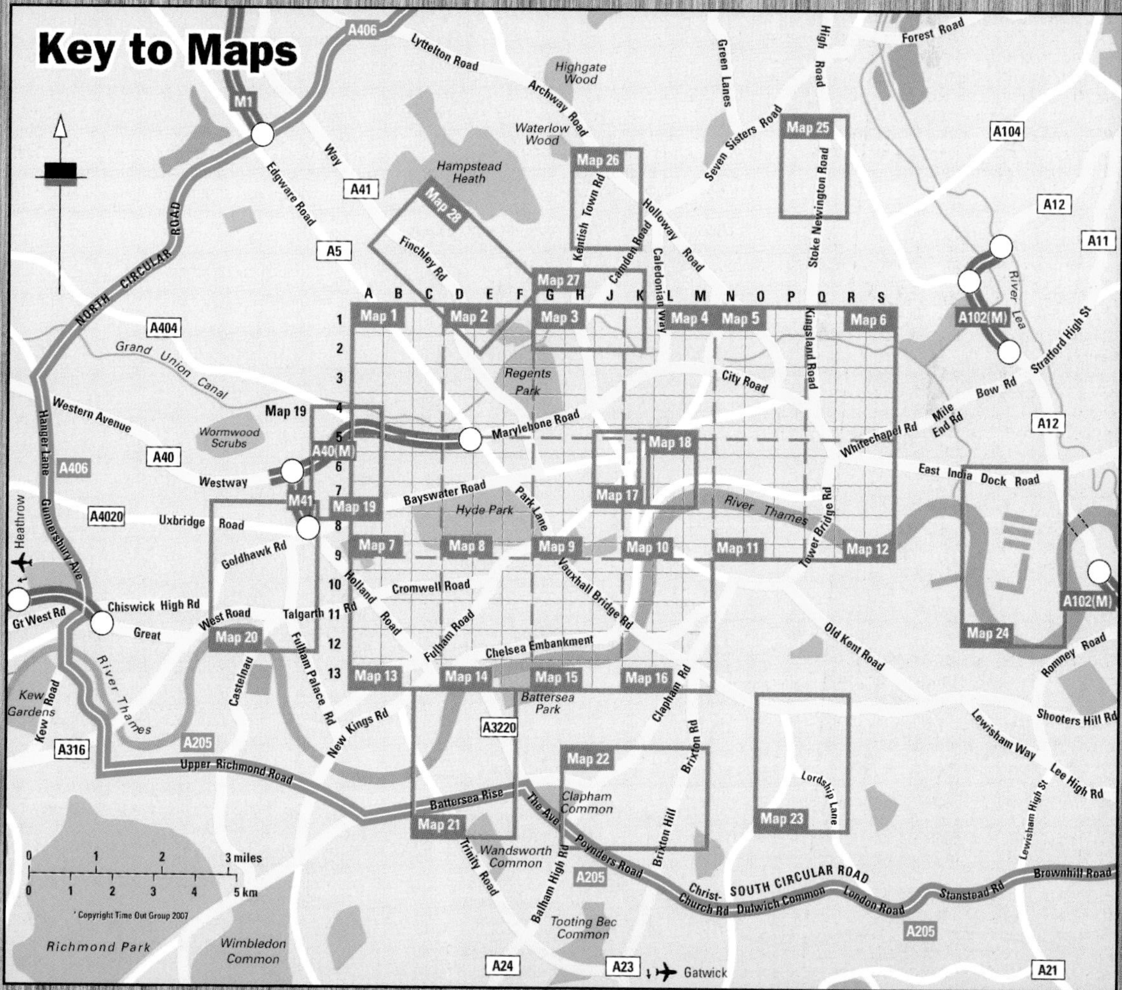

Key to Maps

In association with

Queen's Park & Maida Vale

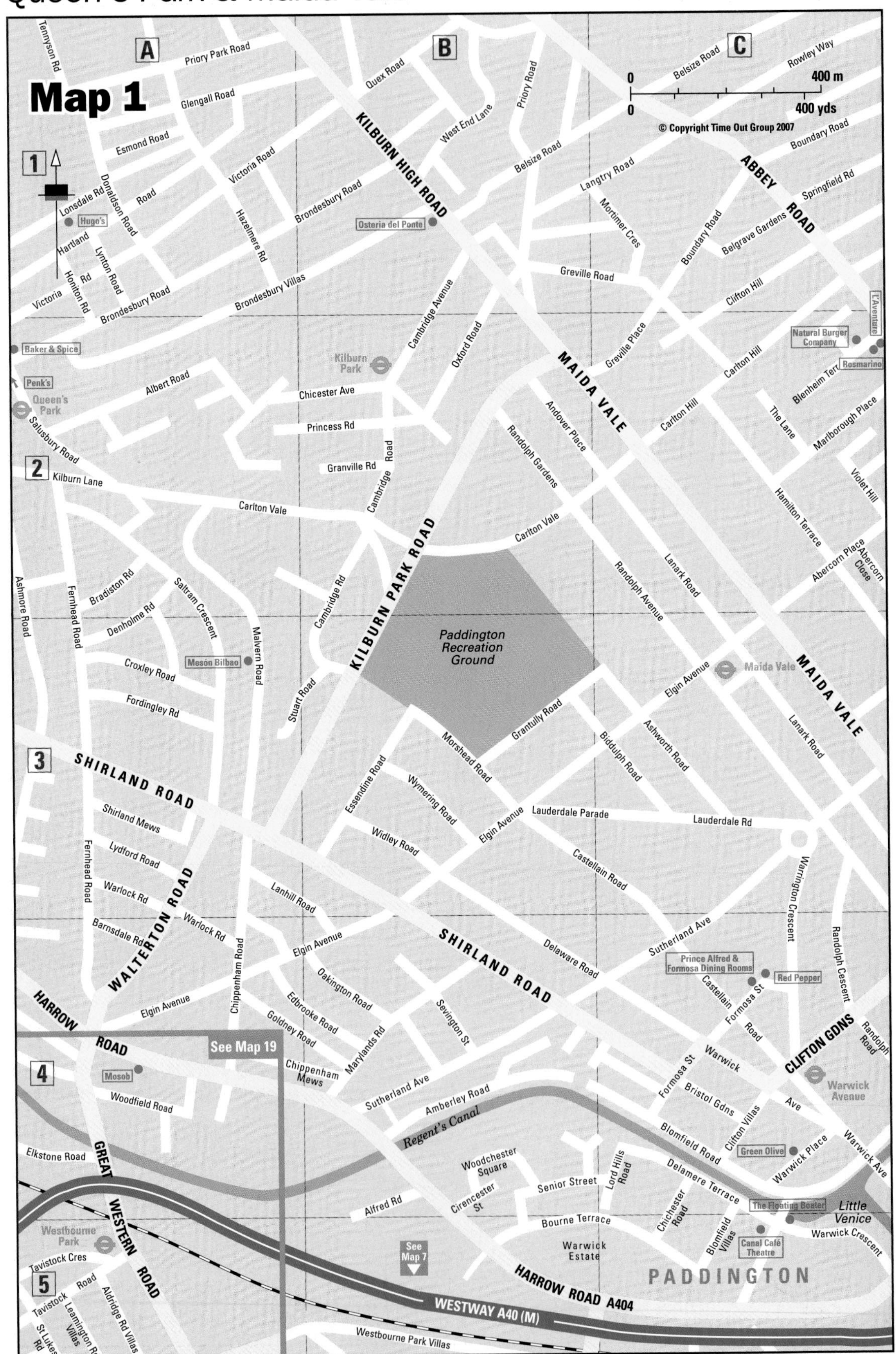
Map 1
A
B
C
1
2
3
4
5
0
400 m
0
400 yds
© Copyright Time Out Group 2007
Tennyson Rd
Priory Park Road
Glengall Road
Esmond Road
Quex Road
West End Lane
Priory Road
Belsize Road
Rowley Way
Boundary Road
KILBURN HIGH ROAD
Victoria Road
Road
Lonsdale Rd
Donaldson Road
Hugo's
Hartland
Lynton Road
Honiton Rd
Rd
Victoria
Brondesbury Road
Brondesbury Villas
Hazelmere Rd
Brondesbury Road
Osteria del Ponte
Langtry Road
Mortimer Cres
ABBEY ROAD
Springfield Rd
Belgrave Gardens
Greville Road
Clifton Hill
L'Aventure
Natural Burger Company
Rosmarino
Blenheim Terr
Baker & Spice
Penk's
Queen's Park
Kilburn Park
Cambridge Avenue
Oxford Road
Albert Road
Chicester Ave
Princess Rd
Granville Rd
Cambridge Road
Greville Place
MAIDA VALE
Andover Place
Randolph Gardens
Carlton Hill
The Lane
Marlborough Place
Violet Hill
Salusbury Road
Kilburn Lane
Carlton Vale
Carlton Vale
Hamilton Terrace
Abercorn Place
Abercorn Close
Ashmore Road
Fernhead Road
Bradiston Rd
Denholme Rd
Saltram Crescent
Croxley Road
Fordingley Rd
Mesón Bilbao
Malvern Road
Cambridge Rd
KILBURN PARK ROAD
Stuart Road
Paddington Recreation Ground
Randolph Avenue
Lanark Road
Elgin Avenue
Maida Vale
MAIDA VALE
Lanark Road
Grantully Road
Biddulph Road
Ashworth Road
Morshead Road
SHIRLAND ROAD
Shirland Mews
Lydford Road
Warlock Rd
Warlock Rd
Barnsdale Rd
Fernhead Road
WALTERTON ROAD
Essendine Road
Wymering Road
Widley Road
Elgin Avenue
Lauderdale Parade
Lauderdale Rd
Castellain Road
Warrington Crescent
Randolph Crescent
Lanhill Road
Elgin Avenue
SHIRLAND ROAD
Delaware Road
Sutherland Ave
Prince Alfred & Formosa Dining Rooms
Red Pepper
Castellain Road
Formosa St
HARROW ROAD
Elgin Avenue
Chippenham Road
Oakington Road
Edbrooke Road
Goldney Road
Marylands Rd
Sevington St
See Map 19
Chippenham Mews
CLIFTON GDNS
Randolph Road
Mosob
Woodfield Road
Sutherland Ave
Amberley Road
Regent's Canal
Formosa St
Warwick Ave
Warwick Avenue
Bristol Gdns
Blomfield Road
Clifton Villas
Green Olive
Warwick Place
Warwick Ave
Elkstone Road
GREAT WESTERN ROAD
Woodchester Square
Senior Street
Lord Hills Road
Delamere Terrace
Chichester Road
The Floating Boater
Little Venice
Warwick Crescent
Alfred Rd
Cirencester St
Bourne Terrace
Warwick Estate
Blomfield Villas
Canal Café Theatre
Westbourne Park
Tavistock Cres
Tavistock Road
Leamington Rd Villas
Aldridge Rd Villas
St Lukes Rd
See Map 7
HARROW ROAD A404
PADDINGTON
WESTWAY A40 (M)
Westbourne Park Villas

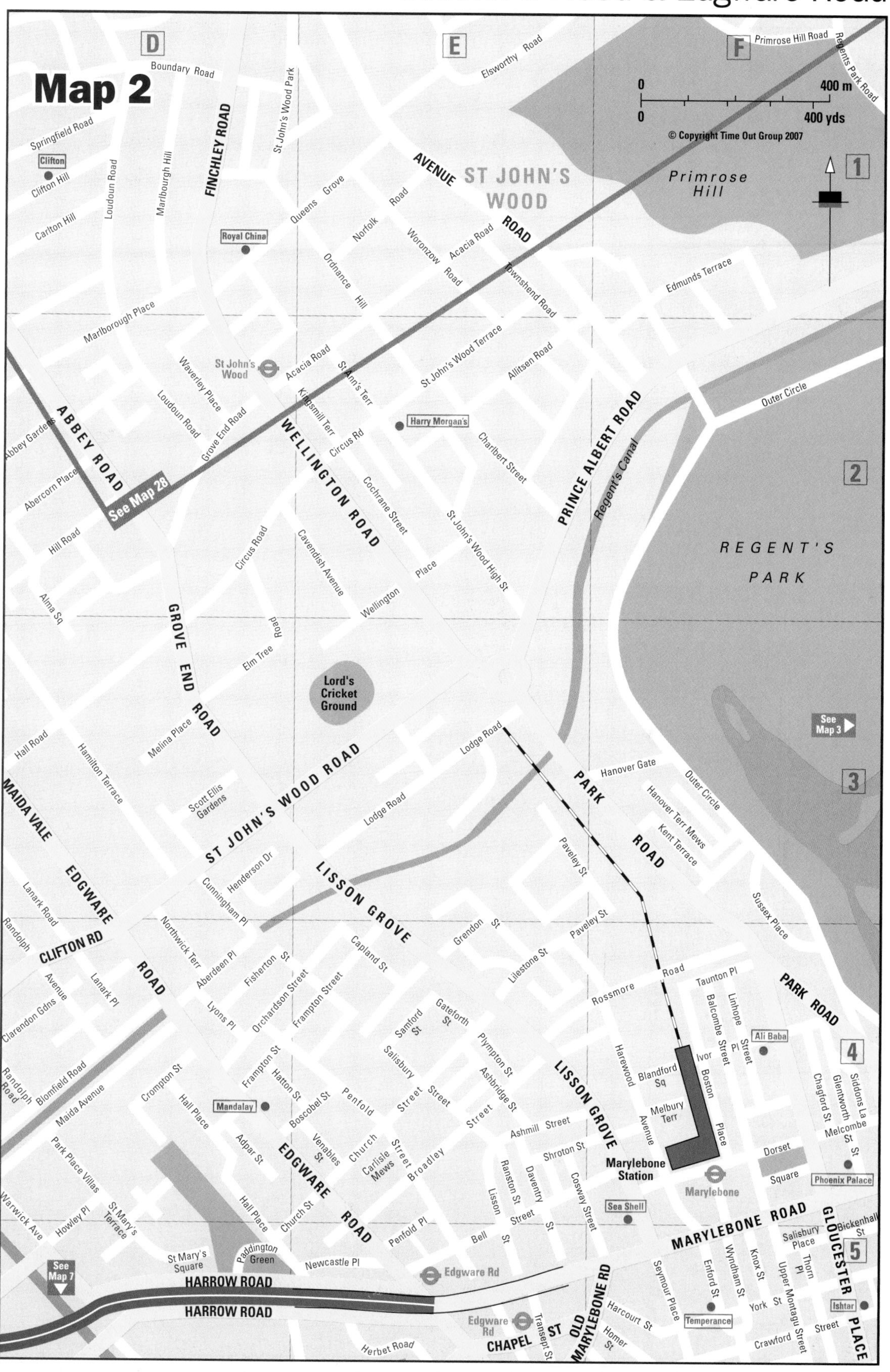

Map 2
© Copyright Time Out Group 2007
ST JOHN'S WOOD
Primrose Hill
REGENT'S PARK
Lord's Cricket Ground
Marylebone Station
See Map 28
See Map 3
See Map 7

Camden Town & Marylebone

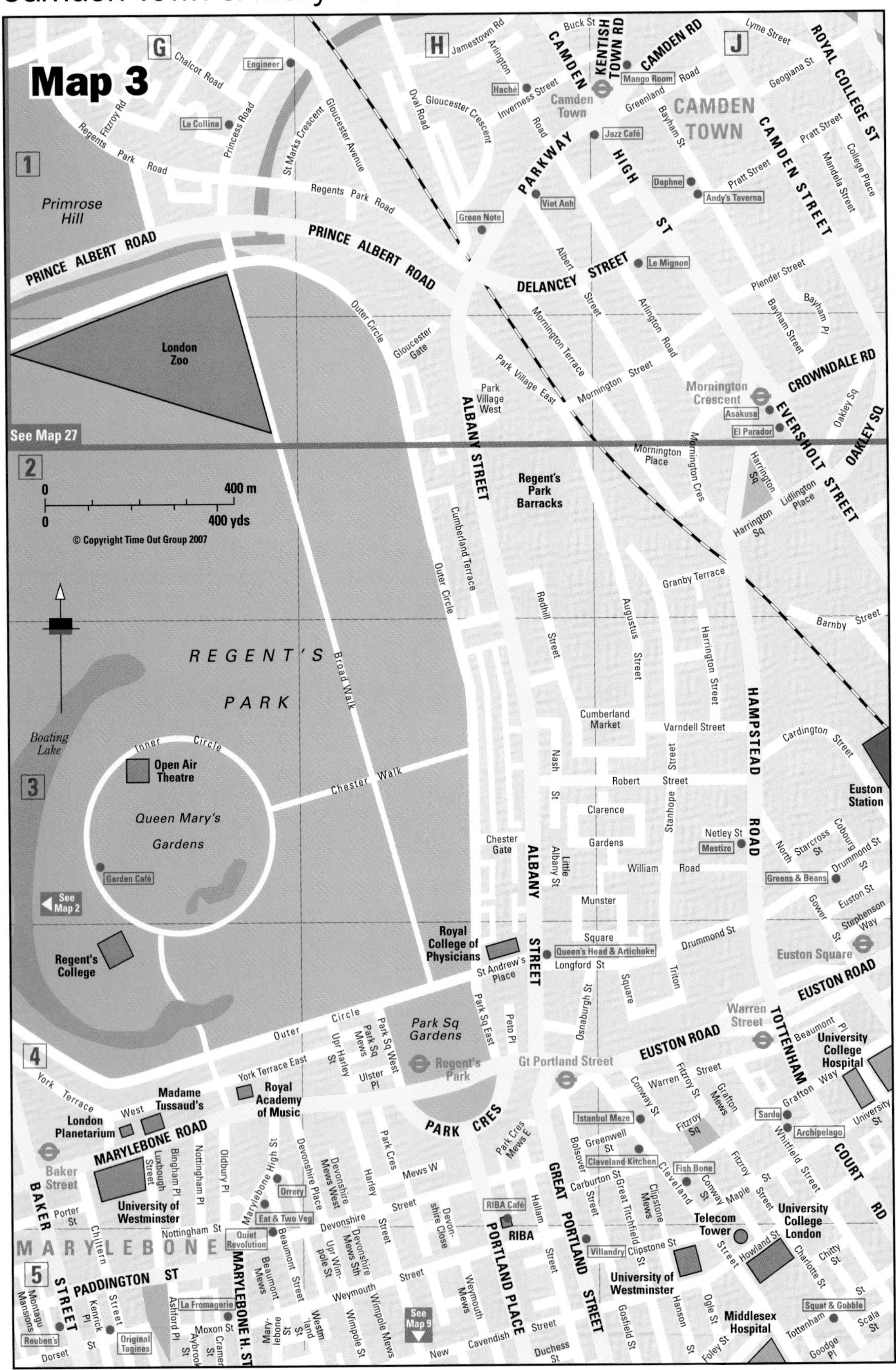

Euston, King's Cross & Bloomsbury

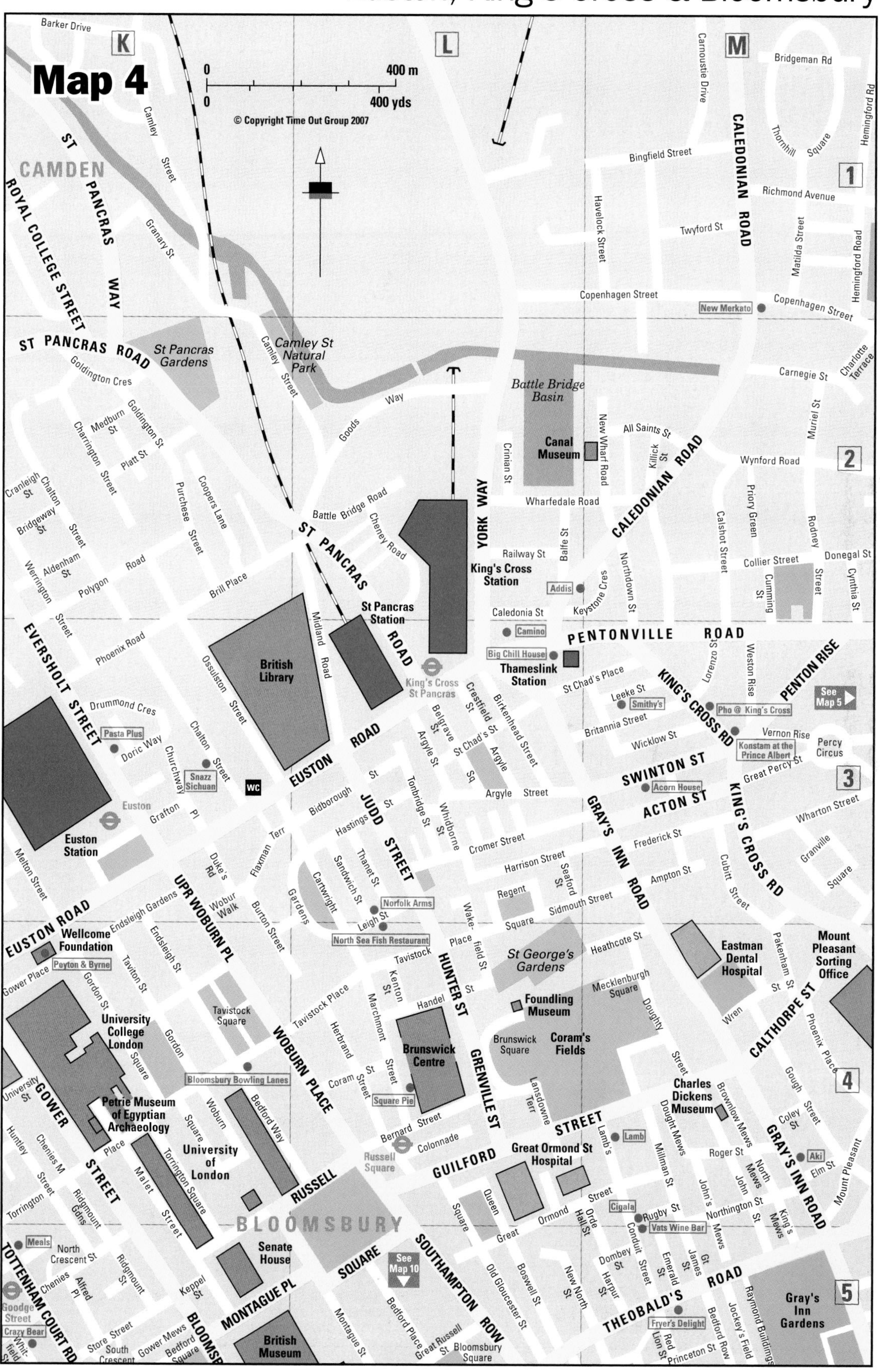

MAPS

Islington, Clerkenwell & Farringdon

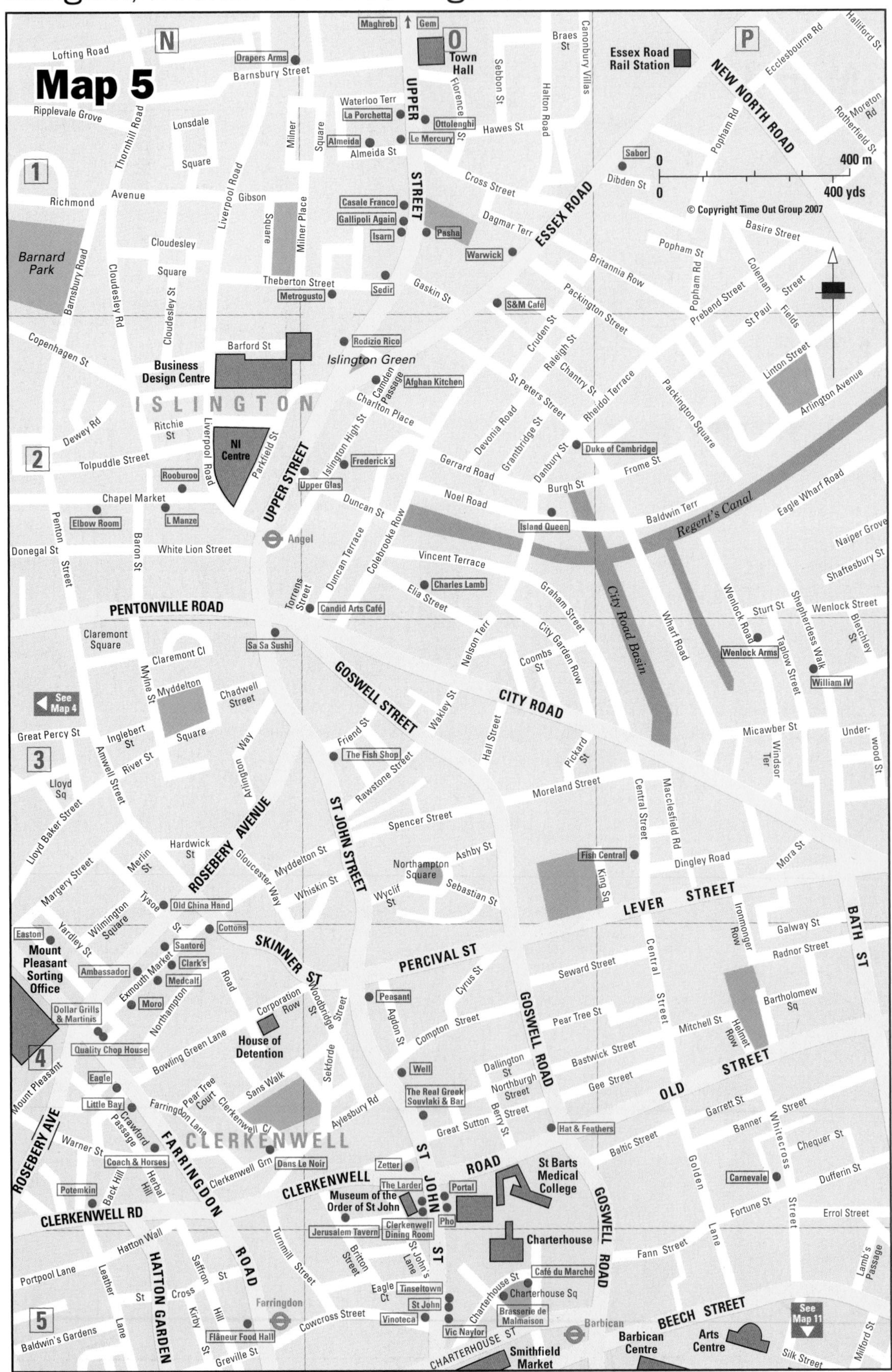

MAPS

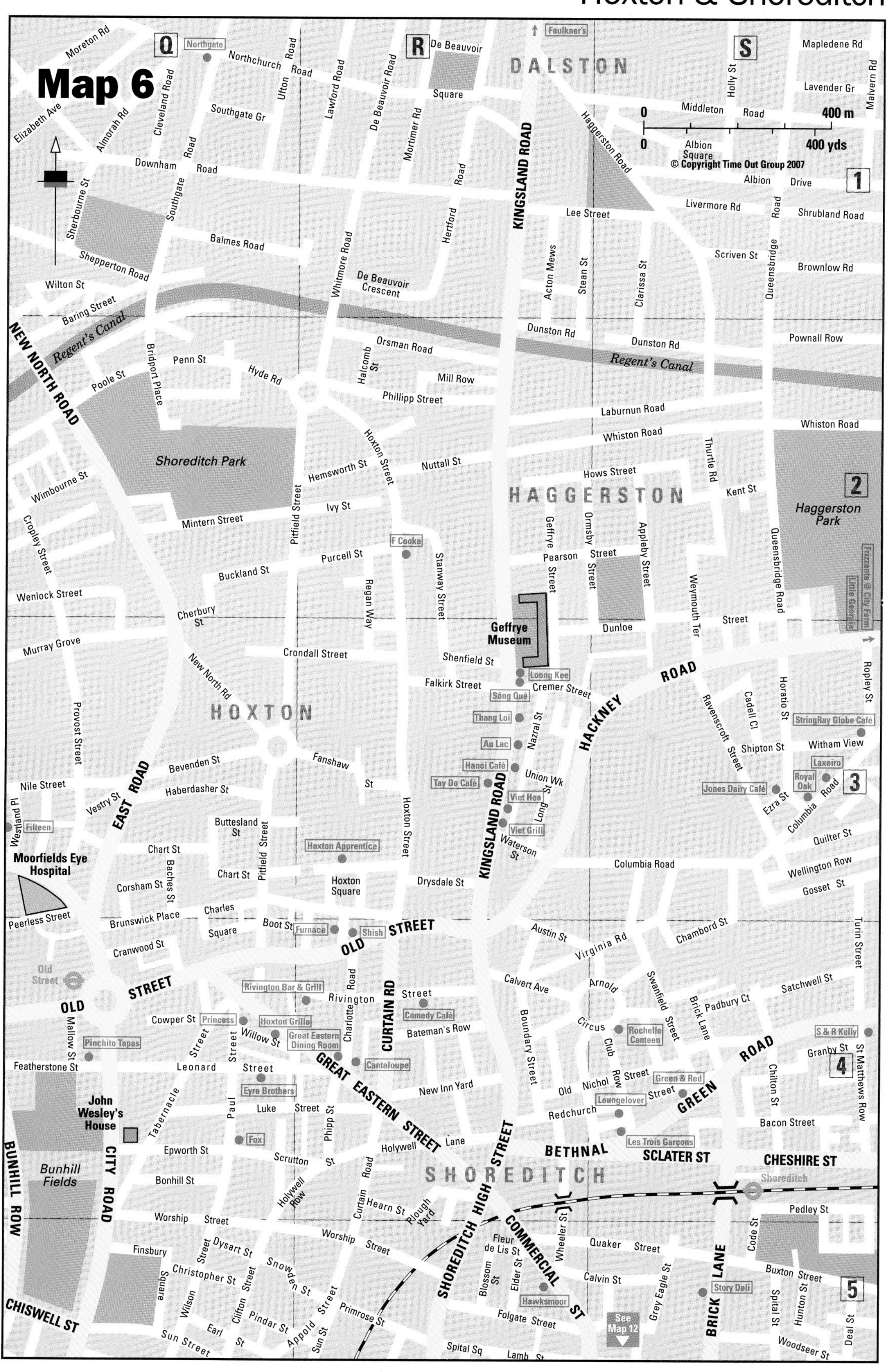
Map 6
DALSTON
HAGGERSTON
HOXTON
SHOREDITCH
Shoreditch Park
Haggerston Park
Regent's Canal
Geffrye Museum
Moorfields Eye Hospital
John Wesley's House
Bunhill Fields
KINGSLAND ROAD
NEW NORTH ROAD
EAST ROAD
CITY ROAD
OLD STREET
HACKNEY ROAD
GREAT EASTERN STREET
SHOREDITCH HIGH STREET
COMMERCIAL ST
BETHNAL GREEN ROAD
SCLATER ST
CHESHIRE ST
BRICK LANE
CURTAIN RD
BUNHILL ROW
CHISWELL ST
0 400 m
0 400 yds
© Copyright Time Out Group 2007
See Map 12
Northgate
Faulkner's
F Cooke
Loong Kee
Sông Quê
Thang Loi
Au Lac
Hanoi Café
Tay Do Café
Viet Hoa
Viet Grill
Hoxton Apprentice
Fifteen
Furnace
Shish
Rivington Bar & Grill
Princess
Hoxton Grille
Great Eastern Dining Room
Comedy Café
Cantaloupe
Pinchito Tapas
Eyre Brothers
Fox
Rochelle Canteen
Green & Red
Loungelover
Les Trois Garçons
Hawksmoor
Story Deli
StringRay Globe Café
Laxeiro
Royal Oak
Jones Dairy Café
S & R Kelly
Frizzante @ City Farm
Little Georgia
Old Street
Shoreditch

MAPS

Notting Hill, Bayswater & Kensington

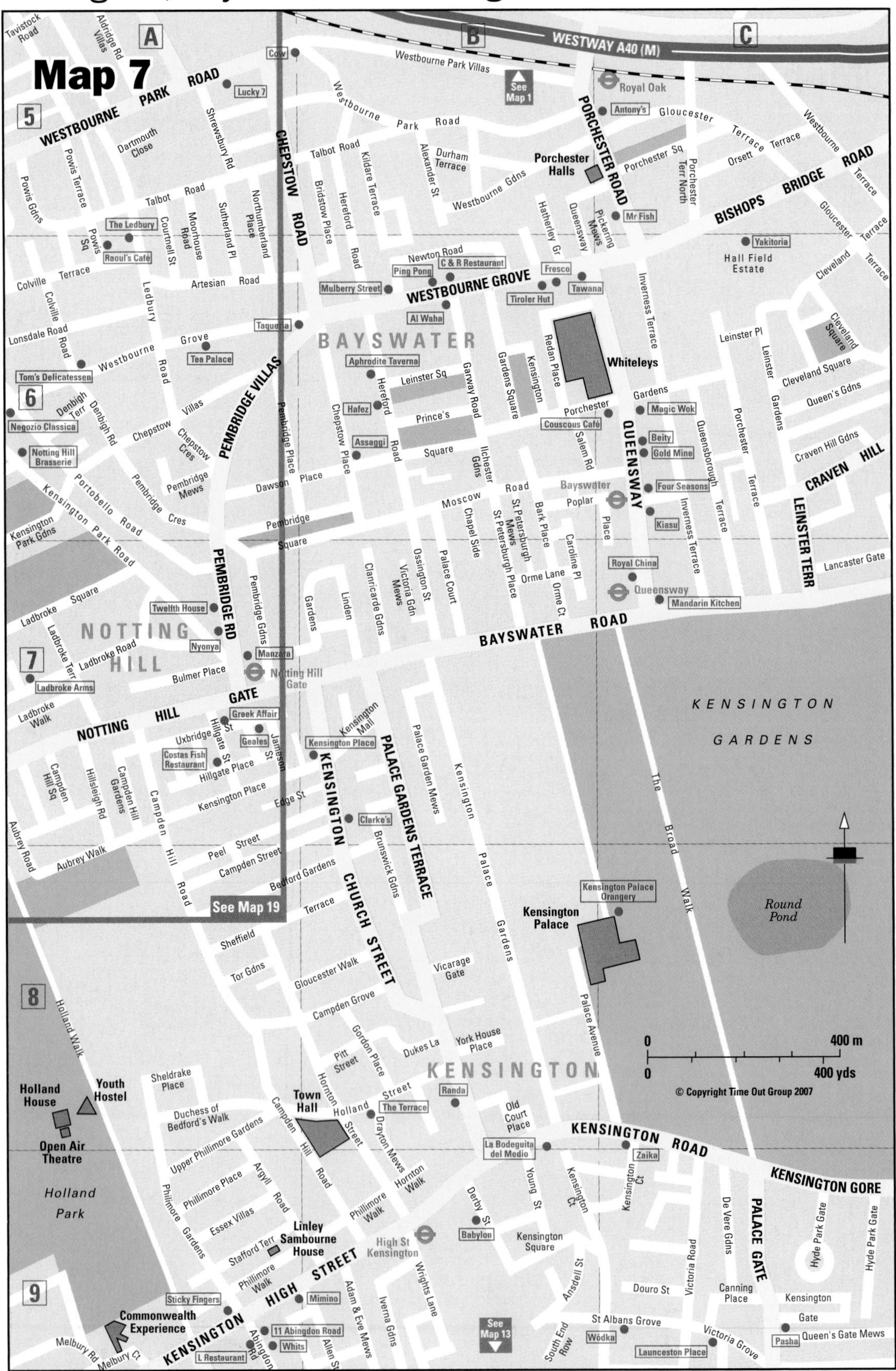

MAPS

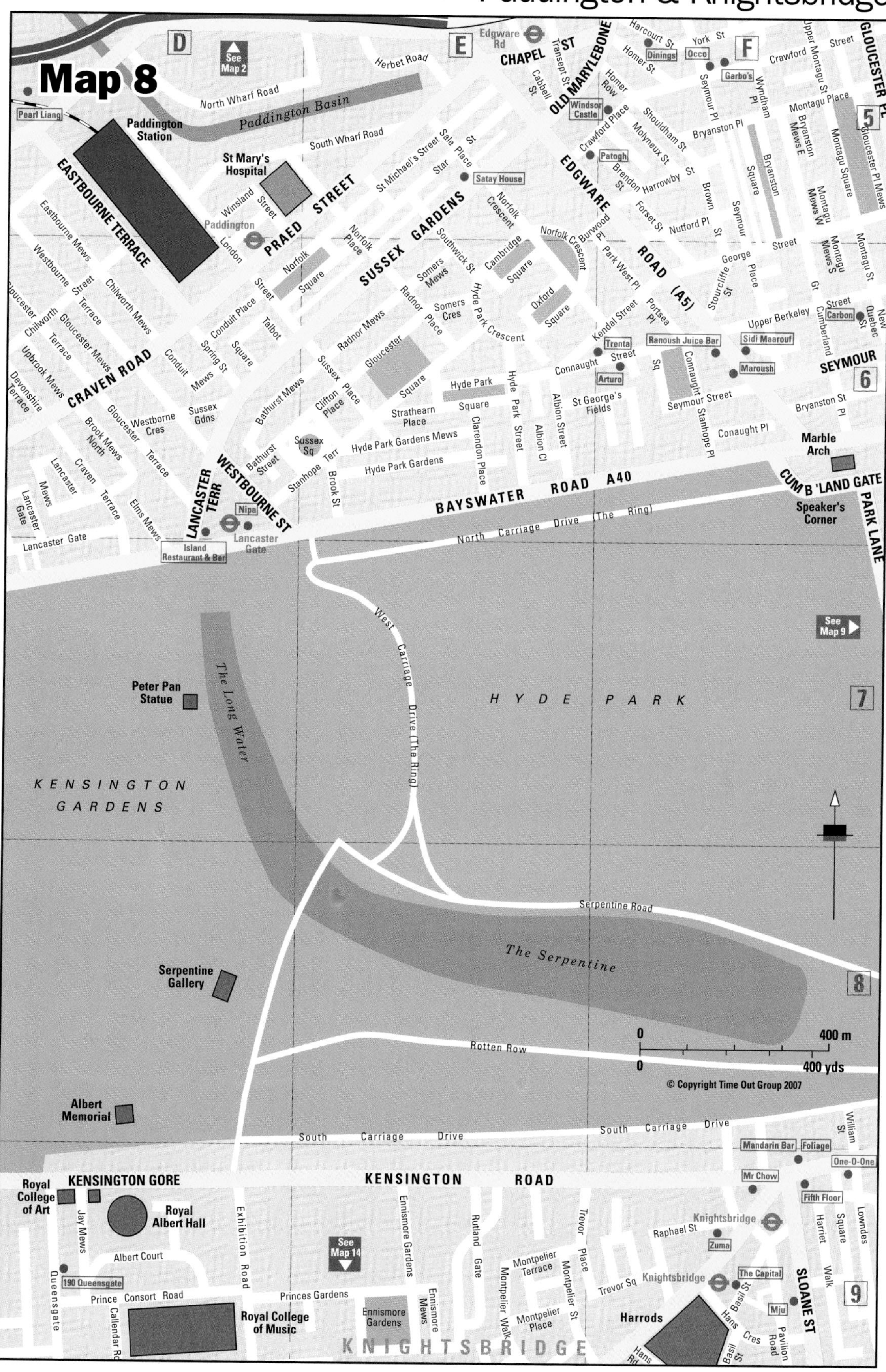
Map 8
D
E
F
See Map 2
Pearl Liang
Paddington Station
North Wharf Road
Paddington Basin
Herbet Road
South Wharf Road
St Mary's Hospital
Edgware Rd
CHAPEL ST
Transept St
Cabbell St
OLD MARYLEBONE
Harcourt St
Homer St
York St
Dinings
Occo
Garbo's
Crawford Street
Upper Montagu St
GLOUCESTER PL
Homer Row
Windsor Castle
Crawford Place
Shouldham St
Molyneux St
Bryanston Pl
Wyndham Pl
Seymour Pl
Montagu Place
Bryanston Mews E
Montagu Square
Gloucester Pl Mews
5
Patogh
Satay House
EASTBOURNE TERRACE
Winsland Street
Paddington
London Street
PRAED STREET
St Michael's Street
Sale Place
Star St
SUSSEX GARDENS
Norfolk Crescent
Norfolk Place
Norfolk Square
EDGWARE ROAD (A5)
Brendon St
Harrowby St
Forset St
Nutford Pl
Brown St
Seymour St
Bryanston Square
Montagu Mews W
Montagu Mews S
Montagu St
George Street
Eastbourne Mews
Westbourne Street
Westbourne Terrace
Chilworth Mews
Gloucester Terrace
Chilworth Street
Gloucester Mews
Craven Terrace
Upbrook Mews
Devonshire Terrace
CRAVEN ROAD
Southwick St
Somers Mews
Somers Cres
Cambridge Square
Burwood Pl
Park West Pl
Stourcliffe St
Great Cumberland Pl
George Place
Conduit Place
Spring St
Conduit Mews
Talbot Square
Radnor Mews
Radnor Place
Hyde Park Crescent
Oxford Square
Kendal Street
Portsea Pl
Upper Berkeley Street
Carbon
New Quebec St
Ranoush Juice Bar
Sidi Maarouf
Trenta
Connaught Street
Arturo
Connaught Sq
Maroush
SEYMOUR
6
Gloucester Square
Sussex Place
Clifton Place
Bathurst Mews
Sussex Gdns
Westbourne Cres
Hyde Park Square
Strathearn Place
Hyde Park Street
Albion Street
Albion Cl
St George's Fields
Seymour Street
Stanhope Pl
Conaught Pl
Bryanston St
Brook Mews North
Sussex Sq
Bathurst Street
Hyde Park Gardens Mews
Hyde Park Gardens
Clarendon Place
Marble Arch
Stanhope Terr
Brook St
Lancaster Mews
Craven Terrace
Elms Mews
LANCASTER TERR
WESTBOURNE ST
Nipa
BAYSWATER ROAD A40
CUMB'LAND GATE
Speaker's Corner
PARK LANE
Lancaster Gate
Island Restaurant & Bar
North Carriage Drive (The Ring)
West Carriage Drive (The Ring)
See Map 9
Peter Pan Statue
The Long Water
HYDE PARK
7
KENSINGTON GARDENS
Serpentine Road
The Serpentine
Serpentine Gallery
8
0
400 m
400 yds
Rotten Row
© Copyright Time Out Group 2007
Albert Memorial
South Carriage Drive
William St
Mandarin Bar
Foliage
One-O-One
Royal College of Art
KENSINGTON GORE
KENSINGTON ROAD
Mr Chow
Fifth Floor
Royal Albert Hall
Jay Mews
Exhibition Road
Ennismore Gardens
Rutland Gate
Trevor Place
Knightsbridge
Raphael St
Zuma
Harriet Walk
Lowndes Square
See Map 14
Albert Court
Montpelier Terrace
Montpelier Walk
Montpelier St
Trevor Sq
The Capital
SLOANE ST
9
190 Queensgate
Queensgate
Prince Consort Road
Princes Gardens
Ennismore Mews
Ennismore Gardens
Montpelier Place
Harrods
Basil St
Mju
Hans Cres
Pavilion Road
Royal College of Music
Callendar Rd
KNIGHTSBRIDGE
Hans Rd

Marylebone, Fitzrovia, Mayfair & St James's

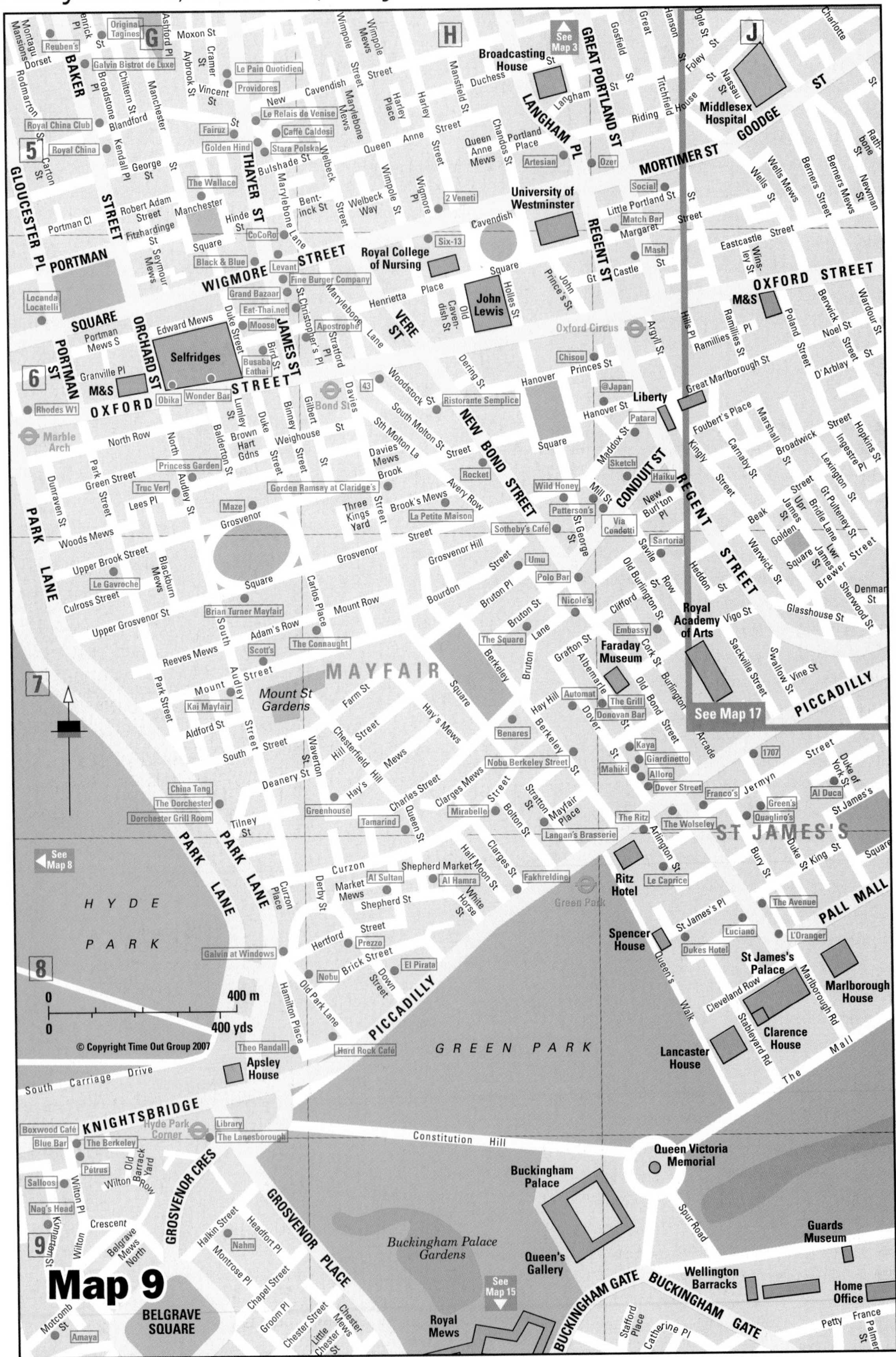

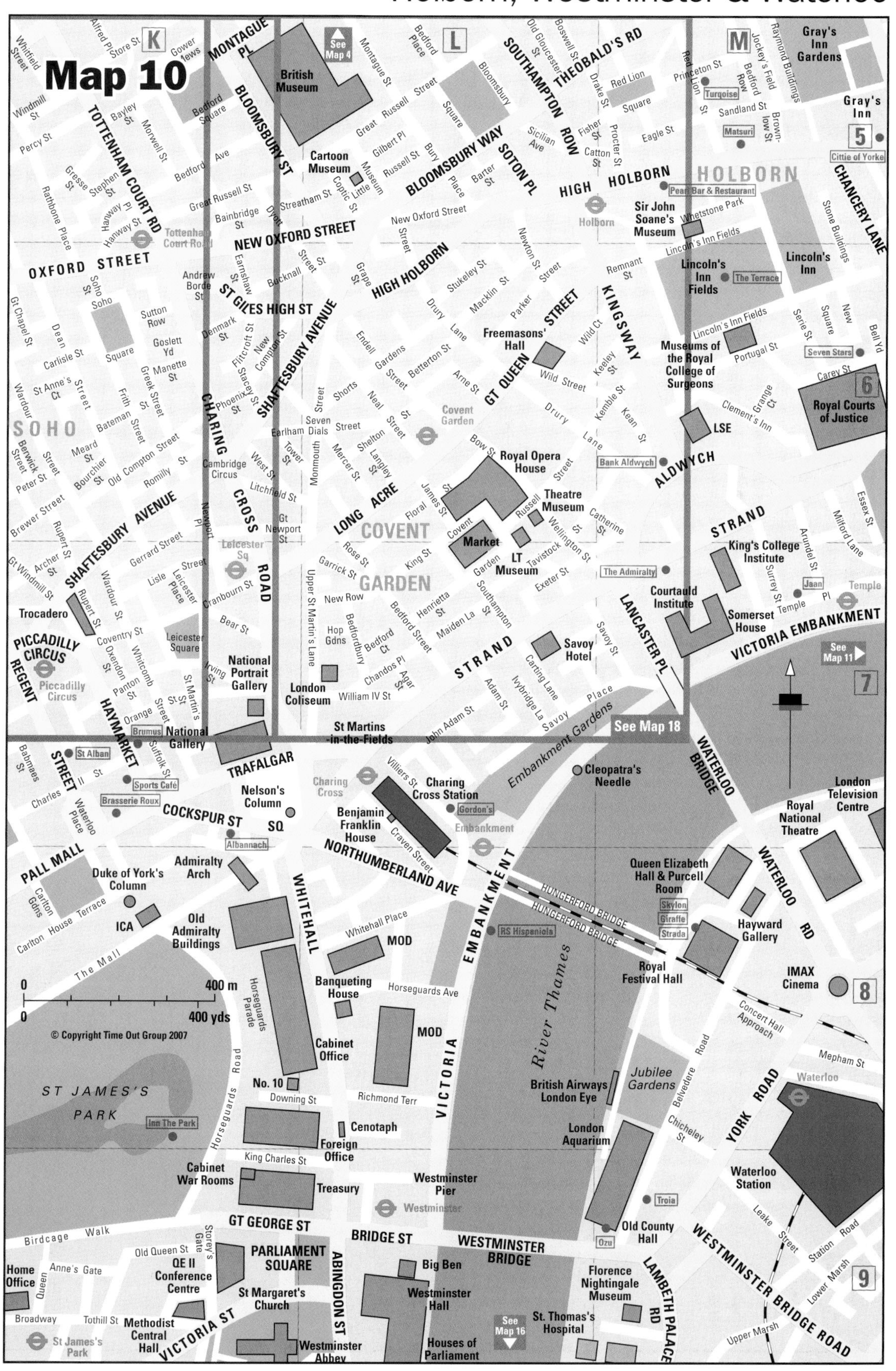
Map 10
British Museum
Cartoon Museum
Sir John Soane's Museum
Lincoln's Inn Fields
Royal Courts of Justice
Freemasons' Hall
Covent Garden
Royal Opera House
Theatre Museum
LT Museum
Somerset House
Courtauld Institute
Savoy Hotel
National Portrait Gallery
London Coliseum
St Martins -in-the-Fields
National Gallery
Trafalgar Sq
Nelson's Column
Charing Cross Station
Cleopatra's Needle
Royal National Theatre
Queen Elizabeth Hall & Purcell Room
Hayward Gallery
Royal Festival Hall
IMAX Cinema
British Airways London Eye
London Aquarium
Waterloo Station
Old County Hall
Westminster Bridge
Big Ben
Westminster Hall
Houses of Parliament
Westminster Abbey
Parliament Square
St James's Park
Cabinet War Rooms
Treasury
Cenotaph
No. 10
Banqueting House
MOD
River Thames
© Copyright Time Out Group 2007

MAPS

City, Waterloo & Borough

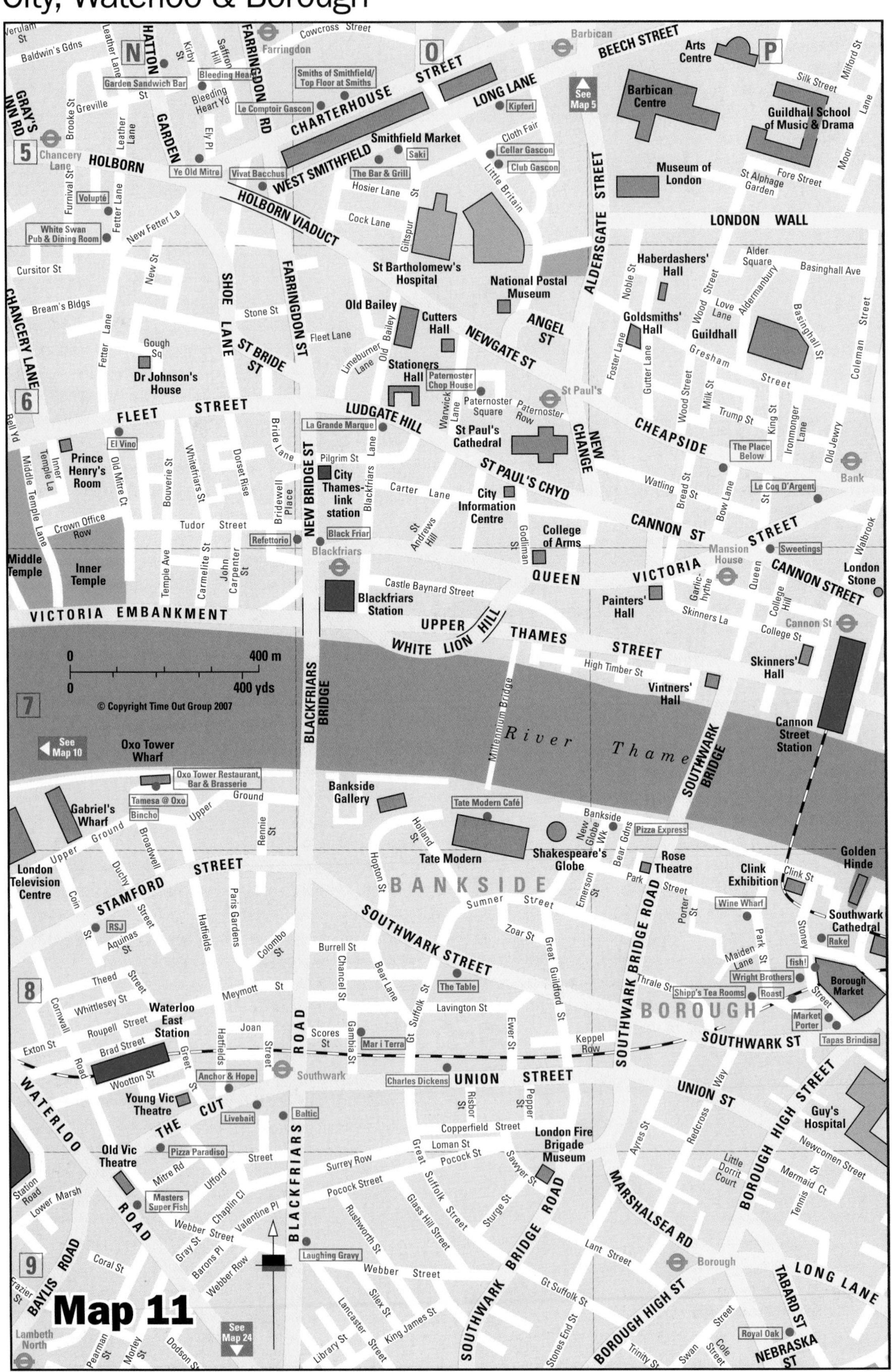

MAPS

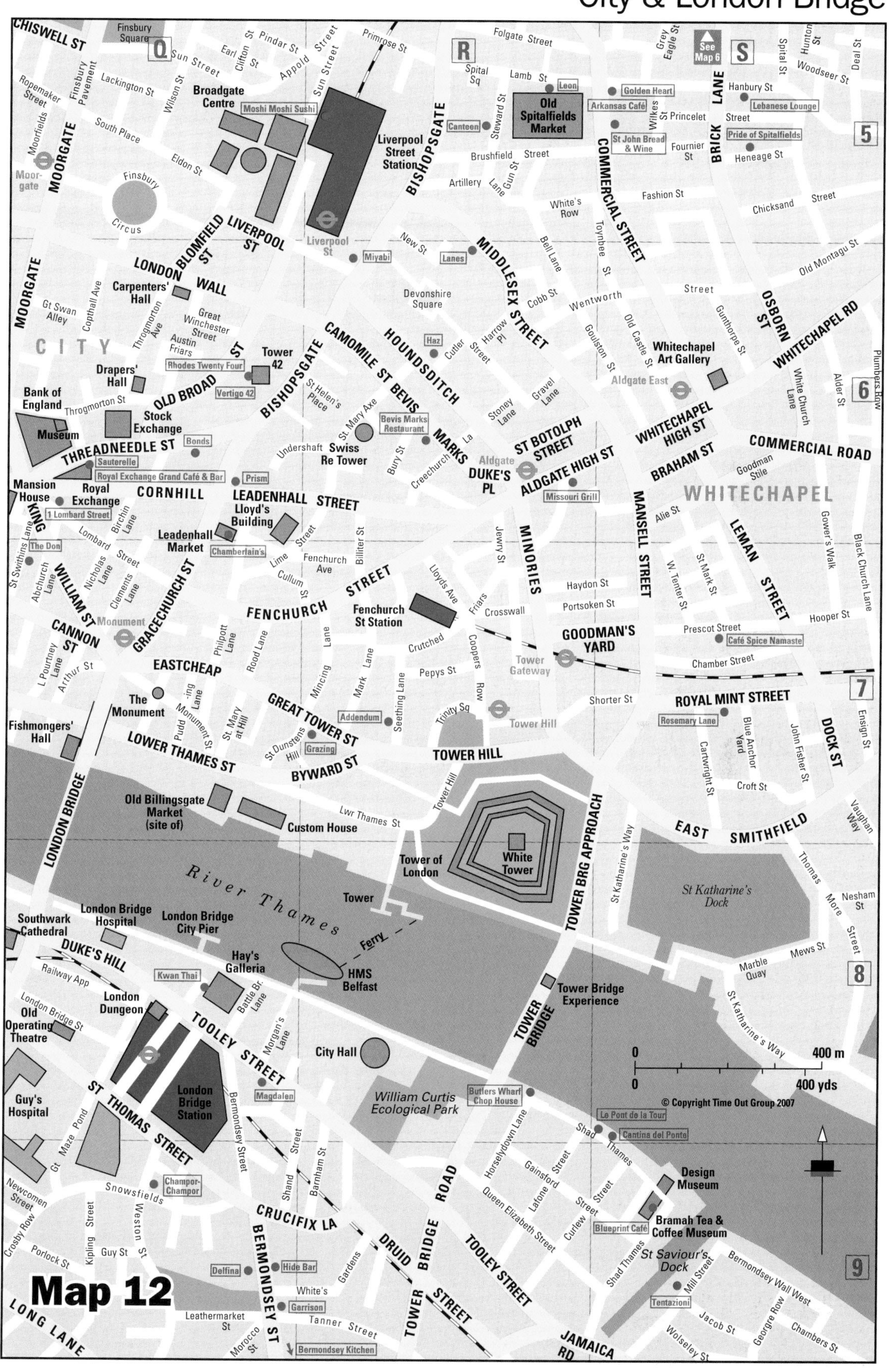
Map 12
Q
R
S
See Map 6
5
6
7
8
9
Chiswell St
Finsbury Square
Sun Street
Earl St
Clifton St
Pindar St
Appold Street
Sun Street
Primrose St
Folgate Street
Grey Eagle St
Spital St
Hunton St
Deal St
Woodseer St
Ropemaker Street
Finsbury Pavement
Lackington St
Wilson St
Broadgate Centre
Moshi Moshi Sushi
Liverpool Street Station
Bishopsgate
Spital Sq
Lamb St
Leon
Old Spitalfields Market
Golden Heart
Arkansas Café
Wilkes St
Princelet Street
Brick Lane
Hanbury St
Lebanese Lounge
Pride of Spitalfields
Moorfields
South Place
Moorgate
Moor-gate
Eldon St
Canteen
Steward St
St John Bread & Wine
Fournier St
Heneage St
Brushfield Street
Commercial Street
Artillery Lane
Gun St
Finsbury Circus
White's Row
Fashion St
Chicksand Street
Blomfield St
Liverpool St
Liverpool St
Miyabi
New St
Lanes
Middlesex Street
Bell Lane
Toynbee St
Old Montagu St
Moorgate
London Wall
Carpenters' Hall
Devonshire Square
Cobb St
Wentworth Street
Gunthorpe St
Osborn St
Whitechapel Rd
Gt Swan Alley
Copthall Ave
Throgmorton Ave
Great Winchester Street
Camomile St
Houndsditch
Harrow Pl
Goulston St
Old Castle St
Whitechapel Art Gallery
Plumbers Row
City
Austin Friars
Old Broad St
Tower 42
Rhodes Twenty Four
Bishopsgate
Haz
Cutler Street
Aldgate East
White Church Lane
Alder St
Drapers' Hall
Vertigo 42
St Helen's Place
St Mary Axe
Bevis Marks
Bevis Marks Restaurant
Stoney Lane
Gravel Lane
Bank of England
Throgmorton St
Stock Exchange
Whitechapel High St
Museum
Threadneedle St
Bonds
Swiss Re Tower
Undershaft
Bury St
Creechurch La
St Botolph Street
Commercial Road
Sauterelle
Royal Exchange Grand Café & Bar
Prism
Aldgate
Duke's Pl
Aldgate High St
Braham St
Goodman Stile
Mansion House
Royal Exchange
Cornhill
Leadenhall Street
Missouri Grill
Whitechapel
King
1 Lombard Street
Birchin Lane
Lloyd's Building
Mansell Street
Alie St
Minories
Jewry St
Leman Street
Gower's Walk
Black Church Lane
St Swithins Lane
The Don
Lombard Street
Leadenhall Market
Chamberlain's
Lime Street
Fenchurch Ave
Billiter St
W. Tenter St
St Mark St
Abchurch Lane
William St
Nicholas Lane
Clements Lane
Gracechurch St
Cullum St
Fenchurch Street
Lloyds Ave
Haydon St
Portsoken St
Fenchurch St Station
Friars
Crosswall
Cannon St
Monument
Philpott Lane
Rood Lane
Mincing Lane
Goodman's Yard
Prescot Street
Café Spice Namaste
Hooper St
L Pourtney Lane
Arthur St
Eastcheap
Crutched
Coopers Row
Tower Gateway
Chamber Street
Mark Lane
Seething Lane
Pepys St
Royal Mint Street
Shorter St
Ensign St
The Monument
Pudd-ing Lane
Monument St
St. Mary at Hill
Great Tower St
Addendum
Trinity Sq
Tower Hill
Rosemary Lane
Blue Anchor Yard
John Fisher St
Dock St
Fishmongers' Hall
Lower Thames St
St Dunstans Hill
Grazing
Byward St
Tower Hill
Cartwright St
Croft St
London Bridge
Old Billingsgate Market (site of)
Custom House
Lwr Thames St
Tower Hill
Tower Brg Approach
St Katharine's Way
East Smithfield
Vaughan Way
White Tower
Tower of London
Thomas More Street
River Thames
Tower
St Katharine's Dock
Nesham St
Southwark Cathedral
London Bridge Hospital
London Bridge City Pier
Ferry
Duke's Hill
Hay's Galleria
Marble Quay
Mews St
Railway App
Kwan Thai
HMS Belfast
Tower Bridge Experience
London Bridge St
London Dungeon
Battle Br. Lane
Tower Bridge
St Katharine's Way
Old Operating Theatre
Tooley Street
Morgan's Lane
City Hall
0
400 m
0
400 yds
Guy's Hospital
St Thomas Street
London Bridge Station
Bermondsey Street
Magdalen
William Curtis Ecological Park
Butlers Wharf Chop House
© Copyright Time Out Group 2007
Le Pont de la Tour
Shad Thames
Cantina del Ponte
Maze Pond
Gt
Shand Street
Barnham St
Horselydown Lane
Gainsford Street
Design Museum
Newcomen Street
Snowsfields
Champor-Champor
Road
Queen Elizabeth Street
Lafone Street
Curlew Street
Kipling Street
Weston St
Crucifix La
Bridge
Blueprint Café
Bramah Tea & Coffee Museum
Crosby Row
Guy St
Druid
Tooley Street
Shad Thames
St Saviour's Dock
Mill Street
Bermondsey Wall West
Porlock St
Delfina
Bermondsey St
Hide Bar
Gardens
Tower
Street
White's
Garrison
Tentazioni
Long Lane
Leathermarket St
Tanner Street
Jacob St
George Row
Chambers St
Morocco St
Bermondsey Kitchen
Jamaica Rd
Wolseley St

Earl's Court, Gloucester Road & Fulham

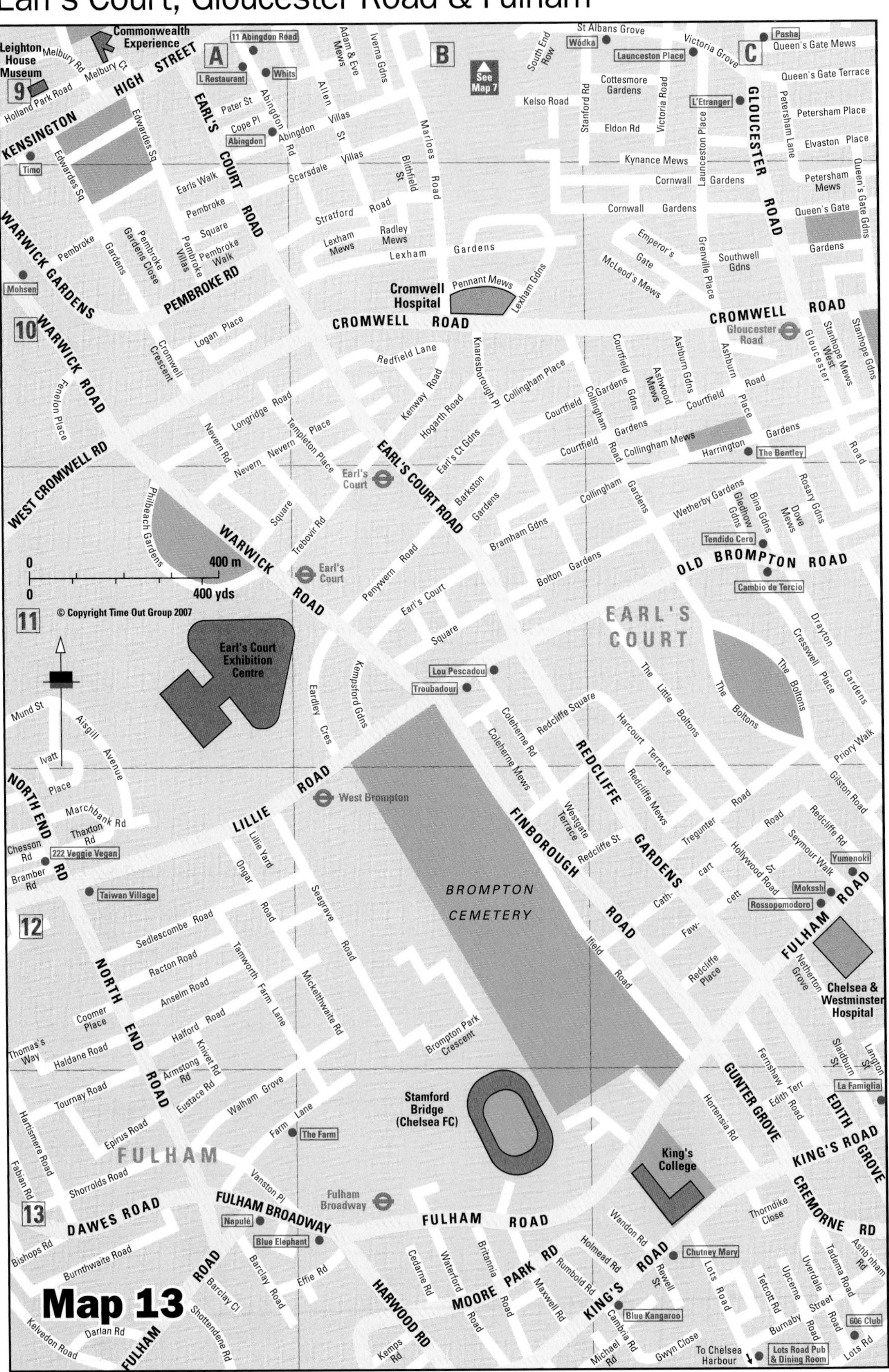

MAPS

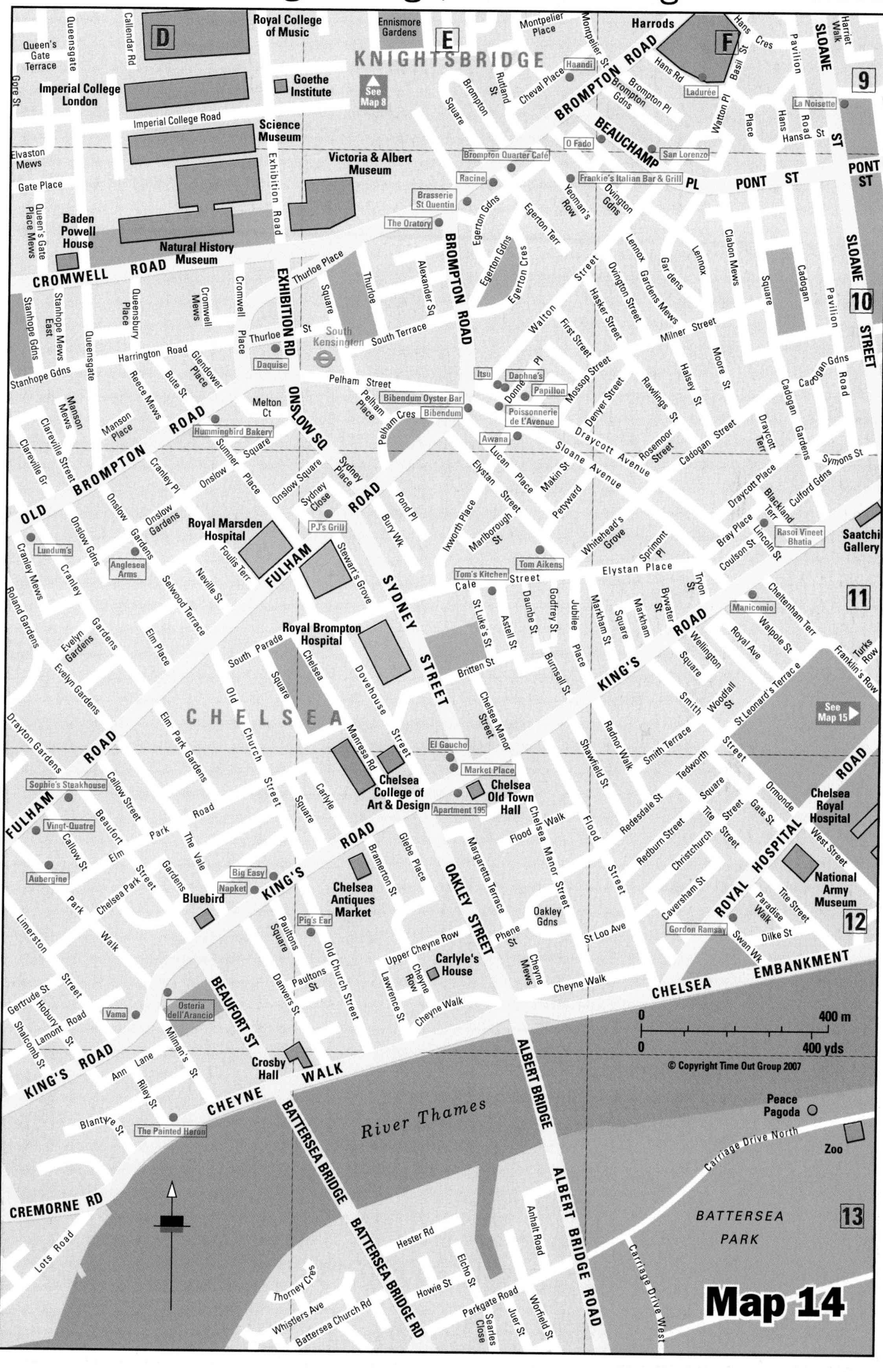

KNIGHTSBRIDGE
CHELSEA
River Thames
BATTERSEA PARK
See Map 8
See Map 15
Map 14
Harrods
Royal College of Music
Imperial College London
Goethe Institute
Science Museum
Victoria & Albert Museum
Natural History Museum
Baden Powell House
South Kensington
Royal Marsden Hospital
Royal Brompton Hospital
Chelsea College of Art & Design
Chelsea Old Town Hall
Chelsea Antiques Market
Carlyle's House
Crosby Hall
Saatchi Gallery
Chelsea Royal Hospital
National Army Museum
Peace Pagoda
Zoo
Haandi
Ladurée
La Noisette
O Fado
San Lorenzo
Brompton Quarter Café
Racine
Frankie's Italian Bar & Grill
Brasserie St Quentin
The Oratory
Daquise
Itsu
Daphne's
Papillon
Bibendum Oyster Bar
Bibendum
Poissonnerie de l'Avenue
Awana
Hummingbird Bakery
PJ's Grill
Lundum's
Anglesea Arms
Tom Aikens
Tom's Kitchen
Rasoi Vineet Bhatia
Manicomio
El Gaucho
Market Place
Apartment 195
Sophie's Steakhouse
Vingt-Quatre
Aubergine
Big Easy
Napket
Bluebird
Pig's Ear
Gordon Ramsay
Vama
Osteria dell'Arancio
The Painted Heron
CROMWELL ROAD
BROMPTON ROAD
OLD BROMPTON ROAD
FULHAM ROAD
KING'S ROAD
SLOANE STREET
PONT ST
BEAUCHAMP PL
EXHIBITION RD
ONSLOW SQ
SYDNEY STREET
OAKLEY STREET
BEAUFORT ST
ROYAL HOSPITAL ROAD
CHELSEA EMBANKMENT
CHEYNE WALK
ALBERT BRIDGE
ALBERT BRIDGE ROAD
BATTERSEA BRIDGE
BATTERSEA BRIDGE RD
CREMORNE RD
0 400 m
0 400 yds
© Copyright Time Out Group 2007

MAPS

Belgravia, Victoria & Pimlico

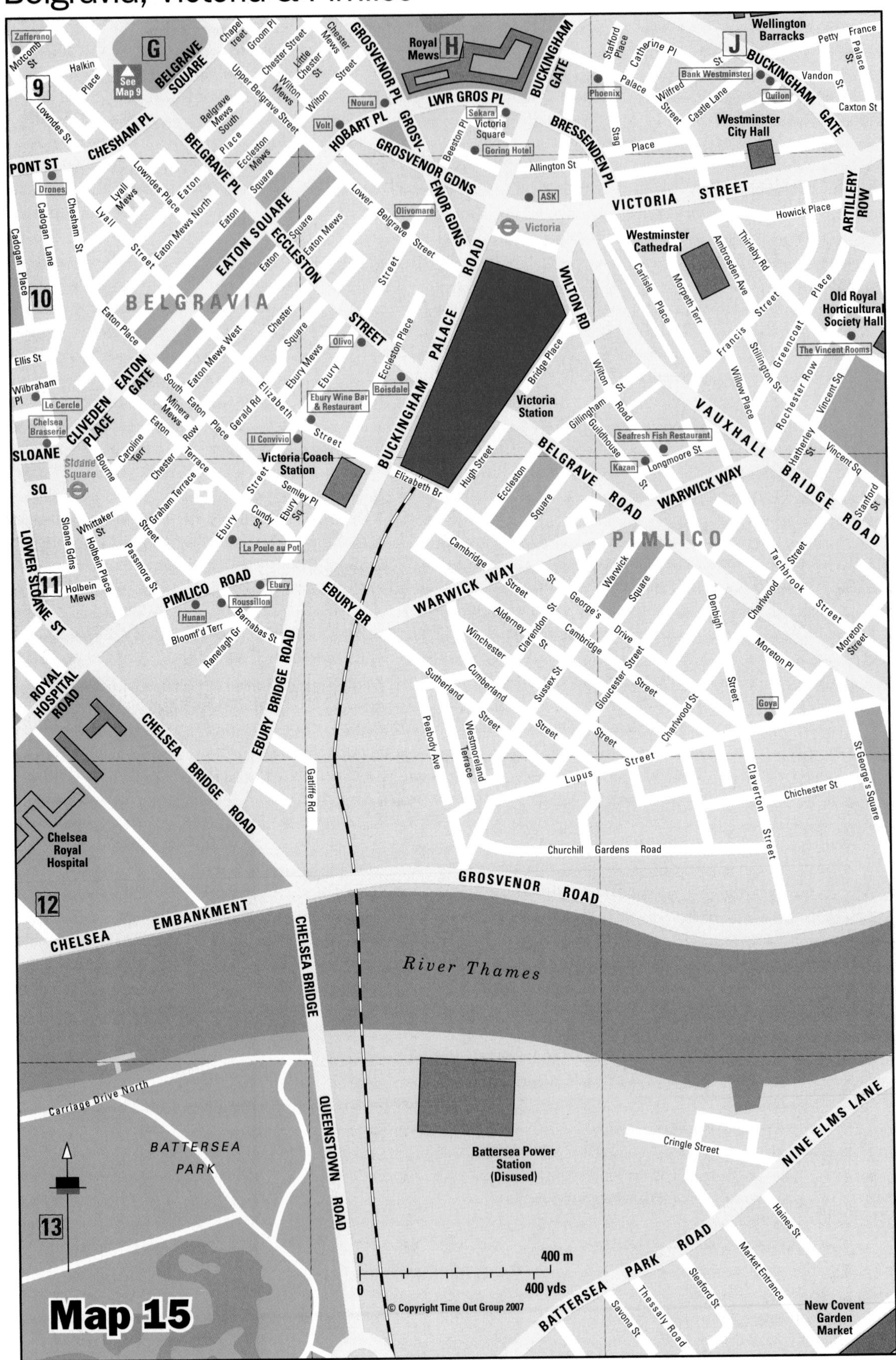

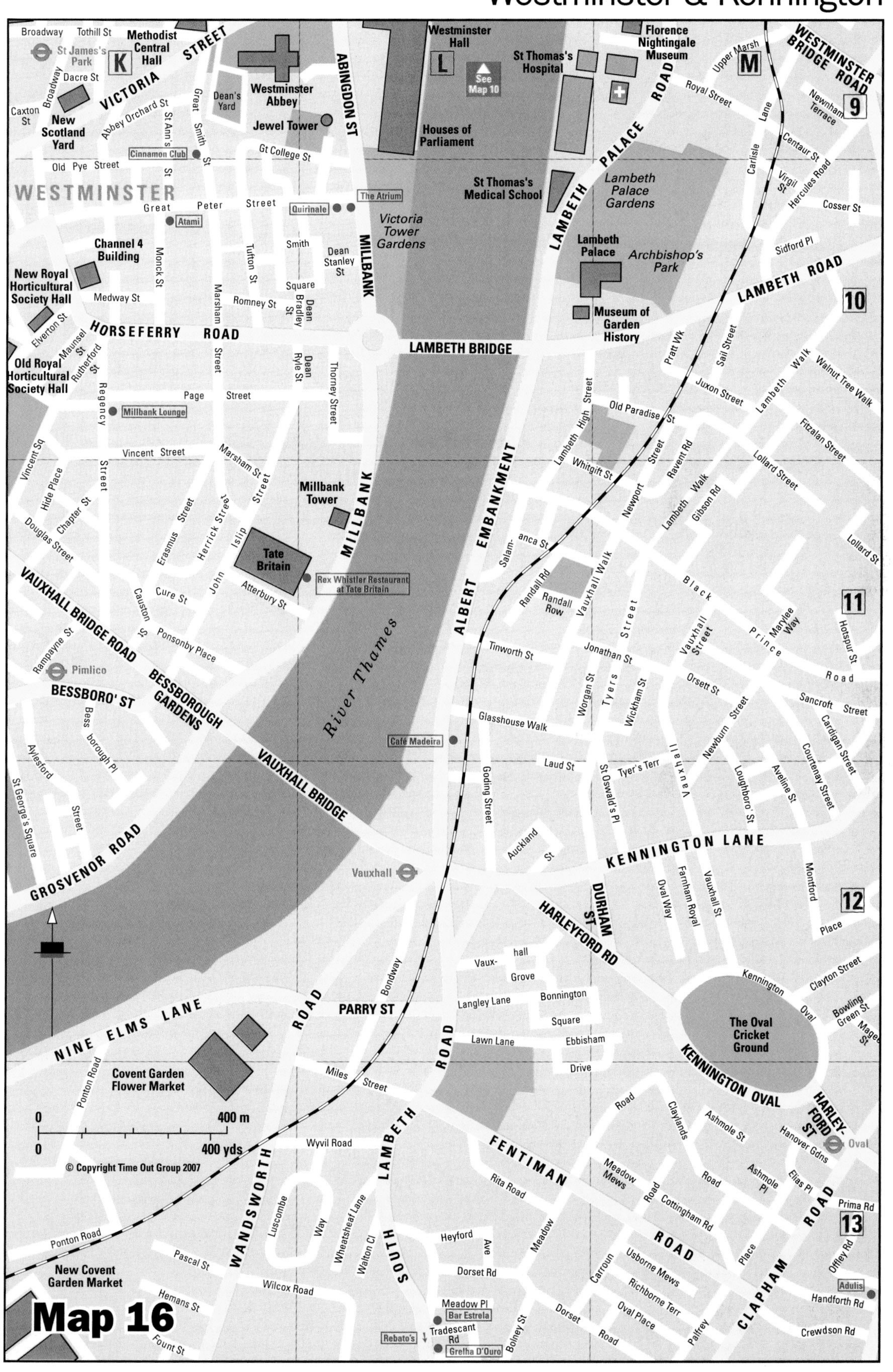
Map 16
WESTMINSTER
Methodist Central Hall
Westminster Hall
St Thomas's Hospital
Florence Nightingale Museum
Westminster Abbey
Jewel Tower
Houses of Parliament
New Scotland Yard
See Map 10
St James's Park
Cinnamon Club
The Atrium
Quirinale
Atami
Channel 4 Building
New Royal Horticultural Society Hall
Old Royal Horticultural Society Hall
St Thomas's Medical School
Victoria Tower Gardens
Lambeth Palace Gardens
Lambeth Palace
Archbishop's Park
Museum of Garden History
LAMBETH BRIDGE
HORSEFERRY ROAD
Millbank Lounge
Millbank Tower
Tate Britain
Rex Whistler Restaurant at Tate Britain
River Thames
Pimlico
Café Madeira
Vauxhall
VAUXHALL BRIDGE
VAUXHALL BRIDGE ROAD
BESSBOROUGH GARDENS
BESSBORO' ST
GROSVENOR ROAD
ALBERT EMBANKMENT
MILLBANK
KENNINGTON LANE
HARLEYFORD RD
The Oval Cricket Ground
KENNINGTON OVAL
Oval
NINE ELMS LANE
Covent Garden Flower Market
New Covent Garden Market
PARRY ST
WANDSWORTH ROAD
SOUTH LAMBETH ROAD
FENTIMAN ROAD
CLAPHAM ROAD
LAMBETH ROAD
LAMBETH PALACE ROAD
WESTMINSTER BRIDGE ROAD
VICTORIA STREET
ABINGDON ST
DURHAM ST
Bar Estrela
Rebato's
Grelha D'Ouro
Adulis
400 m
400 yds
© Copyright Time Out Group 2007

MAPS

Fitzrovia, Soho & Chinatown

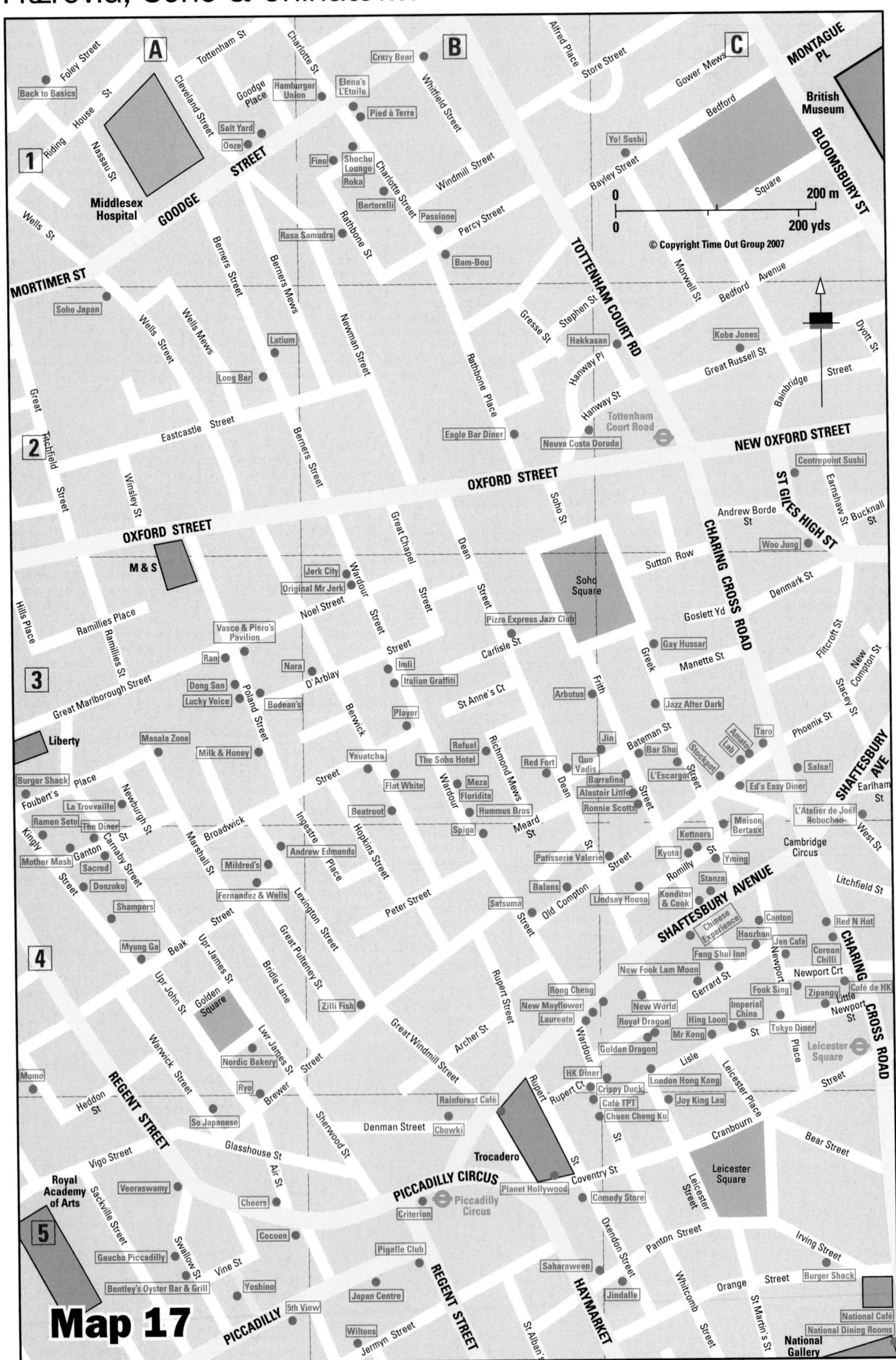

MAPS

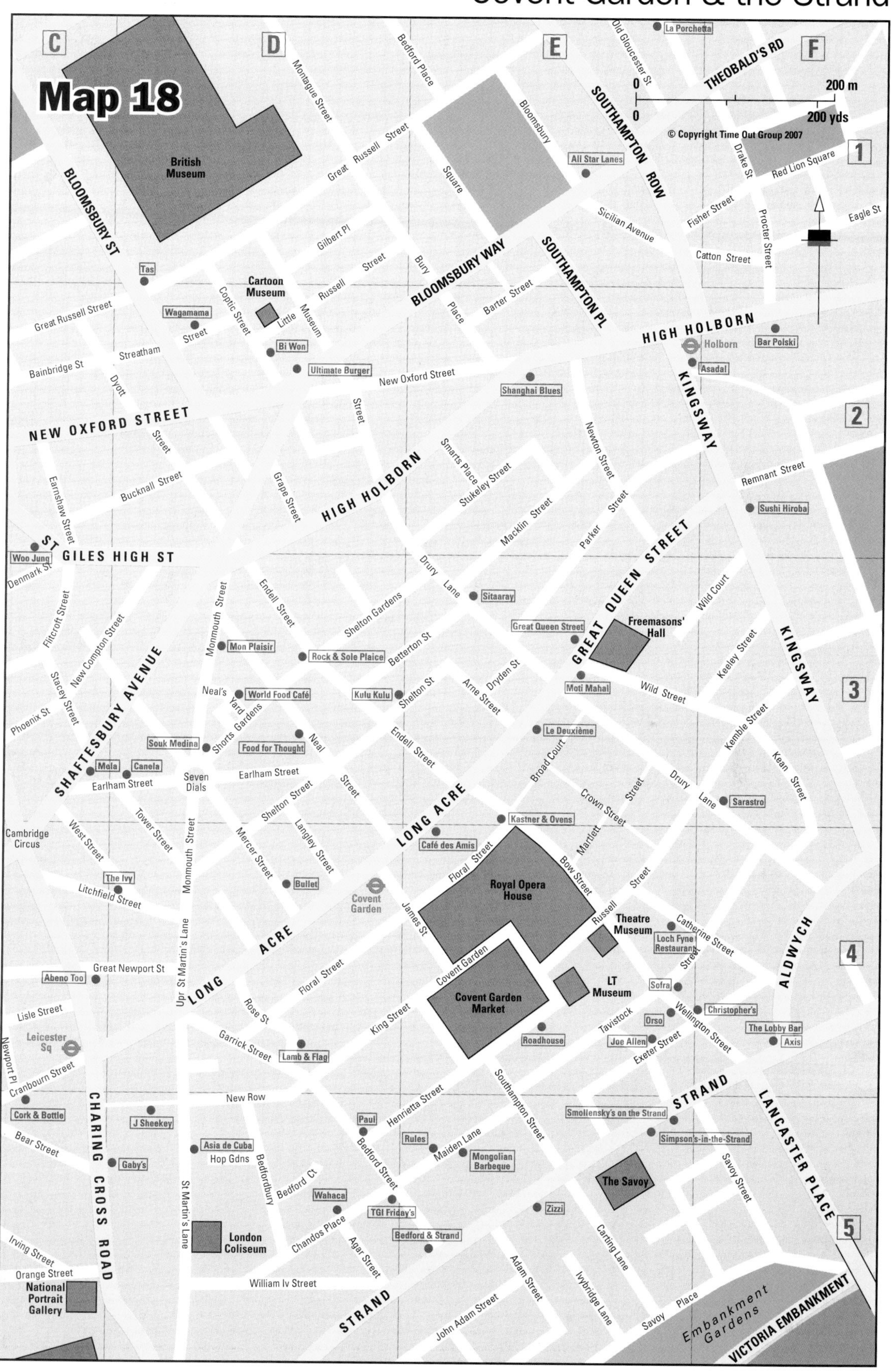
Map 18
© Copyright Time Out Group 2007
British Museum
Cartoon Museum
Freemasons' Hall
Royal Opera House
Theatre Museum
Covent Garden Market
LT Museum
The Savoy
London Coliseum
National Portrait Gallery
Embankment Gardens
La Porchetta
All Star Lanes
Tas
Wagamama
Bi Won
Ultimate Burger
Shanghai Blues
Bar Polski
Asadal
Sushi Hiroba
Woo Jung
Sitaaray
Great Queen Street
Mon Plaisir
Rock & Sole Plaice
World Food Café
Kulu Kulu
Moti Mahal
Le Deuxième
Souk Medina
Food for Thought
Mela
Canela
Sarastro
Kastner & Ovens
Café des Amis
The Ivy
Bullet
Loch Fyne Restaurant
Abeno Too
Sofra
Christopher's
Orso
The Lobby Bar
Axis
Roadhouse
Joe Allen
Lamb & Flag
Cork & Bottle
J Sheekey
Smollensky's on the Strand
Simpson's-in-the-Strand
Paul
Rules
Mongolian Barbeque
Asia de Cuba
Gaby's
Wahaca
TGI Friday's
Zizzi
Bedford & Strand
Holborn
Covent Garden
Leicester Sq
BLOOMSBURY ST
NEW OXFORD STREET
HIGH HOLBORN
ST GILES HIGH ST
SHAFTESBURY AVENUE
LONG ACRE
CHARING CROSS ROAD
STRAND
KINGSWAY
ALDWYCH
LANCASTER PLACE
VICTORIA EMBANKMENT
GREAT QUEEN STREET
SOUTHAMPTON ROW
SOUTHAMPTON PL
BLOOMSBURY WAY
THEOBALD'S RD
MAPS

Hammersmith & Shepherd's Bush

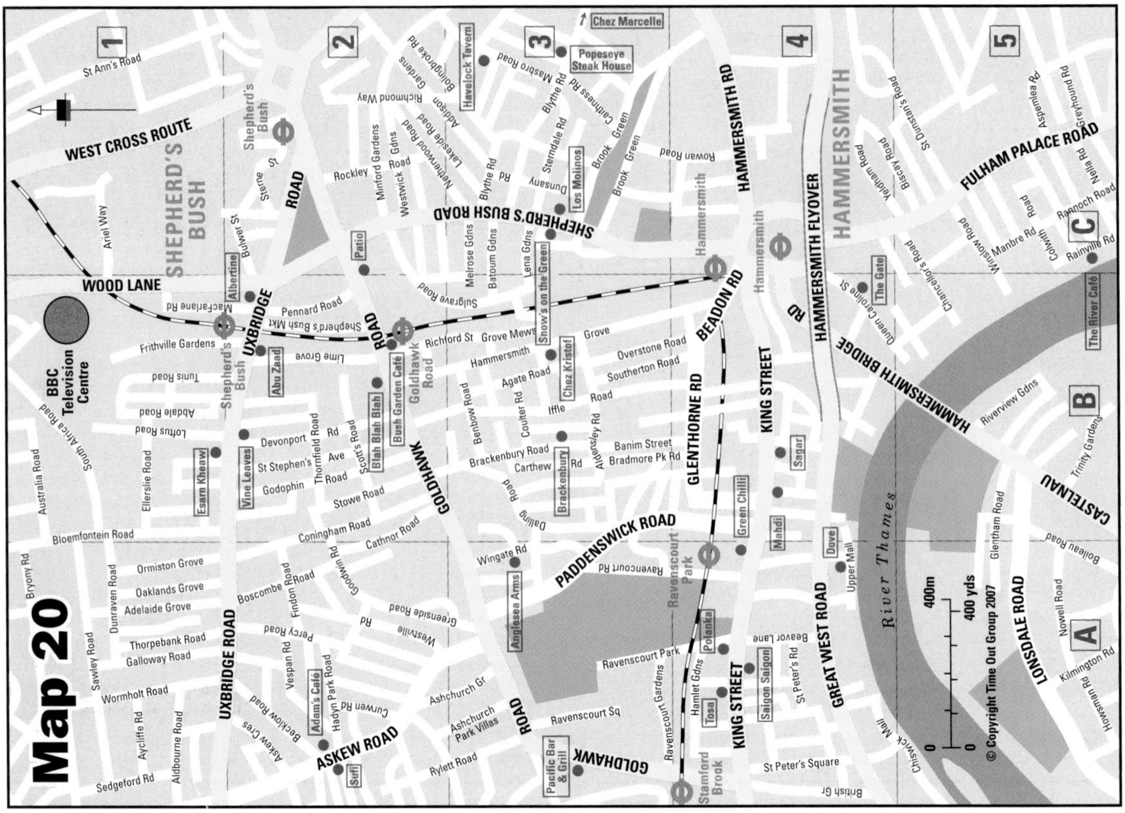

Map 20

© Copyright Time Out Group 2007

Notting Hill & Ladbroke Grove

Map 19

© Copyright Time Out Group 2007

Clapham & Brixton

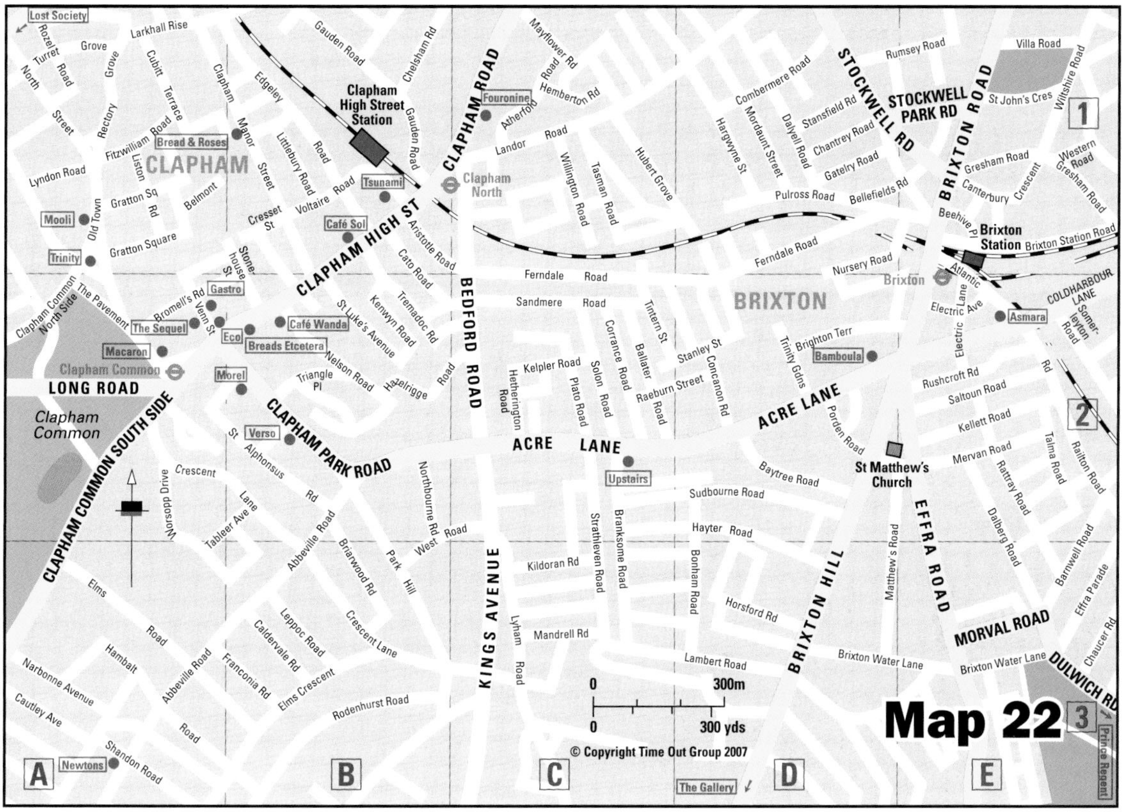

Map 22

© Copyright Time Out Group 2007

Battersea & Wandsworth

Map 21

© Copyright Time Out Group 2007

MAPS

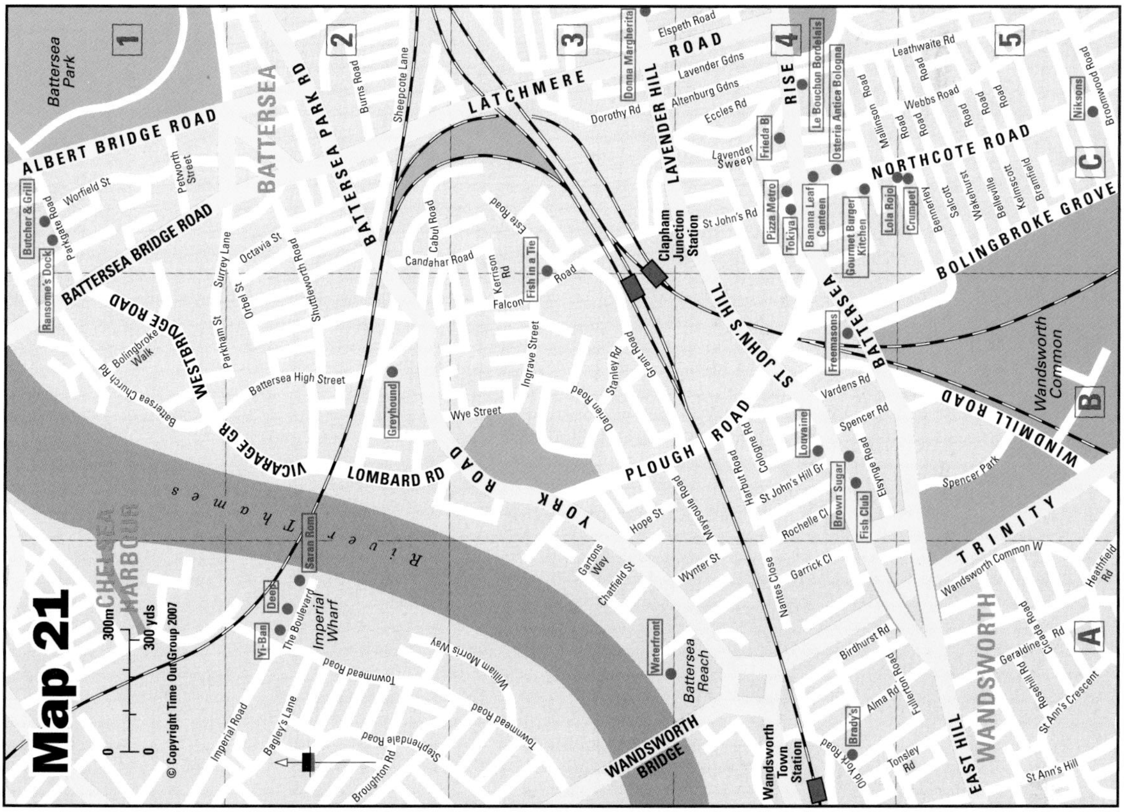

Docklands

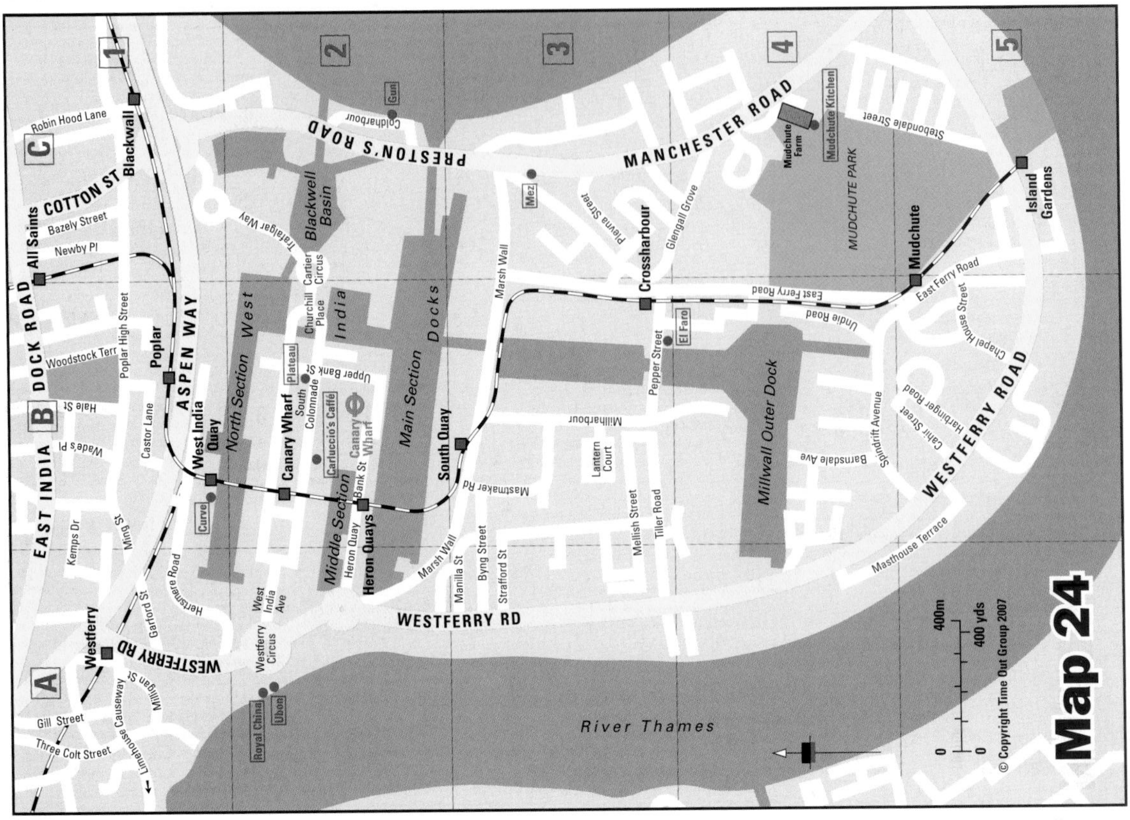

Map 24

Camberwell & Dulwich

Map 23

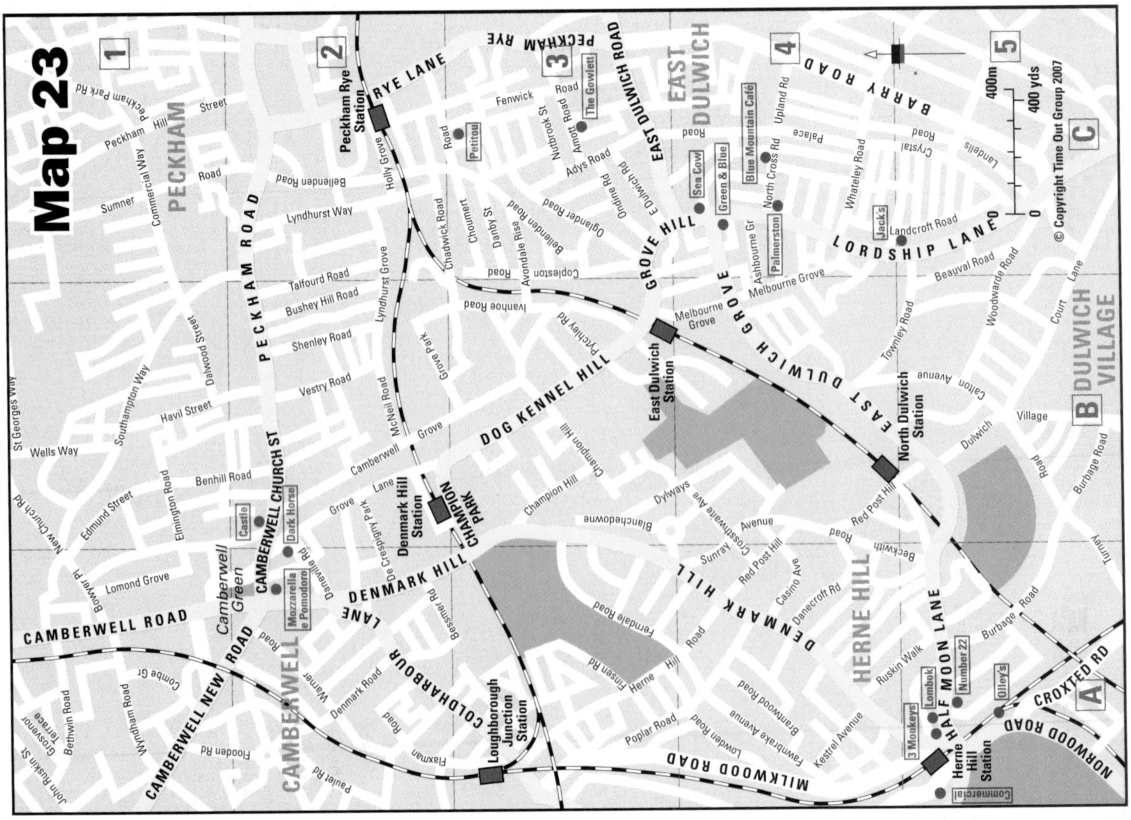

Kentish Town & Archway

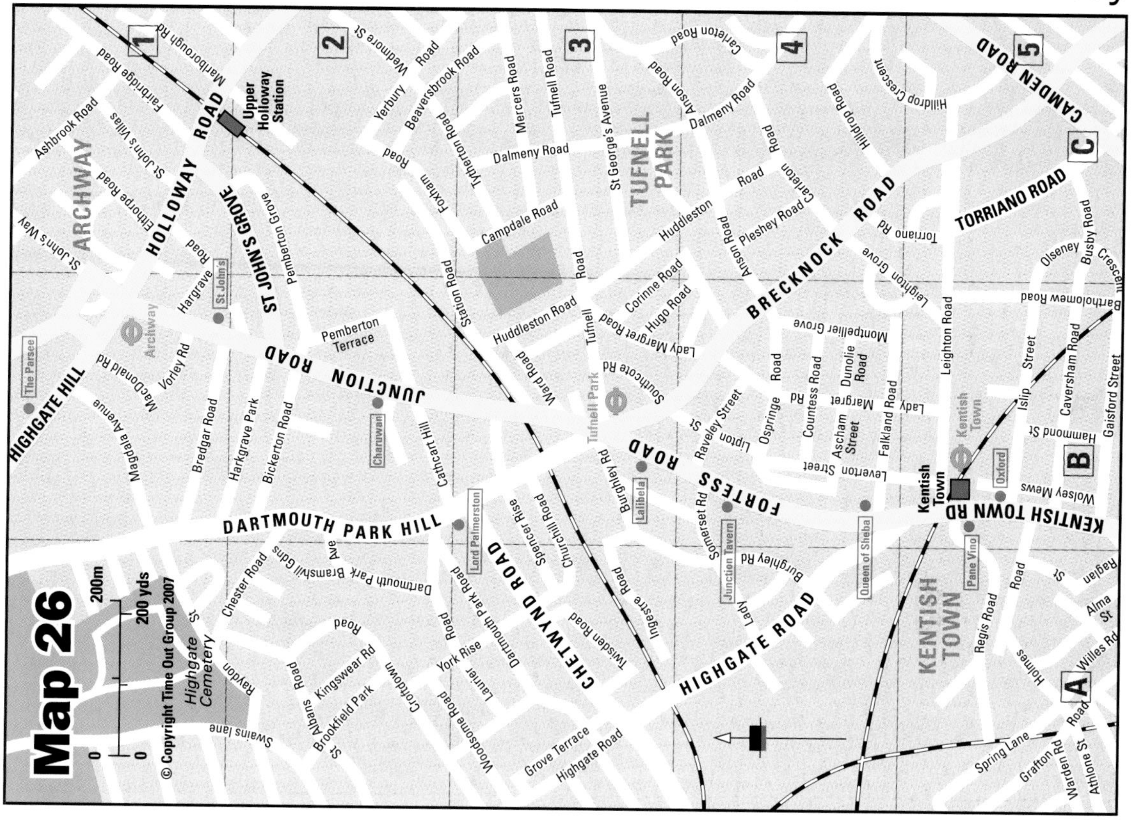

Map 26

0 200m
0 200 yds

© Copyright Time Out Group 2007

Dalston & Stoke Newington

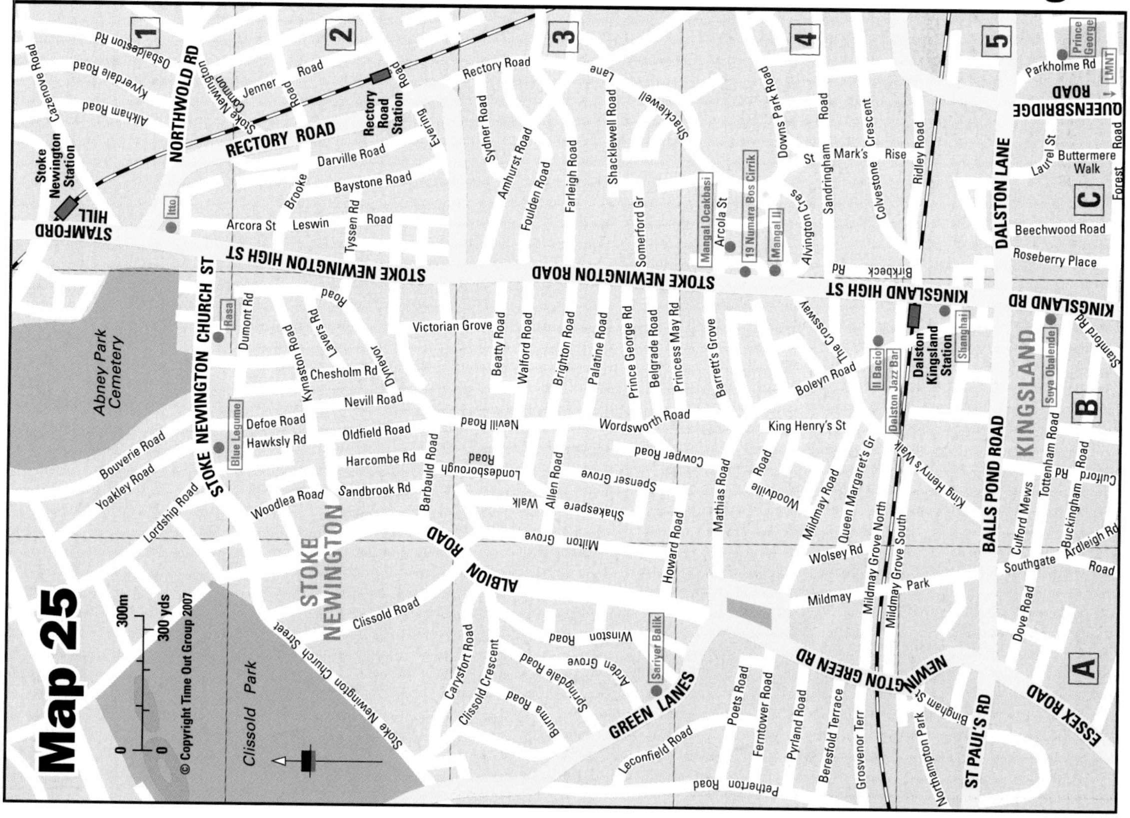

Map 25

0 300m
0 300 yds

© Copyright Time Out Group 2007

Hampstead & St John's Wood

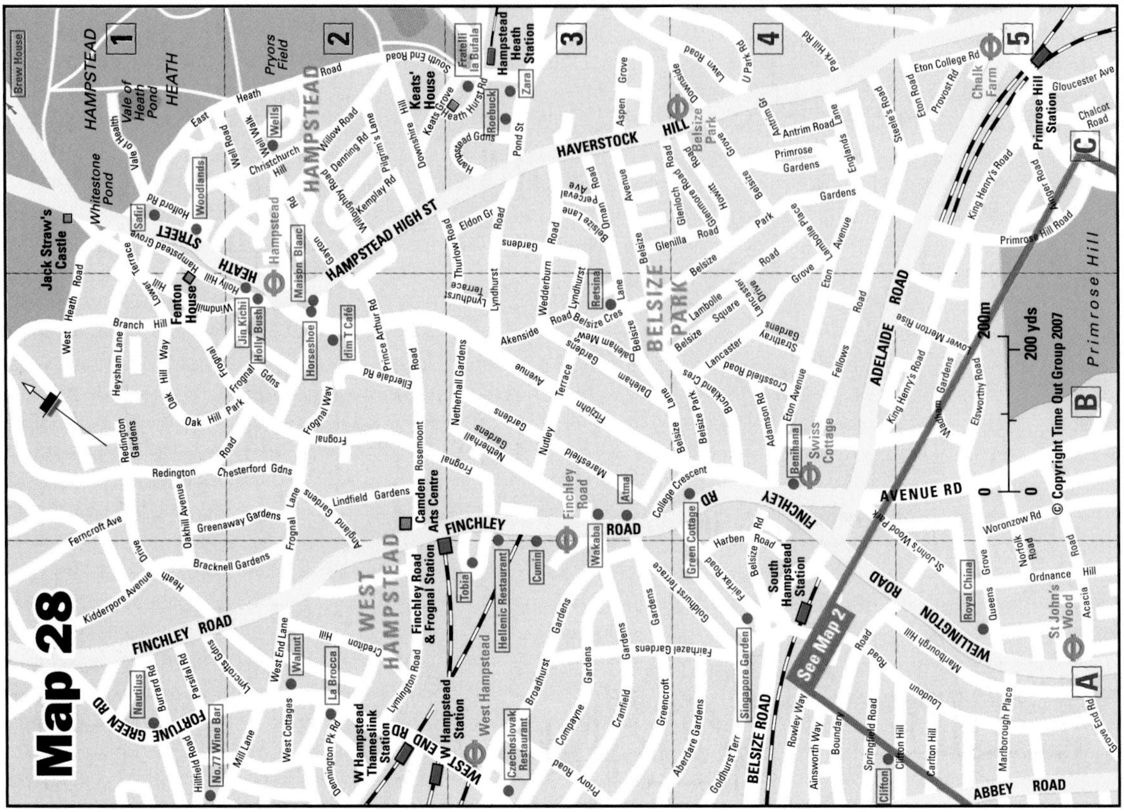

Map 28

Camden Town & Chalk Farm

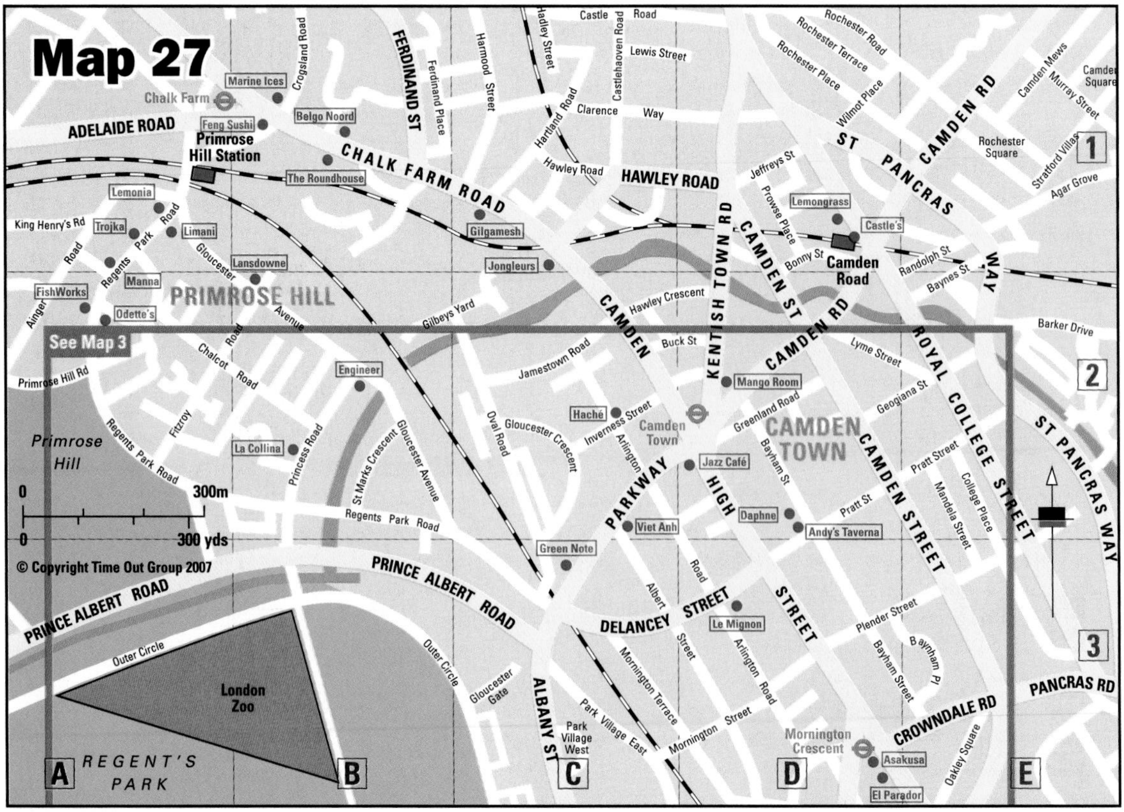

Map 27

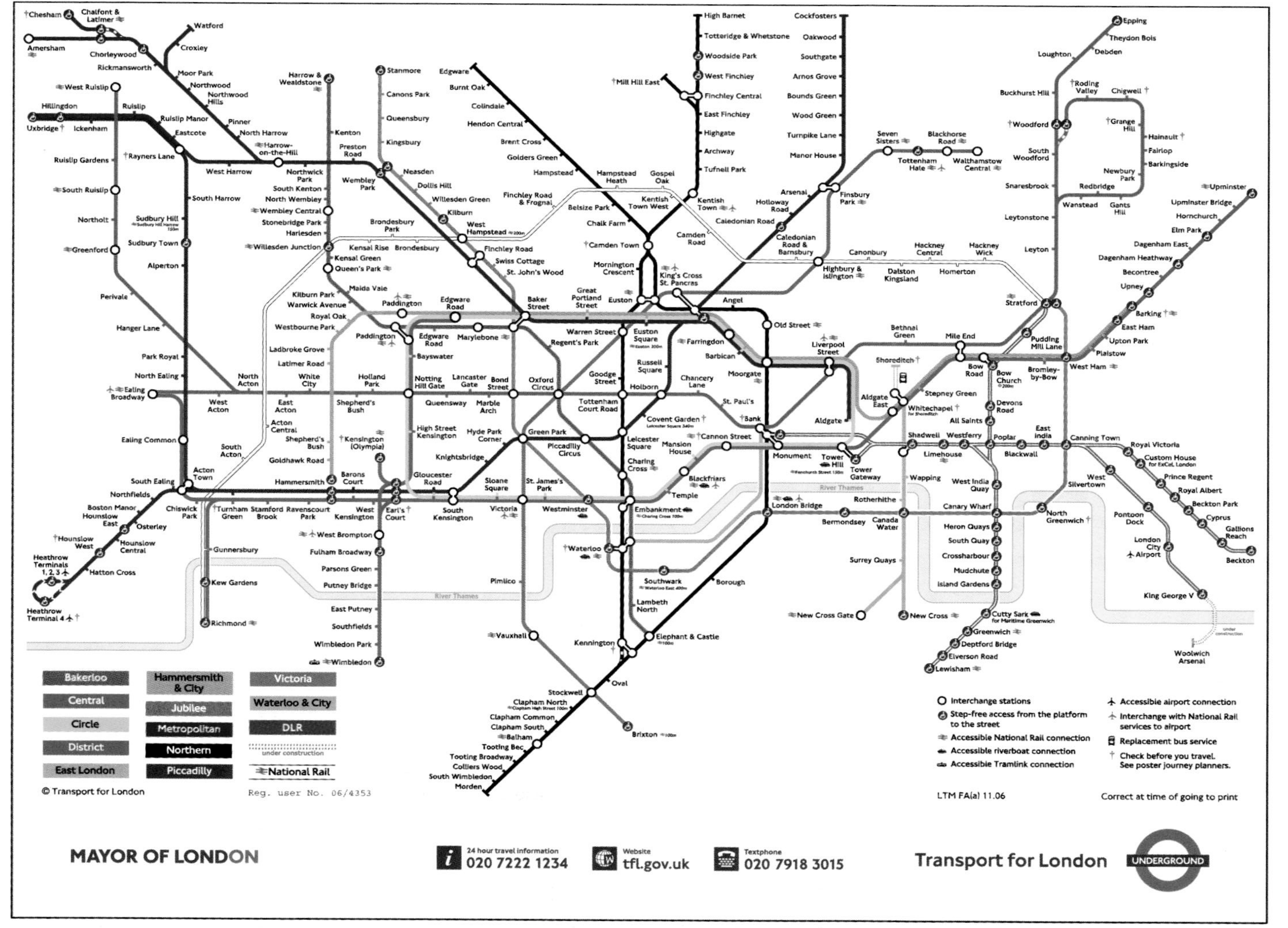
Interchange stations
Step-free access from the platform to the street
Accessible National Rail connection
Accessible riverboat connection
Accessible Tramlink connection
Accessible airport connection
Interchange with National Rail services to airport
Replacement bus service
Check before you travel. See poster journey planners.
LTM FA(a) 11.06
Correct at time of going to print
Bakerloo
Central
Circle
District
East London
Hammersmith & City
Jubilee
Metropolitan
Northern
Piccadilly
Victoria
Waterloo & City
DLR
under construction
National Rail
© Transport for London
Reg. user No. 06/4353
MAYOR OF LONDON
24 hour travel information
020 7222 1234
Website
tfl.gov.uk
Textphone
020 7918 3015
Transport for London
UNDERGROUND

Street Index

Grid references not allocated to a specific map can be found on Maps 1-16, which are contiguous and cover central London. Maps 17-28 cover individual areas, most of them outside the centre. The areas covered by all the maps are shown on p357.

A

B

C

STREET INDEX

STREET INDEX

STREET INDEX

P

Q

R

Advertiser's Index

Please refer to relevant sections for addresses/telephone numbers

Subject Index

SUBJECT INDEX

E

F

G

H

I

SUBJECT INDEX

SUBJECT INDEX

Area Index

Frankie's Italian Bar & Grill
68 Chiswick High Road, W4 1CU (8987 9988)
Giraffe
270 Chiswick High Road, W4 1PD (8995 2100)
Gourmet Burger Kitchen
131 Chiswick High Road, W4 2ED (8995 4548)
Maison Blanc
26-28 Turnham Green Terrace, W4 1QP (8995 7220)
Nando's
187-189 Chiswick High Road, W4 2DR (8995 7533)
Pizza Express
252 High Road, W4 1PD (8747 0193)
Strada
156 Chiswick High Road, W4 1PR (8995 0004)
Tootsies Grill
148 Chiswick High Road, W4 1PR (8747 1869)
Woodlands
12-14 Chiswick High Road, W4 1TH (8994 9333)
Zizzi
231 Chiswick High Road, W4 2DL (8747 9400)

Brasseries

High Road Brasserie p56
162-166 Chiswick High Road, W4 1PR (8742 7474/www.highroadhouse.co.uk)

Budget

Ground p300
217-221 Chiswick High Road, W4 2DW (8747 9113/www.groundrestaurants.com)

Fish

Fish Hook p97
8 Elliott Road, W4 1PE (8742 0766/www.fishhook.co.uk)

French

La Trompette p108
5-7 Devonshire Road, W4 2EU (8747 1836/www.latrompette.co.uk)
Le Vacherin p109
76-77 South Parade, W4 5LF (8742 2121/www.levacherin.co.uk)

Gastropubs

Roebuck p119
122 Chiswick High Road, W4 1PU (8995 4392)

Modern European

Sam's Brasserie & Bar p237
11 Barley Mow Passage, W4 4PH (8987 0555/www.samsbrasserie.co.uk)

City

The Americas

Hawksmoor p42
157 Commercial Street, E1 6BJ (7247 7392/www.thehawksmoor.com)
Missouri Grill p42
76 Aldgate High Street, EC3N 1BD (7481 4010/www.missourigrill.com)

Bars

Hawksmoor p330
157 Commercial Street, E1 6BJ (7247 7392/www.thehawksmoor.com)

Branches

Apostle (branch of Jamies)
34 Ludgate Hill, EC4M 7DE (7489 1938)
Assembly
14-15 Seething Lane, EC3N 4AX (7626 3360)
Balls Brothers
11 Blomfield Street, EC2M 1PS (7588 4643)
Balls Brothers
158 Bishopsgate, EC2M 4LN (7426 0567)
Balls Brothers
King's Arms Yard, EC2R 7AA (7796 3049)
Balls Brothers
5-6 Carey Lane, EC2V 8AE (7600 2720)
Balls Brothers
Bury Court, 38 St Mary Axe, EC3A 8EX (7929 6660)
Balls Brothers
52 Lime Street, EC3M 7BS (7283 0841)
Balls Brothers
Mark Lane, EC3R 7BB (7623 2923)
Balls Brothers
Minster Pavement, Mincing Lane, EC3R 7PP (7283 2838)
Balls Brothers
2 St Mary at Hill, EC3R 8EE (7626 0321)
Balls Brothers
Bucklersbury House, Cannon Street, EC4N 8EL (7248 7557)
Bangers (branch of Davy's)
Eldon House, 2-12 Wilson Street, EC2H 2TE (7377 6326)
Bangers Too (branch of Davy's)
1 St Mary at Hill, EC3R 8EE (7283 4443)
Bertorelli
Plantation Place, 15 Mincing Lane, EC3R 7BD (7283 3028)
Bertorelli
1 Plough Place, EC4A 1HY (7842 0510)
Bishop of Norwich (branch of Davy's)
91-93 Moorgate, EC2M 6SJ (7920 0857)
Boisdale Bishopsgate
Swedeland Court, 202 Bishopsgate, EC2M 4NR (7283 1763/www.boisdale.co.uk)
Caravaggio
107 Leadenhall Street, EC3A 4DP (7626 6206/www.etruscagroup.co.uk)
Cellar
25 Moorgate, EC2R 6AR (7330 0969)
City Boot (branch of Davy's)
7 Moorfields High Walk, EC2Y 9DP (7588 4766)
City Flogger (branch of Davy's)
Fen Court, 120 Fenchurch Street, EC3M 5BA (7623 3251)
City FOB (branch of Davy's)
Lower Thames Street, EC3R 6DJ (7621 0619)
City Pipe (branch of Davy's)
33 Foster Lane, off Cheapside, EC2V 6HD (7606 2110)
Corney & Barrow
10 Paternoster Square, EC4M 7DX (7618 9520/www.corney-barrow.co.uk)
Corney & Barrow
5 Exchange Square, EC2A 2EH (7628 4367)
Corney & Barrow
19 Broadgate Circle, EC2M 2QS (7628 1251)
Corney & Barrow
111 Old Broad Street, EC2N 1AP (7638 9308)
Corney & Barrow
12 Mason's Avenue, EC2V 5BT (7726 6030)
Corney & Barrow
1 Ropemaker Street, EC2Y 9HT (7382 0606)
Corney & Barrow
2B Eastcheap, EC3M 1AB (7929 3220)
Corney & Barrow
1 Leadenhall Place, EC3M 7DX (7621 9201)
Corney & Barrow
37A Jewry Street, EC3N 2EX (7680 8550)
Corney & Barrow
3 Fleet Place, EC4M 7RD (7329 3141)
Davy's
2 Exchange Square, EC2A 2EH (7256 5962)
Davy's
10 Creed Lane, EC4M 8SH (7236 5317)
Davy's at Plantation Place
Unit 8, Plantation Place, Mincing Lane, EC3R 5AT (7621 9878)
Gable
First floor, 25 Moorgate, EC2R 6AR (7330 0950)
Gallery
10-11 Austin Friars, EC2N 2HG (7496 9900)
Gaucho Broadgate
5 Finsbury Avenue, EC2M 2PG (7392 7652)
Gaucho City
1 Bell Inn Yard, off Gracechurch Street, EC3V 0BL (7626 5180)
Giraffe
Unit 1, Crispin Place, off Brushfield Street, E1 6DW (3116 2000)
Gourmet Burger Kitchen
Condor House, St Paul's, EC4M 8AL (7248 9299)
Gow's Restaurant & Oyster Bar (branch of Balls Brothers)
81 Old Broad Street, EC2M 1PR (7920 9645)
Habit & New Waterloo Room (branch of Davy's)
Friday Court, Crutched Friars, EC3 2ND (7481 1131)
Habit (branch of Davy's)
Friary Court, 65 Crutched Friars, EC3 2ND (7481 1131)
Haz
6 Mincing Lane, EC3M 3BD (7929 3173/3174)
Heeltap & Bumper (branch of Davy's)
2-6 Cannon Street, EC4M 6XX (7248 3371)
Jamies
107-112 Leadenhall Street, EC3A 4AA (7626 7226/www.jamiesbars.co.uk)
Jamies
155 Bishopsgate, EC2A 2AA (7256 7279)
Jamies
119-121 The Minories, EC3N 1DR (7709 9900)
Jamies
5 Groveland Court, EC4M 9EH (7248 5551)
Konditor & Cook
30 St Mary Axe, EC3A 8BF (0845 262 3030)
Last
73 Shoe Lane, EC4A 3BQ (7583 8602)
Leon
12 Ludgate Circus, EC4M 7LQ (7489 1580)
Leon
86 Cannon Street, EC4N 6HT (7623 9699)
Number 25 (branch of Jamies)
25 Birchin Lane, EC3V 9DJ (7623 2505)
Orangery (branch of Jamies)
Cutlers Gardens, 10 Devonshire Square, EC2M 4TE (7623 1377)
Paul
Kiosk, Tower of London, EC3N 4AB (7709 7300)
Paul
61 Leadenhall Market, EC3V 1LT (7929 2100)
Paul
147 Fleet Street, EC4A 2BU (7353 5874)
Paul
Paternoster Lodge, Paternoster Square, EC4M 7DX (7329 4705)
Paul
6 Bow Lane, EC4M 9EB (7489 7925)
Pavilion (branch of Jamies)
Finsbury Circus Gardens, EC2M 7AB (7628 8224)
Pizza Express
232-238 Bishopsgate, EC2M 4QD (7247 2838)
Pizza Express
125 Alban Gate, London Wall, EC2Y 5AS (7600 8880)
Pizza Express
150 London Wall, EC2Y 5HN (7588 7262)
Pizza Express
1 Byward Street, EC3R 7QN (7626 5025)
Pizza Express
20-22 Leadenhall Market, EC3V 1LR (7283 5113)
Pizza Express
1 New Fetter Lane, EC4A 1AN (7583 8880)
Pizza Express
7-9 St Bride Street, EC4A 4AS (7583 5126)
Prophet
5-11 Worship Street, EC2A 2BH (7588 8835)
Rocket
6 Adams Court, Old Broad Street, EC2N 1DX (7628 0808)
Saint (branch of Jamies)
Rose Street, Paternoster Square, EC4M 7DQ (7600 5500)
Sterling
30 St Mary Axe, EC3A 8BF (7929 3641)
Strada
88-90 Commercial Street, E1 6LY (7247 4117)
Strada
4 St Paul's Churchyard, EC4M 8AY (7248 7178)
Thai Hut
4 Burgon Street, EC4V 5BR (7213 9884)
Thai Square
136-138 Minories, EC3N 1NT (7680 1111)
Thai Square
1-7 Great St Thomas Apostle, EC4V 2BH (7329 0001)
El Vino
3 Bastion High Walk, 125 London Wall, EC2Y 5AP (7600 6377)
El Vino
30 New Bridge Street, EC4V 6BJ (7236 4534)
El Vino
6 Martin Lane, off Cannon Street, EC4R 0DP (7626 6876)
Wagamama
1 Ropemaker Street, EC2Y 9AW (7588 2688)
Wagamama
22 Old Broad Street, EC3N 1HQ (7256 9992)
Wagamama
Tower Place, off Lower Thames Street, EC3N 4EE (7283 5897)
Wagamama
109 Fleet Street, EC4A 2AB (7583 7889)
Wagamama
4 Great St Thomas Apostle, off Garlick Hill, EC4V 2BH (7248 5766)
Willy's Wine Bar (branch of Jamies)
107 Fenchurch Street, EC3M 5JF (7480 7289)
Wine Tun (branch of Davy's)
2-6 Cannon Street, EC4M 6XX (7248 3371)
Yo! Sushi
Condor House, 5-14 St Paul's Church Yard, EC4M 8AY (7248 8726)

Brasseries

Royal Exchange Grand Café & Bar p54
The Royal Exchange, EC3V 3LR (7618 2480/www.danddlondon.co.uk)

British

Canteen p61
2 Crispin Place, off Brushfield Street, E1 6DW (0845 686 1122/www.canteen.co.uk)
Paternoster Chop House p61
Warwick Court, Paternoster Square, EC4M 7DX (7029 9400/www.danddlondon.co.uk)
Rhodes Twenty Four p61
24th floor, Tower 42, Old Broad Street, EC2N 1HQ (7877 7703/www.rhodes24.co.uk)
St John Bread & Wine p61
94-96 Commercial Street, E1 6LZ (7251 0848/www.stjohnbreadandwine.com)

Budget

Grazing p298
19-21 Great Tower Street, EC3R 5AR (7283 2932/www.grazingfood.com)
Leon p298
3 Crispin Place, E1 6DW (7247 4369/www.leonrestaurants.co.uk)

Eating & Entertainment

Vertigo 42 Champagne Bar p356
Tower 42, 25 Old Broad Street, EC2N 1HQ (7877 7842/www.vertigo42.co.uk)

Fish

Chamberlain's p94
23-25 Leadenhall Market, EC3V 1LR (7648 8690/www.chamberlains.org)
Sweetings p94
39 Queen Victoria Street, EC4N 4SA (7248 3062)

French

Le Coq d'Argent p101
No.1 Poultry, EC2R 8EJ (7395 5000/www.danddlondon.com)
1 Lombard Street p101
1 Lombard Street, EC3V 9AA (7929 6611/www.1lombardstreet.com)
Rosemary Lane p102
61 Royal Mint Street, E1 8LG (7481 2602/www.rosemarylane.btinternet.co.uk)
Sauterelle p102
Royal Exchange, EC3V 3LR (7618 2483/www.danddlondon.com)

Hotels & Haute Cuisine

Addendum p139
Apex City of London Hotel, 1 Seething Lane, EC3N 4AX (7977 9500/www.addendumrestaurant.co.uk)
Bonds p139
Threadneedles, 5 Threadneedle Street, EC2R 8AY (7657 8088/www.theetongroup.com)

Italian

Refettorio p181
Crowne Plaza Hotel, 19 New Bridge Street, EC4V 6DB (7438 8052/www.refettorio.com)

Japanese

Miyabi p196
Great Eastern Hotel, Liverpool Street, EC2M 7QN (7618 7100/www.great-eastern-hotel.co.uk)

Moshi Moshi Sushi p196
24 Upper Level, Liverpool Street Station, EC2M 7QH (7247 3227/www.moshimoshi.co.uk)

Jewish

Bevis Marks Restaurant p211
Bevis Marks, EC3A 5DQ (7283 2220/www.bevismarksthe restaurant.com)

Garden Sandwich Bar p211
32 Hatton Garden, EC1N 8DL (7831 1022)

Modern European

The Don p230
The Courtyard, 20 St Swithin's Lane, EC4N 8AD (7626 2606/www.thedonrestaurant.com)

Prism p230
147 Leadenhall Street, EC3V 4QT (7256 3875/www.harveynichols.com)

Pubs

Black Friar p339
174 Queen Victoria Street, EC4V 4EG (7236 5474)

Golden Heart p339
110 Commercial Street, E1 6LZ (7247 2158)

Turkish

Haz p278
9 Cutler Street, E1 7DJ (7929 7923/www.hazrestaurant.co.uk)

Vegetarian

The Place Below p287
St Mary-le-Bow, Cheapside, EC2V 6AU (7329 0789/www.theplacebelow.co.uk)

Wine Bars

La Grande Marque p345
47 Ludgate Hill, EC4M 7JU (7329 6709/www.lagrandemarque.com)

El Vino p345
47 Fleet Street, EC4Y 1BJ (7353 6786/www.elvino.co.uk)

Clapham

The Americas

Café Sol p53
56 Clapham High Street, SW4 7UL (7498 8558/www.cafesol.net)

Bars

Lost Society p337
697 Wandsworth Road, SW8 3JF (7652 6526/www.lostsociety.co.uk)

Branches

Bierodrome
44-48 Clapham High Street, SW4 7UR (7720 1118)

Bodean's
169 Clapham High Street, SW4 7SS (7622 4248)

Fish Club
57 Clapham High Street, SW4 7TG (7720 5853)

Gourmet Burger Kitchen
84 Clapham High Street, SW4 7UL (7627 5367)

Green & Blue
20-26 Bedford Road, SW4 7HJ (7498 9648)

Nando's
59-63 Clapham High Street, SW4 7TG (7622 1475)

Pizza Express
43 Abbeville Road, SW4 9JX (8673 8878)

Strada
102-104 Clapham High Street, SW4 7UL (7627 4847)

Tootsies Grill
36-38 Abbeville Road, SW4 9NG (8772 6646)

Brasseries

Newtons p58
33-35 Abbeville Road, SW4 9LA (8673 0977/www.newtonsrestaurants.co.uk)

Budget

Gourmet Burger Kitchen p300
44 Northcote Road, SW11 1NZ (7228 3309/www.gbkinfo.com)

Cafés

Breads Etcetera p310
127 Clapham High Street, SW4 7SS (7720 3601/www.breadsetcetera.com)

Macaron p310
22 The Pavement, SW4 0HY (7498 2636)

East European

Café Wanda p90
153 Clapham High Street, SW4 7SS (7738 8760)

French

Gastro p112
67 Venn Street, SW4 0BD (7627 0222)

Trinity p112
4 The Polygon, SW4 0JG (7622 1199/www.trinityrestaurant.co.uk)

International

The Sequel p179
75 Venn Street, SW4 0BD (7622 4222/www.thesequelclapham.com)

Italian

Mooli p191
36A Old Town, SW4 0LB (7627 1166/www.moolirestaurant.com)

Japanese

Tsunami p205
5-7 Voltaire Road, SW4 6DQ (7978 1610/www.tsunamirestaurant.co.uk)

Modern European

Fouronine p243
409 Clapham Road, SW9 9BT (7737 0722/www.fouronine.co.uk)

Morel p243
14 Clapham Park Road, SW4 7BB (7627 2468/www.morelrestaurant.co.uk)

Pizza & Pasta

Eco p322
162 Clapham High Street, SW4 7UG (7978 1108/www.ecorestaurants.com)

Verso p322
84 Clapham Park Road, SW4 7BX (7720 1515)

Pubs

Bread & Roses p342
68 Clapham Manor Street, SW4 6DZ (7498 1779/www.breadandroses pub.com)

Spanish

Lola Rojo p265
78 Northcote Road, SW11 6QL (7350 2262/www.lolarojo.com)

Clapton

Cafés

Venetia p311
55 Chatsworth Road, E5 0LH (8986 1642)

Clerkenwell & Farringdon

African & Caribbean

Cottons p40
70 Exmouth Market, EC1R 4QP (7833 3332/www.cottons-restaurant.co.uk)

The Americas

The Bar & Grill p42
2-3 West Smithfield, EC1A 9JX (7246 0900/www.blackhousegrills.com)

Dollar Grills & Martinis p42
2 Exmouth Market, EC1R 4PX (7278 0077)

Branches

Carluccio's Caffè
12 West Smithfield, EC1A 9JR (7329 5904)

Heads & Tails (branch of Jamies)
64-66 West Smithfield, EC1A 9HE (7600 0700)

Konditor & Cook
46 Gray's Inn Road, WC1X 8LR (7404 6300)

LMNT II
46 Percival Street, EC1V 0HS (7253 2524)

Match EC1
45-47 Clerkenwell Road, EC1M 5RS (7250 4002/www.matchbar.com)

Pizza Express
1 Clerkenwell Road, EC1M 5PA (7253 7770)

Pizza Express
26 Cowcross Street, EC1M 6DQ (7490 8025)

La Porchetta
84-86 Rosebery Avenue, EC1R 4QY (7837 6060)

Puncheon (branch of Davy's)
Unit 5, Cowcross Place, Cowcross Street, EC1M 6DQ (7250 3336)

Strada
8-10 Exmouth Market, EC1R 4QA (7278 0800)

Tas
37 Farringdon Road, EC1M 3JB (7430 9721/9722)

Yo! Sushi
95 Farringdon Road, EC1R 3BT (7841 0785)

Brasseries

Brasserie de Malmaison p54
Malmaison, 18-21 Charterhouse Square, EC1M 6AH (7012 3700/www.malmaison-london.com)

Flâneur Food Hall p54
41 Farringdon Road, EC1M 3JB (7404 4422/www.flaneur.com)

The Larder p55
91-93 St John Street, EC1M 4NU (7608 1558/www.thelarder restaurant.com)

British

Medcalf p63
38-40 Exmouth Market, EC1R 4QE (7833 3533/www.medcalfbar.co.uk)

Quality Chop House p63
92-94 Farringdon Road, EC1R 3EA (7837 5093/www.qualitychop house.co.uk)

St John p63
26 St John Street, EC1M 4AY (7251 0848/4998/www.stjohn restaurant.com)

Top Floor at Smiths p63
Smiths of Smithfield, 67-77 Charterhouse Street, EC1M 6HJ (7251 7950/www.smithsofsmithfield.co.uk)

Budget

Clark's p304
46 Exmouth Market, EC1R 4QE (7837 1974)

Little Bay p298
171 Farringdon Road, EC1R 3AL (7278 1234/www.little-bay.co.uk)

Cafés

Kipferl p305
70 Long Lane, EC1A 9EJ (7796 2229/www.kipferl.co.uk)

Chinese

Old China Hand p76
8 Tysoe Street, EC1R 4RQ (7278 7678/www.oldchinahand.co.uk)

East European

Potemkin p92
144 Clerkenwell Road, EC1R 5DP (7278 6661/www.potemkin.co.uk)

Eating & Entertainment

Dans Le Noir p355
30-31 Clerkenwell Green, EC1R 0DU (7253 1100/www.danslenoir.com/london)

Tinseltown p356
44-46 St John Street, EC1M 4DT (7689 2424/www.tinseltown.co.uk)

French

Café du Marché p102
22 Charterhouse Square, Charterhouse Mews, EC1M 6AH (7608 1609/www.cafedumarche.co.uk)

Club Gascon p102
57 West Smithfield, EC1A 9DS (7796 0600/www.clubgascon.com)

Le Comptoir Gascon p102
61-63 Charterhouse Street, EC1M 6HJ (7608 0851/www.comptoirgascon.com)

Gastropubs

Coach & Horses p115
26-28 Ray Street, EC1R 3DJ (7278 8990/www.thecoachandhorses.com)

Eagle p117
159 Farringdon Road, EC1R 3AL (7837 1353)

Easton p117
22 Easton Street, WC1X 0DS (7278 7608)

Hat & Feathers p117
2 Clerkenwell Road, EC1M 5PQ (7490 2244)

Peasant p117
240 St John Street, EC1V 4PH (7336 7726/www.thepeasant.co.uk)

Well p117
180 St John Street, EC1V 4JY (7251 9363/www.downthewell.com)

Global

Zetter p131
86-88 Clerkenwell Road, EC1M 5RJ (7324 4455/www.thezetter.com)

Greek

The Real Greek p135
140-142 St John Street, EC1V 4UA (7253 7234/www.therealgreek.com)

International

Vic Naylor Restaurant & Bar p175
38-42 St John Street, EC1M 4AY (7608 2181/www.vicnaylor.com)

Japanese

Saki p196
4 West Smithfield, EC1A 9JX (7489 7033/www.saki-food.com)

Modern European

Ambassador p230
55 Exmouth Market, EC1R 4QL (7837 0009/www.theambassador cafe.co.uk)

Clerkenwell Dining Room p230
69-73 St John Street, EC1M 4AN (7253 9000/www.theclerkenwell.com)

Smiths of Smithfield p232
67-77 Charterhouse Street, EC1M 6HJ (7251 7950/www.smithsofsmithfield.co.uk)

Pizza & Pasta

Santoré p319
59-61 Exmouth Market, EC1R 4QL (7812 1488/www.santore-ristorante.co.uk)

Portuguese

Portal p256
88 St John Street, EC1M 4EH (7253 6950/www.portalrestaurant.com)

Pubs

Jerusalem Tavern p339
55 Britton Street, EC1M 5UQ (7490 4281/www.stpetersbrewery.co.uk)

Ye Old Mitre p339
1 Ely Court, Ely Place, at the side of 8 Hatton Gardens, EC1N 6SJ (7405 4751)

Spanish

Moro p258
34-36 Exmouth Market, EC1R 4QE (7833 8336/www.moro.co.uk)

Vietnamese

Pho p292
86 St John Street, EC1M 4EH (7253 7624/www.phocafe.co.uk)

Wine Bars

Bleeding Heart Tavern p345
Bleeding Heart Yard, 19 Greville Street, EC1N 8SJ (7404 0333/www.bleedingheart.co.uk)

Cellar Gascon p346
59 West Smithfield, EC1A 9DS (7600 7561/7796 0600/www.cellargascon.com)

Vinoteca p346
7 St John Street, EC1M 4AA (7253 8786/www.vinoteca.co.uk)

Vivat Bacchus p346
47 Farringdon Street, EC4A 4LL (7353 2648/www.vivatbacchus.co.uk)

Cockfosters Herts

Branches

Prezzo
127-129 Cockfosters Road, Cockfosters, Herts, EN4 0DA (8441 6917)

Colindale

Chinese

Shangri-La Hunan Cuisine Restaurant p87
Oriental City, 399 Edgware Road, NW9 0JJ (8200 9838)

Colliers Wood

Branches

Nando's
Unit 12, Tandem Centre, SW19 2TY (8646 8562)

Pubs

Sultan p341
78 Norman Road, SW19 1BT (8542 4532)

Covent Garden

The Americas

Christopher's p43
18 Wellington Street, WC2E 7DD (7240 4222/www.christophersgrill.com)

Joe Allen p43
13 Exeter Street, WC2E 7DT (7836 0651/www.joeallen.co.uk)

TGI Friday's p46
6 Bedford Street, WC2E 9HZ (7379 0585/www.tgifridays.co.uk)

Wahaca p53
66 Chandos Place, WC2N 4HG (7240 1883/www.wahaca.co.uk)

Branches

Belgo Centraal
50 Earlham Street, WC2H 9LJ (7813 2233)

Spanish

El Faro p267
3 Turnberry Quay, Pepper Street, E14 9RD (7987 5511/www.el-faro.co.uk)

Turkish

Mez p280
571 Manchester Road, E14 3NZ (7005 0421/www.mezrestaurant.com)

Dulwich

Branches

Pizza Express
94 The Village, SE21 7AQ (8693 9333)

Cafés

Blue Mountain Café p311
18 North Cross Road, SE22 9EU (8299 6953/www.bluemo.co.uk)

Jack's Tea & Coffee House p311
85 Pellatt Road, SE22 9JD (8693 0011)

Pavilion Café p313
Dulwich Park, SE21 7BQ (8299 1383/www.pavilioncafedulwich.co.uk)

Fish & Chips

Sea Cow p317
37 Lordship Lane, SE22 8EW (8693 3111)

Gastropubs

Herne Tavern p124
2 Forest Hill Road, SE22 0RR (8299 9521/www.theherne.net)

Palmerston p124
91 Lordship Lane, SE22 8EP (8693 1629)

Rosendale p125
65 Rosendale Road, SE21 8EZ (8670 0812/www.therosendale.co.uk)

Wine Bars

Green & Blue p349
36-38 Lordship Lane, SE22 8HJ (8693 9250/www.greenandbluewines.com)

Ealing

Branches

Carluccio's Caffè
5-6 The Green, W5 5DA (8566 4458)

Gourmet Burger Kitchen
35 Haven Green, W5 2NX (8566 8300)

Nando's
1-2 Station Buildings, Uxbridge Road, W5 3NU (8992 2290)

Pizza Express
23 Bond Street, W5 5AS (8567 7690)

Eating & Entertainment

Bella Italia p356
45 The Mall, W5 3TJ (8840 5888/ www.bellaitalia.co.uk)

Gastropubs

Ealing Park Tavern p119
222 South Ealing Road, W5 4RL (8758 1879)

Japanese

Sushi-Hiro p202
1 Station Parade, Uxbridge Road, W5 3LD (8896 3175)

Earl's Court

Branches

Balans
239 Old Brompton Road, SW5 9HP (7244 8838)

Gourmet Burger Kitchen
163-165 Earl's Court Road, SW5 9RF (7373 3184)

Masala Zone
147 Earl's Court Road, SW5 9RQ (7373 0220)

Nando's
204 Earl's Court Road, SW5 0AA (7259 2544)

Pizza Express
246 Old Brompton Road, SW5 0DE (7373 4712)

Pizza Express
Ground floor, Earl's Court Exhibition Centre, Warwick Road, SW5 9TA (7386 5494)

Strada
237 Earl's Court Road, SW5 9AH (7835 1180)

Wagamama
180-182 Earl's Court Road, SW5 9QG (7373 9660)

Zizzi
194-196 Earl's Court Road, SW5 9QF (7370 1999)

Eating & Entertainment

Troubadour p355
263-267 Old Brompton Road, SW5 9JA (7370 1434/www.troubadour.co.uk)

Fish

Lou Pescadou p98
241 Old Brompton Road, SW5 9HP (7370 1057)

Greek

As Greek As It Gets p135
233 Earl's Court Road, SW5 9AH (7244 7777)

Earlsfield

Turkish

Kazans p280
607-609 Garratt Lane, SW18 4SU (8739 0055/www.kazans.com)

Wine Bars

Willie Gunn p348
422 Garratt Lane, SW18 4HW (8946 7773/www.williegunn.co.uk)

East Dulwich

Branches

Franklins
157 Lordship Lane, SE22 8HX (8299 9598/www.franklins restaurant.com)

East Sheen

Branches

Pizza Express
305 Upper Richmond Road West, SW14 8QS (8878 6833)

La Saveur
201 Upper Richmond Road West, SW14 8QT (8876 0644)

Modern European

Redmond's p241
170 Upper Richmond Road West, SW14 8AW (8878 1922/ www.redmonds.org.uk)

Victoria p241
10 West Temple Sheen, SW14 7RT (8876 4238/www.thevictoria.net)

Eastcote Middlesex

Indian

Nauroz p169
219 Field End Road, Eastcote, Middx, HA5 1QZ (8868 0900)

Edgware Middlesex

Branches

Bloom's
313 Hale Lane, Edgware, Middx, HA8 7AX (8958 2229)

Haandi
301-303 Hale Lane, Edgware, Middx, Middx HA8 7AX (8905 4433)

Nando's
137-139 Station Road, Edgware, Middx, HA8 9JG (8952 3400)

Orli
295 Hale Lane, Edgware, Middx, HA8 7AX (8958 1555)

Jewish

Aviv p215
87-89 High Street, Edgware, Middx, HA8 7DB (8952 2484/ www.avivrestaurant.com)

Ralphy's New York Grill p215
32-34 Station Road, Edgware, Middx, HA8 7AB (8952 6036/ www.ralphys.com)

Edgware Road

Branches

Beirut Express
112-114 Edgware Road, W2 2JE (7724 2700)

Maroush Gardens
1-3 Connaught Street, W2 2DH (7262 0222)

Maroush III
62 Seymour Street, W1H 5BN (7724 5024)

Maroush IV
68 Edgware Road, W2 2EG (7224 9339)

Ranoush Juice
43 Edgware Road, W2 2JR (7723 5929)

Global

Mandalay p131
444 Edgware Road, W2 1EG (7258 3696/www.mandalayway. com)

Middle Eastern

Maroush p224
21 Edgware Road, W2 2JE (7723 0773/www.maroush.com)

Patogh p224
8 Crawford Place, W1H 5NE (7262 4015)

Ranoush Juice p224
43 Edgware Road, W2 2JR (7723 5929)

North African

Sidi Maarouf p248
56-58 Edgware Road, W2 2JE (7724 0525)

Elephant & Castle

Branches

Nando's
Unit 4, Metro Central, 119 Newington Causeway, SE1 6BA (7378 7810)

Chinese

Dragon Castle p84
100 Walworth Road, SE17 1JL (7277 3388/www.dragoncastle.co.uk)

Embankment

Hotels & Haute Cuisine

Jaan p139
Swissôtel London, The Howard, 12 Temple Place, WC2R 2PR (7300 1700/www.swissotel.com)

Enfield Middlesex

Branches

Nando's
2 The Town, Enfield, Middx, EN2 6LE (8366 2904)

Pizza Express
4 Silver Street, Enfield, Middx EN1 3ED (8367 3311)

Prezzo
The Coachouse, 26 The Town, Enfield, Middx EN2 6LU (8366 8817)

TGI Friday's
Enfield Retail Park, Great Cambridge Road, Enfield, Middx, EN1 3RZ (8363 5200)

Euston

Branches

Davy's at Regent's Place
Unit 2, Euston Tower, Regent's Place, NW1 3DP (7387 6622)

Paul
Euston Station Colonnade, Euston Station, NW1 2RT (No phone)

Pizza Express
Clifton House, 93-99 Euston Road, NW1 2RA (7383 7102)

Prezzo
161 Euston Road, NW1 2BD (7387 5587)

Rasa Express
327 Euston Road, NW1 3AD (7387 8974)

Cafés

Peyton & Byrne p305
Wellcome Collection, 183 Euston Road, NW1 2BE (7611 2142/www.peyton andbyrne.co.uk)

Chinese

Snazz Sichuan p76
New China Club, 37 Chalton Street, NW1 1JD (7388 0808)

Pizza & Pasta

Pasta Plus p319
62 Eversholt Street, NW1 1DA (7383 4943/www.pastaplus.co.uk)

Vegetarian

Greens & Beans p289
131 Drummond Street, NW1 2HL (7380 0857/www.greensandbeans.biz)

Ewell Surrey

Branches

Sree Krishna Inn
332 Kingston Road, Ewell, Surrey, KT19 0DT (8393 0445)

Finchley

The Americas

Casa Brasil p51
289 Regents Park Road, N3 3JY (8371 1999)

Branches

ASK
Great North Leisure Park, Chaplin Square, N12 0GL (8446 0970)

Nando's
Unit 2, Great North Leisure Park, Chaplin Square, N12 0GL (8492 8465)

Orli
108 Regents Park Road, N3 3JG (8371 9222)

Pizza Express
820 High Road, N12 9QY (8445 7714)

Zizzi
202-208 Regents Park Road, N3 3HP (8371 6777)

Fish & Chips

Two Brothers Fish Restaurant p318
297-303 Regent's Park Road, N3 1DP (8346 0469/ www.twobrothers.co.uk)

Jewish

The Burger Bar p211
110 Regents Park Road, N3 3JG (8371 1555)

Olive Restaurant p212
224 Regents Park Road, N3 3HP (8343 3188/www.olivekosher restaurant.co.uk)

Turkish

The Ottomans p283
118 Ballards Lane, N3 2DN (8349 9968/www.theottomans.co.uk)

Finsbury Park

Fish

Chez Liline p100
101 Stroud Green Road, N4 3PX (7263 6550)

Turkish

Petek p283
96 Stroud Green Road, N4 3EN (7619 3933)

Yildiz p283
163 Blackstock Road, N4 2JS (7354 3899)

Fitzrovia

The Americas

Eagle Bar Diner p43
3-5 Rathbone Place, W1T 1HJ (7637 1418/www.eaglebardiner.com)

Mestizo p53
103 Hampstead Road, NW1 3EL (7387 4064/www.mestizomx.com)

Bars

Crazy Bear p330
26-28 Whitfield Street, W1T 2RG (7631 0088/www.crazybeargroup.co.uk)

Hakkasan p330
8 Hanway Place, W1T 1HD (7907 1888)

Long Bar p330
The Sanderson, 50 Berners Street, W1T 3NG (7300 1400)

Match Bar p330
37-38 Margaret Street, W1G 0JF (7499 3443/www.matchbar.com)

Shochu Lounge p330
Basement, Roka, 37 Charlotte Street, W1T 1RR (7580 9666/ www.shochulounge.com)

Social p330
5 Little Portland Street, W1W 7JD (7636 4992/www.thesocial.com)

Branches

ASK
48 Grafton Way, W1T 5DZ (7388 8108)

Busaba Eathai
22 Store Street, WC1E 7DS (7299 7900)

dim T café
32 Charlotte Street, W1T 2NQ (7637 1122)

Fresco
34-36 Margaret Street, W1G 0JE (7493 3838)

Harry Morgan's
6 Market Place, W1N 7AH (7580 4849)

Jamies
74 Charlotte Street, W1T 4QH (7636 7556)

Leon
375 Regent Street, W1B 2HB (7495 1514)

Mortimer's
37-40 Berners Street, W1T 3LZ (7436 0451)

Nando's
57-59 Goodge Street, W1T 1TH (7637 0708)

Ping Pong
48 Newman Street, W1T 1QQ (7291 3080)

Ping Pong
48 Eastcastle Street, W1W 8DX (7079 0550)

Pizza Express
4-5 Langham Place, W1B 3DG (7580 3700)

Tootsies Grill
120 Holland Park Avenue, W11 4UA (7229 8567)

British

Notting Grill p67
123A Clarendon Road, W11 4JG (7229 1500/www.awtrestaurants.com)

French

The Belvedere p109
Holland House, off Abbotsbury Road, in Holland Park, W8 6LU (7602 1238/ www.whitestarline.org.uk)

Italian

Edera p189
148 Holland Park Avenue, W11 4UE (7221 6090)

Pubs

Ladbroke Arms p340
54 Ladbroke Road, W11 3NW (7727 6648/www.capitalpubcompany.com)

Holloway

East European

Tbilisi p88
91 Holloway Road, N7 8LT (7607 2536)

Hornchurch Essex

Branches

Mandarin Palace
197-201 High Street, Hornchurch, Essex, RM11 3XT (01708 437 951)

Hornsey

Brasseries

Pumphouse Dining Bar p60
1 New River Avenue, N8 7QD (8340 0400/www.phn8.co.uk)

French

Le Bistro p113
36 High Street, N8 7NX (8340 2116)

Hounslow Middlesex

Branches

Nando's
1 High Street, Hounslow, Middx, TW3 1RH (8570 5881)

Pizza Express
41-43 High Street, Hounslow, Middx TW3 1RH (8577 8522)

Ilford Essex

Branches

Nando's
Unit 1A, Clements Road, Ilford, Essex IG1 1BP (8514 6012)

Chinese

Mandarin Palace p87
559-561 Cranbrook Road, Gants Hill, Ilford, Essex, IG2 6JZ (8550 7661)

Islington

The Americas

Rodizio Rico p51
77-78 Upper Street, N1 0NU (7354 1076/www.rodiziorico.com)

Sabor p53
108 Essex Road, N1 8LX (7226 5551/www.sabor.co.uk)

Bars

25 Canonbury Lane p338
25 Canonbury Lane, N1 2AS (7226 0955/www.25canonburylane.co.uk)

Warwick p338
45 Essex Road, N1 2SF (7688 2882/www.thewarwickbar.com)

Branches

ASK
Business Design Centre, 52 Upper Street, N1 0PN (7226 8728)

Bierodrome
173-174 Upper Street, N1 1XS (7226 5835)

Carluccio's Caffè
305-307 Upper Street, N1 2TU (7359 8167)

Fine Burger Company
330 Upper Street, N1 2XQ (7359 3026)

FishWorks
134 Upper Street, N1 1QP (7354 1279)

Gallipoli
102 Upper Street, N1 1QN (7359 0630)

Gallipoli Bazaar
107 Upper Street, N1 1QN (7226 5333)

Giraffe
29-31 Essex Road, N1 2SA (7359 5999)

Hamburger Union
341 Upper Street, N1 0PB (7359 4436)

Masala Zone
80 Upper Street, N1 0NU (7359 3399/www.realindianfood.com)

Nando's
324 Upper Street, N1 2XQ (7288 0254)

Pizza Express
335 Upper Street, N1 0PB (7226 9542)

La Porchetta
141 Upper Street, N1 1QY (7288 2488)

Strada
105-106 Upper Street, N1 1QN (7226 9742)

Thai Square
347-349 Upper Street, N1 0PD (7704 2000)

Wagamama
N1 Centre, Parkfield Street, N1 0PS (7226 2664)

Yo! Sushi
N1 Centre, 39 Parkfield Street, N1 0PS (7359 3502)

Budget

Candid Arts Café p303
Candid Arts Trust, 3 Torrens Street, EC1V 1NQ (7837 4237/www.candid arts.com)

L Manze p304
74 Chapel Market, N1 9ER (7837 5270)

Le Mercury p303
140A Upper Street, N1 1QY (7354 4088/www.lemercury.co.uk)

S&M Café p303
4-6 Essex Road, N1 8LN (7359 5361/www.sandmcafe.co.uk)

Eating & Entertainment

Elbow Room p356
89-91 Chapel Market, N1 9EX (7278 3244/www.theelbowroom.co.uk)

Fish

The Fish Shop p100
360-362 St John Street, EC1V 4NR (7837 1199/www.thefishshop.net)

French

Almeida p113
30 Almeida Street, N1 1AD (7354 4777/www.danddlondon.com)

Morgan M p113
489 Liverpool Road, N7 8NS (7609 3560/www.morganm.com)

Gastropubs

Charles Lamb p129
16 Elia Street, N1 8DE (7837 5040/ www.thecharleslambpub.com)

Drapers Arms p129
44 Barnsbury Street, N1 1ER (7619 0348/www.thedrapersarms.co.uk)

Duchess of Kent p129
441 Liverpool Road, N7 8PR (7609 7104/www.geronimo-inns.co.uk)

Duke of Cambridge p129
30 St Peter's Street, N1 8JT (7359 3066/www.dukeorganic.co.uk)

House p129
63-69 Canonbury Road, N1 2DG (7704 7410/www.inthehouse.biz)

Marquess Tavern p129
32 Canonbury Street, N1 2TB (7354 2975/www.themarquess tavern.co.uk)

Northgate p129
113 Southgate Road, N1 3JS (7359 7392)

Global

Afghan Kitchen p131
35 Islington Green, N1 8DU (7359 8019)

Upper Glas p134
The Mall, 359 Upper Street, N1 0PD (7359 1932/www.glasrestaurant. co.uk)

Indian

Rooburoo p166
21 Chapel Market, N1 9EZ (7278 8100/www.rooburoo.com)

International

Ottolenghi p180
287 Upper Street, N1 2TZ (7288 1454/www.ottolenghi.co.uk)

Italian

Casale Franco p193
Rear of 134-137 Upper Street, N1 1QP (7226 8994)

Metrogusto p193
13 Theberton Street, N1 0QY (7226 9400/www.metrogusto.co.uk)

Japanese

Sa Sa Sushi p209
422 St John Street, EC1V 4NJ (7837 1155)

Modern European

Frederick's p246
Camden Passage, N1 8EG (7359 2888/www.fredericks.co.uk)

North African

Maghreb p251
189 Upper Street, N1 1RQ (7226 2305/www.maghrebrestaurant.co.uk)

Pubs

Island Queen p344
87 Noel Road, N1 8HD (7704 7631)

Thai

Isarn p277
119 Upper Street, N1 1QP (7424 5153)

Turkish

Bavo p285
105-107 Southgate Road, N1 3JS (7226 0334/www.bavo-restaurant.co.uk)

Gallipoli Again p285
120 Upper Street, N1 1QP (7359 1578/www.gallipolicafe.com)

Gem p285
265 Upper Street, N1 2UQ (7359 0405/www.gemrestaurantbar.co.uk)

Pasha p285
301 Upper Street, N1 2TU (7226 1454/www.thepasharestaurant.co.uk)

Sedir p285
4 Theberton Street, N1 0QX (7226 5489)

Kennington

African & Caribbean

Adulis p37
44-46 Brixton Road, SW9 6BT (7587 0055/www.adulis.co.uk)

Branches

Pizza Express
316 Kennington Road, SE11 4LD (7820 3877)

British

Franklins p67
205-209 Kennington Lane, SE11 5QS (7793 8313/ www.franklinsrestaurant.com)

Fish

Lobster Pot p99
3 Kennington Lane, SE11 4RG (7582 5556/www.lobsterpot restaurant.co.uk)

Kensal

Cafés

Brilliant Kids Café p312
8 Station Terrace, NW10 5RT (8964 4120/www.brilliantkids.co.uk)

Gracelands p312
118 College Road, NW10 5HD (8964 9161/www.gracelandscafe.com)

Thai

Tong Ka Nom Thai p277
833 Harrow Road, NW10 5NH (8964 5373)

Kensington

The Americas

La Bodeguita del Medio p52
47 Kensington Court, W8 5DA (7938 4147/www.bdelmlondon.com)

Sticky Fingers p47
1A Phillimore Gardens, W8 7QG (7938 5338/www.stickyfingers.co.uk)

Branches

ASK
222 Kensington High Street, W8 7RG (7937 5540)

Balans
187 Kensington High Street, W8 6SH (7376 0115)

Black & Blue
215-217 Kensington Church Street, W8 7LX (7727 0004)

The Broadwalk Café
Kensington Gardens, W2 4RU (7034 0722)

Chez Patrick
7 Stratford Road, W8 6RF (7937 6388)

dim T café
154-156 Gloucester Road, SW7 4TD (7370 0070)

Feng Sushi
24 Kensington Church Street, W8 4EP (7937 7927)

Giraffe
7 Kensington High Street, W8 5NP (7938 1221)

Maison Blanc
7A Kensington Church Street, W8 4LF (7937 4767)

Ottolenghi
1 Holland Street, W8 4NA (7937 0003)

Le Pain Quotidien
9 Young Street, W8 5EH (7486 6154)

Pizza Express
7 Rockley Road, W14 0DJ (8749 8582)

Pizza Express
35 Earl's Court Road, W8 6ED (7937 0761)

Pâtisserie Valerie
27 Kensington Church Street, W8 4LL (7937 9574)

Prezzo
35A Kensington High Street, W8 5BA (7937 2800)

Ranoush Juice Bar
86 Kensington High Street, W8 4SG (7938 2234)

Strada
29 Kensington High Street, W8 5NP (7938 4648)

Wagamama
26 Kensington High Street, W8 4PF (7376 1717)

Cafés

Kensington Palace Orangery p313
The Orangery, Kensington Palace, Kensington Gardens, W8 4PX (7376 0239/www.digbytrout.co.uk)

East European

Mimino p88
197C Kensington High Street, W8 6BA (7937 1551/www.mimino.co.uk)

Wódka p90
12 St Alban's Grove, W8 5PN (7937 6513/www.wodka.co.uk)

Indian

Zaika p158
1 Kensington High Street, W8 5NP (7795 6533/www.zaika-restaurant.co.uk)

International

Abingdon p177
54 Abingdon Road, W8 6AP (7937 3339/www.theabingdon restaurant.com)

Italian

Timo p189
343 Kensington High Street, W8 6NW (7603 3888/www.timorestaurant.net)

Middle Eastern

Randa p228
23 Kensington Church Street, W8 4LF (7937 5363)

Modern European

Babylon p238
7th floor, The Roof Gardens, 99 Kensington High Street, W8 5SA (7368 3993/www.roofgardens.com)

Clarke's p238
124 Kensington Church Street, W8 4BH (7221 9225/www.sallyclarke.com)

11 Abingdon Road p238
11 Abingdon Road, W8 6AH (7937 0120/www.abingdonroad.co.uk)

Kensington Place p238
201-209 Kensington Church Street, W8 7LX (7727 3184/www.egami.co.uk)

Launceston Place p238
1A Launceston Place, W8 5RL (7937 6912/www.egami.co.uk)

The Terrace p238
33C Holland Street, W8 4LX (7937 3224/www.theterracerestaurant.co.uk)

Whits p239
21 Abingdon Road, W8 6AH (7938 1122/www.whits.co.uk)

Spanish

L Restaurant & Bar p262
2 Abingdon Road, W8 6AF (7795 6969/www.l-restaurant.co.uk)

Kentish Town

African & Caribbean

Queen of Sheba p37
12 Fortess Road, NW5 2EU (7284 3947/www.thequeenofsheba.co.uk)

Branches

Nando's
227-229 Kentish Town Road, NW5 2JU (7424 9363)

Pizza Express
187 Kentish Town Road, NW1 8PD (7267 0101)

Gastropubs
Junction Tavern p129
101 Fortess Road, NW5 1AG (7485 9400/www.junctiontavern.co.uk)
Oxford p130
256 Kentish Town Road, NW5 2AA (7485 3521/www.realpubs.co.uk)

Italian
Pane Vino p195
323 Kentish Town Road, NW5 2TJ (7267 3879)

Kew Surrey

Branches
Kew Grill
10B Kew Green, Kew, TW9 3BH (8948 4433)
Tapas y Vino
306 Sandycombe Road, Kew, Surrey, TW9 3NG (8940 3504)

French
Ma Cuisine Le Petit Bistrot p114
9 Station Approach, Kew, Surrey, TW9 3QB (8332 1923/ www.macuisinekew.co.uk)

Gastropubs
Inn at Kew Gardens p130
292 Sandycombe Road, Kew, Surrey, TW9 3NG (8940 2220/ www.theinnatkewgardens.com)

Modern European
The Glasshouse p247
14 Station Parade, Kew, Surrey, TW9 3PZ (8940 6777/www.glasshouse restaurant.co.uk)

Kilburn

African & Caribbean
Abyssinia p39
9 Cricklewood Broadway, NW2 3JX (8208 0110)

Branches
Little Bay
228 Belsize Road, NW6 4BT (7372 4699)
Nando's
308 Kilburn High Road, NW6 2DG (7372 1507)

Gastropubs
Salusbury p130
50-52 Salusbury Road, NW6 6NN (7328 3286)

Pizza & Pasta
Osteria del Ponte p326
77 Kilburn High Road, NW6 6HY (7624 5793)

King's Cross

African & Caribbean
Addis p36
42 Caledonian Road, N1 9DT (7278 0679/www.addisrestaurant.co.uk)
New Merkato p36
196 Caledonian Road, N1 0SL (7713 8952)

Bars
Big Chill House p331
257-259 Pentonville Road, N1 9NL (7427 2540/www.bigchill.net/ house.html)

Branches
Big Chill House
257-259 Pentonville Road, N1 9NL (7427 2540/www.bigchill.net/ house.html)
Rasa Maricham
Holiday Inn, 1 King's Cross Road, WC1X 9HX (7833 9787)

Brasseries
Acorn House p56
69 Swinton Street, WC1X 9NT (7812 1842/www.acornhouserestaurant.com)

British
Konstam at the Prince Albert p64
2 Acton Street, WC1X 9NA (7833 5040/www.konstam.co.uk)

Spanish
Camino p261
3 Varnishers Yard, Regents Quarter, N1 9FD (7841 7331/www.barcamino.com)

Vietnamese
Pho @ King's Cross p292
126 King's Cross Road, WC1X 9DS (7833 9088/www.eatpho.co.uk)

Wine Bars
Smithy's p347
15-17 Leeke Street, WC1X 9HY (7278 5949/www.smithyslondon.com)

Kingston Surrey

Branches
Carluccio's Caffè
Charter Quay, Kingston upon Thames, Surrey, KT1 1HT (8549 5898)
China Royal
110 Canbury Park Road, Kingston upon Thames, Surrey, KT2 6JZ (8541 1988)
Gourmet Burger Kitchen
42-46 High Street, Kingston upon Thames, KT1 1HL (8546 1649)
Jo Shmo's
4 Jerome Place, Charter Quay, Kingston, Surrey, KT1 1HX (8439 7766)
Nando's
37-38 High Street, Kingston upon Thames, Surrey, KT1 1LQ (8296 9540)
Paul
3-5 Eden Walk, Kingston upon Thames, Surrey, KT1 1BP (8549 6799)
Pizza Express
The Rotunda, Clarence Street, Kingston upon Thames, Surrey KT1 1QJ (8547 3133)
Strada
1 The Griffin Centre, Market Place, Kingston upon Thames, Surrey, KT1 1JT (8974 8555)
TGI Friday's
The Bentall Centre, Wood Street, Kingston upon Thames, Surrey, KT1 1TR (8547 2900)
Wagamama
16-18 High Street, Kingston upon Thames, Surrey, KT1 1EY (8546 1117)
Zizzi
43 Market Place, Kingston upon Thames, Surrey KT1 1JQ (8546 0717)

Eating & Entertainment
Blue Hawaii p351
2 Richmond Road, Kingston upon Thames, Surrey, KT2 5EB (8549 6989/www.bluehawaii.co.uk)

Fish & Chips
fish! kitchen p318
58 Coombe Road, Kingston, Surrey KT2 7AF (8546 2886/ www.fishkitchen.com)

Oriental
Cammasan p255
8 Charter Quay, High Street, Kingston upon Thames, Surrey, KT1 1NB (8549 3510/www.cammasan.com)

Vegetarian
Riverside Vegetaria p291
64 High Street, Kingston upon Thames, Surrey, KT1 1HN (8546 0609/www.rsveg.plus.com)

Knightsbridge

Bars
Blue Bar p331
The Berkeley, Wilton Place, SW1X 7RL (7235 6000/www.the-berkeley.co.uk)
Mandarin Bar p331
Mandarin Oriental Hyde Park, 66 Knightsbridge, SW1X 7LA (7235 2000/www.mandarinoriental.com)
Zuma p331
5 Raphael Street, SW7 1DL (7584 1010/www.zumarestaurant.com)

Branches
FishWorks Harvey Nichols
Harvey Nichols, 109-125 Knightsbridge, SW1X 7RJ (7245 6029)
Leon
136 Brompton Road, SW3 1HY (7589 7330)
Noura
12 William Street, SW1X 9HL (7235 5900)
Patara
9 Beauchamp Place, SW3 1NQ (7581 8820)
Pâtisserie Valerie
32-44 Hans Crescent, SW1X 0LZ (7590 0905)
Pâtisserie Valerie
215 Brompton Road, SW3 2EJ (7823 9971)
Pizza Express
7 Beauchamp Place, SW3 1NQ (7589 2355)
Ranoush Juice Bar
22 Brompton Road, SW1X 7QN (7584 6999)
Wagamama
Lower ground floor, Harvey Nichols, 109-125 Knightsbridge, SW1X 7RJ (7201 8000)
Yo! Sushi
Fifth floor, Harvey Nichols Food Hall, 102-125 Knightsbridge, SW1X 7RJ (7201 8641)
Yo! Sushi
Harrods, 102-104 Brompton Road, SW3 1JJ (7893 8175)

Cafés
The Berkeley p314
Wilton Place, SW1X 7RL (7235 6000/www.the-berkeley.co.uk)
The Capital p314
22-24 Basil Street, SW3 1AT (7589 5171/7591 1202/ www.capitalhotel.co.uk)
Ladurée p306
Harrods, entrance on Hans Road, SW1X 7XL (7893 8293/ www.laduree.com)

Chinese
Mr Chow p77
151 Knightsbridge, SW1X 7PA (7589 7347/www.mrchow.com)

French
Brasserie St Quentin p105
243 Brompton Road, SW3 2EP (7589 8005/www.brasseriestquentin.co.uk)
Drones p105
1 Pont Street, SW1X 9EJ (7235 9555/www.whitestarline.org.uk)
Racine p105
239 Brompton Road, SW3 2EP (7584 4477)

Hotels & Haute Cuisine
Boxwood Café p141
The Berkeley, Wilton Place, SW1X 7RL (7235 1010/www.gordonramsay.com)
The Capital p141
22-24 Basil Street, SW3 1AT (7589 5171/7591 1202/ www.capitalhotel.co.uk)
Foliage p141
Mandarin Oriental Hyde Park Hotel, 66 Knightsbridge, SW1X 7LA (7201 3723/www.mandarinoriental.com)
Mju p141
The Millennium Knightsbridge, 16-17 Sloane Street, SW1X 9NU (7201 6330/www.millenniumhotels.com)
La Noisette p141
164 Sloane Street, SW1X 9QB (7750 5000/www.gordonramsay.com)
One-O-One p143
101 William Street, SW1X 7RN (7290 7101)
Pétrus p143
The Berkeley, Wilton Place, SW1X 7RL (7235 1200/www.petrus-restaurant. com)

Indian
Amaya p151
19 Motcomb Street, Halkin Arcade, SW1X 8JT (7823 1166/www.real indianfood.com)
Haandi p151
7 Cheval Place, SW3 1HY (7823 7373/www.haandi-restaurants.com)
Salloos p151
62-64 Kinnerton Street, SW1X 8ER (7235 4444)

Italian
San Lorenzo p182
22 Beauchamp Place, SW3 1NH (7584 1074)
Zafferano p182
15 Lowndes Street, SW1X 9EY (7235 5800/www.zafferanorestaurant.com)

Japanese
Zuma p198
5 Raphael Street, SW7 1DL (7584 1010/www.zumarestaurant.com)

Modern European
Fifth Floor p233
Harvey Nichols, Knightsbridge, SW1X 7RJ (7235 5250/ www.harveynichols.com)

Pizza & Pasta
Frankie's Italian Bar & Grill p319
3 Yeomans Row, off Brompton Road, SW3 2AL (7590 9999/www.frankies italianbarandgrill.com)

Portuguese
O Fado p256
49-50 Beauchamp Place, SW3 1NY (7589 3002/www.restauranteo fado.co.uk)

Pubs
Nag's Head p340
53 Kinnerton Street, SW1X 8ED (7235 1135)

Ladbroke Grove

Bars
Montgomery Place p335
31 Kensington Park Road, W11 2EU (7792 3921/www.montgomery place.co.uk)
Trailer Happiness p335
177 Portobello Road, W11 2DY (7727 2700/www.trailerhappiness. com)

Branches
Gourmet Burger Kitchen
160 Portobello Road, W11 2EB (7243 6597)
Hummingbird Bakery
133 Portobello Road, W11 2DY (7229 6446)
Luna Rossa
190-192 Kensington Park Road, W11 2ES (7229 0482)
Mediterraneo
37 Kensington Park Road, W11 2EU (7792 3131/www.mediterraneo-restaurant.co.uk)
Osteria Basilico
29 Kensington Park Road, W11 2EU (7727 9957/www.osteriabasilico. co.uk)
S&M Café
268 Portobello Road, W10 5TY (8968 8898)

Budget
Cockneys Pie & Mash p304
314 Portobello Road, W10 5RU (8960 9409)

Cafés
Books for Cooks p308
4 Blenheim Crescent, W11 1NN (7221 1992/www.booksforcooks.com)

Gastropubs
Fat Badger p120
310 Portobello Road, W10 5TA (8969 4500/www.thefatbadger.com)

International
Palate p179
269 Portobello Road, W11 1LR (7229 4779)

Italian
Essenza p189
210 Kensington Park Road, W11 1NR (7792 1066/www.essenza.co.uk)

North African
Moroccan Tagine p251
95 Golborne Road, W10 5NL (8968 8055)

Oriental
E&O p253
14 Blenheim Crescent, W11 1NN (7229 5454/www.rickerrestaurants. com)

Portuguese
Café Oporto p256
62A Golborne Road, W10 5PS (8968 8839)
Lisboa Pâtisserie p256
57 Golborne Road, W10 5NR (8968 5242)

Spanish
Café Garcia p263
246 Portobello Road, W11 1LL (7221 6119/www.cafegarcia.co.uk)
Galicia p263
323 Portobello Road, W10 5SY (8969 3539)

Leicester Square

The Americas
Planet Hollywood p46
Trocadero, 13 Coventry Street, W1D 7DH (7287 1000/www.planet hollywood.co.uk)

Branches
Burger Shack
147-149 Charing Cross Road, WC2H 0EE (7287 8728)
Hamburger Union
Leicester Square, WC2H 0HA (7839 8100)
Strada
39 Panton Street, SW1Y 4EA (7930 8535)
Wagamama
14 Irving Street, WC2H 7AB (7839 2323)

AREA INDEX

Gastropubs

Queen's Head & Artichoke p117
30-32 Albany Street, NW1 4EA (7916 6206/www.theartichoke.net)

Temperance p119
74-76 York Street, W1H 1QN (7262 1513)

Global

Garbo's p133
42 Crawford Street, W1H 1JW (7262 6582)

International

The Providores & Tapa Room p175
109 Marylebone High Street, W1U 4RX (7935 6175/www.theprovidores.co.uk)

Italian

Caffè Caldesi p184
118 Marylebone Lane, W1U 2QF (7935 1144/www.caffecaldesi.com)

Locanda Locatelli p184
8 Seymour Street, W1H 7JZ (7935 9088/www.locandalocatelli.com)

2 Veneti p184
10 Wigmore Street, W1U 2RD (7637 0789)

Japanese

CoCoRo p198
31 Marylebone Lane, W1U 2NH (7935 2931)

Dinings p198
22 Harcourt Street, W1H 4HH (7723 0666)

Jewish

Reuben's p211
79 Baker Street, W1U 6RG (7486 0035/www.reubensrestaurant.co.uk)

Six-13 p211
19 Wigmore Street, W1U 1PH (7629 6133/www.six13.com)

Middle Eastern

Ali Baba p224
32 Ivor Place, NW1 6DA (7723 7474/5805)

Fairuz p225
3 Blandford Street, W1U 3DA (7486 8108/8182/www.fairuz.uk.com)

Levant p225
Jason Court, 76 Wigmore Street, W1U 2SJ (7224 1111/www.levant.co.uk)

Modern European

Orrery p233
55 Marylebone High Street, W1U 5RB (7616 8000/www.danddlondon.com)

North African

Occo p250
58 Crawford Street, W1H 4NA (7724 4991/www.occo.co.uk)

Original Tagines p250
7A Dorset Street, W1U 6QN (7935 1545)

Pubs

Windsor Castle p340
29 Crawford Place, W1H 4LJ (7723 4371)

Thai

Busaba Eathai p269
8-13 Bird Street, W1U 1BU (7518 8080)

Eat-Thai.net p269
22 St Christopher's Place, W1U 1NP (7486 0777/www.eatthai.net)

Turkish

Grand Bazaar p279
42 James Street, W1N 5HS (7224 1544/www.grand-bazaar.co.uk)

Ishtar p279
10-12 Crawford Street, W1U 6AZ (7224 2446/www.ishtarrestaurant.com)

Vegetarian

Eat & Two Veg p289
50 Marylebone High Street, W1U 5HN (7258 8595/www.eatandtwoveg.com)

Mayfair

The Americas

Automat p45
33 Dover Street, W1S 4NF (7499 3033/www.automat-london.com)

Hard Rock Café p46
150 Old Park Lane, W1K 1QZ (7629 0382/www.hardrock.com)

Bars

Donovan Bar p333
Brown's Hotel, 33-34 Albemarle Street, W1S 4BP (7493 6020/www.roccofortehotels.com)

Library p333
The Lanesborough, 1 Lanesborough Place, Hyde Park Corner, SW1X 7TA (7259 5599/www.lanesborough.com)

Mahiki p333
1 Dover Street, W1S 4LD (7493 9529/www.mahiki.com)

Moose p333
31 Duke Street, W1U 1LG (7224 3452/www.vpmg.net)

Polo Bar p333
Westbury Hotel, New Bond Street, W1S 2YF (7629 7755/www.westburymayfair.com)

Branches

ASK
121-125 Park Street, W1K 7JA (7495 7760)

Balls Brothers
34 Brook Street, W1K 5DN (7499 4567)

Carluccio's Caffè
Fenwick of Bond Street, W1A 3BS (7629 0699)

Chopper Lump (branch of Davy's)
10C Hanover Square, W1R 9HD (7499 7569)

Mulligan's of Mayfair (branch of Balls Brothers)
14 Cork Street, W1S 3NS (7409 1370)

Mô Tea Room
23 Heddon Street, W1B 4BH (7434 4040/www.momoresto.com)

Noura
16 Curzon Street, W1J 5HP (7495 1050)

Pizza Express
23 Bruton Place, W1J 6ND (7495 1411)

Prezzo
15 North Audley Street, W1K 6WZ (7493 4990)

Rasa W1
6 Dering Street, W1S 1AD (7629 1346)

Sofra
18 Shepherd Street, W1Y 7HU (7493 3320)

Strada
15-16 New Burlington Street, W1S 3BJ (7287 5967)

Thai Square
5 Princess Street, W1B 2LF (7499 3333)

Brasseries

Truc Vert p56
42 North Audley Street, W1K 6ZR (7491 9988/www.trucvert.co.uk)

British

Dorchester Grill Room p64
The Dorchester, 53 Park Lane, W1K 1QA (7629 8888/www.thedorchester.com)

Budget

Fine Burger Company p300
50 James Street, W1U 1HB (7224 1890/www.fineburger.co.uk)

Cafés

Claridge's p314
55 Brook Street, W1K 4HA (7409 6307/www.claridges.co.uk)

The Connaught p314
16 Carlos Place, W1K 2AL (7499 7070/www.theconnaught.com)

The Dorchester p314
53 Park Lane, W1K 1QA (7629 8888/www.thedorchester.com)

The Lanesborough p314
1 Lanesborough Place, Hyde Park Corner, SW1X 7TA (7259 5599/www.lanesborough.com)

Sketch: The Parlour p307
9 Conduit Street, W1S 2XJ (0870 777 4488/www.sketch.uk.com)

Chinese

China Tang p78
The Dorchester, 53 Park Lane, W1K 1QA (7629 9988/www.thedorchester.com)

Kai Mayfair p79
65 South Audley Street, W1K 2QU (7493 8988/www.kaimayfair.co.uk)

Princess Garden p79
8-10 North Audley Street, W1K 6ZD (7493 3223/www.princessgardenofmayfair.com)

Eating & Entertainment

Dover Street p353
8-10 Dover Street, W1S 4LQ (7629 9813/www.doverstreet.co.uk)

Fish

Scott's p95
20 Mount Street, W1K 2HE (7495 7309/www.caprice-holdings.co.uk)

French

Mirabelle p106
56 Curzon Street, W1J 8PA (7499 4636/www.whitestarline.org.uk)

La Petite Maison p106
54 Brooks Mews, W1K 4EG (7495 4774)

Hotels & Haute Cuisine

Brian Turner Mayfair p143
Millennium Hotel Mayfair, 44 Grosvenor Square, W1K 2HP (7596 3444/www.millenniumhotels.com)

Galvin at Windows p145
28th floor, The London Hilton, Park Lane, W1K 1BE (7208 4021/www.galvinatwindows.com)

Le Gavroche p145
43 Upper Brook Street, W1K 7QR (7408 0881/www.le-gavroche.co.uk)

Gordon Ramsay at Claridge's p145
Claridge's, 55 Brook Street, W1K 4HR (7499 0099/www.gordonramsay.com)

Greenhouse p146
27A Hay's Mews, W1J 5NY (7499 3331/www.greenhouserestaurant.co.uk)

The Grill p146
Brown's Hotel, 33-34 Albemarle Street, W1S 4BP (7493 6020/www.roccofortehotels.com)

Maze p146
13-15 Grosvenor Square, W1K 6JP (7107 0000/www.gordonramsay.com)

Sketch: The Lecture Room p146
9 Conduit Street, W1S 2XZ (0870 777 4488/www.sketch.uk.com)

The Square p146
6-10 Bruton Street, W1J 6PU (7495 7100/www.squarerestaurant.com)

Theo Randall at the InterContinental p146
1 Hamilton Place, Park Lane, W1J 7QY (7409 3131/www.theorandall.com)

Indian

Benares p151
12A Berkeley Square House, Berkeley Square, W1J 6BS (7629 8886/www.benaresrestaurant.com)

Tamarind p152
20-22 Queen Street, W1J 5PR (7629 3561/www.tamarindrestaurant.com)

Veeraswamy p152
Mezzanine, Victory House, 99-101 Regent Street, W1B 4RS (7734 1401/www.realindianfood.com)

International

Sketch: The Gallery p177
9 Conduit Street, W1S 2XG (0870 777 4488/www.sketch.uk.com)

Sketch: The Glade p177
9 Conduit Street, W1S 2XG (0870 777 4488/www.sketch.uk.com)

Italian

Alloro p184
19-20 Dover Street, W1S 4LU (7495 4768)

Giardinetto p184
39-40 Albemarle Street, W1S 4TE (7493 7091/www.giardinetto.co.uk)

Ristorante Semplice p184
9-10 Blenheim Street, W1S 1LJ (7495 1509)

Sartoria p184
20 Savile Row, W1S 3PR (7534 7000/www.danddlondon.com)

Via Condotti p186
23 Conduit Street, W1S 2XS (7493 7050/www.viacondotti.co.uk)

Japanese

@ Japan p198
7A Hanover Street, W1S 1YS (7629 8801/www.atjapan.co.uk)

Chisou p199
4 Princes Street, W1B 2LE (7629 3931/www.chisou.co.uk)

Nobu p199
1st floor, The Metropolitan, 19 Old Park Lane, W1K 1LB (7447 4747/www.noburestaurants.com)

Nobu Berkeley Street p199
15 Berkeley Street, W1J 8DY (7290 9222/www.noburestaurants.com)

Umu p199
14-16 Bruton Place, W1J 6LX (7499 8881/www.umurestaurant.com)

Korean

Kaya p217
42 Albemarle Street, W1S 4JH (7499 0622/0633/www.kayarestaurant.co.uk)

Middle Eastern

Al Hamra p225
31-33 Shepherd Market, W1J 7PT (7493 1954/www.alhamrarestaurant.co.uk)

Al Sultan p225
51-52 Hertford Street, W1J 7ST (7408 1155/1166/www.alsultan.co.uk)

Modern European

Embassy p233
29 Old Burlington Street, W1S 3AN (7851 0956/www.embassylondon.com)

Langan's Brasserie p233
Stratton Street, W1J 8LB (7491 8822/www.langansrestaurants.co.uk)

Nicole's p235
158 New Bond Street, W1F 2UB (7499 8408/www.nicolefarhi.com)

Patterson's p235
4 Mill Street, W1S 2AX (7499 1308/www.pattersonsrestaurant.co.uk)

Sotheby's Café p235
Sotheby's, 34-35 New Bond Street, W1A 2AA (7293 5077)

Wild Honey p235
12 St George Street, W1S 2FB (7758 9160)

North African

Momo p250
25 Heddon Street, W1B 4BH (7434 4040/www.momoresto.com)

Oriental

Haiku p252
15 New Burlington Place, W1S 2HX (7494 4777/www.bukhara.com)

Pizza & Pasta

Prezzo p327
17 Hertford Street, W1J 7RS (7499 4690/www.prezzoplc.co.uk)

Rocket p321
4-6 Lancashire Court, off New Bond Street, W1Y 9AD (7629 2889/www.rocketrestaurants.co.uk)

Spanish

El Pirata p261
5-6 Down Street, W1J 7AQ (7491 3810/www.elpirata.co.uk)

Thai

Patara p269
3&7 Maddox Street, W1S 2QB (7499 6008)

Mile End

Pubs

Palm Tree p343
127 Grove Road, E3 5BH (8980 2918)

Mill Hill

Branches

Pizza Express
92 The Broadway, NW7 3TB (8959 3898)

TGI Friday's
Pentavia Retail Park, Watford Way, NW7 3JA (8203 9779)

Muswell Hill

Branches

ASK
43 Muswell Hill Broadway, N10 3AH (8365 2833)

Fine Burger Company
256 Muswell Hill Broadway, N10 3SH (8815 9292)

Giraffe
348 Muswell Hill Broadway, N10 1DJ (8883 4463)

Maison Blanc
61 Muswell Hill Broadway, N10 3HA (8883 7520)

Pizza Express
290 Muswell Hill Broadway, N10 2QR (8883 5845)

Prezzo
82 Fortis Green Road, N10 3HP (8883 6198)

Brasseries

Café on the Hill p60
46 Fortis Green Road, N10 3HN (8444 4957)

Fish & Chips

Toff's p318
38 Muswell Hill Broadway, N10 3RT (8883 8656)

South Kensington

The Americas

PJ's Grill p45
52 Fulham Road, SW3 6HH (7581 0025/www.pjsgrill.net)

Bars

190 Queensgate p335
The Gore Hotel, 190 Queensgate, SW7 5EX (7584 6601/www.gorehotel.co.uk)

Branches

Baker & Spice
47 Denyer Street, SW3 2LX (7589 4734)
Carluccio's Caffè
1 Old Brompton Road, SW7 3HZ (7581 8101)
El Gaucho
30B Old Brompton Road, SW7 3DL (7584 8999)
Gourmet Burger Kitchen
107 Old Brompton Road, SW7 3LE (7590 0979)
Hugo's
51 Prince's Gate, Exhibition Road, SW7 2PG (7596 4006)
Kulu Kulu
39 Thurloe Place, SW7 2HP (7589 2225)
Maison Blanc
11 Elystan Street, SW3 3NT (7584 6913)
Nando's
117 Gloucester Road, SW7 4ST (7373 4446)
Patara
181 Fulham Road, SW3 6JN (7351 5692)
Paul
47 Thurloe Street, SW7 2LQ (7581 6034)
Thai Square
19 Exhibition Road, SW7 2HE (7584 8359)
Tootsies Grill
107 Old Brompton Road, SW7 3LE (7581 8942)

Cafés

Hummingbird Bakery p308
47 Old Brompton Road, SW7 3JP (7584 0055/www.hummingbird bakery.com)

East European

Daquise p89
20 Thurloe Street, SW7 2LP (7589 6117)

Fish

Bibendum Oyster Bar p97
Michelin House, 81 Fulham Road, SW3 6RD (7589 1480/www.bibendum.co.uk)
Poissonnerie de l'Avenue p97
82 Sloane Avenue, SW3 3DZ (7589 2457/www.poissonnerie delavenue.co.uk)

French

Papillon p108
96 Draycott Avenue, SW3 3AD (7225 2555/www.papillonchelsea.co.uk)

Global

Brompton Quarter Café p132
225 Brompton Road, SW3 2EJ (7225 2107)
Lundum's p134
117-119 Old Brompton Road, SW7 3RN (7373 7774/www.lundums.com)

Hotels & Haute Cuisine

Tom Aikens p148
43 Elystan Street, SW3 3NT (7584 2003/www.tomaikens.co.uk)

Italian

Daphne's p187
112 Draycott Avenue, SW3 3AE (7589 4257/www.daphnes-restaurant.co.uk)

Malaysian, Indonesian & Singaporean

Awana p220
85 Sloane Avenue, SW3 3DX (7584 8880/www.awana.co.uk)

Modern European

Bibendum p237
Michelin House, 81 Fulham Road, SW3 6RD (7581 5817/www.bibendum.co.uk)

Pubs

Anglesea Arms p340
15 Selwood Terrace, SW7 3QG (7373 7960/www.capitalpub company.com)

Spanish

Cambio de Tercio p262
163 Old Brompton Road, SW5 0LJ (7244 8970/www.cambiodetercio.co.uk)
Tendido Cero p262
174 Old Brompton Road, SW5 0BA (7370 3685/www.cambiodetercio.co.uk)

Wine Bars

Oratory p348
234 Brompton Road, SW3 2BB (7584 3493/www.brinkleys.com)

South Norwood

Thai

Mantanah p275
2 Orton Building, Portland Road, SE25 4UD (8771 1148/www.mantanah.co.uk)

South Woodford

The Americas

Yellow Book Californian Café p49
190 George Lane, E18 1AY (8989 3999/www.theyellowbook.co.uk)

Branches

Prezzo
Elmhurst, 98-106 High Road, South Woodford, Essex E18 2QH (8559 0192)

Fish

Ark Fish Restaurant p99
142 Hermon Hill, E18 1QH (8989 5345/www.arkfishrestaurant.com)

Southall Middlesex

Indian

Brilliant p171
72-76 Western Road, Southall, Middx UB2 5DZ (8574 1928/www.brilliant restaurant.com)
Delhi Wala p171
11 King Street, Southall, Middx, UB2 4DG (8574 0873)
Madhu's p171
39 South Road, Southall, Middx, UB1 1SW (8574 1897/www.madhus online.com)
New Asian Tandoori Centre (Roxy) p172
114-118 The Green, Southall, Middx, UB2 4BQ (8574 2597)

Southgate

Branches

Pizza Express
94 Chaseside, N14 5PH (8886 3300)

Stamford Hill

Cafés

Springfield Park Café p314
White Lodge Mansion, Springfield Park, E5 9EF (8806 0444/www.spark cafe.co.uk)

Stanmore Middlesex

Branches

Pizza Express
55 The Broadway, Stanmore, Middx HA7 4DJ (8420 7474)

Indian

Papaji's Lounge p172
865 Honeypot Lane, Stanmore, Middx, HA7 1AR (8905 6966/www.papajis.com)

Stockwell

Branches

Lisboa Pâtisserie
147 South Lambeth Road, SW8 1XN (7587 1612)

Portuguese

Bar Estrela p257
111-115 South Lambeth Road, SW8 1UZ (7793 1051)
Grelha D'Ouro p257
151 South Lambeth Road, SW8 1XN (7735 9764)
O Moinho p257
355A Wandsworth Road, SW8 2JH (7498 6333)

Pubs

Priory Arms p342
83 Lansdowne Way, SW8 2PB (7622 1884)

Stoke Newington

Branches

Il Bacio
61 Stoke Newington Church Street, N16 0AR (7249 3833)
Il Bacio Express
90 Stoke Newington Church Street, N16 0AD (7249 2344)
19 Numara Bos Cirrik II
194 Stoke Newington High Street, N16 7JD (7249 9111)
Rasa Travancore
56 Stoke Newington Church Street, N16 0NB (7249 1340)
Sea Cow
67 Stoke Newington Church Street, N16 0AR (7249 6566)

Budget

Blue Legume p303
101 Stoke Newington Church Street, N16 0UD (7923 1303)

Indian

Rasa p166
55 Stoke Newington Church Street, N16 0AR (7249 0344/www.rasa restaurants.com)

Oriental

Itto p255
226 Stoke Newington High Street, N16 7HU (7275 8827)

Strand

The Americas

Smollensky's on the Strand p46
105 Strand, WC2R 0AA (7497 2101/www.smollenskys.co.uk)

Branches

Champagne Charlies (branch of Davy's)
17 The Arches, off Villiers Street, WC2N 4NN (7930 7737)
Leon
33 Villiers Street, WC2N 6ND (7240 3070)
Leon
73-76 Strand, WC2R 0DE (7240 3070)
Pizza Express
450 The Strand, WC2R 0RG (7930 8205)
Pizza Express
147 The Strand, WC2R 1JA (7836 7716)
Tappit Hen (branch of Davy's)
5 William IV Street, WC2N 4DW (7836 9839)
Thai Square on the Strand
148 Strand, WC2R 1JA (7497 0904)

British

Simpson's-in-the-Strand p66
100 Strand, WC2R 0EW (7836 9112/www.simpsons-in-the-strand.com)

French

The Admiralty p108
Somerset House, Strand, WC2R 1LA (7845 4646/www.somerset-house.org.uk)

Pizza & Pasta

Zizzi p327
73-75 Strand, WC2R 0DE (7240 1717/www.zizzi.co.uk)

Wine Bars

Gordon's p348
47 Villiers Street, WC2N 6NE (7930 1408/www.gordonswinebar.com)

Stratford

Branches

Nando's
1A Romford Road, E15 4LJ (8221 2148)
Pizza Express
Theatre Square, Stratford East, E15 1BX (8534 1700)

Pubs

King Eddie's p343
47 Broadway, E15 4BQ (8534 2313/www.kingeddie.co.uk)

Streatham

Branches

Nando's
Unit 6-7, The High Parade, SW16 1EX (8769 0951)
Pizza Express
34-36 Streatham High Road, SW16 1DB (8769 0202)

Stroud Green

Branches

Nando's
106 Stroud Green Road, N4 3HB (7263 7447)
La Porchetta
147 Stroud Green Road, N4 3PZ (7281 2892)

Sudbury Middlesex

Indian

Five Hot Chillies p172
875 Harrow Road, Sudbury, Middx, HA0 2RH (8908 5900)

Surbiton Surrey

French

The French Table p114
85 Maple Road, Surbiton, Surrey, KT6 4AW (8399 2365/www.the frenchtable.co.uk)

Sutton Surrey

Branches

Nando's
9-11 High Street, Sutton, Surrey SM1 1DF (8770 0180)
Pizza Express
4 High Street, Sutton, Surrey SM1 1HN (8643 4725)
Zizzi
13-15 High Street, Sutton, Surrey SM1 1DF (8661 8778)

Budget

M Manze p304
226 High Street, Sutton, Surrey SM1 1NT (8286 8787/www.manze.co.uk)

Swiss Cottage

Branches

Elbow Room
135 Finchley Road, NW3 6JA (7586 9888)
Eriki
4-6 Northways Parade, Finchley Road, NW3 5EN (7722 0606/www.eriki.co.uk)
Fine Burger Company
1st floor, O2 Centre, 255 Finchley Road, NW3 6LU (7433 0700)
Hafez II
559 Finchley Road, NW3 7BJ (7431 4546)
Nando's
O2 Centre, 255 Finchley Road, NW3 6LU (7435 4644)
Pizza Express
227 Finchley Road, NW3 6LP (7794 5100)
Yo! Sushi
O2 Centre, 255 Finchley Road, NW3 6LU (7431 4499)

Chinese

Green Cottage p87
9 New College Parade, Finchley Road, NW3 5EP (7722 5305/7892)

Greek

Hellenic Restaurant p138
291 Finchley Road, NW3 6ND (7431 1001/www.gonumber.com/hellenic)

Indian

Atma p167
106C Finchley Road, NW3 5JJ (7431 9487/www.atmarestaurnats.com)
Cumin p167
O2 Centre, 255 Finchley Road, NW3 6LU (7794 5616/www.cumin.co.uk)

Japanese

Benihana p210
100 Avenue Road, NW3 3HF (7586 9508/www.benihana.co.uk)
Wakaba p210
122A Finchley Road, NW3 5HT (7586 7960)

Malaysian, Indonesian & Singaporean

Singapore Garden p223
83A Fairfax Road, NW6 4DY (7624 8233/www.singaporegarden.co.uk)

Teddington Middlesex

Branches

Pizza Express
11 Waldegrave Road, Teddington, Middx TW11 8LA (8943 3553)

AREA INDEX

Fish & Chips

Masters Super Fish p317
191 Waterloo Road, SE1 8UX (7928 6924)

French

RSJ p112
33 Coin Street, SE1 9NR (7928 4554/www.rsj.uk.com)

Gastropubs

Anchor & Hope p123
36 The Cut, SE1 8LP (7928 9898)

International

Laughing Gravy p179
154 Blackfriars Road, SE1 8EN (7721 7055/www.thelaughing gravy.com)

Japanese

Bincho p205
2nd floor, Oxo Tower Wharf, Barge House Street, SE1 9PH (7803 0858/ www.bincho.co.uk)

Ozu p206
County Hall, Westminster Bridge Road, SE1 7PB (7928 7766/ www.ozulondon.com)

Modern European

Oxo Tower Restaurant, Bar & Brasserie p243
Eighth floor, Oxo Tower Wharf, Barge House Street, SE1 9PH (7803 3888/ www.harveynichols.com)

Skylon p243
Royal Festival Hall, Belvedere Road, SE1 8XX (7654 7800/www.dandd london.com)

Pizza & Pasta

Pizza Paradiso p326
61 The Cut, SE1 8LL (7261 1221/ www.pizzaparadiso.co.uk)

Strada p327
Riverside, Royal Festival Hall, Belvedere Road, SE1 8XX (7401 9126/www.strada.co.uk)

Spanish

Mar i Terra p265
14 Gambia Street, SE1 0XH (7928 7628/www.mariterra.co.uk)

Turkish

Troia p280
3F Belvedere Road, SE1 7GQ (7633 9309)

Wembley Middlesex

Branches

Nando's
420-422 High Road, Wembley, Middx, HA9 6AH (8795 3564)

Indian

Dadima p173
228 Ealing Road, Wembley, Middx, HA0 4QL (8902 1072)

Karahi King p173
213 East Lane, North Wembley, Middx, HA0 3NG (8904 2760)

Sakonis p174
129 Ealing Road, Wembley, Middx, HA0 4BP (8903 9601)

Sanghamam p174
531-533 High Road, Wembley, Middx, HA0 2DJ (8900 0777/ www.sanghamam.co.uk)

Middle Eastern

Mesopotamia p229
115 Wembley Park Drive, Wembley, Middx, HA9 8HG (8453 5555/ www.mesopotamia.ltd.uk)

West Hampstead

African & Caribbean

Tobia p39
1st floor, Ethiopian Community Centre, 2A Lithos Road, NW3 6EF (7431 4213/www.tobiarestaurant. co.uk)

Branches

Gourmet Burger Kitchen
331 West End Lane, NW6 1RS (7794 5455)

Nando's
252-254 West End Lane, NW6 1LU (7794 1331)

Pizza Express
319 West End Lane, NW6 1RP (7431 8229)

East European

Czechoslovak Restaurant p88
Czech & Slovak House, 74 West End Lane, NW6 2LX (7372 1193/ www.czechoslovak-restaurant.co.uk)

Fish & Chips

Nautilus p318
27-29 Fortune Green Road, NW6 1DT (7435 2532)

Modern European

Walnut p246
280 West End Lane, NW6 1LJ (7794 7772/www.walnutwalnut.com)

Pizza & Pasta

La Brocca p327
273 West End Lane, NW6 1QS (7433 1989)

Wine Bars

No.77 Wine Bar p350
77 Mill Lane, NW6 1NB (7435 7787)

West Kensington

Turkish

Best Mangal p280
104 North End Road, W14 9EX (7610 1050)

Vegetarian

222 Veggie Vegan p290
222 North End Road, W14 9NU (7381 2322/www.222veggievegan. com)

Westbourne Grove

Bars

Lonsdale p335
44-48 Lonsdale Road, W11 2DE (7727 4080/www.thelonsdale.co.uk)

Branches

Carluccio's Caffè
Westbourne Corner, 108 Westbourne Grove, W2 5RU (7243 8164)

FishWorks
188 Westbourne Grove, W11 2RH (7229 3366)

Cafés

Raoul's Café p309
105-107 Talbot Road, W11 2AT (7229 2400/www.raoulsgourmet.com)

Tea Palace p309
175 Westbourne Grove, W11 2SB (7727 2600/www.teapalace.co.uk)

Tom's Delicatessen p309
226 Westbourne Grove, W11 2RH (7221 8818)

French

The Ledbury p111
127 Ledbury Road, W11 2AQ (7792 9090/www.theledbury.com)

Gastropubs

Cow p121
89 Westbourne Park Road, W2 5QH (7221 0021/www.thecowlondon.co.uk)

Malaysian, Indonesian & Singaporean

C&R Restaurant p221
52 Westbourne Grove, W2 5SH (7221 7979)

Pizza & Pasta

Mulberry Street p321
84 Westbourne Grove, W2 5RT (7313 6789/www.mulberrystreet.co.uk)

Wine Bars

Negozio Classica p348
283 Westbourne Grove, W11 2QA (7034 0005/www.negozioclassica. co.uk)

Westbourne Park

African & Caribbean

Mosob p36
339 Harrow Road, W9 3RB (7266 2012/www.mosob.co.uk)

The Americas

Lucky 7 p47
127 Westbourne Park Road, W2 5QL (7727 6771)

Westminster

Indian

Cinnamon Club p158
The Old Westminster Library, 30-32 Great Smith Street, SW1P 3BU (7222 2555/www.cinnamonclub.com)

International

The Atrium p177
4 Millbank, SW1P 3JA (7233 0032/ www.atriumrestaurant.com)

The Vincent Rooms p177
Westminster Kingsway College, Vincent Square, SW1P 2PD (7802 8391/www.westking.ac.uk)

Italian

Quirinale p187
North Court, 1 Great Peter Street, SW1P 3LL (7222 7080/ www.quirinale.co.uk)

Japanese

Atami p202
37 Monck Street, SW1P 2BL (7222 2218/www.atamirestaurant. co.uk)

Modern European

Bank Westminster p237
45 Buckingham Gate, SW1E 6BS (7379 9797/www.bankrestaurants. com)

Whetstone

Branches

ASK
1257 High Road, N20 0EW (8492 0033)

Pizza Express
1264 High Road, N20 9HH (8446 8800)

Whitechapel

Branches

Grapeshots (branch of Davy's)
2-3 Artillery Passage, E1 7LJ (7247 8215)

Nando's
9-25 Mile End Road, E1 4TW (7791 2720)

Indian

Café Spice Namaste p164
16 Prescot Street, E1 8AZ (7488 9242/www.cafespice.co.uk)

Kolapata p166
222 Whitechapel Road, E1 1BJ (7377 1200)

Willesden

Branches

Shish
2-6 Station Parade, NW2 4NH (8208 9292)

Japanese

Sushi-Say p210
33B Walm Lane, NW2 5SH (8459 2971)

Wimbledon

The Americas

Jo Shmo's p47
33 High Street, SW19 5BY (8879 3845/www.joshmos.com)

Tootsies Grill p47
48 High Street, SW19 5AX (8946 4135/www.tootsies restaurants.com)

Branches

Common Room (branch of Jamies)
18 High Street, SW19 5DX (8944 1909)

Giraffe
21 High Street, Wimbledon Village, SW19 5DX (8946 0544)

Gourmet Burger Kitchen
88 The Broadway, SW19 1RH (8540 3300)

Nando's
1 Russell Road, SW19 1QN (8545 0909)

Pizza Express
104 The Broadway, SW19 1RH (8543 1010)

Pizza Express
84 High Street, SW19 5EG (8946 6027)

San Lorenzo
38 Wimbledon Hill Road, SW19 7PA (8946 8463)

Strada
91 High Street, SW19 5EG (8946 4363)

Sukho
29 Wimbledon Hill Road, SW19 7NE (8947 9199)

Tinseltown
Centre Court Shopping Centre, 4 Queens Road, SW19 8YA (8605 2424)

Wagamama
46-48 Wimbledon Hill Road, SW19 7PA (8879 7280)

Eating & Entertainment

Wimbledon Stadium p353
Plough Lane, SW17 0BL (8946 8000/www.lovethedogs.co.uk)

Gastropubs

Earl Spencer p122
260-262 Merton Road, SW18 5JL (8870 9244/www.theearlspencer. co.uk)

Japanese

Kushi-Tei p203
264 The Broadway, SW19 1SB (8543 1188/www.kushi-tei.com)

Winchmore Hill

Branches

Pizza Express
701 Green Lanes, N21 3RS (8364 2992)

Wood Green

Branches

Mosaica @ the factory
The Chocolate Factory, Wood Green Business Centre, Clarendon Road, N22 6XJ (8889 2400)

Nando's
Hollywood Green, Redvers Road, N22 6EN (8889 2936)

Greek

Vrisaki p137
73 Myddleton Road, N22 8LZ (8889 8760)

Woodford

Branches

Pizza Express
76-78 High Road, E18 2NA (8924 4488)

Prezzo
8 Johnson Road, Woodford Green, Essex 1G8 0XA (8505 2400)

A-Z Index

A

B

Cocoon p333
65 Regent Street, W1B 4EA (7494 7609/www.cocoon-restaurants.com). Bars

CoCoRo p198
31 Marylebone Lane, W1U 2NH (7935 2931). Japanese

CoCoRo Sushi
232 Archway Road, N6 5AX (7935 2931). Branch

La Collina p193
17 Princess Road, NW1 8JR (7483 0192). Italian

Colton Arms p341
187 Greyhound Road, W14 9SD (7385 6956). Pubs

Commercial p342
210-212 Railton Road, SE24 0JT (7501 9051). Pubs

Common Ground p313
Wandsworth Common, off Dorlcote Road, SW18 3RT (8874 9386). Cafés

Common Room (branch of Jamies)
18 High Street, SW19 5DX (8944 1909). Branch

Le Comptoir Gascon p102
61-63 Charterhouse Street, EC1M 6HJ (7608 0851/www.comptoir gascon.com). French

Il Convivio p181
143 Ebury Street, SW1W 9QN (7730 4099/www.etruscagroup.co.uk). Italian

The Connaught p314
16 Carlos Place, W1K 2AL (7499 7070/www.theconnaught.com). Cafés

F Cooke p304
9 Broadway Market, E8 4PH (7254 6458). Budget

F Cooke p304
150 Hoxton Street, N1 6SH (7729 7718). Budget

Cooperage (branch of Davy's)
48-50 Tooley Street, SE1 2SZ (7403 5775). Branch

Le Coq d'Argent p101
No.1 Poultry, EC2R 8EJ (7395 5000/www.danddlondon.com). French

Corean Chilli p216
51 Charing Cross Road, WC2H 0NE (7734 6737). Korean

Cork & Bottle p347
44-46 Cranbourn Street, WC2H 7AN (7734 7807/www.donhewitson.com). Wine Bars

Corney & Barrow
10 Paternoster Square, EC4M 7DX (7618 9520/www.corney-barrow.co.uk). Wine Bars

Corney & Barrow
9 Cabot Square, E14 4EB (7512 0397). Branch

Corney & Barrow
5 Exchange Square, EC2A 2EH (7628 4367). Branch

Corney & Barrow
19 Broadgate Circle, EC2M 2QS (7628 1251). Branch

Corney & Barrow
111 Old Broad Street, EC2N 1AP (7638 9308). Branch

Corney & Barrow
12 Mason's Avenue, EC2V 5BT (7726 6030). Branch

Corney & Barrow
1 Ropemaker Street, EC2Y 9HT (7382 0606). Branch

Corney & Barrow
2B Eastcheap, EC3M 1AB (7929 3220). Branch

Corney & Barrow
1 Leadenhall Place, EC3M 7DX (7621 9201). Branch

Corney & Barrow
37A Jewry Street, EC3N 2EX (7680 8550). Branch

Corney & Barrow
3 Fleet Place, EC4M 7RD (7329 3141). Branch

Costas Fish Restaurant p316
18 Hillgate Street, W8 7SR (7727 4310). Fish & Chips

Cottons p40
70 Exmouth Market, EC1R 4QP (7833 3332/www.cottons-restaurant.co.uk). African & Caribbean

Cottons
55 Chalk Farm Road, NW1 8AN (7485 8388). Branch

Couscous Café p251
7 Porchester Gardens, W2 4DB (7727 6597). North African

Cow p121
89 Westbourne Park Road, W2 5QH (7221 0021/www.thecowlondon.co.uk). Gastropubs

Cow & Coffee Bean
Greenwich Park, Queen Mary's Gate, SE10 8PU (8293 0703). Branch

The Coyote p46
2 Fauconberg Road, W4 3JY (8742 8545/www.thecoyote.co.uk). The Americas

Crazy Bear p252, p330
26-28 Whitfield Street, W1T 2RG (7631 0088/www.crazybear group.co.uk). Oriental, Bars

Cricketers p344
The Green, Richmond, Surrey, TW9 1LX (8940 4372). Pubs

Crispy Duck p72
27 Wardour Street, W1D 6PR (7287 6578). Chinese

Crispy Duck
7 Gerrard Street, W1D 5PH (7434 1888). Branch

Criterion p107
224 Piccadilly, W1J 9HP (7930 0488/www.whitestarline.org.uk). French

Crumpet p310
66 Northcote Road, SW11 6QL (7924 1117/www.crumpet.biz). Cafés

Crusting Pipe (branch of Davy's)
27 The Market, WC2E 8RD (7836 1415). Branch

Cumberland Arms p120
29 North End Road, W14 8SZ (7371 6806/www.thecumberland armspub.co.uk). Gastropubs

Cumin p167
02 Centre, 255 Finchley Road, NW3 6LU (7794 5616/www.cumin.co.uk). Indian

Curve p48
London Marriott, West India Quay, 22 Hertsmere Road, E14 4ED (7093 1000 ext 2622/www.marriott hotels.com). The Americas

Czechoslovak Restaurant p88
Czech & Slovak House, 74 West End Lane, NW6 2LX (7372 1193/www.czechoslovak-restaurant.co.uk). East European

Cây Tre
301 Old Street, EC1V 9LA (7729 8662). Branch

D

Dadima p173
228 Ealing Road, Wembley, Middx, HA0 4QL (8902 1072). Indian

Dalston Jazz Bar p338
4 Bradbury Street, N16 8JN (7254 9728). Bars

Dans Le Noir p355
30-31 Clerkenwell Green, EC1R 0DU (7253 1100/www.danslenoir.com/london). Eating & Entertainment

Daphne p136
83 Bayham Street, NW1 0AG (7267 7322). Greek

Daphne's p187
112 Draycott Avenue, SW3 3AE (7589 4257/www.daphnes-restaurant.co.uk). Italian

Daquise p89
20 Thurloe Street, SW7 2LP (7589 6117). East European

Dark Horse p124
16 Grove Lane, SE5 8SY (7703 9990). Gastropubs

Davy's
31-35 Fisherman's Walk, Cabot Square, E14 4DH (7363 6633). Branch

Davy's
2 Exchange Square, EC2A 2EH (7256 5962). Branch

Davy's
10 Creed Lane, EC4M 8SH (7236 5317). Branch

Davy's at Plantation Place
Unit 8, Plantation Place, Mincing Lane, EC3R 5AT (7621 9878). Branch

Davy's at Regent's Place
Unit 2, Euston Tower, Regent's Place, NW1 3DP (7387 6622). Branch

Davy's at St James's
Crown Passage, Pall Mall, SW1Y 6QY (7839 8831). Branch

Davy's White City
Units 4 & 5, Media Centre, White City Media Village, 201 Wood Lane, W12 7ST (8811 2862). Branch

Davy's Wine Vaults
161-163 Greenwich High Road, SE10 8JA (8858 7204). Branch

Deep p98
The Boulevard, Imperial Wharf, SW6 2UB (7736 3337/www.deep london.co.uk). Fish

Delfina p245
50 Bermondsey Street, SE1 3UD (7357 0244/www.thedelfina.co.uk). Modern European

Delhi Wala p171
11 King Street, Southall, Middx, UB2 4DG (8574 0873). Indian

The Depot p56
Tideway Yard, 125 Mortlake High Street, SW14 8SN (8878 9462/www.depotbrasserie.co.uk). Brasseries

Le Deuxième p175
65A Long Acre, WC2E 9JH (7379 0033/www.ledeuxieme.com). International

Dexter's Grill & Bar p46
20 Bellevue Road, SW17 7EB (8767 1858/www.tootsies restaurants.co.uk). The Americas

dim T café p255
3 Heath Street, NW3 6TP (7435 0024/www.dimt.co.uk). Oriental

dim T café
1A Hampstead Lane, N6 4RS (8340 8800). Branch

dim T café
2B More London, Riverside, SE1 2JP (7403 7000). Branch

dim T café
154-156 Gloucester Road, SW7 4TD (7370 0070). Branch

dim T café
32 Charlotte Street, W1T 2NQ (7637 1122). Branch

The Diner p45
18-20 Ganton Street, W1F 7BU (7287 8962/www.thedinersoho.com). The Americas

Dinings p198
22 Harcourt Street, W1H 4HH (7723 0666). Japanese

Dizengoff's p212
118 Golders Green Road, NW11 8HB (8458 7003/www.dizengoffkosher restaurant.co.uk). Jewish

Dog & Bell p342
116 Prince Street, SE8 3JD (8692 5664/www.thedogandbell.com). Pubs

Dollar Grills & Martinis p42
2 Exmouth Market, EC1R 4PX (7278 0077). The Americas

The Don p230
The Courtyard, 20 St Swithin's Lane, EC4N 8AD (7626 2606/www.thedonrestaurant.com). Modern European

Dong San p217
47 Poland Street, W1F 7NB (7287 0997). Korean

Donna Margherita p322
183 Lavender Hill, SW11 5TE (7228 2660/www.donna-margherita.com). Pizza & Pasta

Donovan Bar p333
Brown's Hotel, 33-34 Albemarle Street, W1S 4BP (7493 6020/www.rocco fortehotels.com). Bars

Donzoko p200
15 Kingly Street, W1B 5PS (7734 1974). Japanese

La Dorada p214
134 Brent Street, NW4 2DR (8202 1339). Jewish

The Dorchester p314
53 Park Lane, W1K 1QA (7629 8888/www.thedorchester.com). Cafés

Dorchester Grill Room p64
The Dorchester, 53 Park Lane, W1K 1QA (7629 8888/www.thedorchester.com). British

Dove p340
19 Upper Mall, W6 9TA (8748 9474). Pubs

Dover Street p353
8-10 Dover Street, W1S 4LQ (7629 9813/www.doverstreet.co.uk). Eating & Entertainment

Dragon Castle p84
100 Walworth Road, SE17 1JL (7277 3388/www.dragoncastle.co.uk). Chinese

Drapers Arms p129
44 Barnsbury Street, N1 1ER (7619 0348/www.thedrapersarms.co.uk). Gastropubs

Drones p105
1 Pont Street, SW1X 9EJ (7235 9555/www.whitestarline.org.uk). French

Al Duca p186
4-5 Duke of York Street, SW1Y 6LA (7839 3090/www.alduca-restaurant.co.uk). Italian

Duchess of Kent p129
441 Liverpool Road, N7 8PR (7609 7104/www.geronimo-inns.co.uk). Gastropubs

Duke of Cambridge p129
30 St Peter's Street, N1 8JT (7359 3066/www.dukeorganic.co.uk). Gastropubs

Dukes Hotel p334
Dukes Hotel, 35 St James's Place, SW1A 1NY (7491 4840/www.dukeshotel.co.uk). Bars

Dusk p337
339 Battersea Park Road, SW11 4LF (7622 2112/www.duskbar.co.uk). Bars

Dylan's Restaurant p246
21 Station Parade, Cockfosters Road, Barnet, Herts, EN4 0DW (8275 1551/www.dylansrestaurant.com). Modern European

E

E Pellicci p302
332 Bethnal Green Road, E2 0AG (7739 4873). Budget

E&O p253
14 Blenheim Crescent, W11 1NN (7229 5454/www.rickerrestaurants.com). Oriental

Eagle p117
159 Farringdon Road, EC1R 3AL (7837 1353). Gastropubs

Eagle Bar Diner p43
3-5 Rathbone Place, W1T 1HJ (7637 1418/www.eaglebardiner.com). The Americas

Ealing Park Tavern p119
222 South Ealing Road, W5 4RL (8758 1879). Gastropubs

Earl Spencer p122
260-262 Merton Road, SW18 5JL (8870 9244/www.theearlspencer.co.uk). Gastropubs

Eastern Fire p169
430 Alexandra Avenue, Rayners Lane, Middlesex, HA2 9TW (8866 8386). Indian

Easton p117
22 Easton Street, WC1X 0DS (7278 7608). Gastropubs

Eat & Two Veg p289
50 Marylebone High Street, W1U 5HN (7258 8595/www.eatandtwoveg.com). Vegetarian

Eat Tokyo p209
14 North End Road, NW11 7PH (8209 0079). Japanese

Eat-Thai.net p269
22 St Christopher's Place, W1U 1NP (7486 0777/www.eatthai.net). Thai

Ebury p115
11 Pimlico Road, SW1W 8NA (7730 6784/www.theebury.co.uk). Gastropubs

Ebury Wine Bar & Restaurant p345
139 Ebury Street, SW1W 9QU (7730 5447/www.eburywine bars.co.uk). Wine Bars

Eco p322
162 Clapham High Street, SW4 7UG (7978 1108/www.ecorestaurants.com). Pizza & Pasta

Eco Brixton
4 Market Row, Brixton Market, Electric Lane, SW9 8LD (7738 3021). Branch

Ed's Easy Diner p45
12 Moor Street, W1V 5LH (7434 4439/www.edseasydiner.co.uk). The Americas

Ed's Easy Diner
362 King's Road, SW3 5UZ (7352 1956). Branch

Ed's Easy Diner
The Trocadero, 19 Rupert Street, W1V 7HN (7287 1951). Branch

Ed's Easy Diner
15 Great Newport Street, WC2H 7JE (7836 0271). Branch

Edera p189
148 Holland Park Avenue, W11 4UE (7221 6090). Italian

Eel Pie p344
9-11 Church Street, Twickenham, Middx, TW1 3NJ (8891 1717). Pubs

805 Bar Restaurant p37
805 Old Kent Road, SE15 1NX (7639 0808/www.805restaurant.com). African & Caribbean

Eighty-Six Bistro Bar p215
86 Brent Street, NW4 2ES (8202 5575). Jewish

Elbow Room p356
89-91 Chapel Market, N1 9EX (7278 3244/www.theelbowroom.co.uk). Eating & Entertainment

Elbow Room
97-113 Curtain Road, EC2A 3BS (7613 1316). Branch

F

G

H

I

J

K

L

M

N

S

A-Z INDEX

T

U

V

W

X

Y

Z

Chicken House

2 Palmer Street, Frome, Somerset BA11 1DS
www.doublecluck.com

First published in Great Britain in 2015
Chicken House
2 Palmer Street
Frome, Somerset BA11 1DS
United Kingdom
www.doublecluck.com

Cover and interior design by Helen Crawford-White
Cover photographs: black ribbon © SeDmi/Shutterstock; broken glass © Patricia Chumillas/Shutterstock; padlock © Svetlana Kuznetsova/Shutterstock; girl © Aleshyn_Andrei/Shutterstock; boy © S-F/Shutterstock
Typeset by Dorchester Typesetting Group Ltd
Printed and bound in Great Britain by CPI Group (UK) Ltd, Croydon CR0 4YY

The paper used in this Chicken House book is made from wood grown in sustainable forests.

1 3 5 7 9 10 8 6 4 2

British Library Cataloguing in Publication data available.

PB ISBN 978-1-909489-81-3
eISBN 978-1-909489-82-0

For my dad

PART I

'Of all forms of caution, caution in love is perhaps the most fatal to true happiness.'

Bertrand Russell, *The Conquest of Happiness*

CHAPTER ONE

THE HONEYPOT

I didn't see it at first, sitting between the cash register and a stack of order pads. It might have been there for hours – or longer – just waiting, while I spent another day of my summer dying of boredom inside Gracewell's Diner.

There were just two of us left to lock up tonight. I was hovering beside the register, drumming my fingernails on the countertop, while Millie, my best friend and partner-in-waitressing, glided around the diner and sang into the broom handle like it was a microphone. Everyone else had left, and my uncle Jack – manager not-so-extraordinaire – had stayed home with a hangover.

The tables stood resolutely in rows, flanked by straight-backed burgundy chairs and the occasional rubber plant. The door was locked, the lights were dimmed and the window booths were clean.

I was trying not to listen to Millie destroying Adele when I noticed it: the jar of honey. I picked it up and studied it.

'I think I'm getting better,' Millie called mid-song-murder from across the diner. The only thing she got right was the faint British accent, but that's only because she *was* British. 'I can hit that high note now!'

'*Big* improvement, Mil,' I lied without looking up.

The jar was small and rounded. Inside, honey dotted with crystals of gold swayed lazily as I tilted it back and forth. A fraying square of cloth covered the lid and, instead of a label, a thin velvet ribbon encircled the middle, finishing in an elaborate bow. It was black.

Homemade? Weird. I didn't know anybody in Cedar Hill who made their own honey, and I knew almost *everyone* in Cedar Hill. It was just that kind of place – a little pocket on the outskirts of Chicago, where everybody knows everybody else's business; where nobody forgives and nobody forgets. I knew all about that. After what happened with my dad, I became infamy's child, and infamy has a way of sticking to you like a big red warning on your forehead.

Millie hit the last note of her song with ear-splitting vigour, then skipped behind the counter and stashed the broom away. 'You ready to go?'

'Where did this come from?' I balanced the jar of honey on the palm of my hand and held it out.

She shrugged. 'Dunno. It was here when my shift started.'

I peered at her through the golden prism, which made her face look distorted. 'It's weird, right?'

Millie rearranged her features into a classic I-don't-really-care-about-this-topic-of-conversation look. 'The honey? Not really.'

'It's homemade,' I said.

'Yeah, I figured.' She pulled her eyebrows together and reached out to touch the glass. 'The ribbon is kind of odd. Maybe a customer left it as a tip?'

'What kind of customer tips with pots of honey?'

Millie gasped, her face lighting up. 'Did you . . .' She breathed in dramatically. 'By any chance . . .' She exhaled. 'Serve . . .'

I leant forward in anticipation.

'. . . a little yellow bear . . .'

I can't believe I fell for it.

'. . . called Winnie-the-Pooh today?'

Her laughter set me off, it always did. That sound – like a duck being strangled – was what drew me to her when she moved to Cedar Hill five years ago. At school we would always find ourselves laughing at the same things. It was the silly stuff – making stupid faces, giggling inappropriately when someone tripped and fell, enjoying long, nonsensical conversations and discussing ridiculous hypothetical situations – that brought us together. Back then I didn't know it would be the only friendship that would survive what happened to my family eighteen months ago, but it didn't matter any more because Millie was the best friend I'd ever have, and the only one I really needed.

We laughed all the way through closing up, until we were outside in the balmy night air. Located on the corner of Foster and Oak, the diner was a modest, low-lying building made from faded brick. It was perfectly symmetrical, its squareness reflected in the boxy windows that dominated the exterior and the small parking lot that surrounded it on all sides. Along the overhanging roof, a scrawling 'Gracewell's' sign was half illuminated by street lights that lined the periphery of the lot. Right across the street, the old library loomed against the night sky, half hidden by a line of neatly clipped trees that continued west past the general post office and on down the sidewalk.

I was still holding the well-dressed pot of honey as we crossed the empty parking lot. It's not like anyone would care, I told myself – with my uncle Jack at home nursing his self-induced headache, there was no one official around to claim it. I'd only done what any jaded, underpaid employee would do in my situation – claimed a freebie that I had no immediate use for and walked away from the diner feeling triumphant because of it.

'So, I've been thinking.' Millie slowed her pace to match mine.

'Be careful,' I teased her.

'Maybe *I* should take the honey.'

'Finders keepers,' I sang.

'Sophie, Sophie, Sophie.' She put her arm around my shoulders and pulled me towards her. We were almost the same height, but while Millie was curvy in all the right places, I was boy-skinny and chipmunk-cheeked like my father, though I had inherited his dimples too, which was somewhat of a silver lining. Millie squished her cheek up against mine, as if to remind me of that. I felt her smile. 'My *best* friend in the *whole* world, *ever.* Oh, how dull would my life be without you in it? The stars wouldn't shine half as bright, the moon would be but a shadow of its former self. The flowers would wither and—'

'No way!' I slithered out of her grip. 'You can't compliment your way in to my honey stash. I'm immune to your charm.'

Millie scrunched her eyes and released a soul-destroying whine. 'You already get the whole freakin' diner. Can't I just have the honey?'

Even though she was right, inheriting the diner when I turned eighteen was hardly my life's greatest ambition. Those were my father's instructions before he went away, which would no doubt be enforced by my gloriously grumpy uncle Jack, who happened to exude a particularly pungent aura of I-don't-take-no-for-an-answer. It didn't matter anyway. Millie and I both knew the diner wasn't something to be excited about. It was just one big dead-end headache waiting to crash into my life. But the black-ribboned honeypot? That was pretty – a nice surprise to lift the monotony of the day.

Millie shuffled behind me. 'Sophie, this is your conscience speaking,' she whispered over my shoulder. 'I know it's been a while since we've talked, but it's time for you to do the right thing. Millie is so nice and pretty. Don't you want to give her the honey? Think of how happy it would make her.'

'I didn't know my conscience had a British accent.'

'Yeah, well, don't read too much into it. Just give her the honey.'

I stalled at the edge of the parking lot, where we would peel off separately into the night. Before my parents' income was halved, Millie and I used to walk in the same direction, to Shrewsbury Avenue, where there were housekeepers and gardeners, giant pools, and crystal chandeliers hanging inside actual foyers. Now my walk home was a whole lot longer than it used to be.

'Millie doesn't even like honey,' I hissed. '*And* she has no respect for bees. I saw her stamp on one three times last week to make sure it was dead.'

'It's not my fault this country is overrun with obnoxious insects.'

'What do you expect? It's the middle of July!'

'It's a disgrace.'

'*And* you were wearing Flowerbomb perfume.'

'He was being inappropriate.'

'So you murdered him.'

Millie shot out her hand. 'Just give me the freaking honey, Gracewell. I need it to bribe my way out of a grounding.'

I raised my eyebrows. We had just completed an eight-hour shift together and she hadn't mentioned this. 'Grounded?'

'Total injustice. *Complete* misunderstanding.'

'I'm listening . . .'

'Alex called me a *braceface.*' Millie paused for effect. 'Can you believe that?'

Well, she did have braces. And they were technically on her face. But I didn't say that. Instead, I did what any best friend would do. I adopted an expression of pure outrage and pretended to linger over what a rude tyrant her not-so-mature-but-definitely-hot brother was.

'He's *such* an ass,' I offered.

'He's literally the worst human being on the planet. Anyway, one thing led to another, and his iPhone fell out of the window . . . well, it sort of fell out of my hands . . . which were coincidentally dangling outside of his bedroom window at the time . . . He *completely* freaked out on me.'

'Oh, siblings . . .'

'Well, you're lucky you don't have to share your house with any douchelords,' she ranted. 'What kind of nineteen-year-old guy *squeals* on his younger sister? I mean, *where* is the honour in that? He's a total disgrace to the Parker name. And how was I even supposed to know his phone would break?'

'Weird.' Honey still in hand, I leant against a nearby street light and watched my shadow curve inside its puddle of light. 'I could have sworn the latest iPhones had tiny built-in parachutes.'

Millie started to swat at the air, like the problem was floating around in front of her. 'If I give my mum that thoughtful jar of honey to use in one of her recipes, then she'll see me as the kind, caring daughter that I am, and take back the unjust grounding, which was unfairly handed out because of my ignorant pigman brother.'

I straightened up. 'That's never going to work. I'm keeping the honey.'

'Whatever,' she said, with an elaborate flick of her poker-straight brown hair. 'It's probably poisoned anyway.'

She stuck out her tongue and flounced off into the darkness, leaving me alone with my hard-won bounty. I slid the jar into my bag, watching the wisps of black ribbon fall away from me.

I crossed the road and paused, trying to decide which way to go. After six shifts in a row, the balls of my feet were throbbing, and because Millie and I had stalled for so long, it was already later than it should have been. The longer way home was usually my preferred option – it was well lit and well travelled – but the shortcut was significantly shorter, bypassing the centre of town, winding up the hill instead and looping around the haunted mansion at the end of Lockwood Avenue.

CHAPTER TWO

THE BOY WITH HAUNTING EYES

The moon was full and high but the evening seemed darker than usual. After fifteen minutes with only the sound of my footsteps as company, the turrets of the old Priestly house climbed into the sky ahead of me, peering over the neighbouring houses like watchtowers.

Beautiful as it was, the mansion had always reminded me of a child's doll's house that had crumpled in on itself. Its white-washed wooden exterior caved in at strange angles, while corners jutted out like knives, piercing the overgrown masses of ivy. A stone wall covered in leaves snaked around the exterior; it was the only house in Cedar Hill that could boast such privacy, but its gothic aura did more to repel intruders than its boundary.

People who knew the house spoke of it with equal amounts

of trepidation and wonder, and would often imagine their own stories about it. When I was seven years old, my mother told me of a beautiful princess who would spend her days high up in the turrets of the old house, hiding herself away from an arranged marriage to a miserable and boring prince. By the time I turned ten, kids in the neighbourhood had decided it was the spellbound home of a wily old witch. She would fill the sprawling rooms with cats and frogs, cauldrons and brooms, and, deep in the night, she would fly out into the sky and scour the neighbourhood for stray children who should have been fast asleep in bed. When I met Millie, she told me about the vampires who stood just inside the cracked windowpanes, peering out with glistening crimson eyes.

Then, at fourteen, when I was completing a school history project about Cedar Hill, I stumbled across the chilling reality of the mansion. There were no witches, no princesses and no vampires – just a story about a young woman named Violet Priestly, a front-line nurse during World War II who had come out the other side as a drastically different version of herself. Traumatic memories haunted her like ghosts until her hallucinations became too strong to ignore. Not long after poisoning her husband and their young son, she hanged herself in the foyer of the old mansion.

Of course, no one wanted to buy it after that.

Nothing could sweep away the darkness that huddled around the Priestly corner. Even during the hottest summer days, when the streets shone with mirages, there was an unmistakable iciness shrouding the mansion. And so it endured for decades, a beacon from another time and place, resolutely empty and utterly unconquerable.

That was, until tonight.

As I drew closer to the mansion, rubbing the warmth back into my suddenly chilly arms and second-guessing my decision to come this way in the first place, I realized with a start that the house had changed entirely since the last time I had seen it. Someone had finally done it – *really* done it. The abandoned Priestly mansion had been dragged into the twenty-first century, and now it was alive again.

I stopped walking.

The rusted wrought-iron gates were wrenched open and pushed against hedges that no longer languished across the garden wall. The weeping willows had been pruned to an almost unnatural neatness, revealing windows on the second storey that I didn't know existed. The ivy had been cut away to reveal sturdy wooden boards and a newly painted red door, lit up by a teardrop lantern on either side. And in the light of the lanterns were two black SUVs parked side by side on freshly strewn gravel.

My phone buzzed against my hip – a text from Millie letting me know she had made it home safe, and an inadvertent reminder that I hadn't. Reluctantly, I moved to continue on my way, but something inside was stopping me. The Priestly mansion, the frozen heart of Cedar Hill, was beating again and, lateness be damned, I had to know more about it.

And that's when I sensed something. I shifted my gaze up past the trees and caught sight of a flickering figure in an upstairs window. It was a boy. I couldn't be sure of his age, but even from a distance his bright eyes were unmistakable. They were too big for his delicate face and as they watched me from what seemed like another world, they rounded into discs that grew unnaturally. He leant forward and pressed his palms against the glass, like he was about to push the pane from the window frame. Was he waving? Or telling me to go?

I raised my hand to him but it stalled, clammy and unsteady, in mid-air. And then, as quickly as I had noticed him, the strange boy was gone, vanished into the darkness behind him until the house, with its brand-new face, was still again.

Frowning, I let my eyes slide down from the empty window-pane across the driveway as the darkness ahead of me came alive. The faint sound of rustling wafted through the air, and I squinted until I could make out another figure behind one of the SUVs. He was hunched over, searching for something inside.

I tried to fight the desire to investigate, but my palms grew shaky at my sides as curiosity overwhelmed me, pushing me towards the house. I shuffled forward from the sidewalk, creeping just inside the open gates, and the rustling stopped. A car door shut and I heard the sound of loose gravel shifting in the darkness. The figure straightened, his head appearing from behind the vehicle, moving in tandem with the noisy gravel until he stood between the house and the gates, watching me watch him.

Even beneath the lanterns, he was just an outline: a tall shadow with broad shoulders and sure movements. He paused and lowered his arm, easing a duffel bag towards the ground with deliberate slowness until it was settled at his feet. He stepped to the side and pushed it with the force of his boot until it disappeared behind the closest SUV and away from my prying eyes. But I had already seen it, whatever *it* was, and we both knew it.

He tilted his head to one side and stepped closer, one purposeful stride and then another, as he closed the space between us. With each step, my heart thumped harder in my chest. My curiosity evaporated, leaving reality in its place: I had been caught trespassing, and now this shadowed figure was stalking towards me.

I turned and stumbled back out on to the deserted street. As the sound of heavy footsteps split the silence behind me apart, I broke into a run, completely unprepared for the cat that hurtled out in front of me with a shrill meow. As I skidded to a halt, my arms flailing at my sides, the stranger crashed into my back, silencing me mid-scream by jolting the wind from my lungs, and sending me flying through the air. I dropped my bag and landed on the sidewalk with a thud. My hands and knees scraped the pavement. Dizziness flooded me, sloshing the contents of my dinner back and forth in my stomach.

Before I could piece together what had happened or just how exactly I was going to be murdered, I was lifted out of my bubble of pain, away from the asphalt and on to my feet again, to where I had been standing seconds before, like someone had pressed rewind.

Only this time, something was different. There was the feeling of strong hands on my waist. They held me upright as I wobbled back and forth, trying to find my balance.

'*Stai tranquillo, sei al sicuro.*' The words were so strange and unexpected, I thought I had imagined them.

I dropped my gaze and found his hands around me and suddenly I saw myself, as if from above, relaxing into the arms of a complete stranger on a deserted street in the middle of the night, in front of the most notorious house in Cedar Hill.

A stranger who had just caught me trespassing and then knocked me to the ground.

I had seen enough romantic movies to appreciate a swoon-worthy moment – but I had also watched a lot of *CSI*. With a start, I pushed the unfamiliar hands away from my body and leapt forwards. I crouched and grabbed my bag from the ground, catching a glimpse of the thick silver buckle on his leather boot before springing back up and hitching my bag onto my shoulder hastily. I looked up at him, wishing I had something weapon-worthy in my handbag, just in case. But he stood still, his face a collection of shadows in the darkness. He didn't make another attempt to attack me, and I didn't wait around to give him the chance.

'Don't follow me.' My voice sounded stronger than I felt.

I turned and started to run.

I heard him call out, but I was already gone.

I didn't turn around, but I was sure I could feel the shadow's eyes – *his* eyes – on the back of my neck as I ran. The distant sound of laughter followed me through the darkness.

I got home in record time. After depositing the pot of honey on the kitchen windowsill and trudging upstairs, I rubbed some ointment on my stinging knees and crawled into bed. After what felt like hours of staring wide-eyed at my ceiling and listening to the urgent thrumming in my chest, I fell into an uneasy sleep during which dreams of boys in windows dissolved into nightmares about shadowed figures and black-ribboned pots of honey.

CHAPTER THREE

THE GOSSIP MERCHANT

There wasn't a whole lot that irritated me. However, the source of such rare annoyance had managed to slither into my house and ruin the sunny morning barely before it began.

'. . . It's not a good omen, Celine. I have a sixth sense about these things . . .'

Rita Bailey's voice, which was shriller than a police siren, had no trouble infiltrating my bedroom despite the fact she was an entire floor below me. I scowled at my ceiling. I didn't want to hear about Lana Green's affair, Jenny Orin's worsening psoriasis, or the Tyler kids' lice scandal. But the volume of the old lady's voice had left me with no other option. I would have to suffer it either way, and, given the depressing messiness of my bedroom coupled with my desire to eat breakfast at some point, I decided to face her head-on and get the most unpleasant part of my day over with.

I rolled out of bed, crawling between crumpled jeans and inside-out T-shirts to fish out a partially obscured bra. Springing to my feet and swivelling around without touching anything – because sometimes I liked to make a game of it – I swooped a pair of denim shorts off the ground and pulled them on before settling on a white tank top and my favourite pair of Converse. After putting on some moisturizer and pulling my hair into a messy braid, I crept downstairs, steeling myself for what I was about to hurtle into, coffee-less and overtired.

Rita Bailey, an old, portly woman with cropped white hair and pinched, shrunken features, hunched over the kitchen table, sipping her coffee in an outrageous pink pantsuit. Beside her, my mother was politely enduring her company, offering a tight smile and a robotic head nod at appropriate times. She had even cleared part of the table, which was usually buried beneath stray sewing projects and piles of fabric samples. Now confined to just one square foot of space, they balanced precariously against the wall, threatening to topple over them.

When we lived in a spacious four-bedroom house on Shrewsbury Avenue, my mother had two whole rooms dedicated to containing the explosions of materials needed for her dressmaking, but here, her works-in-progress always seemed to spill from room to room, following us around our cramped home in every shade and pattern imaginable. Yards of Chantilly and ivory lace stretched along armchairs, jostling for space beneath mannequins in short summer dresses and rich evening gowns. On several scarring occasions since we'd moved here a year and a half ago, I had woken up screaming at the sight of a half-finished dummy bride perched in the corner of my room, or a denim dress that should never see the light of day.

It wasn't that my mother didn't have some sort of system in place, it's just that no one but her could ever figure it out. She was probably the most organized disorganized dressmaker in all of Chicago, and I think she liked it that way. Mrs Bailey, who was staring narrowed-eyed at the teetering pile of fabrics across the table, evidently did not.

I swept into the kitchen, pulling her attention away before her frown became so intense it broke her face. 'Good morning, Mrs Bailey.' *That wasn't so bad.*

She re-fixed her stare on me. 'Good morning, Persephone.'

I winced. It had been a while since I had heard my name in its hideous entirety and, unsurprisingly, nothing had changed – it still sucked. But the way the old lady said it always seemed to make it worse, drawling over the vowel sounds like she was talking to a five-year-old child – *Purr-seph-an-eeeee.*

'I prefer Sophie,' I replied with a level of exasperation that usually accompanied the topic.

'But Persephone is so much nicer.'

'Well, no one calls me that.' It wasn't my name and she knew it. It was just a symbol of my mother's fleeting obsession with Greek mythology, which had, rather unfortunately, coincided with the time I was born. Thankfully, my father had given up on the mouthful within the first year of my birth. It didn't take him long to think of 'Sophie' as a passable alternative – the name I suspect he wanted all along and one that rendered me eternally grateful to him for two reasons: one, that I didn't have to go through life with a barely spellable relic for a name, and two, that he didn't nickname me 'Persy' instead. When my mother conceded defeat, I became 'Sophie' for good. Plain, simple and pronounceable.

'How do you even know to call me that anyway?' I added as an afterthought. For all the times Mrs Bailey had intentionally wrongly addressed me, I had never thought to ask her how she had discovered one of my best-kept secrets. Then again, she was the first person to discover the location of our new house when we moved, despite the fact we had actively tried to hide it from her, *and* it was nearly an hour's walk from Shrewsbury Avenue. Maybe she *was* clairvoyant after all.

'I saw it on a letter once.'

'Where?'

'I can't remember.' She sounded affronted by the question. 'It may have fallen out of your mailbox.'

'Mmhmm.' *Snoop*, I noted mentally.

Beside me, my mother was circling the top of her mug with her finger. 'Sophie,' she chided gently, 'why don't we talk about something else?'

'Why? Are you still trying to shirk the blame for naming me the most hideously embarrassing thing you could think of?' Even though my voice was light, I was only half joking. Not that it seemed to matter to my mother; she found my name-based indignation inexplicably amusing. I guess it made sense. The whole joke was hers in the first place and now it was following me around through people like Mrs Bailey or Uncle Jack, who used it like a weapon when he was angry at me for taking impromptu nap breaks at the diner.

'I think the name Sophie is just as lovely. It suits you,' my mother pandered, smirking into her mug until all I could see were the tips of her delicate pointed brows. I felt a tiny pang of envy for their symmetry. Everything about her was dainty and refined, like a pixie. Through the magic of genetics, she had only passed her sunny blonde hair and her heart-shaped face to me. But, by the wonder of mimicry, I had also acquired her tendency for extreme messiness and her inability to cook properly. I was reserving judgement on where my diminutive height came from, because I was still hoping to miraculously grow another three inches before my seventeenth birthday, which was rapidly approaching.

At the word 'Sophie' Mrs Bailey emitted a long noise of ragged disapproval. It sounded like she was choking – and, fleetingly, a small, morally devoid part of me hoped she was.

I crossed over to the countertop to fill my mug and caught sight of the honey jar on the windowsill. Streaks of sunlight winked at me through the glass, as if to say 'Good morning!' *It would be a shame not to try it*, I resolved. I grabbed a spoon and pried the lid from the jar, setting aside the frayed square of cloth that covered it and taking care not to disturb the black velvet ribbon.

Behind me, Mrs Bailey was practising her favourite hobby – the art of lamenting, 'Persephone is *so* much more elegant. It might not suit her now, but she could always try and *grow* into it.'

'Thanks, but I think I'll just stick with Sophie and continue to live in the modern world.' I dipped a spoon inside the jar and twirled it.

'You look *so* tired this morning, Sophie,' Mrs Bailey informed the back of my head, labouring over my name like it was difficult to pronounce.

Ignoring her taunt, as well as the civilized option to put the honey in oatmeal or on toast, I stuck the heaping spoonful of it straight into my mouth.

'She'll be bright and chirpy once she's had her caffeine fix,' my mother explained over my shoulder. The edge in her usually calm voice informed me that her patience was finally wearing thin. Even after my father's screw-up, my mother had managed to retain her inhuman level of kindness, which meant she was still too polite to turn a sixty-something, lonely, *annoying* Mrs Bailey away, even when her conversation mainly consisted of disapprovals and backhanded compliments.

'Are you sure, Celine? She seems so exhausted. She's a shadow of what a sixteen-year-old girl should look like. She should be out in the sun, getting a tan. She used to be such a pretty little thing.'

Seriously? I would have responded with bitchiness-in-kind but the honey was sticking my teeth together.

My mother released a small sigh – a speciality of hers. It was ambiguous enough to mean anything to anyone – 'I'm tired/happy/disappointed' – but I had a feeling it was intended to politely draw the topic to a close.

Fighting the urge to take my coffee and run, I turned around and seated myself firmly at the kitchen table, dragging the chair legs against the floor as noisily as I could and revelling in the look of discomfort on Mrs Bailey's face.

OK, lady. Let's go. 'I hope I didn't interrupt anything important.' The laboured, honey-laden words masked the sarcasm in my voice. I took my first, glorious sip of coffee and felt the steam rise up and warm my nose.

'Well actually, you *did*.'

Quelle surprise. I always seemed to be interrupting Mrs Bailey's ground-breaking news bulletins.

'I was just telling your mother that a new family have moved into the Priestly house on Lockwood Avenue.'

I was utterly shocked by my unexpected interest in anything Mrs Bailey had to say. But suddenly there I was, glued to Cedar Hill's resident gossip merchant like she was about to announce the finale plot of my favourite TV show. An onslaught of questions formed inside my brain. *Where do they come from? How are they related to the Priestlys? Why are you wearing that crazy pink suit?*

'Well, I bet it will be good to have some new faces around the neighbourhood,' my mother interjected before I could begin.

The old lady shook her head like she was having a seizure. She leant across the table and looked pointedly at each of us in turn as if calling for our undivided attention, which she knew she already had. She dropped her voice. 'You know I have the gift of sight, Celine. I've been seeing things ever since I was a child . . .'

I had to blow into my coffee to hide my smirk.

'I was walking by the old Priestly place a couple of weeks ago and I got the most unsettling feeling. When I saw the renovations and the moving vans, it all started to make sense. The house is full again and I just *know* it's not good.'

'Maybe we shouldn't jump to conclusions,' my mother offered. I could tell by the airiness in her voice that her attention was beginning to wander. She started to pick at a stray thread in her capri pants, frowning.

I considered telling Mrs Bailey to chill out too, but she had already redirected her gaze towards our backyard as if she were looking into another secret dimension. But in reality, she was just staring at the potted plant on the windowsill. She squinted her eyes and sighed, probably noticing it was dead.

'Nothing good will come of having five young men making trouble in the neighbourhood, because that's *exactly* what they'll do, Celine. You mark my words.'

She shook her head again, but every cropped white strand of hair remained perfectly static, like they were frozen in place.

'Wait, did you say *five* guys?' I had already seen two of them. Well, one of them, sort of. The second one had knocked me over. I frowned at the memory. Even after a night of reflection, I still wasn't sure what to make of it.

Mrs Bailey was, of course, scandalized by my interest. Her mouth was bobbing open and closed, like she was trying to find the exact words for how much of a disgrace I was. 'Five young, *troublesome* men,' she heaved at last, clutching at her chest for added effect. 'I saw them move in and I can tell you, they do not seem like the respectable type.'

Isn't that what you said about my father? I wanted to ask, but I stopped myself. The argument wouldn't be worth it. It never was. And besides, I had gotten all the info I needed: there was a new family of boys in the neighbourhood. Millie was going to keel over with happiness when I told her.

Distracted, I got up to take my half-filled mug to the sink. 'I think having new neighbours is pretty cool.'

'What's *cool* about it?' Mrs Bailey threw the question at my back like a dagger.

I turned around. 'What's *not* cool about it? Nobody ever comes to Cedar Hill willingly. This place is so boring. It feels like any minute now we're all just going to fossilize.' *Maybe some of us already have . . .* I stopped myself again.

'There's no need to be so dramatic,' she returned.

I blinked hard to suppress an inadvertent eye roll.

'I'm sure those boys are perfectly fine,' reasoned my mother, who was rifling through her sewing kit. I could tell she was more interested in finding a needle to fix the single thread on the capri pants that had betrayed her.

Mrs Bailey was still wearing a frown that was beginning to twitch from the effort of keeping it in place. 'No, Celine, there's something not right about it. That house has been empty for too long. And we all know the reason.'

'Ghosts,' I whispered dramatically. I wanted to add an '*Oooooo*', but I figured that might be going too far.

Mrs Bailey rose abruptly from her chair, shrugging on her shawl in a show of clumsy indignation. When she spoke again, her voice was low. 'You can make jokes all you like, Persephone, but you just better be careful.'

I glanced at my mother and was surprised to find that she had returned her attention to our conversation.

'Notoriety attracts notoriety,' Mrs Bailey was muttering without looking at either of us. 'And with what your father did, it's best to be aware of—'

'I think that's enough, Rita.' My mother rose from her chair, fixing the old lady with a dark look. 'Sophie can handle herself. She knows how to be careful.'

'Yeah,' I echoed, feeling a million miles away. I was thinking about how I had steered myself into trouble the night before. The stinging in my knees resurfaced at the memory.

CHAPTER FOUR

THE LETTER

Mrs Bailey's words had kindled something I had become all too accustomed to during the last year and a half of my life: Dad-related guilt.

Back in the welcome privacy of my bedroom, I sat cross-legged on my perpetually unmade bed. Clutching the latest prison-issue envelope in one hand, I carefully removed the letter from inside it and dipped back into my father's life, which, for now at least, was confined to the pages he sent me every couple of weeks.

Dear Sophie,

Sorry I haven't written in a while. I like to wait until I have something to say, even if it's not as interesting as life back in

Cedar Hill. I would hate for you to think I'm becoming more boring than I was before I left. In truth, I am trying to make the most of my time here. I want to give you something to be proud of again.

You'll be happy to know that I finished Catch-22 in just two days, which means I am finally getting faster at reading. I will have the knowledge of an English professor by the time I come back, and maybe I'll even write a book of my own.

I hope your summer is going well. Try not to worry too much about not getting out in the sun – you will have the last laugh when all your friends are aging prematurely and you still have the skin of a teenager.

How is everything at the diner? I hope Uncle Jack is looking after you. I know he is really trying his best, so go easy on him. If you ask him, I'm sure he will give you some time off so you can get away with Millie – go on an adventure.

On the subject of your uncle, I was thinking that you should suggest some reading material for him too. It would be a good way for him to de-stress. Maybe something with colourful pictures and big block letters? Just kidding. Don't tell him I said that! I do worry about him, which might sound ironic given the circumstances, but I am relying on you to keep an eye on him and his blood pressure. We are not getting any younger, unfortunately.

How is your mom? Has she remembered to get the dishwasher repaired or have you had to go through with your sink-filling plan? I hope she has stopped over-working herself, but I know how unlikely that is. Please let her know I am thinking about her if she asks, which I hope she does. I haven't heard from her in a while, but I know she is still processing everything. It is difficult for her, as I expect it is for you.

It has been so long since I've seen you. I would really love for you to visit when you get some time off. What about after your birthday, when everything has settled down again? Jack will give you a ride if you ask him. I do miss your teenage sarcasm, despite what you may think.

That's all for now. I look forward to your next letter and, as always, I am thinking of you and counting the days.

Love,
Dad

I slipped the letter back inside the envelope and placed it on the nightstand. I tried to shake the melancholia out of my head. Even after all of my father's letters, I still felt sad reading them, but I knew, too, that not to have them at all would be a thousand times more painful.

With a heavy heart, I propped my notepad against my knees and began my reply, censoring the negative parts of my life and highlighting the positives as I wrote. Even if the world was falling down around me, I would not tell my father, because he, above all the people in my life, needed good tidings in whatever form he could get them. And no matter how angry and frustrated I was, I would give him what he needed to survive.

Hi Dad,

As I write this I am balancing my notepad on two skinned knees and writing with a sore hand. If you're wondering why, it's because on my way home from work last night I face-planted into the pavement.

A freaky shadow chased after me and knocked me to the ground. But it's OK because I didn't let him murder me (you're welcome), and now I'm pretty sure that wasn't his intention in the first place. He was probably just chasing after me like a maniac so he could ask why I was snooping around his driveway in the middle of the night on my own. Teenagers, right?

Luckily I have lived to tell the tale, though I can't say my pride has survived. Still, I think it makes for a fitting opening to this letter, and I bet it made you smile a little.

I hope something good came of the incident, because I bolted home in a state of pain and paranoia.

It's nice to know you are reading. I think writing a book is a great idea. They say it's very therapeutic.

I don't know who 'they' are, or whether that's even true. And I really hope when you say *book* you don't mean an autobiographical one, because I'm not crazy about having to relive the story of your murder trial in paperback format no matter how soothing it is for your psyche. And I don't relish the thought of watching Mom go through another anxiety attack any time soon, either.

I haven't gotten a chance to do very much other than work this summer, which I am getting used to.

I have resigned myself to the current monotony of my life.

Uncle Jack is great. He is still doing his best to step into your role, though he is a little grumpier than you. Maybe that comes with middle age? :) He goes back and forth to the city a lot. Millie and I have developed a theory that he has met a woman there, because what kind of 'city business' would he be attending to so often? What do you think, our Jack, a Casanova? Hmmm . . . food for thought. If it is the case, then I don't think we need to be worrying about his health, as long as his heart is doing OK.

Though, knowing Uncle Jack, I bet it's more of a sordid affair than an epic romance. So far, nothing has coming close to filling the void you left in his life.

Thank you for saying I will have the last laugh when all my friends wrinkle up like prunes in later years for spending the time they have now in the sun.

I am flattered you implied I still have more than one real friend and I hope you really do think that. If you knew how many people turned on me, I think it would break your heart.

And, honestly, I am happy to be out of the sun, because I know my time indoors is all part of the end goal of buying a car. I don't know what I will do to celebrate my 17th birthday, but it will probably be something low-key.

Millie's parents are going away, so she and Alex are going to throw a *huge* house party, complete with all his college friends. If you were here, you would definitely disapprove. But you're not.

I think Mom wants to make me a dress for my birthday. Every time she sees me in sweatpants, I see the light in her eyes dim a little bit. If I don't wear something ladylike soon, she might die inside. Last Saturday morning I caught her measuring me in my sleep.

If I see one frill or even the hint of bedazzling on it, things will get ugly.

She's working more than ever, which she really seems to enjoy.

Most of her friends have deserted her too, in the wake of everything that happened, and those that didn't don't come around much any more. I think Mom has lost her social sparkle.

I know last year was really hard for all of us, but now she seems happier, and I'm sure she is missing you as much as I am.

Sometimes it feels like she hates you and everything your incarceration has put us through. Sometimes I feel that way too.

Mrs Bailey has started to come by on Sunday again. I decided earlier that she is probably the most annoying person to ever live on this planet. Do you think she might be descended from Lucifer? Just a thought.

Annoying is putting it mildly. You don't know any of the crap she's been saying about you. And Millie's probably only told me half of it.

She was here this morning, talking about a new family who have moved into the old Priestly mansion. I guess they must be distant relatives. Weird, huh? I thought that place would be empty for ever.

It's full of boys boys boys!

I will come and see you in a couple of weeks, after my birthday, when I get time off from the diner. I really can't wait.

I am dreading seeing how gaunt and unhappy you look. It makes me want to collapse in tears every time.

That's everything for now. I miss you so much.

Sometimes it physically hurts.

Thinking about you always.

I wish I could turn it off, like a switch.

And counting the days.

Counting the years.

Lots of love and hugs,

Sophie X

CHAPTER FIVE

THE PRIESTLY BROTHERS

I stood face down with my nose pressed against the countertop, willing time to speed up. Even during the busiest hours of the day, the diner was never overrun with customers, but tonight it was unusually quiet. There was just one more hour to go until I could go home, and the minutes were dragging by. To make matters worse, the air conditioner was broken, the stifling humidity was frizzing out the ends of my hair, and the delivery man hadn't shown up for the third day in a row, which meant we were low on some of the menu's ingredients.

Millie hovered behind me, prodding my shoulder. She was, after all, part-female, part-question. 'So if these random Priestly relatives *just* moved in then the shadow guy probably *was* one of the five boys?'

'Yeah,' I replied through a yawn. 'Probably.'

She laughed like it was the funniest thing she'd ever heard. 'How embarrassing for you.'

I lifted my head. 'Better embarrassed than dead.'

She grinned. 'Oh come on, Soph, *where* is your sense of adventure?'

I pretended to contemplate her question. 'I think it's buried deep beneath my natural instinct to survive.'

'You could have made out with a shadow!' Her face was glowing.

'*Or* been brutally murdered by one,' I countered.

'Urgh, you are *such* a killjoy.'

'How about this,' I said. 'Next time I'm in a risky situation with a complete stranger, I promise I'll try and make out with him.'

'Bah! Don't make promises you won't keep. I don't want to get my hopes up.'

The bell above the door jingled and three girls sauntered into the diner. I recognized two of them from school. Erin Reyes and Jane Leder were all bitchiness and long legs, and could have made a full-time career out of judging people. I was surprised to find them at Gracewell's – it was far from the expensive hangouts they seemed to enjoy. Then again, the diner did have their favourite main attraction – me. It might have been nearly a year and a half since my father's incarceration, but it was *still* Erin's favourite topic.

She caught my eye and smirked, and I tried not to flinch as she stage-whispered to the third girl, who was already studying me with rapt attention. 'That's her. She *actually* works here, in the place where it *happened*. Can you believe that?'

The other two giggled, and I felt my cheeks grow hot.

'Ugh,' said Millie, who had as much patience for routine bitchiness as I did. 'I'll get this one. And if they're not careful I'll bring them their menus with a side of my shoe up their . . .' She trailed off, rounding the counter to attend to them.

I smiled graciously at the back of her head. Gracewell's Diner mostly catered for people who worked in town or local families who had been coming here for years. But every so often, nosy vipers from school would stop in to gawk at the infamous Michael Gracewell's restaurant, and Millie would take the hit and serve them so that I wouldn't have to.

Absentmindedly, I started to fix the errant strings on my apron, looping them into an uneven bow.

'Are you going to do *any* work today, Sophie?'

Ursula, the assistant manager, had returned from the kitchen. She was nearly as old as Mrs Bailey but was *infinitely* cooler because she could rock purple hair and was able to have conversations that didn't negatively affect my will to live. She gestured towards Millie, who was handing menus to the three girls.

'Oh, come on. There's no one else here, and I can't exactly wait on ghost tables,' I protested.

Ursula's laugh was husky, betraying her enduring smoking habit. 'I'm just saying you seem distracted tonight.' She pushed her circular spectacles up the bridge of her nose, until they settled, and magnified her eyes twofold. 'Or should I say more distracted than usual.'

'That's because she *is* distracted, Ursula.' Millie was back, and whipping off her apron. She was leaving an hour before me, and in that moment I slightly resented her for it. 'We should tell Ursula.'

'Yes, we should,' Ursula echoed, shuffling sideways so she could prop herself against the wall beside me. We were exactly the same height, so she could bore her eyes right into mine very effectively with little effort.

'But I don't *have* anything to tell,' I swore.

'Lies!' Millie slipped in front of the counter, hoodie in hand. She shrugged it on, smiling so broadly nearly all of her clear braces were visible at once. She zipped it up and her name tag, MILLIE THE MAGNIFICENT – I don't know how she had snuck that one past Uncle Jack – disappeared. Then she leant forward until her hair brushed the countertop, and dropped her voice. Ursula responded like a magnet, coming closer, and training her attention on Millie.

'Well, you probably won't believe this,' Millie began, gesturing subtly at me with her thumb. 'But Sophie has developed a crush on a shadow. A real bona fide shadow-crush. Rare as a solar eclipse, but they do happen. Our Sophie is a shadow-creeper.'

Ursula pulled her eyebrows together until they almost touched. 'What?'

'She's just kidding,' I explained, throwing Millie a death stare.

'Am I, Sophie? Am I?' She smirked suggestively, in the way only Millie could. 'Ursula, I'll need you to take over that table of *wonderful specimens* now that I'm leaving,' she said, gesturing towards Erin and her friends in the corner, before crossing the diner and shouting, 'See you guys tomorrow!'

Once Millie had disappeared, Ursula turned her penetrating gaze back to me. 'So, what's this shadow thing all about?'

'It's nothing, really. There's this new family living in the Priestly place and I think I bumped into one of them the other night, but then I ran away from him, and now Millie thinks it's the funniest and most tragic thing she's ever heard.' I grabbed a cloth and started to wipe down the countertop, which was already gleaming.

Ursula narrowed her eyes as if trying to determine whether there was more to my story, but before she could chase up a line of questioning, the bell above the door jingled.

Against a backdrop of our abrupt silence, two figures swept through the door.

I tried not to gape. One tall, dark, handsome boy is difficult to ignore, but two is near impossible.

They paused inside the door, their broad shoulders brushing as they stood side by side. They began to militarily scan the diner, as though they were looking for something that could have been under any of the tables or swinging from the ceiling fans.

Without meaning to, Ursula and I both took a step forwards.

There was something effortlessly fashionable about them – their dark straight-leg jeans were tailored to break perfectly above expensive leather boots that probably cost more than my entire wardrobe, and they wore designer T-shirts accented by the simple silver chains around their necks.

I studied the boy on the right, feeling something stir inside me. I knew his shape, his height. I dropped my gaze and recognized the silver buckles on his boots.

Ursula and I weren't the only ones hopelessly distracted; fleetingly I noticed how the three girls in the corner had fallen out of their conversation and suddenly looked a lot hungrier than they had been a moment ago. I didn't blame them. The boys were like something out of a Hollywood movie.

Without glancing towards us, they glided – yes, glided – over to a window booth and slid in, keeping their attention on their own whispered conversation.

'Can you take this one, hon?' Ursula sighed. 'I don't think I can stand next to them. It's too depressing.' She made her way across the diner to tend to the girls in the corner instead.

My midnight encounter had seemed like little more than a bad dream, but now that Shadow Boy was here, I realized I would have to confront the reality of the situation – he was Mount Olympus, I was Gracewell's Diner, and I still had no idea why he knocked me over. With any luck, there was every chance he wouldn't even recognize me.

Although their distinct appearances and obvious similarities had led me to assume they were brothers, the fact that they were speaking Italian when I approached their table confirmed it – it was that same lilting dialect that Shadow Boy had spoken to me.

'Hi, my name is Sophie and I'll be your server this evening,' I rhymed off briskly, handing them each a menu.

Shadow Boy snapped out of his conversation. He turned and, up close, he was younger than I expected – still older than me, maybe, with chestnut brown hair that curled beneath his ears and dark, almond-shaped eyes flecked with gold. I was struck just then, not by his handsomeness, but by his familiarity. I couldn't shake the sense that I had seen his face before – long ago – and though it was undeniably handsome, I had the unpleasant compulsion to look away from him. I tried to blink myself out of it. He had just thrown me off. If I had seen him before, I wouldn't have forgotten him.

'Sophie,' he said quietly, meeting my gaze. 'I think we met the other night.'

My face fell. I folded my hands in front of my body as his eyes searched mine with an intensity I was completely unused to. His brother, who seemed completely disinterested in our exchange, was studying his menu in silence.

Shadow Boy smiled. 'I was just trying to help you up, you know.'

'Ah,' I said, returning what I hoped was a nonchalant expression. 'You mean from where you put me in the first place? How kind of you.'

If he was affronted, he didn't show it. 'You stopped running so quickly I didn't have time to slow down . . . And I *did* try to apologize, but, if I recall, you ran away.'

I smiled awkwardly. 'I may have overreacted . . .'

'No harm, no foul,' he offered, holding his hands in the air. 'But are you always so defensive?'

'That depends – are you always so . . . assaulty?'

'*Non lo so,*' he said quietly, and across from him, his brother, who had been concentrating on his menu, released a low chuckle. I was struck by how effortlessly he moved between both languages, and slightly curious about whatever amusement was passing between them.

'That's a loaded question,' Shadow Boy continued after a beat, as if sensing my annoyance. He furrowed his brows and leant across the table. 'I am sorry about the whole thing, Sophie. I just wanted to ask you something. But then you stopped running so abruptly and . . .' He trailed off, doing his best to look ashamed of himself.

'There was a cat, and I didn't want to trample it.'

'Ah, I see.'

'But then *you* went ahead and tried to trample me, so I'm not sure it was worth it.'

'I told you,' he said conspiratorially, 'I wanted to ask you something.'

'Do you always ask your questions so aggressively? I'm not sure you'd make an effective interrogator.'

'Perhaps you're right,' he conceded with a small smile. 'But I'm too impatient for that line of work anyway.'

I zeroed in on the golden flecks in his dark eyes, trying not to lose my train of thought. There was just something about them.

'So what's the question?'

'Well,' he said. 'At first I wanted to know why you were spying on my house. And then I started to wonder why you suddenly decided not to stick around when I noticed you?'

He wasn't smiling any more; he was studying me and I understood what he meant – he knew I had been running away and he knew I was scared of him. But now, looking at him, I couldn't remember why I had felt that way.

'Were you running away from me?'

I shook my head too hard, making my cheeks jiggle. 'Nope, definitely not.'

'Oh, really?' he pressed, smiling broadly this time. It rearranged his face beautifully, raising his brows and softening his jaw.

'I prefer to think of it as casual hobbling.'

He pulled back from me and, slowly, I became aware of the rest of the world again. 'I'd call it frantic sprinting.'

'Semantics.'

'I'm sorry if I hurt you,' he said. 'I'm Nic, by the way, and this is my brother, Luca.'

Even though I was standing between the brothers, I had barely registered Luca. He had stopped studying his menu and was resting his interlocking fingers on top of it. I offered him a smile. 'Welcome to Gracewell's.'

'That was boring for me,' Luca replied. His voice was sharp with impatience, and scratchy too, as though he had a sore throat. 'But it's nice to know you're planning on being somewhat professional this evening, Sophie.'

I blanched. *How rude was this guy?*

He gestured back and forth with his index finger, first at Nic, and then at me, like our conversation was *his* business too. 'Are you ready to focus now, Nicoli?'

Nicoli. His full name suited him. It was beautiful.

Nic shifted in his seat so that he was closer to me, and the two of us were side by side, facing his brother. 'Chill out, Luca.'

Luca's eyebrows climbed. 'My brother, *l'ipocrita.*'

Nic swatted his hand in Luca's direction. '*Stai zitto!*'

'Have you worked here long, Sophie?' Luca cut to me again. He dragged a hand through his hair, settling the unruly black strands away from his face and behind his ears. I found myself entranced by his bright blue eyes, now that I could really see them. They were searing, and seemed to shine unnaturally from his tanned face. Was he the boy from the window, I wondered? No, he was too hard, too unyielding. It wasn't him. I was almost sure of it.

'Well?' he pressed.

'Luca,' Nic rumbled. 'Can you not do this—'

'Let her answer.'

'No, I haven't worked here for long,' I replied quickly, hoping it would ease whatever tension was mounting between them.

Maybe they'd just had an argument before I turned up. Or maybe Luca didn't get out much and this was his idea of socializing. 'It's just a stupid summer job.'

I felt guilty lying about the diner's role in my life and my future, but suddenly I couldn't stand the thought of them thinking I was as ordinary as I was; that my life was bound to a place that hadn't been redecorated in nearly twenty years, a place owned by an incarcerated man, a place where nothing exciting ever happened to anyone.

Nic pulled his arms from the table and folded them. He kept his narrowed gaze on Luca, like he was almost daring him to do something.

Luca appeared unaffected by the death stare. 'Do you like it?'

I shrugged. 'As much as anyone can, I guess.'

'And what about your co-workers? Do you like them?'

'*Smettila!*' Nic hissed, his accent flipping effortlessly again.

'Does it matter if I like them?'

'You tell me,' said Luca.

'Yes, they're nice, mostly,' I returned evenly. 'Why? Are you doing a police survey or something?'

For the first time since our rocky introduction, Luca smiled at me, revealing sharp teeth and pronounced cheekbones.

'Sophie,' Nic murmured. 'Don't worry about my brother. As you can see, he's *completely* socially inept.'

The softness in his voice settled me, and I let myself be charmed by him, if only for a second, before leaving them with their menus.

'Look at those fine specimens!' whooped Ursula when I returned to the counter. 'So *these* boys are the new Priestlys?'

I nodded subtly. Across the way, Nic and Luca were

enthralled in another conversation. They were in their own beautiful little world again. And Ursula and I were on a planet beside that world, stalking them unashamedly.

'Is your shadow crush the black-haired one?' she teased.

'No, the other one.'

Suddenly Nic turned his head a fraction, like he could hear us. I held my breath – without knowing why – and squeezed Ursula's arm, but she didn't notice because she was too busy trying not to drool. And then he was engrossed again. It was as though he'd needed a breather from the intensity of his discussion; now that he had taken it, he was back in. And so was Luca. Their mouths sped up and their gestures became more expressive.

'It's hard to look away,' Ursula teased, undeterred by the mounting anger in their conversation. 'And just *look* at those eyes. Where are they from?'

'Heaven?' I guessed, and we both laughed. They were so exotic, so different from anyone I had ever seen around Cedar Hill.

'Do angels eat?'

That's when I remembered I had completely forgotten to take their order. I slid around the counter and scurried back over. 'What can I get you?' I grabbed the pad from my apron and flicked it open, ripping the bottom of the sheet.

Luca looked alarmed by my interruption, like he had forgotten where they were. He opened his menu again, scanned it for five seconds and pulled back with a frown. 'A coffee. Black. Strong.'

He gestured at Nic.

'I'll have the steak sandwich, rare, with fries. And a glass of milk,' Nic said finally, before shutting his menu and shifting his gaze back to me, 'please.'

'Is that everything?' I held eye contact with him, feeling my lips twitch into a shy smile.

'*Cazzo,* that *is* all!' Luca hissed into the space between us.

By now, I was used to dealing with difficult customers, but Luca's attitude was unparalleled, and I found myself losing my temper quicker than I normally would have. 'I'm sorry, but is my presence in the *place where I work* offending you? Because you don't have to stay here.'

He threw me a contemptuous stare, and I held it.

'Just don't spit in my coffee.'

I bit my tongue and left them again.

After I passed the order through to Kenny in the kitchen, I joined Ursula, who was cleaning up after Erin and co. We busied ourselves wiping down the remaining tables and sweeping the floor as the minutes dragged by. When I served Nic his steak, I caught sight of the beginning of a tattoo above the neckline at the back of his T-shirt, then spent the following ten minutes behind the counter figuring it was probably the top of a large, ornate cross.

Five minutes before closing time, when I was balancing the books for the night, Luca's phone rang, and he got up and left abruptly.

Nic approached the counter timidly, like he was walking into open gunfire. That same uncomfortable flicker of recognition stirred inside me but I pushed it away. *Get a grip.*

'Sorry about my brother.' He swatted his arm at something behind him. 'We think he was dropped on his head as a baby . . . several hundred times.'

'I don't think I've ever met someone so inquisitive,' I noted. It was the only non-negative thing I could think to say about Luca.

Nic jerked his head, like there was a bee buzzing in his ear. Maybe that's how he thought of his brother. 'I guess I'm just used to it by now. Don't let him unnerve you.'

'He didn't.'

'You don't find Luca intimidating?'

I shook my head.

Nic's gaze adopted a sudden fierce intensity, and I was instantly hyperaware of how loud my heartbeat was.

'Good,' he murmured.

'He's definitely weird, though,' I added as an afterthought. 'And unbelievably rude.'

'We should bring him here more often so you can keep him in line.' Nic produced a black credit card that gleamed with a level of affluence I could only dream about, and handed it to me. Suddenly every part of me was standing at attention, and I wondered if he knew it. He was probably used to having this effect on girls.

'So when did you move in?' I asked, trying to keep focused.

'Last week.' Then I couldn't possibly have known him. My mind was playing tricks on me. Nic gestured behind him in the direction of the old house with a casualness that implied it was one of many sprawling mansions frequented by his family. Not that that surprised me; he had a certain look about him, the look of a wealthy kid who could afford European vacations and Aspen ski retreats. He had the kind of bloodline that stretched beyond somewhere as ordinary as Cedar Hill. 'But you probably already know that, since you were spying on our house.'

I felt my cheeks reignite. 'I was *not* spying on your house!'

His smile grew. 'Sure seemed that way.'

I slid the credit card machine towards him and waited as he entered his PIN. My gaze fell on the knuckles of his right hand, which were covered in pooling purple bruises and deep red gashes.

'What happened to your hand?' I asked, startled by the horror in my own voice. It was unpleasant to look at, and I couldn't understand why he wasn't flinching in pain.

Nic pulled his hand away from the machine and stared at it in surprise. 'Oh,' he said slowly, rotating his wrist and studying the injury.

The mechanical printing of the receipt filled the silence.

'Are you OK?'

'I'm fine.'

I got the sense I had upset him. I ripped off the receipt and gave it to him, and this time he took it with his other hand.

'I didn't mean to pry . . .'

'No, of course not.' Nic cleared his throat. 'I had just forgotten about it, that's all. I got locked out the other day and I had to punch in a boarded-up window at the back of our house to get in. The perks of moving and all that . . .'

'It looks painful,' I said, doing my best impression of Captain Obvious.

Nic shook his head a little. 'I've had worse.'

I couldn't tell if he was joking or not, and before I could think of a reply, he was turning from me.

'I should probably go, Sophie.'

'Goodbye,' I offered.

'Maybe I'll see you soon?' he called over his shoulder.

'As long as you don't try and kill me again.'

'I'll try not to, but you're certainly more than welcome to come back and stalk my house.' He winked, the lightness in his voice back again.

'I wasn't stalking it!'

'*Buona notte*, Sophie.'

CHAPTER SIX

THE DROWNED MAN

I arrived home to find a silver Mercedes parked on the street outside my house. I rounded the car, which exaggerated the pitiful state of my mother's battered Ford just by being near it. The Mercedes may have been sleek, but it was empty and unfamiliar. What's more, my mother was usually in bed at this time of night, *not* welcoming rich visitors. I might have been infamy's child, but she was infamy's wife, and that meant her social calendar was a lot more open than it used to be. Now, instead of friends, she had projects.

I began to panic that she *was* welcoming a visitor – the kind of visitor who was going to try and replace my father. Maybe my mother was already tired of waiting. Maybe she didn't want to face the next four years alone, fielding questions from nosy neighbours and fair-weather friends, and spending every

Valentine's Day crying over the night my father was taken away from her. Maybe this was the car of the man who was going to try and fix it all.

I centred myself. There was really only one thing to do. And that one thing was not to stand outside panicking. No. I was going to march inside, muster up every strand of teenage sarcasm and moodiness I had in me, and use it to scare away whoever this mystery suitor was.

I let myself in through the front door and shut it quietly behind me. Deep vibrations were wafting from the kitchen – a man's voice! I padded down the hallway, stopping just behind the door that led to the kitchen. It was ajar.

'I don't know why you're acting so jumpy. You're going to terrify her,' my mother was saying.

'Will there ever be a time when you take my advice, Celine?'

The strained voice of my uncle Jack surprised me more than if it had been a different man entirely. Historically, my mother and my father's brother had never gotten along. In my mother's mind, Jack was always getting in the way. And even when he was getting in the way with concert tickets or take-out pizza, he was still a nuisance. He was about the only person in the world whom she refused to tolerate. He ranked below Mrs Bailey on the I-don't-want-you-in-my-house scale, and *that* was saying something.

Growing up, my father and my uncle only ever had each other – a result of two absent, alcoholic parents – and with Jack being younger, and always refusing to settle down, he had relied a lot on my father, pulling him away for nights at the local bar, or sweeping into his life during private moments that my mother had wanted to keep for just us three. In short, Jack was always there, and was, in my mother's esteem, a bad influence.

But I knew the other parts of him – the man who took me into the city to see *Wicked* at the Oriental Theatre just because I once said in passing that I liked musicals; the man who purposefully lingered around my conversations with Millie at work so he could chime in with his idea of sage advice about our boy problems; the man who ruffled my hair when I was trying to complain about something completely serious, who would buy me the new iPhone on a whim, 'just because', and who would insist on driving me to school when it was snowing so I wouldn't have to walk through the slush to reach the bus. I saw the man who did his best to step in and protect me when my father went to prison, and even though he didn't always succeed in shielding me from the cruel jibes and the rescinded party invitations, at least he tried.

I pressed closer to the door.

'I don't want you getting Sophie involved in your conspiracy stuff,' my mother snapped. 'Haven't you learnt anything?'

'It's my prerogative to look out for her, Celine. I made a promise to Mickey.'

'I think you've already done enough,' my mother replied in a dangerously quiet voice reserved only for her most terrifying moods. I flinched in sympathy for my uncle.

'When are you going to let all this shit go?' Jack spat.

'When you accept your part in it!'

I peeked around the door. My mother stood at one end of the kitchen, wearing her bathrobe and slippers. Her short golden hair lay messy around her face, and her features were pinched in disgust. She had folded her arms and was leaning to one side, her hip hitched up at a defiant angle. Small as she was, nobody wanted to be on the wrong side of Celine Gracewell. I, of all people, could certainly attest to that.

'I'm just trying to keep Sophie safe,' Jack said, his shoulders dropping in resignation. 'Why won't you let me?'

'Because I don't trust you. Not after everything.'

With a frustrated sigh, my uncle stepped back and shook his head. 'You've never trusted me.'

'Oh shut up, Jack.'

Feeling like I had heard enough to make me feel sufficiently uncomfortable for the rest of the year, I kicked the door wide open.

'What the hell is going on?'

Jack's face flooded with relief, settling the high colour in his cheeks. 'There you are!'

'Yeah.' I pointed at myself for added effect. 'Here I am. What's all the yelling about?'

'Nothing, nothing.' He ran his hand along his greying buzz cut, stopping to scratch the back of his head. 'I'm just stressed.'

Jack was always stressed about something.

'What are you doing here?'

'Being dramatic,' my mother hissed before he could reply.

Yikes.

'Is that your new car in the driveway?' I asked, coming to stand between my uncle and my mother and trying to alter the mood. 'If you're making that kind of money from the diner, you should probably give me a raise.'

He wasn't amused by my joke. 'I borrowed it from a friend. I'm not driving my car right now.'

'Feeling too conspicuous these days?' I tried to lighten the mood again.

There really was nothing more uncomfortable than awkwardness. And besides, Uncle Jack drove a red vintage convertible – a homage to his midlife crisis. It was only fair I got to make fun of him for it.

He sighed. 'Something like that.'

My mother moved around me to fill a glass of water. 'Just say what you want to say to her so we can get back to our lives.'

'What are you doing here so late?' I asked again. 'And why haven't you been at work? The delivery man still hasn't shown up.'

My uncle shuffled his feet like a lost child, unsure of where to put himself. 'I know,' he said, his voice thick with weariness. 'Luis died on Friday night.'

'Oh,' I said, feeling a sudden pang of guilt. The delivery man had a name – Luis, yes, I remembered. And now Luis, who was barely forty, was dead. 'What happened to him?'

'He drowned.'

'Drowned,' I echoed. 'At night. Where?'

'In his bathtub,' said Jack, simply, like there wasn't anything bizarre about that statement.

'Oh dear,' said my mother, covering her mouth.

I, on the other hand, was gaping. It just seemed so illogical. 'Was it suicide?' The last time I signed for a delivery, Luis was chattering on about how great the weather was.

'Luis had too much to live for,' Jack replied matter-of-factly. 'He didn't do it to himself.' What did *that* mean? A sudden coldness rippled up my arms. My uncle continued, undeterred by the implication, leaving me to ponder it in silence. 'Eric Cain and I are going to see Luis's family tomorrow. I want to see that they're taken care of while they deal with all of this. His wife is inconsolable.'

I was starting to feel like a royal ass. I had met Luis maybe twenty times and I barely knew his name; my uncle knew his story, his family, and now he was going to go out of his way to make sure they were OK.

'That's really good of you,' I said, looking to my mother for her agreement – surely she would give Uncle Jack credit for this – but she wasn't paying attention to me.

'That poor woman,' she said quietly instead.

'It's the right thing to do,' said Jack, to me.

'Are you OK?' My uncle wasn't one for big displays of emotion, but I could see by his face that he was upset.

'Yeah,' he said, brushing off my concern. 'I just wanted to come by and talk to you before I left.'

'You could have called me,' I ventured, not unkindly, but there's just something so unnerving about people visiting you without calling first. 'I'm permanently contactable.'

'I lost my phone. I have to get a new one.'

My mother circled the table and sat as far away from Jack as she could. She started drumming her fingernails along the table – a not-so-subtle hint – while still keeping a watchful eye on our conversation. If I thought Luis's death had softened her obvious disdain for my uncle, I was wrong.

Jack ignored her exasperation, and I felt like I was the only one left experiencing the full awkwardness of the situation.

'So . . . what's up?' I asked.

He pulled a chair out and sat down, propping his elbows on his knees. His shoulders sagged. 'After I visit Luis's family tomorrow, I'm going to go stay in the city. I won't be back in

Cedar Hill for a while. But I want to talk to you about something before I go away.'

He looked at me with solemn grey-blue eyes – they were my eyes, my father's eyes, and with a sudden pang I was reminded of just how similar they were. Before, they could have been mistaken for twins, but not any more. Prison life had been unkind to my father's appearance, while my uncle's face remained mostly unlined, his hair neat and his skin lightly tanned from being out in the sun.

'What do you want to talk about?' I backed up against the counter and gripped it a lot harder than I meant to, sensing something was wrong. This was what they were arguing about. My mother continued to drum her fingernails on the table.

'A new family have moved into the neighbourhood, and I need you to be careful of them.'

I felt alarm spread across my face. 'What?'

He surveyed me warily. 'Do you know what I'm talking about?'

I nodded slowly, trying to figure out where this was coming from and why it was making me feel panicky all over again. 'What's wrong with the Priestlys?'

I watched my mother's reaction for more clues.

'Theatrics,' she murmured, with a dismissive flick of the wrist. Still, she stayed where she was, monitoring our exchange.

'Persephone,' – I grimaced on instinct. I hated when Jack full-named me. 'I'm not going to get into it,' he said. My uncle's stern voice was so like my father's, it sent a shudder down my spine. For a second I wanted to close my eyes and pretend he was there, that everything was back to the way it should be –

that we hadn't just discussed somebody drowning in their own tub, and that we weren't about to slap a big fat warning sign over the hottest boys in the neighbourhood. 'Just do as I ask.'

I couldn't help but feel sceptical. Even with his bruised hand, there had been something so soothing about Nic's presence.

'When will you be back?'

'I don't know yet.'

Cagey as ever. I wished Millie the High Inquisitor were here. She could get answers from a mute. And she'd enjoy it too.

'So that's all you're going to tell me?'

'That's all there is.' Jack looked away from me, out the window and into the darkness behind our house. 'Do you understand?'

I was about to answer that I didn't really understand *anything* about it, but then the most peculiar thing happened. He sprang to his feet like something had bitten him. The chair tumbled backwards and he darted across the kitchen.

'What on earth?' My mother's chair screeched against the floor.

Jack lunged at the kitchen sink and shot out his hand. I thought he was going to punch through the window, but instead he grabbed the jar of honey from the sill. When he looked at me again, his eyes were red and bulging.

'Where did this come from?'

'The h-honey?' I stuttered. I had never seen someone so freaked out by something so benign. 'I found it.'

He pinched the black ribbon between his fingers, rubbing it. 'Where?'

I shrugged. 'Someone left it at the diner. I found it when I was closing up.'

The colour drained from his face, turning his usually red-tinged cheeks to an eerie paper-white. 'If you find one of these again, I want you to leave it where it is and call me immediately.'

'Jack, it's just honey,' I pointed out.

Why was everyone acting so strangely lately? I had already tasted it and lived to tell the tale, so it's not like it was poisoned.

'Just do it,' he said quietly. 'OK?'

'I thought you said you didn't have a phone,' I reminded him.

'I'll call you when I get a new one.'

'Jack?' In all the strangeness, I had forgotten my mother was still there. 'I think you should go now. You're acting erratically and it's making me very uncomfortable. Sophie probably wants to go to bed.'

I opened my mouth to protest – I wasn't tired – but then I stopped myself. My mother was right.

'OK.' Jack looked at the ground, shaking his head. 'Sorry, Sophie. I've had a very long day.'

'It's fine.' I offered him an encouraging smile. Between managing the diner and taking care of his investments in the city, Jack always worked himself into the ground, but lately he had been more unlike himself than ever; he was exhausted and jittery, and now that Luis had died, his behaviour was stranger than ever.

'Good night, Sophie.'

'Night,' I returned.

Honey still in hand, Jack trudged towards the back door.

Half a second later, the motion censor in our backyard flickered to life, illuminating my uncle's shadow as it faced away from us, staring at the broken patio squares and the overgrown grass.

'What on earth is he—?'

The rest of my mother's question was drowned out by an ear-splitting crash. I pressed my nose up to the window, but Jack was already disappearing from view. I looked down, where the light was winking off a hundred shards of shattered glass.

'That man!' my mother shrieked, coming to stand beside me at the window. 'This is exactly why I don't want him around. Your uncle's behaviour is completely irrational. He's been drinking again, and if he doesn't stop, he's going to wind up doing something he'll really regret . . .' She trailed off and started to rub my arm. 'Are you OK?'

'I'm fine,' I lied, pinning my hand against the window to stop it from shaking.

'I wish your father were here to keep him in line.'

'I think if Dad were here Uncle Jack wouldn't be out of line,' I said quietly.

My mother sighed. 'I'll have to wait until morning to clean up that mess.'

'I'll help you.'

We lingered at the window together, and watched as honey oozed into the pavement cracks like dark gold blood.

CHAPTER SEVEN

THE CRIMSON FALCONS

Millie had an outfit for everything, so when she showed up at the riverside courts on Saturday, I was unsurprised to find her wearing a tiny pair of shorts and the tightest basketball jersey I had ever seen. She pushed her way through pockets of other teenagers, waltzing towards me in an explosion of black and red.

'I didn't know you were a Bulls fan.'

'Oh, didn't you?' She smirked and plonked herself down beside me on the bottom bench of the courtside bleachers.

'Let me rephrase that,' I said as she began to wind her hair into a ponytail. 'I didn't even know you were a basketball fan.'

'I guess you could say I'm more of a *boys* fan.' She snapped the hair elastic into place. 'The top belongs to Alex. It shrank in the wash.' She grinned unashamedly.

I looked down at myself: at my mother's three-quarter-length jogging pants, a plain grey tank top and an old pair of Asics with bright green stripes. My hair was tied high on my head, falling down between my shoulder blades in a straight ponytail. Already I could tell the sun was bleaching the stray baby hairs that were too wispy to be tied back with the rest.

Millie ran her gaze along my outfit, scrunching her nose.

'You look . . .' she began uncertainly.

'. . . normcore?' I finished.

Exercise wasn't exactly my calling in life, but I was grateful to have something to distract me from my uncle's recent behaviour. He had been gone for several days since his whole honeypot-patio freak-out and still hadn't tried to contact me. Ursula was in charge of the diner in his absence. She had reacted the worst to the death of Luis, and had resolved never to take a bath again, just in case she drowned herself. Millie and I were slightly less dramatic about it, but we were still glad to be free of her morbid rants, at least just for the day.

We never usually played in the Cedar Hill Summer Basketball Tournament. Not that the word 'tournament' really summed it up. It was more of a basketball-related gathering hosted by the Cedar Hill Residents' Association every July. As part of an ever-growing agenda that included park maintenance, a neighbourhood watch and outdoor movie nights, the CHRA were always coming up with ideas that would keep us teenagers off the street and out of trouble in a 'socially desirable and positive way' during the summer. The basketball tournament was one of the few that had actually stuck, and over the years it had become a tradition that everyone made fun of but no one wanted to miss. It was really about the only thing the neighbourhood kids actually did together; the rest of the summer we were like lazy suburban tumbleweeds, floating around the town in twos and threes.

For Millie and me, the whole thing had always been more of a spectacle enjoyed from the sidelines while eating ice cream and pointing out hot boys, but in the interest of 'getting back up on the social horse', as Millie called it, we had decided to take part this summer. I was hesitant at best; if nobody wanted to hang out with the daughter of a murderer, who would want to play basketball with one? Thankfully, Millie's brother, Alex, had invited us to be part of his team. I suspected it was a way to make it more of a challenge for him – the trophies from the past three years were probably gathering dust on his bedroom shelf by now.

'We might actually win this thing, you know.' Millie was reclining on the bench, arms splayed out behind her as she scoped out our surroundings.

As always, there were twice as many spectators squishing themselves into the bleachers and spilling out on to the grass that surrounded the courts. Erin Reyes and the rest of her gang had already secured a prime vantage spot at the top of the bleachers. Instead of playing in the tournament, they would most likely be practising how to eat their popsicles as seductively as possible. They were already doing an uncomfortably good job. Just beyond the courts the river flowed lazily, reflecting the clear sky, and along the bank, rows of young trees bowed over the water like they were peering inside for something.

'I remember the last time I played basketball,' said Millie wistfully. She stared up at the sky and I could see the sun was already dusting freckles across her pale cheeks. 'I was trying to pass the ball to Alex, but he missed it and it smashed the kitchen window.'

'Good times,' I remembered fondly.

'What about you?' She snapped her head down.

'Maybe never?'

Little creases rippled along Millie's forehead. 'I'm sure you'll be good at it.'

'You better be,' someone interrupted.

Millie's brother, Alex, was stalking towards us, his grin revealing nearly all of his perfectly square teeth. He was accompanied by two of his friends – the first I recognized as Robbie Stenson, a stockier, *way* less attractive version of a Ken doll, who came complete with floppy brown hair and overly groomed eyebrows. He didn't walk so much as lope around, kind of like a stylish troll. The other boy I had seen once or twice at Millie's house playing video games, but he never seemed to say much. He had bright red hair, gangly limbs and a forehead that was shinier than the rest of him.

Millie bounced to her feet. 'It's about time you showed up. We have a tournament to win.'

'Soph, you know Stenny and Foxy, right?' Alex indicated behind him.

Ah, boys and their stupid nicknames. 'Yeah, hi.' I waved.

Robbie Stenson gave me a too-cool-for-this-introduction head nod – so subtle I barely registered it – while 'Foxy' threw a fluorescent yellow vest at me. I fumbled it and had to bend down to pick it up. They were obviously less than thrilled about having me on their team.

Millie caught her vest on reflex and then dropped it like it was on fire. 'No way. I'm not wearing this. It reeks of sweat.'

'Are you serious?' Alex's voice was already weary with sibling-related fatigue.

Millie curled her lip in disgust. 'I'd literally rather die.' I suppressed my smile. Their British accents made even the most banal exchanges sound way more Masterpiece Theatre than they had any right to be.

Robbie, Foxy and I put our vests on without protest; mine fell to my knees and halfway down my arms, engulfing everything but my luminous kicks. Eventually, and after some not-so-subtle peer pressure on my part, Millie wriggled into hers.

'You're such a tyrant,' she muttered under her breath.

'At least your legs still look good,' I tried to reassure her. But we couldn't hide from the ugly truth. We were both swimming in oversized fluorescence.

'We're up on court one first,' Alex started, clapping his hands and rubbing them together. 'Our team name is the Sharpshooters.'

Millie and I grimaced. 'That's the worst name ever,' we chorused.

'Why don't you come up with something better, then?' Alex challenged.

'Oh, oh, oh!' Millie started hopping up and down. 'What about Victorious Secret?'

Alex's face fell, and Foxy let out a groan.

'That doesn't even make sense,' Robbie cut in.

'How about the Human Highlighters?' I suggested, gesturing at our hideously luminous vests.

'Fine.' Alex threw his hands up in surrender, and Robbie and Foxy nodded their reluctant consent. 'We'll change it.'

Millie cupped her hands around her mouth and made her voice sound crackly. 'That's one small step for Sophie, one giant leap for Alex's sense of humour.'

Robbie sprinted off to reregister our name, leaving us with Foxy and Alex, who was already taking the whole situation a million times more seriously than we were.

'I've done a little recon,' he said, conveying his info like a Navy SEAL. 'A lot of the other players are younger than us this year, which gives us the advantage . . .'

Millie punched me in the arm and my attention fell away from her brother. 'What?'

'Now *you're* literally going to die.' Her eyes had grown to the size of saucers, and I swivelled to follow her gaze. 'That's them, right? The Priestly brothers?'

She wasn't fully wrong about the dying thing. My heart definitely slowed down for at least a couple of beats. Across the far court, the Priestly brothers were coming towards us; there were four of them this time, their connection to each other made plain by their olive skin and dark hair.

'I never thought I'd actually find basketball shorts attractive on a guy,' was all I could manage.

'I was just thinking that,' said Millie.

What the hell are they even doing here? I wondered. Most of us had come for tradition's sake – it was a pleasant enough way to kill time, a last resort on a sunny day for a bunch of kids who had nothing better to do. But these boys weren't like the rest of Cedar Hill. I would have thought them above the idea of attending some lame neighbourhood basketball tournament.

Luca was walking next to Nic, his face stern, and a new brother flanked them on either side. They probably could have nailed a five-legged race if they'd wanted to.

By the way the brothers seemed to zero in on Luca as he spoke, I assumed he was the eldest, though the others, the two I had yet to meet and who were remarkably similar to each other in appearance, could not have been that far behind – maybe eighteen or nineteen years old. They were shorter and more filled out, though they shared the same square jaws and strong cheekbones. I guessed Nic was the youngest of the four, though not by much.

'Holy handsomeness!' Millie was practically salivating. 'Four Italian stallions carved from my dreams. Which one is Nic?'

My eyes hadn't left him. 'The one with the dark hair.'

'Ha ha, very funny.'

'Second from the right.'

'Wow. And Luca?'

'Second from the left.'

Millie whistled to herself. '*Hello*, blue eyes.'

Alex prodded her in the shoulder. 'Are you done? We're trying to talk tactics.'

'Shut up,' she hissed, shaking him off. 'I'm in the middle of something.' She narrowed her eyes, honing in. 'OK, who's on the far right? The one with the slicked-back hair? And is that a *scar*?'

'I don't know. Maybe we should call him Hair Gel.'

The closer they got, the more obvious it became that they were capturing the attention of every girl in the vicinity, and they looked like they knew it too. I wondered where the fifth brother was – the bright-eyed boy from the window who'd raised his hand without a smile – but the thought vanished when Nic's eyes found mine and I nearly exploded with butterflies.

'Hi,' he mouthed.

I smiled back, resisting the urge to clutch my stupid, back-flipping stomach.

'Holy crap, that was seductive.' Millie was hopping from foot to foot. 'They're coming over. Be cool.'

Like helpless magnets, we drifted towards the brothers, leaving Alex and his sidekicks to talk boring strategy behind us, determined, like every boy at the basketball courts, to ignore the new arrivals. My uncle's warning, which had seemed so urgent and important at the time, flittered away on the wind. If these boys were really bad news, as Jack seemed to think, then suddenly I was happy to be Icarus, ready to get all melty from flying too close to the suns.

'Hey,' I called out. 'I didn't know you'd be playing today.'

Nic stopped a couple of feet away and the rest of his brothers closed in around us. 'It was a last minute decision. Now I'm glad we made it.'

Millie pinched me. It was her silent version of an excited squeal.

'Nice vest, Sophie,' said Luca, straight off the bat. 'I can barely see you.'

'Luca.' I tore my attention away from Nic for the amount of time needed to throw his brother a contemptuous glare. 'A pleasure, as always.'

The brother beside him laughed. He had the stupidest hair-style: the top section of his hair was scraped into a short black ponytail, while the sides of his head were shaved, revealing a small golden hoop in his left ear. Despite the ridiculous plant hairstyle, he was attractive, but when he laughed, his eyes widened unnaturally and his opened mouth revealed two chipped front teeth that made him seem slightly maniacal. He reminded me of that one crazy hyena in *The Lion King*.

'Ignore Luca. That's just his bad attempt at trash-talking you,' Nic cut in, sending his brother a glare on my behalf.

'And my way of pointing out that she's small,' Luca added.

'Thanks, Sherlock. I know I'm small.'

'Just making sure.'

'Do you even *have* a brain-to-mouth filter?' I asked.

'I try not to overuse it,' he returned blithely.

'Clearly.'

'Don't cry about it, Day-Glo.'

'Shut up, Luca.' Nic threw his red vest over his head and pulled it down. 'I think you make it look good, Sophie.'

'*Cazzo*, here we go again,' muttered Luca. He rolled his eyes and then leant into Ponytail, adding in a calculated whisper, '*this* is what he was like at the diner. It was so annoying.'

'You know, Luca, you're really good at strategically muttering things just loud enough to be offensive.'

'Thank you, Sophie.' His tone lifted, rendering his false sincerity almost believable. 'I appreciate that.'

'I should get you a medal.'

'Don't bother,' he said, a lazy smirk forming. 'After today, I'll have a trophy.'

I curled my lip. 'I know what you can do with that trophy . . .'

Millie's laugh drowned out the rest of my reply. She hugged her arm around my side, pinching me through the vest. *Squeal, squeal, squeal.*

'So what's your team's name?' Nic cut in, guiding the conversation out of the gutter.

I puffed up my chest and brushed the stray strands of now-white hair away from my face. 'The Human Highlighters.'

Luca snorted.

'What's yours?' asked Millie, but she wasn't directing her question at Nic; she was looking at Hair Gel, her teeth gently pulling at her bottom lip.

I zeroed in on his face – Millie was right, there *was* a scar. It was obviously an old injury, slicing through his left eyebrow and glowing silvery against his tanned skin. On instinct, I glanced at Nic's bruised hand, and felt an uneasiness bubbling in my stomach. I pushed it away.

'The Crimson Falcons,' Hair Gel replied to Millie, falling right into her trap and watching her lips hungrily.

'Intense,' said Millie, her expression entirely coquettish.

'It was either that or the Angel-makers,' Luca added. His humour was so deadpan, sometimes I didn't know if he was funny or just insane.

'Stop it.' Nic punched Luca in the arm with an audible thump, but his brother didn't flinch. If I had received that hit I would have been on the ground screaming for my mother.

'*Calmati!* I think I'd better diffuse this,' Hair Gel cut in, moving easily from one language to the next, just like Nic and Luca did. It was hard to tell which was their real accent – American or Italian. Hair Gel leant over to shake our hands, holding Millie's a little longer than mine and, I noticed, stroking his thumb over hers. Maybe Millie had finally met her flirting match. 'I'm Dominico. You can call me Dom, though.'

Millie broke into the creepiest giggle I've ever heard. 'I'm Millie. This is Sophie. Welcome to the neighbourhood.'

Welcome to the neighbourhood? I'd have to tease her about that later. Maybe she could stop by his house with a basket of muffins.

'Thank you. Do you work at the diner as well, Millie?' Dom lingered over her name like it was a beautiful flower. His charm offensive was almost as powerful as Nic's, but his eyes were darker, his expression intense. I studied his scar as he moved away from me, beginning his own hushed conversation with Millie.

I felt Nic's attention on me again. 'Good luck today,' he offered earnestly.

'Thanks, you too.' There were other things I wanted to say to him, but with Luca and Ponytail watching us I could barely utter a word without feeling self-conscious.

'We don't need luck,' Luca interrupted, prompting another exasperated thump from Nic.

'Luca,' Ponytail whined. His voice was abnormally high and not unlike Marge Simpson's, and for a terrifying moment I thought I was going to laugh in his face. He frowned, and his eyebrows bled into one fuzzy caterpillar above coffee-coloured eyes. 'Can we just go register?'

'Yeah, let's go, Gino. We shouldn't be fraternizing with our competition anyway.' Luca elbowed Nic as he retreated. '*Andiamo,* Loverboy.'

'I should probably go get ready,' Nic offered apologetically. 'Wouldn't want to get on the bad side of our wonderful dictator.'

'Same here,' I said, but both of us still lingered. 'Where's the rest of your team anyway? Don't you have a fifth player?'

He shook his head with more casualness than I was expecting. I was hoping he'd mention the fifth brother, at least give me a clue as to why he hadn't come or even that he did, in fact, exist, and I hadn't imagined a creepy ghost boy at the window that first night. 'We're a foursome.'

'So you're at a disadvantage,' I noted. 'That's a risky move.'

Nic did something with his eyes that made the flecks of gold inside them glisten. I wasn't sure if it was a secret superpower or the effect of the sun, but it was damn effective. And a little jarring, though I still couldn't figure out why.

'You're welcome to be our number five,' he whispered conspiratorially. 'I promise I'll keep Luca away from you.'

I bit my lip to keep my smile from bordering on disturbing. 'I'm not sure Millie would ever forgive me if I jumped ship.'

'Ah, I see.' He feigned the look of a puppy that had just been kicked. 'You're too noble for that.'

'And surely you're too honourable to steal me from her.'

'No, I'm not.'

I felt a blush rise in my cheeks. 'Well, I'll have to be honourable enough for both of us, then. Besides,' I added, trying to justify my refusal to myself, 'we're up in a minute, and we've already missed our strategy session. I don't want to annoy the rest of my team any more than I already have.'

'Where are they?'

I gestured behind me at Alex and the rest of the yellow vests, who were in the middle of an intense set of jumping jacks.

Nic's smile faded. 'That blond guy?'

'That's Millie's brother and two of his friends. I think she bribed them into letting us on their team.'

Nic studied Alex and the others as they started to bend themselves into elaborate stretches. 'I'm sure the bribe wasn't necessary.'

'Soph.' Millie was back and tugging on my arm. 'We gotta go. Our game is about to start.'

Dom had stepped away from her and I caught a glimpse of his scar again. Though he couldn't have been much older than us, something about it aged him, made him other than what he appeared. I couldn't put my finger on what it was. He caught me watching him and smirked, his expression suddenly wolfish.

I looked away, embarrassed.

'See you guys on the court!' Millie pulled me with her, wiggling her butt a lot more than she usually did as she walked.

When I waved at Nic he was still staring at Alex. He didn't wave back.

We won our first game in time to watch the Crimson Falcons play Saved by the Balls on the opposite court. The Priestly brothers were fascinating to watch; even Alex, who had expressed a deliberate disinterest in them since their arrival, was glued to the game. Nic and Dom were the most obviously athletic, whipping up the court in flashes of red. They scored most of their baskets, only occasionally deferring to Gino, who seemed to be more adept at intimidating the other players than actually playing against them. Maybe it was the ponytail.

Luca glided around the sidelines, and when the opportune moment arose, he'd strike from the shadows like a viper, snatching the ball out of the opposition's hands before the other player even had time to notice Luca was there. But that's all he did: intercept. I didn't see him make one single basket. He didn't even break a sweat.

Our game against Don't Hassle the Hoff started before the Priestly game finished, though it was clear that, like us, they would be advancing to the next round. We won by a comfortable margin of 62–39. Alex did most of the work, followed by Foxy and then Robbie. Millie was a very distant last, but she made it clear she didn't care. She was there to make an appearance, and if her fingers happened to brush against a basketball by accident, then fine.

We watched the Priestly brothers win their second game with more ease than we did. In our third game we were up against the Thunder Squirrels. I became acutely aware of Nic's presence on the sidelines and decided to make more of a conscious effort this time. Millie seemed to have concocted a similar plan, because for once she wasn't squealing and running away from the ball. She was actually chasing it.

By the end of our third quarter, the brothers were on the other court, winning their game as well, which meant both of our teams were going to the finals.

CHAPTER EIGHT
THE SWITCHBLADE

'Crap,' Millie said. The short parts of her bangs had frizzed out and she was frantically fixing her hair as we lingered on the court. 'I don't want to play against Dom. He'll see how terrible I am and then he won't come to my house party next week.'

'You invited him to the party already?'

Millie slow-blinked at me. 'Didn't you invite Nic?'

'Um . . .'

'God, Sophie.' She scrunched her eyes and started to rub her temples. 'Sometimes I wonder what goes on in that head of yours.'

'I hadn't even thought about it,' I admitted.

'*I hadn't even thought about it*,' she mimicked in the world's worst attempt at my accent.

'I'm not from the South,' I pointed out.

'It's on your birthday,' she countered, ignoring my jibe. 'You should definitely invite him.'

'I will.' I tried not to feel nervous about the prospect of inviting Nic to a house party taking place on my birthday where a grand total of five people would actually acknowledge me.

'In the meantime, let's hope Dom doesn't lose all respect for me during this game.'

'It's OK,' I soothed, retying my ponytail. 'He's already seen how bad you are.'

She shot me a withering look. 'It's bad enough he's already seen me sweat. It must be over a hundred degrees today.'

Alex, Robbie and Foxy joined us and started stretching again. They were so pumped it was almost laughable. 'Just one more game, guys. We've nearly got this,' Alex said.

'We *so* don't got this,' whispered Millie.

I nodded my head solemnly. 'We are screwed.'

Alex turned his attention to us, his face awash with concern. We were loose cannons, and his awareness of that fact couldn't have been more obvious. 'OK, the Crimson Falcons are a man short, which means Foxy, Stenny and I can take the strongest three. Millie and Sophie, you stay on the tallest guy.'

'I don't want to mark Luca!' I wailed.

'Can I mark Dom?' Millie asked hopefully.

Alex raked his hands through his hair, sweaty strands flopping back around his eyes. 'No. If Luca's free to move around, he'll throw our game off.'

Over Alex's shoulder I could see the Priestly brothers taking up their positions on the court. Nic was passing the ball back and forth between his hands, his expression focused. Beside him, Luca was smirking like it was going out of fashion. I wondered if he even had a facial expression that didn't read as 'smug ass'.

'Earth to Sophie.'

'Huh?'

Alex was staring at me, his big blue eyes as wide as Millie's. Sometimes it was eerie how similar their expressions made them. 'Did you hear what I said?'

I shook my head dumbly. 'Were you speaking?'

He released a sharp sigh and placed his hands on my shoulders, locking gazes with me. Ordinarily I would have been giddy if Millie's hot older brother got this close to me, but my hyperawareness of Nic was distracting me. 'I need you to keep Millie focused. I'll take care of the rest. The Crimson Falcons are going down.'

'You have to stop calling them that. I can't take you seriously.'

He pressed harder on my shoulders, as if to steady my resolve. I watched a stray bead of sweat slide down the side of his face and on to his neck. 'Sophie, can *you* please focus?'

'Hey, man, I think she gets it.'

Alex withdrew his hands and I pulled back to find Nic standing right beside him. He was giving him that look again – that I-don't-trust-you-and-maybe-I-want-to-kill-you look, but it was up close this time, and full of hostility.

'You're so worried about losing that you have to eavesdrop on our huddle?' Alex returned.

Nic arched an eyebrow. 'You're so hyped up about this game that you're going to freak her out about it? Give her a break.'

Alex squared up to Nic; they were almost the same height,

but Nic had the advantage. 'I like to win and so does she.'

'I bet Sophie likes to have fun too. Have you heard of that concept?' Nic clenched his jaw. 'Leave her alone.'

'Who the hell are *you,* anyway?' snapped Alex. 'You don't know either of us, so why don't you get out of our business and worry about yourself?'

Nic didn't move. They stood almost chest to chest, and I could see by the way Alex was flicking his gaze towards Robbie and Foxy that he was angling for backup. Not for the first time I registered Nic's defensive stance, and understood his distrust of Alex was about me. By the way he was staring at him, it looked like Nic was trying to bore a hole through Alex's forehead.

'Boys, chill out!' I squeezed myself into the space between them, pushing them apart with my hands. Alex fell away, but Nic didn't budge as easily. I could practically feel the testosterone seeping through his pores. 'Let's just start this thing, OK?'

'Fine.' Alex's teeth were gritted.

'Fine.' Nic turned on his heel and gestured to his brothers. They huddled up on the other side of the court.

Millie sidled over to me and dropped her voice. 'I think Dom's going to ask me out.'

Alex and Nic were getting into position for the jump ball.

'How do you know?'

A shout went up from somewhere behind us; the ball was in play and Nic had possession.

'He was flirting with me like crazy. And I thought *I* was shameless! I can tell he doesn't want to wait until the party to hang out.'

Nic scored the first basket before I had time to reply.

The game moved so quickly I could hardly keep track. I barely touched the ball, and Millie only managed to bounce it once before Luca zoomed by and dribbled it out from under her. Every time Nic passed me, it felt like he was deliberately slowing down so I could feel him brush against me, and I kept blissfully forgetting I was supposed to be marking Luca. By half-time, we were behind by six points.

At the start of the third quarter, Robbie passed the ball to me – I was standing near the basket, wide open. I sprang up, but the ball was knocked from my hands before I could shoot. It bounced away as Gino barrelled straight into me. I would have flown off the court if Nic hadn't jumped out of nowhere, catching me from behind. I stumbled against him with a thump.

'Careful,' he panted, his breath unsteady on my neck.

'Nic!' Luca yelled. 'Heads up!'

I looked up just in time to see a big orange blur whizzing directly at my face. My head slammed backwards into Nic's chest, and he grabbed me as I slumped against him.

'*Tu sei pazzo!*' Nic screeched over my head.

Tears started to stream down my cheeks, mingling with the blood that was pouring from my nose.

A little crowd formed around me.

'Sorry.' It was Luca's voice, but I couldn't focus on him. 'I did say "heads up", though.'

'Why would you pass the ball to me when her face was in the way?' Nic seethed over me.

'Why would you be feeling her up in the middle of a basketball game?'

'*Vaffanculo!*'

I didn't need to understand Italian to guess what that meant.

Millie whipped off her vest and handed it to me. I started to dab my nose, pinching the bridge with my free hand to stop the bleeding and trying not to smell the years of stale boy-sweat that had been encased in the mesh.

'Can *everyone* just give her some space?' Millie demanded.

Nic pulled his hands from my waist and joined the others, who were all staring at me with various levels of concern. Except Gino, who was tracking the movements of a nearby butterfly and snickering to himself.

'Do you think you can keep playing, Sophie?' Alex asked.

Nic bristled, turning on him. 'Are you serious, dude? That's all you can think to say?'

'What the *hell* is your problem?' Alex shot back.

Before Nic could retort, Millie was stomping her feet on the concrete like the angriest two-year-old imaginable. 'What the hell is wrong with *both* of you? Stupid boys and your *stupid* competitiveness. Just shut up, all of you! Sophie and I are absolutely *not* continuing this *childish* game with you hot-headed *Neanderthals* so you can win some *stupid,* cheap-ass trophy. We want no further part in this pathetic charade.'

'I—' Luca began.

'No!' Millie raised her index finger and pointed it directly into his eye like she was about to poke it. 'Not another word from *you.* If you have something to say, you can write it in a card and send it to Sophie's house with the *nicest flowers* money can buy. And you can say how *sorry* you are for being a *giant* ass and nearly *killing* her. She could have *died.* Do you understand that? *Died!* And all you have to show for it is that smirk. I don't think it's one bit funny, and I'll have you know I am a great judge of humour. So why don't you wipe that smile off your God-awfully perfect face and grow a sense of humanity, you smug douchelord.'

I couldn't quite fathom how everyone was managing not to laugh at Millie's ridiculous dramatics. If I had been in slightly less pain, I would have been doubled over on the ground myself.

'Mil—' Alex tried.

'No, Alex!' she shouted. 'I don't want to hear your excuses either. Where did you even *come* from anyway? I find it hard to believe we crawled out of the same womb. If you're not man enough to go through life without a fake trophy telling you something about yourself, then you're not man enough to speak to Sophie or me. And that goes for *all* of you morons.' She grabbed me by the arm and started pulling me away from everyone. 'We are going to the sidelines, where there is ice cream. And that is *final!*'

I could see the lingering shock in their eyes; they had obviously underestimated Millie. Nic was boring holes in his brother's forehead. If looks could kill, Luca would have been long gone from this world.

'Resume play?' I heard Alex say as we left the court.

'I can sit the game out to make it even.' My heart leapt at Nic's suggestion.

'No way. We finish it like this. We'll still beat you.'

Stupid Alex.

After the game, Nic found me on the sidelines nursing my nose with an unopened popsicle. Millie had gone in search of Dom to try and salvage their burgeoning love after her crazy outburst on the court. Alex had stormed off in a huff, and Luca was probably strolling around somewhere with a giant trophy tucked under his arm.

'Congratulations on your win.'

'Thanks.' Nic sank on to the grass beside me and pulled his knees up, wrapping his arms around them. 'But I don't think a two foot plastic trophy is going to improve my life much.'

'You probably would have lost if I had continued playing,' I teased. I took the popsicle away and wiggled my nose around to restore some feeling, relieved that it didn't seem broken.

'Good as new,' Nic said. He inched closer to get a better look and I noticed a small sprinkling of freckles across the bridge of his nose. 'It's perfect.'

'What is it about you boys and your incessant need to assault me anyway?' I asked. 'Have you got it in for me or something? You could at least be more subtle about it.'

'Must be something about you.' Nic flashed me a roguish grin. 'We're usually very discreet.'

'Four boys and discretion. Those terms don't exactly go together in my mind.'

'Well, actually there aren't just f—' Nic fell away from his sentence when something behind me caught his attention.

I looked over my shoulder.

At the edge of the riverbank, past the last court, I could just make out a ponytailed figure shoving someone with short blond hair behind the trees. Alex and Gino. It was hard to see, but they looked like they were fighting.

Nic sprang to his feet. I tried to keep up, but he was much faster than me.

Within seconds he was at the riverbank, pushing through the trees and pulling Alex off his brother. When I caught up with them, I found Gino doubled over, unmoving, with his head clutched loosely in his hands. Nearby, Nic was pinning Alex on the ground, and the two were trading insults.

Alex jerked his body to the side and kicked out at Nic, making him fall back on to his haunches.

'This has nothing to do with you!' Alex shouted as they both clambered to their feet.

'You just knocked my brother out!' Nic yelled, thundering into Alex and tackling him at the knees. He slammed him into a small tree that bent backwards under their combined weight.

'Stop!' I tried to pull Nic away from Alex, but he wouldn't budge. I stumbled just in time to avoid Alex as he surged forwards, headbutting Nic and knocking him clean over into the dirt.

'Alex!' I screeched. 'Have you gone insane?'

'His brother started it!' He came to stand over Nic. 'You're a family of dirty cheats! Go back to wherever you came from!'

Nic spat a puddle of blood on the ground. 'Don't talk about my family,' he threatened. He stood up with great effort, squaring himself against Alex's attempts to shove him back down. He righted himself and swung out. Alex ducked, leaving him grappling at the air. When Alex shoved him again, Nic didn't budge. Instead, he flung his arm out and pulled Alex into a headlock, dragging him to the ground again.

As Alex cursed and pummelled his hands into his sides, Nic plunged his fist into his back pocket and pulled something out. With a flick of his wrist it doubled in length. He tightened his grip and hunched over Alex until the two were almost nose to the ground. I couldn't see what he was doing, but I registered the glint in Nic's hand as he moved it between their struggling frames, and I screamed as the realization took hold.

'Nicoli, *smettila!*'

I jumped at the sound of Luca's voice. He appeared from behind me, running towards his brother. He grabbed Nic by the back of his neck and tore him away from Alex.

The colour in Nic's cheeks faded as his brother whispered urgently in his ear. I scanned his open hands – the knife he had been holding was gone.

Beside us, Gino was slowly starting to rouse himself. He got to his feet, rubbing the back of his head. He regarded the scene groggily before nearly knocking me over as he stumbled up the bank towards his brothers.

Alex had gotten to his feet as well, and was shaking with anger. He started towards Gino.

'Don't even think about it,' said Luca. 'Just walk away.'

'Two on one isn't fair,' said Alex, starting to circle the brothers, two of whom were completely spaced out. Nic hadn't said a word since Luca pulled him off Alex, and Gino was still having trouble standing upright. I could see Alex sizing them up, zeroing in on their injuries. 'You should fight your own battles next time, Gino.'

I came between them. 'Alex, just go home,' I said. 'This doesn't need to get any worse.'

He narrowed his eyes at Nic and then Luca, considering his options. Then, reluctantly, he relented. 'Fine. Are you coming?' he asked me.

I glanced at Nic. *Not without an explanation.* 'In a minute.'

'They're bad news, Soph,' he said, his voice laced with

confusion. 'Why are you taking their side?'

'I'll just be a minute,' I repeated, trying to ignore the sense of betrayal in his expression.

'Suit yourself. I'm out of here.' Alex started walking away, but not before adding a pointed 'You're lucky!' over his shoulder. I wasn't sure which of the brothers he was talking to.

'No,' said Luca. 'You are.'

Once Alex was out of sight, I turned my attention to the Priestly brothers. Nic was breathing hard, his expression unreadable as he scanned the grass around us. Beside him, Gino's hair was falling unevenly around his ears, like a lopsided mushroom. He held that same crazy look I had seen out on the court: darting and unfocused. Luca was regarding me calmly.

'We're going to go now,' he said, as if he were leaving a party, not a brawl.

'What the hell was that about?' I asked, ignoring his flippancy.

'He called me a cheat,' said Gino slowly, like the memory was just dawning on him. He was obviously concussed, but I couldn't tell what was wrong with Nic, who was still uncharacteristically quiet, his eyes downcast. 'He said I played dirty on the court.'

'So what?' I asked.

'So I had to shut his stupid mouth up!' He raised his voice and I registered his pronounced lisp for the first time. It must have been the effect of his chipped teeth.

Luca rolled his eyes. 'Relax, Gino.'

'Fighting's not the right way to shut someone up,' I said, stopping the phrase *you moron!* before it slipped out. I grabbed Nic's arm and tugged him away from Luca's grip. He pulled his attention from the grass and looked up, the embers in his eyes igniting, at last he seemed to register me.

'I'm sorry you had to see that, Sophie,' he said quietly. 'I was just trying to defend my brother and it got out of control.'

'You think?'

'We're leaving,' said Luca, gesturing for Nic to follow him. 'Come on.'

His dark eyes studied the space around me as he pulled himself away.

'Wait!' I said, following him.

He turned.

'I just saw you pull a knife on Alex. You can't just walk away from that!' As I said it, I couldn't quite believe it was true. It was such a dark thing to do.

Nic shook his head. 'No, I didn't.'

'I saw you,' I countered. 'You took it from your pocket.'

'You don't know what you're talking about,' said Luca without bothering to turn and look at me. 'Come on, Nicoli.'

Nic's forehead creased with concern. 'I think you must have imagined that, Sophie.'

'I didn't imagine it,' I protested.

Nic wasn't listening to me. He was giving me that look – the one that adults use when they're patronizing you – the Mrs Bailey look. 'You had a traumatic incident earlier. I think you need to rest.'

I recoiled from him. 'I know what I saw.'

I was angry now. One minute Nic was being light-hearted and attentive, and the next he was pulling a knife on my best friend's brother and then making me think I was crazy when I questioned him about it.

'We'll talk about this again, OK?' said Nic.

He gave me a brief nod before turning on his heel, leaving me glaring at the back of his head and wondering if I was going nuts or if he was the most convincing liar I had ever met.

I was about to go back across the courts and find Millie when something along the riverbank caught my attention. I followed the glint and in a flash I was combing through the grass and picking up the switchblade I had seen Nic pull from his pocket – so *this* is what he was looking for. And I had thought his downcast expression was a display of remorse. I felt a strange mixture of triumph and nausea as I turned the blade over in my hand. It was six inches long and razor-sharp. I flicked it closed. The handle was heavy and gold and, in the middle near the base, a crest had been etched into it. It was jet black and inside it there was a perched eagle carved in ornate flourishes of deep red. Its half-spread wings brushed along the outline.

Below the crest, there was an inscription:

Nicoli, May 12th

I almost dropped it. This wasn't just any switchblade; this was an expensive, *personalized* switchblade, inscribed with Nic's name and, I guessed, his date of birth. It was important; it had meaning. And I had no idea what that actually meant.

I turned the handle over again, zeroing in on the bird inside the crest. I knew what an eagle looked like, and at a second glance I realized this wasn't one. A hawk, maybe? Then it hit me. The bird inside the crest was a falcon. A crimson falcon. I didn't know what that meant either, but I was sure now, right down in my gut, that it meant something to those brothers, and it sure as hell meant something to Nic.

The realization made me feel panicky, because I knew I wasn't in control of my reaction to it. Even if my uncle *was* right about the Priestly family, I still couldn't help the way my heart flipped every time I thought about Nic's dark eyes – there was something about him, something I couldn't ignore. I was developing feelings for someone who walked around with suspicious bruises on his hands and carried a weapon wherever he went, a weapon he was clearly prepared to *use*. A weapon he would come back for but wouldn't find. I knew I couldn't trust my illogical heart, and that meant I had to do everything in my power to stay away from him so I wouldn't have to.

CHAPTER NINE

THE BREAK-IN

My attempts at avoiding Nic Priestly and his brothers were short-lived.

By the time I arrived home from my dinner shift a couple of days later, the heavens had opened up, giving way to one of the worst summer storms I could remember.

I slumped against my front door as a roll of thunder groaned behind the clouds, raising the hairs on the back of my neck and heralding a fresh onslaught of rain. After rummaging through my handbag for the hundredth time, I conceded defeat. I had forgotten my keys, and since my mother was in the city at a client's dress fitting, I was locked out indefinitely. The battery in my phone had died, so I didn't know when she would be back, and I wasn't about to melt into my stoop waiting for her.

I picked myself up and, trying not to notice how the rain was welding me into my jeans, I hurtled back down the street, hopping over puddles as I ran. If I travelled at just below the speed of light, taking the fastest route, I would make the diner, which was nine blocks away, just as Ursula and the new waitress, Alison, were locking up for the night. Then I could slip inside, find my keys and be out in time to swim back home again.

As I ran, the sky flashed and rumbled, rattling my nerves. It hadn't rained this badly since the night my father went to jail, and I was reminded, with an unpleasant twist in my stomach, of how frightening that storm really was. Ever since that night, the sound of thunder terrified me – it had become a sign of something sinister, something unwelcome. And now, not long after our delivery man was discovered drowned in his own bathtub, here I was, completely alone and trapped in one of the heaviest downfalls Cedar Hill had ever seen.

By the time I finally turned into the diner parking lot, my feet were swimming in shoefuls of water and my nose was completely numb. Inside the diner, all the lights were off. The whole restaurant was just a low concrete square cowering against the night sky.

I was too late.

I sprinted across the lot, hoping to find shelter beneath the awning at the diner's entrance. I could wait out the worst of the storm, then make my way to Millie's house.

If I had been able to open my eyes as normal, and if the storm wasn't whipping my hair around my face in wet lashes, I would have seen the figure outside the entrance before I was charging into it.

'Hey! Watch it!'

I stumbled backwards so that I was half in, half out of the shelter, but not before I'd seen that the stranger was pressed up against the door, his hands against the glass, like he was peering through. He turned and pulled his hood down.

'Nic?'

'Sophie?'

'What are you doing here?' we both asked at the same time.

'I left my keys inside, and I'm locked out of my house.'

Nic nodded thoughtfully. I waited for his answer. After a long moment, he responded quietly, 'I wanted to see you.'

Another flash of lightning ignited the sky, and I saw his face fully. It was solemn, and oddly vulnerable. It was strange to think he had that side to him; I had thought of him as flawless, and confident to his core.

And dangerous, I reminded myself with a start. *Focus, Sophie.*

On instinct, I backed away from him and stood stock-still in the deluge.

'You shouldn't be here,' I said, glad of the steadiness in my voice. 'I don't think it's a good idea for us to hang out.'

'What do you mean?' he asked, his voice suddenly guarded.

'I know you lied to me.' The memory crashed into me, and I reached into my bag. I pulled the knife out. It was closed but I could feel my fingers shake as they clutched the cold metal handle. I didn't think he would snatch it from me, but a part of me wasn't convinced – how could I know for sure? I edged backwards and tightened my grip on it, trying to ignore the rain soaking through my top.

Nic stepped closer. I could see his eyes drift to my hand but he didn't move to take the knife. Cautiously, I edged it higher so that it hovered between us. 'Do you recognize this?'

He watched me with calculated stillness. There was nothing but the sound of his uneven breaths and the distant roll of thunder, as my hand shook.

'Well?' I asked.

The silence endured. His breathing evened out, but his expression remained unchanged, resolute. When he finally answered me, it seemed to take all of his energy. He pressed his lips together and pushed the words out, pronouncing them slowly, like his tongue was betraying him. 'It's mine.'

'I found it in the grass after you left.' It was an unnecessary detail – he had probably come back for it after I left – but I felt compelled to remind him that I had been right and he had been wrong to try and convince me otherwise. He knew I knew it was his, and the less information he offered me, the more suspicious I became.

I lowered my hand and took a step towards him, pushing myself into his personal space beneath the awning, so that the wall between us would shatter.

His shoulders tensed.

'Why do you carry a knife with you?'

He stalled, pulling his fingers through his hair and grabbing at it in clumps so that it stuck out over his ears. When he dropped his hand it was with a sigh of resignation.

'The switchblade was a gift from my uncle,' he began slowly, as though he were reading from a script. 'He can be a bit . . . eccentric.'

I turned the knife over in my hand, tracing my thumb over the falcon crest and the inscription below it. 'That's one word for it.'

'In my family, when we turn sixteen, my uncle gives us a switchblade inscribed with our name and our birth date,' he went on, sounding surer of himself. 'It's something his father, my grandfather, used to do, and so he does it for us. It's just a family tradition.'

'It strikes me as a little unsafe.' I didn't try to keep the judgement out of my voice.

Nic shrugged, and in a quiet voice he conceded, 'Yes, you could say that about Felice.'

'Feh-*leechay*,' I repeated, dwelling on the *leech* part. It suited a knife giver. 'I got earrings for my sixteenth birthday. No weapons, though.'

Nic dragged his thumb along his bottom lip, and I found myself fixating on the way he nipped at it with his teeth.

I shook the thought from my head, and stepped away from him again.

Focus.

'I saw you pull this out during your fight with Alex,' I said. 'Were you going to—?' My voice wavered. 'What were you going to do with it?'

'Nothing,' he said with so much conviction I almost felt compelled to believe him. 'I would never use it on anyone, especially not your friend's brother. But I thought if he saw it he would back off and leave my brother alone. He had already knocked Gino out, but he kept coming back for more. He was so competitive, so angry that we had won, and so convinced that we had cheated. I just wanted to get rid of him before the rest of my brothers got involved.'

'So you were going to threaten him with *a knife*?' I asked, disbelief dripping from my voice.

'No, not like that. I just, I don't know. I was trying to diffuse it . . .' He trailed off.

I had to fight the urge to take his chin between my forefinger and thumb to hold his gaze still enough that he'd level with me. Was this the truth or a well-versed lie?

'Why do you even carry it around?'

'It's hard to explain,' he replied, his expression suddenly sheepish. 'I guess I carry it so I can feel protected, and so I can look out for my brothers if I have to. Ever since my father died, it's been hard for all of us. It changed us. It changed me. I don't know this place or the people in it, and I'm so used to having the blade with me for a sense of security that it's like second nature to keep it in my pocket. I don't really feel safe without it.' He swallowed hard, burying the emotion that was causing his voice to falter. 'I know it's a strange way to cope with something like that, but it helps me.'

The knife suddenly felt heavy in my hand. 'I didn't know that.'

Nic shrugged. Another flash of lightning lit up his face, and I could see it was bleak with the memory. He slumped backwards against the door, his stance defeated. Whatever game of truth we had been playing, I had won, and I felt queasy because of it. 'It is what it is,' he mumbled.

I had to look away from him. I had felt those feelings of grief and sadness, wallowed in them, even, and for what? A father who deserved to be where he was, and who would come back to me eventually. I knew there were things about Nic that might make him bad for me, but there were things about his life that he couldn't change, and that didn't make him a bad person either. 'I'm sorry for your loss.'

'No, I'm sorry.' He straightened up abruptly, as though someone above him was pulling him by strings, and the vulnerability drained from his posture. 'I was an idiot to pull that knife out, but I wouldn't have hurt Alex with it, I promise. I would never do that. Please let Millie know that too.'

'I didn't mention the knife to Millie,' I said, my stomach twisting with guilt. It was a telling revelation.

'Oh,' he said quietly.

'Alex didn't see it, and I didn't want to make the whole thing worse. Besides, he texted me afterwards saying he was sorry things got so heated, so I thought we could all just chalk it up to an isolated incident that got out of hand and maybe you could both just move past it.' I spoke quickly, mashing the words together. Suddenly my cheeks felt like they were on fire. I didn't tell Millie everything. Did that make me a bad friend? Or just an idiot? Because despite knowing I shouldn't care about Nic, I did, and even though I was trying to avoid him, I had been hoping to see him – to give him the chance to explain.

'Thank you,' he said earnestly. 'I'm sorry if I scared you and I'm sorry I lied to you about it. I thought it would be easier, but I knew afterwards it was the wrong thing to do. I wanted to come and talk to you about it.'

'So that's why you're here?' I asked, wondering about the timing of his late-night visit.

Nic smiled, revealing a wedge of white teeth in the dark. 'You got me.'

I stashed the knife back in my bag and moved to peer through the diner door as he had done, not because I thought there was anyone inside, but because I was suddenly feeling shy and I didn't know what else to do.

'Can you get in?' he asked.

My wet hair swung around me like strings as I shook my head. ‘Everyone else has gone home.’

‘Maybe I could do something.’

‘Could you teleport me into my house?’

He took an uneven breath, and coyly asked, ‘Do you want me to try?’

‘To teleport me?’

‘No.’ He cleared his throat. ‘I can try to open the door if you want.’

‘What? How?’

‘Do I have your permission to try?’

I raised my hands in the air. ‘By all means.’

‘Do you mind standing back a little?’

‘Are you really going to do this?’

He set his jaw. ‘Yes.’

I might have agreed to anything he asked right then because, in the rain, he looked incredible. His wavy brown hair was wet and pushed away from his face, revealing the full effect of his chiselled cheekbones. I shuffled backwards.

Nic turned his back to me and pulled something that resembled a fountain pen from his back pocket.

‘What’s that?’

‘Another gift you’d disapprove of,’ he said simply, before moving closer to the door and obscuring it from my view.

For a minute or so all I could see were slight movements in his arm as he went to work on the door – first the upper lock, which yielded with a light click, and then the heavier one lower down, which took longer. Finally, he pulled the handle down and the door swung open in front of us, jingling the bell above it.

My mouth fell open. 'You just broke into the diner.'

'You gave me permission.' He stashed whatever he had been using into his pocket and stepped back so I could enter first. 'After you.'

I stared at him as I shuffled inside to punch in the alarm code before it went off. 'Do you make a habit of that?'

'No,' he said, following me closely. 'My brothers and I used to find tools that we could use to break into one another's rooms when we were younger. It was never anything more serious than bedroom warfare. It was just dumb luck that an old screw-driver could open that door tonight. The locks really aren't what they should be.'

I flicked a switch so that a line of recessed lights sprang to life, illuminating a pathway to the other end of the diner.

'And you just happen to carry that with you because . . . ?'

'I was trying to get into the old barn at my uncle's house tonight so we could use it as a storage unit.'

Nic trailed behind me, his attention wandering around the diner like it was the most fascinating place he had ever seen. 'My mother ordered a truckload of antiques for the new house, but she doesn't want us moving them inside the place until she comes back from overseas in a few weeks. She wants to finish the painting first. So right now we're trying to find a place to stash them.'

I slipped behind the counter and started looking for my keys. 'So your mother's entrusting her sons to handle her expensive furniture in her absence?'

Nic slid in beside me, his arm brushing against mine as we searched side by side. 'Pretty much.'

'I'm not sure I'm completely convinced by that, but it does

seem more likely than my other theories.'

'What kind of theories?'

I tapped my chin. 'How about that you're a notorious jewel thief?'

Nic angled his head to one side and smiled. The tension seeped from his shoulders. 'That actually sounds kind of cool.'

'Or what if you rob little old ladies when they're asleep in their beds?'

'Not cool.'

I stopped searching for a moment and looked at him – his inky-brown eyes, the curve of his upper lip, the way his hair curled beneath his ears. There was something nebulous about him, something dark and uncertain. It ignited a kind of uneasiness in me that I hadn't felt in a long time. I thought of my uncle's warning to me, and not for the first time felt the weight of it on my mind. 'The trouble is,' I said, my voice catching in my throat, 'I don't know *what* you are.'

Nic held my gaze steady. 'Maybe that's half the fun of it.'

Too flustered to respond, I resumed the search for my keys, and Nic broke into a low laugh. I'm sure he didn't mean it to be seductive, but the sound of it coupled with our proximity was having that effect on me.

'So your mom went overseas and left all her sons alone in her new house?' I asked in a bid to distract myself. 'She sounds very trusting.'

'She's not,' said Nic, laughing again. 'It's just that her love for Venetian furniture outweighs the distrust she has in her five sons.'

Five sons! So I hadn't imagined Priestly Boy Number Five and I definitely wasn't seeing ghosts that night.

'We *try* to be respectful of her wishes when she's away,' Nic added as an afterthought. 'Though sometimes we make a mess, and of course we end up fighting, too, as brothers do.'

'I don't have any siblings, so I guess I wouldn't know a lot about the whole rivalry thing.'

Nic nodded thoughtfully. 'That's too bad. My brothers are my best friends.'

'Even Luca?' I couldn't help myself.

Nic's smile was empathetic. '*Even Luca.*'

'That's . . . surprising.'

'He's not so bad.'

I bit my tongue.

'There's nothing more important than the bonds of family,' he went on. 'When my grandfather was alive he would always say, *"La famiglia prima di tutto."* It's written on his mausoleum.'

Rich much? I bit my tongue again. 'What does that mean?'

'Family before everything.'

'Cool,' I said, somewhat ineptly. 'When my mom's dad died, he had "All dressed up with nowhere to go" written on his gravestone.'

Nic's confused expression was unsurprisingly endearing.

'He was an atheist,' I added by way of explanation.

'Oh.' His bewilderment morphed into a wry smile. 'A funny atheist.'

'He died the way he lived – making jokes that pissed off my grandmother.'

I bent down and started rifling through the cabinets behind the counter – there were folded aprons, grimy old sweaters, and somebody's pair of track pants. Probably mine.

Nic continued to rummage through the papers along the countertop. 'Would your manager mind you being in here?'

'My keys aren't up there,' I said, opening another cupboard and fishing around inside – nothing but dust balls and broken pens. 'They're probably in one of these cubbyholes.'

I looked up at Nic. He had picked up a menu and was studying it.

'Would he mind?' he asked again.

'No.' I tried a different nook and felt the tips of my fingers brush against something jagged and metal. 'I'll lock up after us. He won't even know we were here.'

I could hear sheets of paper rustling around as Nic leafed through them, pausing at some before stashing them away again.

'Where is he anyway?'

I shifted my shoulder so I could reach further inside the narrow nook. 'Who?'

'Your manager.'

'His friend died, so he went to visit the family. I don't know where he is now.' I paused as my uncle's disapproving face meandered into my mind, all red and puffy. With a pang I realized I missed him. I hoped he would call me soon.

I closed my hands around the keys, feeling their familiar edges with a flicker of triumph.

Nic had stopped shuffling. 'So he just didn't come back?'

I pulled them out – one brass diner key, another silver one for the smaller lock, my purple house key, and a glitzy Eiffel Tower key ring from Millie. I sprang to my feet and dangled the keys triumphantly in front of me.

'Got 'em!' I dropped them into my bag.

Nic's smile pulled more to one side, pushing against his right cheekbone. We stood a foot apart, no longer distracted by the search, and with nowhere else to look but at each other. Suddenly our surroundings felt a lot more intimate. Standing alone and sopping wet in the diner, my awareness of him spiked, and I was conscious of every exhalation being louder than it should be.

'Do you want me to give you a ride home?' he asked. 'It's still coming down pretty hard out there. I don't want you to melt into a puddle.'

'Are you implying I'm a witch?'

Nic feigned a horrified expression. 'Absolutely not. I am ever the gentleman.'

'Except for when you're knocking over girls outside your house and breaking into diners in the middle of the night,' I pointed out. I thought about adding a switchblade comment but stopped myself, thinking of his father and everything he had just confided in me.

He nodded solemnly. 'Yes. Except for then.'

I hesitated. 'A ride home would be great.'

I followed him back to the other end of the diner, focusing on the lighter streaks of chestnut in his dark hair.

As Nic glided towards the door, his hands stuffed deep into his pockets, he surveyed the diner again. 'This place is so retro.'

'It's an acquired taste.'

'Like my mother,' he surmised with a soft chuckle. 'In fact, sometimes I think I'm still acquiring.'

'I feel that way about certain people too.' I smiled, thinking of Jack and deliberately *not* thinking of his warning. He could be difficult and unpredictable, but once he was in your life, he was there for good, like a mole that makes up part of who you are.

'But I bet no one feels that way about you, Sophie.'

Oh, only about a thousand people in Cedar Hill. 'You'd be surprised.'

'Would I?' Nic turned back to me, hovering across the threshold.

'We should go,' I murmured, forcing myself to focus on all the questionable things about this boy, and not the way he was making me lose my breath just by looking at me.

If Nic was disappointed, he didn't show it. Instead, he unzipped his hoodie.

'Here,' he said, holding it out to me. 'We'll have to run to the car.' He kept his arm outstretched, leaving him in just a black T-shirt and dark jeans. His jaw tightened, and I felt as if he were daring me to refuse the gesture. 'Please.'

'Well, if you insist.'

I took the sweatshirt and shrugged it on. It was at least four sizes too big. When I zipped it up and shook out the sleeves so that they fell over my hands, the severity in Nic's expression faded. I fought the urge to twirl around so that the hoodie would fan out like a cape. *Don't be weird.*

Nic was smirking at me.

'What?' I placed my hands – which were no longer visible – on my waist. 'Have you never seen a drowned rat wearing an oversized hoodie before?'

'None like you,' he laughed.

'Well, you need to get out more.'

'Clearly.'

I shut off the lights, punched in the alarm code and locked up behind us, following him out into the torrential downpour.

No wonder I hadn't seen Nic's SUV earlier – it was parked all the way across the lot, where even the streetlights didn't shine. We sprinted towards it, wobbling under the force of wind that threw buckets of rain across our faces. When we reached the car, I tumbled in, pushing against the storm to shut the door. I fell back against the cool leather seat, wrapping my arms around me while Nic started the engine. Without the added warmth of his hoodie, his teeth were chattering.

I spent the car ride directing him to my house and running my fingers through my hair so it wouldn't frizz out too much in the humidity. I was just melting into the easy conversation between us, and the welcome feeling of dryness, when he pulled up outside my house.

'Thanks for the ride.' I tried not to sound too crestfallen that our time together had ended. I pushed the car door open and it flung outwards under the force of the wind.

'Sophie.' Nic tilted towards me and gripped my leg, holding the lower half of my body in the warmth of the car. 'Wait.'

My heart flipped, and I worried he could hear how loudly it was suddenly beating. I tried not to breathe too quickly, or to stare at his hand on my knee. I looked at him and found him studying my arms, my waist, my – *his* hoodie.

'Oh.' I shook my hair out, scolding myself. 'Your hoodie.'

I began to unzip it.

'No, it's not that,' he replied quickly, keeping his hand on my knee. 'You can give it back to me some other time.'

I dropped my hands into my lap and waited, my breath bound up in the base of my throat. I could see he was steeling himself for something else. My brain began to flash with a thousand possibilities and suddenly my heart was ricocheting off my ribcage like it was trying to punch through it.

He inhaled sharply, his expression suddenly uncertain. 'The switchblade,' he said quietly. 'Can I have it back?'

My face fell, and something inside me – it felt a lot like hope – shrivelled up and died. I reached into my bag and pulled out the knife, dropping it into his outstretched hand in one hurried movement. 'Of course. I forgot.'

His fist closed around it and a flicker of relief passed over his features, relaxing them. 'Thank you.'

'I guess it's for the best. You know, me walking around with a knife isn't exactly a good idea. I'd probably fall on it or something.' The words tumbled out in unbidden, high-pitched sentences, trying to distract from the awkwardness I was feeling. 'I'd probably end up killing myself or something, and I can definitely think of less embarrassing ways to die.' *Could you be any more inappropriate?* I winced right after I said it and then hopped out of the car before I could put my other foot in my mouth. 'Thanks again for everything.'

'Sophie?' Nic leant across the passenger seat, his expression serious. 'Will you do something for me?'

'What?'

'Don't be thinking of ways to die.'

'I won't.'

'Good.'

He pulled back with a small, controlled smile, and I shut the door.

I stood in the rain, watching the car until it disappeared around the end of the street. Then I thought about the boy with the bruised hand and the inscribed switchblade who had just broken into my father's diner, and found myself wondering why the hell I was feeling so sad to see him go.

CHAPTER TEN

THE ARTIST

There was really only one thing to do with Nic's hoodie.

'This is perfect,' Millie said when I called her the following morning to tell her about everything. 'Use it as an excuse to go to his house and invite him to the party on Saturday!'

Because of the fight with Alex, Millie wasn't Nic's biggest fan, but she wasn't a grudge holder either, and given that 'boys will be boys', she resolved that she could certainly 'see potential' in him and that he should still be invited to her house party. I had a pretty good idea of how Alex would react to Nic turning up, but Millie was adamant. Alex didn't get to veto her guests. Especially since she had so few compared to him.

Besides, she took great interest in my pitiful romantic life, and since Nic was new to Cedar Hill and obviously in the dark about my father's recent past, she saw him as a rare judgement-free opportunity for me to fall in love. Whether he might be bad for me or not didn't weigh into it. It only made her more curious about him and his family, especially considering that Dom had asked her out right after the basketball tournament.

'I'm meeting Dom at six for our date, so call me later tonight if you find out anything juicy,' she squealed down the phone. 'And don't forget to take pictures if you make it inside that house. You owe it to me. I'm too young to die from curiosity.'

I decided not to tell Millie that I would not be creepily taking pictures of Nic's house without his knowledge. The idea of inviting him to a party was already terrifying enough. What if he said no? What if he said yes and then found out about my social-pariah status when he got there? 'Only if you find out about Dom's scar,' I countered instead.

'That's a no-brainer. Good luck today. You won't regret it,' she chirped before hanging up.

By the time I reached the Priestly mansion, I was a bundle of nerves. Restored to its rightful regality, the house was like something out of a fairy tale. Beneath the sun's heavy beat, the windows were sparkling like diamonds, and without the ivy that used to slither across the walls, the entire exterior was an unblemished alabaster white.

Just how was I going to do this? *Hey, thanks for lending me your hoodie. By the way, why don't you come to Millie's party on Saturday? It's coincidentally my birthday too, but most people there will just ignore me because my dad's a murderer, which technically makes me the Devil's spawn. So, how about it, will you come?* Smooth. And what if Nic wasn't home and Luca answered instead? *Hey, tell your brother to come to Millie's on*

Saturday, but make sure you don't show up because you suck. If Gino answered I could just distract him with something shiny and hope Nic would come to the door eventually.

With the hoodie draped over my arm and my thoughts spiralling into all the possible ways this could go wrong, I rang the doorbell. When I didn't hear it echo inside the house, I decided to use the brass knocker just to be sure. I waited. I knocked again.

What now? I hadn't come up with any brilliant ideas about what to do if nobody was there. Was I supposed to just leave the hoodie outside the door and let that be the end of it? What an anticlimax. Without thinking, I drifted towards the side of the mansion, where the driveway tapered off into a narrow path that stretched around the house.

When I reached the back, I stopped in surprise. I don't know what I had been expecting – a tennis court or a swimming pool, maybe – but certainly not what I found. Cramped and overgrown, the yard was a far cry from the affluent façade of the house. Around the edges, clumps of weeds tangled into withered rose bushes. The grass was higher than my knees, and was a sickly grey-green colour. At the very back of the ruined garden were the remnants of a fountain with elaborate bird carvings etched into chunks of stone; and in the centre of the grass, a large wooden table balanced on three termite-eaten legs.

Behind me, double doors inlaid with stained glass panes looked out on to the yard. They were slightly ajar.

I rapped my knuckles against the glass, nudging the doors open, and peered into a sprawling kitchen. The walls and cabinets were a stark white, and the pale wood floors looked new. A black cast-iron stove reached up to a high ceiling, which was studded with spotlights.

'Who is it?' A musical voice came from within, startling me from my snooping.

I hesitated. If I didn't know the voice, the voice wouldn't know me, and so what good would my name be?

'It's Sophie,' I said after a beat.

No answer.

'I'm just returning a hoodie.'

I opened the doors another crack. More of the kitchen filtered into my view. On the white walls were several ornately framed oil paintings. I recognized one as da Vinci's *Madonna and Child* – it had been a favourite of my grandmother's – though the others, while also religious in sentiment, were foreign to me. I stared in surprise. I had never seen artwork like this in a home before – it was almost like a gallery, or a church, and I found myself feeling intimidated by the splendour. I considered taking out my phone and sneaking a photo to show Millie after all, but the rational voice inside my head stopped me.

Cautiously, I edged inside.

In the centre of the kitchen was a marble-topped island, and beyond it was a glass table covered with several sheets of paper and scatterings of pencils. Sitting at the table was a boy. He was drawing.

'Hello?' I said again, though I could plainly see he knew I was there.

He looked up and his piercing blue eyes found mine immediately. I zeroed in on them, frowning, as my stomach turned to jelly. 'Luca?'

He didn't respond. He just put his pencil down and sat in

silent contemplation, his elbows atop the table and his chin resting just behind his steepled fingers, as though he were praying.

I felt my breath catch in my throat. 'Oh!'

It wasn't Luca. It was the boy from the window. Just like on that very first night, his eyes grew, but this time in recognition. Set against his olive skin, they were a brilliant, startling blue. They were just like Luca's, but something about them seemed different – warmer, perhaps.

'I recognize you,' he said in that pleasant, lilting voice.

I moved towards him, utterly captivated. He had Luca's searing eyes, his golden skin and his jet-black hair. But while Luca's hair was shaggy, falling in strands across his eyes, this boy's hair was short and clean-cut, combed away from his face entirely, revealing a pointed chin and severe cheekbones. He was thinner, too, and slightly hunched. I couldn't tell if he was older than me – he didn't seem it, but his likeness to Luca made me think maybe he was.

'You were watching my house last week.' He lowered his hands and rested them on the table in front of him, but his eyes remained hooded with caution.

I stopped when I reached the table, hovering uncertainly. I realized then why he hadn't moved towards me, and why he hadn't played in the basketball tournament last week. He was in a wheelchair.

'Yes, that was me,' I replied. I tried not to stare, but he was so like Luca, and yet so unlike him, it was hard to reconcile. 'I was just curious.'

'I believe you fell rather spectacularly just afterwards,' he added, but not unkindly.

'That's a point of contention. Your brother actually crashed into me.'

He smiled, and it made him seem suddenly very young and boyish. 'I hope he apologized.'

'He did – eventually.' I shuffled a little closer until my hands brushed against the edge of the table. 'You're so like him.' It was those eyes – they were so unnatural. That they should exist in two different faces seemed unbelievable to me. 'Luca, that is. I don't mean to stare, but it's really incredible.'

'Well,' he said, 'we may be twins, but we're not the same.'

I was only partly surprised by the revelation. Even though their similarities were startling, all of the Priestly brothers shared the same features, and this boy had an aura of innocence that Luca did not. He seemed sweet, and unblemished by whatever had made his twin such a resounding ass to be around.

'For one thing, he can't manoeuvre a wheelchair half as well as I can.' He tapped the wheel beneath his right hand and released a wry smile. 'And for another, I'm smarter.'

'I don't doubt it.' He seemed appeased by my agreement. 'I'm Sophie. But I said that already.'

'Hello, Sophie.' His smile was a beautiful sight. To think, Luca had the potential to look and act like this and yet he chose not to. 'I'm Valentino.'

He shifted forwards and picked up his pencil again, twirling it between his forefinger and thumb. My attention followed it, and I gasped as the sheets of paper came to life below me. I tried to study them all at once. 'These are incredible.'

Valentino waved his hand over the sketches with a casualness that seemed out of place. They were stunning, and surely he could see that. And more than that, he should be *owning* his talent and agreeing with me. I used to think my father was good because he could draw Mickey Mouse, but this artwork was on a whole other level.

I raked my eyes over the drawings and stopped when I found a side profile of Nic. Drawn in pencil, careful shadows swooped across his creased brow line and gathered beneath his cheekbones. His lips were parted in concentration, his hair twisting in strands below his ear as he looked ahead, focusing on something out of frame.

'You make it seem so real.'

I glanced at Valentino. He was chewing on his lip, thinking. 'I look for the qualities that aren't always apparent at first,' he said. 'The ones that define part of who we are and how we really feel deep down. I try to look below the surface.'

His voice started to bubble with passion, and his hands took on a life of their own. 'This life is so complex that we rarely get to be the people we are truly meant to be. Instead, we wear masks and put up walls to keep from dealing with the fear of rejection, the feeling of regret, the very idea that someone may not love us for who we are deep in our core, that they might not understand the things that drive us. I want to study the realness of life, not the gloss. There is beauty everywhere; even in the dark, there is light, and that is the rarest kind of all.'

I watched the enthusiasm brighten his features. 'I don't know anyone who thinks and talks like that,' I admitted. 'It's . . . refreshing.'

'It's the truth,' he said simply.

'Can I see the others?'

He laid his pencil down and wheeled his chair back. I draped the hoodie over the chair beside me and leant across the table, balancing my weight on my palms.

There was a sketch of Gino and Dom playing a video game; they were sitting on the floor, their legs curled around them like they were little boys again. Controllers clutched in their hands, they were laughing with each other, their shoulders brushing, their heads thrown back towards the ceiling. Their eyes were crinkled at the sides and their noses were scrunched up in amusement. Dom was messing up Gino's ponytail with his free hand.

'It's like the perfect moment,' I breathed.

'Happiness,' said Valentino quietly, his eyes fixed on the scene.

I returned my gaze to Nic's profile. His jaw was set, his expression focused.

'And that one is Determination,' Valentino added.

Beside the sketch of Nic there was a portrait of a woman standing in a kitchen. Her hands gripped the sides of the sink as she looked out the window in front of her. She was willowy and dishevelled, dressed in a silken floor-length robe that pooled around her feet. Streaks of sunlight danced along the tip of her nose, and a spill of dark hair fell freely down her back. Her brows were creased at sharp angles. 'Is this your mother?'

He nodded.

'She's beautiful,' I said.

'She's angry,' said Valentino dispassionately.

I reached out and pulled the next portrait towards me. Luca. He was sitting alone on a stoop, dressed in a black suit. His knees came up to his chest, supporting his elbows. His shoulders were hunched, making his frame appear smaller, like Valentino's. He was looking at the ground, at nothing, and his fingers were scraping through his hair, like he was trying to hurt himself.

I swallowed hard. It was difficult to look at it. I glanced at Valentino and found he wasn't looking at it any more either.

'Pain?' I guessed quietly.

'Grief,' he replied.

'It must be difficult to look beneath the mask,' I said, my throat suddenly tight.

Valentino raised his chin. 'No more difficult than it is to wear one.'

I pulled my hands back and straightened up as a wave of something unpleasant washed over me. I didn't want to look at the portraits any more. It was an uncomfortable feeling, staring into the darkest moments of someone's soul without them knowing. 'Do you think you wear a mask?'

'I'm wearing one right now.' Valentino smiled softly. 'We both are.'

'It's a sad thought.'

'Yes,' he said. 'But sometimes I wonder about the alternative. Imagine if we had no secrets, no respite from the truth. What if everything was laid bare the moment we introduced ourselves?'

The idea swirled around my head. *Hello, I'm Sophie. My uncle's a paranoid loon, my father's in jail for murder, and my mother buries herself in work to distract herself from her broken heart. I'm pretty sure I prefer cartoons over real life and I only have one real friend. I'm terrified of storms and I'm deeply suspicious of cats. I obsess over the cuteness of sloths and sometimes I cry at commercials.*

'It would be terrible,' I confirmed.

Valentino smirked as though he had just listened to my embarrassing inner monologue. 'Absolute chaos.'

I nodded, feeling subdued. Somewhere deep down I was trying to fight the sudden urge to burst into tears. As if sensing my inner struggle, Valentino afforded me a moment of privacy. He deflected his gaze and started to rearrange his sketches into a pile, until I could only see the one he was still working on. It was a man maybe in his mid-forties, dressed impeccably in a glossy dark suit, and staring right at me from the page. For a heartbeat it felt as though I already knew him, that I had seen him somewhere before, but the moment passed, and I knew it was his son I was seeing. He was so like Nic it hit me like a punch in the gut. He had the same dark eyes with lighter flecks swimming inside, the same straight, narrow nose, and the same curving lips. His hair was grey in parts and receding, revealing a forehead etched with worry lines. His expression was grim.

'Seriousness?' I ventured.

'No,' Valentino said without looking up. 'This one is Death.' I watched him smudge the edges. 'I draw my father every day so that I'll never forget him. But there's nothing more to find in him now. He's with the angels and he doesn't need to wear a mask any more. Everything he was is gone.'

'I'm sorry,' I offered weakly. It really was the only thing I could think to say, and still it didn't seem like half enough.

Valentino shrugged, his expression matter-of-fact. 'You can't avoid the inevitability of death. It comes at you one way or another, and takes us all to the same place in the end. To apologize for it is to apologize for the sun shining or the rain falling. It is what it is.'

I wanted to tell him he was lucky for his pragmatism, but I didn't get the opportunity. A door opened behind me. I noticed the smell first: a faint sweetness in the air.

'Valentino?' A man's voice, crisp and gentle, followed.

I turned to find a slim, middle-aged man staring at me with surprise. His skin was olive and his hair the brightest silver I had ever seen. His eyebrows were so light I could barely detect them, but by the way they were denting his forehead, I could tell they were raised.

'Oh my,' he said in a faint accent. 'Hello there.'

He advanced towards me like a well-dressed beanpole, his head tilted to one side. I didn't know much about men's clothing, but I could recognize an expensive suit when I saw one. It was black with thin pinstripes, and beneath it he wore a shiny grey shirt and a silk neck scarf. If he was burning up in the humidity, he didn't show it.

He stuck out his hand and I took it; his handshake was cold and firm. The sweet smell was stronger now that he was so close; it was almost cloying. There was something vaguely familiar about it, too, but I couldn't place it.

'And you are?' he asked, a slow smile forming.

'I'm Sophie, and I just stopped by to—'

'What a pleasure,' he said, silencing me with politeness and releasing my hand militarily.

I tried not to stare at the red marks all over his face: not quite pimples, more like pinpricks – hard to spot when far away but difficult to ignore at close range. It was like he had fallen into a rose garden face first.

'Please excuse my intrusion. I do hope I'm not interrupting anything. I'm Felice,' he said, pronouncing the 'leech-ay' part with a distinct Italian roll. 'Valentino's uncle.'

The switchblade buyer. I tried not to curl my lip in disgust.

'You're not interrupting anything,' Valentino answered from over my shoulder. There was a hint of indignation in his voice.

Felice rounded the table in wide, graceful strides, taking most of the perfumed scent with him. 'I wasn't aware you boys had time to make friends in the neighbourhood.'

'That's not remotely the case,' Valentino replied, his tone acidic. 'Sophie is just returning something.'

I held up Nic's hoodie in a bid to ease the strange tension that had descended upon us.

Felice looked at it sharply. 'Is that Luca's?'

'Unlikely,' said Valentino.

Felice shook his head. 'Of course it's not,' he murmured. '*He* has his priorities in order.'

I wasn't sure if that was a dig at me or a dig at the other three brothers.

'Dom's?' Felice asked with a frown, like it was the world's most important mystery.

'No. He's taking out that girl from the diner.'

'Ah yes, of course.'

My lips parted in surprise. So they already knew about Millie? That news was barely twenty-four hours old! They must have shared everything with each other. And yet they apparently had no idea who I was.

'It's Nic's,' I cut in, feeling marginally insulted. 'I ran into him at the diner last night and he let me borrow it because it was raining.'

Felice stiffened, exchanging a poorly concealed look of alarm with Valentino.

'Nicoli didn't mention that,' he said, regaining his composure in a flash of teeth.

His response landed with a blow. How could they know about Millie already but not a single iota about me? Nic obviously didn't think me important enough to mention, even in passing. The thought made me feel stupid for even being there.

'Well, here it is.' I dropped the hoodie back on the chair carelessly. I had clearly made too much of it already. 'I just wanted to give it back, but then we got to talking about Valentino's artwork and the time got away from me.'

'Ah.' Felice clapped his nephew on the shoulder and glanced at the pile of drawings. 'Exquisite, aren't they?'

'Yes,' I said, wishing I had never come in the first place.

'You know,' said Felice, to no one in particular, 'I've been reading the most incredible things about artistic sensibilities and their connection to great tragedy recently.' He moved away from Valentino and began to pace around the table. 'Did you know that many artists and composers have been known to create their best works following tragedies in their personal lives?'

He didn't wait for either of us to respond, but continued striding around the kitchen, moving his hands around as he spoke. 'Just look at Carlo Gesualdo, a famed Italian prince and widely regarded genius. He murdered his wife and her lover in their bed, mutilated their bodies and then strung them up outside his palace for everyone to see. And *then* he went on to compose some of the most powerful and dark music of the sixteenth century.'

Valentino shifted in his chair.

Felice stopped gesticulating and zeroed in on me for my reaction. 'What do you think of that?'

I tried not to think of how horribly awry my plan had gone.

'It seems to me that the composer's tragedy was brought upon himself,' I ventured, silently wishing I could just dissolve into the ground and slither home through the earth's core. 'So I'm not sure you should count it as something that *happened* to him.'

'A debater, I see.' Felice's expression turned gleeful. 'But surely you could argue that the pressure of having to exact retribution was brought upon him by his wife's actions. To punish her was the societal expectation, but the act of having to do it, for him, I think, may still have been a personal tragedy.'

'But surely he didn't have to kill her.' If only Millie could see me now – debating the intricacies of sixteenth-century murder. All this and headstones in the last twenty-four hours – the calendar said July, but it was definitely starting to feel like Halloween.

'Well, his wife was unfaithful, and in those days, unfaithfulness carried a high penalty.'

'As high as murder?'

'I believe so.'

I crossed my arms, feeling offended on behalf of all sixteenth-century women. 'I don't feel her betrayal justified his response.'

'Ah!' Felice raised his index finger in the air like he had just happened upon the answer to an unsolved riddle. 'But seeing as his response led directly to his musical legacy, perhaps, in the grander scheme of things, it did. All in all, I think it might have made the world a better place. And surely there is justification in that.'

'Uh . . .' I began awkwardly. I was getting confused, and certainly out of my depth. 'I just think the whole thing is pretty messed up.'

'Yes,' echoed Valentino, clearing his throat. 'It *is* messed up. Just like this conversation.'

Felice waved his hand dismissively, his attention now resting on the oil paintings behind us. 'But the point is, the music *was* glorious. You must consider the possibility of an inverse correlation, which would mean a dark deed leading to a deeper connection with creative energy and, as a consequence, a beautiful composition.'

'Hitler was an artist *before* he committed all of his atrocities.' That was about the only thing I had gleaned from history class – and since we were chitchatting about murder, why not throw Hitler into the mix? This day had already hit rock bottom. 'So I don't think you can really say murder leads to better creativity or vice versa.' I wanted to add something along the lines of: *So I wouldn't go killing your wife just yet.* But I thought better of it.

Felice clapped his hands together. 'But isn't it fascinating to think about? That the two parts of one's psyche can coexist like that?'

'There can be light in the dark,' I said, echoing Valentino's words from earlier.

He nodded thoughtfully, but I could sense his discomfort. He was gripping the sides of his chair so hard his fingers were turning white.

Ah, weird relatives. There was something quite sweet about the fact Nic and I shared slightly unhinged uncles. Maybe one day we would get to introduce them.

'Absolutely!' Felice responded to my borrowed maxim after a pause. 'And sometimes a dark path can lead to a bright light.'

I shuffled awkwardly. He'd lost me again, but I was definitely beginning to see how he thought buying knives for his nephews was a good idea. 'I guess it's food for thought.'

Felice's phone buzzed, filling the room with an intense flurry of opera. He closed his eyes and swayed to the music before finally pulling the phone out from his breast pocket and answering the call.

'*Ciao*, Calvino!' He covered the mouthpiece. 'Excuse me for one moment,' he whispered, before leaving the kitchen.

I watched him go. 'Well, he's certainly . . . energetic.'

When I turned back to Valentino, his expression was unreadable.

'Sophie,' he said wearily. 'Thank you for returning Nic's hoodie, but I need to be honest with you. He wouldn't want you here.'

I felt like I had been slapped. 'What?'

'I don't mean to hurt your feelings,' he continued in that same soothing lilt. 'But we're in the middle of a very private family matter.'

Was he referring to their father? His passing was obviously more recent than I'd realized.

'I'll go,' I gulped.

Valentino smiled apologetically. 'Please don't take it personally.'

'It's fine,' I lied, turning from him and hurrying across the kitchen. My gaze fell upon a large black frame to the left of the door. It was hoisted midway up the wall and was unmissable from this angle. Inside the frame was the same crest I had seen on Nic's knife – jet-black with a crimson falcon at its centre. Below the crest, in cursive red script, it read: *la famiglia prima di tutto*. *Family before everything* – Nic's grandfather's words, I remembered.

'It's just the timing of it . . .' Valentino called after me.

I felt tingly all over and I wasn't sure why. Everything felt so intense all of a sudden. Feeling my cheeks prickle as the colour drained out of them, I pulled the double doors of the Priestly kitchen closed behind me.

I had barely made it to the end of the block when someone grabbed the back of my T-shirt. I stumbled backwards and bumped against a small cushioned body with a soft *oomph!*

I sprang around, shrugging away from the vice-like grip.

'Mrs Bailey?' The shrillness in my voice alerted me to an octave I didn't know I could reach. 'What are you doing?'

The old woman contorted her face like she had just bitten into a lemon. 'I could ask you the same question, Persephone Gracewell. What on earth do you think *you're* doing?'

'I'm on my way home. My shift at the diner starts in an hour.' I wrung my hands to keep from shaking her. With the day I was having, this was the last thing I needed. 'And my name is Sophie!'

'I saw you go into that house,' she shot back. 'I told you to stay away from that family. You were in there so long I nearly called the police!'

'Are you serious?'

She stiffened. 'Haven't you been reading the papers?'

'What are you talking about?'

'I'm *talking* about *several* disappearances and *two* strange deaths in the last two weeks – all of whom were members of *this* community, and *you* haven't even noticed. Open your eyes,

Persephone!'

'They are open!' Or so I had thought. I obviously had a lot of googling to do.

Mrs Bailey was still ranting, pointing her finger directly in my face. 'People don't just drown in their own bathtubs, you know. And they don't accidentally fall off roofs either!'

'What are you saying?' I asked, folding my arms to keep the sudden chill at bay.

Mrs Bailey dropped her voice. 'I'm saying there's a wrongness in that house and it's *not* something you should be anywhere near.'

I didn't make an attempt to hide my irritation. Another day, another rumour. 'You can't just go around saying stuff like that, Mrs Bailey!'

'There's a darkness,' she hissed, her resolve unbroken.

I started walking again, quickening my pace so that she had to scurry to keep up. 'It's grief! They're mourning their father.'

She didn't seem the least bit surprised by my response. In fact, she snorted.

I gaped at her. 'Do you find that *amusing*?'

'That man deserves to be where he is.'

I skidded to a halt.

She caught up with me, her chest heaving.

'What did you just say?'

'Listen to me very carefully, Persephone.' She tugged at my arm, pulling me closer so that she could whisper. 'That man deserves to be in the ground. And if those boys are anything remotely like him, then they do too.'

For a long moment I stared at her, my fists clenched at my sides, my nostrils flaring. I was desperately trying to give her the benefit of the doubt, but with the way my emotions had been back-flipping all day, I wanted nothing more than to reach out and throttle her. Was that the kind of stuff she said about *me* behind *my* back? Her thoughts on my father had always been crystal clear. 'How could you say something like that?' I demanded.

Mrs Bailey looked over her shoulder, her eyes darting back and forth. 'Persephone,' she hissed through trembling lips. 'There's a reason that man was called the Angel-maker.'

The Angel-maker. A wave of nausea rolled over me and I wobbled on my feet. 'What does that mean?' I stammered.

'What do you think it means?' she asked. 'I've been doing some digging and I can tell you, their father was a very bad man. I doubt those boys are much better, and you must trust me when I say that you should stay away from them. I don't want to say any more than that.'

What the hell was that supposed to mean? That she actually had an I-better-not-spread-any-more-crap-today threshold. I regarded her warily. What could she possibly gain from saying this? Then again, what did she gain from saying all the stuff she usually said? She was a notorious drama queen and a one-woman rumour mill, and I started to wonder how many people she had warned away from *me*. Nic *wasn't* bad, I was sure of it. And for that matter, neither were the rest of his brothers. They played basketball and video games. They teased each other and flirted with girls. It wasn't fair to tar someone with their father's reputation. I knew all about that, and I wasn't about to make the mistake a lot of my former friends had. Especially when Nic's father was already gone from this world.

I started walking again.

Mrs Bailey picked up her pace. 'I'm trying to warn you.'

'OK.' I swerved around the next corner, swinging my arms out in the hopes they might bring me home faster. 'I appreciate your concern.'

'What were you doing inside that house anyway?'

As much as I didn't want to feed her gossip addiction, I figured the truth might keep her quiet. 'I was returning a sweat-shirt I'd borrowed.'

'You smell funny.'

'Thanks.'

She started to sniff me.

I stopped again. 'What are you doing?'

'Each of my six senses is highly developed. I'm trying to figure out what that smell is.'

I remembered Felice and his sickly scent. 'Is it sweet?' I asked, raising the hand I had used to shake his and smelling it. The faint aroma still lingered on my fingers, but it wasn't as strong as Mrs Bailey was making it out to be. Maybe I'd gotten used to it.

'Yes,' she said, taking my hand and sniffing it. Her whole face furrowed in concentration. 'Is it a new perfume?'

'I'm not wearing perfume.'

'Ah,' she heaved after a moment. Her voice was unbearably smug. 'I know what it is!'

I folded my arms across my chest, pretending impatience, but a cold knot had already settled in the pit of my stomach. I couldn't *not* take the bait. 'What?'

Mrs Bailey arched an incriminating eyebrow, savouring her response. 'It's honey.'

CHAPTER ELEVEN

THE NAME

The rest of the day passed in a blur of monotony. Uncle Jack finally called the diner to check up on me. He gave me the number of his new phone, but before I had time to talk to him about anything at all, he was hanging up again. I spent the rest of my shift wondering exactly what he was doing and why he hadn't come home yet. I wondered, too, about the honey, and whether Felice's strange scent was linked to the jar I had found next to the register.

Ursula had been pulling twelve-hour shifts to fill the void of competency left by my uncle, and Alison and Paul, who spent more time making out in the kitchen than waiting on tables. Millie, on the other hand, had gotten the day off and been spending it wisely. I called her when I left the diner that evening, and we traded stories about how our days had gone.

'So Valentino basically kicked you out?' she asked through a dramatic intake of breath.

'Pretty much,' I said, still feeling a tinge of embarrassment about it. 'The whole thing was weird. Did you get a strange vibe from Dom on your date?'

'Nope!' The excitement in her voice fizzed down the line and I felt an unwelcome twinge of jealousy for how differently things had gone for her and Dom. 'We just hung out and went on a picnic,' Millie chattered away cheerfully. 'Can you believe that?'

I stopped when I reached the edge of the parking lot, wondering which route to take. 'Seriously? That sounds so—'

'Scripted? I know. It's like something out of a movie.'

'And what about his scar?' I asked, crossing the street and opting for the shortcut, unwelcoming Priestly house be damned.

'Boating accident,' said Millie through a yawn.

'Really?' I asked, hearing the scepticism in my voice. Dom didn't seem like the boating type. Then again, his brothers didn't seem like the basketball types either, and I had been wrong about that.

'Yeah, it's a boring story. Something about a fishing hook,' said Millie dismissively. '*Anyway*, we got sandwich wraps and smoothies and took them to Rayfield Park. We just talked for hours. He seemed really interested in me, so I guess that's a good sign.'

'Definitely.' My path home began its slow incline, and my chest started to burn from the effort of walking uphill while trying to explain to Millie everything that had been bothering me at the same time. I mentioned the whole their-dad-might-have-been-a-notorious-murderer thing. Even though I couldn't trust Mrs Bailey, and when I googled every possible variation of 'Priestly Killer Chicago' on my phone nothing relevant to Nic's family had come up, I wanted Millie to know.

'Do you think we should stay away from them, at least until we find out what's going on?' I ventured.

Millie whined in disapproval. 'Soph, Mrs Bailey is, like, a walking gossip magazine. She thrives on ridiculous rumours. Remember that time she told my mum I was pregnant? She's crazy. There's nothing wrong with Dom or his family, trust me.'

'I just think there's something not quite right about it.'

'Then let's figure it out!' she urged. 'Think of it as a mystery. A sexy mystery.'

'What if it's not something we should be trying to figure out?' I asked, thinking again of the cloying honey smell, and the idea that Dom was in a *boating accident*. I just couldn't picture him wearing deck shoes.

'I've seen the way you look at Nic, Soph,' Millie said. 'Tell me he's not worth figuring out.'

Maybe she was right; even if there was something sticking in the pit of my stomach, the way Nic made me feel was undeniable. And Millie knew it. Plus, I didn't want to stomp all over her excitement with hearsay.

'So what did you guys talk about?' I asked instead.

'He told me about how he used to live right in the centre of the city with his family, and how the suburbs are boring in comparison. He's nineteen, which is sexy and totally risqué, though he does go a bit overkill on the whole hair gel aspect of his perfection. I mean, Danny Zuko is only a good look on Halloween. Not that that stopped me from staring at him in a daze when he talked. I had to ask him to repeat himself a lot, which was awkward. Anyway, then the conversation turned to me mostly, but I *am* a pretty fascinating topic. *And* we touched on the subject of you as well.'

I felt my cheeks grow hot. 'Why?'

I turned on to a narrow avenue where gated estates and rows of cherry trees climbed uphill beside me. Halfway up, the street intersected with Lockwood Avenue.

'As much as I *love* talking about you, it was actually Dom who brought you up, by accident.'

'Oh?' I didn't know Dom in the least, except that he was obviously less weird than Gino, and that he ranked far below Luca on the I'm-a-smug-ass scale. 'What did he say about me?'

'He was asking about the diner and stuff. I mentioned you were probably going to take over running it soon from your uncle and that we're best friends, so you will obviously give me a *huge* pay rise.'

'Obviously,' I concurred sarcastically.

'Then I went on a bit of a rant about Jack and what a bad job he's doing running the place now.'

'Mil!'

I turned on to Lockwood Avenue.

'Oh come on, Soph,' she chastised. 'A fact is a fact. He's been totally AWOL. I mean, you can't just disappear whenever you feel like it. For one thing, it's rude, and for another, it's weird. This is the exact kind of behaviour that gives fuel to Mrs Bailey's idiotic rumours.'

'OK.' She had a point and I wasn't going to rile her up about it.

'Anyway, I'm sure Dom will relay the fact that you are going to be sitting on a nice little cash cow someday soon to his brother, and that will no doubt make you seem even more attractive!'

I flinched, thinking of the fib I had told Nic and Luca that first time I saw them, in the diner. Hopefully Nic wouldn't feel cheated by my dishonesty. After all, it *was* technically just my summer job. For now.

As I got nearer I felt my stomach clench uncomfortably at the sight of their house.

'I hardly think they're gold-diggers. You should have seen their house,' I said, looking at it.

'Hopefully someday soon, I will.' I could tell Millie was wiggling her eyebrows suggestively on the other end of the call. 'I'd better go. I'm exhausted from my escapade.'

'Wait! Did you kiss him?'

'If I had, don't you think I would have used that as my opener?'

'Too bad.'

'But he *did* kiss my hand when he dropped me off. Does that count? It was *so* romantic.'

'That definitely counts!' I reassured her as I hurried past Nic's house. 'OK, now you can hang up,' I said once I was safely on the other side and the mansion was stretching into the sky behind me. I turned left and my path began to wind downhill again.

'Text me when you get in. Safe home.'

'Bye!'

'Sophie!' A voice called out just as I was putting my phone back in my bag.

I turned around, feeling a familiar jolt in my stomach. I

recognized him immediately, running towards me with his hood up.

I responded with calculated calmness, trying to keep my dreadful enthusiasm from making me burst into an arms-flailing sprint towards him. 'Nic?'

He came to an easy stop and lowered his hood. His smile lit up his face. 'Hi.'

'What are you doing?' I asked.

'You don't sound too happy to see me,' he noted. Small dents appeared above his brows and his smile faltered. 'Maybe I underestimated how well you would take me chasing after you like a maniac . . .'

'Why? I mean it worked *so well* the last time,' I teased.

His expression turned remorseful but he couldn't hide his smirk. 'I should have learnt my lesson, right? I didn't mean to startle you.'

'It's fine,' I assured him. 'It's just, you came out of nowhere.'

Relief swept across his features. 'I was about to come see you at the diner and then I saw you passing by my house so I figured I'd seize the opportunity.'

'At least you didn't crash into me this time.' I clutched at my chest in feigned relief. 'I might have had to kick your ass.'

'How terrifying,' he said, still smiling.

'Hey!' I punched his arm playfully, revelling in the familiarity that existed between us. 'I'll have you know I can be very intimidating.'

'I'm sure those tiny fists are very powerful.'

I punched him again, but this time he caught my hand beneath his, trapping it mid-assault. 'I heard you came to my house today.' All of a sudden his expression had turned serious, and his eyes had lost their warmth. 'Don't ever come to my house.'

I slid my hand out from under his, turned from him and started walking again. 'Don't worry, I won't.'

'Sophie.' He jogged after me. 'That came out wrong, sorry.'

'I was just returning your hoodie,' I replied, keeping my attention focused ahead of me as I walked. 'It was the polite thing to do. Now I see it was the wrong decision, and before you start, don't worry, your brother Valentino already made it perfectly clear I was unwelcome, so you don't need to bother.'

'Just let me explain.' He sped up, then turned around and began walking backwards so he could face me and keep up at the same time.

I blew a stray strand of hair from my eyes and glowered at him.

'I don't mean your presence is unwelcome. I really like seeing you . . . I'm just wary, that's all.'

'Of me?'

'No, not of you,' he said, pulling at his hair. 'Of my family. Some of them are really strange.'

So he was embarrassed. Well, that wasn't the worst reason not to want me parading through his house.

'I met Felice,' I offered. 'If that's what you're referring to.'

Nic winced. 'I know,' he said. 'He's very intense.'

I decided not to comment on that.

'Does he keep bees?' I asked instead. I had been thinking about the honeyed scent all day; at times I swore I could still smell it. It's not like it was a crime to make your own honey, but there was something about the way my uncle Jack had reacted to that mysterious jar that kept crashing back into my mind.

Nic stopped walking. 'How did you know that?'

'The marks on his face,' I said, stopping as well. 'They're bee stings, right?'

Nic hesitated for a beat, like he was weighing what to say, then simply answered, 'Yes.'

'And he smells of honey.' I paused, wondering if the next sentence would be offensive, but then I decided to say it anyway. 'It's almost like he bathes in it . . .'

Nic laughed. 'Maybe he does. He likes to eat the honeycomb raw, and he harvests and extracts the honey by himself. It's . . . his thing.' A shadow swept across his features, but he broke into another smile before I could decipher it.

'But there aren't any hives at your house?'

'Thankfully!' he replied, a tinge of relief creeping into his voice. 'Felice lives over in Lake Forest. But while my mother's in Europe he makes it his business to check on us, to make sure we're not all killing each other.'

'So he makes his own honey?' I confirmed, trying to stay on topic. I thought of the black-ribboned honey jar again, the one that turned up the week Nic's family moved in.

Nic's answer came slower this time. 'Yes.'

'Does he give his honey away?'

'Why?' His expression changed, and I didn't understand the way he was looking at me. Like he was suspicious of me. Was I asking too many questions about his family? Or had honey just become a universally sore subject for everyone? I had obviously missed the memo.

I shrugged, watching him as carefully as he was watching me. 'A jar of honey turned up in the diner not too long ago. It had a black ribbon around it.'

'OK . . .'

'We were wondering where it came from, and who it was for.'

'Who found it?'

'I did.'

Nic's brows furrowed. 'What did you do with it?'

'I brought it home and tasted it. It was nice . . . Then I dropped it by accident and it broke,' I added. There was no way I was telling him what really happened. It was too weird for even me to understand, and I had known Jack my whole life. One unhinged uncle was enough for this conversation.

Nic's frown deepened, and he shook his head. 'Like I said, Felice doesn't live around here.'

'So that's not something he would do?'

'I highly doubt it,' he said, his attention turning to the stars above us. 'Anyway, I wouldn't worry about it.'

'But I do worry about it,' I said, fighting the urge to tug on his arm so he would look at me again.

As if sensing my request, he returned his gaze to me. 'You worry about honey?' he asked, a smile spreading across his face.

I felt myself blush. When he put it like that, it did seem pretty stupid. 'I just don't like to feel like I'm out of the loop about something.'

'Try being the youngest of five brothers.'

We walked on, our hands swinging side by side, almost touching, as rows of beautiful homes on tree-lined streets bled into smaller, boxy houses along cramped, grid-like blocks.

'So you don't mind having an escort home again?' he asked, following my lead as I crossed a deserted intersection.

'No.' I felt shy looking up at Nic in the moonlight. There was something about the way his eyes were shining, or how his hair was falling in waves, curling beneath his ears, that made my mouth dry.

'I wanted to make sure you weren't upset about earlier. I know Valentino was rude, but he was probably just trying to save you from the Felice train wreck.'

I waved my hand in the air dismissively, even though I felt relieved by his explanation. 'I'll get over it.'

'Good.'

'Speaking of Valentino,' I said, letting my curiosity take over. 'Can I ask what happened to him?'

'You mean why he's in a wheelchair?'

'Well, yeah,' I replied, looking at my shoes. 'If you don't mind me asking.'

Nic didn't seem affronted, and I exhaled quietly in relief. 'I take it you've realized that he and Luca are twins,' he said. I nodded. 'Well, when my mother was pregnant with them, Luca's position in the womb put pressure on the lower half of Valentino's body. He couldn't move properly. His legs became tangled in bands of the amniotic membrane, and when he was delivered he had what they called a "skeletal limb abnormality". His right leg was completely crushed and turned in at the hip. The doctors operated on him when he was a kid, but the leg never developed the right way after that. He can walk for short distances with a cane, but he prefers to use the chair.'

'Has it made him resentful of Luca?' I wondered.

Nic shrugged. 'I think he's just glad Luca didn't decide to eat him in there.' He chuckled at my shocked expression. 'His words, not mine,' he clarified. 'I don't think he resents Luca. Valentino has always been the most intelligent of all of us. He has the most creative mind, and understands people really well – a whole lot better than Luca. They're so close that sometimes it feels like they're the same person. They agree on everything, and if you decide to argue with one, then you're arguing with both, and they will steamroll you before you can even think straight.' He paused for a second, losing himself in a memory that made him smile. I watched him carefully, trying to figure out what was unravelling inside his head. 'I think Luca has always felt guilty about the opportunities he has, but Valentino isn't a victim. They'd die for each other.'

'Wow,' I said, feeling a familiar sense of loneliness for the siblings I would never have. 'Must be nice to have that kind of bond.'

'I think everyone can have that bond with someone,' Nic said quietly. 'Isn't that the whole point of living?'

'I hope you're right.' I studied my nails to keep from burning up under his gaze.

Nic stopped walking, and I stopped too. 'I am right,' he said resolutely.

I looked at him again, shyly, and before the nerves inside me could bubble up and psyche me out completely, I blurted out, 'So, there's this party at Millie's on Saturday, and pretty much everyone is welcome, so I thought maybe you might want to come if you're not doing anything?'

Nic raised his eyebrows – whether it was at the sheer speed of my invitation or the actual meaning of it, I wasn't sure. 'And I take it her charming brother will be there?'

I inhaled through my teeth. 'Yes, but you're definitely still welcome, if that's what you're worried about. They made a rule. They can't veto each other's guests.'

Nic's laugh was soft and low. 'Saved by the power of disallowed vetoes.'

'Exactly,' I said, sounding mellower this time. 'How could you resist?'

'I don't think I could. I take it you'll be there?'

'Of course. It's actually my birthday too.'

'Ah,' he said, smiling. '*Buon compleanno*. I'd love to come.'

I enjoyed a brief inner victory dance while making sure to keep my expression relaxed. 'Cool.'

'I was wondering what kind of stuff you do for fun,' he continued. 'I was thinking about it earlier.'

'So you don't forget about me, then?' I teased. 'When you're playing basketball with your brothers or hanging out in your giant mansion and I'm at the diner wasting away from boredom?'

'Absolutely not.'

'Good.'

'And you're not very forgettable either,' he added, almost as an afterthought.

'I think most people would disagree,' I returned.

'I'm not most people.'

'You're certainly not,' I agreed.

'So tell me about yourself, Sophie. I want to know about you.'

'Why?' No one ever wanted to know about me. Especially not bronze, statue-type people. 'I'm very boring, I promise.'

He laughed again, it was close and intimate this time, and I could feel his breath against my ear as he leant towards me. 'Maybe you should let someone other than you be the judge of that.'

Instead of answering, I kicked a stray pebble and watched as it bounced into the street.

'Well, let's start with what we know' he began, rubbing his chin with his hand. 'You can be a little defensive . . .'

'Hey!'

'It's endearing,' he assured me quickly. 'And what else? You don't like storms. You're thick-skinned, and you blush whenever someone looks at you for too long . . .'

I grimaced. So he had noticed that.

'. . . which makes it more fun to look at you.' He smirked. 'Not that it isn't fun to look at you already.'

I could feel myself blushing again, and I cursed the timing of it.

'Is it just you and your parents at home?' he continued delicately – seamlessly, almost.

'It's just me and my mom,' I answered. 'My dad's been gone for a while, so we do our best not to burn the place down or poison each other with bad food.'

I felt guilty about skimming over the part about my father being in prison, but I didn't want to risk everything so soon.

'Do you get along?'

'Yeah, when we're both at home. But we don't see each other as much as I would like, I guess.'

Suddenly I felt horribly vulnerable, entrusting my innermost thoughts to this beautiful boy, who probably didn't care about my relationship with my mother.

Nic regarded me contemplatively. 'That must be difficult. But maybe your distance makes you closer when it counts?'

'Maybe.' I suddenly felt heavy with emotion. What was it with these Priestly boys? Just this morning I was on the verge of tears with Valentino! And now . . .

'So you're going to be a senior?'

Saved by the conversation change. We fell back into step with each other.

'Yup, starting in September. I have one more torture-filled year of high school to go.' I sighed theatrically, glad to be moving away from the previous topic. 'What about you?'

'Just graduated,' he replied with an edge of triumph in his voice.

'And what will you do with yourself now?'

'I deferred college for a semester; I'm working with my brothers mostly.'

'In Cedar Hill?'

'No,' he replied. 'Not exactly. Not all the time.'

'Do you like it?'

'What I do or where I live?'

'Cedar Hill.' I suddenly felt embarrassed of my association with the place. Especially the part we were in now. It was a far cry from the opulence Nic was used to.

He smiled at me like he could sense my shame. 'I didn't like it at first, but I do now.'

'What do you do here? What kind of work?'

He shrugged, but kept his shoulders rigid. 'Right now? Not a whole lot . . .' he said vaguely, trailing off.

'Do you think you'll miss school?'

Nic shook his head. 'It's only one semester. And I like to be active; I want to feel useful, like what I'm doing is making some small difference in the world. I don't think I'll ever need to use trigonometry in real life.'

'I know,' I concurred enthusiastically. 'Or Shakespeare. *Bleugh.*'

Nic reacted like I had slapped him on the side of the head. He stopped and placed his hands on my arms, pulling me towards him until I was right under his gaze. I thought he was going to start shaking me. 'Did you really just knock the man who gave us *Romeo and Juliet*?'

I frowned. I had never really considered it at length before; I just knew I didn't like school, and for me, Shakespeare was synonymous with school, a place where I didn't feel welcome. 'I guess I'm not a big fan of tragedy.'

'What about love?' he said with such intensity I almost forgot to breathe.

Slowly, he moved his hands up my arms, trailing his fingers across my shoulders until his thumbs were brushing the base of my neck. I felt my skin prickle with anticipation.

'Love is different,' I said.

'Love is weakness.' He studied his fingers as he moved them up my neck in gentle, butterfly touches.

'Weaknesses make us human,' I said, hearing the dryness in my throat.

'And being human makes us fallible.' He was so close.

'Are you fallible, Nic?'

His gaze was on my lips now. 'Of course I am.'

'I find that hard to believe.'

'You shouldn't,' he whispered. He tucked a stray strand of hair behind my ear, leaving his thumb under my chin.

I rose on to my tiptoes and he pulled me into his body, until my nose was almost touching his. His breathing faltered. Then his hands were around my waist, pressing against my lower back, and his lips were on mine.

I couldn't think any more. I was undone, and suddenly

nothing else mattered but Nic and the way he was pressing his mouth against mine and holding me like he never wanted to let me go. Everything around us dulled and, for a heartbeat, it was as if the entire world were holding its breath.

Then a roaring engine split the silence apart. A car sped up the street, pulling us back into reality and away from our kiss.

As the black SUV screeched to a halt on the street beside us, I felt my insides collapse in disappointment. Nic untangled himself from me and lunged forwards to bang on the car's blacked-out window.

'Gino? Dom?' he shouted. '*Cosa vuoi?*'

With a sleek casualness, the window buzzed down and the driver stretched across the passenger seat.

'Luca?' Nic sounded shocked.

Luca, in all his icy-eyed splendour, spat, 'Get in, Nicoli.'

'What the hell is going on?'

Luca threw his arm out and popped the passenger door so that it swung open against his brother's body. 'Get in the car now.'

Nic turned back to me, his expression apologetic. 'He can be a bit over the top sometimes . . .'

'Without her,' Luca interrupted.

'Have you gone insane? Or are you just having an asshole day? I'm not ditching Sophie in the middle of the street!'

Luca rubbed his hand across his forehead and released a sharp sigh. 'I don't know what the hell you think you're doing, little brother, but it's not funny.'

'What are you talking about?'

'Have you spoken to Dom today?'

'No.'

'*Vieni qui.*'

Nic leant into the open window.

Luca dropped his voice and spoke in one endless, hurried thread. Even though I could tell they had switched to Italian, I stood with my arms folded and listened. And though what I heard was mostly an incomprehensible string of syllables, I managed to glean one word successfully. And that word was 'Gracewell'.

The second I heard my name spring from Luca's lips, Nic turned around and regarded me with a poorly concealed display of horror. His mouth, which had been soft against mine just moments ago, was pursed in a hard line. Suddenly he was looking at me like he didn't know who I was.

'What's going on?'

'What's your name?' he asked in a strained voice.

'You know my name,' I replied, feeling scared by how unrecognizable he suddenly seemed. 'It's Sophie.'

'Sophie what?'

'Nic . . .'

'*Sophie what?*' he pressed, his voice growing frighteningly shrill.

'G-Gracewell,' I stammered, my lips trembling.

He looked like he was about to pass out. '*Cazzo!*'

'What does it matter what my name is?' I heard the desperation in my voice, but I didn't care.

He shook his head. 'But it doesn't make any sense.'

'What do you mean?'

'I have to go.' The words seemed forced, but he pushed them out determinedly.

'What does it matter?' I asked again. 'What did Luca say

about me?'

Behind Nic, Luca stared impassively at the road, but his hands were gripping the steering wheel so hard, they looked like marble. 'Get in the car, Nic. Don't drag this out.'

Nic lingered, looking at me like I had just slapped him hard in the face.

'Luca . . .' he pleaded, as if the rug had been pulled from underneath his feet and he had fallen hard on the ground beneath it.

Luca didn't turn his head, and when he spoke again his voice was rough with anger. 'Get. Away. From. Her. Now.'

I grabbed on to Nic's arm. I didn't know where he was going, but I knew I didn't want it to be without me.

'Now!' Luca bared his pointed teeth like a wolf.

There was a moment of nothingness, when my heart crumpled, and then Nic pulled his arm from me, ripped himself out of our bubble, and jumped into the passenger seat, slamming the door behind him.

I leapt forwards and gripped the open window as the engine roared to life beneath me. It was then that I saw there was blood all over Luca's shirt.

'What happened?' I gasped, my stomach filling with dread. If that were his own blood, Luca would have been in the hospital. But he wasn't. He was sitting across from me, seething and unscathed. *Several disappearances and two strange deaths in the last two weeks* – Mrs Bailey's words rang in my ears. 'Where did all that blood come from?'

Luca didn't respond, and Nic spoke instead. 'Get back from the car, Sophie.'

'Is this about my dad?'

Luca and Nic exchanged a loaded glance, and suddenly I felt like a pariah all over again.

'I want to know what he said!' I shouted at Nic. 'Tell me!'

It was Luca who finally responded. Turning his head slowly, he stared at me until his icy blue eyes dominated my world view. 'Gracewell,' he hissed, 'get off my car, or I will remove you from it myself.'

Nic cursed under his breath, but still he wouldn't look at me. Luca, on the other hand, held his hostile gaze until, shattering under the weight of it, I took my hands off the car and stumbled back.

The engine revved twice, and then the Priestly brothers sped off into the night without another glance in my direction. I was left standing alone in the middle of a deserted street as a string of questions exploded inside my brain.

PART II

'It is only in love and murder that we still remain sincere.'

Friedrich Dürrenmatt, *Incident at Twilight*

CHAPTER TWELVE
THE BEE

I stood on the street corner, my hands wrapped tightly around Nic's neck as we clung to each other. We watched the pavement crack beneath our feet. The sound of rushing water roared against my eardrums as a chasm split the ground, giving way to flames that climbed out, licking the sky, and then suddenly Nic was gone and I was sinking. I screamed, but my voice caught in my throat. As air turned to sand that filled my lungs, my whole world turned black, like someone had reached into my head and flicked a switch.

And then there was nothing but my heart pummelling against my chest and the smell of Philadelphia cream cheese. Guided by a distant hum, I hurtled back into reality.

'Sophie . . .'

The sunlight was bouncing off my eyelids.

'Earth to Sophie . . .'

I squinted and waited for the ceiling to shift into focus.

'Guess what day it is?'

I cleared the cobwebs from my throat in groggy squeaks and tried to blink away the memory of my dream – this was the second time I'd had it in as many nights. I propped myself on to my elbows.

'Good morning, Birthday Girl!'

My mother was perched on the end of my bed. There were small crinkles at the sides of her eyes, and her mouth was curved upwards in a grin that could have put the Cheshire Cat's to shame. I was glad to see her smile like that, even if she was just doing it for the sake of the day. I had missed the way it made her eyes sparkle.

In her lap she held a red velvet cupcake, lavished with cream cheese frosting.

'Good morning,' I croaked.

'Happy birthday, sweetheart.'

She fished a Zippo lighter from her cardigan, flicked it open and lit the candle. 'Make a wish!' she said, shoving the cupcake so close to my face I could see tiny wisps of smoke rise above the flame.

I hesitated as it danced across my eye line, taunting me. *Clarity*, I decided at last. *I just want clarity.* I blew purposefully across the flame, extinguishing it in one tiny puff of air.

My mother produced a silver knife from her other pocket. She sliced the cupcake straight down the middle and the two halves fell apart from each other, toppling under the weight of the frosting. She scooped up one half and handed it to me.

'Delicious!' I said, taking a bite. 'Thanks.'

Setting her half on her lap, my mother reached behind her and fished out a present wrapped in glitzy purple paper. 'I made you something.'

I smiled as I wiped the residual cupcake grease from my fingers on to my duvet. I already suspected it was the dress she had been working on in secret. Carefully, I unstuck the tape around the edges and peeled away the paper so that the garment slipped out, perfectly folded, on to the bed. I unfurled it. It was structured but delicate, made from light gold silk that fell in soft waves, and adorned with sequins that glinted in the morning sunlight. I brushed my fingers along the thin straps and felt the dress curve in around the waist as I held it up. 'It's incredible!'

'And it matches your hair!' My mother smiled. 'I thought you could wear it to the party at Millie's later?'

'Great idea.' I felt a pinch of guilt knowing my mother was unaware of Millie's parents' absence. Still, what she didn't know couldn't hurt her, right?

She clapped her hands together. 'Lunch later?' she asked, bouncing up from my bed. 'I want to treat my seventeen-year-old daughter at the Eatery.'

'Really?' I reclined and stretched my body out in one long, angular yawn, blinking up at the ceiling. 'That sounds great.' *And expensive.*

My mother carried the dress across the room with her, hopping over old sweatshirts and unfolded jeans as she went. She hung it inside the closet and, with one final disgruntled – *hypocritical* – look at the floor, she edged back out of the room, leaving me alone with my thoughts, which turned to the strange dream I'd just had. Like a jolt of electricity, the feeling of Nic's kiss took hold of me again and I felt my stomach clench uncomfortably at the memory of how he had left me so suddenly. I hoped I wasn't doomed to relive his desertion in my nightmares too. There were still so many questions floating around in my head, and no way for me to get the answers I desperately wanted. I clutched at the red velvet uneasiness in my stomach and groaned. Maybe a party was exactly what I needed to take my mind off everything.

The black ponytail stuck out of Gino Priestly's head like a noir mini palm tree. Beside him, the lights were dancing off Dom's overly gelled helmet of hair. What the hell were they doing here?

'What is it, sweetheart? Don't you like the quiche?'

I refocused my attention on my mother, who was sitting across from me. 'It's good. I'm just a bit overheated.'

'You've been so quiet since we got here. I thought you'd like this place. Is it too fancy?'

As concern etched across her features, a fresh heap of guilt consumed me. I shook my head more vehemently this time. 'Are you kidding? This place is great.' I gestured around at the Eatery's monochrome décor: the black granite floors were inlaid with intricate floral designs; the tables were covered with expensive white cloths; and all around the restaurant, Romanesque pillars wound towards the ceiling. The walls were decorated with black-and-white photographs of twentieth-century Chicago and dotted incrementally with glass lighting fixtures. 'Makes a welcome change from the diner.'

My mother smiled and took a sip of her Chardonnay. 'Speaking of the diner, I wanted to talk to you about that . . .'

I let my attention fall on Gino and Dom again – or rather, on the backs of their heads – and wondered about the odds of us being at the same restaurant. It was miles away from Cedar Hill, right in the centre of Chicago, *and* since it was one of the best restaurants in the city, it was more of an eye-wateringly expensive, special occasion kind of place. The karma gods must have been enjoying the show.

At least Nic and Luca weren't with their brothers. I tried to remind myself of how horrible Nic had been the other night, but it was difficult to forget all the other things about him: the softer, funnier, kinder things. The way he smiled, the way he had pressed his lips against mine . . . the way he drove away from me in the middle of the night without a second glance. I flinched.

'Sophie?'

'What?' I took another bite of my quiche Lorraine, wondering why I had ordered it. Then again, I didn't understand the majority of the fancy menu and I wasn't convinced I would enjoy 'truffle-infused fries' as much as normal ones.

'I want to talk to you about the diner.'

'OK, shoot.'

Behind my mother, Gino was recoiling from something the bald man sitting across from him had said. Dom sat on his brother's right and there was a narrow, taller man on his left, his back half-turned to me. It was Felice – I would have wagered my meal. Even though they were at the other side of the restaurant, curled around one another in a secluded corner booth, the faint smell of honey was hanging in the air. I was sure of it. Or I was going crazy.

I averted my eyes.

My mother was still talking, her hands flailing animatedly in front of her. '. . . placed unfair expectations on you. You need to get out more and spread your wings, don't you think?'

A buzzing sound tugged at my attention. A bee had found its way inside the restaurant and was circling the table next to us.

'Get out of where?' I asked, dragging my gaze back to my table and scolding myself for being so distractible. I could still see it, though – a small blur of yellow and black in my peripheral vision.

'The diner.'

I jabbed my fork into my quiche. 'What about the diner?'

The man I didn't recognize got up from the Priestly table. He was tall and bald, with a high forehead and a thick black moustache that dominated his angular face. He grunted as he passed a waitress, and then disappeared through the restroom doors.

'I think you should quit. It's too taxing on your energy and you barely have any free time.'

Now that I had heard it in its entirety, I was surprised by her suggestion. I set my fork down and swallowed the mouthful of quiche in one over-zealous gulp. 'But it's Dad's. I thought the whole plan was for me to run it until he gets back.' I didn't know why I was fighting against her idea – the thought of running the diner when I turned eighteen had never excited me; I had always known it wasn't my calling.

The bee whizzed past my face, missing my nose by an inch. My mother dropped her fork and released a small yelp.

'Sorry,' she explained sheepishly, regaining her composure. 'They always give me such a fright.'

'I think bees are kind of cute,' I said, trying to put her at ease.

Across the restaurant, the bee was zigzagging towards the Priestly table. *Probably returning to its 'master,'* I thought, registering the back of Felice's silver head again.

'What's going on with you today? You're all over the place.' My mother grabbed my wrist, tugging at me.

'Sorry.' I shook my head in a futile attempt to settle my wandering attention, and pulled my hand back. 'What were you saying?'

'Why not let your uncle continue to manage the diner after you graduate next year, until your father comes back. That way you can give college your undivided attention – and go to school in Chicago instead of staying here in the burbs. There's a whole world out there, you know.'

I shovelled another forkful of quiche into my mouth. 'I'm still saving for a car. I need the money,' I said ineptly, covering my mouth as I chewed.

I flicked my gaze again. The bald, moustached man had come back from the restroom and was rejoining the Priestly table, sitting down with an audible grunt.

'I can give you a little cash every week to put towards a car. You wouldn't even miss the tips from the diner,' my mother was protesting.

'I don't want to put that strain on you,' I said, my mouth still half full. 'I know we don't have that kind of money any more.'

My mother pushed a square of feta cheese around her plate with her fork. 'Sophie, I'd really prefer it if you left.'

'Did Uncle Jack say something to you? Have you heard from him?' I was starting to get an uneasy feeling in the pit of my stomach again. My mother was acting strange, like just about everyone else in my life.

'No, but maybe we should put some distance between you two. He seems a little more unhinged than usual lately.'

'I think he'd take it pretty badly if I ditched him now. Especially after his friend just died.'

She shrugged and skewered a thin slice of red onion, popping it into her mouth. 'Jack's not even around any more. And he can't always get what he wants.'

My eyes slid across to the Priestly table again. Dom and Gino were arguing with the bald, moustached man. Felice – yes, it was definitely him, I could see now – was sitting perfectly still, his hands clasped on the table in front of him. He was quietly observing the bee that was now swirling perilously close to their table. As the others argued, their voices swelled and travelled through the restaurant.

'What is going on?' My mother swivelled around so she could catch a glimpse of the commotion, but it died down almost as quickly as it had begun and she lost interest.

'Mom?'

She looked at me expectantly.

'Is there something you're not telling me about Dad and Uncle Jack? Or you and Uncle Jack? I get the feeling I'm missing something.'

She leant on to her elbows and knitted her hands under her chin. 'What do you mean?'

'Well, I don't know what I mean. That's why I asked . . .'

There was an almighty *clap!* We jumped in our seats.

'Calvino!' A scream so high it sounded like a woman's. But it hadn't come from a woman, it had come from Felice, who had sprung to his feet and was clasping his hands to his face. Now everyone in the restaurant was looking at them. The bald man

– Calvino – sat back in the booth, casually lifting his palm from the table and wiping it with a napkin, his face placid. He had killed the bee.

Felice's chest was heaving. He said something in amplified Italian, but Calvino didn't bat an eyelid. He tried to wave Felice back into his seat. The calmer he acted, the more incensed Felice became. He began to spit vitriol as he gestured futilely at what I assumed was the squished bee carcass.

I gaped. I had never seen someone so calm flip out so quickly.

Felice reached into his suit jacket, prompting Gino and Dom to pull back in their seats. Calvino shot to his feet and held his hands up, like he was surrendering. He spoke quietly and quickly.

Felice pulled his hand from his pocket and clenched it into a fist by his side. He ran his other hand through his hair, stopping to squeeze the back of his neck, pinching at it.

Slowly, and without taking his eyes off Felice, Calvino sat down.

Felice remained on his feet. He raised his chin so that he appeared even taller than usual, and with one final curse word directed solely at Calvino – but heard by everyone within a one-mile radius – he stormed out of the restaurant like a graceful, seething skeleton.

'What a strange man,' my mother whispered, her hushed words mingling with everyone else's.

'Strange family,' I muttered, watching Gino and Dom resettle themselves at their table, falling back into conversation. Maybe in this one case I was actually *lucky* to have been ostracized. The Priestlys obviously had a lot going on, and I had already reached my drama quota for one lifetime. It was probably for the best. Even if it didn't feel like it.

I shifted back to my mother and found her chewing her bottom lip. 'Sophie, there's a lot you don't know about your father and Uncle Jack,' she said, returning to our conversation like the dramatic interlude hadn't happened at all. 'Sometimes I can't help but think Jack deserves to be in jail more than your father does.'

This was the first time I had ever heard my mother play the blame game about that night – or speak about it willingly, for that matter. It was one of those unsaid, defining moments that was always bubbling beneath the dynamic of our relationship but rarely openly acknowledged by either of us.

'But Jack wasn't even there.'

'I know that,' she conceded. 'But your uncle has always made friends with the wrong people, the sort of people who care more about money than family, and who encourage his paranoid delusions. When your father came to Cedar Hill, it was to make a new life with you and me – a better life than the one he had growing up. He was respectable and successful, but then Jack started coming around. He didn't have a family of his own and so he looked at us like we were his too. It had always been just him and your father growing up, those two boys against the world, and I think your father felt like he owed him a piece of our lives too, so he wouldn't be out on his own.

'But then Jack started putting these thoughts in your father's head. The same thoughts I can see him trying to put in yours – ones designed to make you afraid and anxious. It got to the point where Jack would question everything and everyone who came into the diner, and soon he was making your father paranoid too. The more I think about it, I can't help but feel that if Jack hadn't been getting under your father's skin, then he wouldn't have been so quick to believe that man was a dangerous intruder that night at the diner.'

'And he wouldn't have shot him,' I finished coldly. 'I don't know if you can blame that on Jack.'

'He gave your father the gun.'

'He wanted him to protect himself,' I countered. 'They've always looked out for each other.'

She scooped a tomato wedge on to her fork. 'You're right,' she replied quickly, shaking her head. 'Never mind. I shouldn't have brought it up on your birthday. This day should be about all the good things in your life.'

Suddenly the air between us was awkward and strained. I took a gulp of my Diet Coke and let my eyes wander back to the Priestlys, who had become uncharacteristically silent. Gino sat with his head in his hands, and Dom was leaning back, staring blankly at the ceiling. I knew how they felt.

CHAPTER THIRTEEN

THE PARTY

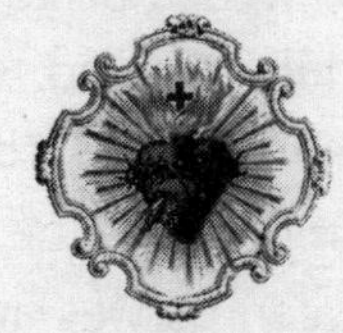

I examined myself in my bedroom mirror, making sure my mother's tinted moisturizer had blended into my skin. I applied some of her bronzer to the high points of my face and added some blush to my cheeks. I rifled through her make-up bag and fished out a deep kohl powder, sweeping it across my eyelids, before applying gooey black mascara to my lashes. Then I stood back and appraised my reflection, marvelling at what the wonders of modern cosmetics could do for sun-starved skin.

My mother shuffled into the room and my gaze fell on the gift in her hands – a large rectangle covered in Disney princess wrapping paper. 'Is that from Millie?'

My mother put the gift on the bed. 'She dropped it off when you were in the shower. Open it. The suspense is killing me.'

I didn't have to be asked twice. I ripped open the wrapping paper to find a grey shoe box. *Carvela* was printed across it in neat black letters.

'How did Millie afford those?' My mother echoed my thoughts.

I shook my head in disbelief. How was it possible to have such an amazing best friend? I eased the lid off the box and pulled the tissue paper away to find a pair of patent-leather nude stilettos. The heel, which was at least five inches high, was coated in a subtle gold gloss, while the front of the shoe slanted downwards into a perfectly rounded peep-toe.

'I think I'm in love,' I groaned.

My mother sighed. 'I've never been so disappointed to have smaller feet than you.'

I slipped my bare foot into the left shoe and teetered upwards. 'How am I going to walk in these without falling on my face?'

My mother grinned as she handed me the second shoe. 'No one really *walks* in high heels. They just get by.'

After fifteen minutes of practising, I shimmied into the gold dress. Twirling in front of my closet mirror, I pulled out the pin that I'd wedged into my hair so that it tumbled down my back in waves. I barely recognized my reflection, but I had a feeling she was going to have a whole lot of fun.

When we pulled up outside Millie's house, I could hear music blaring through the walls. Cars lined the streets and crammed into the driveway. I climbed out on to the curb.

'Are you sure Millie's parents are OK with this?' I watched my mother survey the cars warily.

'Yup.' I turned away from her so she couldn't see my brazen, lying face.

'OK . . .' she relented. 'Have a blast.'

I watched the car until it shrunk to a small blue dot.

When I turned around, Millie was standing at the front door, wearing a short black dress that accentuated her bust and bandaged her in around the waist.

'Mil!' I exclaimed, making my way towards her in high-heel-induced slow motion. 'Thank you so much for the shoes!'

'Holy crap,' she shot back, her red-lipsticked mouth agape.

I hunched my shoulders and covered my dress with my arms. 'Is it too much? Should I change?'

She gestured at my dress, moving her finger up and down in several slow flicks. 'That dress *really* shows off your best assets!' She made a botched attempt at a wolf whistle and then wiggled her eyebrows suggestively.

'Pervert,' I teased, reaching her.

'What?' She raised her hands in a gesture of feigned innocence. 'I meant it really brings out the blue in your eyes . . . So vivid . . .'

'Who are you talking to?' Alex arrived behind Millie at the door. His blond hair was styled in perfect spikes and he wore dark rinse jeans paired with a tight blue shirt. He was smiling goofily and clutching a red plastic cup. When he noticed me hovering in the doorway, he let his jaw drop so that, side by side and wearing the same expression, he and Millie looked like twins.

'Sophie Gracewell,' he spluttered.

'I know,' Millie murmured. 'I know.'

*

Millie and I danced like maniacs across her hardwood floors, throwing our hands in the air and whipping our hair in circles, both of us teetering precariously on our respective sky-high heels. All around us, couples gravitated towards each other like magnets, pushing up against one another or peeling off to other rooms to make out. I barely recognized most of the people – the majority were Alex's college friends, and those who heard about it from Millie were ignoring me, as usual. It didn't matter. Everyone was laughing and having fun, and it was contagious – I was relaxed and energized. But more than that, I was eternally grateful to Millie, who had converted the entire downstairs of her impressive family home into a hub of energy, which meant I could spend my birthday having some much-needed fun.

The front living room had been cleared of its picture frames, knick-knacks and creepy porcelain dolls that usually peered out from glass cases in the corners – an obsession of Millie's mother's. The lights had been dimmed so low that the features of anyone standing more than two feet away were foggy and indiscernible, and the leather couches and upholstered armchairs were pushed back against the wall. Above the fireplace, a fifty-inch TV was blaring music through surround-sound speakers.

'Where's Dom?' I asked, ignoring the dull ache in the balls of my feet.

'He's not coming.' Millie's face crumpled, but she waved her explanation away as though it didn't matter. 'I haven't heard from him since our date. He didn't even return my text.'

'I'm sorry, Mil!' I shouted above the music. 'That sucks!'

'It's fine,' she returned loftily, but I could tell it wasn't. She had been hopelessly obsessed with Dom after their date, and the fact that he hadn't bothered to follow it up was strange, not to mention incredibly rude.

'I hope it's not because of me,' I suddenly realized, feeling the colour drain from my bronzed and blushed face. 'Maybe Nic said something to him.'

Millie's expression soured. 'If it *is* because of you, then Dom is as spineless as his brother and they should both be shunned for judging you for your father's *accident.* I don't want to be with someone like that anyway!'

'It's his loss,' I offered, feeling her anger ignite my own. 'He's an idiot.'

'They both are! I hope they have a really boring time styling their stupid hair and overspending on their stupid Italian clothes while they all grow old together in that creepy mansion!' Millie threw her head back and started swaying her hips, putting an end to the topic of Dom and his brothers for good.

Following her lead, I closed my eyes and let my body melt into the music. But deep down in my private bubble, I couldn't help but imagine Nic's hands around my waist; that he had shown up to apologize for his strange behaviour and that there was a reasonable explanation for his sudden callousness. But when I opened my eyes and twirled around again, I saw a collection of faces I didn't recognize, all red-faced and panting.

After a while, my feet started to throb. I stopped dancing and slipped through the double doors that led into a large marble-fitted kitchen. Inside, a bunch of guys were leaning around a keg, chugging their drinks. At the table, two skinny brunettes in short skirts were squealing their way through a game of beer pong.

I squeezed by a red-haired girl who was inking a henna tattoo on her friend's back, and made my way towards the fridge just as Alex slammed his beer cup across the counter and backed away from his friends with his arms up in victory. 'Losers!' he shouted. 'You can't beat the champ!'

I smiled. Alex had been so uptight at the basketball tournament; it was nice to see him in a lighter mood – even if he was still being abnormally competitive.

When his eyes fell on me, he stuffed his hands down by his sides and hunched his shoulders, adopting a sheepish expression. 'Beer?' he offered, gesturing at the keg behind him. 'Or we have some harder stuff too?'

I pushed the matted hair away from my forehead, feeling beads of sweat underneath my fingers. 'Maybe later,' I said. I was already having a hard time standing up in my heels, I figured I'd better practise some more before adding alcohol to the mix.

'You sure you don't want one?' Alex prompted with a smile that I used to daydream about in school. But something was different now.

'Yeah, I'm sure.' I opened the fridge, pulled out a can of Diet Coke and cracked it open while the boys behind me laughed among themselves. I wondered if they were laughing at me, but I was too chicken to confront them about it. Feeling myself blush, I moved away and shimmied past the girl with red hair, who was inking a dolphin on her own hip now. A ping-pong ball soared past my head and bounced off the marble island in the middle of the kitchen.

I made it back to the living room in one piece, squeezed by a couple who were making out against the door, and danced around someone doing the worm, to get to the nearest couch. When I reached it, I found Millie chatting to Paul and Alison from the diner.

'. . . and then I thought, whatever, I'm going to have fun without him – hey, birthday girl, come sit.' She patted the sliver of space beside her.

'Hey.' I squeezed in between Millie and the armrest, feeling instant relief in the balls of my feet. 'When did you guys get here?' I followed Millie's gaze to Alison's lap and saw that she and Paul were holding hands. They had obviously made it official.

'Just now. Ursula let us off early.'

'Happy birthday, Sophie,' Paul added cheerily. 'Great party.'

'Thanks.' I shrugged. 'It's not mine. I don't know most of these people.'

'Oh, sure it is,' Millie interjected, waving her hand dismissively. 'And if Alex's friends didn't know you before tonight, then they definitely will now, thanks to that dress.' She drained her drink and sighed satisfactorily.

'Yeah,' Paul agreed, causing Alison to dig her nails into his lap. 'Ouch!' he yelped. 'Sorry, I was just saying.'

'Time for a refill, I think.' Millie sprang to her feet and sauntered through the parting crowd with more attitude than Beyoncé. I envied her ability to walk so effortlessly in her heels without experiencing the urge to lie down and chop her feet off.

I went in search of a bathroom. The sound of vomiting from downstairs prompted my journey to the second floor, where, after knocking three times, I swung the door open and came face to face with a half-naked couple. It was a traumatic moment for all of us.

I quickly shut the door and made my way further along the upstairs hallway, stopping outside Millie's parents' room and rapping my knuckles against the door. When there was no answer from inside, I eased my way in, praying I wasn't about to encounter another scarring scene. The bedroom was empty.

The narrow door beside the wall of closets meant my memory had served me correctly and that they did have an en-suite bathroom. But as I approached it, the handle was yanked downwards from the inside and it swung backwards on its hinges. I jumped back and landed against the bed. I shot my hands up and covered my eyes. 'Sorry, I didn't know anyone was in here.'

My explanation was met with a deep laugh. 'Relax, Sophie. I spilt some beer on myself and all the other bathrooms were *ocupado*.'

I unsheltered my eyes and found Robbie Stenson leaning against the doorway, holding a red cup in each hand. 'Do you want one? I've got a spare.'

'Um, thanks.' I was glad to know Robbie wasn't holding our basketball tournament debacle against me. 'I'm not sure if I should drink – it's hard enough to walk in these heels while sober. I don't want to risk my life by doing it drunk.'

He flicked his floppy hair across his forehead and smirked. 'It's just cranberry with seltzer, but it'll give you a nice buzz. I think it's the sugar content or something.'

'Cool.' I reached for the cup in his outstretched hand, feeling hot all of a sudden. 'I am pretty thirsty.'

'No kidding.' He sat on to the bed with a plonk and arched

one of his perfect eyebrows at me. 'You were dropping some killer dance moves earlier. Why didn't you use some of that talent on the court? Then we might have had a snowball's chance.'

I smiled into the cup. 'I'm not sure I could have dribbled the ball and done the robot at the same time.'

Robbie snorted with amusement. 'It might have intimidated our opponents.' He stared unblinkingly at me as I drank. 'You look great, by the way.'

'Thanks.' Suddenly I had a feeling our conversation might mean something different to him than it did to me. What *was* it about this dress?

'I should get back downstairs,' I said, setting the empty cup on the nightstand.

'I thought you had to go to the bathroom?'

'Not really any more. I think I was just feeling overheated.' I rose and teetered to the door as my feet began to ache again.

'Maybe I'll catch you later,' he hollered after me.

'Yeah, maybe,' I said, gripping the banister and lowering myself carefully on to the stairs.

Back in the kitchen, I found Millie cuddling up against a boy with a questionable goatee. She was leaning into his shoulder and giggling like a little girl. Her attempts to forget about Dom were obviously going well.

'Sophie.' She grinned broadly and stood up when she saw me. 'Come meet Marcus. He's so great.' She shuffled closer and dropped her voice. '*So* much more fun than *boring* Dom. I don't know what I was thinking with that guy. Obviously we're not compatible, he's *way* too serious.'

Suddenly she was looming back and forth in front of me, and

I was starting to feel funny. 'Can you stand still?'

'Have you been drinking, Soph?'

Her eyes grew too big for her face and her mouth was hanging open at an unnatural angle. I shook my head and felt it spin.

'You sure?' She came up close until I could see every freckle on her face. They moved around like a puzzle and then disappeared.

'C-course.' I slumped backwards against the wall. 'I don't feel very well, though.' Alarm bells started to go off inside my head, but they got fainter and fainter.

'You sure you didn't do a shot of something?'

The music was thumping against my skull. 'No, I–I just . . .' I paused and scrunched up my face. 'I forgot what I was going to say.'

'I think someone should take you home.' I wasn't aware of much, but I could tell the amusement had drained from Millie's voice, and the guy with the goatee had disappeared.

'I have a headache. C-can you get me something for that?' I heard myself falter over the words and grimaced. They sounded so clear in my head.

'What's going on, Sophie?' Out of nowhere, Alex had appeared and was standing in front of me, holding me up. Suddenly I realized that, if he let me go, I would crumple into a heap on the ground. I fell into him, stubbing my nose on his chest.

'I think she's had too much to drink,' he said, holding me steady again.

'I didn't,' I slurred as the room started to fade into darkness. And then I was lying down in a quiet room at the back of the house, staring at the crystal chandelier above me. Nausea gathered in my stomach. 'I want to go home.'

'Crap,' Millie muttered from somewhere far away. 'Celine is going to kill me if she finds her like this.'

'I'll take her home,' someone suggested.

'You sure, Robbie?'

'Yeah, I know the way. She can't go on her own. Not like this.'

'I don't know.' Alex's face contorted above me, his eyes spinning like little rainbow wheels. 'Maybe we should just call her mum.'

'Alex, I'll take her. I haven't been drinking. You don't want to get this whole rager shut down, do you?'

I groaned and clutched my sides. 'I don't want to go with him,' I whispered into a cushion. 'Get Nic.'

The cushion didn't reply, and Nic never came.

'OK, Sophie, let's go.' Alex placed his arms under mine and lifted me off the couch until I teetered unsteadily against him. The world spun around until the faces of Millie, Alex and Robbie blurred into one strange mosaic of humankind.

'Hang on,' Millie said. 'She can't walk home in those.'

Suddenly there were only two faces in front of me and I couldn't remember who was who. I thought Alex had blond hair, but the other guy was wearing his blue eyes. I shook my head back and forth to get rid of the fuzziness.

'How much did she drink?'

'I bet she polished off that tequila, man.'

And then I was at the front door, wearing a pair of Ugg boots that didn't belong to me. My chin got stuck to the top of my chest, and the ground started pulsating up and down.

'Robbie, get her to call me when she's home, OK? Don't forget.'

And then we were galloping down the driveway and rounding the bend into an empty street that loomed ahead of me like a black river. Suddenly my head was swelling like a balloon.

'I'll fall in.'

I jumped across the cracks in the pavement.

Robbie slid his arm around my waist and scooted me forwards in a straight line. 'Just chill out. You're a little buzzed right now, that's all.'

At the mention of the word 'buzz', I felt something in my ear. I jerked my head and slapped my hand against my face. 'Get off, get off, get off!'

And then I was outside a row of small box houses that looked like they had been punched in.

'They look so sad,' I moaned into Robbie's shoulder.

I blinked my eyes, and when I opened them again I was gliding along the sidewalk and squinting into the overbearing starlight. The Priestly house climbed into the sky ahead of me, like a castle.

'There's a princess in there.' I felt an urgent need to rescue her. And then I forgot what I was thinking about. 'I'm exhausted,' I realized as the world around me became silent and still.

We had stopped walking.

'I know.' Robbie propped me against a wall. I was vaguely aware of the uneven stones scratching against my back.

'I haven't slept for nearly a hundred years,' I remembered. My head lolled until I was looking down at the pavement.

He lifted me back up like a rag doll and squeezed his hands above my waist. 'I've got you.'

'Am I home?' I asked wearily. Everything was so hard to

concentrate on, and I had a bad feeling that any minute now, I would vomit.

'Yeah, just relax, Sophie. Everything is fine.' I felt a finger under my chin, nudging my head. My eyes rolled back as the sensation of warm breath tickled my face. I struggled against my drooping lids, forcing them open. When I did, I found myself staring into two hawk-like grey eyes an inch from my face. And just as my body relinquished control of my limbs completely, I felt his hands start to inch up my dress.

CHAPTER FOURTEEN

THE DARK KNIGHT

Somewhere deep inside me, panic was rising. 'Stop,' I heard myself gasp.

Robbie's eyes shrank to slits in his puffy face. 'Just relax.'

I tried to shake my head, but could only make a sideways figure eight. 'I don't want this.'

He chuckled. 'Then why would you show up to a party wearing *this?*' He tugged at the fabric of my dress. I tried to speak again, but I couldn't conjure up enough energy to push the words out. He moved a rough finger against my lips and I moaned, feeling saliva pool at the back of my throat. He inched closer. Spittle gathered at the sides of his cracked lips as he said, 'Stop playing hard to get.'

His hand moved below my hips and settled on my bare leg, and suddenly it was all I could focus on. He tapped his fingers across my thigh and pressed himself against me, sandwiching my body between his thick frame and the cold wall. He started to run a hand through my hair, tangling it and jerking my head backwards.

I struggled to remember how far I was from home, but everything was a blur. The panic grew and pulsed against my skull until it throbbed. I tried to move my arms, but they were unresponsive, crushed beneath his weight as he walked his other hand up towards the hemline of my dress.

My eyes fluttered back in my head as he pushed his salty lips against my mouth. Fleetingly I thought of Nic: how he had tentatively pressed his lips to my mine like he was trying to savour every part of the moment; how excited butterflies had exploded inside me as his hands gently curled around my waist. But these were not his hands, or his lips. Coarse and dry, they mashed against my mouth, pulling it open beneath the force of a snakelike tongue until I collapsed into Robbie, falling further into the maw that probed mine so relentlessly it began to hurt.

And then the sound of an engine punctured the horrifying silence, and tyres screeched to a halt somewhere nearby. Robbie froze with his lips still on mine, and moved his hands back on to my waist. In my dazed state, I imagined we looked like two wooden puppets, propped against each other in the night.

I don't know how long I leant against the statue of Robbie Stenson, but I rejoiced in the welcome rush of cool air when his body was ripped away from mine. He let out a strangled yelp as he sailed backwards, taking the pressure with him so that my chest expanded again.

Someone was shouting. My body slumped against the wall and slid to the ground beneath legs I could no longer feel. Faraway gravel shifted, and a deep cry rang out. There was a resounding crack and an ear-splitting wail that sounded like a dying cat. Shoes scraped against the ground. High-pitched sobs descended into desperate pleas. I tried to understand, but the words became garbled and indistinct as my body slid towards the ground and my head connected with the concrete.

'Get out of here before I rip your heart out.'

Is he talking to me?

More shuffling.

Why is it so dark?

The sound of footsteps – further and further away.

Am I still alive?

Another set of footsteps, steadier and quieter than the last, moving towards me.

'Sophie? Can you hear me?'

Something gripped my shoulders. My whole body shook gently, but there was no strength left to open my eyes. I was dead to the whole world. Dead to everything, except his voice.

'Sophie? Come on.' More gentle shaking. A finger pressed up against my neck. I could feel my pulse throb against it. There was a sigh – long and relieved. 'Come on, Sophie. Wake up.'

I struggled for the energy, but I was spent, like a deflated balloon. Silence followed, and I found myself trying to remember where I was and what was going on. Had I left the party? Did I fall down?

'Can you try opening your eyes?'

Why couldn't I place that voice? It was so familiar yet so far away. An arm slid around my shoulders and another underneath my knees, lifting me away from the cold ground. My head drooped on to something hard, and I could hear a steady heartbeat drumming against my ear.

I sailed through the air, and into a warm place. The muffled sound of a car door gave way to the comforting hum of an engine, and soon I was rocking back and forth against something soft. The minutes bled into one long stretch of darkness until I was soaring again, through a realm of a hundred distant voices, flashing lights and groaning beeps.

A lone finger trailed along the side of my cheek.

A faraway voice invaded the moment just as I was piecing together where I was, and the thought fluttered away from me before I could pin it down.

'I located her mother. Don't you want to stay until she gets here?'

'I can't.'

Footsteps clicked against the floor, getting softer, until I could hear nothing but the sound of my own breathing as it rattled through my chest. Feeling safe in the complete absence of everything, I fell into nothingness, where half-forgotten memories mingled with harrowing nightmares until I forgot what was real and what was imagined.

I woke to a ceiling entirely different from the one I was used to. It was big and tiled, with fluorescent lights that stung my eyes. The smell of disinfectant hung in the air, and the open curtains of a faraway window were a dull, unfamiliar green. I tried to wriggle my body, but it was constricted under the weight of overly-tucked-in sheets. And yet, despite the warmth that clung to me, I felt a cold stiffness rippling through my left hand.

The bed was edged with bars and the walls beyond were a blinding shade of white. I flexed my fingers against the thick bandage just above them and noticed, with a pinch of horror, that there was an IV drip invading my hand.

'Mrs Gracewell, she's awake.'

My bed shook from the other side. I rolled my head and flinched against a sudden onslaught of pain in the base of my skull. The un-made-up face of my mother was the first thing I saw. Beside her was an exhausted-looking Millie, wearing an oversized hoodie and last night's lipstick, which was just a red stain now. She scooted her chair forwards. 'How do you feel?'

Trying my best not to completely freak out, I wiggled each of my limbs in turn and was relieved to find them unbroken. I checked my body for bandages and found none. Then I dragged my hands through my matted hair and all around my face to make sure there were no stitches.

'What happened?' I croaked. 'This is the worst headache I've ever had.'

'That's OK, sweetheart.' My mother stroked my hand reassuringly. 'That's to be expected.'

Millie looked like she was about to burst into tears. Her foundation was streaked with tear tracks and there were dark smudges of mascara beneath her eyes. She dropped her head into her hands and pulled at her dishevelled brown hair. 'I'm so sorry, Soph.'

My mother squeezed my hand until it stung. 'It looks as though you were drugged at the party.'

It took several seconds for the meaning of the words to connect in my fuzzed brain. Then my heart plummeted into my stomach. 'Drugged?'

'We had no idea,' Millie sniffled. 'One minute you were fine and then the next you couldn't stand up. You kept forgetting where you were and you kept saying you wanted to go home.'

I tried to find them but the memories would not come. 'So you brought me here to get my stomach pumped?'

Millie frowned and traced shapes in the hospital blanket. 'We thought you were just drunk. Someone said you had taken some shots of tequila or something. So we sent you home with Robbie Stenson.'

My mother's features scrunched into a display of disapproval. 'Though Millie now knows she should have called me,' she said. 'Whether you were drinking or not, I still should have been called to make sure you were OK.'

'I'm so sorry, Mrs Gracewell! If I thought for a second someone had slipped her something, I wouldn't have just sent her home like that . . .' Millie broke into sobs that shook her frame with every heave.

My mother rubbed her back in large, circular movements. 'I know,' she said, trying to comfort her.

'What happened?' I felt like I was trying to recall something on the tip of my tongue, but the more I struggled, the more I seemed to forget.

'Robbie hadn't been drinking and he said he knew the way.' Millie was holding back, skirting around something; I could sense it.

My mother cut in, 'I got a call to say a young man had brought you to the emergency room. When I arrived they ran some tests and discovered traces of Rohypnol in your system.'

The word fell into the air like a ton of bricks. 'R-Rohypnol?' I stuttered. 'I was roofied?' Immediately my hands flew to my underwear.

'No, don't worry,' Millie interjected hurriedly. 'He got to you in time.'

'Robbie?'

My mother exchanged a glance with Millie. 'No, not Robbie. The nurse said a young man with tanned skin and dark hair brought you in. She says he wouldn't give his name.'

My head throbbed so hard I could barely think. Where did Nic come into all of this? And why was he being so secretive about his involvement?

'I don't understand . . .'

'He told the nurse he found you with a boy who looked as though he was trying to take advantage of you. He raised his concerns and the boy left. Then he brought you here when he realized what bad shape you were in.'

I felt my hand pinch beneath the drip. 'Where is Nic now?'

'He was gone when we got here,' Millie answered this time. 'The nurse said he stayed for almost an hour, though, while they tried to reach your mom. He wanted to make sure you were OK.'

My mother sat back in her chair and seemed to relax a little. 'Millie and I tried to contact the Priestlys, but they're unlisted. It would be a good idea to have a talk with that boy when we get out of here.'

'So where did Robbie Stenson go when Nic showed up? Was he the one trying to take advantage of me?'

Millie shrugged, her eyebrows knitting themselves together in confusion. 'I guess Nic thought he was trying to kiss you. I thought Robbie might have a crush on you, but I didn't think he'd do something like that when you were so out of it. I mean, you'd vomited twice before you left my house.'

I winced – I didn't remember that.

'Alex has been trying to call Robbie all morning to find out what happened,' Millie continued. 'Maybe Nic just freaked out when he saw the two of you together.'

Memories of how Nic had reacted jealously to Alex at the basketball tournament tugged at my brain, but I was still washed out and confused. I couldn't remember meeting Robbie Stenson last night, though I had a vague recollection he had been at the party somewhere among the crowds.

'So who was it?' I asked, growing hot with anger. 'Who put the Rohypnol in my drink?'

'We don't know, Soph. You were the only victim, as far as we can tell.' Millie could barely look me in the eye. 'Alex says it might have been a cousin of one of his friends. He was mixed up in something like that a couple of years ago. He wasn't even invited in the first place, and now we can't track him down.' Millie's voice turned quiet. She rubbed her eyes, smudging her eyeshadow until she looked like a panda. 'It's all my fault, Soph. I'm sorry for letting the party get so out of hand.'

'It's OK,' I offered, hoping it would ease her guilt. 'It could have been worse, right? I didn't come to any harm.'

'Yes, thankfully,' said my mother.

I clamped my eyes shut and concentrated. I was dancing. I was in the kitchen. I was with Millie. And then, nothing. 'I'm trying to remember.'

My mother rubbed my arm. 'Sweetheart, the doctor says it's unlikely you'll regain your memory of last night. There is a possibility of flashbacks, but they probably won't have all the answers to what happened. We're determined to get to the bottom of it, though. The police will want to speak to you now that you're awake, and we'll talk to this Robbie boy when he surfaces, too, I promise.'

'We'll figure it out,' echoed Millie.

I glanced at the needle in my hand and felt a heightened awareness of the cold liquid entering my body, drip by drip. 'When can I get out of here? Hospitals give me the creeps.'

As if right on cue, a heavyset nurse with short ash-blonde hair sashayed into the room. 'How are you feeling?' she asked.

I had the vaguest feeling I had heard her voice before.

'Confused and headachy,' I told her.

Without looking up, she launched into what seemed like a perfectly rehearsed speech. 'The Rohypnol is leaving your system and the worst of its effects have subsided. You're going to experience residual headaches and possible nausea for another day or two, but after that you should be back to normal. The doctor says you're ready for discharge when you feel strong enough.'

'I'm strong enough.'

The nurse pulled the corners of her plump lips into a frown. 'In the future, I would caution you to keep your drink with you at all times and to have it covered when you're around people you don't know well.'

I opened my mouth to argue, but stopped myself. I was furious, but not at her. I was angry at everything: at the person who'd drugged me, at the boy who'd tried to kiss me when I was so out of it, and at Nic for leaving me here with my mounting confusion.

First, he speeds away with his brother, ditching me in a deserted street, and then he turns up out of nowhere to rescue me, but leaves me with no clue about what happened. Even in his absence, he was still playing games with my head, and one way or another, it had to stop.

CHAPTER FIFTEEN

THE WARNING

I sat with my elbows on the table, watching my phone. It vibrated against the wood and made the peas on my plate quiver. The number on the screen was Jack's.

'He's not going to stop calling.' My mother's words squeezed themselves out through a mouthful of dried pork chop.

'I'll deal with it tomorrow.' I wanted to talk to my uncle, but it was late and I could barely keep my eyes open, save for the hunger. I swallowed the mountain of mashed potatoes in my mouth and scowled. 'Why did you have to tell him so soon anyway?'

'I didn't tell him. I told Ursula because I don't want you going into work tomorrow, and when he called the diner, she told him about it.' My mother shrugged and popped a forkful of peas in her mouth.

My phone started buzzing again, exacerbating the headache that still lingered at the base of my skull. I picked it up and swiped my finger across the screen. 'Hi, Jack.'

'I'm outside, let me in.'

'What?'

'Open the back door.'

He hung up. I crossed to the kitchen window. He was just a shadow lingering by the bushes, carefully out of range of the motion detector, so I could barely make him out at all. Where did he come from?

'Is he here again?' My mother's voice was teeming with bewildered disapproval. She stood up. 'What is he doing?'

I unlocked the door and he slid inside, shutting and locking it behind him.

'Sophie,' he panted, his cheeks blotted with circles of pink.

'Where did you just come from?'

He waved my question away and crushed me into his shoulder so hard I thought I would lose my breath. I hadn't hugged Jack since I was a child. I was used to him showing his affection in other ways – expensive presents, a shift off at the last minute, or random phone calls. But there was something about the hug that made it better than all that – I felt protected. 'I'm so glad you're safe,' he said.

He released me and I stumbled backwards, my hand clutching my chest. I was getting a tight feeling in the base of my throat. I swallowed it, hoping it would go away, but the way Jack was looking at me with my father's eyes, so full of worry and relief, made me want to cry.

'If I had let anything happen to you, Mickey would have broken out of prison just to kill me,' he said, trying and failing to lighten the mood.

'What are you doing here?' I mushed the words together to distract myself from the lump rising in my throat. Behind me, my mother was hovering. I could almost feel the suspicion seeping through her skin.

Jack rubbed the buzzed hair on his head. He was unusually dishevelled, his typical suave suit replaced by loose-fitting jeans and a nondescript black sweatshirt. He didn't look half as important, or affluent, as he usually did. 'I've been calling you all day, Persephone.'

I grimaced. He must have meant business. 'I was in the hospital.'

'I heard. I was going out of my mind with worry.'

'You and me both,' said my mother. She drifted over to the sink and started to fill the kettle for tea.

'How are you feeling?'

'Where have you been?' I asked at the same time.

Jack rubbed his eyes. 'All around the state,' he replied wearily.

'Doing what?'

'Business things.'

He was being curt. He never talked to me about his other business ventures. I knew it had something to do with investments and interest rates, which was why I never bothered to press him about it. The boredom would have overwhelmed me.

'Are you back now? In Cedar Hill?' I was surprised at how childlike the hopefulness in my voice sounded, and felt embarrassed because of it. I had obviously missed him more than I'd realized. He was the only real male presence in my life, and without him, it felt emptier than it should have been.

He shook his head grimly. 'Not yet. Not completely.'

My mother had been busying herself at the stove. She passed a mug of peppermint tea to Jack. He took it with an arched eyebrow for good measure.

'Thank you, Celine.'

'Before you ask, there's no booze in it.'

I winced. It had been going so well. He took a sip without breaking eye contact with her, levelling whatever his response would have been for my benefit.

'Couldn't this visit have waited until a more reasonable hour, Jack?' My mother's voice was edged with disapproval. 'Do you always have to do things in the dead of night?'

He ignored her this time, setting his mug down on the table. 'What happened last night was really serious,' he said to me. 'And on your birthday, no less!'

'I know,' I said, biting my lip to stop it from wobbling.

'Do they know who spiked your drink?'

'No,' I responded, feeling tired of the same question already. The police had already interviewed me at the hospital, and that hadn't exactly been helpful. It's not like there were any leads, and I was pretty convinced I would never regain full memory of the night. I knew, too, that Robbie Stenson, whenever he resurfaced, was going to avoid me for ever. He had finally texted Alex back to say he was out of town for 'family reasons,' and that he didn't realize how out of it I had been. He actually thought I *liked* him and *wanted* to kiss him, and he was sorry my 'boyfriend' got so angry about it and interrupted us. If he was so apologetic, he could have texted *me*, but he didn't even bother. And the only other person who had any knowledge of the forgotten parts of my night was my 'angry boyfriend', Nic, who was already doing a trophy-worthy job of avoiding me.

'Was it someone at the party who spiked it?' my uncle Jack continued his pointless interrogation.

I gave him the same answer I gave the police. 'Yeah, but there were so many people there, it could have been anyone.'

Jack nodded thoughtfully. 'Was there anyone you didn't recognize? What about that new family on Lockwood Avenue?'

'No,' I replied resolutely. 'In fact, if it wasn't for that family, I might have ended up in way worse condition.'

'What?' he snapped, the softness in his voice disappearing.

'One of them found me on my way home and brought me to the hospital.' I left out the part about Robbie Stenson; I didn't want my uncle thinking about me kissing a boy. Besides, I could barely think about it myself without feeling my skin crawl.

Jack set his mouth in a hard line, squaring his jaw. 'How do you know he wasn't the one who drugged you in the first place?'

'What are you talking about?' I didn't bother to keep the mounting irritation from my voice. I would not let Jack taint this good deed with his preconceived notions of Nic's family. 'He didn't drug me. He wasn't even at the party!'

'I don't know,' Jack grumbled. He looked to my mother, but she was staring past him, evidently fed up with his visit. She had done her best; she had lasted four minutes.

I released a sigh that turned into a yawn. 'Even if he *did* drug me by *magical intervention*, then why would he bring me to the hospital and get them to call Mom?'

'I'm sure there are ways he could—'

'Please,' I said. 'Just stop. You're being paranoid.'

'It's exhausting,' added my mother, her voice clipped. She folded her arms across her chest and moved closer to me.

I covered my mouth, stifling another yawn.

'OK,' Jack conceded. 'I'm just worried, Sophie. Can you understand that? I want to make sure you weren't targeted.'

I may have been tired, but I wasn't too exhausted to register the oddness in my uncle's statement. 'Why would someone target me?'

My mother bristled beside me. Her tolerance for Jack's paranoid mutterings had run out a long time ago. After all, it was this habit that had led my father into the mess that had gotten him thrown in prison. 'What are you talking about?'

'I don't know,' he said, more to himself than to us. He dragged his hands across his face and through his hair. I surveyed him: his bloodshot eyes, his week-old stubble, his blotchy skin. Even his lips were pale.

'Sophie's OK, Jack,' my mother said, biting back whatever else she might have wanted to add. It was clear he was troubled about what had happened to me, and there was no point antagonizing him for it. 'I think you need to get some rest. We all do.'

'OK,' he relented. 'I'll go.'

He smiled at me then; it was a sweet, hopeful sort of smile with just a shadow of something darker.

'When are you coming back?' I sounded like a child again, but I couldn't help it. I wanted my uncle close by. He was the unpredictable, wilder half of my calm, measured father, and right now he was doing his best to be both of them for me. He might not have been succeeding very well, but we were still bonded, he and I. And even though my mother would never dare admit it, without my father, we all needed each other.

He ruffled my hair. 'Soon,' he said gruffly. 'I'll call you.'

He paused with his hand on the door. 'And remember what I said. Keep to yourself.'

'I will.' I lied easily this time. Jack's paranoia had only made me more determined to find out exactly what was going on around me. And I suspected some of those answers were in the Priestly house.

CHAPTER SIXTEEN

THE MISUNDERSTANDING

After two days, I had almost fully recovered and was ready to begin my investigation.

I wasn't surprised that Nic hadn't tried to contact me after I was discharged from hospital, because nothing Nic did or didn't do surprised me any more.

I walked to his house in the early afternoon. Pausing outside the wrought-iron gates, I surveyed the mansion with a growing sense of foreboding. There was only one car in the driveway, and suddenly I felt horrified at the thought of coming face to face with any of Nic's other family members. After all, I was still a Gracewell – whatever terrible thing that meant to them – and there was nothing I could do to change that.

Steeling myself, I marched through the open gates and crunched along the gravel driveway. When I reached the red front door, I rapped on the knocker and edged back into the driveway, waiting nervously.

After what seemed like an eternity, the door was unbolted in three metallic thumps, and heaved open to reveal a statuesque figure, darkened by the shadowed hallway behind him. But I knew that outline almost as well as I knew his voice.

'Sophie?' Nic hovered in the doorway, immaculate in faded jeans and a white T-shirt. His feet were bare.

'Hi,' I ventured, watching him clench and unclench his jaw. 'I want to talk to you.'

Anchoring his hands on either side of the door frame, he leant out at an angle and searched the emptiness behind me. 'Sophie,' he said again, but softer this time. 'What are you doing here?'

By the way his eyes searched mine, I knew there was still something between us. The air around us pulsed, and I decided to cut to the chase before it consumed me. 'You don't have to play dumb about the other night.'

His expression turned, his eyes growing. He stepped forwards, slowly, then stopped, wavering, like he was fighting the urge to come to me. 'What are you talking about?'

'The nurse told my mother about you. I know you asked her not to, but she did, so you don't have to lie about it.'

He wasn't stalling any more. He came towards me, bare feet on the gravel. He dropped his voice to a whisper and placed his hands on my arms, gently pulling them – and me – into him. I watched his hands on my skin and my lips twisted in confusion.

'Sophie.' His eyes locked on mine. 'I have absolutely no idea what you're talking about.'

'What? You didn't bring me to the hospital the other night?'

At the mention of the word 'hospital', confusion burnt up into anxiety. 'Why were you in the hospital?' He scanned me up and down. 'Did someone hurt you?'

'You really didn't rescue me?' I asked, suddenly feeling embarrassed.

'*Rescue* you?' he said, horrified.

'But the nurse told my mother . . .'

'Sophie.' He moved his hands to my waist as his voice grew harder. 'Please tell me what happened to you.'

For a second, I could see the Nic I'd first met, standing in front of me. He was right there, within reach, until another figure appeared in the doorway behind him.

'Nicoli?' That was all Luca had to say to make his brother leap away from me like I was on fire.

'What is it?' I demanded. 'What's wrong?'

'I can't,' he half pleaded, backing up. 'I just can't.'

'I don't understand.' I shifted my gaze to Luca, who was leaning against the front of the house, folding his arms across his chest.

He looked through me. 'You should go back inside, Nicoli. Valentino's looking for you.' The last part sounded like a veiled threat, but I couldn't tell why.

Nic hesitated, his fists clenched tight. 'Luca, I'm not leaving until I make sure she's OK.' He was angry, and I was reassured by that, but not reassured enough. 'Something happened to her. She was in the hospital, and I need to know why.'

'I know,' Luca said, striding carelessly towards his brother so they could face each other straight on.

Luca was taller than Nic, but Nic was broader. I wondered who would win in a fight. And then I wondered how Luca knew

I'd been in the hospital.

'How?' Nic and I asked him at the same time.

'Because I brought her in.'

'You what?' I spluttered.

'Are you kidding me, Luca? Why the hell didn't you tell me?' For a second I thought Nic was going to lunge at Luca; take him down, and do us all a favour. But he didn't. He just stood there, seething. I watched his chest rise and fall.

Luca grabbed the back of Nic's neck, bringing him closer so he could mutter something in his ear, and when he pulled away, some of his brother's defiance had shifted.

'You'd better handle it,' Nic snapped before turning back towards the house. 'Because I can't be expected to stand by and do nothing . . .' His sentence died alongside his sudden retreat.

'Um, bye, Nic!' I called sarcastically to his departing figure, scolding myself for letting his desertion hurt me again. 'What a family of *freaks*,' I muttered, making sure it was loud enough for Luca to hear.

His eyebrows disappeared under messy strands of his raven hair. 'Is that what you came here for? To call me names like a child?'

I crossed my arms. 'I thought I was coming here to see Nic.'

He pursed his lips. 'Sorry to disappoint you.'

'You're not sorry.'

'You're right, I'm not.'

I fought the urge to stamp my feet.

'So did you launch yourself on an express mission to thank him and only him? Or do I, the actual person who helped you, merit some kind of gratitude?'

I bit back several curse words. 'This can't be happening.'

'Well, it is.' Suddenly Luca was pulling me by the arm until we were standing on the other side of the SUV, sheltered from the street's view and most of the house's windows.

'Get off me!' I snapped, shrugging him off. 'What's your problem?'

'What's *my* problem? Are you kidding?'

I stepped back, pressing myself against the SUV, and suddenly a memory flashed against my brain. *I was being mashed up against a stone wall.* I shook my head and it flew away. 'Why do you have to be such an ass?'

Luca lessened the gap between us by another half foot. 'Why did you drink yourself into that state the other night?' he countered viciously. 'Have you no regard for your own safety?'

'How dare you,' I snapped. 'You have no idea what you're talking about, so just shut up!'

'I was the one scraping you off the sidewalk!'

'For your information, I wasn't drinking!'

Luca curled his lip, and anger, like a shot of hot metal, rose in my bloodstream. Before I could stop myself, my hands were against his chest, shoving him so hard that he stumbled backwards. I landed against him, pushing him further and further. 'I was roofied, you ass!'

For a moment, we stood against each other, bound by the force of my anger and the sound of our mingled heavy breathing. Then, with exaggerated slowness, he grabbed me by my shoulders and pushed me away from him with ease.

I tried to focus on my breathing, to steady myself, but I was panting hard.

'I see,' he said at last. 'I didn't know.'

I shrugged, feeling deflated. 'I guess I should have been

more careful.'

He scrunched his nose in disgust. 'And he should have been a lot more respectful, regardless of what state you were in.'

I felt a lump form at the bottom of my throat, but I had been keeping it at bay for the last two days and I wasn't about to give in to my tears now, especially not in front of Luca. 'I don't remember anything,' I said, setting my jaw and looking at the patch of grass behind him. 'I'm still struggling to.'

'Don't.' Luca stuffed his hands into the pockets of his jeans. 'Some memories hurt when they hit you.'

'Are you saying it will hurt me to know what Robbie did?'

He shook his head. 'He didn't hurt you, OK? He was just some idiotic drunk guy trying his luck with a pretty girl.'

My eyes widened at the inadvertent compliment.

'I was just making a point about that guy,' Luca went on quickly. 'He was dumb, OK? He shouldn't have tried to take advantage of you.'

'W-where was it? Where were we?' I hadn't imagined talking about the night would be this difficult – and I definitely never thought I'd be talking about it with the obnoxious Luca Priestly – but I had to know.

'A couple of blocks away. I saw him with you sometime before . . .' He stopped abruptly and changed the direction of the sentence. 'I didn't like the look of him, so I drove around to make sure he wasn't doing anything he shouldn't be doing. And when I found you guys, I could see you were pretty out of it, so I decided to intervene.'

'What happened to him?'

'You don't remember?'

'No.'

'I just asked him to leave, and he did,' Luca said simply. 'He was very obliging.'

'So he just walked away in the middle of the night and left me with you, a person he barely knows?'

I studied Luca carefully, waiting for him to elaborate. The sun was making his blue eyes shine, so that he seemed almost friendly, but there was nothing friendly about the edge in his voice when he answered me. 'When I ask someone to do something, I usually don't have to ask twice.'

'That almost sounds like a threat.'

Luca just rolled his eyes and shrugged. 'Do you know who roofied you?'

'No.'

'I'd be interested to know, if that information comes to light.'

'Why?' I asked, feeling a bout of uneasiness.

'You're asking why I want to know the identity of someone who thinks it's acceptable to poison girls' drinks at neighbourhood parties?' His reply conveyed the *duh* sentiment.

'I don't see what difference it would make to you,' I told him plainly.

'No,' he said. 'You wouldn't.'

I could sense the hostility again, the chill I had gotten the night he ordered Nic away from me, and I couldn't stand it. He was so infuriating. 'What have you said to turn your brother against me?'

He shook his head. 'I'm not getting into this.'

'I deserve an explanation.'

'You should leave now. I think I've done enough for you, Gracewell,' he returned evenly. 'I'm not interested in helping you walk off into the sunset with my brother.'

Gracewell? So I wasn't even worthy of my first name now. 'What have I done to make you hate me so much?'

He rolled his eyes again. 'I don't hate you. I *nothing* you.'

His retort stung more than I thought it would. 'You're horrible, do you know that?'

He didn't even flinch.

'And arrogant,' I muttered. 'And smug.'

'Are you done now?' In an instant he had pinned me between his arms against the SUV. 'Let's get one thing straight, OK?' There was a savagery in his eyes. 'This is the last time I want to see you anywhere near this house, got it? When you walk home from work, cross the road. Don't look inside. Don't come in this direction. Don't even *breathe* in this direction. I told you I don't ask twice. If I see you around Nic again, even if you're just saying hi or trailing after him like a lost puppy, then I'll come for you, that chatterbox British best friend of yours, and your mother, and believe me, you're not going to like it. Do you understand me?'

I felt the horror infiltrate my features. Now I saw it. I finally saw the danger that Jack and Mrs Bailey had been warning me about. Not to mention the kind of attitude that must have put blood on Luca's shirt before. Maybe my paranoid uncle and the old busybody had been right about this family all along – certainly about Luca, at least. I wanted to say something defiant and witty, but he was looking at me like he was going to eat me, so instead I nodded like a zombie.

'From here on out, we go our separate ways. *Capisce?*'

My voice shook with anger and fear. 'You can't talk to people like that.'

He moved his hands away from the car and stepped back

from me again. 'Do you understand everything I just said, Gracewell?'

I wrapped my arms around myself and nodded.

'So we are clear?'

'Crystal.'

'Do I frighten you?' He tilted his head.

'Yes,' I said weakly. 'Are you proud of yourself?'

He looked at me for a long moment before replying. 'No, I'm not,' he said, so faintly I had to strain to hear him. Then he turned from me and made his way back to the house.

'Wait!' I called as the rational part of me screamed in protest.

Luca turned around slowly.

'You make a point of keeping your brother away from me and then you bring me to the hospital to make sure I'm OK. And you don't tell the nurse who you are in case I would think you are a *semi-decent* guy. I don't get it.'

'You don't have to get it. You just have to deal with it.'

'Why did you bother *scraping me off the sidewalk,* then? Why do you even care if I was roofied or not?' The question hurtled across the space between us. He blinked twice and his mouth dropped open into an O. For a second, he looked young and innocent, like his twin.

'Are you kidding?' He was dumbfounded. 'I'm not a monster.'

'You could have fooled me.'

He pinched the bridge of his nose and inhaled like he was about to say something. But then he didn't. Instead, he just shook his head. 'You should go, Gracewell.'

'I have a name, you know!'

He laughed, looking up at the sky, like the maniac he clearly was.

'It's Sophie. S-O-P-H-I-E.'

He continued to laugh, but when he returned his attention to me, his voice was utterly flat. 'Are you sure about that?'

I blanched. 'What do you mean?'

'You know what I mean.'

Before I could process the uneasiness grumbling inside me, he spoke again. This time his voice was disturbingly quiet. 'Don't you get it? You're a *Gracewell.* That's all you'll ever be to us.'

'What does it matter to *you* if I'm a Gracewell?' I demanded.

For an interminably long moment, he regarded me pensively. When he finally relented, it was with a determined exhale, like some internal decision had finally been made. He crossed the driveway and reached me in four strides.

'You really have no idea why you're not welcome here?' he hissed. 'Are you seriously that ignorant?'

I swallowed against the sudden dryness in my throat. 'What are you talking about?'

Luca frowned. I didn't understand his question and he didn't understand my response.

'*Cazzo.*' He studied me with an almost violent confusion – it pinched the hollows in his cheeks, making them gaunt. 'I'm not dealing with this.'

'I want answers!' I protested.

'You won't get them here.'

'Then where?' I said half-pleadingly, exasperation sinking into my voice.

Luca ground his jaw in slow clicks, whatever shred of patience he had for our conversation rapidly diminishing. 'Go ask your father, Gracewell. You probably owe him a visit.'

A familiar feeling of dread crept up my spine. *My father.* Everything always came back to my father. Of course it had something to do with him – I would never outrun what he'd done. I would never live it down. But there was something more to Luca's words, something deeper, and it was twisting my stomach. What had my father done to the Priestlys? Before he was arrested he never put a foot out of line. As far as I knew, at least.

Luca wasn't about to wait until I figured it out. He turned away from me once again, storming into the house, and slamming the front door with a deafening bang.

Feeling my cheeks prickle and burn, I looked up and caught sight of Valentino where I had seen him that first night. He was utterly still, his elbows perched along the windowsill as he looked down on me – on everything that had just happened. His face was solemn. Did he hate me too? Did he think it right for his twin to act like that?

He raised his hand and held it up, like a salute. I waved back, my arm feeling as heavy as my heart, and he smiled at me. It was a small moment of kindness – a soft tug at the lips, nothing more.

Then he was gone. And I was left bound up in the realization that if I really wanted answers, I would have to seek them from somewhere I had been avoiding.

CHAPTER SEVENTEEN

THE MEMORY

The following day I called in sick to work and took a bus to visit my father at the Stateville Correctional Centre in Crest Hill. I didn't tell my mother – she had been stressed out ever since the incident at Millie's party, and I figured my father's incarceration was the last thing I should bring up. Besides, I was going there for answers to a problem she seemed to have no knowledge of and, if it was as bad as I was anticipating, I wanted to keep it that way.

The Correctional Centre encompassed several concrete cell blocks and one roundhouse building fenced in by a perimeter with ten walled watchtowers. Beyond the walls, over two thousand acres of barren landscape surrounded the prison, keeping it far removed from anything that might have once resembled normal life for its nearly four thousand inmates, one of whom was my father.

It was the sixth time I had seen him since he had gone to prison almost eighteen months ago, and each time was harder than the one before. I tried not to dwell on the fact that I still had four more years of these visits ahead of me.

After presenting my identification and passing through the security check, I met my father in the visiting room. Around us, other prisoners sat on metal stools at white tables with their families; kids as young as one and two mingled with heavyset grannies and gothic teenagers. Prison guards lingered by the walls, eyes narrowed in pursuit of a forbidden embrace or any other illicit exchange, above or below the tables.

My father was paler than I expected and there were new dark creases under his eyes. I knew it could have been a lot worse. Since my father wasn't gang-affiliated, he was technically, in prison parlance, a 'neutron', which meant the violent inmates mostly left him alone. He could not, however, avoid the effects of meagre food and limited physical exercise. He was losing weight and losing sleep.

'How are you?' I began to chew on my pinkie nail – a nervous habit that usually returned in his company.

My father shook out his scruffy grey hair so it fell across his forehead and hid the faint bruises above his eye – they only *mostly* left him alone. 'Getting by, Soph.' He tried to smile, but it was crooked and yellowed. 'It's so good to see you.'

It took everything in me not to crumple in my cold metal seat. How did my father end up in this place? He was a shadow of the man who had raised me on sweeping fairy tales, swashbuckling adventure movies and faraway hiking trips. The worst things he ever did were yell at me when he lost his temper, forget to wash the dishes, or stay out too late with Uncle Jack every once in a while. He didn't belong in here with murderers. Even if he had killed a man.

'Dad, you don't look so good.'

'We don't get lots of fruit and vegetables in here,' he teased, but the joviality didn't reach his eyes. He leant forward and took my hand in his; I could feel his rough, calloused skin against mine. 'Happy belated birthday, Soph.'

'No contact across the tables!' shouted a nearby prison guard. I resisted the urge to slam my head against the table as we pulled our hands apart. I kept my gaze on my fingernails instead. 'Thanks, Dad.'

'So how is everything at home?' His eyes lit up with interest, brightening his face and pulling my attention away from the new lines that had formed around his mouth.

'Boring, as usual,' I lied, purposefully omitting the part about me being drugged at Millie's house party. I knew he would hear it from Jack or my mother soon, but it wasn't going to be from me.

'I started a new book yesterday . . .' he began.

I listened as he told me all about the books he had been reading. When he finished, I traded some of my own safe topics, including how my mother had gained some new clients in Lincoln Park and Millie's recently formed, hare-brained intention to go Greek-island-hopping after high school. We spoke about Mrs Bailey's weekly visits and touched briefly on my fast-approaching senior year. My father smiled and contributed at all the right times until the conversation drew to a natural close. As much as I wanted to pursue less threatening topics, I knew I had to prioritize my true intentions, because the visit would soon come to an end. As it was, I hadn't even scratched the surface of the real reason I had come to see him.

'Dad,' I interjected before he could launch into another ambling conversation. 'I have a question.'

He perked up in his chair and regarded me seriously. I loved that about him – he had always treated me like an adult worthy of respect, even when I was a small child. I knew that meant he would answer me as best he could. 'What is it, Soph?'

I decided to dive straight in. 'Remember I told you how a new family moved into the old Priestly place? There are five of them and they're all boys.'

His eyelids fluttered, but he kept his mouth closed in a hard line, waiting for me to finish.

'Well, I think you might know them.'

'Have you spoken to this family?' he asked, rubbing the stubble on his chin. 'Have they approached you?'

'Yes,' I said. 'I've spoken to them.'

My father buried his face in his hands and released a heavy sigh. 'Jesus,' he said, half muffled. 'Jesus Christ.'

That horrible sinking feeling came over me again, pricking at my eyes and sticking in my throat. 'Dad?'

'Sophie,' he said, but this time it was weary, and heavy with disappointment. He uncovered his face, letting his hands fall to the table with a heavy *thunk*. 'I thought Uncle Jack told you to stay away from them?'

'How do you know that?'

'Because he came to see me when he found out they had moved in. And we decided—'

'Hold on,' I cut in. 'What do the Priestlys have to do with our family?'

My father double-blinked, his mouth twisting to a frown. 'The Priestlys? Who are the Priestlys?'

'The—' I stopped abruptly. My whole brain shifted. *Think.* Who *were* the Priestlys? We had all just assumed the connection between Nic's family and the old house. After all, it had never been put up for sale, which meant it was inherited or passed down, surely. Even my mother hadn't questioned it. But now . . .

'Sophie,' my father said, his voice so quiet I had to lean towards him. 'I don't know where you got that idea from but they are definitely not Priestlys. They're Falcones.'

He might as well have punched me square in the face.

I slumped backwards in my chair. How could I have been so stupid? So ignorant? Luca was right. I was wrong. I had been wrong all along. They had never identified themselves as Priestlys – I had plucked the name from an old neighbourhood legend and never thought to check whether it was true. The realization came upon me in a succession of lightning bolts. The Mediterranean complexion, the Italian dialogue, the Falcon crest. Nic's face. *Those damn eyes.* The sudden *hatred.*

'Falcone,' I repeated, *Fal-cone-eh*, my voice sounding very far away as I tripped over the word that had just changed everything.

'Yes.' There was a heavy pause, and then, delicately, my father asked, 'Do you remember who Angelo Falcone was?'

It was a painfully unnecessary question. The name was seared in my brain for ever.

'Of course I remember.' I rested my head on the cold metal table. I had looked right at Angelo Falcone's picture fifty times, and yet it hadn't clicked. I had studied Valentino's portrait of him and hadn't even made the connection between his face and the man in all the newspapers when it happened. The man with Nic's eyes. *Oh God.*

I lifted my head. 'He's the man you killed.'

'That's right.' My father had placed his hands in his lap so I could no longer see them, but I knew he was fidgeting. If I concentrated hard enough, I could see the vein in his temple pulse up and down against his skin. He started to grind his teeth – it was a habit he had picked up in prison. For a long moment, neither one of us said anything, but every time his molars rolled against each other, I winced.

I would never forget that name or that day for as long as I lived. But we had never talked about it, not properly. Maybe it was time.

'It happened on Valentine's Day,' I said, breaking the silence. I had gotten a card from Will Ackerman that day at school. He had slipped it into my locker during recess, with his phone number scrawled on the back. It had a teddy bear holding a big heart on the front, and on the inside, a short poem about how he liked my hair. It wasn't the most impressive literary offering, but I could have died and gone to heaven right then. He had been my crush since forever, and all my friends were burning up with jealousy.

'Yes,' he said. 'It was Valentine's Day.'

'There was a storm,' I continued, my thoughts lost in another time and place. 'I had a headache so I took some aspirin and went to bed early. I was just falling asleep when Mom burst into my room. She was crying, and I couldn't understand what she was trying to tell me . . .' I trailed off. I could see it was hard for him to hear it. It was harder for me to say it, but I was going to, because someone had lost his life that night, and I was only beginning to understand the true gravity of it. Nic's father was dead. And all I had ever fixated on was how my father had been thrown behind bars because of a mistake he made when he was in the grip of fear during a dark, stormy night at the diner. 'Mom said you had been closing the diner on your own when a man ran out of the shadows and started yelling things. You thought he was going to try and rob the place, so you took out the gun Jack gave you for Christmas and you shot him.'

'And he died,' he finished.

'Yes,' I echoed. 'He died.'

'And it turned out he wasn't armed.'

God. 'Right.'

'And the gun I used didn't have a permit.'

It gets worse. 'Oh.'

'I shouldn't have been carrying it,' he said, frustration spilling from his voice. 'But it was late and I was nervous. Your uncle had warned me about the gangs around Cedar Hill at that time and I thought I needed the extra protection. I thought that man was going to attack me.'

'So you shot him.' My expression was unreadable. Inside, I was ice cold. 'And now you're doing time for manslaughter while Angelo Falcone's sons—'

'—are living in Cedar Hill beside my daughter,' he finished, biting down on his lip before a curse word slipped out.

I was clenching my fists so hard my nails were digging into my palms. 'And you didn't think to *share* this *massive* piece of information with me?'

'Jack and I didn't want you or your mother panicking about it.'

I almost laughed at the absurdity of it. 'So you thought it would be better if one of Angelo Falcone's *sons* filled in the blanks?'

'I thought Jack would make sure you stayed away from them!' he countered, his mounting anger beginning to match mine. If we kept this up, I'd be asked to leave by one of the prison guards.

'You should have told me,' I said, lowering my voice. 'I wouldn't have freaked out. I could have handled it.' *Probably. Maybe. Eventually.*

'OK, what if you weren't afraid, then?' he said. 'There was always the chance you might approach them, to try to apologize or make amends for what I did. I know you, Soph. You've got a good heart. It's not foolish to expect something like that from you.'

'That's crazy, Dad!' Maybe it wasn't, but I was so riled up I wasn't going to consider the chance he might be right. 'And what about them staying away from me?' I hissed. 'They came into the diner right after they moved in! A less cryptic heads-up would have been nice. I thought Jack was just being weird!'

My father shook his head and sighed, his expression defeated. 'Maybe we should have gone about it differently,' he conceded.

'Yes,' I said. 'You definitely should have.'

He watched me quietly for a moment. His eyes grew big and round until they dominated his weathered face; there was barely any blue left in them now, just stormy grey. 'Sophie, now that you know the truth, please stay away from the Falcones, like Jack told you. There's no knowing how deep their resentment towards me runs, or why they're back in Cedar Hill again.'

'OK,' was all I could muster. I was too spent to argue any more. And besides, it's not like the Falcones were clamouring to hang out with me anyway.

'They're a dangerous family in their own right,' he continued, his breath hitching.

'What's that supposed to mean?' I vaguely remembered something from the time it happened – Angelo Falcone wasn't exactly a stand-up citizen, but I could do with a refresher course on the details, considering I had deliberately avoided reading anything in-depth about my father's victim.

'It means I don't like any of this,' he said, and now there was panic pouring from his expression. Panic I could tell he had been trying to hide from me. 'I don't like that they're near my daughter and there's nothing I can do about it.'

You've already done enough, a part of me wanted to say, but I couldn't be cruel. 'They're just boys,' I said. 'They're the same age as me.'

'Five minutes!' shouted a stocky prison guard standing three tables over.

My father started wringing his hands. 'Will you stay away from them? Please be careful. I'll speak to Jack about this.'

'They're just boys,' I repeated.

He closed his eyes and made an attempt to calm himself. 'This is what prison does to you.' When he opened them again, his face was still creased with worry.

I nodded, feigning understanding. 'Do you think they're back for something?'

'I don't know,' he said quietly. 'I honestly don't know.'

Out of nowhere, the memory of the black-ribboned honey-pot dropped into my mind. I shook it away.

CHAPTER EIGHTEEN

THE ANGEL-MAKER

When I got home, I told my mother I was going to bed with a headache. Fighting the urge to ignore everything and force myself to sleep, I pulled out my father's old laptop and typed 'Angelo Falcone, Chicago' into Google. I found an article from the *Chicago Sun-Times* dating from two Februaries ago, and clicked on it, and suddenly I was drowning in a sea of nausea and incredulity.

A 'WHO'S WHO' OF AMERICA'S INFAMOUS FAMILIES ATTEND FUNERAL OF MOB BOSS ANGELO 'THE ANGEL-MAKER' FALCONE

The funeral of notorious mob boss Don Angelo Falcone took place on Tuesday, February 18 at Holy Name Cathedral, Chicago. Falcone, who was dubbed 'The

Angel-maker' due to his alleged position as a prolific Mafia career assassin, was gunned down at 11 p.m. on February 14.

Falcone was outside Gracewell's, a local diner in the Cedar Hill suburb of Chicago, when he became involved in an altercation with the owner of the establishment. Falcone, who was unarmed, was shot twice in the chest. He died instantly. Michael Gracewell, proprietor of the diner, remains in custody and is awaiting trial. Despite Falcone's position as a Mafia don, police do not suspect underworld involvement in his death.

Angelo Falcone has been well known to police since his ascendancy to the head of the Falcone crime family in the mid-1990s. Despite his arrest on several occasions, he proved questionably fortuitous in avoiding prison when key witnesses either disappeared or retracted their statements before trial. He is believed to be responsible for the recent brutal murders of two pivotal members of the Golden Triangle Gang, an infamous drug cartel based in the Midwest, among others.

Plain-clothes police officers and members of the FBI were among the crowds outside Holy Name Cathedral on Tuesday. While trouble was not expected due to a tradition of respect shared by Mafia families during funerals, law enforcement officials attended to ascertain who might succeed Angelo Falcone as head of the Falcone Mafia dynasty. The identity of the underboss was unknown at the time of Falcone's death.

Police believe that Angelo's younger brother, Felice Falcone, may now succeed him. In a move that seemed to support this assertion, Felice Falcone (pictured above) briefly spoke to reporters while other mourners remained tight-lipped after the service.

The suspected current boss of the Falcone Mafia family said about the deceased: 'Angelo was a true soldier of God. There is no doubt in our minds that he will be rewarded in heaven for his good work here on earth. He goes to Our Savior with honour and dignity, a clear soul, and a noble heart. We will miss him dearly, but he will never be forgotten.'

The 'Angel-maker' was laid to rest in a black marble coffin in the family mausoleum in Graceland Cemetery.

He is survived by his wife – daughter of the rival Genovese mob clan – Elena Genovese-Falcone and their five sons, Valentino, Gianluca, Giorgino, Dominico, and Nicoli (pictured below).

I stared, unblinking, at the final image. In the foreground was Nic: a slightly younger, glassy-eyed Nic, wearing a black suit. His hair was shorter than it was now, absent of the stray, curling strands that fell across his forehead. He was less filled out, making his cheeks seem almost gaunt, and his mouth was pressed into a hard line. He was balancing the front of his father's coffin on his left shoulder.

Luca was supporting the other side of the coffin, the same concentrated expression on his face, his eyes a haunting blue. Gino and Dom stood behind them on either side, their faces crumpled with grief. At the back, I recognized the tall bald man from the restaurant, and the unmistakable Felice, who wore a dark grey scarf and an equally grim expression. Valentino was at the bottom of the cathedral steps, his expression blank, his eyes empty. His mother – the tall, dark-haired woman from his portrait – stood beside him, a netted black veil covering most of her face. Her hand was clenched firmly on Valentino's slumped shoulder as he watched his brothers carry their father away.

I clasped my hand over my mouth to try to keep from vomiting. There was so much to take in, but it was coming at me all at once, like bullets of reality. My father had killed the man in that coffin; he had widowed that weeping woman; and he had taken Nic's father away from him for ever.

But Nic's father was a killer – a notorious mob boss, an *angel-maker* – whose legacy hung over his family like a black cloud. And now Felice was in charge, whatever being 'in charge' even meant, and suddenly he didn't seem harmless or quirky, but terrifying.

My thoughts began to spiral and before I knew what was happening I was sprinting to the bathroom. I stayed there for a long time – curled around the toilet, gasping as every heave shook me violently, as if trying to remind me that my understanding of life in Cedar Hill had changed for ever.

CHAPTER NINETEEN

THE UGLY TRUTH

I stood on the sidewalk, trying to pull my feet away from the mush that rolled over them. I was sinking. A falcon dropped from the sky, circling at close range. It pecked at my eyes until blood began to pour from my pupils, blinding me.

Ping! I blinked hard, and in the sudden darkness I saw my father, crumpled in a heap, his head cradled in his hands. I called out to him, but he was fading from me, and the harder I tried, the more my lungs burnt.

Ping! I woke up, sweating and gasping for air. Behind my curtains, something was bouncing off the window. I grabbed my phone from the nightstand and lit up the screen. It was 1.48 a.m.

Ping! I slipped out of bed and crept up to the window. A tall, dark figure bent low to the ground and picked something out of the untended grass. He lifted an arm into the air, taking aim at the spot where my head was. He paused when he saw I was standing where the darkened curtains had been just seconds before, then dropped the pebble from his hand.

I opened the window and a rush of warm summer air hit my face.

'Sophie?' He came closer, setting off the light censor above the kitchen window.

'Nic?' I closed my eyes and flinched, remembering everything at once. The memory of the funeral photo flashed inside my head, along with the word 'Mafia'. Nic's father had killed people, and my father had killed him.

I wondered what good would come of me going to Nic, looking him in his dark eyes, and seeing the hurt behind them. Hurt he must truly hate me for.

'Sophie,' he said again. 'I need to talk to you.'

I swallowed hard, hoping my voice wouldn't crack. 'OK – I'll come down.'

I flicked on the bedroom light and unearthed a pink cardigan from the floor, wrapping it around me before skirting downstairs. When I reached the backyard, Nic was standing at the back of the garden in the dark, waiting for me.

The light flickered back on as I walked towards him. His expression was inscrutable, his gaze fixed on me.

'Hi,' I said, reaching him. I cradled myself, waiting, as the darkness enveloped us.

'You're probably wondering what I'm doing here,' he said.

'Among other things.' I didn't look at him directly. There was too much guilt inside me and if I looked him in the eyes I knew it would explode right out of me.

'I had to make sure you were OK. Luca told me what happened . . .' He trailed off, then cursed under his breath. 'And I didn't want to leave things like this, not the way my brother made them. He was wrong to say that stuff to you, Sophie.'

I chewed on my lip until it stung. 'I'm not sure what else there is to say.'

'Will you at least look at me?' He inched forward until I could see his feet.

I shook my head, keeping my attention fixed on the grass. There were too many emotions bubbling inside me. I had to keep it together or else I would lose it entirely. I had to focus.

'Sophie, please . . .'

'I can't.' My throat bobbed up and down. I shut my eyes to stop the tears, but I could feel them welling up, ready to fall. I didn't have enough resolve to hold it all in, not any more.

'Why not?' he murmured.

'How can I look at you knowing what I know now?' I lifted my chin and stared at his chest.

'Sophie . . .'

'I visited my dad today,' I continued shakily. 'I know he killed your father. I know that's why you hate me.'

Nic reached out and pressed his index finger under my chin, nudging it softly until I lifted my head and met his eyes.

And then the dam that had been holding my tears for as long as I could remember burst completely. They fell hard and fast down my cheeks, shaking my body with every heave as my breathing hitched, gasping out for air.

Everything I had suppressed – my father's incarceration, my mother's pain, Jack's desertion, the Falcones' disdain for me, and my burning desire for Nic – was bound up in those heavy tears as they fell away from my face and rolled down my neck. I sank to the ground and pulled my body into a ball, hunching over and cradling my head in my hands as I wept uncontrollably for the first time since my father's arrest, not caring about anything but the pain that was springing free from my body at last.

In an instant, Nic was beside me, curling my huddled body into his and enveloping me in his arms until he was all around me. He rested his head on mine and whispered into my hair, 'Please don't cry, Sophie. Please don't cry.'

He held me for a long time, until the rage of tears subsided into quiet streams, and I began to catch my breath again. Then he guided my head into his chest and I buried it in his neck, inhaling his scent.

'How could you not hate me?' I mumbled into his skin. 'You'd be inhuman not to look at me and see what my father did.'

He stroked the back of my hair, his words soft against it. 'It's not like that, I promise.'

'He didn't mean it, Nic. It was an accident,' I sobbed quietly. 'He wouldn't hurt a fly.'

'I know,' he whispered. 'Please don't cry.'

'I'm sorry.' My words were so garbled I could barely understand them.

'You don't have to apologize.'

'Yes, I do. Luca said—'

'Look at me . . . Please just look at me.'

Slowly I raised my head, which was dizzy and heavy all at once. He wiped the wetness from my cheeks.

'Listen to me, Sophie. I want to be very clear about this. Luca had no business saying whatever he said to you. It has nothing to do with you or him, and he knows that. What happened with my father was an accident. It's over now.'

'But it's not over.' I thought of Valentino's drawings, and my father's gaunt, tired face. It would never be over.

'Well, it's not raw any more,' he replied carefully. 'And it's not something I blame you for. When I look at you, I feel happy.' He nudged my chin with his finger again. 'I don't care where you've come from or who you're related to, I knew from that first night when I held you that I didn't want to let go of you. But then you jumped away from me, so I had to . . .' He trailed off and smiled. 'And I felt empty.'

'I don't understand,' I whispered. 'Why would Luca say it if it wasn't the reason you were avoiding me?'

'Because he was trying to get rid of you,' he admitted. 'And he knew that would work.'

'I've never done anything to him,' I protested weakly. 'How could he hate someone he hardly even knows?'

'I know things changed when Dom told him who you were, but Luca doesn't hate you. He's just protective.'

I rolled my eyes, which were damp and sore from crying. 'What's he protecting you from?'

'It's not just about me.' Nic stroked my cheek again. I swallowed hard. I had never wanted to be kissed so badly in my life, and yet I had never felt this desperate for information before.

'Do you always do what he says?' I heard the bitterness in my voice.

Nic tightened his lips; it accentuated the shadows beneath his cheekbones and the circles under his eyes. 'Mostly.'

'Why?'

He pulled his hands away, knitting them together. 'It's complicated.'

'That's why you can't be around me any more,' I pressed, watching his hands and missing their warmth on my skin. 'Because he said so?'

Nic's expression turned rueful. 'You make it sound so simple.'

'Isn't it?'

'No.'

'I don't understand.'

Nic shook his head. 'I know you don't.'

Edging away from him until our bodies were no longer touching, I steeled myself and regarded him coolly. When I spoke again, I said the words as slowly and as clearly as I could so he would understand I knew more than he thought I did, and that I didn't need to be protected from it.

'I guess it must be a Mafia thing.'

The silence that followed was resounding. Nic reacted like I had hit him; his chest was rising and falling unsteadily, his mouth twitching uncertainly. I watched him carefully, keeping my expression blank.

'What do you mean?' he said at last, but the words barely made a sound.

I kept my voice steady. 'I think you know what I mean.'

He glanced over his shoulder, like he was afraid someone was going to jump out of the bushes. He turned his gaze to the grass beside me. A click of his jaw and then – 'I don't.'

'The Angel-maker.' It was a statement, not a question, and it made the balmy summer air seem colder once I'd said it.

He blinked hard. It had wounded him like I knew it would,

and I instantly regretted it.

'So it's true, then?' I asked, fearing and yet needing to hear him say it. 'Your family is part of the Mafia?'

He plucked a long, thin blade of grass and tried to split it in two. 'I do not deny it.'

A familiar wave of nausea rose in my stomach, but it was weaker this time. I had come to terms with most of my horror before falling asleep, and now, his confirmation of something I already knew was more like a dull punch in the gut.

When I didn't answer him he grabbed my hand with violent speed, like he was afraid he had lost me in that one quiet moment. I left my hand in his and pressed on, as carefully as I could.

'Does Felice tell you to hurt people? Do you answer to him the way you answer to Luca?'

'Of course not.' He seemed affronted by the implication, and I was glad of that. If he didn't answer to 'the boss', then he must not be involved in the things his father was accused of.

'What does it mean,' I asked, 'for you and your brothers to be part of the Mafia?'

Nic hesitated, and I could see he was trying to formulate his answer. 'Infamy.'

'And notoriety?' I remembered the article and shivered.

'Yes,' he said plainly, like it didn't bother him the way it would bother me. 'From birth we are stamped with our family's reputation, named after bosses from past generations, and raised with a strong sense of loyalty and honour . . .' He trailed off.

'Do you hurt people?'

He ran his hand through his hair until it hung loosely around his eyes, shielding them. 'It's not like that.'

'What is it like?'

Nic took both my hands in his. 'Sophie, there's a lot I can't say to you. I've taken a serious vow, and to break it would mean violating a code of silence upheld by every member of my family. But if you can trust nothing else, trust this: I am a good person, with good morals. My brothers and I are loyal, to the death. We have been raised with an understanding of right and wrong. We protect and serve our mother so that she may be happy every day of her life, we mourn the death of our father, and we attend church every Sunday to pray for his soul. I want to protect those I love and those who cannot protect themselves. But most of all, I want to make the world a better place by being in it.'

I felt a surge of relief. I didn't know what I had been expecting him to say, but this was so much better.

'You were born into your way of life,' I said, almost as if I were speaking to myself, 'but that doesn't mean you are part of it.' Nic inhaled like he was about to say something, but then he stopped himself. 'We are both living in the shadows of our fathers,' I said, realizing for the first time that it was true.

'I would never hurt you,' he said quietly.

'I know.' I laced my fingers through his. I had seen those hands hurt Alex, I had seen purple bruises along the knuckles, but I had to believe it was different with me. I studied our fingers, his olive skin against the paleness of mine, his grip sure and strong. It felt different. It felt right.

For a while, neither of us said anything. A lot of bandages had been ripped off our psychic wounds and we were both weary with emotion.

'Do you know why I can't be with you?' Nic said at last. 'I want you to know that it's not my choice to walk away.'

I was starting to understand that. 'When Luca found out who I was it changed everything, didn't it?'

'What's in a name, right?' Nic's expression turned rueful. 'It's not a good idea, our being together. Not with what's happened. I don't want to draw any unnecessary attention to you.'

'Am I in danger? They warned me about that . . .' I thought of my uncle, and I understood his concern. A Mafia family moves up the street from the family responsible for their boss's death. I inhaled sharply.

'Jack warned you?' The faintest undertone of animosity tinged Nic's words.

'And my father.'

'You're not in danger.' He tried to sound casual, but there was something new creeping into his voice now, straining it. 'But we think it's best that you're kept far away from us and some of the more . . . unhinged members of our family . . . at least for the time being.'

Nic fell quiet again. He moved his hands to my arms and began to rub them. I hadn't even realized I was cold until I felt the warmth in his touch.

'Should I be scared?' I asked.

'You don't have to be scared of anything,' he said quietly.

I smiled weakly. I was scared of losing him, but I couldn't say so. It wouldn't do any good.

He flicked his gaze to my lips. 'If I knew that night would be the last time I got to kiss you, I wouldn't have stopped.'

My smile faltered. Why couldn't he be someone else, *anyone* but a Falcone?

'I should go,' he said, like he was convincing himself and not me. But he wasn't going, he was leaning in to me. Our fingers were entwining and he was pulling me closer, sliding his arms around my waist.

Slowly, like he was fighting the urge to do so, he nuzzled his forehead against mine. 'But what if . . . what if, in this one moment, you're not Sophie Gracewell and I'm not Nicoli Falcone . . .' He trailed off and let his lips find mine.

Desire raged through me as I pressed my lips against his. His mouth was firm against mine, hot and unyielding, and when our tongues met, I lost myself, wholly and completely, in the passion of his kiss.

All too soon, in the heat of something so intense I found it hard to pull my lips away to breathe, the distant sound of a strange hum dragged us back into our earthly bodies. Breaking away from me and panting heavily, Nic fished his buzzing phone from the pocket of his jeans.

He placed a hand over his heart and clutched at his chest. 'Valentino,' he answered in a shaky voice. 'I'm on my way.' He clicked off and returned his attention to me, but the softness in his eyes was gone, and I realized with a jolt that I was looking at a very different version of Nicoli Falcone.

'You have to go,' I said, still breathing hard.

'I'm sorry.' He took my hand in his. 'Sophie, please don't speak about this with anyone. I've taken a vow and my family wouldn't be pleased with me breaking it, even just a little.'

'I won't,' I said without having to think about it. I could still feel the warmth of his kiss on my lips, and I might have promised him anything just then.

He lifted my hand to his lips, brushing them against it. '*Riguardati,* Sophie,' he murmured. 'Be safe.'

In a fleeting moment of madness, I considered running after him and pulling him back to me, but then I remembered Luca's warning. I didn't want him anywhere near Millie or my mother.

I trudged back upstairs and crawled into bed, thinking of that brief moment in the backyard when everything in my life was heady and blissful. It was just as I was dropping off into nothingness that I remembered something Nic had said.

Jack warned you . . .

How had he known my uncle's name? I had never mentioned it to him – I *knew* I hadn't.

I started to remember other things then, things that were only just beginning to make sense: Luca's strange questions in the diner the first time we met; Dom's interest in Millie's place of work, and how he'd dumped her once he'd gotten information about me; how Nic had been lingering around the diner that night we broke in, his car parked far away in the shadows, as if he was waiting for something or someone.

Suddenly I had a horrible feeling in the pit of my stomach that this certain something or *someone* was the very person who had been avoiding Cedar Hill since the Falcones first arrived – my uncle Jack.

That's when I realized there was more to the Falcone-Gracewell story than I'd thought. And that while Nic may have had feelings for me, they certainly weren't interfering with his ability to lie, and lie hard, to my face.

CHAPTER TWENTY
THE MOVIE

The initial aftermath of my night-time goodbye to Nic was harder than I thought it would be. The things he said had turned my world upside down and made me question everything I thought I knew about my family, and my heart. Every so often, sneaky memories of his dark eyes, the way his tousled hair fell, or how sometimes his smile tugged more to one side would creep into my consciousness and twist the knife deeper into my gut until it felt almost like a real pain threatening to split me in half.

I tried to ignore the unpleasant flickers as much as possible by doubling up on shifts at the diner, coming in early and staying late to cash out. A small part of me hoped Nic might come in, but I knew, deep down, that he wouldn't. I made sure to take the longer route home after work so I wouldn't have to pass the

Priestly – or *Falcone* – house and risk the horrible sinking feeling I had come to associate it with.

Things with my uncle had gone from strange to entirely bizarre. He was completely AWOL. I kept trying his new number, but he never answered. I texted him constantly, but he replied only once, and when he did, it was with two irritating words – I'm fine. More lies.

There was something wrong with him, I could feel it, but I still couldn't pinpoint it. He knew I had questions for him and he had no intention of answering them, through text or otherwise. Now, not only was he avoiding Cedar Hill, he was avoiding me too, and it was making me increasingly anxious. I was beginning to feel like I was screaming into a void and there was no one around to hear me.

'So, you really haven't heard anything from him?' Millie asked as we made our way through the stone archway at the entrance to Rayfield Park. It was outdoor movie night, and she had convinced me to go with her. She wanted me to at least try and put everything out of my mind for a few hours, before I went insane with worry. 'That's really unlike Jack.'

'I know.' Jack had made a promise to my father that he would always look after me, and the fact that he wasn't responding to my attempts to contact him was not a good sign. 'Something must be really wrong if he's avoiding his whole life,' I said.

We followed one of the winding stone pathways that looped around an expanse of open greenery bordered by puffed-out chestnut trees. Ahead of us, a group of pimply teenagers were carrying an array of blankets, picnic baskets and fold-up chairs.

'What if he's actually just run away with all the diner money?' asked Millie.

'What money?'

We both laughed.

It felt good to unwind with Millie after everything. Even though she knew what my father did to Nic's father, I tried not to feel guilty about neglecting to tell her certain details – *Mafia* details – about the situation. I had made a promise to Nic, and I didn't want to be someone who didn't keep promises. Plus, having Millie in the dark was better for her anyway; I didn't want to risk putting her in danger, especially after Luca's threat.

Millie tapped her chin. 'Well, your uncle must get the money for those fancy suits from somewhere.'

'Trust me. I've seen the books. It's not from the diner.'

'Dammit,' Millie lamented. 'And I was still holding out for that pay rise.'

We slipped in behind a throng of people who were following a connecting pathway that led to the park's central square. Up ahead, Erin Reyes and three of her vapid clones were flirting loudly with a bunch of guys from school. She caught my eye and smirked before flipping her hair in her customary I'm-so-much-better-than-you way. Her giggling intensified.

'That has to be a fake laugh.'

'Then it matches her nose,' said Millie, before dragging me away. She trailed her hand along the bark of a nearby oak tree as we walked.

'Trying to reconnect with nature?' I teased.

She nudged me and I teetered off the path, into the mud that lined it. 'Hey!'

'Just trying to get your mind off everything.'

'You're a real gem.'

'Thank you, Sophie,' Millie said, giving me a ridiculous curtsy.

Finally, we entered the square: generous patches of grass divided by criss-crossing stone paths and bordered on all sides by towering trees. At the north end, a huge screen had been erected.

'They have a taco truck this year!' Millie squealed, dragging me by one of the belt loops on my denim cut-offs. 'Let's sit somewhere around here.'

Scores of people were already relaxing on chairs and blankets in front of the giant screen. Families had come out with their children, who were running around with careless abandon, while others were arriving as couples sewn together at the hips and hands and elbows, carrying everything from cushions and picnic baskets to cans of beer and bottles of wine.

'Whoa, people must really love Monty Python,' I observed as Millie fanned out her blanket in a spot equidistant from the screen and the taco truck. She smoothed down all four corners, making sure it was perfectly straight.

'I still can't believe you've never seen this.'

When we were comfortably sprawled out, I emptied the contents of my bag until our makeshift feast was scattered across the quilt in streaks of sugar and chocolate.

Millie ripped into a bag of sour gummy bears and stuffed four into her mouth at once. 'I love these,' she said with swollen cheeks. 'Even though I'm not allowed to eat them.' She grinned, revealing tiny slivers of jelly that were now anchored to her invisible braces.

I laughed at her, and felt good about it. Since the night I fell for Nic, I had been tormenting myself with questions and wallowing in pity, which was doing more harm than good. I had to stop before I drove myself insane thinking of things I knew I couldn't change.

I broadened my smile and then felt it falter at the sudden look on Millie's face.

'But I thought he was out of town,' she said, her voice unnaturally subdued.

'Huh?' I followed her gaze and squinted into the growing crowds. 'Who are you talking about?'

'Robbie Stenson. He's here.'

CHAPTER TWENTY-ONE

THE GUN

I poured all of my concentration into the back of Robbie Stenson's stupid round head. Even though I still couldn't remember anything from that night, I felt angry just looking at him. It was like my skin was burning at the memory and my brain was struggling to catch up. Beside me, Millie's raucous laughter was buzzing in my ears. She was blissfully glued to the movie.

'Why aren't you laughing?' she asked.

I scanned the screen, where a bunch of British knights were harping on in comical French accents. *Strange*. 'I'm distracted.'

'What are you trying to accomplish by staring at Robbie's head like that?' Millie shovelled another handful of caramel popcorn into her mouth. 'Are you trying to make him explode with your mind?'

'I don't know.' I scrunched up my face in an effort to find the memory that was hovering just outside my realm of consciousness. 'I'm trying to remember.'

Millie stuffed another handful into her mouth and chewed thoughtfully. 'Don't,' she said, letting sticky kernels spew across the blanket. 'Just try and forget about it. You're here to unwind, remember?'

I did my best to follow her advice, but still, something wasn't right . . .

After almost an hour, the screen blackened to text, which signalled a short intermission. 'Taco?' I offered, feeling the need to stretch my legs.

'If you insist,' Millie replied, reclining. 'Get me two, please.'

I brushed the crumbs off my clothes and walked across the grass, taking my place at the end of the taco line; soon after, I was wedged between a girl with bright pink hair and an overweight man.

'This register is open!' a wiry voice shouted. A slew of people from behind me parted and shuffled into a second line, and suddenly I was standing almost side by side with Robbie Stenson.

He glanced at me and then quickly looked away, but not before I caught sight of the yellowing bruising around his eye sockets and along his thick jawline. What the hell happened to him?

The register chimed and the line moved forwards, taking me with it. Robbie caught up on his side; he was swirling a red cup in his hands, making the liquid slosh back and forth. He lifted it to his lips, smacked them against it, and began gulping down its contents greedily. The more I saw the red cup bobbing back and forth towards his mouth, the more I fixated on it.

Then it all came flooding back to me.

I remembered going into Millie's parents' room and coming face to face with Robbie Stenson. *I spilt some beer on myself* – wasn't that what he had said? But he had been holding two full cups in his hands. And he told me he hadn't even been drinking. I grimaced as the memory of the sweet, fizzy liquid glided into my mind, reminding me of how he had urged me to drink it and how, as we sat on the bed, I had become uncomfortable with the way he watched me. And then everything in my memory went dark. I realized, just as the register rang again – echoing the alarm bells in my brain – that Robbie Stenson had drugged me that night and then orchestrated our walk home together so that he could assault me. There was nothing innocent or naïve about it.

And worse, I felt sure that if Luca hadn't intervened when he did, things would have gone from bad to awful.

The line pushed forwards.

'Move,' the fat man behind me whined, but I couldn't move. I was rooted to the spot. 'Hey, come on.' He prodded me.

Bile rose in my throat. Beside me, Robbie was shuffling forwards, dangling the empty red cup back and forth in his hand. It had become a pendulum hurling explosive memories at me, one by one, and before I knew what I was doing, I was shoving him out of the line.

'What the hell?' His stocky frame stumbled sideways. He tripped and landed on the grass, clutching at his ribs.

'How could you?' I lunged again, but this time he was prepared. He pulled himself up and backed away from me, away from the crowds. I followed him.

'What the hell is your problem?' he spat through gritted teeth.

'You tried to assault me!' I hissed.

'No, I didn't,' he returned so evenly that I might have doubted the memory if it wasn't pulsating against my brain. 'I was walking you home when your boyfriend beat the crap out of me for no reason. You're lucky I didn't report him.'

So Luca *had* caused Robbie's injuries, and by the looks of things he hadn't held back. But stranger than Luca's likely status as a psychopath was the realization that somewhere beneath my conscience, I felt a wisp of satisfaction. Robbie Stenson hadn't gotten away with trying to violate me.

'I know you drugged me.' I was vaguely aware of hysteria rising inside me. Thanks to Luca Falcone, Robbie might have paid for what he did, but he hadn't paid for what he'd planned to do. 'You set up the whole thing! I remember what you gave me.'

Robbie snorted and his features shrunk into his face. 'Do you?' Still holding his sides, he rounded on me like a vulture circling its prey. 'Well, I doubt that would stand up in court.'

'So you admit it?' I returned furiously.

He shrugged and then I was hurling myself at him again. A sharp pain rippled through my left shoulder as I landed against his chest with a thud. He grabbed me, his hands digging into my ribcage.

'Stop it!' His face contorted in pain. His hands squeezed tighter in warning. 'You're making a fool out of yourself. Let it go.'

I struggled against his arms. 'Get off me!' I shrieked. I dug my nails into his fists as hard as I could until they snapped away.

'Fine,' he replied. 'Just get out of my face.'

I jumped back, widening the gap between us. 'You're a sick freak!' I shouted, raising a fist at him as adrenalin pumped in my veins. 'How could you do that to me? To anyone?'

Robbie's grin stretched into his bruised cheeks. 'Oh, come on. You must know that banging Michael Gracewell's daughter means serious novelty points.'

'You mean *raping*,' I spat, circling him.

'Don't tell me you're going to try and fight me?' he sneered.

He was the ugliest person I had ever encountered. 'I hate you.'

'Relax, Sophie. I wouldn't even touch you now.'

The way he said my name like it was some dirty word made me feel physically ill. 'You'll pay for this!' I watched with satisfaction as the colour drained from his face. His eyes grew wide and he hugged himself tighter. But I was wrong to think my words had suddenly started to scare him, because Robbie wasn't looking at me any more; he was looking over my shoulder.

Out of nowhere, a third voice joined our conversation. It was eerily calm in contrast to our heated exchange.

'*Ciao*, Robert. Long time no see.' I would have mistaken the dulcet tone as familiar – friendly, even – if I weren't so sure it belonged to Luca Falcone. I watched Robbie throw his hands up and recoil as Luca stepped out from behind me like he had just sprung up out of the grass. How long had he been there, listening? I turned around, searching for his brothers, but he was alone. 'I couldn't help but overhear your conversation,' he said calmly. 'I hope I'm not intruding.'

'Get the hell away from me, dude, or I'll call the police.'

Robbie's voice quivered an octave higher than usual and the smugness rapidly vanished from his face.

'Robert,' Luca said. 'I think you need to calm down. You seem very highly strung.'

'You broke my ribs!'

'Only a couple,' said Luca dismissively.

'What do you want?'

Luca's fake-friendly voice was almost more harrowing than his threatening one. 'I just want to talk to you about something, is that acceptable?'

He took another step forwards and Robbie stumbled backwards. 'I don't know you. What the hell would we talk about?'

'Doesn't your dad own a furniture business?'

Robbie's eyes widened. 'How do you know that?'

Luca took another step, closing the gap between them. 'It's common knowledge, right?'

'I guess.'

'And you work for him, don't you?'

By now I could only see the back of Luca's head as he made his way forwards, ignoring my presence completely.

'Yeah, I do,' Robbie said, sounding fractionally more confident.

'Good.' Luca crossed his arms. 'Let's put our little bit of history aside for just a second, OK? The past is the past, and I think we should move on from it. This is really none of my business anyway.'

Robbie nodded like one of those bobble head dogs on car dashboards.

'I'm in the market for some new furniture, believe it or not.'

'Really?'

'And I thought, to make up for our unfortunate run-in a little while ago –' Luca pointed his finger at Robbie's bruised face, twirling it round and round for added effect – 'Do you remember that?'

'Y-yeah.'

'And that?' He indicated towards his ribcage.

'Obviously,' Robbie hissed, cradling himself with his meaty arms.

'Well, I thought, to make amends, that I might send some business your way. I need a lot of stuff.'

Robbie relaxed his shoulders.

'I'm not a bad guy,' Luca continued, and I got the sense he was smiling – an event rarer than a solar eclipse. 'So why don't we talk some stuff over?'

'Now?' Robbie cocked an eyebrow. 'The movie's about to start again. Why don't we do it when I'm at work?'

'The matter is time-sensitive, so let's talk now.' Luca clapped his hand on the back of Robbie's neck. 'Come on.' He pulled him away from the park and towards the trees. 'Wave goodbye to Gracewell,' he prompted. 'She's going to be staying here.'

I sensed the warning in his words, but as I watched them disappear behind the taco truck, I found myself contemplating an unexpected dilemma. *The movie's about to start*, I reminded myself, yet my feet were leading me towards the trees and not back to where Millie was sitting on the lawn, waiting – impatiently, no doubt – for the tacos I now had no intention of buying her.

The way Luca draped his arm around Robbie's shoulders made them seem almost like friends, and I had to admit there was something undeniably convincing about the way he had spoken to him. I, unlike my assailant, was not dumb enough to fall for it. I knew, better than most, that Luca had no need for friends. Or furniture, for that matter. Whatever was going to happen in those trees was unlikely to be a business transaction – for Robbie, at least. But like a bona fide *idiot*, he let Luca lead him away, and I couldn't *not* follow them.

Hurrying my pace so as not to lose them completely, but keeping far enough behind that they wouldn't notice me, I slipped around the back of the taco truck just as the movie flickered to life over my shoulder. Up ahead, I could see Luca and Robbie disappearing between two overhanging trees. I hung back again, tiptoeing across twigs and dry leaves as I followed their voices.

After several minutes of sneaking around, their conversation reached me through a small clearing. They had stopped walking, so I did too. Between the break in the trees, they were standing across from each other; Robbie had his hands folded around his ribs, while Luca's were resting casually by his sides.

I crept closer.

'But I thought you wanted to know about furniture,' Robbie was protesting.

'I just remembered,' Luca replied. 'I don't need any furniture.'

'Then why are we—?' Robbie's breath was knocked out of him before he could finish his sentence.

I watched in muted horror as Luca slammed his fist straight into Robbie's stomach, making him crumple in half on to the ground. He rolled over on to his side and moaned into the dirt.

'We're here, Robert, because I heard what you said to Sophie.' Luca's voice was eerily calm. He stamped down on Robbie's foot, but the dirt muffled his scream. 'And if there's one thing I hate, it's drug pushers.' He rounded on him, obscuring him in his shadow, and kicked him hard in the shoulder. '*Especially* someone who drugs *a girl* and then tries to *rape* her.' He pulled his foot back, and this time he hurled it into Robbie's stomach. There was an audible crack. Robbie screamed into the dirt as Luca used his shoe to roll him on to his stomach. 'I mean, it was bad enough when I thought you were just trying to hit on her, but now?' He stamped down on Robbie's back so that he was spluttering into the dirt and weeds. 'Now you're the *lowest* of the low. You are *scum*.'

I started to stumble forwards, half paralysed by fear yet determined to do *something*. But my attempt to assist the sobbing bundle of cracked ribs was short-lived as another figure entered the clearing.

'Get up!' he roared, and his voice stopped me dead.

'Nicoli, I told you to stay behind!'

But Nic wasn't listening to Luca; he wasn't even looking at him. He was looking at Robbie's crumpled frame, his eyes full of hate as he charged.

'Get up, Stenson!' he yelled in a voice I barely recognized; it was like glass, and edged with a kind of rage I had never known. 'Stand up and look me in the eye or I'll come down there and cut you open!'

Slowly, Robbie heaved himself off the ground. He managed to half lean against a tree by sticking his fingers into the bark and bending his knees in front of him. He puffed hard as Luca moved away from them, clasping his hands behind his back and tilting his head like he was watching a puppet show.

I tried to move, but I couldn't. My legs were shaking violently beneath me and I had to claw against a tree to stop myself from falling to the ground in fear.

'I said *stand*,' Nic seethed.

'Nicoli,' Luca cautioned, but he didn't move. 'Be careful.'

Groaning, Robbie pulled himself up, the strain contorting his face. 'My ribs,' he sobbed. 'Please.'

Nic grabbed him and shoved him into the bark. Robbie's face was beginning to bleed. He closed his hands around Robbie's throat. 'Do you think it's OK to put your hands on someone who doesn't want your hands on them? How is this for you?' He tightened his grip on Robbie's neck.

'Nicoli,' Luca muttered. He stepped closer and put his hand on his brother's shoulder, like a chaperone. '*Stai attento.*'

'What is that?' Robbie gurgled as his face began to turn purple. 'Is that a—?'

A flurry of rushed movements followed, so I could only discern two things. The first was the appearance of a black metal object against the side of Robbie's head. The second was the sound of a click.

And then, in a measured reply, I heard Nic confirm everything I had just witnessed: 'It's a gun, you fucking idiot.'

Robbie tried to scream, but Nic moved the barrel into his mouth so fast it choked it right out of him.

'Listen up, you piece of scum,' Nic snarled. 'This is your final warning. I'll be watching you. If I ever hear of you attempting to handle drugs again, then you're dead. If you try to give a girl any kind of drug, requested or not, you're dead. If you attempt to force yourself on anyone ever again, you're dead. And if you so much as *glance* at Sophie Gracewell again, I'll rip your heart out and stuff it down your fucking throat. Do you understand?'

Robbie nodded.

'The police might not have enough to go on to convict you of attempted date rape, but I do. And I'm not a big fan of trial by jury, Stenson. So I'd advise you to use this final warning as a gift from God. Change your life. And if you so much as breathe a word of this to the police, you'll be shot by one of my brothers before you fall asleep. That, I can *guarantee.*' Nic leant forward in what felt like slow motion. 'Or maybe I'll just shoot you now and do the world a favour.'

I pushed my jelly legs forwards, intent on stopping whatever was about to happen, but Luca got there first.

'*Basta!*' he said, pulling Nic's hand away from Robbie's mouth; Nic let it drop willingly, but he didn't relinquish the gun, and Luca didn't force him. Instead, he kept his hand on his brother's shooting arm, so he couldn't raise it again. I stood frozen in my new spot, half in and half out of the clearing, watching Nic's chest rise and fall as he stared unblinkingly at Robbie's whimpering face.

Nic finally moved his arm away from Luca's hand, uncocked the gun and stashed it in the waistband of his jeans. The movement looked like second nature, and I found myself wondering whether he had been carrying a gun the last time he held me in his arms. He shook out his hair and stepped back, gripping his chest, and turned away from Robbie. 'Luca, get rid of him before I change my mind.'

Luca stepped forwards and slapped Robbie on the cheek in a bizarre show of camaraderie. 'You get all that, Robert?'

Robbie started to wipe the tears from his face with the back of his hand. 'I p-p-promise,' he faltered.

'Good.' Luca lifted his arm and pointed behind Robbie to where the rest of the sprawling park continued. 'Now run like your life depends on it. Because it does.'

And that's exactly what Robbie did. Without sparing another second, he pitched himself forwards and hurtled clumsily through the trees until he was just a dot hobbling into the darkness. When the sounds of his uneven footsteps had disappeared entirely, Luca removed his attention from the space between the trees and settled it on Nic.

'I told you to stay behind.' He sounded weary rather than angry, like he was used to this kind of behaviour.

'You told me he tried to take advantage of her. You didn't tell me he had *drugged* her!'

'I didn't know that then. And you shouldn't have been eavesdropping.'

'You shouldn't have expected me to stay out of it.'

'*Sei un pazzo*, Nicoli.'

'This is different.'

'You always say that.'

'This *is* different.'

'She's not yours.'

'She's mine to protect.'

'You would have *killed* him,' Luca hissed.

'He deserves it,' Nic returned evenly – casually, almost.

'What happened to laying low? You could have ruined everything. And I told you, it's not your concern.'

'*She* is *my fucking concern!*'

'She won't want to have anything to do with you now anyway,' Luca continued, a sudden airiness in his voice.

Nic snapped his head up; his eyes were frantic. 'Why not?'

I felt my heart constrict in agony as I realized what was about to happen; and it was too late, there was nothing I could do to stop it.

Luca raised his arm until he was pointing directly across the clearing. 'Because she's standing right there.'

Nic followed Luca's finger until his gaze found mine and, just like the night he discovered my name, horror possessed his features, warping them as we stood apart from each other, both of us heartbroken for different reasons.

'Sophie . . .' he whispered, but it was too late.

I couldn't speak. I couldn't even open my mouth I was so petrified. I started to back away.

He stumbled forwards.

'Let her go,' Luca cautioned. 'She's terrified.'

I faltered back into the shadows between the trees. My retreat turned to reckless abandon. I careened through the park, racing towards the flickering of the screen. When I passed the final scattering of trees, I sprinted around the taco truck, where I collided with Millie.

'Careful, Soph!' she screeched as I tumbled backwards and landed against the grass beside the taco I had just knocked from her grip. Groaning, she stuck out her hand and hoisted me up from the ground. 'Where the hell have you been?'

'We have to go,' I explained, springing forwards. 'If you knew what I just saw . . .'

'What's going on?'

'Come on!' I pulled her towards the grass. I threw everything back into my bag, watching the trees every few seconds for the reappearance of Nic and Luca. 'I'll explain everything when we're out of here.' And then I was off again, dragging Millie as I raced down the winding paths.

'What's going on?' she whined in between heaves. 'I'm. Too.

Out. Of. Shape. For. This.'

'Just come on!' I navigated our way back through the walkways until the entrance to Rayfield Park edged into view.

Before we passed through the arch, Millie stopped and clutched at her sides like she had been punched in the stomach. 'Stop,' she wheezed. 'I need. A minute.'

'Can we please just keep going?'

'I think. My feet. Are bleeding.' She brushed her hair away from her face, which was glistening with a fresh sheen of sweat. 'What's going on. With you?'

Before I could answer with an explosion of everything I had just witnessed, someone grabbed on to my arm and yanked me away from her.

'Hey!' I protested as Nic pulled me into him.

'Whatever you're about to say to Millie, don't,' he urged in a voice so low only I could hear it. He tightened his hands around my wrists and held them against his. 'Please.'

Behind us, Millie was noticing the sweat stains pooling out from under her arms and the bleeding along the straps of her sandals. 'Gross,' she moaned as she sank to the grass, panting.

'You can't tell me what I can and can't tell my best friend,' I snapped, shaking him off me.

'You promised,' he said quietly. 'That was supposed to mean something.'

'I promised when I thought you were an *inactive* member of the Mafia, which you *clearly* are not! This is completely different. I will not be bound by that!'

'Sophie,' he said, his voice full of strain. 'I really need you to be quiet about what you just saw.'

I could feel my face growing hot with anger. I grabbed his

shirt and pulled him around the side of the arch. 'You lied to me!'

His hands shot up in surrender. 'I didn't lie, Sophie. I just . . . left out certain things. Let me explain.'

I shoved him. 'You made me believe you were good!'

'I am good!'

'No, you're not!' I shoved him again. 'You made me think you were innocent. You made me believe you weren't part of all that crazy Mafia stuff!'

Cautiously, Nic removed my hands from his chest. 'I never said that.'

'You had plenty of time to set the record straight.' I wanted to slap him. It took every ounce of my self-control to curl my hands by my sides.

'I know.'

'But you didn't.'

Purpose and defiance flashed in his eyes. 'I didn't have enough time to explain everything. But I didn't lie to you. Everything I said was true, just not in the way you might have taken it.'

'I asked you if you hurt people! You said no!'

He came closer. 'I said it wasn't like that. And it's not. Everything I do is about protection.'

'Protection,' I scoffed. 'Is that what you tell yourself when you put your *gun* in someone's *mouth*?'

He pulled me into him. 'Listen to me.'

'Don't,' I cried, feeling the tears swarm behind my eyes. 'I'm scared of you.'

He recoiled like I really had slapped him. 'I told you I would never hurt you.'

'How do I know that?'

He stared at me so hard it took my breath away, and after an agonizing moment, he responded quietly. 'Because you're a good person.'

I glowered at him. 'That makes one of us.'

'I'm a good person too.'

'You just put a gun in Robbie Stenson's mouth,' I hissed.

'I'm sorry you had to see that, but it was inevitable.'

'*How* is an assault like that inevitable?'

His eyes darkened, but he didn't respond.

'You must know how totally unacceptable that was. I have to report it to the police.'

'Sophie, it was for *you*. How could I let him walk away from me after I found out what he tried to do to you?'

I backed away from him again. 'Are you insane, Nic? You know you can't just go around *pulling guns on people* for me. I can take care of myself!'

He pinched the bridge of his nose and sighed. 'That was a service to society. Stenson is the type of character who won't stop at just one girl. It was everything I could do shy of actually blowing his head off.'

I gasped. 'Can you not be so graphic?'

He scraped his hands through his hair. 'Sorry.'

'I don't think you are.'

He wasn't looking at me any more and I knew I was right. He wasn't sorry; he was sorry I had seen it. 'I know I have no right to ask anything of you,' he said, 'but please don't tell anyone about what you saw. It will make trouble.'

'No kidding. I witnessed a crime. And even if the victim was someone I hate, it still doesn't make it right. I won't keep it a secret. I won't be your accomplice.'

'Then wait at least.' He grabbed my hands and closed his around them before I could pull them away. I tried to avoid his dark eyes. 'Sophie, I'll break the vow. I'll tell you as much as I can,' he whispered urgently. 'I need you to understand who I am. Please just give me the chance to show you.'

'It's too late,' I said, but my resolve was as unsteady as my voice.

He moved my hand to his heart so I could feel it hammering in his chest. 'I'm not a bad person. I know you can feel it. I admit I lied to you by letting you believe what you wanted to. I needed you to feel happy and secure, and I didn't want to take that feeling away from you after everything you had discovered about our fathers. I'm not ashamed of who I am or where I come from, but I was afraid of you knowing about it and not giving me the chance to help you see what it really means. I was terrified that the truth would change the way you look at me. But you deserve it all, and I'll give it to you if you'll let me.'

My defiance was crumbling and we both knew it. I pulled my hands from him and folded them. I *knew* there had to be more answers, but I didn't think he would admit it so freely after lying to me for so long. Now, the way he was convincing me was working – he was pushing all the right buttons. He had me right where he wanted me. I hated it and I burnt for it.

'You get one chance.'

CHAPTER TWENTY-TWO

THE FALCONE CALLING

Nic offered me a ride to his house from the park but I decided to walk with Millie instead.

'Ah, a lovers' tiff,' she had assumed on our way home. She wasn't half wrong, but she wasn't completely right either. I didn't tell her the truth about the argument in Rayfield Park for the same reason I didn't tell her why I was going to Nic's house after we went our separate ways at Shrewsbury Avenue. I wasn't ready to organize my thoughts about everything, and until I did that, I wanted to make sure she would be safe. The less she knew, the better.

When I turned into his driveway, Nic was already standing in the doorway. 'You came.'

I approached him in silence. He stood against the open door so I could sidle past him. I tried not to notice when I brushed against him, but I could see it register on his face.

The front of the house was entirely different from the modern kitchen at the back. Now, I was hovering in the setting of every horror story I'd ever heard, and it was exactly how I'd imagined it.

A crystal chandelier, still covered in cobwebs, hung from the high ceiling. The wooden floors in the large foyer were discoloured and uneven, creaking with each step. Ahead, a grand staircase lined with a thick burgundy carpet turned sharply to the right and up towards the second floor, while panelled wallpaper fell away from the walls in tattered strips. The hallway continued down the left side of the stairs, branching off into a line of closed rooms with narrow doors. The right side was distinguished by huge, newly varnished doors with heavy brass handles.

'Sophie?' I turned to find Nic looking at me expectantly. 'Do you want to follow me through here?' He led me into a large sitting room, where two dark red leather couches rested around a stately fireplace.

I seated myself on one of the couches, Nic chose the other. I noticed, without an iota of surprise, that there was no TV, just a leather footstool, an old clock on the grand mantelpiece and a built-in bookcase that spanned the entire length of the far wall. It was filled to the brim with Dickens, Defoe, Twain, Swift, and every other great or intimidating novelist I could have imagined. Above the fireplace, an oil painting lorded over the room. It was some kind of avenging angel, rendered in sweeping dark colours and set in a gilded frame. It stretched the entire width of the mantelpiece.

'That's one of Valentino's,' Nic said, following my gaze.

'It's incredible.'

'It's kind of dramatic.'

Dramatic. The thought of Nic holding a gun to Robbie Stenson's head flittered across my memory. 'Well at least he puts *his* time to good creative use.'

Nic cleared his throat awkwardly.

'Well, I'm here,' I said, keeping my thoughts focused on what I needed to know. 'Start talking.'

He leant across the corner of his couch, pinning me with his eyes. 'What I'm about to tell you is not for the faint-hearted,' he said. 'Discussing my family like this is not something I do lightly, and I need to know that you won't use it against me. Against us.'

I hesitated, and he seized my silence.

'Once it's been said, I can't take it back, and I'm risking a lot already.'

I thought about it for a long moment, really considering what he was asking of me, and what he was offering me in return: the unvarnished truth. I didn't want to betray his trust, but I was afraid to offer my silence if what he told me was too big to handle. But I had to know. He wanted to let me in, he wanted to trust me, and despite everything, I wanted to let him.

'OK,' I said. 'I promise.'

'It won't be everything. It can't be.'

'I just need enough to understand, Nic.'

He watched me for a moment more, like he was trying to read something in my eyes. Then he leant back and sighed, finally, after all this time, surrendering. 'Sophie, my family and I are in the business of protection. And what that means is, sometimes we have to hurt people, and sometimes we have to kill people.'

And there it was – out in the open at last. My unspoken fear had come to fruition. Like father, like son: Nic was an Angel-maker too. I covered my mouth with the back of my hand and concentrated on steadying my breathing. I couldn't speak. I felt sick.

'Let me explain,' Nic said. He reached out to me, but I edged away and he dropped his hand. And then he hit me with a fresh bombshell: 'We only go after people who deserve to die.'

I gaped at him. 'Is this some sort of sick joke?' I managed, my mouth still covered by my hand. 'Because it's not funny.'

He just looked at me – defiantly standing by the craziest thing I had ever heard come out of his mouth.

'You mean you go after people like Robbie Stenson?' I pressed after a beat.

He nodded – calmly. Too calmly.

'Would you have killed him if Luca hadn't been there to stop you?'

He didn't miss a beat. 'Without hesitation.'

I thought about getting up and bolting, slamming the door behind me and running far away. But I didn't, I couldn't – not when there was more to know. 'Can't you see how crazy that is?'

This time, Nic looked away from me, his expression twisting. 'He deserves worse than what he got . . . if Luca hadn't been there . . .'

'You'd probably be in jail,' I finished dryly.

'And he'd be six feet under.'

I dropped my hands and ground them into the leather to keep my anger at bay. 'That's what the police are for, Nic. Not normal gun-wielding citizens like you and Luca.'

There was a chasm between us. I studied my lap as the

bitterness stung my throat. Even though Nic had never owed me anything, I felt betrayed, wounded by the truth of his character, and afraid of the feelings that still lingered for him deep down in spite of it.

I thought about leaving again. As if sensing my unease, he slid on to the couch beside me so that his leg brushed against my bare thigh, and I felt charged by his nearness. He rested his elbows on his knees and turned so that all I could focus on was the passion in his voice and the fire in his eyes. 'Do you think Robbie Stenson would have never tried to hurt someone again just because his attempt didn't work on you?' he asked, his voice subdued. 'Because I don't. Someone had to put him in his place before he did what he tried to do to you to someone else. Someone who might not have been as lucky as you were. This is the kind of thing we do, Sophie.'

'What do you mean, the kind of *thing* you do?' I reeled. 'Are you trying to tell me your family is some sort of self-righteous vigilante force?'

Nic laughed unexpectedly; it was a foreign, misplaced reaction, and I wondered how he could be so light-hearted considering what we were talking about. 'When we decide to combat a certain problem, we don't do it within the confines of the law. For us, it's that simple. There's an entire underworld of crime that can't be accessed by the police. Criminals who won't hesitate to kill anyone who gets in the way of profit – the kind of people who have more judges and lawyers in their pocket than cash. They don't play by the rules. *They're* the kind of *things* we deal with.'

I fell back against the couch, groaning under the weight of everything I was being asked to understand. 'But why do you go after people at all? What does it have to do with you?'

Nic dropped his voice, and quietly, like he was revealing a great and terrible secret, he said, 'This has everything to do with us, Sophie. It's in our blood.'

'The same way managing the diner is in my blood?' I would have laughed if I wasn't so full of horror.

'Sort of.' Nic smiled. 'My people are descended from Sicily. From the very beginning every member of my family has been born into the Mafia. Not inducted. *Born.* For us there is no other choice, no alternate way to live.'

I felt a pang of uneasiness in my stomach. Did that mean he was stuck in this life? Did being a Falcone mean he was destined to kill, the same way being a Gracewell made me bad at math? How was that even possible?

He continued, undaunted by my silence. 'The Falcone traditions are unique, our membership confined to blood, and our actions informed by honour and solidarity. We are on earth to make the world a better place. We give everything for the family, and in turn, everything in the pursuit of good.'

'That's all very poetic,' I said after a moment of consideration. 'But when are you going to explain the killing part?'

'Now.' Nic reacted with formidable calmness. He didn't even blink, he just dropped his hand on top of mine and tangled our fingers together on his knee. I let him do it, and I don't know why, but I was trying to look at him as a product of his ancestry and his upbringing, and I wasn't sure whether I could punish him before I understood what that truly meant. I didn't even know if I was safe or not, being there with him, but I felt comforted by his touch, and despite everything telling me to run, I didn't.

'In Sicily, the Mafia came about from the need to protect the local townspeople. It wasn't anything like it is now, different families governed by ruthless behavioural codes and illegal moneymaking schemes. The true and real Mafia, *La Cosa Nostra*, was different.' His voice twisted, turning wistful, like he was remembering something he had once been part of. Maybe that's how he felt. 'After Italy annexed Sicily in the nineteenth century, the lands were taken from the Church and State, and given to private citizens.

'Trading grew and so did commercialism, and out of commercialism came the ugly side of profit: greed, crime, murder. There was no real police force. The townspeople didn't have anyone to protect their homes, their businesses, even their families, so they looked elsewhere. My grandfather used to say it was a simple case of supply and demand. First, small groups of men started to spring up across Sicily; in return for money, they ensured safety by killing those who threatened to destroy it. Word spread, and after a while these groups were hired by wealthier families to settle personal vendettas or offer additional protection.'

'So these groups – these early members of the Mafia – were just a law unto themselves?' I asked. *Sounds familiar.*

'And that was the problem,' Nic replied. 'With no law, apart from their own, temptation got the better of many of them; some organizations turned against the people they protected, falling into violence for violence's sake, extortion, money laundering and racketeering – all the things that make the Mafia as infamous as it is today.

'After that, many of them, who had become formidable families in their own right, emigrated to America. My grandfather's family were among the first immigrants in the early twentieth century.' Nic paused for a moment before continuing with quiet surety. 'But the Falcones never chose the corrupt path of those around them, not in Sicily and not here. We have always tried to protect those who can't protect themselves, to stay on the right side of right and wrong. And sometimes, the right thing is to kill the wrong kind of man.'

Suddenly he seemed so much older. A part of me wanted to cry for him and for the innocence he never really had, but another part wanted to shake him and scream at him for being so idiotic, for not seeing his life's calling as I did – as an insane death wish.

'What are you thinking?' he asked.

I shook my head. 'That you could die at seventeen because you're chasing down vendettas that have nothing to do with you, and I still don't really understand why.'

'It's my job,' he said simply. And then came four horrifying words: 'I'm a career assassin.'

I lost the ability to blink. Suddenly there wasn't enough space in my lungs to fill them with the air I needed to breathe. If I had remembered any curse words in that moment, I would have used them all at once. Nic just waited, politely, while I connected the word 'assassin' with a seventeen-year-old boy who had big, beautiful brown eyes and an easy smile.

'How many?' I stammered, as numbers ran through my mind – five people? Ten? Fifty?

He slow-blinked at me, but I knew he understood. I spelt it out for him. 'How many people have you *killed?*

'I don't know.' *Lie.*

'Ballpark,' I demanded, but my voice wavered. Did I really

want to know? Would it be worse than my guesses?

'Not that many.' His eyes grew, and I caught myself noticing the flecks of gold inside them.

I re-focused. I was not about to let him smoulder his way out of this. 'Anything over zero is "many".'

Nic had the good sense to look away from me, even if he *was* feigning the shame he should have been feeling.

'So how many?' I asked again.

'I can't discuss it, Sophie. I'd get in trouble,' he said, almost pleadingly. 'Just know they were bad people. People a lot worse than Stenson. And it's my job.'

'*How* could that be your job?' I finally managed, though it came out with an eye-watering shrillness.

'It couldn't be anything else,' he replied simply.

'It could be lots of things, Nic!' I was screeching without meaning to. 'You could be a teacher, a doctor, a barista, a fish-monger, an accountant, a—'

'Sophie,' Nic interrupted softly. 'Just calm down . . .'

I clamped my mouth shut until the hysteria subsided, and when I had finally calmed my breathing down, I conceded, 'I'm scared.'

'I told you I would never hurt you,' he said quietly. 'It's just a job.'

'No,' I said, shaking my head. 'How could it be?'

'The Falcones have earned our position as one of the most honourable and respected lineages in the American Mafia. The other families always come to us, for one reason or another, and we always respond. That has been our calling within the underworld. And it is how we operate within *omertà*.' The last word rolled off his tongue.

'What's *omertà*?' My tongue stumbled over the word.

Nic smiled at my botched attempt. 'It's a code of silence. Our people don't speak to the law, but we speak to each other, and that's how we get things done. How we solve certain . . . problems.'

'You mean people,' I pointed out.

'People,' he confirmed.

'So your family is like a special branch of the Mafia?' I ventured.

He considered it for a moment before conceding with a soft smile. 'I suppose it has become that way. We are the part that takes care of the people who shouldn't be dealing on the streets, or trafficking, or killing innocent bystanders . . .' His voice grew hard. 'We take care of the scum.'

He studied me intently as I started knitting the pieces together in my head so I could see the picture he was creating. His family hurt and killed people whose aim in life was to hurt and kill innocents. That was his job, but it was more than that, too: it was his legacy. But how could he justify it to himself, and how could I justify his understanding of it? The idea that I was sitting beside an assassin made me dizzy, and yet when I looked at Nic, I didn't feel afraid, I felt . . . confusion. 'And you get *paid* to do this?'

'Yes, we do.'

'By other families in the Mafia?'

'Yes.'

'Handsomely, I'm guessing.'

'That's not important.' He was right, the answer wasn't important. The mansion spoke for itself.

'Wait.' There was something not quite right about his

explanation. 'Don't members of the Mafia break the law too? I know they're not exactly law-abiding. I've heard about horse heads and secret murders and money laundering and brutal family feuds . . .' I trailed off, hoping Nic wouldn't notice I had just listed a bunch of things I had seen in movies. After all, those stories must have come from somewhere.

He inhaled through clenched teeth. 'Yes, the families are not exactly *angelic*.'

'Well, how do you have their protection if you have to go after at least some of them too?'

Nic regarded me like I had suddenly sprouted horns. 'Sophie,' he said, his tone affronted. 'We *never* go after members of our own culture, whatever they have done.'

All of a sudden I was back on my own planet, watching him from afar and resisting the urge to shake him until all the stupidity fell out. 'Is that a joke?'

'No.'

I pulled my legs underneath me and fell back on my haunches so that I was hovering over him on the couch. 'So you just go after the ordinary, run-of-the-mill criminals? Not the ones on your side?'

'We can't,' he said, looking up at me through thick, dark lashes.

'Why not?'

'Because we'd all have died out by now.' He said it so matter-of-factly it surprised me less than it should have.

'But don't mob families fight with one another all the time?' Another movie-based assertion, but I had a feeling I was right about that.

'Yes, but not with us. We are untouchable.'

'Because most of the time you're doing their bidding, right? You provide them with a service and in return they keep you living in the lap of luxury,' I shot back. 'That is so messed up.'

Nic shifted so that he was sitting up straighter, putting us at the same height again. 'We are eliminating the worst kinds of people in society. Can't you see that?'

I shook my head. How could he be so naïve? 'You only kill their competition, Nic. The Mafia can still do whatever they want.'

'It's still a service to society.'

'It's a selective one.'

'Better than none at all.'

'Doesn't it bother you? Don't you think about the hypocrisy of it all? Murderers paying you to murder other murderers?' My mind was starting to spin again.

'I try not to think about it.'

'You should.'

'What?' he asked, his voice wounded. 'Consider that my whole family are going to hell for trying to make Chicago a better place for people like you to live in? Consider that, no matter how much freedom and protection we have, our hands are still tied by others in our culture?'

'Yes!' I urged. 'Think about that!'

'Sophie, there's nothing I can do about it!' His voice escalated with anger. 'This is my life. It's everything I've ever known. It's what I know is right. It's *all* I know.'

I settled my hands in my lap and fell back from him, recognizing the losing battle I was fighting. 'It shouldn't be all or nothing.'

'I know,' he conceded, exasperated. 'But what can I do?'

'You could walk away.'

'The only way to leave this way of life is in a coffin,' he said with chilling finality.

Silence descended. Part of me understood. I wanted to cry for him and the future he was bound up in, but I didn't. I was too numb, too afraid to consider the possibility that maybe Nic didn't *want* to walk away from his way of life, that he enjoyed the feeling of punishing people, of watching them quiver and beg before him. I studied my cuticles while he studied me.

'It's suicide,' I muttered.

Nic sat back and smiled, and for a second he looked like the teenager he was supposed to be. Happy and carefree, not dark and hardened. 'My brothers and I, we have been training for this life since we could walk,' he said. 'We can read situations unlike anyone else. We can break a man's neck ten different ways. We have the knowledge to infiltrate gangs and the skill to shoot their leader from one hundred feet away.' He spoke like he was listing a set of everyday skills on his résumé, and not reeling off his special mob-related activities.

'Do you have to answer to the boss of your family?' I asked.

'Yes,' Nic said slowly, as though he was starting to realize something. 'We follow his instructions.'

'Who is he?'

He shook his head like he was coming out of a daze. 'Sophie,' he said hesitantly, 'I've already said far too much. I got carried away . . . I always seem to with you . . .' He trailed off. 'You could ruin me now.'

'I won't,' I said automatically. I hadn't even thought about it, but my heart already had an answer. Despite everything, I didn't want to ruin him. He was already being ruined by the people around him. By his own family. If only he could see that, maybe I could get through to him.

'I can't say anything else,' he said.

It didn't matter; I already knew who the boss was.

How could their father have OK'd this when he was alive? My father saw me pretending to smoke a candy cigarette once and nearly grounded me over it. But Nic's father probably bought him his first gun, taught him how to load it, how to aim it, how to kill with it. And now Felice? Surely he had a responsibility to look out for these boys, not use them to kill people.

I fell back against the couch, suddenly feeling exhausted. 'You don't have to say anything else,' I said softly.

Nic sank down so that our eyes were level when he looked at me. 'Are you frightened, Sophie?'

I did my best to ignore how close he was. 'I don't know.'

'You didn't run away.'

'Not yet.'

His smile was a soft tug at the lips.

I was beginning to feel intoxicated again; dizzy with desire. 'You do bad things,' I reminded myself aloud, making the mistake of looking into his eyes. How many people had spent their last seconds on earth looking into those eyes?

'Only sometimes,' he said quietly.

'Do you have to be so casual about it?'

'I don't feel bad about what I do.' He brushed his finger along my neck, and my spine started to tingle. How many necks had he broken with those fingers? 'But I feel bad that you dislike this part of me, and this part is almost all of me, Sophie.'

'But there's so much kindness in you, Nic,' I whispered.

'Kindness for the right people.' He watched my lips as he

trailed his finger beneath them. 'For people like you.'

I felt a familiar rush in the air. *Don't get distracted.* What were all those things I'd wanted to say? Suddenly I couldn't remember a single one. 'You shouldn't break the law.'

He pulled my chin towards him and brushed his nose against mine. 'I know,' he hummed against my lips. His breath was as unsteady as mine. '*Bella mia,*' he moaned softly into my mouth, and that was all it took to make my resolve implode.

This time, our kiss was deeper than before. Nic tangled his hands in my hair, pulling me into his body and moulding my shape to his. He dragged his mouth along my skin, intoxicating me with his kisses. 'Staying away from you is too hard,' he groaned into my neck. 'I don't want to be good any more.'

'Then don't be,' I said, clutching him tighter and feeling the muscles in his back flex against my fingers. Gently he dipped my head back and found my mouth again, parting my lips with his tongue as he pushed me down across the couch, holding me beneath him.

When the sound of the front door slamming against its hinges made the couch jump under us, we were shocked back into reality. I pulled myself up just in time to see the look of unbridled horror on Nic's face. He shot up, his cheeks flushed with pink, his eyes darting.

CHAPTER TWENTY-THREE
THE UNDERBOSS

Luca stalked into the room.

'Nic, have you heard from Val— What the hell is she doing here?' The beginning of his sentence differed drastically from its end, which rose substantially in pitch.

Nic raised his hands in the air like he was surrendering to a police officer, positioning his body protectively in front of me as though Luca might lunge and tear my throat out.

He came to tower over us. Fury and shock mingled in his eyes, but there was something else there too, something I couldn't place. 'Nic, I am going to rip your heart out and make you eat it, you stupid . . .' His sentence descended into the worst combination of expletives I had ever heard in one single breath.

Nic jumped to his feet and squared up to his brother. 'I had to explain what she saw.'

Luca's icy blue eyes flashed with fury. 'So you *brought her here*?'

Nic balled his fists. 'Don't start.'

Feeling dangerously close to losing it, I sprang to my feet and pushed past Luca. I couldn't handle being on the edge of a conversation that would undoubtedly slide right over my head, but still be close enough to drive me insane with questions. I shouldn't have been there with them anyway, and now that my clarity was back, I was going to use it. 'I'm going to get out of here.'

Nic reached for me, but Luca slapped his hand away. 'Let her go,' he warned. 'Unless you want this whole thing to get worse.'

Nic didn't protest, and I wondered why. I stepped away from him, sliding across Luca's stiffened frame without another look at either of them and banging the front door behind me in my own display of hostility.

As I crunched through the gravel of the driveway, my mind erupted with questions about how I had gotten back into the same situation all over again. I had just begun to move on and now I was back at square one, feeling confused and jilted by a mafioso who was as good for me as a syringe full of poison.

I started to run, skidding over the gravel, but I didn't get far before something wrapped itself around my arm and I was twirled unceremoniously into the unyielding frame of the last person I wanted to see.

I removed myself from where I had landed against Luca's chest. He gripped my shoulders and pushed against me until I was backing up against the stone wall at the end of the driveway, pinned between his hands just like before. His face adopted the angry, feral appearance I was already so familiar with. 'I thought I told you I don't ever want to see you in my house again.' He was so close I could see a small white scar above the right side of his lip. It occurred to me, pretty inappropriately, that I was probably one of very few people alive who knew it was there.

I blew a stray strand of hair from my eyes. Now armed with the knowledge that he wouldn't hurt an innocent girl, I felt fractionally more confident about how I could speak to him. 'Nic invited me.'

'I don't care if the Pope invited you. You're not welcome here.'

'Well, take it up with your brother. I don't respect your authority.'

My reply provoked his temper, which was etched above his eyebrows in deep dents. 'You know you shouldn't be with him.'

'I can handle it.'

'You can't.'

'I know you won't hurt me.'

Luca's eyes flashed in warning, but when he spoke again it was quiet – gentle, almost. 'That doesn't mean you won't get hurt.' He scrunched his eyes in frustration, and when he opened them again they were blazing. 'Just tell me what I need to do to get rid of you, since rehashing your father's crime didn't help!'

I pushed my face forwards and clenched my jaw. 'Tell me what you're doing in Cedar Hill.'

Luca regarded me warily, hesitating, then – 'No.'

'Then I guess I'll just stick around here.'

'I wouldn't do that if I were you,' he threatened.

'What are you going to do, Luca?' I clenched my fists at my sides. 'Pull a gun on me?'

'If that's what it takes.'

'How brave!' I exploded. We were so close to one another now. 'You can't use your words, but you're more than happy to use your gun.'

'I'm not going to be responsible for ruining your innocence!'

I tilted my face towards him to show I wasn't afraid, or as innocent as he clearly thought. 'Go ahead,' I whispered. 'Shatter it.' We were nose to nose. 'It *almost* worked last time, when you told me about my dad.'

'I don't care,' he replied resolutely. 'I'm not punching Bambi in the face.'

I raised my voice again. 'Tell me what you're doing in Cedar Hill!'

Luca moved his unblinking stare from my eyes to my lips and then shook whatever thought was forming out of his head. 'No,' he said calmly.

I prodded him in the chest, pushing him away. 'I know you're in the Mafia. If you think I can't handle that, then you're wrong.'

He shook his head again, in disbelief, his voice pulsing with a level of anger that far eclipsed my own. 'Of course he told you. That idiot. And you're still here, which doesn't make you any smarter than him.'

I glowered at him. 'I know you don't hurt innocent people. You're all about "honour" and "morals" . . . skewed as they are,' I added venomously.

He pulled back, his expression suddenly unreadable. There was a beat of silence and then, in a cold, calculated voice, he said, 'And revenge.'

'What?'

He narrowed his eyes. 'You forgot about revenge.'

'What about revenge?' I faltered, thinking about my father. His father. Our history.

Luca's sudden smile sharpened his cheekbones. 'Oh, Nicoli left that part out? Figures he'd be selective.'

I started to chew on my lip, searching internally for the bravery I had just summoned, but I had spent it all screaming in his face. 'He said you're different from the other families.'

'Yes.' Luca remained perfectly still, watching me like a hawk circling its prey. 'Except when it comes to revenge. Like the other families, the Falcones *always* exact revenge, regardless of whether it's morally sanctioned.'

'No,' I said, jutting out my chin and shaking my head.

'No?' Luca laughed freely; I gathered it was his real laugh, and it was a strange, silvery sound. 'Gracewell, you really are something else. What did you think?' he asked bemusedly. 'That we're gun-toting, knife-wielding avenging angels without fault or sin? You saw Nic put that gun in Robbie Stenson's mouth. You heard him cock the trigger. Do you really believe that the idea of revenge is above a dynasty of temperamental, hot-blooded, territorial assassins who have appointed themselves the underworld distributors of a kind of karma that shouldn't be policed by anyone else on this earth? Do you think that everything we do is the right thing?'

He shook his head disbelievingly, and I cursed my naïvety. I had been stupid to get swept up in romantic notions of Nic as some sort of vigilante; he was a killer, plain and simple, prone to the same tempers and temptations as the rest of us.

I slid along the wall so I was out from under Luca. He let me, and I felt a pinch of relief. 'You're not going to hurt me . . .'

'No,' he replied. 'I'm not.'

'Then why are you being so dramatic about it?'

Luca's voice grew dangerously quiet. 'Listen very carefully to what I'm about to say.' I had to watch his lips as he spoke because the shards of turquoise in his eyes were suddenly too intense. 'I am the underboss of the entire Falcone dynasty, and if I'm telling you to keep your head down and stop coming around here, then you'd better believe I have a damn good reason. You need to get away from this house and as far away from Cedar Hill as you can. Nic might have deluded himself into thinking he can shield you from what's going to happen, but he can't. My father was a made man, and that means your family owes us a blood debt, Sophie.'

A blood debt. The air left my lungs in a swift gasp. Luca's expression faltered, but he twisted away from me before I could catch the real emotion behind it. When he reached the door again, he turned around. I was rooted to the same spot, like he knew I would be.

'Do you know what that jar of honey meant?' he asked.

My stomach twisted at his tone, at his knowledge of the honey. Although I think I had always known, deep down, that there was a connection, it suddenly felt more sinister now than I ever could have imagined.

I shook my head.

'It wasn't a gift.'

'I didn't think it was,' I lied.

There was nothing in Luca's voice or on his face now; it was completely void of emotion. He looked past me into the night sky. 'There's a reason people in the underworld call my uncle

Felice "The Sting", you know.'

I didn't respond. I just stood there, trying to get my legs to work, as memories of his uncle's bee-stung face crept across my mind.

'When Felice Falcone gives someone a sample of his black-ribboned honey, it means he's going to come back for the jar.'

I tried to swallow the tightness in my throat, but it was unyielding.

'And when he does, he brings his gun. That jar of honey is the Falcone Gift of Death.' Luca shifted his gaze again, pinning me beneath his stare. 'Let that be your final warning. Get out of here while you can.'

I blanched, my mind whirling frantically. I had all the pieces, I just had to make them fit. 'But what are—?'

'Talk to your uncle, Gracewell,' Luca cut in. 'Or should I say, *Persephone*?'

Before I could respond, he was slamming the door in one deafening bang, leaving me shaking from head to toe.

CHAPTER TWENTY-FOUR
THE INTRUDERS

I started home, pulling out my phone and dialling my uncle's number. It rang and rang and went to voicemail. *Come on.* I could have smashed my phone in frustration. I called four more times in a row and still, nothing. I left two voicemails and finally I sent a text:

> I know what the honey meant. We need to talk about the Falcones. Call me ASAP.

I was almost home when my phone started ringing.

'Jack,' I answered. 'I think I'm in danger.'

'Sophie, I just read your text. Is everything OK?' His voice was edged with panic, and it was taking hold of mine too.

'Where the hell have you been? I've been calling you!' I exploded.

'Focus, Sophie,' he snapped. 'I'll explain all that later. Where are they now?'

'I don't know,' I said. There were so many of them they could be anywhere, doing anything. I told him about Luca's threats, about the blood debt and the honey, my words catching between breathless gasps as I spoke.

'Where are you now?' he asked once I had finished.

I skidded up my driveway. 'I'm home,' I said.

'Go inside, lock all the doors. I'm sending someone for you.'

'Uncle Jack?' I was struggling with my keys. I only had three on the chain, but they kept escaping from my shaky grasp. 'Are they going to hurt me?'

'No,' he answered too quickly. 'Of course not,' he added after a beat.

'What's going on?' The million-dollar question, and I still hadn't put all the pieces together.

'There really isn't enough time to explain, Sophie.' I could hear him barking orders at someone in the background.

I slotted the right key into the lock. The click inside flooded me with relief. 'If you knew I'd be in danger, why would you take off like that?'

Now that my fear was ebbing away, I was getting angry. Jack had been avoiding Cedar Hill like the plague for his own safety, and he hadn't bothered to tell my mother and me to do the same. So much for that promise he had made to my father. I made a mental note to call my mom after I was done with Jack. She was in the city at a series of bridal fittings until tomorrow evening, but I knew she'd freak out at being left out of the loop. Especially this one.

'Sophie,' Jack was saying, his words edged with one big,

constant sigh, 'they're not going to hurt you. I wouldn't have left you behind if I thought that. Those boys are just shooting their mouths off. That family love the sound of their own voices.'

'They want revenge, Jack.' I slammed the door behind me and fixed the chain in place. 'They want a blood debt for what Dad did. Luca told me himself!' I skirted into the kitchen and climbed on to the countertop. I clamped the phone between my shoulder and my ear so I could lock the windows shut.

The phone line buzzed with Jack's defiance. 'Ignore what Luca said. He's just trying to frighten you.'

I slid off the counter. 'But why?'

'Listen. The Falcones' problem is with me. *Just* me. Not you.'

'What do you mean, with you?' I jiggled the back door handle to make sure it was locked.

'I can't go into it now. I've sent Eric Cain for you. He'll keep you safe. You've met him before, at my birthday a few years ago.'

'I remember,' I said, vaguely recalling a small, effeminate man with enviable dark-red hair. How exactly was he supposed to keep me safe?

'I'll meet you somewhere outside of Cedar Hill and we'll talk about it.'

'What about Mom?' I asked.

My uncle had the audacity to laugh. I balled my fist until my nails dug into my palm.

'They wouldn't go near Celine,' he said dismissively. 'She's got nothing to do with me. It's common knowledge your mother loathes the ground I walk on. And they're not interested in punishing your dad, Sophie. Have you locked the doors?'

'Yes.' I was in the hall again. I took the stairs two at a time, deciding to lock all the second-floor windows just in case. 'Why are you taking me away if I'm not in danger? At least tell me something so I can be prepared.'

'It's a precaution, Sophie.' He laboured over the word 'precaution' like it would make me feel better. It didn't. 'They would never go after you for what your dad did. The very idea is ridiculous. And even if they *did*, which they *wouldn't*, the Falcone Mafia doesn't hurt innocents. It's one of their almighty, crap-loaded, self-righteous rules. And they just *love* being self-righteous.'

I could practically taste the venom. So Jack knew everything I did, and he had decided to be coy about it. And did that mean he *wasn't* innocent? What exactly had he done to make it on to the Deserves-to-Die list? 'Sounds like you know a lot about them. Thanks for the heads-up.' *You could have saved me a whole lot of time and swooning.*

'I did give you a heads-up.'

'Yeah. A *crap* one.'

I sprinted back downstairs, my feet hammering against the steps like thunder.

'Sophie, I really can't get into this now.' His voice was weary. 'Just sit tight. I've sent someone.'

'I'm trying.' I slid through the open door into the living room and snapped the window shut. I was in the middle of pulling the curtains closed when I heard a voice behind me.

'Hello, Sophie.'

I dropped the phone. Gino and Dom Falcone stood up from the couch at the same time, moving towards me with matching gaits.

'How did you get into my house?' I tried to find where my

phone had fallen, but the room was almost pitch black. They both shrugged, their faces disguised by the darkness. Had they rehearsed this?

'You should go.' I folded my arms in what I hoped was an act of defiance. I raised my voice too, hoping Jack was still listening. 'I'm expecting visitors.'

Gino's laugh was a rasping bark. Dom stopped two feet away from me, and his brother hovered behind him, his ponytail adding two solid inches to his height. They smirked the same menacing smile.

'What do you want, Dom?'

'Ideally, Jack,' he said. Behind him, Gino nodded animatedly in agreement. 'But we can't waste any more time trying to find him. We're done chasing.'

'And following you has gotten us nowhere,' added Gino, his unibrow furrowed above fathomless eyes. 'It's been so *boring*.'

I stumbled backwards, hitting the backs of my knees against the window ledge. 'You've been *following* me?'

I prayed Jack was still listening from wherever my phone had landed.

'Yes,' said Dom matter-of-factly. 'When we found out who you were, it was a stroke of luck. We thought you'd eventually lead us to your uncle . . .' The way he said it made it sound like he was disappointed in me for failing at a task I had no idea I was doing. 'But you didn't.'

Gino started sniggering through his nose.

'You've been following me,' I said again. My voice sounded far away; it was buckling with incredulity. 'For how long?'

'Too long,' they said together.

'Nic was against it, if that makes it any easier to stomach.

He's been fighting to leave you out of this,' Dom said with mock sympathy. 'But it is what it is.'

'Out of what?'

'Fighting and *losing*,' Gino sneered, ignoring my question.

'But,' added Dom, 'if we hadn't been following you, you probably would have been raped that night after the world's most boring party.'

'Oh my God.' Horror curled in my stomach. 'That's how Luca found me.'

'He wasn't supposed to intervene,' said Dom, his voice suddenly disapproving. 'We weren't allowed to do anything that would disrupt your day *unless* your uncle made an appearance, but Luca broke the rules, like he always does. We didn't even know about it until you came around shouting in our driveway.'

I blanched. Gino seemed to disengage from the conversation, and his attention started to wander around the darkened room. At a sound from outside, Dom glanced past me through a crack in the curtains. I seized the brothers' momentary distraction and slid around the wall until I was nearer to the door.

They drifted with me like tracking drones.

'I wouldn't if I were you,' lisped Gino. 'I don't want to hit a girl. Even if it is you.'

'You're going to have to come with us.' Dom sounded almost apologetic, but it did little to soothe my slow-burning hatred for him. Not only had he broken into my house, and was trying to take me somewhere against my will, but he had obviously used Millie and then dumped her, and that made him a *total, unredeemable asshole*. I slid into the open doorway, but Gino blocked me in an instant. He shot his arm out, covering the sliver of space.

Dom curled around the other side of me, closing in. He glanced at his brother and gave him a controlled nod. Gino dropped to his hands and knees and slithered across the floor like a reptile, swiping his hand around as he crawled. It was completely, unnecessarily dramatic.

I tried to run, but Dom grabbed my arm and pulled me back. 'Don't.'

Finally, Gino fished out my phone from underneath the armchair and sprang to his feet, dangling it in the air between us. 'Gotcha,' he said triumphantly to Dom.

Dom took the phone and held it to his ear. 'Jackie boy?' he sneered. The distant sound of shouting filled my ears. 'I think it's time we finished this.'

Laughing to himself, Gino shuffled to my side. 'Time for Sophie to say bye-bye.' His smile revealed his two chipped teeth, and his tongue poked out beneath them. I was still straining to hear what Jack was saying when Gino's hands disappeared from my view.

Dom covered the mouthpiece and redirected to his brother. 'Hurry up,' he said.

The damp rag came out of nowhere.

PART III

'And where the offence is, let the great ax fall.'

William Shakespeare, *Hamlet*

CHAPTER TWENTY-FIVE

THE VALENTINE VENDETTA

I could hear buzzing. It made the world vibrate, pulsing inside my eardrums until it felt like the bees were coming from inside my skull. I twitched awake. The sweetest cacophony of smells hung in the air, coaxing me from the darkness that had engulfed me so completely. I opened my eyes to a white ceiling and felt a horrible tightness in my chest.

I groaned.

'Ah, you're awake at last. I was wondering how long that would take to wear off.'

I didn't have to turn my head in the direction of the voice to know who it belonged to. It was unusually soft for a man's tone, and each syllable was pronounced with over-exaggerated precision, betraying his faint Italian accent.

'Felice,' I said. I tried to sit up, but I couldn't. My arms and legs were bound together by cable ties; they cut into my wrists and squeezed the bottom of my bare ankles uncomfortably. 'Where am I?'

'Generally? You are in Lake Forest. Specifically? You are reclining on my couch.'

The leather squeaked as I heaved my clasped hands towards my bound legs and pulled them together, crunching into an upright position. I swivelled my body around, dropping my knees over the couch and placing my hands in my lap as a streak of white sunlight slashed across my vision, making my eyelids flutter.

I was almost level with an open bay window across the room. The sun was beginning to dip in the pink-tinged sky – I must have been out for a long time. I could tell I was at least one storey up. Outside, there was an old wooden barn tucked behind a sprawling garden with vibrant flowers that faded into open fields. About fifteen small sheds dotted the grass in regimented lines.

'Beehives,' I realized aloud. I could just about make out the swarms of bees droning in the distance, and there were at least two more buzzing somewhere inside the room.

'Well noted, Persephone,' said Felice. He was sitting bolt upright in an armchair directly across from me, one impossibly long leg crossed over the other.

I rolled my eyes over him and frowned. Everything about him – from his silver slicked-back hair and his Mediterranean complexion to his expensive pin-striped suit – screamed *creepy Mafia dude*. And judging by the house so far, not to mention its location, he was rich.

'It's Sophie,' I replied.

'Apparently it is. If only we had been aware of that sooner, it would have saved us quite the confusion. We would have known you from the outset.'

From what I could see we were the only ones in the room. Aside from the black leather couch on which I sat, there was nothing else but Felice and his bees. They were flying in wide circles around his head as though they were defending him, and I felt my skin prickle uncomfortably at the sight.

'I must say I'm surprised you haven't screamed yet.' He settled an elbow on each armrest and brought his hands together in the middle so that each finger touched its correspondent.

'Would there be a point in screaming?'

He shook his head. 'We are far removed from civilization. It is just you and the bees, Persephone.'

I felt a vague semblance of fear somewhere deep inside, but my head was still fuzzy from whatever had put me to sleep. It was hard to arrange my emotions appropriately, and even more difficult not to say the wrong thing. I knew I had been kidnapped, but I couldn't determine the correct response. I zeroed in on the pockmarks along Felice's neck and face. They were shiny and red, and bubbling angrily in places.

'So this is where you live with all your bees? How romantic.' I knew I shouldn't have said it, but my brain had disengaged from keeping my actions appropriate. 'Pity they sting you so much.'

He raised his eyebrows, causing ripples along his forehead. 'It is my personal choice not to wear a mesh veil when in the company of my bees. I feel it separates us needlessly; I prefer to be close to them, to feel them on my skin.' He flicked his gaze to the bee flying nearest his head and smiled like a proud parent. 'It is an honour to be stung by such noble creatures. That they would lay down their lives for a fleeting moment of my attention is extraordinary. There is no creature more majestic than the honeybee.'

'If you say so,' I said, without registering what I meant. My brain was so cloudy, and the buzzing was making it worse.

'I do say so. The honeybee is already dying out and it is my contention that we must do our very best to protect nature's noble children.'

Nature's noble children? I could have knocked myself out again just to keep from dealing with the crazy in front of me. 'What do you want with me?'

Felice pursed his lips. It made his chin look unnaturally sharp. He didn't answer. He just stared at me, and I got the sense I had offended him by moving the topic away from his bees.

'Can you at least loosen these ties? They really hurt.' My wrists and ankles were red-raw and stinging.

He shook his head; it was almost imperceptible this time. 'Not quite yet, Persephone.'

'My name is Sophie. I don't call you Fabio.'

Felice threw back his head and laughed until his eyes began to water. 'Of all the things you could be angry about,' he said, wiping them with the back of his hand. 'You are a funny one.'

I didn't feel humorous, I felt drugged. 'I got your honey, by the way. Thanks *so* much.'

'I think we both know it was not meant for you, but for the sake of clarity, since I cannot fathom whether you are playing dumb or actually *being* dumb, I shall elucidate. The honey was intended for your uncle.'

'I don't think he appreciated it.'

'Oh, no?' Felice contorted his features into the most elaborate smile I had ever seen. It was as terrifying as it was disingenuous.

'He smashed it,' I said, setting my tone to serious. Whatever delirious desire I had to be a smart-ass was fading. I was coming to my senses again.

'It happens.' Felice waved his hand in the air dismissively. 'I know you're not supposed to tip off your victims, but I just can't help my flair for theatrics. And I'll have you know I prepare the honey myself and it is positively delicious, not that anyone ever bothers to try it.'

'I tried it. It tasted off,' I lied.

'That's an incredibly rude thing to say.' Felice made a point of grimacing at me before continuing. 'Still, it does its job. I do think everyone deserves a fair warning so they can get their affairs in order.'

'Before you kill them?' I asked. Though I already knew, I wanted him to say it, so it would kick my fuzzy brain into gear.

'Of course.' Felice smiled, revealing two long rows of sharp teeth. 'Head start or no head start, we always catch up in the end. And sometimes, I dare say, the chase is the best part.'

A shudder rippled up my spine. Finally, and unpleasantly, the urgency of the situation had settled on me; I had more people than just myself to think about. 'Why did you send my uncle the Gift of Death?' My voice cracked, and a wave of fear careened over me. 'If it has something to do with revenge for what my father did, he didn't mean it.'

Felice raised his finger to hush me. 'The death of my beloved brother, Angelo, at the hands of your father was, of course, regrettable, but I don't believe there was any ill intent on your father's part.'

I felt my shoulders dip. 'That's good.'

'That is not to say, however, that this situation is not about revenge. Because,' he said, standing to his full height, 'of course, it is.'

Felice's tallness suddenly seemed so much more formidable. He began pacing up and down, and I got the sense he did this all the time – intimidation by theatrics. He probably had a special suit for every occasion. His neck scarf cascaded behind him as he glided back and forth.

'I think it is reasonable to ascertain now that you are clearly unaware that your uncle, Jack Gracewell, is a pivotal member of the biggest drug cartel in the Midwest. The Golden Triangle Gang, as they so eloquently call themselves. Would I be correct in assuming so?'

I gaped at him. It couldn't be true. It had to be part of his 'theatrics'.

'Among other things, they have recently begun dealing a hybrid narcotic that, when taken, elicits effects similar to those associated with extreme intoxication, and can lead to an array of unfortunate after-effects, including paranoia, memory loss, paralysis, and – my personal *least* favourite – death.' He shook his head at the world outside, like all the birds and flowers had let him down at once.

'No,' was all I could muster. Words were failing me. I was dumbfounded and Felice could see it; worse than that, he was thriving on it, like a well-dressed parasite.

He started pacing again. 'Of course, we've been monitoring

your uncle and his not-so-esteemed business partners for nearly four years – right back to the time when he began using the diner, your homey family establishment, to stash drug shipments between deliveries.'

'What?' I spluttered back into life. 'Jack used my father's diner for drug trafficking?'

'Well, I would have thought those two dots would have been easy to connect, but maybe I'm too close to the situation, so it's easier for me.' Felice hunkered down so he could be closer to me. 'Initially, there were just three pivotal members of the Golden Triangle Gang operating on this side of the Atlantic; each one positioned at a different key point in the Midwest; points that, when drawn together on a map, form a perfect triangle' – he made a triangle in the air with his fingers – 'of ill-earned profit.'

I felt a bee buzzing dangerously close to my ear and jerked my head on reflex.

'Careful,' Felice warned. He sprang to his feet again. 'As the Falcone boss, my brother Angelo was principally in charge of ending this chain of unlawful activities. It was no mean feat, but as we have always said, "the falcon does not hunt flies". Together, we were to change the face of the Midwest narcotics underworld.'

Felice's movements turned fluid, one hand tucked behind his back wistfully, as though he were taking an evening stroll down a quiet street.

'My brother was successful in coordinating the demise of founding fathers one and two of the Golden Triangle Gang in relatively quick succession, not to mention several key members of their respective crews.' He widened his colourless eyes and looked towards the ceiling like he was talking to someone beyond it. 'And if I may say, the family made *quite* an artful job of them, but I would hate to offend your sensibilities, Persephone, so I won't go into the details.'

I remembered the newspaper article with a jolt. It had mentioned the Golden Triangle Gang. Angelo Falcone had been suspected of their murders – their *brutal* murders – but was never charged. I didn't know whether I could bring myself to believe it, but before I could stop myself I was saying, 'And Jack was number three.'

'And Jack Gracewell was the elusive third point on said triangle,' Felice confirmed, his expression suddenly sombre. He cracked his knuckles, one by one, and I noticed they were stung just as badly as his face. 'Miss Gracewell, I have yet to meet a more slippery, unconscionable individual as your uncle.'

Me too, I realized as nausea rose in my stomach. If everything Felice said was true, I didn't know my uncle at all. Sure, I knew Jack was capable of acting out of line: he drank too much, he had a short fuse, and he had a tendency to disappear sometimes. But these accusations were something else entirely.

'We almost did it, you know – wiped them all out – and that might have been the end of it, but of course it wasn't. Because Angelo ran into the wrong brother that fateful Valentine's night, and then everything changed in the blink of an eye.'

I could taste the bile rising in my throat. I thought of my father all alone in the dark outside the diner and how scared he must have been when Angelo Falcone approached him, yelling. He had no idea who was coming for him. He couldn't have. He would never be involved in something like that. Right? I clenched my fists to stop my hands from shaking. Just how many people in my life weren't who they said they were?

'I didn't know Jack had a brother who looked *so* like him until the night I saw him shoot *my* brother. That's terrible research, is it not? I can tell you, a lot of heads rolled after that unfortunate mix-up.' Felice allowed himself a fleeting smirk before adding, 'Literally.'

'You were there?'

He sighed, his bravado diminishing. 'It was dark, and Angelo approached the wrong Gracewell. The plan was for my brother to subdue Jack and drag him back into the alley behind the diner so that I could shoot him in private – it was my personal request, you see – but we never got that far, and that is something you do know, at last.'

I flinched at the thought of him shooting Jack.

Felice wagged his finger at me, back and forth like a metronome, until I wanted to rip it off and spit it back in his face. 'You mustn't conceptualize me as the monster. It was Jack who was *and is* contributing to society's underbelly in the worst way. And it was *Jack* who got your father into such an unfortunate position. If I were ever to traffic drugs, which *of course* I would not, I certainly wouldn't use one of my brother's family establishments for storage.'

'Jack isn't into that stuff.' Doubt caused my words to falter. They fell out of my mouth, unsteady and forced. 'My father would never let him do that. I don't believe you.' I would have crossed my arms and stormed off if I could have. Not because I was angry, but because I was afraid of the truth, and what it meant for my understanding of family, of right and wrong.

'Well fortunately for me, it is of no concern whether you choose to believe me. It does not change the truth of the matter.'

The more I thought about it, though, the more I teetered towards his version of events. After all, it was strange to think that Angelo Falcone would be skulking, unarmed, around a small suburban diner in the middle of the night. And stranger still was all of Jack's mysterious business in the city. And the money he always seemed to have, the fancy cars and the exquisite suits. There was always something a little off about him: something that caused my mother to keep him at arm's length, something that had kept him from settling down with a family of his own. And then there was his vehement hatred of the Falcones. The more I pieced everything together, the less ridiculous it was beginning to sound. 'So if it is true . . .' I began.

'It is,' clarified Felice.

'Well, why am I here now, if this isn't about my father? I haven't done anything wrong.'

'After the unfortunate death of my beloved brother, Jack's activities experienced a significant decline, so much so that we believed the Golden Triangle to be finished entirely. Of course, we were always going to finish what we started with him – after the appropriate mourning period, that is. I must admit Angelo's death took a heavy toll on all of us, the boys especially. But when we discovered our intel was incorrect and that Jack is now *spearheading* the entire gang from the city, we realized we would have to dispatch him sooner rather than later. We procured a residence in Cedar Hill, and from there, we have been picking off your uncle's key associates one by one.'

Did that explain the drowned delivery man – was Luis part of this too? And all the other mysterious disappearances Mrs Bailey had been so eager to point out – the ones I had been so quick to ignore? All this time, and right under my nose, they were killing people.

'That's horrible,' I said, feeling dazed.

'Actually, it's competence,' Felice corrected me. 'And now, with Jack proving to be the final piece of the puzzle – and weakened without his most trusted henchmen – we must end him sooner rather than later, before he can regroup. It must finally come to an end the way my brother intended it to.'

I panicked at the thought of what they would do to Jack, wondering just how many of his 'associates' had been killed over the past few months, and trying not to think about which ones had met their deaths at the end of Nic's gun. 'So you're going to kill him.'

'Yes.' Felice eased himself into the chair like his bones would snap if he wasn't careful. 'And that, lovely *Persephone*, is where you come in.'

I bristled. 'That's *not* my name.'

'I don't see why you have chosen to cast it off.' He paused as if expecting me to justify something that seemed so unbearably trivial to me now. When I didn't answer, he continued with obvious bewilderment. 'Why wouldn't you want to associate yourself with the majestic and beautiful Queen of the Underworld, the wondrous and infernal Goddess of Death? Sophie is so *plain* in comparison.'

'Do you really expect me to answer that?'

'The significance of such a name is amusing to me. You have even found your Hades.' He smirked, and I got the feeling he was expecting me to be impressed by his knowledge of Greek mythology. I wasn't.

When I didn't reply, he continued. 'It was Dominico who found out who you were, when he was with that trivial British waitress, trying to gather information on Jack. By the time Nicoli realized that you were, in fact, *Persephone* Gracewell, he tried to pull away from you, but it was too late. Suddenly you had become the most viable way to lead us to our intended target at a time when we were running out of patience.'

I thought of Nic and frowned. All this time he was fighting his desires for my safety, and he was losing. And lying.

'But you didn't see the danger, did you? Because you see only the parts you want to see, and you are blind to all else.'

I glowered at him. 'I'm not blind to anything.' *Except my uncle's secret life as a drug kingpin. And my crush's secret life as a killer.*

'Of course, of course,' Felice replied dismissively. 'How would an old fool like me know anything about that? I have no doubt you are perfectly in love and that you've counted all the notches on his trigger hand *lovingly*.' He leered at me and I hated him for it; but most of all, I hated him because he was right. I hadn't reconciled myself with that part of Nic; I had tried to ignore it. I had even tried to justify it.

'So you see,' Felice purred on, 'when Jack fled, he foolishly left *you* behind, the very thing that will cause his undoing. We expected you might lead us to him. However, since your uncle is smarter than your average deckchair and has inexplicably been able to outrun us thus far, we must move on to a more improvised plan, in which you are *bait*.' He clapped his hands together. 'If Jack doesn't present himself to us at the abandoned auto parts warehouse in Hegewisch before midnight tonight, then things will take a very unfortunate turn.'

'So you're going to kill me?' I asked, feeling completely hollow inside. Was this really how it was going to end? I had fallen down a tunnel of lies, and now there was a gun to my head?

Felice stared at me impassively. 'The idea of killing a teenage girl just doesn't appeal to me, but I think you'll really have to ask someone better qualified to answer, Persephone.'

'Like who?'

Felice rose to his feet again. 'Our boss.'

My mouth dropped open. 'You're not the boss?'

'Me?' A shadow passed across his face, but before I could focus on it, he lit up until he looked like a children's cartoon character. 'I am not. But thank you for assuming so. I'm flattered.'

'What are *you*, then?'

'Me? I'm just a simple beekeeper.' As he said it, one of his bees droned into my eye line, just a foot away from my face, as though he had programmed it to do so.

'And a murderer,' I reminded him.

'I do feel we can all be defined by more than one thing.'

'Unless you're a killer. Then that's pretty much all you amount to.'

'Maybe you should tell that to your father. Or to your handsome Hades, between kisses.'

If I could have jumped out of my seat and ripped his face off right then, I would have.

'In any case,' he continued in his patronizing way, 'I'm just the Falcone *consigliere*. I offer advice, which is usually ignored. I'll find someone more equipped to answer your question. Frankly, I've grown weary of your teenage sarcasm.'

CHAPTER TWENTY-SIX

THE BOSS

I heard him before I saw him – the hardwood floors rumbled as he glided into my eye line, his hands barely touching the wheels to make them move. He turned with a series of expert flicks and then he was facing me. His frame was narrow, but not hunched as I'd remembered; he was dressed in black pants and a crisp black button-up shirt that pulled across his shoulders. The occasion? My doom.

He shifted his left leg so that it stretched out towards me, grazing the floor. His right leg, which was bony and turned in at the hip, slumped against it so that he looked twisted from the waist down. He released his hands from the wheels and entwined his fingers in his lap. The first time I saw him, he was behind a table, coaxing the emotion from his absentee subjects and showing me a different world with his pencils. Now he was watching me through that delicate azure gaze, his lips set in a hard line.

'You wanted to see me?' That musical voice. I struggled to believe it could be the commanding force of an entire fleet of assassins.

'Valentino,' I said, my voice surprisingly steady. I spoke like I had known him for years, but his expression didn't break. It was unreadable. 'Please tell me this isn't true.'

He shifted in his wheelchair, pulling himself up, and he was taller all of a sudden, his shoulders broader than before. I realized I had been a fool to think him weak. 'What isn't true?' he asked.

'You're the boss of this whole thing?' I said.

He raised his jet-black brows. 'By "thing" do you mean family?'

'Yes.'

'Is it so hard to believe?' he countered.

I leant forward, like I was trying to pierce the invisible wall between us. 'Yes. It *is* hard to believe.'

He tapped the right wheel of his chair with his finger. 'Because of this?' There was a hint of bitterness in his response.

'No. Because you seemed so . . . empathetic before.'

'I am empathetic,' he replied. 'It's one of my more prevalent traits.'

'But you kill people.' My voice was wavering.

Again he tapped his chair by way of explanation. 'I *order* kills.'

'That's not much better.'

'It is a necessary evil for a greater good,' he answered evenly. 'It is what it is.'

'Are you really going to kill me?' My voice cracked and a string of tears slid down my cheek on to my neck, dampening it uncomfortably. Still I kept my chin up. If nothing else, I would be brave.

Valentino was slow to respond. He shifted his gaze out the window. 'Yes.'

'Even if Jack shows up?' I couldn't believe what I was asking; I shouldn't have even entertained the possibility of anyone's life being forfeited for mine, but it turns out my survival instincts were crueller than I was.

Valentino turned back to me. He smiled, just a little. 'Even then.'

I opened my mouth to speak, but a strangled cry escaped instead. Shaking, I buried my head in my bound hands and wept hard, trying to get it all out at once. I had to pull it together, to try and find a way out of this, but my shoulders were convulsing and my breathing was coming in thick gasps.

'If you would allow me to explain,' he said. I wouldn't look at him, but his tone was entirely unaffected by my emotional meltdown. 'I don't want to be anything other than fair in this role that was given to me. I try to be as logical as I can when making decisions about life and death.'

'But you're *not* fair,' I sobbed. 'None of this is fair. I'm not a drug dealer! I'm just a girl!'

'A Gracewell girl. And a loose end, I'm afraid.'

He let me cry in silence, and he didn't speak again until I finally lifted my head.

'Jack's debt is owed because of his prolific drug activity and the destructive, far-reaching effects it has had. That much is plain to see. But your father's debt to us is owed because of what he did to my father.'

'Your father was trying to kill him!' I shouted. I was shaking so bad I felt like I was going to combust. 'Of course he defended himself! The whole thing was an accident. Even Felice admits my father didn't do anything on purpose!'

'How do you know?' The impassive nature of Valentino's response caught me off guard. For a laughable moment I found myself feeling foolish for reacting so violently, when he could have had this conversation the same way he would have talked if he were ordering a pizza for dinner.

'What do you mean?' The words quivered in my throat.

'How do you know your father was innocent?' he asked, studying my reaction. 'How do you know your uncle didn't confide in him? That he wasn't prepared to do the unthinkable to defend his family?'

'Because . . .' I faltered.

Valentino narrowed his eyes, and I felt colder all of a sudden.

'Because my father would never hurt someone deliberately,' I said with renewed confidence. I wasn't sure of much, but I was sure of that. 'He's not capable of such a thing.'

'Did you think your uncle was capable of masterminding an entire drug cartel before today?'

I hesitated.

'Did you think I was capable of overseeing a dynasty of assassins before the moment in which we now find ourselves?'

I looked away from him, but he didn't relent.

'Did you think, the first time he kissed you, that Nic was capable of drowning a man in his own bathtub?'

'Stop,' I pleaded, feeling an overwhelming urge to vomit. 'Just stop.'

'Masks,' said Valentino. 'Look what happens when we take them off.'

'It's horrible.' I buried my face in my hands again so he wouldn't have the satisfaction of watching his words burn right through me.

'Absolute chaos,' he reminded me calmly, like he had not just annihilated my family's reputation. 'Since it is principally my decision, I think when we have apprehended your uncle at the warehouse, the correct course of action is to settle your father's blood debt, once and for all.'

I lifted my head again, feeling dizzy and nauseous. 'So you're going to use me to lure him out and then kill me anyway?'

Valentino shrugged. 'It is the best plan.'

I thought of my mother and Millie and had to choke back another sob. My mother wouldn't survive this, she was barely hanging on as it was. And Millie – she had given up entire friendships to stick by me after my dad went to prison. She didn't have anyone else, not any more. We only had each other.

When Valentino spoke again his voice was clinical, though the musical edge endured, lilting his words as they stung. 'Nic won't come for you, Sophie. He doesn't know about any of this.'

I didn't say anything. I just sat there, feeling the hollowness inside me harden.

'Do you want a handkerchief?' He pulled a silken red square from the pocket of his shirt. His initials were monogrammed in black thread in the corner.

I ignored the gesture. 'I thought you liked me. I thought we understood each other.'

'I do like you.' He tucked the handkerchief back in place,

unaffected by my refusal. 'If the circumstances were different, I think we'd be friends.'

'But you're all set to kill me?'

He spoke matter-of-factly. 'The reason I was appointed to this position by my father was because I have always been adept at keeping my personal feelings separate from the Falcone mission. I have the ability to compartmentalize.'

'Congratulations,' I spat.

'I'm not sure what Nic told you about me.' His left leg twitched against his right in a sudden spasm. 'But Luca and I were appointed together, did you know that? Two bosses. It was a decision that was unheard of in underworld circles, but for our family it made sense. We have done everything together since before birth, each of us a half of one whole. I would remain cool and collected, making the decisions from afar, and he would ensure they were carried out effectively. That was the idea of it. Together we would be the perfect boss: fair and efficient. Removed and yet completely involved.'

'But he's not the boss. He's the underboss,' I argued pointlessly.

If Valentino was surprised by my knowledge of their infrastructure, he didn't show it. 'That's right.' He smiled, revealing a glimpse of his teeth. 'He deferred to me entirely shortly after our father's death. He stepped back from his part in this role.'

'Why?' I gaped. If any of the five brothers fit the definition of a mob boss, it was Luca. Or so I'd have thought.

Valentino raised his hands, gesturing at the room and everything it encompassed: me, him, a black leather couch, my impending death. 'Perhaps because of this. These kinds of manoeuvres are particularly difficult to stomach.' He paused for a moment, ruminating on something. 'Or,' he ventured, 'perhaps he felt like he owed me.' He casually fanned his fingers towards his mangled leg, but his face flashed with something else. 'In any case, Luca and I had always worked together in perfect harmony, until this situation came upon us. Of course, I argue with Nic all the time, so it's no surprise we've had to keep him out of this, but this is the first time in my life that I have ever disagreed with my twin brother over anything. And the fact that it's about the fate of a Gracewell girl he doesn't even know is truly beyond me.'

I felt an unexpected heave in my chest.

'But I'm the boss,' Valentino surmised, the lyrical lilt of his voice veiling the bluntness of his statement. I got the sense he didn't want the flicker of hope inside me growing any stronger.

'So the final decision rests with you,' I realized.

'It does,' he said solemnly. 'And Luca will respect that.'

And just like that, the flicker died.

'Have you heard from my uncle?' I wished I could call Jack and tell him not to bother coming for me. If they were going to kill me anyway, the whole thing would be a trap.

'It's difficult to persuade a drug baron, who is selfish by nature, to trade his life for another's, even if that other is someone very dear to him. But I'm sure when he sees our video of you, he will understand the true gravity of the situation.'

'What video?'

Valentino dipped his head, turning from me. 'Be brave for Calvino or he will go harder on you.'

He left, and I was alone again.

CHAPTER TWENTY-SEVEN

THE VIDEO

Sometime later, a door opened and closed behind me, and the sound of heavy footsteps punctuated the silence. A bald, stern-looking man with a thick black moustache stalked across the room. I remembered him from that day at the restaurant – Calvino.

He seated himself in Felice's vacant armchair, contorting his angular features until they looked like prosthetics, and stared right through me.

'I saw you at The Eatery a few weeks ago,' I said, hoping that kindling a conversation might offer a way out of whatever he was planning to do to me. 'You killed the bee.'

His smirk curled into a grimace. 'And I'm still paying for it.' His voice was rasping and deep, and it occurred to me – however absurdly – that he might make a good radio announcer. If killing people didn't work out, that is.

'What are you going to do to me?'

'Much the same.' His expression darkened, and he moved his stare back to the door behind me just as it swung open.

A boy of around twelve came to stand behind Calvino, resting his hand across his shoulder like some creepy family portrait set-up. The boy was obviously his son. They shared pointy chins that jutted out below thin, pale lips, and hooked noses that dominated their faces. Their eyes were dark with heavy lids, and, like all of the Falcones, they shared an olive complexion.

Calvino gestured at the boy, and in response he whipped out a phone – *my phone* – from his pocket.

'Hey!' I yelled, startling myself. They both turned to me, identical looks of surprise making their faces seem impossibly long. 'That's my phone, you little shit. Give it back.'

'No,' the boy hissed.

'CJ,' his father cautioned him. 'I said no talking to her.'

CJ frowned. 'Tell me when you want me to start recording,' he said to his father, clicking into the camera feature on my phone and making the flash on the back of it light up.

Of course. They were going to send the video to Jack from my own phone. Calvino stood and rolled up his black shirt-sleeves until the end of a tattoo peeked out on his right bicep. Instinctively, I pushed back against the couch and brought my legs higher in front of my huddled frame.

'Should I start now?' CJ was hopping from foot to foot.

'Yeah.' Calvino whipped a knife out of his pocket and flicked the blade open. I recognized it as a Falcone switchblade – it was identical to Nic's.

'Should he be witnessing this?' I gestured at his son as he moved towards me. 'He's just a kid.'

Calvino raised his thick eyebrows – they matched his caterpillar moustache perfectly. 'He is a Falcone.'

He retained his shocked expression for five full seconds, as if to indicate that great offence had been taken at my question. I used the time to grapple against the couch; I brought my legs up until they blocked the rest of my torso, and tried to push myself over the top as the knife-wielding madman and his son moved towards me.

'Do you want to introduce it?' his son asked.

Calvino seemed surprised by CJ's apparent ingenuity. 'Good idea.'

A wide grin spread across the boy's acne-fied face.

I pushed against the couch with my bound feet as Calvino zeroed in on me, casually, like he knew no matter how hard I tried, he would get the better of me. He stowed the blade and grabbed on to my arm. I sailed back towards the middle of the couch with one stiff yank. Then he shuffled in beside me so we were both under the phone's lens. He dropped to his haunches and pulled me by the collar of my T-shirt so CJ could zoom in.

The pungent smell of aftershave rolled over me. I noticed, with horror and an irrepressible sliver of intrigue, that a thick white scar rippled along where Calvino's hairline might have been once upon a time. As he tilted closer towards me, it glowed beneath the lights, making the top of his head look like a lid.

'Jack Gracewell' – like steel claws shredding a bass drum, every syllable scraped at his throat – 'I hope this video finds you gravely unwell.'

CJ gave him a thumbs-up from behind the phone. I tried to inch away from his father's shiny head, but he squeezed the back of my neck until he broke the skin with his fingernails, and I let out a yelp of pain.

'As you can see, we have your beloved niece, Miss Persephone Gracewell.' He patted my hair in one long sliding motion. I tried to jerk my head away again, but he grabbed my jaw and pulled me back so that it unhinged itself with a small *pop.* I closed my eyes and tried not to scream as I set it back into its socket in one agonizing click.

'As you are aware,' he continued to the camera, swatting my flailing hands down in a painful blow, 'we were not happy with our conversation earlier and feel your hesitance should result in escalation on our side.'

Escalation? The word rang in my head like a car alarm.

Calvino grabbed my hair and twined his fingers in it, pulling roughly. I threw my arms against his chest, pummelling it as hard as I could, but he angled away from me so I was punching at the air.

'Please!' I screamed.

He kept twisting his fingers through my hair, yanking so hard it felt like he was trying to rip my scalp off.

'You have until midnight to come alone and unarmed to the abandoned warehouse on the outskirts of Old Hegewisch, where we will talk about the terms of your business activity and the girl's release.'

So they were misleading him twofold: once about his own fate and once about mine. 'You lying assholes,' I spat.

Calvino flung his hand across my face. The blow stung the tears out of my eyes. Bucking wildly, I hit him in the shoulder;

he recoiled and cursed under his breath. Seizing the moment his distraction allowed me, I rolled off the couch and struggled to my feet, hopping towards the door.

Calvino lurched forwards and grabbed my shoulders, pulling me back to him and that godforsaken couch. I covered my face with my bound hands as he loomed over me, breathing raggedly through his nose. He bent down until I could feel his breath across my hair, ruffling it away from my forehead as he forced my hands from my face.

He slammed the heel of his hand against my nose, and my upper teeth imprinted on the inside of my lips. The taste of salt and rust oozed away from my gums, mixing with the stream of blood coming from my nose. I wheezed as it trickled out over my lips and down my chin.

'Stop,' I begged. I started to claw up over the couch, but Calvino yanked me back again. My head landed against his chest with a thud and he held it there.

'If you don't show up, Jack,' he resumed his psycho video voice-over, 'we'll kill her. And then we will come for you with every man we have until you are hanging from the ceiling of your restaurant.' He pushed me away and I fell back against the couch, aching and trembling.

CJ scurried up until there was less than a foot between the lens and me, and I could make out every pus-filled zit on his greasy face.

'You see what you make me do, Gracewell?' Calvino paused as if he was expecting Jack to respond. My crying filled the silence. I hadn't even realized I was sobbing until I heard myself. He gestured to CJ to turn it off.

'Nailed it!' his son chimed. 'It's good.' Like he had just gotten an A on a test instead of a video documenting the abuse of a defenceless seventeen-year-old girl.

I spat a pool of blood on to Calvino's silk shirt. 'You're a monster!'

He raised his hand at me and I flinched away from it. 'Watch your tongue,' he cautioned. 'Or I'll take it from your mouth.' Then he stood up and laid a heavy hand on his son's shoulder. 'Bring the video to Felice and send it through. He'll be leaving soon to set up for Gracewell's arrival. I'll follow later with the girl.'

'Can I go too?' CJ asked excitedly.

'Next time.'

Nice to know this kind of thing was a regular occurrence in the Falcone family.

The boy disappeared, leaving me alone with my torturer. I fell back into a seated position and pulled my limbs into my body.

'Nothing's broken,' Calvino informed me in a way that implied I was being overdramatic. He sauntered back to the chair and relaxed into it with a deep sigh.

I wanted to shout profanities at him, but my energy was dying with each breath. I knew I had to escape – if not for me, then for my mother, and my best friend, and my father. And even Jack. Deep down I was still hoping for something that would explain this, something that would make it less horrific than it seemed.

Calvino was watching me, his gaze unblinking. I flicked my attention around the room. I could jump through the window, but I would probably break my leg on landing. And then there were all those bees to think about. Even if I could somehow get the ties off, I'd have to run through the fields at the back or take a chance going through the front of the house. I didn't know how many people were here or how big the place was. The door was behind me. If I was lucky, maybe Calvino would get bored and fall asleep. It was dark out now.

My thoughts were still whirling when he stood again. He re-rolled his sleeves.

'What are you doing?' I tried to hop off the couch, but the binds on my legs tripped me.

'I wasn't finished,' Calvino replied as I landed against the floor and tried to slither away from him, using my butt and my legs like a caterpillar. 'I just needed a rest.'

He rounded on me. I scooted furiously until my head banged against one of the walls. He brought his foot back like he was going to kick a ball, but I rolled over at the last second.

I pulled myself across the floor with my hands. He kicked me again, and this time it landed on my right side. I heard a faint crack as the wind left my lungs. Twinkling stars began to cloud my vision as I clawed at the rough wooden floors. There was a laboured grunt from somewhere above and I crumpled as another blow hurtled into me.

Waves of nausea rocked back and forth inside me. I pulled my knees into my chest and cradled myself into a foetal position as shrieks of uncontrollable pain ripped through my body. Calvino began circling my frame. This time, instead of kicking me, he flipped me over with his shoe so that I landed under the force of my own body. He started to press against my back with his heel.

'Stop,' I wheezed. I tried to claw across the wood, but he stamped down harder, and then I heard the flick of his switchblade from somewhere above me.

'Please,' I panted, but to whom, I didn't know. I was on my own, and I had to do something before it was too late.

He rolled me over again, until I lay flat out under the glaring ceiling lights, squinting as his angular face came back into focus.

He brandished the blade, running his thumb along the edge. Slowly I pushed myself on to my side and pulled my legs back behind me, bending them a little at the knees. This was my last hope. I prayed he wouldn't move before I could swing them forwards again, and he didn't; he was too busy staring amorously at the blade as it glinted above me.

It was my only chance: I pushed against the floor with my bound hands and swung the lower half of my body forwards with as much force as I could muster, using my elbow and my hips to propel myself. My legs swooped in a semicircle, and by the time Calvino noticed what I was trying to do, they were already knocking his legs out from under him.

In what felt like slow motion, he careened backwards, tumbling from his tremendous height. The blade landed with a *ping* beside my shoulder. His head hit the wall behind him with a deafening thump. He crumpled and slid towards the floor a couple of feet away from me, and then, apart from one brief twitch in his leg, he lay perfectly still.

I crunched into an upright position, biting hard on my bottom lip to stop the screams of agony building inside me. I grabbed the knife and got to work on my leg binds, sawing through them as quickly as possible, and glancing at Calvino every few seconds to make sure he wasn't about to lunge at me and choke me out. His eyes were shut, but his chest was still rising and falling, so I knew I was short on time. The ties around my ankles came away.

I curled my hand around the knife and tried to cut backwards into the binds on my hands, but I couldn't find the right angle and each attempt was useless. But I had come too far to fail now, with tied wrists or not. I held the knife between my hands and rocked back and forth until I could push up on to my feet.

When I stood up, the pain in my chest tore through me like a flame. I doubled over, clutching the knife inside my fist. Using the wall as my anchor, I slid forwards against it, one baby step and then another, forcing my screams into breathless sobs. The door was close enough to touch. Behind me, Calvino's breathing was growing steadier.

Slowly, I started to slump against the wall. I held my ribs tight against my bound hands, but the strength was petering out of my body. I was shuddering with pain, and suddenly escape seemed impossible. He was going to catch me.

I couldn't lift my head, and I couldn't see the door any more. But I was close enough to feel the surge of air that rippled inside when it swung open in front of me. With every last ounce of strength, I forced my chin away from my chest and fixed my gaze forwards.

'Sophie?'

I opened my mouth to yell, but the words came out in breathless puffs. 'You. Asshole.'

CHAPTER TWENTY-EIGHT

THE ESCAPE

Luca and I stared at each other for a long, agonizing moment.

I watched his expression darken. I tried to speak again, but I couldn't. I knew I was teetering on the edge of unconsciousness; flashes of pain were pulsing through my ribcage, and every breath was more difficult than the one before. But I knew, too, if I let myself fall into the darkness that was licking at my mind, then I might never wake up again – because Luca was Valentino's underboss, and he had orders to extract a blood debt from me.

I unballed my fist and pushed onwards, holding the knife as far from my body as I could and using my shoulder as an anchor to keep me upright.

'Get out of my way.' Brandishing the switchblade, I tried to shove against his chest with my other shoulder.

Luca curled his hand around my back and yanked the knife easily from my grip with the other. He flicked it closed and threw it on to the couch, far from my reach. 'You can't go through me.'

I looked up at him, glaring. I had seen enough of those piercing eyes to last me a century. 'Let go of me.'

He didn't. He moved his gaze across the room and let it rest on Calvino's flat-out form. 'You do that to him?' he asked evenly.

I nodded.

He studied me, first the dried blood on my chin, and then where I was trying to clutch at my ribs. '*Cazzo,*' he muttered, shaking his head.

My legs buckled, but he caught me. He lowered me to the floor so that I was sitting. I wanted to tell him to get his hands off me, but I didn't because, for a nanosecond, I felt a respite from pain. It was almost manageable in this position, but I knew I couldn't remain in it. I had to escape.

Without taking his eyes off me, Luca pulled out his phone, punched in a number and lifted it to his ear. 'She's still here.' A short silence, and then, 'An hour.' He clicked off and returned the phone to his pocket.

'What's in an hour?' My voice was breathless with pain.

Luca didn't respond, and I winced as another ache spread along my chest. He got to his feet and crossed over to where Calvino was beginning to stir on the floor.

'*Svegliati,*' he said, nudging his shoulder with his shoe. Calvino groaned, but he didn't open his eyes. 'I'm taking her to the warehouse,' Luca continued, as though talking to a semi-conscious, moaning man was entirely normal. 'I'll try not to let everyone know a seventeen-year-old, tied-up girl with no formal training managed to knock you out. In the meantime, you might want to sleep this off.'

Calvino's leg twitched as Luca walked away from him. '*Pezzo di merda,*' he muttered, before returning his attention to me.

'I'm not going anywhere with you,' I said.

'It's not up to you.'

'Nic will never forgive you.' My voice cracked and I cursed the weakness it betrayed, but Luca didn't seem to notice. Or care. He flicked his gaze to Calvino again. 'Nic is not my concern right now.'

He peered around the open door, into the next room. When he turned back I was already on my feet again, swaying. I stumbled forwards.

Luca cocked his head. 'You're coming with me, Sophie.'

'No,' I heaved, pushing forwards until we were standing together at the threshold once more. 'I told you I don't respect your authority.' I staggered on and nearly tripped.

Luca caught me again. I tried to hit his shoulder, but I faltered and he grabbed me by the waist, anchoring me to him so that I was half floating and half standing. 'That doesn't change anything.'

I tried to wriggle free, but he wouldn't let go of me. 'I hate you,' I heaved.

'Then this probably won't help,' he replied. Before I could respond, he swung my legs upwards and caught them beneath one arm, pulling my body into his with the other. I kicked out as hard as I could, but he only held me tighter, crushing me against his chest.

He carried me through a second, larger room. It was a dimly lit sitting area strewn with empty pizza boxes and cans of Coke. There was a muted poker tournament playing on a huge flat-screen TV, which was surrounded by wide leather armchairs.

I continued to struggle as agony coursed through my body, pushing through my vocal cords in banshee moans.

'Shut up,' he cautioned as he opened another door and we plunged into the darkness along the second-storey landing. I didn't shut up. I screamed until my voice cracked and my throat stung.

We reached the top of a winding staircase that parted into two identical paths. Luca descended quickly, his footfalls tapping against the marble until we were at the very bottom, standing in a large circular foyer with a white stone floor. In the centre, a glass chandelier illuminated a mosaic of the Falcone family crest carved into the stone at our feet. My kicks were getting weaker and weaker.

'Please,' I said, looking up at him. My head lolled against his shoulder as exhaustion crashed over me. 'Please don't do this.'

Luca's mouth was a hard line, stretching the faint scar above his lip. He didn't look at me.

We reached the front door and stepped out into the night. Luca hurried into a jog. The house rose into the sky behind us; it was a gargantuan three-storey mansion made of white stone. In the middle, the roof rounded and protruded from the rest of the house, supported by a semi-circular row of columns.

The driveway was torturously long and dark. When we finally stopped, Luca hitched me away from his body and opened the door of his SUV, propping me into the passenger seat and shutting me in before I could try and tumble out. He jumped into the driver's seat and started the engine. It roared to life beneath us. The clock on the dashboard read 10.04.

'Where are we going?' I already knew. I just wanted him to speak to me, to acknowledge what he was doing. Even yelling was better than the stony silence that stretched out between us. The quiet meant he was too focused on what he had to do, and that my pleas weren't causing him to waver.

We drove in silence for a long time, speeding along deserted roads I didn't recognize, until finally, strands of civilization edged back into view. I tried to stay alert, but I could feel myself slipping in and out of consciousness as the pain ebbed and flowed through my body.

I tried everything to get through to Luca: I cried, I pleaded, I yelled, but he never replied. He never even looked at me. He just stared, face forwards, at the road, grinding his jaw and gripping the steering wheel so hard his fingers turned white.

And then when the clock read 10.57, almost an hour after leaving Lake Forest, we stopped. Luca turned off the highway and pulled around the back of a small service station. He parked the car, and for the first time since we had started driving, he turned to me. I stared back into his fathomless blue eyes, and waited as he shifted in his seat. He pulled something out of his back pocket, and my stomach curled with terror as he leant towards me. He dropped it into my lap and for a moment I felt no pain, just surprise. It was a fifty-dollar bill.

Then he spoke quickly and quietly: 'I took you from Felice's house against your will. When we made it into town, I stopped at a red light and you escaped. You ran into a service station. I couldn't come after you because there were too many people inside. I couldn't risk getting caught. You called a cab to pick you up. You went home to your mother and you both fled Cedar Hill immediately.'

I started to shake, first my hands and then the rest of me. He was setting me free. He wasn't going to kill me. 'What about my uncle . . .' I said as tears pricked the back of my eyes.

Luca's expression was unyielding, his voice dark. 'You will not return home until after your uncle's funeral. Valentino won't keep us in Cedar Hill just for you. He won't like it that you escaped, but he will be able to move past it once Jack Gracewell's debt is settled.'

'But if—'

'Sophie,' Luca cut me off. 'You will never see your uncle again.'

'Please,' I whispered. 'Please, you have to help him.'

'There are certain mistakes I can afford to make,' he replied evenly. 'And certain mistakes I can't.'

'Do you mean they'd kill you if you tried to help him? But they're your family.'

'I mean I wouldn't try,' he said plainly.

I swallowed my words. Not only could Luca not help Jack, I knew he wouldn't. In his heart, he believed he should die, and there was nothing I could do to change that. How could a boy who was raised to believe that bad people are wholly bad possibly understand the idea that within bad there can be good and, more important, the potential for good? Luca and his family were looking at the world in black and white.

With a quick glance over my shoulder, Luca pulled his switchblade out of his pocket and cut the ties around my wrist. I watched as they fell apart limply. He pressed the handle of the blade into my hand and closed my fingers around it. 'You stole my knife and took it with you in case you needed protection.'

I looked down at the inscription:

Gianluca, March 20th

He was really giving me his blade, his personalized blade. And what's more, he was trusting that I wouldn't use it against him. It felt cold and unnatural in my hands, but I kept it, stuffing it in a pocket of my shorts alongside the fifty dollars.

'Thank you,' I said, because I couldn't manage anything else. I didn't know whether to be grateful or horrified. I was exhausted, I was numb, and I was shaking. But he was setting me free, and whatever else was happening around us, that meant something. He was going against his family. He was giving me my life back.

'You'll never see us again, Sophie.' There was a devastating finality in his words, but there was still nothing in his expression. It was, as ever, carefully controlled.

Before I could respond, the handle of the passenger door clicked and I turned to find Nic standing there, in the small parking lot at the back of the service station, holding it open for me. I stepped out of the car. We looked at each other, and I could see every shred of heartache bound up in his dark eyes.

He studied me – the bruising on my face and the lopsided way I was holding myself, my hands clutched beneath my ribs. He shut his eyes, there was a sharp intake of breath, and I swore both our hearts cracked just a little in that moment.

'I'm sorry,' he said, opening his eyes again.

I couldn't tell him it was OK. It was a million miles away from being OK. But I offered him something small: a soft, watery smile for the boy who had kissed me like I had never been kissed before. He had goodness in him, even if it was buried far beneath the codes he lived his life by.

I stood back from Nic and he brushed by me, taking his place beside Luca in the car. He reached out for my hand and I gave it to him. He held it carefully, like it was made of porcelain, and traced the red marks on my wrist with his thumb. Then he lifted it to his lips and kissed it. '*Riguardati,*' he murmured against my skin.

And then the Falcone brothers were gone from me, and I was doubled over on the ground, crying so hard I could barely breathe.

CHAPTER TWENTY-NINE

THE WAREHOUSE

The more I cried, the more I thought about everything that had happened, and slowly my resolve grew steadier than all the pain swimming inside me. If all the Falcones did was put people in the ground, then how could they know the benefits of second chances and what they can do for someone? How much good were they doing by ripping the potential out of a man before he could find the good in himself?

Luca and Nic might not have had a choice about killing Jack, but *I* did. I didn't know his number to call him – never mind that my phone was presently in the possession of thug-in-training CJ – but I knew where they were going, I had a weapon, and I had money to get there. If I abandoned my uncle now, I would never forgive myself, and I would never think of Nic with anything other than contempt. I had made a promise to my father to look after Jack, and if his brother died like this I knew he would never recover. He was barely hanging on already.

But there was still time, I could still do something. I could stand between Nic and my uncle, I could stop him from killing him. I might not have been able to convince Luca, but I knew Nic would listen to me. He wouldn't devastate my family so completely, not after everything we had shared with each other.

I picked myself up and did my best to clean my face, wiping the blood from my chin and pulling my hair around my eyes to hide the bruising. I forced my body to straighten, walked into the service station, and broke the fifty-dollar bill so that I'd have one measly quarter to call a cab. I waited in the service station bathroom until it arrived, studying my reflection. I pulled my matted hair back from my face and stifled a horrified gasp. Deep bruises pooled out from under my swollen eyes. The bridge of my nose was crooked, and my cheeks and chin were raw from where I had scrubbed the blood away. I gripped the sides of the sink as the pain in my ribs surged. A few weeks ago, my biggest problem was the stifling July humidity. How had it come to this?

Somewhere along the way, there had been a gross misunderstanding. Everything had spiralled out of control. I couldn't just think about the drugs or the money or the dark parts of my uncle's soul without thinking about the good parts of him too, the parts I knew existed. My uncle was not the one-dimensional villain the Falcones thought he was – how could they make allowances for themselves and not him? It wasn't right. Even if I couldn't convince them of that before it was too late, I still had to try.

Twenty minutes later, and to the bewilderment of the cab driver, I got out at a vacant lot on the outskirts of Old Hegewisch. Along the periphery, plastic bags floated like ghosts over sideways shopping carts. The old auto warehouse was halfway across the lot; it was a huge, faceless structure, its cracked concrete walls stained with rust and pigeon crap. On either side, shipping containers were precariously stacked like giant LEGO bricks, orange, beige and blue. Along the top, a worn sign reading GREENE'S AUTO SUPPLIES swung precariously from its final screw. I walked briskly towards it, feeling less scared than I should have been. I was running entirely on adrenalin now, and I could feel my pulse in my fingertips.

I walked along a row of corrugated steel containers until I found an alley barely wider than a car. It was pitch black and completely hidden from the entrance to the parking lot. At the end of the alley, I turned right and found two of the Falcones' SUVs, parked and empty. So Luca and Nic were here already, but who had come in the other car? It was obvious why they had chosen the spot. It gave them a secret entrance and an immediate upper hand for when Jack arrived.

At the back of the warehouse, a small door was hidden behind several stacks of wooden crates. It was partially ajar. The lock had been broken, but I doubted its necessity – the door itself was already crumbling at the edges, and probably could have been kicked in by a child.

I tiptoed between the crates and slid through the door. The space inside was mostly empty; it was cold and dirty, and damp. The smell of mould hung in the air, and more stacks of termite-eaten crates were piled haphazardly around the edges, regurgitating strips of plastic packaging. A single wire cage lamp illuminated a circular space at the front, and another smaller light bulb had been strung near the centre, where the Falcones were standing, partially shielded by a tower of crates that came up to their chests. Luca was arguing with Felice, while Gino and Dom hovered behind them, fidgeting with their guns. Nic was several yards away, waiting just inside the front entrance. If only I could get his attention, maybe he would listen to me without being influenced by his brothers.

I started moving around the side of the warehouse, clutching at my sides as I bent low behind the boxes. Rats scurried in and out of crates, and I had to bite hard on my tongue to keep from yelping every time one skittered by my sneakers.

I stopped creeping and listened as the faraway rumblings of a car grew louder.

The activity in the warehouse fell deathly quiet.

The engine cut somewhere beyond the front entrance. I heard a car door shut. *Jack.* My heart was pounding hard and fast in my chest. Suddenly all I could think about was my uncle's face when he walked into the guns that were about to be levelled at his head.

Then something unexpected happened: I heard another door shut, and another, and finally a fourth. Jack wasn't alone.

Nic peered around the warehouse entrance and then pulled his head back in a blur. 'He's got company,' he announced to the others, backing away from his post and coming to stand beside Luca. Both of them looked uneasy, but no one seemed particularly surprised. I don't know why I was so shocked: walking into a dark warehouse alone was suicide. Jack was smarter than that, and, to my dismay, he was obviously used to this world and how things worked in it.

'They'll have guns,' said Dom casually.

'Classic Gracewell,' said Felice with a mirthless laugh. 'There is never any honour in his agreements. We always knew he would come heavy. How many are there?'

'It's too dark, I couldn't tell.' Nic's voice was tight with frustration. He pulled out his gun and double-checked to make sure it was loaded. How could I get to him now, when he was so close to his brothers? Maybe if I made it to Jack before he came inside, it would stop him from trying to come in at all. All this time I had been so worried about my uncle that I hadn't stopped to think about the possibility that he might come prepared too. And that meant Nic and Luca weren't any safer than he was.

Stupid vendetta.

I became more deliberate about my steps as the crates grew fewer and further between. They were getting trickier to hide behind and, with each shallow breath like a stab in my cracked ribcage, I was finding it harder to exert myself. If I could just make it through that front door before anyone came in, I might be able to stop a massacre.

'I knew this would get messy,' Felice was ranting. 'And if he sees we don't have the girl any more, then he won't hesitate to shoot first. We need to be on our guard – we've lost the upper hand.'

The shadows of Dom and Gino murmured their agreement. Luca's voice was too low to hear, but by the way his hands were gesturing, I guessed he was protesting his innocence. From my vantage point, it looked convincing. I hoped it was.

'And you're not even fully protected.' Felice motioned towards Luca's and Nic's chests. 'Go out back before you get injured. Valentino's angry enough already. We can't afford to have anything else go wrong.'

Neither of them moved. 'We'll see this through,' said Luca.

Nic rolled his neck around until it cracked. He squared his shoulders and clenched his jaw. If this was him in soldier mode, it was damn effective. And that made me want to pull my hair out of my scalp, because he was preparing to kill my uncle.

The Falcones fell out of their conversation; no one wanted to argue any more. They grew silent, each of them boring holes in the door with their eyes, waiting for Jack to make his move. They knew he was out there; he knew they were inside. Both sides had backup and both sides, presumably, had guns. And I was stuck, crouching in rat piss behind a stack of mouldy crates in a warehouse in the middle of nowhere, wondering which of the people I cared about would die first, and whether I would survive long enough to try and forgive the ones that didn't. If this wasn't rock bottom, I shuddered to think what was.

I was trying to sneak across a gap between two toppled crates when the door to the warehouse creaked open, first one notch, and then another. I froze. The Falcones raised their guns at the entranceway. I was too late. I had failed.

'Hello,' said a quiet, nervous voice.

My whole body turned to ice.

No one answered her.

'Hello?' she said again, the word just a wavering tinkle in this huge, barren space.

In one echoing click, they set their guns ready to fire, and aimed them at my mother as she edged into the warehouse.

CHAPTER THIRTY

THE CHOICE

Her hair was falling in messy strands across her ashen face, and she'd pulled her old cardigan over her pyjamas. She was still wearing her slippers.

Suddenly it felt like all my nightmares were colliding with each other and exploding into one dreadful spectacle. And this? *This* was my rock bottom.

If I thought I'd known anger before, this was something else entirely. Heat surged through me, and I could barely keep from screaming. What was Jack *thinking*? How could he do this to my own *mother*? To his brother's *wife*? I felt sick, and suddenly I didn't know which side I was on any more. Luca was right; I should have gone home. I should have left Cedar Hill with my mother. I should have kept her safe. She was the only person in my family I could rely on, and I had been a fool to think anything different.

When she saw the guns that were pointed at her, my mother let out a strangled gasp. Her hands flew to her mouth and she stumbled backwards.

The Falcones hesitated, glancing at one another, but they didn't lower their guns. I couldn't understand why they would see anything remotely threatening about her. She was five feet tall, a hundred pounds, and shaking like a leaf.

I bit the back of my hand and tried to centre myself, but I was screaming on the inside. I crept closer – as close as I could get to her before I couldn't hide behind the dwindling crates any more. It still wasn't close enough. I desperately wanted to spring from the shadows and pull her out of there, but I knew I'd probably be shot before I got to her.

My mother shuffled forwards again, cradling herself. 'I'm here for my daughter.' The fear made her voice unrecognizable. 'I'm here for Sophie.'

Luca lowered his gun. 'What the hell does Gracewell think he's doing?'

The others didn't move.

'Keep your defences up,' cautioned Felice. 'This is clearly a trap.'

'It's her mother,' said Nic, turning to spit on the ground. 'He's using her goddamn mother.'

'There are more of them outside,' said Felice. He narrowed his eyes and started scanning my mother as if making sure she wasn't an illusion. 'I don't know what this is, but if Jack Gracewell thinks we won't shoot you, then he's sorely mistaken.'

'W-where is my daughter?' My mother wasn't focusing. Her

attention had fallen away from the guns and she was whipping her head around, searching the warehouse frantically. For me. 'Where is she?' she asked, dread drowning out the fear in her breathless voice. 'He said she was here. What have you done with her?'

'Where is Jack Gracewell at this moment?' Felice started towards her, levelling his gun at her forehead. 'Tell me what he's planning or I'll kill you right now.'

'Stop!' shouted Nic. He flung his arm out across his uncle's chest and Felice skidded to an unexpected halt.

'Nicoli,' he hissed. 'You need to learn to pick your battles.'

'She's not part of this,' he snapped.

'Of course she's part of this, she's standing right here!'

'We said no more innocents. You're as bad as Valentino!'

'Nonsense,' said Felice indignantly. 'Of course we should kill her.'

Luca stepped between Nic and Felice. 'Do you really wish to derail this family further, Felice?' he asked, his voice carefully controlled. 'This is not what my father would have wanted, and we all know it.'

'Then perhaps you shouldn't have shunned his last request. You would certainly be in a better position to complain now.'

Luca's expression grew faintly hostile, but his voice remained unchanged. 'I'm sure I don't need to remind you, Felice, that regardless of my decision, I still outrank you.'

Felice grimaced and lowered his gun slowly. The feeling returned to my jelly legs.

'S-Sophie?' My mother inched forwards, craning her neck to see behind the crates ahead of her. But she wouldn't find me there, and the more she tried, the harder it was to watch her fail. Silent tears were streaming down her cheeks, catching in the half-light. 'Sophie?'

'Where is Jack Gracewell?' Felice repeated. He was so caught up in studying her that he didn't hear the dim thud coming from the back of the warehouse. None of them did.

I felt myself jump and the pain in my ribcage soared, as if an invisible hand had decided to braid my insides. I fell back on to my haunches and followed the noise. Four figures were sneaking through the hidden back door. They started navigating their way through the crates, crouching low to the ground. A shock of crimson hair alerted me to Eric Cain's position. Of course Jack's best friend was involved in this, just like everybody else seemed to be. Beside him, I recognized the gait of my uncle as he pulled himself across the ground, stalking towards the Falcones.

I started to panic, caught between shouting out to draw attention to Jack so that Nic and Luca could be forewarned and keeping quiet so Jack could save my mother from Felice's increasingly steady aim. Maybe he did deserve this, but she didn't. I patted my hand against Luca's knife in my pocket and the angriest part of me imagined using it on Jack. What good was showing up to rescue me if he was prepared to use my own mother, knowing she could get hurt too?

'Enough of this!' It was Gino; Gino the Unstable. He lunged forwards, barrelling past Felice and Nic, his gun held high.

My mother yelped, stumbling backwards, and almost tripping over herself.

'Gino!' Nic's scream drowned out my own, and no one seemed to notice the threads of our voices intertwining. Luca lunged at the same time and in a heartbeat he was standing in front of my mother, his palms raised towards his brother.

'Gino, no,' he echoed, but calmer.

'She's a distraction,' Gino lisped, madly waving his gun in the air. 'And she's Michael Gracewell's wife! At least this way we can get the blood debt that you and Calvino screwed up.'

'Watch what you say, Gino,' Luca said without budging.

The shadows at the back were lurking ever closer. I caught a glint of Jack's buzz cut several crates across from me. I decided to go for him. If he knew I was OK, maybe he could sneak away, and then Luca could convince them to let my mother go too.

I dragged myself across the cement, glancing over my shoulder as I crept as quickly as possible. My mother had buried her face in her hands and her sobs were echoing around the warehouse. I watched Luca turn and whisper something to her. She straightened up and began to wipe her face with shaking hands. She said something in return. He nodded and she released a watery smile, her face twitching with relief. She knew I was alive.

When I turned back, my uncle was no longer in my sights, and the lurking shadows were no longer shadows. They were men. And they were standing up, arms outstretched and guns in hand. I screamed at the top of my lungs, but it was too late.

In the movies it's always so dramatic when someone gets shot. Time slows, the music ebbs and flows around the moment. When the bullet hits, the body buckles – each limb reacting in perfect unison – as it sails backwards through the air, and even though it's supposed to be horrifying, there's always something quietly artistic about it too.

It wasn't like that with Luca. He just crumpled. One minute he was on his feet, standing in front of my mother, and the next he was lying on the ground in a pool of his own blood.

The pop was still echoing in my eardrums when she started screaming, and then the shouting followed, and all hell broke loose.

Eric Cain, the man who had shot Luca, dropped to the ground and rolled behind a line of broken crates. Dom started shooting at him, putting holes in the crates as he sprang up and leapt between them like a gazelle, weaving towards the back of the warehouse. Another man – who was little more than a curtain of white-blond hair – was trying to dart in wide circles around Gino, while Felice cornered the fourth, all of them firing at one another between crates.

Nic went straight for Jack, his gun readied, but Jack shot first. The bullet lodged in the crate beside Nic's head. He shot back, but Jack dodged it, leaping behind a tower of crates and disappearing from my view. And then I couldn't see them any more, but their shouts rose up with the others'.

I slithered across the cold cement, following Luca's blood like it was a trail and ignoring the pulsing pain in my ribcage. My mother was already crouched down, trying to drag him away from the chaos with one hand and protecting her head from stray bullets with the other. Someone screamed my name, and I braced myself for the impact of a bullet that never came.

Behind us, a door slammed and most of the shouting moved outside. I reached Luca and threw my hands on to his waist to stop the bleeding that was coming thick and fast from an entry wound in his side. It bubbled angrily beneath my hands as blood oozed over my fingers, coating them in sticky warmth.

'Sophie!' my mother cried, grabbing on to my shoulders.

'Sophie, you have to leave!'

'No.' I pressed down harder, feeling my own ribs shriek in protest. Luca's eyelids were fluttering and his complexion was drained. It was strange to see him so pale. 'Call an ambulance.'

My mother released me and started patting her sweater frantically. 'I don't have a phone. I didn't think,' she dithered. 'Everything happened so fast, and Jack said we had to leave urgently if we were to have any chance of . . . oh, and I was so worried I could barely think . . .' She trailed off into senseless mutterings. We were close to the front of the warehouse now. She started pulling nearby crates around us – building a makeshift barrier.

There was no sign of Nic or Jack. Before, I could hear them barking at each other, but now there was nothing. Inside, the rest of the shooting had ceased. Someone had had the sense to lure the chaos away from us, and I couldn't be sure which side had thought to do it, and whether it was for my benefit or for Luca's, but in that moment I was profoundly grateful.

Outside, three more shots rang out and an engine roared to life. Someone was leaving in a car at the front of the warehouse, and I didn't know whether to be relieved or terrified.

'We have to get help.' I started to drag Luca towards the entrance with my free hand. He gurgled and a stream of blood bubbled from his discoloured lips, staining his chalk-white skin.

'It's too dangerous, Sophie,' my mother whispered. 'We don't know what's going on out there.'

The sound of another engine startled me. It was further away, coming from the back of the warehouse. Tyres squealed, and I knew it meant at least one Falcone was taking off.

'Those bastards,' I spat. 'They're leaving him here to die.'

'They probably think he's already dead.' The way my mother said it betrayed her own grim expectations. 'He very nearly is.'

The tears stung my eyes, but I blinked quickly so they would fall away from them and clear my vision. 'If you hold the wound, I could try to find—'

The front entrance was kicked in. Jack stomped into the warehouse, his shirt pooling with sweat and his face blotchy and red. He had his gun raised in front of him, his eyes darting around the warehouse for possible threats.

'You're safe,' he said without looking at my mother and me. He was still scanning the warehouse. 'We have to go.'

'Where are the others?' I asked.

'Carter's dead. They got him twice in the head. Grant's still out there with one of them. Cain's been shot in the arm, but he rallied and—'

'The Falcones,' I interrupted. 'Where are the Falcones?'

Jack didn't register the urgency in my question; he probably thought it was fear. 'Cain's leading them on a wild goose chase across the city; those dumb goombahs think they're chasing me. They thought it would be so easy, but once again they've underestimated me. They have no idea what they've started. I'm going to pick those little shits off one by one. No one lays a hand on my niece and gets away with it.' The pride in his voice was horrifyingly misplaced; I guessed it often was in this strange underworld, where morals were warped beyond reason. 'We've got to get you two to safety before that other Falcone comes back in here. I've called Hamish and he's on his way; we're meeting him at the edge of the lot. We'll just have to write Grant off as an expense. He was new any—'

Jack stopped mid-rant. For the first time, his attention

focused on our little heap behind the crates. He zeroed in on Luca, his eyes growing. 'Shit,' he said, grimacing. 'Move aside.'

He pointed his gun at Luca's head.

'Stop!' I screeched, shifting so I was in his firing line instead.

He came closer, stomping through Luca's blood like it was a puddle of water. He softened his voice in an effort to comfort me. 'You don't have to look.'

'Jack!' my mother cried hysterically. 'Don't shoot the boy!'

Jack didn't understand. Luca was just another fallen chess piece, and he was distracting me from our getaway. 'Celine, if she doesn't come now, we won't get her to safety.'

Luca was unconscious, but I could still hear laboured wheezes seeping from his chest. I pulled my body over his, bringing our foreheads together so that my hair fell around his head, shielding him. I stretched my free hand across his body, covering his heart, while keeping the other one tight against his wound. 'No.'

'He has to go, Sophie. He's the underboss.' The gentleness in my uncle's voice was turning to frustration, his patience to urgency. 'Don't make me pry you off him.'

'Jack,' my mother tried again. 'We need to help him.'

I could hear his knees crack as he hunkered down beside me. 'Don't be ridiculous, Celine.'

I held on tighter.

'Come on, Soph.' He grabbed me by the shoulder and pulled me away from Luca's body in one stiff yank. 'Turn away.'

I clawed forwards, but he pushed me back, sliding me across the ground until my bare legs were stained with Luca's blood and I was too far away to stop him. I screamed as he cocked the gun at his head.

There was an almighty pop. It was louder this time, and it seemed to change the particles in the air around me, pushing them against each other in small vibrations. My mother and I screamed, but Luca, who was barely Luca now, remained intact.

Instead, the gun flew out of Jack's hand, and skidded along the floor past me.

'Son of a bitch!' he cursed. His head was lolling, his expression dazed. The bullet had gone right through his hand, and now the tear was pumping blood down his arm. Jack shrunk to the floor, gasping and clutching his crimson fingers. I kicked his gun away. It slid to a stop between two bullet-riddled crates, far from his reach.

At the back of the warehouse, Nic was sprinting towards us, his face spattered with dirt, his clothes soaked with what must have been someone else's blood. The gun was still in his hand, half raised at my uncle, like he was planning to shoot at him again. I guess he wasn't kidding about that perfect aim.

'Both your friends are dead!' he shouted.

Jack started scrabbling backwards towards the entrance, pulling himself across the floor with his uninjured hand. 'Sophie!' he shouted, but he wasn't focusing; he couldn't see me. But I could see him; his pale face was awash with terror and his blood was mixing with Luca's as he dragged himself through it.

Nic stopped running and raised his gun again. 'Stop!' he commanded.

'Nic, don't!' I yelled. 'He's not armed. Just let him go!'

Nic's head twitched like there was something buzzing around it. He hesitated. Jack was at the door now; he stuck his good hand through and tried to pull himself up. He was almost there.

And then Nic shot him.

My mother and I screamed. Jack slumped against the doorway, and a blood-red star started to swell across the left side of his shirt.

Nic skidded to a stop beside Luca. He didn't even look at Jack. He stowed his gun and crouched down beside his brother, checking the pulse in his neck. 'We need to get him to the hospital,' he said to my mother. She was visibly shaking, but she was still plugging the wound.

I was too numb to move. I was still staring at my uncle and the new, terrified expression in his eyes. He was still alive, and he was looking at me, his body slumped half in and half out of the warehouse. I scanned the entry wound – it was just below his left shoulder. Not quite his heart, although it could easily have been. By all appearances, from where my mother and Nic were huddled, my uncle seemed very much dead, but I could see the alertness in his expression, and the fear in his eyes. Had Nic shot to kill or to wound Jack? And if he knew what I knew then – that the bullet had missed my uncle's heart, then would he finish the job?

'Sophie,' my mother said, her voice heaving. She and Nic had started to hoist Luca between them. 'Can you help us? We need you to plug the wound while we move him.'

Did Jack deserve my forgiveness? No. Did he deserve to die? That wasn't my decision to make; it wasn't anyone's. I didn't have any time to think. I stood up without saying anything, sticking my hand out to help, and blocking their view of my uncle's body as I came towards them. Then we moved quickly, all three of us in tandem, towards the back of the warehouse, away from all the blood. I didn't turn around to see if Jack was still there.

My mother and Nic carried Luca into the remaining SUV, while I stumbled along beside them, clutching my ribs with one hand and plugging his wound with the other. And then we took off, Luca and I lying side by side in the back seat, my hand pressed tight against his torso as our laboured breathing mingled in the air between us.

As Nic sped through the darkness, lost in hurried conversation with my mother, I drifted away from the pain inside me, and into the darkness that had been creeping up on me all evening.

CHAPTER THIRTY-ONE

THE HOSPITAL

For the second time this summer, I awoke in a hospital room. Everything around me was strange and discoloured. Cartoonish images danced back and forth in my brain as I lay still, feeling a million miles above the earth. I pulled my hand up around my chest and felt a subtle pinch as my eyes rolled back in my head.

'Sophie?' A tinkling bell infiltrated my bubble.

I rolled my head around and landed on my right cheek, which throbbed dully beneath me, like the pain was just outside of my body, looking in. I tried to groan, but it caught in my throat and wheezed out in pathetic puffs of nothingness.

'Sweetheart?' My vision sharpened until my mother's face loomed just inches from my own. Her eyes were glassy and her face was drawn. 'How are you feeling?'

I tried to speak, but I couldn't find the words, and I knew even if I could, I wouldn't be able to push them out. I scrunched up my face and blinked over and over until my mother's movements became disjointed.

'The doctor has given you morphine. You have two broken ribs and a broken nose. Don't worry if you feel a little strange.' She reached over to my un-obscured hand and squeezed it tightly. The sensation was little more than a slight tickle.

For every moment I lay there, feeling high and low all at once, memories flashed across my addled brain. I remembered the pain of every Calvino-inflicted blow, the argument with Luca at Felice's mansion, a long, meandering drive to nowhere. I pulled my hands under the blankets and, dimly, I became aware of the hospital gown I was wearing. Beside me, on the bedside locker, my tank top and cut-offs were folded in a pile. The top of a switchblade peaked out from my front pocket. There were more flickers of confusion and then something real, another disjointed memory. It was Luca's knife. But why did I have it again? I scrunched my eyes shut and tried to reach inside the darkest parts of my mind.

When I opened them, Nic had appeared inside the room, looking like he hadn't slept in a very long time; his hair was tousled across his forehead and dark circles had spread out under his eyes. He handed a paper cup of coffee to my mother and sat next to her so that their faces appeared side by side. For a second I could have sworn they were nothing more than floating heads, but then the morphine crest subsided enough for me to register some level of reality.

'You're awake.' He released a small smile.

I moaned breathlessly in response.

Nic leant in until his dark eyes dominated my limited field of vision. 'You are stubborn, Sophie Gracewell,' he chided softly. 'I don't know what I would have done if something had happened to you.'

I tried to remember more. The faint memory of shouting filled my brain, but it floated away again. I stared at Nic so hard I felt tears stream from my eyes and slide back into my hair.

He gently traced his forefinger under my swollen eye; I desperately wanted to feel his touch, but I couldn't. 'I'll make this right,' he said. 'I promise.'

I closed my eyes, remembering the old, dank smell of the warehouse with a start. I saw a line of scattered crates stretch out before me into the darkness. Nic and his brothers were standing in a solitary patch of light, arguing.

When I opened my eyes, Nic was lifting his hand away from my face, but his attention was still trained on me. 'Forgive me,' he whispered.

In my botched peripheral vision, I could make out my mother; pools of tears were spilling into the corners of her eyes. 'Sweetheart, I'm so sorry. I didn't know about any of this. I thought you were with Millie until Jack came banging on the door. I had no idea what he was doing. I had no idea about any of this.'

I could see her then, in another time and place, weeping as she was now, wearing the same pyjamas, and the slippers I had gotten her for Christmas.

I reached out and patted her arm in what I hoped was reassurance, but I could barely feel the gesture because of the morphine. When I felt satisfied with the feeble attempt, I tried to sit up.

'Stop,' Nic murmured, putting his hand on mine. 'Don't try to move just yet, OK?'

Stop. Nic had yelled that in the warehouse. That was right before he shot Jack. *Jack.* 'Jack,' I wheezed. It barely made a sound, but my mother understood.

'It appears your uncle made it out alive.' There was no emotion in her voice. I wasn't sure if she was relieved or disappointed. Cautiously I flicked my gaze to Nic. His expression was unreadable. I couldn't tell if he was surprised by the news or not, but he wasn't looking at me any more. I looked away from him too, but our fingers remained entwined.

When my head hit the pillow again it seemed to lift the rest of the fog in my brain. My memory flashed; the bullets were raining down around me as I huddled with my mother on the floor. I saw Jack, first holding a gun, and then clutching his hand as spurts of blood ran down his arm. Below us, Luca's eyelids fluttered, his chest heaving unsteadily. He was lying in a pool of his own blood, and my fingers were *inside* his body, holding him together.

Suddenly the image of Luca crumpling to the ground crashed into my mind, and every single harrowing memory of our escape littered my thoughts. I gasped so hard it stung my chest. I threw my hands out, flailing them helplessly, until Nic returned his attention to me. He grabbed them and settled them by my side, brushing his fingers across mine. 'It's OK,' he soothed.

'Luca?' I wheezed. 'Where is Luca?' My breathing quickened to match my heart rate and suddenly the room began to spin. Nic was reaching for something in his pocket. The pain in my ribs resurfaced and rattled against my skin. A strangled scream sprang from my chest.

My mother was on her feet, settling me. 'He survived,' she said. 'He's alive as well, sweetheart. He's alive.'

Nic unfolded the piece of paper he was holding. 'He's down the hall. He lost a lot of blood, but he's recovering. We got him here just in time.'

'You saved him,' I said, feeling myself smile. It felt heavenly not to have to worry any more. 'You shot Jack's gun out of his hand.'

'It really was remarkable,' my mother echoed. I could tell by her tone that she couldn't decide whether to be impressed or disapproving.

'*You* saved him,' said Nic. His expression was sheepish, his eyes dark. 'You stopped the bleeding.'

'You were so brave, sweetheart.' My mother started to stroke my forehead. 'I'm so proud of you.'

'Here,' Nic said, handing me the note he'd already opened. 'He's not able to walk around yet, but he wanted me to give this to you when you woke up.'

I grabbed it more fiercely than I intended to, almost ripping it. It was simple and short, written in neat black lettering. It took me a while to read it:

I told you to go home.

I felt myself grin. Nic was watching me intently; two dimples punctured the skin above his brows and his mouth was pursed. I caught his eye and the sternness disappeared. He smiled at me encouragingly.

'Pen?' I asked him.

My mother rustled around in her purse and handed me one. I turned the note over and wrote on the back. It took me far longer than it should have, and when I finished, the morphine-guided script was wobbly and disjointed, veering up and down the paper like a six-year-old had written it:

Aren't you glad I have no respect for your authority? ☺

I folded it over and handed it to Nic. 'Will you give this to him, please?'

His frown returned, and this time he didn't hide it. 'Sure,' he said, glancing at the piece of paper as he stepped out of the room. 'I'll be right back.'

My mother leant over me and dropped her voice. 'The police were here earlier asking questions. I expect they'll be back.'

'No statements,' I replied, falling back into my pillow. I wanted to say more, but I was losing my energy again.

My mother didn't appear surprised by my answer. She shook her head. 'No, I don't think so either.'

'Welcome to *omertà*,' I murmured. My tongue was thick and heavy in my mouth.

'*Omertà*,' she repeated quietly, and I could tell by her tone she already knew what it meant.

ACKNOWLEDGEMENTS

Thank you to Samantha Eves – you have been an instrumental part of this journey. I can't tell you how much I appreciate your tireless enthusiasm, your honest feedback and your readiness to read the book over and over . . . and *over*, at every stage. Thank you for the midnight Skype sessions and Niagara dinners where many of the characters and their journeys took shape.

Thank you to Jessica Hanley, Katie Harte and Susan Ryan for flat-out refusing to acknowledge my fear that you wouldn't embrace my book, and for insisting on being my first readers. From the start, you have been the greatest friends and supporters I could have asked for.

Thank you to my dad for thinking so convincingly like a Mafia boss and for rivalling my excitement at every step of this process. I am only sorry I couldn't have a winking cartoon bee on the cover, like you so desperately wanted.

Thank you to my mom, for making me take part in many library read-a-thons as a child, and for ensuring I actually *read* the books instead of just ticking them off the list . . . like my brothers did. I am especially grateful for the way you sneakily convinced me to accompany you to those creative writing courses two years ago. I see now, with perfect clarity, you were not going for yourself – you never even did the homework! You were really introducing me to a world I always wanted to be a part of but was too scared to enter alone. You are an amazing mother, and a truly talented meddler.

Thank you to my brothers. Conor, I know you wanted to write your own acknowledgement to yourself but this will have to do instead. You have been such a great CEO. Thanks for personally appointing yourself the Boss of My Life. You were the first person I told about my publishing deal, and even though you insisted on making a sandwich before celebrating with me, I can't think of anyone I would have rather told first. Really, you are a great brother . . . but don't let it get to your head. Colm, thank you for your unwavering belief in me, and your insistence on spurring me on when I felt like giving up. Thank you for your cheerful company on all my London visits, for giving me your bed, your time and your optimism . . . and for not letting those birds eat me at the zoo!

To Claire Wilson, thank you for making my dream come true, and for being an incredible agent. To Lexie and everyone else at Rogers, Coleridge & White, thank you for championing *Vendetta* so well. Thank you to my fellow STAGS, Alice Oseman, Lauren James and Melinda Salisbury, for sharing your journeys with me and for being part of mine. I see a lot more magical moments and beach Pimm's ahead!

Thank you to everyone at Chicken House – to Barry Cunningham and Rachel Hickman for welcoming me so wonderfully and offering my book an incredible home. Thank you to Rachel Leyshon, for adding your magical editorial touch to *Vendetta*, and making it better than I ever thought it could be. Thank you to Jasmine Bartlett, Laura Myers and Laura Smythe for introducing *Vendetta* to the world, and for being so amazing along the way.

Thank you to Siobhan McGowan for your humorous and insightful copy-edits, and to Emellia Zamani and the Scholastic team for championing *Vendetta* on the other side of the Atlantic.

Thank you to Aoife, my soul sister-cousin and fellow writer, for all the late night conversations about bees and dragons, and everything in between. Thanks to Sinéad for introducing me to Young Adult fiction all those years ago in school and for not hounding me too much about all the books I still have to give back. Aidan, thanks for *that* line and for the ones I'm sure I'll be 'borrowing' from you in future. Remember our deal – you're not allowed to sue me.

Finally, I am so grateful to everyone at Salmon Poetry, and to all my amazing friends and extended family, for being part of this journey and for sharing in the excitement with me at every stage. I feel very fortunate to have you all in my life! ❤

Bertrand Russell, *The Conquest of Happiness* (Liveright, 1996), © 1930 by Horace Liveright, Inc.; copyright renewed 1958 by Bertrand Russell

Friedrich Dürrenmatt, *Incident at Twilight* (1952)

The publisher has made reasonable effort to contact the copyright-holders for permission, and apologizes for any errors or omissions, which will be rectified at the earliest opportunity.

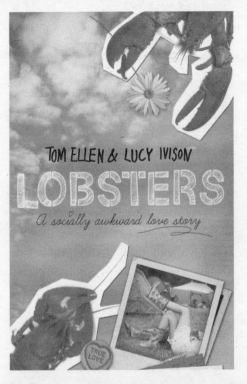

TRY ANOTHER GREAT BOOK FROM CHICKEN HOUSE

STOLEN by LUCY CHRISTOPHER

It happened like this.

I was stolen from an airport.

Taken from everything I knew, everything I was used to. Taken to sand and heat, dirt and danger. And he expected me to love him. This is my story.

A letter from nowhere.

'A vivid new voice for teens.'
MELVIN BURGESS

'Tautly written and hard to put down . . .'
INDEPENDENT ON SUNDAY

Paperback, ISBN 978-1-908435-75-0, £7.99 • ebook, ISBN 978-1-908435-18-7, £7.99